Since 1900

THE MACMILLAN COMPANY
NEW YORK · CHICAGO
DALLAS · ATLANTA · SAN FRANCISCO
LONDON · MANILA

IN CANADA
BRETT-MACMILLAN LTD.
GALT, ONTARIO

SINCE 1900

A History of the United States in Our Times

OSCAR THEODORE BARCK, JR.

Professor of History,
Syracuse University

NELSON MANFRED BLAKE

Professor of History,
Syracuse University

THIRD EDITION

NEW YORK
THE MACMILLAN COMPANY

Kenneth Rudd

THE ☼ SUN

VOL. CLXIII—NO. 133   101,501   BALTIMORE, MONDAY MORNING, NOVEMBER 11, 1918   14 PAGES.   PRICE TWO CENTS

EX-KAISER FLEES TO HOLLAND; REVOLUTIONISTS NOW SUPREME; ARMISTICE SIGNING IS AWAITED

Period Of Grace May Be Extended Owing To Chaotic Conditions In Conquered Country.

BERLIN EXPECTS TERMS

YANKS ATTACK IN LORRA

General Bull
Army Take 2 Villages
In Initial Offensive

EMPEROR SIGNED WITH A SHIVER

London, Nov. 10—(8.04 P. M.)—Emperor signed a letter of abdication Saturday morning at the German Grand Headquarters in the presence of Crown Prince Frederick William and Field Marshal Hindenburg, according to a dispatch from Amsterdam to the Exchange Telegraph Company.
The German Crown Prince signed his renunciation to the throne shortly afterward.

People's Government Formed With Chancellor Ebert At Head And Steps Taken To Restore Order. Frontier Guards To Prevent Escape Of Wealthy Persons.

Chicago Daily Tribune

2 CENTS PAY NO MORE   THE WORLD'S GREATEST NEWSPAPER   FINAL EDITION

VOLUME LXXIX—NO. 224. C.   FRIDAY, SEPTEMBER 17, 1920.—30 PAGES.   ★ ★ PRICE TWO CENTS

RED BOMB IN N. Y. 31 KILLED; 300 HURT

McKinley Leading; Small 13,000 Votes Ahead

INFERNAL MACHINE SLUGS TAKE TOLL IN WALL STREET

DRYS PREPARE BLACKLIST OF CANDIDATES

SOCIETY GIRL TAKES LOOP JOB FOR ART'S SAKE
Lydia Brown, "Clerk," Surprises Aunt.

ANTI-TAMMANY GETS MOST OF STATE OFFICES

THE CAMPAIGN MANAGER HAS TO BE AN OPTIMIST

Wide Hunt On for Anarchist Band.
New York, Sept. 16—(Special.)—A mysterious explosion at

BASIS FOR BELIEF BLAST WAS PLOT BY ANARCHISTS

ST. LOUIS POST-DISPATCH

Trade for Something Useful

The Only Evening Paper in St. Louis With the Associated Press News Service.

CITY EDITION

VOL. 75, NO. 329.   ST. LOUIS, FRIDAY EVENING, AUGUST 3, 1923—32 PAGES.   PRICE 2 CENTS

COOLIDGE SWORN IN; SPEEDING TO WASHINGTON

Harding Funeral Party Starts for Capital Tonight

DEATH CAME TO THE PRESIDENT WITH

PRESIDENT'S BODY WILL BE BURIED

1865—WARREN GAMALIEL HARDING—1923

FATHER ADMINISTERS OATH OF NEW OFFICE

ST. LOUIS POST-DISPATCH

Classified Advertising
REAL ESTATE ....PART 9
WANTS—FOR SALE PART 9
HELPS, SERVICE....PART 10

VOL. 79. No. 237.   PART ONE   ST. LOUIS, SUNDAY MORNING, MAY 22, 1927.   PAGES 1—16   PRICE 10 CENTS

CAPT. LINDBERGH LANDS SAFELY ON PARIS FLYING FIELD

BEATS HIS SCHEDULE, SETS NEW NON-STOP RECORD IN 33 HOURS, 28 MINUTES

EXCITED CROWD PRESSES AROUND AIRMAN AND TEARS MEMENTOS FROM PLANE

PARIS REJOICES IN SAFE ARRIVAL OF THE AMERICAN

Crowds Line Roads to Le Bourget Field Where He Landed — Waiting for News of Him.

U. S. FLAGS OUT

CLOUDY AND SHOWERS LIKELY; TEMPERATURE ABOUT SAME
THE TEMPERATURES

ST. LOUIS PLANS ROYAL WELCOME FOR LINDBERGH

Mayor to Direct Arrangements for Flyer's Reception on His Return to This City.

WHISTLES GREET

Lindbergh Tells How He Made Trip

By ARNO DOSCH-FLEUROT
A Staff Correspondent of the Post-Dispatch and the New York World.

PARIS, MAY 21.

THE first man of a breathless mob rushing across Le Bourget flying field tonight thrust his head into the cockpit of Lindbergh's monoplane and cried:
"How are you?"
"Who, me?" replied Lindbergh. "Oh, I'm all right."

"WELL, HERE WE ARE; I AM VERY HAPPY," HE SAYS ON ARRIVAL

Keeping Awake Sole Difficulty—Ate Only a Sandwich and a Half and

Preface to First Edition

The pitfalls in writing contemporary history are obvious, but the values of its study outweigh them. Never before has intelligent understanding of the role of the United States in world affairs been so much needed; never before has it been so imperative that the American government and the American economy be wisely guided. We are under no illusion that we know all the answers to urgent present day problems, but we are convinced that no one will ever find the answers without a study of the historical development of the issues—particularly since the turn of the century. This consideration has guided our choice of materials and greatest attention has been devoted to the problems that are of current importance. We are well aware of the significance of recent social and cultural trends and we have tried to give them ample treatment. But we have reserved a major portion of our space for the two lines of development which seem to us most impressive—the steady expansion of the functions of government to deal with the complex problems of a new age and the increasing involvement of the United States in global politics.

As far as is humanly possible, we have tried to keep this account free from partisan bias. Desirable in any case, this policy has been a practical necessity with us since we belong to different political parties and hold opposing convictions on many subjects; we have tried to state the facts and leave final judgments to the reader. This does not mean that we have shunned all responsibility for interpretation. On the contrary, we have tried to prepare the ground for fruitful discussion and thought by suggesting the most pertinent arguments for and against the more controversial propositions advanced during the period.

We are indebted to numerous colleagues and professional associates for encouragement and help in this enterprise. We wish to express particular gratitude to artists and newspapers all over the country for generous permission to reproduce cartoons. The opportunity to use these has greatly pleased us, since we are convinced that studying such material is one of the very best methods of projecting oneself back in time and seeing issues as they appeared to intelligent contemporary observers. To our loyal wives we want to pay sincere tribute both for their good sportsmanship in putting up with many inconveniences while we have been at work and for the long hours which they themselves contributed to helping us with proofreading and preparing the index. We of course must accept full responsibility for all errors of fact and judgment.

OSCAR THEODORE BARCK, JR.
NELSON MANFRED BLAKE

Syracuse University
August 21, 1947

Preface to Third Edition

Those who venture to write of relatively recent events always have to wrestle with the problem of perspective. Since 1947, when the first edition of this book was published, the passage of time and intervening developments have inevitably modified our estimate of the significance of many earlier episodes. Moreover, there has been a wealth of recent scholarship, devoted particularly to the presidencies of the two Roosevelts and of Wilson. Consequently we are grateful to our publishers for giving us the opportunity to revise the book from beginning to end. In addition to bringing the book as nearly up to date as possible, we have somewhat reduced the political coverage to make room for additional chapters on social and cultural developments. We have also included more on nineteenth century background, more on the progressive movement, and more on the Wilsonian domestic program, while cutting down slightly on the domestic transactions of the 1920's and 1930's. For the post-World War II period we have emphasized foreign policy problems as providing the context in which domestic policies have had to be formulated.

In making this revision we have been greatly aided by many suggestions from those who have used the book in earlier editions. For the interest and help of these friends we wish to express our gratitude.

Oscar Theodore Barck, Jr.
Nelson Manfred Blake

Syracuse University
May, 1958

Contents

Since 1900

1
Looking Backward

The closing years of the nineteenth century and the opening ones of the twentieth were vastly significant in American history. In 1898 the United States abruptly announced its advancement to the rank of a first-class world power by waging war on Spain, liquidating that country's imperial possessions in the Caribbean Sea, and compelling her to cede the Philippine Islands, 8,000 miles across the Pacific from San Francisco. Three years later an assassin's bullet cut short the life of President William McKinley and ended an era in American domestic politics as well. The genial McKinley, like all his predecessors, Republican and Democratic, for thirty years, had been a conservative who believed that the nation's economic life should be subject to as little interference as possible at the hands of government. Theodore Roosevelt, his colorful successor, was sympathetic to new demands which were sweeping the country—demands that government should be more responsive to the popular will and that the state should intervene in economic affairs where necessary to protect the public interest.

Thus were clearly foreshadowed the three themes that were to run through the history of the United States during the next two generations. A people largely indifferent to international politics were to be pushed by men and events into a position of dominating power in world affairs. They were to be compelled not only to defend democracy as a way of government and of life, but to re-examine their own institutions to see whether they squared with the democratic ideal. And finally the American system of capitalism was to be subjected to acid testing. A new generation was to raise the insistent cry that to produce wealth was not enough; a just economic system must provide security

1

as well. Politics were to orient themselves around the rival claims of the parties to foster the economic well-being of the people.

What kind of a nation was the United States in 1900? What was the nature of the legacy handed down to twentieth century Americans from the preceding age?

The Momentum of American Growth

The emergence of the United States as a world power was an inevitable result of its astounding growth. In 1790 the new nation, extending westward to the Mississippi, had contained about 900,000 square miles of territory. By the end of the nineteenth century, the Americans had extended their rule over a vast empire covering 3,738,000 square miles. The population growth had been even more remarkable. In 1790 the United States had less than 4 million inhabitants. By 1860 the population had increased to 31 million. The census of 1900 showed that there were 76 million people in continental United States and some 9 million living under the American flag in outlying territories.

Many factors had contributed to this remarkable record. By conquest, annexation, and purchase the United States had extended its domain over the sparse populations of Louisiana, Florida, Texas, Oregon, California, and New Mexico by 1860. After the Civil War, the imperialist impulse began to find outlet in the annexation of non-contiguous territories. Thus it was that Alaska, Hawaii, Puerto Rico, the Philippines, and various smaller areas had been acquired.

Although by European or Asiatic standards much of the United States was thinly settled in 1900, the rate of American population growth had been extraordinary. For most of its history America had had a rural society wherein early marriages and large families were customary. Yet the rapid increase in population was more directly traceable to large-scale immigration than to any other single factor. That the Americans of 1900 were an immigrant people, a glance at the census figures clearly proved. Over one third of the population was of immediate foreign stock—either foreign-born or of foreign parentage. The rest of the population was descended, almost without exception, from the immigrants of earlier generations. Of the country's 76 million inhabitants, about 66.8 million were descended from white Europeans; some 8.8 million were of African Negro stock; and approximately 115,000 were of Oriental origin. The only truly 100 per cent Americans were some 237,000 Indians, mostly living on their scattered reservations.

For three hundred years this stream of immigration had been flowing to America, but it was not until the middle of the nineteenth century that it reached huge proportions. For thirty years after 1850 foreigners entered the country at the rate of about 250,000 a year; then from 1880 to 1890 the annual average jumped to approximately 400,000. As recently as 1880, about 80 per cent of the foreign-born Americans had come from Germany, Ireland, England, and Canada, but thereafter the proportion of immigrants from these traditional sources declined while more and more newcomers from Italy, Russia, and Austria-Hungary arrived. The so-called new immigration outnumbered the old for the first time in 1896.

As characteristic of America as the entrance of foreigners had been the movement of the population from section to section. Since the days of Jamestown and Plymouth, the frontier had been one of the most persistent influences on American life. After the Civil War came the final great frontier movement, which populated the vast area lying between eastern Kansas and such earlier-settled states as California and Oregon. The lure of gold and silver, abundant pasturage for cattle and sheep, and rich prairie soil attracted miners, cattlemen, sheepherders, and farmers in successive waves that finally erased the frontier line from the census map in 1890. By 1900 the roster of the forty-nine states was almost complete: three states (Idaho, Wyoming, and Utah) had been admitted into the Union during the nineties; only four more (Oklahoma, New Mexico, Arizona, and Alaska) remained to be added in the twentieth century. But the closing of the frontier during the 1890's was more theoretical than real. Much of the West was sparsely settled; there still remained millions of acres of virgin soil to be broken to the plow or of fresh grazing lands to be opened up. With farmers continuing to seek new land, manufacturers moving to promising industrial sites, and the sick and the old seeking sunnier skies, the westward impulse still persisted.

Meanwhile, the nation was being transformed from a predominantly rural country to an urban one. In 1860, 83 per cent of the people had lived in communities of less than 2,500 inhabitants; by 1900 the percentage declined to 60. Urban population increased by over 16 million between 1880 and 1900; rural population by less than 10 million. This disparity of growth resulted from numerous factors, prominent among which were the thronging of immigrants to the cities and the tendency of farmers' sons and daughters to seek employment in the towns. The degree of urbanization was by no means the same throughout the nation. Whereas Rhode Island, Massachusetts, and New York had respectively 95, 91, and 73 per cent of their population living under urban conditions in 1900, Idaho, North Dakota, Oklahoma, Mississippi, and Arkansas were still more than 90 per cent rural. American politics inevitably reflected the conflict between the points of view to which these far different environments gave rise.

Industry's Giant Steps

The most significant events of the period between the Civil War and World War I occurred not in diplomacy or in the halls of Congress, but in the economic sphere. Among the industrial nations of the world, the United States rose from fourth place in 1860 to first place in 1894. Between 1860 and 1899 the value of products manufactured in American factories rose from less than $2 billion annually to more than $11 billion.

Industries that in 1860 had scarcely existed at all grew to husky manhood by the end of the century. In earlier years steel had been made by hand processes, so costly that the product could only be used for fine weapons and tools. The mass-production processes, developed by William Kelly in the United States and by Henry Bessemer in England, were first adopted in this country in 1864 and 1865. These methods made possible the production of steel at a price that opened up hundreds of new uses. Steel railroad locomotives now drew steel cars over steel rails and steel bridges—with great gains in speed and safety over the older iron equipment. Steel armor plate transformed naval vessels; steel girders revolutionized commercial architecture; barbed steel wire provided an ideal fencing material for the treeless prairies and plains; tin-plated steel furnished the cheap containers needed for the preservation of foods. Small wonder that American steel production expanded from less than 69,000 tons in 1870 to over 10 million tons in 1899.

No less remarkable was the growth of the oil industry. In earlier years petroleum had been known only as a disagreeable substance sometimes befouling streams and wells. Except to a few ingenious quacks who bottled it, the stuff seemed to have no value. During the 1850's, however, two revolutionary discoveries had been made. One was that by distilling petroleum, it was possible to manufacture kerosene, a cheap and satisfactory fuel for lamps and lanterns. The other was that by drilling wells, abundant supplies of underground oil could be brought to the surface. Thereafter, events followed rapidly. Drillers and speculators swarmed into the oil districts of western Pennsylvania, and thousands of oil wells were soon in production. These provided the raw product from which a booming refining business evolved in Cleveland, Philadelphia, and other cities. Kerosene lamps soon displaced tallow candles and whale-oil lamps in millions of American homes. By the end of the century, American kerosene was being exported to foreign markets as remote as China. Meanwhile, the value of lubricating oils and other by-products was becoming evident, although the importance of gasoline was scarcely recognized until after 1900.

The harnessing of electricity to a variety of practical uses gave birth to a cluster of closely related industries. The electric telegraph, whose practicability had been demonstrated by Samuel F. B. Morse in 1844, provided an exciting new method of instantaneous communication. As early as 1861 San Francisco had been linked with the rest of the country by telegraph; five years later the first successful trans-Atlantic cable was laid. These seeming miracles were followed by Alexander Graham Bell's patenting of the telephone in 1876 and its rapid extension during the next quarter century. Thomas A. Edison's invention of the incandescent electric lamp in 1880 was followed two years later by the introduction of electric lighting into the homes and offices of downtown New York City. Later in the 1880's the first successful electric streetcars were introduced. So well adapted was this new method of transportation to the needs of the growing cities that there were 850 local streetcar lines in the country by 1895. These multiplying uses of electricity offered great opportunities to manufacturers of generators, motors, and other types of electrical equipment and also to the power companies that supplied current to the public.

The Railroad Age

The rise of the United States to industrial supremacy resulted from the fortunate concurrence of many different factors: abundance of natural resources, political and economic freedom, widespread educational opportunities, common acceptance of the middle-class virtues of thrift and industry, and the accumulation of investment capital. Most important of all, perhaps, was the golden opportunity provided for the manufacturer to buy his raw materials and sell his product in a great national market. In striking contrast to Europe, where national boundaries divided the continent into a score of independent sovereignties separated by tariff walls and other legal barriers, the United States offered a vast market, protected, of course, by its own tariff barriers, extending from the Atlantic Ocean to the Pacific in one direction and from the Canadian border to the Gulf of Mexico in the other.

To move raw materials and finished goods over great distances, the nation depended largely upon the railroads. Although the first few miles of American railroad had been opened in 1830, the new mode of transportation was of minor importance during the next two decades, for the early, locally owned lines operated over short distances only. Differences in track gauge and separate terminals made it necessary for passengers to change trains frequently, while the transfer of freight was slow and costly. The railroad age did not really commence until after 1850, when trunk lines linking one section of the country with another began to operate. After the Civil War the process of consolidating short lines into great systems went steadily forward under the driving leadership of masterful men like "Commodore" Vanderbilt, Tom Scott, and Jay Gould. In the Far West, where railroad construction preceded rather than followed settlement, Federal land grants and loans encouraged the building of the Union Pacific and the other so-called transcontinentals—long systems from the start.

Accompanying the process of consolidation was feverish new construction. In 1865 the United States had only 35,000 miles of track; by 1900 it had 193,000. On the technological side, progress was equally impressive. Steel equipment, new coupling devices, air brakes, and automatic signals added greatly to the safety of the railroads, while the development of sleeping, parlor, and dining cars made travel comfortable and even luxurious for those who could afford extra services.

The railroads gave the nation the tremendous advantages of a continental economy. Massachusetts shoes, New York clothing, and Illinois plows found their way to customers thousands of miles distant. Western cattle raisers and wheat farmers fed the nation and still had a surplus for export. Yet as producers everywhere became dependent upon the railroads, they began to fear the economic power of these great corporations. At first wholly arbitrary in their rate policies, the railroads might discriminate against entire communities, impoverish farmers or other economic groups by excessive charges, or bankrupt small businessmen by special concessions to their larger competitors. Out of this fear arose the demand for government regulation of the railroads that swept the Middle West during the 1870's and 1880's, leading to the enactment of numerous state laws and the first great Federal regulatory measure, the Interstate Commerce Act of 1887. This measure provided for the establishment of the Interstate Commerce Commission, which was empowered to investigate the management of railroads engaged in interstate commerce. Such lines were required to file annual reports of financial operations and adopt a uniform system of bookkeeping. Unfortunately, Commission orders had to be supplemented by court orders, which were seldom granted. Despite these various statutes, abuses in railroad management continued, and the problem of effective government regulation was still urgent in 1900.

The Trust Problem

The growth of big business, first exemplified in the railroad field, was paralleled in many other areas of the American economy. The telegraph business, for example, had a natural tendency toward monopoly. The early situation, with competing lines between cities, resulted in a wasteful duplication of facilities, and the weaker telegraph companies had to go out of business or sell out to their stronger rivals. In this competition the Western Union Telegraph Company steadily forged ahead, thanks particularly to the mutually profitable contracts with the railroads, under which Western Union enjoyed the right to erect poles and wires along railroad rights of way and to have telegraph offices in the railroad stations in return for providing free wire services for train orders. As Western Union came closer and closer to achieving complete monopoly, many farmers' organizations, labor unions, and local trade associations demanded that the Federal government enter the field. Before 1900, some seventy-five bills for the establishment of a government telegraph service had been introduced into Congress and seventeen different investigating committees had recommended such action, but no legislation was passed. Unlike most European countries, the United States left this important means of communication under private

A Dream of Empire. The desire of the trusts to dominate the world.
(By Opper in the *New York Journal*.)

ownership. The telephone business followed a somewhat similar process of evolution. Although there were many small, locally owned telephone companies in various parts of the country, the control of long-distance lines was closely held by the American Telephone and Telegraph Company, a large holding corporation organized around the Bell system in 1900.

In the field of manufacturing, the same degree of monopoly was impossible, but the tendency toward consolidation was nevertheless strong. In 1860, industry was almost exclusively managed through partnerships and small corporations—organizations of modest capital, largely local in influence. By the opening years of the twentieth century the situation was strikingly different. Through giant corporations, a major portion of the national economy had come under the control of relatively small groups of powerful men. To be sure, there continued to be many small businesses; indeed as late as 1914, 88 per cent of the manufacturing establishments of the country were factories or shops with an annual output worth less than $100,000. The remaining 12 per cent, however, employed three quarters of the workers and turned out four fifths of the nation's manufactures.

The most famous example of these consolidation tendencies was provided by the oil industry. In 1863, when John D. Rockefeller entered the refining business in Cleveland, the industry was characterized by hundreds of fiercely competing small businessmen. It was an ideal situation for Rockefeller's particular type of organizing genius. Within five years he had built his refinery into the largest such establishment in the world. In 1870 he established the Standard Oil Company of Ohio and began to buy out his competitors in Cleveland and other cities. By 1882 the Rockefeller combine controlled over 90 per cent of the refining capacity of the country. Many factors contributed to this spectacular achievement. Rockefeller pleased customers by providing a product of dependable quality. He cut his costs at every point through efficient management and the utilization of by-products. Most important of all, through hard and often unscrupulous bargaining with the railroads, he obtained preferential rates his competitors could not match.

While Rockefeller's near monopoly of refining provided the most important example of horizontal combination, Andrew Carnegie was patiently piecing together a vertical integration of the steel industry. During the 1890's—twenty years after Carnegie entered the steel business—the Carnegie Steel Company was obtaining iron ore from its own mines in the rich Mesabi range of Minnesota, carrying it across the Great Lakes in its own steamships, and transporting it from Lake Erie to Pittsburgh on its own railroad. To provide fuel for the blast furnaces, Bessemer converters, and open hearths of its plants in the Pittsburgh suburbs, the Carnegie Company relied on rich coke fields under its control at Connelsville, Pennsylvania. Although Carnegie's share in the nation's steel production was only about two fifths, it was an extraordinarily profitable share —enough to make the one-time Scotch immigrant one of the wealthiest and most powerful men in the United States.

During the 1880's, Americans began to worry over the "trust" problem. The original trust, in the strict sense of the word, was the Standard Oil Trust, organized in 1882 when the stockholders of some forty companies were induced to surrender their stock to nine trustees and accept in its place trust certificates entitling them to share in the profits of the combined operations, but not in their management. Through this device John D. Rockefeller and his fellow-trustees were enabled to rule a huge economic empire. Similar trusts soon appeared in several other lines of business.

This form of organization speedily fell under attack. In 1890 Congress passed the Sherman Antitrust Act, which declared illegal "every contract, combination in the form of trust or otherwise, or conspiracy in restraint of trade" in interstate or foreign commerce. For the next twelve years this Federal law was ineffective because of lax enforcement and narrow interpretation in the courts. But the trust form of organization received more damaging blows in the state courts, where abdication to trustees on the part of the stockholders was ruled to violate corporate charters.

Confronted with these legal setbacks, promoters devised new types of combination, made possible by changes in corporate laws of New Jersey and other states hospitable to big business. In outright consolidations, individual competing companies were merged or amalgamated into a single giant corporation and lost their separate identities. In holding companies, the constituent concerns preserved their separate names and organizations, but were integrated in management by a parent corporation which owned a controlling interest in the stock of each of them.

The word "trust" was now used in a loose sense to describe any industrial combination, whatever its form of organization, that sought to avoid competition by absorbing, controlling, or forcing out of business its competitors, or by acting together with them to fix prices or to regulate output. Absolute monopoly was difficult to achieve and seldom sought. The essential aim was the stabilization of the industry and the maintenance of prices. The trust movement entered its most aggressive phase between 1897 and 1903, when 234 combinations were formed, including such giants as the Standard Oil Company of New Jersey, the American Telephone and Telegraph Company, and the Amalgamated Copper Company. Particularly bold was the organization of the United States Steel Corporation by J. P. Morgan in 1901. The great Carnegie Company was purchased for $400 million; to this were added some nine other large corporations owning mines and manufacturing steel, tubes, wire, tin plate, sheet steel, steel hoops, and bridges—about three fifths of the steel business of the country. The par value of United States Steel's stocks and bonds totaled some $1.4 billion, making it the nation's first billion dollar corporation. Yet since the market value of such securities was less than $800 million, in actuality about half of the capitalization was "water." Such over-capitalization was characteristic of big business methods of the period.

Finance Capitalism

The big corporations dominated American economic life, but who dominated the big corporations? Not, as a usual thing, the experienced steelmaker or the expert in railroad transportation. The era was one of finance capitalism. Money was the lifeblood of the large combinations, and it was the private bankers who had access to the vast funds of accumulated wealth of the nation. The great corporations could not sell their securities without the services of the investment bankers, who took a large part of their compensation in blocks of stock and demanded a leading voice in management to protect their own interests and those of their clients.

To the ordinary American of 1900, the name J. P. Morgan suggested vast, but ill-understood, economic power. Morgan's leadership in his field began in 1860, when he became the New York agent for a London banking house of which his father was a partner. In 1871 the young banker made an advantageous alliance with the Drexel family of Philadelphia, another well-established bank-ing dynasty. After the panic of 1873, when the meteoric career of Jay Cooke ended, the Morgan firm became the strongest banking house in the country. Wealthy Englishmen wishing to invest in American government bonds or other securities gave Morgan much of his early business. In 1879 the New York banker sold a large block of New York Central stock to English investors and accepted a position on the railroad's board of directors to represent the inter-ests of the new holders.

Over the next twenty years, Morgan's influence in the railroad field steadily mounted. The pattern of events was fairly predictable. A railroad company, guilty of reckless financing and overexpansion, would find itself in serious trouble, particularly during depression years. Unable to straighten out its own affairs, the railroad would have to accept a reorganization plan drafted by Morgan. Through painful surgery—a scaling down of bondholder claims, assess-ments against stockholders, and the sale of new securities—the railroad would be saved from liquidation, and the Morgan firm would collect liberal compensa-tion for its services. Moreover, to protect the new investors, Morgan-designated directors would join the boards of the reorganized companies and Morgan-approved executives would be placed in charge of operations.

By 1900 Morgan's influence, in one form or another, was strong in the New

J. P. Morgan, Sr., (with cane) in France. (Brown Bros.)

York Central, the Erie, the New Haven, the Reading, the Norfolk and Western, the Lehigh Valley, and the Southern Railway System. In alliance with James J. Hill, Morgan's power extended into the affairs of the Great Northern, the Northern Pacific, and the Baltimore and Ohio.

During the 1890's Morgan also became a key figure in the consolidation of industry. For several years before he achieved his masterpiece of corporate architecture in the United States Steel Corporation, he had been active in organizing holding companies like the Federal Steel Company, the National Tube Company, and the American Bridge Company. The House of Morgan undertook to sell the securities and mobilize the capital needed for these new ventures; inevitably, therefore, it became a powerful voice in the management of the companies.

Although Morgan was the most famous banker in the country, he was not the only man in his field any more than Rockefeller and Carnegie were in theirs. Such banking houses as Lee, Higginson & Company of Boston, and Kuhn, Loeb & Company of New York were private firms of great prestige, while commercial banks like the First National Bank and the National City Bank of New York were also deeply involved in the growth of finance capitalism.

Whether big business and finance capitalism were regarded as good or bad depended on the point of view. The large corporations were usually able to produce more efficiently. The standardization of products and the frequent lowering of their prices[1] raised the standard of living for the whole population. Banker control was often a conservative, rationalizing influence. Despite all this, millions of Americans were uneasy in the realization that so much power rested in so few hands. Farmers, workers, consumers, and small businessmen shared this fear and looked increasingly to the government to bring these giants under some control.

The Lot of the Worker

By comparison with Europe, where conditions admittedly were not so favorable, the United States was a land of good wages and advantageous working conditions. Opportunities for employment in American mines and factories appeared sufficiently attractive to draw millions of immigrants from Europe and even to tap the rural population of the United States itself. By present-day standards, however, the workers' share in American prosperity was a modest one. Hours were long: blast furnace laborers in the steel mills worked 84 hours a week; most factory employees were at their jobs 60 hours a week; and even the relatively fortunate construction workers put in a 48-hour week. Wages were low; one careful estimate is that the average annual earnings of all employed workers (excluding farm laborers) in 1900 was only $490—comparable to perhaps $2,000 in today's prices.

Throughout the nineteenth century the wage earners had made sporadic efforts to improve their position by forming unions and attempting strikes and boycotts. But labor's attempts to organize had been subject to many setbacks. Every period of economic boom brought a mushroom crop of local unions; every serious depression killed off all but the hardiest of these as the workers competed frantically for the few available jobs. The labor movement also suffered through confusion as to ends and means. Middle-class reformers sought working-class support for a variety of panaceas—utopian communities, producers' cooperatives, hard money, workingmen's parties, and the like.

After the Civil War, labor demonstrated increasing restlessness, but still had

[1] Sometimes the formation of combinations resulted in higher prices. For example, United States Steel set and maintained a $28 a ton price on steel rails, which was $10 higher than the competitive price in the late 1890's.

difficulty in establishing stable organization. The National Labor Union enrolled an impressive membership around 1870, but then was shattered by a bungling attempt to establish a third party. The Knights of Labor claimed 700,000 members in 1886 and appeared to have achieved a stronger position than any preceding American labor organization. In the wave of strikes that resulted from this growth, however, the Knights revealed unsuspected weaknesses. Having enrolled a heterogeneous company of skilled and unskilled workers, farmers, physicians, small businessmen, feminists, and miscellaneous reformers, the Knights had neither the financial reserves nor the singleness of purpose necessary to impose the principle of collective bargaining upon militant employers. The Haymarket Square bombing (1886), for which the Knights were wrongly held responsible by many Americans, was another important factor in the decline of the organization.

The organizing genius who led American labor out of this wilderness of frustration was Samuel Gompers. Himself a skilled cigarmaker, Gompers believed that permanent organization could only be built upon the foundation of the many local craft unions that had grown up in the country despite the vicissitudes of national organization. His first attempt to federate these bodies in 1881 was not very successful. He persisted, however, and in 1886 the American Federation of Labor was established on a basis destined to be permanent. President of the AFL every year except one until his death in 1924, Gompers formulated the philosophy of "pure and simple unionism" that came to dominate all but a small segment of the American labor movement. He was uncompromising in his assertion of labor's right to organize—and, when necessary, to strike—in order to obtain higher wages, shorter hours, and better working conditions. By other standards, however, his leadership was conservative. Gompers advocated organization along the lines of skilled crafts, a procedure that proved to be impossible for many of the mass-production industries. Unlike most European labor leaders, he was completely hostile to socialism. He opposed, moreover, the formation of an independent labor party, preferring that the Federation limit its political activities to endorsing or refusing to endorse candidates of the established parties. In seeking legislation, Gompers was also cautious because he feared making labor's position too dependent on government. The AFL dominated the organized labor field by 1900; of the 800,000 union members in that year, some 550,000 were part of the AFL.

The leadership of Gompers was not accepted in all quarters. The railroad employees, for example, maintained the independence of their own prosperous and powerful Brotherhoods, while on the left of the labor movement were numerous small radical organizations.

Despite Gompers' achievement, the American labor movement was weak in comparison with its European counterparts. How did it happen that in a highly industrial nation, where perhaps 15 million persons were working for wages in non-agricultural jobs, only 800,000 were organized for collective bargaining? Or that the number of union members was only slightly higher than at the end of the Civil War despite a doubled national population? In part, the answer lies in Gompers' preference for organization along trade lines. Except for a few industrial unions like the coal miners' and brewers', the AFL had all its strength in occupations where the old tradition of craftsmanship still persisted, such as the building trades, the printing trades, and the metal industries. In the great mass-production industries like steel or textiles, where the bulk of the employees were unskilled or semiskilled workers, the unions were either non-existent or impotent.

Other fundamental factors had handicapped the American labor movement. In many parts of Europe there was a more or less stable working class, composed of men who spent their whole lives in their jobs and whose children expected to do the same. Such men fitted well into the Marxian concept of an industrial proletariat and were easily organized for militant action. But the American labor force had different characteristics. Many native-born workers were fresh from American farms and villages; the more ambitious were likely to work themselves up to the rank of foreman or superintendent; the less successful would sometimes drift back to the rural environment whence they had come. Enjoying this mobility, the native workers rarely thought of themselves as permanent members of the toiling masses. On the other hand, foreign-born wage earners were likely to accept meekly whatever conditions of employment were offered them and to turn an indifferent ear to the union organizer.[2] The proportion of these recent immigrants among the workers in Pennsylvania coal mines, Pittsburgh steel plants, and New England textile mills was very high in 1900; indeed, many employers deliberately preferred the newcomers as even less apt to make trouble than the older groups. Any American factory was likely to contain a miscellaneous collection of employees, each feeling more kinship with others of his own nationality group than with the working class as a whole.

Still another formidable obstacle to the growth of labor unions was the dominant American philosophy of individualism. Employers argued that labor relations should be based on what they called "freedom of contract." They offered terms of employment to prospective employees, and the latter were free as individuals to accept or reject the proferred conditions. From the worker's point of view, this freedom of contract was a fiction. Employers and individual employees were hardly on an equal basis, since the industrialist who employed men by the hundreds could offer terms on a take-it-or-leave-it basis, while the em-

---

[2] However, John Mitchell of the United Mine Workers asserted that he found it easier to organize immigrants than native Americans in southern Illinois.

ployee—particularly in a company town where there was a single great industry —had to accept these terms or allow his family to go hungry. Yet strong though the logical case for collective bargaining was, most employers refused to concede its justice. They strongly opposed both labor unions that attempted to bargain for groups of employees and social reformers who sought to have working conditions regulated by law.

The prevailing faith in individualism assured the employer that most middle-class Americans would share his prejudice against unionism. The "walking delegate" or professional labor leader was regarded as nothing but a trouble-maker, and strikes, picket lines, and boycotts were condemned as threats to private property and public order. Government's intervention in labor disputes was almost invariably on the side of management. When President Cleveland helped to break the Pullman strike of 1894 with Federal court injunctions, the arrest and imprisonment of Eugene V. Debs and other strike leaders, and the use of Federal troops, his one-sided action won wide applause from the general public. Middle-class opinion was not yet ready to accept the labor unions as truly respectable institutions.

Problems of Agriculture

Changes in agriculture between 1861 and 1900 were scarcely less revolutionary than in transportation and industry. In an age of railroads, steamships, and cities, the farmer no longer thought primarily in terms of feeding and clothing his family from the produce of his own acres. Agriculture became increasingly commercial, with the farmer devoting most of his energy to the production of staples for distant markets while he purchased goods for his family at nearby stores or from mail-order houses. The new agriculture demanded new methods. To grow wheat or corn in profitable volume, the farmer needed many acres of land and horse-drawn harvesters and other machines. Most Middle-Western farmers went heavily into debt during and after the Civil War, to buy land and equipment. Although the growing of cotton in the South was not mechanized in anything like the same degree, the Southern farmer also struggled with the problem of debt. Thousands regularly mortgaged their crops to country merchants in exchange for seed and provisions.

The large volume of agricultural debt made American farmers particularly resentful of falling prices. Unfortunately for the rural population, the general trend of agricultural prices after the Civil War was downward, with especially serious declines during the priods 1872–1878 and 1887–1896. Many factors contributed to this situation. Because of increased acreage and mechanized methods, the supply of agricultural commodities expanded more rapidly than the market for them. In the world market, moreover, American farmers came into increasing competition with the producers of Russia, Argentina, Australia, and other countries.

In their own analysis of their difficulties, American farmers placed the principal blame on the businessmen with whom they dealt. They accused the railroads of fixing unfair rates, manufacturers of exacting monopolistic prices, middlemen of excessive handling charges, land speculators of controlling the best acreage, and bankers of usurious interest rates. Equally condemned were the state and Federal governments, whose monetary and fiscal policies were believed to favor bankers and industrialists while penalizing workers and farmers. In spite of criticism from many quarters, there was considerable truth in their analysis.

More than once during these years of agrarian discontent the farmers attempted concerted action to improve their lot. During the 1870's, thousands joined the Patrons of Husbandry, popularly called the Grange. Through group purchasing and the establishment of cooperatives, the Grangers attempted to free themselves from dependence on established merchants and middlemen. The aroused farmers even tried to manufacture machinery and tools in their own factories. Most of the ventures failed, but they partly served their purpose by scaring businessmen into treating their rural customers more fairly. Meantime, a number of "Granger" political parties sprang up in the Middle West, where they succeeded in obtaining state laws regulating railroad rates. This moment of power was brief. The railroads soon secured repeal of most of the regulatory laws, but the precedent of policing business in the public interest was of prime importance for the future, as indicated by the passage of the Interstate Commerce Act in 1887.

Although better times in the early 1880's temporarily quieted agrarian agitation, the widespread agricultural depression of 1887–1896 resulted in new and stronger movements of protest. The Farmers' Alliances established cooperatives and agitated for a broad program of government intervention to curb land speculation, nationalize the railroads, and provide more money and easier credit for farmers. Entering politics, these farmers' organizations won numerous local victories in the Middle West and the South, although their attempts on the national level, both under the Populist banner in 1892 and under the Democratic party label in 1896, failed. After the excitement of Bryan's Free Silver campaign had died down, the agrarian ferment largely subsided. Business conditions improved, and attention was diverted from economic issues to war with Spain and the acquisition of a colonial empire. The larger quantity of money demanded and, in fact, needed by the farmers was partly met by new discoveries of gold. By 1900 agriculture was entering a happier period of good crops and gradually rising prices.

The fundamental agricultural problem, however, still remained unsolved.

The farmer was an individualist, who confidently believed that hard work and investment in more land and equipment would assure greater income. Yet the very energy with which millions of farmers sought to increase their output threatened to destroy their security. Again and again during the twentieth century American agriculture was destined to produce more than the world market could absorb at profitable prices. The precariousness of the farmer's position was increased by the rising cost of the things he had to purchase and heavier taxes and interest charges. The farm problem became a perennial political issue, as some legislators of both parties struggled to obtain measures that would help the farmer to borrow money on better terms, maintain prices on staple crops, and control production.

The Dominance of Laissez Faire

Ideas exert an influence in history perhaps no less compelling than material circumstances. As Americans in the twentieth century confronted the perplexing problems arising out of the growth of big business and mechanized agriculture, their beliefs about how government ought to deal with these issues were powerfully shaped by traditional patterns of thought.

Americans inherited a dislike for too much government. The tall figure of Thomas Jefferson still cast a long shadow. In his inaugural address in 1801, the third President had argued that American happiness and prosperity depended upon "a wise and frugal Government, which shall restrain men from injuring one another, shall leave them otherwise free to regulate their own pursuits of industry and improvement, and shall not take from the mouth of labor the bread it has earned." Jefferson had been particularly insistent that the national government should restrict its activities to an essential minimum, leaving primary responsibility for internal affairs to the states. Though the Democratic party under Bryan in 1896 had asked for such departures from laissez faire as regulation of the railroads and telegraph and manipulation of the currency, in 1900 it still claimed Jefferson as its patron saint.

This Jeffersonian philosophy had from the beginning been challenged by another point of view, first articulated by the brilliant Alexander Hamilton and maintained with more or less consistency by the Federalists, the Whigs, and the Republicans. Less fearful of government and more nationalistic, the Hamiltonian tradition had favored positive Federal action to promote economic prosperity.

After the Civil War the dominant business classes skillfully extracted what was most useful to their interests from both the Jeffersonian and Hamiltonian traditions. In their opposition to government regulation of economic affairs, business leaders could cite the warnings of Jefferson, while in their requests for protective tariffs, land grants to railroads, and government loans they could quote Hamilton. The orthodox philosophy was one of laissez faire, that is, a hands-off policy by government which would allow businessmen a maximum of liberty to run their own affairs—but it was a strictly American version of laissez faire with ample leeway for business to get what positive government assistance it could. To put this American version another way, the business leaders scrupulously preserved laissez faire for the farmers and the workers, while they tried to avoid its perils by private consolidations and government assistance.

The traditional Jeffersonian argument for laissez faire was powerfully buttressed during the 1880's and 1890's by a vein of thought known as Social Darwinism. Social evolution was depicted as resulting from a struggle for existence among fiercely competing individuals. In this contest, the strong and efficient won out; the weak and inefficient fell by the wayside; only thus could progress be achieved. Legislation to hamper the strong or to the help the weak was, therefore, both futile and harmful. Wise statesmanship should permit a maximum of individual liberty, restricting the function of government to the protection of lives and property and the enforcement of contracts.

Conservative—or so-called "hard"—Social Darwinism received its first persuasive statement in the works of Herbert Spencer, an English philosopher with an amazingly large American following. The American writer who stated the case most forcefully was William Graham Sumner, famous Yale professor, who rebuked all projects for social reform that involved limiting the liberty of the rich in order to equalize the opportunities of the poor. "Let it be understood," said Sumner, "that we cannot go outside of this alternative: liberty, inequality, survival of the fittest; not liberty, equality, survival of the unfittest. The former carries society forward and favors all its best members; the latter carries society downwards and favors all its worst members." As a consistent Social Darwinist, Sumner also condemned the tariff with its indirect subsidy of business. Overlooking this aspect, successful captains of industry like Andrew Carnegie and John D. Rockefeller eagerly proclaimed the Social Darwinist philosophy.

Still a third support for laissez faire was to be found in the traditional social values preached from Protestant pulpits. Since the days of John Calvin, most Protestants had emphasized a doctrine of extreme individualism. Each man had the moral obligation to work hard in his chosen occupation or "calling," to save his money, and to abstain from waste or luxury. The rich man was assumed to have been blessed by God with rewards appropriate to his superior industry and thrift; the poor man suffered the consequences of his own laziness and lack of foresight. To Americans schooled in these simple precepts, the idea that government had a responsibility to protect the poor from exploitation and to restrain the rich from using their power unjustly seemed almost impious.

Challenges to Laissez Faire

Strongly entrenched though the philosophy of laissez faire appeared to be, it was under attack during the 1880's and 1890's on both the popular and intellectual fronts. Grangers and Populists demanded government intervention to regulate the railroads and other powerful businesses with which the farmers had to deal. Sumner's hard Social Darwinism was countered with the soft, or liberal, Social Darwinism of thinkers like Lester Frank Ward, who emphasized the idea that men could use their intelligence to direct social evolution toward definite goals. Ward repudiated laissez faire and argued for a program of bold government action to promote the general welfare.

The philosophy of pragmatism, given its first persuasive statement by William James, was destined to erode many of the piers upon which laissez faire and other orthodoxies rested. Pragmatism rejected the idea of a single, absolute truth. All ideas, according to James, must be tested by their practical results. In its origins, pragmatism supported extreme individualism, but in the hands of John Dewey the new philosophy became an instrument of social criticism and an encouragement to social experimentation.

In provoking Americans to consider whether there might not be serious flaws in the existing social system and whether government might not be utilized to remedy these flaws, two writers of the late nineteenth century were particularly important. In *Progress and Poverty* (1879), Henry George dealt with the paradox of the increasing want that accompanied increasing wealth. He found the cause in the private ownership of land—the natural resource to which all men ought to have equal right as they had to air and sunlight. As the remedy, he advocated the so-called "single tax," a levy to take away from the landlord for the benefit of society the increase in the value of land that was created by no labor of its owner, but arose through the growth of cities, proximity to markets, or the discovery of mineral resources. The collection of this single tax, George maintained, would obviate the need for tariffs or taxes on the products of human labor. It would destroy monopoly, speculation, inflation, and depressions. Even those who regarded George's remedy as oversimple found his graphic description of the inequalities of American life profoundly moving.

Similarly provocative of thought and discussion was Edward Bellamy's *Looking Backward, 2000–1887* (1888). This fascinating novel contrasted the injustices of contemporary society with an Utopian America of the year 2000, where all industry was merged into one great trust or national syndicate. Everyone had a job; no one was permitted to live off the labor of others. Repudiating the ideas of class struggle and proletarian dictatorship, Bellamy made socialism appear respectable to many middle-class idealists who shied away from the more ruthless aspects of Marxism.

Meanwhile, certain religious leaders were taking an increasingly serious interest in social issues. During the 1880's, Washington Gladden, pastor of a Congregational church in Columbus, Ohio, began to attract attention by defending labor's right to organize and strike and characterizing John D. Rockefeller's fortune as "tainted money." Gladden advocated a more Christian social order based upon cooperation rather than competition. In 1889 the Reverend W. D. P. Bliss, an Episcopalian, founded a Society of Christian Socialists, and in 1892 Bishop F. D. Huntington of the Episcopal Church, became president of the Christian Social Union. Also in 1892 Walter Rauschenbusch, a minister of the German Baptist denomination, organized the Brotherhood of the Kingdom, a group committed to the belief that the Kingdom of God was to be achieved in this world rather than in the next. As yet the Social Gospel movement was only in its incipient stages, but the new demand for a more Christian social order had great significance for the future.

Within the Roman Catholic Church a somewhat similiar reorientation was in progress. Cardinal Gibbons, the leading American churchman, was a moderate on social issues, quietly combatting the influence of more conservative Church leaders who condemned all projects for social change. The famous encyclical *Rerum Novarum*, issued by Pope Leo XIII in 1891, balanced its condemnation of socialism with criticism of the evils of unregulated capitalism. The Pope appealed for a Christian social order and a living wage for all workers.

On the eve of the twentieth century the United States was a rapidly expanding nation with a proud record of growth and bright prospects for the future. Since the Civil War the American economy had undergone tremendous changes that had greatly increased national wealth. But the process of expansion had brought troublesome problems that the new generation would have to face. The older philosophy of laissez faire taught that, left alone, economic maladjustments would be self-correcting; government intervention could only make matters worse. The newer lines of thought pointed toward different conclusions. In a democracy, it was argued, the people had every right to use their government as an instrument to protect the public interest and to promote with positive measures the general welfare.

2
The Passion for Reform

From 1901 to 1917 center stage in American politics was increasingly domi-nated by what became known as the progressive movement. Theodore Roose-velt and progressivism became synonymous to millions of Americans, but in reality the progressive movement was something older and bigger than the popular President. On almost every level of life a ferment was at work that found its outlet in a demand for reforming whatever seemed corrupt and unjust in American government and economic life.

Business and Politics

During the presidency of William McKinley, the millionaire Ohio industri-alist Mark Hanna played the role of national Republican boss and kept the Federal government safely quarantined from the contagion of crusading reform. Hanna's prominence in national politics dramatized a situation that was far from new. Since the Civil War, businessmen had exerted a dominant influence over both state and national government. This was in contrast to the pre-Civil War situation in which the agrarian interests had usually been para-mount.

The shift in power, which mirrored new economic developments, was has-tened by the Civil War. Taking advantage of the absence of legislators from the agricultural South, Republicans from the Northeast and the Middle West had enacted a series of laws that benefited business. The low-tariff policy pre-vailing since 1846 was reversed, and high protection was extended to Northern industry. By purchasing government bonds with depreciated wartime currency,

Northern investors assured themselves a profitable return for many years to come. In thousands of communities, local businessmen obtained charters under the National Banking Act of 1864 empowering them to engage in banking and to issue bank notes upon the security of their government bonds. Railroad promoters, moreover, profited greatly from Congressional generosity in the form of land subsidies and loans for new construction.

With the end of the Civil War, the business interests felt some uneasiness lest a premature revival of the Democratic party should endanger their gains. Radical Reconstruction policies, however, kept at least a part of the South under Republican dominance until the last Federal troops were withdrawn in 1877. Thereafter resentful Dixie voted solidly Democratic for many years. This development weakened Republican control of the national government, but did not destroy it. The balance of power was closest in the House of Representatives. During the thirty-six years between 1865 and 1901, the Republicans controlled the House twenty years and the Democrats sixteen. Republicans sat in the White House twenty-eight of these thirty-six years; they controlled the Senate thirty-two of them. Yet the political distinction between the two parties was misleading. There was during these years considerable cooperation between Southern Democratic conservatives and Republicans in Congress. Furthermore, the northern wing of the Democratic party was dominated throughout most of this period by conservatives like Tilden and Cleveland. As a result, Republican legislative policies were in the main secure until the end of the century.

Obviously, Republican success was based on something more than alliance with the business interests and the tenuous cooperation of conservative Democrats. The party was usually supported by the farmers of the East and Middle West, grateful for Republican-sponsored homestead legislation, land grants for the support of agricultural colleges, and creation of the Department of Agriculture. The labor vote was divided, but the Republicans convinced a substantial proportion of the industrial workers that a high protective tariff was their guarantee of high wages and "a full dinner pail." Probably a majority of the voters of every class were politically regular, casting their ballots for the party that had always held the loyalty of the family. The Democrats could thus depend upon many groups in the large cities of the North—particularly those of recent immigrant origin. Similarly, millions of Northern and Midwestern families were traditionally Republican—still loyal to the "Grand Old Party" that had saved the Union. Veterans of the Union army were particularly likely to be vociferous Republicans and received their rewards in generous pensions.

Prominent in both Republican and Democratic party circles were the political bosses. These experienced politicians obtained campaign gifts from corporations and wealthy individuals and levied assessments upon public employees. By manipulating the machinery of nomination, they saw to it that none but "safe" men became candidates for public office. Party regularity demanded that legislators vote for or against bills as the bosses commanded. Governors were expected to give jobs to faithful party workers. Describing the situation in New York, Elihu Root once said:

> They call the system—I do not coin the phrase, I adopt it because it carries its own meaning—the system they call "invisible government." For I do not remember how many years, Mr. Conkling was the supreme ruler in this state; the governor did not count; the legislators did not count; comptrollers and secretaries of state and what not, did not count. . . . Then Mr. Platt ruled the state; for nigh upon twenty years he ruled it. It was not the governor; it was not the legislature; it was not any elected officers; it was Mr. Platt. . . . The ruler of the state during the greater part of the forty years of my acquaintance with the state government has not been any man authorized by the constitution or by the law.

The state bosses exercised much influence over the Federal government as well. Their particular citadel was the Senate—until 1913 elected by the state legislatures rather than directly by the people. Such bosses as Roscoe Conkling, Thomas C. Platt, and David B. Hill of New York, and Matthew Quay and Boies Penrose of Pennsylvania sat in the Senate themselves, while many of their fellow-Senators were wealthy men enjoying this reward for generous campaign contributions. As members of the Upper House, the bosses and their lieutenants not only exercised a veto on unwanted legislation, but used their power to control the Federal patronage. Through the device of "Senatorial courtesy," the Senate refused to confirm presidential appointments unless they were acceptable to the Senator from the state concerned. Also useful to the bosses in curbing excessive independence in the White House was the institution of national party conventions. Politicians controlling large blocs of votes exerted their influence to name candidates for President respectable enough to get elected, but not so independent as to challenge the party machines. In the House of Representatives, the dictatorial rule of speakers like "Czar" Reed and "Uncle Joe" Cannon speedily schooled Congressmen in the virtues of party regularity and the perils of insurgency.

So long as political machines did not overreach themselves and engage in crude graft that raised taxes and antagonized the voters, many businessmen welcomed their existence. To the boss the businessman made his campaign contribution; to the boss he went when he wanted some law enacted, or—as more frequently happened—when he wished some legislative proposal defeated. All proposals for regulating rates or wages, for fixing maximum hours, or for compulsory arbitration of labor disputes were opposed as unsound interference with natural economic laws. On the other hand, businessmen never allowed their laissez-faire principles to inhibit them in seeking from government such positive aids as protective tariff duties, land grants, and franchises.

Practical politicians had to temper their ardor for the business interest with occasional concessions to other groups. Thus the farmers' demand for more money resulted in such mildly inflationary laws as the Bland-Allison Act of 1878 and the Sherman Silver Purchase Act of 1890. Similarly, widespread indignation over the spoils system led to the Pendleton Act of 1883, authorizing the establishment of a merit system in the Federal civil service, while the protests of farmers and small businessmen brought about the passage of the Interstate Commerce Act in 1887 and the Sherman Antitrust Act in 1890.

Such concessions as these were only small breaches in the conservative dike. The silver purchase laws fell far short of the wholesale issuance of greenbacks and the free coinage of silver demanded by Western inflationists. The Federal civil service system was dependent upon presidential action for its implementation and still left much patronage under the control of the political leaders. The powers of the Interstate Commerce Commission were so circumscribed that shippers found themselves without adequate remedy against the unfair rates and other forms of discrimination still practiced by the railroads. At the same time, the Sherman Act became almost a dead letter through the unwillingness of the Attorneys General to initiate suits and the narrow interpretations given the law by the courts. In United States v. E. C. Knight Company, *et al.* (1895), a case arising out of the formation of a trust controlling some 95 per cent of the country's sugar production, the Supreme Court ruled that a monopoly in manufacturing was not conspiracy in restraint of trade within the meaning of the Sherman Act. Later decisions of the nineties, while upholding the Act, did so in terms that encouraged lawyers to believe that industrial holding companies would not be disturbed.

Indeed, the conservatism of state and Federal courts proved to be one of the most important lines of defense against legislation unwanted by the businessmen. The Fourteenth Amendment to the Federal Constitution provided somewhat uncertain protection to Negroes against discrimination, but it was interpreted to give corporations immunity from many types of "unreasonable" regulation of their rates and labor relations. Similarly, the Sherman Act, although ineffective in breaking up trusts, proved a useful weapon for prosecuting leaders of strikes and boycotts for "conspiracy in restraint of trade." In one of the most controversial decisions in its history (Pollock v. Farmers' Loan and Trust Company), the Supreme Court in 1895 held a Federal income tax to be unconstitutional.

Industrialists were deeply disturbed by President Grover Cleveland's campaign to reduce the tariff, but they were not greatly injured because the Democratic Wilson-Gorman Tariff of 1894 incorporated no consistent policy, and was not long on the books in any case. Except on the tariff issue, moreover, business-men had no reason to complain of Cleveland's policies. As conservative as any of his Republican predecessors, the New York Democrat fought staunchly for the gold standard and broke the Pullman strike with Federal troops and in-junctions.

The defeat of William Jennings Bryan in the free silver campaign of 1896 and the election of William McKinley appeared to complete the capture of the Federal government by the business interests. The great victory was widely attributed to the shrewd generalship of Mark Hanna, who had adopted McKin-ley as his political protégé. Hanna had many admirable qualities. He was intelligent, honest—within the standards of his day—loyal, and more sympa-thetic to organized labor than most contemporary businessmen. These sides of Hanna's character, however, were largely unknown. Cartoonists portrayed him as a heavily jowled figure wearing a suit covered with dollar signs—the embodi-ment of predatory big business. Unfair though this was, it remained true that industrialists and financiers had good reason to rejoice in the McKinley-Hanna regime. The Dingley Tariff of 1897 was a return to the doctrine of high protec-tion; the Gold Standard Act of 1900 seemed to settle the troublesome monetary issue; the Spanish-American War distracted public attention from domestic problems, provided some short but exciting campaigns, and opened up new markets. Best of all, the period of hard times appeared to have ended in a new wave of prosperity and economic advance.

The Rising Tide of Protest

Although business appeared to be firmly in the saddle of government, it was in reality insecurely mounted. For three decades there had been rising dis-content with certain aspects of American political and economic life. During the late sixties and seventies, resentment against conservative control of the two major parties led to attempts to organize third-party movements. "Granger" parties gained power in some Middle-Western states and passed regulatory laws in the interests of the farmers. "Greenback" and "Greenback-Labor" candi-dates for President were nominated in 1876, 1880, and 1884. Although they attempted to win the support of both Eastern workers and Western farmers, their vote was usually small. In 1878, however, the soft-money men polled a million ballots and sent fifteen representatives to Congress.

Henry George and Edward Bellamy, whose intellectual influence has been stressed in the preceding chapter, had an impact on politics as well. In 1886 George ran for mayor of New York City on a third-party ticket supported by many labor union leaders and middle-class reformers. Alarmed by this threat, Tammany Hall nominated Abram Hewitt, an unusually able and respectable businessman, but even so the election was exciting and close. Hewitt won by a narrow margin, with George second, and the youthful Theodore Roosevelt the Republican candidate, a poor third. A decade later, in 1897, Henry George again ran for the New York mayoralty, but died before the election. No comparable personal movement gathered around Bellamy, but during the period when *Looking Backward* reached the height of its popularity, hundreds of local Bellamy or Nationalist clubs were founded to agitate for Bellamy's ideas.

Meanwhile, agricultural hard times had resulted in the Farmers' Alliance movement. After their encouraging successes at the state level in 1890, the agrarians entered the field of national politics in the election of 1892 when the People's party, better known as the "Populists," was organized. The Populist platform was a challenging document.

> Corruption [said the preamble] dominates the ballot-box, the Legislatures, the Congress, and touches even the ermine of the bench. . . . The newspapers are largely subsidized or muzzled, public opinion silenced, business prostrated, homes covered with mortgages, labor impoverished, and the land concentrating in the hands of the capitalists. . . . The fruits of the toil of millions are boldly stolen to build up colossal fortunes for a few, unprecedented in the history of mankind; and the possessors of these, in turn, despise the Republic and endanger liberty. From the same prolific womb of governmental injustice, we breed the two great classes—tramps and millionaires.

To fight these evils, the Populists demanded the issuance of more money (both paper and silver), a graduated income tax, government ownership of railroads and telegraph, conservation of the national domain, a "subtreasury" plan for farmers, restriction of immigration, election of Senators by direct vote of the people, adoption of the initiative and referendum, and use of the secret ballot. James B. Weaver, the Populist candidate for President, received more than a million popular votes and twenty-two electoral ballots. This impressive gesture of protest would have been greater still if the industrial workers had given wholehearted support to the movement.

In 1896 agrarian radicals captured the Democratic party. William Jennings Bryan made a spirited campaign for the presidency on a platform that incorporated many of the Populist demands of 1892, although it subordinated all other planks to the demand for unlimited coinage of silver. Despite sweeping victories in the West and South, Bryan went down to defeat, and the revolt of the farmers subsided during the ensuing period of prosperity. Although free silver was dead as a political issue, a vestige of Populism survived. The farmers had been imbued with fear of corporate wealth and monopoly, and this fear of big business was destined to be one of the principal ingredients in the progressive movement after 1900.

The citadels of American capitalism were being vigorously assaulted from

William Jennings Bryan. (Brown Bros.)

another direction as well. For decades a few Americans had been familiar with the teachings of Karl Marx. During the 1860's a segment of the American labor movement associated itself with the short-lived First International, and local socialist groups were formed in various parts of the country. In 1877 the latter were merged into a national organization, the Socialist Labor party—at first more a propagandist group than a political party. From 1900 to 1914 the Socialist Labor faction was dominated by the brilliant Daniel DeLeon. Opposing all halfway measures, DeLeon demanded a proletarian revolution aimed at the "unconditional surrender of capitalism." His militancy and hostility to the established labor union movement repelled all but a small faction of fanatics.

More moderate was the program of the rival Socialist party, organized by Eugene V. Debs and others in 1901. Debs, a familiar figure through his leadership of the workers in the Pullman strike of 1894, became a convert to socialism through reading Marx, Bellamy, and other authors during his prison term. A sincere and eloquent Middle-Westerner, Debs was well equipped to present socialism in a way that largely cleared it of the taint of foreign ideology. As presidential candidate of his party, Debs' popular vote steadily increased from 95,000 in 1900 to 900,000 in 1912.[1]

By other standards also, the Socialists seemed to be making themselves an important force in American life. Victor Berger, who had helped found the

[1] In 1900 Debs ran as the candidate of the Social Democratic party, founded in 1898 and superseded in 1901 by the more broadly based Socialist party.

party, was sent to Congress as representative from Wisconsin; a Socialist mayor, Emil Seidel, was elected in Milwaukee. Many Socialist periodicals were published, and there was a large Socialist faction within the American Federation of Labor.

Although the ultimate goal of the Socialists was the establishment of a co-operative commonwealth, they presented a series of immediate demands that were in reality only an advanced brand of Populism. In addition to public ownership of railroads, public utilities, and mines, they sought government relief for the unemployed, a shorter work week, abolition of child labor, social security legislation, income and inheritance taxes, equal suffrage, initiative and referendum, proportional representation, and abolition of the Supreme Court's power to pass upon the constitutionality of legislation.

While never more than a minority of Americans called themselves Socialists, the followers of Debs, like the Populists, helped to educate the American public to the idea that government should intervene in American economic life to promote social justice.

The Muckrakers

Grangers, Greenbackers, Single-Taxers, Bellamyites, Populists, and Socialists all challenged the conservative control of government. Despite their vigor, however, these groups were indisputably minority movements, regarded by general middle-class opinion as visionary and dangerous. What was chiefly to distinguish progressivism from these earlier manifestations of protest was its broad appeal—its respectability in the eyes of a majority of the people.

After 1900, the reform movement gained much of its impetus from the activities of a talented group of writers generally known as the "muckrakers." This label was intended to convey a rebuke when it was applied to these authors by President Theodore Roosevelt in 1906, and the more irresponsible among them, who placed sensation above facts, may have deserved such condemnation. The more important muckrakers, however, were scrupulously honest and thorough in their research. They painted a dark picture of contemporary political and economic life only because they had discovered unpleasant truths.

The earliest of the great exposures appeared in *McClure's Magazine*. Eager to increase the circulation of this popularly priced periodical, S. S. McClure, its publisher, employed the most capable journalists he could find and advanced thousands of dollars for their investigations. In October, 1902, appeared the first of Lincoln Steffens' revealing articles on municipal corruption. St. Louis, Minneapolis, Philadelphia—one city after another provided shocking case studies for what the author called *The Shame of the Cities*. Only a month after the first Steffens article, *McClure's* began the publication of Ida M. Tarbell's *History of the Standard Oil Company*—a muckraking classic based upon five years of patient research into the devious transactions that had built up that great monopoly. In Ray Stannard Baker, McClure discovered still another talented fact-finder who wrote such effective articles as *The Right to Work*, a study of labor relations, and *The Railroads on Trial*, which explored the rate problem.

Other magazines soon followed *McClure's* lead. *Everybody's Magazine* created a sensation in 1904 with the publication of *Frenzied Finance*, in which Thomas W. Lawson revealed how stockmarket operators like himself gambled with the savings of others The next year the same magazine published Charles Edward Russell's exposé of the meat industry, *The Greatest Trust in the World*. *Collier's* most notable muckraking series was Samuel Hopkins Adams' *The Great American Fraud*, which revealed how patent medicine manufacturers cheated and poisoned their credulous customers. Most sensational of all was the publication in Hearst's *Cosmopolitan* of David Graham Phillips' *The Treason of the Senate*—an exposé of the close ties between well-known legislators and the vested interests. This was the series that prompted Roosevelt's stinging denunciation of the muckrakers at a Gridiron Club banquet in April, 1906.

Roosevelt's disapproval was not enough to kill the literature of exposure. Able writers in a dozen periodicals continued to demand reform. Muckraking articles were still an important political influence during Taft's administration. Several factors, however, finally brought muckraking to an end. The earlier writers had exhausted the richest veins of material; later investigators found less rewarding subjects and often did their work less carefully. Exposure of corruption lost some of its novelty and was less effective in selling magazines. Financiers and advertisers exerted an increasingly effective pressure against the muckraking periodicals. Several had to suspend publication; others stopped printing articles offensive to big business. The final blow was World War I, which diverted attention from domestic issues and divided the reformers themselves into prowar and antiwar factions.

Although muckraking found its most characteristic medium in magazine articles, it flowed through other channels as well. Gustavus Myers' three-volume *History of the Great American Fortunes* was based on years of thorough research by a scholarly Socialist. Edwin Markham's poem. "The Man with a Hoe" (1899), antedated the main muckraking movement, but Markham contributed other influential appeals for social justice in both prose and verse during the next decade. One of the most effective documents of the period was Upton Sinclair's novel, *The Jungle* (1906)—a shocking revelation of labor relations and sanitary conditions in the meat industry. The muckraking spirit also pervaded much of the fiction written by Jack London, Brand Whitlock, and David Graham Phillips. In diluted form it influenced several of the later novels of the very popular Winston Churchill (not to be confused with the English statesman of the same name).

Municipal Reformers

Muckraking was both cause and symptom of the growing demand for reform—a demand that became effective at the local and state level before it did in national politics. When James Bryce wrote his famous study, *The American Commonwealth* (1888), he expressed the opinion that the most conspicuous American failure had been in the field of municipal government. The muckraking writings of Lincoln Steffens indicated that conditions had not materially improved by 1902.

The most famous—or infamous—political machine in the country was New York City's Tammany Hall. Through their control of the local Democratic party, the Tammany politicians were in a position to practice graft in all its varieties. By awarding contracts for the construction of public buildings and the paving of streets to favored businessmen, the insiders could enjoy a cut in the profits at the taxpayers' expense. Through control of the city council the machine could extort money from individuals and companies who either wanted ordinances that would favor their interests or feared hostile action. Tammany judges could be influenced in their decisions; Tammany-controlled police captains gladly tolerated gambling houses, brothels, unlicensed saloons, and other illegal establishments when "protection money" was paid through the proper channels.

Tammany could not have remained in power, of course, without winning elections. To keep its henchmen in power, the machine resorted to whatever trickery might be necessary. Immigrants just off the boat were illegally naturalized; false names and names of dead men were placed on the voting lists; votes were bought with money or whiskey; "repeaters" were allowed to vote again and again; ballot boxes were stuffed and counts falsified. Yet such desperate measures were in ordinary years unnecessary, because the great majority of the voters willingly gave their support to Tammany candidates. A large part of the electorate was composed of foreign-born families, poorly paid and poorly educated. To these people the Tammany district leader appeared to be and often was a valuable friend, who could aid destitute families with loads of coal or free groceries, hand out jobs in municipal departments or with private contractors, speak a good word to the judge when one was in trouble with the law, or break humdrum monotony by arranging a large-scale free picnic. Small wonder that the unthinking gladly cast their ballots for the machine. Only the middle class seemed to realize that the Tammany fairy godmother supported herself by selling political favors at their expense; this element, in New York

City and elsewhere, consequently led the movement for "clean government."

With local variations, Tammany's misgovernment of New York was paralleled in most of the other major cities of the country. Chicago, Philadelphia, St. Louis, Boston—all had their political machines, some of them Democratic, some Republican. Some of the most notorious, far outdistancing Tammany in brazen viciousness, were in the smaller cities.

If men of action wanted to attempt the purification of American politics, they could obviously find abundant opportunity at the local level. Stirring examples of what might be done were soon provided.

Samuel M. Jones, a successful factory owner, was elected mayor of Toledo, Ohio, in 1897 through the efforts of the local Republican boss and certain business interests. The new mayor soon discovered that he was expected to show his gratitude by granting a favorable franchise to a certain street-railway company. He rebelled against becoming a party to such graft, thereby provoking a bitter fight with the Republican machine. As a result, he was denied the Republican nomination for re-election; but he ran as an independent, won, and continued in office until his death in 1904. Jones had gained the nickname of "Golden-Rule" because he endeavored to apply that Christian principle in his business dealings; he carried the same spirit into his administration of the city government. He took night sticks away from the policemen, introduced free kindergartens into the public schools, and established public playgrounds for the children. Jones fought unsuccessfully for public ownership of the utilities of the city. The stock of the Toledo street-railway company jumped twenty-four points the morning after his death—good evidence of the fear he had instilled in the hearts of his opponents.

The Toledo reform movement did not die with "Golden-Rule" Jones. The following year his disciple and former secretary, Brand Whitlock, became mayor. During his four terms, Whitlock continued to battle against machine politics. His most notable achievement was the obtaining of a new city charter which provided for initiative, referendum, recall, and direct nominations.

Events followed a similar course in Cleveland. Tom L. Johnson had had a typically American business career during the eighties and nineties, when he amassed a fortune through the steel industry and the manipulation of street railroads. A monopolist himself, Johnson enlisted in the crusade against monopoly after reading the works of Henry George. In 1901 he was elected mayor of Cleveland, where he gave the people an administration so energetic and efficient that Lincoln Steffens described him as "the best mayor of the best-governed city in America." Johnson brought the street railways under municipal regulation, forced a reduction of their fares to three cents, and attacked tax assessment abuses. After eight years in office, Johnson was defeated, but in 1911 a new reform mayor, Newton D. Baker, was elected to continue Johnson's ideals.

Jones and Johnson were the most picturesque of the municipal reformers, but there were many others. Attempts were made to clean out such Augean stables as Chicago, St. Louis, Minneapolis, Jersey City, San Francisco, Denver, and even New York. Many brave victories were won, but unfortunately few of them proved to be permanent. All too often the grafters took to cover while public indignation waxed strong, only to emerge again, almost as evil, when the voters returned to complacency.

One of the weaknesses in the municipal reform movement was that the crusaders for decency often limited their indignation to the crooked politicians, shutting their eyes to the fact that the bribe-givers were as responsible as the bribe-takers for the low state of city government. Realistic reformers like Tom Johnson recognized that their most powerful enemies were respected business-men who manipulated city councilmen, tax assessors, and judges to gain profit-able streetcar franchises, low tax assessments, and similar special privileges. Johnson therefore believed that the jailing of a few political grafters was much less important than fundamental changes like government ownership of rail-roads and city transit lines and the elimination of land monopoly through the single tax. Yet the average American, traditionally respectful of the rights of private property, was reluctant to consider these more radical remedies.

A second shortcoming of moralists who focused all their wrath on individual malefactors was that they failed to give serious consideration to the structure of municipal government. Most cities had antiquated charters providing for large, unwieldy city councils, weak mayors, and a dispersion of executive responsibil-ity among separately elected departments heads and independent boards. The machinery of municipal government was so rusty that the temptation to grease the works with bribe money was understandably great.

Many reformers believed that the solution to the problem lay in new forms of city government. Galveston, Texas, devised one such innovation following the disastrous hurricane and flood of 1900, which took the lives of one sixth of the population and destroyed one third of the city's property. To meet the emergency, extraordinary powers were placed in the hands of a commission of five. The experiment was so successful that a new city charter was presently drafted to make the commission form of government permanent. Interest in the Galveston venture led to the inauguration of similar plans in other cities. The scheme worked out in Des Moines, Iowa, which combined the superior effi-ciency of commission government with certain democratic checks, served as a model for many other communities. Another widely copied plan was that de-vised by Dayton, Ohio, under which a commission acted like a board of directors for the city, while the actual municipal administration was entrusted to a city manager, a non-political executive hired to run the government along lines of business efficiency. In one form or another, commission government had been introduced into 210 American cities by 1912, with varying degrees of success.

Progressivism in the States

While these years witnessed efforts to achieve a multitude of individual reforms, all of them may be reduced to two general principles. The progressives— and the word is used here in an inclusive sense to cover liberals of all parties who were seeking to advance social justice through political action—wanted to purify politics and to eliminate the worst abuses in American business life. The cleansing of politics required the destruction of "invisible government," or government dominated by the bosses; this overthrow, the progressives believed, could be achieved by devising means whereby all the voters could participate in all the processes of government. The elimination of economic abuses entailed government regulation of business. Some progressives believed that this was as far as government should depart from laissez faire; others, however, were of the opinion that government should move further from laissez faire in order to promote human welfare by positive measures.

In attempting to achieve these fundamental principles, the progressives found a particularly fruitful field for activity within the forty-eight states. The major political bosses maintained themselves through their control of state governments; they could best be forced to abdicate by popular revolts within their own feudal preserves. In these years, moreover, it semed that the bulk of the necessary regulation of business might be obtained through state legislation enacted under the so-called police power—that is, the power that enables a state legislature to pass laws for the protection of the public health, morals, safety, or general welfare.

The campaign against the bosses is best exemplified in the career of Robert M. LaFollette of Wisconsin. Entering politics as an ambitious young lawyer, he first became a district attorney and then a Congressman. In the latter role he discovered he was supposed to take orders from Senator Philetus Sawyer, wealthy lumber man and political boss. LaFollette not only asserted his independence of the machine, but threw his energy into a fight against Sawyer. The rebel's conduct kept him out of office for nine years, but during that period he worked doggedly to build up an anti-Sawyer bloc within the Republican party of the state. To defeat the old machine it was necessary to create a new one, committed to the interests of the people as against those of the great corporations. LaFollette's triumph finally came in 1900 when he was elected governor by the largest majority in Wisconsin history. He was re-elected in both 1902 and

The Robert M. LaFollettes, Junior and Senior. (World Wide Photos.)

1904; from 1906 until his death in 1925 he represented his state in the United States Senate.

The program that LaFollette carried into effect in his home state was given wide publicity as the "Wisconsin idea." To curb the power of the bosses, he secured a law that took the naming of candidates out of the control of party caucuses and conventions and gave it to the voters in direct primary elections. The privileged position of the railroads and other corporations was attacked in legislation that required the corporations to pay a larger share of the taxes, enlarged the power of the state railroad commission, and prohibited the acceptance of railroad passes by public officials. Other laws subjected inheritance to a progressive tax, provided for workmen's compensation in case of industrial accidents, and aimed at the conservation of the forests and water power.

No less important than Wisconsin as a laboratory for trying out new ideas in government was the state of Oregon. In 1891 the Australian or secret ballot was adopted; in 1899 a new registration law was passed; in 1902 the initiative and referendum were introduced; in 1904, 1908, and 1910 respectively a direct primary law, a corrupt practices act, and a measure providing for the recall were placed on the statute books. The successful fight for all these reforms was led by William S. U'Ren, a quiet man who avoided public position and campaigned for reform through the agency of voters' organizations.

In almost every state the party Goliaths found themselves challenged by youthful Davids. Among the men who gained recognition as anti-machine governors were Joseph W. Folk of Missouri, Albert B. Cummins of Iowa, Hiram W. Johnson of California, Theodore Roosevelt and Charles Evans Hughes of New York, and Woodrow Wilson of New Jersey. Franklin D. Roosevelt was much younger than these men and his part in the progressive movement was a minor one; but it is worthy of note that he first attracted attention in 1910, when, as a New York state senator, he led a fight of independent Democrats in the legislature against the party bosses.

Everywhere the progressives placed great importance on the adoption of new devices of democratic government. The direct primary in some form was eventually introduced into all of the states; twenty-one states adopted initiative and referendum procedures; eleven states made provision for recall of state officials. Women's suffrage also became a part of the progressive program; by 1914 the male monopoly of the voting booth had been broken in eleven states—all west of the Mississippi. The direct election of United States Senators was an almost universal progressive demand. Since, as a constitutional amendment, it required a two-thirds vote of the very chamber it sought to reform, direct election was not finally achieved until 1913. Prior to that time, however, twenty-nine states adopted Senatorial preference primaries, which in effect took the power of election out of the hands of the state legislators and put it into the hands of the people.

This was a period of significant progress in social legislation. Much of the impetus for the new laws came from professional social workers—dedicated women like Jane Addams and Florence Kelley of Chicago, and Lillian Wald and Frances Perkins of New York. Such able leaders, who had forsaken well-to-do homes to live and work in settlement houses in the city slums, soon became impatient with the inhibitions of laissez faire. They prodded state legislatures into action to deal with the worst abuses of child labor and the exploitation of the workers through long hours, sweatshop pay rates, and uncompensated industrial accidents. Future national leaders like Alfred E. Smith, Robert F. Wagner, and Franklin D. Roosevelt received their first indoctrination in the cause of social justice at the hands of determined social workers.

Humanitarians were particularly disturbed by the prevalence of child labor—an evil that seemed to be on the increase. In 1900 more than 1.7 million children—almost one out of five in the 10 to 15 age bracket—were gainfully employed. New Jersey berry fields, Kentucky coal mines, Vermont granite quarries, and Carolina textile mills were all employing children, usually for long hours at pitifully small wages. In 1904 a National Child Labor Committee was organized to press for reform. During the next ten years a great deal was accomplished. Virtually without exception, the states set minimum ages for employment, ranging from twelve to fifteen years; maximum hours for youthful employees were specified; night work and work in certain dangerous jobs were forbidden; educational requirements were set. Yet much remained to be done: some states had set higher standards than others, thereby risking an exodus of industries to their more lenient neighbors. Many reformers believed that a Federal law was required, and Senator Albert J. Beveridge of Indiana introduced such a bill in 1906. Not until the Wilson Administration, however, did Congress take the desired action.

A second area of significant progress was in protecting industrial workers against the hazards of injury on the job. Until the 1890's victims of industrial accidents found it almost impossible to recover damages from their employers. Under the commonly prevailing law, the burden of proof was on the employee to prove that the employer had been negligent. If either the worker himself or one of his fellow-laborers had been careless, the employer usually escaped liability. A new crop of employers' liability acts passed during the 1890's and early 1900's corrected some of the old injustices: the fellow-servant doctrine was abolished and the burden of proving that he had not been negligent was thrown upon the employer. Even these laws, however, required the injured worker to collect his claims through expensive litigation in the courts. A more thorough-going reform was provided by workmen's compensation acts, under which employers were compelled to carry insurance against industrial accidents. Some thirty-five such measures were passed in various states between 1910 and 1917. Since insurance rates were determined by the frequency of accidents, a powerful incentive was created for placing guards around machinery and removing other job hazards.

Similar advances were made in other areas. During the first thirty years of the century all except five states enacted laws limiting the number of hours that women could work. Statutes limiting the work day for men were less frequent, but several states restricted the hours of labor in certain occupations, such as mining. About one third of the states enacted measures embodying minimum-wage standards for women and children. Conditions that long had been taken for granted suddenly aroused the public conscience and brought remedial legislation. Thus in the three years between 1911 and 1913, twenty states passed mothers' assistance acts, providing pensions for widows with dependent children. The first state to set up an old-age pension system was Arizona in 1914, but the state supreme court found the act unconstitutional.

Judicial Conservatism

The fate of the Arizona old-age pension law was illustrative of one of the most serious obstacles encountered by the progressives. Peculiar to the American system of government, both state and Federal, was the tremendous power wielded by the courts in holding laws invalid on the grounds of unconstitutionality. Since judges were appointed or elected from the ranks of successful lawyers, they were likely to be social conservatives, both by training and by professional ties.

In giving judicial blessing to the doctrine of laissez faire, the judges found a handy formula in the familiar words: no person shall be deprived of life, liberty, or property without due process of law. These or similar words were to be found in three significant places: in the Fifth Amendment to the Federal Constitution, where they constituted a limitation upon Congress; in the Fourteenth Amendment, where they limited the states; and in most state constitutions as restraints upon the legislatures. Originally intended as a guarantee that men should not be punished nor have their property confiscated without fair trial in the courts, judicial interpretation had extended the "due process" clauses to mean that certain types of legislation were invalid. In 1885, for example, the New York Court of Appeals had declared unconstitutional a state statute prohibiting cigar-manufacturing in tenement houses on the ground "that it arbitrarily interferes with personal liberty and private property without due process of law." A similar fate befell an Illinois eight-hour law for women in 1895, a Colorado eight-hour law for smelting workers in 1899, and a New York workmen's compensation act in 1911.

Even when states laws successfully leaped the hurdles erected by the state courts, they were often invalidated by the United States Supreme Court. Although the highest tribunal had in the Granger cases of the 1870's laid down the general principle that when private property was devoted to public use it was subject to public regulation, it had subsequently qualified this in ways that made effective action difficult. Corporations were held to be "persons" entitled to the protection of the due process clause; they had the right to appeal to the courts as to the "reasonableness" of rates fixed by state legislatures or commissions; rates that did not provide a fair return on the investment were set aside as deprivations of property in violation of the Fourteenth Amendment.

The extreme to which the Supreme Court was ready to go in reading the philosophy of laissez faire into the Constitution is best illustrated by the case of Lochner v. New York, decided by a 5 to 4 vote in 1905. Here the issue was the validity of a New York law limiting the hours of labor for bakery employees to ten a day or sixty a week. Speaking for the majority, Justice Rufus Peckham emphasized that the right to make labor contracts was "part of the liberty of

the individual protected by the Fourteenth Amendment of the Federal Constitution." The act in question was "an illegal interference with the rights of
individuals, both employers and employees, to make contracts regarding labor
upon such terms as they may think best. . . ." In his famous dissent, Justice
Oliver Wendell Holmes pointed out that laws restricting liberty of contract
were not uncommon:

> Some of these laws embody convictions or prejudices which judges are likely
> to share. Some may not. But a constitution is not intended to embody a particular
> economic theory, whether of paternalism and the organic relation of the citizen
> to the state or of laissez faire. It is made for people of fundamentally differing
> views, and the accident of our finding certain opinions natural and familiar, or
> novel, and even shocking, ought not to conclude our judgment upon the ques-
> tion whether statutes embodying them conflict with the Constitution of the
> United States.

The Supreme Court was by no means uninfluenced by the changing temper
of the times. On the question of maximum-hour laws it gradually gave way. In
Muller v. Oregon (1908), a ten-hour law applying to female factory workers
was upheld on the grounds that women might need this special protection. The
Muller case was memorable because of the forceful presentation of Louis D.
Brandeis, a wealthy Boston lawyer who was gaining fame in these years as "the
people's attorney." Brandeis' brief dealt with the legal precedents in two
pages, but devoted more than a hundred pages to mustering economic and
sociological data drawn from both American and European sources to demonstrate that protective legislation for women was reasonable to protect the health
and welfare of the people. The Brandeis-type or sociological brief became the
most useful weapon in the arsenal of the progressive lawyers. When a general
ten-hour law applying to men as well as women was upheld in Bunting v.
Oregon (1917), another significant victory for the advocates of state regulation
was achieved.

Yet the state and Federal courts continued to antagonize the progressives
on many issues. In his attempts to reform tax assessments and to force down
street railroad fares, Mayor Tom Johnson was frustrated again and again by the
conservative Ohio courts. In his autobiography, Johnson refers to more than
fifty injunctions "which hampered the progress of the people's movement in
Cleveland." Organized labor complained that the courts were lax in enforcing
the antitrust laws against business, but vigorous in using the same laws to
prohibit boycotts and picketing and to jail union leaders who violated injunctions.

For progressives determined to make government more responsive to the
popular will, this situation was hard to tolerate. Moderate reformers placed
their hope on the appointment and election of more liberal judges who would

understand the needs of the new age. But to many other progressives this process was too slow. They advocated machinery either for the recall of judges whose behavior displeased the voters or for the recall of their decisions. By permitting the voters to re-enact laws that had been held unconstitutional by the courts, the recall of judicial decisions promised a new and speedier method of constitutional amendment by popular referendum.

No part of the progressive program was more resolutely opposed by conservatives than the proposals for tampering with the court system. The power of judicial review and the independence of the judiciary were defended as the greatest safeguards of constitutional rights of liberty and property. The struggle between the progressives and the conservatives on this issue was deeply significant because it involved the whole conflict between the older and the newer views of the proper function of government.

3

Theodore Roosevelt in the Saddle

An exciting period in American politics began on September 14, 1901, the day when the young and colorful Theodore Roosevelt became President of the United States. During the course of the next seven and a half years, Roosevelt became the dominant figure on the national and international scene. At home he won fame as the first Chief Executive to achieve many of the aims and objectives of progressivism. True, there was little that was new in his program, for he was merely promoting some of the proposals advocated by late nineteenth century third parties, notably the Populist. Nor was his zeal for reform as great as that of many other leaders of the same period; by comparison with such crusaders as Robert LaFollette or William U'Ren, Roosevelt was almost conservative. Yet the "Rough Rider" with his passion for publicity aroused the American people to the dangers attendant upon the "unholy alliance" of amoral big business and corrupt politics. As a result, Roosevelt became the popular symbol of the early twentieth century progressive movement. In the international field, he completed the task of making the United States a world power through his efforts to obtain the right to build the Panama Canal, his "Big Stick" interpretation of the Monroe Doctrine, his mediation of the Russo-Japanese War, and his attempts to maintain world peace.

Road to the White House

And yet, in a sense, Theodore Roosevelt was a political accident. To be sure, this member of a prominent old New York family had been in a hurry from the start. In 1880 he was graduated from Harvard; in 1881 he was elected to the New

York Assembly; the following year he published his first book, *The Naval War of 1812*. After three years in the legislature, Roosevelt purchased two cattle ranches in the Bad Lands of North Dakota. Although this venture was not an economic success, his residence in the West helped to develop his philosophy of "the strenuous life." What was just as important, this tenderfoot made many friends and acquired a staunch enthusiasm for the traditions and virtues of the frontier.[1]

The young Roosevelt bitterly opposed the nomination of James G. Blaine for the presidency in 1884. The *New York Times* of June 7, 1884, quoted him as declaring: "To say I am satisfied with the nomination of Mr. Blaine would be false." After wrestling with his conscience for some time, however, he concluded that party loyalty must be upheld, and he refused to join other Mugwumps in supporting Grover Cleveland.

Following the failure of his North Dakota venture, Roosevelt turned his major attention to politics again and was nominated as Republican candidate for mayor of New York City in 1886. About the only result of this effort was to keep his name before the public, for he ran a poor third to Abraham Hewitt, the successful Democratic candidate, and Henry George, who had the support of labor. Not disheartened by this ignominious defeat, Roosevelt found new outlets for his energy in further writing and in a period of service on the Federal Civil Service Commission, to which he was appointed by President Benjamin Harrison and reappointed by President Cleveland. To that post he brought a vigor that had been lacking, and he helped make the public conscious of the evils of the spoils system; Roosevelt himself announced within a month and a half of taking the office that he had already made the Commission "a living force." Yet in that position he showed a certain propensity for stepping on the toes of those who opposed him. His next post of importance was the presidency of the New York City board of police commissioners, where he displayed independence, vigor, and a flair for provoking controversy.

In the election of 1896, Roosevelt campaigned actively for William McKinley, for which he was rewarded with appointment as Assistant Secretary of the Navy. There he played a conspicuous part in helping to build up the strength of the service and to prepare it for effective participation in the war with Spain—a conflict which Roosevelt welcomed with enthusiasm. Not content with a desk job during that struggle, the young politician resigned to obtain a commission as lieutenant colonel of the First Volunteer Cavalry—the famous Rough Riders, composed in large part of recruits from Roosevelt's beloved West. After chafing restlessly in the United States, the new colonel finally saw

[1] In 1889, Roosevelt published the first section of a four-volume history, *The Winning of the West*, which has been considered the best of his historical writings. Even though he was more concerned with individual heroic exploits than with the influence of the frontier, he did antedate Frederick Jackson Turner in public expression of an interest in the West.

Theodore Roosevelt. (Brown Bros.)

action in Cuba, particularly in the battle of San Juan Hill, where a disproportionate share of the glory fell upon his willing shoulders. Indeed, when he
published his account of the fighting in Cuba, Finley Peter Dunne, in his
inimitable "Mr. Dooley" column, asserted: "If I was him, I'd call th' book
'Alone in Cubia.'"

Roosevelt returned to the United States a hero, and Boss Thomas C. Platt,
taking advantage of his popularity, succeeded in having him elected as governor
of New York. Platt soon repented of his action, however, for while he and the
new governor did not quarrel openly—Roosevelt was too aware of the requirements for practical political achievement to do this—they did not get
along well. Roosevelt refused to give the boss anything approaching a free hand;
he insisted on reasonably honest appointments and he advocated certain reforms that Platt disliked. From the boss's point of view, the governor was irresponsible and impulsive. This was the situation when the campaign of 1900
opened.

The Election of 1900

So far as the Republicans were concerned, progressivism was not intended to be the issue in the 1900 campaign. Astutely manipulated by Mark Hanna, the Republican convention renominated the safe and respectable William McKinley and adopted an equally safe and respectable platform, which praised the administration's foreign and domestic policies and pledged the party to the gold standard, the protective tariff, the maintenance of American rule over Hawaii and the Philippines, and the construction and control of an interoceanic canal by the United States.

At only one point were Hanna's wishes ignored. Vice President Garrett Hobart had died in 1899, thereby leaving the race for the second post wide open. Hanna wanted to dictate this nomination also, but a number of factors took the decision from his hands. Matthew Quay, Republican boss of Pennsylvania, disliked Hanna and welcomed this opportunity to oppose him. Platt had no quarrel with Hanna, but longed to remove Roosevelt from the governorship of New York, a post Platt preferred to see occupied by some less impulsive and more "regular" politician. Thus several state bosses decided to support Roosevelt, whom the disapproving Hanna referred to as that "damned cowboy." When news of this plan to "kick him upstairs" came to the governor's ears, he objected strenuously. He felt he was too young to take an office traditionally regarded as a dead-end street in politics, and he discussed with numerous friends whether he should seek instead a second term in New York or try to be appointed as Secretary of War. The rank and file of convention delegates—particularly those from the West—took up the idea of Roosevelt for Vice President with marked enthusiasm and refused to allow his name to be withdrawn. The reluctant candidate, flattered by this impressive acclaim, accepted the nomination, much to the displeasure of Hanna, who regretted—according to reports—that there would be only one life "between this madman and the Presidency."

To oppose this Republican ticket of McKinley and Roosevelt, the Democrats nominated William Jennings Bryan and Adlai E. Stevenson (grandfather of the Democratic presidential candidate in 1952 and 1956). Their platform once again demanded the free coinage of silver and reduction of the tariff, but this time placed major emphasis on the issue of imperialism. Warning the nation that "imperialism abroad will lead quickly and inevitably to despotism at home," the party pledged itself to grant independence to the Philippines as soon as a stable government could be established in the islands.

Among the third parties, there appeared in the political arena for the first time the recently formed Social Democratic party. Its nominees were Eugene V. Debs and Job Harriman. To all intents, the Populist party was dead by this time.

As in 1896, Bryan conducted an energetic campaign, visiting every section of the country, while McKinley repeated his front-porch tactics. Despite the apparent popularity of the Republicans as a result of the overwhelming victory over Spain and the emphasis upon the full dinner pail, some of the party leaders were worried. A threatened strike of anthracite coal miners was an indication that Republican prosperity was not shared by all Americans, and there was considerable apprehension about possible inroads made by Bryan's anti-imperialist speeches and his condemnation of the Dingley Tariff as a trust-breeder. Therefore Hanna, again as in 1896, flooded the country with speakers who denounced the Democratic candidate as a dangerous visionary. One of the most articulate was Roosevelt, who traveled almost 22,000 miles to make more than a thousand speeches before audiences estimated at three million. Nearly always he spoke in the same vein: Bryan was backed by the forces of anarchy, as well as cowards, knaves, and lunatics; a vote for McKinley was a vote for American honor, an unsullied flag, and continued prosperity. Bryan still retained his magnetic charm, but his following was a restless, disorganized collection of groups; when he advocated one issue, he would lose the support of one element; when he stressed something else, another group would turn away.

Consequently, the election resulted in a more decisive victory for McKinley than he had achieved over the same opponent in 1896. In the electoral college the vote was 292 to 155; in the popular total, it was 7,200,000 for McKinley, and 6,360,000 for Bryan.[2] Thus Hanna and his big-business friends had reason to hope that the threat of popular revolt against their dominance had been thoroughly smashed. There were two weaknesses, however, in the conservative optimism. One was that the country's desire for reform was much stronger than the electoral vote—reflecting national pride in the military victories and joy over the return of prosperity—seemed to indicate. For example, to Bryan's popular vote must be added the nearly 100,000 ballots cast for Debs. The second was that only one life lay between the presidency and Theodore Roosevelt, who already perceived the new direction from which the political winds of the twentieth century were likely to blow.

McKinley served only six months of his second term. On September 6, 1901, while the President was attending a Pan-American Exposition at Buffalo, New York, he was shot by Leon Czolgosz, a demented Polish fanatic. After an eight-day fight for life, McKinley succumbed to the wound.

Roosevelt the Man

Thus Theodore Roosevelt achieved the presidency at the age of forty-two, the youngest man to assume that position. He brought to it a certain fearless

[2] In 1896, it had been 271 to 176 in the electoral college; the popular vote was 7,036,000 to 6,470,000.

and independent judgment that was imbued with a spirit of self-righteousness. Roosevelt always believed he was in the right, and consequently had little use for those who opposed him. In his quest for a "square deal" he made enemies, but the range of his popular appeal was nevertheless extraordinary. He was as much at ease with a king as with a cowboy, with a scholar as with a professional pugilist. Not a profound nor particularly original thinker, he had the happy faculty of anticipating the trend of public opinion, thereby appearing to be leading it. Not basically a progressive, he steered a course which made the progressive movement popular and alive. Roosevelt could cleverly avoid taking up matters of which he had little—or even superficial—knowledge, notably in the field of economics, and yet on other issues he was ready to rush in where others feared to tread. Although a firm believer in the party system, he bitterly fought party bosses who placed selfish interests above national welfare. Yet he realized that party backing was essential to the success of many of his objectives, even if this involved compromise. Consequently he liked to regard himself as a practical idealist. Basking in the limelight of the publicity he loved, he is said to have wanted to be the bride at every wedding, the corpse at every funeral. Despite the fact that he frequently preferred words to deeds, that he glittered in undeserved spotlights, and that he often claimed credit where it was not due, Roosevelt was one of the most versatile men to occupy the White House: a college graduate, an historian, a one-time rancher, an editor, an explorer, a big game hunter, a naturalist, and a soldier.

After taking the oath of office, President Roosevelt immediately announced: "I wish to say that it shall be my aim to continue, absolutely unbroken, the policy of President McKinley for the peace, the prosperity, and the honor of our beloved country."[3] In line with this assertion, he asked his predecessor's cabinet to continue in office.[4] This initial decision to tread cautiously in another man's footprints was not typical of Roosevelt, but he was wise enough to realize that he must feel his way at first in order to make sure that he would obtain the

[3] *New York Times*, Sept. 15, 1901.

[4] There were eventually many changes. The cabinet officers under Roosevelt were: Secretary of State, John Hay of Ohio followed by Elihu Root of New York in 1905 and Robert Bacon of New York in 1909; Secretary of the Treasury, Lyman J. Gage of Illinois followed by Leslie M. Shaw of Iowa in 1902 and George B. Cortelyou of New York in 1907; Secretary of War, Elihu Root followed by William H. Taft of Ohio in 1904 and Luke E. Wright of Tennessee in 1908; Secretary of the Navy, John D. Long of Massachusetts followed by William H. Moody of Massachusetts in 1902, Paul Morton of Illinois in 1904, Charles J. Bonaparte of Maryland in 1905, Victor H. Metcalf of California in 1906, and Truman H. Newberry of Michigan in 1908; Attorney General, Philander C. Knox of Pennsylvania, followed by William H. Moody in 1904 and Charles J. Bonaparte in 1906; Postmaster General, Charles E. Smith of Pennsylvania followed by Henry C. Payne of Wisconsin in 1902, Robert J. Wynne of Pennsylvania in 1904, George B. Cortelyou in 1905, and George von L. Meyer of Massachusetts in 1907; Secretary of Agriculture, James Wilson of Iowa; Secretary of the Interior, Ethan A. Hitchcock of Missouri followed by James R. Garfield of Ohio in 1907; Secretary of Commerce and Labor (post created in 1903), George B. Cortelyou followed by Victor H. Metcalf in 1904 and Oscar S. Straus of New York in 1906.

support of party leaders and of the public before he ventured out in new directions.

Roosevelt Challenges the Trusts

The new President, however, was not for long content to sit idly by while big business and the political bosses ran the country. One of the earliest signs that the Roosevelt regime was shifting from the policies of the McKinley era came on December 5, 1901, when the President sent his first annual message to Congress. This document, some twenty thousand words long, seemed on the surface to be following a course which would not antagonize any group, particularly the Old Guard and the big business interests. Yet while it did not condemn trusts as such, the message indicated that there must be some form of regulation. The inimitable Mr. Dooley poked characteristic fun at Roosevelt's on-the-fence position: " 'Th' trusts,' says he, 'are heejious monsthers built up by th' enlightened intherprise iv th' men that have done so much to advance progress in our beloved country,' he says. 'On wan hand I wud stamp thim undher fut; on th' other hand not so fast.' " A deeper and more thorough study of the message, however, would have revealed that there were warnings of things to come. Roosevelt specifically asked for the establishment of a Department of Commerce and Labor that would have authority to investigate the earnings of corporations, as well as to protect the rights of workers. He also indicated his opposition to "men who seek gain, not by genuine work . . . but by gambling." This was a not-so-veiled attack upon stock speculators.

These warnings materialized into open assault on February 18, 1902, when conservatives were shocked to learn that the administration had decided to prosecute the recently organized Northern Securities Company as a combination in restraint of trade. Immediately prices on the stock market fell sharply, and J. P. Morgan hurried to Washington in an unsuccessful attempt to induce the President to halt the proceedings.

In attacking the Northern Securities Company, Roosevelt was challenging the interests of the great Morgan himself, as well as those of two of the country's most powerful railroad magnates, James J. Hill and Edward H. Harriman. This $400 million holding company was the device through which these three titans had made peace after a famous financial battle of 1901. At that time Hill and Morgan, who dominated the Great Northern and North Pacific Railroads, had aroused the anger of Harriman, who controlled the third of the large transcontinental lines, the Union Pacific, by buying the Chicago, Burlington, and Quincy, on which all three of the systems were dependent for connection with Chicago. Harriman fought back by purchasing enormous blocks of Northern Pacific stock. Since Morgan's domination over this company rested upon an insecure minority interest, he became involved in a wide buying campaign to prevent control from passing into the hands of his ambitious rival. The struggle became so violent that the price of Northern Pacific stock was run up from 110 to 1000 and a panic was precipitated in the stock market, where shorts were fighting desperately to fulfill their contracts. So confused did the situation become that only through court litigation would it have been possible to determine which party had won. Characteristically, the contestants abruptly decided to join hands rather than to continue their costly contest. In November, 1901, the three principals organized the Northern Securities Company as a holding corporation to unify the management of the Great Northern, the Northern Pacific, and the Chicago, Burlington, and Quincy. The best legal talent available was obtained to insure that this giant combination would not be a victim of the Sherman Antitrust Act.

Morgan was especially enthusiastic about this creation. It was a step toward peace in the transportation field, for it would end vicious stock market battles that had threatened panics and attendant loss of investments to thousands of security owners, large and small. Moreover, the new company would be in line with the trend toward a sounder financial structure in the whole railroad business, a trend that Morgan himself had initiated some fifteen years earlier. In addition, the move would help the new imperialism, for Morgan and his associates envisioned the time when these railroads would link up with trans-Pacific merchantmen to reach the Far East.

The government did not share these views, but charged that the new combination would obtain an illegal monopoly over transportation in the whole Northwest. Proceeding cautiously because of the hitherto conservative attitude of the courts, Attorney General Philander Knox spent two years collecting evidence against the company. Roosevelt also did his part by appealing for popular support in a speaking tour which took him to New England and the Middle West in the late summer and fall of 1902. His general theme was that a distinction should be made between good and bad trusts; he let it be known that the bad ones must be regulated, but "wisdom and restraint" must be shown in dealing with the whole problem. A second presidential step was to take advantage of a vacancy on the Supreme Court to appoint one of the outstanding jurists of the twentieth century, Oliver Wendell Holmes of Massachusetts, whom Roosevelt believed was "absolutely sane and sound on the great national policies for which we stand in public life." In other words, the President fully expected that Holmes would share his views on all the great issues of the day, including the trust problem.

When the Supreme Court finally handed down its decision in 1904, the government's case was sustained—but by the narrowest of margins. Justice Harlan, speaking for five judges, ordered the dissolution of the Northern Securities Company. "If the Anti-Trust Act is held not to embrace a case such as is now before us, the plain intention of the legislative branch of the Government will be defeated." A minority of four judges, headed by Holmes, dissented. "Great cases like hard cases make bad law," the new appointee wrote. The mere organization of a holding company, he believed, could not be illegal even though the intent of the incorporators was to end competition between competing railroads.

Roosevelt was annoyed by Holmes' stand. "I could carve out of a banana," the President snapped, "a judge with more backbone than that." But his unhappiness with the dissenters did not mar his feeling of triumph over the majority opinion. To his non-legal mind the Knight case of 1895 was now dead. "This decision," he subsequently wrote, "I caused to be annulled by the court that had rendered it."

The President's victory was actually less sweeping than he believed. Many monopolies still found shelter behind the Knight case doctrine that manufacturing was not part of commerce, while the recently rebuked Hill, Morgan, and Harriman found ways to evade the intention of the administration. By "community of interest," or unwritten agreement, they achieved most of the purposes that they would have gained through the forbidden holding company. Even so, the Northern Securities decision was important in giving a new direction to public policy. The Sherman Act, which had appeared to be moribund, was brought back to life. The government's vigorous effort had demonstrated to a

The Fatted Steer: "I just wonder what he is going to do?"
(By Rehse in the *St. Paul Pioneer Press*.)

doubting citizenry that even the rich and powerful were answerable to the laws. As a result, President Roosevelt gained a new and popular title, "the trust-buster." Capitalizing on this, he lashed out in his speeches at the "malefactors of great wealth."

Even while the Northern Securities case was under consideration, three statutes were enacted—all in February, 1903—to strengthen the government's hand in dealing with big business. One measure authorized the establishment of the Department of Commerce and Labor, in line with Roosevelt's request in his first annual message, and its head was given cabinet status. Within this new Department, a Bureau of Corporations was organized to gather facts and figures concerning the great industries of the nation—information that might provide evidence needed by the Justice Department in antitrust suits. While the Bureau had no regulatory authority, its first head, James R. Garfield, so capably publicized the facts he collected that popular opinion helped to make "evil" corporations reform themselves. The second law was the Expediting Act, passed at the request of Attorney General Knox, to prevent delays in prosecutions under the antitrust and interstate commerce laws by giving government cases a preferred place on the circuit court calendars.

The last of the three was the Elkins Anti-Rebate Act, which struck at the abuse of railroad rebates. This practice had come to be regarded as a nuisance by the railroads themselves. Some less ethical carriers had refused to respect the anti-rebate provisions of the Interstate Commerce Act by paying shippers for fictitious damages in transit, renting the spur tracks of the shippers, refunding storage charges, and other subterfuges. Hence it was the roads injured by the illegal actions of their competitors, rather than the Roosevelt administration, that successfully demanded the passage of this measure. The new law made no mention of the establishment of reasonable rates; departure from the existing published rates became the sole test of discrimination, and shippers who accepted rebates were made subject to fines, as well as the railroads that gave them. Federal courts might issue injunctions to prevent such practices.

Thus armed, the Roosevelt administration brought a number of powerful lawbreakers to book—though it waited until after the election of 1904 had given the President impressive evidence of popular support. In Swift & Company v. United States (1905), the Supreme Court ordered the dissolution of the so-called "Beef Trust"—a combination of leading packers who had agreed not to bid against each other in the livestock market, to restrict the output of meat in order to raise prices, and to secure illegal rates from the railroads to the exclusion of competitors. In the decision in this case, Justice Holmes, speaking for the unanimous court, asserted the "stream of commerce" doctrine. Even when the stockyards were entirely within a single state, the buying and selling of cattle were to be considered as transactions in interstate commerce since the cattle had been shipped in from different states and were destined for eventual use in still other states. This "stream of commerce" doctrine provided a concept under which a much wider Federal regulation of business would eventually be possible. The government also instituted proceedings to obtain a dissolution of the American Tobacco and Standard Oil Trusts—cases that were not finally decided until the Taft administration.

A number of prosecutions were attempted under the Elkins Act. In the most spectacular of these, the Standard Oil Company was found guilty of accepting rebates on 1462 separate counts and was fined $29,240,000 by Judge Kenesaw Mountain Landis. This verdict was, however, set aside upon appeal to a higher court. In another notorious instance, officials and employees of the American Sugar Refining Company were convicted of tampering with their scales in order to avoid import duties. The Federal government recovered more than $4 million, plus a fine of $300,000, from the guilty corporation.

The significance of these activities has sometimes been overrated. Fewer suits were instituted under the long Roosevelt administration than during the four years when Taft was President. Moreover, Roosevelt emphasized constantly that not all trusts were bad; the good ones that were the result of natural developments in the business world should be left alone so long as they operated within the law. Roosevelt came increasingly to believe that regulation rather than destruction was the answer to the trust problem. "We do not wish to destroy corporations," he asserted, "but we do wish to make them subserve the public good." He advocated measures that would require all businesses engaged in interstate commerce to be licensed by the Federal government, but the idea never received sufficient support to be enacted into law.

Roosevelt and Labor

In the period following the Civil War, the several administrations, both Republican and Democratic, had shown a certain degree of hostility toward organized labor. This attitude had its most dramatic illustration during the Pullman strike of 1894. In his first annual message to Congress, President Roosevelt struck a somewhat more sympathetic note toward the rights of labor. He was soon given an opportunity to demonstrate his sincerity as a result of a serious strike in the Pennsylvania anthracite coal fields in 1902.

This upheaval was not entirely unexpected, for the miners had been unhappy with their lot for a number of years. The mines of Ohio, Illinois, West Virginia, and Pennsylvania were largely owned by the big coal-carrying railroads. The miners worked long hours for pay that lagged behind the rising cost of living; they had to patronize company stores where they paid tribute in the form of higher prices to their employers; living quarters in the mining "patches" left much to be desired. Resentful of these conditions, the miners joined the United Mine Workers, then under the able leadership of energetic young John Mitchell.

In the summer of 1900, Mitchell threatened to call a strike unless wages, stationary since 1880, were increased 10 per cent. Mark Hanna, who disliked labor troubles in an election year when his party was stressing the "full dinner pail," exerted pressure upon the operators to yield to the miners' demands. Considering the raise inadequate, the miners broadened their demands in the spring of 1902, this time seeking a 20 per cent wage increase, an eight-hour day, improved working conditions, and union recognition. The operators, headed by George F. Baer, president of the Reading Railroad, were determined not only to resist these demands, but to break the obnoxious union. Baer's opinion of collective bargaining was immortalized in a widely quoted letter in which he asserted that the interests of the workers would be taken care of not by "labor agitators," but by "the Christian men to whom God in His infinite wisdom has given the control of the property interests of the country."

The strike involving 140,000 men began on May 12, 1902. By mid-September no progress had been made toward a settlement, the price of anthracite had risen from $5 a ton to over $30, and worried householders started to fear a coalless winter. The public placed most of the blame on the operators, for Mitchell, not making the mistake of some earlier labor leaders, prevented the strikers from engaging in acts of violence. Even to conservative politicians it seemed imperative that the President do something about the situation, although neither law nor precedent offered any satisfactory basis for executive action. At Roosevelt's behest, Mark Hanna conducted secret negotiations with Mitchell and J. P. Morgan, who had extensive interests at stake and was worried lest the continuation of the strike bring more regulatory legislation for big business. But "Divine Right" Baer refused all proposals for compromise.

Finally the President summoned representatives of both sides to meet with him at a White House conference on October 3. Mitchell there offered to submit the miners' demands to an impartial commission to be appointed by Roosevelt, but Baer and his colleagues not only refused this suggestion, but rebuked the President for his unwillingness to use Federal authority to break the strike in the same way that Cleveland had ended the Pullman strike of 1894.

In the days following the White House conference, Roosevelt made no secret of his disapproval of the conduct of the operators. He allowed it to be known that he was contemplating calling out the army to take possession of the mines and operate them. If this were a bluff, the mine owners did not care to call it. After negotiations conducted by Secretary of War Elihu Root with J. P. Morgan, the operators finally consented to submit the controversy to arbitration. They insisted, however, that the President's commission should include no representative of organized labor. The miners protested against this reservation and a new deadlock was threatened. But Roosevelt adroitly overcame the difficulty by appointing E. E. Clark, the head of the railway conductors' union, describing him as an "eminent sociologist" rather than a representative of labor.

The commission, headed by Judge George Gray, spent four months questioning more than five hundred witnesses before it handed down its decision in March, 1903. Only some of the miners' demands were granted. They were given a 10 per cent raise, a nine-hour day, and the right to submit future grievances to a board of conciliation, representing both owners and miners,[5] but were refused union recognition and other concessions. The miners' victory was a modest one, yet Roosevelt's departure from earlier precedents was important. For the first time the Federal government intervened in a labor controversy not to uphold the employers against their rebellious workmen, but in a way calculated to protect the interests of the general public and bring about a peaceful solution without prejudice to either party. The President's action was sharply criticized in conservative circles.

Roosevelt's sympathy with the miners did not indicate an unqualified approval of labor unionism. On the contrary, he publicly opposed the closed shop and denounced the radicalism of more aggressive labor leaders. He frequently expressed the opinion it was his duty to steer a middle course, in order to save the country from socialism by punishing the excesses of predatory wealth on the one hand and of lawless agitators on the other.

The Election of 1904

As President, Roosevelt continued the policy that he had followed as governor of New York in alternately defying and appeasing the Republican bosses and the wealthy business interests. He did many things of which the Old Guard disapproved, and yet he shrank from any break serious enough to endanger his chances for re-election or the success of his legislative program. Despite this presidential caution, there was some talk that the Republican nomination in 1904 should be given to a less impulsive politician. The one most often mentioned was Hanna himself, although the Ohioan refused to avow his candidacy. The conservatives would not take Hanna's refusal seriously, but on February 15, 1904, the powerful boss died, and the President's control over the party machinery became complete. The Old Guard no longer had anyone who could seriously challenge the popular Teddy.

Consequently, when the convention met at Chicago, Roosevelt was nominated without opposition. The naming of Charles W. Fairbanks, Senator from

[5] If the conciliation board were unable to reach a decision, the final settlement would be made by the Federal circuit judge of the district. Under this arbitration agreement, there was comparative peace in the anthracite coal fields until after World War I.

Indiana, as his running mate was a sop to the conservative wing. The platform was largely confined to recounting the achievements of the administration, with emphasis upon trust busting and the acquisition of canal rights, rather than on specific pledges for the future.

Bryan's defeats made his renomination in 1904 unlikely. Many Democrats now wanted a more conservative candidate. There was even talk of drafting Grover Cleveland once again, for it was said that big business, normally Republican, would support him as an antidote to Roosevelt. The ex-President, however, refused to allow his potential candidacy to develop; instead, he threw his backing to Judge Gray, who had headed the coal arbitration commission. The Bryan element, on the other hand, favored William Randolph Hearst. In the end, the convention, meeting at St. Louis, nominated Judge Alton B. Parker of New York, a representative of the conservative Cleveland wing of the party. Although Parker was rather colorless, the Democrats felt that he might be able to defeat Roosevelt in New York State, a requisite for victory. The platform was also negative and notably failed to endorse a silver plank, because of Parker's refusal to run unless the gold standard were "firmly and irrevocably established."

A dull campaign followed, enlivened only near the end by Parker's charge that George Cortelyou, who was both Secretary of Commerce and Labor and Republican National Chairman, had used information gained from the Bureau of Corporations to extort money from monopolistic corporations for the benefit of the Republican campaign fund and had promised immunity from antitrust prosecutions as a reward. Roosevelt did not deny that his party had accepted the usual donations from corporations, but indignantly asserted that the charges of blackmail were "monstrous"; he was, he said, "unhampered by any pledge, promise or understanding of any kind, save my promise, made openly to the American people, that so far as in my power lies I shall see to it that every man has a square deal, no less and no more."

Roosevelt won a sweeping victory in November. Parker did not carry a single state outside of the Solid South, and even lost Missouri, which had been in the Democratic column consistently since the Civil War. The Roosevelt popular vote was 7,628,834 to Parker's 5,084,491, while the electoral count was 336 to 140.

The successful candidate immediately made an important announcement; according to the *New York World* of November 9, 1904, he said: "On the 4th of March next I shall have served three and a half years and this . . . constitutes my first term. The wise custom which limits the President to two terms regards the substance and not the form; and under no circumstances will I be a candidate for or accept another nomination." This statement helps to account for the Congressional opposition Roosevelt encountered during his second term, despite his great popular victory in 1904.

Rooseveltian Reforms

Conscious now of the full extent of his popularity, Roosevelt moved further toward progressivism. In this he was clearly responding to the mood of the nation, now insistently demanding reform of the abuses exposed by the muckrakers. Moreover, although Bryan had never won the presidency, he had greatly influenced the Democratic party, a majority of whose legislators were now committed to government regulation of business.

As in earlier upsurges of popular protest, the railroads were the most conspicuous targets for criticism. The Interstate Commerce Act, the Elkins Act, and various state regulatory laws had been ineffective in curing the long-existent abuses of exorbitant rates, discriminations, disregard of public safety, and excessive political influence. Roosevelt called for greater regulation, but was opposed by the conservative Senate leadership of his own party. The Townshend-Esch Bill, incorporating presidential recommendations, passed the House early in 1905, but died in the Upper House. A year later, the President gave his support to a stronger bill introduced into the new Congress by Peter Hepburn of Iowa. Although the measure speedily passed the House by a vote of 346 to 7, it was bitterly opposed in the Senate. Since Republican leaders like Aldrich of Rhode Island, Elkins of West Virginia, and Foraker of Ohio were against effective regulation, Roosevelt had to ally himself with men like "Pitchfork Ben" Tillman of South Carolina, the famous Populist-Democrat, and Jonathan Dolliver of Iowa, a progressive Republican. In the end, the President felt compelled to compromise with the conservatives and the bill passed, 71 to 3, in a form somewhat disappointing to the progressives. The Hepburn Act expanded the Interstate Commerce Commission from five to seven members and extended its authority to cover express companies, sleeping-car companies, pipe lines, and railroad terminals. The most important new power bestowed upon the commission was that of nullifying rates found, upon complaint of shippers, to be unreasonable and, in such cases, stating the maximum rate that would be reasonable. The orders of the commission were to be binding upon the carriers unless set aside by the courts, with the burden of initiating such litigation being transferred from the commission to the carriers. Free passes, except to railroad personnel, were forbidden, and the act attempted to compel the lines to give up other forms of business.

Progressive Westerners criticized the Hepburn Act because it permitted the courts to delay and reverse the orders of the commission and because it did not authorize the commission to appraise the value of railroad properties—a step that Senator LaFollette argued was an essential preliminary to determining whether rates were bringing more than a fair return to the carrier. Whatever may have been its shortcomings, the Hepburn Act saved the Interstate Commerce Commission from oblivion and gave it its first really important powers. It was the most important piece of economic legislation of the Roosevelt administration, since it established Federal regulation as a major influence on the operation of the American transportation system. Shippers were prompt to take advantage of the Hepburn Act; more complaints—some 1500—were registered with the commission in the two years after its passage than in the nearly two decades before. Within a few years, a number of rates were reduced, sometimes through commission action, sometimes through voluntary decision of the carriers. Yet these reductions did not result in bankruptcy for the railroads, as had been widely predicted by the conservatives during the fight over the Hepburn Bill; instead, the carriers adjusted themselves to the new conditions and discovered they were not so badly off.

Another act of 1906 made the railroads engaged in interstate commerce liable for injuries sustained by their employees. Although this measure was invalidated by the Supreme Court, a law somewhat more strictly drawn was passed in 1908 and upheld. Moreover, under the Immunity of Witnesses Act of 1906, officials could be compelled to testify about the operations and conduct of their corporations without running the risk of self-incrimination.

Popular demand for reform, at a peak in 1906, focused particularly on the problem of pure food and drugs. Dr. Harvey W. Wiley, chief chemist of the Department of Agriculture, had been warning the public of abuses in this field for many years and urging remedial legislation. He found some of his most energetic co-workers among women like Alice Lakey of the Consumers' League. Publicity for the cause was gained through experiments of the "poison squad"— a group of Wiley's assistants who permitted themselves to be used as human guinea pigs to test the effects of harmful patent medicines and adulterated foods. Even more effective was an exhibit at the St. Louis Exposition of 1904, where visitors could examine textiles and woods vividly dyed by coloring materials extracted from preserved foods. The usually conservative Edward Bok crusaded against patent medicines in the *Ladies' Home Journal*, while Samuel Hopkins Adams applied the muckrake in articles in *Collier's*.

Despite all this agitation, pure food bills passed by the House were not even permitted to come to a vote in the Senate. The National Wholesale Liquor Dealers' Association and the Proprietary Medicine Association fought all such proposals both through direct lobbying and through threatening the newspapers with advertising boycotts. Early in 1906, by a disheartening shift of tactics, the conservatives allowed a Pure Food Bill to pass the Senate, but bottled it up in committee in the House.

The final burst of indignation that overrode this obstructionism resulted from the publication of Upton Sinclair's novel, *The Jungle*. Intended primarily as a plea for socialism, the book had its greatest effect in acquainting the public with the shockingly unsanitary conditions under which meat was slaughtered and prepared for market. At first skeptical of the book's accuracy, President Roosevelt was moved to action when Sinclair's charges were largely confirmed by investigators from the Department of Agriculture. Responding to pressure both from the White House and the nation, Congress passed the Pure Food and Drugs Act on June 23, 1906, and the Meat Inspection Act a week later. The former prohibited the manufacture, sale, or transportation of adulterated, misbranded, or harmful foods, drugs, or liquors, and required that medicines containing dangerous drugs should carry a label stating the character of the contents. The latter authorized Federal inspectors to examine meat shipped in interstate commerce and to enforce adequate sanitary standards in the slaughtering houses. Although the laws fell short of the demands of the progressives for penalties against false and misleading advertising, they represented a significant advance for the principle of regulation of industry in the public interest.

President Roosevelt also tried during his second administration to help the cause of the worker, although he had considerably less success than in other areas. For example, he urged a thorough investigation of the child labor situation; he warned that the use of injunctions in labor disputes might result in "grave abuses" to the strikers; and he proposed a workmen's compensation measure for Federal employees. None of these suggestions was given legislative approval. The President's only victory came with the passage of a measure in 1908 for the regulation of hours for telegraph operators and trainmen employed by railroads crossing state lines.

Conservation

Theodore Roosevelt's most enduring contributions may have been made in the field of conservation. For decades the national domain had been passing out of the hands of the Federal government into those of private owners. With careless generosity, not only agricultural lands, but forest regions, mineral deposits, oil fields, and water-power sites had been given over to ruthless exploitation, without thought for the future needs of the country. Roosevelt's great love for the outdoors and the West ideally equipped him for the task of laying down a new policy.

Early in his presidency, Roosevelt threw his support to a bill sponsored by Senator Francis G. Newlands, a Nevada Democrat, for a Federal reclamation program. The resulting Newlands Act of 1902 provided that the proceeds of Western land sales should be applied to the construction of dams and other works necessary to irrigate arid tracts. Settlers on the reclaimed land were to repay the government, and these revenues would constitute a revolving fund for further irrigation projects. Under this important law great dams like the Shoshone in Wyoming and the Roosevelt in Arizona were built and nearly 1.2 million acres of land were opened to cultivation by 1920.

Taking advantage of legislation that had been on the books since 1891 but applied only on a small scale by his cautious predecessors, Roosevelt withdrew from public sale 150 million acres of forest land—an area considerably larger than France. Roosevelt's adviser and most enthusiastic lieutenant in this policy was Gifford Pinchot, chief of the Forestry Service in the Department of Agriculture. The President was equally interested in protecting mineral and water-power sites. In 1903 he vetoed a bill awarding to private interests the right to build a dam and generating system at Muscle Shoals—a location destined to be famous in future debates on the public versus private power issue. Despite questionable legal authority, he ordered the withdrawal from public entry of millions of acres of coal and phosphate lands and water-power sites.

Roosevelt had a great flair for publicity; by numerous expedients he succeeded in making the American public conservation-conscious. In December, 1907, his annual message to Congress contained a striking survey of the whole problem of conservation and the development of the nation's resources. The next year an important conservation conference was held at Washington, with governors, legislators, scientific experts, and prominent citizens from all parts of the country in attendance. The resulting declaration of principles urged the extension of the forest fire fighting service, protection for sources of navigable waterways, control of timber cutting on both public and private lands, and government retention of subsoil rights, especially in coal, oil, and natural gas. Inspired by this conference and other factors, forty-one state conservation commissions were established before 1909. To coordinate these activities and compile an inventory of national resources, Roosevelt appointed a National Conservation Commission with Pinchot as chairman. Just before Roosevelt left office, an international conference, representing several of the countries of North America, agreed to cooperate in preserving the natural resources of the continent.

The conservation program ran into increasingly formidable obstacles. Lumbering firms and other economic groups eager to exploit the national domain lobbied actively against the new policy; many Western politicians opposed it as retarding the growth of their section; Congressmen resented the President's failure to gain legislative authorization for many parts of his program. Laws were passed to prohibit further reservations of forest lands in certain states and to deny funds for the continuance of commissions established without Congressional approval. Despite such harassments, Roosevelt succeeded in advancing the ideal of conservation to the point where public opinion would countenance no major reversal of policy after he left the White House.

The Panic of 1907

In 1907 the country suffered a brief interruption to the unrivaled prosperity it had been enjoying for ten years. The stock market began to decline in March as a warning of troubles ahead. Later in the year several railroads went into receivers' hands, thirteen New York City banks failed, and elsewhere serious unemployment and wage cuts were to be found. It was largely a bankers' panic brought about through speculation and rash management, but conservatives did not miss the opportunity to lay their troubles upon the shoulders of the President; they asserted that the depression had been caused by the business community's lack of confidence in the policies of the administration. This responsibility Roosevelt denied, but certain concessions to Wall Street were, nevertheless, made.

One morning during the worst phase of the panic, Roosevelt was called away from his breakfast table to meet two envoys from J. P. Morgan. They confided to the President that a large New York financial institution would fail unless a quantity of shares in the Tennessee Coal and Iron Company were taken off its hands. The United States Steel Corporation stood ready to make the purchase, but its management desired to know whether this action would be viewed by the government as a violation of the Sherman Antitrust Act. The President replied that he did not feel it his duty "to interpose any objections." Thus did the "trust buster" give his tacit blessing to a transaction whereby the country's largest corporation acquired control of one of its most important competitors.[6]

The panic focused attention on two major deficiencies of the national banking system: the inelasticity of the national bank notes, whose volume depended not on the needs of business but upon holdings of government bonds, and the lack of an adequate system of reserves upon which banks could draw in time of stringency. As a first step toward reform, the Aldrich-Vreeland Act of 1908 permitted national banks to form associations for the issuance of temporary currency in time of financial emergency. The Act also authorized the establishment of a National Monetary Commission to investigate the currency systems of the United States and foreign countries. Thus was the ground prepared for the establishment of the Federal Reserve System in 1913.

The economic setback of 1907 was brief and the country soon resumed its normal pursuits—one of which was to debate the virtues and vices of its colorful Chief Executive. One episode after another—many of them now almost for-

[6] United States Steel obtained some $80 million worth of Tennessee Coal and Iron stock for approximately $45 million.

gotten—became matters of heated controversy. Toward Roosevelt few could be neutral. When he invited Booker T. Washington, prominent Negro educator, to lunch at the White House, Roosevelt provoked bitter denunciation from Southern whites, as he did by appointing Negroes to Federal offices in the South. But the Negroes themselves later found occasion to condemn the President for his hasty and indiscriminate punishment of Negro soldiers unjustly accused of provoking a racial affray in Brownsville, Texas. When news was scarce, reporters could always play up the President's latest vigorous pronouncement, whether it be condemnation of "nature-fakers" or "race suicide," or a boost for "simplified spelling."

On issues more clearly within his field of responsibility, Roosevelt was both praised and blamed. Admirers made much of his support for civil service reform, where the number of positions filled through competitive examinations was materially increased, while corrupt or dishonest officials were summarily removed. On the other hand, critics accused the President of using his power of appointment to build up the strength of his party and his own personal machine.

The more advanced liberals were often disappointed in Roosevelt. He refused to be drawn into any really serious quarrel with the "standpatters" of his party, men like Speaker "Uncle Joe" Cannon of the House and Senator Aldrich. He shunned the cause of tariff revision, which was, in the opinion of many progressives, the most promising way of attacking monopoly, although there was, in truth, no widespread popular demand for such reform. Obviously Roosevelt was no radical. He was by his own description an intelligent conservative, seeking to preserve free enterprise by curbing the most flagrant abuses in the system, abuses that were likely to lead to revolutionary discontent. He had numerous defects of character—vanity, bellicosity, impulsiveness. But his faults were easily forgotten by the great American public, which loved him for his youthful energy, his zest for adventure, his gift for vivid phrasemaking, and his staunch patriotism. Above all, they praised him because he was the first President to make them fully aware of the existing evils of big business and to try to remedy some of those evils.

4

Taft and the Battle of the Progressives

The progressive movement, heralded before 1900 by prophets in advance of their time and by rumblings of protest among the farmers and laborers, became a popular religion during the presidency of Theodore Roosevelt. During his seven and a half years in the White House, the Rough Rider promoted the new faith at the national level, and provided as well some of the incentive for similar advances in the states and municipalities. The crusade had not gained all its objectives, however, and William Howard Taft, Roosevelt's more or less hand-picked successor, undertook to carry it on. Unfortunately, he did not have his predecessor's happy faculty of being able to conciliate both supporters and opponents of progressivism. As a result, the progressives within his own party, growing steadily in strength, set up such a clamor as virtually to disrupt the regular Republican organization. By constantly keeping the reform issue before the public, these insurgents helped to force the movement to a climax in the campaign of 1912, when three parties fought for the approval of the voters, each claiming to be more devoted to the cause of true reform than were its rivals.

The Crown Prince

Such was Roosevelt's popularity and power that he could have easily secured a third term for himself, but he had publicly renounced any intention of seeking such an honor immediately after his electoral triumph of 1904. Like other strong Presidents before him, however, Roosevelt was able virtually to name his successor, something to which he gave serious consideration.

There were several men who might have been chosen to take over his mantle.

Many believed that Elihu Root was the greatest intellectual force in the Roosevelt Cabinet, but the President realized that the Secretary of State's earlier career as a corporation lawyer would be held against him, especially by the progressives. As far as Charles Evans Hughes was concerned, his brilliant record as a lawyer, as the successful investigator of insurance rackets, and as governor of New York was offset by Roosevelt's distrust of his uncompromising attitude and the belief that the governor might pursue his own policies, rather than those of his predecessor. Consequently, the outgoing President threw his support to William Howard Taft, who came from a prominent Ohio family, had an excellent academic record at Yale and in law school, and had gained renown in several judicial positions. Taft also had done outstanding work in the Philippines, both as a member of the Second Commission and as governor-general. When he succeeded Root as Secretary of War, he performed his new duties in able fashion. Fat and genial, Taft was judged to have good potentialities as a vote getter—even though he had never run for an elective office. Roosevelt also respected Taft's administrative ability and his loyalty to the cause of reform. Yielding to both presidential and family pressure, Taft agreed to seek the White House instead of the Supreme Court post that would have been his own preference.

William Howard Taft, *third from left*. (Brown Bros.)

At the Republican national convention in Chicago, Taft was nominated on the first ballot, thanks largely to Roosevelt's backing, with James S. Sherman of New York as his running mate. The platform was a moderately progressive document that gave no hint of any intraparty strife. It highly endorsed the Roosevelt regime, with emphasis upon the war against the trusts and the quest for social justice. It also called for a strengthening of the Interstate Commerce and Sherman Antitrust Acts, for conservation and good roads, for a postal savings system, and even for tariff revision. Not accepted, however, were the more radical planks advocated by LaFollette and his friends, which would have pledged the party to legislation requiring public reports of campaign expenditures, the valuation of railroad properties, and the direct election of United States Senators.

The Democrats, having suffered an overwhelming defeat with a conservative candidate in 1904, returned to the leadership of Bryan, nominating him on the first ballot at their Denver convention—a remarkable tribute to a two-time loser. The platform condemned the Republican party as the organization of "privileges and private monopoly." It demanded laws prohibiting corporations from contributing to campaign funds, new antitrust legislation, and measures limiting the issuance of injunctions in labor disputes. Especially firm was the plank advocating a reduction of the Dingley Tariff.

The Labor Issue

The election of 1908 was notable for the more prominent part taken by organized labor. Samuel Gompers had always placed the achievement of collective bargaining above the enactment of legislation, but by 1908 a situation had arisen that could only be met by political action. The utilization of Federal court injunctions to break strikes had become increasingly common since Attorney General Richard Olney's well-publicized success in dealing with the Pullman strike of 1894. Indeed, the interference of the courts with labor union activities took extreme forms after 1900.

A notable instance was in 1902, when the hatters' union, attempting to support a strike by the employees of D. E. Loewe and Company of Danbury, Connecticut, declared a nation-wide boycott against the Loewe Company's products. The next year the company filed suit in the Federal district court for triple damages of $240,000 against the officers and members of the United Hatters of America, asserting that this boycott had been a conspiracy in restraint of trade under the Sherman Act. Although the case was not finally disposed of until 1917, the union lost the principal bastions of its defense in February, 1908, when the Supreme Court ruled in the so-called Danbury Hatters' case (Loewe v. Lawlor) that such a boycott constituted an interference with interstate commerce under the Sherman Act. The implications of the decision were most alarming to organized labor. Not only might a union be rendered liable for civil damages for its strike and boycott activities, but individual union members might be held responsible for the actions of union officers and might suffer the attachment of their homes and savings.[1]

Another evidence of the vulnerability of labor-union activity to attack through the courts came in the Buck's Stove case. A controversy between the foundrymen's union and the Buck's Stove and Range Company resulted in the inclusion of the company's name among the eighty or more firms on the *American Federationist's* list of concerns deemed unfair to labor and from whom members of the AFL should not buy. The company thereupon appealed to the courts and in December, 1907, the Supreme Court of the District of Columbia issued an injunction ordering the American Federation of Labor and its affiliated bodies to desist from further prosecuting their boycott. Like the Danbury Hatters' case, subsequent litigation kept the issue before the courts for years. In 1909 jail sentences were imposed upon Samuel Gompers and two other officers of the AFL for contempt of court in violating the injunction. Gompers was saved from serving his sentence through a technicality, but the whole issue of the use of the injunction and the boycott in labor controversies and of labor's status under the Sherman Act was brought once again into the center of the stage.

Gompers and other labor leaders traveled first to Chicago and then to Denver in an endeavor to insert planks in the Republican and Democratic platforms of 1908 promising the enactment of legislation limiting the issuance of injunctions in labor disputes and requiring trial by jury in contempt cases where the alleged contempt did not occur in the presence of the court. The Republican response to these demands was not satisfactory; indeed, the platform upheld "the authority and integrity of the courts" and insisted that "their powers to enforce their process and to protect life, liberty, and property . . . be preserved inviolate." On the other hand, the Democrats received the Gompers delegation cordially and incorporated most of its requests in the party platform.

The American Federation of Labor followed its traditional non-partisan policy to the extent of refraining from a formal endorsement of the Democratic party, but the inadequacy of the Republican platform and Taft's personal shortcomings were emphasized. Therefore, labor's rank and file could hardly mistake which candidate was favored by the Federation leaders. The issue was given more prominence by the fact that Taft was alleged to have been an "injunction judge" during his earlier years on the bench.

Gompers' support of Bryan, however, was a poor counterweight to Roose-

---

[1] The case was finally settled for $234,000 in 1917; the greater part of this amount was raised by organized labor.

velt's support of Taft. The campaign started off in dull fashion, but eventually became more interesting than the preceding one. Both candidates went on long speaking tours, with Bryan's oratory being more than offset by Taft's patent honesty and infectious chuckles. Thus, when the votes were counted in November, the crown prince's victory appeared to be scarcely less sweeping than that of his sponsor four years before. The electoral count was 321 to 162; the popular vote, 7,700,000 to 6,410,000; and the Republicans continued in secure control of both Houses of Congress. Yet there were storm clouds on the Republican horizon. Even though Taft's popular total was about 75,000 larger than Roosevelt's in 1904, the Democratic vote was 1,375,000 higher than four years earlier. Moreover, Taft had found it difficult during the campaign to hold together the conservative and progressive wings of his own party. The progressive elements, who were sometimes highly critical of Taft's stand on important issues, had become stronger in Congress. And the Democrats had gained control of several Midwestern and Western states that Roosevelt had easily carried in 1904.

An Unfortunate Beginning

The enthusiasm of victory, however, made the Republican party overlook the danger signals, and Taft took office with every prospect of a peaceful, successful term. Roosevelt and the rest of the country assumed that the personnel and policies of the new administration would be almost identical with those of the old. This belief was accentuated when Taft, in his inaugural, promised to carry on his predecessor's policies. Shortly after the ceremony was over, Roosevelt departed for Africa on a big-game hunt, confident that the nation was in good hands.

To follow Roosevelt in the White House, however, was far from easy. The new President was not a good mixer and, if anything, he shunned the publicity that his predecessor sought. He did not believe he should be given praise for doing the job for which he was elected. Whereas Roosevelt could further the progressive objectives by obtaining the support of the party liberals, without losing the backing of the conservatives, Taft, faced by a growing party schism, was compelled to choose between the two factions. Though sympathetic to the progressive movement and doing much for it, he cast his lot chiefly with the Old Guard—which proved to be an error. Roosevelt had refused to consider the Constitution as a "strait jacket"; to him, the executive branch was all powerful. Taft, on the other hand, believed in the separation of powers; with his legal training, he was of the opinion that the Constitution was sacred and that the executive branch was one of three co-equals. Consequently, his approach to progressivism was very different from that of Roosevelt, and, with his failure to retain the support of the American people generally, he was bound to encounter stormy times.

The first real doubts of the progressives about the new administration came when Taft made his cabinet selections. Only two of them, Secretary of the Navy George Meyer and Secretary of Agriculture James Wilson, had been serving under Roosevelt. The outgoing President was unhappy about the situation because he had been under the impression that it was Taft's intention to retain at least five of the Roosevelt cabinet. He particularly resented Taft's rejection of Secretary of the Interior James R. Garfield, a great champion of conservation, and of Attorney General Luke Wright, to whom Roosevelt had offered this post in 1908 with the assurance that he would be retained in the official family of the incoming President. In making the new selections, Taft drew largely on members of the legal profession. Philander Knox of Pennsylvania, the new Secretary of State, had been Roosevelt's Attorney General, but the progressives now remembered principally his earlier career as a big corporation lawyer. George B. Wickersham of New York, the new Attorney General, had a similar background and was regarded as a partisan of big business.[2] Taken as a whole, this cabinet did not consist of men of unusual force.

The Tariff Battle

The Republican party had pledged itself to revise the tariff, and Taft quickly called the new Congress into special session to redeem this promise. Evidences of party discord immediately appeared in the House, where twelve progressive Republicans, discontented with the extreme control over rules and procedure exercised by Speaker Cannon, a leader of the Old Guard, tried to prevent his re-election. Even though they had the support of most of the Democrats, they could not muster sufficient strength to accomplish their purpose; but their refusal to knuckle down to party discipline was an augury of things to come.

With the revolt of these insurgents apparently squelched, the House Ways and Means Committee, under the chairmanship of Sereno Payne of New York, prepared a bill that, though far from radical, provided for considerable reductions, particularly on steel and iron, from the rates of the Dingley Tariff and also placed more raw materials on the free list. Generally overlooked in the partisan discussions that followed were certain definitely progressive inclusions: partial free trade with the Philippines; provision for a tariff commission to study the effect of the tariff in scientific fashion and to suggest changes; and an

[2] Other cabinet members were: Franklin MacVeagh of Illinois, Secretary of the Treasury; Jacob M. Dickinson of Tennessee, Secretary of War; Frank H. Hitchcock of Massachusetts, who had managed the Taft campaign, Postmaster General; Richard A. Ballinger of Washington, Secretary of the Interior; and Charles Nagel of Missouri, Secretary of Commerce and Labor.

income tax on corporations engaged in interstate commerce, which would be another step toward greater control of big business and a measure that Roosevelt had strenuously advocated. The Payne Bill passed the House in practically its original form, but in the Senate it had to run the gauntlet of the Finance Committee headed by the powerful Senator Aldrich, a rigid protectionist. Amendments to a total of 847 were made, generally in the direction of higher rates. Debate on the floor of the Senate was unusually acrimonious. Western Republicans led by LaFollette denounced what they regarded as a betrayal of the campaign pledge, while the Aldrich faction countered with the assertion that only "a revision" of the tariff had been promised and that the legislators had a free hand to change it either upward or downward. Ten insurgents carried their revolt to the point of voting with the Democrats against the amended measure, but they could not prevent its passage.

The Temptation of William. Speaker Cannon and Senator Aldrich attempting to persuade President Taft to support high protection. (By Rehse in the *St. Paul Pioneer Press*.)

Since the House and Senate had passed the bill in different forms, a conference committee was necessary. Warned by President Taft that he would veto the measure unless reasonable concessions were made, the conferees reduced a few of the Senate schedules. Nevertheless, as finally passed and signed by the

President on August 5, 1909, the Payne-Aldrich Tariff was a bitter disappointment to progressives. Since every tariff measure covers thousands of items, it is
difficult to compare one act with another. This is especially true of the Payne-
Aldrich Tariff, because the Aldrich faction had succeeded in substituting
specific duties for the previous ad valorem charges; it can only be said that
despite reductions in some schedules and raises in a few others, no significant
change had been made in the system of high protection maintained since the
Civil War.

Taft did not like the measure, but, considering the dissension within Republican ranks, he believed that his signature might avoid further strife and restore
party harmony. The reverse was the case, for the insurgents, most of them
ardent admirers of Roosevelt, asserted that Taft had sold out to the Old Guard.
Their indignation was only intensified when the President attempted to defend
the act in a speech at Winona, Wisconsin. "I would say without hesitation,"
Taft told his audience, "that this is the best tariff bill that the Republican party
has ever passed, and therefore the best tariff bill that has been passed at all. . . ."

The Struggle over Reciprocity

That Taft did desire to lower the tariff wall and at the same time to restore
the harmony disrupted by the ill-fated Payne-Aldrich Act was shown in the
reciprocity agreement signed with Canada on January 21, 1911. More than one
hundred items were to be placed on the free list and the tariff was to be reduced
on more than four hundred others. In the President's opinion, this arrangement
promised many advantages. Its effect would be to modify the unpopular Payne-
Aldrich Tariff—which should commend it to Democrats and insurgent Republicans; on the other hand, it would make for closer ties with the neighbor to the
north and widen the market for American manufacturers—considerations likely
to appeal to regular Republicans.

To his surprise, Taft found himself involved in one of the most heated battles
of his administration. Instead of receiving the expected support from the progressives, the President was promptly opposed by LaFollette and his followers
who charged that the reciprocity arrangement would benefit only Eastern industrialists, while Western interests would be injured by the importation of
Canadian cattle, hides, and grain. A strange alliance of insurgents and ultraconservatives opposed the treaty, while Republicans loyal to the President and
many Democrats united to support it.

Due to the well-known difficulties of obtaining a two-thirds Senate majority
for the approval of formal treaties, it had to be stipulated that the tariff changes
should be made by independent but parallel legislation in the two countries. In
the United States, the House of Representatives passed the necessary bill in

February, 1911, but the Senate failed to take action before it adjourned on March 4. The President refused to be thwarted and called the newly elected Congress into special session in April. Once again the House, now controlled by the Democrats, approved the measure, but in the Senate a bitter fight developed. The National Grange and other farm organizations lobbied against reciprocity, while Taft sought to enlist public support for it. In vigorous speeches in New York and Chicago he charged that the opposition was inspired by a "contemptible union" of the lumber and paper interests and "those who claimed vociferously to represent the whole farming industry of the United States." On June 21, 1911, the Senate finally passed the bill by a vote of 53 to 27. For the moment it was a great triumph for Taft, although one that would have been impossible without the support of the Democrats; of the President's own party members, 12 insurgents and 12 regulars voted against the measure.

But the ill fate that pursued so many of Taft's ventures overtook this one as well. For almost half a century Canadian statesmen had sought a reciprocity treaty with the United States in order to enjoy again the benefits that had followed an earlier agreement between the two countries in effect from 1854 to 1866. Now that such an agreement had been actually worked out and accepted by the American Congress, the whole project was wrecked through its involvement in Canadian domestic politics. The treaty had been the work of the veteran Liberal Prime Minister, Sir Wilfrid Laurier; it was opposed by Sir Robert Borden and the Conservatives. The latter asserted that reciprocity would injure the British mother country, that it would result in American exploitation of Canadian resources, and, above all, that it would pave the way for the eventual annexation of the Dominion by the United States. The Conservatives pointed out that the Hearst papers had been agitating for such an annexation for many years and that Speaker Champ Clark hoped "to see the day when the American flag will float over every square foot of the British North American possessions," which he believed could be accomplished by gradual economic means. Even President Taft had spoken of the "light and imperceptible" ties that bound Canada to the mother country. The issue forced a dissolution of the Canadian Parliament and, in the resulting general election, the Liberals and the cause of reciprocity went down together in humiliating defeat. To make matters worse for Taft, in the United States the Western progressives charged the President with full responsibility for the failure—although they themselves had not favored the project.

The Ballinger Affair

While the controversy over the Payne-Aldrich Tariff was still raging, the administration fell under violent attack for its alleged sabotage of Rooseveltian conservation policies. The new Secretary of the Interior, Richard A. Ballinger, was, like the President, a cautious lawyer. He believed that the Roosevelt administration in its enthusiasm for conservation had sometimes exceeded its legal authority. With Taft's support, Ballinger proposed to proceed in the future with much more scrupulous regard for legal niceties. The ardent Gifford Pinchot was still head of the Forestry Service, and such circumspection immediately aroused his suspicions that the new Secretary was in league with large corporate interests greedy to gain control of the nation's mineral reserves and water-power sites. A month after Taft's inaugural, Pinchot was protesting vigorously against the action of Ballinger in opening again to private entry extensive water-power sites that Roosevelt had set aside during his last days in office. On this occasion Taft took Pinchot's side and ordered the lands in question to be restored to the Forestry Service, but the friction between the Secretary of the Interior and the Chief Forester continued and deepened.

Ballinger's integrity was also doubted by one of his own subordinates, Louis R. Glavis, the young chief of the Field Division. Ballinger insisted upon approving the claims of one Clarence Cunningham and others to extensive coal and timber lands in Alaska. Glavis had been investigating these claims and had become convinced that they were fraudulent and that the whole affair was a conspiracy designed to enable a Morgan-Guggenheim syndicate—the embodiment of sinister big business—to gain control of a valuable portion of the public domain. Rebuffed in his protests to Ballinger, Glavis confided his suspicions to Pinchot, who took the unusual step of sending the young man directly to the President. Unmindful of the explosive possibilities of the affair, Taft dealt with it in a hasty and superficial manner. Accepting the assurances of the accused Ballinger that Glavis' charges were unfounded, the President wrote a public letter to the Secretary, exonerating him and requesting him to dismiss Glavis.

Conservation—already a holy cause to millions of Americans—now had a martyr. The insurgent bloc in Congress took up the case of Glavis with enthusiasm, while sensational attacks upon the Interior Department were published in the great muckraking magazines: *Hampton's*, *McClure's*, and *Collier's*. Much was made of the fact that, before his appointment to office, Ballinger had upon one occasion acted as private counsel for the Cunningham group. Pinchot, taking up the issue with characteristic zeal, finally took the serious step of writing an indignant letter to the insurgent Senator Dolliver of Iowa, which was read on the floor of the Senate. Suffering the same fate as Glavis, the Chief Forester was dismissed for insubordination. This was a much more serious matter. Glavis' name had been known to only a few; Pinchot's was a household word and had become synonymous with the whole cause of conservation. Furthermore, Pinchot, as everyone knew, was the intimate friend of Theodore Roosevelt.

This was not the end of the embarrassing ramifications of the Ballinger affair. During 1910 a Congressional committee held extended hearings, in which the Glavis-Pinchot charges were pressed by the brilliant liberal lawyer, Louis D. Brandeis. Although the investigating committee's standpat majority supported the conduct of Taft and Ballinger, the administration's victory was a hollow one since a minority report sharply criticized the President and advised the censure and removal of the Secretary. Moreover, some new facts about the case, brought to light under the sharp questioning of Brandeis, provided ammunition for additional newspaper attacks upon the administration. In March, 1911, Ballinger decided that his health would not permit him to continue in office and he was replaced by a conservationist of the more zealous school, Walter Fisher of Chicago. Under the new Secretary the controversial Cunningham claims were withdrawn by the government.

In the judgment of most recent historians, Secretary Ballinger was the victim of considerable injustice in the attacks which finally drove him from office. Apparently he was a real, though legalistic, friend of the conservation cause and innocent of any corrupt dealings in connection with the Cunningham claims. His principal accusers, Glavis and Pinchot, were honest and sincere, but mistaken. Whatever the merits of the controversy, however, the immediate effect of the affair was most damaging to the Taft administration.[3] Both the Ballinger incident and the Payne-Aldrich Tariff contributed to Republican humiliations at the polls in 1910. For the first time in eighteen years the voters sent a Democratic majority to the House of Representatives, while the Republican majority in the Senate was reduced from twenty-eight to ten.

Republican Insurgency

The political dexterity of Theodore Roosevelt had prevented any serious schism within the Republican ranks while he remained in the White House. Each succeeding month of the Taft administration, however, widened the gulf between the party conservatives and the extreme progressives. In the Senate, serious insurgency dated from the fight over the Payne-Aldrich Tariff, while in the House the incident most clearly foreshadowing a party split was the fight of 1910 over the powers of Speaker Cannon. Following precedents laid down by Speaker "Czar" Reed in the early nineties, Cannon had ruled the House with an iron hand since he first gained the Speaker's post in 1901. He appointed the Republican majority on all committees and named their chairmen, being thus enabled to reward the faithful and discipline the rebellious. Moreover, he himself served as chairman of the powerful Rules Committee, which deter-

---

[3] Lending credence to the charge against the administration was evidence that Taft had predated a document in the case.

mined procedure and made whatever special orders might be necessary. To call up a bill, a Representative had to negotiate humbly with the Speaker in his private chambers. Otherwise measures never emerged from committee, nor did their sponsors obtain permission to address the House.

Not discouraged by the earlier failure, Representative George W. Norris, a Republican from Nebraska, launched a new and sudden attack upon the Speaker's autocratic powers in March, 1910. He moved that the Committee on Rules be henceforth elected by the House and that the Speaker be excluded from membership upon it. Although caught momentarily off guard, Cannon fought desperately to retain his full powers, and he had the support of all the standpatters. But after an excited debate that continued without interruption for almost thirty hours, the Speaker was beaten. About forty insurgent Republicans voted with the Democrats for Norris' motion. Cannon thereupon dramatically offered to vacate the Speakership, but the insurgents, including Norris himself, voted to retain the old veteran, personally a likeable character. The following year the Democrats, placed in a majority by the election of 1910, voted still further restrictions upon the Speaker's powers. All committees were henceforth to be chosen by the Ways and Means Committee, which, in its turn, was made up of members designated by the caucuses of the majority and minority parties.

As Republicans approached the parting of the ways, the President elected to stand with the conservatives. In his private correspondence he alluded to men like LaFollette and Norris as "yellow dogs," and he discriminated against the whole insurgent group in distributing patronage. Despite Taft's attempt to read them out of the party, all the progressives except Senator Beveridge triumphantly survived the election of 1910, while many of the conservatives were repudiated by the voters.

Taft and Reform

Despite dissension within Republican ranks and reviving Democratic strength, the Taft administration achieved not a little for the cause of reform. Even the unfortunate Ballinger had to his credit several new conservation laws enacted by Congress upon his advice. The President was given authority to withdraw from entry other lands in addition to forest reserves; the public lands were reclassified according to a scientific survey of their resources, and the title of surface holdings was separated from the coal, oil, natural gas, asphalt, or phosphates below surface, rights to which were to be leased rather than sold. In 1911 the Appalachian Forest Reserve Act was passed, appropriating $8 million over a period of four years for the purchase of lands controlling the sources of important streams in the White Mountains and the southern part of the Appalachian chain.

As far as trust control was concerned, President Taft urged the enactment of a measure to provide for Federal incorporation of firms engaged in interstate commerce. Such companies would be compelled to submit complete reports of their operations to the Department of Commerce and Labor, and would be prevented from buying stock in other businesses. Through injunctions and court decisions threatening them with dissolution, such corporations would be competently regulated. Congress took no action upon the President's suggestion and the proposal died.

Consequently, the administration resorted to the methods of the Roosevelt regime. In the Justice Department Attorney General Wickersham, though accounted a conservative, demonstrated great zeal in the enforcement of the Sherman Act, initiating some eighty suits against the trusts. His most notable victories came in 1911 when the Supreme Court ordered the dissolution of the American Tobacco Company and the Standard Oil Company of New Jersey in the forms that these combinations had then attained. Gratifying though these decisions were to those who feared the trusts, jubilation could not be complete. These corporate monsters, chopped into pieces, showed a discouraging vitality in their dismembered parts; indeed they often continued to act like single organisms. Moreover, the Standard Oil decision revealed an inclination upon the part of Chief Justice White and a majority of his colleagues to narrow the scope of the Sherman Act by judicial interpretation. Because of the Act's broad and general terms, said the Chief Justice, it seemed clear that their application "necessarily called for the exercise of judgment"; "the standard of reason" should be resorted to in determining whether or not the statute had been violated in any given case. In a dissenting opinion by Justice Harlan, the so-called rule of reason was condemned as a usurpation of power upon the part of the Court; in effect, argued Harlan, the Court was amending the statute. Many legislators became convinced that new antitrust legislation was imperative. The Senate Committee on Interstate Commerce reported that, although it respected the intelligence and integrity of the Supreme Court, it felt an "unwillingness to repose in that court, or any other court, the vast and undefined power which it must exercise in the administration of the statute under the rule which it has promulgated." Taft, however, defended the principle laid down by the Court.

New railroad legislation was passed in 1910. Under the procedures of the Hepburn Act, railroad rates fixed by the carriers were collected by them until some shipper complained that they were unreasonable and the commission, after investigation, ordered them to be changed; meantime, shippers had to continue paying the high charges. By the new Mann-Elkins Act, the commission was empowered to suspend newly announced rates for a period not exceeding ten months and to decide during that time whether the rates were reasonable. Furthermore, the commission might act upon its own initiative without waiting for some shipper to complain. Other provisions of the new measure extended the jurisdiction of the commission over means of communication as well as transportation and revived the old prohibition against charging more for the short haul than for the long haul over the same route. A Commerce Court was instituted to expedite appeals from the orders of the commission, but the court proved unpopular and was abolished by Congress before Taft left office. LaFollette failed in 1910, as he had before in 1906, to have the commission authorized to appraise the property of railroads as a basis for determining rates, but this principle was finally incorporated in the Physical Valuations Act of 1913.

With President Taft's approval Congress passed the Sixteenth (1909) and Seventeenth (1912) Amendments to the Federal Constitution. The former granted to Congress the power to lay and collect taxes on income from whatever source derived; the latter provided for the direct election of United States Senators. Both of these proposals had long been on the program of American progressives. In 1913 both amendments, having been ratified by the required number of states, were proclaimed in effect. The Payne-Aldrich Tariff had, in a sense, anticipated the Sixteenth Amendment by applying a 1 per cent tax on corporation earnings over $5,000.

Another demand of the progressives was met by a law of 1910 requiring publication of the names of persons who contributed to campaign funds in Federal elections, the amounts given, and a detailed account of the expenditures of the candidates and the purposes for which they were incurred. In 1910 Congress established postal savings banks, which proved of great benefit to small investors who were suspicious of large private banks. Two years later the parcel post system was begun, a blow at the monopolistic express companies. Taft gave his approval to both these measures despite charges by the banks and express companies that they were socialistic. A special commission was appointed to promote increased efficiency and economy in the national government, and the Department of Commerce and Labor was divided, with two new cabinet posts resulting. In an effort to publicize the child labor problem, as well as other related issues, a Federal Children's Bureau was established. The merit system was extended to include the lesser postmasterships, and Alaska was granted a greater degree of self-government through receiving territorial status.

But these good deeds were not enough to make Taft a hero to the progressives. Two things in particular brought political disaster to the President. In the first place, Taft was not Roosevelt; he lacked the explosive energy and colorful personality of his famous predecessor and he failed to publicize his own good works. More important still, the reform movement had turned toward new objectives. The Taft administration was progressive according to the standards of 1900 or 1905; it was not when judged by those of 1910—the standards of Senators LaFollette and Beveridge, or of Governor Hiram Johnson of California.

Illustrative of the limits beyond which Taft's progressivism would not go was the Arizona constitution issue. In 1911 both Arizona and New Mexico, having drawn up constitutions imbued with the liberal spirit then pervading the West, applied for statehood. A joint measure, the New Mexico-Arizona Enabling Resolution, was approved by Congress, but President Taft vetoed it in August, 1911, because the Arizona document provided for the recall of judges. He regarded that clause as "so pernicious in its effect, so destructive of independence in the judiciary, so likely to subject the rights of the individual to the possible tyranny of a popular majority," that he could not give his assent. Not until Arizona removed the objectionable provision was it granted admission—along with New Mexico—in 1912. Once in the Union, the Arizona citizens proceeded to add the questioned clause and there was nothing Taft could do about it. To the progressives, this presidential opposition to the recall of judges placed Taft definitely in the conservative, standpat category.

The Progressives Organize

On January 21, 1911, the National Progressive Republican League was organized by a group that made clear its intention of opposing Taft for renomination in 1912. Senator Jonathan Bourne of Oregon was elected president of the League, but it derived most of its energy from the tireless LaFollette. The evangelical spirit of the movement was sounded by Louis D. Brandeis, one of its founders, who declared: "We are confronted in the twentieth century, as we were in the nineteenth century, with an irreconcilable conflict. Our democracy cannot endure half free and half slave. . . ."

Throughout 1911 a LaFollette-for-President boom appeared to be making great progress. In April a conference of Congressional insurgents passed a resolution inviting the Wisconsin Senator to become a candidate for the Republican nomination. At a progressive convention held in October in Chicago, informally chosen representatives from many states gathered and endorsed LaFollette's candidacy. Lincoln Steffens of muckraking fame was active in this movement, as were Gifford Pinchot, his brother Amos, and James R. Garfield, Roosevelt's Secretary of the Interior. A group of millionaire liberals, including Medill McCormick of Chicago, Joseph Fels of Philadelphia, and Rudolph Spreckels of San Francisco, gave financial support, while LaFollette poured out his energy in touring the country and making innumerable speeches.

Splitting. The break between Republican regulars and insurgents.
(From the *Brooklyn Eagle*.)

Roosevelt Returns to Politics

How would Theodore Roosevelt stand in the coming contest? No question in American politics aroused such interest as this. Following Roosevelt's hunting trip to Africa, he toured Europe, where he was treated like visiting royalty by emperors, kings, politicians, and educators. But the most gratifying tribute of all was the enthusiastic welcome he received from his own people when he returned to America in June, 1910. While he was still abroad, standpatters and insurgents had bombarded him with indignant accounts of their opponents' conduct and, with the popular hero home again, these efforts were redoubled. Both the supporters of Taft and those of LaFollette made pilgrimages to Oyster Bay, Roosevelt's Long Island home, to enlist his backing in the intra-party conflict.

Although no longer feeling the cordial friendship that had once marked his relations with Taft, Roosevelt for many months refrained from any public criticism of his successor. Without taking sides between the two factions, he participated in the campaign of 1910—with unhappy results. Induced by his friends to accept nomination as chairman of the New York Republican state convention, he found his election opposed by conservatives and only secured the post after a close vote of the delegates. His friend, the progressive Henry

L. Stimson, won the nomination for governor, but was defeated in November by the Democrat, John A. Dix.

The former President's western speaking tour in behalf of his party was equally ill-starred. His references to Taft were so noncommittal as to offend both standpatters and insurgents, while conservative opinion was deeply shocked by his speech on the "New Nationalism," delivered at Osawatomie, Kansas, on August 31, 1910. Here Roosevelt said that property, which man's labor had created, must be "the servant and not the master of the common-wealth." The people "must effectively control the mighty forces which they have themselves called into being." The New Nationalism put national need before sectional or personal advantage, regarded the executive power as the steward of the public welfare, and demanded of the judiciary that it "be inter-ested primarily in human welfare rather than in property." To make these things possible, he advocated a number of "square deal" reforms, including greater regulation of corporations, a revision of the tariff, income and inherit-ance taxes, broadened conservation, compensation legislation for workers, regu-lation of child labor, and the direct primary. He was not ready, however, to champion completely the cause of the initiative, referendum, and recall.

Despite these ultraprogressive expressions, Roosevelt declined to join the Na-tional Progressive Republican League after its organization in 1911. Through-out most of the year he remained silent in the face of pleas from his liberal friends that he become a candidate for the Republican presidential nomination. LaFollette still stood unchallenged as the hope of those who wanted to deny renomination to President Taft.

All this time Roosevelt's growing irritation with Taft was revealed in his private conversations with his friends. Not until November 16, 1911, did the general public read words from the ex-President's pen severely critical of his successor. On that date *The Outlook*, of which Roosevelt was now one of the editors, carried his caustic comments on the recently announced antitrust suit brought by the Taft administration against the United States Steel Corporation. He took violent exception to the government's contention that he had been mislead during his presidency when he gave approval to the Steel Corporation's purchase of control in the Tennessee Coal and Iron Company.[3] Moreover, he criticized the whole direction that the Taft antitrust campaign was taking. Nothing was to be gained, he said, "by breaking up a huge industrial organiza-tion which has not offended otherwise than by its size." Unless they were guilty of wrongdoing, the large corporations should be handled by regulation, not by "destructive litigation" in the courts.

This public blast at the administration revived the hopes of Roosevelt's admirers that he would try for the nomination. By January, 1912, it was clear

[3] See above, p. 58.

that the progressive rank and file, as well as most of its leadership, would swing over from LaFollette to Roosevelt if the latter said the word. The Wisconsin Senator's fortunes were already sinking fast when they were finally destroyed by a tragic incident. On February 2, 1912, LaFollette spoke at a banquet given by the Publishers Association in Philadelphia. Overtired from his numerous activities and worried over the illness of one of his daughters, the insurgent leader shoved aside his prepared manuscript and indulged in a two-hour tirade against the big newspaper interests represented by his listeners. His disgusted audience walked out on him and the rambling, repetitive speech came to an end at last with the orator slumping to his seat and allowing his head to sink to the table. LaFollette's loss of self-control was only temporary, but the incident provided an opportunity for progressives who wanted to shift their support to Roosevelt to assert that they had no choice in the matter because of LaFollette's condition.

The truth was that Roosevelt had already decided to seek the nomination for himself. During January he dispatched his devoted follower, Frank Knox of Michigan (later to be Secretary of the Navy under another Roosevelt), to obtain the signatures of seven progressive governors to a letter—composed by the Rough Rider himself—begging him to make the race against Taft.[4] On February 24, 1912, Roosevelt's reply to the appeal of the seven governors was made public: "I will accept the nomination for President if it is tendered to me, and I will adhere to this decision until the convention has expressed its preference." This was the formal announcement of his candidacy, but his campaign to secure it had actually begun three days before. In his so-called Charter of Democracy speech at Columbus, Ohio, he had come out for the initiative, the referendum, and the recall of judicial decisions. The same day he had replied to a reporter's question with the vivid phrase: "My hat is in the ring, the fight is on and I am stripped to the buff."

Taft versus Roosevelt

The quarrel between the former President and the man he had put in the White House now became a bitter one. Speaking of extreme progressives, Taft condemned them as "neurotics"—a word that Roosevelt indignantly assumed was aimed at him. In April the President denounced his predecessor in an angry two-hour speech at Boston, while Roosevelt replied twenty-four hours later in a meeting at Worcester, Massachusetts; Taft, his opponent declared, had been "disloyal to every canon of decency and fair play"; he would never have become

[4] The governors were Walter R. Stubbs of Kansas, Chase S. Osborn of Michigan, Herbert S. Hadley of Missouri, Chester H. Aldrich of Nebraska, Robert P. Bass of New Hampshire, W. E. Glasscock of West Virginia, and J. M. Carey of Wyoming.

President had not Roosevelt kept his promise in spite of infinite pressure to break it. "It is a bad trait," the Colonel cried, "to bite the hand that feeds you."

Throughout the spring there was a feverish campaign to gain delegates for the national convention. Within the Republican rank and file Roosevelt's popularity was still great. In thirteen states where presidential primaries were held, he secured 281 delegates as against 71 for Taft and 36 for LaFollette. In the remaining states, however, the delegates were chosen by older, less democratic means. There the Old Guard was able to muster most of the delegations for Taft.[5] Preconvention polls indicated that Taft had about 550 delegates, enough to nominate him, while Roosevelt had about 100 less. Twelve days before the convention, the Republican National Committee convened to decide 238 cases in which there was a dispute as to who were the properly chosen delegates from a particular state; some of the challenged delegations were for Roosevelt, some for Taft. The progressives hoped to win enough of the cases—many of them trumped up for this purpose—to overturn the Taft majority. But the National Committee was dominated by the conservatives and decided against the Rooseveltians in almost every contest.

The Progressives refused to surrender. Two days before the convention opened, Roosevelt went to Chicago, the convention city, where he received a fervent welcome from his admirers. That night he addressed a crowded mass meeting at the auditorium. His closing words were so moving that they were quoted throughout the country:

> We fight in honorable fashion for the good of mankind; fearless of the future, unheeding of our individual fates, with unflinching hearts and undimmed eyes; we stand at Armegeddon, and we battle for the Lord.

On June 18 the convention began its sessions and was immediately thrown into an uproar by two issues. The progressives challenged the right of seventy-two Taft delegates to their seats and moved to substitute seventy-two Roosevelt adherents. This motion was declared out of order and the Taft delegates were allowed to occupy their places while the convention voted for a permanent chairman; their ballots helped to elect the conservative Elihu Root by a vote of 552 to 502 over the progressive Francis E. McGovern, governor of Wisconsin. This was an all-important victory for the Old Guard because it kept them in control of the convention machinery. When the Rooseveltians then renewed their attempt to unseat the Taft delegates, Root, following good legal precedents, allowed the latter to vote on their own cases despite angry cries of "theft," "fraud," and "steam-roller" hurled at him from the floor and the galleries. Most of the Roosevelt backers, on orders from the candidate himself,

---

[5] The results in the states holding primaries do not prove that Roosevelt would have carried the other states if he had had a democratic chance. The states having primaries were usually the most advanced progressive territory in any case.

refused to recognize the legitimacy of the convention and declined to vote either in the adoption of the platform or the balloting for candidates. Consequently, Taft was nominated on the first ballot, and James Sherman was again selected as his running mate.[6]

The Republican platform recognized the popular demand for reform by advocating maximum-hour laws for women and children, workmen's compensation acts, reforms in legal procedure, a simpler process than impeachment for the removal of judges, additions to the antitrust laws, revision of the currency system, publicity of campaign contributions, and parcel post.

On June 22, the night following the nomination of Taft, the defeated faction held an informal meeting. Roosevelt addressed the assembly in moving terms and announced plans for the organization of a new party—the Progressive. The delegates were directed to return to their homes, ascertain the sentiments of their communities, and reconvene on August 5 in a representative convention to adopt a platform and name a candidate.

The Rise of Wilson

With a Republican split assured, Democratic hopes soared and the nation watched with eager interest the proceedings of their national convention, which opened at Baltimore on June 25. The leading contenders for the nomination were Champ Clark of Missouri, the popular Speaker of the House, Governor Judson Harmon of Ohio, Representative Oscar W. Underwood of Alabama, and Governor Woodrow Wilson of New Jersey. The first three were politicians who had been in the public eye for many years. Wilson, on the contrary, had been chosen for his first public office only two years before.

The New Jersey governor, who was destined to snatch the coveted nomination from his more experienced rivals, had been born in Staunton, Virginia, in 1856. His ancestors were of Scotch-Irish stock and his father was a Presbyterian clergyman—facts that go far toward explaining the austere sense of duty, the frequent stubbornness, and the deep religious conviction that were to be so characteristic of Wilson as President. After graduating from Princeton and studying law, Wilson set up practice in Atlanta, Georgia, but he disliked his first-chosen profession and turned to teaching. After receiving his doctorate at Johns Hopkins and teaching at several other institutions, he returned to Princeton as professor of government and history. He was successful as an author, his ablest book, *Congressional Government*, going through twenty-four editions between 1885 and 1913. A competent scholar and prolific writer,

[6] Sherman died before election day and Nicholas Murray Butler, president of Columbia University, was substituted.

Wilson's real genius, however, was in his command of the spoken word. He was a lecturer and public speaker of captivating grace and power.

In 1902 Wilson was chosen president of Princeton and henceforth enjoyed a wider audience for his talents. His career as an university administrator was anything but placid. Faculty politics, usually spirited enough in any institution, took a particularly bitter form at Princeton, where Wilson and Graduate Dean Andrew F. West fought a seven years' war over the administration and expansion of the graduate school. Another controversy arose when Wilson attempted to democratize undergraduate social life by eliminating exclusive eating clubs. The president's activities alienated many of the rich patrons of the university and created a powerful opposition among the trustees. By 1910 Wilson's position had become so difficult that he required little urging to accept the Democratic nomination for governor of New Jersey, thus launching out on a new career.

The idea of nominating Wilson was sold to the Democratic state bosses by Colonel George Harvey, the publisher of the *North American Review* and *Harper's Weekly*. As early as 1906 Harvey had publicly expressed his conviction that the gifted head of Princeton would make an excellent President of the United States. What attracted the publisher was not Wilson's liberalism but his apparent conservatism. Up to this point in his career Wilson had given little indication of sympathy with the aims of the progressives; he had condemned the regulatory legislation under Roosevelt and opposed Bryan's leadership of the Democratic party as dangerously radical. All this, thought Harvey, was excellent; through Wilson he hoped that conservative Easterners would regain control of the Democratic organization. Harvey, it should be noted, was the friend of some of the most powerful figures in Wall Street.

The election of Wilson to the New Jersey governorship was the necessary preliminary to Harvey's further plans, and to this end he obtained the cooperation of ex-Senator Jim Smith and Jim Nugent, the state's Democratic bosses. The machine men at first hesitated to back a candidate with such an unorthodox background, but they realized that an eminently respectable name might bring victory. Wilson also hesitated, but finally gave his assent. In a dramatic acceptance speech, he declared that his unsolicited nomination would enable him to take office "with absolutely no pledges of any kind" to the bosses. In November, 1910, Wilson was one of twenty-six Democratic governors elected in the great uprising against the Republicans.

Although the New Jersey progressives at first regarded Wilson with suspicion, his sturdy independence soon won them to his side. First of all, the governor successfully prevented Jim Smith from stealing the Senatorship from James Martine, whom the voters had supported in a preferential primary. Next, Wilson prevailed upon the state legislature to enact a drastic election reform law, a public-utility regulation act, and a workmen's compensation measure. New Jersey's corporation laws, so hospitable to big business that the state had become known as the "mother of trusts," were now radically amended. Moreover, during an effective speaking tour in the West during the summer of 1911, Wilson advocated the initiative, referendum, and recall—all favorite demands of the progressives.

In this swing toward liberalism, Wilson found Harvey's support embarrassing, and in December, 1911, he practically asked Harvey to stop advocating his nomination for the presidency. Thereupon the governor selected Colonel Edward M. House, a prominent Texas politician who was anxious to enter the national field, to serve on his inner board of strategy. House was a quiet man of refinement and wealth who loved to play the political game from behind the scenes; unlike Harvey, his sympathies were with the progressives. Relying heavily on House's advice, Wilson made a complete break with Harvey and began to court the Western faction of the party in general and Bryan in particular. Fortunately for the governor, Bryan forgave him for having one time expressed the wish that the Great Commoner might be knocked "once for all, into a cocked hat."

Although having no chance to be nominated himself, Bryan proved to be a powerful figure at the Baltimore convention. While he failed to gain the chairmanship, he did succeed in having adopted a bold platform that called for immediate downward revision of the tariff, strengthening of the antitrust laws, presidential preference primaries, prohibition of corporation contributions to campaign chests, a single term for the President, and revision of banking and currency laws. Bryan's most dramatic maneuver came on the third day when he unexpectedly offered a resolution that read in part: "As proof of our fidelity to the people, we hereby declare ourselves opposed to the nomination of any candidate for President who is the representative of or under obligation to J. Pierpont Morgan, Thomas F. Ryan, August Belmont, or any other member of the privilege-hunting and favor-seeking class. . . . We demand the withdrawal of any delegate or delegates constituting or representing the above-named interests." This direct challenge to Tammany and Wall Street threw the convention into an uproar. While Bryan consented to delete its most offensive parts, the resolution was overwhelmingly adopted in amended form.

Champ Clark led in the early balloting and had an actual majority on the second day of voting when Charles Murphy, boss of Tammany, shifted the New York delegation to the Missourian at the expense of Harmon. But a variety of circumstances kept Clark from receiving the two-thirds vote necessary for nomination. Murphy's move to Clark was countered when Bryan—unwilling to be on the same side with Tammany—shifted his support from Clark to Wilson. More important than Bryan's action, however, were certain backstage maneuvers of the Wilson managers. By alliance with the Underwood group the Wilson supporters were able to beat back the Clark threat. Gradually they won away some of the Speaker's more fickle followers; finally, by gaining the votes of the Illinois delegation, controlled by Chicago boss Roger Sullivan, a Wilson band wagon was put in motion that gave the New Jersey governor the nomination on the forty-sixth ballot. Governor Thomas R. Marshall of Indiana was selected as the party's candidate for vice president.

The Bolt Complete

The first national convention of the National Progressive party opened in Chicago on August 5 in a unique atmosphere of religious enthusiasm. "John Brown's Body" and "Onward Christian Soldiers" were sung by the inspired delegates, and Albert Beveridge delivered a passionately eloquent keynote address. In the same spirit was Roosevelt's speech the next day accepting the nomination of the new party. Hiram Johnson was given the second place on the ticket. The platform called for the whole calendar of reform: direct primaries, direct election of Senators, initiative, referendum, and recall, a speedier method of amending the Constitution, women's suffrage, limitation of campaign expenditures, prohibition of child labor, a "living wage," the eight-hour day, a Department of Labor, conservation, strong regulation of interstate corporations, and the establishment of a Federal industrial commission comparable to the Interstate Commerce Commission.

Republicans throughout the country now had to choose between loyalty to the historic party or alignment with the secessionists. Naturally the bulk of the machine politicians as well as the businessmen supported Taft, while idealists and reformers rallied happily to the so-called Bull Moose standard. Many individuals, however, took an unpredictable course. Such outstanding insurgents as LaFollette and Borah refused to support the third-party movement, while among Roosevelt's most active supporters were Boss Bill Flinn of Pittsburgh, millionaire publisher Frank A. Munsey, and George W. Perkins, former partner of J. P. Morgan, who became chairman of the Progressive National Committee.

The Election of Wilson

The campaign was a curious one. All three major candidates claimed to be friendly to the cause of reform; all three party platforms were liberal documents. That Taft's liberalism was more cautious than that of the others was fairly obvious, but what was the difference between the New Nationalism proclaimed by Colonel Roosevelt and the New Freedom promised by Governor Wilson?

Actually the similar-sounding slogans reflected some rather fundamental differences in point of view. Roosevelt's program was frankly Hamiltonian, based on the assumption that a bold enlargement of Federal functions was necessary to meet new economic and social conditions. On the trust issue, for example, Roosevelt enlarged upon his old distinction between good and bad trusts. What was needed, he now insisted, was not new legislation and prosecutions designed to break large corporations into small, but Federal regulation of the trusts to preserve their good points and eradicate their evil.

Wilson, on the other hand, considered himself a faithful disciple of Jefferson. He feared the growth of the Federal government and wanted to see the progressive objectives achieved as largely as possible through state action. Moreover, he still hoped for a minimum of government intervention in economic life and pinned his hopes on the restoration of competition. Wilson rejected Roosevelt's contention that bigness in business might sometimes be a good thing. He believed, on the contrary, that excessive size was in itself bad because it often produced inefficiency and gave the corporations too much power, both economic and political. The antitrust laws should therefore be strengthened and clarified, the tariff should be drastically reduced, and the national banking system should be reformed to free farmers and small businessmen from the clutches of the money trust.

Both Roosevelt's New Nationalism and Wilson's New Freedom showed the influence of other men's thinking upon the issues of the day. Roosevelt's convictions had been fortified by the arguments of Herbert Croly, whose influential book, *The Promise of American Life*, had appeared in 1909; Wilson accepted many of the ideas developed by Louis D. Brandeis in his studies of the interrelations of finance and business.

Perplexed by these conflicting brands of progressivism, the voters considered the contest as one of personalities. They were impressed by Wilson's eloquence and his lofty idealism; they were entertained by the vigor with which the former friends, Taft and Roosevelt, ripped into each other. They were shocked by the near tragedy of October 14, when Roosevelt was wounded by an unbalanced person in Milwaukee.

Yet all the oratory and unexpected drama of the campaign could not alter the election results. The Democrats had only to hold their ranks to vanquish their divided enemy. By an overwhelming electoral majority Woodrow Wilson was chosen President; he had 435 ballots, Roosevelt 88, and Taft 8. Of the popular votes, Wilson received 6.3 million or 42 per cent; Roosevelt, 4 million or 27 per cent; and Taft, 3.5 million or 23 per cent. The schism had enabled a candidate with a minority of the popular votes to win. Almost a million Americans showed their distrust of all three major candidates by backing Euguene V. Debs, the Socialist. The new Congress also showed the effects of the Republican split; the House would consist of 290 Democrats to 145 Republicans and Progressives; the Senate, 51 Democrats to 45 of the opposition.

5

The American Empire

The closing years of the nineteenth century were climactic ones in American diplomatic history. They marked the end of an era of comparative isolation and the beginning of an epoch during which the United States emerged as a world power. Although the conclusion of the war with Spain is generally accepted as the dividing line between the two periods, actually the shift was gradual; the war merely hastened and accentuated it.

As a result of that war, the United States gained several insular possessions and, appetite whetted, secured others in which it had been previously interested. The administration of some of the newly acquired lands overseas—particularly those in the Far East—raised unusual problems and turned American diplomatic interest again toward that part of the world. In order to settle these problems, the United States became involved with other nations and thus emerged from its shell of isolation.

The Rise of Imperialistic Thought

Since 1890 a series of events had combined to bring an end to comparative isolation and to make the United States a world-minded nation. By this time the American frontier was disappearing. While it is true that there were still millions of acres available for homesteading, American citizens were beginning to look about for new opportunities. Industry, growing mightily since the Civil War, had reached a point where it was producing more goods than the home market could sustain. Consequently, new markets were being sought to buy the surplus. At the same time, these mercantile interests were looking for new sources of raw materials to keep their ever expanding factories going. This combination of desire for new markets and for new areas for investment could not long be held in check.

"Manifest Destiny," dormant since the early 1870's as Americans moved into the West, rehabilitated the South, and promoted industry, once more emerged; but it was a new form of destiny, one motivated both by economics and by needs of national defense. The foremost proponent of expansion was a prominent naval officer and writer, Captain Alfred Thayer Mahan. Captain Mahan firmly believed that the bulwark of American defense was a strong navy—and to be strong, the navy must have additional bases from which to operate. Therefore he restored to life the theories that had been advocated by William Seward, Secretary of State during the Lincoln-Johnson era: the United States should extend its control over potential bases in both the Caribbean and the Pacific. To Mahan, the original Monroe Doctrine was not so important now. Since the United States could not adequately defend southern South America, he felt that the nation should concentrate primarily upon the West Indies and the Gulf of Mexico. He was also a firm believer in an interoceanic canal under complete American control. This canal, strongly protected by Caribbean bases, would furnish the avenue to the Pacific, where the United States must also have naval outposts.

Captain Mahan was likewise convinced that this country must develop markets in the Far East, and that China, the center of that trade, must be kept politically independent. He did not believe in territorial expansion as such, for the United States had enough land as it was; but the acquisition of bases was an essential adjunct for the maintenance of the United States as a world power. By the middle 1890's Mahan was a firm supporter of close cooperation with Great Britain, whose outlook, he believed, was similar to that of the United States.

A vociferous apostle of these views was the young Henry Cabot Lodge of Massachusetts. He lacked Mahan's breadth of vision and was much less cautious. In many ways he was like the War Hawks of 1812. Lodge felt that Canada should be annexed, Cuba taken by force from Spain, and the islands of the Pacific snatched from the grasping hands of European nations. Yet Lodge did not comtemplate the means by which those objectives could be obtained—nor the effects. He was an out-and-out jingoist at this time and had considerable influence among the younger generation.

Combining the strategic intuitions of Mahan with the rashness of Lodge was Theodore Roosevelt, who first made his presence felt on the national scene while serving as Assistant Secretary of the Navy under President McKinley.

Like Mahan, he was a crusader for a bigger and better navy, and the efficiency that the naval forces showed during the war with Spain resulted in part from his efforts.

The larger navy demanded by the expansionists was beginning to materialize. Among the factors that favored increased appropriations for this purpose were the prosperous condition of the treasury around 1890, troubles with Chile that made the nation realize its naval deficiencies, and difficulties with Great Britain and Germany over Samoa.

In the 1890's political scientists, sociologists, and religious leaders were teaching doctrines which tended to support imperialism. From Darwin's theory of evolution, students of society drew the analogy that there was a world struggle for existence and that the fittest races were destined to survive and dominate. From this premise it was an easy step to conclude, as did Professor John W. Burgess of Columbia, that the Teutonic nations like England, Germany, and the United States were especially endowed with "the capacity for establishing nation states." It was, therefore, their historic mission "to carry the political civilization of the modern world into those parts of the world inhabited by unpolitical and barbaric races." In similar fashion, clergymen like the Reverend Josiah Strong believed that the expansion of Anglo-Saxon rule and Protestant Christianity throughout the world was the will of God.

Many newspaper editors pounded the drum for Manifest Destiny. Some liked the increased circulation that followed war-scare stories; others joined the jingo parade because this seemed to be what their readers wanted. Thus the demand for colonial expansion increased in intensity throughout the 1890's, as naval leaders, politicians, educational and religious leaders, investors, and industrialists all added their voices to the chorus.

True, there were vigorous opponents of imperialism. President Grover Cleveland in his second term (1893–1897) indicated his opposition by withdrawing the Hawaiian annexation treaty from Senatorial consideration. Many New Englanders were strong in their denunciation of expansion. Critics of big business could see in imperialism only another medium for promoting greater profits for the capitalists. Some of the businessmen themselves, on the other hand, opposed colonial adventures as likely to involve the nation in war and heavy taxes. Isolationists warned against distant annexations that might entangle the United States in the meshes of world politics.

If the advocates of expansion were to have their way, they needed a cause to unite their varied, scattered forces. The event that served to coalesce those forces, to win new converts, to launch the nation definitely upon an imperialist course, and to make it, as a result, a world power was the Spanish-American War.

The War with Spain

The "splendid little war," as John Hay called it, had both deep and surface roots. For a century Americans had been interested in Cuba, while Spaniards had feared that the United States might seize that rich and strategic island. The situation brought numerous diplomatic crises, particularly during the 1850's and 1870's. But the more immediate causes for the war grew out of the Cuban revolt that broke out in 1895. Spanish measures of repression were harsh, and the atrocity stories that horrified America had an unfortunate basis in fact, although they were frequently exaggerated in the propaganda of the Cuban juntas and the columns of the "yellow" press. American investments amounting to $50 million and trade worth $100 million were imperiled by the insurrection; American health was threatened by the plague conditions in Cuban "reconcentration camps." Public opinion in the United States demanded that the Spanish government cease hostilities and grant the Cubans their own government. President McKinley tried to withstand the pressure of the war party and achieve these ends without hostilities, but in the end he failed. The DeLôme letter episode, in which the Spanish ambassador's unflattering description of McKinley made its way into the American newspapers, and the tragic explosion that destroyed the battleship *Maine* in Havana harbor, aroused an American war spirit that neither McKinley nor Congress could withstand.

On April 11, 1898, McKinley asked Congress for authority to intervene; on April 19 Congress responded with the passage of four resolutions that amounted to a declaration of war. The fourth of these, the so-called Teller Amendment, however, was a concession to the anti-imperialists since it disclaimed any intention on the part of the United States to annex Cuba; the ultimate objective of American policy was declared to be "to leave the government and control of the Island to its people."

Judged by twentieth century standards the Spanish War was not a great military struggle. The American army was woefully unprepared so far as leadership, manpower, and equipment were concerned. The navy, greatly increased in size and efficiency since 1890, was in much better shape than the army and, thanks to the foresight of Secretary of the Navy Long and his assistant, Theodore Roosevelt, the various fleets were at strategic points when hostilities started. Fortunately for the United States, Spain was worse off, despite an apparent supremacy on paper.

The fighting began on May 1, when Admiral George Dewey, who had been ordered to the Far East shortly after the blowing up of the *Maine*, successfully attacked the Spanish fleet in Manila Bay. What was considered the major campaign did not open until about June 1, when the Atlantic fleet under Admiral Schley and Admiral Sampson succeeded in bottling up the Spanish navy at Santiago, Cuba. Not until three weeks later did the American army invade that island. After several misfortunes, Santiago was captured and the Spanish fleet was destroyed while attempting to escape. By the middle of July the Americans were in practical control of the whole of Cuba. General Miles had an even easier time dominating nearby Puerto Rico. While the fighting around Manila continued, the disastrous blows of the Americans, added to political and economic troubles in the homeland, compelled Spain to ask for armistice terms on July 26.

This speedy victory made Americans forget that their country was still largely unprepared. Instead, they felt a new sense of power; had not a European power been brought to its knees in less than three months? Now it was the destiny—perhaps even the duty—of the United States to assume its rightful place in world affairs and to make its wishes and interests felt everywhere.

The Treaty of Paris

This feeling of world-mindedness and new-found power was expressed at the peace conference, held in Paris from October to December, 1898. Although the United States had entered the war ostensibly only to obtain freedom for Cuba, she emerged from the conference with Puerto Rico, Guam, and the Philippines, together with a guardianship over Cuba until its inhabitants were ready to govern themselves.

The decision to annex the Philippines, heavily populated and located on the other side of the world, was a momentous one. Although most of the American public, including President McKinley himself, scarcely knew where these islands were when Dewey won his dramatic victory, a demand to bring them under the American flag soon developed. American businessmen were interested in the trade both of the Philippines themselves and of nearby China; naval experts stressed the islands' strategic importance; missionaries were inspired by the rich harvest of souls to be garnered in. McKinley, a cautious man by nature, was won over to the idea of annexing the islands largely because of the lack of any attractive alternative. To turn the islanders back to Spanish rule seemed unjust in view of recent evidence of Spain's inability to govern her colonies, but, on the other hand, the Filipinos were not believed ready for independence. Unless the United States would accept the responsibility of ruling the islands, it appeared likely that they would fall under the domination of some other imperial power like Germany, England, France, or Japan. McKinley himself related how he agonized in prayer over the issue until late one night it had come to him "that there was nothing left for us to do but to take them all, and to educate the Filipinos and uplift and civilize and Christianize them, and by God's grace do the very best we could by them, as our fellow-men for whom Christ also died."

The treaty ran into difficulties in the Senate, where the anti-imperialists rallied under the leadership of George Hoar of Massachusetts to delay ratification. They argued that for the United States to hold colonies was inconsistent with the Declaration of Independence, which asserted that all governments derived their just powers from the consent of the governed. The administration forces, basing their support of the treaty upon a variety of arguments, finally won the day, aided in part by William Jennings Bryan. Bryan, a professed anti-imperialist, wanted to bring the war to an end and deliver the Filipinos from Spanish rule as a first step toward granting them independence. He influenced some of the treaty opponents to change their minds, saying that the issue of imperialism could be settled by the people themselves in the election of 1900. Even so, the treaty just squeezed through by a vote of 57 to 27 on February 6, 1899. Forty of the supporters were Republicans; twenty of the opponents were Democrats.

Before the century was over, imperialism had gained additional triumphs. In 1898 the United States annexed Hawaii by joint resolution of Congress and similar action by the Hawaiian legislature; the following year diplomatic agreements among Great Britain, Germany, and the United States resulted in a partition of the Samoan Islands, with the United States receiving Tutuila, where the excellent coaling station and naval base of Pago-Pago was located.

Thus, as the twentieth century opened, the United States had given up its previous isolation. Through its recent victory, it had obtained insular territories in the Caribbean and the Pacific. Additional bases in the Pacific had been acquired by peaceful diplomatic action. The European powers were showing an unaccustomed respect for America. The nation was now definitely a world power, and with that position came new responsibilities and new interests. Dealing with those responsibilities and interests became the major task of American diplomacy in the opening years of the new century.

Keeping the Pledge with Cuba

The Teller Amendment of April, 1898, mentioned above, had stated: "That the United States hereby disclaims any disposition or intention to exercise sovereignty, jurisdiction, or control" over Cuba "except for the pacification thereof, and asserts its determination, when that is accomplished, to leave the government and control of the Island to its people." With the conclusion of the war with Spain, however, the United States was not ready to put this pledge into immediate effect. Fear of a counterrevolution by the Spanish residents, the appalling illiteracy, the lack of training in self-government, and the fear that

Cuba, the Beginner. Uncle Sam getting Cuba ready for self-government.
(By Bart in the *Minneapolis Journal*.)

were the United States to withdraw at once some other power, perhaps Germany, might step in delayed fulfillment of the promise.

An American military regime was therefore established, with General Leonard Wood eventually serving as governor general. Wood's administration brought many benefits to the Cubans. The construction of a road from one end of the island to the other and other public works improved transportation facilities; the activities of the Army Medical Corps, and particularly Major Walter Reed's demonstration of the role of mosquitoes in transmitting yellow fever, cut down the death rate; and the American-organized educational system reduced illiteracy and prepared the Cubans for new responsibilities.

By the middle of 1900 Governor Wood, after conferring with the Cuban leaders, felt that the islanders were ready for self-government. A constituent assembly, selected by a limited franchise, convened in November. By February, 1901, this group, guided by Wood, had drawn up a constitution that provided for three branches of government and separation of powers, but made no mention of Cuba's relationship with the United States. When the War Department refused to approve the document as it stood, Secretary of War Root and General Wood collaborated in drawing up the so-called Platt Amendment, which was made a rider to the Army Appropriation Act of March, 1901. Of the seven articles of this amendment, the most important were: (1) the "Government of Cuba shall never enter into any treaty or other compact with any foreign power . . . which will impair . . . the independence of Cuba, nor in any manner authorize . . . any foreign power . . . to obtain by colonization or for military or naval purposes . . . control over any portion of the said island"; (2) Cuba shall not "assume or contract any public debt to pay the interest upon which . . . the ordinary revenues . . . shall be inadequate"; (3) Cuba agrees "that the United States may exercise the right to intervene for the preservation of Cuban independence, the maintenance of a government adequate for the protection of life, property, and individual liberty"; (4) Cuba will continue the sanitation program; and (5) Cuba will lease or sell coaling stations and naval bases to the United States to aid in Cuban defense.

Acceptance of the Platt Amendment, with its limitations upon sovereignty and its recognition of the right of a foreign power to intervene, meant that Cuba would be a protectorate of the United States, enjoying something less than full independence. This the Cubans resented. But the islanders knew that unless they complied with American wishes they could not hope to achieve the cherished goal of self-government. Therefore, with many misgivings, they made the necessary additions to their constitution. To strengthen the right of American intervention, the Platt Amendment was also made the basis of a treaty between Cuba and the United States in 1903.

As soon as the Cuban constitution was approved by the American Congress, preparations were made for the first election. The presidency was gained by Thomas Estrada Palma, whose long exile in the United States had acquainted him with democratic procedures. Following Palma's inauguration in May, 1902, American troops were withdrawn and the island left to its destiny. The ending of the military occupation of Cuba was a great surprise to most Europeans, who had not believed that the United States would relinquish such a valuable prize. Naturally, the self-denying step occasioned some grumbling among the more zealous American imperialists and those who had investments in Cuba. Most Americans, however, realized that the honor of the United States was at stake, since a promise of Cuban independence had been made and reiterated.

During Palma's first administration Cuban progress continued with friendly assistance from the United States. President Roosevelt realized that the Dingley Tariff rates were so high that they tended to exclude Cuba's principal crop, sugar, from its natural American market, so he asked Congress to grant preferential rates to the new republic. Despite the opposition of the Louisiana sugar interests and other protectionists, Congress eventually took the requested action in December, 1903. Rates on imports from Cuba were reduced from 20 to 40 per cent, and sugar reciprocity agreements with other nations were terminated. Cuba was greatly aided by this policy, and American exporters also bene-fited, since the nearby republic became one of the leading purchasers of Ameri-can goods.

When Palma was re-elected in 1905, the Cuban opposition, charging him with dictatorial tendencies, threatened to start a civil war. To meet this threat, American troops were sent to the island in 1906, and military government was re-established. American annexationists were eager to believe that the independ-ence policy had failed, and even Roosevelt wrote to a friend: "I am so angry with that infernal little Cuban republic that I would like to wipe its people off the face of the earth."

During this period of intervention the governorship was chiefly in the hands of Charles Magoon of Nebraska, who had had experience as an executive in the Canal Zone. Magoon undertook to stimulate Cuban economic life, to build roads, to strengthen the educational system, and to improve the electoral laws. This paternalism did not commend him to the Cubans, who accused the governor of extravagance, abuse of the pardoning power, and even of corruption —charges that were dismissed as groundless in a subsequent American investiga-tion.

When the Cubans were again thought ready to govern themselves, an elec-tion was held, resulting in victory for the Liberal, José Gomez. In January, 1909, the American intervention was ended. Once more the United States lived up to its promise to abstain from annexation, yet American policy clearly demon-strated that the Platt Amendment was no empty formula. Cuban independence was contingent upon the Cubans' behaving themselves—from the American point of view.

The Puerto Rican Experiment

Puerto Rico, with its 3,435 square miles of territory and population of a million, was another responsibility assumed by the United States after the war with Spain. The islanders were largely illiterate, with no training whatever in the field of self-government. The treaty provided that "the civil rights and political status of the native inhabitants . . . shall be determined by Con-gress." Since no promise concerning the future had been made, the case of Puerto Rico was obviously radically different from that of Cuba.

At the time of annexation the island was in a bad way economically, and the situation was made worse by a severe hurricane during the summer of 1899. The several military governors sent out during this period did commendable work in laying the foundations for improved economic, educational, and sanitary con-ditions.

In April, 1900, permanent civil government was established under the Foraker Act. There was a governor and an executive council of eleven, named by the President with the consent of the Senate. At least five councillors were to be Puerto Ricans. Six executive departments were created, each of which was headed by a council member, usually an American. The insular legislature was made up of the council, which served as the upper house, and the House of Delegates, elected by the qualified voters. The court system was based on the United States model. The inhabitants were designated as "citizens of Puerto Rico," entitled to the protection of the United States but not to all the privileges of American citizenship. The form of government bore a striking resemblance to that which the Americans themselves had once "enjoyed" under British rule.

The system thus established, which represented the views of the dominant Republican party in the United States, remained in force without essential change until 1917, despite the fact that the political arrangements did not work altogether smoothly. The Puerto Ricans were dissatisfied because they seemed to be placed in a position of inferiority through the denial of American citizenship, and they were especially distressed because the control of the executive departments was kept from the assembly. The result was friction and a series of petty quarrels between the governor and his council on the one hand and the House of Delegates on the other, which are reminiscent of the eighteenth century conflict between British colonial executives and the American colonists. Just as in those cases, the popular branch of the legislature tried to tighten the purse strings. The Congress of the United States foiled such tactics, however, by passing a law in 1909 providing that the amount approved for the preceding year would be collected if the House of Delegates failed at any time to vote the necessary appropriations. Although better administrators were sent out and the government now worked more smoothly, it cannot be said that the Puerto Ricans were any more enthusiastic over American control.

In spite of political bickering, there is no doubt that under American rule Puerto Rican economic conditions—though still far from prosperous—developed beyond anything the island had previously known. It is true that the advantages did not affect all lines of production equally and that the important coffee industry even declined somewhat, but the total exports and imports were considerably larger than in the past. In addition, Puerto Rico obtained improved means of transportation, modern sanitation that thwarted the dread hookworm, and better schools that decreased the widespread illiteracy. The United States assuredly was showing its good intentions, but the primary problem of civilized government under normal conditions is to obtain the consent of the governed, and in that regard she was deficient.

Philippine Difficulties

The most novel immediate question raised by the war with Spain was that of control of the Philippines, consisting of seven thousand islands of varying size and inhabited by seven million persons, many of them uncivilized. Many dialects were spoken in the islands and a variety of religions practiced. The great majority of the American people regarded the rule of the islands as a trust and desired to educate the Filipinos to self-government in the American sense as soon as possible, although it seemed to leading Republicans that a long course of education would be necessary before the natives could be trusted to conduct a modern administration. It was, of course, inevitable that the Filipinos, after their experience with Spain, would not appreciate the American point of view and that unhappy consequences would result.

After the surrender of Spain, American control did not extend beyond the environs of Manila and, when it became evident that the United States did not intend to recognize the Philippine Republic under Emilio Aguinaldo, that leader and his supporters resorted to arms. Two days before the treaty of peace was ratified, the Filipino insurgents attacked the American troops at Manila. As their forces were numerous and fairly well equipped, the situation became serious.

In regular warfare, however, the Filipinos proved unable to offer very effective resistance to the Americans who were soon heavily re-enforced, with the volunteers for the Spanish War being replaced as quickly as possible by regulars. In a few months the insurgent government was broken up and all its chief officers captured except Aguinaldo, who eluded his pursuers. In this struggle the American forces showed efficiency and zeal, but the campaigning was most difficult because of the delays occasioned by the rainy season, the character of the country, and the trouble in controlling large districts with small garrisons.

The spirit of the insurgents was not broken. Realizing at length the strength and weaknesses of the Americans, they decided in November, 1899, to disband their organized forces and resort to guerrilla warfare exclusively. This decision increased the problems of the Americans, and the fighting was now carried on with mounting ferocity. Public opinion at home became disturbed by the persistent reports of outrages committed by American troops against Filipino captives, and this sentiment finally forced a Senatorial investigation. The testimony clearly showed that the methods of American soldiers had in many cases been ruthless. Yet in extenuation it appeared that the situation was very trying and that the officers as a rule had tried to prevent the atrocities. Such incidents are unfortunately the almost inevitable result of guerrilla warfare.

Meantime, the military operations were actively pushed and, in February,

1901, Aguinaldo himself was tracked down and captured by General Frederick Funston as a result of a daring ruse. Contrary to expectation, Aguinaldo's capture had little effect on the insurgents, but the end was a matter of time; the last resistance ceased in April, 1902.

The earliest American rule in the archipelago was necessarily military, with first General Otis and then General MacArthur[1] serving as military governor. Even before the ratification of the peace treaty, however, President McKinley named a commission of five to study conditions in the islands and to report on the best means of control. In January, 1899, this First Philippine Commission, headed by President Schurman of Cornell University, began its careful investigation and subsequently presented an elaborate report. The commission concluded that the natives were as yet incapable of self-government; the report included a very useful account of the conditions and resources of the Philippines, about which Americans knew little.

Acting on the commission's recommendation, McKinley therefore named a second commission made up of Chairman William Howard Taft and four other members in March, 1900. Unlike the first board, this was to be a permanent administrative body and was especially charged with the delicate task of organizing a system of government beginning with the municipalities and then extending to the provinces. When the commissioners believed that a civil, as distinct from a military, central government could be established, they were to submit the necessary recommendations. The Second Philippine Commission became the supreme legislative authority in the islands, subject to the President through the Secretary of War, but the military governor was retained as chief executive. All these important steps were taken by President McKinley by virtue of his military power as commander-in-chief.

Since it was felt that a firmer legal basis was desirable for such an important action, Congress in March, 1901, added the Spooner Amendment to the Military Appropriation Act. This conferred upon the President complete military, civil, and judicial power over the Philippines until Congress should provide otherwise. The measure, although filling an immediate practical need, constituted a rather remarkable step for a Congress acting under the American system of government, for it made President McKinley virtually a dictator of the archipelago.

Taking advantage of his new power, McKinley wisely made certain alterations in the government of the islands. Taft was appointed civil governor and the authority of General MacArthur was limited to the districts in which the insurrection had not been crushed. A little later three native members were added to the commission, and the administration was divided into four executive departments, each in charge of one of the American commissioners.

[1] The father of General Douglas MacArthur of World War II fame.

In carrying out his difficult assignment, Governor Taft gained a reputation for executive ability that later helped make him President. To train the natives in civic responsibilities, Taft organized a system of local government in which elected officials served under careful American supervision.

These arrangements having worked well, on the whole, Congress in July, 1902, confirmed what the President and the commission had done, although specifying that the civil governor and other executive officers named by the President were thereafter to be approved by the Senate. The same measure also prepared the way for further progress: a census of the islands was to be taken, and two years later elections were to be held for a general assembly. When this body convened, it assigned the legislative power in the islands to a bicameral congress, with the elective assembly as the lower house and the commission as the upper. The act further declared the natives to be citizens of the Philippines and extended to them nearly all the provisions of the American Constitution. Life, liberty, and property were guaranteed, but not trial by jury.

Although the work was carried out rather slowly, the plans for the elections were finally completed. More than 100,000 Filipinos voted and, in the fall of 1907, eight years after the institution of American rule, the Philippine Assembly met. Nothing revolutionary happened, although the Nationalist party, which stood for speedy independence, gained a majority over the Progressives, who favored evolution under American rule. The Nationalists, while expressing their desire for freedom, wisely refrained from following an aggressive or violent course, and the existence of the assembly did not greatly complicate the situation.

The duty of creating the best possible system of government for these new wards was, however, only one of the numerous tasks that the possession of this vast and populous archipelago entailed. Particularly important were the settlement of the question of the Friars' land and the introduction of a new system of education.

The Friars' land problem was vital because the dominant position that had been held under the Spanish regime by the three prominent religious orders— the Dominicans, the Augustinians, and the Recollectos—had much to do with the discontent of the natives. The Friars held about 400,000 acres of the best land in the islands and had established a system under which the Filipinos could cultivate it only by renting it on shares for long periods. The revolt against Spain in 1896 had been largely the outgrowth of Filipino hostility to this condition, as well as the alleged immorality among the members of the religious orders. During the revolt the Friars had been largely dispossessed, but they still continued their claims, while the native holders naturally regarded the captured soil as their own. The best way out, according to the commission, was to purchase the disputed acreage—which it was authorized to do under the Act of

1902—but the Orders demanded too high a price. Lengthy negotiations were needed, including a trip by Taft to the Vatican, before the price was lowered to $7,239,000, a sum that was admitted to be more than the actual value of the land; but the commission regarded this concession to the diplomatic skill of the Holy See as a proper one to gain the consent of all concerned. Further problems remained, however, for the plan was to sell the land on fair terms to the tenants, and the feeling was prevalent among the Filipinos that they were already entitled to the property. As time passed, the titles were granted to the natives upon very liberal terms.

Perhaps no aspect of American control deserves more praise than the successful effort to develop an educational system. The next organized invasion after that of the army was one of American teachers, who promoted a school plan vastly superior to that of the Spaniards. Because of the differences in tribal speech and the absence of a written literature, English was made the basis of instruction. Normal schools were quickly established for the training of native teachers, and a university on the model of American state universities was founded at Manila. Under the Spanish regime, manual toil of all kinds had been regarded as something to be avoided, but, in the face of the most deep-seated prejudice, the American schools made commendable progress in their efforts to popularize technical and agricultural education.

Nevertheless, the results should not be exaggerated. The difficulties to be faced were still great. An Oriental people change slowly, and some of the measures devised to force upon the Filipinos a premature enthusiasm for "American liberty" had exactly the opposite effect. Moreover, the refusal of Congress to grant adequate financial aid to the Filipino schools retarded the work and limited to a disappointing degree the numbers reached.

The Insular Cases

Meantime, the outcome of the Spanish War had brought the United States face to face with some of the most complicated questions of political theory and constitutional law that Americans have ever had to meet. While the United States had often acquired territory before, with the exception of Alaska it had been land contiguous to the United States and clearly destined to be admitted some day to the Union. The case of Alaska caused little trouble since most of it remained so long unoccupied, but it seemed absurd to many Americans that distant islands, inhabited by races so dissimilar as those of the Philippines, should ever become states. On the other hand, the idea of the Stars and Stripes waving over permanently subject peoples was abhorrent to many of the best and wisest, like Senator Hoar, Carl Schurz, and other leading anti-imperialists.

Nor, after the deed was done, did the complications cease. Many well-informed men held that the new lands had at once become parts of the United States, and their inhabitants were citizens just like those of the older American territories. It seemed indeed absurd that Moros and headhunters should have all the privileges of the Bill of Rights and the Fourteenth Amendment, yet there were not a few thinking Americans who contended that under the American form of government nothing else was possible. The Constitution spoke nowhere of subjects, but only of citizens.

In the opposing view, the Constitution did not extend automatically to the new lands, because they were "dependencies" subject to the rule of Congress, and the Constitution would not apply to them until it was extended by act of the "sovereign legislature." This view appeared to be good common sense, but it was not easy to find basis for it in the Constitution. Especially was it hard to think of Congress bound by the limitations of the Constitution within the continental United States, but doing anything it pleased regarding life, liberty, and property outside of those geographical limits.

These vital questions came before the Supreme Court in the so-called Insular Cases of 1901. The first case, DeLima v. Bidwell, turned on whether duties on goods from Puerto Rico could be collected under the Dingley Tariff Act. The court held, but only by a vote of five to four, that Puerto Rico was not a foreign country and therefore the duties could not be collected. This, however, did not reach the real heart of the matter. Although it was settled that the Dingley Act did not apply automatically, it was not decided whether Congress had the right to place special duties on merchandise imported from the islands.

This further question at once arose. When the Foraker Act was passed, the President and many other people wished Puerto Rican products to come in free. The sugar interests, however, were opposed and were able to insert a provision that placed a 15 per cent duty on imports from Puerto Rico until 1902. The validity of this requirement was now tested in Downes v. Bidwell, decided in May, 1901. The crux of the matter lay in this question: did the provision of the Constitution that all duties must be uniform throughout the United States apply to Puerto Rico? By upholding the validity of the Foraker Act, the Supreme Court ruled that the Constitution did not automatically follow the flag; it was only extended to the outlying territories when Congress so ordered. In many ways Downes v. Bidwell was an unsatisfactory decision; the judges divided five to four and the majority could not agree on their reasoning even when concurring in upholding the validity of the Act. Nevertheless, the imperialists welcomed the outcome of the litigation. The way now seemed open for American rule to be extended over peoples regarded as inferior without any tiresome requirement that these wards must be granted full rights of citizenship. But even decisions of the Supreme Court could not govern irrevocably the thinking of the American people. In the minds of many, permanent American domination over colonial populations was inconsistent with American principles, nor could the implied pledge to prepare the Filipinos for eventual independence be forgotten.

Generally speaking, the issue was drawn between the major political parties. The Republicans, susceptible to the influence of big business and rather inclined to view with complacency the peculiar virtues of American progress, regarded independence for the Philippines as impracticable until the remote future. The Democrats, more or less committed against imperialism by William Jennings Bryan, favored early freedom for the islands.

American Interests in the Far East

The occupation of the Philippines and, to a lesser extent, of Hawaii, Guam, and Samoa, revived American interest in the Far East, an interest that had been largely dormant since before the Civil War, when Secretary of State Daniel Webster and his immediate successors had worked for equality of privileges and commercial facilities for all nations doing business with China.

Following the Civil War that interest had lagged and, even as late as March, 1898, a British proposal for joint action in the Far East to protect the open door was sidetracked in the United States official quarters. Then came the war with Spain and the resultant annexation of Far Eastern territory. Very speedily the American attitude changed. Part of the reason was economic: American exporters in quest of new markets and importers in search of new sources of supply wanted their full share of Far Eastern commerce. Part of it was strategic: that region must be kept at peace so that the new insular holdings could be defended more easily and at less cost.

The major trouble spot was China, whose weakness had been clearly demonstrated by her overwhelming defeat in the Sino-Japanese War of 1894–95. Japan and the major powers of Europe were quick to seize advantage by acquiring spheres of influence in Chinese territory. France obtained a ninety-nine-year lease to Kwangchow-wan; Britain gained Wei-hai-wei and Kowloon; Russia took over Port Arthur; Germany secured Kiaochow; Japan was showing interest in Fukhien and Korea; and Italy was striving to keep pace with the rest. It was no coincidence that these spheres centered around important ports. The United States did not share in those spoils, but she was concerned over what might follow. Suppose each trespassing power closed its ports to the commerce of all but its own ships? Certainly, then, American trade would suffer increasingly. Furthermore, the closed-port theory might lead to antagonisms, war might follow among the contestants, and the American hold on the Philippines might be lost. At the least, the United States would have to increase her military and naval establishments in that part of the world.

Although Britain was participating in the scramble for concessions in China, she greatly preferred the traditional policy of the Open Door under which English merchants had gained a major share of Far Eastern trade. On several occasions, therefore, the British government pressed upon the reluctant McKinley administration proposals for some kind of joint action in the Chinese situation. An active propagandist for this point of view was Lord Charles Beresford, a popular British naval hero who visited the United States in February, 1899, after a tour of the Far East. Meanwhile, American businessmen interested in the China trade were clamoring for a change of American policy.

Finally responding to these various pressures, Secretary of State John Hay adopted as his own certain ideas that had been in the process of formulation by W. W. Rockhill, one of his American advisers who had spent years in the Far East, and by Rockhill's friend, Alfred Hippisley, an Englishman employed in the Chinese customs service. On September 6, 1899, Hay sent similar notes to Great Britain, Germany, and Russia, and two months later to France, Italy, and Japan. The gist of these messages was that no country should interfere "with any treaty port or vested interest within any so-called 'spheres of interest' or leased territory it may have in China"; within each sphere the Chinese government should collect all duties provided for in its tariff treaties; and each power was asked not only to approve these statements but to try to persuade the others to agree also.

Hay's notes, it will be observed, gave only a strictly limited definition to the Open Door. No attempt was made to halt the partition of China; all Hay asked was that in any such partition American treaty rights in Chinese ports should be respected. Even for this modest program he obtained only faltering support. The replies from most of the powers were equivocal, with assent made contingent upon approval by all the other powers. The Russian answer, indeed, was practically a rejection. Secretary Hay was displeased with the result, but he determined upon a bold stroke. On March 20, 1900, he publicly announced that all the nations concerned had given their support in "final and definitive" terms to his proposal. None of the powers cared to challenge his statement, lest the others consider it grasping. Thus Hay enjoyed a diplomatic victory which had some real significance, although much less than that credited to him by the enthusiastic American press.

Hay carried his policy a step further within a few months. In June, 1900, a faction of Chinese nationalists, popularly known as the "Boxers," began a fanatical attempt to drive the invaders from their precious land. Several hundred of the "foreign devils" were killed, and the British legation at Peking, where many found refuge, was for weeks besieged by the Boxer forces. An international army of 20,000, of whom 2,500 were American troops from the Philip pines, had to be dispatched to effect a rescue. By the middle of August the siege was raised and the Boxer rebels dispersed.

Again the United States had to go to China's aid. On July 3, 1900, Hay added to the Open Door principle the additional policy of preserving the territorial integrity and independence of China. The other powers did not formally accept Hay's principles, but the dismemberment of the empire was prevented by working one country's territorial greed against that of another. Furthermore, the possible bankruptcy of China through payment of a billion-dollar indemnity was avoided when the United States persuaded the other nations to cut their demands by two thirds. China showed her gratitude by signing a commercial treaty particularly favorable to her benefactor. The good relations were further accentuated when the United States later returned most of her $24 million share of the Boxer indemnity. In turn, China used this money for scholarships in the United States granted to outstanding Chinese students.

Hay was not always consistent in his policies. At the close of 1900—the very year in which he made his public statements about preserving Chinese territorial integrity—the Secretary secretly tried to obtain a naval base for the United States in Southern China. The deal was frustrated through the opposition of the Japanese government, which chided Hay for his forgetfulness.

Hay's little flirtation with imperialism was fortunately not revealed until many years after his death, and the Secretary continued to enjoy a great reputation as the disinterested statesman who had saved a helpless China from the ravenous clutches of the other powers. This reputation was partly deserved and partly not. Hay had in truth showed considerable diplomatic skill in serving notice to the world that the United States stood committed both to equality of trading opportunity in China and the preservation of that nation's independence. Yet the policy was not primarily altruistic; it was designed more to promote American trade and investment and to preserve the general peace in the Far East than to safeguard China's territorial integrity as an end in itself. Moreover, other factors were probably more important than Hay's diplomacy in saving China from further encroachments. The United States was not prepared to fight to protect China in 1900, and all the world knew this. Much more important in calling a recess to the march of imperialism was, first, the warning of outraged nationalism sounded by the Boxer Uprising itself and, second, the balance of power that was taking shape in the Far East with Russia and France on one side and England and Japan on the other.

Relations with Japan

After 1900 English and American proponents of the Open Door watched with growing concern while Russia extended more and more complete domination over Manchuria and even made gestures toward Korea. The British government, with the approval of most Americans, countered Russian imperialism by promoting an alliance with Japan in 1902. This diplomatic development encouraged the Nipponese suddenly to attack Port Arthur in 1904, thus precipitating the Russo-Japanese War. Toward this contest the United States government maintained an official neutrality, but there was little attempt to disguise the strongly pro-Japanese character of its sympathies. Indeed, according to Roosevelt's own story—which has been questioned—he went so far as to warn France and Germany that the United States might go to the assistance of Japan were either of them to enter on the side of Russia. Whatever the truth of this tale, it is certain that Roosevelt responded eagerly when the Japanese government intimated to him in ultrasecrecy that it would welcome his good offices in bringing the war to an early conclusion, whereby the fruits of initial Japanese victories would be ensured. Fortunately for the President, Russia—convulsed by internal revolution—was also secretly eager for peace. Roosevelt was therefore upon sure ground when he issued his public invitation to the belligerents for a peace conference to be held in the United States. The resultant Treaty of Portsmouth of 1905 pleased the President, since it was moderate enough to maintain a balance of power and since he subsequently received the Nobel Peace Prize for his part in bringing it about.

The surprising military strength displayed by Japan impressed upon the Roosevelt administration the desirability of an understanding to safeguard American interests in the Philippines. Accordingly, President Roosevelt authorized Secretary of War Taft, upon completing a special mission to Manila, to proceed to Tokyo to sound out Japanese plans. Toward the close of July, 1905, Taft and Prime Minister Katsura concluded the so-called Agreed Memorandum. Under this arrangement the United States was to allow Japan a free hand in Korea in return for a promise that Japan had no designs upon the Philippines. Before the year was over, Secretary Root indicated his full support of this memorandum by telling the Japanese ambassador that in the future the United States would deal with Korean problems only through Japan.

This Agreed Memorandum was kept secret from the American people for many years. Certainly it was not in accord with the announced policy of the Open Door. Later, Root tried to defend this act of secret diplomacy by saying that the only way to have stopped the Japanese trespass in Korea was through war. He inferred that Congress would not have made a declaration and, if it had, the people would not have stood for it. Therefore, "all we might have done was to make threats which we could not carry out."

Although the Agreed Memorandum normally would be considered an indication of full cordiality between the two nations, actually beneath the surface there were signs of ill-feeling. Japanese jingoists, unacquainted with the initiative taken by their own government, believed that American diplomatic intervention in their war with Russia had deprived them of territory and large financial indemnity. On the other hand, Americans along the Pacific coast were worried over increased Japanese immigration, particularly of unskilled workers with a low standard of living. While a Congressional bill for complete exclusion of the Japanese failed because of Roosevelt's opposition, the San Francisco local authorities enacted in October, 1906, an ordinance preventing Orientals from attending the regular city schools. Immediately Japan objected on the ground that a treaty with the United States gave her nationals the same rights as those enjoyed by the most favored nation.

"Get Out O' There, Ye Foolish Boy." Uncle Sam trying to
prevent California from antagonizing Japan.
(From the *Cleveland Plain Dealer*.)

President Roosevelt supported this contention, but the Constitution gave him no authority to act in a local matter. The President, however, used other means to end this "wicked absurdity." He called the Republican leaders of California to a White House conference in which he persuaded them to use their influence to have the obnoxious statute repealed. And in this stand he was backed by most of the press of the nation, which feared war, so great was the Japanese resentment. The San Francisco authorities, influenced by the higher-ups and the absence of public backing, amended the school law so that Japanese children "of proper age and preparation" could attend the regular schools.

Then, in an effort to stop further local or state actions of a similar nature, Roosevelt arranged with the Japanese government the so-called "Gentlemen's Agreement" of 1907. By an exchange of notes Japan promised to refuse passports to the United States to Japanese laborers. By this face-saving device the Japanese government assumed responsibility for halting the type of emigration that had aroused antagonism.

Roosevelt did not wish the Japanese to take his intervention in the school law case as a sign of weakness. Indeed, he wrote to one of his friends in July, 1907: "I am none the less anxious that they would realize that I am not afraid of them and that the United States will no more submit to bullying than it will to bully." Consequently, he decided to send the American battle fleet of sixteen battleships with numerous smaller craft around the world. This would warn Japanese jingoists that the United States, with the world's second largest navy, was prepared for any trouble. When the announcement was made in the summer of 1907 there were immediate protests. The press in the East asserted that it was a foolhardy move that would leave the Atlantic shores unprotected and expose the fleet to a possible Japanese attack. Congress at first refused to furnish the money necessary for the venture. The President, however, bluntly declared that there were enough funds available to get the fleet to the Pacific where it would stay until Congress changed its mind. And thus Roosevelt had his way.

The spectacular voyage had more behind it than simply a brandishing of the sword under the nose of Japan. Roosevelt, still the eager promoter of naval expansion, hoped both to give the fleet practice in large-scale operations and to publicize the need for larger appropriations both for the navy itself and for the Panama Canal. So far as Japan was concerned, the expedition appeared to work out well. The fleet accepted a Japanese invitation to visit Tokyo, where it received an enthusiastic welcome. Roosevelt could therefore congratulate himself that his policy had promoted the cause of peace. Whether it had really done so, however, is questionable. Secretly resentful of the American demonstration of strength, the big-navy faction in Japan redoubled its efforts to build up Japan's own naval strength to the point where she would dominate the Far East.

While the fleet was still on the high seas, Secretary Root effected a promising agreement with Japanese Ambassador Takahira in November, 1908. Its terms provided for mutual support for the Pacific status quo, non-interference with each other's possessions, mutual backing of the independence and territorial integrity of China, and general reiteration of the Open Door principle. Unfortunately this was not a treaty, but simply an executive arrangement; yet under it Japan gave her most adequate endorsement of the Hay theory up to that time.

Despite the measures that had been taken to ease Japanese-American tension, a growing antagonism between the more nationalistic factions in the two countries was evident. Among a certain class of Americans it was popular to depict Japan as the inevitable enemy of the future and to ask whether the United States should not embark upon a preventive war before her rival became too strong. This attitude was accentuated during the Taft administration when a Japanese syndicate sought to gain control of Magdalena Bay in the Lower California area of Mexico in 1911. Immediately the cry was raised that the syndicate was really a Japanese governmental agency which wanted the Bay as a future naval base from which to attack the United States. So great was the furor that the syndicate dropped its plans. To make sure that a similar threat would not arise in the future, Senator Henry Cabot Lodge introduced into the Upper House the so-called Lodge Corollary to the Monroe Doctrine, which was approved by a vote of 51 to 4 in August, 1912. This resolution declared that "when any harbor or any other place in the American continents is so situated that the occupation thereof for naval or military purposes might threaten . . . the safety of the United States, the Government of the United States could not see without grave concern the actual or potential possession of such harbor or other place by any Government, not American." While this corollary was not endorsed by President Taft, the American people welcomed it as a twentieth-century version of the hallowed Monroe Doctrine. This attitude did not improve relations between Japan and the United States.

Dollar Diplomacy in China

The Open Door was supposedly in jeopardy again during Taft's presidency. In 1910 occurred the Chinese revolution, which overthrew the Manchu Dynasty and made China nominally a republic. The immediate result was to submerge the Chinese in problems of reorganization, particularly economic. Taft, along with Secretary Knox, became worried over the proposal of French, German, and British bankers to enter the picture by constructing the Hukuang Railroad through Southern and Central China. Taft felt that the building of this line might destroy the Open Door. Consequently, the State Department prevailed upon J. P. Morgan to establish an American syndicate to participate in the railway development. About the only effect of this action was to make the European powers suspicious of American designs, and even the Morgan interests were not enthusiastic about entering the project.

Taft was also fearful of the Russo-Japanese railroad interests in Manchuria, the extension of which the President believed was endangering the territorial integrity of China. Therefore he proposed to the several European powers and to Japan that their bankers combine with those from the United States to loan China sufficient money to buy the railroads in question. The other powers were not in sympathy with the proposal, and the American bankers had to be practically forced to participate. They finally worked out a six-power arrangement for lending $125 million to China; but before the loan could go through, Woodrow Wilson became President. In March, 1913, he publicly announced through the press that such a loan would weaken China's sovereignty and might lead to future interventions. If the American bankers wanted to go ahead, they would do so at their own risk; they could expect no backing from his administration. Thus did Taft's efforts at so-called dollar diplomacy in China fail. His honesty of intention could not be doubted, but his methods only served to promote closer Russo-Japanese accord and to weaken the status quo arrangements that Theodore Roosevelt had made with Japan.

In administering its new empire, the United States showed considerable ability and restraint. There was little effort made to subjugate the inhabitants in the style of earlier European imperialism. While there were complaints from those inhabitants, actually they were far better off in every way than they had been.

But in plunging into Far Eastern problems the United States was inviting serious future trouble. Since in a showdown the American government would have neither the popular support nor the military strength necessary to back up its policies with force, it had to rely upon diplomatic maneuvering and the game of playing off one nation against another. This worked so long as the elements were available upon which a balance of power could be based. When the European nations became locked in titanic struggles like World War I and World War II, the American position became increasingly untenable. Finally, during the crisis of 1941, the United States found itself in a position where it was compelled either to retire in humiliation or to fight.

6

Search for Security and Peace

American diplomacy in the first decade of the twentieth century was not limited to problems of colonial administration or efforts to maintain the Open Door in China and peace in the Far East. There were other matters that demanded equal attention. In order to maintain its newly won position as a world power, the United States felt the need of constructing an interoceanic canal, of seeing that the approaches to that waterway were protected, and of developing a closer spirit of accord in the Western Hemisphere. Likewise, the United States assumed the responsibility of promoting world peace. She continued to be a prime supporter of the doctrine of arbitration for settling international disputes.

Clearing the Way for the Panama Canal

The idea of a canal to pierce Central America and link the Atlantic and Pacific Oceans was a magnificent dream that had appealed to Spanish imagination during the Age of Discovery. In later days Thomas Jefferson had proposed such a waterway, and mid-nineteenth century supporters of Manifest Destiny had taken up the idea as a means of speeding transportation to California and Oregon. Indeed, in 1846 Minister Benjamin Bidlack concluded a treaty with New Granada, the predecessor of Colombia, granting the United States and its citizens a right of way across the Isthmus of Panama. Although no canal was built at this time, an American-controlled Panama railroad did result from the Bidlack diplomacy. During the late 1840's the rivalry of England and the United States in Central America threatened serious trouble, but the two nations eventually reached a compromise in the Clayton-Bulwer Treaty of 1850, by which the signatories agreed that neither would seek to fortify or exercise exclusive control over any isthmian canal.

In 1879, when French promoters sought to follow up their triumph in building the Suez Canal with the organization of a Panama Canal Company, it appeared that the long-dreamed-of waterway might soon become a reality under a control neither British nor American. Acquiring a concession from the Colombian government, the French promoters began construction in a great burst of energy. Long before the project could be completed, however, the company, plagued by graft and mismanagement, went into bankruptcy—to the immense relief of jealously watching Americans.

Meantime, the United States had become thoroughly dissatisfied with the limitations of the Clayton-Bulwer Treaty. In 1880 President Hayes declared that any canal connecting the Atlantic and the Pacific must be under exclusive American control because it would form "a part of the coastline of the United States." During the administrations of Garfield and Arthur efforts were made to modify the Clayton-Bulwer Treaty, but Great Britain refused to waive her rights—greatly to the displeasure of American expansionists who threatened to have the United States tear up the old treaty and proceed on its own willful way. The anti-imperialist Cleveland sternly opposed proposals for unilateral action, but he impressed upon the English the desirability of modifying their position. By 1897 the latter were beginning to face up to the realities of the new situation. Eager to improve Anglo-American relations and desirous of encouraging the construction of a canal that would benefit English commerce as much as American, the British government was now ready to negotiate on the issue.

This was the situation when the Spanish-American War provided dramatic evidence of the need for building the waterway without further delay. The sixty-eight-day voyage of the *Oregon* around Cape Horn and the acquisition of the Pacific islands demonstrated the need for linking the Atlantic and Pacific Oceans, if the new possessions were to be adequately protected.

Under these new circumstances Secretary Hay was able with relatively little difficulty to reach an agreement with Lord Pauncefote, the British ambassador. The so-called First Hay-Pauncefote Treaty provided that the United States might build and manage a canal through Central America, but specified that the canal must be neutralized and unfortified under approximately the same rules as those governing the Suez Canal. The United States Senate refused to ratify this document as it stood. Instead, the Upper House made a number of changes, the most important of which denied the international character of the canal and provided for American defense of the proposed waterway. Since Britain would not accept these amendments, Hay had to start all over again.

On November 18, 1901, a compromise was reached in the Second Hay-Pauncefote treaty: the Clayton-Bulwer arrangement was definitely superseded;

the United States could build and manage a canal which, although theoretically neutralized, would be under the protection of the United States; and the clause barring fortifications was removed. The only restricting article of importance provided that the canal be open to the nations of the world on terms of equality. This time the Senate offered no opposition to ratification. Somewhat later, Britain conceded the right of the United States to fortify the canal since there was nothing in the treaty to forbid such action. These British concessions indicated the growing accord between the two nations. Another sign of friendly feeling was the gradual reduction of the British fleet and garrisons in Caribbean waters, tacit admission of American supremacy in that area.

Meanwhile, a spirited controversy had developed over the route to be used for the canal. The most promising alternatives were a plan that would connect the various natural waterways of Nicaragua and one that would cut directly across the narrow waist of Panama. For various reasons the American preference had always been for the Nicaragua project, but the partisans of Panama were now engaged in a great campaign to call public attention to what they claimed were the superior advantages of their shorter route. Deeply interested in the issue was the New Panama Canal Company, which had taken over the assets of the old corporation. The stockholders' only hope of salvaging something from the financial wreck was to sell their rights to the United States government for as much as they could get. In Philippe Bunau-Varilla, a French engineer who had worked for the old company, and William Nelson Cromwell, an astute New York lawyer, the new company had two highly ingenious lobbyists.

To study the problem of the competing routes, President McKinley had appointed a commission headed by Admiral John G. Walker. In a report submitted two days before the Second Hay-Pauncefote Treaty was concluded, the Walker Commission recommended the Nicaragua route. The chief reason for this decision was that the stockholders of the New Panama Canal Company were demanding $109 million for their rights across the isthmus. Were this amount to be paid by the United States, the total cost for a Panama canal would be considerably higher.[1]

The chief executive, now Theodore Roosevelt, was most anxious to begin construction of the canal, a project in which he had long been interested. While he probably preferred the Panama route, he refused to pay the outrageous sum the New Panama Canal Company was asking. Consequently, in December, 1901, he gave his outward blessing to the Hepburn Bill for a Nicaragua canal, which passed the House of Representatives early in January, 1902, by the one-sided vote of 308 to 2. Meantime, the Panama Company stockholders, realizing

[1] The Walker Commission reported that construction costs alone would be: for Panama, $144 million; for Nicaragua, $190 million. The addition of $109 million to the Panama construction cost would therefore make the total $60 million more than for the Nicaraguan canal.

that the Hepburn Bill would pass unless something were done and knowing that their own rights would be worthless were a canal built through Nicaragua, forced out their officers who had made the $109 million claim. The stockholders then offered to sell their privileges for $40 million. According to the Walker Commission, this was a reasonable sum. Therefore the Spooner Amendment was added to the Hepburn Bill in the Senate, substituting the Panama route if the United States could get the company's rights for the $40 million figure and obtain satisfactory permission from Colombia. Thanks to administration pressure and volcanic eruptions near the site of the proposed Nicaragua route, the amended Hepburn Bill passed both Houses by overwhelming majorities and was signed by President Roosevelt on June 28, 1902.

The remaining obstacle, Colombian permission, was the most difficult of all. After long negotiations, Secretary Hay finally concluded the Hay-Herrán Treaty in January, 1903. Under the terms of this convention, the United States was to lease a six-mile-wide strip across the Panama Isthmus with full construction rights in return for a cash payment of $10 million and an annual rental of $250,000. The United States Senate ratified this arrangement on March 17, despite the protests of some members that the treaty did not give the United States sovereign authority over the canal zone.

In Colombia the treaty proved highly unpopular. Suspicious Latin Americans looked upon the lease arrangements as merely an ingenious lever by which the imperialistic Yankees were attempting to pry Panama away from Colombia; moreover, they regarded the proferred compensation as niggardly. Colombian national finances were in wretched condition, and it was desperately hoped that either the United States could be induced to raise its price or the New Panama Canal Company might be required to share some of its $40 million with Colombia. In view of the explosive state of Colombian public opinion, President José Marroquín decided that it would be prudent to share responsibility with the Colombian Congress, even though for several years his dictatorial regime had been getting along without that body. Special elections were therefore held, and for several weeks the legislators engaged in feverish debate on the issue. In the end, the Colombian Senate rejected the treaty by an almost unanimous vote.

Although this step was quite within Colombia's rights as a sovereign nation, President Roosevelt was incensed with men whom he described as "the foolish and homicidal corruptionists at Bogotá." Even though he still had the alternative of the Nicaraguan route, he was reluctant to give up the Panama project, to which he was now strongly committed.

The Colombian rejection of the Hay-Herrán Treaty was also greatly resented by the inhabitants of the Panama Isthmus, a region largely isolated from the rest of Colombia and long addicted to dreams of secession. Fear of losing the

The Man Behind the Egg. The intrigue promoting the Panama
Revolution. (By Drake in *The New York Times*.)

economic benefits that the canal would bring now stirred the Panamanians to
active plotting for revolt. Such was the disparity of strength between Colombia
and Panama, however, that any insurrection would be hopeless unless the
rebels could count on immediate protection from the United States. It became
the delicate mission of Bunau-Varilla, eager to help a movement beneficial to
the New Panama Canal Company, to sound out the Roosevelt administration
to see what its attitude would be in case of a Panama revolt. Although Roosevelt and Hay carefully avoided any definite commitment, Bunau-Varilla left
Washington with the distinct conviction that the conspirators had nothing to
fear.

With the ground thus prepared, events moved rapidly. On November 2,
1903, the U.S.S. *Nashville* arrived at Colon, the Atlantic terminal of the
Panama railroad. This was the first of several naval vessels that the Navy Department had ordered to move to the expected trouble spot. The day after her
arrival, the rebels struck against the weak Colombian garrison at Panama City
on the Pacific Coast. There were enough Colombian troops at Colon to have
suppressed the movement, but they were not permitted to use the railroad.
Cowed by the guns of the *Nashville*, the Colombian commander accepted a
Panamanian bribe of $8,000 and two cases of champagne and evacuated the city.
By November 5 the rebels were in complete control of the isthmus and any
possibility that Colombia might land forces to reconquer the territory was
ruled out by the warning that this would not be permitted by the American
naval vessels now guarding both coasts of Panama. The American government
justified its intervention by the old Bidlack Treaty, under which the United

States had guaranteed the neutrality of the isthmus "with the view that the free transit from one to the other side may not be interrupted." Naturally, Colombia did not concede that it was a rightful interpretation of these words for the United States to deny the right of a sovereign nation to put down an insurrection on its own soil.

Brushing aside Colombian protests, the Roosevelt administration recognized the new Republic of Panama on November 6, 1903, and on November 19, Bunau-Varilla, who had been designated as special envoy by the Panama government, signed a new canal agreement.[2] Under the terms of this Hay-Bunau-Varilla Treaty the United States guaranteed the independence of Panama, obtained a perpetual lease to a ten-mile-wide canal zone, and agreed to pay Panama the same amounts that had been offered Colombia in the rejected Hay-Herrán Treaty.

Although the Senate approved the treaty without serious opposition, Roosevelt's conduct in the Panama affair was severely criticized not only by Colombians, who felt that they had been outrageously treated, but by many Americans as well. The President denied that he had any direct complicity in the revolt and justified the measures that had been taken on the grounds of the Bidlack Treaty, American national interests, and the need of the world for the canal. In later years, however, Roosevelt described his action more bluntly. In a speech in 1911, for example, he said: "I took the Canal Zone and let Congress debate." Quite apart from the moral issue of whether the end justified the means, Roosevelt's Panama policy cannot escape condemnation on other grounds. American conduct damaged the reputation of the United States in the eyes of Latin America, causing injury that took many years to repair.

With the diplomatic problems surmounted, those of construction now had to be faced. Differences of opinion concerning the type of canal, Congressional red tape, disputes over control and methods, and the search for an efficient labor supply held up the work during the initial years. Finally, in 1907, President Roosevelt, anxious to see "the dirt begin to fly," placed the construction in the hands of army engineers commanded by Lieutenant Colonel George W. Goethals. Colonel William Gorgas of the Army Medical Corps supervised in competent fashion the improvement of sanitary and health conditions in the Canal Zone. The work then began in earnest and, despite many landslides and other obstructions, the Panama Canal was opened to traffic on August 15, 1914. The cost, $375 million, was higher than had been anticipated; however, considering the advantages of the waterway to the United States and to the world,

---

[2] The fact that the rights of the New Panama Canal Company would expire in 1904 helps to account for Colombia's desire to delay negotiations and for Bunau-Varilla's (and perhaps Roosevelt's) wish for haste in obtaining United States recognition of Panama's independence. Those rights, of course, were worth $40 million.

it was more than worth the price. Roosevelt regarded obtaining the route and actual construction of the canal as his greatest achievement.

In anticipation of the opening of the canal, Congress passed the Panama Canal Act in August, 1912. This measure established the toll rates to be charged the users of the canal. It exempted, however, American ships engaged in the coastwise trade from any payment. Britain immediately protested that this exemption was contrary to the clause of the Hay-Pauncefote Treaty providing that the canal should be open to the nations of the world on terms of equality. Not until March, 1914, was President Wilson able to persuade Congress that treaty obligation went ahead of national self-interest and that the exemption should be removed.[3]

Caribbean Diplomacy

One of Theodore Roosevelt's favorite maxims was: "Speak softly but carry a big stick." In his own eyes the soft-speaking was as important as the big stick, but to other people it usually seemed that the latter was much more characteristically Rooseveltian than the former. At all events, the President believed that, while bluff and bluster were to be avoided, a readiness to use force if necessary was a vital element in foreign policy. In no field was this more evident than in Roosevelt's dealing with the Caribbean region. The importance of this area to American security was magnified by the construction of the Panama Canal. No potentially dangerous foreign power must be allowed to obtain a foothold near the approaches to this waterway; no little hemisphere republic must be permitted to reach such a condition of bankruptcy or disorder as to provoke foreign intervention. The Monroe Doctrine must be brought up to date to meet such threats.

Roosevelt was not the first to employ big-stick diplomacy. During the 1890's American nationalists became fearful lest, under the guise of a dispute over a boundary between British Guiana and Venezuela, the British might extend their control over territory in a strategically important Caribbean area. Cleveland's Secretary of State, Richard Olney, demanded that this controversy be submitted to arbitration, and flatly stated: "Today the United States is practically sovereign on this continent, and its fiat is law upon the subjects to which it confines its interposition." The British at first denied that the United States had any right to intervene but, after Cleveland backed his Secretary with a stern special message to Congress in which he said that all the power of the United States would be used to prevent British encroachment on Venezuelan territory, Great Britain began to retreat. Not that Britain feared the United States—her navy, for instance, was five times larger than the American—but as Minister

[3] See Chapter 8 for more details on this issue.

Bayard wrote, "The United States is the last nation on earth with whom the British people or their rulers desire to quarrel." The English were worried about the European situation, and Britain's traditional isolation was now looking much less splendid.

Britain consequently submitted to the American demand, with a few face-saving safeguards, and the arbitral tribunal of 1899 awarded her most of the disputed territory. Through her acquiescence in the new and broadly extended interpretation that Olney had given to the Monroe Doctrine, Britain was paying the price of American friendship by accepting the supremacy of the United States in the Western Hemisphere. One of the chief evidences of this acceptance was the British ratification of the Hay-Pauncefote Treaty in 1902.

Even while the negotiations for a canal were proceeding, Venezuela again became a trouble center, this time over debts owed to the citizens of at least ten countries. British and German creditors, tired of being refused payment of either interest or principal, appealed to their respective governments in 1901 to intervene in their behalf. Germany took the lead among the creditors by offering to submit the debt problem to the Hague Court for arbitration, but Venezuelan dictator Cipriano Castro, who was in part responsible for the extravagance that had caused the debt, refused the proposition. Consequently, Great Britain, with more at stake financially than the other creditors, suggested forcible collection, a move which President Roosevelt did not oppose. He accepted British and German assurances that such action would not result in annexation of territory and therefore the Monroe Doctrine would not be at stake; furthermore, he felt that Venezuela was in the wrong in not agreeing to arbitration. Indeed, he wrote in 1901 that if a Latin-American country misbehaved, "let the European country spank it."

Encouraged by Roosevelt's policy of non-interference, Great Britain and Germany, followed eventually by Italy, began a blockade of Venezuela in December, 1902. Although there was no declaration of war, ships of the little Venezuelan navy were captured and two were sunk. Castro now abruptly changed his tune and through the United States requested arbitration. The creditor states agreed in principle, but insisted on maintaining the blockade until all the details could be arranged. An agreement to arbitrate finally was signed in February, 1903. The blockade, thus continued for over two months, was extremely irritating to American public opinion, especially when it resulted in incidents like the bombardment of a Venezuelan coastal town. Significantly the Germans rather than the British were the targets of most of this indignation. Even Roosevelt became restive and suspicious, urging the German ambassador to have the arbitration settlement arranged and the blockade ended as soon as possible. Although professing faith that the Kaiser would keep his pledge and refrain from any attempt to obtain South American territory, the

President kept the navy mobilized at Puerto Rico as an additional insurance that the Monroe Doctrine would be respected. In later years Roosevelt asserted that he compelled the Kaiser to accept arbitration by an ultimatum in which he threatened to send the fleet to Venezuela, but the contemporary evidence to support this story is not convincing. Be that as it may, the importance of the whole affair was that the European powers did not institute the blockade until they learned it would not be opposed by the United States, and their decision to accept arbitration was hastened by the knowledge that the blockade was resented by American public opinion. This so-called second Venezuela affair, like the first, resulted in an impressive recognition of the strength of the United States in the Western Hemisphere.

President Roosevelt was made wary by this affair. With the diplomatic negotiations for the canal concluded, he did not want similar incidents to develop in other Latin-American countries which might enable creditor nations to intervene and perhaps obtain a foothold dangerous to the security of the canal. The United States, he believed, must use its police power to prevent chronic wrongdoing within the republics bordering on the approaches to the isthmus. This need was brought to the fore in 1903 when the Dominican Republic, following years of dictatorship and civil war, found herself unable to meet financial obligations owed to several European countries, notably France and Italy, and to the American-controlled San Domingo Improvement Company. After numerous efforts at settlement by arbitration, the United States signed a protocol stipulating that if the republic did not pay what it owed, the American government would have to take over the administration of Dominican customs receipts. The Dominican authorities failed to heed the warning, no payments on the debt were made, and both France and Italy considered the possibility of intervention. Consequently, in October, 1904, a financial agent of the United States was placed in charge of the customhouses under a temporary arrangement.

President Roosevelt justified his action in his annual message to Congress in December, 1904, and again a year later. Telling passages in these two messages were:

> If a nation shows that it knows how to act with reasonable efficiency and decency in social and political matters, if it keeps order and pays its obligations, it need fear no interference from the United States. Chronic wrongdoing . . . in the Western Hemisphere . . . may force the United States, however reluctantly, in flagrant cases of wrongdoing or impotence, to the exercise of an international police power. . . . We must make it evident that we do not intend to permit the Monroe Doctrine to be used by any nation on this Continent as a shield to protect it from the consequences of its own misdeeds against foreign nations. . . .

This was the so-called Roosevelt or Big Stick Corollary of the Monroe Doctrine, which was the logical extension of the Olney interpretation of the previous decade. Its promulgation offered further proof that the United States realized it had become a world power; in view of the deferring of the European powers to that Doctrine in the second Venezuela affair, it was perhaps only natural that the United States should expect the big-stick theory also to be recognized.

Under this doctrine of hemisphere police power and to make the temporary arrangement with the Dominican Republic more satisfactory and permanent, Secretary Hay sought a treaty that would give the United States the right to collect Dominican duties and pay the creditors. In February, 1905, President Morales approved the suggestion that 45 per cent of the customs be used for Dominican government expenses and the rest to take care of the debt. Furthermore, the United States was to be empowered "to restore the credit, preserve the order, increase the efficiency of the civil administration, and advance the material progress and welfare of the Dominican Republic." This agreement was not approved by the United States Senate, largely because of the belief that the executive branch was overstepping its authority. President Roosevelt, however, put the protocol into effect by executive order.

Under this agreement, the United States did excellent work in the Dominican Republic. The Dominican government received more income from its 45 per cent share of the customs than it had previously from the full receipts, and at the same time its debt was scaled down materially. In 1907 the American Senate, seeing this progress and having temporarily put aside partisan bickerings, ratified a treaty providing that the Dominican debt, now fixed at $17 million, should be paid with the aid of a $20 million loan advanced by American bankers. That debt could not be increased and an American receiver of customs was appointed to collect all receipts. This financial protocol lasted until 1924.

During the remainder of Roosevelt's administration and throughout the greater part of Taft's four years in office, the Dominican Republic was peaceful politically. The republic's trade developed rapidly and her program of public works was beneficial to the inhabitants. No effort was made by the United States to exploit the Dominicans in any way. Yet by 1911 the political leaders, tired of political peace, began to chafe under restraint. An era of rebellions started, which subsequently led to the establishment of American military and political control.

This intervention in the Dominican Republic under Theodore Roosevelt was the forerunner of the so-called dollar diplomacy that reached its zenith under Taft. As in later cases of dollar diplomacy, a chaotic and nearly bankrupt country, facing possible intervention by a European nation, had to be saved from such a fate by the United States, using the Roosevelt Corollary as justification. A fairly standard procedure came to be followed. The United States would set up a financial protectorate and prevail upon private bankers to lend money to the backward state, and the bankers in turn would demand that their loans be protected. The United States therefore would establish a political protectorate as well, usually with the aid of American marines. Elections would be supervised and this would result in the selection of a president favorably disposed toward the United States and the American banker creditors. Owing his position to American favor, this president would then grant concessions to American investors who would subsequently reap the profits. This dollar diplomacy insofar as it affected Latin America was promoted under the guise of safeguarding the Panama Canal. As Taft's Secretary of State Knox said: "Thus the malady of revolutions and financial collapse is most acute precisely in the region where it is most dangerous to us. It is here we seek to apply a remedy." But at another time Knox tried to place such diplomacy on a higher plane: "If the American dollar can aid suffering humanity and lift the burden of financial difficulty from states with which we live on terms of intimate intercourse and earnest friendship, and replace insecurity and devastation by stability and peaceful self-development, all I can say is that it would be hard to find better employment."

The remedy that Knox and Taft advocated was administered to Honduras in 1909. That Central American republic could not pay the interest on its bonds, most of which were held by British investors. Fearing the possibility of British intervention, Knox finally persuaded American bankers to take over the Honduran debt in 1911. Similar trouble coupled with political chaos in Nicaragua led to the placing of that state's customhouses under an American collector, a move aided in no small measure by the presence of an American warship and marines. The Taft administration then refused to recognize the new Nicaraguan president until he obtained American loans sufficient to pay off his country's foreign debt. As the people of Nicaragua did not like these high-handed actions, it was only through threats of force that the financial protectorate was established. Haiti, one of the insular republics, was also beginning to show signs of economic troubles. Consequently, the State Department in 1910 prevailed upon four American banks to buy up a large number of the bonds of Haiti's National Bank. This opened the way for further intervention under Wilson.

Dollar diplomacy was a form of economic imperialism. While Taft used the excuse that only through American interventions and investments could the backward republics be made stable, peaceful, and civilized, one of the primary motives was to give American bankers and investors a profit. And it cannot be said that dollar diplomacy improved Pan-American relations.

Pan-Americanism

An attempt to bring the republics of the hemisphere more closely together diplomatically, economically, and culturally—the objectives of Pan-American-ism—had originated under James G. Blaine, who served as Secretary of State under Garfield and Benjamin Harrison. The first modern Pan-American meet-ing, held in Washington in 1889–90, discussed arbitration agreements, a cus-toms union, uniform weights and measures, copyright and patent laws, and a trade dollar, but did not accomplish a great deal. The novelty of the plan, suspicion of American motives, and mutual jealousies all combined to prevent the Washington conference from attaining its objectives. However, the meeting did smooth the way for future sessions and established the forerunner of the Pan-American Union, a clearinghouse for varied information of value to the republics.

The first conference of the new century, held at Mexico City in 1901–2 did not open auspiciously. The United States had just finished its war with Spain, a war that, to the Latin-American mind, had turned from an altruistic battle to free Cuba into an imperialistic contest. It was feared that American imperialism had not been satisfied, and that the next objective might be the smaller states of the Western Hemisphere. The United States delegates tried to quiet these apprehensions by proposing that all international disputes be submitted to arbitration. Unfortunately, this suggestion did not receive unanimous backing, although a goodly minority supported the proposition. A majority, however, did support the view that financial problems which could not be settled by normal diplomatic procedure should be submitted to arbitration, through the channels suggested at the Hague Conference of 1899.

Nor did the next session, held at Rio de Janeiro in 1906, begin on a friendlier note. The forcing of the Platt Amendment upon Cuba, the Panama revolu-tion, intervention in the Dominican Republic, and the promulgation of the Roosevelt Corollary created suspicion of American intentions. Furthermore, Argentina, rival of the United States for hemisphere leadership, had her own solution for the controversial debt problem. This Drago Doctrine stated that armed force must not be used to collect financial obligations, a theory in a sense opposed to the Roosevelt Corollary. Disagreement over the issue might have broken up the meeting had it not been for the conciliatory attitude of Elihu Root, chairman of the United States delegation. Root agreed to have the matter of debt collection submitted to the Second Hague Conference, scheduled to meet the following year. He was also able to keep diplomatic discussions at Rio to a minimum and to concentrate on the promotion of economic and cultural accord.

Following this meeting, Root visited seven other Latin-American countries in an effort to promote better relations within the hemisphere through greater sympathy and understanding. He was well received in each of the republics as he stressed the need of cooperation for peace and security. President Roosevelt, commenting on Root's trip, wrote: "We in this country do not realize how wonderful it was and how much good he has done." It was also Root who prevailed upon Andrew Carnegie to contribute a large sum of money toward the construction of the building in which the Pan American Union is housed.

The Buenos Aires Conference of 1910 gave evidence of greater harmony among the now twenty-one republics than heretofore. All the members signed a pact to arbitrate any financial differences that arose among them. The Pan American Union was reorganized in a way that proved satisfactory to most of the previous objectors. Such matters as uniform patents, copyrights, and trademarks, the improvement of communications, health and sanitation, and the interchange of students and professors occupied the major attention of the delegates.

The United States also used its good offices in trying to effect accord among the Central-American republics, which were constantly battling with each other. After a war between Guatemala on one side and El Salvador and Honduras on the other in 1906, President Roosevelt, aided by President Díaz of Mexico, sought a solution. But opposition from Dictator Zelaya of Nicaragua, who believed the United States was trying to dominate Central America, prevented a satisfactory settlement and the strife broadened. Consequently, in 1907, Roosevelt and Díaz again called a conference of the republics, which was held in Washington. This meeting resulted in the establishment of the Central American International Bureau to promote unity, and in the organization of the Central American Court of Justice, which was to serve as a tribunal to arbitrate future quarrels among the members. The International Bureau did excellent work along the lines of the Pan-American Union; unfortunately, the tribunal was not a success.

Arbitration Efforts

The growing interest of the United States in world affairs and, more particularly, in the pacific settlement of controversies, was well demonstrated under both Roosevelt and Taft. The first sign of this attitude had been shown at the first Hague Conference, which was called by the Tsar of Russia in November, 1899. The United States was one of the twenty-six nations represented, with Ambassador to Germany Andrew D. White as head of the American delegation. A "Convention for the Peaceful Adjustment of International Differences"

was drawn up, under which disputes between nations might be settled by mediation, by international tribunals of inquiry, or by the Permanent Court of Arbitration (which was not a court in the real sense, but a panel of jurists from
which arbiters could be chosen for any specific controversy) for which the
Hague conferees provided. White played a prominent part in overcoming
Germany's opposition. In ratifying the work of the Hague meeting, however,
the United States Senate insisted that incidents arising under the Monroe
Doctrine were outside the scope of the permanent court.

The first case that came before the Hague Court concerned the so-called
Pious Fund. In the seventeenth century the Catholic Church had established
a trust fund to convert the Indians of California to Christianity. When the
fund's administrators, the Jesuits, were expelled from the Spanish Indies, the
King of Spain assumed the dispensing of this fund until the Wars of Independence. Then the new Mexican government took charge. In 1848, the
United States gained California and the Catholic bishops sought control of the
money. Mexico, however, refused to turn it over, and the bishops subsequently
brought the case before a mixed commission, which decided in their favor.
Mexico then paid some of the interest, but stopped after a few years. In the
1890's the United States government interceded at the behest of the archbishop
of San Francisco and the bishop of Monterey, and Mexico promised to abide
by the decision of the anticipated Permanent Court. In 1902 the judgment was
handed down in favor of the clerics, a judgment to which Mexico conformed.
Thus the combined efforts of the two neighboring nations showed that arbitration could work under the Hague plan.

The Alaska Boundary Settlement

Another long-standing difference settled by peaceful means was the controversy over the boundary between southern Alaska and Canada. The Klondike
gold rush at the end of the century made Canadians ambitious to obtain control
of the Lynn Canal and the port of Skagway. The United States insisted, however, on an interpretation of earlier treaties which would maintain exclusive
American domination of this stretch of coast.

Since 1899 Secretary Hay had tried to effect a settlement, but without success.
The British government, at the insistence of Canada, argued that the issue
should be submitted to an arbitration in which some foreign umpire would have
the deciding voice, but the American government maintained that the Canadian claims had so little basis that the American rights should not be thus
jeopardized. Instead, Hay suggested that the question be decided by a commission of three American and three British members. No decision could then be

reached unless one of the commissioners voted against the contentions of his own government. When in 1903 Britain finally consented to this proposition, President Roosevelt turned not to impartial jurists for his appointments to the commission, but to politicians: Secretary of War Root, Senator Lodge, and ex-Senator George Turner of Washington, on whom he could depend to hold out for the claims of the United States. The British government named Lord Alverstone, the Lord Chief Justice of England, and two prominent Canadians. Given this tribunal, the United States could scarcely lose its case, but Roosevelt took aggressive steps to assure a clean-cut victory. By every possible channel he sought to impress upon the British government how unfortunate the conse-quences might be if Lord Alverstone did not cast his vote against the Ca-nadian contentions. In the end the British jurist did vote with the Americans for a decision that ruled out most of the Canadian claims. Despite Canadian protests, the issue was ultimately settled on this basis.

The Hay Arbitration Treaties

After taking so prominent a part in the establishment of the Permanent Court at the Hague, the Roosevelt administration not only showed the way in referring special cases to it, but tried hard to establish agreements with other nations to submit to this tribunal all cases coming within what international jurists then regarded as the scope of arbitration. The First Hague Conference as part of its work had prepared a model treaty through which the contracting parties would promise to refer all such problems to the Permanent Court.

Secretary Hay negotiated fourteen treaties on this model, chiefly with Great Britain, France, and Germany, by December, 1904. They all excepted from arbitration questions affecting the vital interests, independence, or honor of the contracting parties. As these exceptions were precisely the things that caused war, the negotiation of such instruments did not go very far. And as far as Great Britain was concerned, the United States had already arbitrated to great mutual advantage matters that might fairly be called vital. Nevertheless, the action of Hay helped at least to advertise the idea of arbitration.

When these treaties were submitted to the Senate for ratification, there was trouble. The Upper House feared that its power over all treaties as laid down in the Constitution was being threatened. Some Senators also professed doubt lest questions arising out of the repudiation of debts by some of the states would be subjected to arbitration. The Upper House therefore amended the treaties in such a way as to alter the "special agreements" under which the various ques-tions were in each case to be arbitrated into special treaties subject individually to the advice and consent of the Senate. Angered by this action, Roosevelt withdrew the treaties from further consideration. He said at the time:

I think that this amendment makes the treaties shams, and my present impression is that we had better abandon the whole business rather than give the impression of trickiness and insincerity which would be produced by solemnly promulgating a sham.

The Second Hague Conference

The Second Hague Conference of 1907, also called by the Tsar, was signalized by the fact that the nations of Latin America were invited to attend at the insistence of Elihu Root. The United States delegation was headed by Joseph Choate and General Horace Porter. In respect to limitation of armaments and formation of a real world court, this meeting accomplished little more than had the first. The American representatives exerted their efforts largely toward obtaining guarantees of the rights of neutrals and of neutral commerce during war. But such differences of opinion arose that the best that could be done was to have the matter referred to a supplementary naval conference, which was scheduled to meet at London in 1908.

That naval gathering produced in 1909 the famous Declaration of London, which was practically a maritime code defining absolute and conditional contraband, blockades, and the right of search. It also laid down clear rules for the conduct of belligerents and neutrals during wartime. Great Britain, however,

The Angel of Peace: "Help Help!" Can the Big Stick work at the Second Hague Conference? (From the *New York World*.)

refused to ratify this declaration. Thus, at the outbreak of World War I, the Declaration could be regarded as international law only by a tremendous stretch of imagination.

The Second Hague Conference likewise took up a problem of special interest to the United States and its Latin-American neighbors—the Drago Doctrine. The delegates refused to accept that doctrine as it stood, but instead amended it to read that armed force should not be used to collect debts unless the debtor country refused to arbitrate.

Shortly after the 1907 meeting adjourned, Secretary of State Root began to negotiate arbitration treaties similar to those engineered by Hay. During the remainder of Roosevelt's second term he was able to complete twenty-five of them with all the leading powers except Germany. Since they guaranteed the rights of the Senate in each individual case, these treaties were duly ratified.

The Taft-Knox Treaties

Taft and his Secretary of State, Philander Knox, were ready to go further than to adopt documents rendering lip service to arbitration but actually excepting everything that might cause war. As Taft said in October, 1911:

> We now have treaties of arbitration . . . in which we agree to submit all questions that do not affect our national honor and do not affect our vital interest. Well, that seems to me to be an agreement to arbitrate everything that is highly unimportant. . . . If arbitration is worth anything it is an instrumentality for avoiding war. But, it is asked, would you arbitrate a question of national honor? I am not afraid of that question. Of course I would.

Following this theory, Knox negotiated two remarkable treaties with France and Great Britain, popularly known as the "Taft-Knox Treaties," which went the whole way in providing for the submission to arbitration of all justiciable disputes whatsoever. Again there was much criticism from the more nationalistic elements. Former President Roosevelt became an outspoken opponent of agreements which might involve "national honor." And the Senate proceeded to emasculate the documents by exempting from arbitration questions involving immigration, state debts, and the Monroe Doctrine. Thoroughly disgusted, Taft thereupon withdrew the treaties from further consideration.

However disappointing was the progress toward general arbitration, the peaceful settlement of specific controversies through arbitration continued. In 1909 the United States and Great Britain agreed to submit to the Hague Court the troublesome question of the rights of American fishermen in Newfoundland waters—a question that had been vexing the diplomats since 1782. The Court's decision in 1910 provided a workable compromise that safeguarded the rights of both the Americans and the Newfoundlanders.

The Algeciras Conference

In 1905 President Roosevelt became deeply involved in a tangled web of European diplomacy. By a dramatic visit to Tangier, Morocco, in that year, the German Kaiser made clear the objections of his government to the steps that France was taking to extend a protectorate over that North African country. Germany brusquely demanded that the Morocco question be submitted to an international conference. France, strongly supported by Great Britain, refused and there was grave danger of a European war over the issue. The Kaiser, who had been courting Roosevelt ever since he became President, urged the American chief executive to back Germany in her conference demand. Roosevelt at first refused to take the problem seriously and ridiculed the "pipe dreams" of the German emperor. But when he became convinced that the danger of war was actually great, he sought to mediate between the angry governments. Fortunately Roosevelt was on terms of closest intimacy with both the French ambassador at Washington, Jules Jusserand, and the German envoy, Baron Speck von Sternburg, and through them he finally suggested an acceptable formula under which the conference could be held.

Is Miss Morocco Worth It? (From the *Minneapolis Journal*.)

Early in 1906 the diplomatic representatives of the powers interested in the Morocco question met at Algeciras, Spain. Roosevelt sent an American delegation, headed by Henry White, the ambassador to Italy. American participation was justified on the grounds that the United States had treaty rights in Morocco and some slight trade to protect, as well as on the more defensible principle that America had an important interest in the preservation of world peace.

White at Algeciras and Roosevelt at Washington worked hard to bring about a settlement. Although the President strove to maintain his role as friendly mediator between the European rivals, he had from the beginning believed that France was in the right. Consequently, on crucial issues the American weight was thrown to the side of France and England. The resulting General Act of Algeciras saved the face of Germany by paying lip service to the independence of Morocco and to the principle of the open door for trade, but actually left France free to increase her influence over the disputed country. A typically Rooseveltian flourish marked the conclusion of the conference. The President sent word to the reluctant Kaiser that if he would accept the settlement, Roosevelt would pay public tribute to the German monarch's contribution to peace. The Kaiser agreed, and within the next few days the President received a delegation of German war veterans at the White House. In their presence he gave William credit for the Moroccan settlement.

Roosevelt's action during this crisis was subjected to some criticism as a departure from the traditional American policy of non-involvement in European affairs. The President, however, was intelligent enough to see how dangerous to all Western civilization a general European war would be.[4] Both he and his successor were working earnestly during these years to dispel the mutual fears and suspicions that were threatening world peace—and to them peace was more important than tradition.

---

[4] While conceding Roosevelt's good intentions in the Algeciras affair, some historians consider the effects of his action to have been unfortunate. They contend that he failed to understand the justice of Germany's complaints against French and English policy. Furthermore Germany, having been compelled to back down on this occasion, might be more stubborn in the future—thereby increasing rather than decreasing the likelihood of war.

7

The Good Old Days

To millions of Americans still living, the years between 1900 and 1917 are warmly remembered as "the good old days." Back before American involvement in World War I, our parents tell us, America was a happier place. Men were more honest, women were more ladylike, and children behaved better. Young lovers strolled down country lanes or rode "a bicycle built for two" instead of racing madly over the countryside in convertibles. Skies were bluer—and provided pathways for birds and kites, not for bomb-carrying planes and guided missiles.

Most of this is simple nostalgia—the longing of an older generation for the golden days of youth. If we seek to discover what these years were really like, the picture will contain both sunlight and shadows—like every other period of history. For many Americans these were years of peace and promise, but for others they were years of tension when old institutions fell under criticism and the need for change was strongly felt.

High Tide of Immigration

Except for brief setbacks, the period from 1900 to 1917 was one of prosperity and economic expansion. Never had America seemed so inviting to the humble people of other lands, discouraged by the limited opportunities of the Old World. During the first decade of the twentieth century almost 8.8 million immigrants entered the country—more than twice as many as during the preceding ten years. The peak year in the whole history of American immigration was

1907, when almost 1.3 million foreigners arrived, but this was only slightly more than the influx in five other years, 1905, 1906, 1910, 1913, and 1914, in each of which there were more than a million immigrants.

What were the sources of this vast stream? In simplified form, the following table tells the story:

Immigrants Arriving in the United States, 1901–1910[1]

Country of Last Permanent Residence	Millions of Immigrants
Europe	
Old Immigration Countries (England, Ireland Germany, Sweden, etc.)	1.90
New Immigration Countries (Italy, Austria-Hungary, Russia, etc.)	6.23
Total Europe	8.13
North and South America	
Canada	.18
West Indies and Latin America	.18
Total North and South America	.36
Asia	
China	.02
Japan	.13
Other Asiatic countries	.09
Total Asia	.24
All Other Countries	.06
Grand Total	8.79

[1] Based upon *Statistical Abstract of the United States, 1920* (Washington: Government Printing Office, 1921), pp. 100–101.

More than 92 per cent of the immigrants came from Europe. Of these, three quarters were from the countries of southern and eastern Europe. Among these, three groups bulked with formidable size. The first was that from southern Italy, an area impoverished by an archaic land system and burdensome taxes. More than half the South Italian immigrants were illiterate, unable to read or write even their native language. A second group was Slavic, consisting of Poles, Czechs, Croats, and other subject peoples who had been living under either Austrian or Russian rule. These people were also largely of poor peasant stock with a high percentage of illiterates. The third group was Jewish, principally refugees from the persecutions of Tsarist Russia. They too were desperately poor, badly educated, and bore the further stigma of differing in appearance and custom from earlier American stocks.

Italian Immigrants Arriving in the United States. (Brown Bros.)

Even more than the old immigration, the new arrivals huddled together in the slums of the large cities. In 1910, about 40 per cent of New York's population was foreign-born, and another 38 per cent was second-generation stock—native-born, but with one or both parents foreign-born. For Chicago the corresponding figures were 36 per cent foreign-born and 42 per cent second-generation stock. In each of the three other largest cities of 1910—Philadelphia, St. Louis, and Boston—more than 50 per cent of the population was of foreign birth or parentage.

Gloomy critics asserted that the Slavic, Latin, and Jewish peoples of eastern and southern Europe were of racial stock inferior to that of the northern Europeans who had been predominant in the older generation. Such assumptions have since come to be seen as unscientific and dangerous, and even at the time there were many who questioned them. A more valid indictment of the recent newcomers could be made: many of them manifested no intention of becoming naturalized and making America their permanent home. Indeed, nearly one half of the 13 million immigrants admitted between 1901 and 1914 returned to the old country after a few years.[2] To the American wage earner, it

[2] A number of those who went back home had accumulated enough money to live quite comfortably in the old country. Likewise, however, there were many who returned to Europe disillusioned by the fact that the United States was not the "promised land."

seemed unfair that he should have to compete with this type in the labor market.

American attitudes toward immigration were changing. Before the Civil War it had been generally believed that an open door to foreigners should be maintained to provide the population needed for national growth. Although there were, to be sure, strong nativist groups like the Know Nothings, they concentrated on making naturalization more difficult or on forbidding the foreign-born from holding office rather than on curbing immigration directly. After 1870, however, American wage earners became more and more concerned lest the uncontrolled flood of immigrant labor undermine wage scales and hamper unionization of the workers. All the large national labor unions—the National Labor Union, the Knights of Labor, and the American Federation of Labor—included some restriction of immigration as one of their objectives. Most employers of this period still favored unrestricted immigration, but a few were changing their minds along with other worried members of the middle class. There was a growing fear of the serious social problems arising out of the poverty and ignorance of these unassimilated masses. Optimists placed their faith in the American "melting pot"; pessimists feared that the elements would never adequately blend. A more particular fear was that alien ideas as well as alien persons were entering the country; such anarchist-connected crimes as the Haymarket affair and the assassination of President McKinley instilled a fear of alien radicalism.

Congress responded to this growing pressure with a policy of qualitative restriction, barring from the country the groups to which there was the greatest objection. Prostitutes, lunatics, idiots, convicts, paupers, contract laborers, and anarchists were denied admission in a series of laws passed between 1868 and 1903.

Although Oriental immigration had never been large in comparison with European, it provoked a disproportionate clamor of opposition among jealous native workers. Chinese laborers were excluded in 1882, but the Japanese did not arouse much alarm until after 1900. In 1880 there were scarcely 2,000 Japanese in the United States; by 1900 their number had increased to 24,000, and by 1910 to 72,000—largely living in the Pacific Coast states. An Asiatic Exclusion League, formed in 1905, gained the support of organized labor and many farmers with its demand for the barring of all Oriental immigration. Unable to ban the Japanese directly, Western legislatures and municipal bodies passed harassing legislation, limiting the right of Orientals to own land or segregating their children in the schools. The issue was a delicate and dangerous one, since it involved the relations of the United States and Japan, the other new great power of the twentieth century. The Gentlemen's Agreement, de-

The New Gate. The Senate and the House viewing with delight
the effect of the literacy test upon immigration.
(From the *Minneapolis Journal*.)

scribed in an earlier chapter, provided a temporary solution, but it failed to
satisfy the rabid exclusionists.

So far as the larger immigration problem was concerned, advocates of drastic
action pressed with increasing vigor for a literacy test, which would exclude
all foreigners who could not read or write some language. The restrictionists
frankly admitted that such a test would sharply reduce the new immigration
while affecting the old very little. Congress passed literacy test bills three times
—in 1897, 1911, and 1915—only to have them vetoed by Presidents Cleveland,
Taft, and Wilson, all of whom believed that the proposed test was unfair because it penalized would-be immigrants for not having had earlier the very
opportunities that they were seeking in America. But in the end the restrictionists won their battle; in 1917 Congress enacted the literacy test over another
Wilson veto.

Status of the Negro

In 1910 there were more than 9.8 million Negroes in the United States, composing almost 11 per cent of the entire population. For the most part they

were still living in the regions where their ancestors had once toiled as slaves. Almost 81 per cent of the Negroes were to be found in the eleven states that had made up the Southern Confederacy;[3] another 7 per cent lived in the four border states of Delaware, Maryland, Kentucky, and Missouri.

During Reconstruction days the Radical Republicans had attempted to guarantee to the freedmen the right to vote and full equality of citizenship, but this effort had failed. Federal troops had been withdrawn from Southern soil, the "carpetbag" state governments overthrown, and white supremacy restored. Weary of the issue, politicians of both parties had tacitly acquiesced in Southern policies that to all intents and purposes nullified the Fourteenth and Fifteenth Amendments to the Federal Constitution and reduced the Negro to a kind of second-class citizenship.

For a time the Ku Klux Klan and similar groups had used force and intimidation to keep the Negroes from the polls. These rough methods were later subordinated to more subtle means of controlling the Negro vote. White landlords and employers were in a position either to discourage their colored tenants and workers from voting at all or to influence how their ballots would be cast. Thus manipulated, the Negro vote became an instrument for maintaining the rule of the so-called Bourbons. Therefore the complete disenfranchisement of the Negro became one of the prime objectives of the poorer farmers during the 1890's, when the Populist ferment was convulsing the Democratic party of the South. Bourbon loss of power was followed by a spate of state laws providing literacy tests, poll tax requirements, and other devices by which Negroes could be denied the ballot.

Southern white opinion also placed great emphasis on preserving the separateness of the races. Interracial marriages were forbidden; segregation was maintained in schools, public transportation systems, theaters, hotels, restaurants, churches, labor unions, and other organizations. The Federal Supreme Court cooperated by carefully circumscribing the Fourteenth Amendment to the narrowest limits. The Court ruled that the kind of private discrimination practiced by innkeepers or theater owners could not be forbidden by Federal law (Civil Rights Cases, 1883), and that state laws requiring the separation of the races in schools and on public conveyances were not unconstitutional so long as the accommodations provided were "separate but equal" (Plessey v. Ferguson, 1896). Behind this convenient separate but equal formula, state segregation laws were destined to enjoy more than fifty years of immunity despite the fact that the equality between Negro and white schools or between Negro and white railroad cars was often fictional.

[3] Alabama, Arkansas, Florida, Georgia, Louisiana, Mississippi, North Carolina, South Carolina, Tennessee, Texas, and Virginia.

The two races did not enjoy the equal protection of the laws. By tacit consent of Southern authorities, Negroes were kept off the jury lists. The courts dealt severely with Negroes accused of killing or assaulting whites, whatever the provocation, but were singularly indulgent toward whites accused of similar crimes against Negroes. Even with the scales of justice thus tilted by white prejudice, ugly mobs frequently took the law into their own hands, wreaking swift and terrible vengeance against Negroes suspected of misdeeds. More than one hundred Negroes were lynched in 1900 and in 1901, and there were between fifty and one hundred such incidents annually thereafter until 1917.

Outside the South the Negro's position was somewhat more secure. He enjoyed the right to vote and general equality before the law. Yet private discrimination was almost universal. The Negro found many jobs closed to him; he was unable to buy real estate and to rent except in certain districts; he was often excluded from hotels and restaurants. From the Negro's point of view the situation in the early twentieth century was particularly discouraging. Most of the idealism that had sought to combat prejudice in the Civil War generation seemed to have spent itself; even in the North discrimination seemed to be increasing rather than declining.

By 1910 two basically different Negro strategies for dealing with the situation had evolved. One was that of Booker T. Washington, the best-known Negro leader of the time. He believed that the Negro's best hope lay in demonstrating his worth through hard work and thrift. Consequently, Washington had developed at Tuskegee Institute in Alabama an excellent industrial school where colored students were taught to be good farmers and mechanics. In a famous speech delivered at the Atlanta Exposition in 1895, the educator offered his formula for amicable relations between his own race and the whites: "In all things that are purely social we can be as separate as the five fingers, yet one as the hand in all things essential to mutual progress."

Washington's apparent willingness to put up with unequal political and social status and to concentrate on economic improvement became increasingly distasteful to a militant Negro minority. William E. B. DuBois, who had earned a doctorate in history at Harvard University, argued that vocational education was not enough. The "talented tenth" of the race ought to be able to obtain the classical and professional training essential to leadership, while the race as a whole should press for full equality of rights. In 1905, DuBois and a small group of Negro intellectuals met at Niagara Falls, Canada, to formulate their demands. This Niagara Movement was at first small and little-noticed, but eventually it won the interest of an influential group of white liberals. With this broader backing the National Association for the Advancement of Colored People was founded in 1910.

Economic Progress

The consolidation of industry reached a peak of intensity around the turn of the century when the United States Steel Corporation, the Amalgamated Copper Company, the American Telephone and Telegraph Company, the Northern Securities Company, and other giant holding companies were organized. After the 1903–4 recession, this passion for trust-building slackened off perceptibly. One reason was the change of political climate in Washington, with its threat of antitrust prosecutions; another was a cooling-off in investor enthusiasm for the new securities flooding the market. The most promising fields for consolidation had already been exploited; some of the new trust proposals were ill-disguised stock-jobbing schemes.

Investor confidence was shaken by several episodes indicating that some of the leading financial institutions of the country were not above sharp dealing. In 1905 a committee of the New York legislature, with the able Charles Evans Hughes serving as counsel, uncovered shocking conditions in the life insurance field, where the executives of such leading companies as the Equitable, the Mutual, and the New York Life had jeopardized the interests of their policy holders by diversion of funds into highly speculative investments—sometimes for the executives' personal benefit. During the panic of 1907, some of the large New York banks were forced to close their doors because stock-market plungers had wormed their way into positions where they could use depositors' savings to finance their ventures. Even the great J. P. Morgan suffered a loss of confidence when the Morgan-controlled New York, New Haven, and Hartford Railroad went into liquidation in 1913 after a giddy decade that the Interstate Commerce Commission characterized as "one of the most glaring instances of maladministration provided in the history of American railroading."

Yet neither these unsettling episodes nor the mild depressions of 1900, 1904, 1907–8, 1911, and 1913, which occurred at intervals so regular as to seem a built-in characteristic of American capitalism, could shake popular faith in the American future. The setbacks appeared to be minor as compared with the general upsurge of American industry and business. Between 1899 and 1914 the annual value of products manufactured in American factories more than doubled, rising from $11 billion to $24 billion. American railroads appeared to be enjoying a golden age. The laying of new track, largely halted during the depression of the 1890's, was resumed; between 1900 and 1915 total American railroad trackage increased from 193,000 to 260,000 miles.

The greatest figure in the railroad world was Edward H. Harriman. Beginning as an office boy in a Wall Street brokerage firm, Harriman had used his shrewd intelligence first to push forward in the financial field and then to move into railroad management. After achieving an outstanding success with the Illinois

Central Railroad during the 1880's, he formed an alliance with the powerful banking house of Kuhn, Loeb and Company to rehabilitate the historic but hitherto unprofitable Union Pacific Railroad. This success in turn helped Harriman gain control of the great Southern Pacific-Central Pacific system. After this, he extended his influence into the Pacific Northwest—first bucking Morgan and Hill and then collaborating with them in the Northern Securities Company scheme. Roosevelt's victory over this trust[4] was only a minor setback for the triumvirate, since interlocking stock-holdings and community of interest prevented any destructive competition among the various transcontinental lines. The restless Harriman now invaded the eastern railroads, gaining substantial holdings in the New York Central, the Central of Georgia, and the Baltimore and Ohio. By this time his influence in American transportation had become nation-wide, and he was seeking new worlds to conquer in regions as remote as Manchuria.

Harriman's death in 1909 was followed by the sale of many of his holdings, so that the control exercised by his heirs was much less Napoleonic in scope. The case of Harriman, although exceptional, typifies a general tendency toward railroad consolidation throughout the 1900–1917 period.

In retrospect, the railroad prosperity of these years appears to have been built upon shaky foundations. Railroad mileage reached its maximum in 1916; thereafter, there was to be very little new construction and the gradual abandonment of many miles of unprofitable trackage.

Challenges to the Railroads

Rival means of transportation that would cause serious problems for the railroads were in process of development during pre-World War I days. Most of the older waterways gave the railroads little to worry about, but the tremendous increase in shipping on the Great Lakes was a different matter. Between 1899 and 1916 the total annual shipments on the Lakes grew from 25 million to 125 million tons—most of it coal and iron. Interurban electric streetcar lines enjoyed a mushroom growth for a few years. Indeed, in 1914 travelers could go from New York City to Sheboygan, Wisconsin, in one direction, or to Portland, Maine, in another, entirely by electric roads.

The streetcar fad was short-lived, but a much more serious threat to the railroads was implicit in the birth and growth of the automobile industry. The motor car was a European invention. About 1800, experiments in steam-propelled road vehicles had been made both in England and on the Continent, but without enough success to displace the horse and carriage. The key discovery of the internal-combustion engine powered with gasoline came through the

[4] See Chapter 3.

experiments of French and German engineers between 1860 and 1890. By the eighties it had been demonstrated that such engines could successfully propel vehicles along the roads.

Ingenious Americans soon entered the field. The nineties were a period of endless experimentation with all types of vehicles—steam, gasoline, and electric. It required many years for the superior advantages of the gasoline-driven cars to be generally recognized. Indeed, as late as World War I the Stanley Steamer was still considered by many to be the last word in mechanical perfection. Pioneer builders of gasoline vehicles in America were Charles E. Duryea, who built the first such car in the United States, Henry Ford, Ransom E. Olds, Elwood Haynes, and the Apperson brothers. The new contraptions were extremely crude and undependable, but a moderate demand for them developed among people able to indulge themselves with rather expensive playthings. At first this trade was served by small shops where the horseless carriages were built to order. Production in quantity began in 1898 when the Mitchell-Lewis Motor Car Company of Racine, Wisconsin, manufactured five-hundred three-wheeled motor vehicles for the European market. Better known companies founded during the next few years were the Locomobile Company of America, the Olds Motor Works, and the Cadillac Company.

The Ford Motor Company, destined to revolutionize the industry, was organized in 1903. Like other manufacturers, Ford at first experimented with a variety of motor types—two-, four-, and six-cylinder. In 1908, however, he began turning out the famous four-cylindered Model T. These "tin Lizzies," as the Fords were affectionately called, were ugly to behold, clumsy to drive, and uncomfortable to ride in, yet they provided transportation at a price the average American could afford to pay. In 1908 the Model T was priced at $850; by 1917 it cost only $360. Ford was able to produce cars cheaply not only because he concentrated on a single model, but because he pioneered in many techniques of production. Standardized, interchangeable parts had been basic in American industrial success since Eli Whitney started manufacturing guns in 1798, but the assembly-line method of organizing production was largely a Ford innovation.

The General Motors Corporation, the other great giant of the industry, was organized in 1908 through the promotion of William C. Durant of the Buick Company. Durant was brilliant but reckless, expanding the company rapidly through the purchase of more and more separate concerns engaged in some phase of automotive manufacturing. He lost control of the company in 1910 when it had to be rescued by the bankers, regained command in 1915, and was finally ousted during the depression of 1921. The corporation thereafter was dominated by Morgan and DuPont interests. As late as 1917, Ford was producing nearly four times as many cars annually as General Motors.

Despite the strength of Ford and General Motors, the automobile industry was still strongly competitive, with scores of independent companies producing for a rapidly expanding market. The extraordinary rapidity with which the new means of transportation was taken up by the public is evidenced by the fact that in 1895 there had been only four registered automobiles in the entire United States; in 1900 there were 8,000; in 1915, almost 2,500,000.

By 1917 the automobile's threat to the railroad industry was already alarming, but the challenge of the airplane still lay in the future. The famous experiments of Wilbur and Orville Wright at Kitty Hawk, North Carolina, had demonstrated the possibility of flying in heavier-than-air machines as early as 1903, but for the next decade only the most venturesome took to the skies. Not until 1911 did an airplane fly across the United States, and then the exploit required nearly seven weeks and was interrupted by numerous forced landings.

Better Times for the Farmer

From 1900 to 1920 American farmers were relatively free from those worries that had beset them throughout the preceding generation. The decline in farm prices was halted, and a modest upward movement was in progress even before the dramatic rise resulting from World War I. The farmer's relative prosperity was reflected in the estimated value of farm lands and buildings, which rose from a total of $16.6 billion in 1900 to $34.8 billion in 1910. The average price of farm land increased at an unprecedented rate: from $19.81 per acre in 1900 to $39.60 in 1910. For once agricultural prices went up more than the prices of manufactured goods, thereby adding to the farmer's feeling of well-being.

Several factors had combined to bring these benefits to agriculture. Many theorists emphasized the inflationary influence of discoveries of gold in the Klondike and South Africa and the new cyanide process of extracting the metal from low-grade ores. By 1914 the world's monetary stock of gold was about twice that of 1896. More fundamental, however, was the fact that the demand for agricultural commodities was at this time expanding more rapidly than the supply. Despite reclamation projects and new methods of dry farming, the opening of new lands in the West was proceeding at a rate much slower than in earlier decades. The production of staple crops continued to increase, but at a modest rate. Meantime, the number of consumers was rapidly increasing. The non-rural population of the country grew by 40 per cent from 1900 to 1910, thereby providing some twelve million more bodies to be fed and clothed with the products of agriculture. Indeed, the demands of the domestic market were such that the exports of American farm products were falling off sharply until World War I reversed this trend.

In other ways, also, life on the farm was becoming easier. The hard days of the first pioneers were over. Thousands of farmers lived in comfortable homes near established villages with stores, churches, and schools. The railroad, rural free delivery, and the telephone had already taken much of the isolation and loneliness from rural life, and the cheap automobile offered even more promise for the future.

There were, nevertheless, still dark shadows in the picture. In New England, where agriculture had been in the doldrums for decades, the number of acres under cultivation declined by over 10 per cent between 1900 and 1910. In the South, the lot of the small farmer and the sharecropper was a hard one. In the West, the rapidly diminishing supply of good cheap land made it obvious that agriculture would have to rely increasingly on intensive, scientific methods.

The Unions Gain Ground

The American Federation of Labor enjoyed a dramatic growth around the turn of the century. Total membership in the organization, which stood at only 278,000 in 1898, increased to 1,676,000 by 1905. Thereafter, the rate of expansion was much slower, but by 1914 AFL membership had passed the 2 million mark. Some 500,000 more workers were members of unions not affiliated with the Federation.

The United Mine Workers, founded in 1890, increased steadily in power during these years. In 1897 the UMW won its first significant victory when it forced the operators of the so-called central bituminous field—western Pennsylvania, Ohio, Indiana, and Illinois—to recognize the union and enter into arrangements for periodic bargaining. The anthracite operators of eastern Pennsylvania were bitterly opposed to the union, but Roosevelt's intervention during the strike of 1902[5] helped the UMW, now under John Mitchell's able leadership, to win important concessions for the miners. Formal recognition of the union was not conceded at this time, but by 1916 the UMW was strong enough to obtain an important contract with the anthracite operators that granted recognition, the eight-hour day, and increased pay.

Elsewhere the UMW was less successful. In the West Virginia bituminous mines, the operators, enjoying strong support from state and local government, were able to limit the union to small gains. The UMW's most costly defeat was in its attempt to organize the bituminous coal fields of southern Colorado. Here underpaid workers—80 per cent of them unable to speak English—lived under almost feudal conditions in primitive company towns without decent homes or sanitary provisions. The strike that began in September, 1913, and dragged on for some fifteen months, was one of the most bitter conflicts in labor history. In the Ludlow massacre of April 20, 1914, six men, two women, and eleven children were killed when the National Guard attacked a strikers'

[5] See Chapter 3.

tent colony. After appealing in vain to John D. Rockefeller, Jr., who controlled one of the principal coal companies, to submit the dispute to arbitration, President Wilson had to send two-thousand Federal troops into Colorado to restore order. The strike was a complete failure, but it served to dramatize the seriousness of the labor problem for many Americans.

Unionism also made striking gains in the clothing industry. Most of the ready-made garments of the country were manufactured in New York City by immigrant women working under sweatshop conditions. Hitherto these underpaid seamstresses had been largely unorganized, but under the leadership of the International Ladies' Garment Workers' Union they waged two successful strikes in 1909 and 1910. As a result, immediate gains were achieved, machinery for the arbitration of future disputes was erected, and the ILGWU became a powerful arm of the labor movement.

Businessmen confronted by the increased strength of organized labor showed a variety of responses. Mark Hanna was prominent among those who believed the unions should be recognized as respectable American institutions. Hanna, John D. Rockefeller, Jr., Samuel Gompers, and John Mitchell were all associated with the National Civic Federation, founded in 1901 to promote industrial peace by the acceptance of collective bargaining and the trade agreement, as well as the promotion of mediation and conciliation.

This compromising spirit was, however, alien to most employers. The labor movement suffered a severe setback when the newly-established United States Steel Corporation defeated the workers in two long strikes and freed itself from any need of dealing with the unions. This conspicuous victory encouraged the management of other heavy industries to pursue antiunion policies. In 1915 a Federal investigating committee reported:

> Almost without exception the employees of the large corporations are unorganized as a result of the active and aggressive "non-union" policy of the corporate management. Furthermore, the labor policy of the large corporations almost inevitably determines the labor policy of the entire industry.

Equally determined opponents of unionism were to be found among small employers. The National Association of Manufacturers, founded in 1895, turned its attention to the labor problem eight years later and was aggressive in its opposition to unions. The American Anti-Boycott Association, organized in 1902, specialized in harassing the labor organizations through court actions like the Danbury Hatters' case.[6] Employers could usually count on the support of general middle-class opinion. Labor organizers were denounced as troublemakers, and vigilantes were frequently called upon to run them out of town or to break up meetings that they tried to address.

The unions had many unhappy experiences in the courts. The issuance of

[6] See Chapter 4.

injunctions in labor disputes rapidly increased. Federal judges were particularly generous in granting such orders, basing their action on the contention that picketing, boycotting, and other union activities were conspiracies in restraint of trade under the Sherman Act.

An employer's antiunion policy did not always indicate a desire to subject labor to ruthless exploitation. This was dramatically illustrated on January 5, 1914, when Henry Ford announced that he had established a minimum wage of $5.00 per eight-hour day for his 13,000 employees. Ford's motives in proposing to pay twice the going rate for labor were not understood at the time. But eventually a definite theory was worked out to justify payment of high wages. Industries like the automobile business depended on a large market. How better could such a market be created than through lifting the income of American workers above subsistence level? Ford's example was subsequently followed by numerous other employers, and the payment of good wages was combined with honest efforts to improve working conditions in the factories. This became known as "welfare capitalism." It was a trend still in its infancy in 1914, but it served to strengthen the conviction of many middle-class Americans that workers would be better off if they ignored the siren song of the labor-union organizer and placed their faith in the good intentions of management. The wide acceptance of this belief hampered the work of union organizers and strengthened the position of antiunion employers, whether or not they were practitioners of welfare capitalism.

Meantime, the Gompers philosophy of conservative unionism had come under bitter attack from more radical leaders who wanted to mobilize all the workers, skilled and unskilled, into one big union, dedicated to the overthrow of capitalism. In 1897 the Western Federation of Miners seceded from the AFL and attempted to organize a rival movement. At first these efforts were not very effective, but in 1905 the leaders of the Western Federation joined with other radical unionists and with such prominent socialists as Eugene V. Debs and Daniel DeLeon to found the Industrial Workers of the World (IWW). "The working class and the employing class have nothing in common," the preamble of the IWW constitution asserted. "Between these two classes a struggle must go on until all the toilers come together . . . and take hold of that which they produce by their labor through an economic organization of the working class, without affiliation with any political party."

The IWW was rent with factionalism from the beginning, and Debs, DeLeon, and several other leaders either dropped out or were expelled. At the height of its power around 1912, the union probably had no more than 60,000 members. Despite these handicaps, the "Wobblies" were much in the public eye in pre-World War I days, when they were under the leadership of the militant "Big Bill" Haywood, a one-eyed former cowboy and miner. Revolutionary syndicalism was flaunted in rousing songs like the one that boasted:

> We hate their rotten system more than any mortals do,
> Our aim is not to patch it up, but build it all anew,
> And what we'll have for government, when finally we're through,
> Is ONE BIG INDUSTRIAL UNION!

The IWW had its greatest success in the West, where poorly paid workers in the logging camps, mines, oil fields, canneries, and grain fields—many of them immigrants—were easy converts to a philosophy of sabotage and violence. In towns where the local police banned public meetings, IWW agitators would stage "free speech" demonstrations, sending in hundreds of Wobblies to make speeches and get themselves arrested, until the authorities had to reverse their policy in order to empty the overcrowded jails. In 1912 the IWW invaded the East and became involved in bitter strikes in Lawrence, Massachusetts, and Paterson, New Jersey.

Although here and there the IWW won striking victories, the movement was too radical in its objectives and methods to win over the rank and file of American workers. The AFL, still committed to Gompers' philosophy of "pure and simple unionism," continued to constitute the main stream of the American Labor movement.

Religion in a Changing America

The religion of an earlier, largely rural America had manifested itself through rival denominations and forms of worship as diverse as the noisy frontier revival and the quiet Quaker meetinghouse. But certain generalizations could, nevertheless, be made. The predominant faith was Protestant, Bible-centered, and dedicated to the salvation of individual souls.

Since the 1870's, this old-time religion had been under assault by new intellectual forces. Faith, founded upon a literal interpretation of the Bible, felt itself threatened by Darwin's theory of evolution and "the higher criticism"—a new type of critical study of the Scriptures that had originated in Europe. In the light of the new knowledge, Colonel "Bob" Ingersoll and other prominent agnostics of the late nineteenth century doubted whether belief in God was any longer possible.

Yet those who thought that the churches were dying underestimated religion's basic resilience and adaptability. Many churches responded to the challenge of the city by broadening their programs to include the sponsorship of scout troops and other youth groups, vocational classes, fresh-air camps for slum children, nurseries for the babies of working mothers, and temporary jobs for the unemployed. These so-called "institutional churches" built additions or

separate parish halls to house gymnasiums, social rooms, and classrooms necessary for their seven-day-a-week activities.

The bolder religious leaders went further than this. They asserted that it
was not enough to preach salvation to the individual and to temper the lot of
the poor with charitable good works, but that Christians should try to reform
society itself. Walter Rauschenbusch, now teaching at the Rochester Theological Seminary, was at the height of his influence during these years. In books like
Christianity and the Social Order (1907) and *Prayers of the Social Awakening*
(1916), he condemned contemporary American economic life as un-Christian
in its motivations and advocated the establishment of a truly Christian society
based upon socialist principles.

Only a minority of churchmen went as far as Rauschenbusch, but less
sweeping expressions of the "social gospel" were frequent. In 1908 a general
conference of the Methodist Episcopal Church asserted that the organization
of labor into unions was not only the right of the workers, but "of great
benefit to society at large." Several other denominations established associations or committees to study labor problems, while the Federal Council of
Churches, organized in 1908 through the cooperation of thirty-three Protestant
bodies, adopted a "social creed" that urged the abolition of child labor, the
reduction of the work day, the establishment of old-age insurance, and the
"most equitable division of the products of industry that can ultimately be
devised."

Meanwhile, many Protestant theologians had modified their teachings to
accommodate the theory of evolution and other findings of modern science.
In most of the leading Northern theological seminaries Biblical study was now
influenced by the spirit of higher criticism. Young ministers, thus trained, were
likely to be "modernists." Although Protestant congregations were often more
orthodox than were their pastors, the sermons of the young liberals usually escaped criticism—provided they were not too long. Protestantism in the urban
areas was being quietly guided toward a milder and more tolerant creed.

In the rural districts, neither the social gospel nor modernism was popular.
Asserting their faith in the "fundamentals" of old-time religion, rural preachers
condemned the evils of the new day and warned of the wrath to come. When
the local pastor's efforts seemed to falter, some traveling evangelist would visit
the town to call sinners to repentance in highly emotional revival meetings.
Most prominent among the revivalists after 1900 was the Reverend William
A. ("Billy") Sunday. An ex-baseball player, Sunday preached in a way so
sensational and energetic that he attracted tremendous crowds. He invaded
the cities and inspired thousands of converts to throng to the front of the
specially constructed tabernacles in which his meetings were held—to "hit
the sawdust trail," in the slang phrase of the evangelist himself. Those who

retained something of the old Puritan spirit were shocked at urban manners and morals. Dancing and card playing, long denounced as snares of the Devil, became increasingly popular, while newspapers, baseball games, moving pictures, and "joy riding" all intruded upon the quiet observance of the Sabbath.

The American religious situation was profoundly altered by immigration. The Roman Catholic Church enjoyed an extraordinary growth. In 1840 the Church claimed about 600,000 members; by 1860 it had over 3 million; by 1910 about 16 million. Although still outnumbered by Protestants almost two to one, the Catholics had a unity that contrasted sharply with the multitude of sectarian lines among the Protestants. Crowded churches, large hospitals, imposing parochial schools, and numerous colleges and seminaries gave impressive evidence of Catholic strength. Fearful that the "Papists" were about to "take over" the government, excitable Protestants gave support from time to time to anti-Catholic movements like the American Protective Association of the late 1880's. Such manifestations of nativism were usually shortlived, however, and the prevalent spirit was one of tolerance.

Although the problem of modernism troubled the Catholics much less than the Protestants, the Roman Church could not avoid the challenge of new economic conditions. The study of social problems had been encouraged by the encyclical *Rerum Novarum* (1891), in which Pope Leo XIII condemned the evils of the industrial system and advocated a Christian social order. The foremost American champion of Catholic social action was Father John A. Ryan of Catholic University. In *A Living Wage* (1906), Father Ryan deplored the fact that so many American workers were receiving wages inadequate to support their families in decent comfort and advocated the enactment of minimum wage laws.

Immigration also greatly increased the number of Jews. During the middle nineteenth century most Jewish immigrants had been from Germany. Many of these organized "reformed" congregations, where numerous departures from strict Hebrew law and tradition were permitted. Of the 1.5 million Jews who entered the country in the new immigration of 1880–1910, over 70 per cent were from Russia and Russian Poland. Victims of persecution in the old country, most of the newcomers were strongly attached to orthodox Judaism. A substantial number of Jews took a middle stand between the reformed and orthodox congregations and attended "conservative" synagogues.

Among the reform causes taken up by religious people before World War I, none aroused more enthusiasm than the crusade against alcoholic beverages. So tragic were the broken homes and broken lives caused by intemperance that millions of well-intentioned people determined to drive the liquor business out of American life. While all the churches advocated temperance, the extreme goal of legislative prohibition gained most of its support from evangelical Protestants. Organized in 1874, the Woman's Christian Temperance Union had been conspicuously successful in obtaining state laws requiring that instruction in the evils of intemperance be given in the public schools. Even more powerful was the American Anti-Saloon League, founded in 1893. By 1914 the League was employing hundreds of agents and speakers, and spending hundreds of thousands of dollars annually in a many-pronged offensive against "Demon Rum." The League kept a careful record of the votes of all legislators and was singularly successful in rewarding its friends and punishing its enemies.

The prohibition movement enjoyed particular success in the South, where many were eager to keep liquor from the Negroes, and in the Midwest, where the Methodists and Baptists had their greatest strength. By the end of 1914 the sale of intoxicants had been declared illegal in nine states, while five others had voted to put prohibition into effect within the next two years. In many states where the dry forces had not yet gained state-wide prohibition, there were local-option laws permitting towns or counties to outlaw the trade. By one device or another, the saloon had been driven from most of rural America. In the cities, however, the enemy was still firmly entrenched.

It was obviously difficult to make local prohibition effective when liquor could be ordered by mail from neighboring communities. The Anti-Saloon League therefore concentrated its activities on obtaining Federal legislation. In March, 1913, the Webb-Kenyon Act, passed over the veto of President Taft, made illegal the shipment of intoxicating liquors into any state, territory, or district where their consumption was in violation of local law. In December of the same year the prohibition forces induced Senator Morris Sheppard of Texas and Representative Richmond P. Hobson of Alabama to present to Congress a resolution providing for national prohibition by Constitutional amendment. The proposal did not emerge from committee during that session, but it did serve to mark out an objective toward which all the militant foes of liquor could thenceforth drive.

Science and Health

Although the churches were still potent influences in shaping American society, they no longer dominated intellectual life. Much of the prestige which in an earlier generation had been attached to the theologians now belonged to the scientists. Until the late nineteenth century American science had been backward by European standards. Although ingenious in discovering practical applications like the telegraph or anesthesia, the Americans had been lacking in the well-equipped laboratories and institutional support required for fundamental research. By 1900 the situation was changing rapidly, and a talented generation of American scientists—most of them European-trained—were beginning to make contributions of great significance.

Among these scholars Albert A. Michelson of the University of Chicago enjoyed an international reputation for his ingenuity in measuring the speed of light and other experiments—some of which had a direct influence on Einstein's famous theory of relativity. Of comparable stature was Thomas Hunt Morgan of Columbia University, upon whose experiments in breeding fruit flies the modern science of genetics was largely based.

Much of this scientific research was along lines that seemed remote from the daily life of the average citizen. He could hardly fail to be impressed, however, by the work of the chemists. When the man in the street learned that coal tar was being transformed into coloring matter for cake frosting, and wood pulp into sausage casings and rayon underwear, he was willing to concede that synthetic chemistry was working miracles.

It was when science joined hands with medicine that the most obvious contributions to human welfare were made possible. Dr. Walter Reed's heroic experiment demonstrating that yellow fever was carried by mosquitoes saved thousands of lives and helped make possible the building of the Panama Canal. Medical scientists, working first in Puerto Rico and then in the South, discovered that the hookworm was one of man's insidious enemies, an enemy that did not kill its victim but sapped his energies, leaving him tired, indolent, and despondent. A widespread campaign, aided by Rockefeller money, was waged to eradicate this disease and thus contribute to the rehabilitation of whole districts. Preventive medicine was meanwhile making smallpox, typhoid fever, and diphtheria very rare, instead of very common, diseases.

No speedy magic was discovered to dispel the terrors of tuberculosis. But the work of Edward L. Trudeau at Saranac Lake, New York, demonstrated that nature would cure many cases if patients were treated at sanitariums where rest, good food, and proper amounts of sunlight were provided. Early diagnosis of the ailment was found to be of prime importance. Through the activities of public health authorities and of the National Tuberculosis Association, founded in 1904, the annual death rate from tuberculosis of the lungs was reduced from 181.8 per hundred thousand population in 1900 to 128.2 in 1914.

The Study of Politics and Society

The years between 1900 and 1914 marked the development of many new viewpoints in the social sciences. Social thought, hitherto largely directed to a rationalization of existing institutions, became critical and provocative. This challenge to academic orthodoxy was related to the contemporary progressive movement both as cause and as effect.

Oliver Wendell Holmes and Louis D. Brandeis. (Brown Bros.)

Of particular importance was the new pragmatic approach to law. The idea that the law should be deduced from fixed, immutable principles was challenged by a new emphasis upon the necessity of a fluid legal system constantly adapting itself to the changing needs of society. Long before Oliver Wendell Holmes, Jr., was appointed to the Supreme Court, he had emphasized this point of view. "The life of the law has not been logic," Holmes wrote in 1881;

"it has been experience." Although himself skeptical of the possibility of social reform through legislation, Holmes believed that, in the absence of specific constitutional prohibitions, the majority will should prevail and legislative experiment should proceed without judicial interference. Louis D. Brandeis, both as a lawyer and as a Supreme Court justice, combined Holmes's pragmatic philosophy of the law with a conviction that judges should acquaint themselves with the changing conditions of society. The new sociological jurisprudence invaded the law schools, particularly under the patronage of Roscoe Pound, dean first of the University of Nebraska Law School and later of the Harvard Law School.

For many years the progressive jurists were a minority, and courts, both Federal and state, continued to disallow regulatory laws. This conservative citadel gained much of its strength from the almost religious veneration in which the Federal Constitution was held by the general public. An audacious challenge to the prevalent piety was offered by J. Alden Smith, professor of economics at the University of Washington. In his book, *The Spirit of American Government* (1907), Smith described the Constitution as the creation of a faction of property owners whose deliberate purpose had been to prevent genuinely democratic government.

Smith's controversial theory was given impressive documentation by *An Economic Interpretation of the Constitution* (1913), written by Charles A. Beard, brilliant young history professor at Columbia University. To the conservatives, Beard's cold-blooded analysis of just what material interests the framers of the Constitution had at stake in their handiwork was an outrage; to the progressives, it was an inspiration to override constitutional scruples and push ahead with their program.

Beard's book on the Constitution and his *Economic Origins of Jeffersonian Democracy* (1915) reflected the outlook of historians no longer satisfied with the narrow political and military themes of the past, but eager to broaden their investigations to cover man's economic and intellectual activities as well. Frederick Jackson Turner's influential essay, "The Influence of the Frontier in American History" (1893), had taken a long stride in this direction; James Harvey Robinson's *The New History* (1912) revealed the exciting prospects that lay ahead.

In the field of economics the forces of change were also at work. In 1899 Thorstein Veblen, then of the University of Chicago, published *The Theory of the Leisure Class*, an irreverent book which depicted the businessman as a sort of economic parasite, dominated by a passion to make money to be expended in ostentatious living. Other leading economists of the day, like Richard T. Ely of the University of Wisconsin and Wesley C. Mitchell of the University of California, were less extreme than Veblen in their criticism of the existing system, but they treated their subject not as a set of arid deductions from fixed principles, but as the investigation of fluid forces subject to human direction and control.

Some of the most challenging political writing of the period was done by non-academicians. Herbert Croly, whose book *The Promise of American Life* (1909), with its anti-Jefferson bias fortified the "New Nationalism" of Theodore Roosevelt, was a magazine editor. Walter Lippmann, just beginning a distinguished career in journalism, attracted wide attention with *A Preface to Politics* (1913), in which he argued that statesmen should not try to deduce their policies from abstract moral principles, but should discover what men really needed and then act on those findings. Croly and Lippmann were both prominent in the *New Republic*, a weekly journal founded in 1914 with the provocative purpose of starting "little insurrections" in the convictions of its readers.

Agencies of Education

The most influential American philosopher of the first half of the twentieth century was John Dewey, a gaunt Vermonter who taught first at the University of Chicago and then at Columbia. Dewey rejected belief in absolutes. Truth, he asserted, was the successfulness of ideas which men framed as instruments for the achievement of their purposes—or, in other words, as plans for solving problems. Dewey's greatest influence was in the field of education. Since reality was not fixed or complete, authoritarian methods of teaching fell into disrepute and stress was placed on the importance of learning through experience. Social efficiency, and not mere knowledge, it was asserted, should be the aim of education.

By 1914 Dewey's ideas of education had been put into practice in scores of private, so-called "progressive" schools. Their penetration into teachers' training institutions and through these into the public schools had begun, although the period of their greatest influence still lay in the future.

Although Dewey's philosophy of education always encountered a substantial amount of conservative opposition, most Americans shared his faith that the solution of almost every national problem lay in improved schooling made available to more and more young people.

The statistics of educational expansion were impressive. Between 1898 and 1914 enrollment in elementary schools grew from 16 million to more than 20 million, while that in high schools and colleges more than doubled. Much of this increase was in the South. As the number of students who went to high school and college increased, there were significant changes in the courses offered. Latin and Greek received less emphasis, and vocational training along many different lines was now available.

Colleges and universities became much less dependent on the churches for support than they had been a generation before. New patrons were found among men who had gained wealth in banking or industry. The Rockefellers generously endowed the University of Chicago; Edward Stephen Harkness bestowed princely gifts on Yale; George F. Baker gave $6 million to found the Harvard Graduate School of Business Administration.

Although such gifts were of inestimable value to the cause of higher education, they were not without their dangers. Some university presidents and deans, it was suspected, placed more importance on keeping the money rolling in from wealthy benefactors than in defending academic freedom. In 1915 a Federal commission asserted that there was developing "a degree of control over the teachings of professors in our colleges and universities which constitutes a serious menace." While this may have been an overstatement, it was true that in several well-known incidents college instructors had lost their jobs, not because they were poor teachers, but because they were suspected of being unorthodox in their economic or political views. Concern over this situation was one of the things that led in 1914 to the organization of the American Association of University Professors.

The desire to learn often continued past the years of formal schooling. Many American women found an opportunity to widen their intellectual horizons through lectures and study classes sponsored by women's clubs. Large and small communities alike received annual concentrated doses of both entertainment and education when traveling Chautauqua companies set up their big tents in town. There such notables as Theodore Roosevelt and William Jennings Bryan might be seen and heard.

The most powerful influence working upon the adult mind was the periodical press. In the fourteen largest cities alone daily newspapers had reached a circulation of over 40 million by 1914, while the circulation per issue of all periodicals—daily, weekly, monthly, and quarterly—went over the 200 million mark.

Americans might take pride in many of the achievements of their journalists. The newspapers were larger, contained more news, and were more readable than most English or European papers. They introduced to the public such talented humorists as "Mr. Dooley" (Finley Peter Dunne), George Ade, Don Marquis, and Franklin P. Adams. Courageous crusades were frequently made for good causes. The *New York World*, for example, forced the legislature to investigate the mismanagement of the life insurance companies, exposed police corruption in New York City, and aroused the public conscience on the issue of campaign contributions by the large corporations. Through the weekly and monthly magazines many evils in the political and business world were pointed out.

There was, unfortunately, another side to the picture. American liberals were disturbed by the heavy dependence of the periodical press upon advertising. In 1911 Will Irwin revealed in a series of magazine articles that newspapers often shaped their editorial policy and either played up or suppressed news stories to meet the wishes of their advertisers. The desire to expand their circulation led many publishers to give an unwarranted amount of space and emphasis to stories of scandal and crime. Paradoxically, the same Joseph Pulitzer who made the *New York World* an outstanding champion of reform contributed much to the development of "yellow journalism." He was speedily outdone, however, by William Randolph Hearst. By 1914 Hearst was the owner of papers in New York, Chicago, Boston, Atlanta, San Francisco, and Los Angeles. Wherever they appeared, they were easily identified by their cheap sensationalism, their pseudo-radicalism, and their irresponsible jingoism.

The newspapers expanded their circulation not only by featuring murders and divorces, but by introducing so-called features—comic strips, recipes and menus, puzzles, bedtime stories, and advice to the lovelorn. Many of these features were syndicated. This development, combined with the growth of newspaper chains and the increasing dependence of all papers on the great news services like the Associated Press and the United Press, imposed a monotonous similarity upon most American papers. The day of colorful editors like James Gordon Bennett, Horace Greeley, Henry J. Raymond, and Charles A. Dana, and of famous reporters like Richard Harding Davis, was passing; the newspapers were gradually becoming impersonal products of machinelike journalism.

Literature and Art

The same demand for easy, rather than profound, reading material carried over from the world of newspapers into the realm of books. Historical novels had a tremendous vogue around the turn of the century; by 1914 the trend was toward sentimental stories like those by Kate Douglas Wiggin and Gene Stratton Porter, entertaining studies of American character like those of Booth Tarkington, red-blooded tales of the North like those of Rex Beach, and earnest narratives conveying a rather obvious moral like those of Harold Bell Wright. Probably the best of the popular writers was Winston Churchill. His historical novels, *Richard Carvel* and *The Crisis*, had enjoyed great success in 1899 and 1901, and his popularity was still great in 1913 and 1914 when his fictional appeal for Social Christianity, *The Inside of the Cup*, led the list of best sellers.

The minority of readers who were repelled by the shallow romanticism of the popular novelists applauded the growth of realism. The pioneers of the new school, William Dean Howells and Henry James, were firmly established by 1900. The former's most important work was already done; the latter wrote three of his greatest novels, *The Wings of the Dove*, *The Ambassadors*, and *The Golden Bowl*, early in the twentieth century. Of the younger writers, Edith Wharton and Willa Cather were outstanding. Most of Mrs. Wharton's novels were penetrating studies of New York society, but her masterpiece, *Ethan Frome* (1911), was a powerful tragedy laid in a rural New England setting. Miss Cather attracted the attention of the discerning in 1913 with *O Pioneers*, a finely written story of Bohemian and Scandinavian immigrants in Nebraska. Two promising careers were cut short in 1900 and 1902 when Stephen Crane and Frank Norris died after writing a few works of real power. Jack London lived longer, but his early promise was not fulfilled; he could not resist the temptation to gain wealth by giving the public the romantic stuff it craved. The author who most stubbornly resisted the popular taste for an unvaried diet of sweetness and light was Theodore Dreiser. His first novel, *Sister Carrie* (1900), dealt with illicit love in so frank a fashion that the first editions were suppressed. Later novels, *The Financier* (1912) and *The Titan* (1914), told the story of a ruthless American businessman. *The Titan* was so brutally direct that Dreiser's publishers became frightened again and attempted to suppress the book.

American poetry suffered from the same shallowness as American fiction. The popular poets were such genial versifiers as James Whitcomb Riley. Largely unrecognized by the general public, however, a young and singularly gifted generation of poets was learning its craft just prior to World War I. The oldest of the new school was Edwin Arlington Robinson, who was helped by the patronage of President Theodore Roosevelt. Less fortunate was Robert Frost. His early work was rejected by American editors and publishers. Not until *A Boy's Will* (1913) and *North of Boston* (1914) were published and acclaimed in England did Frost find honor in his own country. Both Robinson and Frost wrote poems that were remarkable for their insight into life and for their beauty of diction, but their work showed no radical departure from earlier verse forms. These poets were New Englanders, but the Midwest also shared in the revival. Vachel Lindsay, Carl Sandburg, and Edgar Lee Masters, all from Illinois, were just beginning to attract attention with their bold and free techniques.

To serious readers this was an exciting period in which American literature seemed to be gaining a vitality and freedom that had been all too scarce since the 1840's and 1850's. Yet the "little renaissance," as the literary movement was sometimes called, never achieved broad recognition from the American public.

American achievement in the fine arts was still small. Painters were hardly recognized as useful members of society and indeed they often preferred to live abroad. This was the case with John Singer Sargent, who studied art in Paris and for most of his life practiced his craft in England. Some of the most notable of Sargent's work, nevertheless, was done in the United States. He accepted lucrative commissions to paint the lords of Wall Street and their wives and daughters. Boston was vastly proud of the murals with which Sargent decorated her Public Library and her Museum of Fine Arts. While the name of the fabulous Sargent had become a household word, many scarcely less talented and much more authentically American artists were appreciated only by a discerning few. There were, for example, Winslow Homer, who conveyed to canvas the rugged beauty of the Maine coast, Albert Ryder, who was to art what Poe was to literature—a creator of dark, mysterious fantasies—and Thomas Eakins, who not only painted many notable portraits but discovered significant new themes in Negro life and in the world of sport. And there were John Sloan and George Bellows, who recorded colorful scenes of New York City—its bars, prize fights, and slums.

Although the lot of the serious artist was not easy, there were fortunate individuals who won both fame and fortune through their dexterity with pencil and brush. The magazine illustrations of Charles Dana Gibson, James Montgomery Flagg, and Howard Chandler Christy enjoyed tremendous vogue. The "Gibson girl" was indeed an influence to be reckoned with. She was the lovely, smartly dressed young lady every American girl imagined herself to be.

Sculpture interested the general public more than did painting. After all, a people proud of its history could not fail to think it appropriate that the figures of its famous statesmen and generals should be carved in stone for the adornment of its parks and public buildings. Fortunately, a generation of talented American sculptors was available for the task. The most prominent of these was Augustus Saint-Gaudens, but memorable work was also done by George Gray Barnard, Daniel Chester French, and Lorado Taft.

American cities were losing some of their earlier ugliness with the development of fine parks and broad avenues and by the erection of impressive buildings. The prevalent taste in architecture was for the traditional styles, either neo-classical or Gothic. Monumental structures like the Pennsylvania Station in New York City found their inspiration in ancient Roman buildings. Many of the new "skyscrapers," like the 57-story Woolworth Building, completed in 1912, were given a Gothic cloak. Largely unrecognized by the general public were the two Chicago architects destined to exert a great future influence. Louis Sullivan and Frank Lloyd Wright rejected the prevalent traditionalism and advocated using steel, concrete, and other new building materials to achieve a more "functional" or "organic" style.

The state of American music was peculiar. Millions of little Americans were industriously practicing Schumann's "Happy Farmer" on the parlor piano;

thousands of Caruso records were being purchased for the new phonographs; the Metropolitan Opera Company of New York was the finest in the world; the symphony orchestras of Boston, Philadelphia, Chicago, and New York were among the world's greatest. These facts suggested that the United States was a nation of music lovers. But piano playing was mostly a polite accomplishment with which young ladies were expected to impress their young gentlemen callers; the phonograph was a novelty; the opera and symphonies brought real pleasure only to a select few. Before World War I Americans seldom became great musicians, more seldom still great composers.

But Americans did thoroughly enjoy music in a lighter vain. Operettas and musical comedies had long runs and millions of Americans hummed their tunes. The public taste for this type of music was well served. In all the world there was no more skilled creator of captivating melodies than Victor Herbert.

Americans also loved to dance, and the new type of dance music that was to conquer the world was just evolving in 1914. Irving Berlin's "Alexander's Ragtime Band" was published in 1911; W. C. Handy's "Memphis Blues" and "St. Louis Blues" appeared around 1912. The birthplace of jazz was New Orleans; thence it spread to the big excursion boats that played the Mississippi River ports. Jazz captured Chicago, and then moved east to New York. The first prominent jazz orchestra, the Dixieland Band, was organized in New Orleans around 1905, moved from city to city, and finally took both New York and London by storm in the years following 1916.

These then were the "good old days." Viewed in close perspective, they do not seem a golden age. The United States was prosperous, but its prosperity did not extend to all groups. The nation was religious, but its church members did not invariably practice righteousness. The country was full of schoolhouses, newspapers, and books, but popular taste in literature, art, and music was shallow. The days between 1900 and 1917 linger in affectionate memory, not because they were perfect, but because they were untroubled by the most acute of present anxieties.

8

The New Freedom

Many Americans had been so absorbed by the Taft-Roosevelt feud in 1912 that they paid scant attention to the Democratic candidate. With his spare, angular body, thin face, and pince-nez glasses, Woodrow Wilson seemed to fit perfectly the popular stereotype of a college professor. It was easy to assume that such a man would be a spineless intellectual, certain to be dominated by the practical politicians of his party. Such a judgment, however, showed little knowledge of Wilson's actual record as college professor, university president, and governor of New Jersey. The new President possessed an inflexible will and a fighting heart. He had fervent democratic convictions, which he wished to see carried into effective action.

As a close student of American government, Wilson had become convinced that strong leadership was necessary to make the system work. In his earlier years he had favored adoption of the British cabinet plan, but by the time he reached the White House he had come to believe that the President already had ample power if he would only use it boldly. From the beginning of his presidency Wilson acted as the leader of the Democratic party. He formulated an ambitious legislative program, consulted regularly with the Congressional leaders, exerted personal pressure to bring wavering party members into line, and frequently went over the heads of the legislators to appeal directly to the country on important issues.

In the early years of his administration, Wilson was strikingly successful. With wide support both in Congress and from the general public, he was able to move toward his objectives in both the domestic and foreign fields. In later years, however, he encountered an increasing amount of opposition. Much of this was inevitable in the American system, yet some of it resulted from the hostility aroused by certain traits in Wilson's character. Wilson had great virtues—high-mindedness, faith in the democratic process, respect for human rights, and lofty eloquence; but he also possessed certain closely related defects. In his certainty that he was always right he was likely to attribute unworthy motives to honest opposition. Even his associates complained that the President seemed cold and aloof, that he resented criticism and bore grudges, and that he was stubborn and reluctant to compromise.

The New Administration

Influenced by Colonel House, who was somewhat fearful that in an excess of idealism the new President might ignore orthodox Democrats and fill his cabinet with independents, Wilson selected an official family that rewarded the various sections of the country and the different factions within the party in a traditional way. Steeling himself to what the situation seemed to demand, he bestowed the Secretaryship of State upon William Jennings Bryan, the man whom in earlier years he had sharply criticized. Sophisticated Easterners were inclined to ridicule the new Secretary, to laugh at his dinners where parched diplomats found nothing stronger than grape juice in their glasses, and to be vastly amused when he took time off from his official duties to lecture in Chautauqua tents. But Wilson quickly learned to respect Bryan's sincerity, to value his sturdy common sense, and to accept gratefully his advice on political matters—a subject on which the Secretary certainly spoke from experience whatever the deficiencies in his diplomatic education. The ablest man in the new cabinet was probably William Gibbs McAdoo, originally a Georgian, who had moved to New York City where he achieved a striking business success by promoting the construction of railroad tunnels under the Hudson River from New York to New Jersey. As Secretary of the Treasury, McAdoo demonstrated both administrative skill and an ability to formulate policy.[1]

Besides his Cabinet, Wilson consulted regularly with certain unofficial ad-

[1] Bryan was succeeded as Secretary of State by Robert Lansing of New York in 1915 and by Bainbridge Colby of New York in 1920; McAdoo was succeeded as Secretary of the Treasury by Carter Glass of Virginia in 1919. Other Wilson cabinet officers were: Secretary of War, Lindley M. Garrison of New Jersey followed by Newton D. Baker of Ohio in 1916; Secretary of the Navy, Josephus Daniels of North Carolina; Attorney General, James C. McReynolds of Tennessee, followed by Thomas W. Gregory of Texas in 1914, and A. Mitchell Palmer of Pennsylvania in 1919; Postmaster General, Albert S. Burleson of Texas; Secretary of the Interior, Franklin K. Lane of California, succeeded by John B. Payne of Virginia in 1920; Secretary of Agriculture, David F. Houston of Missouri, followed by Edward T. Meredith of Iowa in 1920; Secretary of Commerce, William C. Redfield of New York, succeeded by Joshua W. Alexander of Missouri in 1919; Secretary of Labor, William B. Wilson of Pennsylvania.

Woodrow Wilson. (Brown Bros.)

visers, who often exerted more influence on administration policies than did the department heads. Colonel House was the President's closest friend of these years, often acting as Wilson's spokesman in conferring with both politicians and businessmen. When World War I began in 1914, House acted as an unofficial roving diplomat visiting the various belligerent capitals.

Another powerful adviser was Louis Brandeis. Wilson had wanted the Boston lawyer in his cabinet either as Attorney General or as Secretary of Commerce, but any such appointment was strongly opposed by practical politicians on the ground that Brandeis was a late convert to the Democratic party, whose supposed radicalism would antagonize businessmen. Nevertheless Brandeis' keen legal mind was extremely useful to the administration in framing its legislative program. In 1916 Wilson risked the ire of the conservatives by appointing Brandeis to the Supreme Court. The nomination was bitterly opposed, no fewer than six former presidents of the American Bar Association, including Taft and Root, contending that Brandeis was "not a fit person to be a member of the Supreme Court of the United States." President Wilson stuck by his nominee, however, and obtained Senate confirmation after a hard fight.

Although the new President was firmly committed to a program of progressive reform, he avoided any declaration of war against old-line Democrats whose votes he would need. By courting Speaker Champ Clark and Representative Oscar W. Underwood, he sought to heal the wounds left by the Baltimore convention. Moreover, he learned to acquiesce while Postmaster General Burleson dispensed patronage with a practised hand and Secretary of State Bryan found posts for "deserving Democrats."

If much of the old in political practice survived under Wilson, much that was strikingly new was introduced. His inaugural address was both eloquent and bold. After itemizing the need for tariff and currency reform, for further regulation of business, and for measures benefiting labor and agriculture, he concluded with these stirring words:

> This is not a day of triumph; it is a day of dedication. Here muster, not the forces of party, but the forces of humanity. Men's hearts wait upon us; men's lives hang in the balance; men's hopes call upon us to say what we will do. Who shall live up to the great trust? Who dares fail to try? I summon all honest men, all patriotic, all forward-looking men, to my side. God helping me, I will not fail them, if they will but counsel and sustain me!

Scarcely a month after taking office, Wilson gave a striking demonstration of the role which he believed the chief executive should play. When the new Congress convened in special session, Wilson appeared in person before the legislators and packed galleries to appeal for tariff revision. By delivering his message in this way instead of sending the written document to be droned out by a reading clerk to an indifferent and largely empty chamber, the President was boldly breaking a precedent established by Thomas Jefferson and followed religiously by succeeding executives for more than a century. This was only the first of such appearances. Again and again over the next eight years Wilson went before Congress to ask for legislation or to outline his policies.

Tariff Reform

At the special session thus dramatically opened, Congress provided the first dividend from the Democratic victory—the Underwood Tariff of 1913. During the last two years of the Taft administration a Democratic-Insurgent coalition had passed several bills that would have materially altered the Payne-Aldrich schedules had they not been vetoed by President Taft. After Wilson's election, the House Ways and Means Committee under Chairman Underwood began framing a general tariff measure, and the preliminary work was well advanced by the time the special session began. The new bill was designed to reduce the cost of living by placing wheat, corn, sugar, meat, eggs, and milk on the free list, along with raw wool, flax, and shoes. Duty-free also were iron ore, pig iron, steel rails, rough lumber, paper, and wood pulp. On hundreds of other items the protective principle was maintained, but rates were reduced in accordance with President Wilson's theory that "the object of tariff duties henceforth laid must be effective competition, the whetting of American wits by contest with the wits of the rest of the world." On luxuries, such as precious stones, furs, perfumes, and fashionable garments, the old rates were left unchanged. Taken as a whole, the Underwood Bill was by no means a radical abandonment of protection, but it did propose the first genuine downward tariff revision since the Civil War.

Under Underwood's skillful leadership the bill passed the House in May without significant change. In the Senate, however, a hard fight developed. There the Democratic margin of control was small, and many Senators were tempted to seek amendments that would continue the protection enjoyed by their own constituents. So active were the lobbyists that the President had to enter the struggle. By conference and letter he implored the Democrats to stand firm, and when still stronger action seemed necessary, he took the unusual step of appealing to the public. In a statement given out to the press Wilson said:

> It is of serious interest to the country that the people at large should have no lobby and be voiceless in these matters, while great lobbies of astute men seek to create an artificial opinion and to overcome the interests of the public for their private profit. . . . Only public opinion can check and destroy it. . . .

In the end, wavering Democrats were kept in line, and the measure was passed in substantially its original form—indeed, in some schedules the final rates were even lower than those first proposed. As signed by the President on October 3, 1913, the Underwood Tariff lowered the average ad valorem rates from the Payne-Aldrich level of over 40 per cent to about 25 per cent, besides providing an extensive free list. One of the most important features of the new law was its provision for a graduated income tax, made possible by the Sixteenth Amendment, ratified in February, 1913. The rates adopted were moderate—disappointingly so from the point of view of Senator LaFollette and the more advanced progressives. Incomes of less than $3,000 for unmarried persons and of less than $4,000 for married ones were exempted; incomes in excess of these figures were subject to a normal tax of 1 per cent and graduated surtaxes reaching a level of 6 per cent on incomes in excess of $500,000. The principal architect of the income tax clauses had been Representative Cordell Hull of Tennessee. Altogether, the Underwood Tariff was a tremendous victory for Wilson—one gained on an issue that Roosevelt had avoided and Taft had taken up to his own hurt.

Economists watched with interest to see how American economic life would be affected by the new tariff policy. They were prevented, however, by the course of events from obtaining adequate data. Within ten months after the Underwood schedules went into effect, international trade was completely disrupted by the outbreak of World War I. Conditions continued to be highly abnormal as late as 1921, when the Republicans returned to power and promptly rewrote the tariff laws according to their own doctrines.

The income tax was at first disappointing as a revenue producer, but it did disclose interesting data on the concentration of wealth in the country. Of 120 individuals paying taxes on income of $1 million or more in 1916, 100 lived in three states: 74 in New York, 16 in Illinois, and 10 in Pennsylvania.

The Federal Reserve System

Wilson was a hard taskmaster. While the tariff debates were still in progress, Congress was given a new assignment—the complicated and difficult task of banking and currency reform. Serious faults in the banking structure of the country had been obvious for years. National banks still operated under antiquated legislation passed during the Civil War; state banks went their own way under a hodgepodge of conflicting statutes; over the system as a whole there was no agency of control. Bank reserves were not mobilized in a manner to meet depositors' runs on fundamentally sound institutions. Small-town banks followed the practice of depositing their reserve funds principally in the banks of larger cities; these in turn deposited in the great New York City banks. Since the funds of these banks were available for speculative loans, the banking structure of the entire country was likely to be jeopardized by trouble in the securities market. The system furthermore tended to drain funds from rural districts where credit was badly needed and concentrate them in the cities where they encouraged speculation. Credit was inelastic. Banks unable to borrow themselves were often compelled to refuse to make new loans to their clients or to renew old ones, even when perfectly good security was offered. Currency was also inelastic. Instead of expanding and contracting as business increased or diminished, national bank notes were fixed in amount by the number of government bonds available for purchase by the banks.

Following the bankers' panic of 1907, a National Monetary Commission, under the chairmanship of Senator Aldrich, had studied the problem for four years. The Commission's analysis of the situation proved of the utmost value, but its suggested remedy, a strong central banking association controlled by private bankers, was politically impossible. Aldrich was regarded by the progressives as ultraconservative and a spokesman for special interests; the great bankers, moreover, were in particular disrepute because of revelations concerning the "money trust" that had been made in 1912 by a special Congressional committee headed by Representative Arsene Pujo of Louisiana.[2]

An inner circle of Democratic leaders began an intensive study of the banking problem soon after the 1912 election. Colonel House, a former banker himself, conducted private discussions with the leading financiers of the country, while the task of actually drafting a bill was taken up by Representative Carter Glass of Virginia, the chairman of the House Banking and Currency Committee, assisted by Paul Warburg, a big banker, and Professor H. Parker Willis of George Washington University. The bill that Glass first drafted was so conservative that it aroused the excited hostility of Secretary Bryan as a surrender to the "money trust." A countermeasure representing Bryan's demand for strict government control was drawn up by Senator Robert L. Owen of Oklahoma, chairman of the Senate Banking and Currency Committee, with the assistance of the progressive lawyer, Samuel Untermeyer of New York. President Wilson's first impulse was to side with the Glass version, but Brandeis, to whom he turned for advice, strongly supported Bryan and Owen in some of their main contentions. In the end, the President accepted two important principles for which the Westerners had been contending: that the central governing board of the new system should be made up exclusively of government appointees, and that the new currency should be an obligation of the United States government rather than of the banks.

Out of all these discussions a compromise measure was at length prepared. The Glass-Owen or Federal Reserve bill provided most of the facilities of a central banking system, but at the same time brought banking under a form of government control. Despite misgivings on the part of both Western radicals and Wall Streeters, the bill, with its essential principles intact, became law in December, 1913.

Instead of a single central bank, the new legislation provided for the establishment of twelve regional banks to serve so-called Federal reserve districts. The stock of these Federal reserve banks was to be entirely owned by the mem-

[2] The Pujo Committee had revealed that three New York banking institutions—J. P. Morgan and Company, the First National Bank, and the National City Bank—had combined resources of over $600 million and control of seven other New York banks as well as of the Equitable Life Assurance Company. Direction over the investment of funds totaling some $2 billion thus lay within the power of a few individuals. The banking triumvirate was represented by 341 directors in 112 corporations having aggregate resources exceeding $22 billion. This so-called money trust included banks, insurance companies, transportation systems, public utility corporations, and manufacturing establishments.

ber banks—that is, all the national banks of the country and such state banks and trust companies as cared to join.

The Federal reserve banks were primarily bankers' banks. They received deposits from the member banks and these had to be large enough to cover the reserves the law required to be maintained against the deposits in the member banks. The banking reserves of the country were thus concentrated in a few large reservoirs, where they could not be used for speculative purposes.

Member banks might borrow from the Federal reserve banks through the rediscounting of commercial paper. This meant that the member banks could use highgrade notes, drafts, and bills of exchange on which they had advanced money to their own customers as the basis for obtaining loans for themselves. Unexpectedly important were the open market operations, under which reserve banks could deal in government bonds and domestic bills of exchange. A special Open Market Committee, chosen by the reserve banks, could sell such bonds and bills to the member banks, thereby increasing their reserves and enabling them to extend more credit; when the Committee was purchasing such bills, the member banks sold, thus reducing their reserves and decreasing their ability to give credit. Thus credit could be eased or tightened, depending on the economic situation. Likewise, through these processes the banking funds of the country became mobile; they moved quickly to the places of greatest business activity.

One of the most important functions of the Federal reserve banks was to put into circulation a new kind of currency, the Federal reserve notes. As Bryan had insisted, the new notes were made a direct obligation of the United States government, redeemable in gold and acceptable for all public dues. In issuing them, the government received and held as security commercial paper, which the Federal reserve banks had taken in through their rediscounting activities. Although the law required a 40 per cent gold reserve to be maintained, the new currency possessed to a large degree the elasticity so lacking in the old national bank notes. When business flourished, commercial paper increased in volume. This paper, through the process of discounting, flowed into the Federal reserve banks and was available to serve as collateral for the issuance of Federal reserve notes. When business activity lagged, this process was reversed and the volume of notes in circulation was reduced.

The Federal reserve banks also received the deposits of the Federal government and acted as the government's financial agents. This permitted the eventual abandonment of the unsatisfactory system of keeping Federal funds in independent treasuries.[3]

Despite strong opposition from the bankers, an independent agency, the Federal Reserve Board, was created to supervise the new system. The board

---

[3] The independent treasury system was finally terminated by act of Congress in 1920.

consisted of the Secretary of the Treasury, the Comptroller of the Currency, and five other members appointed by the President with the consent of the Senate and serving ten years each. Each Federal reserve bank was to have a board of nine directors, six of whom were elected by the member banks and three appointed by the Federal Reserve Board. That board was given extensive powers to examine the books of the Federal reserve banks, to remove their officers, and even to order them to suspend operations. Probably the most important function of the board, however, was to approve the rediscount rates fixed by the Federal reserve banks. This power provided a governor on the economic machinery of the country: a low discount rate encouraged borrowing and business expansion; a high discount rate discouraged them.

The Federal Reserve Act on the whole proved to be very satisfactory. The shock of World War I to American economic life was cushioned by the new system, while the Federal government could scarcely have financed American participation in the hostilities had not the new organization of banking been substantially completed by 1917.

Even after the reform of 1913, however, there still remained many weaknesses in the American banking system. The country had many more state banks than national; for the former, membership in the Federal Reserve System was not compulsory, and a majority of them stayed outside. Non-member banks outnumbered member banks two to one, even though 80 per cent of the combined banking resources of the nation were held by the latter. Proposals that membership be made compulsory for all institutions were opposed on the ground that such action would violate states' rights. Even over the banking practices of the member banks themselves the Federal Reserve Board had too little control, as banking abuses of the 1920's revealed.

The Trust Problem

On January 20, 1914, President Wilson appeared once again before Congress, this time to ask for new antitrust legislation. The issue thus posed was a perplexing one. During the 1912 campaign Roosevelt and Wilson had taken positions that seemed sharply opposed. The former's New Nationalism assumed that big business was here to stay and should be strongly policed by the Federal government; the latter's New Freedom held out the hope that competition could be restored through a vigorous antitrust policy without expanding Federal power at the expense of the states. Now that they were faced with the responsibility of office, however, the Democrats found this antithesis entirely too simple. The legislative program they eventually evolved was neither as broadly Hamiltonian as Roosevelt's proposals nor as purely Jeffersonian as Wilson's. Instead the new laws found a kind of middle ground between the two.

The original antitrust bills, drafted by Henry D. Clayton of Alabama, chairman of the House Judiciary Committee, were Jeffersonian in philosophy. The vague and general language of the Sherman Act was now to be fortified with a series of explicit prohibitions against interlocking directorates and other monopolistic practices, while a new interstate trade commission was to have investigatory rather than regulatory powers. These proposals were criticized on a variety of grounds. Businessmen felt that the new prohibitions were so sweeping that they would hamper legitimate corporate growth; union leaders protested that the proposed law would not give labor its promised exemption from antitrust prosecution; many progressives repeated their conviction that what was needed was not more antitrust suits, but Federal regulation.

In his perplexity Wilson turned for guidance to Brandeis. The Boston lawyer's own thought upon the trust problem had been changing, and he had now come over to the strong Federal commission approach. In collaboration with George L. Rublee, a New York lawyer friend, Brandeis drafted a new bill to which the President swung his powerful support.

The resulting Federal Trade Commission Act of September, 1914, provided for a bipartisan commission of five members, to be appointed by the President with the approval of the Senate for a seven-year term. The commission was given extensive powers to compile information concerning the organization and conduct of corporations engaged in interstate commerce. Furthermore, it was to investigate the manner in which corporations that had been adjudged guilty of violating the antitrust laws carried out the decrees of the courts. Unfair methods of competition were declared to be unlawful, and the commission was empowered to issue orders requiring any person or corporation believed to be using unfair methods to "cease and desist" from doing so. The orders of the commission, however, were subject to review in the Federal courts.

As the trade commission approach gained ascendancy, enthusiasm for equipping the Sherman Act with a new and sharper set of teeth declined. The Clayton Act, finally signed in October, 1914, was considerably weaker than the original bill had been. Although there was an imposing list of prohibitions against price discriminations, exclusive selling or leasing contracts, and the purchase by one corporation of the stock of a competing corporation, the bans were not absolute but were limited to cases where the effect of such action might be "to substantially lessen competition or tend to create a monopoly in any line of commerce." Similarly limited were the prohibitions on interlocking directorates. No person might be a director or officer of more than one bank, if one of the banks had assets of more than $5 million; nor could a person be a director of more than one corporation if the corporations were competitors and if one of them had assets of more than $1 million. In contrast with the Sherman Act, the new law was designed to be primarily preventive rather than punitive.

The forbidden corporate practices were declared illegal per se without proof of actual monopoly or conspiracy.

Particularly important were the provisions of the Clayton Act dealing with the rights of workers. "The labor of a human being," the measure declared, "is not a commodity or article of commerce." Neither labor unions nor farmers' organizations were to be considered illegal combinations in restraint of trade under the antitrust laws, provided they were engaged in lawful pursuit of their objectives. The rights of laborers to strike, to picket peaceably, to pay out strike benefits, or to boycott an employer were recognized. No Federal judge was to grant an injunction in any case growing out of a labor controversy unless necessary to prevent irreparable injury to property; trial by jury was to be granted in contempt cases unless the contempt was committted in the presence of the court. Samuel Gompers hailed these provisions as a "Magna Carta" for labor, but time was to prove that the rights obtained had definite limitations. Judicial interpretation of the Clayton Act narrowed its scope so that many antilabor injunctions continued to be granted by the Federal courts.

The underlying philosophy of the Federal Trade Commission Act and the Clayton Act was obvious. The liberals of 1914 refused to accept the socialist assumption that the trend toward monopoly was inevitable and that the public could only safeguard its interests through nationalizing the trusts. They believed, on the contrary, that competition was the answer to the country's economic ills. If the corporations could be compelled to compete, and the competition kept open and fair, monopolies would be impossible, small business would survive, and consumers would be protected. The legislation of 1914 was no more successful than the Sherman Act in halting the trend toward business consolidation; but it did protect the public against the squeeze of economic power in many of its cruder forms.

In administering the new laws Wilson showed a desire not to alarm the business world unduly. From the beginning the Federal Trade Commission was criticized by LaFollette and the advanced progressives as lacking in reforming zeal and all too eager to cooperate with the corporations that it was supposed to be policing. Nevertheless, the Department of Justice brought a number of important antitrust suits, while the Federal Trade Commission between 1914 and 1921 issued 379 "cease and desist" orders against such practices as false advertising, false statements against competitors, bribery, adulteration of goods, and misbranding of fabrics. The Commission, together with the Justice Department, obtained the dissolution of the International Harvester Company in 1918 and the Corn Products Refining Company the following year.

American involvement in World War I had an inevitable influence. With popular attention focused on new issues, the antitrust crusade lost much of its fervor. Moreover, the economic mobilization of the nation tremendously accelerated the rate of corporate growth. Evidence of the changing course of events was the failure of the government's case against the Steel Trust in 1920. The Supreme Court refused to order the breakup of the United States Steel Corporation upon the ground that, despite its huge size, it was not following monopolistic practices.

Benefits for Agriculture and Labor

By creating the Federal Reserve Board and the Federal Trade Commission, the New Freedom had taken two cautious steps in the direction of the New Nationalism. In extending Federal authority to benefit agriculture and labor the Democrats departed still further from their traditional states' rights philosophy.

Increased appropriations were obtained from Congress for the support of the Department of Agriculture, which now took on enlarged activities including a market news service. New Federal legislation provided for the uniform grading of staple crops, for regulating trade in agricultural staples, and for developing a better system of warehousing. The Agricultural Extension Act of 1914 made it possible through Federal and state cooperation to place in each of the 2,850 rural counties of the nation two agents to do farm demonstration work. Road-building was stimulated by the Federal Highway Act of 1916, under which the Federal government expended money for rural roads on condition that its appropriations be matched by those of the states.

One of the most urgent of the farmer's demands was for facilities whereby he might obtain loans upon more favorable terms. The Federal Reserve Act provided a measure of improvement in the situation, but the need for long-term credit required new machinery. During the early years of his presidency, Wilson's laissez-faire scruples prevented him from accepting the idea that the Federal government should take on this additional function, but by 1916 he had changed his mind. The Federal Farm Loan Act, passed in that year with the President's strong support, established twelve Federal Land Banks in the various sections of the country. These were authorized to loan money to cooperative farm-loan associations made up of farmers who wanted to borrow. The farmer gave a mortgage on his real estate to the association; the association in turn deposited the mortgage with the Land Bank. The initial capital of the Land Banks was to be subscribed by private investors, with the government making up any deficiency. Additional funds were to be raised by the sale of tax-exempt bonds secured by the mortgages held by the Land Banks. Supervision of the system was lodged in a Federal Loan Board, composed of the Secretary of the Treasury and four other members appointed by the President.

Although private capital was at first suspicious of the project and supplied but $200,000 of the $9 million required to set up the system, a steadily larger proportion of private investment developed until by 1930 the government had disposed of almost all the stock it had originally subscribed. Local farm-loan associations numbered 4,659 in 1930, while the Federal Land Banks held about $1 billion worth of farm mortgages.

The Wilson administration was also responsive to the demands of labor. The American Federation of Labor leadership had given its support to Wilson in 1912, as it had to Bryan in 1908. Its most appreciated reward came in the amendment of the antitrust laws to protect labor union activity from judicial interference, but other legislation in which labor was deeply interested was also passed. Despite the objections of certain State Department officials who feared complications with other maritime nations, the President gave his support to the La-Follete Seamen's Act of 1915, designed to protect merchant sailors from many injustices. In 1913 a Board of Mediation and Conciliation was established to deal with railroad labor controversies, while in 1916, under circumstances that will be discussed in a later chapter, the Adamson Act, to institute an eight-hour day for railroad employees, was pushed through Congress under Wilson's urgings.

The movement for a Federal child labor law, a project that Senator Beveridge had vainly urged during the Roosevelt administration, became more and more insistent after the Democratic victory of 1912. On this issue as on others, Wilson changed his mind. At first he believed that such a law would be an unconstitutional invasion of states' rights, but he later overcame these scruples and brought the full weight of his influence to bear to obtain Congressional approval of the measure. The Keating-Owen Child Labor Act of 1916 excluded from interstate commerce goods produced in factories where child labor was employed. After this measure was held unconstitutional by the Supreme Court (Hammer v. Dagenhart, et al., 1918), a second child labor act was passed in 1919. But this statute, which levied a 10 per cent tax on the income of factories and mines employing children, was likewise held invalid (Bailey v. Drexel Furniture Company, 1922).[4]

By the time of the 1916 presidential election, the Democrats had enacted a large part of the Progressive party platform of 1912. To some extent this heavy borrowing from the program of the New Nationalism was political, a conscious bid to win the progressive vote in this important election. But undoubtedly Wilson's drift away from states' rights and laissez faire toward federalism and regulation was also based upon an enlarged understanding of how government must respond to the changing conditions of modern life.

---

[4] As a result a child labor amendment to the Constitution was proposed. It was approved by both Houses in 1924, but was never ratified by the states.

Wilson and the Dependencies

The spirit of the New Freedom was carried into the administration of the outlying possessions. In one of his early messages to Congress, Wilson asserted that the United States must move toward granting independence for the Philippines "as steadily as the way can be cleared." In naming the Philippine Commission the President gave a majority of places to Filipinos, while as governor general he appointed Francis Burton Harrison of New York, who administered the islands in a liberal spirit that aroused the nationalist ambitions of the natives. Wilson and Harrison were severely criticized by Taft, who had been the first governor of the islands, and by other prominent citizens on the ground that the Filipinos should not be encouraged to expect an early grant of independence for which they were not ready.

The administration, however, refused to deviate from its course. In 1916, after a hot debate, Congress passed the Jones or Philippine Organic Act, which stated in its preamble that "it is, as it has always been, the purpose of the people of the United States to withdraw their sovereignty over the Philippine Islands and to recognize their independence as soon as a stable government can be established therein. . . ."[5] To speed that day, the act reorganized the government of the archipelago in a manner designed to increase native participation and responsibility. The old Philippine Commission and Assembly were abolished and legislative power was now lodged in a senate and house of representatives, both to be elected by Filipino citizens who could meet certain property or literacy qualifications. Executive power was to be exercised by a governor general appointed by the President of the United States with the consent of the American Senate. Most of the other executive officers were to be appointed by the governor general with the consent of the Filipino senate.

The Jones Act took a long step toward delivering the islands to native rule, despite extensive veto powers retained by the governor general and the President. In execution the new organic law proved even more liberal than it appeared on paper because of the policies followed by Harrison. By executive order, he created a council of state consisting of the governor general, the presidents of both legislative houses, and the six Filipinos who headed the executive departments.

The New Diplomacy

President Wilson aspired to bring the same spirit of reform into the conduct of foreign affairs that he applied to domestic problems. Ever an idealist, he

---

[5] An attempt by some Democratic Senators to amend the measure to provide independence within four years was defeated.

hoped to base his foreign policy on enduring principles of justice and morality. He was deeply suspicious of professional diplomats, who all too often advocated what was expedient rather than what was right. Wilson was particularly disturbed by the close alliance of the State Department and Wall Street that had grown up during the Taft administration—the era of frankly avowed dollar diplomacy.

Scarcely two weeks after his inauguration, Wilson had occasion to make plain his intention of repudiating this alliance. At the invitation of the Taft administration, a group of American bankers had arranged to cooperate with bankers of five other powers in a consortium or international loan to the Chinese government. Representatives of J. P. Morgan and Company sought from Secretary Bryan a statement of the attitude of the new administration toward the project. In a statement to the press on March 19, 1913, Wilson expressed his emphatic disapproval. The conditions of the loan, he said, threatened the administrative independence of China; the United States government might, through connection with the project, become involved in a forcible intervention. Altogether, the plan was "obnoxious to the principles upon which the government of our people rests." The American bankers, unenthusiastic about the proposition anyway, acquiesced in the President's position and withdrew from the consortium.

Economic imperialism in Latin America was even more bluntly condemned. First in a statement to the press on March 11, 1913, and later in a speech at Mobile, Alabama, the following October, Wilson lashed out at "special groups and interests." At Mobile the President said of the relations of Latin-American governments with foreign capitalists:

> They have had harder bargains driven with them in the matter of loans than any other people in the world. Interest has been exacted of them that was not exacted of anybody else, because the risk was said to be greater; and then securities were taken that destroyed the risk—an admirable arrangement for those who were forcing the terms! I rejoice in nothing so much as in the prospect that they will now be emancipated from these conditions, and we ought to be the first to take part in assisting that emancipation.

Wilson went on to make an important statement of policy: "I want to take this occasion to say that the United States will never again seek one additional foot of territory by conquest."

Such were the standards upon which Wilsonian foreign policy was based. Like most idealists, however, the President often found the practical application of his principles a matter of most perplexing difficulty. More than once, indeed, the Wilson administration became involved in a line of conduct quite incompatible with Wilsonian ideals.

In Behalf of Peace

Despite the striking differences between Wilson and Bryan, they saw eye to eye on many issues. The Secretary of State was delighted by his chief's repudiation of imperialism, and the President in turn gave hearty support to a project Bryan had been sponsoring for many years. The essence of the latter's plan was that the United States should enter treaties with as many other nations as possible, pledging that all questions in dispute between the signatories that did not yield to diplomacy should be submitted to an international commission. The nations should agree not to resort to force until the commission had had an opportunity to investigate and report—a proceeding that must be completed within one year. The agreements embodying these principles became known as "cooling-off treaties," since one of the advantages of the plan was believed to be the unlikelihood of two nations going to war over an issue if they had waited a year for the report of an international commission. England, France, and most of the other great powers were included among the thirty nations entering into such treaties with the United States. But Germany rejected the proposition; other governments, she objected, would request similar treaties with her, and to sign them would deprive her of the advantages to be derived from her superior military preparedness.

Bryan negotiated with the Senate as successfully as with the foreign diplomats and obtained assent to all but one or two of the treaties. Only twenty-two of them went into effect, however, because of ratification difficulties with the signatory states.

Like all of Bryan's activities, the "cooling-off treaties" were subjected to considerable ridicule, and they were, to be sure, frail bulwarks against the whirlwinds of war that were to be unloosed in 1914. As late as 1938, however, nineteen of them were still in force, and they did have some influence on the thinking of diplomats struggling to build more effective peace machinery.

A more ambitious proposal was pushed by the administration in 1915 and 1916, after Bryan had been succeeded as Secretary of State by Robert Lansing. This was for a Pan-American pact in which the twenty-one republics should mutually guarantee the independence of the member states under republican forms of government, as well as their territorial integrity. The project, which was the brain child of Colonel House, failed largely because of Chile's opposition. Even more than the Bryan treaties, however, the pact idea influenced Wilson in his later work on the Covenant of the League of Nations.

Wilson and the Canal

The great Panama Canal, opened to traffic in 1914 although not fully completed until 1920, continued to involve the United States in a tangle of diplomatic problems. The Colombian government had never ceased to protest the steps by which Theodore Roosevelt "took" the Canal Zone. The Taft administration had attempted without success to placate this neighbor, and the problem was still acute when Wilson and Bryan took over. In 1914 a treaty between the United States and Colombia was arranged whereby the United States expressed "sincere regret" for the incident of 1903 and promised to pay Colombia $25 million. This typically Wilsonian effort to right an old wrong was blocked in the United States Senate, where friends of Roosevelt indignantly opposed any American acknowledgement of guilt. Not until 1921, when Roosevelt was dead and Wilson had left the White House, did a similar treaty, although without the expression of regret, obtain ratification—this time under the sponsorship of a Republican administration probably not unmindful of the recent discovery of oil in Colombia.

Another diplomatic problem inherited from the Taft regime was the tolls issue. In 1912, it will be recalled, Congress had enacted legislation fixing the tolls to be charged when the canal was opened. This act stipulated that American ships sailing from one American port to another should be permitted to use the waterway without charge. The British government protested that this exemption violated the Hay-Pauncefote Treaty of 1901, which stated that the canal should be "free and open to the vessels . . . of all nations . . . on terms of entire equality." President Taft and Secretary Knox, both excellent lawyers, had held that the words "all nations" meant all nations other than the United States and that the American government was within its rights in giving preference to its own citizens. Foreign experts in international law almost unanimously disputed this, however, and many thoughtful Americans also believed that the United States had promised not to make such a discrimination. Elihu Root, who had assisted Hay in the negotiations of 1901, was among those who believed that the Taft-Knox interpretation was wrong. The British took a serious view of the controversy and were particularly resentful of Taft's refusal to submit the case to arbitration.

Wilson had not given the subject any particular attention before he became President, but he gradually became convinced that the United States was in the wrong and that the exemption clause was a breach of good faith with Great Britain. Despite the embarrassing fact that the Democratic platform of 1912 had upheld the exemption principle, Wilson made a personal appearance before Congress on March 5, 1914, to request "a voluntary withdrawal from a position everywhere questioned and misunderstood." "I ask this of you," the President concluded, "in support of the foreign policy of the administration. I shall not know how to deal with other matters of even greater delicacy and nearer consequence if you do not grant it to me in ungrudging measure." This somewhat cryptic language probably referred both to Wilson's general aspiration to bring the United States to a position of moral leadership in world affairs and to his more specific need of enlisting Britain's support for his Mexican policy, presently to be discussed. The bill to repeal the exemption clause precipitated a stormy debate, but it was finally passed. Wilson's policy raised the reputation of the United States for fair dealing in foreign, and particularly British, eyes.

Protecting the Caribbean Life Line

Despite Wilson's repudiation of imperialism in theory, the exigencies of canal diplomacy drew him into more than a little imperialism in fact. Indeed, his administration became involved in more armed interventions in Latin America than had any of its predecessors—interventions in Mexico, Cuba, Haiti, and the Dominican Republic. It followed policies that tended, like those of the Roosevelt and Taft administrations, to reduce the Caribbean states to the ranks of protectorates of the United States. The American empire was enlarged, moreover, by the addition of the Danish West Indies—promptly renamed the Virgin Islands—purchased from Denmark in 1917 for $25 million.[6] The administration's Carribbean policy, seemingly so inconsistent with Wilsonian principles, is to be explained in part by the outbreak of World War I. Both the State and Navy Departments were seriously alarmed lest Germany or some other belligerent seize territory that might be used as a base of operations against the Panama Canal. American intervention was also motivated by the aspiration to help Latin American populations achieve genuinely democratic government—an idealistic goal that Wilson and Bryan shared.

The most serious of the Wilsonian interventions was in Haiti. In that island republic, conditions approaching anarchy had developed by 1914. Politics were characterized by civil war, assassination, and mass executions. The situation endangered the lives and property of foreigners and threatened to bring about intervention by some European power. In particular jeopardy were certain American financial interests, specifically those which the National City Bank of New York held in the National Bank of Haiti. In order to protect the gold reserve of the latter institution, American naval officers landed in December, 1914, and removed $500,000 from the bank's vaults. The money was then deposited in the National City Bank of New York pending a reform of Haitian finances. Meantime, pressure was exerted on the insular government to accept a financial arrangement with the United States like that of the neighboring Dominican Republic. This pressure brought no result, and affairs arose to a

[6] Sporadic negotiations for such a purchase had taken place since the Civil War, but had failed for a variety of reasons. Wilson insisted that a plebiscite be conducted before the deal was completed. The inhabitants of the islands voted overwhelmingly in favor of American annexation.

climax on July 27 and 28, 1915. On the first of these days President Vilbrun Guillaume Sam infuriated the opposition party by summarily executing some 160 political prisoners; this bloody massacre was followed the next day by a mob uprising, in which the Haitian executive was hunted down in the French legation and literally torn limb from limb. That afternoon United States marines landed and began an occupation destined to last for nineteen years.

Under the vigilant eye of Admiral W. B. Caperton of the American Navy, the Haitian legislature elected a president acceptable to the United States. The new government then entered into a treaty whereby provisions were made not only for American receivership of Haitian finances, but for the organization of a constabulary trained and officered by Americans and for restrictions upon Haitian sovereignty more extensive than those embodied in the famous Platt Amendment. In 1918 the island republic, cowed by the new constabulary, obediently voted 69,377 to 355 for the adoption of a new constitution in whose drafting Americans had taken a leading part.[7]

American intervention brought many material reforms to Haiti. A sanitary program to improve health conditions was instituted, roads were built, the currency was stabilized, and the government's financial house put in order. But there was a darker side to the picture. Haitian resistance to foreign control brought drastic action; more than two thousand Haitians were shot by American marines in pacifying the country. American public opinion was shocked by stories of atrocities and forced labor.

Events in the Dominican Republic followed a similar, if less spectacular, course. Financial receivership proved insufficient by itself to assure stable political conditions. Civil war resulted in intervention by American marines in 1916, which continued until 1924. Once again the establishment of an American protectorate meant material benefits for the population, but brought uneasy consciences to United States citizens who believed in "government by the consent of the governed." In 1917 the United States once again sent troops into Cuba, where they remained until 1922. They did not, however, establish military rule as in 1906, but merely served as a warning to the Cubans to maintain order.

Nicaragua had been one of the most active fields of Taft's dollar diplomacy, and at the end of his term a treaty embodying striking advantages for the United States was drafted. By this agreement the latter was to obtain a renewable ninety-nine-year lease of the Great and Little Corn Islands, the privilege

[7] Assistant Secretary of the Navy Franklin D. Roosevelt said in the course of a campaign speech in 1920: "You know, I have had something to do with the running of a couple of little republics. The facts are that I wrote Haiti's constitution myself, and if I do say it I think it is a very good constitution." Actually, however, Roosevelt had nothing to do with drawing up this constitution, and the Republicans used his statement against him throughout the remainder of the campaign.

for a like period of establishing a naval base on the Gulf of Fonseca, and a grant in perpetuity of the exclusive right to build an interoceanic canal across Nicaraguan territory. In return, the United States would pay Nicaragua $3 million, but the consent of the United States would be necessary to the disbursement of this payment, a stipulation obviously in the interest of American bankers who had loaned money to Nicaragua. The advantages of thus guaranteeing that no foreign government should gain control of a water route rivaling the Panama Canal were so obvious that Wilson and Bryan decided to support the treaty. They even agreed to a Nicaraguan suggestion that clauses similar to the Platt Amendment should be incorporated. But the Senate revolted at the proposal to establish so undisguised a protectorate and rejected the treaty. In 1916, however, a new agreement, the Bryan-Chamorro Treaty, incorporating the original terms without the protectorate clauses, was approved by the Senate and carried into effect.

The Acid Test: Mexico

Although the events just related seemed to belie the sincerity of Wilson's repudiation of imperialism, the President's forbearance in dealing with a difficult situation in neighboring Mexico marked a really sharp departure from the methods of dollar diplomacy.

From 1876 to 1911 Mexico was ruled by Porfirio Díaz, a military dictator who maintained strict order and encouraged foreign investment. To Americans resident in the country or doing business there, Mexico under Díaz seemed in happy contrast to strife-ridden nations elsewhere in Latin America. But the beneficence of the dictator's rule was more apparent to foreigners exploiting Mexico's resources and to the privileged few among the Mexicans themselves who had amassed fabulous wealth than it was to the masses. The peasants, sunk in ignorance, remained in a condition of peonage that was almost slavery, and much of the land was monopolized by wealthy aristocrats who owned enormous estates.

Revolution broke out in 1910, and the following year Díaz fled to Europe where he soon died. His successor as president was Francisco Madero, an idealist and reformer, but a gentle soul hardly equipped to control the explosive forces now unleashed. Civil war swept the country, and foreigners, fearing for their lives and property, remembered longingly happier days under Díaz.

In February, 1913, Madero was the victim of shocking treachery. One of his generals, Victoriano Huerta, rebelled against him, imprisoned him, and proclaimed himself president instead. A few days later Madero was killed, almost in cold blood. Foreign diplomats in Mexico shrugged off the murder as an unfortunate, but understandable, act of Latin violence and recommended that their home governments recognize the new regime—a step which seemed likely to restore the conditions of the Díaz dictatorship. Most of the European powers, including Great Britain, acted upon this advice. Had it not been the last month of Taft's term, the United States would undoubtedly have followed the same course, but instead the decision was left to the incoming administration.

Wilson believed that the circumstances of Huerta's seizure of power created grave doubts as to whether his government should be recognized. He regarded Huerta as a murderer and suspected that he was much more popular with foreign, expecially British, oil interests than he was with the Mexican people. Evidence of this was the continuing civil war in which Venustiano Carranza, governor of the northern state of Coahuila, was showing himself a formidable rival. Despite widespread American criticism that denial of recognition to a de facto government was against American diplomatic precedent dating back to the days of Thomas Jefferson, Wilson let the months slip by without according recognition to the Huerta regime. Through unofficial channels he sought to have Mexican factions accept a plan providing for an armistice in the civil war, an early, free election to be supported by all groups, a pledge by Huerta that he would not be a candidate in this election, and the agreement of all parties to abide by the election results. Characteristically, Wilson chose for his agent to present these proposals, not a professional diplomat, but ex-Governor John Lind of Minnesota, one of Bryan's friends.

When Huerta refused this invitation to remove himself from Mexican politics, Wilson fell back upon a policy known as "watchful waiting"—that is, refusing recognition to Huerta but resisting at the same time the loud demand set up by eager American jingoes for United States military intervention to set the Mexican house in order. By refusing recognition, Wilson expected that Huerta could not long remain in power. Defending this policy before Congress on August 27, 1913, Wilson declared:

> We can afford to exercise the self-restraint of a really great nation which realizes its own strength and scorns to misuse it. It was our duty to offer our active assistance. It is now our duty to show what true neutrality will do to enable the people of Mexico to set their affairs in order again, and wait for a further opportunity to offer our friendly counsels.

Waiting proved scarcely a popular policy in many quarters, especially since Mexican civil strife resulted in damage to American property and death to more than seventy American citizens between 1913 and 1915. Theodore Roosevelt demanded intervention, and Wilson's policy was vigorously denounced in Congress. Senator Albert Fall of New Mexico, who had close connections with American oil magnates, was one of the President's leading critics.

At the end of 1913 Wilson modified his own policy to the extent of adopting active measures to try to force Huerta out. The British government, grateful for Wilson's leadership in the fight against the Panama tolls exemption clause, agreed to withdraw its support from Huerta. Moreover, in February, 1914, the President lifted the arms embargo, imposed the preceding year, thus greatly assisting the rebels, Carranza and Francisco Villa. Despite these blows, Huerta still clung to power. Indeed, his defiance of the "Colossus of the North" was an important factor in winning for him a considerable backing among his own people.

In April, 1914, a crisis developed that seemed almost certain to bring about the full-scale American intervention Wilson had been trying to avoid. On the ninth of the month, American sailors engaged in loading supplies for an American naval vessel were arrested at Tampico by a Mexican force and paraded through the streets to jail for having allegedly violated martial law. The men were soon after released by the Mexican commanding officer, who apologized for the ignorance of his subordinate in making the arrests. But Admiral Henry T. Mayo, in command of the American fleet at the scene, was not satisfied with this verbal expression of regret. He demanded that within twenty-four hours the Mexican authorities should submit a formal apology and disavowal of the act, together with an assurance that the officer responsible for the incident would receive severe punishment. As a further measure, the admiral's ultimatum demanded that the Mexicans "publicly hoist the American flag in a prominent position on shore and salute it with twenty-one guns, which salute will be duly returned by this ship." The expression of regret that Mayo demanded was transmitted, but Huerta balked at giving orders for the salute.

Wilson could scarcely refuse to back up his admiral, despite the dubious wisdom of the latter's unauthorized ultimatum. On April 20 the President went before Congress to ask approval for using the armed forces of the United States "in such ways and to such an extent as may be necessary to obtain from General Huerta and his adherents the fullest recognition of the rights and dignity of the United States . . ." After a two-day debate, Wilson was voted this authority: 323 to 29 in the House and 72 to 13 in the Senate.

Full-scale war now seemed likely. "I'd make them salute the flag if we had to blow up the whole place," asserted Senator Chilton of West Virginia, while Senator Borah said: "This is the beginning of the march of the United States to the Panama Canal." Indeed, events beyond Wilson's power to control seemed to be forcing his hand. Even before the authorization to use force had passed Congress, the President was informed that a German merchant ship was about to deliver a cargo of arms to the Huerta faction at Vera Cruz. Fearful lest possession of more munitions should strengthen the Mexican usurper and provide him with equipment to use against the United States, Wilson gave the order for armed action. On April 21, Vera Cruz was bombarded and occupied by American marines after considerable bloodshed.

Since the seizure of Vera Cruz served only to strengthen the defiance of Huerta, further military operations seemed inevitable, when a way out of the situation was offered from an unexpected quarter. On April 25, the diplomatic representatives of Argentina, Brazil, and Chile, the so-called ABC powers, called at the State Department with an offer to mediate in the Mexican imbroglio. Wilson's immediate acceptance of the proposal brought him enthusiastic praise throughout Latin America. Not only did it show friendly deference by the United States to the opinion of the republics to the South, but it indicated that Wilson's repudiation of aggressive designs toward Latin America was sincere. It was, in the opinion of the Springfield (Mass.) *Republican,* "worth dozens of Pan-American conferences. . . . It establishes a precedent; possibly it opens an era."

The chief contribution of the mediation proposal to the actual Mexican situation was to ease over the crisis caused by the Tampico and Vera Cruz incidents. The plan for a general Mexican settlement, which was worked out at a conference of representatives of the ABC powers, the United States, and Mexico at Niagara Falls, Canada, failed because Carranza refused to accept it. The United States, however, evacuated Vera Cruz without receiving the demanded salute, and in July, 1914, Huerta gave up the struggle to hold the Mexican presidency and fled the country. To Wilson's admirers, Huerta's final downfall seemed complete vindication of both the President's policy and his tactics in pursuing it.

Unfortunately, however, the potentialities of the Mexican situation for creating embarrassing complications had not yet been exhausted. A new civil war resulted from the rival claims of Carranza and Villa to wear the mantle of the martyred Madero. Although Carranza held the stronger position, the Wilson administration for some months gave its encouragement to the Villa movement in the mistaken belief that Villa would be more cooperative than his stiff-necked opponent. By October, 1915, Carranza's growing power became so great that Wilson had to reserve his policy and grant *de facto* recognition to the Carranza government. Villa, resentful of this action and gambling desperately to discredit Carranza by provoking American intervention, began a policy of deliberate provocation. In January, 1916, Villa's followers murdered a party of sixteen American engineers at Santa Ysabel, Mexico. Once again a demand for military action swept the United States, and when, on March 9, 1916, Villa led one of his companies on a raid across the border and sacked Columbus, New Mexico, killing seventeen Americans, Wilson had to act. General John J. Pershing was ordered to lead a cavalry force into Mexico and capture Villa dead or alive.

For the next eleven months the situation was explosive. Villa proved to be extraordinarily elusive, and Pershing was several times reinforced, to the great distress of Carranza who had given grudging consent to the original expedition but now wished to get the Americans off Mexican soil as quickly as possible. With American public opinion turning strongly against Carranza for his unwillingness to cooperate in suppressing Villa and with Mexican opinion becoming more and more bitterly anti-American, the danger of full-scale war between the two countries was great.

The situation was particularly worrisome to Wilson because of World War I. If the United States were destined to become involved in war in Europe, it would not do to have a major portion of its small army tied up in Mexico. The sudden worsening of German-American relations in February, 1917, finally convinced the administration that Pershing's forces must be withdrawn. Once again Wilson's critics denounced his failure to adopt a policy of wholesale intervention and thorough housecleaning in Mexico, asserting that the Villa episode had been humiliating to the prestige of the United States. Ironically, at the same time that many Americans were criticizing Wilson for not being sufficiently vigorous, Mexicans of all parties were denouncing the American President for having interfered too much.

Although the continuance of the Mexican revolution after 1917 involved still more diplomatic problems, the entry of the United States into World War I shifted American attention away from the maelstrom of Mexican politics. Whether the whole course of American policy was to be praised or condemned depended largely on the partisan sympathies of the critic. Wilson's own evaluation of his policy was embodied in his message to Congress in December, 1916:

> We have been put to the acid test in the case of Mexico, and we have stood the test. Whether we have benefited Mexico by the course we have pursued remains to be seen. Her fortunes are in her own hands. But we have at least proved that we will not take advantage of her in her distress and undertake to impose upon her an order and government of our own choosing . . . that we seek no political suzerainty or selfish control.

Reform Interrupted

For leadership in domestic reform, Wilson had possessed unusual training. He was a student of government and of the new economic and social problems with which government had to deal. For leadership in foreign affairs, his training was much less adequate. His interests had been to a large degree focused on purely American issues. Yet through one of history's ironies it was destined that Wilson should be compelled to deal not only with vexatious issues in Latin America, but with problems of world politics more momentous than those any

President had faced before his time. In August, 1914, Germany invaded Belgium, and Europe became involved in the first general war since the defeat of Napoleon a century before. From that time on, America's relationship to the great conflict increasingly absorbed the attention of both the President and the nation.

The progressive movement did not end abruptly with the advent of war. Liberal legislation continued to be enacted and, as late as 1920, the Nineteenth Amendment granting women's suffrage was added to the Constitution. But the crusading spirit of the earlier years was gone. After the United States belatedly entered the war, the country passed into a period of indifference and then of hostility to the progressive point of view. For fifteen years after the conclusion of hostilities this conservative reaction continued. Not until the country was engulfed by the Great Depression did a new demand for reform and change make itself heard.

9
The Road to War

The outbreak of World War I came as an unexpected shock to the American people, for little attention had been paid to the European scene during the years preceding 1914. The first reaction was that the United States would not be affected by hostilities on the other side of the Atlantic, and President Wilson immediately issued the traditional proclamation of neutrality, along with an unusual request that Americans be impartial in thought as well as in action. As the contest in Europe progressed, however, the United States discovered that its diplomatic and economic reverberations were felt in all parts of the world. America's industrial output was in growing demand; its struggle to obtain recognition of its conception of neutral rights was not successful; and its efforts to mediate the war were thwarted. While the Allies were the greater culprits as far as infringements of international law were concerned, it was Germany that caused the loss of American lives. This fact, plus the natural affinity for England and France and the belief that the Allies were the European guardians of democracy, helped to promote a growing feeling in the United States that the Central Powers must be defeated. Only by American entrance into the war could this be accomplished; but the road to war was slow and tortuous.

European Rivalry

The war in Europe found the American people ill-prepared to understand its causes and implications. For many years they had been concerned primarily with matters of domestic importance—the tariff, banking reform, antitrust legislation, and social justice generally. Their chief diplomatic interests centered

on affairs of the hemisphere: the construction of the Panama Canal, intervention in the smaller republics, and, more immediately, the Mexican problem.

Consequently, the public did not realize that since about 1870 dangerous antagonisms had been growing among the European powers and that alliances had
been formed that needed but one little incident to arouse long-engendered
animosities to a state of war. One alliance included Germany, Austria, and Italy;
the other, France, Russia, and Great Britain. Balance of power, spheres of influence, nationalism, and commercial rivalry were motivating factors in laying
the groundwork for growing unrest between the two rival groups.

The assassination of Austrian Archduke Francis Ferdinand at Sarajevo, the
capital of Bosnia, on June 28, 1914, was the incident that touched off the spark.
It made the headlines in the United States for a day or two, but the average
American thought it was just another local flare-up following the Balkan Wars.
If trouble were brewing, it would soon blow over. Nor did the State Department
seem especially anxious about the whole affair; no reports from the diplomatic
corps overseas warned that anything serious would develop. Secretary Bryan was
busy with his "cooling-off" treaties, while President Wilson was concentrating
on the mediation of the Mexican trouble. True, he asserted he was "deeply
shocked at the atrocious murder," but there is no indication that he then realized its potentialities.

Wilson and His Diplomatic Advisers

President Wilson might be called a practical idealist. As a student of political
science and history, he became firmly convinced that the United States had a
mission to perform in the world. It must serve as a model of righteousness—a
theory that may have grown as well from his Calvinistic background. If the nation boldly promoted international law and adhered to all its precepts, then
other countries would be compelled to follow suit. Force should be used to protect American citizens in their international rights only as a last resort. Diplomacy, plus the firm assertion of right, would accomplish more than arms. A
streak of stubbornness, added to a reluctance to accept advice, prevented the
President from accomplishing as much as he might have under other circumstances.

The State Department was largely staffed by men with little experience in
the field of diplomacy. William Jennings Bryan became Secretary of State as a
reward for his prominence in the Democratic party and his support of Wilson
in the 1912 convention. Although not an unconditional pacifist, he thoroughly
disliked war. Bryan's major assistant and eventual successor, Robert Lansing,
was a specialist in international law. Although Lansing outwardly posed as a
vigorous champion of American rights, he inclined more and more toward

sympathy with the British as the war went on; consequently, when controversies arose with England, he plunged them into an endless tangle of legalisms so that there would be little embarrassment to the Allied cause.

The United States was not particularly well represented in the belligerent capitals. Walter Hines Page, ambassador to Great Britain, was so convinced England was entirely in the right that he did his best to bring the United States into the war on her side. James Gerard, ambassador to Germany, was a wealthy socialite who did little to improve German-American relations. Despite greater diplomatic experience, Myron Herrick, the envoy in France, displayed no real understanding of the European situation.

Neither the State Department nor the ambassadors abroad, however, played as prominent roles as might have been expected. More than most Presidents, Wilson himself decided questions of foreign policy and even drafted many important diplomatic documents. Moreover, the President distrusted conventional diplomacy and relied upon unofficial agents. His close friend, Colonel Edward M. House of Texas, was entrusted with important confidential missions to foreign capitals.

As animosities grew in Europe in the spring of 1914, Colonel House, believing that a war could be prevented by mediation, persuaded Wilson to send him across the Atlantic. The Texan wanted to establish a concert of powers, with the United States as a member, to ensure a long-range peace. He also planned to divert attention from rivalries in Europe toward colonial expansion. Despite his visits with leaders of the major powers during the hectic days of June and July, his correspondence with President Wilson made no mention of the archduke's assassination. After the dam of peace broke, House soon concluded that the Allied cause was just, thus seeing eye to eye with Page and Lansing.

The Decision for Neutrality

On July 26, 1914, came the first intimation for Americans that war in Europe might develop, when the newspapers announced Austria's severance of relations with Serbia because the latter had not acceded to the terms of a twenty-four-hour ultimatum. Worried by the grave illness of his wife (who died on August 6), President Wilson paid little attention to this report. Not until July 28, when Ambassador Herrick described the situation as "the gravest in history," did the Chief Executive realize the urgency of the problem, and even then he contacted Page before taking any positive step. During this interval, Austria declared war on Serbia, Germany on Russia, France, and Belgium, and Britain on Germany. The unforeseen hostilities had burst in full fury.

No American doubted the wisdom of neutrality at this point. European troubles should no more concern the nation in the twentieth century than they

Play in Your Own Back Yard. Uncle Sam, backed by the ABC powers, attempts to promote neutrality with a 60-mile zone along the Atlantic coast. (From the *San Francisco Chronicle*.)

had when Washington issued his famous proclamation in 1793. As a student of history, the President believed he must preserve the American tradition; furthermore, he had been elected on a platform that stressed domestic reform. His achievement of the New Freedom might depend in large part upon the absence of other absorbing interests.

Consequently, on August 4 he announced that since "a state of war unhappily exists," no one in the United States "shall take part, directly or indirectly, in the said wars, but shall maintain a strict and impartial neutrality." There would be no interference, however, "with the free expression of opinion and sympathy, or with the commercial manufacture or sale of arms or munitions of war." Belligerents were strictly warned against using American waters and territory for hostile purposes.

The President did not believe the conflict would seriously implicate the United States; he constantly spoke of World War I at the outset as one "which cannot touch us" or "with which we have nothing to do." Nonetheless, as the most important neutral nation, the United States might stem hostilities by using its "influence for peace." Therefore, on August 4 and 5 Wilson offered his good services as mediator, only to be promptly rejected.

At this time American opinion was strongly behind the President. Even Theodore Roosevelt praised Wilson's stand and wrote that Americans should be thankful that they lived in a nation at peace, safe from the horrors of war. Despite this support, Wilson knew that about one third of the nation's 92 million inhabitants were of foreign birth or had one or both parents foreign born. Consequently he tried to reinforce his policy by directly appealing to the people on August 19 to

> act and speak in the true spirit of neutrality, which is the spirit of impartiality and fairness and friendliness to all concerned. . . . Some will wish one nation, others another, to succeed in the momentous struggle. . . . Such divisions amongst us would be fatal to our peace of mind and might seriously stand in the way of the proper performance of our duty as the one great nation at peace. . . . The United States must be neutral in fact as well as in name during these days that are to try men's souls. We must be neutral in thought as well as in act. . . .

Again Theodore Roosevelt supported Wilson when he wrote: ". . . Nothing but urgent need would warrant breaking our neutrality and taking sides one way or another."

Pro-Ally Trends

While the majority of Americans probably did honestly strive to be "neutral in fact as well as in name," there was a definite swing in favor of the Allied cause as the war progressed. Although the Germans as a people were not disliked, their leaders' demands for their rightful place in the sun, their boasts of the supremacy of Germanic civilization or *Kultur*, the strutting of Prussian officers, and the Kaiser's "Me und Gott" proclamations did not appeal to the average American. What was worse in American eyes were the Germanic acts of violence. The disregard of Belgium's neutrality was the most heinous of all and was accentuated by Chancellor Bethmann-Hollweg's reference to the nearly century-old neutrality treaty as a mere "scrap of paper." Furthermore, the atrocity stories about the mistreatment of Belgian civilians were wholly believed by most Americans. While it has since been proved that most of these stories were propagandist fabrications, Americans were then so shocked by the invasion of Belgium that they were ready to believe anything.

On the other side of the picture, the kinship of Americans to Britons, based on common language and institutions, was strong. The friendship between the two countries in recent years was bearing full fruit, aided in no small way by the American feeling that Germany had tried to hurt the United States during the same period. The accounts of the progress of World War I came chiefly from

Allied sources and were undoubtedly colored to play up Allied victories and heroism. The taxicab-transported French army, the first "hundred thousand" Britons who went to Belgium's defense, the slogan "They Shall Not Pass," all stirred up American emotions in favor of the Allied cause. The Allies definitely had the advantage in these battle reports: they had cut the cable between Germany and the United States early in the war; except for brief wireless dispatches, German accounts had to come by mail that followed a circuitous route; most American correspondents were with the Allied armies, not only because of preference, but because of speedier means of filing their stories.

Monetary considerations also closely linked the two great English speaking countries. American bankers loaned money to Britain and naturally felt that an Allied victory would result in speedier repayment. While munition makers would have sold their wares to both groups of contestants, British control of the seas made delivery to Germany impossible. The American munitions trade was entirely with the Allies and brought a pro-Ally feeling; the same can be said for trade in general.

The British were not content to rely entirely on these factors. They maintained a well-organized propaganda distribution center, referred to as Wellington House, under the leadership of the prominent publisher, Lord Northcliffe. The articles from Wellington House kept pounding at German atrocities, the righteousness of the Allied cause, the danger of a possible German victory to the whole world, and the duty of the United States to enter on the Allied side to aid the triumph of democracy. Sir Gilbert Parker, a Canadian novelist whose writings were well known in the United States, was in charge of propagandist activities directed toward America. Through free news service, pamphlets written by prominent Britons, and lectures, Parker did effective work.

The German-American author, George Sylvester Viereck, aided by Frederick Schrader, tried to offset the work of Wellington House with the newspaper *The Fatherland, Fair Play for Germany and Austria-Hungary*. The effort was amateurish, feeble, and un-American in comparison, and before long Viereck confessed defeat. Other German attempts, liberally supported from the Embassy, had no greater success because they were inadequate and suffered in translation.

France was probably better liked by most Americans than was Britain. They still remembered their history sufficiently to know that France had aided the United States during the Revolution. Perhaps the time had now come to repay that debt. There was also a feeling of sympathy because France was regarded as the victim of vicious invasion. Russia, on the other hand, was little known or liked by the general public.

In the long run, however, the invasion of Belgium, the German submarine warfare with its destruction of American lives, and the belief that the Allied cause represented democracy and right were the prime factors in the gradual swing from neutrality in thought and action to a definite feeling that the Allies must win.

Economic Effects of the War

As the foremost maritime and industrial neutral, the United States was bound to be affected by World War I, despite Wilson's assertion that the conflict would not touch the American people. Even the President realized that American trade would boom. The warring countries must necessarily seek supplies of all kinds from the United States; there would be orders from European neutrals who previously bought from nations now at war; and markets all over the world would look to America to stock their larders.

To meet the expected shortage of shipping facilities, Congress passed in August, 1914, the Ship Registry Act that enabled foreign-built vessels owned by American corporations to be more easily and speedily admitted to United States registry. Two weeks later the Bureau of War Risk Insurance was set up with a fund of $5 million to provide insurance for American merchant vessels and their cargoes unable to obtain reasonable terms from private firms. Congress was not ready at this time, however, to authorize the government to buy, build, or lease ships.

The expected increase in American exports did not materialize at once. Instead there was a decided drop, particularly in wheat and cotton. The growers of these staples were especially hard hit because their large exports in 1913 had encouraged them to produce more during the first year of the war. For example, wheat production was about 20 per cent higher in 1914, but in August none was exported to Germany. In August, 1913, nearly 260,000 bales of cotton were sold abroad; a year later less than 10 per cent of that amount was exported, and the decrease was even greater in September. Consequently the price of cotton dropped from 12½ cents a pound to 7¼ cents. An effort was made to peg the price at 10 cents; another, to subsidize the growers; and still another, to persuade patriotic citizens to buy bales to preserve the price. The demand for copper and steel likewise fell off, and the textile industry was hurt when German dyes became unavailable. As Seth Low, president of the New York Chamber of Commerce, said in mid-August, 1914: "Europe has placed an embargo on the commerce of the world."

When the first shock of war wore off, however, and the nation realized that events in Europe would help, rather than hurt, American industry, confidence was gradually restored by the spring of 1915. The Allies, turning their industrial efforts primarily to the war effort and expending their backlog of prewar commodities, sought more and more supplies from the United States; an increasing number of ships became available to take care of that demand; and in turn

American production in many fields was speeded up. Germany could have used the American output as well, but British control of the seas precluded delivery. Indeed, only one German ship, the large submarine *Deutschland*, reached the United States and returned home after the British blockade was established.

The growth of American exports is shown in the following table:

	Exports to Europe	Imports from Europe	U.S. Favorable Balance
1913	$1,449,573,000	$864,666,000	$ 584,907,000
1914	1,399,296,000	788,517,000	610,779,000
1915	2,573,408,000	546,362,000	2,027,046,000
1916	3,813,278,000	633,317,000	3,179,961,000
1917	4,061,729,000	551,144,000	3,510,585,000
1918	3,858,698,000	318,121,000	3,540,577,000

The one-sided character of this trade is revealed by these figures:

	Exports to Allied Nations	Exports to Central Powers
1914	$ 824,861,000	$169,290,000
1915	1,990,748,000	11,879,000
1916	3,214,481,000	1,160,000

Thus exports to the Allies nearly quadrupled in that three-year period, whereas in 1916 the Central Powers obtained less than 1 per cent of their 1914 imports from the United States.

The biggest export increases were in so-called war necessities. In 1914, about $6 million worth of explosives were sold; in 1917, more than $800 million. Iron and steel exports rose from $25 million in 1914 to more than $1 billion in 1917. The value of wheat sent abroad mounted from $88 million to nearly $300 million in the same period. Prices rose almost in the same proportion as export values. For example, wheat sold for less than $1.00 at the opening of the war; shortly after the United States entered hostilities, the price rose to nearly $3.00 a bushel. American production of iron ore grew from 40 million tons in 1914 to approximately 75 million tons in 1917; copper production in the same period increased from 1.1 billion pounds to 1.8 billion; wheat, from 760 million bushels to nearly 900 million.

The Germans, embittered by the export situation, asserted that since only the Allies were being helped, the United States should lay an embargo, at least on munitions. But, as the Wilson administration pointed out, to impose such an embargo during wartime would obviously be an unneutral act. Under the principles of international law, the fact that the Allies could obtain goods from America and Germany could not was simply the fortunes of war. Even Ambassador Bernstorff had to admit that "under the general principles of international law, no exceptions can be taken to neutral states letting war materials go to Germany's enemies."

Stocks and Loans

Fear that the $2.7 billion European-owned American securities would be dumped in the United States market caused the New York Stock Exchange to close down on July 31, 1914. Not until December 12 was the danger deemed sufficiently eased to allow limited trading, although not until the following April did full regular stock dealings resume. Thereafter, prices of stocks, especially of the so-called "war babies," mounted rapidly, but whatever European-owned securities were sold did not materially affect the American exchange.

Nevertheless, the enormously expanded purchases of American commodities threatened serious trouble. The Allies could not afford to ship all their gold to the United States to pay for what they bought, nor did the United States want to dislocate both its own and the European monetary economy by such a transfer. Thus only about $1 billion in gold found its way to America. Approximately $1.5 billion worth of European-owned American securities were sold to offset the unfavorable balance, but not for long could the Allies count on these limited resources to pay for their purchases in the United States.

If the trade were to continue, the Allies would have to obtain loans in America. When the issue was first raised, however, Secretary of State Bryan wrote to J. P. Morgan in August, 1914: "There is no reason why loans should not be made to Governments of neutral nations, but, in the judgment of this Government, loans by American bankers to any foreign nation which is at war is inconsistent with the true spirit of neutrality." At first the bankers considered the Bryan statement as official, but, as the war progressed and the realization grew that loans would also help the American economy, they felt it was no longer binding. By the summer of 1915 Wilson had approved of the shift, and on September 6, Lansing, the new Secretary of State, and Secretary of the Treasury McAdoo announced that "the flotation of large bond issues by the belligerent countries" was the only solution to the overfavorable balance of trade. Another indication of the move away from the Bryan position had been shown nearly a year before. In October, 1914, President Wilson indirectly informed the bankers that he would not oppose commercial short-term loans to belligerent nations.

As these short-term loans were not sufficiently large to meet the needs, the bankers, taking advantage of the changed position of the administration, reopened negotiations with the Allies. Before the close of September, 1915, Morgan, representing a syndicate of more than sixty New York banks with some fifteen hundred affiliates throughout the nation, subscribed to a $500 million loan for the French and British governments through the Reading Commission. The only collateral was the promise of those governments to repay—a sure indication that American bankers were convinced of eventual Allied victory. In

1916 four more Allied loans were floated, totaling another $500 million and backed by American securities still owned by the Allies. In addition, $75 million in Russian bonds were sold in the American market. A warning from the Federal Reserve Board about the effect of these sales brought a suspension of loans for the rest of the year, but in January, 1917, England sold $250 million worth of gold notes, and two months later France disposed of $100 million in similar securities.

On the other hand, Germany was able to sell less than $20 million worth of short-term bonds in the early days of the war. Since she could not obtain war supplies in return, she used a substantial part of the proceeds for propaganda and sabotage.

Anglo-American Controversies

Although relations between the United States and Great Britain had been unusually friendly for nearly two decades, that friendship was sorely tried early in World War I. Insular Britain insisted from the outset that she must dominate the seas to maintain her lifeline and to prevent supplies from reaching the enemy. Therefore she refused to accept the Declaration of London of 1909, the maritime code drawn up under the auspices of the Second Hague Conference, which had defined what belligerent nations could and could not do on the high seas.

On the other hand, the United States, as the outstanding champion of neutral rights, had agreed to the Declaration, and, with the advent of World War I, insisted that the belligerents observe its terms. These two positions were bound to result in frequent controversies as Britain, the mistress of the seas, formulated her own conception of international maritime law and the United States, with the largest neutral carrying trade, sought to safeguard what were considered the legal rights of her citizens and their cargoes.

One of the first controversies involved the various types of cargoes, which had been defined at London as: (1) absolute contraband, consisting of actual war materials destined for the enemy and seizable, even from a neutral vessel, without compensation; (2) conditional contraband, made up of goods that might be used for purposes of both war and peace, but which were contraband only if proven they were destined for enemy governments and their military forces; and (3) non-contraband or free goods, including commodities like food, wood, and certain ores, which were essential to the life and industry of civilain groups.

When, in August, 1914, Britain first announced the list of commodities she would consider absolute and conditional contraband, the United States had no cause for complaint because the items were practically the same as those in the Declaration of London. As the war progressed, however, and England's posi-

"Scat!" President Wilson trying to protect American commerce from
British interference. (By Carter in *The Sun*, New York.)

tion became precarious, she gradually added to the absolute list a number of materials previously conditional—notably gasoline, cotton, and rubber. Her argument was that new methods of warfare had been adopted since the opening of
hostilities, with the result that the added commodities were now being used directly by the fighting forces. The most unusual addition was food, because of
the German order commandeering all wheat, flour, and corn within Germany.
Britain concluded that this was done to ensure edibles for the German army;
ipso facto, food must be contraband and could be seized by British blockaders.
The ultimate was reached in April, 1916, when Britain removed all distinctions
between absolute and conditional contraband; thereafter more than 225 commodities might be seized from neutral ships.

Had the Wilson administration taken a firm stand in the beginning, Britain
might not have acted as she did. But the administration's only response was to
warn England that her actions were "highly prejudicial to the neutral rights of

commerce" and might stir up "bitter feeling among the American people." And Ambassador Page, when he delivered this warning to Foreign Minister Sir Edward Grey, said that he did not agree with its tenor and that England could easily find some means of getting around it. Nor did Wilson's immediate advisers approve of this warning, and American exporters did not complain about subsequent British seizures of their cargoes because England gave them adequate compensation.

Why did the President, with his strong views on neutral rights, temporize until it was too late to force a change in the British position? Some observers feel that a strong anti-British move would have jeopardized Democratic chances in the elections of these years; others have reasoned that he did not wish to interfere with American exporters, who were making money in spite of the seizures; and, finally, it has been asserted that Wilson from the beginning wanted the Allies to win—therefore, as long as American lives were not lost through British infringements, he would only protest, not act.

Blockade and Search Problems

Another source of disagreement centered upon the definition of a blockade. According to the Declaration of London, it must be effective and impartial; it must be announced in a formal decree; it must be established in the vicinity of the area under blockade; and it must not prevent access to neutral ports nor allow capture of ships going to non-blockaded ones. Nor did the Declaration recognize the doctrine of continuous voyage or ultimate destination—that is, that goods could be seized on the way to neutral ports if it could be proved that they were ultimately destined for enemy territory.

Britain proceeded to disregard all of these provisions. Her blockade, never formally announced, was not established near the German coast because of the submarine menace, but at the mouth of the North Sea. Her blockading ships could thereby control all traffic to the neutral countries of Northern Europe and could apply the doctrine of continuous voyage. Wilsonian protests were disregarded as Grey asserted that British measures did "conform to the spirit and principles of the essence of the rules of war." He also pointed out that the United States had applied the doctrine of continuous voyage during the Civil War and had been upheld by the Supreme Court. Was the present British position any different?

Although American protest notes were sent as late as April, 1916, the British refused to back down on their decision to exclude Germany from as much commercial contact as possible with the rest of the world. In fact, the British position was stated simply: "We have necessity on our side; you have the law—what is left of it—on your side; we'll not seriously quarrel."

Closely related to the blockade issue was that of visit and search. Under the

Declaration of London, a belligerent ship that stopped a neutral merchantman suspected of carrying contraband must make the search on the scene. Were any contraband discovered, it could be removed but the merchantman must then be allowed to continue its voyage. Again Britain defied this procedure. German submarines made it dangerous for British destroyers to conduct searches at sea, so merchantmen were usually taken to British ports for examination. This might entail a delay of a week or more, but the ship owners were usually compensated for it. Another reason for a search in port was that contraband goods were sometimes cleverly concealed and could not be discovered without X-ray machines and the like. Still another argument for taking neutral ships into British ports was the claim that pilots were needed to steer such vessels through the mine fields in the North Sea. British patrol vessels persuaded merchantmen, regardless of their destination, to pick up the pilots in British ports. Once there, the ships were searched and goods alleged to be destined for the enemy were seized. American governmental protests were as unavailing as in other controversies.

Another source of complaint was the British practice of raising the American flag over their ships to escape from German submarines. The first American protest was made in February, 1915, against the "general use" of the flag, but Bryan weakened the objection by admitting that "occasional use" of the flag as a *ruse de guerre* might be condoned. Nor did Wilson's statement that the protest was sent only because he did not wish to strengthen the "hands of Germany in their extraordinary threat to destroy commerce" help the situation. Lord Grey's reply asserted that Britain was merely following common usage; indeed, Union ships had flown neutral flags during the Civil War. Consequently, Britain would not abandon the practice, and nothing further was said about the issue.

British and French censoring of American mail also gave rise to protests. During the first sixteen months of the war, the Allies only examined letters going through their territory, but by the end of 1915 the inspection was broadened to include mail on ships merely stopping at their ports. In this particular controversy, most complaints came not from the government but from businessmen who asserted that Britain obtained valuable trade information and also delayed completion of American bids on contracts. President Wilson, on the other hand, refused to allow Lansing to send a note that categorically demanded a change in Allied conduct and virtually admitted the belligerent right to seize merchandise in packages. Thus in the absence of forceful official demand on America's part, Britain and France continued their widespread censorship.

The British practice of arming merchantmen for defense against submarine attacks led to three delicate problems. First of all, did Germany have to give warning before trying to sink such armed vessels? Second, what was the status of American passengers on those ships? And, finally, could such vessels rightly enter an American port? Even Lansing, pro-Ally though he was, admitted that "merchant vessels . . . carrying an armament . . . should not possess the immunities attaching to private vessels of belligerent nationality. . . ." But all the administration efforts to make England see its position were equally unavailing.

A particularly irritating issue arose in July, 1916, when the British published a "blacklist" of more than four hundred firms located in neutral countries, including over eighty in the United States, which were suspected of doing business with the Central Powers. No loyal Briton could therefore have any dealings with those companies. The Wilson administration was highly incensed; the President believed this British step was "the last straw" and he privately alluded to those responsible for the blacklist as "poor boobs." Congress authorized retaliatory measures, but Wilson, primarily occupied with the campaign of 1916 and mediation plans, did not put them into operation.

For several weeks in 1916 England lost much ground in American public opinion through her mishandling of events in Ireland. Radical nationalists in Ireland sought to take advantage of Britain's involvement in war to gain full independence; some even urged a military alliance with Germany to attain this goal. Because the aspirations of the radicals obviously depended on a German victory, their supporters among Irish-Americans tried to prevent the United States from going to England's assistance. They cooperated with German-American groups in mass protest meetings against the Wilson policies, which they considered pro-British. Moreover, a small group of Irish-American leaders tried to gain the backing of Ambassador Bernstorff for the proposed Irish revolt. The German reply was encouraging, and for the first few months of 1916 leaders of the Clan-na-Gael, the radical nationalist society, were in close touch with the German Embassy. But a succession of disasters befell the Irish volunteers, who made their bid for independence during Easter week, 1916. The British quelled the uprising, 15 of the Irish leaders were executed, 145 were sentenced to long prison terms, and 1,841 were interned in England.

This severe British retribution shocked many Americans. In the eyes of all Irish-Americans, the executed Irish leaders were martyrs in a holy cause. Even the staunchly pro-Ally *New York Times* pronounced the executions to be "incredibly stupid." The Senate expressed hope that the British government would extend clemency to Irish political prisoners. David Lawrence, the journalist, wrote: "The truth is, Great Britain in a few days has alienated many of her sympathizers—almost as many as Germany alienated when the *Lusitania* was sunk." Consequently, pro-Ally elements for the time being found it difficult to use their most effective argument—the contrast between the brutality of the Hun and the humane principles of the British and French.

Although several of these controversies threatened to get out of hand, this did not happen for several reasons. In the first place, there was the growing pro-Ally feeling in the United States as the war progressed; if British hands were tied by American conceptions of international law, the Allies would be weakened. Secondly, British infringements may have resulted in loss of time and inconvenience for American shippers, but not in loss of American lives and seldom of money; consequently, even though President Wilson might send vigorous notes of protest, he did not enjoy the wholehearted backing of the American people. Moreover, when Ambassador Page delivered those notes, he usually softened them with a statement that they were written primarily for the American public and not to thwart British actions. Finally, when England committed some flagrant deed which might have aroused the United States to a truly antagonistic mood, Germany would commit an inhumane act that would overshadow the British violation; or Britain would skillfully time the extension of her blockade tactics to coincide with German-American crises.

German Sabotage

Despite the numerous British infringements of international law, it was Germany that stirred up most resentment in the United States because her actions led to loss of lives and property. Very early in the war, agents of the Central Powers tried to disrupt American industrial life, especially in the fields of munitions and transportation. This sabotage was asserted to be in retaliation for American shipments to the Allies, but American resentment against such German activities played no small part in the growth of pro-Ally feeling.

Directed chiefly from the German Embassy with money supplied by the German government, the sabotage leaders were German Ambassador Count Johann von Bernstorff, Austrian Ambassador Constantin Dumba, Captain Franz von Papen, the military attaché to the German Embassy, Captain Karl Boy-Ed, the naval attaché, and Dr. Heinrich Albert, commercial attaché.

Espionage and sabotage took many forms. German agents tried to send their government information about the quantity of munitions produced in the United States. They attempted to prevent the exportation of military supplies or to destroy the ships that carried them. Strikes were fomented in munitions plants. False passports were obtained so that German reservists might reach the Fatherland in the guise of American citizens. Manifests were forged to get supplies, like fuel, to German warships and submarines that were attacking Allied merchantmen. German agents also cooperated with Irish revolutionists in America and, through such organizations as the American Embargo Conference and the German-American National Alliance, tried to persuade Congress to pass measures inimical to the Allies.

American newspapers had a field day playing up sabotage cases, real or fanciful. Many incidents blamed upon German agents were normal accidents, but, as in the case of Belgian atrocities, the public was more than ready to accept every large fire or explosion as another instance of sabotage. Consequently, the hostility toward Germany grew; Lansing likened this attitude to the witch-hunting of colonial days.

Yet there is no doubt that saboteurs were responsible for some of these incidents, for the millions of dollars dispensed from the German and Austrian embassies could not all have been wasted. When the British seized the luggage of the lecturer-journalist James F. J. Archibald as he landed at Falmouth, they found numerous letters indicating the scope of the plans. One of these written by Ambassador Dumba read in part:

> It is my impression that we can disorganize and hold up for months, if not entirely prevent, the manufacture of munitions in Bethlehem and the Middle West, which . . . is of importance and amply outweighs the comparatively small expenditure of money involved. . . .

This message, plus Dumba's unfortunate reference to President Wilson's "self-willed temperament," forced the administration to demand the Austrian's recall in September, 1915. Another document revealed that von Papen had referred to "these idiotic Yankees." He escaped dismissal on this occasion, but by the end of the year both he and Boy-Ed proved so obnoxious that Wilson insisted they leave the country. And the briefcase of Dr. Albert, absent-mindedly left on a New York City elevated train, contained documents showing that Germany was trying to foment strikes and prevent munitions shipments.

The watchfulness of the American secret service nipped most of the German plots in the bud. At least two attempts to blow up the Welland Canal were frustrated, as were bomb plots against numerous Du Pont plants, the Bethlehem Steel Works at Newcastle, Pennsylvania, and many others. On the other hand, the explosion on the evening of July 30, 1916, at the Black Tom (New Jersey) docks of the Lehigh Valley Railroad brought death to two persons and property damage of $22 million. Subsequently Germany admitted her responsibility and paid for this destruction.

On the whole, whatever the extent of these and other disruptive actions, Germany did not achieve her objective—to cripple American industry. Indeed, she lost ground because opinion in the United States turned against her, and this prepared the way for America's entrance into the war.

The Early Submarine Threat

Much more important than sabotage in causing the ultimate break with Germany was her submarine warfare, which threatened the safety of American lives on the high seas. The German proposal to isolate the British Isles by means of the submarine was first made in the fall of 1914, but some German leaders objected because there were not enough U-boats to establish an effective blockade and vigorous American protests would undoubtedly follow.

By January, 1915, however, the British navy was establishing a tighter ring around Germany, which had to seek means to prevent being strangled. In consequence, several British merchantmen were torpedoed without warning before the month was over. Encouraged by this success, on February 4, Germany officially announced that after the 18th "the waters surrounding Great Britain and Ireland including the whole English Channel are hereby declared to be comprised within the seat of war. . . . All enemy merchant ships found in these waters . . . will be destroyed although it may not always be possible to save crews and passengers. . . ." Because British ships were wont to fly neutral flags, vessels of non-belligerents would expose themselves to danger if they entered this zone.

Anticipating American protest, Ambassador Bernstorff quickly informed the State Department that his country was forced to retaliate because Britain had flouted "all the principles of international law"—something in which neutrals had "generally acquiesced" to the detriment of Germany. While Germany would try "to avoid violence to neutral ships," she might make mistakes.

To Wilson and his advisers, this new German policy presented a delicate problem. As an ardent advocate of neutral rights, Wilson felt he must nip the plan in the bud. In his note to Germany of February 10, he stated that the sinking of any merchant ship, even one owned by a belligerent, without preliminary visit and search, was "unprecedented in naval warfare." Were Germany to sink an American ship, even by mistake, the United States must regard the act as an "indefensible violation of neutral rights" for which the perpetrator would be held to "strict accountability."

This message was received in Germany with mixed feelings. Chancellor Bethmann-Hollweg and Foreign Secretary Gottlieb von Jagow wanted to placate the United States; the naval leaders, on the other hand, thought that a month and a half would end the British blockade. The Kaiser made the ultimate decision: the submarine war on enemy merchant ships must continue, but U-boat captains must abstain "from violence to American merchant ships when they are recognizable as such." Thus the Kaiser tried to show that it was not his country's intention "to destroy neutral lives and neutral property . . . as the American Government appear to have erroneously understood."

President Wilson then tried to effect a compromise to end the submarine menace. He suggested that if all American food shipments to Germany were distributed only to civilians by American agents, England should promise not to interfere with the shipments. Germany, in turn, would give up her proposed submarine warfare, and both sides would stop indiscriminate mine laying and the use of neutral flags. The replies to these proposals were anything but satisfactory. Indeed, the situation became more discouraging because Britain tightened her own blockade.

American Lives Are Lost

Although many Allied ships were torpedoed after this compromise failed, the first incident to arouse the American public was the sinking of the British *Falaba,* carrying both passengers and munitions, on March 28, 1915, with the loss of one American life. Warning had been given by the submarine captain, who also allowed 23 minutes for the passengers to get off. The fatal torpedo was fired before they were all safe because other British vessels were in the vicinity.

Wilson, Bryan, and Lansing could not agree on the protest to be sent. While Lansing favored severing relations and Wilson believed that the German act was "an unquestionable violation of the just rules of international law," Bryan felt that Americans who traveled on belligerent ships did so at their own risk. He wanted the President to forbid such travel, but Wilson was convinced that citizens of a neutral country had a right to travel on the seas, even aboard a belligerent-owned merchant vessel.

During these discussions, the *Cushing,* a clearly marked American steamer, was attacked by a German plane, but without loss of life, and three days later, the *Gulflight,* owned by the Gulf Refining Company, was torpedoed. While the tanker reached port, two of the crew were drowned and the captain died of shock. In the latter case the submarine captain may have believed the *Gulflight* was part of a British convoy; the tanker was seeking information from several British trawlers about obtaining a pilot, and she broke out the American flag at the last moment.

Germany was prompt to admit her errors, saying she "very much regretted" the "unfortunate, unintentional" incidents, for which she promised "full recompense." In addition, at Chancellor Bethmann-Hollweg's insistence, the German Admiralty grudgingly agreed that future attacks on neutral ships would be avoided "under all circumstances"; thus no more American ships were torpedoed until February, 1917.

The "Lusitania" Tragedy

While this discussion was going on, the British liner *Lusitania* was sunk off the coast of Ireland on May 7, 1915, with the loss of 1,198 lives, of which 124 were American. Immediately a demand for war developed in the United States. The press made much of the deaths of helpless women and children, and Theodore Roosevelt called the sinking an act of piracy. While it has since been shown that the sinking was not planned, the fact that warnings against neutral citizens sailing on belligerent ships had been printed in American newspapers by the German Embassy, and telegrams similar in nature had been sent to those who had booked passage on the *Lusitania*, convinced many Americans that it was a deliberately plotted crime.

President Wilson refused to be influenced by the war element or by pressure from the British. Instead, on May 14 he made known his position in a Philadelphia speech:

> . . . The example of America must be the example not merely of peace because it will not fight, but of peace because peace is the healing and elevating influence of the world and strife is not. There is such a thing as a man being too proud to fight . . . a nation being so right that it does not need to convince others by force that it is right.

Many Americans condemned his stand, with Theodore Roosevelt as his most severe critic. The former President referred to Wilson as a "Byzantine logothete," surrounded by "flubdubs, mollycoddles, and flapdoodle pacifists." Yet these and other attacks failed to swerve the President.

On May 13, Secretary Bryan signed the first *Lusitania* note with the greatest reluctance. It stated that Germany had been previously warned against such incidents, and then emphasized that a submarine could not adhere to the following points of international law: the right of visit and search, the right to take prizes, the ability to take care of passengers and crews, and the need to give adequate warning before opening fire. Therefore Germany must prevent "the recurrence of anything so obviously subversive to the principles of warfare. . . ." Bryan offset to some degree the severity of the note by informing Austrian Ambassador Dumba that it was sent merely to satisfy American public opinion.

The German reply was noncommital, although it did say that since the *Lusitania* was armed and carried munitions, the sinking was perfectly justified. To this a second American note was drafted with Wilson's approval, denying that the ship was armed and carried explosives.[1] It also refused to concede that Germany might violate "the rights of humanity" in retaliation for England's

---

[1] There has been great controversy about whether the *Lusitania* was armed; the most thorough investigator asserts definitely that it was not. The fact is, however, that the submarine captain did no know whether it was armed, nor did he make any effort to find out. And he did break the rules of war by not giving warning. Therefore the question is merely academic. There is no doubt it carried several thousand cases of rifle cartridges, but they were not "Explosives" in the terminology of international law.

non-observance of property rights; the two violations had nothing in common. Nor was it a valid excuse that the submarine was a new weapon, not covered by the Declaration of London.

Secretary Bryan refused to approve this draft, asserting that the United States could not remain neutral if it failed to protest England's failure to abide by international law while severely proclaiming its rights against Germany. When the rest of the Cabinet would not support him, Bryan resigned on June 8, to be succeeded by Robert Lansing, definitely pro-Ally and certainly less of a pacifist. Then the second note, practically in its original form, was sent to Germany. Again the German reply failed to meet the American points, much to the disgust of many citizens like Theodore Roosevelt, who believed there should be less writing and more fighting.[2]

The "Arabic" Promise

Notes were still being exchanged in the fruitless endeavor to dispose of the *Lusitania* problem when news came of the sinking of the British *Arabic* on August 19, 1915, with the death of two Americans. So belligerent was American opinion that Bernstorff, on his own responsibility, promptly gave the State Department what has been called the *Arabic* pledge: "Liners will not be sunk by our submarines without warning and without safety of the lives of non-combatants, provided that the liners do not try to escape or offer resistance." Even though he was subsequently reprimanded for his promise, he had succeeded in temporarily quieting American opposition. When the State Department renewed its protests of the violations of the "rights of humanity," Bethmann-Hollweg expressed regret for the *Arabic* sinking, promised an indemnity, and assured the United States that such stringent orders had been given to submarine captains "that a recurrence of incidents similar to the *Arabic* case is considered out of the question."

President Wilson regarded the *Arabic* pledge as a victory for his note-writing diplomacy. The war spirit quickly died down; even the belligerent Roosevelt accepted the result as "most gratifying." And Wilson could write toward the close of September: "The country is undoubtedly back of me in the whole matter. . . ." Yet Germany still had not admitted that search must precede an attack upon a merchant vessel that did not try to resist, nor that such an attack must not cause death or injury to neutral citizens. Moreover, the American

---

[2] In February, 1916, Germany did agree to pay indemnity for the American losses in the *Lusitania* sinking, thereby admitting her liability. But since this offer was not accompanied by a statement that the act was illegal, Wilson refused to accept its adequacy. Therefore the affair was still unsettled when the United States entered the war.

contention had been pressed to the point where the United States could hardly avoid drastic steps were German sinkings resumed.

The House-Grey Memorandum

Meantime, while the controversies with both belligerent groups were mounting, President Wilson still hoped that he might act as peacemaker. Encouraged by certain statements by Sir Edward Grey in the early fall of 1915, the President sent Colonel House to learn whether Allied leaders were ready for a peace based upon justice. Were they interested, Wilson would send invitations to a peace meeting. If Germany accepted the olive branch and, at a subsequent conference, an adequate accord were reached, hostilities would end, prewar boundaries would be re-established, and future peace assured through disarmament and a league of nations.

House sailed forth on another "great adventure" in December, 1915, and for the next two and a half months he conferred with British, French, and German officials. His Berlin reception was none too cordial, and he became convinced that German authorities did not favor a peace satisfactory either to the Allies or to Wilson. In the French capital, he found the government noncommittal, largely because of the belief that Germany would never submit to Allied wishes. In London, however, there was the expected hearty reception. After lengthy conferences, Grey and House agreed on February 22, 1916, to the famous House-Grey Memorandum, the heart of which was:

> Colonel House told me [Grey] that President Wilson was ready, on hearing from France and England that the moment was opportune, to propose that a Conference should be summoned to put an end to the war. Should the Allies accept this proposal, and should Germany refuse it, the United States would probably enter the war against Germany.
>
> Colonel House expressed the opinion that, if such a Conference met, it would secure peace on terms not unfavorable to the Allies; and, if it failed to secure peace, the United States would leave the Conference as a belligerent on the side of the Allies, if Germany were unreasonable. . . .

When House returned home, Wilson approved the memorandum with one significant amendment: he inserted the word "probably" before Grey's statement that in case Germany were unreasonable at the proposed conference, the United States would leave the meeting as a belligerent. Wilson hoped the Allies would now support him in a peace move, but not even the assurance that the United States might enter the war was tangible enough to induce the British government to act upon the proposal. The abortive negotiations, which were kept secret, only made it more difficult for Wilson to obtain concessions from the Allies on such issues as the blockade and the arming of merchant ships.

The Gore-McLemore Resolutions

Although Congress did not know about the House-Grey negotiations, there were some members who believed Wilson's shift toward preparedness and his more vigorous position in regard to Germany meant he was planning to bring the nation into war. Moreover, there was a disposition among some Democratic leaders to challenge Wilson's leadership in anticipation of the 1916 election; were they to force the President to reveal his policy toward the war, they might make a strong case against him with the voters.

While numerous resolutions concerning control of munitions makers, embargoes on armaments exports, and the like were introduced in Congress by those seeking to embarrass the administration, the real fight was staged over the so-called Gore-McLemore Resolutions. On the premise that the loss of American lives on belligerent ships might bring the nation into war, the anti-Wilson faction asserted that American citizens must be barred from such travel. On January 5, 1916, Democratic Senator Thomas P. Gore of Oklahoma proposed to deny passports to citizens contemplating sailing on belligerent-owned ships; several days later he added the principle that American non-contraband must be fully protected on the high seas. While the Senate was discussing these propositions, Representative Jeff McLemore of Texas was working on a similar proposal to forbid Americans from traveling on armed belligerent ships.[3]

The President vigorously opposed these Gore-McLemore Resolutions because they would restrict the neutral rights for which he had been struggling since the beginning and because a defeat on this issue would undermine his leadership. On the other hand, many Congressmen, especially Democrats, were just as insistent that the resolutions be passed. By mid-February it appeared that the President might be defeated. Secretary Lansing was "very much alarmed," and Speaker Champ Clark felt that if the resolutions came to a vote, the House would support them by at least a two-to-one vote.

Wilson still had a strong string to his bow. In a series of conferences with the party leaders[4] and in a number of letters to key men in Congress, he made the defeat of the resolutions a matter of party loyalty. One letter specifically explained the President's position:

[3] The only American lives lost on American ships prior to severance of diplomatic relations with Germany were the three aboard the *Gulflight*. This fact would lend support to these resolutions.

[4] One of these conferences may have been the much-publicized "Sunrise Conference" with Democratic leaders that was supposed to have been held some time between February 22 and early April; the most likely time was February 25. There is so much disagreement about this meeting and what is said to have taken place at it that the authors have not seen fit to include it in the main text.

. . . I shall do everything in my power to keep the United States out of war. I think the country will feel no uneasiness about my course in that respect. . . . But in any event our duty is clear. No nation, no group of nations, has the right . . . to alter or disregard the principles which all nations have agreed upon in mitigation of the horrors and sufferings of war; and if the clear rights of American citizens should ever unhappily be abridged . . . we should . . . have in honor no choice as to what our own course should be. . . . We covet peace, and we shall preserve it at any cost but the loss of honor. . . .

As a result of these efforts by the President, the Senate turned down the Gore-McLemore proposals by a vote of 68 to 14, and the House by 276 to 142. The disappointed Gore then tried to force the administration's hand by resolving that when American lives were lost as a result of submarine action without warning, war should be declared. But the President, still in the driver's seat, had this proposal tabled.

The "Sussex" Pledge

Scarcely had this opposition at home been stilled when the unarmed French *Sussex*, plying across the English Channel, was torpedoed without warning on March 24, 1916. Although the ship limped into port, a number of lives were lost and many passengers, including several Americans, were injured. Secretary Lansing promptly drew up a memorandum advocating an immediate rupture of diplomatic relations with Germany.

Wilson refused to take this action, which he believed would mean war with Germany. He did yield sufficiently, however, to warn Bernstorff that a break would come unless Germany mended her ways. While the President was considering what to do about the *Sussex* case, Germany explained that the submarine captain claimed not to have attacked a merchant ship, but a war vessel. Wilson, however, declared that this was a "direct untruth," and since Germany was not contrite, the first *Sussex* note was sent on April 18. After calling the submarine attacks the "most terrible examples of . . . inhumanity," it warned that unless Germany immediately abandoned "its present methods of submarine warfare against passenger and freight-carrying vessels, the Government of the United States can have no other choice but to sever diplomatic relations with the German Government altogether." This would be done "with the greatest reluctance," yet such a step would be necessary "in behalf of humanity and the rights of neutral nations."

Many Americans in the East believed that the *Sussex* note meant war was in the immediate offing—and welcomed it. Westerners and the great majority in Congress, on the other hand, felt that the *Sussex* incident did not warrant hostilities. Germany thought that war might soon come, and Bernstorff was instructed to sabotage German ships in American ports. And Britain, in an effort to build up the German-American crisis, cautiously apologized for her actions against which the United States had protested.

Germany, anxious to keep the United States out of the war, replied on May 4 that she would do her "utmost to confine the operation of war for the rest of its duration to the fighting forces of the belligerents." No more merchantmen would be sunk without warning or without an effort to save lives unless such ships resisted or tried to escape. To put this pledge into operation, however, the United States must insist that Britain end her restrictions upon neutrals; otherwise Germany "would then be facing a new situation in which it must reserve [to] itself complete liberty of decision."

Wilson was not satisfied with Germany's apparent change of heart and refused to promise that he would take up again with Britain her infringements of neutral rights. Instead, he insisted that American rights be respected by Germany regardless of what other countries did. "Responsibility in such matters," he concluded, "is single, not joint; absolute, not relative."

Since Germany made no reply, Wilson assumed she would keep the Sussex pledge, temporarily at least, without the proviso. The war spirit among Easterners again faded as no more American lives or property were lost until the following year. Consequently, relations with the German Empire perceptibly improved during the remainder of 1916 as the submarine policy was removed from its dangerous phase. Most Americans realized, however, that the balance between peace and war was still precarious and that a change of policy might occur in Berlin at any time.

The Preparedness Struggle

From the beginning of hostilities in Europe, Americans had been sharply divided on the question of how the United States could best avoid involvement. Some thought that the best solution was not to supply the belligerents with war materials, thereby preventing antagonism from developing against the United States. Others considered that the proper preventive was to work for mediation between the antagonists to bring an early peace. Still another group felt that America should turn the other cheek to belligerent infractions of neutral rights and to various insults. And another element asserted that preparedness was the best method of avoiding war; an increase in American might would cause other powers to think twice before antagonizing the United States. These conflicting points of view had been vigorously debated during the early days of the European conflict.

There were numerous organizations devoting their energies against war when World War I broke out, notably the Carnegie Endowment for International Peace and the World Peace Foundation. The number of such peace societies grew after hostilities started. In addition to the American Society for the Judicial Settlement of Disputes, the American School Peace League, and the Church Peace Union, there were the Women's Peace Party, with Jane Addams and Carrie Chapman Catt as sponsors, the Anti-Militarist League, which obtained its backing chiefly from the colleges, and the National Peace Council. The majority of these peace societies were fully loyal and patriotic. Not all were against preparedness, but preparedness must be aimed at keeping the country out of war. That might be a difficult task, however, because an increased army and navy could promote a martial spirit among American citizens; or belligerents, seeing America arming, might attack before preparedness was complete. Therefore, said these proponents of peace, the best course would be to keep preparedness at a minimum and concentrate upon mediation between the warring groups.

In another category was the American Embargo Congress, which had the support of those with pro-German sympathies and which attempted to influence Congress to ban shipments of munitions and supplies to the belligerents. Germany would be helped were the United States to remain neutral, and the more Americans were influenced to join any peace organization, the less would be the chance that the United States might join the Allies.

Considerable publicity attended the mediation efforts of Henry Ford. Announcing his conviction that "the fighting nations are sick of war," Ford chartered the Scandinavian liner *Oscar II* and set out for Europe in December, 1915, to "get the boys out of the trenches before Christmas." The sixty delegates who went along were a heterogeneous group, and the accompanying newspapermen had a field day poking fun at the "Peace Ship." Although Ford's motives could not be questioned, the movement, needless to say, did not accomplish its purpose; indeed, it served only to hurt later peace projects, which were exposed to ridicule because of the derision which the Ford plan had previously engendered.

The outstanding pacifist was William Jennings Bryan, particularly after he left the State Department in June, 1915. In speeches and in the columns of his paper, *The Commoner*, he preached the folly of both war and preparedness. He hurt his case, however, by becoming more bitter with the passage of time—and thus less convincing. Moreover, he unwittingly played into the hands of the pro-German elements, so that suspicious patriots questioned his loyalty.

On the other hand, the first prominent advocate of preparedness as an antiwar measure was Henry Cabot Lodge's son-in-law, Congressman Augustus P. Gardner of Massachusetts. On October 15, 1914, Gardner requested Congress to form a National Security Commission to determine how close the army and navy were to war strength. He warned that the United States was totally unprepared to defend itself and that the belligerents might some day attack

America. The legislature, perhaps persuaded by the administration, refused to approve the Gardner project. The Congressman, however, kept alive the plan by frequent public appeals and by helping to establish preparedness organizations.

Two of the earliest of such agencies were the National Security League and the American Legion, Incorporated, both promoted by General Leonard Wood and Theodore Roosevelt. The League had as its chief objective to "insure for the nation an adequate system of national defense." The American Legion organized a military training program and advocated the enrollment of a variety of specialists like engineers, automobile drivers, and telegraph operators. Thus several hundred thousand trained volunteers would be available in case of attack; if war did not materialize, they might be used to prevent sabotage.

Backed by many prominent Americans, Wood started his plan for voluntary military training for businessmen at Plattsburg, New York, in the summer of 1915. At the outset this was a small-scale project attracting only about 1,200 men. The following year the movement was expanded; at least four camps were attended by some 12,000 men. Even so, the Plattsburg plan touched only a small number of Americans and never gained the support of the Wilson administration.

Meantime, Theodore Roosevelt, tired of what he called the milk-and-water policy of President Wilson, became the outstanding critic of the administration and the most vigorous advocate of preparedness. In January, 1915, he explained the need for adequate defense in *America and the World War*, and followed this the next year with *Fear God and Take Your Own Part*, in which he decried the folly of turning the other cheek. This thesis was also upheld by Hudson Maxim in *Defenseless America* and by Frederick L. Huidekoper in *The Military Unpreparedness of the United States*. The latter pointed out that in past wars many American soldiers had needlessly been slaughtered because they lacked military training. After war started was too late to prepare; in addition to greater loss of life, there was larger monetary expense, not to mention the danger to the nation.

Because Wilson believed at first that the preparedness movement might weaken America's role as potential peacemaker, he opposed the efforts of the National Security League; in his view, it wanted an increase in military strength as a prelude to American entrance into the war. In a speech to Congress in December, 1914, Wilson said: "We shall not alter our attitude . . . because some amongst us are nervous and excited. Such a change would merely mean that we had lost our self-possession." He continued to place national reliance upon a "citizenry trained and accustomed to arms," rather than on a large standing army. The navy should be a medium for defense, not for attack. Thus without executive approval of preparedness, military appropriations were kept at the low prewar level.

As the war progressed, however, the President gradually changed his position. With American rights increasingly denied on the high seas, perhaps the preparedness advocates were correct in their belief that armed force would do the most good in upholding international law. By May, 1915, Wilson was beginning to talk about the need for improved national defense, though it was not until the end of the year that he asked Congress for larger appropriations for the army and navy, as well as increased control over the merchant marine. In support of his new position, the President insisted that he was not seeking war, for "we regard war merely as a means of asserting the rights of a people against aggression. . . . But we do believe in a body of free citizens ready and sufficient to take care of themselves. . . . At least so much by way of preparation for defense seems to me to be absolutely imperative now."

The First Preparedness Measures

To test whether his new thesis had popular support and in anticipation of the election of 1916, Wilson made a series of speeches in key cities, especially in the Middle West, during January and February, 1916. Important sentences from some of the addresses were: "We must be ready . . . upon the shortest possible notice . . ."; "This country should prepare herself, not for war . . . but for adequate national defense"; we must build "a great navy second to none in the world." The enthusiasm with which these opinions were received, even in the supposedly antiwar Middle West, convinced Wilson that he must press for preparedness legislation from Congress without further delay.

Consequently, early in March, 1916, there were introduced in both Houses similar bills to increase the armed forces. Delayed by disagreement over details but aided by Villa's raids on American territory, the Hay or National Defense Act was finally signed by the President on June 6. It provided for a gradual increase in the regular army from the existing 90,000 to a minimum of 175,000 and a maximum of 220,000 men; federalization of the National Guard, which was to be built up to a complement of 400,000; establishment of officers' reserve corps; and compulsory training for youths over the age of sixteen in high schools and colleges. General public support for the Hay Act was shown by the numerous preparedness-day parades throughout the land. That there was some opposition, however, was indicated at San Francisco where, on July 22, Thomas Mooney and Warren Billings were accused of throwing a bomb among the paraders. Their subsequent trial and imprisonment became a *cause célèbre.*

With this successful opening wedge, it was easy to pass several other preparedness measures. On August 29, 1916, the Naval Construction Act was placed on the books, under which more than $500 million would be spent during the next three years to build at least five battle cruisers, together with numerous lesser craft. About a week later, Congress, after nearly two years of debate, established the United States Shipping Board, with power to lease, buy, build, and operate merchant ships through an Emergency Fleet Corporation. The original operating fund for this purpose was $50 million.

The Adamson Act

The preparedness campaign carried the national government much further than ever before into the field of labor relations. In March, 1916, the four railway brotherhoods sought an eight-hour day and additional overtime pay. When the operators refused to agree and likewise failed to arbitrate the differences, the unions scheduled a strike to begin on Labor Day. The government, fearful lest the proposed walkout tie up national transportation facilities and thereby delay the general preparedness program, tried its best to settle the controversy through the Board of Mediation and Conciliation, established under the Newlands Act of 1913, but without success. President Wilson also failed to persuade the operators to grant the eight-hour day, which, he said, had "the sanction of the judgment of society in its favor."

Consequently, Wilson went before Congress on August 29, explained the gravity of the situation, and quickly obtained the passage of the Adamson Act four days later. This statute granted the union members the working day they sought, although the overtime pay was to be prorated. Furthermore, a fact-finding commission was set up to consider a general overhauling of the Interstate Commerce Commission and the Newlands Act. This measure satisfied the brotherhoods and the strike was called off. The President was widely criticized by business for surrendering to the threats of labor, but Wilson felt justified in his action to keep preparedness rolling and to prevent an embarrassing strike in the midst of his presidential campaign.

The Campaign of 1916

Even while Congress was passing these preparedness measures, the politicians were appealing to the nation's voters in anticipation of the presidential election of 1916. Wilson's election in 1912 had been possible only because of the quarrel within the Republican ranks and the subsequent formation of the Progressive party. The Progressives, however, proved to have little vitality except as they drew upon that of the dynamic Theodore Roosevelt—and Roosevelt's interest in quixotic politics rapidly subsided. Much though the former President hated the Republican Old Guard, he detested Wilson more. The Congressional elections of 1914 had shown clearly that the Progressive party was dying; some supporters went over to the Democratic ranks and others returned to the Republican fold. Although that election strengthened the Democratic control of the Senate from 51 seats to 56, the administration majority in the House was sharply reduced from 290 to 231.

During the next two years the disintegration of the Progressives continued. Roosevelt was still the party's idol, but he wanted no new three-way contest such as that which had led to Wilson's victory in 1912. He hoped rather that the split might be healed and that he would be triumphantly returned to the White House as the candidate of both the Republicans and Progressives. But the Old Guard, still bitter about the quarrel of 1912, wanted the Progressive vote but not the Progressive hero. Another obstacle confronting Roosevelt was that no man in America was more hated by the German-Americans, whose votes were needed to beat Wilson.

What the Republicans required was a candidate who had not bolted, but whose record, nevertheless, was sufficiently liberal to attract the Progressives. He must not have alienated the German vote, yet at the same time he could not be open to the charge of being pro-German. Automatically ruled out were such prominent statesmen as ex-President Taft, Elihu Root, and Henry Cabot Lodge. The field, in fact, soon reduced itself to one—Justice Charles Evans Hughes of the Supreme Court. Hughes had first gained prominence in 1905 by his fearless investigation of insurance company scandals in New York; from 1907 to 1910 he had been a successful governor of that state. This part of his record would appeal to liberal voters. On the other hand, conservative Republicans noted with approval that Hughes had been appointed to the Supreme Court by Taft in 1910, that he had been a sound judge, and that his judicial position had prevented his taking any stand in the party quarrel of 1912. Both conservative Republicans and German-Americans noted with distinct satisfaction one final fact about Hughes—it was common knowledge that Roosevelt did not like him.

Early in June, 1916, the Republicans and the Progressives held their separate conventions in Chicago. The younger party marked time to see whether the Republicans would accept Roosevelt after all, but the voting soon demonstrated Hughes' strength and he was nominated on the third ballot. The platform was brief; it denounced the Democratic administration for failure to protect the rights of American citizens, especially in Mexico, stressed the need for preparedness, and attacked both the Underwood Tariff and the merchant marine program.

The Progressives then nominated Roosevelt on a platform which repeated the slogans of 1912 and attacked Wilson's foreign policy, while demanding military and naval preparedness. But the party the Rough Rider had created in

1912 was killed by its own parent. A letter from Roosevelt, declining the nomination and announcing his intention to support Hughes, was made public too late for the convention to name another candidate. The Progressive National Committee, by a divided vote, endorsed Hughes and then adjourned, never to meet again. Most of the Progressives returned to the Republican fold; a minority became Democrats.

The Democratic convention, assembling later in June at St. Louis, proved a triumph for the President. Not only was he renominated by a vote of 1092 to 1, with Marshall again chosen as his running mate, but the platform was largely his handiwork. It pointed with pride to the legislation passed by two Democratic Congresses and acclaimed the administration's patient Mexican policy. It praised American neutrality in the European war, but proclaimed it was the duty of the United States to join with other countries in an association of nations.

Because Wilson believed there was "disloyalty active in the United States" which "must be absolutely crushed," he wanted to fight the campaign on a ringing assertion of Americanism linked with a denunciation of "hyphenism" —the divided loyalty of some German-Americans and other groups of recent foreign stock. Events in St. Louis, however, proved the greater popularity of a different slogan. In his keynote speech, Martin H. Glynn of New York defined the avoidance of war as the paramount issue of the campaign. He cited numerous historical instances when dangerous controversies had arisen between the United States and some other nation; in each case Glynn hammered home the point: "But we didn't go to war." The delegates gave their enthusiastic approval and it was obvious that Wilson's strongest political asset was his success in keeping the United States insulated from the world conflagration. A sentence in the platform capitalized on this: "In particular we commend to the American people the splendid diplomatic victories of our great President, who has preserved the vital interests of our Government and its citizens, and kept us out of war." As a summary of the President's past policy, the slogan "He kept us out of war" was true enough; yet it was a dangerous one when regarded as a guarantee for the future. Wilson had already told one of his advisers: "I can't keep the country out of war. . . . Any little German lieutenant can put us into war at any time by some calculated outrage."

The campaign that followed was more notable for colorful incidents than for the quality of the debate on the issues. Several of these incidents involved the hyphenate problem. Radical Irish- and German-Americans claimed credit for persuading the Democratic voters of New Jersey to renominate Senator Martine in September despite Wilson's opposition. Jeremiah O'Leary, head of the rabid Anglophobe organization known as the "American Truth Society," dispatched an exuberant telegram to the President:

Senator Martine won because the voters of New Jersey do not want any truckling to the British Empire nor do they approve of dictatorship over Congress. Your foreign policies, your failure to secure compliance with all American rights, your leniency with the British Empire, your approval of war loans, the ammunition traffic, are issues in this campaign.

Wilson's reply was immediate and crushing:

Your telegram received. I would feel deeply mortified to have you or anybody like you vote for me. Since you have access to many disloyal Americans and I have not, I will ask you to convey this message to them.

This O'Leary incident captured headlines all over the country, and the Democratic National Committee sought to capitalize further upon it by charging that Hughes had made a deal with the wicked O'Leary and a group of German-Americans and Irish-Americans. Hughes admitted he had been interviewed by such a group, but denied he had promised them anything or had known who O'Leary was when he met him. *The New York Times*, supporting Wilson, chortled: "A few days ago who would have suspected in the bustling Jeremiah O'Leary the successor, as a candidate slayer, of the grave and reverend Burchard."

Hughes's campaign was full of other embarrassments. His speeches, while vigorously critical of the President, were vague as to any alternative policy. His cautious dealing with the submarine issue was in sharp contrast with the fiery speeches of Roosevelt, who likened the President to Pontius Pilate, and then apologized to Pilate. Roosevelt's language was such as to dismay the Irish and German groups working for Hughes. Ambassador Bernstorff indeed informed German-Americans who looked to him for advice that Germany had more to lose than to gain in a Republican victory.

The costliest blunder of the campaign was committed in California, where Hughes, complying with the wishes of the conservative bosses, shunned Governor Hiram Johnson, who had been the Progressive vice-presidential candidate in 1912 and who was now running for the United States Senate. Therefore Johnson made no effort to have his own followers support Hughes. When the ballots were counted in November, it was revealed that Johnson carried the state by almost 300,000 votes, while Hughes was losing it by 4,000.

The first editions of the newspapers on the morning after election announced that Hughes had won, for he had carried all the large Eastern states—upon which victory had hitherto always hinged, as well as the strategic Midwestern states of Illinois, Indiana, and Michigan. To win all these and yet lose the election seemed impossible, but Hughes did it. To Wilson went the Solid

South, plus Maryland, New Hampshire, and Ohio; the balance of power proved to be the states west of the Mississippi, all of which the President carried except Oregon, Iowa, South Dakota, and Minnesota. After several days of uncertainty, the final electoral vote was revealed as: Wilson, 277; Hughes, 254. The popular totals gave Wilson 9.1 million, Hughes, 8.5 million, and Benson (Socialist), 585,000.

The defeat of Hughes in such a close contest obviously depended on other factors than the snub of Johnson. Had he carried states like Ohio or Kansas, he could have afforded to lose California. The general weakness of his campaign was that it depended on appealing both to the elements that desired a more genuine neutrality than that of the Wilson administration and to those who wanted a more energetically pro-Ally course of action. On domestic issues also Hughes was unconvincing. Wilson, on the other hand, derived effective political support from organized labor, which liked the Adamson Act, and from farmers, grateful for the Farm Loan Bank Act. Furthermore, women now voted in most of the Western states, and they were particularly responsive to the slogan: "He kept us out of war." The effect of the O'Leary incident is not clear; the President's condemnation of hyphenism probably won him many votes, but he lost the six states—New York, Pennsylvania, New Jersey, Massachusetts, Connecticut, and Illinois—in which the largest number of Irish votes were concentrated.

The Democrats, with 53 seats, maintained their control of the Senate. In the House, however, 216 Republicans were elected to 210 Democrats. Enough of the nine independents, who held the balance of power, allied with the Democrats to permit the latter to re-elect Champ Clark as Speaker when the new Congress convened in April, 1917.

The Appeal for Peace

From the time of the initial shots of World War I, President Wilson had tried to act as peacemaker or mediator. Even though his early offers of good services were rejected, he continued his attempts. House's second "great adventure," including his memorandum with Lord Grey, was the most notable example.

It was after his re-election that Wilson made his most vigorous effort. One reason was that Germany showed an apparent change of heart, during the summer of 1916, by authorizing Bernstorff to say that his country was ready to ask the President to call a peace conference. More important was Wilson's realization that the longer the war lasted, the more difficult American neutrality would become; indeed he had said during the political campaign that "this is the last war . . . that involves the world that the United States can keep out of. . . . I mean this, that war now has such a scale that the position of neutrals sooner or later becomes intolerable." And he had privately informed Colonel House that unless peace were soon restored, America would "inevitably drift into war with Germany upon the submarine issue."

Determined to make a strong move despite the lack of sympathy of his close advisers, Wilson sent identical notes on December 18, 1916, to each belligerent government, asking it to state the specific terms upon which it would agree to conclude hostilities and what it would require for future security. Were each to reply favorably, then all might learn, neutrals as well as belligerents, "how near the haven of peace may be for which all mankind longs with an intense and increasing longing."

The responses were anything but satisfactory. The Allied reply of January 10, 1917, placed all the blame for the war on the Central Powers and insisted that the peace settlement must protect Europe from another outbreak of such "brutal covetousness." To do this, the Central Powers must be deprived of all lands they had conquered and the peoples they had enslaved must be liberated.

Despite the fact that Germany had spoken in favor of peace negotiations just before Wilson sent the notes, she now refused to state any specific terms. Perhaps she was concerned about a tactless statement by Lansing that the dispatch of the notes "will indicate the possibility of our being forced into the war." While the Secretary of State later disclaimed this statement, the damage had been done. Perhaps it was because Germany knew that Wilson's mediation would prevent the annexations she desired. At any event, she announced she would deal only with Allied delegates in some neutral European city where peace negotiations would be free from "American indiscreetness and intermeddling."

Faced with this situation—with Germany refusing to state any peace terms at all and with the Allies giving terms so far-reaching as to make immediate peace impossible—Wilson reacted in a way completely characteristic of his own conception of democratic leadership. His carefully prepared address to the Senate on January 22, 1917, was really a direct appeal to the peoples of the warring nations over the heads of their governments. He took it for granted, he said, that mere terms of peace between the belligerents would not satisfy those belligerents for long. Any lasting peace must be "a peace without victory. . . . Victory would mean peace forced upon a loser, a victor's peace imposed upon the vanquished. . . . Only a peace between equals can last." Also a durable peace must be based on the principles of government by the consent of the governed, freedom of the seas, and disarmament. Most important of all, something must be done to guarantee the permanency of a settlement, a guarantee so powerful that no nation or combination of nations could break it. In other words, "peace must be followed by some concert of powers which will make it virtually impossible that any such catastrophe should ever overwhelm us again." And such a league must include the United States, for otherwise it would not be sufficiently strong.

By many critics this is considered the greatest of Wilson's public papers—a message of prophetic power which, had it been heeded, might have saved the peoples of all countries from untold suffering. But, despite the heartfelt approval of much American opinion and that of liberals even in the belligerent countries, the speech was denounced in many quarters. Several leading Republican Senators attacked bitterly the idea of American participation in a league of nations which would employ force to maintain peace. The phrase "peace without victory" greatly offended the Allies; that of government by the consent of the governed seemed dangerous to the Central Powers.

The desperate odds against Wilson's success in his campaign for a negotiated peace were becoming daily more obvious, but the President did not give up. On the contrary, he renewed pressure upon the German government to state the terms on which it would be willing to bring the war to an end.

End of the "Sussex" Pledge

Germany, however, wanted peace only if it could be made on her own terms. As January, 1917, progressed, her military leaders were won over by the admirals to the cause of resumption of ruthless submarine warfare. Consequently, on January 9, the Kaiser issued the fateful command that was to be kept secret as long as possible: "I order that the unrestricted submarine warfare be launched with the greatest vigor on the 1st of February." In taking this step, the German authorities knew that it would most probably bring the United States into the war on the Allied side, but that was a risk that had to be chanced. Some Germans even believed America would remain neutral; had not the American voters given a mandate to their government in the recent election to stay out of war? And what if the mandate were broken? The assistance that the United States could give the Allies over and above what she had already furnished in the way of supplies and loans would, in the opinion of the German military leaders, "amount to nothing." On the other hand, ruthless submarine warfare would bring England to her knees in a few months, and with England defeated the Allied cause would be lost.

It was not until January 31 that Bernstorff handed Lansing a brusque note: after February 1, Germany would forcibly prevent all navigation, that of neutrals included, in a zone around Great Britain, France, and Italy, and in the eastern Mediterranean. All ships within that zone would be sunk on sight. As a concession to the United States, however, one American steamer, not carrying contraband, might sail to and from Falmouth, England, each week, provided three "vertical stripes, one meter wide," alternately red and white, were painted on the hull; furthermore, that ship must fly a red-and-white checkered flag from both stern and masthead, it must be lighted at night, and it must follow a course mapped out by German authorities. To indignant Americans reading this note in their newspapers, this patronizing concession seemed the ultimate in insult.

In a desperate effort to prevent a diplomatic break, Bernstorff on this same day confided to Colonel House the specific German peace terms the President had been asking. But Wilson was no longer interested; for the Germans to expect him to continue his peace efforts when they were tearing up the Sussex pledge was a mockery.

His answer was to appear before Congress on February 3 to announce the severance of all diplomatic relations with the German Empire. Yet he added, "I refuse to believe that it is the intention of the German authorities to do in fact what they have warned us they will feel at liberty to do. . . . Only actual overt acts on their part can make me believe it even now." Should such acts occur, however, Wilson would ask Congress for the authority necessary "for the protection of our seamen and our people." The popularity of his position was indicated when the Senate quickly endorsed his action by a vote of 78 to 5.

Armed Neutrality

Although the only two American ships sunk by submarines in February were given warning so that no lives were lost, American shipping was badly demoralized. Many vessels remained in port, and an insistent demand went up that the government should provide navy guns and gunners for their protection. At first Wilson opposed such a step, which would obviously bring the nation closer to war.

Just at this critical moment the President learned of an act of intrigue that more than any other single thing destroyed all his trust in German good faith. In the middle of January, 1917, German Foreign Minister Zimmermann had dispatched to the German minister to Mexico a coded message telling of the decision to resume unrestricted submarine warfare. If war with the United States resulted, the minister was to propose an alliance with Mexico on the following basis: the two countries should make war and peace together; Germany would give Mexico financial support; and Mexico would use the war against the United States "to reconquer the lost territory in New Mexico, Texas, and Arizona." The Zimmermann note further proposed "that the President of Mexico on his own initiative should communicate with Japan suggesting adherence at once to this plan; at the same time offer to mediate between Germany and Japan."

British intelligence officers had intercepted this message when it left Germany; the British government, however, had shrewdly refrained from handing it over to American officials until German-American relations had approached a breaking point. On February 25, this Zimmermann note was in Wilson's hands; the next day he asked Congressional approval to arm American merchant ships.

To understand the President's indignation over this German invitation for Mexico and Japan to attack the United States, it must be remembered that the document had been prepared at the very time German officials were urging Wilson to continue his peace efforts. All this was bad enough; what made it worse was that the German Foreign Office, granted the unusual privilege of exchanging cipher messages with Bernstorff through State Department channels, had abused this courtesy by sending the Zimmermann note to the German Embassy in Washington for transmission to Mexico. British intelligence officers had unblushingly intercepted it en route between the American Embassy in Berlin and the State Department.

After some hesitation, Wilson made public the note. It immediately aroused great excitement and contributed to the growth of a war spirit. Although some Americans insisted that the Zimmermann note was a British forgery, calculated to bring the United States into the war on the Allied side, this possibility was ruled out when Zimmermann admitted his authorship.

Despite Wilson's personal appeal and the militant mood prevading the country, the armed ship bill did not become law. True, it passed the House by a vote of 403 to 14, but in the Senate eleven legislators, headed by LaFollette and Norris, successfully filibustered to prevent the measure from coming to a vote before Congress adjourned on March 4. The President bitterly condemned these obstructionist Senators as "a little group of willful men, representing no opinion but their own," who "have rendered the great Government of the United States helpless and contemptible." Consequently, much against his original wish but because of the need for speedy action, Wilson on March 12 ordered the arming of merchant ships on his own responsibility, using as his authority a statute originally passed in 1797.

By this time most American opinion was clamoring for still more drastic action. The events of the past six weeks had already aroused great indignation; now news of the sinking of several American ships, mostly without warning, and the resultant loss of American lives, brought the nation to a fighting pitch.

Just at that moment the dramatic information came that the Russian people had forced the abdication of the Tsar and established a constitutional government. America emphatically approved; indeed, the United States was the first to recognize the new regime. The event also seemed to clarify the issues of the war; now the Allied cause appeared to be truly that of democracy struggling against absolutism. No one felt this more keenly than did Wilson, who said: "If our entering the war would hasten and fix the movements in Russia and Germany, it would be a marked gain to the world and would tend to give additional justification to the whole struggle."

With these two developments—the sinking of more American ships and the Russian Revolution—Wilson at last concluded that this country must enter the war. To make doubly sure he was right, he called a special Cabinet meeting on March 20 and, without telling the members his own position, he asked them what course the United States should now follow. With but little discussion they quickly supported a declaration of war against Germany. Immediately Wilson called the new Congress into special session because of "grave questions of national policy."

Since this could mean but one thing—war—it was an impressive assembly that Wilson faced in the House chamber on the evening of April 2. Directly in front of the Speaker's desk sat the Justices of the Supreme Court. On one side were the Cabinet officials and, immediately behind them, the diplomatic corps, sitting for the first time on the floor of the House. Other distinguished visitors crowded the galleries. After the Representatives had taken their places, the Senators filed in, most of them wearing or carrying little American flags.

Wilson's address was worthy of the occasion. First, he reviewed the history of the submarine controversy, stressing not the loss of property involved, but "the wanton and wholesale destruction of the lives of non-combatants, men, women, and children, engaged in pursuits which have always, even in the darkest periods of modern history, been deemed innocent and legitimate." Property could be paid for, the lives of peaceful and innocent people could not be. Therefore he asked that Congress declare the recent course of the Imperial German Government to be in fact nothing less than war against the government and people of the United States and that it formally accept the status of belligerent. Then followed an eloquent statement of America's war objectives. With the German people, Wilson asserted, the United States had no quarrel; it was not upon their impulse that their government had acted in entering the war. The United States would fight for the ultimate peace of the world and for the liberation of its peoples, the Germans included. "The world must," he said, "be made safe for democracy." After admitting that it was a fearful thing to lead a great peaceful people into war, he concluded with these stirring words:

> But the right is more precious than peace, and we shall fight for the things which we have always carried nearest our hearts,—for democracy, for the right of those who submit to authority to have a voice in their own Governments, for the rights and liberties of small nations, for a universal dominion of right by such a concert of free peoples as shall bring peace and safety to all nations and make

the world itself at last free. To such a task we can dedicate our lives and our fortunes, everything that we are and everything that we have, with the pride of those who know that the day has come when America is privileged to spend her blood and her might for the principles that gave her birth and happiness and the peace which she has treasured. God helping her, she can do no other.

The President's address was frequently interrupted by wild applause; there was no question but that Congress and the country would follow his leadership. The opponents of war were beaten and they knew it. On April 4 there was a spirited, but brief, debate in the Senate. Despite the opposition of LaFollette, supported by Norris and Stone (of Missouri), the war declaration was passed late that evening by a vote of 82 to 6. All the next day the House debated and the final ballot was not taken until three o'clock on the morning of the 6th. The Representatives approved the declaration by a vote of 373 to 50; Miss Jeannette Rankin, the only woman in Congress, voted with the minority. That afternoon of April 6, 1917, Wilson signed the declaration, and the United States was at war with Germany.

Why America Fought

In later years much was said and written about why the United States went to war in 1917. One school of thought held that Americans had been tricked by British propaganda; another, that bankers and munitions makers had insisted upon the country's active participation to save the money that they had loaned to the Allies and to make bigger profits; a third, that Wilson had from the beginning wanted war and that he had deliberately adopted policies to bring about this result.

British propaganda there was, and in abundance, but the Germans were scarcely less active. Why did the majority of Americans believe the British and not their opponents? Fundamentally, it was because the Allies had the stronger case. Although many atrocity stories were exaggerated or untrue, the deeds that most hopelessly damned the Germans in American eyes were incidents that could not be denied—like the violation of Belgian neutrality and the sinking of the *Lusitania*. These actions seemed to show that Germany was utterly ruthless in seeking to fulfill her ambitions. Moreover, educated and influential Americans, particularly if they lived in the East, tended to see the issues of war in exactly the same light as did similar people in England. The best spokesmen for the Allied cause were respected citizens like Theodore Roosevelt, Elihu Root, Leonard Wood, Henry Cabot Lodge, and ex-President Charles W. Eliot of Harvard, men of whom it would be absurd to think as paid propagandists of Great Britain.

It is undeniable that American financial involvement in the war had become very great by 1917. And American industry had boomed on war orders, while British control of the seas resulted in American munitions going almost exclusively to the Allies. Furthermore, when the Allies ran out of money, they procured loans through American bankers. Undoubtedly these economic factors did stimulate strong pro-Ally sentiment among industrialists and financiers, but the sentiment of those individuals would not have been much different had such trade and loans been prohibited. The charge that Wilson himself was influenced by the bankers to ask Congress for a declaration of war is absurd. Not only does it receive no support from the documents, but it entirely misrepresents the character of a man who placed much more value in ideals and principles than he did in dollars, and who was particularly suspicious of suggestions from Wall Street.

Nor does the theory that Wilson plotted from the beginning to get the country into war hold together. To be sure, he was pro-Ally and anti-German, but he was less so than almost any other public man who had a similar background. He accepted the idea that the United States might eventually have to enter the war and, if it did so, it should be on the Allied side. But he much preferred that the United States should keep out and use its great influence to bring a just and durable peace. Instead of becoming more pro-Ally, Wilson had, by January, 1917, become "really neutral," an admission that came from Ambassador Bernstorff himself.

The conclusion is inescapable that it was the submarine issue that was decisive. Had not the German government resumed unrestricted submarine warfare, the United States might easily have remained neutral; but with that German decision, there was nothing honorable left for Wilson to do except ask for war, particularly after the stand he had taken in the Sussex affair. Only through war, Wilson believed, could the United States maintain the long-cherished doctrine of freedom of the seas.

A more effective criticism of Wilson is that, although he really desired to keep the United States out of war, he followed policies which defeated his purpose. This was the accusation of Senator LaFollette in the debate on the declaration of war. According to the Wisconsin legislator, the Democratic administration made a fatal mistake. It had "assumed and acted upon the policy that it could enforce to the very letter of the law the principles of international law against one belligerent and relax them to the other." That thing, LaFollette continued, no nation could do without losing the rights that went with "strict and absolute neutrality."

The question that must be answered in the final analysis is this: Was World War I a struggle of such character that the United States could afford the kind of "strict and absolute neutrality" that LaFollette was thinking about? Such neutrality might have resulted in a crushing defeat of Britain and France and so resounding a victory for the Central Powers that the German military caste would have been encouraged to seek further triumphs. Would such an outcome to the war have been desirable from the standpoint of American interests? Looking back from our present vantage point, the answer seems obvious. Complete German dominance of Europe, followed as it must inevitably have been by mastery of the Atlantic Ocean, would have created such a new situation in world politics as to affect most seriously the security of the United States. Since this was so, "strict and absolute neutrality" was as unrealistic in the years following 1914 as it was in the years following 1939.[5] Wilson may be criticized for not having stressed the issue more in his war messages. Probably he himself did not see it clearly. It was characteristic of him that he thought and talked more in terms of legal rights and moral principles than in those of national interest.

Once having accepted the idea of war, Wilson laid great stress on the ends he hoped to gain: the furtherance of democracy, insurance of the rights and liberties of small nations, and the establishment of a league of nations. He assumed that he spoke for the entire nation in stating these war aims, and in the exaltation of the moment it seemed that he did. As time went on, however, it became apparent that many Americans, while accepting the necessity of war against Germany, rejected the Wilsonian conception of the ultimate war objectives.

[5] Many scholars, however, still regard American involvement in World War I as a tragic mistake, since by contributing to total Allied victory Wilson lost the chance of achieving the just peace—"the peace without victory"—of which he had been dreaming. Such critics deny that Germany would necessarily have won if America had persisted in its neutrality. The more likely outcome of the war, they believe, would have been a stalemate. This school of thought believes that Wilson could have avoided the pitfalls implicit in his position on submarine warfare if he had simply warned Americans not to travel on belligerent ships.

10
The War for Democracy

The United States was at war, but what did war under such circumstances mean? How did one nation fight another 3,000 miles away? Americans both in official positions and in civilian life were not sure. There was no precedent to follow, for this was the first major struggle involving the United States that entailed sending military forces outside the Western Hemisphere. Moreover, the navy was still in the process of enlargement, while the National Defense Act of 1916 provided for a maximum army of only 220,000, together with a possible 400,000 national guardsmen. Neither branch of the armed services had had any experience in the modern type of warfare being waged in Europe. Transportation facilities for troops and supplies were as yet inadequate, and the German submarine menace was potent. Perhaps, as Germany believed, the United States would be limited in its role to a continuation of its prior efforts—providing loans and supplies to the Allies. Despite all these obstacles, however, the desperate needs of the hour spurred the nation to greater and greater efforts.

First Aid to the Allies

The navy was thrown into the struggle at once. Indeed, even before the actual declaration of war, Rear Admiral—soon to become Vice Admiral—William S. Sims had been quietly sent to England; by April, 1917, he was already planning joint operations with the British navy. In May the first flotilla of American destroyers reached British waters, gradually to be followed by a large part of the growing navy. These ships were desperately needed by the English to help in destroying submarines, which were sinking several hundred thousand tons of Allied shipping each month.

The Allies were not slow in making other needs known. Within three weeks of the declaration of war, British and French missions arrived in the United States, where the members were enthusiastically received. The first Allied need was money. The British had served as Allied bankers for almost three years; now, however, they were hard pressed for further assets to purchase food and munitions. Anticipating the requests of the missions, Congress had already passed the Emergency Loan Act, which authorized the issuance of $5 billion worth of bonds bearing 3½ per cent interest. Three billion of this amount might be loaned to nations "engaged in war with the enemies of the United States." Many more loans—to a total of $7 billion—were to follow during the next year and a half, not only to England and France, but to Italy, Russia, Yugoslavia, and Cuba as well. Most of the money was spent by the borrowers in the United States for the products of American factories and farms.

Naval support, money, and goods—these the United States could obviously contribute to the campaign against the Central Powers, but most observers in April, 1917, felt this was about all the nation could do. It seemed fantastic to believe that the United States could create a large army, train it, equip it, and transport it across 3,000 miles of submarine-infested waters to the western front. Yet such an army was needed, for the French were dangerously weary of war, and their burdens seemed too heavy to be borne much longer. During the visit of the French war mission, Marshal Joffre appealed for an American token force, which might stiffen sagging morale.

As early as May 8, 1917, President Wilson and Secretary of War Baker decided to respond to this appeal, and Major General John J. Pershing was placed in command of the proposed American Expeditionary Force. On June 26, the first American regiments, numbering about 14,500 men, disembarked at St. Nazaire, France. While this handful received a joyous welcome, it was not sufficient to enable the Allies, weakened by three years of war, to launch a winning offensive. Concluding that only a large-scale American intervention could break the stalemate and crush the enemy, Pershing informed the War Department on July 6 that plans "Should contemplate sending over one million men" by the spring of 1918, with additional millions to follow. In short, the impossible would have to be accomplished.

Raising an Army

Although the project of sending a million soldiers to France was a new and breath-taking one, the idea that a state of war would require a greatly enlarged army for national defense was not. When war was declared, the General Staff advocated immediate conscription, and President Wilson and Secretary Baker concurred at once, for they believed that in a democracy the obligation for military service should be universal. Furthermore, they knew of the difficulties involved in recruiting as a result of the recent experience of the British, who had depended on volunteers during the first years of the war. The greatest weakness of the system had been, not that it failed to bring a large number of recruits into the armed forces, but that all too often it brought the wrong men, or the right men at the wrong time. There was a wastage of manpower as volunteers gave up vital production jobs, or as fine potential officer material left school to serve as privates and to become an appallingly large proportion of the early casualties of the war. As a result of this British experience, Wilson said: "The idea of a selective draft is that those should be chosen . . . who can be most readily spared from the prosecution of the other activities which the country must engage in and to which it must devote a great deal of its best energy and capacity."

The Selective Service Bill,[1] introduced in April, 1917, was based upon the principle that the draft should be administered by public-spirited civilians serving in their own communities. Despite this suggested democratic machinery, the bill was not passed without a struggle. Speaker Champ Clark expressed the blunt judgment that "in the estimation of Missourians there is precious little difference between a conscript and a convict," while the Democratic chairman of the House Military Affairs Committee vigorously opposed the measure. One controversial point concerned the age limits for registrants; the War Department preferred men from 19 to 25; Congress, rebelling at drafting youths too young to vote, placed the limits at 21 to 30.

The most bitter issue involved an amendment proposed by admirers of Theodore Roosevelt, which would have made it mandatory to accept volunteer units under their own officers. This project reflected the patriotic ambition of the ex-President to raise a division of volunteers just as the Rough Riders had been recruited in 1898. The idea aroused the enthusiastic support of many Americans, but the army was thoroughly opposed. Modern warfare was for professionals; to commission a civilian to command an expeditionary force would be a disastrous precedent. Therefore Congress left the President at liberty to accept or reject volunteer units.

The Selective Service Bill finally became law on May 18, 1917. Without delay the President settled the Roosevelt issue by bluntly stating that this was "not the time for compliment or for any action not calculated to contribute to the immediate success of the war." Many critics attributed Wilson's action to petty jealousy and partisanship. Similar accusations were made when it was

---

[1] It was written largely by Captain Hugh S. Johnson, who had recently been with Pershing in Mexico and was destined sixteen years later to be one of the most colorful figures in the early days of the New Deal.

learned that General Leonard Wood was not to be given active command in France; but here again civilian heads of the army were basing their policy upon professional advice. Pershing was chosen for the European command because he had had more experience, was younger, and in better health. Given a free hand in selecting his subordinates, Pershing opposed using Wood in any capacity.

Selective Conscription Will Pan Out Well.
(From the Chicago Tribune.)

Registration day, June 5, was awaited with considerable anxiety. Memories of Civil War draft riots haunted certain gloomy souls; Senator Reed of Missouri predicted that enforced conscription would cause the streets of American cities to run with blood. Nothing of the kind occurred, however, and on the appointed day more than 9.5 million young men filled out their registration blanks and received their serial numbers at 4,557 local selective service boards. On July 20, Secretary Baker drew from a large bowl the first serial number—258; the registrants having that number in each local district were to be the first called for classification. The drawing continued until each registrant had been assigned a call number. Eventually all were grouped into five classes, based upon their availability for armed service, their obligations toward dependents, and the degree of importance attached to their civilian occupation. A total of 3,706,544 men was placed in Class I—subject to military duty. Later, when the needs of the services increased, all men between the ages of 18 and 45 not previously registered were enrolled in September, 1918. All told, 24,234,021 were registered under Selective Service during World War I.

Thousands of men did not wait for the draft, but enlisted in the Regular Army, the National Guard, the Navy, or the Marine Corps. This continued until August 9, 1918, when the government discontinued volunteering for all services. On April 2, 1917, just before Wilson's war message to Congress, the total number in the armed forces was 378,619; on Armistice Day, 1918, the number had grown to 4,791,172.

Training the Armed Forces

Finding the men was comparatively easy, but transforming these civilians into soldiers was immeasurably more difficult. First of all, the men had to be housed. In June, 1917, construction was begun on sixteen camps—each camp to be a complete city, equipped to quarter and feed 48,000 recruits. Impatient critics sniffed at the wooden barracks, recreation centers, and modern plumbing. Soldiers pampered with these luxuries, they asserted, would be too soft for the conditions of the battlefield. The experience of other wars, however, had taught that unhealthy training centers were likely to kill more soldiers than enemy bullets. The building of the camps was a miracle of speedy construction. Even so, they were far from completed by September, 1917, when the first men of the new National Army were mobilized. Not all of the first 687,000 draftees were in cantonments by Christmas.

The problem of finding sufficient instructors to teach the new methods of warfare was difficult. In part it was solved by the employment of British and French officers, loaned to the American Army for this purpose. One of the most serious needs was for officers. The process of giving officer training to intelligent civilians had been started under the Plattsburg plan, well before the country's involvement in the war. The War Department set up special officer training camps where university students and other young men, carefully selected, were given intensive three-month courses, after which those found competent were commissioned as second lieutenants.

Economic Mobilization

Under the Army Appropriation Act of August 29, 1916, there had been created a Council of National Defense, comprising six cabinet officers—the Secretaries of War, Navy, Interior, Agriculture, Commerce, and Labor. With advisory powers only, this council was charged, among other things, with the "coordination of industries and resources for the national security and welfare," and with the "creation of relations which will render possible in time of need the immediate concentration and utilization of the resources of the Nation." To provide essential information for this council, the President appointed an Advisory Commission of seven specially qualified persons to serve without compensation: Daniel Willard of the Baltimore and Ohio railroad, who advised on transportation problems; President Hollis Godfrey of Drexel Institute, engineering and education; Howard Coffin, a leading automotive engineer, manufacturing and munitions; Dr. Franklin H. Martin, medicine and surgery; Bernard Baruch, a successful Wall Street operator, raw materials; Julius Rosenwald of Sears Roebuck, supplies; and Samuel Gompers, president of the AFL, labor relations.

By March, 1917, the commission had developed into a considerable organization, consisting of experts drawn from varied lines of industry. But in guiding the transition of the national economy from a peace- to a wartime basis, the National Defense Council and its dollar-a-year advisers labored under serious handicaps. They lacked authority, their advice was often ignored, and the various agencies of government worked at cross-purposes. Moreover, there was criticism that in counseling the government while remaining on the payrolls of private corporations, the members of the Advisory Commission were serving two masters, whose interests did not coincide. Gradually more and more work was assumed by new independent administrative bodies, staffed by men who had cut their ties with private business. These agencies in turn were eventually dominated by individual administrators with vast power.

One such independent agency was already in existence when war was declared. This was the United States Shipping Board, organized in January, 1917, under the chairmanship of William Denman of California, and empowered to buy, lease, or build ships and operate them through the Emergency Fleet Corporation. The increasing emphasis placed on expansion of the merchant marine may be measured by the growth of government-supplied capital poured into the enterprise; originally fixed at $50 million, it was enlarged to $1,934 million by October, 1917.

Ships were bought, leased, and built. As soon as war was declared, 105 enemy-owned vessels interned in American ports were turned over to the Shipping Board. Although they had been sabotaged by their crews, they were quickly repaired and put in service within a few months. The Emergency Fleet Corporation also commandeered some four-hundred ships being constructed in American shipyards, mostly for British and Norwegian buyers.

The necessity of building new ships in large volume led to a bitter controversy between Chairman Denman, who believed that wooden ships could be built quickly and cheaply, and Major General George W. Goethals of Panama Canal construction fame and now manager of the Emergency Fleet Corporation, who asserted that steel ships should be given priority. Eventually the President had to replace both men with Edward N. Hurley, a Chicago businessman. Under his leadership, not only were both steel and wooden ships now built, but even concrete vessels. Many new shipyards were opened, the largest being at Hog Island, near Philadelphia, and many ingenious new methods of speeding construction were devised. Ship design was standardized, many parts were prefabricated in various factories, and the work of the shipyards simplified to the point where it was primarily one of assembly. As a result, by the fall of 1918, 44 steel ships and 96 wooden ones were coming off the ways each month. Despite these striking achievements, not many new ships actually went into service before the armistice. The most effective work of the Shipping Board was coordinating the use of existing vessels in efficient fashion.

A second powerful agency of economic mobilization was the Food Administration. As early as April, 1917, the Council of National Defense created a committee on food supply and prices with Herbert C. Hoover as chairman. Successful as a mining engineer in the United States, China, and Australia, he was representing extensive business interests in London at the outbreak of the war. Heading a committee organized to aid American tourists caught in Europe, Hoover handled the job so effectively that he was placed in charge of the newly created Belgian Relief Commission. Within a few weeks he became a world figure because of his success in helping the Belgians without arousing the opposition of either the Allies or the Germans. When the United States abandoned neutrality, Hoover had to terminate his work in Belgium and return to the United States. His recent experience made him the ideal man to head the American food administration.

Hoover at once objected to the purely advisory character of his committee. In May, 1917, he was named Food Commissioner and made independent of the Council of National Defense, but he still did not have sufficient legal authority to take the drastic steps he believed necessary. Therefore, on August 10, 1917, after two months of extensive debate, Congress passed the Lever Act, granting unprecedented powers over a broad area of American life. The President was authorized to establish controls over food, feeds, fuel, and fertilizers, as well as over the machinery and equipment for producing them. A minimum of $2.00 a bushel was fixed for the 1918 wheat crop, with the President to set in advance the minimum price for succeeding years. A striking victory for the antiliquor forces was included in the section that prohibited the use of food to manufacture "distilled spirits for beverage purposes" or for "'malt or vinous liquors." The Lever Act was chiefly criticized by the farmers who claimed it established a "dictatorship"—a result of the administration's subservience to organized labor.

Hoover now became Food Administrator, and his volunteer organization was given legal basis. Much of the agency's activity was educational. Housewives were not subjected to formal rationing, but they were enjoined to use leftovers, to substitute dark bread for white, and to observe wheatless Mondays and Wednesdays, meatless Tuesdays, and porkless Thursdays and Saturdays. The menfolk were exhorted to plant victory gardens even at the sacrifice of the front lawn. The activities of millers were conducted under a strict licensing system, and hoarding and profiteering were severely dealt with. Farmers were encouraged to produce more wheat by fixing its price at $2.20—twenty cents above the minimum guaranteed by the Lever Act. To stabilize the market, a government-owned Grain Corporation was established, and it was soon followed by the Sugar Equalization Board. Increased production and conservation made possible the exportation to the Allied nations of three times the amount of foodstuffs shipped to them before 1914.

Another war agency set up under the Lever Act was the Fuel Administration, headed by Harry A. Garfield, son of a former President of the United States and himself president of Williams College. The price of coal was fixed sufficiently high to stimulate production and the public was implored to use fuel sparingly. The importance of gasoline to modern warfare was reflected in the ban, enforced by public opinion alone, upon all but essential driving on Sundays.

The fuel problem was closely linked with that of transportation. One of the voluntary organizations under the Council of National Defense had been a Railroads War Board, made up of prominent railroad executives. This board did much to coordinate the operations of the independent lines, and a system of freight priorities expedited the movement of vital supplies. Yet serious problems arose when tremendous quantities of freight, moved to the Atlantic coast for shipment to Europe, could not be unloaded fast enough. As a result the yards of Eastern terminals were jammed with full cars while the rest of the country was starved for "empties." Therefore, on December 28, 1917, the President, under authority of the Army Appropriation Act of 1916, placed the management of all rail lines of the country in the hands of William Gibbs McAdoo, who was named Director General of the Railroads. McAdoo then proceeded to operate them as a single consolidated system.

Meantime, these transportation tie-ups had caused thirty-seven ships loaded with munitions to be held up in New York harbor for lack of coal. Before the public became aware of the seriousness of the situation, Garfield announced that for five days starting January 18, 1918, all factories east of the Mississippi, except plants making munitions or other essential supplies, were to be closed and that thereafter "heatless Mondays" were to be observed for the next nine weeks. At first denounced as both arbitrary and unnecessary, Garfield's order was soon conceded to be essential for the success of the war effort. "Daylight saving" was one of the lasting features of Garfield's program to conserve coal and electricity.

Less known to the general public than the well-advertised activities of Hurley, Hoover, Garfield, and McAdoo was the work of the War Trade Board, headed by Vance McCormick. A number of laws, culminating in the Trading-with-the-Enemy Act of October, 1917, gave it control over all American exports and imports. Through a system of licenses and black-listing of firms in neutral countries, the British blockade of Germany was powerfully implemented and each month the economic strangulation of the enemy came closer to fulfillment.

Bernard Baruch: Economic Dictator

Meantime, the need for arming and equipping a vast military machine had made the government the most important customer of American industry. The difficulty was that the government contracted for the products of the nation's factories not as a single unit, but through numerous separate and competing agencies. The confusion was increased by the separate purchasing activities of the Allies and by shortages that inevitably developed as one industry bid against another for essential raw materials. After struggling with various expedients, the Council of National Defense finally created the War Industries Board in July, 1917, with Frank A. Scott, a Cleveland manufacturer, as its first chairman, to set up a system of priorities and fix prices for necessary raw materials.

The War Industries Board had at first merely advisory powers, and neither government purchasing agencies on one side nor businessmen on the other were legally obliged to follow its orders. The need for independent status having become increasingly apparent, in 1918 Bernard Baruch was named chairman

And, By Ginger, He Can Play 'em All! But it keeps Uncle Sam busy these days. (By Donahey in the *Cleveland Plain Dealer*.)

and given vast powers, while the board was made an administrative agency directly responsible to the President.

In the end, Baruch's organization served as a clearinghouse to which all government purchasing bureaus and those of the Allies submitted their requirements. The board then planned how these were to be met and which needs were to be given priority. The search for new sources of critical raw materials led Baruch's lieutenants to survey not only the resources of the United States, but those of the rest of the world. The construction of new industrial plants was made possible, and existing ones were guided in their conversion from civilian to war production. The country had passed for the time being under a planned economy, and Baruch, affable and diplomatic though he was, wielded the broad powers of an economic dictator.

Continued criticism of governmental inefficiency by Democrats and Republicans alike led to the passage of the Overman Act in May, 1918, which empowered Wilson to reorganize the wartime agencies and consolidate more effectively their functions. Making prompt use of this authority, the President met regularly with the Secretaries of War and the Navy and the heads of the six most prominent boards; in effect this group could be considered a war cabinet, which operated more efficiently than had the previous more or less separate agencies.

There were many disappointments in war production. To create a vast aircraft industry proved much more difficult than was anticipated. By Armistice Day about 1,100 planes and 32,000 "Liberty" motors had been manufactured, but only 200 of them reached American combat aviators. Not until three months before the armistice were Browning machine guns available in quantities sufficient to equip the American troops at the front, while the war was over before American-made artillery appeared in France. In many lines, as in shipping, American production was just beginning to achieve large volume when hostilities ceased. This led to pointed criticisms of the administration in both Congress and the press, but to the Germans the wonder was not that the Yankees produced so little, but that they produced so much. When the Kaiser's generals undertook in later years to explain why the Fatherland lost the war, they gave full credit to American industry, and they uttered the name "Baruch" with regretful awe. Strangely enough, it had remained for the United States— antimilitary in tradition though it was—to develop the organization of "total war."

Labor and the War

One of the country's greatest assets during 1917 and 1918 was the patriotism and loyalty of Samuel Gompers. Not only did the president of the AFL efficiently combat radical socialists who sought to convince the workers that the war was merely for capitalistic aggrandizement, but he prevented many strikes and allayed the natural uneasiness with which union men saw women and non-union labor streaming into war-plant jobs. The general public, observing Gompers fraternizing with important industrialists of the Council of National Defense, was as much amazed as if the vision of the wolf dwelling with the lamb had suddenly become reality.

On the issue of wages, however, labor's patience had definite limits. With the cost of living rapidly rising and the country's wage scales none too generous to begin with, there were demands for pay increases on every side. In taking over the railroads, the government found itself faced with a particularly serious situation. Despite increases during 1916 and 1917, 80 per cent of the railroad employees received only $100 a month or less. The government proceeded to grant substantial raises, not only to meet the rising cost of living, but "to find a just and equitable basis which would outlive the war and which would give a living wage and decent working conditions to every railroad employee." The war had made the government the country's greatest employer, with thousands of workers receiving pay in government-owned shipyards and war plants. More-over, many private construction companies and factories were working on war contracts on a cost-plus basis. On every hand, the payment of higher wages seemed infinitely preferable to serious labor controversy.

Since disputes and strikes still threatened production in many quarters, a National War Labor Board was appointed in April, 1918, with ex-President Taft and Frank P. Walsh, a prominent labor lawyer, as joint chairmen. During the first year the board held more than a thousand hearings and made recommenda-tions when all other methods of settlement had failed. In the few instances where the rulings were ignored, the President used or threatened coercion. Thus the War Department commandeered the Smith and Wesson plant at Spring-field, Massachusetts, after non-compliance by its management, and workers at Bridgeport, Connecticut, were threatened with cancellation of their draft deferments for resisting orders of the Taft-Walsh Board.

Other important new agencies were the War Labor Policies Board with Felix Frankfurter as chairman, which worked out uniform labor standards for government employees, and the United States Employment Service, which found jobs for 3.7 million men and women.

Where the Money Came From

Waging modern war involved the expenditure of money in amounts which seemed fabulous to Americans accustomed to peacetime national budgets of less than $750 million annually. Between July 1, 1917, and June 30, 1920, the outlays of the United States government averaged $12.5 billion each year.

A few prominent citizens believed that the war could be financed on a "pay-as-you-go" basis. The American Committee on War Finance advocated such a policy, and Senator LaFollette urged it in the Senate—largely because it would penalize war manufacturers whom he suspected of having forced the country into hostilities. Most Americans, however, believed that taxes sufficiently heavy to pay current war bills would paralyze national economic life. Secretary of the Treasury McAdoo eventually recommended that one third of the costs be met by taxation and the remainder by loans. Most businessmen preferred the ratio of taxes to loans to be about one to five—the ratio of Federal financing during the Civil War.

The Revenue Act of 1917 levied excise taxes on nearly everything in sight; in addition to such familiar tax victims as tobacco and alcoholic beverages, the list now included transportation, communications, insurance, automobiles, pianos, phonographs, amusements, jewelry, patent medicines, and even chewing gum. The principal controversy was over rates for income and war profits taxes; no one knew just how much the recipients of large incomes could or should pay. After allowing $1,000 exemption for unmarried persons and $2,000 for heads of families, the final schedule provided for graduated taxes that rose from 2 per cent on the lowest taxable incomes to 67 per cent on incomes in excess of $2 million. Corporations were taxed 6 per cent of their net income, while profits in excess of what was considered normal both on the basis of invested capital and prewar earnings were taxed at rates graduated from 20 to 60 per cent.

Never before had the government laid such heavy taxes directly on individuals and corporations, yet the war machine demanded still more. The Revenue Act of 1918 raised income taxes to 6 per cent on the lowest brackets and to 77 per cent on incomes of the highest level—over $1 million. The corporation income tax was doubled, while excess profits were subjected to an 80 per cent levy in the highest bracket.

Meantime, the government was borrowing from its own citizens in amounts hitherto deemed impossible by practical financiers. When the first Liberty Loan drive was being planned, J. P. Morgan advised $1 billion as the goal, but the optimistic McAdoo decided to seek twice that amount. When the books were closed on this loan, the McAdoo quota was oversubscribed by more than $1 billion. Succeeding loans were equally successful and the four Liberty Loans and the Victory Loan—sold just after the armistice—brought into the Treasury almost $21.5 billion. School children and others of small means contributed another $800 million by buying thrift stamps and war-savings certificates.

The Liberty Bond campaigns were skillfully organized through committees in every city, town, and village. Moving-picture programs were interrupted so that patriotic appeals could be made from the stage by "four-minute" speakers, while in the larger cities, stage and screen celebrities contributed their services to sell bonds. So successfully was the message hammered home that more than 21 million individuals purchased bonds during the fourth drive.

The United States spent almost $22 billion in direct war expenditures and loaned another $10 billion to its cobelligerents. Just about one third of the total outlay was raised by taxes and the remainder by loans; war financing, in short, followed closely the recommendations of Secretary McAdoo.

Witch-Hunting

As soon as war was declared, many Americans became acutely spy-conscious. They imagined they saw mysterious lights at night, or asserted that German agents were plotting to poison Red Cross bandages or to wipe out entire communities by planting germs in the public drinking water. Such hysterical ideas were not entirely unnatural, since there had been some evidence of German sabotage activities during the days of neutrality. German-Americans were suspected of disloyalty and were the victims of numerous local persecutions.

Congress enacted new laws empowering the government to deal drastically with treasonable activities. The Espionage Act of June, 1917, provided penalties running to $10,000 fine and twenty years' imprisonment for those who willfully caused or attempted to cause insubordination in the armed services or obstructed recruiting. Also subject to punishment were persons who willfully made false reports and statements with intent to interfere with the operation or success of the military or naval forces. The Postmaster General was authorized to bar from the mails any letter, pamphlet, book, or newspaper that violated any provision of the act or that advocated treason, insurrection, or forcible resistance to any law of the United States.

Drastic though the Espionage Act was, especially as vigorously administered by Attorney General Gregory and Postmaster General Burleson, still more powers were granted in the Trading-with-the-Enemy Act of October, 1917. In addition to its sections dealing with the control of foreign trade, the law authorized the appointment of an Alien Property Custodian to take over and administer the property of enemy aliens resident in the United States and that of corporations controlled by enemy nationals. Furthermore, it empowered the President to set up a censorship over all channels of communication between the United States and other countries, and widened the Post Office Department's powers to exclude material from the mails in a manner that amounted to an effective censorship of the foreign-language press. In April, 1918, the Sabotage Act was passed, making it a Federal offense to damage or destroy war material, utilities, or transportation, whether public or private.

Still the advocates of ruthless suppression of all subversive activities were not satisfied. In May 1918, the so-called Sedition Act amended the Espionage Act to provide penalties for saying or doing anything to obstruct the sale of Liberty Bonds; for uttering, writing, or printing "any disloyal, scurrilous, or abusive language" about the form of government of the United States, the Constitution, the armed forces, or the flag, or language intended to bring these institutions into contempt or disrepute; or for advocating curtailment of war production. The Postmaster General's powers were further extended to exclude any written matter of this description from the mails. The Sedition Act was far more drastic than the Espionage Act because the government now only need prove that an accused person had used disloyal language; it was no longer necessary to establish that some harmful consequence to the war effort had resulted.

The Department of Justice took vigorous action under these laws. 1,532 persons were arrested for disloyal utterances, 65 for threats against the President, and 10 for sabotage. Actual plots, however, were few. Now that the unwanted war had come, all but a few German-Americans proved thoroughly loyal. Such pro-Germanism as survived was not often expressed where unsympathetic neighbors might hear.

The principal victims of these laws were Socialists and other radicals who opposed war on ideological grounds, rather than because of sympathy for the enemy. Mrs. Rose Pastor Stokes was sentenced to ten years' imprisonment for asserting, "I am for the people and the government is for profiteers." A higher court set aside her conviction, but Eugene V. Debs was not so fortunate. Before he was finally pardoned by President Harding on Christmas Day, 1921, the veteran head of American Socialism served thirty-two months of his ten-year sentence for a speech in which he referred to the war as the supreme curse of capitalism. Leaders of the IWW, accused of using the war situation to destroy the existing economic system, were dealt with even more severely. One hundred of them were brought to trial in the Chicago court of Judge Kenesaw Mountain Landis. Although the trial lasted 138 days, the jury took but four hours to find them all guilty. Judge Landis sentenced the fifteen most prominent leaders to twenty-year terms, thirty-five others to ten years, and the rest to less drastic penalties. The fines aggregated $2,300,000—a blow from which the IWW never really recovered.

Freedom of the press suffered even more than freedom of speech. The watchful eyes of Postmaster General Burleson's assistants were everywhere. Papers accused of violating the espionage acts were penalized, not only by having the single offending issue barred from the mails, but by being declared unmailable for the future no matter how circumspect their conduct. Such was the fate of German-American newspapers like the Philadelphia *Tagenblatt*, Irish-American papers like the *Gaelic American*, and radical periodicals like the *Masses* and the *Milwaukee Leader*. Although the witch-hunting record of the Wilson administration was inconsistent with its notable progressive achievements of earlier years, it must be remembered that the government was acting in response to insistent public opinion and was widely criticized as being too lenient. "Disloyalty"—a word of dangerously vague meaning—was for the time being considered the most heinous of crimes.

The unpopularity of all things German reached ludicrous extremes. Public demand compelled the statue of Frederick the Great in Washington to be taken down and ignominiously stored away in the basement of a War Department building. Local officials ordered instruction in German to be halted in many public schools; German operas and opera singers were boycotted; the great violinist, Fritz Kreisler, was not allowed to play in a concert at East Orange, New Jersey. To the ultrapatriotic, German measles became "liberty measles," dachshunds "liberty pups," and sauerkraut "liberty cabbage."

Advertising America

Soon after the United States entered the war, the Army and Navy Departments urged that there be strict censorship of the news to prevent vital information from reaching the enemy. The newspapers, however, violently protested against the establishment of such controls. In his perplexity, Wilson turned with relief to the suggestion of George Creel, a dynamic free-lance journalist and editor, who asserted that what was needed was not censorship in the conventional sense of the word, but an agency that should provide the press with the fullest possible information, relying upon voluntary cooperation of the newspapers to refrain from publishing material that might help the enemy.

The President promptly appointed a Committee on Public Information, with the Secretaries of State, War, and the Navy as members and Creel as executive head. Like so many other war agencies that had started as committees or boards, the Committee on Public Information speedily became a one-man affair. Unencumbered by his fellow committeemen and loyally supported by Wilson, Creel built up a vast organization engaged in a great variety of activities.

The first modest function assumed by Creel's staff was to serve as a liaison agency between the various government departments and Washington reporters. The CPI's offices were open twenty-four hours a day, grinding out mimeographed releases for the newspapers, releases that were soon given a more pretentious form by being published daily in a new periodical, the *Official Journal*.

But Creel soon organized more ambitious projects. His job, as he conceived it, was to sell the war to the American people and Wilson's ideals of a democratic peace to the world. On the domestic front, leading American illustrators, men like Charles Dana Gibson, James Montgomery Flagg, Howard Chandler Christy, and Joseph Pennell, contributed their efforts to preparing a remarkable series of war posters. College professors under the leadership of Guy Stanton Ford, Professor of History at the University of Minnesota, wrote popular pamphlets explaining the nation's war aims. The varied talents of novelists, dramatists, musicians, actors, and motion-picture directors were all employed in arousing the patriotic enthusiasm of the country. Perhaps the most remarkable of Creel's feats at home was the enlistment of 75,000 speakers or "Four-Minute Men." These privates in the CPI army fired 7,555,190 speeches at their fellow-countrymen assembled in moving-picture theaters, lodge meetings, schools, and churches; they even invaded lumber camps and Indian reservations where they found some of their most enthusiastic audiences. The Four-Minute Men sold Liberty Bonds, explained the draft, urged food and fuel conservation, and attacked rumor-mongers.

Creel was a devoted disciple of Wilson. He believed that the great war speeches in which the President gave expression to his abiding faith in democracy, his hatred of militarism, and his hope for future peace should be given the widest possible circulation. Through CPI agencies abroad, the speeches were translated and published in almost every country. A volume of Wilson's messages became a best seller in China, and the text of one address was used as a schoolbook in Madrid.

But the audiences that Creel most of all wanted to reach were the German army and the German home front. Therefore CPI pamphlets printed in German were showered down from airplanes and shot over no man's land from guns. Some of the propaganda bombs consisted of facts, figures, and pictures designed to impress the enemy with the size of the American war effort and the hopelessness of further resistance; others were translations of Wilson's speeches offering a just peace if the Germans rebelled against their war lords. The effectiveness of these tactics was evidenced by the frantic efforts of the German government to prevent its subjects from reading the CPI literature.

Creel made mistakes. He believed truth was his best weapon; yet under the pressure of war psychology, he sometimes distorted the facts. He sold Wilsonian-idealism so completely to the common people of the world that they were bitterly disillusioned when the peace settlement fell short of perfection. He was worse than tactless in dealing with Congress, where he made dangerous enemies for both himself and Wilson. Despite these shortcomings, Creel's accomplishments were remarkable. He was a pioneer in the field of political warfare and, as truly as Pershing and Baruch, he was one of the architects of German defeat.

The War Fronts

The German High Command had resorted to unlimited submarine warfare in the twin beliefs that this weapon would bring speedy victory and that the United States, even though it might enter the war, could not exert any effective military pressure. During the spring and summer of 1917 both premises seemed all too sound. The submarine campaign was dangerously effective, while America's unreadiness for real fighting was evident to friend and foe alike.

Unless the seas could be rendered safe for Allied shipping, Germany's defeat seemed impossible. When Admiral Sims took over his European command, a convoy system had not been instituted because the British did not have enough destroyers for the task, and they doubted, moreover, that merchant ships could be kept in formation and moving at the same speed. Even the antisubmarine patrols then in use needed many more ships. In answer to frantic appeals from Sims, the Navy Department hurried into service every vessel that could be used against U-boats, and the building of destroyers and subchasers was given priority in naval construction.

The ensuing battle against underwater raiders became a grim contest in which new methods and tactics were constantly tried. Improved means of detection and more powerful depth charges helped in this struggle. Despite the difficulties, more and more shipping moved in convoys protected by destroyers and other small craft. The most ingenious stratagem was that of bottling up the submarines in the North Sea with a string of mines from Scotland to Norway. This gigantic task had not been completed when the war ended, but already it had proved effective. One out of every ten German submarines trying to cross the barrier was destroyed, and many more were so badly damaged that they had to return to port. The morale of the crews was thereby seriously shaken.

The success of the antisubmarine campaign was to be measured not alone by the steadily declining toll of Allied shipping losses after April, 1917, but also by the safety in which American soldiers were ferried across the Atlantic. It was the proud boast of the navy that not a single troopship was lost on the way to Europe. Three troopships, however, were torpedoed on the return voyage, and the Cunard liner *Tucania* was sunk off Ireland in February, 1918, with the loss of about 175 American lives.

Pershing had asked for a million men by the end of May, 1918, but it seemed impossible that he would get them. Up to March 1, 1918, only 291,000 had been sent across. The delay was caused partly by the necessity for building camps and training the men in America, and partly by the scarcity of shipping to carry the troops. American facilities were entirely inadequate, and the British found it difficult to help because of their losses. They could spare vessels for transporting

American soldiers only by diverting them from carrying vital supplies to England itself. This they were at first most reluctant to do.

This British hesitancy was closely linked with a delicate issue that was being violently contested behind the scenes: the disposition of the troops when they reached France. From the beginning, General Pershing had insisted on a separate American army, fighting on its own sector of the front under its own commanders. The British and French authorities opposed this proposition, however, because they feared Pershing would hoard his men until he had enough for an effective army; thus Germany might achieve victory before the Americans were ready. Moreover, with the troops untested and the officers inexperienced, it might be actually dangerous to entrust any sizable section of the front to Pershing. Instead, the Allies wanted American units to support the British and French armies already in the field. Despite direct appeals by Lloyd George and Clemenceau to Wilson, the President stood by his commander. So long as this difference of opinion continued, the British hated to gamble their precious shipping on the American Expeditionary Force.

Pershing was not unwilling to loan units to the Allies for limited periods or to meet special emergencies, because this would provide valuable training for his troops. Consequently, battalions of the American First Division participated in combat with the French forces in Lorraine as early as October 21, 1917. The experience gained enabled the Americans under Major General Robert L. Bullock to take over a quiet sector near Toul in mid-January, 1918.

In early 1918 the Germans staged a drive they hoped would win the war, and their hopes were re-enforced by several factors. The Bolsheviks, who had overthrown the Kerensky government in November, 1917, were forced to agree to the harsh terms of the Treaty of Brest-Litovsk in May, 1918, which took Russia out of the war and gave Germany access to the agricultural wealth of Ukraine. Moreover, the bulk of the Kaiser's armies were shifted to the western front to add weight to the offensive. For four months the Allied lines were subjected to terrific hammer blows that threatened complete disaster. The peril of the situation was increased by the lack of British and French reserves, by the fact that they were still under separate commands, and by the hesitancy of one army to divert units to rescue some sector held by another.

The German offensive, beginning along the Somme River on March 21, drove more than thirty miles in six days—greater gains than either side had achieved since 1914, and a wide gap was torn in the Allied lines. Desperate British countermeasures were required to stabilize the front. Ludendorff threw a second juggernaut into motion on April 9, this time in the Flanders region. Although deep penetrations were made, the Germans failed to keep their offensive rolling.

These near-disasters drove home to the Allies both the necessity of unified command and the desperate need for American reinforcements. After a series of conferences, General Ferdinand Foch was designated Commander-in-Chief of the Allied Armies in April. Pershing at once offered him all American resources overseas and agreed to delay the establishment of a separate American army until the military situation improved.

Herculean efforts were now made to move American troops across the Atlantic, with the British diverting as much of their shipping to this service as possible. Thus 85,000 soldiers were transported to France in March, 120,000 in April, and a monthly average of 263,000 for the next six months. The first million men arrived by July 1, and a million more had come by Armistice Day. The new arrivals required more training behind the lines before they were ready for active combat, but by summer more and more Americans were moving to the fighting zones.

Neither friend nor foe had had as yet the opportunity to measure the quality

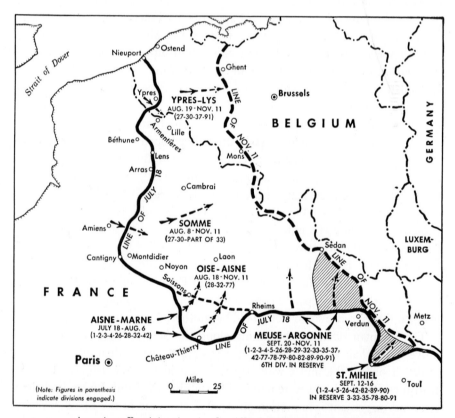

American Participation in the Allied Offensives of 1918. Based on map in *The War With Germany, A Statistical Summary,* Washington, 1919. (By permission of the Central Statistical Office, Office of the Chief of Staff.)

of the American forces. The first real test came when the First Division attacked Cantigny, strategically located near the tip of the Somme salient. Not only did the Americans take the village on May 28, but they held it against seven German counterattacks during the next two days.

Meantime, the third and most dangerous of the German drives had been struck against the French left flank west of Rheims. In the first three days the offensive reached Chateau-Thierry on the Marne River, only fifty miles from Paris. Once again American troops—this time the Second Division and units from the Third and Twenty-eighth—were thrown into battle, and with the French they halted the advance. After a week of desperate fighting, the Americans regained Belleau Wood and thereby stabilized the line again.

The Germans, still maintaining the initiative, launched two more offensives. The first, directed west of the Marne salient in June, was halted after a gain of six miles. The second, begun on July 14 in the Champagne sector around Rheims, hoped to roll down the Marne Valley to Paris. "If my offensive at Rheims succeeds, we have won the war," declared Ludendorff; but once again a combination of American and French troops prevented a break-through.

Foch Strikes Back

This was the final turning point of the war. The Germans had thrown all their resources into these five mighty blows; thereafter the preponderance of strength lay with the Allies as more and more American divisions became ready for action. As soon as the enemy had been stopped at Rheims, Foch directed his first great counterblow at the Marne salient. American troops, now well regarded, were used to spearhead the drive on July 18, and after three weeks of fighting they controlled the entire salient.

At long last on August 10, Pershing gained command of an army of his own, the First American Army, made up of divisions that for the past crucial months had been strengthening the French and British lines. This new army was assigned to eliminate the St. Mihiel salient east of Verdun, which the Germans had held since 1914. Thirty-six hours after the opening attack on September 12, the salient was wiped out.

General Pershing hoped to keep his offensive rolling toward the great fortress of Metz, a vital nerve center in the German communications system, but Foch had other plans. His earlier limited offensive had aimed at eventually launching a grand assault on the Hindenburg Line, the deep defense zone the Germans had been preparing for four years. The new task of the American First Army was to attack west of Verdun in the Meuse-Argonne sector through a heavily fortified terrain filled with hills, ravines, rivers, and forests. It was a vital zone because not far beyond lay the Mézières-Metz railroad on which the whole German front was dependent.

On September 26, Foch's grand assault began, with the Americans holding 24 miles of the flaming 200-mile front. The First Army found the initial going desperately difficult, its attack soon bogged down, and a reorganization of forces became necessary. The offensive was renewed on October 4, and continued for the next four weeks. This was the greatest battle in which Americans had ever been engaged. The weight of ammunition fired was more than that used by the Union forces in the entire Civil War, and each day's gains were to be measured in yards, not miles. But by October 20 the Argonne Forest lay behind and Pershing's men were ready for their next task—that of cutting the Mézières-Metz railroad. This new attack, opening on November 1, brought decisive results. Within a week the German line was broken, the outskirts of Sedan were reached, bridgeheads were established across the Meuse River, and the vital railroad had been cut.

Elsewhere along the broad front the French, British, and Belgians had been equally successful. The Hindenburg Line was everywhere broken, and the Germans had been pushed back toward their own borders. Disasters even more catastrophic had befallen the Central Powers in the Balkan and Italian theaters. On September 29 Bulgaria accepted Allied armistice terms, Turkey followed suit October 30, and Austria-Hungary surrendered on November 3.

Acknowledging that the war was lost, the German High Command had urged as early as October 1 that an armistice be sought. Preliminary negotiations began on October 3 and were hastened along by the crumbling of the western front and the spread of revolution throughout Germany. On November 7, German delegates passed through the lines to receive Foch's terms. On November 11, in a dramatic meeting in the forest of Compiègne, the armistice was signed and, at 11 A.M. that day, the military phase of World War I ended.

This victory was not achieved without cost. The total American casualties were 321,000, of whom 39,000 were killed in action, 62,700 died of disease, 201,000 were wounded, and 4,400 were taken prisoner. Seven per cent of all those mobilized were on the casualty list. Compared to the 73 per cent casualties suffered by the French and the 36 per cent by the British Empire, American losses were extremely light. It should be remembered, however, that American troops were in the front lines only a few months. The actual battles in which the Yanks engaged were among the most bitterly fought and most bloody in American history.

11

The Treaty of Versailles—
Made and Rejected

With the military battle won, the next great challenge to the world's states-men was to negotiate a satisfactory peace. Woodrow Wilson's dearest dream was to be the architect of a new world order, which would be founded upon jus-tice and buttressed by a universal league of nations. Of all the goals to which the President had dedicated himself, this proved to be the hardest to achieve. First, he had to struggle with the heads of the Allied governments, each eager to ad-vance as best he could his own nation's special interests. More formidable still was the opposition to Wilson's program to be found in his own country, espe-cially among certain Republican Senators. The American enemies ultimately gained the upper hand and destroyed most of Wilson's handiwork.

Evolution of War Aims

As soon as the European war began, shocked Americans started to consider the means by which such conflicts might be prevented in the future. On June 17, 1915, the League to Enforce Peace was organized at a large meeting in Inde-pendence Hall, Philadelphia. This new association, under the leadership of former President Taft and President A. Lawrence Lowell of Harvard, advocated the establishment of an international court of justice to which all "justiciable" questions arising between nations should be submitted and a league of nations that would employ its joint forces against any state rejecting these procedures.

Local chapters of the League to Enforce Peace were founded throughout the country, and hundreds of speakers urged its program.

Even before the formation of the new association, President Wilson had been thinking along the same general lines and, as time went on, he made it abundantly clear that he considered the establishment of some kind of league of nations to be the essential foundation to any permanent peace after the war.[1] Sir Edward Grey's correspondence with Colonel House indicated that the British government also favored the organization of such a league. Indeed, British public opinion appeared to demand it.

By January, 1917, Wilson had formulated other principles necessary to undergird a durable postwar settlement. In his "Peace without Victory" speech he asserted that it must be a peace between equals and one that recognized the ideal of government by the consent of the governed, freedom of the seas, and disarmament. His war message three months later declared that the United States was entering the contest to make the world safe for democracy.

By the end of 1917, there arose an insistent public demand for a much more specific statement of war aims than anyone had yet made. The demand was partially the result of the publication by the newly established Bolshevik government in Russia of secret treaties found in the Tsarist archives. These treaties pointed to an old-fashioned division of spoils in case of an Allied victory. Repudiating these pacts, the Bolsheviks gave wide publicity to their own ideals for a just peace: no annexations nor indemnities, and self-determination for subject nationalities. The effect of these developments was to raise searching questions. To what end were the peoples of all the belligerent nations being called upon to make such terrible sacrifices? Was it simply to serve the territorial ambitions of the rival powers? Or was there some happier alternative—some hope that, when the guns were stilled, a better world would emerge?

Wilson's answer to these questions was embodied in the most famous of all his state papers, the speech to Congress on January 9, 1918, in which the "Fourteen Points" were set forth. As the basis for an enduring peace, Wilson advocated:

1. "Open covenants of peace, openly arrived at. . . ."
2. "Absolute freedom of navigation upon the seas . . . alike in peace and in war," except as the seas may be closed by international action for the enforcement of international covenants.

---

[1] Although Roosevelt, Taft, and Wilson were all interested in maintaining world peace, their conceptions of how it could be attained were basically different. Roosevelt believed that such peace could be preserved by some type of international police power that would enforce peace. Taft, through the League to Enforce Peace, desired to codify international law and thereby make it more definite. Then some type of international agency or court, using such law as authority, would attempt to conciliate differences. Were it unsuccessful, it could resort to economic sanctions or military power to force a hostile nation to return to peace. Wilson, on the other hand, concluded that the best way to preserve world peace was by resolving international conflict by discussion, publicity, and compromise through an association of all nations—that is, through a form of international democracy.

3. "The removal, as far as possible, of all economic barriers and the establishment of an equality of trade conditions. . . ."

4. Reduction of armaments "to the lowest point consistent with domestic safety."

5. Impartial adjustment of all colonial claims in which "the interests of the populations concerned must have equal weight with the equitable claims of the government whose title is to be determined."

6. Evacuation of all Russian territory and an unhampered opportunity for Russia to determine her own political development and national policy.

7. Evacuation and restoration of Belgium without any attempt to limit her sovereignty.

8. All French territory to be freed and the invaded portions restored, "and the wrong done to France by Prussia in 1871 in the matter of Alsace-Lorraine . . . should be righted . . ."

9. Readjustment of the frontiers of Italy "along clearly recognizable lines of nationality."

10. Freest opportunity of autonomous development for the peoples of Austria-Hungary, but without destroying the country.

11. Rumania, Serbia, and Montenegro to be evacuated and restored, Serbia accorded free and secure access to the sea, and the relations of the several Balkan states to one another determined "along historically established lines of allegiance and nationality . . ."

12. An independent Polish state including "the territory inhabited by indisputably Polish populations, which would be assured a free and secure access to the sea. . . ."

13. Secure sovereignty for the Turkish portions of the Ottoman Empire, but other nationalities then under Turkish rule should be assured security of life and an opportunity for autonomous development, and "the Dardenelles should be permanently opened as a free passage to the ships and commerce of all nations under international guarantees."

14. "A general association of nations must be formed under specific covenants for the purpose of affording mutual guarantees of political independence and territorial integrity to great and small states alike."

This speech made a tremendous impression—not because it contained many novel or unfamiliar ideas, but for the contrary reason that it stated in memorable phrases the thoughts running in the minds of people in many countries. Indeed only three days earlier, Prime Minister Lloyd George had stated British objectives in very similar terms.

Wilson discussed the bases of a just peace in several other speeches during 1918. On February 11 he added to the Fourteen Points "Four Principles." The second and fourth were particularly appealing: the former asserted "that peoples and provinces are not to be bartered about from sovereignty to sovereignty as if they were mere chattels and pawns in a game . . ."; the latter stated "that all well-defined national aspirations shall be accorded the utmost satisfaction that can be accorded them without introducing new or perpetuating old elements of discord and antagonism. . . ." In a Fourth-of-July address at Mount

Vernon, the President spoke of the "Four Ends" for which the United States and the Allies were fighting. The first of these called for "the destruction of every arbitrary power anywhere that can separately, secretly, and of its single choice disturb the peace of the world . . ." All four objects, Wilson declared, could be summed up in a single sentence: "What we seek is the reign of law, based upon the consent of the governed and sustained by the organized opinion of mankind."

The last of the great war speeches was that of September 27, 1918, when President Wilson spoke at the Metropolitan Opera House in New York City on the occasion of the opening of the Fourth Liberty Loan. To the Fourteen Points and its corollaries were now added "Five Particulars." Those meriting special mention were the first: "The impartial justice meted out must involve no discrimination between those to whom we wish to be just and those to whom we do not wish to be just . . ."; and the third, stating that "there can be no leagues or alliances or special covenants and understandings within the general and common family of the League of Nations."

Armistice Negotiations

In the fall of 1918 when the German officials acknowledged to themselves that they had lost the war, they turned to the Fourteen Points in the desperate hope that they might obtain lenient treatment. Accordingly, it was to the American President that Prince Max addressed his request of October 3 for an armistice. Wilson, however, proved to be not so naively eager for immediate peace as the Germans thought that he would be. While Foch hammered back the German lines, the President exchanged notes with the enemy government, demanding categorical acceptance of the principles that he had laid down in his war speeches, a promise to evacuate all Allied territory, a cessation of submarine attacks upon passenger liners, and an assurance that the arbitrary power of the Kaiser and of the German generals had been placed under constitutional checks. Only after his adroit diplomacy had secured these things did the President consent on October 23 to transmit the German armistice request to the Allies.

Now the problem was transferred to the European capitals. The military commanders had to decide whether it was expedient to halt hostilities, and, if so, on what terms. The British General Haig thought that mild armistice terms should be offered so as to ensure their acceptance; Pershing preferred that there should be no armistice at all; Foch, whose decision was final, favored an armistice with terms so drastic that Germany could not possibly renew the war. Meanwhile, the heads of the Allied governments were debating whether or not they would accept the Fourteen Points as the basis of peace. They were at first reluctant to do so, and Colonel House had to warn them that refusal might result in the United States dropping out of the war. Finally, after studying an interpretation of the famous document prepared by Frank I. Cobb and Walter Lippmann, two able journalists who were acting as advisers to Colonel House, the Allied statesmen accepted the Wilsonian principles with one reservation and one elucidation. The second of the Fourteen Points, relating to freedom of the seas, they asserted, was "open to various interpretations, some of which they could not accept. They must, therefore, reserve to themselves complete freedom in this subject when they enter the peace conference." This reservation obviously reflected the ideas of the British; those of the French were represented in the stipulation that Germany must not only evacuate invaded territory but compensate "for all damage done to the civilian population of the Allies and their property by the aggression of Germany by land, by sea, and from the air."

On November 5, President Wilson informed the German government of the Allied reply; if the Germans wanted to proceed, they could learn the actual armistice terms by sending representatives through the lines to meet General Foch. The Germans did so at once; their envoys received Foch's terms on November 8, appealed to Berlin for further instructions, and finally signed the armistice agreement on November 11. This agreement provided for a cessation of hostilities, German evacuation of all non-German territory, Allied occupation of both banks of the Rhine, and German delivery to the Allies of vast quantities of military equipment. Compliance with such terms would make it virtually impossible for the Germans to renew hostilities.

The first Armistice Day was one of delirious rejoicing. Wilson's own happiness was reflected in an exultant statement he gave out to the newspapers:

> Everything for which America fought has been accomplished. It will now be our fortunate duty to assist by example, by sober friendly counsel and by material aid in the establishment of a just democracy throughout the world.

It is no wonder that the President used such phrases. The triumph of his principles appeared to be as complete as the victory of the Allied arms. Not only had the Fourteen Points been accepted as the basis of peace by friend and foe alike but German military autocracy seemed utterly vanquished. The peace-hungry German people, convinced that the Kaiser's continued presence on the throne was a barrier to the granting of an armistice, had risen in revolt. On November 9 the government was turned over to the Socialists, who proclaimed a German republic, and the emperor fled across the border into Holland. It was another great victory for the American statesman who had called for "the destruction of every arbitrary power."

The Rise of Republican Opposition

Actually, however, Wilson's position was less impregnable than these diplomatic victories would indicate. Not only in Europe but in America powerful elements resented his leadership and were waiting for the first opportunity to make their opposition felt.

The most influential Republican was still Theodore Roosevelt, and his hatred for Wilson had become more intense with the passing of the years. Thoroughly loyal and patriotic, Roosevelt supported the war in vigorous public speeches, but at the same time he maintained a constant barrage of criticism of the Wilson administration. He was particularly contemptuous of the President's peace program, although as early as 1910 he himself had expressed the idea that world peace must be backed up by force. Even after the war had begun, Roosevelt said that if the idea of an international police power was utopian, then we must choose between "Utopia or Hell." Yet by 1918 his dislike for Wilson had taken him so far that he tried to sabotage Wilson's October negotiations with Germany by calling upon the Senate to repudiate the Fourteen Points. "Let us dictate peace by the hammering guns," he declared, "and not chat about peace to the accompaniment of clicking typewriters. . . ."

Equally hostile was Senator Henry Cabot Lodge of Massachusetts. He and Roosevelt were close friends, and for years in their private correspondence they had heaped scorn upon the professor in the White House. Like Roosevelt, Lodge thought that an association of nations to enforce future world peace was an excellent idea. In 1915, for example, he had asserted: "The great nations must be so united as to be able to say to any single country, you must not go to war, and they can only say that effectively when the country desiring war knows that the force . . . is irresistible. . . ." A year later he repeated and elaborated on this conviction in a notable address before the League to Enforce Peace. But following Wilson's fervent plea for a league in his "Peace without Victory" speech of January, 1917, the Massachusetts Senator reversed himself completely, warning the Senate that such an international organization might force Oriental immigration upon the United States or "might plunge us into war at any moment at the bidding of other nations."

The Republican leaders were naturally eager to return to power in the national government. They believed that the country was normally Republican and that the Democrats had enjoyed their brief hour of glory only because of animosities within the ranks of the dominant party. With the Congressional election of November, 1918, approaching, strenuous efforts were made to patch up the old quarrel. A new and energetic national chairman, Will H. Hays of Indiana, was appointed, while Roosevelt, Taft, and Root appeared together on public platforms as a visible demonstration that the schism of 1912 was ended. Wilson was accused of desiring a negotiated peace with the Kaiser rather than unconditional surrender, and the third of the Fourteen Points was depicted as a threat to the protective-tariff system. Democratic Congressmen, worried by the aggressiveness of the opposition, beseeched the President for help. Somewhat reluctantly, he issued an appeal to the voters through the newspapers on October 24. Among other things, he said:

> If you have approved of my leadership and wish me to continue to be your unembarrassed spokesman in affairs at home and abroad, I earnestly beg that you will express yourselves unmistakably to that effect by returning a Democratic majority to both the Senate and the House of Representatives. . . . The leaders of the minority in the present Congress have unquestionably been pro-war, but they have been anti-administration. At almost every turn since we entered the war they have sought to take the choice of policy and the conduct of the war out of my hands and put it under the control of the instrumentalities of their own choosing. . . . The return of a Republican majority to either house of the Congress would . . . be interpreted on the other side of the water as a repudiation of my leadership.

Wilson's appeal proved to be a blunder. It offered the Republicans the excuse for casting off the restraint that they might have felt over attacking the President during wartime. Chairman Hays denounced Wilson's words as "ungracious . . . wanton . . . mendacious." The President, it was charged, had cast a slur upon Republican patriotism.

When the votes were counted on November 5, it was learned that the new House of Representatives would have 237 Republicans, 191 Democrats, and 7 Independents, while in the Senate there would be 49 Republicans and 47 Democrats. It was a defeat for the President's party and also for the President himself since, in his own words, Wilson had defined confidence in his leadership as one of the issues of the campaign. The exultant victors asserted that the President had been decisively repudiated. In reality, it was by no means certain that this was so. The war was nearly over, and many voters expressed with their ballots their impatience with wartime restrictions or their sentiments on local issues rather than their opinion of Wilson. Republican victory under the circumstances was probably inevitable, but it was made more damaging to the President than it needed to have been by the role he had assumed during the campaign.

Wilson Goes to Europe

Before November was over, the names of the American peace commissioners were announced. Wilson had long before decided to attend the peace conference in person; to go with him he now named Secretary of State Lansing, Colonel House, General Tasker H. Bliss, and Henry White. It was a competent group. Next to the President himself, Lansing and House were obviously the two best informed men in the country on recent diplomatic developments. Bliss was not only a military expert, but a scholar with an excellent grasp of European economic and political problems, and White had had an unusually distinguished diplomatic career, having held important posts in London, Paris, and Rome.

The President's opponents, however, criticized the appointments severely. Natural though it might seem that the President should wish to go to Paris himself, he was breaking a precedent. Earlier Chief Executives had left to other men the actual work of negotiating treaties of peace. Wilson's decision to head his own delegation was attributed to his vanity or to his "Messiah complex." The commission was further criticized as giving inadequate recognition to the Republicans. True, White was a Republican, but not an active partisan. Why had the President ignored such distinguished leaders as Hughes, Taft, and Root? Finally, the absence of Senators on the delegation was resented as a slight to the body that must give its consent to the ratification of any peace treaty. Although much of the criticism was mere partisanship, it does appear that Wilson's failure to take with him to Paris at least one prominent Senator from each party was a serious mistake—a mistake that played directly into the hands of his enemies.[2]

On December 4, 1918, the liner *George Washington* left New York, bearing the peace commission and scores of advisers and experts on various problems. Key men from the war administration were aboard, as well as numerous college professors and other specialists in history, geography, and economics. These experts had been assembled by Colonel House over the course of the past year. Known as "The Inquiry," they had been gathering facts and figures at their headquarters in New York City for many months. Even this evidence of earnest preparation for the serious tasks ahead was ridiculed by unfriendly newspapers, which sneered at "Colonel House's troupe of performing professors."

The *George Washington* docked at Brest on December 13, but not for another month did the peace conference begin its work. During this period of waiting, President Wilson visited Paris, London, and Rome, where he received a most extraordinary welcome. The enthusiasm of the crowds lining the streets surpassed anything that men could remember. With pathetic trust, common people in all countries were counting on the American President to achieve an impossible goal—a perfect peace settlement.

Lions in the Path

At the very moment when Wilson was enjoying his greatest triumphs, the dangers that confronted him were clearly evident. Behind him in America his

[2] Thomas A. Bailey, *Woodrow Wilson and the Lost Peace* (New York: Macmillan, 1944), pp. 87–105, gives the best account of the selection of the members of the peace delegation and the arguments pro and con as to why Wilson took no member of the Senate and no prominent Republican.

opponents were ceaseless in their activity. Even before the President sailed, Theodore Roosevelt had warned in a statement to the press:

> Our allies and our enemies and Mr. Wilson himself should all understand that Mr. Wilson has no authority whatever to speak for the American people at this time. His leadership has just been emphatically repudiated by them. . . . Mr. Wilson and his fourteen points and his four supplementary points and his five complementary points and all his utterances every which way have ceased to have any shadow of right to be accepted as expressive of the will of the American people. . . .

This bitter document was one of Roosevelt's last contributions to American public discussion. The former President was a desperately sick man, fighting a losing struggle with a tropical ailment he had contracted during a trip to the Amazon in 1913. On January 6, 1919, he died.

But Henry Cabot Lodge remained very much alive. On December 21, 1918, he addressed the Senate at length, stating his belief that the Allies should be permitted to make any territorial settlement they desired without Wilson's intereference, and that the League of Nations should not be included as a part of the peace treaties. The Senate, he said, could, and often had, refused to ratify treaties; many other agreements—and these were significant words—had been "virtually amended." Without waiting to see what kind of league of nations would be proposed, Lodge was already laying careful plans to oppose it. He even went to the extreme of suggesting to Henry White that the latter should communicate these ideas to leading Allied statesmen in order to encourage them to oppose the President; but White honorably refrained from acting upon the suggestion.

On the European front, several major obstacles lay in the President's path. Four years of bitter struggle had created a great public demand for stern punishment of the country that almost universal Allied opinion held guilty for the war. There had been a 1918 election in England as well as in the United States; Lloyd George was victorious, and the most popular electoral appeals were such incendiary slogans as "Hang the Kaiser," "Squeeze the Germans until the pips squeak," and "Make Germany pay for the war." In France, Clemenceau had received an impressive vote of confidence from the Chamber of Deputies under circumstances that indicated popular expectation that he would demand vigorous handling of the hated *Boche.*

Equally dangerous to Wilsonian idealism was the network of secret treaties that had been formulated by the Allied governments before the United States declared war. Italy, as her reward for abandoning neutrality in 1915 and entering the struggle against her former allies, had been promised a strategic frontier in the Alps and along the Adriatic, which would extend her rule not only over "unredeemed" Italians but over thousands of Germans and Slavs as well. Rumania had been promised a large section of Hungary, while Russia, France, and Great Britain had planned a partition of the Turkish Empire. Japan had secured from her hard-pressed Allies their assent to her keeping Germany's Pacific islands north of the equator, as well as German political and economic rights in the Shantung Peninsula on the China coast.

Wilson had long been aware of the existence of most of these documents. Indeed, his appeal for "open covenants of peace, openly arrived at" expressed his disapproval of such bargains. But he refrained from any study of their details. Wilson considered that the entry of the United States into the war, as well as the negotiations leading to the armistice, created a new situation in which the secret treaties should be ignored. Each part of the settlement should be made on the merits of that particular case, without regard to previous agreements. Wilson soon discovered, however, that the Allied statesmen were determined to insist stubbornly on the fulfillment of these old pledges.

The work of peacemaking had to be carried on in an atmosphere of haste and confusion hardly conducive to long and patient consideration of any single problem. Treaties of peace had to be made not only with Germany, but also with Austria, Hungary, Bulgaria, and Turkey. The new states that were making their appearance on the map had to be committed by a separate series of treaties to the decent treatment of their minorities. But these were not the only anxieties of the Peace Conference. All Europe appeared to be tottering on the edge of chaos. A score of petty wars had broken out—both civil wars between rival factions and wars between neighboring nations over disputed boundaries. There were, moreover, unemployment, hunger, and discontent everywhere.

Such unrest seemed doubly dangerous because of the situation in Russia. Might not the wildfire of Communism spread west across the whole continent? This was the greatest of all the fears haunting the peacemakers and impelling them to make important decisions in frantic haste.

In other ways as well, the work of the Peace Conference was hampered by affairs in Russia. That great country was convulsed by civil war, and the Allies were uncomfortably involved. After the Soviet government had made its separate peace with Germany, Allied expeditionary forces were sent into various parts of Russia to try to prevent military supplies from falling into the hands of the Germans. American troops were involved in these operations, both around Archangel and Murmansk and in eastern Siberia. The armistice of November, 1918, ended the necessity for trying to protect the military supplies, but by then the Allies had become entangled in virtual alliances with anti-Bolshevik armies resisting the authority of the Soviet government in various sections of the country.

No question confronting the statesmen at Paris was more perplexing than that of trying to shape a Russian policy. The French government favored all-out military action to suppress the Communist regime, but Lloyd George and Wilson urged instead that Bolshevik and anti-Bolshevik leaders be brought together around a conference table to see whether their differences could be compromised. When this effort failed, President Wilson, with Lloyd George's approval, sent the youthful William C. Bullitt to Moscow on an unofficial and highly confidential mission. Bullitt brought back to Paris a Bolshevik offer to make an armistice, come to a conference, and acknowledge Russia's debts to the Allies, if the latter would restore diplomatic relations and terminate their intervention in Russian internal affairs. When news of these negotiations leaked out to the French and British press, there was such loud condemnation that the whole matter had to be dropped.

The consequence of these failures was most unfortunate. The Allied policy of supplying and encouraging the anti-Bolsheviks continued—not with sufficient volume or energy to be effective, but just enough to plant in the hearts of Soviet leaders a bitterness and suspicion of the Western democracies that would plague international relations for the next generation. The Wilson administration, reluctant from the beginning to send American troops into Russia, began evacuating them from North Russia in May, 1919, and from Siberia in January, 1920. Not until 1933, however, did the United States accord diplomatic recognition to the Soviet government. The hated regime, which had overthrown capitalism in Russia and accepted a separate peace with Germany, was unrepresented at the Peace Conference. Not only did this make it impossible for the Allied statesmen to draw boundary lines in eastern Europe but, what was still more important, no place was provided for vast Russia in the new League of Nations or in the concert of powers which would have an interest in preserving the peace settlement.

Planning the League

On January 18, 1919, the Peace Conference held its first plenary session. Open meetings such as this one, where the delegates of all the nations that had broken relations with Germany were represented, were held on only a few occasions thereafter, and then merely to ratify decisions reached elsewhere. All the important work of the conference was done by smaller groups. From January to March the most important of these was the Council of Ten, which Wilson and Lansing attended along with the two highest ranking delegates from Great Britain, France, Italy, and Japan. Even this proved too cumbersome a body, and from March to June, while the most important issues were being threshed out, the Council of Four, Lloyd George, Clemenceau, Wilson, and Orlando (Premier of Italy), dominated the scene. Most of the work of the conference was done behind carefully guarded doors, with only brief and juiceless communiqués being issued to the press. Critics protested that this was hardly the open diplomacy that Wilson had advocated. But, although the President tried to secure more privileges for the journalists, the other leaders prevailed with their contention that full publicity would advertise each occasion of difference between the victors and stiffen the resistance of the vanquished.

The Big Four at Paris—Lloyd George, Orlando, Clemenceau, and Wilson. (Brown Bros.)

Wilson won two important points early in the negotiations. Against the wishes of France and such British Dominions as Australia and South Africa, the American President prevented outright annexation of the German colonies and the Arab territories of the Turkish Empire. Instead, the mandate principle was accepted. This meant that those areas should be held under a form of trusteeship; the mandatory power should administer them under conditions that would protect the rights of the natives and provide for general supervision by the League of Nations. The President's second early achievement was securing immediate consideration for the League of Nations and an acceptance of the principle that the League should be made an integral part of the peace treaty instead of postponing this issue for a later conference.

A League of Nations Commission, with Wilson as chairman, began the task of drafting a constitution for this new international body. Much preliminary work had already been done by British, French, and American experts and, after long and exhausting night sessions, the document was finally whipped into such form that it could be presented to a plenary session of the conference on February 14.

The proposed Covenant provided for an Assembly in which every member state, large or small, would have one vote, and for a Council on which the Big Five—Great Britain, France, Italy, Japan, and the United States—would have permanent representation with non-permanent seats allotted to four of the smaller powers. In addition to the Assembly and the Council, which were to meet at stated intervals and might be specially convened to deal with emergencies, there was to be a permanent Secretariat to assemble information for the use of the League and to receive and publish the texts of any treaties signed by the member states. Many functions were to be undertaken by the League, including the establishment of a Permanent Court of International Justice, the formulation of plans for international disarmament, the supervision of mandates, the safeguarding of world health, and the promotion of fair conditions of labor. But the League's most important responsibility was to preserve peace. Any future war or threat of war was to be considered a matter of concern to the whole League; members of the League agreed to submit any controversy between them likely to lead to war either to arbitration or to inquiry by the Council, and not to resort to war until three months after an award or report had been made; moreover, if all the members of the Council other than those representing parties to the dispute agreed to certain recommendations, members of the League were bound not to go to war against any nation that complied with these recommendations. Should any member of the League resort to war in disregard of these pledges, it was to be punished by economic sanctions; and the Council, as a last resort, might recommend joint military action against the offending power. What President Wilson regarded as "the heart of the Covenant" was Article 10, which read:

> The Members of the League undertake to respect and preserve as against external aggression the territorial integrity and existing political independence of all Members of the League. In case of any threat of danger of such aggression the Council shall advise upon the means by which this obligation shall be fulfilled.

The day after this draft of the Covenant was presented, Wilson embarked on the *George Washington* for America. Congress was about to adjourn and the President had to be available to sign bills and attend to various affairs that had accumulated during his absence.

At Colonel House's suggestion, Wilson entertained the members of the Senate Foreign Relations Committee at a White House dinner on the evening

Getting a Taste of It. Wilson giving Congress the first sample of the
League of Nations. (By Donahey in the *Cleveland Plain Dealer*.)

of February 26. Until nearly midnight the President explained the Covenant
to the Senators and answered their questions. The Democratic members of
the committee were much impressed; the Republicans were not. It was hard to
say whose attitude was most ominous: that of Senator Brandegee of Connecticut, who cross-examined Wilson like a district attorney; that of Senator Lodge,
who kept silent most of the evening; or that of Senators Borah of Idaho and
Fall of New Mexico, who refused to attend at all.

The President's failure to win over the skeptics was made all too clear less
than a week later. On March 4, the last day of the session, Senator Lodge
requested unanimous consent for consideration of a resolution, asserting that
"the constitution of the League of Nations in the form now proposed to the
peace conference should not be accepted by the United States" and that the
whole proposal should be postponed until after peace was made with Germany.
Immediate objection was registered by a Democratic member—just as Lodge
had hoped. This gave him his opportunity to read into the Congressional
Record the names of thirty-nine Republican Senators, or Senators-elect, who
would have voted for the resolution had they been given the opportunity. This
challenge to the President, henceforth known as the "Round Robin," had been

the idea of Senator Brandegee; its support by thirty-nine Senators was of serious import, since only thirty-three votes were required to block the ratification of a treaty.

The President was entirely unwilling to yield to the Round Robin threat insofar as that maneuver sought to compel him to separate the League Covenant from the peace treaty. If this were done, he feared that the world's best opportunity to secure a league would be lost and the project would be subjected to indefinite delay. On the evening of the same March 4, Wilson and Taft addressed a huge and enthusiastic audience in the Metropolitan Opera House in New York City. In a fighting speech, the President accepted the gauge of battle flung down by his opponents. When the treaty was completed, he said, not only would the Covenant be in it, but so many threads of the treaty would be tied to the Covenant that the Covenant could not be dissected from the treaty without destroying the whole vital structure. That the treaty itself might be rejected, the President apparently had no fear.

On the other hand, Wilson was not hostile to really constructive criticism. Following his return to Paris, a careful study was made of all the suggestions that had been offered by prominent Republicans like Taft, Lowell, Hughes, and Root, and by Democrats like Bryan and Senator Hitchcock of Nebraska. Lodge also had been urged to make specific recommendations, but had refused to do so. Although the President believed that the plan as already drafted adequately safeguarded American rights, he decided to ask for a number of amendments in order to satisfy hesitant Senators. The League of Nations Commission was reconvened, and numerous concessions to the United States were written into the Covenant. The right of a member state to withdraw from the League was recognized, as was the right to refuse a mandate. Domestic questions such as immigration control and tariffs were specifically exempted from League jurisdiction, and provision was made that, for all important questions, the Council and the Assembly would have to agree unanimously upon any course of action. Finally, and most important, it was stated that nothing in the Covenant should be deemed "to affect the validity . . . of regional understandings like the Monroe Doctrine. . . ." The formal recognition of this historic American policy represented a striking diplomatic victory.

Wilson thus fought for and won safeguards that had been demanded by American opinion, but in order to do so he found it necessary to moderate his opposition to certain things that the other powers were seeking.

Completing the Treaty

The period from March 14, when the President returned to Paris, to June 28, when the Treaty of Versailles was finally signed, was one of great and exasperating difficulties. Always frail in health, Wilson aged perceptibly during these weeks of anxiety and overwork. For several days in April he was confined to his bed with an attack of the deadly influenza that had been sweeping both America and Europe.

Clemenceau fought savagely for drastic treaty provisions that he believed vital to French security: French annexation of the coal-rich Saar Basin, detachment of the strategic Rhineland from Germany and its establishment as an independent buffer state, French military occupation of bridgeheads across the Rhine for thirty years, and a crushing reparations burden for the defeated foe. Wilson opposed this program as not only inconsistent with the Fourteen Points, but as providing the seeds of future war. Except on the reparations issue, Lloyd George supported the President. Compromises were finally arranged. In the Saar only the coal mines went to France; administration of the area was entrusted to the League of Nations for fifteen years, after which a plebiscite would determine final disposition of that territory. The Rhineland remained a part of Germany, but was to be permanently demilitarized. Allied troops were to occupy territory along the Rhine for fifteen years. In order to obtain Clemenceau's consent to these decisions, security treaties were signed under which Great Britain and the United States promised to come to the support of France in case she were the victim of unprovoked aggression.[3]

On the reparations issue Wilson was opposed by both Lloyd George and Clemenceau. The American delegation contended that a definite sum should be fixed in the treaty, that it should be based upon a reasonable estimate of Germany's ability to pay, that the period of payments should not extend longer than thirty years, and that Germany's responsibility should be limited to paying for the restoration of devastated areas. Although the President successfully withstood pressure to have Germany's obligations stretched to cover the whole cost of the war, he had to give in to the British contention that Allied pensions bills should be added to civilian damages. In the end, the Treaty of Versailles compelled Germany to sign a blank check—a promise to accept a bill that would be compiled and presented to her by a Reparations Commission in 1921. Thirty-three billion dollars, the sum eventually demanded, proved to be far more than Germany could or would pay.

Two issues that provoked particular anxiety were the Italian demand for Fiume and the Japanese determination to take over Germany's political and economic rights in the Shantung peninsula. Wilson believed that to permit Italy to annex Fiume would be a gross injustice to the new state of Yugoslavia, whose economic position would be highly insecure without this important Adriatic port. He attempted to appeal over Orlando's head directly to the

[3] The treaties never went into effect since they were to remain inoperative unless both Great Britain and the United States ratified them. The American treaty was never reported out of the Senate Foreign Relations Committee.

Italian people, but the gesture failed. Orlando absented himself from the conference for several weeks, returning to Rome where he was given impressive evidence of popular backing in his struggle with Wilson. The Fiume question had to be left unsettled in the Paris treaties.[4] On the Shantung question, the President's sympathies were all with the Chinese spokesmen, who argued that the German leasehold at Kiaochow and the German railroad and mining properties should revert to China. Japan, however, had a very strong case. She was in actual possession, having ousted the Germans by military force when she entered the war in 1914; she had compelled the Chinese government to confirm her rights in 1915 and 1918, she had gained the assent of Great Britain and France to these arrangements by secret treaty in 1917. Fearful lest Japan might quit the conference and refuse to join the League, Wilson gave in. The treaty assigned Germany's economic rights and holdings in Shantung to Japan, although in a separate unsigned declaration the Japanese promised that they would eventually withdraw their troops and restore sovereignty of Shantung to China, keeping only the economic concessions. The Chinese representatives registered their indignant protest by refusing to sign the treaty .

At last, after many stormy sessions, the victorious powers agreed on the terms, which were presented to the German representatives on May 7, 1919. No oral discussion was permitted, but the Germans were allowed to file written protests and counterproposals. At the urging of Lloyd George, a few concessions were made, although Wilson agreed on the whole with Clemenceau that the Germans should be required to accept the treaty as written without further change or delay. The final crisis came in June, when the German cabinet resigned rather than approve the document. Foch was then ordered to march into the heart of Germany unless the Allied terms were accepted within three days. The Germans bowed to this ultimatum and on June 28 the treaty was signed at a dramatic ceremony in the Hall of Mirrors at Versailles.

The Treaty of Versailles has been severely criticized both by those who think it was too soft and by those who think it was too harsh. The former regret that Wilson interfered with Clemenceau's program for the complete crippling of the enemy; the latter denounce the President for not having compelled the other leaders to accept his ideas in every detail. To the first line of criticism it may be answered that a document providing for the almost complete disarmament of the defeated enemy as well as for the absolute demilitarization of his western frontier should have given ample security to France and the rest of Europe. That it did not resulted not from deficiencies in the treaty itself, but from divisions of opinion and weakness of will, which permitted Hitlerite Germany to flout its provisions with impunity.

[4] In 1924 Yugoslavia finally acquiesced in Italian annexation of Fiume in return for certain Italian concessions giving Yugoslavia port facilities and an outlet to the Sea.

A more valid indictment of the Treaty of Versailles is that it broke faith with Germany, which had accepted the 1918 armistice after receiving an explicit stipulation that the Fourteen Points and the other Wilsonian principles should serve as the basis of the peace settlement. As finally drafted, the treaty sinned against the spirit if not the letter of the Fourteen Points. Although most of the points can be said to have been given embodiment in some part of the document, the terms imposed upon the vanquished nation were in the aggregate severe: loss of her entire colonial empire, loss of sizable portions of her territory and population within Europe, loss of important economic resources, limitations on her sovereignty, acknowledgement of war guilt, and a crushing reparations obligation. Two unfortunate results followed from this severity: German opinion was easily aroused by demagogues to regard the whole settlement as so intolerable as to require repudiation at whatever cost; on the other hand, a guilt-complex came to obsess English and American liberals who became so acutely conscious of the shortcomings of the treaty that they failed to see how dangerous it was not to insist upon the fulfillment of its terms. But, if the treaty were too harsh, this at least can be said: it would have been harsher still had not Wilson gone to Paris to fight for his principles. That the great idealist had to compromise on many points was unfortunate, but not to be avoided under conditions as they existed in 1919.[5]

The Treaty of Versailles has, unhappily, been more closely examined for its sins than its virtues. Yet it did not lack for the latter. More nearly than on any preceding map of Europe, boundary lines now followed the principle of nationality.[6] Moreover, the Covenant of the League of Nations offered a more promising opportunity for international cooperation than the world had ever known. Indeed, the President, whose eyes were not blind to the treaty's faults, consoled himself with the thought that whatever was unjust in the settlement might eventually be adjusted through procedures provided in the Covenant. That the League did not in practice function this way was not his fault.

Shortly after the signing of the treaty, the weary President embarked on the *George Washington* for home, leaving Colonel House at the conference to deal with the great volume of still unsettled business. Months of bitter controversy with the Senate lay ahead.

[5] Some writers have questioned why Wilson, in an effort to gain his objectives, did not threaten to withdraw American troops and to withhold rehabilitation loans unless the Allies gave in. But to have taken such a position would have been a contradiction to Wilson's whole conception of international relations. He certainly did not believe, as Theodore Roosevelt had, in resorting to the threat of force to win his way.

[6] Yet in drawing these boundaries, some of them thousands of miles long, the peacemakers sometimes had to put other considerations, such as strategic and economic ones, ahead of self-determination. Wilson was severely criticized for such compromises by many observers, notably two Englishmen, Harold Nicolson and John Maynard Keynes.

Delay on the Treaty

The President's confidence that the concessions he had obtained during his second stay at Paris would disarm his opponents proved to be entirely unwarranted. Lodge announced to the country that the League in its revised form was worse than before and went ahead with his plans to attack the whole Wilsonian settlement.

The Republican leader was a master strategist. His first achievement was to secure the organization of the newly elected Senate in a way certain to create difficulties for the President. Through a well-planned filibuster the Republicans had held up the passage of necessary appropriation bills before the old legislature adjourned on March 4, 1919. This action made it necessary for Wilson to call the new Congress into special session in May. Thus the opposition was given ample opportunity to form its battle lines before the President returned to American with the completed treaty. Not only was Lodge chairman of the powerful Senate Foreign Relations Committee, but the latter was packed with anti-League Republicans.

On July 10, the day after his return, the President appeared before the Senate to submit the treaty and to make a personal appeal for its approval. His position still seemed strong. Even his most bitter opponents were of the opinion that if the treaty came to an immediate vote it would probably be accepted without change. Therefore their strategy had to be one of delay. The Foreign Relations Committee began a leisurely consideration of the document that held it up for the next two months. Lodge killed two weeks by reading the entire treaty line by line, sometimes to an empty committee room. Six weeks more were devoted to public hearings during which self-appointed spokesmen of Ireland, China, India, Egypt, Italy, Persia, and the Ukraine, together with many others claiming to be experts on specific problems, were allowed to register their protests against various details in the settlement.

The committee then requested the President to place all his records of the Paris negotiations at its disposal. This Wilson refused to do—a refusal that gave credence to the charge that he was concealing something. Instead, he invited the committee to confer with him at the White House on August 19. There, after reading a prepared statement in which he tried to answer the various arguments that had been offered against the treaty, he permitted himself to be questioned for more than three hours during which he was asked about every controversial issue. Article 10 of the League Covenant, already under bitter attack, was carefully considered. Of this undertaking "to respect and preserve as against external aggression the territorial integrity and political independence of all Members of the League," Wilson pointed out that the League Council could only "advise upon" the means by which the obligation should be carried out in any particular case. Unless the United States were already involved in the controversy, no advice at all could be given without the assent of the American representative. Moreover, the vote of the Council was only advice, which each government would be free to reject if it pleased. Article 10 created "a moral, not a legal obligation." If left Congress absolutely free to put its own interpretation upon the commitment in all cases that called for action. Notwithstanding this fact, Article 10 seemed to Wilson "to constitute the very backbone of the whole Covenant. Without it the League would be hardly more than an influential debating society."

Concerning reservations to the treaty, he could see no objection to the Senate's passing resolutions interpreting the sense in which the United States accepted the obligations of the Covenant, provided they were not made part of the formal ratification itself. He did, however, strongly oppose reservations that would have to be accepted by other signatories. Not only would they indefinitely delay final ratification, but they would cause other governments to follow the American example so that "the meaning and operative force of the treaty would presently be clouded from one end of its clauses to the other."

But the President made no converts. As in the February conference, the Democrats went away convinced that Wilson had met every reasonable objection, while Lodge and his followers persisted in their contention that the treaty should be ratified only with important reservations, if at all.

Public Opinion and the League

Both supporters and opponents of the League counted upon the creation of a vast tide of popular sentiment that would overwhelm the opposing faction. At first the pro-League forces seemed to have the better of it. Out of 1,377 newspaper editors polled by the *Literary Digest* in April, 1919, 718 unconditionally favored the League, 478 favored it conditionally, and only 181 opposed it. Thirty-two state legislatures passed resolutions favoring the entrance of the United States into some form of international organization, thirty-three governors were similarly on record, while pro-League sentiment was also very strong among Protestant clergymen. The League to Enforce Peace, at the height of its power and influence, staged meetings throughout the country to urge ratification of the treaty without reservations. Prominent in this movement was Taft, who sharply denounced the partisan maneuvers of his fellow Republicans.

But the anti-Leaguers were also active. A self-constituted general staff held frequent meetings—usually in the Washington home of Senator Brandegee, occasionally in that of Mrs. Alice Roosevelt Longworth, T. R.'s energetic daughter. Important in the so-called cabal were Senators Borah of Idaho, Johnson of California, Knox of Pennsylvania, and McCormick of Illinois, and Colonel Harvey, publisher of the influential *Harper's Weekly* and bitter enemy of the President since their break in 1911. Two Pennsylvania multimillionaires, Henry Clay Frick and Andrew W. Mellon, provided the group with ample funds. The Hearst press was already engaged in violent denunciation of the League; its efforts were now supplemented by a great mass of literature warning against the perils of foreign entanglements. A League for the Preservation of American Independence held protest meetings against "the evil thing with a holy name."

Opponents of the League found willing allies among the American Irish. The latter would probably have regarded the League as a sinister Anglo-American alliance under any circumstances, but a series of events in 1919 intensified their hostility. In February, a Philadelphia convention of Irish-Americans from all over the country adopted a resolution asking the Peace Conference "to recognize the right of the people of Ireland to select for themselves . . . the form of government under which in the future they shall live." Shortly afterward, a distinguished Irish-American commission, headed by Frank P. Walsh, former co-chairman of the War Labor Board, went to Paris to demand that Eamon de Valera, president of the so-called Irish Republic, be allowed to present the cause of his government to the conference. Wilson, not unsympathetic to the idea of Irish nationalism, tried to persuade Lloyd George to meet this delegation. He might have been successful had not the Walsh commission visited Ireland, where it conveyed American greetings to the Irish Republic— thus demonstrating its support of the idea of an independent government rather than of the limited Home Rule the English favored. When the commissioners returned to Paris, Lloyd George refused to confer with them and Wilson did not press the issue to avoid offending the British. Disillusioned, the Irish-Americans returned to the United States, convinced that Wilson and the other peace negotiators were spurning the rights of small nations for which the war had supposedly been fought.

Naturally the anti-Leaguers increased this Irish-American hostility by portraying the League as a menace both to Irish and American independence. The Friends of Irish Freedom spent thousands of dollars in an advertising campaign against ratification of the treaty. Likewise helping the cause was the visit to the United States of de Valera, whose presence became the symbol for the whole nationalist movement. While it is true that he was less bitterly anti-League than many others, the mass meetings greeting him in city after city inevitably become the centers of violent anti-League and anti-Wilson demonstrations.

Alarmed by the success of his opponents in delaying action and beclouding the issues, Wilson set out in September on a speaking trip to carry his cause directly to the people. He visited the states of the Midwest, of the Pacific coast, and of the Rocky Mountains. During the space of 22 days he traveled more than 8,000 miles and delivered 37 speeches averaging an hour in length. For a frail man of 63, already overtaxed by his labors, this was too much. After his speech at Pueblo, Colorado, on September 25, Wilson suffered a serious breakdown. All thought of further activity had to be abandoned, and the President's special train speeded back to Washington. Stricken with partial paralysis the day after his return, Wilson was never again a well man. During the crucial rounds of the battle over the treaty, he was desperately sick, confined to his bedroom where he received little news from the outside world except through his wife and his doctor. Observers disagreed as to whether or not the heroic effort that had cost the President his health strengthened his cause. He had been greeted by large and enthusiastic crowds, many of his speeches were remarkably eloquent, thousands of listeners were impressed by his impassioned earnestness; but he gained no additional support in the one place where he most needed it—in the Senate—and big crowds also applauded the anti-League speeches of Borah, Johnson, and McCormick who pressed hard on the President's heels during the tour.

The Defeat of the Treaty

The Senate Foreign Relations Committee finally made its recommendations on September 10, 1919. The majority report, concurred in by nine of the ten Republican members, advocated no less than forty-five amendments and four reservations to the treaty. On the other hand, six of the seven Democrats signed a minority report calling for ratification without change. The stage was now set for a long debate on the floor of the Senate.

For purposes of clarity and convenience, the members of the Upper House may be divided into four major groups. All but about seven Democrats were willing to vote for the treaty without change—either out of devotion to the League idea itself or out of loyalty to Wilson as party leader. The Republicans, on the other hand, were divided into three factions, roughly equal in size. Some fourteen were staunch isolationists—the so-called irreconcilables, determined to vote against the treaty as long as it incorporated the League in any form. A second faction, headed by Lodge, consisted of strong reservationists; some of them believed basically in an association of nations, but felt that the Wilson version must be drastically amended to safeguard American interests; others were probably against any league, but believed that it was more strategic to emasculate the treaty with amendments than to attempt to obtain its outright rejection. The remainder were mild reservationists, at heart pro-League, yet believing that Wilson's work needed some clarification.

The initial advantage appeared to lie with the friends of the treaty. All of the amendments originally recommended in the majority report of the Foreign Relations Committee were voted down by an alliance of the Democrats with the mild reservationists. But Lodge made an extraordinary recovery from this setback. He now presented a battery of fourteen reservations and, by adroit political generalship, won a majority of the Senate to their support. The strong reservationists favored the Lodge proposals as minimum safeguards if the United States were to accept the suspect treaty; the irreconcilables voted for them because they wanted to weaken the treaty in any way possible even if they could not kill it outright; the mild reservationists accepted Lodge's leadership because they wanted to get the treaty ratified and believed that the reservations would serve that end. The Democrats made their worst tactical error in not developing a rival program that would hold the support of these pro-League Republicans.

Senators were impelled to support the reservations for a variety of motives. Staunch Republicans were reluctant to let Wilson's treaty go through without change lest the Democratic party get too much credit with the voters. Sticklers for Congressional prerogatives feared that League membership might weaken Congress' sole authority to declare war. The bogy that Article 10 constituted an entangling alliance impressed isolationists generally and particularly the Irish, who argued that the United States might become involved in helping suppress the Irish Republic. Much was made of the contention that the British Empire had six votes in the League Assembly to one for the United States (although English influence over the votes of South Africa or Canada was in reality not likely to be as great as that of the United States over the votes of Panama or a dozen small neighboring republics). Wilson was accused of insulting the Senate in the choice of his peace commission, of thwarting the aspirations of the Italians and the Chinese, and of lying in his denial that he had known about the secret treaties before he went to Paris.

In the end, the Lodge reservations were approved by a majority of the Senate. All but one of the Republicans voted for them; most but not all of the Democrats voted against them. The most important of the reservations was the one practically nullifying Article 10 of the Covenant: the United States would assume no obligation under it unless Congress decided to act in a particular case. Other reservations claimed for the United States complete freedom to declare any issue a domestic one and as such excluded from the jurisdiction of the League; the sole right to interpret the Monroe Doctrine; refusal to agree to the Shantung settlement; and refusal of the United States to be bound by any League decision in which member states of the British Commonwealth cast in the aggregate more than one vote.

Lodge's motives in pushing through these reservations are still a matter of controversy. Those who believe in the Senator's sincerity contend that he really wanted an association of nations such as he had championed in earlier years and that he was seeking only to protect vital American interests that Wilson's project had jeopardized. Those who doubt Lodge's sincerity regard him as a bitter partisan determined to kill Wilson's project by maneuvering its Senate approval in such mutilated form that Wilson would not attempt to obtain its ratification by other powers. They point out that Lodge had taken a leading part in killing arbitration treaties in 1905 and 1911 by just this device.

The question now was: would the treaty with the Lodge reservations obtain the two-thirds vote essential for final Senate approval? Wilson's position on the issue was made clear in a letter to Senator Hitchcock of Nebraska, the Democratic leader. The President expressed hope that the friends and supporters of the treaty would vote against this proposal because it provided not for ratification, but "rather for nullification of the treaty."

On November 19, when the important roll call was finally taken, only 39 Senators voted to approve the treaty with the Lodge reservations, while 55 opposed it. The nays were cast by 42 Democrats, most of them guided by the advice from the White House, and 13 Republican irreconcilables, who were opposed to a League whatever the safeguards. The sentiment of the Senate on ratification without reservations was then tested, but only 38 Senators, all but one of them Democrats, would support the treaty in unadulterated form, while 55 opposed it, both groups of reservationists joining forces with the irreconcilables.

It seemed fantastic that, although there were only 17 Senators who were completely opposed to the treaty, ratification could not be obtained. Moderates from both parties sought to discover an escape from the impasse through a bipartisan conference in January, 1920. The Democrats offered to accept several reservations, including one to Article 10 that had been drafted by Taft. The conference made such apparent progress that the irreconcilables became alarmed and threatened to bolt the party if Lodge gave ground. In the end, the Massachusetts Senator refused all terms except complete Democratic acquiescence in the Lodge reservations, and the attempt at compromise failed.

On March 19, 1920, the Senate took the final vote on the treaty. The fourteen Lodge reservations had been strengthened rather than weakened and a fifteenth reservation of Democratic parentage had been adopted, stating that in the judgment of the United States Senate the Irish people were entitled to a government of their own choice. The treaty with its fifteen reservations came within seven of the two-thirds vote necessary for ratification; now 49 Senators voted for it and 35 against it. Half of the Democrats who had voted against the treaty with reservations the previous November now voted for it, convinced that approval in this form was better than no ratification at all. But the other half voted against it, following the advice of Wilson. Once again it was their votes, added to those of the irreconcilables, that killed the treaty.

An interesting speculation is whether the result would have been different if Wilson had retained his health. Perhaps pro-League public opinion would have been more effectively rallied. Perhaps the President, more conscious of the realities of the situation, might have seen the need for Republican votes and, by timely compromise, have won the support of the more reasonable reservationists. Such an outcome of the struggle should have been possible if the good offices of Taft and other pro-League Republicans had been employed. But to compromise was impossible for the Wilson of 1920; many critics considered this to be his fatal weakness, although his admirers have insisted that compromise would have been equivalent to surrender.

Failure to ratify left the United States legally at war with Germany. The Republicans, anxious to end Wilson's wartime powers, passed the so-called Knox Resolution that simply repealed the declaration of war, but the President returned it to Congress with a stinging veto stating that this expedient was an "ineffaceable stain upon the gallantry and honor of the United States." Consequently, the official state of war continued until Harding was in office.

President Wilson never lost faith that American opinion would eventually rally to the League in such volume as to override the obstructionists. He looked forward to the 1920 election as "a solemn referendum" on the issue. But as will be shown later, the election proved to be meaningless as such a referendum. What the American people really thought of the League is difficult to determine. Undoubtedly time worked to the advantage of the anti-Leaguers. Over the course of the months, the combined efforts of the irreconcilable Senators, the nationalist press, the Irish, and other groups succeeded in convincing millions of Americans that the League was a sinister plot against American independence. Millions of others did not lose their faith in the ideal, but they became hopelessly divided in opinion as to how to realize it. Taft and other leaders of the League to Enforce Peace shifted their ground, giving up their fight to obtain the treaty without change and urging ratification with the Lodge reservations, even though they considered some of them "harmful." On the other hand, many believed that the President was right and that the Lodge reservations were impossible to accept because they nullified the treaty.[7] Baffled and confused, more and more Americans became tired of the whole debate and more than willing to forget the war and the League. Sadly commenting on this, Wilson declared: "They will have to learn now by bitter experience just what they have lost. . . . We had a chance to gain the leadership of the world. We have lost it, and soon we shall be witnessing the tragedy of it all."

[7] Whether other signatories of the treaty would have accepted the reservations is uncertain, although there is some evidence that they were willing to do so.

12

Problems of the Postwar Period

The country was also deserting Wilson's leadership in domestic affairs. For months the President's attention had been absorbed by the Peace Conference and the subsequent struggle with the Senate. Then his physical collapse and long illness prevented his giving effective attention to important problems of domestic reconstruction. The loneliness of Wilson's position was accentuated by estrangement from his long-time advisers. In February, 1920, Secretary Lansing was asked to resign—ostensibly because he had called unauthorized Cabinet meetings during Wilson's illness, actually because the two men had not agreed on fundamental policies for many months. This quarrel was inevitable, but Wilson's break with Colonel House is less easy to understand. Perhaps it arose out of House's fondness for compromise at a time when the President hated to make concessions to his opponents.

Quite apart from Wilson's physical inability to provide his old-time leadership, the nation was in no mood to accept his advice. Already disillusionment was widespread. The returning soldier found little glamour attached to his recent experiences; the mud of France, trench warfare, wholesale death and destruction left vivid and unpleasant memories. Those who had stayed at home were disgusted by the greedy scramble for the spoils of war at the Peace Conference. They were irritated by continued wartime controls and unchecked rising prices. Veterans and civilians alike wanted nothing so much as the return of prewar standards of living, but the road back was a rocky one.

Postwar Reforms

The reaction against idealism did not prevent certain prewar reform movements from achieving their goals in the months after the armistice. Indeed, the demand for both prohibition and women's suffrage had been accentuated by the war itself.

The Anti-Saloon League and its allies, already strong, took immediate advantage of the opportunity offered by the war. The brewery business was denounced as unpatriotic because it was dominated by German-Americans, while great stress was laid upon the danger of the liquor trade to the morals of the soldiers and upon the iniquity of diverting scarce grain into the manufacture of intoxicants. The Lever Act of 1917 included clauses prohibiting the use of grain for the manufacture of distilled liquors and making it permissive for the President to extend the ban to beer, ale, and wine. Acting under this authority, Wilson ordered the breweries to close in October, 1918. Ten days after the armistice a law—curiously known as the "War Prohibition Act"—was passed, making it unlawful to sell intoxicating beverages after June 30, 1919, until the President should proclaim the end of the war and demobilization period.

This date was, in fact, destined to be the last day on which intoxicating beverages were legally sold in the United States for more than fourteen years. Before "war prohibition" was over, prohibition by Constitutional amendment had been declared in effect. On December 18, 1917, Congress had passed and sent to the states the Eighteenth Amendment by which "the manufacture, sale or transportation of intoxicating liquors within, the importation thereof into, or the exportation thereof from the United States and all territory subject to the jurisdiction thereof for beverage purposes" was to be prohibited. Congress and the several states were to have concurrent power to enforce the amendment by appropriate legislation. Ratification was obtained with surprising speed and ease. By January 16, 1919, the necessary thirty-six states had approved the amendment, which was proclaimed in force one year later. Eventually all the states except Connecticut and Rhode Island joined in ratification.

The actual definition of intoxicating beverages, as well as drastic penalties for their manufacture or sale, was provided by the Volstead Act, passed by Congress over Wilson's veto in October, 1919. The banning of all liquors containing more than 0.5 per cent alcohol was criticized by many who denied that light wines and beer were in fact intoxicating, but the Supreme Court upheld the law (Hawke v. Smith, 1920, and Rhode Island v. Palmer, 1920). The enforcement of legislation that a large section of the public considered a violation of personal liberty proved to be one of the most troublesome problems of the 1920's.

Meantime, the nation's participation in a crusade to make the world safe for democracy and the magnificent support given by women to the war effort had undermined male resistance to the demand for women's suffrage. In June, 1919, Congress accepted the Nineteenth Amendment, which specified that the right of citizens to vote should not be denied by the United States or any state

Can She Live Up to Expectations? (By McCutcheon
in the *Chicago Tribune.*)

"on account of sex." Ratification met some opposition in the South, where Alabama, Maryland, and Virginia rejected the amendment. The fact, however, that 1920 was an election year worked to the advantage of the suffrage advocates. Republicans vied with Democrats for the political credit of having given women the vote, and in August, 1920, the consent of the thirty-sixth state was gained. The amendment was declared in effect in time for the ladies to cast their ballots for Harding or Cox. The feminine vote under the Nineteenth Amendment did not bring the immediate purification of politics that the more ardent suffragettes had promised, but neither did it produce the dreadful consequences predicted by the misogynists.

Demobilization

The task of demobilizing more than four million men in the armed services was accomplished quickly. By the middle of April, 1919, four-thousand men a day were being discharged, and nearly half of those in training camps in the United States had been dismissed. Even before Wilson returned with the completed treaty of peace, a million and a half members of the AEF were back on American shores. This was almost as spectacular an achievement as getting them overseas, because only American ships were used on the return voyage. Thanks to the speedy conversion of cargo ships into transports and the use of various types of naval vessels, the homecoming of the troops was surprisingly rapid. With the exception of less than twenty thousand men under General Henry T. Allen, serving as an American Army of Occupation in the Rhineland, all of the expeditionary forces were once more in the United States by January, 1920.

It is questionable whether so rapid a demobilization was wise. Soldiers were discharged by military units, without any consideration of employment opportunities in their home communities. As a result, many veterans faced weeks without work because of local conditions. The problem was accentuated by the abrupt and planless termination of war contracts, which threatened many industrial units with bankruptcy. Thousands of war workers, moreover, were seeking new jobs along with the returned veterans. All this resulted in a serious situation during the early months of 1919. According to Labor Department estimates, there were a million unemployed on January 30, 1919, and that number increased at the rate of a hundred thousand a week for more than two months thereafter.

The Federal government did little to help during the crisis. In Wilson's message to Congress of December 2, 1918, he expressed the opinion that the American people knew their own business, were quick and resourceful in making adjustments, and were self-reliant in action. He advocated, therefore, a minimum of governmental direction over the processes of reconstruction. The President's principal adviser on economic matters, Bernard Baruch, concurred in this judgment, and by January 1, 1919, the powerful War Industries Board had closed shop. Even the limited program that the President did recommend was largely jettisoned by the Republican-dominated Congress. The United States Employment Service, which had placed more than 4.5 million workers in jobs over the course of sixteen months, was compelled to scrap 80 per cent of its machinery in March, 1919, just when it was most needed for the reconversion period. The service was killed by the refusal of Congress to make sufficient appropriations to support it, due both to the general impulse to cut down the huge expenditures of the government and the unpopularity of this particular agency with employers who accused it of being staffed with doctrinaire social workers, oversympathetic with the cause of labor unionism. The Congressional drive for economy led also to the rejection of proposals for the expansion of public works and for grants to rehabilitate the railroads, which were in bad condition because of overuse during the war.

Similar motives combined with the opposition of the National Grange to defeat the so-called Lane Plan, a scheme sponsored by the Secretary of the Interior for Federal and state cooperation in a bold reclamation project to provide both employment and farms for returned veterans. One of the few measures actually passed by Congress was the Vocational Rehabilitation Act of June, 1918, which set up a Federal Board of Vocational Education to train disabled veterans for jobs. Several thousand men were placed in colleges and schools throughout the country, but the program, nevertheless, proved a great disappointment because it never benefited more than a small percentage of the 230,000 Americans disabled during the war.

Many states and municipalities took a broader view of their responsibilities during the reconstruction period. States like New York, Oregon, and Indiana made generous appropriations for state employment services to serve both veterans and displaced civilian workers. Employment bureaus were also maintained by welfare agencies all over the nation. The task of coordinating these activities for the benefit of the discharged servicemen was entrusted to Colonel Arthur Woods, formerly police commissioner of New York City and at this time Assistant to Secretary of War Baker. In the end more than a million men were placed in jobs through these channels. Massachusetts, Minnesota, and fifteen other states passed bonus acts for the benefit of the veterans; New York and Oregon voted grants to assist veterans in obtaining an education; California and New York provided for an expanded program of public works; several Western states passed legislation promising cooperation with the Lane Plan for settling veterans on reclaimed lands and, when Congress failed to act, California went ahead with a land settlement program of its own.

The greatest help, however, in carrying the country safely through the period of demobilization came from an unexpected quarter. By the summer of 1919 the post-armistice depression was giving way to an extraordinary postwar prosperity. Because the war had ruined for the time being the German export trade and seriously injured the British, American exports soared to dizzy heights for several months. They totaled slightly less than $8 billion in 1919 and considerably more than that in 1920—over three times their 1913 level. The domestic market was similarly active. There was an orgy of spending as wartime savings were poured out for commodities that had been difficult to buy during the period of hostilities. Particularly prosperous was the automobile business. The boom, however, was an unhealthy one. With all Europe impoverished by the war, the export business was cut in half as sharply as it had risen. With wartime controls relaxed, domestic prices jumped to such an unreasonable level as to dry up demand, while warehouses bulged with the huge inventories carried by overoptimistic businessmen. During 1921 the country suffered a serious economic depression. But the short-lived prosperity of the fall of 1919 and the following winter did at least ease the problems created by the rapid demobilization of the armed forces.

Getting the Government out of Business

During the war advanced liberals had watched with approval while the Federal government not only built and operated millions of tons of shipping, but took over the management of the railroad, telegraph, telephone, cable, and radio systems of the country. Some at least of these economic activities, they hoped, would remain permanently nationalized or at least subjected to much more rigorous public control than before the war. Conservatives, on the other hand, had acquiesced in government operation of these enterprises with great misgivings and, as soon as the armistice was signed, they demanded that business be turned back to private control as speedily as possible. In the case of electrical communications they had a complete victory. At midnight, July 31, 1919, these properties were returned by act of Congress to their owners without any condition attached other than that the rates established by the Postmaster General should be continued for four months unless changed by authority of the government.

The railroads, however, constituted a somewhat different problem. Although high wartime costs resulted in the Railroad Administration suffering a loss of $1 billion during the twenty-six months of its existence, government operation by certain other standards proved an interesting and not unsuccessful experiment. Particularly impressive was the greatly improved efficiency made possible by operating the railroads as a single system without wasteful duplication of facilities. Progressives demanded either the continuance of government operation or the return of the roads under conditions that would consolidate the wartime gains. McAdoo, who headed the Railroad Administration until January, 1919, and Walter D. Hines, his successor, both recommended that Federal control be continued for five years while the whole railroad problem was subjected to intensive investigation. The Railroad Brotherhoods vigorously supported a plan, drafted by Glenn E. Plumb, their legal representative, under which the government would purchase the roads and operate them through a tripartite board representative of the government, management, and employees. One half of the net earnings would be set aside for the payment of the bonds issued to finance the government purchase; the other half would be paid to the employees and executives as dividends on wages.

Congress, however, turned its face against all such proposals. On March 1, 1920, the lines were turned back to private management under the terms of the Esch-Cummins or Transportation Act of 1920. This important law not only provided for government support to the railroads during the difficult transition period, but laid down significant principles governing the future regulation of transportation. For a period of six months after the return of the lines, the government guaranteed to the carriers a net return equal to the rentals they had been receiving from the Railroad Administration; rates, fares, wages, and salaries were all to be frozen at existing levels during the guarantee period unless changes were authorized by the government. As a further help to the carriers, a revolving fund of $300 million was set up from which the railroads might obtain loans, upon approval of the Interstate Commerce Commission, for a period of two years after the resumption of private control.

The commission was enlarged from nine to eleven members and was given important additional powers. Its consent was now needed to issue new railroad securities and construct or abandon track. It could fix both minimum and maximum rates, and could set aside rates fixed by state authorities if these were found to be prejudicial to interstate commerce. For the purpose of rate-fixing the commission was authorized to divide the country into districts, in each of which rates were to be fixed at such a level that the carriers of the district would earn a fair return upon the aggregate value of their properties. Since, however, under the same rates strong railroads might earn unreasonable profits while weaker lines were suffering losses, a controversial "recapture clause" was written into the act. Any carrier earning more than 6 per cent on the value of its property was required to put one half the surplus in its own reserve fund and the other half in a general contingent fund. This fund would be used by the commission either to make loans to the weaker companies for capital expenditures or to purchase equipment that would be leased to them.

The most striking change of policy in the railroad legislation of 1920 was that under which cooperation and consolidation of the carriers were favored. Not only could the Interstate Commerce Commission relax the long-short haul clause under certain circumstances and permit forms of pooling formerly prohibited, but it was directed to prepare a plan under which the railroad properties of the country would be consolidated into a limited number of systems. Thus it was frankly recognized that enforced competition as the panacea for all railroad abuses had failed and that the public interest would best be served by encouraging the strong carriers to take over the weak under strict government regulation.

Finally, the Transportation Act provided new machinery for handling labor problems. There had been considerable Congressional support for compulsory arbitration and the outlawing of railroad strikes; indeed, the Senate had passed the Esch Bill in a form incorporating these principles. The House rejected this extreme procedure, however, and the act provided instead for the establishment of both railroad boards of labor adjustment and a national Railroad Labor Board. The former, to be set up by agreement between the carriers and their employees, were to hear grievances over rules and working conditions. Wage disputes and any grievances not settled by the adjustment boards were to be referred to the Railroad Labor Board, composed of nine members appointed by the President; three of these were to be chosen from a list nominated by the employers, three from a list drawn up by the employees, and three appointed without restriction to represent the public. The board was given wide powers to compel testimony, but its finding were not binding upon either party. A discussion of the problems that confronted the board during its short life and that killed it in 1926 is included in a later chapter.

In many ways the shipping problem was even more complex than the railroad situation. Here it was not a question of the government's returning to private management enterprises that had all along been privately owned; rather it was a problem of deciding what should be done with some two-thousand ships built or purchased with government money. During the export boom of 1919 the problem was not acute; some three-hundred operating companies willingly kept existing routes in operation and developed new ones on a cost-plus basis under the supervision of the Merchant Fleet Corporation and the Shipping Board. But the collapse of international trade in 1920 brought unpleasant results. Since there was no longer enough business to provide attractive commissions to the operating companies, their number fell from three hundred to forty. Often government-owned ships were simply abandoned in foreign ports. The losses to the government from its shipping operations reached $16 million a month by 1921.

Once again the formula favored by Congressional conservatives was a speedy return to private enterprise. The Merchant Marine Act of 1920 directed the Shipping Board to transfer government-owned ships quickly and on easy terms to private ownership. Except under special circumstances, the ships might be sold only to corporations in which a majority of the stock was held by American citizens; indeed, if the ships were to be used in the coasting trade, the companies had to be at least 75 per cent American controlled. The Merchant Fleet Corporation was to operate the ships that could not be sold; it was to establish new shipping routes and maintain them until private capital could be induced to take them over; it was given a revolving fund of $25 million and empowered to make loans to companies willing to operate the new routes.

The shipping problem was too complex to be solved by any single wave of the wand. The methods by which the Shipping Board carried out its mandate under the act of 1920 provided material for controversy for many years. The nub of the problem was this: high costs made it unprofitable for American shipping to compete with foreign lines; yet an American merchant marine was vital to national defense. The only possible answers were government operation at a loss or private ownership and operation with subsidies. It required many years for American opinion to accept the inevitability of choosing between these alternatives.

Labor Unrest

During the war labor relations had been abnormal. The AFL leaders were fairly successful in preventing strikes. At the same time, however, workers demanded substantial wage increases and the Federal war administrations favored their demands in order to keep industrial peace and maintain production. From the standpoint of most employers, labor became entirely too assertive, and it seemed imperative to resist firmly the trend toward increased power for labor-union leaders once the war was over. The unions, on the other hand, were determined not only to preserve their wartime gains, but to obtain new concessions. They pointed out that the cost of living after the armistice was constantly rising and that many workers, even after pay raises, were worse off than they had been before the war. With both management and labor in an uncompromising mood, all the elements for serious industrial warfare were present. During 1919 more than four million American workers were at one time or another out on strike, and the number of such disputes reached 3,630.

In many of these contests labor was victorious. Such was the result of walk-outs of the New York clothing workers, the New York harbor workers, the New England textile employees, the New England telegraph operators, and the New York actors. But these victories—mostly won early in 1919—hardened public opinion against labor, and the strikes later in that year were much less successful.

Particularly damaging to the cause of unionism was the alarm felt all over the country when Seattle, Washington, became the scene of a general strike in February. The trouble, starting in the shipyards, reached serious propor-tions when sixty-thousand workers in all trades struck on February 6 to support the demands of the shipworkers. Strict order was maintained by the strikers and an attempt was made to carry on essential services. But even though the strike was called off after five days, the spectacle of the economic life of a large city being thus tied up was widely cited as evidence of the danger of Bolshevism in the country—an interpretation of the event given wide publicity through the speeches of Seattle's Mayor Ole Hansen. This feeling that labor was getting out of hand and was threatening revolution received additional impetus from the occurrence of a more serious general strike in May across the border in Winnipeg, Canada.

The Steel Strike

Against this background the story of the three most important labor con-troversies of 1919 must be considered. In the steel industry the workers were very discontented over their conditions. Their working day was frequently twelve hours, and the average in some plants was about sixty-nine hours for a seven-day week. Nor was it unusual for the operators to call upon the men to labor on twenty-four-hour shifts.

In an effort to remedy the situation, twenty-four unions of the AFL estab-lished a steelworkers' organizing committee which attempted to unionize the men during the summer of 1919. Prominent in the movement was William Z. Foster, who was reputed to be anything from a Communist to a syndicalist. When the organizing committee demanded an eight-hour day, a six-day week, the ending of the twenty-four-hour shift practice, and collective bargaining, Judge Elbert H. Gary, chairman of the board of the United States Steel Corporation and general spokesman for the whole industry, refused to recognize the right of the group to speak for the men.

Consequently, a strike was scheduled for September 22. President Wilson's effort to avert the danger failed when the union officials rejected his plea to postpone the walkout. On the appointed day, approximately 280,000 men left their jobs, chiefly in Chicago, Youngstown, Ohio, Buffalo, New York, and several plants in Pennsylvania. Gradually more workers joined the walkout until there were at least 300,000 in the strikers' ranks. There was disorder around some of the steel mills and, during the disturbances, at least four persons were killed and more than fifty wounded. At one time Federal troops under General Leonard Wood were moved into Gary, Indiana, where martial law was declared and picketing limited.

Public opinion, influenced in no small part by an antilabor press, turned more and more against the strikers. The feeling was widespread that Foster was promoting un-American agitation and also that the workers had gained enough during the war itself. A back-to-work movement gained momentum by January, 1920, the strikers' committee acknowledged failure, and the strike was declared at an end.

The strike had a curious aftermath. Public opinion, which had been so generally adverse to the workers while the dispute was in progress, showed signs of a reversal after it was over. In large part this was because of the harrowing picture of actual labor conditions in the steel industry contained in the report of a special investigating committee of the Interchurch World Movement. This report, signed by an impressive list of Protestant churchmen headed by Bishop Francis J. McConnell of the Methodist Episcopal Church, denied that the strike had been Red-inspired and asserted that it had been the natural result of the labor policies of the United States Steel Corporation—policies that were based not alone on low wages and long hours, but included arbitrary management, bribery, spying on the workers, and stirring up of racial animosities to prevent employees from forming a common front. The corporation indignantly denied the truth of this indictment, but under the pressure of public opinion and after proddings by President Harding, the twelve-hour day was eliminated from the steel industry in 1923.

The Boston Police Strike

Boston policemen after the armistice were in a rebellious mood. Their station houses were crowded, they were compelled to buy their own uniforms, and, worst of all, with the cost of living soaring they continued to be paid according to prewar scales based upon a minimum of $1,100. In the summer of 1919 the Boston Social Club, to which the police had belonged for thirteen years, applied for a charter from the AFL. Since Police Commissioner Edwin U. Curtis had forbidden any such affiliation, he now proceeded to take stern disciplinary action against the officers of the club. Nineteen men were threatened with suspension from the force, bringing the situation to a crisis. Mayor Andrew J. Peters, a Democrat, and a Citizens' Committee sought to mediate under the following formula: the leaders who were in trouble were to be reinstated, the police were to be permitted to maintain a union but without outside affiliations, and an opportunity should be provided for the men to present their grievances. But the commissioner refused to compromise; instead he carried through the threatened suspensions and, by a vote of 1,134 to 2, the men decided to strike.

When the Policeman Strikes. (Kirby in the *New York World*.)

On September 9 the police left their posts and shortly thereafter ruffians, hoodlums, and lawbreakers of every description took advantage of the situation. Stores and homes had to be boarded up to prevent looting. The next day Mayor Peters called out that part of the state guard resident in Boston, over which he shared authority with the governor, and this action proved effective in restoring order. On the third day of the strike, Calvin Coolidge, the Republican governor of Massachusetts, intervened and took the situation into his own hands. He called out the rest of the state guard and appealed to the Secretary of War for a promise of Federal troops in case an attempt were made to stage a general strike.

The policemen, realizing their defeat, were ready to return to work, but Curtis refused to take back any strikers and proposed enlisting an entirely new force. Samuel Gompers tried to intercede, but Coolidge, standing firmly behind his commissioner, rebuked the AFL head with a stinging public telegram. "There is no right," Coolidge asserted, "to strike against the public safety by anybody, anywhere, any time."

It reveals much concerning the prevailing mood of the country that Coolidge's rebuke to Gompers and his stern disciplining of the Boston policemen made him a national hero and a possibility for the Republican presidential nomination in 1920. Even President Wilson added his congratulations to those showered down upon the Yankee champion of law and order.

Enter John L. Lewis

John L. Lewis, destined to be a prominent figure in labor circles for the next four decades, became president of the United Mine Workers in 1919. His first task was to lead the workers in the bituminous coal fields in their struggle to achieve a program of far-reaching demands, which included a national contract, a 60 per cent wage increase, and a thirty-hour minimum work week. The pay demand was large because the bituminous miners, unlike the anthracite workers, had had no wage increase since September, 1917, even though the cost of living had risen sharply.

When the operators rejected these terms, a strike was called for November 1, 1919. Lewis was solidly supported by the miners, but the Federal government permitted the dispute to continue only a little over a week before intervening. On November 9, Attorney General Palmer obtained from a district court judge in Indiana a sweeping injunction based on the Lever Act, the law still on the books under which the government had been given its extraordinary wartime powers over food and fuel. The officers of the UMW were ordered to cease all activities tending to encourage and maintain the strike in the bituminous coal industry. To the reporters Lewis commented, "We cannot fight the government," and an order declaring the strike officially at an end was duly issued.

Despite Lewis' gesture of compliance, the miners did not actually go back to work until a month later when the union accepted President Wilson's proposal that the issues in controversy be submitted to arbitration. After extended hearings the arbitral body awarded the miners a 27 per cent wage increase, but no shortening of hours.

The Red Scare

In itself the strike epidemic would have been enough to convince many conservative Americans that dangerous radicalism was rampant in the land. This feeling was many times intensified by events in Europe. The Bolsheviks had seized control of Russia in November, 1917, and made a separate peace with Germany the following March. Despite counterrevolutionary attempts and foreign interventions the hated Reds had not only clung to power in Russia, but had boldly raised the banner of world revolution. For a time during 1919 universal proletarian revolt seemed a possibility both to hopeful radicals and trembling conservatives. The German Communists held the city of Berlin for a few days; the Hungarian Communists ruled their country for five months; unrest boiled high in Italy and elsewhere in Europe; there were ominous rumblings in India and the British Empire.

There was an intoxicating quality in the news that led a few extremists in the United States to the point of dangerous action. Late in April, 1919, a bomb was found in the mail of Mayor Ole Hansen of Seattle, a conspicuous Red-baiter. A day later the colored maid of Senator Thomas R. Hardwick of Georgia, an advocate of immigration restriction, had her hands blown off when she opened a mysterious package addressed to her employer. Timely investigation in the New York City Post Office disclosed sixteen packages containing bombs addressed to prominent persons in public life. Some twenty other deadly bundles were discovered passing through the mails elsewhere. Among the prominent citizens marked for death were Attorney General Palmer, Postmaster General Burleson, Supreme Court Justice Holmes, Federal Judge Landis, J. P. Morgan, and John D. Rockefeller. A month later several bomb explosions occurred in widely scattered parts of the country, one of them wrecking the Washington home of Attorney General Palmer. The most sensational of these outrages took place on September 16, 1920, when a terrific blast in noonday-crowded Wall Street caused the death of thirty-eight persons, injury to hundreds of others, property damage to the extent of $2 million, and untold harm to the nerves of the masters of capital.

These and other similar incidents were more an index of the unusual strain of the times than of the real strength or intensity of the revolutionary movement in the United States. Actually radical ranks were divided and confused by the turn of events. A right-wing minority of the Socialists led by John Spargo had withdrawn from the party when it went on record in 1917 as condemning American participation in the war. This loss had not been serious, but in 1919 a more important crisis developed. Left-wing Socialists sought to capture the party machinery and affiliate with the Communist Third International; when this attempt failed, the extremists split off into two new groups: the Com-

The Wall Street Explosion, September 16, 1920. (Brown Bros.)

munist party and the slightly less radical Communist Labor party. On orders from Moscow the two were united in the spring of 1920 as the United Communist party. Meantime, the Socialist Labor group continued to regard itself as the true Marxian party, the Industrial Workers of the World continued on its separate way, and the Anarchists would have nothing to do with any of the others. The total number of all these radical groups has been estimated at less than 0.2 per cent of the American population. There could be little menace from that small a minority.

To middle-class Americans, however, a Red was a Red. They were ignorant of or indifferent to the fact that the Socialists had purged Communists from their own ranks or that Anarchists were anti-Bolshevik in sentiment. All radicals were branded as un-American because of their hostility to the war and because of the preponderance of recent immigrant stock in their ranks. In Weirton, West Virginia, 118 foreigners, members of the IWW and involved in the steel strike, were compelled by the police to kiss the flag. In New York City a mob of ex-soldiers and civilians wrecked the office of the *New York Call*, a leading Socialist newspaper. Most serious of all was the clash at Centralia, Washington, on Armistice Day, 1919. Three parading members of the American Legion were killed by gunfire from IWW headquarters and another lost his life during the ensuing turmoil. The affair was surrounded by great controversy. The Legionnaires asserted that the attack was unprovoked; the IWW members claimed to have been defending their hall against an attempt to wreck it as it had been wrecked the year before. Guilty or innocent, the IWW was severely punished. Of twelve men accused of complicity in the shooting, one was taken from his cell by a mob, mutilated, and brutally lynched, while the others were given prison sentences ranging from 25 to 40 years. But this was not all. Throughout the Northwest IWW halls were demolished by irate citizens; over one thousand of the detested group were arrested and it was difficult to find lawyers willing to undertake their defense.

Prosecution of individuals for merely belonging to the IWW or any other radical organization was made possible by the enactment of criminal syndi-calist laws in thirty-two states declaring it illegal to belong to organizations advocating the overthrow of the government by force. Twenty-eight states made it a punishable offense to display the Red flag as a political emblem.

Although ultrapatriots were unsuccessful in their attempt to have passed a new Federal sedition act even more severe than the wartime legislation, the Federal government did enforce existing laws drastically against the radicals. President Wilson could not forgive the Socialists for their opposition to the war and refused to pardon Debs and others who had been sent to prison for their activities. Not until Christmas Day, 1933, were the Federal prisons finally cleared of the last of the fifteen hundred originally convicted.

A particularly effective antiradical weapon was a law passed by Congress in October, 1918, authorizing the Secretary of Labor to arrest and deport any alien who advocated revolution himself or belonged to any organization that advocated the overthrow of government by force, assassination of public officials, no human government, or the unlawful destruction of property. In 1920 the Secretary's authority was extended to permit the deportation of aliens who had been convicted under the wartime espionage laws. The first wholesale deportation occurred in December, 1919, when the *Buford*, popularly referred to as the Red or Soviet Ark, left for Russia with 249 radicals aboard.

Meantime, Attorney General Palmer was preparing a drastic blow. For many weeks during 1919 Department of Justice operatives gathered data on Communists and Anarchists. Spies were employed to attend secret meetings of these radicals and obtain the names of the leaders. In the absence of Secretary of Labor Wilson, who was ill, a subordinate in the Labor Department obligingly supplied Palmer with three-thousand deportation warrants, which were served on January 2, 1920, in carefully prepared simultaneous raids upon radical meetings in all parts of the country. Everyone found on the premises was arrested whether or not the agents actually had a warrant for the particular individual, whether or not he was a member of the Communist party, and whether he was an alien or a citizen. Other radicals were apprehended in their homes. Even persons attempting to visit the jailed suspects were themselves arrested on suspicion of affiliation with the proscribed groups. Some four-thousand persons in all were rounded up. Their treatment after arrest was often harsh, and the deportation hearings were conducted without counsel or other judicial safeguards. Only 556 of those arrested were in the end deported; some of the others were turned over to state authorities for punishment under the criminal syndicalist laws, but the majority were eventually released for want of evidence. Palmer's high-handed procedure was enthusiastically applauded by the great mass of the public who hated and feared the alien radicals; a few thoughtful citizens, however, were seriously disturbed by the un-American conduct of the government itself. Charles Evans Hughes spoke gravely of "violations of personal rights which savor of the worst practices of tyranny."

While the country was still excited over the arrest of the alien radicals, the New York Assembly attempted to outdo the Attorney General in its assertion of 100 per cent Americanism. Five regularly elected assemblymen, representing districts in New York City, were expelled simply because they were members of the Socialist party. Hughes led the New York Bar Association in a vigorous, but ineffective, protest against this action. The former Supreme Court justice and presidential candidate wrote:

> This is not, in my judgment, American government. . . . I count it a most serious mistake to proceed, not against individuals charged with violation of the law, but against masses of our citizens combined for political action, by denying them the only resource of peaceful government; that is, action by the ballot box and through duly elected representatives in legislative bodies.

The Assembly attempted to follow up its action by passing several drastic anti-radical laws proposed by the Lusk Committee, but the measures were vetoed by Governor Alfred E. Smith.

The Federal Congress also refused to be contaminated by the presence of Socialists. Victor Berger, second only to Debs in prominence in the party, had been an outspoken opponent of American participation in the war. His activities led to a trial under the Espionage Act in December, 1918. He was convicted and sentenced by Judge Landis to twenty years in prison, but this conviction was later set aside by the Supreme Court because of the judge's prejudicial conduct. In the spring of 1919 Berger appeared in the House of Representatives to which he had been duly elected by the voters of his district the preceding November. But his right to sit in the House was promptly challenged. The case was referred to a special committee that reported against him, and on November 11, 1919, the seat was declared vacant. The next month the voters of Berger's district named him again in a special election, even though Democrats and Republicans had united on a single candidate to oppose him. His case went back to the House and once again that body voted to exclude him, despite the plea of Representative James R. Mann of Illinois, the Republican floor manager, who said:

> I do not share the views of Mr. Berger, but I am willing to meet his views in an argument before the people rather than to say we shall deny him the opportunity to be heard when selected by the people in the legal form and invite them, in effect, to resort to violence.

Not until Berger was elected for a third time in 1922 did the House allow him to occupy a seat.

Thus in an atmosphere of narrow nationalism and intolerance, the Wilson administration, which in better days had been dedicated to much different ideals, drew to a close.

13

The Republican Restoration

The decade of the 1920's opened while the United States was still in the throes of reaction against anything that was deemed un-American, while the nation was demanding a return to full peacetime conditions, and while the feeling was still growing that the League of Nations was not the cure-all for world ills. Under the circumstances, it was only natural that the electorate in 1920 and again in 1924 turned to the party that had opposed the New Freedom and that had done so much to defeat the Treaty of Versailles. Consequently the decade of the twenties saw the Republican party firmly entrenched in power, with first Harding and then Coolidge occupying the White House. This Republican restoration catered to the natural conservatism of the period when laissez faire and materialism were the order of the day. Both Presidents favored a return to tariff protection, supported immigration restriction, opposed government competition with private industry, and were firm advocates of lower taxes and economy. To be sure, these policies provoked discontent in various sections of the country, but the cries of the dissatisfied elements were drowned by the growing waves of support for a return to the days before Wilsonian liberalism.

The Republican Convention

Realizing that the political trend that had started with the Congressional elections of 1918 was now running at full tide in their favor, the Republican delegates gathered in Chicago on June 8, 1920, on a note of optimism. The Progressive-Conservative split had been largely healed; the death of Theodore

Roosevelt in January, 1919, meant that the Progressives had no chance for revival; mutual animosities within the various party factions were largely forgotten in the desire to bring defeat to Wilsonian Democracy. Indeed, Keynoter Lodge set the convention stage when he said: "Mr. Wilson and his dynasty, his heirs and assigns, or anybody that is his, anybody who with bent knee has served his purpose, must be driven from all control of the government and all influence in it."

Since the Republican presidential nominee would probably win the November election, there was a spirited contest for delegates to the convention. Indeed, so numerous were the Republican seekers of that nomination that as early as February, 1920, Harry M. Daugherty, a small-town Ohio lawyer who hoped to emulate his fellow Ohioan, Mark Hanna, by becoming a President-maker, had wishfully predicted a deadlock. Then, "at the proper time . . . some fifteen men, bleary eyed with loss of sleep and perspiring profusely with the excessive heat, will sit down at a big table. I will be with them and will present the name of Senator Harding to them, and before we get through they will put him over." As it turned out, Daugherty was substantially correct in his prediction, but in "putting over" Harding, he was aided by numerous circumstances.

Had Theodore Roosevelt lived, he probably would have had the nomination easily, possibly by acclamation; but his death threw the race wide open. The man originally expected to win was General Leonard Wood; many Republicans believed he had inherited the Roosevelt mantle, and the fact that Wilson refused him permission to go overseas in World War I made him an excellent choice to turn the Wilson regime out of office. Opposed to his selection were his military background and advocacy of military preparedness; among an electorate desirous of a speedy return to prewar conditions, Wood was not the ideal candidate. Second in line was Governor Frank Lowden of Illinois, a self-made man with an excellent record in Congress and in the governorship; a detrimental factor was his connection by marriage with the Pullman millions. Hiram Johnson had the backing of the Western Progressives and his strong fight against the League made him popular among isolationist elements. Governor Coolidge, Herbert Hoover, President Butler of Columbia University, and Senator Warren G. Harding of Ohio were among the other possibilities.

One of the main factors leading to the deadlock grew out of the expensive contest between Wood and Lowden for delegates. The more or less self-appointed manager of the Wood campaign was Colonel William C. Procter, a prominent soap manufacturer, who set out to raise a million dollars from his wealthy friends. Nothing loath, the Lowden supporters likewise started a huge fund. Hiram Johnson, whose own war chest was far from full, became incensed over the lavish sums expended for his rivals and, through his fellow irreconcilable, Senator Borah, an investigation of campaign expenditures was conducted in the Upper House by the Kenyon Committee. This committee's report, made public just before the convention, revealed that the Wood forces had spent $1,773,303, while the Lowden-for-President group had expended $414,000. From that time on, the chances of General Wood for the nomination dwindled rapidly, while the Lowden hopes, although not so badly damaged, were materially impaired.

Contributing also to the Wood failure was the fact that the general would not bow down to the "interests"—both big business and senatorial. Yet he led on the first ballot, with Lowden a close second. On the next three ballots there was considerable vote lending and jockeying of forces; when it was conceivable that Wood might obtain the necessary majority, the Lowden group would go all out against him, and in similar fashion the Wood adherents cut Lowden's presidential hopes. The party's elder statesmen did not wish the potential deadlock to continue over the week end; were it to do so, the voters at large would realize the disunity within the Republican ranks. Therefore, at four o'clock Friday afternoon, Chairman Lodge, through a successful parliamentary maneuver, gained adjournment until Saturday morning.

During the interim, the leaders were in almost constant conference in the Blackstone Hotel. They all agreed that the choice must be a man who had opposed the League as Wilson fashioned it, but who had backed the Lodge reservations; he must also be a strict organization man who had not joined the revolt in 1912 but who had not antagonized the Progressives; he must not be like the cold, reserved Wilson; and most of all he must follow the orders of the party leaders. Around two o'clock on Saturday morning the word circulated that Harding was the choice of the inner circle.

While more ballots were taken on Saturday, the result was not long in doubt. The Harding votes increased with each successive canvass until finally on the tenth he received the coveted nomination. For the vice-presidency, Governor Calvin Coolidge was named on the first ballot. A *New York Times* editorial expressed the opinion of many Americans about the Harding nomination:

> The Chicago convention presents a candidate whose nomination will be received with astonishment and dismay by the party whose suffrage he invites. Warren G. Harding is a very respectable Ohio politician of the second class. . . . Senator Harding's record at Washington has been faint and colorless. He was an undistinguished and indistinguishable unit in the ruck of Republican Senators who obediently followed Mr. Lodge. . . . Governor Coolidge for Vice President really shines by comparison with the head of the ticket.

Yet Harding was the type the party leaders wanted. It mattered not that some wit quipped that the ticket should be "stood on its head."

The platform was no more distinguished than was the presidential candidate.

On the important League issue, it carefully avoided a definite position. After asserting that the party stood "for agreement among the nations to preserve the peace of the world," which could "be done without the compromise of national independence," the platform denounced Wilson's Covenant because it contained "stipulations not only intolerable for an independent people but certain to produce the injustice, hostility, and controversy among nations which it proposed to prevent." The platform writers undoubtedly hoped to retain the allegiance of the irreconcilable element by denouncing the Covenant and of the Taft-Root group by promising to work for the preservation of peace. The platform endorsed the return of the railroads and the merchant marine to private ownership, increased immigration restriction, and greater protection for American manufacturers. It also advocated an adequate army and navy, effective aid for the farmer, increased Federal support for education, and a sound, economical administration.

The Democratic Candidate and Platform

There is evidence that Wilson hoped to run for a third term in order to carry into operation his League of Nations, but his illness and the turn of public opinion made this impossible. Indeed, by the summer of 1920 he was opposed by several factions within his own party. Thus the quest for the nomination rested chiefly among Attorney General A. Mitchell Palmer of Red-baiting fame, William Gibbs McAdoo, and Governor James Cox of Ohio. Probably McAdoo was the ablest, but the fact that he was Wilson's son-in-law reacted against him in the long run. For thirty-nine ballots at the San Francisco convention the issue was in doubt. Then the shift toward Cox began, and he was finally victorious on the forty-fourth. As his running mate, Assistant Secretary of the Navy Franklin D. Roosevelt was nominated, partly to capitalize on the magic Roosevelt name.

The Democratic stand on the League was unequivocal: "We advocate the immediate ratification of the treaty without reservations which would impair its essential integrity." The domestic features of the New Freedom, with specific emphasis upon "adherence to the fundamental progressive principles of social, economic, and industrial justice," were endorsed, along with economy and reduction of taxation. Women's suffrage, additional Federal educational aid, statehood for Puerto Rico, and independence for the Philippines were other prominent planks.

The Socialist party had been hard hit by the war. Splits within the ranks were numerous, and public opinion largely assumed that the Socialists had been un-American during the contest. Nevertheless, Eugene V. Debs was nominated again, although he was serving a term in Atlanta prison for his antidraft activities. The Farmer-Labor party also entered the campaign with a platform urging government ownership of natural resources, railroads, and mines, repudiation of the Treaty of Versailles, restoration of diplomatic and economic relations with Russia, and a series of social-economic reforms reminiscent of Theodore Roosevelt's New Nationalism. With Parley P. Christensen of Utah as the standard bearer, the Farmer-Laborites hoped to gain the support of liberals, labor, and farmers.

No Solemn Referendum

The Democrats, following Wilson's advice, tried to make the election a "solemn referendum" on the League. Cox's swing around the circle, however, during which he came out boldly for Wilson's international policies, made little impression on the electorate.

The Republican leaders, fearful of what Candidate Harding might say, kept him in his Marion, Ohio, home for a front-porch campaign. Harding's position vacillated. He condemned the Wilsonian League with sufficient vigor to retain the support of the Johnson-Borah faction, while ambiguous references to the desirability of a real "association of nations" encouraged internationally minded Republicans to remain loyal. To prevent pro-League Republicans from voting for Cox, Root, Hughes, Hoover, Stimson, and other respected leaders issued a statement denying that the issue was "between a league and no league," and implying that a vote for Harding was a vote for the League with reservations. Thus the issue continued to be confused, and voters who wanted the League supported Harding as well as those who did not. But it made little difference because the League was a dead issue among most voters.

The electorate wanted a change, and believed that it would come sooner and more completely under Republican rule. Thus Harding was swept into overwhelming victory. He received 16 million popular votes to Cox's 9 million; the 61 per cent of the total that the Republican candidate obtained was one of the most impressive majorities in American history.[1] The electoral totals gave Harding 404 to 127 for Cox. The Republican sweep was complete in the new Congress as well. In the Upper House, they had a majority of 22; in the Lower, of 167. But the victory was not one of party; it was brought about by war-born resentments and the desire to repudiate Wilson.

Harding and His Helpers

The new President readily admitted he was poorly fitted for his position. Born and brought up in rural Ohio, he had finally settled down in Marion,

---

[1] The Republican vote was double that of 1916, while the Democratic total was approximately the same as in the previous election. Debs received 900,000 votes, and Christensen, 26,000.

married an ambitious, fairly wealthy widow who urged him on to greater things, and became owner-editor of the local *Star*. Eventually he entered state politics, where at first he was affiliated with the Foraker or Standard Oil faction. He served in the state legislature and as lieutenant governor, but was defeated for the governorship in 1910. During the 1912 split, he remained a thorough conservative; indeed, he made the nominating speech for Taft. In partial reward and aided by a factional quarrel in Ohio, he was elected to the United States Senate in 1914. During his term in the Upper House he voted as he was told—and thus opposed the League as drafted, but favored it with the Lodge reservations.

Harding presented a good appearance and was an effective orator of the old school, although his speeches were more remarkable for their verbosity than for their content. He was not a deep thinker; he knew little about domestic problems and less about international ones. He was genial and easygoing to the point of weakness. The new President thought everyone was his friend—and friends were to be rewarded and trusted—but some of them let him down. That was one of the fatal errors of the new regime.

For his Secretary of State Harding wanted his fellow Senator, Albert Fall of

Governor Fuller of Massachusetts, President Harding, and Senator Lodge. (Acme.)

New Mexico; the suggestion aroused so much protest that the post went instead to Charles Evans Hughes, who did a remarkably fine job. Another good appointment was that of Herbert Hoover as Secretary of Commerce. The Treasury post was given to Andrew D. Mellon, a Pittsburgh millionaire affiliated with the aluminum interests. He proved a good choice for managing the nation's finances smoothly and economically, but his ideas on taxation were vigorously attacked by liberals. The desire to give plums to his friends, however, caused Harding to appoint what proved to be some of the worst elements within the party. To his backer, Harry Daugherty, went the Attorney Generalship, while Fall was made Secretary of the Interior.[2]

The Return to Tariff Protection

One of the first steps in the return to normalcy was to raise the tariff schedules above the levels of the existing Underwood Act. In addition to the wish to overthrow everything connected with the Wilson regime and to return to Republican protectionist principles, more tangible factors were at work. As part of the postwar reaction there developed a stronger feeling of nationalism, and with it a desire for greater self-sufficiency. And how could that self-sufficiency be better promoted than through a higher tariff? Then, too, a new American chemical industry had resulted from the war, while other industries, especially metallurgical enterprises, had grown rapidly. Were they now to be sacrificed on the altar of free competition? There was the feeling they would not survive were German-made competing products allowed to enter the American market with little or no duty.

The farmers joined in the demand for higher import duties. The farmers admittedly had made money during the wartime boom, but they had used their additional income to buy more land or more equipment. With the cessation of hostilities, however, the bottom dropped out of the agricultural market, and the farmers were left with a huge surplus that they could not sell at prices adequate to meet their overhead. Those who had borrowed from the banks or who had mortgaged their property were threatened with bankruptcy or foreclosure. Their dissatisfaction was quickly reflected in Congress, where their representatives had established the so-called Farm Bloc by the spring of 1921. Under the leadership of Republican Senators William S. Kenyon of Iowa and Arthur Capper of Kansas, Representatives and Senators of both parties from

[2] Will Hays of Indiana, chairman of the National Committee, received the usual Post-master Generalship; he was succeded by Hubert Work of Colorado in 1922 and by Harry S. New of Indiana in 1923. James J. Davis of Pennsylvania, Secretary of Labor; John W. Weeks of Massachusetts, Secretary of War; Edwin Denby of Michigan, Secretary of the Navy; Henry C. Wallace of Iowa, and Hubert Work, who succeeded Fall in the Interior Department in 1923, were the other cabinet members.

agricultural communities combined to demand aid for their constituents. So great was the voting strength of this bloc that unless some remedial legislation were passed, it might disrupt the agenda of the party in power.

Even before President Wilson returned from Versailles the movement to raise the Underwood rates had begun. The President sought to thwart this trend by sending a special message to Congress in which he pointed out that Europe was, and would be for years to come, in the process of rehabilitation and without the means for developing quickly along industrial lines. Therefore, he concluded, "no serious danger of foreign competition now threatens American industries."

In December, 1919, Wilson again attempted to combat protectionism by stressing the changes that the war had brought. The United States, now a creditor nation, could only maintain its exports to Europe by one of three policies. It could demand payment in gold, which would be unfortunate since it would adversely affect the economies on both sides of the Atlantic; it could extend further credit, which was unwise since Europe's indebtedness to America was large enough already; or it could exchange goods. The last was the most beneficial policy to all parties concerned. Therefore, Wilson sensibly concluded, "If we want to sell, we must be prepared to buy."

The American groups, especially the farmers, who were hard hit by the depression of 1920, were not content to listen to presidential moralizing. They wanted action to alleviate their troubles, and the action they sought was an upward tariff revision. In this stand they were aided by the growing dissatisfaction with Wilsonianism, by the Republican majority in Congress, by the decisive election results of 1920, and by the rapidly forming Farm Bloc. In anticipation of the incoming Harding regime, the House Ways and Means Committee, under the chairmanship of Joseph W. Fordney of Michigan, opened hearings in January, 1921. Anxious to rush through a temporary measure to quiet the farmers, a bill was introduced in February to increase the rates on agricultural imports. After quickly passing both Houses, it fell before Wilson's veto on March 3.

The advent of Harding, however, brought a speedy change in administration policy. In a special message to Congress on April 12, 1921, the new executive said: "I believe in protection of American industry, and it is our purpose to prosper America first." Consequently, the Wilson-vetoed measure was revived, again rushed through Congress, and signed by the President on May 27 as the so-called Emergency Tariff. Under it the duties on corn, wheat, meat, wool, and sugar were raised to about the Payne-Aldrich levels.

The tariff law of 1921 was only a temporary measure, to last until a broader and more definitive act was worked out. The House Committee on Ways and Means, still presided over by Representative Fordney and continuing to have a Republican, protectionist majority, now went to work in earnest. The Fordney bill, establishing rates considerably higher than in the Underwood Tariff, was passed by the House in July, 1921, very much as the committee had submitted it. The Senate Finance Committee, headed by Porter McCumber of North Dakota, was even more protectionist. It worked until April, 1922, on the Fordney bill, adding more articles to the dutiable list and raising the rates on the already taxable commodities. In the Senate debate, which lasted for four months, two-thousand amendments made the rates higher still. Strong lobbies were at work to help special interests. This was especially true of the dye industry, backed by the advocates of greater military protection, because many ingredients used in that industry were also required for the manufacture of explosives.

In conference, the House usually gave way to the Senate changes; as finally approved on September 22, 1922, the measure—now called the Fordney-McCumber bill—gave the United States its highest import rates in peacetime history. The duties on wheat, rye, corn, beef, lamb, sugar and wool were now higher than under the Payne-Aldrich Tariff. Chinaware, jewelry, cutlery, dyes, chemicals, toys, laces, and cotton goods were given substantial increases. By means of such changes, Congress hoped to keep the cost of production abroad plus the duty equal to the cost of production in the United States. Because production costs were constantly changing, the Tariff Commission was to keep vigilant watch over those foreign and domestic costs in order to maintain the precarious balance. When any inequalities arose, the commission would so advise the President, who might raise or lower the existing rates as much as 50 per cent to achieve stability.

The protection afforded by the Fordney-McCumber Tariff did not bring all the expected results. Since agricultural surpluses at home made protection ineffectual, the farmers were no better off and sought other cures. American exports did not materially increase because European countries raised their own tariff barriers in retaliation. The net result was to start tariff wars, which adversely affected international trade, and to develop greater nationalism. As the decade progressed, more and more American manufacturers, seeking broader markets for their products, established branches in foreign countries to escape the higher import levies. In the United States the lessening of foreign competition encouraged the concentration of industrial control in fewer hands. European debtor nations, unable to sell in the American market, found it increasingly difficult to pay their wartime obligations.

The Tariff Commission became a target of criticism. The industrial interests felt that its reports to the President were neither fair nor sound. The Democrats, particularly after 1926, charged that the members were motivated by political partisanship. In attempts to maintain the production-cost balance, Harding and Coolidge together raised the duties on thirty-two commodities and lowered them on but five (the latter being items in great general demand: bobwhite quail, cresylic acid, milk feed, paintbrush handles, and phenol).

Yet there was no organized demand for a general revision of the Fordney-McCumber Tariff during the rest of the twenties; indeed, in the campaign of 1928 both major parties urged continued protection. Important factors in this complacency were: the prosperity that the United States enjoyed until 1929 and the fear that a tariff change might disturb it; the industrialization of the South, originally the opponent of protection; and the attitude of the farmers who, although still unhappy, did not blame protection for their troubles. As a source of revenue, the Fordney-McCumber Tariff was bringing in more than $500 million annually, a jump of $200 million over the Payne-Aldrich receipts.

The Budget Act

In the quest for more efficient and economical administration, a better budget system for the Federal government had been urged for many years. The existing practice was wasteful, extravagant, and haphazard; the various executive departments, quite unrelated to one another and without cooperation, tried to obtain for themselves as large a share of the annual appropriations as possible.

Not until the Treaty of Versailles had been concluded, however, did President Wilson give ear to the reformers. Then the need to deal with the postwar problems of debt and tax reduction led him to ask Congress to provide for the more efficient planning of Federal expenditures. His particular suggestion was that the responsibility for drawing up the budget be placed in the hands of the executive branch, which would obtain estimates from the different departments of government for the ensuing fiscal year. The only changes that Congress should make would be through a special appropriations committee of each House.

In the fall of 1920 the legislature passed a measure that conformed in general with Wilson's wishes, but the President vetoed it because of a clause he believed placed an unconstitutional check upon the executive. Although the House quickly removed the objectionable part, the Senate did not act before the session ended. Nevertheless, Wilson continued to press the demand. In December, 1920, he once more made a plea for the passage of his original plan, saying: "I cannot overemphasize the necessity of economy in government appropriations and expenditures."

Shortly before his inauguration, Harding took up the issue in the Wilsonian form and there followed the passage in June, 1921, of the Budget and Accounting Act, which provided that each department, bureau, and agency of government should submit to the President its fiscal needs. He would then consider the feasibility of each and present the amended total budget to Congress on the opening day of every regular session, along with a financial report on the nation. That report would include an estimate of income and expenditures for the coming year and the financial picture for the preceding year. Only through a special committee of each House could departments appeal for a change. To assist the President in his work, a new Budget Bureau was to be established, and a Director of the Budget was to be appointed for fifteen years.

The executive budget system was much better than the old haphazard method, for it attempted to work out some relationship between receipts and expenditures. To be sure, there were still many weaknesses, for Congress frequently did change materially some of the executive proposals. Charles G. Dawes of Illinois, who had gained fame as purchasing agent of the Expeditionary Forces in World War I, was the first Director of the Budget, a position that he filled both colorfully and efficiently for about a year. Then in 1922 his place was taken by the equally firm and able General H. M. Lord.

The Harding administration also faced numerous other problems of the postwar era. Immigration restriction, the politically dangerous bonus issue, the equally troublesome farm problem, the matter of tax reduction and its attendant complication of lowering the debt were all given initial consideration. Completion of the formula for each, however, was not achieved during Harding's term, which was suddenly and unexpectedly shortened by death.

The voters were disturbed by the delays in settling various important matters and by the failure of the country to return to prosperity as speedily as had been anticipated. Thus in the Congressional elections of 1922 the Republican majority in the Senate was cut from 22 to 6, and in the House from 167 to 15. It is doubtful, however, whether even a stronger President could have accomplished much more during the period of reaction.

The Death of Harding

The presidency was a hardship for Warren Harding. Accustomed as he was to a life of comparative ease and freedom, he did not readily take to his burdensome task. In his own way he did try to fulfill the obligations of his office, but the more time he spent in dealing with the affairs of the nation, the more hours he devoted to golf, poker, and other diversions. The combination of harder work and more strenuous play was bad enough for a constitution that had been allowed to run down, despite its outwardly robust appearance; the situation became worse when Harding eventually realized that his supposed friends, whom he had appointed to public office, were betraying his trust in them. By early 1923 rumors were circulating that all was not well in certain administration quarters. Harding did not know how long it would be before the storm would break, and his nature was such that he blamed himself for what his appointees did.

As a release from his mental and physical troubles, he decided upon a speechmaking tour, which might serve as well the purpose of bolstering his position with the people. The trip began on June 20, 1923. Enthusiastic audiences in St. Louis, Kansas City, Denver, Salt Lake City, and other Western communities greeted his speeches on farm problems, taxation, railroad reorganization, the World Court, and prohibition. He drove a binder in Kansas, visited miners in Montana, saw the glories of Zion National Park, and participated in rodeos and pageants. Little time was allowed for relaxation; he was constantly in the limelight. All this took additional toll of a mind and body already close to the breaking point. By the time of embarkation for Alaska, the President showed definite signs of strain, which were augmented by news of the deceit of his friends. The sea voyage did not help him and, after his return to Seattle on July 27, his advisers urged him to cancel the remainder of his itinerary. This Harding refused to do. That evening, however, after a strenuous speech under a broiling sun, his physician, Dr. Charles Sawyer, had to be called because the President was suffering from what was diagnosed as ptomaine poisoning, supposedly the result of eating none-too-fresh crabs.

Harding was hurried to San Francisco, where consultants were called in. His condition failed to improve as pneumonia developed, followed by a stroke of apoplexy that brought death on August 2. The nation's grief was sincere. The funeral cortège from San Francisco to Washington, and then to Marion, was watched by mourning millions. Hundreds of eulogies were delivered for the man who was a martyr to the burdens of the presidency. Not until some time after his burial did the expected storm break, and only then did the public realize that the scandals of his administration were the worst in American history. It was then, too, that all sorts of rumors cropped up about his "mysterious" death; among them was the story that his wife had poisoned him. In all probability the strain of office, his weakened constitution, and the absence of will to live combined to bring Harding's death.

President Calvin Coolidge

The oath of presidential office was administered to Calvin Coolidge by his father early on the morning of August 3, 1923, in the family home at Plymouth, Vermont, where the Vice President had been vacationing. A graduate of Amherst College and trained for the law, Coolidge had made politics practically his vocation. He capably filled a number of local posts, served in the Massachusetts state legislature, and finally as governor. His stand in the Boston police strike made him a national figure and brought him the vice-presidential nomination in 1920.

There was nothing spectacular about Coolidge. He lacked the energy of Roosevelt, the idealism of Wilson, and the glad-handedness of Harding. He made up for those deficiences, however, by having the confidence of the people, to whom he appeared as an average American—the type who could steer the nation along its normal road in sensible fashion.

The new President was primarily a party man of the conservative school. Laissez faire was his doctrine, and he relied for advice, not upon the Republican liberals, but upon businessmen and lawyers. Economy in government was the general theme of his nearly six years in office, and he vetoed many a bill because of the proposed expenditures involved. Little social legislation was enacted during his administration, and there was little effort to enforce the existing regulatory measures against big business. This seemed to fit the mood of the country, for there was no widespread public demand for continuation of the Square Deal or the New Freedom. The vast majority of Americans were concerned with matters materialistic rather than idealistic, and Coolidge was the man who would assist them. The ship of state was never to be in danger while he was on the bridge, but the skipper never was to venture into uncharted seas.

The Harding Scandals

The first problem that President Coolidge faced arose out of the scandals connected with the administration of his predecessor. As has been said, Harding had an inkling that all was not well in the spring of 1923, but the facts of corruption were for the most part not brought to light until after his death. Whether Coolidge, who had attended frequent cabinet meetings during his vice-presidency and was in close contact with the men responsible for some of the misdeeds, knew what was taking place it is impossible to judge. After he became President, however, he kept Harding's official family until Congressional pressure and the force of public opinion compelled the resignation or removal of those involved in scandal, and he hesitated to press the cases against them until the evidence was so strong that to have failed to approve an investigation would have weakened his chances for the 1924 Republican presidential nomination. The only charitable thing that can be said about Coolidge's laxity is that he may have believed the charges against Fall, Daugherty, and others were primarily political, brought by the opposition to weaken his party.

The most spectacular of the Harding scandals involved the naval oil reserves. Back in 1912, President Taft had ordered set aside for the use of the navy some 70,000 acres of oil lands in the Elk Hills region of California, and three years later Wilson had added nearly 10,000 acres at Teapot Dome, Wyoming. Both of these acts were part of the general conservation program; the oil in those reserves was to be maintained until some future time when the navy might find difficulty in obtaining it from other sources.

When the operations in privately owned neighboring fields endangered the naval reserves during the latter part of the Wilson regime, Congress passed the General Leasing Act of 1920. This empowered the Secretary of the Navy, at his discretion, to "use, store, exchange or sell the oil . . . from lands in the Naval Reserves, for the benefit of the United States." Secretary Daniels then did lease a small percentage, but he kept the vast majority under naval control.

Shortly after Harding's inauguration, Secretary of the Interior Fall persuaded him to issue a secret executive order transferring the reserves to the Interior Department, and the amenable Denby concurred without question. Fall's excuse was the continued draining of the reserves; if he could lease them to private companies, the government would profit from the rentals. He also

Will It Prove More Than a Tempest in a Teapot?
(From the *San Francisco Chronicle.*)

subsequently intimated that the move would benefit national preparedness—in what way he did not specify.

It was in 1922 that Fall leased the reserves to two powerful oil operators: Teapot Dome to Harry F. Sinclair, and Elk Hills to Edward L. Doheny. Again these were secret transactions, but rumors of Fall's actions eventually circulated. Senator LaFollette, to whom any government deal with big business smacked of corruption, thereupon forced through the Upper House a resolution calling for an investigation, which was placed in the capable hands of Thomas J. Walsh of Montana.

Walsh required a year and a half of preparation before he was ready to start the open hearings on October 9, 1923. The testimony was long and complicated. Navy Secretary Denby was shown not to have committed any corrupt act, but the furor aroused over his complacency and lack of responsibility caused him to resign in March, 1924, to relieve Coolidge of further embarrassment.[3]

At first Fall made a good impression before the Senate committee; his answers seemed straightforward and convincing. Additional testimony from other witnesses, however, disclosed that he had recently spent some $170,000 on his New Mexico ranch. Walsh then pressed him as to the source of his sudden wealth. Only after weeks of questioning did the truth come out. Fall had received "loans" of $100,000 from Doheny and of nearly $250,000 from Sinclair—who also contributed lavishly to the Republican campaign chest. Fall's resignation did not save him from prosecution, along with Doheny and Sinclair, on criminal charges of conspiracy against the United States. Since the Department of Justice was under fire at the time, special government prosecutors, Owen J. Roberts of Pennsylvania and Atlee Pomerene of Ohio, were named in February, 1924, to press the cases. At this point Coolidge, who now strongly backed the investigations, made his only public statement about this particular scandal; he said that the guilty ones would be punished and the interests of the government fully protected.

Indictments for conspiracy and bribery were brought against Fall, Doheny, and Sinclair in June, 1924. Delays of various kinds held up the trials for years. All were found not guilty of conspiracy to defraud, but finally in October, 1929, Fall was convicted of accepting a bribe and sentenced to one year in prison and a fine of $100,000. Doheny and Sinclair were both acquitted on the bribery charges. The latter, however, who had been a most unwilling witness throughout, was found guilty of contempt of the Senate—for refusing to answer questions—and also of contempt of court—for having his jurors shadowed; he was fined $1,000 and sentenced to nine months in jail. In June, 1924, the govern-

---

[3] The Senate had demanded that Coolidge dismiss him. This he refused to do, partly because of his belief that Denby was not guilty of any malfeasance, partly because the Senate had no right to make the demand.

ment instituted proceedings to cancel the leases. Appeals delayed the final decision of the Supreme Court until December, 1927, when the tribunal invalidated the leases on the grounds that they had been obtained through fraud and corruption.

The tendency has been to emphasize the lurid incidents in the oil scandals, but equally significant was the revelation that men in high government posts apparently were willing to sabotage the conservation and defense programs of the nation. The appointment of Fall should never have been made, for he was known to be an opponent of conservation; and Denby was little more than a "yes man" who knew nothing about the needs of the navy. It likewise throws a strange light on the workings of American justice that the public official who took bribes was punished, while Doheny and Sinclair, who did the bribing and stood to profit to the tune of at least $100 million from the leases, should have escaped so easily.

Other betrayals of the public faith were revealed. Custodian of Alien Property Thomas W. Miller, a member of the so-called Ohio gang that trailed Harding to Washington for spoils of office, was found guilty of having obtained $50,000 through disposal of patents and other property in his care; he was fined $5,000 and sentenced to eighteen months in prison. Jess Smith, Harry Daugherty's right-hand man, committed suicide when he became involved in the scandal. The Department of Justice was likewise under suspicion of collaboration with certain corrupt big business interests. Indeed, Daugherty was accused of conspiracy to defraud the government. For some months Coolidge resisted pressure to remove him from the Attorney Generalship, but when he refused to answer the questions of a Congressional committee on grounds that he might incriminate himself, the President felt compelled to demand his resignation in March, 1924. Only jury disagreement kept Daugherty out of prison. His department was involved in the withdrawal of liquor from government warehouses for the benefit of other members of the "gang." Colonel Charles R. Forbes, Director of the Veterans' Bureau, was found guilty of diverting at least $250 million from his agency into the pockets of himself and his friends through corrupt contract and building practices.

The Republican party might have been critically affected had Harding still been President when the investigations and trials were taking place. While it is true that Coolidge did not do much to bring the perpetrators to account, he did enough to satisfy the voters, who showed in 1924 that they blamed the individuals involved, rather than the party. The easy complacence with which the general public shrugged off not only the evidence of governmental corruption but the sabotage of the conservation, veterans' aid, and preparedness programs is impressive evidence of the postwar retreat from idealism. The country seemed to have lost its capacity for indignation on such issues. And, to make matters worse, individuals connected with the prosecutions were hounded unmercifully and subjected to trials on fraudulent charges; fortunately, they all survived the attempts to besmirch them.

America for Americans

Among the problems of the twenties, none was more significant than formulation of a new immigration policy. Although the arrival of foreigners had been reduced by the literacy test of 1917 and the disturbed conditions of World War I, immigration seemed likely to assume huge volume again after the end of hostilities. The AFL and other worker groups demanded more effective dikes against the anticipated flood and they now found strong allies elsewhere. Before the war most employers' associations had opposed legislation that would bar sturdy foreign workers; now employer opinion tended to swing over to restriction—largely because of the fear of communism and labor violence that swept the country during the Red scare of 1919 and 1920. Also alarmed were the Daughters of the American Revolution and other patriotic organizations. An early evidence of this fear of alien radicalism was the amendment of the immigration laws to provide for the exclusion or expulsion from the United States of "aliens who are members of the anarchistic and similar classes."

The demand for more drastic laws became urgent in 1920 when consular reports warned that millions of war-weary Europeans were clamoring for transportation to the land of the free. In February, 1921, Congress passed a bill that would have fixed quotas for each European country, but Wilson vetoed the measure. Harding strongly favored this proposal, however, and in May, 1921, the Emergency Quota Act received the new President's approval. This first effort to apply a radically different principle in immigration policy provided that the number of aliens of any nationality who might be admitted to the United States in any year should be limited to 3 per cent of the foreign-born population of that nationality resident in the United States according to the census of 1910. Not more than 20 per cent of the annual total were to be allowed to enter in any one month, and the measure was "in addition to and not in substitution for" the previous immigration statutes.

The effects of the Emergency Quota Act were felt almost immediately. For the year ending June 30, 1921, 805,228 immigrants were admitted; for the following year, the first in which the act was in effect, the number dropped to 309,556. The restrictionists, however, were far from satisfied. They considered the total volume of immigration still excessive; they believed that the quotas assigned to southern and eastern European countries, although smaller than those allotted to western and northern countries, were yet too large.[4] President Coolidge voiced his sympathy with the restrictionist demands in his message to Congress of December 6, 1923: "New arrivals should be limited to our capacity to absorb them into the ranks of good citizenship. America must be kept American. For this purpose, it is necessary to continue a policy of restricted immigration. . . ."

Therefore on May 26, 1924, the Johnson Immigration Act fixed the quotas at 2 per cent of the foreign-born of each nationality according to the census of 1890, thus reducing the total number from about 350,000 to 164,000, while discriminating much more drastically against southern and eastern Europe. The new immigration, which had contributed 75 per cent of the total between 1901 and 1910, was now restricted to less than 15 per cent. Immigration from nations in the Western Hemisphere was not brought under the quota system. An excellent provision of the new law placed responsibility for the primary selection of immigration on United States consuls in the ports of embarkation, rather than on officials in American immigration stations like Ellis Island. This eliminated many earlier abuses: competition among steamship companies to land their passengers before the monthly quotas were filled, turning back immigrants after they crossed the ocean, separation of families, and frequent petition to Congress for special legislation to take care of hardship cases.

Certain provisions of the Act of 1924 created serious controversy. Anti-Japanese agitation in California and elsewhere was responsible for a clause excluding all aliens ineligible for citizenship. Since the Supreme Court as recently as 1923 had ruled that the Japanese, being neither "free white persons" nor persons of African nativity and descent, might not be naturalized under existing statutes, the purpose of the exclusion clause was obvious. President Coolidge and the State Department opposed this affront to Japanese national pride, while Japanese Ambassador Hanihara warned that "grave consequences" might follow this termination of the Gentlemen's Agreement to which Japan had adhered faithfully. But the Hanihara note only stiffened the determination of the exclusionists, despite the fact that the Japanese quota would have been a mere one-hundred immigrants a year in any case. Senator Kenneth McKellar of Tennessee probably expressed the opinion of a majority of the legislators when he said: "Whenever we permit a quota . . . , we have established a principle by which in the future Japanese can come in here as the subjects of other nations can come in. To that I am opposed . . . because we can never assimilate that race with ours." The day the act went into effect was one of mourning in Japan, punctuated by ominous anti-American demonstrations.

---

[4] Under this law, 198,082 were to be allowed to enter from western and northern countries and 158,200 from southern and eastern Europe. In the first year of the law's operation, only about 46 per cent of the quota came from the former, while 95 per cent of the latter's quota arrived.

A second highly debatable provision of the Johnson Act stipulated that the quotas based on 2 per cent of the foreign-born population in 1890 should be temporary. After July 1, 1927, the annual quota for each country should be "a number which bears the same ratio to 150,000 as the number of inhabitants in continental United States in 1920 having that national origin . . . bears to the number of inhabitants in continental United States in 1920. . . ." To the Secretaries of State, Commerce, and Labor was delegated the virtually impossible task of determining the national origins of the entire American population of 1920. Although these unhappy officials more than once asked to be relieved of responsibility for attempting a quantitative analysis of the American melting pot after three-hundred years of immigration and intermarriage, Congress refused to repeal the national origins clause.

When the preliminary findings of the experts were announced, the general public gained its first real understanding of what was involved in the national origins quotas. The effect of this formula would be to almost double the quota allotted to Great Britain, while reducing the German and Irish quotas by almost one half and the Scandinavian by two thirds. A cry of protest arose from the affected groups, and Herbert Hoover and Alfred E. Smith both advocated repeal of the national origins provision during their presidential campaigns of 1928.

All efforts to change the troublesome formula were bitterly opposed. Patriotic organizations cooperated through the so-called American Coalition in popularizing the slogan "Keep America American." Organized labor opposed any change that might increase the total volume of immigration. After several postponements, the new quotas finally became effective on July 1, 1929.

Total quota immigration, fixed at about 350,000 in 1921 and reduced to 164,000 in 1924, was established at about 150,000 in 1929. Yet even this number was not destined to enter. The Great Depression strongly discouraged immigration, while in 1931 President Hoover, fearing that incoming aliens might swell the ranks of the unemployed, reduced the total quota to 48,500 by executive order. At the same time, Mexican immigration, normally exempted from the quota system, was drastically reduced by bans against "floaters" who crossed the border in search of jobs. Through rigid screening of newcomers and a severe deportation policy, the Hoover administration actually permitted less than 36,000 aliens to enter the country in 1932, while more than 103,000 were leaving either voluntarily or involuntarily. Depression and war continued to hold immigration to small proportions for more than a decade. Not until 1946 did annual arrivals again exceed 100,000.

The radical curtailment of immigration was one of the most decisive events in recent American history. It brought certain obvious advantages: American workers no longer had to fear competition of cheap immigrant labor, and cities might expect some alleviation of the serious social problems involved in large-scale assimilation of people brought up in a foreign culture. On the other hand, the new immigration laws were open to sharp criticism. For example, a quota system that admitted over 65,000 immigrants from Great Britain in a year but less than 6,000 from Italy and none at all from Japan was based upon racial assumptions that had their foundations not in science and reason, but in nativist prejudice. Therefore it was felt in many quarters that a more rational policy would have been to hold total immigration within manageable limits, but to permit the selection of actual immigrants on the basis of individual merit.

The Veterans and the Bonus

Even before the armistice was signed, Colonel Theodore Roosevelt, Jr., son of the ex-President, had dreamed of a vast veterans' organization to be formed not from the AEF alone, but from all men who had been in uniform during the great conflict. On February 16, 1919, Roosevelt entertained twenty officers at a dinner party in Paris where he enlisted their support for his plan. One month later an organization meeting attended by a thousand soldiers was held in the same city. There the name "American Legion" was adopted. Later organization gatherings were staged in St. Louis and in Minneapolis. On September 16, 1919, the American Legion was chartered by act of Congress. The new organization was a powerful champion of the ideal of patriotism, a vigilant guardian of the cause of national defense, a promoter of many worthy charities, and a sponsor of an active social and recreational program for its members. But to the general public the Legion became best known as a tremendously effective pressure group seeking legislation to benefit the service-men.

Through the efforts of the Legion's lobbyists, the Fordney bill passed the House in May, 1920, by a vote of 289 to 92. The measure proposed to provide the veteran with "adjusted compensation" in one of four ways: land settlement, aid in the purchase of a city or country home, vocational training, or bonds on the basis of $1.50 for each day of military service. The bill was buried in the Senate Finance Committee, but the issue of the bonus, as the proposal was soon popularly tagged, became one of the most controversial political issues of the twenties.

Shortly after Harding became President it came up again. To Congressmen the issue was a delicate one. Most of them wanted to cut down expenses and taxes, but to vote against the bonus would mean antagonizing their many con-stituents who had served in the armed forces. Furthermore, despite the im-portance of the economy program, the argument of the veterans seemed sound; they had served in the armed forces for approximately $1.00 a day. Those who had remained in civilian life had benefited financially from the large wage increases of the wartime boom. Were not the veterans entitled therefore to some "adjusted compensation" for the time they had spent in their country's service? The payment need not be in cash; it could be made in long-term bonds or certificates.

President Harding was able to delay the movement for a time, but in 1922 the veterans' demands could no longer be denied. In March, Representative Fordney reintroduced his 1920 measure, together with a plan to pay the adjusted compensation by issuing paid-up twenty-year endowment policies or certificates. The value of these policies would be determined at the rate of $1.00 a day for military service in the United States and $1.25 for service overseas. A veteran might borrow up to one half the face value of his policy; he could then use this amount to purchase land or a home. On March 23, the Fordney bill was approved by the House by the one-sided vote of 333 to 70, and the galleries, packed with members of the Legion and other veterans, cheered as each affirmative vote was cast. The Senate was slower to act, and the general feeling in the Upper House was that the tariff should be completed first. The power of the veterans' lobby was so greatly feared, however, that the bonus proposal was given precedence; on August 30, 1922, the Senate gave its approval by a vote of 47 to 22.

The President refused to sign the measure, and in his veto message—which has been called Harding's most impressive state paper—pointed out that Congress had made no provision for paying the bonus. He admitted that he was in accord "with the avowed purpose of the bill to give expression of a nation's gratitude to those who served in its defense"; yet the cost, estimated at $3 billion—one sixth of the public debt—should not be added to the already heavy financial burdens of the total population to help less than five million persons. To do so "would undermine the confidence on which our public credit is builded and establish the precedent of distributing public funds whenever the proposal and the members affected make it seem politically appealing to do so."

The House quickly overrode Harding's veto, 258 to 54; the Senate sustained it, although only by four votes—44 to 28. This defeat of the Fordney bill served only as a temporary check upon the demands of the veterans; thereafter they redoubled their efforts.[5] The problem was presently dumped in the lap of President Coolidge. In March, 1924, the World War Adjusted Compensation bill, better known as the Soldiers' Bonus, was quickly approved in the House by a vote of 355 to 54. The Senate accepted the principle, but not the form,

[5] Not all veterans favored the bonus. Indeed, in 1922 an Ex-Service Men's Anti-Bonus League was established. This organization asserted that the veterans had received all they had been promised, as well as the unexpected $60 discharge pay. Were a bonus paid, the veteran would be "pauperized in body and spirit."

of this proposal with a similarly overwhelming ballot, 67 to 17, in April. In the ensuing conference early in May, a compromise was reached: twenty-year paid-up endowment policies were to be given to veterans on the basis of $1.00 a day for home and $1.25 a day for overseas service; those who were entitled to $50 or less were to be paid in cash; the certificates, which averaged $1,500 and bore interest of 4 per cent, were expected to total $3.5 billion; veterans could borrow up to 22½ per cent of the face value of their certificates.

Coolidge, following the precedent of Harding, vetoed the bill, using economy as the reason, along with the failure of the measure to provide the wherewithal to finance it. The President criticized the bonus as class legislation and insisted that its payment would not end future pension demands. Congress promptly repassed the bill over this veto by overwhelming votes. The legislature was not under Coolidge's thumb, and 1924 was an election year. Few members cared to endanger their chances of re-election by voting against the measure.

The bonus or adjusted compensation was not the only form of assistance given the veterans of World War I. In August, 1921, Congress established the Veterans' Bureau, which consolidated the work of three hitherto separate agencies: the Federal Board for Vocational Training, the Bureau of War Risk Insurance, and the Soldiers' Health Service. Colonel Charles R. Forbes of Washington was named as first administrator of this new bureau. Eventually more than forty hospitals and a dozen soldiers' homes were supervised by the Veterans' Bureau through its numerous regional branches. Unfortunately, the agency gained a bad name early in its career because of the misdeeds of Forbes; following a change in administration, however, the bureau performed excellent service for those who sought its benefits.

By 1931 the number of veterans receiving compensation was nearly 300,000; approximately 100,000 widows were being helped; 230,000 men were on disability allowance; and more than 500,000 had received hospital treatment. The cost of this care, the borrowings on the certificates, and the administration of the vocational program raised the price of World War I considerably. By 1931 the amount paid out through the Veterans' Bureau was $14 billion. While this sum was for a worthy cause, it helped to complicate Republican plans for economy and lowering the public debt—plans that Coolidge and Mellon devoted themselves to fulfilling, particularly after the election of 1924.

The Triumph of Calvin Coolidge

The Republican party entered the campaign of 1924 with some misgivings. There had been signs of discontent with the regime in the Congressional elections of 1922 when the party's majority had been materially cut. Coolidge's support in Congress was shaky, as the overriding of his bonus veto and the rejection of some of his legislative proposals demonstrated. Finally and most serious, continued revelations of scandals had besmirched the party with an oily brush.

The nation, however, did not blame Coolidge for the weaknesses of his predecessor. He seemed to have given the nation a Midas touch—and growing prosperity covered a multitude of the party's sins of omission. Full purses made many a voter indifferent to the ideals of social justice that had appeared so important a decade before.

When the Republican Convention met in Cleveland early in June, the nomination was already signed, sealed, and all but delivered to Calvin Coolidge. This was not simply because the President had the confidence of the nation, but because Coolidge had planned it that way. Shortly after he assumed office, he started the machinery moving. By Thanksgiving, 1923, he had obtained the support of most of the Republican wheelhorses. Not content, he then turned to the business interests and, with the assistance of William M. Butler, a textile industrialist of Massachusetts, he received their backing. Consequently, Coolidge was overwhelmingly named on the first ballot. There were, however, a few incidents to mar the President's triumph: some of the LaFollette backers from Wisconsin and North Dakota refused to make the nomination by acclamation, and the demonstration after the nomination seemed singularly lacking in enthusiasm and spontaneity.

The position as running mate was offered to Frank Lowden, largely as a sign of revolt against the dictatorship of Butler. Much to the chagrin of the convention, however, Lowden refused to run. After several substitutes had been considered, the nomination went, apparently by default, to Charles G. Dawes, former Director of the Budget.

The Republican platform emphasized the "record unsurpassed" in economy and debt reduction, and asserted that the Fordney-McCumber Tariff was in part responsible for the excellent national recovery. Public utilities must be regulated, but government ownership was out of the question. The Railroad Labor Board, a relic of the Wilson regime, was denounced, along with compulsory arbitration of labor disputes. The eight-hour day was supported, as well as a constitutional amendment to end child labor. Conservation of natural resources, promotion of the merchant marine and aviation, immigration restriction, help for disabled veterans, and an army and navy strong enough for national defense were likewise advocated. In the diplomatic field, the platform praised the work of the Washington Conference as a move toward world peace and favored joining the World Court. The only mention of the scandals came when all corruption was denounced. The platform, like the candidate, was unexciting, but comfortably safe.

The Democratic Marathon

The Democratic party was by no means united when its convention opened in Madison Square Garden, New York City, on June 24, and the cleavages that developed during the long gathering accentuated still more the diverse elements within the organization. The death of Woodrow Wilson in the preceding February left no one strong enough to handle the situation—and it is doubtful whether even Wilson could have. The Southern delegates, fearing Negro and labor problems, vigorously opposed the revival of anything that savored of the New Freedom; the eastern elements of the party tended to be heavily Catholic and bitterly attacked the Ku Klux Klan, which had considerable backing among fundamentalist southern and western Protestants. The South, with its growing industrialization, was losing interest in the principle of tariff for revenue only, and with that defection one of the few remaining Democratic issues died. The delegates from urban districts were against prohibition, but those from rural sections were "drys."

The two leading candidates were William Gibbs McAdoo and Governor Alfred E. Smith of New York. The former had the backing of the West and the South; he appeared to be the knight who might lead the charge against Eastern big business interests. Detrimental were his relationship to Wilson and his

How Could McAdoo Hope to Win? (By Darling
in the New York Tribune.)

legal activities in behalf of Doheny and the oil group. Smith was regarded by Eastern liberals as the man best fitted to carry on the quest for social justice; his record as governor was excellent in the field of progressive legislation. But, as a Catholic and a "wet," he was anathema to the Klansmen in general and the South in particular.

Each man had enough backing to prevent the other from gaining the nomination; neither would yield to the other. Ballot after ballot was taken without a decision being reached. The delegates' nerves were on edge, the galleries, vociferously for Al Smith, got out of hand, and the heat was terrific. Not until more than ninety ballots had been taken was there a movement in favor of a compromise candidate, John W. Davis, a wealthy New York corporation lawyer and diplomat. On the one-hundred-third ballot the tired, worn-out, divided delegates selected him. Although able and distinguished, Davis could scarcely be advertised as a great liberal who would appeal to the anti-Coolidge vote. The nomination of Charles W. Bryan, brother of William Jennings, did not strengthen the ticket.

The making of the platform also showed the divisions within the ranks. A plank calling for American entry into the League of Nations was defeated by more than two to one; denunciation of the Klan as un-American failed by the close vote of 546 to 541—and that closeness served to widen the breach; the differences over prohibition were indicated when the only step taken was to criticize the Republicans for failure to enforce the amendment. The 1922 tariff law was denounced as an aid to monopolies and a detriment to trade. The Transportation Act of 1920 must be revised, and the merchant marine must once more come under government control. The farm aid and labor planks were little different from those in the Republican platform, but Republican corruption was roundly condemned. War was frowned upon as "a relic of barbarism"; disarmament was a possible solution. All in all, this document was no more constructive than that of the opposition.

LaFollette Runs Again

Senator LaFollette had long been disappointed in the trend away from liberalism. To stem this reaction, he formed the Conference for Progressive Political Action in 1922, reminiscent of his National Progressive Republican League of a decade before. He hoped through this new organization to capture the Republican party and obtain the 1924 nomination for himself.

When Coolidge nevertheless won the party designation, LaFollette charged that it was the result of intrigue on the part of Butler and Coolidge's cabinet advisers. Even before the delegates departed from Cleveland, he planned to call a second Cleveland convention on July 4, at which he would consolidate the various progressive forces and revive the movement for reform and social justice.

This convention quickly named LaFollette for the presidency by acclamation, with Democratic Senator Burton K. Wheeler of Montana, who had played a prominent part in bringing to light some of the Harding scandals, as his running mate. This Progressive ticket was endorsed by the Socialist party, the Farmer-Labor party, and the AFL. The Communists tried to lend their support also, but LaFollette refused it.

The brief fourteen-point platform was the handiwork of LaFollette. The power of the Federal government, it asserted, must be used to crush, not foster, monopolies. Public ownership of water power must be established, as well as control over all natural resources. Rapidly progressive taxes must be assessed upon large incomes and inheritances. An immediate farm-relief program should be enacted, together with reform of the Federal Reserve System. Direct election of Federal judges and Congressional power to override judicial decisions were sponsored. The child labor amendment should be quickly ratified, and injunctions denied in labor disputes. The foreign policies of the Harding-Coolidge regime were denounced as mercenary, primarily in the "interests of financial imperialists, oil monopolists and international bankers." There should be a general revision of the Treaty of Versailles to bring it more in line with the armistice. Disarmament should be speedy, war outlawed, and a referendum taken before the United States could become involved in hostilities.

Coolidge Victorious

The campaign did not arouse public enthusiasm. Davis made a swing around the circle during which he played up the national scandals and promised that such things would not be found in his administration; yet he did not try to link Coolidge with the Harding corruption. He tried to debate the issues, but the listeners were not interested and the Republicans did not challenge his arguments. They centered their attacks on LaFollette and warned that a vote for him was a vote for revolution and overthrow of the government. Coolidge, hard hit by the recent death of his son, did not show much interest in the election until the early fall. His speeches were few and stressed the economic phase. "This is a business country," he declared, "it wants a business government." LaFollette concentrated his appeal on voters of the Middle and Far West.

The Republican slogan, "Keep Cool with Coolidge," satisfied the listless electorate. The general question seemed to be, "Why swap horses in the middle of prosperity?" and no adequate reason could be found by the voters. The November returns gave Coolidge 15.7 million votes, Davis nearly 8.4 million, and LaFollette 4.8 million. Coolidge had 2.5 million more than the combined opposition. The electoral college showed Coolidge with 382 votes, Davis with 136—all from the South—and LaFollette with 13 from his native Wisconsin. The good showing of LaFollette in twelve states of the West, in which he ran ahead of Davis, indicated that old-fashioned progressivism was not entirely dead, but it was not sufficiently strong to support a third party. Coolidge's triumph, though impressive, was largely a negative one; only about half of the qualified electorate bothered to cast their votes.

The Republicans also maintained their control of the new Congress. The Senate would consist of 50 Republicans, 40 Democrats, and 6 LaFollette men; the House would be made up of 232 Republicans, 183 Democrats, and 20 in the LaFollette bloc.

The inaugural of March 4, 1925, was a simple one, in line with President Coolidge's desire to avoid ostentatious show. Yet more people heard his speech than had listened to any previous inaugural, for it was broadcast by radio. And

President Coolidge and His Cabinet. *Seated, left to right:* Secretary of War Weeks, Secretary of State Hughes, President Coolidge, Secretary of the Treasury Mellon, Attorney General Stone, Secretary of the Navy Wilbur; *standing,* Secretary of Agriculture Wallace, Secretary of Commerce Hoover, and Secretary of the Interior Work. *Not shown:* Postmaster General New and Secretary of Labor Davis. (Acme.)

that speech, considered the ablest of Coolidge's career, set the keynote for the next four years. "I favor the policy of economy," he said, "not because I wish to save money, but because I wish to save people." Then he continued:

> Economy is idealism in its most practical form. . . . The wise and correct course to follow in taxation and all other economic legislation is not to destroy those who have already secured success but to create conditions under which everyone will have a better chance to be successful. . . . We are not without our problems, but our most important problem is not to secure new advantages but to maintain those which we already possess.

His was to be an administration in which the government did its best to encourage private enterprise and to keep government control at a minimum.

Congress Balks

There were a number of changes in the official family after Coolidge took office. Only Herbert Hoover, Andrew Mellon, and James Davis held their original posts in the Cabinet throughout the remainder of the Coolidge regime.[6] Secretary of State Hughes retired in March, 1925, to be replaced by Frank B. Kellogg of Minnesota, who had been serving as ambassador to Great Britain. Although Kellogg was a hard-working lawyer and was considered competent for the post, he lacked the ability and farsightedness of Hughes.[7]

President Coolidge had many difficulties with Congress, despite its Republican majority. He was the nominal leader of his party, but his following was to be found among the rank and file, rather than in Congress. The Progressive legislators usually combined with the Democrats to attack administration measures, sometimes with success. Furthermore, Congress tended to believe that the executive branch was infringing on its prerogatives, and in turn Coolidge resented Congressional efforts to dominate his office. Yet the President did not try to dictate to the legislature as Theodore Roosevelt and Woodrow Wilson had done; he was content, after a few flare-ups, to maintain the separation of powers.

One of Coolidge's first conflicts with Congress came when he nominated Charles B. Warren of Michigan as Attorney General to succeed Harlan Stone, recently appointed to the Supreme Court. Even though the Senate Judiciary Committee approved this nomination in February, 1925, a storm of protest developed when Warren's name came before the whole Senate. Democrats and Progressives, led by George Norris of Nebraska, asserted that Warren's Michi-

---

[6] Hoover, however, did resign shortly before his nomination for the presidency in 1928.

[7] Other cabinet changes were: William M. Jardine of Kansas became Secretary of Agriculture on the death of Henry C. Wallace in 1924; Curtis Wilbur of California succeeded Denby as Secretary of the Navy; Harlan F. Stone replaced Daugherty as Attorney General.

gan State Sugar Trust had broken the antitrust laws and that the nominee had defended his company's actions. When Coolidge saw he would have a fight on his hands, he requested postponement of the final vote; at the same time, however, he denounced the charges of the opposition as false.

On the opening of the new session of Congress, Coolidge again submitted Warren's name. When the vote was taken on March 10, Vice-President Dawes was absent, and without his guiding influence the appointment was turned down, 41 to 39. Coolidge was furious; contrary to the advice of his party leaders, he resubmitted the nomination a week later, only to be turned down once again by the more decisive vote of 46 to 39. The President then offered Warren a recess appointment, which would not need Senate approval, but Warren refused to accept it. Consequently, Coolidge nominated John Garibaldi Sargent of Vermont, with whom the Senate found no fault and who performed the functions of the Attorney General's office in competent fashion. Thereafter, Coolidge tried to ascertain beforehand whether his appointees were acceptable. While he did not like this procedure, he realized that he lacked the capacity for forceful leadership of some of his predecessors. Although some lesser appointments were rejected, the Upper House generally supported the President in his nominations from this time on.

Factional Differences

The Republican regulars took steps to punish those who had bolted the party to support LaFollette. The Progressives, headed by Smith Brookhart of Iowa, lost their key positions on committees, had no chance for chairmanships, or were demoted to the bottom of committee lists. This attack was continued when the Republican Senators refused to grant Brookhart his newly won seat and substituted a Democrat. This virtual purge of the Republican insurgents accounts in part for the factional strife Coolidge encountered during the first half of his second administration. The insurgents held the balance of power in Congress and, to gain support for the measures they sponsored, they frequently allied with the Democrats to form an effective opposition to administration bills.

The elections of 1926 showed a definite swing toward the left, especially in the Middle West. Brookhart, seeking vindication, defeated the administration-backed Albert Cummins in the Iowa Senatorial primaries and then went on to defeat his Democratic opponent in the November ballot. Gerald Nye of North Dakota also was re-elected over a presidential favorite. Robert LaFollette, Jr., took the seat of his famous father, who had died in June, 1925. In the East, the reaction was likewise shown when a Democrat, David Walsh of Massachusetts, defeated William Butler for the United States Senate, despite Coolidge's active support.

While the Republicans retained a majority of 40 members in the House of Representatives of the Seventieth Congress, their hold over the Senate was extremely precarious. At the opening session, the line-up indicated that there would be 48 Republicans, 47 Democrats, and 1 Farmer-Laborite. Therefore, in order to maintain the small majority, the Republican regulars had to restore the purged insurgents to their committee posts and to promise them legislative concessions.

The matter was further complicated by the fact that two recently elected Republican Senators—William S. Vare of Pennsylvania and Frank L. Smith of Illinois—were denied their seats. Their chief opponent was Senator Norris,[8] who won his battle when an investigating committee of the Upper House eventually disqualified both Vare and Smith because they had spent too much money in winning their elections. It was shown that Vare spent at least $800,-000, and Smith practically as much—which probably came from the Insull utilities group. In the Pennsylvania case, Norris' triumph was short-lived, as the governor named the reactionary Joseph Grundy to the vacant position.

Government and Business

Meantime, the Coolidge administration showed an increasing tendency to give business a free hand. One of the early indications of this laissez faire attitude was in appointments to governmental departments and agencies entrusted with the regulation of big-business activities. The Interstate Commerce Commission, with its composition changed, no longer favored curbing practices deemed inconsistent with the antitrust laws; as a result, laissez faire flourished. The most notable addition to this commission was Thomas F. Woodlock of New York, who had made his money from railroad stocks. The liberals, led again by Senator Norris, failed to thwart his appointment; they believed that henceforth the railroads would dominate the commission.

In similar fashion the appointment of William E. Humphrey of Washington to the Federal Trade Commission gave the advocates of big business a majority, and that majority proceeded to change the former policy of regulating big business to a more limited one of giving advice. Moreover, the Tariff Commission underwent an overhauling, with the new appointees proving to be sympathetic to the wishes of manufacturing groups.

Under the circumstances, businessmen had little reason to complain of

[8] Norris had persuaded his liberal friends in Pennsylvania to vote for Vare's Democratic opponent, William Wilson. Despite this liberal support and the fact that he carried almost every county outside of Philadelphia, Wilson was beaten by Vare's Philadelphia machine.

governmental interference with their activities during the Harding-Coolidge period. On the contrary, the Department of Commerce tried to help industry in as many ways as possible. Secretary Hoover gave the trade association movement his enthusiastic support; in the stabilization of production through voluntary cooperation he saw hope for the survival of small business. The Commerce Department published a handbook designed to promote the movement and sponsored many industrial conferences. Much statistical information was collected and printed by the Department itself, even though the exchange of such data was one of the chief devices through which trade associations hoped to induce their members to restrict production and maintain prices.

What one branch of the government was actively promoting, other branches regarded for a time with suspicion. The Federal Trade Commission condemned certain trade association practices, and Attorney General Daugherty prosecuted the concerns using the Hardwood Manufacturers' Association for price-fixing activities. In this case the Supreme Court ruled that the gathering of information and statistics among members of such an association violated the Sherman Antitrust Act. The Court took a similar stand two years later in the Linseed Oil case.

For the moment these decisions discouraged the trade association movement, but presently the situation changed. The Supreme Court greatly weakened the antitrust laws in a series of five-to-four decisions. In 1925, for example, it decided in the Maple Flooring Manufacturers' Association and the Cement Manufacturers' Protective Association cases that exchange of statistical information not involving any agreement as to production or prices was legal.

The Justice Department became more lenient, although the several Attorneys General in the 1921–1929 era did bring a total of 138 antitrust cases to the courts. Public indifference, plus the attitude of the judiciary, resulted in fewer convictions after 1925, and the opinion was frequently expressed that the Sherman and Clayton Acts were outmoded and should be repealed. Indeed, the Department adopted the practice of advising organizers of trade associations in advance on the legality of their activities.

There was also a definite change in the policy of the FTC after the appointment of Humphrey in 1925. "So far as I can prevent it," announced the new chairman, "the Federal Trade Commission is not going to be used as a publicity bureau to spread socialistic propaganda." And almost at once he began revising the rules. These changes were vigorously fought by the Commission's minority members and by the liberals generally. Senators Borah and Norris asserted that the FTC might as well be dissolved, so completely was it dominated by big-business interests. And it is true that the commission, instead of aiding in the prosecution of concerns under the antitrust laws, actively participated in drafting codes of ethics and trade-association practice agreements under which members of an industry promised not to use unfair methods of competition such as bribery, misbranding, misrepresentation of products, refunds, discounts, freight allowances, and the like. Sometimes clauses forbidding price cutting more directly were added in secret by the producers; in any case, the general tendency of these associations was toward restrictions on production and price fixing. So far indeed was this true that even while the Republicans were still in power the government somewhat modified its policy toward such activities. In 1930, the Department of Justice brought suit against eight of the associations; the next year Assistant Attorney General John Lord O'Brian reported that an investigation of fifty trade associations revealed that the majority of them were violating the Sherman Act.

By that time, however, the trade association movement had grown too strong to be wiped out easily. The encouragement of the several agencies of government—the Supreme Court, the Department of Commerce, the Department of Justice, and the FTC—and their preference for modifying questionable business practices through quiet admonition and conferences rather than through the use of more aggressive methods had built up a huge network of business associations. The government practice of cooperating with business rather than regulating it was widely praised by industrialists large and small.

Debt and Tax Reduction

The struggles between the conservatives and liberals during the twenties were best exemplified in the issues concerning tax reduction, the disposition of Muscle Shoals, and the farm problem.

The peak of gross United States debt was reached on August 31, 1919, with the then staggering total of $26.6 billion. President Wilson and his successors regarded the reduction of this amount as one of the principal duties of the Federal government. At the same time, however, the several administrations deemed it essential to decrease taxes, which had mounted steadily in size and in number during the war period. The latter problem became a political as well as an economic issue during the twenties The conservatives desired the burden to be lifted most quickly from the wealthy, who could thereby use the amounts hitherto earmarked for taxes to develop national industry and national income. The liberals, on the other hand, believed that high rates should be continued on excess profits, incomes, and inheritances, with the primary alleviation given those in the lower brackets in order to stimulate purchasing power. President Coolidge and Secretary Mellon were subjected to bitter attacks for not sharing this view.

Despite this controversy, the Federal government not only lowered taxes materially, but by June 30, 1930, had reduced its debt to $16.2 billion. This decrease of approximately one third of the national debt in a decade led his conservative admirers to describe Andrew Mellon as the greatest Secretary of the Treasury since Alexander Hamilton.

In his postwar messages President Wilson favored giving some tax relief to business, but at the same time emphasized his belief that the first step should be to help the average taxpayer and to eliminate the nuisance levies, while retaining the income tax, the excess-profits tax, and the estate tax as the mainstays of government income. The Revenue Act of 1919 followed in general the Wilsonian principles.

With the advent of President Harding, conservative influences predominated. In a series of recommendations to Congress from April through August, 1921, Secretary Mellon urged repeal of excess-profits taxes, a compensatory increase in corporation levies, ending most of the nuisance taxes, and gradual reduction of both normal and surtaxes on individual incomes. Harding supported Mellon in strongly urging repeal of the excess-profits tax.

Congress did not follow Harding's wishes in the Revenue Act of 1921. The excess-profits levy was slightly raised, some of the nuisance taxes were ended, income, surtax, and corporation taxes remained unchanged, although the exemption for married persons was raised from $2000 to $2500. The members of the Farm Bloc and the Democrats were largely responsible for thwarting administration plans.

Although government revenue from internal taxes fell off in 1922 because of the depression and lowered tax rates, the Treasury Department reported a surplus. Consequently Mellon urged in 1923 a revision of the whole tax program. He argued that the wealthy would not invest their money in industry when the government was taking so large a percentage of their profits. Without investments by the rich, new fields of economic enterprise could not be developed. Instead, the rich were investing more and more in tax-exempt securities or in foreign fields to avoid payment of income obligations. President Coolidge upheld these views in his Congressional message of December, 1923, and even suggested a Constitutional amendment to abolish the issuance of tax-exempt securities.

Once more the combination of the Farm Bloc and Democrats prevented the administration from having its way. The Revenue Act of 1924 did, it is true, lower taxes in the lower brackets and allow a 25 per cent rebate on earned income, but it left corporation taxes unchanged and raised estate levies. An unusual clause provided for the publication of the name of everyone making a tax return, together with the amount paid, under the assumption that such publicity would make tax evasion more difficult.

Although Coolidge signed this measure, he was highly critical of it. To him the law was "tax reduction, not tax reform," and both reduction and reform should be promoted "upon an economic and not a political basis." He attacked the publicity feature as an "unwarranted interference with the right of a citizen to privacy," which would not attain its objective because evaders would conceal their assets more cleverly. All in all, he concluded, the act would throttle initiative and new enterprise.

The Republican victory in the election of 1924 and the prosperity of the years immediately ensuing helped to bring success to the Coolidge-Mellon tax theories in the several revenue measures from 1926 to 1928. Normal taxes, surtaxes, and corporation taxes were lowered, the estate tax was cut approximately in half, and the excess-profits levy was wiped out along with most of the remaining "nuisance taxes." Another administration victory came when the clause requiring publicity of tax returns was repealed. Despite Democratic charges that the majority wanted only to relieve the wealthy, the administration succeeded in keeping the existing income-tax exemptions, thereby following the Mellon theory that as many citizens as possible should contribute to the running of the government.

Although the administration anticipated a drop in revenue as a result of the tax cuts, such a drop did not materialize. Surpluses continued to pile up as the government became the beneficiary of payments on the war debts, back taxes, and the like. The opposition took advantage of the surplus to denounce the administration for not cutting taxes even more.

From the standpoint of later theory, both the Republicans and Democrats were wrong in this controversy. A new school of economists argued that tax policies should follow the ups and downs of the economic cycle. In depression times the government should reduce taxes to encourage investment; it should spend more than it received in revenues in order to create purchasing power. During boom times, according to this line of reasoning, tax rates should be raised and government expenditures reduced as a curb upon inflation. It may therefore be argued that the whole effort to reduce taxes during the twenties was misdirected. Much of the money saved by wealthy taxpayers went not into healthy investment but into speculation in land and securities, thereby contributing to the cycle of inflation and the crash of 1929. Sounder policy would have been to retain high rates and to retire even more of the public debt. Conservatives, however, have never accepted this contention. They have continued to regard the Coolidge-Mellon policy as a model of sound government finance.

Whatever the merits or deficiencies of Republican tax policy may have been, the government was run efficiently from a purely business standpoint. The following table indicates various phases of government economy:

	Receipts from Income and Excess-Profits Taxes	Total Government Receipts	Total Government Expenditures
	(in millions of dollars)		
1921	$3228	$5625	$5538
1922	2087	4109	3795
1923	1691	4007	3697
1924	1842	4012	3506
1925	1762	3780	3529
1926	1974	3963	3585
1927	2220	4129	3493
1928	2175	4042	3643
1929	2331	4033	3848

The Battle over Muscle Shoals

As part of the preparedness program, the National Defense Act of June, 1916, had empowered the President to construct and operate power facilities for the manufacture of explosives and fertilizers. Nothing was done until February, 1918, when Wilson ordered the 35-mile Muscle Shoals section of the Tennessee River in Alabama to be used for those purposes. The Wilson Dam was almost completed before the end of Wilson's second term and plants were constructed for the production of atmospheric nitrogen.

Such was the situation when Harding became chief executive. As another step toward normalcy, Harding was determined that the government must retire from the hydroelectric power business. Consequently, work on the Wilson Dam was stopped and Secretary of War Weeks, hoping to dispose of the nitrate plants and the uncompleted dams on which the government had already spent more than $100 million, asked for bids from private industry. One of the first to reply was Henry Ford, who in July, 1921, offered to take a hundred-year lease of Muscle Shoals at a rental of 4 per cent of the construction costs, to buy the nitrate plants which he promised to have constantly available for the manufacture of explosives, and to provide 40,000 tons of nitrogen annually for fertilizer if the government would complete the dams already started.

This proposal was well received by the administration, especially by Secretary Hoover, by the Republican and Democratic leaders in Congress, and by the farm groups—who looked forward to the promise of cheap fertilizer. Senator Norris, however, was vigorously opposed to granting the lease, and he began a long fight, against tremendous odds, to defeat it. Norris believed that Ford was using the cloak of fertilizer manufacturing to obtain hydroelectric power for his own purposes at a ridiculously low price. Were that done, the aims of the Federal Power Act of 1920 would be defeated. The government should complete the Muscle Shoals dams and plants and then operate them for the manufacture of power, explosives, and fertilizers for the primary use of the army and navy. A special government corporation should be set up to supervise Muscle Shoals and to sell any surplus power to either public or private corporations. Norris did not make this suggestion on the spur of the moment. He had been studying the power problem for years and had reached the conclusion that public-run plants could produce electricity more cheaply than could private concerns. He had figures to show that the government-operated hydroelectric company of the Province of Ontario furnished electricity to local consumers at about one seventh the rates charged in Washington, D.C., by privately owned utility companies.

While the struggle over the two plans was going on, the new executive, Calvin Coolidge, urged in his message to Congress of December, 1923, that the Muscle Shoals property and equipment be sold to the highest bidder, who could then operate the power and fertilizer facilities under private control. It seemed as if this laissez faire doctrine would prevail when in March, 1924, the House approved the Ford lease by a vote of 227 to 143. But by that time the issue was complicated still more when several private utility companies formed the Associated Power Companies of the South and offered to rent Muscle Shoals for $3 million a year, to produce 50 million tons of fertilizer yearly, to spend $1 million on a research project that might lower the cost of fertilizer to the farmer, and to accept regulation in the production of electricity by the Federal Power Act.

Norris, however, persuaded his fellow Senators not to act upon either the Ford or Associated Power proposals and succeeded in shelving Coolidge's plan. Indeed, before 1924 was over, Ford withdrew his offer in the face of certain defeat, saying, "We have lost our interest in Muscle Shoals. Productive business cannot wait on politics." Nevertheless, President Coolidge and the conservatives in Congress were also able to frustrate Norris' advocacy of government operation. In 1928 the two Houses of Congress did accept a resolution embodying the Norris proposition, but Coolidge killed it with a pocket veto.

This Muscle Shoals controversy was the most notable battle between conservatives and liberals during the twenties. By 1928 the contest had developed into a stalemate, with neither Coolidge nor Norris able to have his way. The issue did not die, however; it was to be very much alive during the Hoover regime and to result in eventual victory for Norris under the New Deal.

The failure of the various Muscle Shoals proposals did not prevent other ventures in related fields. The continued spring floods in the Mississippi Valley, culminating in the disastrous one of 1927, made the Coolidge administration realize the need for action. Consequently, a special commission was appointed to supervise the alleviation of suffering and to propose new methods of flood control. Its chairman, Herbert Hoover, personally visited the devastated areas and, with Red Cross aid, provided relief and prevented potential epidemics from developing.

Congress, sensitive to the widespread demand that something be done to prevent future occurrences, finally passed the Jones-Reid Act of May, 1928, under which more than $300 million was appropriated to construct levees, drainage basins, and spillways along the dangerous parts of the river. Coolidge urged that the states concerned bear one fifth of the costs, but Congress, believing that they had spent enough, placed the whole financial burden upon the Federal government.

Combining flood control, hydroelectric power development, and irrigation was the movement to regulate the waters of the Colorado River. In the summer of 1921, Congress authorized seven states[9] to try to effect an aggreement as to how the waters of that river might be apportioned. Although a tentative arrangement was approved by those states in the late fall of 1922, Congress did not sanction it until six years later. There were numerous reasons for this delay: Arizona and California quarreled over their respective water allotments; engineers differed over method; there was controversy over means of operation; and a struggle developed over the "twilight zone" of Federal-state authority.

Finally, however, these problems were disposed of and, just before Christmas, 1928, Congress passed the Boulder Dam Project Act. This provided for construction of a 750-foot dam near Las Vegas, Nevada, capable of storing at least 20 million acre-feet of water, for building a canal to carry water to the arid Imperial Valley of California, and erecting hydroelectric power plants. The cost of the undertaking, estimated at $165 million, would eventually be taken care of through the sale of electric power and water privileges to the neighboring states during the next half century. In such sales, local government agencies were to be granted preference over private concerns. The passage of this act marked the beginning of the Federal government's active participation in the production of hydroelectric power, a participation which was to grow during the next decade. It also indicated a partial breakdown of the laissez faire attitude that had been so characteristic of the Coolidge regime.

The Farm Problem

In many ways American farming showed remarkable progress in the twenties. New methods permitted the cultivation of the semiarid belt of the Great Plains, where much land was brought under the plow during World War I and another great area during the twenties. Agriculture was being transformed by another mechanical revolution. Gasoline-powered equipment was taking the place of the horse-drawn machinery of prewar days; the number of tractors in use increased

---

[9] Colorado, Arizona, New Mexico, Utah, Nevada, California, and Wyoming.

from 230,000 in 1920 to 920,000 in 1930. With new combines that cut, bound, threshed, and sacked wheat as they were pulled through the fields, one man could harvest forty acres in a day and do work that formerly would have required the labor of fifty men. In planting, similar if less dramatic economies were introduced through the use of disk plows and power drills. Nor was wheat the only crop thus mechanized. The corn belt witnessed the increasing use of such machines as the three-row planter, the four-row cultivator, the picker-husker, and the husker-shredder, and through the use of sleds in the cotton fields one man could harvest as much as fifteen hand workers.

The seed which the farmer sowed was much improved. Hybrid corn, for example, grew more quickly than older varieties, yielded heavier crops, and was resistant to many of the diseases that had earlier plagued the farmer. Similarly improved strains of wheat, sugar, and cotton seed were developed, as well as better fertilizers and both materials and methods for insect control.

Parallel progress was made by livestock raisers. Partly as a result of scientific breeding, but more because of better care and nutrition, hogs produced more pork and lard, steers more beef, and cows more milk. Important work was also done to control animal diseases.

But as agriculture became more scientific, it likewise became more expensive. Full advantage of the new methods could be taken only by farmers cultivating many acres, who could afford large capital investments. Corporations appeared upon the agricultural scene. Largest of these was the Campbell Farming Corporation, which owned a domain of 100,000 acres in Montana on which it produced 500,000 bushels of wheat a year. Similar if smaller enterprises were engaged in the cotton-growing or fruit-raising business. In 1928 there were 9,000 corporation-owned farms in the United States.

The corporate organization of agriculture, however, was unusual. Most farms continued to be owned by individuals, but they were becoming larger. By 1930 the average size of farms in the corn belt was already 239 acres, and experts were advocating 640 acres as the minimum desirable size for a family enterprise, while for maximum efficiency they were saying that a farmer would require 1,000 or even 2,500 acres. The small farmer, usually tilling the less desirable land, found it increasingly difficult to make a living. Many of these small farmers lost their holdings through mortgage foreclosures, or sold or abandoned them and became tenant farmers, agricultural laborers, or factory workers in the cities. More and more chose the third of these alternatives. During the seven years after 1921 the nation's agricultural population declined by some three million.[10]

The mechanization of agriculture, however, more than made up for the

[10] Farm tenancy increased 4 per cent during the decade, so that by 1929 more than 42 per cent of the farmers were tenants. Also in 1929 more than one sixth of the national bankruptcies involved farmers.

decline in the number of farmers. Acreage under cultivation had greatly increased during the war under the stimulation of large export markets and government-guaranteed prices. During the twenties not only did this expanded acreage not decline, but it actually increased. Production of all the great staples remained at high levels.

Yet, while the supply of American farm products remained large, effective market demand for them declined soon after the war was over. Between December, 1919, and December, 1920, wheat dropped from $2.15 a bushel to $1.44, corn from $1.25 to $0.68, and cotton from $0.36 a pound to $0.14. Nor did foreign market prospects improve during the ensuing years. The age was one of economic nationalism; by tariffs and bounties the various countries, often in reprisal for American tariffs, were striving to promote their own agriculture and to cut down dependence on imports. In this shrinking market, moreover, American foodstuffs were competing with those grown in Canada, Australia, and Argentina.

The domestic demand for agricultural products failed to expand as in earlier generations. Immigration restriction and a declinging birth rate meant fewer new Americans to be fed and clothed. Changes in diet and style likewise influenced the market. As a larger proportion of the population followed sedentary callings, less bread and meat were eaten. To be sure, a vitamin-conscious generation consumed more vegetables and fruits, but the contraction of one type of agriculture and the expansion of another was not an easy transition. The cotton grower as well as the textile manufacturer was injured as women began to wear less clothing and rejected cotton in favor of silk and rayon. Finally, the displacement of perhaps 8 million horses by automobiles, trucks, and tractors profoundly affected the agricultural situation. Some 35 million acres had been required to grow feed for these animals, and most of this acreage was now planted with crops suitable for human consumption.

Denying the urgency of the problem, some critics pointed out that farm prices during the twenties were 25 to 50 per cent higher than they had been in pre-war days and that agricultural exports maintained a substantially higher level than before 1915. Spokesmen for the farmers, however, emphasized a number of important points. In the first place, the prices of manufactured goods had risen much more than had the prices of farm commodities. The farmer's real income, therefore, was less than before the war. Moreover, a substantial proportion of the nation's farmers had bought land at the inflated values of the war years. The collapse of prices in 1921 not only gave these farmers a very small return upon the capital they had thus invested, but when they had borrowed the money to purchase the land, low prices made it extremely difficult for them to make their interest and principal payments. Indeed, the growth of mortgage indebtedness on American farms from $3.8

billion in 1912 to $9.2 billion in 1930 was one of the most serious aspects of the situation. The high costs of agriculture were reflected not only in the increased prices of the things the farmer had to purchase and his higher interest burdens, but in higher taxes, higher wages for farm labor, higher freight rates, and higher distribution costs.

The spokesmen for the farmers insisted that prices must be raised to save American agriculture from disaster. But the problem was a difficult one. Tariff protection was ineffective because of the annual surplus that had to be sold in the world market. To raise prices, either the surplus would have to be reduced or exports would have to be subsidized in some manner. The various legislative projects whereby the farmers sought to obtain these ends occupied much of Congress' attention during the Coolidge administration.

Legislating for the Farmer

The Emergency Tariff of 1921 did not stop the fall in agricultural commodity prices, and even before this was demonstrated the Packers and Stockyards Act was passed through the efforts of the Farm Bloc in August, 1921. This statute attempted to help the raisers of livestock by declaring it unlawful for packers to monopolize the market, to control prices, to establish territorial pools, or to otherwise engage in unfair practices. Were the Secretary of Agriculture to consider any charges or practices as unfair, he was empowered to issue "cease and desist" orders to packers and stockyard operators in somewhat the same fashion as the Federal Trade Commission. Less than two weeks later Congress enacted the Grain Futures Act, which gave the Secretary of Agriculture similar control over the dealers in wheat and other grains. At the same time, the Agricultural Credits Act broadened the powers of the War Finance Corporation to allow greater loans to agriculture, so that farm surpluses could be more effectively handled. During the life of this measure (until 1924), nearly $300 million was loaned to farm associations.

Still not satisfied, the Farm Bloc forced through the Capper-Volstead Cooperative Act in February, 1922, after ten months of debate. This act reinforced the Clayton Act by once more exempting agricultural organizations from the provisions of the Sherman Antitrust Act. Furthermore, farm associations were allowed to process and market their staples in interstate commerce under the watchful eye of the Secretary of Agriculture.

None of this legislation provided the expected relief, nor did the Fordney-McCumber Tariff; hence the Farm Bloc tried again with the Federal Intermediate Credit Act, passed on March 4, 1923. Under this measure, the Federal Farm Loan Board established twelve new banks—known as the Federal Intermediate Credit Banks—separate and distinct from the Land Banks even though they were located in the same towns and had the same officials. The government contributed the $5 million capital for each institution, and each bank had the right to rediscount agricultural paper and to loan money to farm co-operatives for as little as six months and as long as three years. The collateral for these loans comprised the agricultural products the cooperatives had in their warehouses. In addition, the farmers' associations were allowed to establish their own credit corporations, which could also loan money, while the maximum loans permitted to be made by the Farm Loan and Federal Reserve Banks were increased. By the end of the decade, farmers had borrowed more than $3 billion from these various sources.

Other concessions to agriculture came when the Fordney-McCumber rate on imported wheat was raised to 42 cents a bushel in 1924, and on butter to 12 cents a pound in 1926. Yet the farmers were coming to the conclusion that a tariff increase would not help a product that was available for export. The price of such a commodity was established primarily by the demand in the world market. A different type of farm relief was advocated by George Peek and Hugh S. Johnson—who were to become more famous under the New Deal—president and attorney respectively of the Moline Plow Company of Illinois. Briefly, the Peek-Johnson plan, first advocated in 1922, proposed that the exportable surplus of an American staple like wheat should be purchased by some government agency at a fair domestic price and then sold abroad at the world market price. The losses incurred in pegging domestic prices above their world level could be covered by a special tax or equalization fee levied upon the producers of the staple.

This proposal was the basis for several measures sponsored in Congress by Senator Charles McNary of Oregon and Representative Gilbert Haugen of Iowa. The McNary-Haugen bills provoked stormy controversy, and the original plan was several times amended between 1924 and 1928.[11] Each new amendment brought additional support. Originally the plan had the backing primarily of the Middle West. Gradually the Southern representatives joined the other members of the Farm Bloc as cotton and tobacco were added to the staples whose price was to be protected, and more votes were gained among the Congressional members from the Far West. Moreover, an increasing number of liberals and men prominent in government circles like Vice-President Dawes, Secretary of Agriculture Wallace, and Frank Lowden added their names to the growing list of McNary-Haugen adherents.

Despite the increased backing for the plan, President Coolidge consistently

[11] The first bill was introduced in January, 1924, and, after months of debate, was defeated in the House on June 3 by a vote of 223 to 153. The second version was voted down in May, 1926, 167 to 112. The third effort passed the House 214 to 178 and the Senate 51 to 43, but was vetoed by President Coolidge. The fourth attempt likewise passed—the House vote was 204 to 121, the Senate, 58 to 23—but again encountered a presidential veto which could not be overridden.

refused to give his approval, and he was supported in his stand by Secretary of Agriculture Jardine and Eastern conservatives generally. In addition to the economic problems involved, the situation had political ramifications. Here was an issue that crossed party lines and threatened to develop sectional differences as well. The threat of another Populist revolt alarmed the conservative wing of the Republican party. It was a phase of the contest between the advocates of laissez faire and the proponents of governmental control and regulation.

In February, 1927, the McNary-Haugen bill passed Congress, but Coolidge vetoed it with a caustic message. He asserted that the scheme benefited the growers of only a few staples like wheat, cotton, tobacco, and corn, but did not help agriculture in general. It provided for price fixing by the government—which was not in accord with his laissez faire theories. It was unconstitutional[12] because it enabled the Farm Board to levy a tax—the equalization fee—and that power was reserved to Congress under the Constitution. The President also argued that the plan would result in further overproduction of the staples involved and would lead to dumping of foreign crops in the American market to take advantage of the artificial prices. Finally, he declared that the Farm Board personnel throughout the country might develop into "an enormous bureaucracy . . . offering infinite opportunities to fraud and incapacity." The President admitted that the lot of the farmer was an unhappy one. He said:

> The evidence is all too convincing that agriculture has not had its fair share of the national income since the war. Farmers and business men directly dependent upon agriculture . . . are entitled to and will receive every consideration at the hands of the government. To saddle agriculture with unjust, unworkable schemes of government control is to invite disaster worse than any that has yet befallen our farmers. A real farm relief measure must be just and impartial. . . . I have frequently urged such legislation. I wish again to renew my recommendation that some such plan be adopted.

The McNary-Haugen advocates paid little attention to the President's preachments. Instead they tried to get support for still another version of their own project. This measure, passed by both Houses in May, 1928, contained the major parts of each of its defeated predecessors. It provided for the establishment of a Federal Farm Board, which would have a $400 million revolving loan fund available for agricultural cooperatives in the marketing of staples. If losses were to be suffered when the surplus was sold in the world market, then an equalization fee would be collected. To explain briefly and as simply as possible how the measure was expected to work, it can be assumed—in a purely hypothetical case with figures reduced for ease in comprehension—that the wheat produced in a given year was 100 million bushels. Of that amount the

---

[12] His veto message was accompanied by an opinion of Attorney General Sargent supporting this contention.

American market could take care of 75 million bushels. Under the Fordney-McCumber amendment of 1924 the import tax on wheat was $0.42 a bushel. Even though the world wheat price might be only $1.00, the American farmer, taking advantage of this protection, would desire to sell as near the $1.42 level as possible—say for $1.40. Therefore the Farm Board would lend the wheat cooperatives enough to buy the 25 million exportable surplus at the protected price ($1.40)—and the total farm income from wheat would be $140 million. However, the exportable amount could be sold at only $1.00 a bushel, or at a loss of 40 cents a bushel. This total loss of $10 million (25 million bushels at 40 cents loss) would be made up from an equalization fee, levied upon those farmers who produced the total wheat supply, which would amount to 10 cents a bushel. The farmers would not object to this tax, for the plan would enable them to get a net of $1.30 a bushel for their whole crop, whereas they would receive only $1.00 if they competed in the world market.

Using the same arguments as in his 1927 message, Coolidge vetoed this new version, and the legislature again could not muster the necessary votes to override him. Laissez faire had once again triumphed. President Coolidge still contended that government aid for a particular class was un-American.[13] Moreover, he felt that the farm situation was gradually improving. That improvement would be speeded if the farmers used more scientific methods and resorted to voluntary crop reduction. Consequently, both Harding and Coolidge urged the farmers to establish cooperative associations through which they could work out their own problems in the true laissez faire manner. Both Presidents were willing to help. For example, in 1921 the first in a series of Commissions on Agricultural Inquiry was established, and the following year a National Agricultural Conference was called under government auspices. The Farm Bureau Federation was given government blessing, while the Department of Agriculture was constantly sending out bulletins offering suggestions on forming more competent cooperatives and giving various types of advice.

Yet at the end of the Coolidge regime the farm problem was by no means solved. Farm income had dropped from 15 per cent of the national total in 1920 to but 9 per cent in 1929. The farmer's purchasing power was steadily diminishing. The political effect of the resulting unrest was indicated by the fact that both major parties were forced to bid for the votes of the farmers by incorporating promises of agricultural aid in their platforms of 1928.

The Coolidge period was one of conservative supremacy. But the liberals had developed a counterprogram on taxation, power, and agriculture. So long as prosperity continued, the country generally was not greatly interested in these issues, but the economic collapse of the next few years was to transform completely the balance of political power.

[13] Actually, of course, government aid for a particular class—manufacturers—had been defended as "American" since the days of Alexander Hamilton.

14

Foreign Affairs, 1921–1929

While economic materialism was holding sway at home, the United States was playing a varied role in the world of diplomacy. Numerous inconsistencies developed, which were to be expected in a country that had never had any well-defined, long-range international policy. The League was rejected and membership in the World Court postponed, yet the United States attempted to find some other road to world peace. Extreme nationalism was shown in the erection of high protective walls against imports and immigrants on the one hand, although, on the other, the United States showed willingness to make concessions in the matters of debts, reparations, and disarmament. In Latin-American affairs, Uncle Sam also played a dual role as dollar diplomat and as good neighbor.

The Knox Resolution

President Harding's Secretary of State Hughes was immediately faced with the problem of ending the state of war with Germany, Austria, and Hungary, not only as a diplomatic necessity, but as a means of answering the public demand that domestic wartime controls be concluded. There was no interest in reviving the Treaty of Versailles issue. Indeed, President Harding was undoubtedly voicing the opinion of the American majority when he said on April 12, 1921, that while he desired to prevent war, "We can have no part in a committal to an agency of force in unknown contingencies; we can recognize no super-authority."

Consequently, the Knox Resolution, which Wilson had vetoed successfully the year before, was passed again and signed by Harding on July 2, 1921. The resolution asserted the state of war "to be at an end," and it reserved for the United States "all rights, privileges, indemnities, reparations, or advantages" accruing from its part in the war and the armistice arrangements, as well as those which it would have obtained had it ratified the Treaty of Versailles.

To Hughes this was a one-sided arrangement that might not stand up in a court of international law. Therefore, in August, 1921, treaties were drawn up with Germany, Austria, and Hungary, which reiterated the rights claimed by the United States without any commitment to the Treaty of Versailles. They were all duly ratified before the year was over. Hughes subsequently asserted in support of this method of getting out of the war:

> It was in the interest of the Allies, as well as of ourselves, and it was essential to the cause of peace that we should dispose of the matter by separate treaty; and this was accomplished in a manner confirming our rights and not derogating from those of the Allies.

The World Court

So terrorized by the Republican irreconcilables was the administration that at first the State Department declined even to acknowledge receipt of communications from the League of Nations. Gradually, however, this extreme policy gave way to one of quiet cooperation with many of the activities of the new body. Unofficial observers, sent to the League sessions from the beginning, were frequently called upon for advisory consultation on non-political matters. Then in 1924 the country was officially represented at the Second Opium Conference. Thereafter, the United States participated actively in nearly fifty meetings of a similar non-political nature. In addition, five envoys were permanently stationed at Geneva to take care of American interests at League headquarters.

The Harding and Coolidge administrations hoped to take the further step of associating the United States with the Permanent Court of International Justice provided for in Article 14 of the League Covenant. A stimulus for American admission to this so-called World Court was the decision of the League Council that membership would be open to all nations of the world, regardless of their membership in the League.

The Court represented an idea in which Americans had been interested since at least 1832, when the Massachusetts State Senate advocated the establishment of a tribunal for the peaceful settlement of international disputes. In 1899 John Hay had instructed the American delegates to the Hague Conference to propose the organization of a permanent tribunal. The American government was disappointed in the makeshift substitute that was then adopted and attempted— again unsuccessfully—to establish a real World Court during the Hague Conference of 1907. As Secretary of State, Elihu Root had been particularly inter-

ested in the project, and in 1920 when the protocol establishing the postwar tribunal was drafted, he took a leading part. Far from being a sinister foreign
conspiracy, therefore, the Court was peculiarly American in its philosophy and
origin. John Bassett Moore, a leading American expert on international law, was
one of the eleven judges chosen in the first election to the Court bench. Later,
Charles Evans Hughes and Frank B. Kellogg, both former Secretaries of State,
as well as Manley O. Hudson, a prominent professor of international law, served
terms as World Court judges.

Enter Uncle Sam, with Escort. (By Harding in the *Brooklyn Eagle*.)

As Secretary of State, Hughes was an ardent supporter of American entrance
into the World Court and succeeded in gaining Harding's backing. However,
Hughes believed that the United States should append certain reservations to
the World Court protocol which would further guarantee the American position. On February 17, 1923, four such reservations were announced: (1) American membership must not commit the United States to any Treaty of Versailles or League obligations; (2) the United States must have equality with
League members in the selection of judges to the Court; (3) the United States
would pay its fair share of Court expenses; and (4) the Court protocol could not

be amended without the approval of the United States, which could withdraw from the Court at any time.

A week after Harding received these Hughes reservations, he submitted the Court plan to the Senate for its consideration, saying: "Our deliberate public opinion of today is overwhelmingly in favor of participation"; but Henry Cabot Lodge cared little for public opinion and kept the project shelved in the Foreign Relations Committee, of which he was still chairman. Disappointed, the President renewed his pleas in public speeches in both April and June, but the committee still took no action. Harding's death did not end the matter, for Coolidge took up the issue again in his first annual message to Congress in December, 1923, with an even more urgent request for Senatorial support. By that time other factors underlined the need for joining. Several of the bilateral arbitration treaties were up for renewal, and the other signatories, notably Great Britain, France, and Japan, were requesting that disputes might be submitted to the World Court for adjudication.

Public opinion came out more strongly for admission as the Senate continued to refuse to act. Prominent citizens of both parties voiced the necessity for speedy consent; the American Bar Association, the Federal Council of Churches, the American Federation of Labor, and the United States Chamber of Commerce went on record in favor of the action.

Both major parties advocated joining the Court in their 1924 platforms. Lodge died during the year, but the chairmanship of the Senate Foreign Relations Committee fell to an even more determined obstructionist, Senator Borah. The issue was still postponed, despite a resolution advocating membership overwhelmingly adopted by the House of Representatives on March 3, 1925, and despite the stress which Coolidge gave to the cause in his inaugural address the next day when he said: "We ought not to withhold our own sanction because of any small and inessential difference . . . The weight of our enormous influence must be cast upon the side of a reign, not of force but of law; and trial, not by battle but by reason."

Not until December, 1925—two years and ten months after Harding's original message on the subject—did the Court issue reach the floor of the Senate. There the so-called battalion of death—Borah, Johnson, Reed, and their followers—put up a bitter fight, but the measure was finally accepted by the one-sided vote of 76 to 17. Suspicious Senators had, however, added to the original Hughes reservations a fifth, which constituted a veritable omnibus of safeguards for American sovereignty and dealt particularly with the issue of the Court's power to give advisory opinions.

Immediately Secretary Kellogg forwarded the reservations to the Court members and to the League Council. The Council concluded that some of the reservations might "hamper the work of the Council and prejudice the rights of the members of the League," and therefore asked that the United States meet with the League members to arrange a compromise. This Council opinion made the battalion of death jubilant since it provided support for their charge that the Court was merely a League tool. Kellogg refused the proposed meeting because "the reservations are plain and unequivocal." Nevertheless, at a conference held at Geneva in December, 1926, it was finally agreed to accept the American reservations with the exception of that part of the fifth which read: ". . . nor shall it, without the consent of the United States, entertain any request for an advisory opinion touching any dispute or question in which the United States has or claims an interest."

The Senate refused to approve this compromise, and President Coolidge stood by the Upper House, saying in his December, 1926, annual message that he considered the whole matter closed. Perhaps he was motivated by the election results of the previous month; ten out of fifteen Senators seeking re-election who had voted for the World Court were defeated in campaigns that were interpreted in some quarters as referendums on the issue. Although this was not the case, the League's refusal to approve all the American reservations actually did increase isolationist sentiment. The matter was then dropped until after the election of Herbert Hoover in 1928.

The Washington Conference

Even though the United States refused to associate itself with the League and the Court, it did try other means to promote world peace during the twenties. The first effort was through the Washington Conference of 1921–1922. This conference was the brain child of Senator Borah, who as early as December, 1920, became worried about existing conditions. Japan was already beginning a broad naval construction program calculated to place her on a par with, or possibly superior to, Great Britain and the United States. Borah feared lest this lead to a world-wide naval armaments race that might bring on another war— and war would end the American isolation for which he had struggled.

In December, 1920, Borah succeeded in adding to a pending naval appropriation bill a rider authorizing the President to call a conference among the United States, Great Britain, and Japan in order to secure a mutual agreement for yearly naval reductions over a five-year period. Not until July, 1921, however, was this bill enacted into law. By that time the new Secretary of State Hughes realized that naval armament was only one phase of potential trouble. As he subsequently said: "Without better understanding of the Far East, it would have been idle to deal with proposals of limitation of armament." The State Department was disturbed by the aggressive foreign policy Japan had followed during the war when she had entrenched herself in the Shantung peninsula, secured additional rights in Manchuria, and generally threatened the principles of the

Open Door and the territorial integrity and independence of China. Nor was the United States satisfied—despite the safeguards in the League of Nations Covenant—that Japan would actually refrain from fortifying the former German islands in the Pacific that she had received as mandates. One of these islands in particular, Yap, Hughes hoped to have internationalized because of its importance as a cable station.

The British government desired a conference on Pacific affairs even more than did the American. Its particular problem was whether to renew the Anglo-Japanese alliance. The British were well aware that the alliance was unpopular in America despite British declarations that their country would never join Japan in a war against the United States. Canada and Australia, suspicious of Japan and hoping for closer relations with the United States, were outspoken in their demand that the alliance be discontinued. Indeed their insistence on the issue at an imperial conference in June, 1921, led to the British government's suggesting a conference of Pacific affairs to Washington even before Hughes' project could be presented in London.

Thus President Harding's formal invitations to the naval limitations conference included the proposal to discuss as well the problems of the Far East and the Pacific. That being the case, the list of the invited was expanded to include France, Italy, the Netherlands, Portugal, Belgium, and China. All accepted the invitation, although Japan did so with much less enthusiasm than the others.

On November 12, 1921, an impressive group of delegates gathered in Washington. Secretary Hughes, Henry Cabot Lodge, Oscar W. Underwood, and Elihu Root made up the United States delegation. Arthur Balfour headed a prominent British group that included envoys from the Dominions; Premier Aristide Briand, René Viviani, and Jules Jusserand were the French delegates; Sao-Ke Alfred Sze, Minister to the United States, and Wellington Koo, Minister to Great Britain, were the Chinese representatives; and Baron Tomosaburo Kato, Minister of the Navy, and Masanao Hanihara represented Japan. The prominence of these envoys indicated the importance each country attached to this conference.

After a welcoming address by President Harding, Chairman Hughes took over the leadership of the conference. His initial speech proved a bombshell. "The time has come," he said, "and this Conference has been called, not for a general resolution or mutual advice, but for action." And the action he then proposed was drastic reduction of naval armaments. The building of all capital ships should cease for ten years; this holiday must affect not only the building programs, but the ships still on the ways. Moreover, old ships in service above a certain total tonnage must be scrapped.[1] The comparative naval strength of the

---

[1] The United Sates should scrap fifteen old ships and stop work on fifteen new ones having a total tonnage of 845,740; Great Britain, nineteen old and four new totaling 583,375 tons; and Japan, ten old and seven new of 448,958 tons.

nations concerned must be maintained, and the capital ship tonnage of the several countries should be approximately 500,000 for Great Britain and the United States, 300,000 for Japan, and 175,000 for France and Italy. Hughes hoped that this 5:5:3:1.75:1.75 ratio would also be observed for lesser naval craft.

This proposition to scrap almost two million tons of combat ships came as a decided surprise to the audience. British delegates, with their country's long tradition of naval supremacy, and the Japanese envoys, who had hoped for naval equality with the other two powers, did not at first seem to favor the plan. A British observer, Colonel Repington, is said to have exclaimed: "Secretary Hughes sunk in thirty-five minutes more ships than all the admirals of the world have sunk in a cycle of centuries." But the galleries, filled with prominent persons from many countries, were more than enthusiastic. Taking advantage of the shock which his speech had occasioned, Hughes quickly obtained an adjournment over the week end before there was an opportunity for the delegates to praise or criticize. And before the conferees met again, newspapers in all parts of the world came out in favor of the Hughes proposition.

On November 15 the discussions began in earnest among representatives who, on the whole, were very cooperative. The main exception was the French delegation, which opposed the extension of the quota system to lesser naval craft and refused to consider the proposal for reduction of armies and land fortifications. Otherwise, there was considerable unanimity of opinion on general terms, although there were some differences over detail.

During twelve weeks of discussion, several important agreements were reached. The foremost was the Five-Power Naval Treaty, signed February 6, 1922. This listed the capital ships built or building of the United States, Great Britain, Japan, France, and Italy that were to be scrapped. For a period of ten years no new capital ships were to be built except as replacements for vessels twenty years old. The total capital-ship replacements were not to exceed 525,-000 tons for the United States and England, 315,000 tons for Japan, and 175,-000 tons for Italy and France. Nor were the replacement vessels to exceed 35,-000 tons each or carry guns of more than 16 inches. Aircraft-carrier tonnage was also limited for each of the contracting parties,[2] and none of these carriers was to be larger than 27,000 tons. No lesser naval ships, excepting transports, should exceed 10,000 tons, and merchant vessels should not be prepared for possible armaments.

Britain, Japan, and the United States also agreed to maintain the status quo on fortifications and naval bases in the Pacific, except for the islands lying off their respective mainland holdings and certain of the larger island groups. The primary American exception from this ban was the Hawaiian Islands. This

[2] Great Britain and the United States, 135,000 tons; Japan, 81,000 tons; Italy and France, 60,000 tons.

Naval Treaty was to remain in force until the end of 1936 unless a signatory gave a two-year notice of intention to terminate it.

Another important agreement was the Four-Power Pact, signed by Great Britain, France, Japan, and the United States. This provided for mutual recognition of insular rights in the Pacific. Were any controversy to arise during the ten-year life of the pact that might result in war, the signatories promised to hold a joint conference to promote adjustment of the differences. In case the rights of the signatories were threatened by some other power, the contracting parties agreed to communicate with each other in order to agree on proper measures to be taken. Upon ratification of the Four-Power Pact, the Anglo-Japanese alliance was to be terminated.

More Up to Date. The Four-Power Treaty replaces the cloak of isolation.
(By Harding in the *Brooklyn Eagle*.)

The Nine-Power Treaty, agreed to by the United States, Great Britain, Japan, France, Italy, the Netherlands, Belgium, Portugal, and China, had as its purpose the desire "to stabilize conditions in the Far East, to safeguard the rights and interests of China, and to promote intercourse between China and the other Powers upon the basis of equality of opportunity." Therefore the signatories promised to respect the political independence and territorial integrity of

China and to preserve the Open Door, while China agreed not to discriminate against the nationals of any other power using her railroads or otherwise passing through her territory.

Lesser arrangements at Washington provided that: (1) the United States should have free access to the island of Yap, as well as equality with Japan in the matter of cable communications there; (2) Japan gave up her political rights in the Shantung peninsula and withdrew from Siberia; (3) the Lansing-Ishii agreement was to be abrogated;[3] and (4) a commission was to be appointed to consider the matter of extraterritorial rights in China.

The achievements of the Washington Conference seemed great at the time and won the immediate acclaim of almost all Americans. Actual limitation of armaments by international agreement was a goal often sought but never before achieved. Subsequent events, however, have made a later generation dubious of the wisdom of many of these decisions. Japan's navy, though smaller than those of Great Britain and the United States, was large enough to dominate the western Pacific. After Japanese militarists gained control of Japanese destinies during the thirties, it became painfully obvious that the Naval Treaty had rendered Britain and the United States impotent to challenge her. Disarmament proved a feeble foundation for peace without some effective system of collective security that would prevent an aggressor state from taking advantage of the military and naval weakness of other powers.

The Geneva Conference

The failure of the Washington meeting to extend the quota system to destroyers, cruisers, and submarines led to a race among some nations in those fields of construction. The United States, primarily interested in domestic matters, did not participate in this race and even failed to keep its capital-ship tonnage up to the allotted ratio.

Yet by early 1927, President Coolidge became concerned about the increase in lesser naval armament, as well as about the strained relations that had been developing between his country and Japan since passage of the immigration law of 1924. These were potential causes for war. Therefore, would it not be wise to hold another disarmament conference? Accordingly, on February 10, 1927, he invited the other four signatories of the Washington Treaty to another discussion to be held at Geneva.

The Geneva Conference, which opened June 20, 1927, proved a disappoint-

[3] The Lansing-Ishii agreement of November, 1917, was a wartime attempt to find a formula that would reconcile the conflicting China policies of the United States and Japan, then cobelligerents against Germany. This agreement pledged mutual adherence to the principles of the Open Door and the territorial integrity and political independence of China, but recognized that "Japan has special interests in China, particularly in that part to which her possessions are contiguous."

ing failure. France and Italy refused to attend at all, while the United States, Great Britain, and Japan were unsuccessful in their search for a formula to extend the quota system to the smaller naval craft. Great Britain, with world-wide commitments and a network of island bases, asserted her need for a large number of small cruisers, while the United States—poor in overseas possessions —held out for a small number of large cruisers. The conference's difficulties were multiplied through the failure of the governments concerned to canvass these controversial questions in preliminary discussions, through the presence of professional naval officers opposed to the whole principle of limitation, and through the activities of lobbyists like the American Willam Shearer who were working to sabotage the project in the interests of munitions and armament firms.

The conference's failure had serious results. Anglo-American relations were more strained than they had been for many years, and American isolationism and nationalism were given strong nourishment.

War Debts

Another matter of controversy was the payment of war debts. While the war was still in progress, the United States had loaned to seven countries that were fighting Germany a total of over $7 billion. After the armistice, about $3.3 billion more was granted to these nations and thirteen others hard hit by the ravages of war and in need of cash and supplies to speed rehabilitation.

These twenty debtor states started a movement as early as 1919 to have this $10.3 billion obligation canceled or at least reduced. The debtors asserted that these loans were, in effect, America's contribution to the war effort before she participated actively in the military conflict. Furthermore, the borrowers had used the loans primarily to buy supplies in the United States. The profits accruing to American industry from those sales should be considered sufficient repayment. Then, too, it would be impossible to pay back in gold; most of the bullion had been drained to the United States in the early days of the war. What little was left in Europe was essential for currency stabilization. The only way to repay, therefore, was in goods, but American tariff barriers precluded that possibility. France had her own reason for requesting cancellation. During the American Revolution she had loaned the young United States what were then considered large sums. This amount had not been fully repaid, and France had not dunned America for it. Was it not the time now for the United States to reciprocate?

The United States refused to heed these arguments. President Wilson succeeded in averting a discussion of inter-Allied debts at the Peace Conference, and both he and his successors refused to concede that there was any relationship between German reparations to the Allies and the Allied obligations to the United States. Since the money had been loaned by the United States government to European governments without any strings attached, the debtors had both a legal and moral obligation to repay in full. Nor did assertions that the American loans constituted her contribution to the war effort hold good for the postwar aid. Moreover, at the Peace Conference the other victors had obtained land and promises of reparations, while the United States had obtained nothing tangible.

The debtors considered the American position greedy, and there were numerous references to Uncle Shylock and the pound of flesh he was collecting from unfortunate Europe. Yet it was not until December 6, 1921, that President Harding requested Congressional authority to effect a settlement of the debt principal and interest of 5 per cent that was in default. The legislature answered on February 9, 1922, with a measure providing for the appointment of the World War Foreign Debt Commission, which was empowered

> to refund or convert, and to extend time of payment of the principal or the interest, or both, of any obligation of any foreign government now held by the United States, or any obligation of any foreign government hereafter received by the United States arising out of the World War.

The commission[4] immediately started holding conferences with envoys of the debtor nations, trying to reach a compromise in each case based on the debtor's ability to pay. Great Britain, the first to reach an agreement, promised to pay her whole indebtedness of more than $4 billion in semiannual installments over a period of 62 years at interest of 3.3 per cent. During the next three years twelve other borrowers made varied arrangements with different rates of interest.[5] One of the most stubborn negotiators was France, who did not come to terms until 1926, when she agreed to pay the low interest rate of 1.6 per cent. Italy appeared to make an even better bargain with a 0.4 per cent interest charge.

From the point of view of Americans who looked upon the war debts as purely commercial transactions, the United States was more than generous in these debt settlements. Some of the unpaid interest that had accumulated was forgiven, thereby reducing a paper indebtedness of $12 billion to $11.6 billion. More important, the original interest rate of 5 per cent was reduced to an average of 2.1 per cent, despite the fact that the United States was paying 4.25 per cent interest on the Liberty Bonds held by its own citizens. Figured over sixty-two years, the debt had been reduced to approximately one half the original obligation.

[4] The members were Secretary Andrew Mellon, who served as chairman; Secretary Hughes, Secretary Hoover, Senator Reed Smoot of Utah, Representative Theodore Burton of Ohio, Representative Charles Crisp of Georgia, and Richard Olney, formerly in Cleveland's cabinet.

[5] Of the remaining seven debtor states, Russia, Greece, and Armenia had not had their new governments recognized by the United States and thus no envoys were received by the commission; Cuba and Nicaragua had already repaid most of their obligations; Liberia was about to receive an American loan to take care of her debt; and there was an agreement to postpone consideration of the Austrian debt for twenty years.

Yet the fact remains that these were not ordinary commercial debts. Rather they were American expenditures in support of American foreign policy, comparable to foreign aid grants made during and after World War II. From the European point of view, the United States was exacting sixty-two years of tribute from her former allies, thereby adding to their already desperate postwar problems. English voters, in particular, had good reason to complain that their government had obligated itself to the United States well beyond the nation's capacity to pay. Furthermore, Europeans complained with justice that the American high tariff policy was completely inconsistent with insistence upon war debt payments.

Many American liberals could understand and sympathize with the European attitude, but politically any talk of further war debt cancellation was anathema. The American majority considered the Europeans as virtual defaulters. The isolationist trend was strengthened; if war brought repudiation, the best American policy was to stay out of European troubles. Whether wise or unwise, however, the temporary settlement of the debt question did at least clear the air and contribute to better international relations.

The Dawes and Young Plans

Despite the continued American insistence that the European obligations were not contingent upon the payment of German reparations, the United States did assist in drawing up a plan whereby the reparation payments were speeded up. In turn, the United States would benefit because the sooner the reparations problem was taken care of, the sooner the European debtors would reach an agreement with the United States on war debts. Thus on August 12, 1924, Germany and the Allies ratified the Dawes Plan, for which three Americans were largely responsible.[6] This agreement provided that Germany the following year should pay the Allies $250 million out of income from railroads, industry, and loans, with larger amounts in ensuing years. American and Allied bankers would loan Germany $200 million in gold to facilitate the first payments, to speed up industrial recovery, and to back a new currency issue.

The Dawes Plan worked well at first, but as the payments became larger and Germany realized that no ultimate date had been set for the completion of her reparations, she urged a new program. Again the United States played a leading role in finding a solution—this time through the Young Plan of December 22, 1928. Germany was to pay $153 million a year for fifty-nine years, plus a varied scale of "conditional payments" determined by her prosperity. In turn, the Allies agreed to evacuate all German territory by 1930 and to end the supervision

[6] Charles G. Dawes, Henry M. Robinson, a prominent banker, and Owen D. Young, an outstanding industrialist.

of her actions. Were the United States to lower the obligations of her own debtors, Germany would be relieved of some of her reparations.

As to claims of the American government and American citizens against Germany, Austria, and Hungary, these were taken care of in a complicated series of agreements, culminating in the War Claims Act of March, 1928. Various commissioners and umpires awarded—with interest—some $233 million to settle those claims.

Non-recognition of Russia

The one nation with which the United States did not negotiate for a debt settlement was the Soviet Union. Ever since the Bolsheviks had gained control in November, 1917, and repudiated all debts contracted by previous regimes, relations with the United States had been strained. The immediate cause for the failure of the United States to recognize the Soviet government was the latter's refusal to admit responsibility for an American loan of $178 million to the Kerensky administration, the confiscation of American property in Russia valued at $443 million, and the failure to pay either principal or interest on the $75 million worth of bonds of the old regime sold in the United States. But there were other factors as well. Americans generally were shocked by the way in which the Communists had come to power and did not believe that the regime represented the will of the Russian people. Furthermore, the United States charged that the Soviet was spreading propaganda in America calculated to overthrow the existing government. Wilson's Secretary of State Colby said: "We cannot recognize, hold official relations with, or give friendly reception to the agents of a government which is determined and bound to conspire against our institutions, whose diplomats will be the agitators of dangerous revolt."

This non-recognition policy, originating under Wilson, continued throughout the twenties despite the fact that European neighbors did accept Russia into the family of nations. True, there was considerable pressure from American liberals to change this attitude, but Secretaries Hughes, Kellogg, and Stimson, backed by majority opinion including organized labor, refused to be swerved.

The Paris Pact

Even before the Geneva Conference had demonstrated that naval limitation was not a sure path to peace, some Americans were urging that the nations of the world band together to legislate against war. This view was also upheld by Aristide Briand, the French Foreign Minister. To publicize his belief, he devoted part of his address to the American people on April 6, 1927—in commemoration of the entrance of the United States into World War I—to a proposition that the two nations agree to outlaw war beween themselves.

Secretary Kellogg was not quick to accept the Briand proposal. Perhaps he was not interested; perhaps he felt that it was too limited in scope to do much for world peace. Yet there were a number of prominent Americans led by President Butler of Columbia University who gave their support. The press played it up, and the public became enthusiastic. The isolationists saw in the Briand suggestion a way to avoid war without the commitments of the League of Nations. The arch-isolationist Senator Borah urged making the agreement multilateral. Petition after petition was sent to the administration with signatures reaching into the millions. The Grange went on record in favor of outlawing war.

This enormous tide of opinion forced Kellogg to change his hesitant policy, but it was not until the end of December, 1927, that he agreed to consider the Briand suggestion if it were broadened to include other nations. France consented to extend the invitation, and thus at Paris on August 27, 1928, Britain, her Dominions, Germany, Japan, Poland, Belgium, and Czechoslovakia joined with France and the United States in signing the Paris or Kellogg-Briand Pact. Under its terms the signatories "solemnly declare . . . that they condemn recourse to war as an instrument of national policy in their relations with one another." Furthermore, "the settlement or solution of all disputes or conflicts of whatever nature or of whatever origin they may be, which shall arise among them, shall never be sought except by pacific means." No termination date was provided—the obligation was expected to be perpetual.

The ratifying agencies of the fifteen signatories[7] subsequently gave their approval, usually with reservations. The chief American reservations were that the pact did not cover defensive wars and that the United States regarded the safeguarding of the Monroe Doctrine as necessary for its "national security and self-defense." Backed by overwhelming public opinion, the Senate approved in January, 1929, by the one-sided vote of 85 to 1.

In many ways the Pact of Paris appears to have been a pious fraud. In the first place, since most nations reserved the right to defend not only themselves but certain cherished spheres of interest, the agreement "outlawed" not all wars, but only wars of aggression. Any student of history knows that aggressor states never admit the fact of their aggression; they invariably justify their military measures as defensive. Therefore, it is not surprising that the aggressors of the 1930's—Japan, Germany, Italy, and Russia—were all solemn signatories of the Paris Pact. An even more fatal weakness in the new treaty was that it provided no means of enforcement. It represented in purest form the isolationist dream that war could be abolished merely by the general acceptance of a pledge not to go to war.

Absurd though all this seems today, the Pact of Paris was accepted by the gen-

[7] By 1935 only five countries of the world had failed to sign the pact.

eral American public with all seriousness as a major achievement in the search for peace. Secretary Kellogg sought to capitalize on the spirit by reviving the Root arbitration-treaty plan. Eighteen such bilateral treaties were negotiated before 1931. Each committed the contracting parties to submit all justiciable differences to some international tribunal, preferably the Hague Court. The Senate, still jealous of its prerogatives, continued to insist on the right to determine what matters should be submitted to arbitration. Yet by 1931 the Upper House was ready to allow more cases than had its predecessors under the Root-Knox-Bryan treaties.

The United States and Latin America

At the immediate close of World War I, relations between Latin America and the United States outwardly appeared to be more friendly than ever before. For the time being the United States had assumed first place among the nations exporting to and importing from the Latin-American states. The total value of exports and imports had grown from approximately $700 million in 1913 to about $3 billion at the opening of 1919. United States loans and investments in Latin America more than kept pace with the commercial interchange. Influenced in large part by the actions of the United States, eight other hemisphere republics had declared war on Germany, with five others severing relations. President Wilson's decision to try to make the world safe for democracy and his subsequent Fourteen Points were well received in the rest of the hemisphere and tended to help the other republics lose for the time being their fear of the "Colossus of the North."

The League of Nations was regarded as an additional safeguard for Latin America, and seventeen of the states joined it at once. They saw in the new organization an opportunity to participate in world affairs, to settle international differences by peaceful means, and to have their independence and territorial integrity better protected. The one dark spot was Article 21 of the Covenant, which asserted that nothing in the document should be "deemed to affect the validity of international engagements . . . such as the Monroe Doctrine." All efforts of the Latin-American republics to amend that article were unavailing. The most publicized was the amendment proposed by Honduras:

> This Doctrine, which the United States of America have maintained since the year 1823, when it was proclaimed by President Monroe, signifies: All the republics of America have a right to independent existence; that no nation may acquire by conquest any part of the territory of any of these nations, nor interfere with its internal government or administration, nor do any other act to impair its autonomy or to wound its national dignity. It is not to hinder Latin American countries from confederating or in any other forms uniting themselves, seeking the best way to realize their destiny.

Most of the states also joined the World Court.

By 1920, however, the old fear of *Yanqui* imperialism was returning. The failure of the United States to join the League seemed to indicate that she was not sincere in her wish for international cooperation. Then, to make that fear doubly strong, came the repudiation of Woodrow Wilson by Congress and by the people in the election of 1920. The wartime trade boom gradually diminished with the return of world peace. This decline of business with the United States was in part due to the failure of American exporters to live up to promises of speedy delivery and of high quality goods. Latin America consequently turned again to European markets or, as a result of wartime specialization in that part of the hemisphere, to the neighboring republics. The Americans felt they should sell to, not buy from, Latin America.

Mexican Oil

Throughout the greater part of the twenties there was tension between the United States and Mexico, brought on by the instability of Mexican politics and complications arising out of the extremely liberal Mexican constitution of 1917.

In 1920, Alvaro Obregón became President of Mexico by revolt and subsequent election. Immediately American investors in Mexican oil and land worried lest he make retroactive Article 27 of the constitution, which asserted that subsoil rights belonged to the Mexican nation. They demanded that the new executive approve a treaty that would guarantee their property rights. This Obregón would not do because, as he said, foreigners would in that event have more security than Mexican citizens. Furthermore, Mexico seemed unable to pay her debt, much of it owed abroad, which had been greatly increased by the recent political chaos. Consequently, the United States refused to recognize the new president.

American non-recognition not only weakened Obregón's position, but made it difficult for Mexico to obtain new loans. Therefore in 1922 the Mexican Supreme Court decided that Article 27 could not affect oil leases acquired prior to 1917, a decision given greater weight by a similar executive decree in the spring of 1923. This decree was soon followed by provision for a meeting of an American-Mexican joint commission to be held in the early summer. This commission decided that subsoil rights gained by Americans prior to 1917 would not be interfered with, that Americans owning land in Mexico who lost their property through expropriation proceedings—also provided for in the 1917 constitution—should be paid a fair price, and that American monetary claims would be settled through future joint commissions. These promises were satisfactory to the United States, which recognized Obregón in August, 1923. Other major powers were quick to follow America's lead in this respect.

The next year Plutarco Calles was elected to the presidency. At first it appeared as though the improved relations would continue, but the new American Ambassador, James Sheffield, perhaps persuaded by the petroleum interests, informed Secretary Kellogg that Mexico was ignoring American rights. Kellogg presently charged through the press that Mexico was not taking sufficiently strong or active steps to indemnify American citizens for seized property. In addition, he hinted that the Calles administration was threatened by revolution and warned:

> . . . it is now the policy of this government to use its influence and its support in behalf of stability and orderly constitutional procedure, but it should be made clear that this government will continue to support the government in Mexico only so long as it protects American lives and American rights and complies with its international engagements and obligations. The government of Mexico is now on trial before the world.

Calles, angered by Kellogg's implied threat, apparently decided that if his country had a bad name it might as well live up to its reputation. Thus in December, 1925, the so-called Petroleum Law and the Land Law were passed, placing so many conditions on oil leases and property rights that they made Article 27 in effect retroactive. Although the smaller American oil companies and landowners complied with the provisions of this legislation, the more important ones refused to do so and appealed for United States protection. Secretary Kellogg, backed by President Coolidge, was inclined to support them. There followed a year of vigorous note writing between the two governments that did not ease the situation. To many Americans it looked as if war might break out, especially when in January, 1927, Kellogg informed the Senate Foreign Relations Committee that he had proof that Mexico was the center of Bolshevik activities in the Western Hemisphere.

The Senate, following the lead of the press, refused to believe these charges; both President Coolidge and his Secretary were definitely repudiated when the Upper House on January 27, 1927, approved without a dissenting vote a resolution to arbitrate the whole oil problem. The administration realized it had gone too far. In June, Ambassador Sheffield resigned, to be succeeded by Dwight Morrow, who, though a business associate of J. P. Morgan, was an able conciliator, as indicated by his statement that "we shall not fail to adjust outstanding questions with dignity and mutual respect." Morrow's friendly spirit, plus the need of the Calles administration for money, brought a change in Mexican policy. In December, 1927, the Mexican legislature rescinded most of the 1925 and 1926 measures to which American interests objected; in effect, Article 27 was no longer retroactive. Moreover, a Mexican statute prohibiting the purchase of American goods was repealed. With tensions eased, Morrow was able to obtain some justice for Americans whose Mexican lands had been seized and to help temporarily in the troublesome religious situation in Mexico. Another step in the improvement of relations was the goodwill flight to Mexico City by Charles Lindbergh,[8] soon to be Morrow's son-in-law.

Thus the air was cleared and friendship restored between the two neighbors. But the problems of debts, oil, and land were not settled; they were to cause more controversy during the next decade.

Meddling in Nicaragua

American dollar diplomacy in Nicaragua proved to be a constant source of trouble throughout the twenties. Only the presence of American marines could keep political peace there, and at times even they were unable to preserve order. In an effort to end the chaos, Nicaragua was persuaded in 1923 to adopt for use in the next year's balloting a new election law, which had been drawn up by an American. This reform, plus the fact that Nicaraguan finances were in much better shape, thanks in part to the efficient American collector of customs, brought the promise of Secretary Hughes that the marines would be withdrawn after the inauguration of the new president. The 1924 election, asserted to be the most fair and honest in the history of Nicaragua, brought victory to a "Conservative-Liberal" coalition. In August, 1925, the American troops left the country. Scarcely had they been withdrawn, however, when a revolt took place, forcing President Solórzano to resign and Vice-President Sacasa to flee. The rebel leader, Emiliano Chammoro, set himself up as executive, but the United States would not recognize him.

Heartened by the American position, Sacasa, avowedly a Liberal, returned and civil war broke out anew. Therefore in June, 1926, American troops, in greater numbers than before, were sent in. After considerable political maneuvering, hostilities ceased in the early fall, and a new election resulted in victory for "Conservative" Adolpho Díaz, who was recognized by the United States. But Sacasa, still claiming the presidency and supported by Mexico, established his own administration, and the fighting broke out again. More American troops were then landed to protect Díaz, despite protests from other Latin-American republics and from liberals within the United States. Much of the tension in United States-Mexican relations during these years grew out of the conflicting Nicaraguan policies being pursued by the two governments.

In the spring of 1927, President Coolidge sent Henry L. Stimson, who had been Secretary of War under Taft, to Nicaragua to solve the imbroglio. Stimson concluded that Díaz should remain in power throughout the remainder of his term and that the American marines, now nearly 6,000 strong, should keep the opposition in check. Sacasa had to bow to the inevitable, although his fellow "Liberal," Augusto Sandino, kept the revolt alive in defiance of the American

[8] Mexico reciprocated by sending her leading aviator, Emilio Carranza, to the United States. Unforunately, he was killed during a storm on his return flight.

forces. Then Stimson arranged for a new election law, under which the 1928 campaign was held. José Moncada, a "Liberal," won in balloting supervised by American troops. He promised to establish a national guard, trained by an American officer. When this force was competent to police the country, Coolidge agreed to withdraw the marines. Sandino, however, continued to be a source of trouble, even though Moncada disavowed his actions.

Military intervention in Nicaragua did not help the position of the United States in the Western Hemisphere. The Coolidge excuse for it, however, was indicated on January 20, 1927:

> The United States cannot fail to view with deep concern any serious threat to stability and constitutional government in Nicaragua tending toward anarchy and jeopardizing American interests, especially if such state of affairs is contributed to or brought about by outside influence or by any foreign power.[9]

Growing Neighborliness

Fortunately for United States-Latin-American relations, there were a number of incidents during the twenties that offset the ill-feeling promoted by affairs in Mexico and Nicaragua. Mention has already been made of the satisfactory settlement of the long-standing differences with Colombia through an American payment of $25 million and the granting to Colombia of equal rights with the United States in the use of the Panama Canal. Senate ratification of this conciliatory act in April, 1921, by the overwhelming vote of 69 to 19, indicated a definite change of opinion. American oil interests, desirous of obtaining leases in the rich Colombian fields, played a prominent role in this solution, which was followed by a rapid increase of American investments—between 1922 and 1929 more than $260 million in American capital was so invested—in that Latin-American republic, and by the signing of a commercial treaty advantageous to both parties.

In 1924 the last of the American marines were withdrawn from the Dominican Republic. The Dominican government promised to continue the political and economic improvements achieved during the American protectorate and to allow the American collector of customs to supervise local finances until the American loans were repaid.[10] And in Cuba, the American General Enoch Crowder drew up new election laws that temporarily ended chaotic political conditions there without the use of military force.

The long-standing problem of the Tacna-Arica territory, which had alienated Chile and Peru for decades, was presented to the United States for mediation in

---

[9] President Coolidge was referring to charges that Communists from Mexico were contributing to the Nicaraguan unrest.

[10] In September, 1940, the United States ended its control over Dominican finances when that government signed an agreement that the payments due American bondholders would form the first lien on general government revenues.

1922. For the next seven years the American State Department struggled with the problem, suggesting procedures for settlement that ranged all the way from a plebiscite of the inhabitants of the disputed zone to direct negotiations between the two claimants. Finally, in May, 1929, the disputants asked President Hoover to submit his own solution for resolving their differences. This was accepted and at last the United States had succeeded in acting as impartial mediator in a prominant South American dispute.

Two regular Pan-American conferences were held during the twenties. The first, delayed since 1914 by the war, convened at Santiago, Chile, in 1923. Although the United States refused to make the Monroe Doctrine multilateral, she did give her unqualified support to the so-called Gondra Treaty. This provided for the peaceful settlement of all disputes arising among the American republics. Should a conflict develop, a commission of inquiry was to be initiated as quickly as possible. While the findings of this commission were not binding upon the disputants, they might lead to a settlement.

The second meeting was at Havana, Cuba, in 1928. A feature was the opening speech by President Coolidge, in which he emphasized the importance of hemisphere cooperation for the development of human rights and pledged that the United States would do her part. Coolidge asserted: "All nations here represented stand on an exact footing of equality," but this principle was not carried to its logical conclusion. When the right of one republic to intervene in the affairs of another was questioned, former Secretary of State Hughes vigorously opposed discussion of the issue since it involved not only the recent activities of the United States in Mexico and Nicaragua, but the whole trend of its Caribbean policy since 1905. The United States was supported by Brazil, Bolivia, Chile, and Peru, and the explosive proposal was dropped. Another suggestion that the Governing Board of the Pan American Union serve as a hemisphere court of justice was likewise turned down, largely through American opposition. Despite the contrariness of the United States in these matters, Hughes proved an able conciliator in other respects. It was primarily through his efforts that the delegates agreed to hold a special conference in Washington the following December to consider possible extension of arbitration in the hemisphere.

This Washington meeting, called the Pan-American Conference on Conciliation and Arbitration, resulted in long steps toward peaceful settlement of disputes among the republics. First of all, the Gondra Treaty was reaffirmed with an amendment providing that disputing nations would not resort to war while the commissioners of inquiry were making their investigation. To this was added a General Treaty of Inter-American Arbitration, under which the states agreed to submit to arbitration all disputes of a juridical nature, but not domestic differences or those arising under the Monroe Doctrine. The decisions of the arbitral tribunal were to be final. And the Protocol for Progressive Arbitration attempted to set the stage for the abandonment of exceptions to arbitration. Shortly after this session, Argentina offered her South American Anti-War Pact, similar in content to the Paris Pact. All the republics signed this agreement to outlaw war.

While these efforts were taking place, President Coolidge requested J. Reuben Clark of the State Department to draw up a document that would define the proper scope of the Monroe Doctrine. Although this Clark Memorandum was not published until 1930, it did much to improve inter-American relations. It asserted: (1) that the Doctrine was still unilateral—that is, that the United States alone would determine when it was being violated; (2) "the Doctrine does not concern itself with purely Inter-American relations"; (3) "the Doctrine states a case of the United States versus Europe, not of the United States versus Latin America"; (4) "so far as Latin America is concerned, the Doctrine is now, and always has been, not an instrument of violence and oppression, but an unbought, freely bestowed and wholly effective guaranty of their freedom, independence, and territorial integrity against the imperialistic designs of Europe"; and (5) "it is not believed that this [Roosevelt] corollary is justified by the terms of the Monroe Doctrine, however much it may be justified by the application of the doctrine of self-preservation." These statements, especially the repudiation of the Roosevelt Corollary, were welcome news to the other republics. The fulfillment of the promises contained in the Clark Memorandum could be called the basis for better relations—relations subsequently known as the "Good Neighbor Policy."

Colonial Unrest

The people of Puerto Rico had served their guardian well during World War I by participation in military service, buying war bonds, and aiding the Red Cross. Therefore it was a distinct shock to them when they were rewarded with the appointment of the ill-fitted E. Mont Reily as governor by President Harding in 1921. Reily's failure to consider the wishes and needs of the Puerto Ricans, his replacement of competent judges and other local officials by his own untrained friends, and his increases in the budget to raise the salaries of these newcomers brought protest after protest from the inhabitants. The threat of a Congressional investigation resulted in Reily's resignation early in 1923, and he was succeeded by Horace Towner, who has been described as "one of the best governors the island has ever had."

The Puerto Ricans realized that Towner could not remain in office indefinitely and that he might eventually be replaced by a man of the Reily type. Therefore, in 1924, a delegation went to Washington with Towner's full approval to seek a greater degree of autonomy, including the right of the Puerto

Ricans to elect their own governor, who should have considerable power to appoint local officials. Although President Coolidge was in partial sympathy with this request, he would not approve all of it, saying "Puerto Rico has a greater degree of sovereignty over its internal affairs than does the government of any State or Territory of the United States." And Congress, through failure to agree, did not give its support to the insular requests.

Then in 1928, the Puerto Ricans asked that they become a "free state," and employed the services of Charles Lindbergh to send the request to Washington. Nothing came of this petition. Coolidge again asserted that they had a more liberal government than was to be found in the United States proper, something they did not seem to realize—but he did not try to explain how citizens of one of the states would react to having their governor appointed by the President.

But if the Coolidge administration showed little sympathy for changes in the administrative system, it was not lacking in humanity. When a disastrous hurricane swept over the island in the fall of 1928, killing hundreds of people, rendering several hundred thousands homeless, and destroying millions of dollars worth of property, the United States government quickly appropriated $8 million for repairs and for loans to hard-hit farmers. At the same time the Red Cross sent over workers and spent more than $3 million to alleviate the suffering. Although the Puerto Ricans were grateful, this gratitude did not make them forget their desire for greater autonomy.

The Harding-Coolidge regime also turned deaf ears toward Filipino demands for independence. Harding appointed General Leonard Wood as governor of the Philippines, and he proceeded to undo most of the liberal work of his predecessor, Governor Harrison. With the Philippine Organic Act of 1916 as his authority, Wood used his veto power extensively and thwarted the plans of his department heads. The Filipino legislators, who had enjoyed comparative freedom under Harrison, did not like this suppression. Therefore, in October, 1923, they approved a resolution calling for the dismissal of Wood. But Coolidge gave Wood his unlimited backing in the use of the veto power, saying, "You are entitled to the support of the Administration and shall have it."

Undismayed by this rebuff, the Filipinos then asked that one of their number be appointed as governor, and at the same time asserted that the arbitrary actions of Wood made it impossible for Filipinos to work with him in any capacity. These resolutions concluded with the statement "that the immediate and absolute independence of the Philippines, which the whole country demands, is the only complete and satisfactory settlement of the Philippine problem."

Coolidge's answer took the same form as his reply to the Puerto Ricans. Under American rule, he asserted, the Filipinos were much better off than if they wholly governed themselves. They did not have sufficient experience for independence and they failed to consider that they would not have the advantage of free trade with the United States.

On Wood's death early in 1928, Coolidge named Henry L. Stimson to the governorship. Before the year was over, Stimson established another Council of State consisting of himself, the heads of the Philippine Senate and House, together with the majority leaders, and the chairmen of the executive departments. Its purpose was to serve as an advisory board for the governor when he felt disposed to call it into session. While this council was not so free or powerful as the one for which Harrison had provided, it was the first step in almost a decade toward autonomy—and additional steps were soon to follow.

On the whole, the diplomacy of the twenties was not vigorous. President Harding left most of the duties in that field to the State Department—fortunately under the capable administration of Charles Evans Hughes. The Washington Conference was more of a paper than an actual victory for peace, and the settlement of the debts and reparations problems was only temporary. Coolidge, during his early years in office, based his diplomacy on the same laissez faire principles on which his domestic policies were based. When he did act, he favored American business interests. Toward the close of his administration, however, he took a more liberal view of colonial and world affairs, thereby setting the stage for the more international-minded Hoover and Roosevelt regimes.

15

Reactionaries and Rebels

American social and cultural life during the twenties displayed conflicting tendencies. It was a period of intolerance and narrow nationalism, when the Ku Klux Klan and all that it represented flourished. At the other extreme it was an age of revolt, when women bobbed their hair and took up smoking, when flaming youth drank excessively and went mad over jazz, and when the intelligentsia sneered at the conventions of earlier days. But probably to most Americans it was simply a happy, carefree period—a period of apparent prosperity—when the exploits of Babe Ruth, Jack Dempsey, Red Grange, and Bobby Jones seemed infinitely more interesting than the activities of the politicians.

The Unions Lose Ground

Labor shortage and governmental favor had helped labor unions to almost double their membership between 1914 and 1920. In the latter year more than five million workers were affiliated with unions; four fifths of these belonged to groups included within the American Federation of Labor, the remainder to the Railroad Brotherhoods and various other independents. These gains, however, proved impossible to hold. By 1923 total trade-union membership had dropped to about 3.6 million.

The losses of the early twenties were to a certain degree natural. Many workers had joined unions during the period of rapid growth simply because of temporary factors and neglected to pay their dues afterward. The depression of 1921, moreover, hurt the unions. Labor was then abundant, and employers could give preference to non-union men, while the unions lost their popularity when they could not prevent wage cuts and layoffs. Of equal importance was the aggressive campaign waged by many businessmen to curb what they regarded as labor's excessive power. Trade associations, chambers of commerce, and farmers' groups gave support to a well-organized open-shop movement. In January, 1921, representatives from twenty-two manufacturers' associations met in Chicago and adopted the name "American Plan" for their campaign to combat the unions. During the next several months organized labor suffered a number of bad defeats. A strike by merchant sailors against a proposed wage cut in 1921 tied up shipping for almost two months, but failed with disastrous results for the International Seamen's Union, whose membership fell from nearly 100,000 in 1921 to 18,000 in 1923. Most of the progress made during the war toward organizing the meat-packing industry was similarly lost through an unsuccessful strike in 1922. An open-shop drive in San Francisco undermined the position that organized labor had gained in the building industry of that city, while a similar movement in Chicago made great temporary progress.

The unions also suffered serious setbacks in the courts. The provisions of the Clayton Act, which Samuel Gompers had greeted as "Labor's Magna Carta", were interpreted very narrowly. In the Duplex case of 1921, the Supreme Court ruled that the immunities granted by the act applied only to employees directly involved in a dispute and that it was illegal for fellow unionists to attempt to support those employees by refusing to service the employer's products. In another case of the same year (American Steel Foundries v. Tri-City Trades Council), labor's right to picket was rigorously limited, while in Truax v. Corrigan, also in 1921, the Supreme Court upheld the right of state courts to issue injunctions in labor disputes, even when such injunctions had been forbidden by the state legislature. Such orders continued to be issued extensively by both Federal and state courts. Particularly hated by the unions were the "yellow-dog" contracts—agreements under which employees were obliged to promise that they would not become members of any union during their employment. The courts used the existence of such contracts as grounds for issuing injunctions forbidding union organizers to make any attempts, however peaceful, to enlist new members.

For the unions to lose membership during periods of depression was natural; the remarkable thing during the twenties was that they failed to make up their lost ground during the ensuing years of prosperity. Instead, their total membership in 1929 was only 3.45 million, about 150,000 less than in 1923.

Organized labor's most conspicuous failure was its inability to penetrate such major industries as iron and steel, food packing, automobiles, rubber products, chemicals, and electrical equipment. This failure resulted on one side from the determined opposition of the employers; on the other, from the union leaders' uncertainty as to what tactics should be pursued. Since these were mass-production industries, employing for the most part workers without marked individual skills, the old-line unions that constituted the major strength of the AFL were ill-suited to the task of organizing them. Although the Federation did have a few industrial unions like the United Mine Workers, the attempt to establish new ones aroused the jealousy of existing craft unions that feared an infringement upon their jurisdictions. The AFL witnessed many sharp fights between the progressives who advocated more aggressive tactics and the conservatives who counseled caution. Throughout the decade the latter faction, led by Gompers, Matthew Woll, and William Green,[1] kept control of the national organization.

The cause of the progressives was injured by Communist attempts to capture existing labor unions by "boring from within." William Z. Foster of steel-strike fame organized the Trade Union Educational League to serve this purpose. Gompers was determined to keep Communists out of the AFL and proceeded to take stern measures, ousting from conventions individuals who had sided with Foster and revoking the charters of unions that had fallen under Communist control. So far did the Federation go in its anti-Red campaign that it put itself repeatedly on record as opposing recognition of the Soviet government by the United States; in 1930 it even asked for an embargo on imports from Russia because they were "convict made." Although most of the progressives within the AFL were scarcely less opposed to the Communists than were Gompers and Green, their efforts to advance industrial unionism fell into disrepute when the Communists began to demand the same things.

The United Mine Workers under John L. Lewis had many difficulties during the decade. In 1922, when the operators sought to cut wages, there were prolonged and bitter strikes in both the hard- and soft-coal fields. So high did feeling run at Herrin, Illinois, that twenty-five men, most of them strike-breakers, were killed. Although the miners won satisfactory settlements in 1922, during later years they proved unable to hold their gains. Despite Lewis' slogan, "No backward step," the bituminous miners were compelled to take severe cuts and to suffer much unemployment because of competition with the non-union fields in West Virginia, Kentucky, and Alabama. Attempts to organize these areas were sternly opposed by hired mine guards and company-controlled local officials. When the miners also resorted to violence, gun battles and bloodshed resulted. Such was the case in Harlan County, Kentucky, where three deputies and a miner were killed in a pitched battle on May 5, 1931; seven of the miners were sentenced to life imprisonment as an aftermath of this affray. The defeats suffered under Lewis led to rebellions against his leadership. Rival unions were formed, and the IWW and the Communists took their turn in organizing campaigns, but they had no greater success.

[1] Gompers died in 1924. William Green succeeded him as president of the Federation.

Serious strife also developed in the textile field. The workers in the woolen mills of Passaic, New Jersey, rebelled against low wages and poor working conditions in a strike that began January 21, 1927, and did not finally come to an end until March 1, 1928. The trouble was punctuated by clashes between the police and the strikers. Strike leaders were arrested, as well as outsiders like the Socialist, Norman Thomas, when they protested against violations of civil liberties by the authorities. The vigorous role played by radicals tended to divert attention from the legitimate grievances of the workers, and eventually the Communists, who had been leading the strikers, consented to retire from the struggle. But even after the workers were adopted by an old-line union, the United Textile Workers, they found it impossible to obtain any important concessions from their employers.

During 1929 there were bitterly contested strikes in the Tennessee textile town of Elizabethton and in the North Carolina towns of Gastonia and Marion. The first of these was notable for the mob violence employed against labor organizers; the second, for the drastic tactics used by the local authorities against the strikers and the resulting clash in which the chief of police was killed; the third, for an incident in which the sheriff and his deputies fired upon unarmed pickets, killing three and wounding twenty-one others, two of whom later died. Against the alliance of company, local governmental authorities, and antiunion mobs, all campaigns to organize the southern textile workers broke down, whether led by Communists as at Gastonia, or by the United Textile Workers as at Elizabethton and Marion.

Welfare Capitalism

The weakness of the labor-union movement during the twenties is not to be completely explained either by the shortcomings of the union leadership or by the determination of the antiunion forces. Much of labor's docility resulted from the fact that many workers seemed to be bettering their lot without organization. Wage cuts there were during the depression of 1921, but usually pay remained substantially higher than before the war. The farmers' bad fortune, moreover, was to a certain extent the workers' good. Food prices, though higher than in 1914, rose proportionately less than wages; the result was a gratifying increase in purchasing power. According to the calculation of a leading economist, the workers' real earnings averaged 32 per cent higher in 1929 than in 1914.

The better wages of the twenties were sometimes a price grudgingly paid to keep workers reasonably satisfied and indifferent to the union organizers. On the part of many businessmen, however, they reflected a new philosophy that defended high wages not merely as a necessary evil, but as a positive good since they attracted the more enterprising and efficient workers to a particular plant and since they helped build up the purchasing power which gave industry a mass market for automobiles, radios, electric vacuum cleaners, and the like. Similarly, employers were converted to the shorter work week as a contribution to higher labor efficiency and more leisure time for the workers to consume the products of industry.

Welfare capitalism sought also to improve the conditions under which laborers worked. Highly trained personnel departments hired and fired with more discernment than had old-fashioned foremen and superintendents. Piece rates and working rules were more carefully drafted, and provision was sometimes made for vacations with pay. Recreation halls and cafeterias likewise played their part in keeping the employees contented.

A favorite device of employers during the twenties was the company union. The number of corporations supporting such plans increased from 145 in 1919 to 432 in 1926, when the movement reached a peak of popularity. The company union provided a mechanism under which representatives could be elected to confer with the management on behalf of their fellow workers and through which grievances could be voiced. But such unions were kept strictly under the control of the employer and the extent of their activities was rigidly restricted.

In order to prevent the extension of the company-union movement, many of the old-line unions felt the necessity of cooperating closely with management. Under the Baltimore and Ohio plan, for example, President Daniel Willard agreed to have as much work as possible done by union labor in the Baltimore and Ohio shops, while the machinists' union pledged to make the work of the shops as efficient and economical as possible. The plan's success led to its adoption by several other railroads. Another outstanding experiment in management-union cooperation was that developed in the men's clothing industry by the Amalgamated Clothing Workers under the leadership of Sidney Hillman. William Green asserted:

> We are cooperating with the managements in the elimination of waste because the working man suffers most of all as a result of waste. We are also cooperating with the managements in the elimination of duplication of effort, and we are not opposing the introduction of improved machinery.

Despite such conservative statements of policy, employers in industries not already organized continued to recognize only company unions and to base their labor policies upon the tenets of welfare capitalism. Often they sought to ensure the loyalty of the men through stock-purchase plans—a policy that had sometimes unfortunate repercussions when stock prices collapsed in 1929.

Suppressing Radicalism

The anti-Red hysteria of 1919 gradually subsided as the extremely small number of real radicals in the country became more apparent. But the IWW and the Communists continued to be highly unpopular. The criminal syndicalism laws remained on the books and at least in California were actively enforced. In that state there were 504 arrests under the law between 1919 and 1924 and, when juries began to refuse to convict, the state attorney general obtained a court injunction under which IWW organizers could be arrested and tried for contempt of court, without a jury, merely for soliciting new members for the outlawed organization.

Radicals who fell into the toils of the law on any charge were likely to find judge and jury prejudiced against them. Such at least was the conclusion of thousands of Americans who interested themselves in the Sacco-Vanzetti case. Nicola Sacco and Bartolomeo Vanzetti, two anarchists who had been active in strikes during earlier years, were arrested in 1920 on the accusation of having held up and murdered the paymaster of a shoe factory in South Braintree, Massachusetts. During their trial the strong distaste of the presiding judge, Webster Thayer, for anarchists in general, and these two in particular, was made clear by his comments outside the courtroom. The district attorney was permitted not only to drive home to the jury the radical beliefs of the defend-

Sacco and Vanzetti (second and third figures walking
in front row). (Brown Bros.)

ants, but also the fact that they had fled to Mexico in 1917 to evade the draft. After the two men were found guilty and sentenced to death, defense lawyers started a long campaign to obtain a new trial on the ground that the first had been unfair. Despite the weakness of the case against the two radicals and the discovery of new evidence pointing to others as the guilty parties, Judge Thayer refused all motions for a new trial and was upheld in his rulings by the highest court in the state. The controversy over the case reached a climax in 1927. Professor Felix Frankfurter of the Harvard Law School had become convinced that the men had not had a fair trial. He incorporated his findings in a book that provided disturbing reading to thousands of citizens, even many who had no sympathy for radicalism. Nevertheless, Governor Alvan T. Fuller allowed the executions to be carried out on August 23, 1927, basing his decision upon his own investigation and that made by a governor's committee headed by President A. Lawrence Lowell of Harvard University. Prominent in efforts to save the two had been newspapermen like Heywood Broun, literary figures like Edna St. Vincent Millay and John Dos Passos, and outstanding lawyers like Frank P. Walsh and Arthur Garfield Hayes. News of the executions brought demonstrations thousands of miles away—in England, France, Italy, Russia, and Latin America. Rightly or wrongly, countless people throughout the world were convinced that Sacco and Vanzetti had gone to the electric chair because of their unpopular opinions and not because they had been conclusively proved guilty of murder.

In California two radical unionists, Thomas J. Mooney and Warren K. Billings, escaped death but nevertheless suffered long imprisonment for a crime of which many Americans also believed them innocent. Accused of participating in a bomb outrage that took the lives of eight persons in a San Francisco Preparedness Day parade in 1916, Mooney was convicted and sentenced to be hanged, while Billings was given a life term. As a result of President Wilson's intercession, the governor of California commuted Mooney's sentence to life imprisonment. The two men remained in prison despite the fact that the convictions had been obtained on flimsy evidence and perhaps on perjured testimony. As in the Sacco-Vanzetti case, the circumstance that thousands of liberals were demanding their release only seemed to stiffen the determination of the state authorities to allow the law to take its course. Not until 1939 were the California prisoners granted a pardon.

The Ku Klux Klan

On Thanksgiving night, 1915, Colonel William Joseph Simmons and some thirty friends gathered under a fiery cross on top of Stone Mountain near Atlanta, Georgia, and swore allegiance to the Invisible Empire, Knights of the Ku Klux Klan. During the next ten years such weird scenes were repeated thousands of times in every part of the country. Simmons' attempt to found a new organization employing the name and paraphernalia of the old Klan of Reconstruction days had no great success at first. Up to June, 1920, the Klan had gained only four or five thousand members and was still to be found mostly in the South. The organization was given a new lease on life when Edward Clarke and Mrs. Elizabeth Tyler were put in charge of its promotional activities. The country was divided into domains headed by Grand Goblins, and realms or states each supervised by a King Kleagle. At the bottom of the organizational pyramid were thousands of local Kleagles who rounded up new members and collected their $10 initiation fees. Four dollars of the latter was retained by the local Kleagle, while $1.00 went to the King Kleagle of the realm, $0.50 to the Grand Goblin of the domain, and the remainder to the Atlanta oligarchy. With this streamlined machinery well lubricated with money, the Klan had a marvelous growth. Its days of greatest prosperity were from 1922 to 1925, during the regime of Simmons' successor, Hiram Wesley Evans, a Texas dentist.

Defenders of the Klan asserted that it was simply a fraternal order devoted to the praiseworthy ideals of patriotism and Christian morality. Many of its members were attracted either by these professed objectives or by the opportunity which the Klan offered for dressing up in mysterious robes and hoods, for participating in melodramatic rituals, or for talking a strange jargon that featured words starting with the letter "K."

Yet the movement, which had gained perhaps four of five million adherents by 1925, had many sinister aspects. It was fed by group hatreds—white hatred of the Negro, Christian hatred of the Jew, and, above all, Protestant hatred of the Catholic. Klan spellbinders convinced many Americans who should have known better that nuns in convents were prisoners against their will, that the Pope was about to transfer his headquarters from Rome to Washington, and that arms and ammunition were being stored in cathedrals preparatory to the Catholics seizing control of the government. The ends to which the Klan was devoted and the methods it used depended upon the local situation. In some areas its activities were confined to burning crosses at night, holding mysterious konklaves, and parading through the streets; in others it acted as a vigilance committee, sending warning messages to bootleggers, persons accused of immorality, Negroes lacking in humility, or labor-union organizers. Spokesmen for the Klan always denied that it was guilty of violence, but there appears little doubt that local groups using the costume of the Klan were involved in floggings, tar-and-feather parties, mutilations, and even killings.

Physical violence, however, was less characteristic of the Klan than were other methods. Catholic and Jewish merchants found themselves boycotted. Schoolteachers who failed to present their subjects in the way prescribed by the

Klan were spied upon by their own students, badgered by their superiors, and often dismissed by local school committees. Ministers brave enough to condemn the intolerance of the Invisible Empire found their congregations evaporating and were forced to resign. More and more the Klan became involved in politics, rewarding its friends and punishing its enemies until it was a power in states as widely scattered as Oregon, Texas, Oklahoma, Louisiana, Maine, and Kansas. Particularly notorious was the situation in Indiana, where David C. Stephenson used the Klan to establish a virtual dictatorship. But Stephenson's fall was as dramatic as his rise. The suicide of a girl whom he had abducted led to his arrest and conviction for murder. With its state leader condemned to prison for life under such circumstances, the Klan's reputation as the guardian of morality and the champion of law and order was shattered. This scandal was followed by revelations of corruption involving the Klan-elected governor of the state and several other prominent members of Stephenson's machine. Good citizens who had been taken in by the Klan organizers resigned in haste, while others sought to cut their connection with a group so thoroughly in disgrace.

Elsewhere the decline of the organization was not so rapid, but by 1926 the peak of the movement had passed. Two years later the Klan was so much in public disfavor that Imperial Wizard Evans tried to rescue it through banning the use of masks and visors. Yet the removal of much of the secrecy simply marked a further step in the Klan's disintegration. The Invisible Empire's greatest success had come through convincing misguided individuals that its activities were somehow patriotic; its collapse followed the belated discovery of what should have been evident from the first—that, whatever the Klan's professed ideals, its actual objectives and methods were the antithesis of "good Americanism" and standards of human decency.

Fundamentalists versus Modernists

Among the dangerous ideas that certain Americans hoped to repress in postwar years were those that challenged old standards of religious orthodoxy. The tendency of a younger generation of Protestant clergymen to doubt the Virgin birth of Jesus, the reality of the Devil and Hell, and the literal truth of every word in the Bible, alarmed conservatives who believed that the essential foundations of Christianity were being undermined. As early as 1910 an influential pamphlet entitled *The Fundamentals, A Testimony of Truth* had been published and, with the backing of two wealthy laymen, millions of copies were distributed. This encouraged the growth of a faction calling themselves fundamentalists, who sought to purge the churches of hated modernism. The fight was taken to the floor of religious conventions, where the conservatives tried to have the unorthodoxy of the liberals condemned, to denominational schools where the two factions struggled for control, and even to individual congregations where fundamentalist and modernist cliques took shape.

Most prominent of fundamentalist laymen was William Jennings Bryan, a Presbyterian. The Great Commoner devoted his last years to crusading against modernism with the same zeal that he had shown in his earlier struggles against the gold standard, imperialism, war, and liquor. Due in large part to Bryan's compaigning, bills to forbid the teaching of evolution in the public schools were introduced in the legislatures of almost half the states. In Tennessee, Mississippi, and Arkansas the proposal actually became law.

The Tennessee anti-evolution act of March, 1925, led at once to interesting consequences. The American Civil Liberties Union announced that it would back any schoolteachers who would test the law. Enterprising citizens of Dayton acted quickly to obtain a promising show for their own home town. A young high school biology teacher, John Thomas Scopes, readily agreed to cooperate. According to the testimony of one of his pupils, Scopes told his class "that the earth was once a hot molten mass, too hot for plant or animal life to exist upon it; in the sea the earth cooled off; there was a little germ of one-cell organism formed, and this organism kept evolving until it got to be a land animal, and it kept on evolving, and from this was man." For teaching this departure from the story "of the divine creation of man as taught in the Bible," Scopes was arrested and brought to trial in Dayton during July, 1925.

The young defendant was largely forgotten in the battle of legal giants drawn into the case. William Jennings Bryan threw all his energy into the prosecution, while the defense was in the hands of Clarence Darrow, the most famous criminal lawyer in America, who was ably seconded by Arthur Garfield Hayes and Dudley Field Malone. The courtroom was crowded with reporters and photographers from all parts of the country, as well as telegraph operators, radio broadcasters, and throngs of curious Tennesseans who promptly took sides and cheered loudly whenever a telling point was scored.

The trial's most dramatic moment came when the defense summoned Bryan to the stand to testify as an expert on the Bible. Under Darrow's sharp questioning, Bryan proclaimed his belief that the whale swallowed Jonah, that Joshua made the sun stand still, and that the world was created in the year 4004 B.C. The Commoner's defense of the literal truth of the Bible was greeted with loud hurrahs and amens from the courtroom audience, although Darrow contended that the examination had exposed "fool ideas that no intelligent Christian on earth believes." The defense attempted to bring to the stand religious-minded scientists who would have testified that the doctrine of evolution was not inconsistent with Christianity, but the presiding judge ruled that the only question at issue was whether Scopes had taught evolution. Since this was admitted, his conviction was a foregone conclusion.

Hearing the case upon appeal, the Supreme Court of Tennessee upheld the constitutionality of the anti-evolution law, but set aside Scopes' hundred-dollar fine on the grounds that the judge had exceeded his authority in imposing it. By this technicality the door was closed to carrying the case to the United States Supreme Court as the defense had hoped. Bryan was not on hand to witness the final disposition of the case. About a week after the end of the Dayton trial he suddenly died—his demise no doubt hastened by overexcitement and overwork.

Fortunately for the churches, a large middle party existed between the fundamentalist and modernist factions. This group was more interested in the church's work than in its doctrines and helped to prevent the quarrel from reaching the point of schism. The controversy gradually quieted down without a clear-cut victory for either side.

Just how strong the churches really were is difficult to say. A poll of newspaper readers taken in 1927 indicated that nearly 91 per cent professed a belief in God and that this belief was more nearly unanimous among college students than among their elders. Open skepticism was rare—rarer than during some earlier periods of national history. Despite this fact, the number of Americans who were casual and indifferent in their religious attitudes seemed to be growing. No longer was it taken for granted that a solid citizen would be found sedately occupying the family pew each Sunday morning. He was, indeed, as likely to be found on the golf course, in his car speeding through the countryside, or in bed reading the Sunday paper. Nor would college students any longer tamely accept the institution of compulsory chapel; on campuses everywhere student newspapers were campaigning—usually with success—for making chapel attendance voluntary. Statistically the churches made a good record: the number of church members continued to grow, the churches gained in wealth and enlarged their social program at home and their missionary efforts abroad; the kind of work represented by the Young Men's Christian Association, the Young Women's Christian Association, and the Knights of Columbus was greatly expanded. To many spiritually minded individuals, nevertheless, it appeared that the majority of their countrymen were more interested in making money and having a good time than they were in seeking the Kingdom of God.

Problems of Prohibition

Millions of good people believed that the ratification of the Eighteenth Amendment had miraculously ended the liquor problem; the sale of intoxicants would at once cease and, with that cessation, poverty and crime would largely disappear and America would enter upon a golden era.

But millions of other Americans had an entirely different attitude toward alcoholic beverages. They had been brought up in households where beer or wine was served with the family meal, where birthday and wedding celebrations were incomplete without a few rounds of drinks, and where the problem of how much an individual should imbibe was a question of personal morals. To such people national prohibition was an interference with personal liberty. They felt that the law was unreasonable and that they were justified in continuing to buy liquor wherever it was available. Many who did not drink themselves, moreover, believed that the prohibition laws were not deserving of the same respect as statutes that dealt with crimes like burglary or arson. Hence they did not feel under any obligation to report Volstead Act violators to the police or to vote for city officials who would carry out vigorous enforcement measures.

This hostility or indifference to the law—particularly to be found in the large cities—was the nub of the enforcement problem. With millions of thirsty citizens ready to pay high prices for any kind of alcoholic beverage, it was not long before other citizens decided to run the not very great risk involved in catering to this demand.

An abundant supply of illegal liquor was available from many sources. In the first place, there were 18,700 miles of border—land, sea, lake, and river— across which foreign beverages could be smuggled. Some of the nation's largest cities were nearby. For example, ships could stand off Long Island, outside United States territorial limits, while motorboats and fast launches ran their illegal cargoes onto deserted beaches only an hour's drive from New York City. In the second place, wholesale manufacture within the country soon developed. Illicit stills long antedated prohibition; their earlier use had been in evasion of the revenue laws. Now they simply multiplied to meet the new demand. Stills were inexpensive and easily constructed—in fact thousands of householders experimented with their own apparatus in the kitchen or the cellar. Finally, a large amount of liquor was available through diversion from legitimate channels. The rapidly growing chemical industry used 28 million gallons of alcohol annually. Although this was supposed to be rendered unfit for human consumption, large quantities passed secretly into the hands of bootleggers. Breweries supplying the near-beer industry had to produce the real product as the first step, and much of this was not actually dealcoholized as the law required. Physicians, furthermore, were issuing eleven million prescriptions annually under which patients might obtain alcoholic beverages for medicinal purposes. Many doctors were more than generous in handing these out, while druggists often diluted their medicinal stock and sold the balance illegally.

The distribution of this vast supply of illicit liquor was in the hands of bootleggers who retailed their wares to the doorsteps of customers or who disposed of it wholesale to speakeasies. How openly the latter often operated in the large cities was described in 1923 by Governor Gifford Pinchot of Pennsylvania, a dry. Reporting on a personal investigation in Philadelphia, he said:

> In one saloon the law-breaking drinkers surrounded the illegal bar four deep. It was easy to find, for there was as little secrecy about it as there is about the Washington Monument. Crowds walked in and out. A policeman stood at the very door.

Assigned to combat all this was the Prohibition Bureau of the Treasury Department, employing about three-thousand agents. The exploits of at least two of these, Izzy Einstein and Moe Smith, became legendary in the New York area. In order to collect evidence against lawbreakers, Izzy and Moe disguised themselves as automobile dealers, milkmen, fishermen, horse dealers, streetcar conductors, Palm Sunday churchgoers, football heroes, trombone players, and turkey salesmen. But no amount of ingenuity could alter the fact that the bureau was too small and too poorly supplied with money to plug up the real sources of the illicit supply. General Lincoln C. Andrews, one of the many administrators who attempted to direct the bureau during its troubled history, testified in 1925 that only about 5 per cent of the liquor smuggled into the country was being stopped and that only about one out of every ten stills in operation was being seized. To add to the difficulties of the service, the extraordinary opportunities for corruption made it necessary to dismiss in disgrace about one out of every twelve agents hired. Prosecutions under the law created forty or fifty thousand cases annually. For such an increase in their business the Federal courts were not ready; the congestion in their dockets could only be cleared by accepting pleas of guilty in return for a light penalty; over 90 per cent of the cases were disposed of by such "bargain-day" procedures.

The states, to be sure, had been granted concurrent power with the Federal government in enforcing the Eighteenth Amendment. All but six of them passed state enforcement acts, some of them more severe than the Volstead Act itself. But they showed great reluctance to spend money in the war against liquor; their appropriations were only one eighth the sum they were spending for the enforcement of their fish-and-game laws. Of course, in traditionally dry territory the local police arrested prohibition law violators, but in wet communities they did nothing except under heavy pressure from their superiors— and such pressure was rarely forthcoming. Wherever local sentiment was strongly antiprohibition, police, judges, and juries all reflected the situation.

Despite the shortcomings of enforcement, the drys claimed that prohibition had brought important benefits. The open saloon had disappeared in most places, and drinking, particularly by the poor, had been materially reduced. The highly respected economist, Professor Irving Fisher of Yale, believed that prohibition had contributed largely to the prosperity of the twenties, and many employers noted a gratifying decline in the absenteeism and inefficiency that had been a problem—particularly on "blue Mondays"—in pre-Volstead days. Other businessmen praised prohibition because of the added purchasing power which was created when money formerly spent for liquor was available for Fords and radios.

But the wets asserted that the defects of prohibition far outweighed its merits. They emphasized the widespread violation of the law as evidence that the experiment had been a complete failure, and they claimed that only through repeal of the amendment could the mistake be rectified.

Organized Crime

The consolidation of business so characteristic in legitimate lines was duplicated in business carried on in defiance of the law. Gambling and prostitution were already highly organized, bootlegging increasingly so. The profits to be made by monopolizing the illicit liquor trade were fabulous, and hardened criminals were prepared either to beat up speakeasy proprietors who refused to buy from them or to wreck their property, while with competitors they were ready to employ even more drastic methods. Such men naturally interested themselves in politics, bribing their friends and intimidating their enemies until they gained such power that they often seemed to have obtained complete immunity from the law.

The most spectacular criminal career of the twenties was that of Al Capone. Capone was brought from New York City to Chicago in 1920 by Johnny Torrio, who needed a lieutenant to handle his competitors in the struggle to gain control of the illegal liquor business of Chicago. By 1929 Capone had replaced Torrio as the "big shot"; he had at his command several hundred ruthless gunmen armed with submachine guns and sawed-off shotguns; he largely controlled the sale of liquor to Chicago's ten-thousand speakeasies; he was in complete political control of the suburb of Cicero; and he had useful ties with many Chicago politicians and judges. How much money he had made and concealed no one knew, but Federal agents estimated the sum at $20 million.

Capone's wealth and power had not been achieved without the plentiful spilling of blood. Particularly bitter was the gang war fought between Capone's henchmen and those of his ambitious rival, Dion O'Banion. O'Banion himself was shot to death in his own florist shop by gunmen masquerading as customers, but his gangsters continued to oppose Capone and made a grand attempt to assassinate him in 1926, when in broad daylight eight touring cars paraded slowly past his headquarters in Cicero, raking the building with machine-gun fire. Unfortunately the effort failed. In the most gruesome of all the killings, the St. Valentine's Day Massacre of 1929, seven of the O'Banions were lined up against a garage wall by strangers disguised as policemen and then mowed down with machine guns. Between 1920 and 1929 there were more than five hundred gang murders in Chicago, and few of those responsible were ever brought to justice. Not until 1931 did Federal officers finally arrest Capone—and then the charge was not murder, extortion, bribery, or violation of the Volstead Act, but merely tax evasion.

Capone and his numerous imitators in New York, Detroit, and other cities gained much of their wealth through the opportunities created by prohibition. They showed ingenuity, however, in expanding into other lines. They operated or demanded tribute from gambling houses, dog tracks, houses of prostitution, dance halls, and roadhouses. The ancient crime of kidnapping was given an unpleasant revival, with wealthy adults often victims. Innumerable were the so-called rackets of the decade. Small businessmen were compelled to pay for "protection"; those who thought that they did not need this commodity were speedily disillusioned when their trucks were wrecked, their shops bombed, or they themselves were beaten up or killed. Unfortunately for the reputation of the legitimate labor-union movement, these rackets were often operated through the connivance of corrupt union leaders who permitted established unions to be used in this way. Sometimes new unions were organized for no other purpose than to levy tribute upon unfortunate workers and employers. Only less common than the racketeering labor union was the racketeering trade association terrorizing small businessmen until they signed up and meekly paid their regular assessments.

The crime wave that caused so much alarm during the twenties was more a change in the character of criminal activities than an absolute increase in their amount. Murder, robbery, assault, and extortion America had always had, and statistics showed no greater increase in the aggregate number of such offenses than might have been expected with the growing population and urbanization of the nation. What was new and alarming was the large degree of organization among criminals and their wholesale use of high-powered automobiles, machine guns, and explosives. Crime had become big business—and to many thoughtful citizens the most serious aspect of the prohibition problem was that by turning the liquor business over to criminals, vast new opportunities to make crime pay had been opened up.

Flaming Youth

Worry over children must be as old as human parenthood, but the older generation of the twenties perhaps worried over the young rather more than usual. They were shocked in the first place at the revolution in women's dress. Corsets were discarded along with numerous other articles of apparel no longer considered essential. The amount of cloth necessary to garb a woman declined from 19¼ yards in 1913 to 7 yards in 1928. During 1919 and 1920 much shorter than ankle-length skirts had appeared, to the great alarm of moralists. Fashion ordered them down again, but women proved reluctant to obey, and by 1925 the designers had surrendered; skirts became shorter and shorter until they reached the knee in 1927. To aggravate the scandal, many bold young ladies began to roll their stockings.

Not content with abbreviating their skirts and exposing their knees, the flappers—as the pert young females of the decade were called—abbreviated their tresses as well. Short-haired women in 1918 were assumed to be Bolsheviks, but by 1924 a vogue for bobbed hair was sweeping the nation. Barbers relegated the cuspidor and the *Police Gazette* to the closet and tidied up their shops to please their new customers—but in the end most of the business went to "beauty shoppes."

Before the war convention had decreed that no nice woman used rouge or lipstick, or, if she did, she tried to conceal the fact. During the postwar decade, however, the use of these and other cosmetics increased until their manufacture and sale became a billion-dollar business.

The young woman of the twenties not only looked different; she acted differently. Back in Theodore Roosevelt's time, when his daughter Alice wanted to experiment with tobacco she sought to escape parental wrath by blowing her smoke rings carefully up the chimneys of the White House fireplaces. Only the most sophisticated of women used cigarettes. But during the postwar decade the taboo against feminine smoking to a large extent broke down. Shocking as this was to the older generation, women's increasing use of alcoholic beverages was even more so. Among the smart set it became the accepted thing for men and women to drink together at domestic cocktail parties, at country club dances, and at speakeasies.

All this was a final stage in the feminine revolt that had been in progress for many decades. Women had successfully rebelled against their inadequate educational opportunities, against their unfavorable legal status, against their disenfranchisement. Now they were asserting their right to smoke and drink because men did, and to cut their hair, rouge their cheeks, and wear scanty clothing because it symbolized their independence. Not for long, moreover, were the new manners found solely among the young. To an increasing degree older women occupied and held the territory the younger shock troops had captured.

Though many parents were seriously troubled over such issues as these, what kept them awake nights was their children's rebelliousness in other matters. Sons boldly demanded the use of the family car, daughters hotly asserted their intention of driving off with their boy friends without chaperonage. Often the youngsters did not get home until almost morning and indignantly refused to divulge where they had been or what they had been doing. Or what was perhaps worse, they told exactly what they had been doing and then asked belligerently what their parents intended to do about it.

Significantly enough, Samuel Hopkins Adams, one of the muckrakers of prewar days, found a theme in this rebellion. Under the pseudonym Warner Fabian, he wrote the lurid novel, *Flaming Youth*, which had a huge popular sale and was syndicated in many newspapers. Shocked parents read about wild parties where young people enjoyed the intoxication of both gin and jazz, of midnight swimming excursions, and of petting parties on lonely lanes. Similarly upsetting were *The Plastic Age* by Percy Marks and—on a distinctly higher literary level—the novels of F. Scott Fitzgerald. A sensation of another sort was provided by Judge Ben B. Lindsey, who believed that the breakdown in old moral conventions was so serious that the situation should be frankly faced and a system of "companionate marriage" legalized—a sort of trial marriage that could be terminated at any time by mutual consent, provided there were no children.

Undoubtedly the situation was exaggerated by such writers as these. For the most part, the great revolution in morals probably amounted to simply this: girls were easier to kiss than they once had been, and the automobile offered a much better opportunity. But many of the petting parties went further; just how large a proportion is a matter of dispute. The flouting of older conventions regarding the relations of unmarried young people was to a large extent inevitable and to be explained as still another aspect of the new freedom that women were demanding. The war, however, with its philosophy of seizing the pleasures of the moment in a world of uncertainties, accelerated the movement.

Disputed though the facts might be as to the actual state of sexual morals, one thing was crystal clear. The new generation talked about sex with a frankness that would have been unthinkable to the old. The subject was endlessly discussed, not only because of its interest, but because of its fashionableness. The teachings of Sigmund Freud had been familiar to American psychologists since the beginning of the century; his ideas were being popularized for the first time, however, during the postwar decade. Exactly what they meant would have been a little hard for most people to explain, but this did not prevent glib usage of such fascinating new expressions as "Oedipus complex," "inhibition," and "libido." In general, laymen gathered the impression that scientists had decided that sex was not only exciting but important, and that it was dangerous to repress sexual impulses. This offered a comforting rationalization to those who thought it smart to defy the old conventions.

The Changing Family

For better or worse, American family life was being transformed from old to newer patterns. The home was less important as an economic, educational, and recreational center. Functions once performed by the family were more and more being taken over by outside agencies, and whether the change was good or bad was a matter of dispute.

Married women, particularly those of the middle-income groups, were now relieved of much of the drudgery that had always been their lot. Bread was a highly commercialized product purchased in stores instead of a masterpiece laboriously fashioned in the kitchen, while many other foods hitherto prepared in the home were now secured at bakery shops or delicatessens. Commercial laundries did an increasing share of the nation's washing. Many tasks, to be sure, still remained to the housewife, but the use of electrical appliances permitted them to be performed more quickly and easily.

Husbands and children too had their crowded schedules of activities, and the result was that many homes became scarcely more than a place where the members of the family checked in for a few hours of sleep each night and had their breakfasts—though rarely together.

An increasing number of American marriages were ending in divorce. In 1900 there were 20 divorces for each 10,000 married persons; in 1930 there were 36. By the latter year the chances that any particular marriage would eventually break up were about one in six. Divorce was more common in the United States than in any other country for which statistics were available, with the possible exception of the Soviet Union. But the conclusions to be drawn from this fact were disputed. Many regarded it as evidence that unhappiness in marriage was much greater than ever before. Others asserted that there had always been a great many unhappy marriages and that the high divorce rate meant only that more people were taking this way out of the unfortunate situation. Few denied that there was some connection between the increasing number of broken homes and the youth problem.

Another fact about family life that was undeniable, though given varying interpretations, was the declining birth rate. The rate had been 26.6 per thousand population in 1910 and had fluctuated within narrow limits until 1921, when it was 27.1; thereafter it fell until it was 19.7 in 1931—a decline of one quarter during the decade. Many Americans considered this a healthy development, asserting that a prime cause of poverty would be removed were birth control practiced by the poor as well as by the well-to-do. The American Birth Control League, organized in 1917, carried on an active propaganda under the crusading leadership of Margaret Sanger. Her attempt in 1921 to open a clinic in Brooklyn where birth control information might be given to low-income groups led to her arrest, but the New York courts ruled that such information could be given legally by physicians for health reasons. A permanent clinic was opened in New York City in 1923, and others followed in many cities, although in some states they were not permitted. Protestant churchmen disagreed on the moral issues involved. The Committee on Marriage and the Home of the Federal Council of Churches recommended in 1930 that "the church should not seek to impose its point of view as to the use of contraceptives upon the public by legislation or any other form of coercion; and especially should not seek to prohibit physicians from imparting such information to those who in the judgment of the medical profession are entitled to receive it." The General Assembly of the Presbyterian Church, however, criticized this statement of policy as dangerous to morals.

The Roman Catholic Church was uncompromising in its condemnation of both divorce and birth control. The papal encyclical, *Casti Conubii*, issued by Pope Pius XI in 1930, asserted that marriage was a "perpetual and indissoluble bond which cannot be dissolved by any civil law"; that companionate and experimental marriages were "hateful abominations . . . which reduce our truly cultured natures to the barbarous standards of savage people"; and that contraceptive devices were "an offense against the law of God and nature."

Literature during the Twenties

The postwar reaction from idealism, notable in so many different areas of American life, markedly affected literature. The nation had an unusually talented group of novelists and poets during the twenties, but their gifts were used in large degree to attack contemporary American culture.

The reading public had its first rude jolt in 1920 with the publication of Sinclair Lewis' *Main Street*. The small midwestern town, usually sentimentalized in literature, was here depicted as dreary, narrow, and hypocritical. Inasmuch as the character of American life was still so largely reflective of such small towns, Lewis' attack appeared to be a general disparagement of American civilization. A succession of other brilliant, but caustic, novels from the same author broadened the indictment. *Babbitt* (1922) satirized the self-satisfaction and crude self-advertisement of the American businessman. In the young doctor of *Arrowsmith* (1925), Lewis created a hero whom he could admire, yet he found at the same time much to criticize in the medical profession. *Elmer Gantry* (1927), the novelist's caricature of a go-getter religionist, gave ample proof—if any were needed—that the church could expect no immunity from his idol-smashing.

The great city, no less than the small, was subjected to literary attack. John Dos Passos in *Manhattan Transfer* (1925) depicted life in New York City as hard and meaningless for the individuals thrown together in the vast net of urban society. An earlier Dos Passos novel, *Three Soldiers* (1921), struck the note of revulsion against war that was to recur through the decade.

Disillusionment not only with the war but with the general complexity of modern life was reflected in the novels and short stories of Ernest Hemingway. *The Sun Also Rises* (1926), *Men Without Women* (1927), and *A Farewell to Arms* (1929) reflect apparent indifference to idealistic aspirations or to the problems of society. The Hemingway characters found life's fleeting pleasures only in the most elemental experiences, particularly in physical combat and sex. Hemingway was one of the not inconsiderable group of American intellectuals who spent most of the twenties in Europe.

Both the outer shell of sophistication and the inner kernel of unhappiness characteristic of sensitive young people of "the lost generation" were exposed in the novels of F. Scott Fitzgerald. Early works like *This Side of Paradise* (1921) and *The Beautiful and the Damned* (1922) were regarded by the critics as little more than popular fiction, but *The Great Gatsby* (1926) demonstrated that Fitzgerald had one of the finest talents of his generation.

One of the great literary vogues of the period was for the work of James Branch Cabell. His *Jurgen* (1919) received magnificent advertising when it was banned from the mails as obscene. The charge was unfounded in the opinion of most readers, who believed the treatment of sex in this exotic fantasy to be witty and sophisticated, yet hardly likely to undermine the country's morals.

Of the older generation of novelists whose reputation had been well established before the war, Theodore Dreiser enjoyed most favor with those who were looking for ruthless realism. To these, Dreiser's *The American Tragedy* (1925) was the greatest novel of the decade. Other readers, repelled by the crudities of Dreiser's style, took delight in the beautifully written and thoughtful works of Willa Cather, Edith Wharton, and Ellen Glasgow.

The revival of poetry, which had been just beginning in 1914, more than fulfilled its early promise. Edwin Arlington Robinson and Robert Frost reflected their New England background in the austere beauty of their writing; they often found their themes in the frustrations and tragedies of life, but they differed from most of the novelists of the period in upholding the dignity of man in the face of suffering. Carl Sandburg and Vachel Lindsay spoke in the more strident cadences of the Midwest. Cruelty and injustice they attacked fiercely, yet they displayed a basic love for America and a faith in its destiny. The same qualities were to be found in Stephen Vincent Benét, whose attempt at an American epic, *John Brown's Body*, aroused great interest in 1929.

Poetry was not immune, however, to the spirit of the times. Indeed, no work of literature more completely reflected the generation's disillusionment and lack of faith than T. S. Eliot's *The Wasteland* (1922). Ezra Pound's contempt for American democracy was so complete that he not only lived the life of an expatriate, but ended up as a glorifier of fascism. Thus there disappeared from the American scene one of the boldest experimenters with new verse forms.

More frequent than such complete repudiation was poetry written in a spirit of detached cynicism and sophistication. In such a vein was Edna St. Vincent Millay's *A Few Figs from Thistles* (1920). Other works by this poet displayed higher sensitivity to beauty and a larger sense of social responsibility, but failed to enjoy the popularity of this lighter work.

Writing for the American stage has rarely won lasting acclaim as literature, yet that distinction was realized by Eugene O'Neill. His plays, *Emperor Jones* (1921), *Desire under the Elms* (1924), *The Great God Brown* (1925), and *Strange Interlude* (1929), showed great psychological insight and much ingenuity in the use of dramatic innovations to carry his meaning. Like so many of his contemporaries, however, O'Neill's emphasis was on the least healthy aspects of American life.

A great influence on the literary life of the twenties was exercised by H. L. Mencken, the editor of the *American Mercury*. This vigorous and outspoken critic of the American scene regarded most of his fellow countrymen as "boobs," "morons," and "yokels," and said so month after month to the delight of his sophisticated readers. One of the leading features of Mencken's magazine was "Americana," a department made up of excerpts from the press chronicling the more idiotic deeds and pronouncements of Americans. A moderate sampling of Mencken's criticism often proved a healthy antidote to the reader's complacency, but an excessive dose was likely to leave him with a cynical contempt for democracy.

High- and Low-brow Reading

The number of Americans who prided themselves on reading good books increased during the decade, but they showed a certain timidity in choosing their reading matter for themselves. The Book-of-the-Month Club broadened its list of subscribers until by the end of the twenties some hundred-thousand Americans were accepting the judgment of its board of experts in making their periodic purchases. The Literary Guild and other organizations distributed books on the same basis. To be selected through this system was to guarantee the success of any book. One of the unfortunate results, however, was that many scarcely less worthy books that had failed to appeal to the experts were doomed to small sales.

On the other hand, many readers chose books for their entertainment value and were indifferent to their rating as literature. The detective stories of Mary Roberts Rinehart, S. S. Van Dine, and others enjoyed a tremendous popularity, as did sexy romances like *The Sheik* by Mrs. E. M. Hull. There was also a good audience for biographies, which varied in treatment from Albert J. Beveridge's highly scholarly *Life of John Marshall* (1916–1919) and Carl Sandburg's beautifully written *Abraham Lincoln: The Prairie Years* (1926) to popular works that attempted to psychoanalyze their subjects, to "debunk" national heroes, and to glamorize national villains. Astonishingly successful was *The Man Nobody Knows* (1925), in which Bruce Barton, an expert in advertising promotion, portrayed Jesus as a model businessman.

Self-improvement continued to be the aim of many earnest readers. For them a diversified fare was offered during the twenties, ranging from excellent popularizations like Will Durant's *Story of Philosophy* (1926) to the fabulously successful Emily Post's *Etiquette* (1922).

No other reading matter, however, was so widely distributed as daily newspapers, whose aggregate circulation in the United States and Canada reached forty million in 1929. The trend away from personal journalism and toward standardized, large-scale production methods, already pronounced in 1914, was much accelerated during the next fifteen years—due in part to the rising cost of paper. Newspapers became increasingly dependent upon syndicated material, advertising revenue, and mass distribution. Since costs could be reduced by operating several papers under a single ownership, the number of newspaper chains doubled between 1923 and 1927. Within each city, moreover, the tendency was toward the merger of competing journals; five out of seven Chicago morning papers disappeared in fifteen years, while in Detroit the number of morning papers dropped from three to one. There were two-thoussand fewer publications in 1929 than in 1914.

Sensational stories of crime and scandal still provided a dependable formula for making a paper popular, as was demonstrated by the striking growth of the New York *Daily News*. This first New York tabloid, which began publication in 1919, achieved a circulation of 1.3 million ten years later. The success of this brash pioneer invited competition; Hearst's *Mirror* and Bernarr MacFadden's *Evening Graphic* entered the New York field, while similar papers multiplied in other cities.

Magazines also increased their sales. The periodicals that catered to the literary-minded or those interested in fundamental social problems had little share in this prosperity. Muckraking articles, so popular a generation earlier, rarely appeared in the magazines of large circulation like the *Saturday Evening Post*, *Collier's*, *The American Magazine*, or the *Ladies' Home Journal*. Instead, their pages were devoted to fiction, light but frequently excellent within its limitations, and to articles praising the achievements of American businessmen. The counterpart to the tabloid was the "confession" magazine. Bernarr MacFadden's *True Stories* and its imitators built up an enormous sale through endless variations on such simple formulas as that of the innocent girl corrupted by the bright lights of the big city and involved in amorous adventures, but reformed and safely married by the final paragraph.

Education and Learning

The goal of most American parents was to provide their children with greater educational opportunities than they themselves had received. The result was a remarkable increase in the number of pupils attending public high schools: in 1900 public secondary-school enrollment stood at 519,000; in 1910, 915,000; in 1920, 2,199,000; and in 1930, 4,399,000. With rapidly expanding attendance went important modifications of curriculum to meet the needs of the new pupils. Whereas in 1900 over 50 per cent of high-school students studied Latin and over 56 per cent algebra, the percentages were only 22 and 35 respectively in 1928. Furthermore, many subjects that had not been part of the old high-school course of studies were now offered. Most of these were vocational in character like home economics, manual training, bookkeeping, shorthand, typewriting, and agriculture, but others, notably art and music, were cultural by any definition.

The advent of the automobile made it possible to close many of the one-room schoolhouses of the nation. The children from rural families were now transported by bus to well-equipped consolidated schools where each grade could be taught in a separate room. In order to improve and enrich elementary education in the higher grades, many communities organized junior high schools to include the seventh, eighth, and ninth grades, the senior-high-school course being then reduced to three years.

Colleges and universities also grew rapidly. In 1900 college enrollment was 168,000; in 1910, 266,000; in 1920, 517,000; and in 1930, 1,085,799. Some critics believed that this expansion made advisable a division of higher education between the first two and the last two years. Junior colleges, of which there had been only 132 in 1917, numbered 450 in 1930. This tendency was deplored, however, by those educators who believed that the traditional four-year college course had a unity that should not be destroyed. An increasing number of students now devoted more than four years to their higher education. Training in theology, medicine, dentistry, law, engineering, and business administration was based to an increasing degree on a foundation of three or four years of general education in a liberal arts college. A growing number of graduate degrees were granted; the annual crop of Ph.D.'s quadrupled during the decade. Most of this increase resulted from the demand for more and better trained college instructors, but a growing number of positions in industry were available to men who had graduate training—notably in chemistry.

University faculty members placed increasing emphasis on their responsibility to develop the body of knowledge rather than merely to transmit the cultural heritage. To catalogue the significant achievements of research in all the specialized branches of learning would be impossible, but a few landmarks must be noted because of their importance to general American thought during the decade. The whole field of American history was surveyed from a fresh and stimulating point of view by Charles and Mary Beard in *The Rise of American Civilization* (1927). Of equal significance as an interpretation of the roots of American culture was Vernon L. Parrington's *Main Currents in American Thought* (1927). The reader who wished to learn how people of every income level and background lived in a typical American community was fascinated by *Middletown* (1929), by Robert S. and Helen Lynd. Profoundly influential in its effect upon thinking in such diverse fields as education, morals, criminology, and philosophy was the purely mechanistic explanation of human behavior presented by John B. Watson in his *Behaviorism* (1925).

In the field of physical sciences, Americans like Robert A. Millikan and Arthur H. Compton helped to fill in the details of the newer conceptions of the universe that were taking shape during the twenties following the pioneer work of the great German, Albert Einstein. Two important astronomical observatories in California, Mt. Hamilton and Mt. Wilson, provided international science with data of great value in testing the new theories.

Medical research was generously endowed and achieved many goals. Important advances in surgical technique grew out of the work of the doctors during the war. New uses for the X ray were developed both in diagnosis and therapy. The importance of vitamins in nutrition was demonstrated, and the consumption of these miraculous health-givers later became a national fad. Public-health measures virtually eliminated typhoid fever, while diphtheria, scarlet fever, and tuberculosis came under steadily increasing control. Life expectancy was raised from 49.24 years in 1901 to 59.1 years in 1927—largely through the reduction of the death rate among infants and children. New techniques for treating burns produced almost miraculous recoveries; at the Johns Hopkins Hospital in Baltimore the use of the new gentian violet treatment resulted in cutting the mortality in such cases from 42 to 5 per cent in two years.

The Arts

The prosperity of the twenties encouraged construction, and many of the new edifices displayed striking beauty. Some American architects continued to find their inspiration in classical and medieval models. Henry Bacon's Lincoln Memorial in Washington, D. C., for example, demonstrated anew the appeal of the Greek qualities of simplicity, balance, and proportion. Ralph Adams Cram was deeply interested in promoting the use of Gothic style in ecclesiastical architecture, and many of his ideas found their embodiment in the Cathedral of St. John the Divine in New York City. The suitability of the Gothic style for university buildings was emphasized by Cram-designed buildings at Princeton and West Point, as well as by many beautiful structures at Yale.

America's most distinctive contribution to architecture, however, lay along more original lines. The ten years that followed the armistice were the great age of the skyscraper. In 1922 architects from all countries were invited to submit their designs for the *Chicago Tribune* Tower. The competition, which attracted 260 plans from 23 nations, was won by the Gothic design of John Mead Howells and Raymond Hood, but the second-prize design submitted by the Finnish architect, Eliel Saarinen, rivaled the winner in the degree of interest it created. New York City, where the technical requirements of the building ordinances had much to do with the development of setback architecture, prided itself on the loftiness and grandeur of the great buildings constructed there during the twenties. The culmination of the movement was the Empire State Building, designed by Shreve, Lamb, and Harmon.

Outside the boundaries of the United States the best known American architect was Frank Lloyd Wright, who boldly discarded older conventions and carried functional design to its logical limits. Wright advocated taking full advantage of new materials and fitting each building both to its use and environment. His "prairie houses" with their emphasis on horizontal lines close to the earth pointed toward a revolution in residential design. Wright's influence was international in scope, but during much of his career he was too bold for the majority of his timid countrymen.

American painters lacked the originality of American architects. Many took their cues from European art during this era and found an outlet for their talents in cubism, expressionism, and surrealism. Yet despite the weakness of the Americans for imported fads, a number of capable artists were at work. Among these were John Marin, Max Weber, and Georgia O'Keefe.

Musical appreciation seemed to deepen after the war. The radio brought concerts by the country's great orchestras and soloists into millions of homes, and individuals like Walter Damrosch worked tirelessly to educate the people to understand and enjoy good music. American-born singers like Marion Talley, Carmela and Rosa Ponselle, and Lawrence Tibbett sang with the Metropolitan Opera Company, and leading symphony orchestras like those of New York, Philadelphia, and Boston attained extraordinary virtuosity. In the field of light music, Sigmund Romberg, Rudolf Friml, and Jerome Kern proved worthy successors to Victor Herbert.

Jazz during the twenties began to demand attention as an authentic form of musical expression. Orchestras playing in the new rhythms became increasingly pretentious, with Paul Whiteman's taking the lead in presenting jazz in "symphonic" arrangements. A furious debate was provoked between musical fundamentalists, who regarded jazz as merely unpleasant noise, and modernists, who proclaimed it to be as important an American contribution to art as the skyscraper. One of the best assets of the modernist school was George Gershwin, whose unusual talent and success in speaking through the new idiom were hard to resist. Gershwin wrote the music for a number of successful musical comedies during the twenties, but he was eager to express himself in more ambitious forms. Therefore he composed such symphonic works as *Rhapsody in Blue, Concerto in F*, and *An American in Paris*. The first enjoyed the widest success, but many discerning critics much preferred the third. That Gershwin was gifted few denied, although there was no final judgment possible as to whether his work would endure.

There Were Giants in Those Days

Despite the cynicism of the intellectuals, the age was one of hero worship. Rudolph Valentino, the great screen lover, died in 1926, and the crowd attracted to the New York undertaking parlor where he lay in state extended for eleven blocks. "Shipwreck" Kelly achieved transient glory by sitting on top of a Baltimore flagpole for twenty-three days and seven hours. The whole country wept when efforts were unavailing to extricate Floyd Collins alive from a Kentucky cave where he had been trapped. And when the Lone Eagle, Lindbergh, flew nonstop from New York to Paris the nation went wild.

Perhaps the most typical heroes of the twenties were to be found in the world of sport. Shrewd promotion, willingly abetted by newspaper and radio reporters, aroused the American people to a unique enthusiasm for athletics. Their work was made easier by the circumstance that the sports world had an unusually large number of competitors who were not only capable performers, but colorful personalities as well.

In 1919 "Babe" Ruth, playing for the Boston Red Sox, set a new record by hitting twenty-nine home runs in a season. The New York Yankees sensed the opportunity for making a profitable investment and purchased the young pitcher-outfielder for $125,000. The Babe's employers never regretted their decision, nor did they refuse the slugger's eventual demand for a salary almost as large as that of the President of the United States. The exploits of Ruth, who hit fifty-nine homers in 1921 and sixty in 1927, brought customers to the Yankee Stadium by the thousands and enabled baseball to retain its popularity despite the growing interest in other sports.

College football was followed avidly by the public. So great was the demand to see games that new stadia were built, many of them large enough to accommodate seventy or eighty thousand spectators. Despite the sputtering of faculty members who complained that the game had become professionalized, alumni insisted on highly paid coaches who could produce winning teams, and

Babe Ruth. (Brown Bros.)

the coaches in turn demanded athletic scholarships and other inducements to attract promising material. The best players, men like "Red" Grange of Illinois, and the most successful coaches like Knute Rockne of Notre Dame received unlimited publicity.

Sports taste was catholic, however, and thousands of Americans who did not know the difference between a mashie and a putter followed breathlessly the progress of the great golf amateur, Bobby Jones, through various tournaments. Tennis, once thought like golf to be a high-brow game, became pop-

The "Long Count"—Tunney-Dempsey Fight
at Chicago, 1927. (Acme.)

ularized through the dynamic play of Big Bill Tilden, while women's athletic
prowess was demonstrated by another fine tennis player, Helen Wills. In most
sports, women's performances could not be compared with those of the stronger
sex, but when the American Gertrude Ederle swam the English Channel in
1926, her time was better than that of any of the five men who had completed
the difficult journey before her. Even horses had their triumphant careers. Man
o' War was a sporting sensation in 1919 and 1920. As late as 1945 he was reported to be living "in luxury" on a beautiful farm in Kentucky—which was
more than many of his human rivals for acclaim could say twenty-five years
after their peak of glory.

No sport of the twenties could secure more publicity for a single contest
than heavyweight boxing. The golden days of the prize ring were attained when
the master promoter, Tex Rickard, had as his drawing card the superb per-
former, Jack Dempsey. On July 4, 1919, Dempsey gained the heavyweight title
by knocking out the giant Jess Willard at Toledo, Ohio. The new champion,
colorful and aggressive, seemed to carry dynamite in his gloves. Attending
prize fights became suddenly respectable, and the crowds that saw Dempsey
knock out Georges Carpentier in 1921 and Luis Firpo in 1923 were notable not

only for their tremendous size but for the extraordinary number of politicians and socialites who were to be found among the spectators. After Dempsey lost his title unexpectedly to Gene Tunney in 1926, the stage was set the next year for what was perhaps the most highly publicized sports spectacle of the decade, the second Tunney-Dempsey fight at Chicago, when the gate receipts totaled $2,650,000. Newspaper reporters had sent daily stories from the training camps of the two great men for weeks; after the fight was over they devoted endless columns to the important question of whether Tunney had been the beneficiary of a "long count" in retaining his title.

Such were the twenties. American prosperity was built on a shaky foundation that threatened to collapse. The rest of the world struggled with problems too difficult to be solved and that were destined to involve the United States. But oblivious to the storm clouds on the horizon, the average American had a wonderful time during the age of the supercolossal.

16
Prosperity

When, in his speech accepting the Republican presidential nomination in 1928, Herbert Hoover said, "We in America today are nearer to the final triumph over poverty than ever before in the history of any land," he was expressing the belief of almost all Americans. The United States had enjoyed seven years of extraordinary prosperity and few indeed were the gloomy prophets who ventured to predict danger ahead.

Economic Trends, 1914–1929

When the European war broke out in 1914, the United States was in what seemed to be the incipient stages of a serious depression. At first hostilities abroad simply increased the nation's economic troubles, but French and English war orders reversed the trend in 1915 and produced a great wartime prosperity, which was intensified by actual American participation in 1917. The effect of the armistice was temporarily upsetting, and serious unemployment prevailed for several months. This gave way, however, to a postwar boom lasting from the late spring of 1919 to the middle of 1920. This bubble burst suddenly, to be succeeded during the last half of 1920 and most of 1921 by a severe depression. In the latter year some seven million unemployed were walking the streets. National income fell from $75 billion in 1920 to $59 billion in 1921.

This depression, although grave, was short-lived. Recovery set in during 1922; by 1925 national income had passed the 1920 level, and it continued to rise until it reached more than $84 billion in 1929. In a proud catalogue of progress that Candidate Hoover recited in 1928 these items were listed: over

25 per cent increase in the production of goods since 1921; the construction of more than 3.5 million new dwellings; the electrification of nearly 9 million homes; the installation of 6 million telephones; the manufacture of 7 million radio sets; the production of 14 million automobiles; and the building of parks, playgrounds, and highways. And in human terms Hoover reported:

> We have doubled the use of electrical power and with it we have taken sweat from the backs of man. The purchasing power of wages has steadily increased. The hours of labor have decreased. The twelve-hour day has been abolished. Great progress has been made in stabilization of commerce and industry. The job of every man has thus been made more secure. Unemployment in the sense of distress is widely disappearing.

Such was the impressive evidence of prosperity during the twenties. It was small wonder that few Americans were seriously troubled by darker aspects of the picture that Hoover had omitted to mention.

America Takes to the Road

Much of the prosperity of the period reflected the rapid growth of new industries, and, of these, the automobile business was the most astonishing in the degree of its expansion.

Henry Ford continued to be the dominant personality in the industry. Still producing the famous Model T that had brought the price of an automobile down to a figure the ordinary farmer or workingman could afford, Ford built upon the success that he had achieved in prewar years. In 1924 a Ford could be bought for $290—if its owner was not too proud to crank it by hand. The Ford joke had become a staple commodity in American humor, and the canny Detroit industrialist accepted without complaint this free advertising, continuing to roll out cars and roll in money until he had amassed one of the greatest American fortunes.

Yet Ford's position was not impregnable. The General Motors Corporation, now allied with the powerful DuPont and Morgan empires and producing a well-balanced line of cars, grew rapidly during the twenties. The Chevrolet, which GM manufactured at a price to compete with the Ford, was equipped with conventional gear shift, good body lines, and other features that made it more attractive than the ugly Model T. For a time Ford's famous business acumen seemed to have deserted him, as he stuck with his old model despite sharply declining sales. In 1928, however, he finally acknowledged changing times and brought out his new and more conventional Model A.

Between 1903 and 1926, 181 companies at one time or another manufactured passenger cars, but the mortality was exceptionally heavy. By 1926 the number of automobile manufacturers had been reduced to 44; during the next few

Henry Ford with His First and Ten-Millionth Ford, 1924. (Acme.)

years many more had to quit. By 1930, 90 per cent of the business was being done by six companies.

The "big two" became a "big three" after the organization of the Chrysler Corporation in 1923 and its purchase of Dodge Brothers five years later. In 1929 Chrysler brought out the Plymouth to compete for the business being so profitably divided between Ford and Chevrolet. That year Chrysler produced about 450,000 cars as compared with Ford's 1,950,000 and General Motors' 1,900,000, but its share in the business was destined to become larger during the thirties.

Annual production of motor cars in the United States rose from 1.9 million in 1920 to a peak of almost 4.8 million in 1929. The number of automobiles registered in the country climbed from 8 million in 1920 to 23 million in 1929. By the latter year there was one car for every six inhabitants. The automobile industry had become the nation's leading business as measured by the value of its annual product; in 1929 that value was nearly $3.5 billion.

The production of motor cars required vast quantities of steel, plate glass, rubber, leather, aluminum, and copper, while their operation consumed the lion's share of the nation's petroleum products. In terms of labor the automobile industry not only provided direct employment to some 350,000 factory executives and employees, but gave indirect employment to workers in accessory and tire factories, salesmen, repair men, filling station operators, truck drivers, and the like. In fact, in the calculation of one authority, some five million persons had jobs in some way dependent upon the automotive business. This was one out of every nine persons gainfully employed in the United States.

Because the nation's roads were pitifully inadequate to an automobile age, Federal, state, and local governments found it necessary to spend close to $10 billion on highway construction during the twenties. So heavy was the traffic that only well-built macadam or cement roads would hold up at all. The cost was great, but the major part of it was borne by the motorists. Not only did they have to pay heavy registration and license fees, but between 1919 and 1930 every state followed the example of Oregon, which pioneered in the levying of a gasoline tax. In 1930 direct and indirect taxes upon those who used the roads accounted for approximately four fifths of the income expended on state highways.

The economic, political, and social implications of the expansion of the automobile industry would be difficult to catalogue completely. Regions like New England, whose agriculture and industry were less prosperous than formerly, found partial compensation in new opportunities of selling their scenery and climate to motorists on vacation. Although Americans traveled more, they depended less on older modes of transportation. The horse and buggy became symbols of the quaint past; even the electric streetcar and the railroad seriously felt the competition of the motor vehicles speeding across the countryside, particularly when bus companies and commercial trucking concerns began to expand their operations greatly. Many new problems were posed for government. Not only was there highway construction to be organized and financed, but the alarming number of serious accidents involving motorists underlined the necessity for new traffic legislation and strict policing. The automobile made the prohibition and immigration laws more difficult to enforce and helped murderers and bank robbers to make their getaways. For the farmer the new means of transportation brought many benefits; it lessened his isolation and provided an admirable means for him to carry his product to market. Many parents of teen-age boys and girls worried greatly, however, because of the ease with which the younger generation escaped the supervision of the elder through using the new vehicles.

As Americans took to the road, enterprising businessmen made an earnest bid to secure their money. The new state highways were lined with billboards, ornate filling stations, tourist camps, and hot-dog stands. To most citizens this was merely another evidence of the healthy competition of rugged individualism; but the more sensitive complained bitterly that the beauty of the American countryside was being destroyed.

The Age of Electricity

Another rapidly expanding industry contributing to the prosperity of the twenties was the electrical business. In 1902 less than 5 billion kilowatt-hours of electricity were produced in the United States. This rate of production had more than tripled by 1912, when 17 billion kilowatt-hours were generated. This, however, was only a small beginning. In 1920, 43 billion, and in 1929, 97 billion kilowatt-hours of electricity flowed through the wires into American homes and factories. Capital investment in the industry was less than $6 billion in 1910, over $12 billion in 1920, and more than $23 billion in 1930.

Who was using this current? Much of it was consumed in domestic lighting. In 1912, only 16 per cent of the population lived in electrically lighted dwellings, but by 1927 this convenience was enjoyed by 63 per cent. And once the home was wired for electricity, the housewife was almost certain to demand some of the electrical appliances that were then available to lighten her domestic chores. According to a calculation of 1926, of 16 million households equipped with electricity, 80 per cent had electric irons, 37 per cent had vacuum cleaners, and more than 25 per cent washing machines, fans, or toasters. Electric refrigerators, clocks, and stoves likewise became more and more common. Obviously, the rapidly increasing use of electricity offered a huge volume of business for manufacturers of household appliances.

But the factory no less than the home was being transformed. In 1914 only about 30 per cent of factory machine equipment had been electrified; by 1929 approximately 70 per cent was run by electrical power. This permitted a much more efficient organization of production without cumbersome and dangerous systems of belts and pulleys. One of the industrial marvels of the day was the photoelectric eye, which counted products, detected flaws, and performed many other functions with uncanny accuracy. Electricity also had important special uses in the metallurgical and chemical industries.

The rapid growth of the power business presented new problems for government. Advanced liberals insisted that the public stake in the production and distribution of electricity at the cheapest possible rates was so great as to require public ownership. For a time there seemed to be a considerable trend in that direction. In 1902, 815 American municipalities operated their own utility systems; by 1922 the number had increased to 2,581. During the balance of the twenties, however, the number declined, largely because power could be more economically generated by large plants serving many cities and industries than by smaller local plants. What was required, in the opinion of advocates of public control, was the generation of hydroelectric power in large volume by state or Federal authorities and its transmission and sale at reasonable rates to municipal distributing systems. Senator George Norris believed that a reasonable amount of public power production would provide a "yardstick" for measuring the rates of the private companies, and he hoped to have the Muscle Shoals project developed in this way. Other widely discussed plans called for the production of public power in connection with the building of a proposed St. Lawrence seaway, as well as for combined irrigation-power projects along the Colorado, Columbia, and Missouri Rivers. Private power corporations naturally opposed such government competition with private enterprise, and they had the support of the Coolidge and Hoover administrations. Not until the thirties were the advocates of public power development given much opportunity to try out their theories.

Meantime, the private power industry was being consolidated into larger and larger units. Not only did local distributing companies find that they could purchase power from the larger producing companies more economically than they could generate it themselves, but all operating companies were to an increasing degree brought under the control of holding corporations. The holding companies themselves were often controlled by other holding companies, and this process of pyramiding was carried so far that oftentimes six or more companies were piled on top of one another. By 1929 twelve large systems controlled approximately 76 per cent of the electricity generated in the United States. Finance capitalism was well illustrated in the industry, since corporations in which the influence of Morgan and National City Bank of New York was strong controlled some 37 per cent of the business, while companies within the sphere of influence of the Chase National Bank of New York accounted for about 11 per cent more. A third major group was controlled by Samuel Insull of Chicago. The Insull empire, comprising 10 per cent of the industry, was a fantastic affair. A labyrinth of holding and investment companies had been built up to include concerns serving 4,741 communities in thirty different states. Insull himself was chairman of the board of directors in sixty-five concerns and president of eleven others.

Although consolidation through holding companies served some economic purpose when judiciously carried out, much of the pyramiding characteristic of the twenties was against the public interest. The market was flooded with grossly watered securities on which small investors lost millions of dollars during and after the Wall Street crash of 1929. Control of local operating companies, furthermore, was placed in the hands of bankers remote from the scene and often insensitive to the interests of the consumers. Finally, the overcapitalization of the industry and its control by holding companies incorporated in many different states made the problem of rate regulation by state public-utilities commissions extremely difficult.

A cautious beginning toward Federal regulation had been made in 1920 when Congress provided for the establishment of a Federal Power Commission to include three cabinet members—the Secretaries of War, Interior, and Agriculture. The commission was empowered to issue fifty-year licenses for electric projects on the public lands, reservations, and navigable streams. It could regulate rates on power moved across state lines by the licensed companies and their subsidiaries. The results were not very satisfactory. The cabinet members were too busy with their own departments to give the commission's activities much attention, while only a very small proportion of the country's power was being produced under Federal license. Legislation in 1930 provided for the reorganization of the commission; it was now given five full-time members and increased funds, but was granted no additional regulatory authority. Although the demand that the FPC should be given control over the rates of all electricity crossing state lines was not met during the twenties, the liberals did succeed in bringing about an important investigation of the whole utilities problem by the Federal Trade Commission. The most sensational revelation was that utilities companies were spending millions of dollars every year to secure newspaper comment favorable to the private control of the electricity business and opposing government ownership. Similar propaganda was being artfully introduced into the educational system at every level from the kindergarten to the university.

Movies and Radio

Electricity made possible the development of two new forms of entertainment that gained wide popularity and influence, and themselves became big business. The first of these to evolve—largely through the experiments of Thomas A. Edison—was the moving picture. Crude machines capable of throwing animated pictures upon a screen were developed by 1896. In that year an audience in a New York music hall saw the first short movie show—some breaking waves, a bit of a prize fight, and a dancer. Thereafter short subjects occasionally were interspersed with the regular program in vaudeville houses, but the pictures were too hard on the eyes to have much popularity except as a curiosity. They improved, however, and in 1903 the first screen story was made under the intriguing title of "The Great Train Robbery." Two years later a Pittsburgh real-estate operator, one Harry Davis, had the inspiration of putting a movie projector, a piano, and ninety-nine seats into a vacant storeroom and charging 5 cents to see a one-reel show. The idea caught on and by 1907 there were five-thousand similar "nickelodeons" in various parts of the country. After 1910 movie theaters became more pretentious; the Strand Theater, which opened on Broadway, New York City, in 1914, was the first of the really large ones.

As the motion picture began to capture the popular fancy, the business of producing films grew. The first large studios, those of the Biograph Company and the Edison Company, were opened in 1906. Within the next decade such favorite stars as Mary Pickford, Charlie Chaplin, Norma Talmadge, and Lillian and Dorothy Gish had emerged. David Wark Griffith was the most celebrated of the early directors. In 1915 he produced "The Birth of a Nation," an exciting story of the Civil War and Reconstruction. Although the picture fostered race prejudice and exalted the old Ku Klux Klan, it enjoyed huge popularity. Cutting loose from stage conventions, Griffith demonstrated the dramatic possibilities of such screen techniques as distant views and close-ups, fade-outs and switchbacks, mob and battle scenes, and exciting flights and pursuits.

Mary Pickford in an Early Movie Studio. (Acme.)

The industry had at first been located largely on Long Island, but the superior photographic advantages of California sunlight, as well as certain legal complications, resulted in a wholesale removal to Hollywood. There in 1922 the producers sought to avoid threatened public censorship by organizing the Motion Picture Producers and Distributors of America. Postmaster General Will H. Hays was induced to resign from Harding's cabinet to head the new project. Under the guidance of the so-called Hays office the industry sought zealously to avoid offending public taste. Overpassionate love scenes, the ridicule of any religious group, the portrayal of crime or sin in which the culprit escaped just retribution were sternly forbidden.

The problem of making the movies talk was a difficult one, but eventually successful systems for synchronizing picture and sound were developed. "The Jazz Singer" starring Al Jolson in 1927 was the first great hit in the new medium. Some two years more elapsed before the wiring of theaters for sound became general.

By the end of the twenties all but the smallest American communities had motion-picture theaters, and between eighty and one-hundred million customers each week were paying their money to ride the Western ranges with William S. Hart and Tom Mix, to sigh through the romances of Rudolph Valentino, John Gilbert, Greta Garbo, Gloria Swanson, and other popular screen lovers, or to be instructed concerning the magic power of a quality mysteriously known as "It," supposedly possessed in overpowering quantity by Clara Bow. The popularity of these actors and actresses was in fact international. A large export business in films developed and a majority of the pictures shown in almost every country were American-made.

As early as 1903 Reginald Fessenden was demonstrating the possibility of radio telephony in experiments at Washington, D. C. Other pioneers were also at work in the field, and in 1910 Dr. Lee De Forest successfully broadcast Enrico Caruso's voice from the Metropolitan Opera House. Six years later De Forest began experimental broadcasting from High Bridge, New York. Then in August, 1920, the Detroit *Daily News* started the practice of broadcasting news bulletins regularly over its own transmitter for the benefit of amateurs in the Detroit area.

Meantime, in Pittsburgh, Pennsylvania, amateurs had become interested in tuning in the experimental broadcasts made by the transmitters of the Westinghouse Electric and Manufacturing Company. A department store in the city started selling receiving sets, and the Westinghouse Company presently decided to provide daily programs for the general public. Radio station KDKA was built and began regular broadcasting on November 2, 1920. The Harding-Cox election returns provided the first program material. The success of this venture induced Westinghouse to erect other stations the next year in Springfield, Massachusetts, Newark, New Jersey, and Chicago. Interest in the new form of entertainment swept the country and, by 1929, ten million sets were in use in the United States.

The problem of who was to pay for the expenses of broadcasting was solved in 1922 when the American Telephone and Telegraph Company's New York station, WEAF, utilized advertising sponsors for its programs; the first "commercial" was one in behalf of the Queensboro Realty Company. The broadcasting business promptly became highly remunerative; by 1927 there were some seven hundred stations in operation. Chaos on the air waves threatened, and the government had to intervene by establishing the Federal Radio Commission with authority to grant licenses to broadcasting stations and fix their wave length and hours of operation.

The almost inevitable trend of all business toward consolidation was evident in the organization of the Radio Corporation of America in 1919. This company, largely controlled by General Electric and Westinghouse, achieved a commanding position in the sale of radio sets and equipment. In 1926 the National Broadcasting Company, dominated by RCA, was established and soon controlled a chain of broadcasting stations from coast to coast. The rival Columbia Broadcasting System was organized the following year.

More Boom Industries

The manufacture of chemicals was scarcely a new industry in the sense that the automobile, movie, and radio businesses were. During the seventeenth century the colonists had begun the production of such commodities as potash and saltpeter. By 1900, moreover, there was extensive manufacture of the so-called heavy chemicals, products like sulphuric acid, soda ash, and caustic soda that were put to important industrial use. Up to 1914, however, the United States was almost completely dependent on imports from Germany for aniline dyes and other synthetic supplies.

The outbreak of war in Europe brought great opportunities. With imports from Germany practically cut off, American textile manufacturers had to turn to American-made dyes, poor though they were at first. A vast amount of important technical information was made available when the Alien Property Custodian seized and assigned to the newly organized Chemical Foundation some four-thousand enemy-owned patents for dyes, drugs, and other products. Chemical companies were prospering, meanwhile, through the huge wartime expenditures for explosives and fertilizers; some 40 per cent of all the explosives used by the Allies were manufactured by E. I. Du Pont de Nemours and Company of Wilmington, Delaware. Wartime contracts permitted vast plant expansion and provided ample funds for research.

The industry, already in a powerful position as it entered the postwar period, was given additional stimulus by the high rates of the Emergency Tariff of 1921 and the Fordney-McCumber Act. By 1929 four of the great American chemical concerns were larger than any of their European rivals. Greatest of all was Du Pont, which in 1930 was making eleven-hundred different products in eighty different factories located in thirty different states.

It seemed that the chemical industry had almost limitless possibilities. Plastics had increased in number and utility since the pioneer discovery of celluloid by an American in 1869, until an appropriate product was now available for radio panels, fountain pens, buttons, combs, and hundreds of other uses. Although rayon was not satisfactory at first, it improved in quality and grew rapidly in popularity. New lacquers made of synthetic resins permitted the application of a fine finish to automobiles in two days insteads of the twenty-six days formerly required. Other applications of chemistry made possible cheaper fertilizers for the farmer and more durable aluminum pots and pans for the housewife.

Wholesale industrial expansion afforded large profits to the construction business during the twenties, while the prevailing optimism of the period was reflected in the erection of ever higher skyscrapers. New York City, with its Chrysler Building (77 stories) and its Empire State Building (102 stories), led the country, but throughout the nation local pride was served by the construction of lofty office buildings. The erection of homes also boomed, particularly since very little house-building had been done during the war. Suburban developments were particularly popular as automobiles became more common and city workers accepted this opportunity to acquire homes in quieter, more country-like surroundings. On the other hand, the building of luxurious apartment houses was evidence that many families preferred to live in the cities and escape the inconvenience of commuting. Like the automobile industry, the construction business was notable for the stimulus it gave to other industries—to steel, cement, lumber, electrical appliances, plumbing, and heating concerns, for example.

The Sick Industries

There were a few industries that appeared not to share in the prevailing prosperity. This was notably true of agriculture, which has been discussed in an earlier chapter, but it was true also of bituminous coal mining and cotton textile manufacture.

A combination of factors kept the bituminous coal industry in the doldrums. Fundamentally, the situation was one of overexpansion and overproduction. Furthermore, coal was feeling the competition of newer sources of energy. Whereas 87 per cent of all energy utilized in the United States at the end of the nineteenth century had been derived from coal, the use of petroleum, natural gas, and hydroelectric power had reduced the proportion of coal-produced energy to 45 per cent by the thirties. The price of bituminous coal dropped with disastrous results to the high-cost mines; there was much bankruptcy and unemployment. To make matters worse, many of the older mines that had accepted the union contracts stipulating the payment of reasonably good wages found themselves unable to compete effectively with newer mines, opened in West Virginia, Kentucky, and elsewhere, where an aggressive antiunion policy made it possible to pay low wages.

The cotton textile industry suffered in part from loss of export markets. The growth of textile manufacturing in Japan, India, South America, and China had serious repercussions both in England and the United States. To this blow was added certain changes in feminine apparel. Women wore shorter skirts, less clothing, and preferred silk or rayon to cotton for most of their lingerie and dresses. The total number of spindles actively employed in cotton textile manufacturing in the United States declined by 4.2 million, or about 12 per cent, between 1920 and 1930. Prices fell, mills went bankrupt, and unemployment grew. As in the bituminous coal industry, Northern industrialists found themselves at a very serious disadvantage in competing with newer Southern concerns. The latter had the advantage of proximity to the source of raw material, an abundant labor supply willing to work long hours for a low wage, and the use of new machinery, much more efficient than the old equipment of New England factories. Thus the Southern mills were able to expand despite the unfavorable circumstances in which the industry as a whole was placed; the number of spindles in the South was 4.3 million in 1900, 15.2 million in 1920, and 18.5 million in 1930. This development, of course, multiplied the troubles besetting the industry in New England, where spindles in operation declined by almost one third during the decade.

Subsidized Industries

Businessmen fervently pledged their allegiance to laissez faire, but few interpreted the term to mean that government should abstain from measures directly helping them. The high tariffs of the twenties provided in reality a subsidy paid by the consumer to thousands of industries. Where it seemed necessary, moreover, the Republican administrations of the day did not hesitate to have the government itself pay out money to private business enterprises. This proved to be the case with both the merchant marine and the aviation industries.

The need for a large and healthy merchant marine in case the United States became involved in war was obvious, yet the difficulties in maintaining one proved great. In conformity with the provisions of the Merchant Marine Act of 1920, the Shipping Board sold 1,141 government-owned ships to private corporations between 1920 and 1928. Ships that had cost during the war as much as $200 a ton to build were sold for $30, $20, and occasionally as low as $8 a ton. Even at these bargain prices, several hundred ships found no purchasers. Almost five hundred of these were allowed to lie idle; the remainder were operated by private companies under contracts so drawn that the companies could not lose but the government could—and did in sums fluctuating between $12 million and $50 million annually. The concerns that had purchased government ships had scarcely better success. They were competing with foreign shipping companies that enjoyed government subsidies, had lower operating costs, and used newer, faster, more efficient vessels. In 1921 almost 43 per cent of American foreign trade was carried in American ships; by 1928 the proportion had dropped to 32 per cent.

Congress tried to rescue the industry with new legislation, the Jones-White Act of 1928. To modernize American shipping, the Shipping Board's loan fund was increased to $250 million, from which advances could be made at very low interest rates to private concerns for the construction of new ships or the rehabilitation of old ones. Furthermore, the government was authorized to enter into long-term contracts with the shipping companies for carriage of the mails. It was well understood that these contracts would provide a generous if indirect subsidy. By 1933 these payments to shipping concerns for carrying mail reached about $23 million annually, many times what it actually cost to perform the service. Meantime, the government continued to sell its own ships to private companies at a great loss and to loan large sums of money for new construction. Such measures managed to keep the American merchant marine alive and even to provide it with a few new ships, but the situation was obviously far from healthy. Many stockholders and executives connected with the shipping business had grown wealthy on government money, yet the nation had not acquired an effective merchant marine.

Aviation was a new industry, but it was far from being a boom enterprise like the automobile business. World War I had speeded its development immeasurably; planes had to be produced in quantity, and thousands of young Americans were trained as aviators. In 1918 the first regular air-mail service in the world was instituted between New York and Washington, and the following year an United States Navy seaplane, the NC-4, made the first crossing of the Atlantic by air.

The early postwar years were, nevertheless, discouraging ones for the industry. The government was no longer a customer for any substantial number of planes; indeed it was dumping its own surplus aircraft on the market. General William ("Billy") Mitchell preached earnestly the importance of aviation to national defense and even demonstrated that aerial bombing could sink a battleship. His superiors were unimpressed, however, and, when he became disrespectful in the heat of his campaign to unify the army and navy air forces, he was first demoted in rank, then court-martialed and forced to retire from the service. Nor was there any extensive market for aircraft among private citizens. Aviation to them was still largely a curiosity; its principal vocational opportunity was to reckless young "barnstormers" who looped the loop and did barrel rolls for the edification of the patrons of county fairs and then sold rides to anyone courageous enough to go up in the air with them.

The Post Office gradually expanded its air-mail service, but up to 1925 the

flying was done by its own pilots. In that year the Kelly Act was passed, authorizing the government to make contracts for carrying the mail with private lines.
In further recognition of the importance of the new industry, the Air Commerce Act of 1926 vested extensive powers over commercial aviation in the Department of Commerce.

The year 1927 was a turning point for the industry. On May 20 of that year
Charles A. Lindbergh took off in his plane, "The Spirit of St. Louis," from the
New York airport; thirty-three and a half hours later he landed safely at Le
Bourget Field in Paris. The flight, so quietly and competently performed, captured the imagination of the American public and demonstrated the possibilities of aviation as no previous event had done. The "Flying Colonel" became
a national hero overnight, and aviation securities took off on a seemingly nonstop flight themselves; in nineteen months the Wright Aeronautical Company's stock soared from 25 to 245. The air-mindedness of investors was stimulated still further by several other notable flights of these years; in 1926 Commander Richard E. Byrd and Floyd Bennett flew over the North Pole; the next
year Byrd organized a trans-Atlantic flight; in 1928 he flew over the South Pole.
Meantime, the Atlantic had been crossed also by Clarence Chamberlain and
Charles A. Levine and by the famous woman pilot, Amelia Earhart. Two Army
Air Corps pilots, Lieutenants Maitland and Hegenberger, flew from San Francisco to Honolulu in June, 1927.

By the end of 1928, there were forty-eight air lines in the United States with
a combined length of 20,000 miles that served 355 cities. Licensed aviators
numbered eleven thousand.

To an extraordinary degree, however, the industry was dependent upon the
patronage of the government. Between 1927 and 1933 over 50 per cent of the
output of the aircraft factories was purchased by the army and the navy, and as
late as 1931, 85 per cent of the income of the transport companies came not
from carrying passengers or freight, but from the Post Office Department on
mail contracts. The rates of payment permitted under the Kelly Act were
judged to be inadequate and Congress raised them several times. Finally in
1930 the McNary-Watres Act empowered the Postmaster General to make
contracts under which the companies would be paid for providing space for
mail irrespective of the weight or volume of the mail actually carried. By 1932
payments on these contracts had risen to nearly $20 million annually, some
three times what the Post Office was taking in through the sale of air-mail
postage.

The development of aviation was probably important enough to the national
welfare to justify a policy of subsidies, but the actual administration of the system brought much criticism. Not only were the payments often excessive, but
there seemed to be favoritism in their distribution. Hoover's Postmaster Gen-

eral, Walter F. Brown, was accused of having evaded the clauses in the McNary-Watres Act that required competitive bidding, of having allotted the contracts in such a manner that 90 per cent of the government payments were made to three major groups in the industry, and of having brought pressure to bear upon the smaller independent companies to compel them to merge with the larger one.

The Railroads

The development of air transportation was a potential, rather than an actual, threat to the railroads during the twenties. Their more immediate difficulties lay in the growth of other forms of competition. Fords and Chevrolets were scurrying over the roads on innumerable errands that a decade before would have provided business for the trains. The problem became still more serious as bus lines and trucking companies expanded their activities. Railroad executives complained bitterly that, whereas their companies had to expend huge sums of money in maintaining their tracks and roadbeds, these new competitors were enjoying the use of highways built at the taxpayers' expense. To make matters worse from the railroads' point of view, interstate motor transportation was not yet subject to Federal regulation.

The railroads also felt increased competition from waterways. The building of the Panama Canal stimulated interest in similar projects within the nation's borders. In 1918 the new New York State Barge Canal, superseding the historic Erie Canal, was opened to traffic. The Federal government expended large sums of money in projects designed to improve navigation along the Ohio, Missouri, and Mississippi Rivers. Once again there was bitterness in the comments of the rail executives; most of these projects, they charged, did not pay for themselves; the railroads were being injured by a form of government-subsidized competition.

The long-range prospects of the railroads looked anything but promising and the carriers were hard hit by the depression of 1921. Yet the day of reckoning was for a little while postponed during the period of Coolidge prosperity. Despite the continued falling off of passenger receipts, freight revenues reflected the satisfactory state of general business activity. Substantial economies in operation, moreover, were effected. Freight cars were increased in capacity and locomotive design was improved so that longer trains could be pulled. Important experiments were made in the use of diesel engines, electrification, automatic systems of sorting cars in freight yards, and streamlining. One million and a half railroad employees were operating the country's lines in 1930, whereas two million had been required a decade before.

Increased efficiency, however, was not enough to save the carriers from the devastating effects of the Great Depression that started in 1929. During the next few years most of the railroads failed to earn their fixed charges, while over 40,000 miles were in the hands of receivers by 1933. Had it not been for life-saving loans by Hoover's Reconstruction Finance Corporation, bankrupt mileage would have been much greater—greater, in fact, than in any previous period of railroad history.

The Transportation Act of 1920 proved in certain of its provisions hard to administer. The organization of labor adjustment boards proceeded very slowly because of differences between the carriers and their employees. This added to the crushing weight of the problems confronting the National Railroad Labor Board. The board gained the hostility of the unions by recommending wage cuts in 1921 and 1922. When the shopmen walked out in protest against the latter cut as well as against other grievances, their strike was broken with the assistance of an injunction secured by Attorney General Daugherty.

Labor's wholesale opposition to the Labor Board, combined with an attack upon it headed by the Pennsylvania Railroad and several other lines, resulted in the passage of the Railroad Labor Act of 1926. The old board was abolished; in its place was established a permanent Board of Mediation composed of five members chosen by the President. The board's primary duty was to attempt to mediate in railroad labor disputes not settled by direct negotiations or by adjustment boards; if the board's effort at settlement also failed, it was then to urge the parties to submit the dispute to arbitration. The employers and employees could not be compelled to arbitrate, but if they did agree to this form of settlement, the findings of the arbiters were to be binding at law. Should either or both the parties refuse to arbitrate and an interruption in interstate commerce be threatened, the President was empowered to appoint an emergency board to investigate and report to him. The parties were required not to make any change in conditions until thirty days after the emergency board's report. Despite pessimistic predictions by those who remembered the failure of similar legislation passed in 1913, this machinery worked surprisingly well.

The portion of the Transportation Act of 1920 that dealt with the consolidation of the nation's railroads caused difficulties. In the early twenties the Interstate Commerce Commission issued a tentative plan calling for consolidation into nineteen great systems; the railroads protested many details and a revised plan providing for twenty-one systems was published in 1929. Once again the railroads were dissatisfied; they suggested certain regional consolidations based upon their own ideas, but the commission's approval of these was given upon conditions that were unacceptable to the roads. As a result of this deadlock, none of the consolidation contemplated in the legislation of 1920 was actually achieved.

For a time the railroads appeared to have found in holding-company organization a device for securing their own kind of consolidation—one that would escape the regulatory powers of the Interstate Commerce Commission. Particularly notorious were the activities of the Van Sweringen brothers of Cleveland, Ohio, who used pyramided holding companies to gain control over railroads having aggregate assets of $2.5 billion with an investment of less than $20 million. Similarly bold were the operations of the Pennroad Company through which the Pennsylvania Railroad sought to extend its influence into new fields. The ICC was threatened with the undermining of much of its power until the situation was remedied by legislation in 1933.

The "recapture clause" in the Transportation Act also proved hard to administer. The law required that one half of the earnings of the lines in excess of a fair return on their property should be paid into a railroad contingent fund. The commission fixed 6 per cent as a fair return, but commission and carriers disagreed sharply on the valuations of railroad property on which fair return should be figured. The commission laboriously worked out valuations for each railroad, based largely upon what it would have cost to reproduce it in 1914; the railroads contended for a "reproduction cost new" formula that would base valuations upon what reconstruction would cost under the prices of the twenties. In the so-called O'Fallon case (1929), the Supreme Court refused to uphold the commission; the result was to throw the whole issue into great confusion, from which the country was finally delivered by the repeal of the recapture clause in 1933. Since these valuation problems also made it difficult for the commission to base rates upon the formula laid down in the law of 1920, this likewise had to be modified in 1933.

The railroad question continued, obviously, to be one of the major national issues. As time went on, however, the nub of the problem changed from protecting the public against railroad abuses to keeping the roads operating in reasonably solvent fashion.

Business Becomes Bigger

As has been stressed already, the decade of the twenties was an age of consolidation. Not since the years 1897 to 1903 had political, economic, and social factors blended in an atmosphere so exhilarating to the promoters of vast enterprises. The movement profited particularly from the increasing number of Americans eager to invest in stocks and willing to buy up almost any new issue of securities thrown upon the market.

The extent to which business concentration had gone is shown by the fact that in 1930 the 200 largest non-financial corporations of the country—45 railroads, 58 public utilities, and 97 industrials—had gross assets of $67 billion. This was almost one half of all the assets owned by corporations of this character in the country. By 1930 there were 15 companies each of which had assets of over $1 billion. Mergers resulted in the disappearance of 6,000 manufacturing and mining enterprises between 1919 and 1928, while 4,000 public utilities and more than 1,800 banks were absorbed by other concerns.

Retail trade had been revolutionized as giant chain stores like the A & P, Woolworth's, the United Cigar Stores, and Walgreen's Drug Stores spread across the country. In 1929, 27 per cent of American food sales, 19 per cent of drugstore sales, and 93 per cent of variety-store sales were made through these chains.

Although outright mergers were frequent, the most popular device for consolidating business during the decade was the holding company. This form of combination had lost its popularity following the adverse decisions of the Supreme Court in the Northern Securities case in 1904 and the Standard Oil case in 1911, but after 1920, when the Court refused to order the dissolution of the United States Steel Corporation, corporation lawyers returned to it with great enthusiasm. Not only were about one quarter of all the nation's industrial concerns brought under holding-company organization during the next twelve years, but the method was used with increasing frequency in the railroad and banking fields.

As corporations became larger, they fell more and more under management control. So numerous were the stockholders and so small was the proportion of stock that most of them held that few ever tried to influence or control the policies of the company; instead they willingly mailed in their proxies to be voted by a committee of the management. Unwilling to run even a remote risk of a stockholders' revolt, moreover, corporation lawyers specialized in so organizing the companies that the investing public put up the capital through the purchase of bonds, preferred stock, and non-voting common stock, while control of the enterprise was tightly held by a little group of insiders owning a small issue of voting stock never put on public sale. The growing divorce between corporate ownership and control sometimes made for irresponsibility and bad management.

Despite this trend toward consolidation, the single corporation threatening to monopolize a whole field of economic endeavor was less characteristic of the twenties than it had been of the early years of the century. The various Standard Oil companies, for example, controlled only about 43 per cent of the oil business in 1926 as compared with the 80 per cent that had been theirs in 1911, while the United States Steel Corporation's output declined from 65 per cent of the nation's total in 1902 to approximately 40 per cent. But this did not mean a revival of small business. What was developing instead was a situation wherein there were three or four great companies in a field, competing with each other but far outdistancing smaller rivals. This condition, called by the economists oligopoly, was illustrated by the dominance of the automobile field by Ford, General Motors, and Chrysler; in the chemical field by Du Pont, Allied Chemical and Dye, and Union Carbide and Carbon; in motion pictures by Famous Players-Lasky, Metro-Goldwyn-Mayer, Fox, and Universal; and by similar situations in the oil, steel, cigarette, aviation, and electrical industries.

The competition of the giants was a great boon to the advertising business. Enormous sums of money were spent in an attempt to impress upon the buying public the sterling merits of Lucky Strike, Camel, and Chesterfield cigarettes, or the prodigious power of Socony, Good Gulf, or Texaco gasoline. Advertising, however, emphasized the quality of the competing products, rather than their price. Indeed, it was taken for granted that the popular brands of cigarettes would all sell at the same price, as did the leading brands of gasoline, bread, and milk. Businessmen came to look upon price cutting as unethical. It was assumed, for example, that the figure set by Standard Oil would fix the price charged for gasoline by all the other major companies. Similar price leadership was exercised by the United States Steel Corporation, the International Harvester Company, the National Biscuit Company, and many others.

The desire to stabilize business was reflected also in the organization of trade associations. Such groupings had been in existence since the days of the Civil War, but they increased greatly in number and importance during and after World War I. In 1925 there were approximately a thousand of them. Trade association activities took many different forms. Sometimes advertising was done in the interests of the whole industry. For example, when the American Tobacco Company made extensive use of the slogan, "Reach for a Lucky instead of a sweet," the candymakers' association published a series of advertisements emphasizing the healthful food values in their products. Sometimes industrial research was promoted, as at the University of Chicago under the patronage of the Institute of American Meat Packers. Many trade associations undertook to simplify the prevalent business practices in their fields or to standardize products. In such activities they had the full cooperation of Secretary of Commerce Herbert Hoover. The varieties of paving brick were thus reduced from 66 to 4, of sheet steel from 1,819 to 261, and of range boilers from 130 to 13.

The temptation was great, however, to direct trade association activities into less legitimate channels—channels tending toward price fixing, restriction of production, and restraint of competition. Particularly controversial was the so-called open-price movement, which had its original impetus in 1912 from a book entitled *The New Competition*, written by a Chicago lawyer, A. J. Eddy. Upon its title page were these words: "Competition is War and 'War is Hell.'" Eddy's thesis was that cutthroat competition could be avoided and business stabilized if producers would provide each other with complete information about all their transactions—about sales, customers, shipments, production, and prices. By 1921 there were more than one hundred open-price associations engaged in collecting and distributing such information.

Foreign Trade and Investments

About one tenth of the annual production of goods in the United States was sold abroad. As compared with the proportion disposed of in the domestic market these sales were not large, but to many industries they represented the difference between prosperity and depression. Hoover, as Secretary of Commerce, was particularly zealous in promoting American export trade. Requests to his department for information about foreign markets rose from 700 to 10,000 a day, and a large corps of commercial attachés and trade experts were sent abroad to advance the interests of the exporters. Other agencies for promoting foreign trade were some fifty export associations, which had been granted exemption from the antitrust laws by the Webb-Pomerene Act of 1918, and numerous American banks, which were permitted under the Federal Reserve Act to maintain foreign branches.

Thus encouraged, American exports rose from their depression low of $3.8 billion in 1922 to $5.2 billion in 1929. Certain interesting trends were to be noted. Up to 1900 the leading exports had been cotton, wheat, and meat; by 1929 only cotton maintained its leading place—wheat and meat exports being far surpassed by petroleum products, machinery, and automobiles. In 1900, about two thirds of sales abroad had been agricultural products; by 1929 the proportion of these was not more than one third. In 1900, moreover, over three quarters of American exports went to Europe; by 1929 less than one half did so because of increased sales to Canada, Latin America, and Asia.

Imports, no less than exports, were important to the nation's economy. Increasing industrialization led to large purchases of newsprint, vegetable oils, rubber, and certain metals like copper, nickel, and tin. As in the case of sales abroad, American purchases from Europe were becoming proportionately less, while those from Canada and Asia were showing notable increases. Republican tariff policies, however, were reflected in the continued excess of exports over imports. In 1929, goods entering the United States were valued at only $4.4 billion, which fell short by $800 million of balancing the country's sales abroad.

Such an annual excess of exports over imports had been usual before World War I. Then it had served a useful function, since the United States was a debtor country and required funds to pay dividends and interest to foreign investors who had loaned their money for building American railroads and otherwise furnished capital for the rapid economic development of the country. But the war radically altered the situation. Many foreigners had to liquidate their holdings of American securities, while American bankers and the

United States government itself loaned large sums to the belligerents. Even excluding the huge intergovernmental debts, the change in the situation was striking; foreign investments in the United States between 1914 and 1919 fell from $6.75 billion to $2.2 billion, while investments abroad increased from $3.5 billion to $6.5 billion. The United States, in short, had become a creditor nation.

Ten years after the war, conditions were still more radically altered. Foreign investment in the United States had risen again to $6.7 billion—attracted by the dazzling prospects of American industry. But it by no means kept pace with American investment abroad, which, with the blessing of the American State Department, had risen by 1929 to $15.4 billion. The excess of American exports over imports provided funds for American loans to many foreign governments, as well as for the financing of tin-mine operations in Bolivia, oil development in Mexico, Venezuela, and Iraq, rubber plantations in the Netherlands East Indies, banana plantations in Central America, and sugar plantations in Cuba. Particularly notable was the large amount of American capital—$1.5 billion—invested in manufacturing enterprises in foreign countries, often in foreign branches of American companies. The export of American capital to build foreign factories was so extensive as to threaten the export markets for goods manufactured in the United States.

So long as American capital continued to flow into foreign investments, world economic conditions appeared to be in a state of healthy convalescence. Germany successfully met the reparations payments fixed under the Dawes Plan of 1924, and her creditors in turn made their war-debt payments to the United States. American exports continued in large volume since they were in truth being financed by expanding American investments. But the foundation of this convalescence remained precarious. Should American loans abroad cease, disastrous consequences would be inevitable.

The Balance Sheet for the Twenties

Seen in perspective, the prosperity of the twenties was by no means fictitious. On the contrary, there was much solid economic achievement. Not only was there a substantial increase in the gross national income, but there were measurable gains both in per capita real income and in the real wages of American laborers. Particularly impressive was the increased efficiency to be found in manufacturing, mining, transportation, and agriculture. Scientific management and improved machinery had made human labor more productive than ever before.

Unfortunately, however, certain other developments of the period proved in the long run so unhealthy as to threaten the whole economic structure. The failure of agricultural prices to maintain an equitable relationship with other prices undermined the security of millions of Americans, while sick industries like bituminous coal mining and cotton textile manufacture involved hardship for many others. Particularly disquieting was the growth of technological unemployment; new machinery seemed to be taking away jobs faster than it created them. It was cold comfort to the man thrown out of work to assure him that his plight was temporary and that ultimately he might expect a new and better job from expanding industry. The transition period was often long and painful, and the rugged individualism of the twenties was entirely opposed to the principle of compulsory unemployment insurance to provide for such cases.

During the Coolidge era men liked to dream that the business cycle had been broken and that the country had entered a period of perpetual prosperity. But the continuance of good times required that distribution keep pace with production, demand with increased supply. Since this was fundamental, the seri-

The Progress of Civilization. Pioneers of the nineteenth and twentieth centuries. (From the *Rochester Democrat and Chronicle.*)

ousness of a situation in which millions of farmers, miners, and workers failed to secure an ample and stable income is obvious. The price policies of many manufacturers added to the difficulty. The comparative stability of the general price level during the twenties is misleading, suggesting as it does that there was no general inflation. Yet in many lines reductions in cost were effected that failed to be reflected in reductions in price; the result was a species of concealed inflation. Instead of the savings beings handed on to the consumers, they were largely diverted to increased profits. Many businessmen preferred to take a large profit on a small volume of business rather than a small profit on a large volume. But prices higher than they needed to be seriously reduced the purchasing power of the consumers upon which continued prosperity depended. The inflexibility of prices, of course, reflected the restraints upon competition that were so common during the twenties—monopoly, oligopoly, price leadership, and trade association agreements.

In certain other lines the inflation was not concealed at all. By 1927 the price of most common stock was purely speculative and had lost all contact with the actual earning power of the corporation involved. Yet the great bull market was merely gathering momentum; up and up it went until it reached the fantastic peaks of September, 1929. The housing and real-estate boom of the earlier twenties likewise drove prices to unnatural levels; the most notorious situation was that in the Florida land market, where thousands of Northerners were feverishly engaged in buying and selling real estate, much of which they had never seen. Before the hurricane of 1926 and other factors combined to cool the excessive ardor of the speculators, prices had been pushed to grotesque levels.

Speculation in stocks and real estate was particularly dangerous to the continuance of prosperity because it was carried on largely upon credit. The investor preferred to borrow from his broker and buy a large amount of stock on margin rather than purchase a smaller amount outright; the real-estate buyer gave a mortgage for most of the sales price and obligated himself for an indefinite period in the future to make heavy interest payments based upon an inflated valuation of his property. The overextension of credit was, in fact, to be seen on every hand. Hard to resist was the ubiquitous salesman perpetually urging his prospect to "buy now and pay in easy installments." Many a young couple was making payments simultaneously on a bungalow, household furniture, radio, washing machine, vacuum cleaner, and automobile. It was an expensive process because it involved large interest payments; it was precarious since illness, unexpected expenses, or loss of one's job might make it impossible to continue the payments, in which case the unhappy householders might lose both their purchases and the payments they had already made. But the great banker was often as imprudent as the small householder; many of the securities

—particularly the foreign ones—that he bought for himself and sold to his customers proved to be worthless.

The final weakness in the prosperity of the twenties was its narrow base. In 1929 there were 16,350,000 families in the United States receiving less than $2,000 in annual income. This was nearly 60 per cent of all the families in the country, yet they received less than 24 per cent of the national total. A still greater drag on the country's economy was the lowest income group—the 21 per cent of American families who received less than $1,000 a year and less than 4 per cent of the national income. Here were the customers who would have to secure greater purchasing power before the nation would really achieve Hoover's noble goal, "the final triumph over poverty."

17

Hoover and the Depression

In October, 1929, a calamitous break in the New York stock market occurred. This was the dramatic beginning of the greatest depression in world history. Its repercussions were momentous both in domestic and international politics. In England, a Labor government was swept from power; in Germany, the political parties upholding the republic were overwhelmed by their anti-republican enemies; in France, no ministry could remain long in authority; in ten of the Latin-American states there were revolutions. And in the United States the Great Depression blasted the political fortunes of Herbert Hoover, despite the fact that few American presidents have entered the White House with greater prestige than was his in March, 1929.

The Election of 1928

On August 2, 1927, reporters assigned to cover President Coolidge's vacation in the Black Hills of South Dakota were provided with an unexpected scoop when the President handed out the terse statement: "I do not choose to run for President in 1928." It was big news because the country was prosperous and contented, Coolidge was at the height of his popularity, and political experts were freely predicting that he would run for a third term and be easily elected. Some of the President's most enthusiastic admirers refused to take his announcement as final and hoped that the movement to renominate him would assume such proportions that he would accept after all. In the absence of any encouragement from the White House, however, the "draft-Coolidge" plan foundered; it lasted only long enough to induce Coolidge's Senate opponents

—Democrats and Republican progressives—to pass a resolution on February 10, 1928, stating that any departure from the time-honored custom established by Washington of retiring after two presidential terms "would be unwise, unpatriotic and fraught with peril to our free institutions." Coolidge did not give his reasons for not seeking reelection. His decision may have been based upon respect for the anti-third-term tradition, on the knowledge that his health was failing, or upon a canny recognition that prosperity might not last forever.[1]

Coolidge's announcement was the signal for various Republican factions to start promoting their candidates. Former Governor Lowden of Illinois had a faithful following, but his chances for the nomination were injured by his age (68) and by the scars left from the Lowden-Wood struggle in the convention of 1920. Vice-President Dawes had demonstrated executive ability during his career and possessed an unusually colorful personality, but the Senators had never forgiven him for lecturing them on the obsolescence of their rules when he took up the gavel in 1925. Senator Borah of Idaho was a hero to thousands of Republican liberals, yet his name was anathema to most of the conservative Eastern leaders. The aspirations of all these rivals were doomed to defeat by the irresistible tide that set in for the nomination of Herbert Hoover. The Secretary of Commerce was unpopular with many of the Republican leaders, but he had tremendous strength among the party rank and file. His administration of Belgian war relief had established his reputation as a great humanitarian, his work as wartime Food Administrator had made his name a household word, and his long term as Secretary of Commerce had given him thousands of influential contacts with the business community. Hoover was assured of administration support when he issued a statement in praise of Coolidge's veto of the McNary-Haugen bill.

At the Republican convention at Kansas City, Hoover won the nomination on the first ballot. The vice-presidential candidate was Senator Charles Curtis of Kansas, who had been serving as majority leader in the Upper House. The platform was a cautious document, promising a continuance of the sound Republican policies that were asserted to be responsible for the nation's prosperity. The troublesome farm problem was recognized in a plank promising governmental assistance in the establishment of a farm marketing system, while prohibition was dealt with in a passage pledging the party to "the observance and vigorous enforcement" of the Eighteenth Amendment. In international affairs the platform advocated the outlawing of war and the further limitation of armaments, but opposed American entry into the League of Nations.

Several candidates, among them Governor Albert J. Ritchie of Maryland and Senator Thomas J. Walsh of Montana, were backed for the Democratic nomination. Their support was weak, however, compared with that of Governor

---

[1] Later, in his autobiography, Coolidge asserted that it was the anti-third-term tradition that caused his statement.

Alfred E. Smith and Herbert Hoover. (Acme.)

Alfred E. Smith of New York. Since his unsuccessful bid for the nomination
four years before, Smith had continued to grow in political stature. In 1924 he
had been re-elected governor despite the fact that Coolidge carried the state by a
large majority; in 1926 he was elected for an unprecedented fourth term. Not
only had he proved himself an effective campaigner, but his reform of the New

York state government and his advocacy of progressive measures secured him nation-wide publicity. He was still disliked in the South as a Catholic and a wet, but no bitter-end opposition to him—such as had wrecked the party's chances in the 1924 campaign—was allowed to develop. Instead, the "Happy Warrior," as he had once been described by Franklin D. Roosevelt, received a first-ballot nomination at the Houston convention. An attempt to sugar-coat the pill for the South was made by naming Senator Joseph T. Robinson of Arkansas as his running mate.

The Democratic platform of 1928 was no more inspiring than the Republican. The League of Nations was not mentioned and prohibition was dealt with only in a pledge to make "an honest effort to enforce the Eighteenth Amendment and all other provisions of the Federal Constitution and all laws enacted pursuant thereto." Even on the tariff the Democrats demanded no radical change of policy, promising, on the contrary, duties which would maintain legitimate business and a high standard of wages while permitting effective competition and ensuring against monopoy. Coolidge's farm policy was severely criticized, but the Democratic alternative was left vague.

Fortunately the candidates proved somewhat less evasive than the party platforms. Governor Smith promised to enforce the prohibition laws so long as they were on the books, but he advocated speedy modification of the Volstead Act and eventual repeal of the Eighteenth Amendment. His alternative was a system under which each state would handle its own liquor problem, yet he opposed the return of the saloon and urged the sale of liquor through state stores. Hoover, on the other hand, defended prohibition as "a great social and economic experiment, noble in motive and far-reaching in purpose." Smith made his bid for the farmer's vote by accepting the principle of the McNary-Haugen bill; he advocated also the public operation of the Muscle Shoals project and gained thereby the support of Senator Norris. Hoover outdid Coolidge in his condemnation of such proposals, warning solemnly: "You cannot extend the mastery of the government over the daily working life of a people without at the same time making it the master of the people's souls and thoughts." Despite his stand on prohibition, farm relief, and public power, Smith was no radical. He sought to reassure the country that he would do nothing to interfere with prosperity, and in particular that he would not press for drastic tariff revision. The Smith campaign was essentially conservative, deriving its tone perhaps from the unusual circumstance that a wealthy General Motors executive, John J. Raskob, was serving as Democratic campaign manager.

The contest was a heated one, but not because of any widespread interest in the issues. What created excitement was the unorthodox background of the Democratic candidate. A product of Tammany Hall, boasting of his affection for "the sidewalks of New York," he was viewed with inevitable suspicion by millions of small-town Americans. That suspicion was doubled by the knowledge that he was a wet and multiplied many times over by the knowledge that he was a Roman Catholic. Never before had a member of that faith been nominated for the presidency by a major party, and many narrow-minded Protestants—their prejudices heightened by recent Klan propaganda—predicted terrible consequences if Smith were successful. A vicious whispering campaign was directed against the New York governor.

The Republicans' best argument was prosperity, for which the party orators naturally took complete credit. And the election returns showed the strength of that argument. Hoover received 444 electoral votes to Smith's 87. The unusual degree of hostility to the Democratic candidate in the South was demonstrated by Hoover's victory in Florida, North Carolina, Texas, and Virginia— states never carried by a Republican since Reconstruction days. Smith suffered further disappointment when he lost his own home state, although he did carry nearby Massachusetts and Rhode Island. Despite the fact that the Democrats won only eight states, Smith's popular vote of 15 million compared very favorably with the 9 million votes given to Cox in 1920 and the 8 million to Davis in 1924. Hoover's popular vote was over 21 million; the minor party candidates, Thomas (Socialist) and Foster (Workers or Communist) received only 267,000 and 48,000 respectively. The Progressives made no effort to revive their party during this campaign. As in 1900, the election results were somewhat deceptive. The conservatives seemed completely triumphant, yet the onset of depression was soon to restore progressivism to all its old vigor.

Hoover: Assets and Liabilities

The President who took office on March 4, 1929, had many assets. Before he became a well-known public figure, he had had years of experience in the business world. Trained as an engineer at Stanford University, he had begun in his profession at the bottom, but speedily acquired a fortune as a mining and railroad expert and promoter. He spent many years abroad in China, in South Africa, and in England. Both as businessman and government executive, he developed a passion for facts. He campaigned by quoting statistics; as President, he was continually organizing commissions of experts to study and report on problems. Many of these bodies prepared studies of great interest and importance as, for example, the Committees on Recent Economic Change, on Child Health and Protection, and on Recent Social Trends. Most famous of all was the Commission on Law Enforcement, better known as the "Wickersham Commission," which prepared an exhaustive report on prohibition and related problems. Another outstanding talent of the new President was for organizing cooperative enterprises. As a cabinet officer under Harding and Coolidge, he had been conspicuously successful in helping businessmen to help themselves. In the White House he sought the solution of important national problems through the same method. Hoover had, moreover, a well-formulated philosophy of government, which he upheld with sincerity, if not always with consistency. He objected to government intervention in the business world as not alone injurious to economic life, but to liberty. "Economic freedom," he asserted during the campaign, "cannot be sacrificed if political freedom is to be preserved."

But Hoover had serious liabilities as well. His convictions regarding the proper functions of government were destined to be much more popular during days of prosperity than during the depression. Moreover, the new President's training, rich in so many respects, was dangerously weak in the field of practical politics. Never before had he held an elective office; never before had he had to deal intimately with a legislative body, jealous of its prerogatives. He was sensitive to criticism, stiff in his personal contacts, cold to newspapermen, and colorless in his public appearances. Most serious of all perhaps, he—like so many products during the golden age of salesmanship—had been overadvertised to the electorate. Depicted as a sort of superman, Hoover's popularity evaporated rapidly when the depression did not disappear at the magician's wand; by 1932 the words "Great Engineer" were usually uttered in a tone of bitterness.

The New Administration

Hoover's inaugural address listed the ideals to which he had devoted his leadership. They included:

> The preservation of self-government and its full foundations in local government; the perfection of justice whether in economic or in social fields; the maintenance of ordered liberty; the denial of domination by any group or class; the building up and preservation of equality of opportunity; the stimulation of initiative and individuality; absolute integrity in public affairs; the choice of officials for fitness to office; the direction of economic progress toward prosperity and the further lessening of poverty; the freedom of public opinion; the sustaining of education and of the advancement of knowledge; the growth of religious spirit and the tolerance of all faiths; the strengthening of the home; the advancement of peace.

In selecting his cabinet, the new President retained two of his associates in the Coolidge administration, Secretary of the Treasury Mellon and Secretary of Labor Davis. Of the new appointments, the most cherished prize, the Secretaryship of State, went to Henry L. Stimson, who had been Secretary of War under Taft and Governor General of the Philippines under Coolidge. Hoover's good friend President Ray Lyman Wilbur of Stanford University became Secretary of the Interior, while the chairman of the Republican National Committee, Walter F. Brown of Ohio, received the traditional post of Postmaster General.[2]

The retiring Vice-President, Charles G. Dawes, became Ambassador to Great Britain, an important post at any time and in 1929 particularly so due to Anglo-American disagreement on the issue of naval limitation.

The Great Bull Market

During Coolidge's presidency stock-market prices had risen almost without interruption. Up to 1927 the advance had been normal since business was expanding and profits were increasing. Thereafter an unnatural and unhealthy trend developed. Business activity leveled off, commodity prices tended to decline, but the price of common stocks soared up and up. On several occasions the market threatened to break, yet in a few days it would steady itself and then leap upward again. Hoover's victory in November, 1928, led to one of the most enthusiastic of these spurts. On September 3, 1929, the bull market reached its final, fantastic peak. Over the course of eighteen months—taking account of split-ups and the issuance of special rights—the stock of United States Steel and Union Carbide had more than doubled in price, that of General Electric, Westinghouse, and Montgomery Ward had tripled, that of Radio Corporation of America had quintupled. Such prices obviously represented speculative, rather than investment, values. American corporations, though enjoying good profits, were not earning the gigantic sums that alone would have justified these transactions. Stock purchasers were gambling recklessly, buying in hope of making a huge profit as the market continued to rise.

The situation was as remarkable for the number of people who were involved as for the strange behavior of prices. Back in 1919 when an earlier bull market had been in progress, there had been only six days on which as many as two million shares had been traded on the Exchange. During 1928 and 1929, however, five-million-share days were frequent, and on September 3, 1929, when prices were at their highest, over eight million shares were traded. Before World War I the realm of stocks and bonds was a mysterious area into which the average citizen did not care to venture. The great Liberty Bond drives of war days gave thousands of Americans their first interest in other forms of investment than savings-bank accounts. Further education was provided when large companies like the United States Steel Corporation encouraged stock purchases by their own employees as a form of welfare capitalism. As interest in the stock

[2] Other cabinet members were: James W. Good of Iowa, Secretary of War, succeeded during Hoover's first year by Patrick J. Hurley of Oklahoma; William D. Mitchell of Minnesota, Attorney General; Charles Francis Adams of Massachusetts, Secretary of the Navy; Arthur M. Hyde of Missouri, Secretary of Agriculture; Robert P. Lamont of Illinois, Secretary of Commerce, succeeded in 1932 by Roy D. Chapin of Michigan. The Coolidge holdovers eventually resigned: Mellon was succeeded by Ogden L. Mills of New York in 1932, while William N. Doak of Virginia followed Davis as Secretary of Labor in 1930.

market grew, Wall Street brokerage houses opened branch offices in all the large cities, while important banks like the National City Bank of New York had closely affiliated investment branches aggressively scouring the country for new customers. Investment trusts were organized on the plausible principle that purchase of their securities would permit small investors to share in the ownership of diversified holdings chosen by experts. Never before had so many people owned corporation securities. Between 1912 and 1931 the number of stockholders in the Pennsylvania Railroad multiplied three times, in the United States Steel Corporation five, and in the American Telephone and Telegraph Company over thirteen. Some of the political conservatism of the twenties is probably to be explained by this development.

The most disquieting aspect of the period was the increasing proportion of stocks held on margin—that is, not owned outright, but purchased through a loan from one's broker who held the stock as security. The technique fascinated the uninitiated since one could apparently buy a great deal of stock with a small investment and then pay for it from the profit realized by its rise. Too late did many small investors discover the catch: if the price of the stock went down they had to put up more and more margin to keep their equity; when they were

Hold On There, Sonny! Ma Columbia fears inflation may cause an
explosion (From the *Rochester Democrat and Chronicle.*)

no longer able to do so, they lost both investment and stock. The banks were involved in these transactions through extensive loans made to the brokers for the financing of marginal buying. Such brokers' loans rose from $3.5 billion in June, 1927, to over $8 billion in September, 1929.

The Coolidge administration had watched the bull market with equanimity. Speculators from time to time drew fresh courage from Secretary Mellon's optimistic comments on business conditions, while the usually close-mouthed Coolidge gave the inflationary forces new strength in January, 1928, when he stated publicly that he did not consider brokers' loans too high. The Federal Reserve Board, moreover, took steps during the summer of 1927 to loosen rather than tighten credit. The motive was worthy, since the action was taken at the request of the central banks of England, France, and Germany to assist European business through a threatened crisis. The effect of the lowered interest rates, however, was greatly to increase speculation in Wall Street. So powerful, indeed, was the magnet of the stock boom that Americans began to reduce their investments and loans in Europe in order to buy stocks; worse still, Europeans sent their own funds to America for this purpose. This trend, long continued, presaged disaster for the shaky European economy.

Worried by what was occurring, the Federal Reserve Board tried to stem the trend in 1928 by raising the rediscount rates several times. Yet the bull market continued—fed by more and more brokers' loans. Two days after he took office, President Hoover conferred with the Federal Reserve officials and the conference resulted in an unprecedented action—the board decided to refuse credit to banks which were directly or indirectly financing speculation. Shortly thereafter Secretary Mellon gave out a curiously veiled warning: "The present situation in the financial markets offers an opportunity for the prudent investors to buy bonds. Bonds are low in price compared to stocks." These actions and warnings halted the bull market only temporarily. Many of the banks, including Federal reserve banks, defied the board's program by offering large credits to the stock market. The government's action resulted in boosting stock-exchange loan rates up to 15 or 20 per cent, but these high rates only encouraged the diversion of money to the call market in preference to less remunerative investments. Even corporations were making such loans from their surplus funds. Throughout the first half of 1929 the Federal Reserve Board maintained its policy of raising the rediscount rates, but the bankers and other moneylenders would not heed the warning.

The American people continued to refuse to believe that disaster lay ahead, and for the most part this was as true of experts as of laymen. Businessmen and college professors talked convincingly of "a new economic era"; the old truism that "what goes up must come down" was amended to read that what goes up will remain on "a permanently high plateau."

The Crash

The stock market began to hesitate in September. On the third, prices were at a peak, then they went down but recovered so quickly that on the nineteenth some established new highs. This respite was short-lived. For a month prices fluctuated, but the trend was strongly downward. The decline was not considered alarming and the papers were full of reassuring statements. When Mitchell of the National City Bank arrived in New York from Europe on October 22, he assured the reporters: "I know of nothing fundamentally wrong with the stock market or with the underlying business and credit structure."

On October 23 the situation became suddenly serious when stocks suffered drops averaging 18 points. The next day panic developed. There were over 12 million transactions on the Stock Exchange and a $240 million bankers' pool, hurriedly organized by the largest financial institutions in the city, had to come to the rescue. Prices were temporarily stabilized, but a few days later they began plunging down again. The blackest day in stock market history was Tuesday, October 29, 1929. An all-time record of 16,410,030 transactions took place; the average prices of fifty leading stocks, as compiled by the *New York Times*, fell nearly 40 points. Brokers were deluged with orders to sell from customers who wanted to unload before the market dropped any lower. Many of the sales were involuntary. Traders who had been operating on margin were unable to raise enough money to save their accounts and were sold out. Thousands of Americans saw their life savings thus disappear.

After this terrible day there was no further panic. A stabilizing influence was the welter of comforting statements coming out of Washington and Wall Street. John D. Rockefeller announced: "Believing that fundamental conditions of the country are sound and there is nothing in the business situation to warrant the destruction of values that has taken place on the exchanges during the past week, my son and I have for some days been purchasing sound common stocks." Even with confidence somewhat restored, the process of liquidating the unfortunate marginal traders continued to depress the market and on November 13, prices reached their 1929 lows. In seventy-one days since September 3, American Telephone and Telegraph had fallen from 304 to 197¼, General Electric from 396¼ to 168⅛, Montgomery Ward from 137⅞ to 49¼, and Radio Corporation of America from 101 to 28.

Depression

So persistent was the belief that America was in a new economic era of perpetual prosperity that even the catastrophe in the stock market failed at first to shake it. On New Year's Day, 1930, Secretary Mellon declared: "I see nothing in the situation which warrants pessimism." And Secretary of Commerce

Lamont predicted "for the long run" a continuance of prosperity and progress.

It soon became apparent, however, that the stock market collapse was merely the opening crash of thunder for an economic storm of hurricane proportions. Manufacturers found their orders falling off alarmingly, and price cuts failed to revive them. The net income of the 550 largest industrial corporations of the country declined 68 per cent during the next two years. Weak companies were forced out of business, stronger ones operated part time and with sharply reduced personnel. By 1932 industrial production was not more than half what it had been in 1929. The construction business was even harder hit as residential and commercial building fell to one fifth of its 1929 volume. The railroads, dependent upon a high level of business activity for adequate revenues, were placed in a desperate situation. One third of the nation's mileage passed into receivership. National income dropped from $82 billion in 1928 to $40 billion in 1932.

Wage workers suffered greatly. Until September, 1931, employers generally avoided wage cuts in the belief that their effect would prolong the depression. But even while hourly rates were maintained, the take-home pay of labor was sharply curtailed either because the factories were operating only part time or because what work was available was being spread to provide for as many employees as possible—a practice that was encouraged by the American Federation of Labor. Despite this staggering of employment, more and more workers found themselves laid off. Accurate statistics on unemployment were not obtained and estimates varied widely according to the political leanings of the estimator. Apparently at least 10 million Americans were jobless in 1932, however, while in the spring of the following year the number increased to somewhere between 13 and 15 million. Moreover, between 1931 and 1933 substantial wage cuts were suffered by those who were fortunate enough to have jobs. The reductions in hourly rates were in most cases less than the reduction in the cost of living, but only a small proportion of the workers enjoyed steady enough employment to benefit by this.

People in all walks of life found themselves either without income at all or with income sharply reduced. Ministers, teachers, salesmen, salaried executives, and farmers suffered along with industrial workers. Savings painfully accumulated were soon exhausted. People in debt—and there were millions of them— were confronted with especially serious problems. Thousands of farmers and home owners lost their property, and there would have been many more foreclosures had not the real-estate market been so depressed that the creditors postponed taking action. Stock that had been given as collateral for loans was sold when the debts could not be paid, while furniture and automobiles were repossessed by the finance companies.

If it was a hard time to owe money, it was no great privilege to be a creditor either. Banks were placed in great jeopardy when their debtors defaulted whole-sale at a time when stock and real-estate values were so low that the collateral the banks held was often insufficient to cover their outstanding loans. Even during the years of prosperity American banks had failed with alarming fre-quency, averaging about 700 a year. In 1930, the number almost doubled when 1,326 institutions had to close their doors, while in 1931 the figure rose to 2,294 and in 1932 to 1,456. It was the smaller state banks, unaffiliated with the Federal Reserve, that failed most frequently, but large city institutions often found themselves in very serious difficulty. Their troubles were multiplied when frightened depositors began to withdraw and hoard their money.

Unfair though it was, the farmers, who had shared very little in the pros-perity of the twenties, were particularly hard hit by the depression. Agricultural prices had been considered low in comparison to other prices in 1929, yet by the spring of 1933 the former had fallen 64 per cent from their 1929 level, while the prices of manufactured goods had gone down only 34 per cent. Farmers' cash income dropped from $11 billion in 1929 to $5 billion in 1932. The industrialists were able to maintain prices to some extent by reducing pro-duction, but the farmers, doing business under ruthlessly competitive condi-tions, were unable to follow suit. Instead, the warehouses groaned with agri-cultural surpluses.

Causes of the Disaster

The economic collapse, it should be stressed, was world-wide. Some of its roots were to be found in the maladjustment brought about by the war. Mil-lions of lives had been lost and untold property damage caused. A tremendous volume of debt, both internal and intergovernmental, had been created in all the belligerent countries. Europe was criss-crossed by new political frontiers along which economic barriers were speedily erected. Fear for each nation's security led to the maintenance of expensive military establishments. For a few years the seriousness of the fundamental situation was shrouded from view by the fictitious prosperity created by American loans. When the stream of Ameri-can investment dried up, due in part to the superior attractions of the stock market, the European situation deteriorated very rapidly. Stocks fell off in price, unemployment grew ominously, and the debts were defaulted. America felt the repercussions in many ways, but most directly by a 69 per cent decline in the dollar value of her exports between 1920 and 1932.

Another factor of importance in the world situation was the enormous ex-pansion of production that occurred during the twenties in the primary indus-tries. For a time international cartels and marketing agreements succeeded in maintaining prices, but in 1929 and thereafter the market broke disastrously.

Coffee fell off one third in price in three months, wool nearly 40 per cent in a year. Other prices declined less rapidly, but eventually all foodstuffs and raw materials showed the same extreme downward trend. Such great primary producing countries as Canada, Australia, and Brazil were grievously hurt, and their difficulties reacted on the entire world.

America's economic troubles could not all be blamed on outside forces. Factors already discussed—speculation, overextension of credit, inflexible prices, the faulty balance between agriculture and the rest of the economy, the inadequate income of millions of American families—all contributed to the debacle. The country's economic difficulties were increased by abuses in the banking system that permitted dangerous credit inflation during prosperity and endangered the savings of depositors during depression.

During the late thirties much discussion was provoked by the explanation of the depression advanced by Professor Alvin H. Hansen of Harvard University. Adapting an analysis derived from John Maynard Keynes, famous English economist, Hansen stressed the fundamental changes brought about in the American situation by the closing of the frontier, the restriction of immigration, and the declining birth rate. All of these factors tended to reduce the opportunities for private investment. The housing shortage caused by World War I and the new industries of the twenties offered outlets for the time being, but their possibilities were largely exhausted by 1929. Nearly all the homes that people could afford had been built, skyscraper office buildings could not find tenants, factories had been expanded to such an extent that their output could not be disposed of in a market where income did not keep pace with production. Automobiles, radios, refrigerators, and the like had been purchased by most Americans who could afford them—and by some who could not. These were relatively durable goods for which the market in the future would have to be largely a replacement one. Therefore there was little inducement to invest in plants for expanding their production. Savings lay idle in the banks or were gambled in Wall Street because investment outlets were so largely saturated. And as capital expenditures declined, the market for basic goods like steel contracted and the country fell into a declining economic spiral. This "mature economy" theory drew the conclusion that capitalism could only be preserved by government planning and government investment. The Hansen thesis was one of the most powerful influences at work during the later period of the New Deal.

The Federal Farm Board

In April, 1929, six months before the stock-market crash, Congress met in special session to redeem Republican campaign pledges for farm relief. The administration program called for increased tariff protection and for the establishment of a farm board to promote orderly agricultural marketing. Discussion of the former proposal was protracted and it was not until June, 1930, that the Hawley-Smoot Tariff was passed. The Agricultural Marketing Act, however, was rapidly whipped into shape and received the President's signature on June 15, 1929.

The new law provided for the creation of a Federal Farm Board of nine members to be appointed by the President. A revolving fund of $500 million was made available for loans to cooperative marketing associations, owned and controlled by the farmers themselves. In case more drastic measures were necessary, the Farm Board was authorized to establish stabilization corporations to buy and take off the market a sufficient portion of the crop to maintain prices. The Farm Bloc was dubious of the effectiveness of the measure and attempted to amend it by providing for export debentures—a plan whereby the government would pay a subsidy on agricultural exports equivalent to one half the American tariff rate. Hoover so vigorously opposed this that the act was passed in the form he approved. On the occasion of signing the bill, the President pronounced it "the most important measure ever passed by Congress in aid of a single industry." As chairman of the new Farm Board, he appointed Alexander Legge, president of the International Harvester Company.

The basic idea incorporated in the Agricultural Marketing Act was typical of Hoover. He hoped to help the farmers to help themselves or, in his own words, "with government assistance and an initial advance of capital to enable the agricultural industry to reach a stature of modern business operations by which the farmer will attain his independence and maintain his individuality." The board began its operations in this spirit. Existing cooperative associations were strengthened and enabled to expand; local and state bodies were merged into nation-wide organizations like the Farmers National Grain Corporation, the American Cotton Cooperative Association, the National Livestock Marketing Association, and the National Wool Association. From the revolving fund the cooperatives were permitted to borrow money to build storage facilities, creameries, canning, packing, and processing plants, as well as to finance the marketing of members' crops.

Such activities, however, would benefit farmers more in the future than immediately, and by the end of 1929 the stock-market crash had so upset agricultural prices that the problem of immediate relief was paramount. To an increasing degree, therefore, the Farm Board was diverted from a program of long-range assistance to desperate piecemeal efforts to halt the ruinous fall of prices. Willy-nilly, it had become the first of the great emergency agencies.

In October, 1929, the Farm Board authorized the marketing associations to make loans upon wheat and cotton at fixed prices, and later to purchase some of these commodities. The board felt sufficiently encouraged by this first venture to enlarge its price-pegging policy in 1930. A Grain Stabilization Corporation and a Cotton Stabilization Corporation were established and the two began large-scale operations in the market. During the next three years, 370 million bushels of wheat and 1.3 million bales of cotton were purchased with money advanced by the Farm Board.

During the first two years of these operations the Hoover administration was able to defend the Farm Board activities on the ground that, although they had by no means prevented a drastic fall in prices, they held American prices at a level somewhat higher than those prevailing in the world market. But as time went on the board's activities became progressively less effective. The huge surpluses purchased by the stabilization corporations hung over the market with depressing effect. Moreover, the farmers, trying desperately to maintain their income despite falling prices, continued to produce a large surplus. The Farm Board sought to correct this by asking the farmers for a voluntary reduction of their acreage by 30 per cent. Since each farmer hesitated to reduce his own plantings unless he were sure that all farmers were going to do so, the plan inevitably failed. More instead of less acreage was planted in 1932.

By the spring of 1932 the necessity of disposing of the Farm Board's surplus holdings was obvious. Special sales to China, Germany, and Brazil were made, and about one half of the board's stocks was turned over to the Red Cross for distribution to the victims of the depression.

The Farm Board was eventually abolished by executive order of Hoover's Democratic successor. Losses sustained through loans that could not be recovered and through the disposal of its wheat and cotton holdings brought the total cost of the experiment to about $345 million. This was not large compared with other relief expenditures that the government was destined to make, but the Farm Board policy was, nevertheless, a failure since it brought no solution to the fundamental agricultural problem: that of either reducing production or opening up new markets where American staples could be disposed of under conditions which would provide farmers with an adequate income.

The Hawley-Smoot Tariff

The other measure of farm relief promised by the Hoover administration was an increase in the tariff schedules covering agricultural products. The President hoped that the revision would be a limited one and that the rates on industrial goods would be changed only in those exceptional cases where existing duties did not conform with his favorite tariff formula, "the difference in the cost of production at home and abroad." Once the issue was before the House, however, the familiar process of logrolling was soon in evidence. Out of a thousand tariff raises proposed in the so-called Hawley bill, 75 were on farm products and

925 on manufactured goods. A farm paper warned that if the farmer was not careful he would find himself "paying out $2.00 in increased tariffs on manufactured products, which he must buy, for every $1.00 gain received on farm products." Such warnings were ineffective. Agricultural pressure groups vied with manufacturers' lobbyists in seeking benefits.

Hoover's principal anxiety was to keep the bill free from farm-relief riders and to expand the "flexibility" of the measure through the enlargement of the powers of the Tariff Commission. On both these issues he had difficulty with the Senate. The Farm Bloc succeeded in amending the House bill to include the export debenture plan, while Senator Borah, ever fearful of encroachments by the executive on the legislative branch of the government, headed a Progressive-Democratic-Old Guard-Republican campaign to compel all recommendations of the Tariff Commission to be passed upon by Congress. When, however, a deadlock between the House and the Senate versions of the bill necessitated the appointment of a conference committee, the President succeeded in getting the debenture plan out of the bill and the flexible provisions in.

Progressive strength in the Senate had been sufficient to obstruct some of the more excessive demands of the manufacturers' lobbies. Senator Joseph W. Grundy of Pennsylvania, the spokesman of the ultraprotectionists, was disappointed because the measure did not go far enough. Nevertheless, the country's leading economists believed that the new rates were far too high. Over one thousand of them signed a manifesto appealing to the President to veto the bill. They asserted that the measure would raise prices for the American consumer, would hamper the export of both agricultural and manufactured goods, would be ineffective in helping the producers of staples that had to be sold in the world market, would make it difficult for the interest and principal on American loans abroad to be paid, and would lead to reprisals by foreign governments. Prominent bankers and spokesmen for the export industries also opposed the measure, but it was defended by the American Farm Bureau, the National Grange, the American Federation of Labor, and the National Association of Manufacturers. On June 15, 1930, the measure became law with the President's signature.

The Hawley-Smoot Tariff raised the general average of duties from the 33 per cent of the Fordney-McCumber Act to 40 per cent. Rates on farm products were increased from less than 20 per cent to more than 33 per cent. The advantage of this to agriculture, however, was dubious. On the most important staples where an exportable surplus was produced, the tariff was ineffective in raising prices, while the farmer's cost of living was affected by higher duties on shoes, harnesses, saddles, shovels, spades, lumber, shingles, bricks, and cement. Moreover, the retaliatory measures in foreign countries against which the economists had warned followed speedily. The road of extreme economic nationalism on

Careful You Don't Upset Things! A warning against the Hawley-Smoot
Tariff. (Reproduced by permission of the *New York World-Telegram*.
Copyright, 1929.)

which the United States had elected to journey was crowded with fellow travelers.

Fighting the Depression

More than once in American history the Republicans have had the good
fortune to witness the beginning of a great upsweep of prosperity coinciding
with the passage of one of their tariff measures. Such, however, was not the
happy experience of the architects of the Hawley-Smoot Act. On the contrary,
the business indexes continued their relentless downward spiral.

The President had already responded to the crisis with a program typically
Hooverian. On November 21, 1929, Henry Ford, Alfred P. Sloane of General
Motors, Owen D. Young of General Electric, Walter Gifford of the American
Telephone and Telegraph Company, Pierre Du Pont of the great chemical
company, and other important leaders met the President in a confidential
White House conference. He asked for their cooperation in maintaining existing wage rates, in continuing construction, and in spreading available work as
widely as possible among employees. The industrialists agreed—contingent
upon the President's securing from organized labor a pledge not to seek pay increases and to avoid strikes during the crisis. A group of prominent trade-union
officials, including William Green and John L. Lewis, met with Hoover later
the same day and gave the required assurances, even going so far as to agree to

withdraw certain demands already made. Announcement of this promise of cooperation between industry and labor was given to the press, and two weeks later the President's program was ratified at a White House conference attended by several hundred representatives of the employers and the labor unions.

The pledges were substantially kept by both parties for almost two years. During 1930 an average of only seven out of each hundred firms reporting to the Bureau of Labor Statistics recorded pay cuts as against ninety-two cuts per hundred firms during the depression of 1921. The workers' record was equally good. Early in October, 1930, President Hoover, speaking to the American Federation of Labor, congratulated the unions on having held strikes to less than three hundred since their agreement of the preceding September.

Since 1921 Hoover had been an advocate of expanding public works during periods of depression. In November, 1929, he telegraphed governors and mayors all over the country requesting them to increase rather than contract governmental construction, while in his message to Congress the next month he asked for increased Federal appropriations for this purpose. Public-works expenditures by the Federal government rose from their predepression level of around $250 million annually to $412 million in the fiscal year ending June 30, 1930. Thereafter they increased until they reached almost $728 million for the year ending June, 30, 1933.

To coordinate the relief activities of private charities and local and state agencies, Hoover established in October, 1930, the President's Committee for Unemployment Relief under the chairmanship of Colonel Arthur Woods of New York City. Similar committees of prominent citizens to mobilize relief activities were set up in the various states and local communities.

In September, 1930, the President announced his determination to stop all immigration into the United States, on the ground that under existing conditions the newcomers were likely to become public charges. Over the course of the next eight months the influx of foreigners, already sharply cut by the legislation of 1924, was reduced from a monthly rate of about 22,000 to one of 3,000. Meantime, departures from the country, both voluntary and involuntary, reached 7,000 monthly. This latter figure reflected the rigorous deportation policy of the administration. For the four years, 1929–32, the annual immigration and emigration totals were as follows:

	Immigration (inward)	Emigrants (outward)
1929	279,678	69,203
1930	241,700	50,661
1931	97,139	61,882
1932	35,576	103,295

This revolution in immigration resulted not solely from the policies of the Hoover administration, but from the disillusionment of foreigners with the United States as a land of unlimited opportunity.

The Depression Grows Worse

The President and his advisers hoped that these initial steps would be successful in tiding over the crisis until recovery could set in. At times victory seemed within grasp; confidence revived and production climbed. Inevitably, however, a relapse would occur. Stocks would plunge down again, factories would lay off more men, farm prices would decline once more. By the fall of 1931 wage cuts were the rule everywhere. The world-wide character of the depression became steadily more apparent, and Hoover struggled during 1931 with the crises caused by the threatened economic collapse of Central Europe and England's departure from the gold standard.

As conditions grew worse, new problems arose. Bank failures and general business uncertainty led to large-scale hoarding both of currency and of gold, while foreigners withdrew funds from the country in alarming volume. This embarrassed the operations of the Federal reserve banks. Although the law required them to maintain only a 40 per cent gold reserve against the Federal reserve notes, the scarcity of eligible commercial paper made it necessary in practice to increase the gold reserve to 75 per cent. This combination of circumstances threatened to force the nation off the gold standard—a possibility as terrifying to Herbert Hoover as it had been to Grover Cleveland in the early 1890's.

Elsewhere the contraction of credit brought serious consequences. Home owners and farmers faced foreclosures. Manufacturing concerns and railroads could not borrow. The banks themselves found it difficult to obtain additional funds since they could not present eligible collateral to the Federal reserve banks.

Confronted with this situation, the Hoover administration was obliged to expand greatly the range of its activities. At the urging of the President, the banks of the country organized in October, 1931, the National Credit Association with a capital of $500 million. Its functions were to rediscount bank assets not eligible in the Federal Reserve System in order to assure the stability of banks against runs and to make loans against the assets of closed banks so that dividends to the depositors might be made. But the situation was too serious to be met adequately by this form of self-help. Therefore, in January, 1932, Congress accepted the President's recommendation for the creation of the Reconstruction Finance Corporation (RFC). Capital to the amount of $500 million was advanced by the government, while additional sums up to $1.5 billion might be borrowed by the new agency, whose function was to loan money to railroads, banks, insurance companies, and industrial corporations. The RFC's first head was Charles G. Dawes, former Vice-President and ambassador to Great Britain. In July, the Emergency Relief and Construction Act gave the RFC greatly extended powers. The amount it could borrow upon the credit of the United States was doubled, and the purposes for which it could advance money were broadened to include the establishment of agricultural-credit banks, loans to states, counties, or cities unable to handle their own relief problems, and loans for public or private construction projects that would be self-liquidating.

The Hoover policy of easing the credit situation was further developed through extending the activities of the Federal Land Banks and creating a new system of Federal Home Loan Banks. Since the latter could only loan up to 50 per cent of the appraised value of the mortgagor's property, however, they did little business. To assist the Federal reserve banks and the member banks of the system, the Glass-Steagall Act was passed in February, 1932. This measure permitted the Federal reserve banks to accept a much larger variety of collateral from their borrowers; it served the double purpose of freeing vast amounts of gold being held in excess of the legal reserve behind the Federal reserve notes and at the same time making available to the member banks large amounts of credit. The Federal reserve banks engaged in vast open-market operations, buying more than $1 billion worth of government bonds during the next few months; this operation was designed to expand credit for the benefit of the whole country. Simultaneously, a vast antihoarding campaign was organized at Hoover's request by Colonel Frank Knox, a prominent Chicago publisher.

Progressive and Democratic Opposition

The continuance of the depression despite all that Hoover had done naturally turned public attention more and more to the President's critics. During the first two years of the administration, the conservative Republicans were in control of the House, but in the Senate their position was not so fortunate. About a dozen of the 56 Republicans in the Upper House were progressives; they held the balance of power and by allying with the 39 Democrats and the sole Farmer-Laborite, they could outvote the administration supporters. The strength of the coalition was demonstrated when Senators Norris and Borah opposed the appointment of Charles Evans Hughes for Chief Justice of the United States in February, 1930, on the ground that his recent legal work had been largely in the employ of the great corporations. Hughes was confirmed, 52 to 26, but the size of the opposition vote was a warning of discontent with the conservative trend of recent Supreme Court decisions. Hoover's second appointment to the

Court created a still greater controversy. The nominee, John J. Parker of North Carolina, was opposed by organized labor because of decisions he had handed down as a circuit court judge upholding "yellow-dog" contracts. Negro groups also protested the appointment, and in the end it was rejected, 39 to 41. Hoover then substituted Owen J. Roberts of Pennsylvania, who was confirmed by unanimous vote. When another vacancy occurred in 1932, the President obviated the possibility of another bitter fight by naming the liberal and universally respected Benjamin N. Cardozo of New York.

Hoover's difficulties with Congress were greatly increased by the elections of 1930. The new Senate contained 48 Republicans, of whom 12 were progressives, 47 Democrats, and 1 Farmer-Laborite. On the face of the election returns the Republicans appeared to have maintained their control of the House by a very narrow margin, but a number of deaths occurred before the Seventy-Second Congress finally convened in December, 1931. The Democrats found themselves with a majority of four and were able to organize the House, electing John Nance Garner of Texas to the speakership.

The progressives found the political currents running in their direction for the first time since the Wilson administration. Even during the "lame-duck" session of the old Congress, they showed their strength by pushing through Norris' bill for government operation of Muscle Shoals. The President, however, subjected the measure to a stinging veto:

> This bill would launch the Federal Government upon a policy of ownership and operation of power utilities upon a basis of competition instead of by the proper government function of regulation for the protection of all the people. I hesitate to contemplate the future of our institutions, of our government, and of our country if the preoccupation of its officials is to be no longer the promotion of justice and equal opportunity but is to be devoted to barter in the markets. This is not liberalism, it is degeneration.

The Senate upheld the veto, but the insurgents were unabashed by this setback. A week after the adjournment of Congress in March, 1931, a conference of progressives met in Washington to formulate a program. Prominent in the movement were Senators LaFollette, Norris, and Borah, historian Charles A. Beard, future New Dealers Harold L. Ickes of Chicago and Mayor Frank W. Murphy of Detroit, and labor leader Sidney Hillman. Among the proposals discussed were such anti-Hooverian ideas as a large public works program, compulsory unemployment insurance, minimum wages, a five-day week, a six-hour day, wider distribution of wealth, social security, child labor laws, and a national economic council.

Neither the Democrats nor the progressives had any opportunity to attempt to attain their objectives until December, 1931, because Hoover ignored their demand that he call the new Congress into special session to deal with the emergency. When the Seventy-Second Congress finally met, conflicts between the legislators and the President were frequent. Hoover regarded the balancing of the budget as an essential step toward recovery. To this principle few of the Congressmen openly objected, because deficit spending as a weapon for combatting depressions had as yet few proponents. Nevertheless, it required months of discussion to frame a new revenue bill. The Southern Democrats advocated a manufacturers' sales tax, but the progressive Republican, Representative Fiorello H. LaGuardia of New York, secured enough votes to defeat the proposal. In the end, income-tax rates were raised and nuisance taxes were imposed; the new bill was calculated to increase revenues by $1 billion, but it fell short of what the President requested by some $400 million. The President and Congress similarly agreed in principle upon the necessity for economy, but differed on where the axe should be applied. In the end, Congress reduced appropriations by only $300 million instead of by $700 million as Hoover had asked.

During this stormy session the President's Congressional opponents raised many issues. One group attempted to challenge the Hawley-Smoot Act with bills that would have made the Tariff Commission answerable to Congress instead of to the Executive, would have directed the President to invite other powers to an international tariff conference, and would have authorized him to negotiate reciprocal trade agreements. Another faction advocated the issuance of more money. The Goldsborough bill, for example, which passed in the House but failed in the Senate, would have directed expanded currency and credit until prices rose to the averages prevailing between 1921 and 1929. A third faction insisted that the Federal government make large appropriations to provide either work or relief for the unemployed. Speaker Garner and Representative Rainey of Illinois were sponsors of a bill providing a vastly expanded program of public works, while Senators Wagner of New York, LaFollette of Wisconsin, and Costigan of Colorado, along with Representative LaGuardia of New York, were outspoken in their demand for a more adequate program of unemployment relief. All of these measures, however, were successfully blocked by the President.

Not all the work of the progressives was frustrated. They enjoyed an important triumph in obtaining the passage of the Norris-LaGuardia Anti-Injunction Act in March, 1932. By this law the public policy of the United States was thus stated:

> Whereas, under prevailing economic conditions, . . . the individual unorganized worker is commonly helpless to exercise actual liberty of contract and to protect his freedom of labor, and thereby to obtain acceptable terms and conditions of employment, wherefore, though he should be free to decline to associate with his fellows, it is necessary that he should have full freedom of association, self-organization, and designation of representatives of his own choosing, to negotiate the terms and conditions of his employment, and that he shall be free

from the interference, restraints, or coercion of employers of labor . . . in the activities for the purpose of collective bargaining or other mutual aid or protection. . . .

Yellow-dog contracts, whereby employees agreed not to join a labor union as a condition of employment, were declared to be against this public policy and were not enforceable in any Federal court. Then followed a listing of specific union activities that might not be prohibited by any Federal court injunction. Such orders in labor disputes were not entirely banned, but the circumstances under which they could be issued were strictly defined and provision was made for jury trial in any contempt-of-court case arising out of such instances, unless the alleged contempt occurred in the presence of the court. By this important law, organized labor obtained the substance of rights of which the Clayton Act of 1914 had provided only the shadow. With some signs of reluctance Hoover signed this measure.

The Bonus Issue Revived

From the World War I veterans came an appeal for immediate payment of the bonus. A year before, Congress had enacted a measure over Hoover's veto permitting the veterans to borrow up to 50 per cent on their certificates. In 1932, when the depression was even more severe, a demand went up for payment of the whole amount. A bill to this end, introduced by Representative Wright Patman of Texas, passed the House of Representatives but, under pressure from the President, was rejected by the Senate in June, 1932. The incident had an unhappy sequel. Starting in May, an increasingly large "Bonus Army" made up of unemployed veterans congregated in Washington to lobby for the Patman bill. On July 16 Congress adjourned without conceding the veterans' demands, but the Bonus Army lingered on disconsolately in their shanty villages on the outskirts of the capital. Hoover tried to get rid of the unwelcome horde through using government funds to pay their fares home. Some six thousand availed themselves of this help, but five thousand others remained in the city, many of them with their wives and children.

On July 28 they became involved in a fracas with the police in which two veterans were killed and several policemen were injured. Acting immediately upon a request from the District Commissioners, the President called out the army to restore order. Under command of General Douglas A. MacArthur, four troops of cavalry, four of infantry, a machine-gun squadron, and six tanks completely dispersed the Bonus Army and evicted the men from their camps. Whether by accident or design, the shacks in which they had lived were set on fire and burned to the ground. Hoover's defenders stressed the patience the President had hitherto shown in handling the situation and the fact that no lives were lost in the final eviction; they asserted that a large proportion of the demonstrators were Communists or hoodlums—not veterans at all. Moreover, they said, the shanty village was becoming a menace to the health of Washington. Whatever justification there might have been for the action, however, the incident did untold damage to the President's reputation as a great humanitarian and gave shocking evidence of the seriousness of the nation's economic situation.

Between President Hoover and his liberal critics there was a clear-cut difference of principle. Hoover believed in using Federal funds and credit to combat the depression, but he thought that the proper place for the money to be expended was in strengthening banks, railroads, and other corporations. By so doing, small depositors and investors would be protected, employment would be maintained and expanded, and a process of economic recovery set in motion that would in the end benefit everyone. His philosophy also accepted public works so long as they fulfilled a real need, the distribution of food and clothing to prevent actual physical suffering, and the advance of Federal funds to the states under careful restrictions. But he opposed the direct expenditure of Federal funds to relieve either the unemployed or the farmers. He held that such direct relief would create a burdensome bureaucracy and destroy the initiative and self-reliance of the recipients.

But Hoover's critics contended that by 1931 and 1932 a condition and not a theory confronted the nation. Panhandlers lined the streets, and discouraged men sold apples on the corners. Long breadlines were everywhere to be seen outside private and local relief headquarters. Private charity was near the end of its resources, local governments were threatened with insolvency, the states were without adequate resources. The problem was too big for any lesser agency than the Federal government itself. Moreover, these opponents of the President asserted that money poured into the financial pyramid at the top through the Reconstruction Finance Corporation never seeped down to the bottom. A demand arose for measures that would put purchasing power into the hands of the individual victims of the depression.

As the election of 1932 approached, it was obvious that not only the harassed President but bankers and businessmen generally had suffered an enormous loss of prestige. A revolution in public opinion had occurred, and those who had been the lords of creation in 1929 were now in disrepute.

18

Hoover's Quest for World Stability

In dealing with the international situation, Hoover showed bolder qualities of leadership than he did in his domestic policies. His earlier experience as engineer and relief administrator had given him an unusually broad knowledge of world affairs, and, as Secretary of Commerce, he had become a leading authority in the field of international economics.

During his four years in the presidency, Hoover attempted to use his position to promote world peace. In the course of the 1928 campaign he set the stage for his administration when he said: "Our foreign policy has one primary object, and that is peace. We have no hates; we wish no further possessions; we harbor no military threats." And in his inaugural he promised that the United States would take "a practical part in supporting all useful international undertakings. We not only desire peace with the world, but to see peace maintained throughout the world. We wish to advance the reign of justice and reason towards the extinction of force."

In working toward these goals Hoover seemed to make real progress. The extension of naval disarmament, the moratorium on reparations and war debt payments, and the more liberal Latin-American policy were all first-class achievements. Yet ironically the structure of world peace was torn down in other parts of the world much more rapidly than Hoover could build it up. Even while he was still President, Japan began its course of aggression and Germany fell under the rule of Hitler. To deal with such challenges as these, neither the prevalent American isolationism nor Hoover's cautious internationalism was adequate.

Further Rejection of the League and the Court

President Hoover did not believe that the League of Nations was a satisfactory agency for the promotion of the peace he desired. In his inaugural address he asserted:

> Our people have determined that we should make no political engagements such as membership in the League of Nations, which may commit us in advance as a nation to become involved in the settlement of controversies between other countries. They adhere to the belief that the independence of America from such obligations increases its ability and availability for service in all fields of human progress.

Thus Hoover rejected what he considered an entangling alliance, and during his term of office there was no public demand for a change in policy.

On the other hand, he was willing to have the United States participate directly or indirectly in certain of the League's activities that were not of a political nature. For example, American adherence to the World Court was strongly urged by Hoover in his inaugural address:

> American statesmen were among the first to propose, and they have constantly urged upon the world, the establishment of a tribunal for the settlement of controversies of a justiciable nature. The Permanent Court of International Justice in its major purpose is thus peculiarly identified with American ideals and American statesmanship.

Then he concluded with the hope that "we may take our proper place in a movement so fundamental to the progress of peace."

This action was to be based upon the so-called Root formula, worked out by a League-sponsored committee of which Elihu Root was a leading member. The formula, completed by the fall of 1929, attempted to solve the differences of opinion that had developed between the United States Senate and the League Council back in 1926. First of all, it provided that all requests for advisory opinions be submitted to the United States. Next, any American objections to these opinions might be discussed with and among the parties concerned. Finally, the United States might withdraw from Court membership without endangering its interests, were the other members to refuse to admit that the United States had a "vital" interest.

Both the League members and the American State Department found this formula satisfactory. As early as December, 1929, Secretary of State Stimson signed the protocols for the admission of the United States into the World Court with the Root reservations. Not until a year later, however, did Hoover submit the protocols to the Senate with an urgent request for speedy approval. The President wrote:

The provisions of the protocols free us from any entanglement in the diplomacy of other nations. We cannot be summoned before this Court, we can from time to time seek its service by agreement with other nations. These protocols permit our withdrawal from the Court at any time without reproach or ill-will. . . . Through the Kellogg-Briand Pact we have pledged ourselves to the use of pacific means in settlement of all controversies. Our great nation, so devoted to peace and justice, should lend its cooperation to this effort of nations to establish a great agency for pacific settlements.

But like his predecessors, Hoover found it difficult to induce the Senate to approve even this small step toward international cooperation. Although a majority of public opinion and 75 per cent of the press supported the President's plea, another battalion of death was formed in the Upper House, sufficiently large to prevent the issue from coming to a vote. These opponents of internationalism were backed in their obstructionist tactics by the isolationist press, headed by the Hearst papers, which once more headlined charges that the Court was nothing more than an agency of the League with a membership consisting of "international robbers."

The Renewal of Naval Disarmament

Following the failure of the Geneva Conference of 1927, the so-called Butler Cruiser bill was introduced into Congress in November, 1927, providing for the construction of 25 cruisers, 5 aircraft carriers, and other craft at a cost of $725 million. It was stipulated, however, that the building of the cruisers and carriers was subject to the provisions of the Washington Treaty and that if another limitation conference were called the President might suspend all or part of this construction program.

While Congress was debating this measure, the British announced that they had abandoned two thirds of their proposed naval-building projects. To many Americans, especially the advocates of a big navy, this step came too late. The United States should complete the Cruiser bill provisions within five years and follow a replacement program during the next twenty years. This opinion did not go unchallenged. Senator Borah led the attack upon the bill, asserting it would lead to "immediate and inevitable war." He was supported by Quakers, the Federal Council of Churches, and many other groups. This opposition had its way; the Butler bill was withdrawn in favor of a substitute that cut the program to fifteen cruisers and one carrier at a cost of $274 million.

The new Navy Cruiser bill passed the House in March, 1928, but the Senate, due to Borah's continued opposition, held it up until February, 1929. While this measure avoided a direct challenge to Great Britain, it did threaten a new naval race.

Such was the situation when Hoover assumed the presidency. The problem was further complicated by the fact that England and France were having their troubles over parity definitions, while the League was facing the difficult task of trying to arrange a general disarmament conference. True to his inaugural promise, Hoover began negotiations for another meeting of the nations that had signed the Washington Treaty. First he authorized Charles Dawes, now ambassador to England, to confer with the new Labor Prime Minister, Ramsay MacDonald, over the possibility of complete naval parity between the two nations. Through these talks most of the difficulties that had appeared at Geneva were ironed out before the end of the summer of 1929. To carry on the rapprochement, MacDonald accepted an invitation to visit President Hoover in early October. Substantial agreement on many issues was reached during their conferences, and even before they were over Great Britain formally invited France, Italy, Japan, and the United States to another disarmament meeting to be held at London. Acceptances from all were quickly received.

Navalism. Japan tilts the scales in her own favor despite the 5–5–3 ratio.
(By Bishop in the *St. Louis Star-Times*.)

The London Naval Conference opened on January 21, 1930. The seven-man American delegation, headed by Secretary Stimson, was carefully selected.[1] There were high hopes of success because the preliminary discussions between Great Britain and the United States had developed an understanding that had been lacking at Geneva. Moreover, the admirals and other big-navy advocates

[1] The other members were Ambassador Dawes, Ambassador Hugh Gibson, Secretary of the Navy Charles Francis Adams, Republican Senator Reed of Pennsylvania, Democratic Senator Robinson of Arkansas, and Dwight Morrow.

who had helped to sabotage the efforts in 1927 were conspicuous by their absence.

Despite the favorable auguries, the conference did not go smoothly at the start. There was wrangling over unessential details, and France almost broke up the meeting when she sought defensive military agreements with the others before she would consider continuing the naval limitations program.

Gradually, however, the three largest naval powers found a satisfactory solution to the limitation problem. The London Naval Treaty of April 22, 1930, provided first of all for foregoing the construction of the capital ships allowed under the Washington Treaty[2] and for having Great Britain scrap five capital ships, the United States three, and Japan one before the end of 1931. Thus the total capital-ship tonnage would be: for Great Britain, 474,750 (15 ships); for the United States, 464,300 (15 ships); and for Japan, 272,070 (9 ships). Aircraft-carrier tonnage was also agreed to at approximately the same ratio. Class A cruisers carrying 8-inch guns were limited to 10,000 tons each, with the United States allotted 18, Great Britain 15, and Japan 12. The number of Class B cruisers with 6-inch guns was not allotted, but the total tonnage for each power was limited; the same was true of destroyers and submarines.[3]

An unusual feature was the "escape" or "escalator" clause, which allowed any signatory to build above treaty limits if some other power, not bound by this London agreement, started a construction program that tended to threaten the safety of the signatory. The treaty was to continue in operation until December 31, 1936, with another conference called for 1935 to discuss the feasibility of extending the arrangements beyond that date.

The London Naval Treaty had serious weaknesses. France and Italy, having found fault with the negotiations and with the proposed ratios, refused to enter the agreement. This threatened to upset the whole settlement since either French or Italian construction might cause one of the signatory powers to invoke the escalator clause and embark upon a new building program. American admirals and naval experts, moreover, warned that the limitations would prevent the American navy from satisfactorily defending the United States and its outlying possessions.

On the other hand, the long-desired parity with Great Britain in all naval categories was at last achieved. Moreover, if the signatories lived up to the agreement, the menace of a naval construction race was ended during the life of the London Treaty. Savings of at least $300 million were thereby assured to American taxpayers. Actually the United States did not build up to treaty strength and

[2] The United States had been authorized to lay down ten capital ships, Britain ten, and Japan five before 1936.

[3] The tonnage of Class B cruisers was: for the United States, 143,500; for Great Britain, 192,200; and for Japan, 100,450. The advantage for Great Britain was offset by the American superiority in the larger Class A cruisers. For destroyers, the ratio was 10:10:7. For submarines each of the nations was allowed 52,700 tons, but the maximum size was limited.

thus lost much of its naval superiority over Japan, which took full advantage of her quota.

In the United States, the reception of the London Treaty was, on the whole, good. True, there was some complaint about the cost of bringing the nation up to parity, but that quickly disappeared. Navy men opposing the agreement were backed by the jingo press, which asserted that the American envoys had become the dupes of Britain and Japan. Some newspapers even avowed that the United States had become involved in a secret entangling agreement with the other signatories.

When the treaty was submitted to the Senate early in July, 1930, some members demanded that President Hoover turn over to them all the documents concerning the London meeting. This Hoover refused to do because it was contrary to precedent and might impede future treaty making. Further Senatorial requests for information led him to agree to allow certain key Senators to see all the private papers. Enough of the members were satisfied to approve the treaty on July 21 by a vote of 58 to 9. To make doubly sure that there were no strings attached, the Senate then proceeded to resolve that the nation was not bound by any secret commitment.

President Hoover was not content to stop with the London Treaty. When the World Disarmament Conference, sponsored by the League of Nations, met in Geneva in 1932, the American delegates sought international approval for scrapping all offensive weapons of war. The reception of this proposal was by no means enthusiastic. France led the way in tabling it; she refused to reduce her military arm without adequate guarantees that she would not be attacked. Hoover continued his quest for limitation by asking that all nations represented at Geneva reduce their armaments approximately 30 per cent. Although there seemed to be widespread support for this proposal, nothing came of it. Even while this disarmament meeting was in session, the peace of the world was threatened by hostilities between Japan and China on the other side of the globe.

The Moratorium

The quest for improved international relations was complicated by a series of events in the economic field that disrupted the war debts and reparations settlements. By the summer of 1931, France feared that a proposed customs union between Germany and Austria might develop into a political and military alliance. In an attempt to prevent such action, France withdrew her credit from a large Austrian bank, already hard hit by the depression. That bank was compelled to close its doors and, with its failure, a number of financially associated German institutions, both banks and insurance companies, tottered on the brink of bankruptcy. In turn, foreign credit, particularly American, was quickly withdrawn from Germany to escape engulfment in the threatened economic collapse. American banks holding large amounts in German short-term notes became alarmed by the situation.

Fearing an economic catastrophe greater than the stock-market crash of 1929, Hoover acted quickly to avert it. Congress was not in session at the time, but the President gained the consent of twenty-one Senators and eighteen Representatives, all key men and from both parties, to a proposition which he made public on June 20, 1931. This proposed "the postponement during one year of all payments on intergovernmental debts, reparations and relief payments, both principal and interest."[4] On July 6 Hoover was able to report that the European nations concerned had given their approval to the proposal and about two weeks later, at the London Conference on Recovery from the Depression, the international bankers agreed to a similar moratorium on private international obligations.

There is little doubt that this moratorium did ease the international situation. Moreover, for the first time the United States recognized a relationship between war debts and reparations, but there were still dangers ahead. German banks were in bad straits as a result of the earlier difficulties. A number of foreign banks, including the Federal Reserve of New York, loaned a total of approximately $100 million in short-term notes to the ailing institutions. While this action saved some of the German banks, it did not prevent the withdrawal of gold from one country after another. Nation after nation was forced to go off the gold standard, culminating in the September, 1931, decision of Great Britain that she too must cease redeeming her currency with that bullion. Thereafter it seemed as if nothing could be done to avert international disaster. Each nation thought primarily of itself. Tariff walls were raised higher to protect domestic conditions, and the local currency inflated to spur a return to prosperity.

While the moratorium was in effect, the French premier, Pierre Laval, visited President Hoover in late October, 1931. After a series of conversations, during which the President soothed Laval's troubled feelings over American failure to confer specially with France before the moratorium was declared, they both agreed that the question of intergovernmental debts must be reconsidered before the moratorium was over in order to alleviate the depression and save the gold standard. While there were no actual commitments, Hoover and Laval pledged themselves to do all in their power to assist in a solution. The initiative, they asserted, must be taken by Europe in connection with German reparations.

Acting upon the Hoover-Laval proposal, Germany's creditors met with German representatives at Lausanne, Switzerland, in June, 1932. By July 8 they had agreed to wipe away more than 90 per cent of the original reparations demands,

---

[4] In December, 1931, Congress approved this moratorium: the Senate vote was 79 to 15, the House, 317 to 100. This act stipulated that the suspended payments should be paid over a ten-year period at 4 per cent interest.

Now If He Just Doesn't Try to Bring His Trunk Along.
(Copyright, 1931, by the *Chicago Tribune*.)

cutting down their claims to approximately $700 million, payable in 5 per cent German bonds. This Lausanne agreement, however, had a string attached to it. The creditors of Germany said they would not ratify until they had made a satisfactory arrangement for scaling down their own obligations to the United States.

The appeal for war-debt reduction reached the United States during the vigorous presidential contest of 1932. The Democrats had already gone on record against cancellation of those debts. Moreover, neither party dared to come out in favor of the European proposal because they feared that the American voters, hard hit by the depression, regarded the payment of the war debts as a means of alleviating their own economic distress.[5] Likewise linked with the issue was the matter of reducing armaments and, since the European nations showed no inclination to conform to American wishes on that subject, the Americans were all the more unwilling to follow up the Lausanne proposition with parallel reductions.

When Great Britain asked the United States for an opportunity to discuss a reduction of the December, 1932, payment, President Hoover and President-elect Roosevelt could not agree as to the method of conference. Thus nothing was done. Consequently, France and four other nations defaulted on their pay-

---

[5] Actually, everything pointed to the fact that public opinion favored a benevolent policy toward these debts.

ments. Great Britain and the remaining debtors did send the full amounts of their semiannual obligations, but they warned that this might be the last time they could do so unless a new arrangement were made. None was, and thereafter the whole problem was left for the new administration to deal with.

As things worked out, Hoover's moratorium, which had been intended merely to postpone war debt and reparations payments for one year, resulted in a permanent halt to all but a small trickle of installments. From the economic point of view, this was an excellent thing because reparations and war debts had hung like millstones around the neck of the postwar world. From the political point of view, however, the outcome was bad. The United States had not made the generous gesture in cancelling the debts that might have earned her some gratitude in Europe. Instead, Europe had simply ceased to pay, thereby playing straight into the hands of the American isolationists who warned the United States to go its own way and turn its back on the world's troubles.

The New Pan-Americanism

The same spirit President Hoover showed in trying to ease world tensions was evinced in his Latin-American policy. Shortly after his election in 1928, he visited many of the Latin-American countries, where he made contacts that were to prove important later on. Indeed, it was while he was on this trip that he was approached by the leaders of Peru, Bolivia, and Chile on the subject of the Tacna-Arica controversy. Partly through the knowledge he acquired during his visit, he was able to find the solution to that long-standing problem. Moreover, this journey aided in bettering the relations between the United States and Latin America; the citizens of the other republics appreciated the fact that such a prominent American had visited them.

During his term in the White House, Hoover did his best to remove the fears and suspicions that Latin America held toward his country and thereby fostered an improved feeling of cooperation and friendship in the Western Hemisphere. True, he was aided in this respect by some of the incidents near the close of Coolidge's administration—the naming of Dwight Morrow as minister to Mexico, the drawing up of the Clark Memorandum, and the Washington Conference on Conciliation and Arbitration were the most notable—but they would not have helped the situation for long had Hoover not carried on and extended the policy of neighborliness.

The first official pronouncement of this desire came in Hoover's inaugural address. He said:

> I have lately returned from a journey among our sister Republics of the Western Hemisphere. I have received unbounded hospitality and courtesy as their expression of friendliness to our country. We are held by particular bonds of sympathy and common interest with them. . . . We wish only for the mainte-

nance of their independence, the growth of their stability, and their prosperity. . . . Fortunately the New World is largely free from the inheritance of fear and distrust which have so troubled the Old World. We should keep it so.

Yet it was difficult for President Hoover to allay distrust completely because the depression hit some of the Latin republics hard and, to make matters worse, the Hawley-Smoot Tariff reacted unfavorably upon Latin-American commerce. Half of the republics witnessed the overturn of their governments, largely as a result of economic troubles. Several of the Latin-American states had to announce suspension of interest payments on their foreign obligations in October, 1931. President Hoover did not press for payment, however, nor did he threaten military intervention for forcible collection as some of his predecessors had done under similar circumstances. Moreover, the new governments established by these revolutions were almost immediately recognized by the United States.

Withdrawal from Haiti

It was Hoover's attitude toward countries in which the United States had previously intervened, and in some of which marines were still stationed, that proved the sincerity of his professions of good will. In Haiti, for example, President Louis Borno, serving his second term, became increasingly unpopular as 1929 progressed because of the popular belief that he was subservient to American wishes. In December, a strike of students, supported by Haitian politicians, brought the matter to a climax. An attack was made on the American marines near Port-au-Prince, and in the ensuing struggle six Haitians were killed and some thirty wounded.

A few days before this affray, President Hoover had referred to Haiti in his annual message to Congress, suggesting that a commission be sent to the island preparatory to clarifying American policy toward the protectorate. When the news of the outbreak reached him, Hoover sent a special message to the legislature, asking for immediate action. Congress quickly responded by appointing the so-called Forbes Commission in February, 1930, to conduct a thorough investigation of Haiti's problems, to ascertain how the obligations of the United States could be fulfilled, and to suggest when the American troops might be withdrawn.

After a two-month study the Forbes Commission reported its findings to President Hoover. Although they praised the work done by American officials in the field of transportation, health, and sanitation, the commissioners concluded that little progress had occurred in training the Haitians to govern themselves, the American policy being based "upon the assumption that the occupation would continue indefinitely." They recommended that the 1915 treaty rights remain in force until 1936 except where mutual agreement might modify them, that the military high commissioner be replaced by a civilian leader, that the Haitians be trained to take over control of their civil administration and national guard, that a new president be elected by the Haitian legislature, and that the American marines be gradually withdrawn.

With the backing of Congress, President Hoover quickly carried these recommendations into effect. The little-liked Borno was replaced by Provisional President Eugene Roy toward the end of April, 1930, and in October the legislature selected Stenio Vincent as the regular executive. Meantime, High Commissioner General Russell was replaced by Dana G. Munro, a civilian authority on Latin-American affairs. Then, under an agreement of August, 1931, Americans were gradually withdrawn from the various government departments. Differences over financial control, the national guard, and the withdrawal of the marines delayed a settlement until September, 1932, when a treaty was drawn up for complete civil and military retirement from Haiti by the end of 1934, although the United States might continue to keep a watchful eye on Haitian finances after that date. Some Haitian opposition to this treaty delayed its acceptance until after Hoover left office. President Roosevelt, however, was able to effect a solution, primarily based on the 1932 treaty, and the last of the marines left Haiti on August 15, 1934.

Ending Military Intervention in Nicaragua

Shortly before Hoover entered office, Nicaraguan President Moncada agreed to substitute a national guard for the army, and the United States promised to withdraw its marines when that guard was ready to police the country.

In April, 1931, the difficulty of the American position was increased when the rebel leader, Augusto Sandino, began an open attack upon the Moncada administration. All the efforts of the national guard and the American marines could not curb his raids on Nicaraguan communities. At least nine American civilians lost their lives. So serious did the problem become that Secretary Stimson was compelled to advise Americans residing in the interior to retire to coastal settlements because of the inability of the marines to protect them. Stimson's action aroused a storm of debate in Congress, with some Senators supporting the Secretary and others condemning what they regarded as a confession of weakness. Stimson replied to his critics by explaining that the marines were not equipped for jungle fighting; he promised, however, that the American navy would stand off the coast, ready to protect "the lives of our nationals wherever they may be found."

When Sandino's men killed five marines during a raid in April, 1932, there were new Senatorial protests against risking the lives of American troops merely to protect a handful of American businessmen. A resolution was introduced, calling for the immediate withdrawal of the marines. Since the American forces had already been reduced from almost 6,000 to less than 1,000, complete evacuation might have been ordered had not the American government previously committed itself to the supervision of the Nicaraguan election, scheduled for the following fall. Living up to that pledge, 500 marines guarded the polls on election day, November 6, 1932, and prevented the disorders that had been so characteristic in the past. Rear Admiral Clark Woodward of the United States Navy served as head of the election board.

Victory was gained by Liberal Juan Sacassa. Despite the fact that Sandino asserted he would not recognize the new executive, Sacassa took office without incident on January 2, 1933. Shortly after this installation, the last of the American marines left the country. Another venture in dollar diplomacy was thereby concluded.

Mexican Problems

Emilio Portes Gil became provisional executive of Mexico in November, 1928. He was not particularly well liked, being considered nothing more than a puppet of the powerful Plutarco Calles. Shortly after, a regular election was scheduled for November, 1929. The political opponents of the administration, feeling that they would not have a chance in the ensuing campaign, appealed to the element that had become dissatisfied with the anti-church attitude of the government to participate in a revolution. The Catholic group agreed and on March 3, 1929, the day before Hoover took office, the uprising occurred.

President Hoover promptly acted in support of the Gil government. Not only did he proclaim an embargo on all exports of arms and ammunition to the rebellious forces in line with the Arms Embargo Resolution of 1922, but he allowed the Mexican government to buy military supplies in the United States. The State Department refused to consider the rebels as belligerents or to receive any of their representatives. Thanks in part to this American attitude, the Mexican administration was able to crush the uprising by the beginning of May, 1929.

Hoover also helped to improve relations by naming the able J. Reuben Clark to succeed Dwight Morrow as American ambassador. Clark continued the policy of friendship Morrow had instituted. Moreover, the United States immediately recognized Ortiz Rubio, victor in the election of November, 1929. The new executive showed his gratitude by visiting the United States, where he was well received.

Just before Hoover left office, another move to strengthen the accord between the two nations was taken. On February 1, 1933, a treaty was signed providing for the settlement of some of the differences that had arisen in connection with control over the Rio Grande in the El Paso region, a step which, it was hoped, would end the danger from floods.

Non-Intervention in Cuba

The Cuban situation was difficult during the Hoover administration. Cuban President Gerardo Machado had become practically a dictator with the result that popular unrest grew, much aggravated by the falling price of sugar during the depression. Unfortunately, Hoover appointed as envoy Harry Guggenheim, an inexperienced diplomat. The ambassador did his best to keep Machado in office, aiding him financially and otherwise.

As the Cuban unrest mounted, it became evident that civil war might break out at any time. Consequently, some Senators urged the United States to intervene toward the close of 1930. Secretary Stimson, however, refused to heed the proposal. He asserted that only actual chaos warranted such intervention; until that chaos developed, the United States would merely maintain a "close watch" of the situation. In the summer of 1931 an abortive revolt did take place, but the Hoover administration refused to use the Platt Amendment as an excuse for re-establishing military control. Instead, a "hands off" policy was followed, with no effort being made to establish an arms embargo.

Many Cubans criticized Hoover's policy. Although pleased that there was no intervention, they felt that the United States was trying to maintain the dictatorial Machado in office. In both countries a demand arose for the abrogation of the Platt Amendment.

For Latin America generally, Hoover followed the policy of recognizing *de facto* presidents without examining the means by which they obtained office. While no regular Pan-American conferences were held, he helped the cause by proclaiming on May 28, 1930, that thereafter April 14 would be celebrated as Pan-American Day.

President Hoover tried to alleviate conditions in Puerto Rico. Indeed, he even visited the island and saw at first hand its great poverty. On his return to the United States, the President secured from Congress increased appropriations for the improvement of insular conditions. Theodore Roosevelt, Jr., new governor general of the island, showed great energy and vigor in attempting to end the sickness, hunger, and economic hardships that prevailed throughout the island. The Puerto Ricans appreciated this assistance, with the result that there were few political controversies during the Hoover regime.

The Movement toward Philippine Independence

The question of Philippine independence arose once again during Hoover's term. This time, however, the impetus came largely from the United States, with the depression, rather than altruism, playing no small part in revival of the issue. American farmers, their income falling rapidly, did not like to face competition from Filipino cottonseed oil, sugar, dairy products, and cordage, which were allowed to enter duty free. Nor did American workers care to see their jobs taken by cheap Filipino laborers. Moreover, the threat of Japanese aggression in the Far East caused many Americans to believe that the Philippines could not continue to be protected without the expenditure of vast sums, which the American taxpayers were not eager to pay.

This combination of anti-imperialists, farmers, and workers was able to exert sufficient pressure upon Congress to pass the Hawes-Cutting bill on January 12, 1933, despite the objections of another bloc, consisting of American investors in Filipino resources, big navy advocates who saw in the retention of the islands an opportunity to press their cause, and the supporters of imperialism.

The Hawes-Cutting bill provided for the framing of a constitution by a specially convened Philippine convention, which was to be submitted to the Filipino voters for approval, along with the question of whether independence was desired. Were approval given, the Philippines would then begin a ten-year intermediate or probationary period, during which the position of governor general was to be abolished and the American civil control ended except for the supervisory powers exercised by a new American official, the high commissioner. Throughout the probationary period, however, the President of the United States was to be allowed some regulation of Philippine legislation, the Supreme Court could review legal cases, and the foreign problems of the islands would be supervised by the United States. The right to send commodities to the United States duty free was to be gradually reduced and the competitive commodities placed under a quota system. Immigration to the United States was practically to end.

After the ten-year probation was concluded, complete independence would automatically begin. Then all free trade with the United States would end, unless some commercial arrangement between the two nations effected reciprocity. The United States would be allowed to maintain military establishments and naval bases in the islands and would try to secure an international agreement for the neutralization of the Philippines.

President Hoover wrote a long veto message on January 13, 1933, in which he criticized the bill because of its economic provisions, which he believed would lead to "a degenerating economic and social life, with all its governmental difficulties." He also asserted that during the probationary period American civil control would be weakened "to a point of practical impotence." Nor did he think that the Philippines were prepared to provide the military forces necessary for the preservation of internal order or external defense.

The opposing factions were sufficiently strong to pass the Hawes-Cutting bill over the executive veto. When the plan was presented to the Philippine legislature, however, it was rejected, primarily because of the restrictions on immigration and the failure to continue free trade with the United States. Therefore, although Hoover favored Philippine independence, the failure of Congress to follow his suggestions delayed the enactment of a mutually satisfactory plan until the next administration.

Far Eastern Troubles

Hoover's quest for international cooperation and peace received a rude jolt in the Orient. Throughout the 1920's revolutionary ferment and civil war in China resulted in incidents that threatened to bring outside intervention reminiscent of the days of the Boxer Rebellion. For example, there were riots in both Shanghai and Canton in 1925 that endangered the property of foreigners. Two years later the British concession in Hankow was attacked by Chinese mobs. Later in 1927 Chinese Nationalist or Kuomintang troops captured Nanking and looted the foreign holdings, with resulting loss of life to foreigners, including Americans. The United States, along with other powers whose nationals had suffered, demanded punishment for the guilty, but unsatisfactory replies were received. Some of the nations, notably France, Britain, and Italy, urged economic sanctions against China until complete restitution was given. The United States, however, refused to cooperate and the matter was dropped.

Coolidge and Secretary Kellogg undoubtedly realized that Chinese domestic unrest would not end until a single leader had won out in the civil war and that it would be useless to try to effect any settlement until that time. The adminisration's general policy was to cooperate with Chiang Kai-shek, the head of the Nationalist element, in order to hasten the return of peace. For example, in July, 1927, a treaty was made with Chiang under which the United States recognized China's complete control of her tariff. Yet the Coolidge administration was ready to protect the lives and property of Americans in China, as indicated by the constant presence of American gunboats in Chinese waters.

By the time of the American election of 1928, Chiang had defeated most of his domestic foes except the Communists and had secured recognition of his government by many of the great powers, including the United States. To show his good faith and desire for peace, Chiang signed the Kellogg-Briand Pact in August, 1928. Yet these incidents did not settle all of the problems, particularly the controversy between China and Russia over North Manchuria, from which Russia refused to withdraw its dominant influence.

The Sino-Russian Controversy

A series of incidents in the spring and summer of 1929 widened the breach between the two countries. The Chinese, aided by the Manchurians, raided Russian consulates in several Manchurian cities, arresting the consuls and Communists who were charged with breaking a 1924 treaty by spreading anti-

Chinese propaganda. This was followed by the seizure of the communications systems of the Chinese Eastern Railways, hitherto under joint management, the substitution of Chinese for Russian officials, and the deportation of Russian employees.

Russia quickly sent an ultimatum to Chiang, demanding a prompt conference to settle the problem. She insisted that a solution could not be reached until China revoked her action and restored Russian control over the railway. Since Chiang's answer was considered unsatisfactory, on July 17, 1929, Russia severed diplomatic relations with the Nanking government. There was an immediate mobilization of armed forces along the border, with every indication that war would soon break out.

The Kellogg-Briand Pact, which both the Soviet and China had signed, left the responsibility of maintaining peace to each signatory; there was no machinery set up for conciliation and mediation. Secretary of State Stimson, however, insisted that the Pact "necessarily carries with it the implication of consultation" and urged both countries to settle their troubles by peaceful means. The major powers of Europe backed Stimson in this request. Both potential contestants answered that they would not fight except in self-defense. Thus it appeared that Stimson had won a victory for peace under the Pact.

The ensuing Sino-Soviet conference broke down, however, because of differences over the future of Manchuria, and neither side would accept outside mediation. Consequently, fighting broke out, the Manchurian provincial forces were defeated, and Chiang was compelled to recognize Russian rights in North Manchuria.

Meantime, Stimson was hard at work trying to effect mediation. Though Germany and Japan refused to join the United States in applying pressure, Britain, France, and Italy agreed to cooperate. The four nations then sent identical notes to the two disputants on December 2, tracing the course of the peacemaking efforts since the beginning of the trouble and stressing the importance of abiding by the promises of the Paris Pact.

In answer to this multilateral request for peace China refused to admit that it had broken the Pact and insisted that it was ready to submit the differences to mediation. The Russian reply was even less satisfactory. The blame for the failure of negotiations was placed squarely at the doors of China and the United States; China was blamed for not being conciliatory, the United States for meddling after the joint conference was under way. Moreover, said the Russian reply, the issue could not be settled by a third party, particularly when that third party was the United States, because

> The Soviet Government cannot forbear expressing amazement that the Government of the United States, which by its own will has no official relations with the Soviet, deems it possible to apply to it with advice and counsel.

Thus, despite the energetic efforts of Secretary Stimson to resolve this particular Manchurian problem, he ended in failure. The first test of the Paris Pact had shown the weakness of that agreement—the absence of any machinery to force a settlement of international disputes. Moreover, external interference, especially by the United States, helped to cause Russia to insist, even by force, upon regaining her former rights in North Manchuria and obtaining additional privileges.

The Menace of Japan

Soon after this American failure in the Far East, another problem arose that indicated still more clearly the weakness of both the Paris Pact and the League of Nations.

Beneath the surface, the relations between the United States and Japan had not been satisfactory for many years. Japan blamed the United States for its inability to obtain all of the Twenty-One Demands from China in 1915, for the retreat from Shantung after the war, and for its inferior naval position in the Washington Treaty. Nor did the breaking of the Gentlemen's Agreement in the Johnson-Lodge Immigration Act of 1924 help the situation. On the other hand, the Japanese intention to dominate the Far East was clearly shown in 1923 when Baron Ishii asserted on the occasion of the abrogation of the Lansing-Ishii agreement: "Japan's special interests in China continue to live in all their vigor." He insisted that they did not result from "benefits conferred upon Japan by the United States," but from "realities deriving from nature and geography."

Although maintaining a facade of parliamentary institutions, Japan was by no means a democracy. The government was dominated by aristocratic old families, by the officers of the army and navy, and by the groups that controlled the country's highly concentrated industrial and commercial activities—particularly the Mitsui and the Mitsubishi families. All of these dominant elements were ambitious to extend Japanese power and influence, although they differed considerably on methods. The moderates, particularly to be found among Japanese big businessmen, thought in terms of economic penetration. By a "friendship policy" toward China, a subtle mixture of diplomatic pressure oiled by judicious bribery, they hoped to win an increasing share in the trade and investment opportunities of the undeveloped country, while they avoided serious trouble with the Western powers through a reasonable degree of collaboration with the League of Nations and the various international conferences. The moderates maintained an uneasy ascendancy through most of the twenties, but they were increasingly threatened by the militarist factions who were impatient with these tactics. The extremists were ambitious to extend Japanese political control; they wished to dominate the more valuable parts of China and to expel the hated Occidentals from the western Pacific area. China's progress toward unification and modernization late in the twenties was not at all to their liking.[6]

The moderates' position was greatly weakened by events after 1929. The Great Depression accentuated Japanese economic problems, already serious because 70 million people were endeavoring to make a living in a small and essentially poor country. The extremists regarded this as final proof of the need for Japanese expansion. Their discontent was increased by the refusal of Britain and the United States to grant Japan naval parity at the London Conference of 1930. The temptation to embark upon an aggressive program was great because of the obvious demoralization of the Occident, where monetary chaos, governmental deficits, debt and armament controversies, and general loss of nerve made it unlikely that the Western powers could take any decisive step. As for the United States and its Open Door policy, Japanese realists believed that it had been largely based on bluff since its first pronouncement.

The showdown came in Manchuria—long a Far Eastern trouble spot. Since the war with Russia, Japan had had extensive treaty rights in the southern part of that province—particularly in the South Manchuria Railroad zone. A quiet struggle for power had been for some time in progress between the Japanese who wanted to extend their influence and the Chinese who wished to interpret Japanese rights very narrowly. The incident that gave the Japanese army its excuse for drastic action was the alleged blowing up of a section of track along the main line of the South Manchuria Railroad, just a few miles from the important center of Mukden, on the evening of September 18, 1931. Immediate blame was placed upon the Chinese, despite the latter's denial. Japanese troops guarding the line under the provisions of the Treaty of Peking of 1905 quickly attacked the small Chinese force in the vicinity, and just as promptly the Japanese army in Manchuria seized Mukden and several other strategic points. Although the Japanese authorities asserted that the military forces were acting in self-defense, it appeared to many observers that this was but the beginning of a well-laid plan to conquer Manchuria.

Three days later China appealed both to the League and to the United States

[6] In 1931 Chinese authorities made public the so-called Tanaka and Honjo Memorials, which they asserted to be ultrasecret Japanese documents representing the real intentions of the Japanese government. Their authenticity is questionable, but they have considerable interest, nevertheless, in view of subsequent developments. The first, allegedly drafted for the emperor by Premier Baron Tanaka in 1927, urged the construction of strategic railroads throughout Mongolia and Manchuria to tap the valuable resources of these areas and give Japan economic control. This in turn would prepare the ground for political domination of these regions and would be a steppingstone for the eventual conquest of all China. The Memorial of General Honjo, head of the Japanese army in Manchuria, also allegedly prepared in 1927, included proposals for the conquest of Australia, the Philippines, and the East Indies, as well as China, and went on to plan for Japanese domination over Africa and most of Europe. Japan and the United States would then divide the world and, if the United States should prove hostile, Japan would be strong enough to crush this rival as well.

to try to effect a settlement. Secretary Stimson immediately announced that he was following the problem closely to ascertain whether the Mukden incident contravened the Paris Pact and the Nine-Power Treaty. At the same time he notified Sir Eric Drummond, the League's Secretary General, that the United States would cooperate with the League in its efforts to settle the strife. Stimson gave little credence to the statement of the Japanese ambassador that the attacks had been made without the knowledge of the Tokyo government.

Is He In or Out? (By Fitzpatrick in the *St. Louis Post-Dispatch.*)

For the next few days Stimson took no further action, hoping that the two Far Eastern nations might be able to reach a satisfactory settlement, but on September 25 he addressed similar notes to both parties in which he urged them not to extend the conflict. Neither the League nor the American request for a peaceful solution succeeded, for although both Asiatic parties asserted they were moving toward that objective, fighting broke out anew in early October. Consequently, on October 5, Stimson decided that the United States should conduct an independent investigation to uphold both the Pact and the Treaty, while at the same time cooperating with the League "to reinforce what the League does." With the latter purpose in mind, Stimson secured the consent of President Hoover to have the American consul at Geneva, Prentiss Gilbert, sit in on the meetings of the League Council to consider the enforcement of the Paris Pact. This promise to cooperate with the League and the participation of an American in open League meetings was a far cry from the American attitude of the previous decade, but three quarters of the American press supported the policy.

Despite Sino-Japanese charges and countercharges, the United States came to the conclusion on October 8 that Japan was the aggressor. On that date Japanese planes bombed the unfortified city of Chinchow, bringing death to a number of civilians. Almost at once Secretary Stimson sent a sharp note to the Japanese Foreign Office:

> The Secretary of State cannot understand how the bombing of Chinchow can be minimized . . . Chinchow is more than 50 miles from the Japanese railway zone and it is situated in territory where the Chinese have an entire right to maintain troops. . . . Bombing of an unfortified and unwarned town is one of the most extreme of military actions, deprecated even in time of war . . .

No attention was paid to this note, nor did Japan heed the League warning that she was breaking the Paris Pact. Moreover, it was her negative vote that prevented the League Council from approving a resolution calling for the retirement of Japanese troops from the Manchurian region outside of the railway zone before November 15 and for the prompt beginning of direct peace negotiations between Japan and China.

Since Gilbert's attendance at the League sessions appeared not to be accomplishing very much, the United States returned to what was called the policy of independent cooperation. Ambassador Dawes was instructed to be in Paris during the Council sessions for purposes of consultation. And on December 10, 1931, the League decided on still another method of attacking the problem. It set up a commission, headed by Lord Lytton of Great Britain, to make an on-the-scene study of the Sino-Japanese conflict and report to the Council on its findings.[7]

On the same day that the Lytton Commission was set up, President Hoover delivered his annual message to Congress. In it he asserted that the United States was committed to the maintenance of China's territorial integrity. This could best be done through full cooperation with the League, rather than through independent action, for "unity of effort to maintain peace" would thereby be achieved. Yet he insisted that such cooperation would not lead to American membership in the League because "in all the negotiations the Department of State has maintained complete freedom of judgment and action as to participation in any measures which might finally be determined upon."

The threat of League action, even in cooperation with the United States, did not deter Japan from her objective. By early January, 1932, all of South Manchuria was in her hands. The United States refused to recognize this conquest, and on January 7 Secretary Stimson notified the signatories of the Nine-Power Treaty that his country

[7] The other countries represented were Italy, France, Germany, and the United States. The American member was General Frank R. McCoy.

can not admit the legality of any situation *de facto* nor does it intend to recognize any treaty or agreement entered into . . . which may impair the treaty rights of the United States or its citizens in China, including those which relate to the sovereignty, the independence, or the territorial and administrative integrity of the Republic of China, or to the international policy relative to China, commonly known as the open-door treaty; and that it does not intend to recognize any situation . . . brought about by means contrary . . . to . . . the pact of Paris. . . .

This became known as the "Stimson Doctrine," despite the fact that the policy of non-recognition did not originate with Hoover's Secretary of State. Yet Stimson tried to make it international in scope by basing it in part upon the Paris Pact, which so many of the nations had signed.

At home the doctrine was received with mixed feelings. Some believed it was worthless because there was no real force to back it up. Another faction feared it might lead to trouble for the United States. To others, however, it was the natural sequel to the Paris Pact; it was a means through which an aggressor might be actually deterred from waging war.

Stimson believed that his announcement would be well received by the European powers. He was in for a rude shock, however, when a spokesman for the British government expressed confidence that Japan's promises to respect the Open Door would be carried out. As a result of British complacency, the impact of the Stimson Doctrine was weakened because Japan realized that her opposition was divided. Moreover, she concluded that the United States, torn by partisan strife and hard hit by the depression, was in no position to force her to back down. While it was true that most Americans thought that China was being mistreated, this opinion did not carry beyond the extension of expressions of sympathy. Nor was the State Department ready to make an issue of the Stimson Doctrine. Indeed, the more vigorous notes to Japan were not published until some time after they were sent and the press was cautioned not to play up the troubles in the Far East.

Encouraged by the lack of cooperation among the Western powers, Japan broadened her aggression. In late January, 1932, she attacked Shanghai and in the ensuing bombing thousands of civilians lost their lives. Only then did American public opinion really express itself against Japanese actions. Stimson likened the feeling to that expressed in 1914 when Germany invaded Belgium. Even Britain was stirred because Japan was striking closer to the British spheres of influence.

When Stimson requested the British Foreign Secretary to collaborate in a stern and forceful note to Japan, stressing this time simply the breaking of the Nine-Power Treaty, Sir John Simon's reply was noncommittal. This may have been because Britain still had faith in the League and the Lytton Commission, and thus did not wish to join in any other project, particularly when the proposer was not a member of the League and had never been willing to undertake any responsibility for the actual enforcement of international obligations. Or it may have been because of the British desire to appease Japan, and thereby save Hong Kong and the British interests generally in Central China.

Realizing that unilateral action by the United States would not bring results, Secretary Stimson decided to express the American position in an open letter to Senator Borah, chairman of the Foreign Relations Committee. This letter would be widely published, would probably be read by the officials of the governments concerned, and, Stimson hoped, might stir up public opinion in many parts of the world in support of the American position. And since it was a letter to an American rather than an official note to Japan, failure would not be so injurious to American prestige.

On February 23, 1932, this long letter to Borah was released. After tracing the history of Far Eastern relations from the Open Door through the attack on Shanghai, Stimson stressed the importance of upholding the Nine-Power Treaty and the Paris Pact. Then he continued:

> That is the view of this Government. We see no reason for abandoning the enlightened principles which are embodied in these treaties. We believe that this situation would have been avoided had these covenants been faithfully observed, and no evidence has come to us to indicate that a due compliance with them would have interfered with the adequate protection of the legitimate rights in China of the signatories of those treaties and their nations. . . . If a similar decision should be reached and a similar position taken by the other governments of the world, a caveat will be placed upon such action which . . . will effectively bar the legality hereafter of any title or right sought to be obtained by pressure or treaty violation.

The American press in general praised the policy expressed in this letter, and on March 11, 1932, the League Assembly approved of a resolution that was similar to the Stimson Doctrine without a dissenting vote. Many believe that the Stimson letter played a part in influencing Japan to effect a compromise with China, under which Japanese troops withdrew from Shanghai at the end of May, 1932.

Yet Japan was still in control of Manchuria. True, she attempted to forestall criticism by establishing a government that declared itself independent of China. Early in March, 1932, this "independent" state adopted the name of "Manchukuo" and selected Henry Pu-yi, deposed emperor of China, as regent. But the other powers, including the United States, refused to recognize the new state. They knew that Pu-yi was nothing more than a puppet of Japan and that Japan had been responsible for the "independence" movement.

The next six months witnessed efforts by Japan to defend her actions and continued refusals of the other powers to change their positions. On September 15, 1932, Japan made a more definite break by recognizing the new state and concluding an alliance with it. Then on October 1 the long-awaited Lytton

Report was published. After condemning Japan for its actions in defiance of existing commitments, the Report refused to accept Manchukuo as a sovereign state. Manchuria should be returned to China, but certain rights of Russia and Japan should be recognized. The League Assembly approved of these findings, and Secretary Stimson asserted he was in substantial agreement. Japan, however, refused to follow the wishes of the League and maintained her dominant control over Manchukuo.

During the whole controversy, the United States consistently upheld the Paris Pact and the Nine-Power Treaty. Throughout she was ready to cooperate with the League or with other powers generally. When collaboration was not forthcoming, the United States was ready to play a lone hand in supporting the Stimson Doctrine of non-recognition. Whether the American public would have supported the administration if force had been attempted is problematical; in all probability it would not. The whole affair showed that as a medium of peace the Kellogg-Briand Pact was powerless and the League was not much better.

Throughout the Hoover regime, the United States showed a greater degree of international cooperation than previously. The support of the London Naval Conference, the granting of respite on debts, the improved relations with Latin America, and the efforts to settle Far Eastern problems were all indications of that. Nevertheless, the United States refused to consider actual membership in the League and even failed to act upon the World Court proposal. The machinery of international cooperation was far too fragile to deal with the rude forces that were rising in Japan, Germany, Italy, and Russia.

New Deal Triumphant

Politics during the thirties revolved in a strikingly different orbit from the politics of the twenties. Old issues that had seemed dead during the complacent years of prosperity suddenly came to life again, while a multitude of new demands made themselves felt. Out of this conflict of forces came the New Deal—a simple name to describe a complex thing, composed of emergency measures, fundamental reforms, practical politics, and idealistic experiments. So heated was the partisanship evoked by the New Deal that most men either praised it as wholly good or damned it as entirely bad; balanced judgments were rare. Fully as controversial as the measures themselves was their sponsor, the only man in American history to be elected four times to the presidency.

The Emergence of Franklin Roosevelt

Franklin Delano Roosevelt was born January 30, 1882, at Hyde Park, New York. He was descended from the same seventeenth-century Dutch ancestor, Nicholas Roosevelt, from whom Theodore Roosevelt also traced descent. James Roosevelt, his father, was a wealthy landowner and businessman. His mother, Sara Delano, belonged to a still wealthier family. Instructed by private tutors until the age of fourteen, young Franklin then attended the exclusive Groton School and received his collegiate training at Harvard. He subsequently studied law at Columbia University Law School and, after being admitted to the bar, accepted employment with a Wall Street legal firm.

Yet his chosen profession had small appeal for him. He spent much time at the family home at Hyde Park and, when an opportunity arose to enter local politics, he took it eagerly. The assignment was not a promising one—to run as Democratic candidate for the State Senate in a district where no Democrat was supposed to have a chance for election—but the twenty-eight-year-old candidate threw himself wholeheartedly into the contest. His vigorous campaigning and the strongly anti-Republican trend of 1910 combined to win for Roosevelt his first public office. Soon after he took his seat at Albany an opportunity arose for him to earn a reputation for progressivism by leading an insurgent revolt against the Tammany boss, Charles E. Murphy.

In 1913 he received his first introduction to the Washington scene. Because he was an asset to his party in a day when the name Roosevelt possessed political magic and also because he had been an energetic campaigner for Wilson, the young politician was named to the post of Assistant Secretary of the Navy—a position once held by Theodore Roosevelt. Unusual opportunities now came his way, particularly when the country became involved in war with Germany. He performed his duties in competent fashion, made important friends, and received an invaluable education in national politics.

In 1920, at the age of 38, he was nominated for the vice-presidency. It was an honor that many shrewd politicians would have declined since the Democrats were confronted with certain defeat, but Roosevelt accepted it as an opportunity. He made a long campaign tour during which thousands of people came to know him as a handsome young man with a fascinating smile and an attractive voice. Despite the humiliating defeat of the party, many predicted a brilliant future for this candidate.

The next year, however, Roosevelt was stricken with infantile paralysis. For months he was a helpless victim of this disease, and it was generally assumed that his political career was ended. Yet the disaster was not without its compensation. Although his legs were never again strong enough to permit him to walk without support, his struggle with invalidism both demonstrated and deepened the courage that proved to be his most valuable asset in days of crisis.

Rest and exercise at Warm Springs, Georgia, restored Roosevelt's health and in 1928, at the urging of the Democratic presidential candidate, Al Smith, he consented to run for governor of New York. Gaining election in the year of a Republician landslide, Roosevelt returned quickly to a central place on the political stage. When he was re-elected in 1930 by a margin greater than any previously won by the popular Smith, Governor Roosevelt became a leading contender for the presidency.

Long before the Democratic convention of 1932, an astute campaign to obtain the nomination for the New York governor was in progress. James A. Farley was traveling through the country, making friends and lining up delegates; Roosevelt's secretary and shrewd political adviser, Louis M. Howe, was coaching his protégé in practical politics; and a group of college professors—presently to be known as the "Brain Trust"—was assembling for Roosevelt the data on government and economics he was eager to have. The Governor himself was the movement's best asset. In a speech of April 7, 1932, he put his finger upon what many felt was the fundamental fallacy of the Hoover policies when he called for plans "that build from the bottom up and not from the top down, that put their faith once more in the forgotten man at the bottom of the economic pyramid." Even more did he identify himself with the mood of the hour when he declared on May 22, 1932, at Oglethorpe University:

> The country needs and, unless I mistake its temper, the country demands bold, persistent experimentation. It is common sense to take a method and try it. If it fails, admit it frankly and try another. But above all, try something. The millions who are in want will not stand by silently forever while the things to satisfy their needs are within easy reach.

The Election of 1932

On June 14, 1932, the Republican National Convention opened its session at Chicago. There was no question of President Hoover's renomination—he was still titular head and, in the face of probable defeat, no one seriously challenged him. The party platform was largely devoted to praise of the Hoover record. Not only was the Hawley-Smoot Tariff upheld, but a pledge to extend the protectionist principle was incorporated. The policies of the Federal Farm Board were defended, and the party went on record in support of "any plan which will help to balance production against demand, and thereby raise agricultural prices, provided it is economically sound and administratively workable without burdensome bureaucracy." A sharp fight developed over the prohibition issue. The majority report favored a vague formula under which the voters were to pass upon a proposed amendment "which, while retaining in the Federal Government power to preserve the gains already made in dealing with the evils inherent in the liquor traffic, shall allow States to deal with the problem as their citizens may determine. . . ." Opposing this, a minority report advocated immediate repeal of the Eighteenth Amendment. After a bitter fight, the majority report—the so-called wet-dry plank—was carried by a vote of 690 to 460. Hoover was renominated on the first ballot with only a light and scattered opposition. The renomination of Vice-President Curtis, however, precipitated a real contest. While he did win on the first ballot, he received only 634 votes as compared with 513 cast for other candidates.

The Democratic Convention also met in Chicago. The party platform proved to be in refreshing contrast to most such documents. It was comparatively brief, and the commitments were clear—embarrassingly clear in the case of those that later failed to be carried out. The document called for repeal of the Eighteenth Amendment, the reduction of government expenses by 25 per cent, an annually balanced budget, an enlarged program of public works and unemployment relief, the enactment of state unemployment and old-age pension laws, regulation of the sale of securities and banking reform, a modification of the tariff through reciprocal trade agreements, aid for the farmer through control of crop surpluses, and the independence of the Philippines.

Roosevelt had the support of more than half the delegates, but this did not assure his nomination because the two-thirds rule was still in effect. The most formidable candidate was Alfred E. Smith, eager for vindication after his defeat of 1928 and strongly supported by a faction of wealthy conservatives, headed by the party chairman, John J. Raskob. A third figure with strong backing was Speaker of the House John Nance Garner of Texas. The anti-Roosevelt forces hoped to block the nomination of the New York governor and obtain the prize for some compromise candidate. But after Roosevelt's vote had climbed from 666 to 682 on the first three ballots, Speaker Garner decided to withdraw in order to prevent any such disastrous deadlock as that of the 1924 convention. Two powerful delegations, those of Texas and California, now swung to the support of Roosevelt. Senator William Gibbs McAdoo of California enjoyed his revenge against Smith, who had blocked his nomination in 1924, by announcing the shift of the California delegation's vote from Garner to Roosevelt; this was the break that set the Roosevelt band wagon into triumphant progress. On the fourth ballot the New York governor gained the coveted prize with 945 votes to 190½ cast for Smith and 13 scattered among other candidates. Garner's reward came at once; he was unanimously nominated for the vice-presidency.

Roosevelt demonstrated his impatience with meaningless tradition by flying at once to Chicago to accept his nomination instead of waiting for the customary notification ceremony. He brought the tired delegates to a high state of enthusiasm with an aggressive speech concluding with these words:

> I pledge you, I pledge myself, to a new deal for the American people. Let us all here assembled constitute ourselves prophets of a new order of competence and of courage. . . . Give me your help, not to win votes alone, but to win in this crusade to restore America to its own people.

By this bold gesture Roosevelt captured the attention of the electorate, and he never lost it during the long campaign. His speeches made the most of the weaknesses in the Republican record, while offering only the outlines of an alternative policy. They were progressive enough on the issues of farm relief and public utilities to win the support of Republicans like Senators Norris,

Hiram Johnson, and Bronson Cutting of New Mexico, as well as the Progressive LaFollette, son of "Fighting Bob" of earlier days. But at the same time the candidate's promise to balance the budget and his cautiousness on the tariff held in line the conservatives of his own party. Throughout the campaign he demonstrated a mastery of the difficult art of maintaining the backing of widely divergent elements.

Late in the campaign President Hoover became conscious of the precarious position of the Republicans. He abandoned his own front-porch tactics and made an extensive tour, climaxing his efforts with a fighting speech in Madison Square Garden, New York. Were the Democratic tariff proposals to be put into effect, he asserted, grass would grow in the streets of a hundred cities. The Democratic promise to put the unemployed to work he characterized as "cruel" because it was "absolutely impossible of realization." He defined the issue of the campaign as whether or not the "American system" was to be maintained.

Election day gave convincing evidence of the revolution in American public opinion. Hoover, who four years before had carried forty states, now took but six: Connecticut, Delaware, Maine, New Hampshire, Pennsylvania, and Vermont. The electoral vote was: Roosevelt, 472, and Hoover, 59; the popular vote: Roosevelt, 22,821,857, and Hoover, 15,761,841.[1] The Congressional election results were equally decisive. The Democrats won 59 seats in the Senate to 36 for the Republicans and 1 for the Farmer-Laborites; in the House the division was 313 Democrats, 117 Republicans, and 5 independents. Political observers commented that these results were not so much a Democratic victory as they were a Republican defeat. So dissatisfied were the voters with existing conditions that they cast their ballots for Roosevelt in order to turn the Republicans out, believing that a change could not be for the worse and might conceivably be for the better.

The Lame Ducks

During the twenties Senator Norris had conducted a long crusade for a Constitutional amendment that would provide for the inauguration of the President in January rather than in March and also eliminate lame-duck sessions of the old Congress. Despite the obvious merits of the proposal and the fact that the Senate passed it five times between 1923 and 1931, it failed to obtain the approval of the House, largely because of the hostility of Speaker Nicholas Longworth and the Republican Old Guard. After the election of Speaker Garner, however, the amendment passed both chambers and was submitted to the states in March, 1932. Less than a year later, more than three quarters of the

[1] The minor party figures showed Norman Thomas (Socialist) with 884,781, and William Foster (Communist) with 102,991.

states having ratified it, the Twentieth, or "Lame Duck," Amendment was declared in effect on February 6, 1933.[2]

Unfortunately the reform came too late to prevent the most glaring illustration of the evils of the old system. For four months after a decisive vote of no confidence had been registered, the Hoover administration continued in office, and for three of those months a Lame Duck Congress was in session. It is little wonder that the resulting confusion and uncertainty plunged the nation into the most critical phase of the whole depression.

Congress and the President could not agree on measures for balancing the budget nor on banking reform. Among the few legislative acts of a positive character was the approval of the Twenty-first Amendment to the Constitution. This provided for repeal of the Eighteenth Amendment, but prohibited the transportation or importation of intoxicating liquors into any state in violation of the laws thereof. The amendment was unique among such proposals in stipulating that its ratification must be obtained through special conventions in the several states.[3]

Within a week after election, Hoover began to feel the embarrassment of his position. A world disarmament conference was intermittently in progress, a world economic conference was in prospect, and the question of war debts was pressing for settlement. On November 22, 1932, the President and Secretary of the Treasury Ogden Mills conferred on these problems with the President-elect and his adviser, Professor Raymond Moley of Columbia University. Neither in this meeting nor in subsequent correspondence did Hoover and Roosevelt achieve a good understanding. Hoover felt that he could not initiate

[2] The text of the Twentieth Amendment is as follows:

Section 1. The terms of the President and Vice-President shall end at noon on the 20th day of January, and the terms of Senators and Representatives at noon on the 3rd day of January, of the years in which such terms would have ended if this article had not been ratified; and the terms of their successors shall then begin.

Section 2. The Congress shall assemble at least once in every year, and such meeting shall begin at noon on the 3rd day of January, unless they shall by law appoint a different day.

Section 3. If, at the time fixed for the beginning of the term of the President, the President elect shall have died, the Vice-President elect shall become President. If a President shall not have been chosen before the time fixed for the beginning of his term, or if the President elect shall have failed to qualify, then the Vice-President elect shall act as President until a President shall have qualified; and the Congress may by law provide for the case wherein neither a President elect nor a Vice-President elect shall have qualified, declaring who shall then act as President, or the manner in which one who is to act shall be selected, and such person shall act accordingly until a President or Vice-President shall have qualified.

Section 4. The Congress may by law provide for the case of the death of any of the persons from whom the House of Representatives may choose a President whenever the right of choice shall have devolved upon them, and for the case of the death of any of the persons from whom the Senate may choose a Vice-President whenever the right of choice shall have devolved upon them.

[3] In March, 1933, the next Congress amended the Volstead Act to permit the sale of beer and wine with an alcoholic content not greater than 3.2 per cent. The final termination of prohibition came with the ratification of the Twenty-first Amendment on December 5, 1933.

policies without a pledge from the President-elect that these would not be repudiated after March 4; but Roosevelt asserted in a letter to Hoover: "I think you will realize that it would be unwise for me to accept an apparent joint responsibility with you when, as a matter of constitutional fact, I would be wholly lacking in any attendant authority." Both men were right; the difficulty lay not with them, but with the Constitutional provision that required so long an interregnum. This did not mean, however, that there was no cooperation at all between the outgoing and incoming administrations. On the contrary, there was agreement on many points, and Hoover received assurances that there would not be any major reorientation of American foreign policy.

Banking Chaos

Problems of foreign relations were as nothing compared with the crucial issues of domestic policy that arose during the last month of Hoover's term. Depositors who had lost confidence in banks withdrew their savings; many who trusted the banks did not trust the incoming administration and the result was the same—they hoarded their money. The situation threatened disaster for the whole country. The Federal reserve banks were under great strain, being compelled to put constantly larger amounts of currency into circulation while their gold stocks were seriously depleted. Gold was not only being hidden away by domestic hoarders, but was being exported in large volume.

The danger was great that sound institutions would be pulled under along with unsound ones. State governments struggling with the situation resorted to temporary bank holidays—periods during which all transactions between the banks and the public were halted while the situation eased. During 1932 there were several such local bank holidays in the Middle West. But these incidents did not begin to alarm the general public until February, 1933. On the fourth of that month the governor of Louisiana had to proclaim a week-end bank holiday for New Orleans; on the fourteenth the governor of Michigan announced an eight-day state-wide holiday in order to save the banks of Detroit from disaster. The Michigan crisis had a serious effect on the situation in other states.

To President Hoover the crisis reflected nothing but the country's alarm over what the new administration might do. On February 17, 1933, he wrote to the President-elect requesting him to assure the nation "that there will be no tampering or inflation of the currency; that the budget will be unquestionably balanced, even if further taxation is necessary; that the Government credit will be maintained by refusal to exhaust it in the issue of securities." The demand was an astonishing one, and indeed its implication was fully realized by Hoover, for he wrote to Senator Reed of Pennsylvania: "I realize that if these declarations be made by the President-elect, he will have ratified the whole major program of the Republican Administration; that is, it means the abandonment of 90 per cent of the so-called new deal." Roosevelt refused to allow his hands to be thus tied. He did, however, choose this occasion to announce that the two most important cabinet posts in the new administration would be held by men who could by no stretch of the imagination be portrayed as radicals: Senator Cordell Hull of Tennessee was to be his Secretary of State and William H. Woodin of New York, president of the American Car and Foundry Company, his Secretary of the Treasury. Many days before the inauguration of his chief, Woodin and a group of Democratic experts were in earnest conference with Secretary Mills and other Treasury officials over the banking crisis.

Meantime the situation went from bad to worse. By March 3 over twenty states had to place restrictions on bank withdrawals. The night before Inauguration Day the officials of the outgoing administration and the new agreed that the banking holiday must be made general and together they exercised pressure on Governor Lehman of New York and other state executives to proclaim temporary holidays. By noon of March 4, when Roosevelt took the oath of office, scarcely a bank in the country was engaged in normal operations.

The New President

Throughout the morning of March 4, 1933, news of the crisis spread across the nation, and the groups who crowded around radios at noon to listen to the new President's inaugural were bewildered and somber. What they heard was tonic not only in phraseology, but in the calm and courageous manner of its delivery.

> This great Nation will endure as it has endured, will revive and will prosper. So, first of all, let me assert my belief that the only thing we have to fear is fear itself —nameless, unreasoning, unjustified terror which paralyzes needed efforts to convert retreat into advance.

Roosevelt announced that Congress would meet at once in special session and stated his confidence that he could obtain the passage of necessary measures. If Congress should fail to act, however, he would ask that body "for the one remaining instrument to meet the crisis—broad Executive power to wage a war against the emergency, as great as the power that would be given me if we were in fact invaded by a foreign foe."

Roosevelt appointed his cabinet with the usual geographical and political considerations in mind. Besides Hull and Woodin, important appointments went to Farley, the Democratic campaign manager, who became Postmaster General; to Henry A. Wallace of Iowa and Harold L. Ickes of Illinois, two converted Republicans, who became respectively Secretary of Agriculture and Secretary of the Interior; and to Frances Perkins of New York, who became

Secretary of Labor and first woman cabinet member.[4] The new President showed a lively interest in the ideas presented by college professors and young lawyers—many of the latter being recommended to him by Professor Felix Frankfurter of Harvard Law School. Roosevelt's "Brain Trust" gained a horrendous reputation among businessmen and old-line politicians for radicalism, but in reality Moley, who was the most powerful of Roosevelt's advisers in 1933, was conservative on most issues and the others were less radical than they were generally painted.

The action that Roosevelt had promised began at once. On the day after his inauguration the President called the new Congress into special session. Pending that event, he issued a sweeping executive proclamation ordering a national bank holiday, with all banking transactions suspended except those that might be permitted by the Secretary of the Treasury. By the time Congress convened on March 9 an Emergency Banking bill had been drafted; the measure was passed almost unanimously by the two Houses and received the President's signature the same day. It confirmed all of the measures already taken and gave the President further emergency powers to control foreign exchange, gold and currency movements, and banking in general.

Throughout the week the Treasury Department worked day and night on the banking problem. With the cooperation of the Federal reserve banks, the financial condition of institutions all over the country was reviewed to discover as speedily as possible which ones might be permitted to reopen and which must remain closed while their affairs were set in order. It was decided that on Monday, March 13, the sound banks located in the twelve Federal reserve bank cities should be permitted to open, to be followed the next day by those situated in some 250 cities where there were recognized clearinghouse associations; those elsewhere would be licensed on succeeding days as rapidly as their condition could be determined.

These measures represented a bipartisan effort. The teamwork had begun well before Inauguration Day and it continued for many days thereafter, the outgoing Treasury officials working side by side with the new staff. But after all

---

[4] Original and subsequent Roosevelt cabinet appointments were as follows: Secretary of State Cordell Hull, succeeded by Edward R. Stettinius, Jr., of Virginia in 1944; Secretary of the Treasury William H. Woodin, succeeded by Henry L. Morgenthau, Jr., of New York in 1934; Secretary of War George H. Dern of Utah, succeeded by Harry H. Woodring of Kansas in 1936, and Henry L. Stimson of New York in 1940; Secretary of the Navy Claude A. Swanson of Virginia, succeeded by Charles Edison of New Jersey in 1940, Frank Knox of Illinois in 1940, and James Forrestal of New York in 1944; Attorney General Homer Cummings of Connecticut, succeeded by Frank Murphy of Michigan in 1939, Robert H. Jackson of New York in 1940, and Francis Biddle of Pennsylvania in 1941; Postmaster General James A. Farley, succeeded by Frank C. Walker of Pennsylvania in 1940; Secretary of the Interior Harold L. Ickes; Secretary of Agriculture Henry A. Wallace, succeeded by Claude Wickard of Indiana in 1940; Secretary of Commerce Daniel C. Roper of South Carolina, succeeded by Harry L. Hopkins of Iowa in 1939, Jesse Jones of Texas in 1940, and Henry A. Wallace in 1945; Secretary of Labor Frances Perkins.

possible safeguards had been provided, there still remained a grave psychological obstacle to be surmounted. When the banks reopened, would the public have confidence in them? Or would bank runs and hoarding bring on a new crisis? It was at this point that the new President made his own most important contribution. On Sunday evening, March 12, he delivered the first of his so-called fireside chats—an informal radio talk addressed directly to the common man. Simply and clearly he explained the measures that had been taken and promised his listeners that they might trust the institutions that would begin operations again during the next few days. "I can assure you," he said, "that it is safer to keep your money in a reopened bank than under the mattress."

The reopening proved successful. Within three days about 76 per cent of the member banks of the Federal Reserve System were doing business again. Non-member banks had to be licensed by the state banking authorities and the process took longer, but 72 per cent of them had reopened by April 12. More than 4,000 banks failed to obtain licenses during these early weeks; many of these reorganized and opened later, sometimes with no loss to their depositors, sometimes with partial loss. Hundreds were so hopelessly insolvent that they had to be liquidated, but even here the loss to depositors was rarely 100 per cent.[5] As gratifying as the successful reopening of so large a proportion of the banks was the renewed confidence shown by the public. Hoarding ceased, paper currency and gold flowed back to the banks, and deposits by the middle of April increased over $1 billion.

First aid had been successfully rendered to the banking system, but as yet the abuses that had led to the crisis remained uncorrected. It was a problem to which the administration returned at a later date.

The executive orders under which the banks had been closed and reopened contained several important restrictions. No gold, gold bullion, or gold certificates might be paid out by the banks without the authorization of the Secretary of the Treasury, nor could gold in any form be exported without a Treasury license. The purpose of these regulations was not only to conserve the gold stock of the country, but to permit the dollar to depreciate in its relationship to foreign currencies so as to raise the domestic price level and stimulate exports. For the first time since 1879 the currency of the United States could not be redeemed in gold.

The Hundred Days

The special session of the Seventy-third Congress that opened on March 9, 1933, adjourned on June 16, only 104 days after Roosevelt's inauguration. During these "Hundred Days," Congress passed more important pieces of legisla-

---

[5] Nevertheless, more than 1,700 banks failed with losses to their depositors of over $1 billion.

tion than any previous legislature in American history. This unusual record was possible because of the great prestige of the new President and the willingness of a Congress sobered by the emergency to accept a large amount of executive leadership. Public opinion throughout the nation favored a maximum of action and a minimum of debate.

Two days after the enactment of the Emergency Banking Law, the Economy Act was passed. The President was given wide powers to cut the salaries of Federal employees by as much as 15 per cent and to reduce as well the pensions and allowances of war veterans. Roosevelt made prompt use of his authority and his courage in braving the wrath of politically powerful groups did much to restore business confidence.

Inconsistent though it seemed to many, Federal emergency appropriations were increased at the same time that other expenditures were being reduced. The President was able to gain early Congressional approval for a project that would have appealed to the first Roosevelt in the White House as much as it did to the second. The Civilian Conservation Corps (CCC) was created to give temporary employment to about 300,000 men—250,000 unmarried men between the ages of 18 and 25, 25,000 veterans of World War I, and 25,000 experienced woodsmen. Most of the young men received but $30 a month, $25 of which was sent to their families. They were taken off the streets, given board and lodgings in camps, and put to work on useful projects in the national forests.

Since the funds made available in 1932 through the Reconstruction Finance Corporation for loans to the states for relief activities were now almost exhausted, Congress made a new appropriation of $500 million. A few significant changes were introduced. Money was advanced to the states in the form of grants rather than loans, and a new agency, the Federal Emergency Relief Administration (FERA), was created to carry out the provisions of the law. To head the FERA President Roosevelt summoned to Washington Harry L. Hopkins of Iowa, long engaged in social work, who had directed the New York State Unemployment Relief Administration when Roosevelt was at Albany.

Meantime, advocates of a large public-works program impressed upon the President the benefits that would flow from their proposals. Not only would employment be given to many workers, but a demand for steel, cement, and other materials would be stimulated. The final appropriation, embodied in Title II of the National Industrial Recovery Act (NIRA), was $3.3 billion—a larger amount than any earlier peacetime appropriation by any government. The Public Works Administration (PWA) was placed under the chairmanship of Secretary of the Interior Ickes, an outspoken and honest official, whose deliberation and care in perusing each project was the despair of many other New Dealers.

The unemployed were not the only group who needed immediate help. The problem of unmanageable private debts threatened to crush debtors and creditors alike. The Emergency Farm Mortgage Act authorized the Federal Land Banks to undertake a wholesale refinancing of farm mortgages. The law not only enabled many thousands of farmers to escape foreclosure proceedings, but served equally the interests of banks and insurance companies holding defaulted obligations. Similar in purpose was the Home Owners Loan Corporation (HOLC), created by the national legislature to relieve both mortgagors and mortgagees of residential real estate. In the three-year priod during which it was authorized to make loans, the HOLC advanced more than $3 billion to over a million home owners.

The Reconstruction Finance Corporation was not only continued by the Roosevelt administration but was given much broader powers. Besides loaning money to banks in distress, it could now strengthen them by purchasing capital stock. Money was made available for payments to depositors who had funds tied up in closed banks. Direct loans to small businessmen were permitted, while advances to farmers on the security of their crops attained large volume. Loans from the RFC proved to be the lifeblood for almost every phase of the recovery program.

It will be noted that the measures so far discussed differed from the Hoover depression policies more in the scale upon which they were carried out than in the underlying philosophy. Like Hoover, Roosevelt was trying to bolster up the credit structure of the country and prevent wholesale liquidation. Capitalism had been granted a reprieve.

The New Dealers believed, however, that all such measures to save the banks, the corporations, the railroads, the home owners, and the farmers would be futile unless economic activity could be stimulated and maintained. The income of millions of farmers and workers must be substantially raised if real recovery were to be attained. This was the primary purpose of the two most controversial measures passed by Congress during the Hundred Days—the Agricultural Adjustment Act and the National Industrial Recovery Act.

The First AAA

Four days after his inauguration, Roosevelt took steps to carry out the party's pledge to aid the farmers. A speedily gathered conference of some fifty representative farm leaders formulated a set of recommendations that were presented to the President on March 11. These suggestions together with those of various braintrusters and legislators were finally combined in the Agricultural Adjustment Act of May 12, 1933. By one section of this measure the President was given broad inflationary powers to be discussed later in this chapter. Principal interest, however, lay in Title I, which gave the Secretary of Agriculture extraordinary powers to raise the farmers' income. The purpose was to give agricultural commodities a purchasing power with respect to articles farmers bought equivalent to the purchasing power of agricultural commodities in the base period, 1909–14. To gain this end, two principal methods were provided. In the case of seven basic commodities,[6] the Secretary was authorized to make agreements with individual farmers under which the latter would receive benefit payments for reducing the acreage of their crops or their production of live-stock. The revenue for these payments was to be raised through a "processing tax"—an excise paid by the manufacturers on the first processing of the basic commodities for the domestic market. The other method was to authorize the Secretary of Agriculture to enter into marketing agreements with processors, farmers' associations, and others engaged in the handling of farm products. Steps could thus be taken through voluntary agreements—exempt from the antitrust laws—to establish marketing quotas that would maintain prices by curbing the sale of surpluses. The Secretary was also granted broad powers to loan money on the security of crops, to purchase surplus commodities, and to subsidize exports.

To carry out the provisions of the act, Secretary Wallace set up the Agricultural Adjustment Administration (AAA). George N. Peek, one of the authors of the bill and an advocate of farm-relief measures since McNary-Haugen days, was appointed to head the agency. Peek disagreed with Wallace, however, on fundamental issues of policy. The former was an economic nationalist who believed that emphasis should be placed on an aggressive campaign to sell the agricultural surplus abroad. He favored benefit payments but opposed curbs on production. Secretary Wallace believed that American farm production must be immediately curtailed, although he was hopeful that this might be temporary and that reciprocal trade agreements and tariff concessions might eventually restore foreign markets for American farm products. Increasing friction between the two men led to Peek's resignation in December, 1933, and the appointment of Chester A. Davis as administrator.

The first steps taken under AAA were particularly controversial because they involved destruction of commodities already growing. This was believed to be necessary since the program began too late in the year to prevent the planting of crops and the breeding of livestock that threatened to glut the market. Cotton growers were asked to rent to the Secretary of Agriculture at least one quarter of their acreage. Over one million such contracts were made, and cotton plants on about 10.4 million acres of land were plowed under. For not producing an estimated 4.4 million bales of cotton, the growers received approximately $113 million in benefit payments. Even more shocking to Eastern conservatives were

---

[6] These basic commodities were wheat, cotton, corn, hogs, rice, tobacco, and milk. The act was amended in 1934 to add sugar, beef and dairy cattle, peanuts, rye, flax, barley, and grass sorghums.

How Would They Like to Trade Doctors? (By Darling
in the *New York Herald Tribune.*)

the purchase and slaughter of thousands of little pigs and pregnant sows to
prevent a hog surplus.

The plowing up of crops and the slaughtering of animals were only emergency
procedures. The long-range plans of AAA called for limitations upon production in advance. During the next three years the system had an extensive trial.
Reduced production and better prices plus benefit payments increased farm
income from $4.5 billion in 1932 to $6.9 billion in 1935. Even allowing for a
substantial rise in the prices the farmer had to pay for his purchases, this was
equivalent to a 35 per cent increase in his real income. The effect of AAA
policies upon the production and prices of certain of the basic commodities is
indicated in the following chart:

	Cotton		Corn		Wheat	
	Net Output (mil. bales)	Price ($ per bale)	Net Output (mil. bus.)	Price (¢ per bu.)	Net Output (mil. bus.)	Price (¢ per bu.)
1932	13.0	32.60	587.2	31.9	548.5	38.2
1933	13.05	50.85	437.0	52.2	401.6	74.4
1934	9.64	61.80	170.1	81.5	360.1	84.8
1935	10.64	55.45	409.5	65.5	455.6	83.2

The reduced output and increased prices could not, however, be attributed solely to AAA. Since government spending for relief, dollar devaluation, the creation of increased purchasing power through NRA, and natural forces of recovery were all at work, it is impossible to isolate the effect of any one factor. Of great importance, also, was the serious drought of 1934, which reduced production more drastically than AAA had planned.

Farmers grumbled about many aspects of the program. Despite efforts to administer it democratically, the experiment interfered with the American farmer's cherished individualism and established precedents that might lead to more disasteful forms of regimentation in the future. Some farmers were worried about the ultimate effect on exports of a policy reducing production and raising prices. Not all farmers shared equally in the benefits of the act. Producers of the basic commodities usually gained more than growers of other products, while large farmers gained more than small. Whatever the farmers' misgivings, however, referendums revealed that the overwhelming majority desired to have the AAA experiment continued at least until something better could be devised.

Consumers were less enthusiastic. They were required to contribute to the rehabilitation of agriculture both in increased prices and in the processing taxes, which the manfacturers passed on to them. But spokesmen for agriculture promptly pointed out that for many decades consumers had been paying a similar, if less obvious, subsidy to manufacturers through the operations of the protective tariff. And they also asserted that "the economics of scarcity" had not originated with them, but with industrialists who sought by fair means and foul to control production in order to maintain prices.

The New Deal was also interested in another type of agricultural legislation. Following the Emergency Farm Mortgage Act of 1933, Congress approved the Farm Mortgage Foreclosure Act of June, 1934, enabling farmers to borrow money from the government to forestall the loss of their holdings in foreclosure proceedings. At the same time the Frazier-Lemke Bankruptcy Act was also placed on the statute books. This controversial measure permitted a farmer to demand a reappraisal of his property lost through foreclosure and buy it back at the new figure, paying for it over a six-year period with interest rates of only 1 per cent. Were the creditor to object, the law gave the farmer the right to halt proceedings and to keep his property for five years at a reasonable rental. This act led to bitter struggles in the Middle West between bankrupt farmers and the mortgage holders, and eventually the Supreme Court in 1935 found the measure in conflict with the Fifth Amendment (Louisville Joint Stock Co. v. Radford). The following year the Frazier-Lemke Act was passed again in an amended form that changed the retention period to only three years. Thanks in part to personnel changes in the Supreme Court, its validity was now upheld.

NRA: Experiment in Industrial Self-Government

During the election campaign, Roosevelt had expressed interest in a movement for industrial self-government that had been enlisting the support of many business leaders. Competition, at least in its most aggressive forms, had grown unpopular—particularly during the depression. This led to a demand that the trade associations be expanded in membership and allowed to organize measures for stabilizing production, prices, and marketing practices. Since such activities were not permitted under the antitrust laws, it was proposed that the latter should be amended, suspended, or repealed. A concrete proposal based on these principles was put forward by Gerard Swope, president of the General Electric Company, in the autumn of 1931, and a somewhat similar plan was developed under the auspices of the United States Chamber of Commerce. Hoover had been cold to the movement, but Roosevelt was disposed to give the idea his sympathetic consideration.

Meantime, labor leaders were insisting on the need for shortening the work week. They asserted that the principal cause of the depression was unemployment brought on by the increased productivity of the individual worker. In order to create purchasing power, hours should be radically shortened and employment spread as widely as possible. To achieve this end Senator Hugo L. Black of Alabama had introduced as early as December, 1932, a bill that would have limited work in factories to thirty hours a week. Although strongly opposed by the Chamber of Commerce, the Black Thirty-Hour bill passed the Senate in April, 1933. In the House the proposal had the support of Representative William P. Connery of Massachusetts, the chairman of the Committee on Labor, who suggested strengthening amendments. Secretary of Labor Perkins intervened to advise that any bill fixing maximum hours would be dangerous to labor unless it also dealt with minimum wages.

As this Black-Connery-Perkins project took form, businessmen became greatly alarmed. Bowing to the opposition, the President disassociated himself from the Thirty-Hour bill and set his advisers to drafting a measure that would reconcile the demands of the industrialists with those of labor.

The result was the National Industrial Recovery Act, which provided for drafting of "codes of fair competition" by industrial groups or associations. These codes were to be submitted to the President or to some representative designated by him, whose duty it was to make sure that the associations were "truly representative," and that the proposed codes were "not designed to promote monopolies, or to eliminate or oppress enterprises." When the President was satisfied with a particular code, he would give it his formal approval; then all units in the industry were bound to the code and might be punished for violations, whether or not they had participated in its formulation. Protection to labor was provided by Section 7-A, which required that every code and agreement must guarantee to employees the right of collective bargaining by representatives of their own choosing, free from restraint or coercion by employers. The measure was to be in force for two years and, during that period, approved code activities were to be exempt from the antitrust laws.

Although the bill encountered opposition from old-line progressives who disliked the relaxation of the antitrust laws, the measure became law on June 16, 1933. President Roosevelt displayed his enthusiasm for the experiment in a statement issued the same day:

> History probably will record the National Industrial Recovery Act as the most important and far-reaching legislation ever enacted by the American Congress. It represents a supreme effort to stabilize for all time the many factors which make for the prosperity of the Nation, and the preservation of American standards.

With the launching of this experiment, the New Deal veered sharply away from the traditions of Wilson's New Freedom toward those of Theodore Roosevelt's New Nationalism. The inevitability of big business was accepted, and the protection of the public was entrusted, not primarily to trust-busting and strict regulation, but to enlightened cooperation between business and government.

To carry out the provisions of the act the President established a National Recovery Administration (NRA) with General Hugh Johnson as its head. The general had a colorful personality, great zeal for work, and a flair for pungent expression. The high point of his previous career had been reached during World War I when he had organized the draft and then served as one of Baruch's lieutenants on the War Industries Board. As NRA administrator, he sought to use the methods that had made these earlier ventures successful.

There were more than two hundred codes submitted to NRA during July, 1933, alone, making it obvious that it would be many months before the whole field of industry could be covered. A short cut for achieving at once the agency's more important objectives was provided by the President's Re-employment Agreement (PRA) of July, 1933, to which all employers were invited to subscribe. This pledged them to abstain from employing children, to limit hours of labor in stores and banks to forty and in factories to thirty-five, and to pay minimum wages of not less than 30 cents per hour. This document was popularly referred to as the Blanket Code—a misleading term since it was an entirely voluntary agreement entered upon by the individual employer with the President. Its purpose was to create purchasing power to sustain the industrial recovery that had developed on a somewhat speculative basis during the summer of 1933.

Employers who agreed to abide by either the PRA or the code for their particular industry were entitled to display an official symbol featuring a blue eagle and the words "NRA—We do our part." The dynamic General Johnson organized a vast Blue Eagle campaign patterned on the Liberty Loan drives of World War I. Within four months, Johnson claimed that 96 per cent of commerce and industry were displaying the Blue Eagle, 2.8 million workers had been put back on payrolls, and annual purchasing power had been increased by $3 billion.

It had been hoped that the Blue Eagle drive would encourage the drafting of specific codes to substitute for the rather rigid requirements of the PRA. This proved to be the case, and eventually 557 basic codes received NRA approval. By February, 1934, the code-making process was virtually completed and all but a very small segment of American industry had been covered. Not only manufacturing, but such economic activities as wholesale trade, retail trade, construction, and the service industries were all operating under NRA organization.

The codes differed greatly, yet some of their more characteristic features may be listed. They always forbade child labor; maximum hours of work were variously fixed at between thirty-five and forty-eight weekly, with the average about forty; minimum wages were established usually at about 40 cents an hour; and the right of collective bargaining was recognized as required by Section 7-A. Most of the codes banned false advertising, commercial bribery, harassing litigation, and the like—practices that were already unlawful but that still prevailed in certain areas. More controversial were the provisions permitting control of production or limitations on pricing. The cotton textile code limited the number of hours the plants could operate. Several codes forbade the acquisition of new machinery or the entry of new units into the industry without special authorization. In a few natural-resource industries like lumber, copper, and petroleum, definite production quotas were set. In the lumber, bituminous coal, and petroleum codes, moreover, prices were fixed. Most codes merely provided that goods must not be sold "below cost"—a formula that proved difficult of application. Contrary to the advice of NRA officials, the tendency of the sponsors was to make the codes increasingly elaborate, dealing with trade practices in bewildering detail.

The Tennessee Valley Authority

During the second month of his administration, the President appealed to Congress to carry out Senator Norris' Muscle Shoals project in a form that surpassed the dreams of that veteran progressive. Instead of a single power plant, Roosevelt called for a program that would develop the full resources of the region. He asked Congress to create a Tennessee Valley Authority, "a corporation clothed with the power of Government but possessed of the flexibility and initiative of a private enterprise," to be "charged with the broadest duty of planning for the proper use, conservation and development of the

Senator George Norris at Norris Dam, Part of TVA. (Acme.)

natural resources of the Tennessee River drainage basin and its adjoining territory for the general social and economic welfare of the Nation."

Congress passed the requested legislation and on May 18, 1933, the Tennessee Valley Authority Act received the President's signature. Arthur E. Morgan, president of Antioch College, served as chairman until 1938, when a quarrel between him and his fellow directors led to his removal and the elevation to the chairmanship of David E. Lilienthal of Wisconsin, who had been an influential figure in the TVA since its organization.

The first great activity of the agency was dam building. Thirty dams eventually came under TVA's control, and of these twenty were new ones constructed by TVA itself.

Highly controversial was the authority given TVA by Congress to generate and sell electricity. The private power companies would not have objected so much if the power had been sold wholesale to them for transmission and distribution. But Congress laid down a very different policy. TVA was directed to "give preference to states, counties, municipalities, and cooperative organizations of citizens or members. . . ." Against this effort to promote a public power business in competition with private industry, the utility companies put up a stubborn fight in the courts. Although the constitutionality of the provisions permitting TVA to sell surplus electric power was upheld by the Supreme Court in 1936 (Ashwander v. TVA), this did not end the legal battle. A score of issues was raised, sweeping injunctions were issued in the lower courts, and several cases were taken to the Supreme Court. On every major issue TVA was sustained, but the litigation cost millions of dollars and hampered the agency's activities for years. Eventually, in 1939, Commonwealth and Southern, the holding company whose subsidiaries were most affected, accepted a negotiated settlement. For $78.6 million the company sold its Tennessee electrical properties to TVA and local public agencies. It was a substantially larger sum than the public power representatives had wanted to pay, and Wendell Willkie, president of Commonwealth and Southern, received nation-wide publicity because of his fight in behalf of the investors. Parallel negotiations led to the purchase of other private utility properties in Mississippi and Alabama.

The agency did not deal directly with domestic consumers. Instead it sold its power wholesale to municipalities and cooperative associations. In 1950 it was doing business with 95 of the former, including the cities of Knoxville, Nashville, Memphis, and Chattanooga, and 50 of the latter. Since it also sold directly to big industrial plants, many new enterprises were attracted to the area, particularly during World War II.

One of the most interesting aspects of the TVA experiment was its pioneering with a radically low rate structure. Reduced rates encouraged the much wider use of electricity. In twelve communities served by TVA from 1934 to 1942 the consumption of electricity in homes increased by 196 per cent as compared with 63 per cent for the nation. Public power advocates contended that the TVA experiment provided a "yardstick" whereby the reasonableness of private-utility rates all over the country could be measured. Private industry spokesmen replied that the comparison was unfair since TVA and the public agencies with which it dealt did not have to pay taxes and make a profit. This was not entirely true, since TVA made annual payments of some $2 million to state and county governments in lieu of taxes, while the municipalities and co-operatives followed similar practices. Although the conditions under which TVA was doing business were more nearly similar to the private utilities than the latter were willing to admit, it nevertheless remained true that the comparison between TVA rates and private rates was sometimes misleading, and that the fairness of the rates in any particular part of the country had to be judged on the basis of the local situation.

Whether TVA had provided a fair yardstick or not, private utilities responded to its challenge. An emphasis on rate reduction and increased consumption characterized the entire industry during the thirties. According to TVA Chairman Lilienthal, electric rates dropped only 2 per cent in the seven years before TVA as compared with a decrease of approximately 33 per cent during the seven years after 1933.

Public attention was largely concentrated on TVA's power program because of its challenging and controversial character. Less known were its other activities. The great TVA dams were multipurpose structures. One of their principal objectives was to promote navigation. Great artificial lakes connected by a system of locks provided 650 miles of navigable waterways. The dams also prevented floods. No major river in the world was so fully controlled as the Tennessee. By holding back or releasing the waters impounded behind dams on the main stream and its tributaries, a vast region could be protected against inundation. Moreover, TVA manufactured fertilizer, rehabilitated impoverished farmers, educated them in better agricultural methods, and promoted reforestation.

Monetary Policy

Nothing better illustrates the difference in viewpoint between Hoover and Roosevelt than their attitudes toward the country's monetary system. The Republican President had regarded the maintenance of the gold standard as perhaps his most important trust; he viewed with horror the slightest deviation from it. Roosevelt refused to adopt this fetish. In his campaign speeches he pledged himself to "sound money," but it was obvious that he was leaving himself free to deviate from conventional views if a moderate and controlled inflation seemed advisable. Money was, in the new President's philosophy, a means to an end rather than an end in itself. If one kind of money contributed more to recovery than another, then by pragmatic test the "soundness" of that money was demonstrated.

If Roosevelt's ideas on money were unorthodox, they were moderate when contrasted with the extreme inflationary demands of many members of his party. Senator Burton K. Wheeler of Montana had revived Bryan's old demand for the free and unlimited coinage of silver at the ratio of sixteen to one. An amendment to the Agricultural Adjustment Act that would have established the Wheeler policy failed of adoption in the Senate by only ten votes and would have passed had the administration not used its influence against it. Other inflationists sought to compel the Treasury to issue several billion dollars in greenbacks. Some form of currency or monetary experimentation was inevitable, and Roosevelt met the situation by inducing Congress to grant him wide powers with discretion to choose whatever procedure seemed best.

Having obtained a grant of power over the monetary system unprecedented in American history, Roosevelt proceeded cautiously. He shunned both the greenback and free-silver panaceas. Instead, he continued with the policy upon which he had embarked during the first week after his inauguration—that of passive devaluation of the dollar. It will be remembered that the Emergency Banking Act had given the President power to control transactions in gold. On April 5, 1933, Roosevelt ordered all persons owning gold coin, gold certificates, or gold bullion to deliver the same to the Federal reserve banks and receive in exchange an equivalent amount of any other form of coin or currency. On April 19 the Treasury announced that no further licenses for the export of gold would be granted.

These steps had a dual purpose: to reduce the value of the dollar in foreign exchange and to raise the domestic price level. The first of these goals seemed essential to the President because of the abnormal conditions of 1933. England and most of the other countries of the world had abandoned the gold standard. So long as the United States clung to it, the American dollar was expensive in terms of these foreign currencies, thus making it difficult for foreigners to buy American goods. To reduce the foreign exchange value of the dollar, therefore, would encourage American exports. The raising of the domestic price level seemed equally necessary. The downward spiral of prices made it more and more difficult for debtors to meet their obligations, besides discouraging industrialists from manufacturing for future sale and merchants from buying more than they could quickly sell. The 1933 price level could be fairly described as deflated; the policies undertaken to raise that level were more accurately labeled reflationary than inflationary. In Roosevelt's words:

> The Administration has the definite objective of raising commodity prices to such an extent that those who have borrowed money will, on the average, be able to repay that money in the same kind of dollar which they borrowed. We do not seek to let them get such a cheap dollar that they will be able to pay back a great deal less than they borrowed. In other words, we seek to correct a wrong and not to create another wrong in the opposite direction.

Obviously the cheapening of the dollar would result in a windfall to creditors if they could force their debtors to pay in gold rather than in currency. To prevent this, Congress by joint resolution of June 5, 1933, voided any clause requiring payment in gold in any past or future obligation, whether government or private. Congress' power to enact such a provision was upheld by the Supreme Court in the Gold Clause cases of 1935.

The London Economic Conference—discussed more fully in a later chapter —made it necessary for Roosevelt to decide early in July, 1933, whether recovery could best be served by entering a stabilization agreement with other nations or by continuing his policy of lowering the value of the dollar and raising the domestic price level. He chose the latter path despite its lethal effect on the Conference.

Until October, 1933, the administration's policy was one of passive devaluation. That is, the dollar was simply divorced from gold with the intention of allowing its value to sink in terms of other currencies. But during the autumn the President, presumably under the influence of Professor George F. Warren of Cornell University, initiated a more aggressive campaign to achieve his aims. The Reconstanction Finance Corporation began to buy gold at a price substantially above the world market. The first purchases were at $31.36 per ounce. The price was gradually raised until in January, 1934, it reached $34.45. In view of the fact that an ounce of gold before March 4, 1933, had been worth $20.67, this was equivalent to a devaluation of the dollar by approximately 40 per cent.

This experiment was terminated by the Gold Reserve Act of January 30, 1934.[7] By presidential proclamation of January 31 the weight of the gold dollar was finally fixed at 15 5/21 grains nine-tenths fine. Measured by the old gold dollar (25.8 grains), the new dollar was worth 59.06 cents; gold was priced at $35 an ounce as against the old price of $20.67.

Although the President still retained power to change the weight of the dollar within a designated range, he abstained from any further action. Instead, administration policy was now to hold the dollar steady through the operations of a stabilization fund. When in 1936 a new wave of competitive currency depreciation threatened to develop, the United States joined Britain and France in an agreement to cooperate in maintaining an equilibrium among their respective currencies.

It is impossible to say that the gold policy either succeded or failed. Domestic prices rose and exports increased, but many factors other than monetary policy were at work. Furthermore, prices did not follow a uniform course. While manufactured goods held their price gains of the spring and early summer of

---

[7] Title to all gold owned by the Federal reserve banks was transferred to the United States Treasury in return for dollar certificates; gold coin was abolished as a component of the American monetary system, but gold in bullion form was to be held in the Treasury as a reserve against the currency; the President was authorized to fix the gold content of the dollar between 50 and 60 per cent of its old weight; $2 billion of the profit accruing to the Treasury through the revaluation of its gold holdings was to be utilized as a stabilization fund to enable the Treasury to maintain the dollar at a reasonable ratio with foreign currencies through operations in the foreign exchange market.

1933, agricultural prices, after a rapid upward spurt, drifted downward again for the balance of the year. Experience with the gold-purchase plan seemed to indicate that the general price level did not respond as directly to a change in the gold value of the dollar as the Warren school of theorists had believed. Too many factors—among them the volume of credit, the rate of government spending, the supply of and demand for goods, the activities of speculators—were at work.

Perhaps the most serious criticism to be made of the gold policy is that it represented a type of economic nationalism all too common in the world of 1933. To be sure, the steps that the United States took in the foreign exchange market were essentially defensive since most of the other nations had already resorted to currency depreciation, but the American policy was, nevertheless, a source of anxiety to other countries. Despite world-wide restrictions on transactions in gold, the purchasing program drew an abnormally large proportion of the world's gold supply to the United States. In terms of domestic policies, Roosevelt's unorthodoxy on the monetary question cost him much of the business support he had enjoyed during the early weeks of his administration. Conservatives never forgave the President for abandoning the gold standard in favor of what Al Smith called the "baloney dollar."

On the other hand, monetary experimentation had at least one healthy result. Most of the predictions regarding the dire results that would follow any deviation from the old gold standard proved to be groundless. When Americans learned that life went on as usual even when they could not redeem their currency in gold coin, another inhibiting fear that had shackled the country in 1932 was conquered.

The administration's silver policy, although bearing points of resemblance to the gold plan, had this fundamental difference: it was forced upon the President somewhat against his will. Senators and Represenatives from silver-producing states were anxious to remonetize silver in order to rescue the white metal from its disastrously low price at the beginning of 1933. Their position in Congress was strong because they held the balance of power between the inflationists and the anti-inflationists. When the President showed little inclination to use his optional powers, the silverites demanded mandatory legislation. They soon compelled Roosevelt to make important concessions out of fear that, if he failed to do so, some much more drastic step might be forced upon him.

The silverites won their most important victory in the passage of the Silver Purchase Act of June 19, 1934. Congress fixed the objective of increasing the proportion of silver to gold in the national monetary stocks until one quarter of such stocks was in silver. The Treasury was directed to purchase domestic and foreign silver until either the prescribed proportion of the two metals was reached or the price of silver rose above its monetary value of $1.293 per ounce.

As a result of this legislation, the Treasury was obliged to buy the entire output of the domestic silver mines at an artificially high price and to make extensive purchases of foreign silver as well. The policy made grave difficulties for China, Mexico, and other countries on a silver standard. Among its few satisfactory results was that of creating foreign purchasing power for the benefit of American exporters.

The Second New Deal

The nation's psychological response to the Hundred Days was striking. Most of the dark pessimism of the preceding winter was overcome, and there was general belief that recovery would now be both speedy and complete. Stock-market prices rose rapidly, and industrial activity expanded greatly. Much of this activity, however, was speculative in character. Manufacturers and merchants, anticipating higher costs, were filling their warehouses with products they hoped to sell at higher prices. Since purchasing power had not yet been created to sustain this higher level of production, business activity began to decline again during the summer and fall of 1933.

The failure of the New Deal to bring an immediate restoration of prosperity had inevitable consequences. Roosevelt felt under compulsion to move on to further experiments in priming the economic pump. Meanwhile, business was in a state of cranky convalescence—no longer fearing the worst, but irritable with Doctor New Deal because recovery was not more rapid. It soon became evident that the era of good feeling under which the Democratic administration had begun could not last much longer.

In November, 1934, the voters had their first opportunity to register their opinion of the New Deal. The results were a Roosevelt triumph. The Democratic majority in the Senate increased from 22 to 42 and in the House from 191 to 209.

Strengthened by this victory, Roosevelt obtained from Congress in 1935 and 1936 the enactment of a legislative program comparable in importance to the measures of 1933. But not for this reason alone were the policies now instituted often described as the Second New Deal. They represented an important shift of emphasis. The First New Deal had been dedicated primarily to recovery, and only incidentally to reform. The emphasis was now reversed. "When a man is convalescing from illness," Roosevelt declared in his first message to the new Congress, "wisdom dictates not only cure of the symptoms, but removal of their cause." The administration had shifted to the left by this time; under increasing attack from business, it derived its most dependable support from labor. The shift had its visible embodiment in the resignation of such conservative advisers as Raymond Moley, General Johnson, and George Peek.

Most prominent among the newer faces were Harry Hopkins and two able protégés of Professor Frankfurter, Thomas Corcoran and Benjamin Cohen.

Many factors now contributed to shaping a more far-reaching program of reform. The hope that the social objectives of the administration could be largely achieved through NRA was destroyed by increasing discontent with that agency and its overthrow through an adverse Supreme Court decision. Still dissatisfied with the degree of economic recovery, the administration felt the need for more aggressive moves to create purchasing power. There was, moreover, growing danger that discontented groups would abandon the New Deal and throw their support to such extremist programs as those being agitated by Huey Long, Dr. Townsend, Upton Sinclair, and Father Coughlin.

Among the fruits of the Second New Deal were the establishment of a large work-relief program, the passage of the National Labor Relations and Social Security Acts, and the enactment of strict regulation of the electrical utilities business.

Work for the Unemployed

One of the most troublesome problems confronting the Roosevelt administration was continued large-scale unemployment. Although the number of workers in private industry rose slowly from depression lows, the population was meanwhile increasing and jobs were not being created as rapidly as new workers were available to fill them. Throughout the eight years, 1933–40, unemployment figures did not drop below 8 million and they averaged about 10 million.

As measures for dealing with unemployment, both PWA and FERA had serious limitations. Large public-works projects were expensive, they were not always available in the areas of greatest economic need, and they gave employment almost exclusively to construction workers, whereas many of the unemployed were to be found among the white-collar group—clerks, teachers, musicians, actors, artists, and even doctors and nurses. On the other hand, most of the locally administered FERA money went for direct relief—doles that provided only a bare subsistence. Such relief was cheaper in money than any other form of assistance, but it was expensive in other terms. The reliefers were given no real purchasing power that would stimulate the country's economy, while protracted idleness deprived them both of the will to work and whatever skills they might once have possessed.

A short experiment in still a third method of dealing with the unemployment problem had been attempted during the winter of 1933–34, when faltering recovery had seemed to need a shot of adrenalin. Given charge of a so-called Civil Works Administration (CWA) in November, 1933, Harry Hopkins provided work for more than 4 million men by January, 1934. Administered directly by Federal employees, the CWA offered temporary employment in painting and repairing school houses, resurfacing highways, building flood control works, and similar projects of civic value.

The CWA experiment, terminated in the spring of 1934, had been sufficiently successful to serve as the inspiration for a much more ambitious program during the period of the Second New Deal. On May 6, 1935, the Works Progress Administration (WPA) was created with Hopkins as Administrator. Hopkins acted with characteristic speed in setting up his organization; by December almost 2.7 million were receiving employment through this new agency. Up to October 1, 1937, the WPA built 11,000 public buildings and repaired 30,000 others, laid over 43,000 miles of roads and repaired 116,000 miles, and constructed thousands of bridges, culverts, sidewalks, athletic fields, playgrounds, swimming pools, dams, levees, and sewers. Women were given work on sewing and canning projects; doctors and nurses operated clinics; musicians were organized in WPA orchestras, which gave free concerts; actors, writers, and teachers were given similar opportunities to practice their professions. Those employed in these multifarious activities received wages which were substantially higher than the payments under the FERA had been, but

Harry Hopkins and Daughter, Diane, President Roosevelt, Secretary of State Hull, and Secretary of the Treasury Morgenthau. (Acme.)

not so high as under either the PWA or CWA projects, on which the general rule had been to pay the prevailing rate. The lower wages of WPA were set both as a measure of economy and as an inducement to the workers to obtain private employment wherever possible.

A particularly disquieting problem was that of young people in families on relief. The number of these was estimated to be about 2.9 million in 1935. The natural course for such youngsters was to quit school and look for jobs. But this was deplored both because it aggravated the unemployment problem and because it interrupted the education of the young people, with potentially serious results for themselves and the community. To deal with this situation, a National Youth Administration (NYA) was established within the WPA. High-school and college students were given part-time employment on projects helpful to the institutions they were attending. The amount that could be earned was small, but it was enough in many cases to make it possible for the students to stay in school.

New Deal spending was hotly attacked and as resolutely defended. Critics asserted that much of the work relief was expended for what some cynic named "boondoggling"—made work of no real value. Popular jokes depicted the WPA worker as leaning on his shovel much more than he dug with it. It was alleged that relief spending jeopardized the solvency of the Federal government and was manipulated to serve political purposes. But New Deal supporters, while not claiming that all WPA projects were worthwhile or all WPA workers were conscientious, asserted that no government responsibility was more important than that of preventing suffering. The great justification of the Hopkins program was that it served this end and at the same time produced in the aggregate an immense amount of useful work. The cost was well within the capacity of the government and small enough when compared with what would be expended in a wartime emergency. Politics and graft undoubtedly existed in some local WPA situations, but defenders of the agency argued that such abuses were really not very great in view of the magnitude of the program.

The End of NRA

Only for a brief period did NRA enjoy almost universal support. As time went on, the experiment was the target for increasingly serious criticism. Employers protested that the agency was pro-labor; union leaders that it was pro-management. Small businessmen were divided in their attitudes. Many operators of small coal mines and sawmills were saved from disaster; many small merchants were grateful for NRA protection against loss leaders and other cutthroat competitive practices. Nevertheless, the codes were often bitterly resented. The wage and hour requirements were more burdensome to small employers than to large, while big business was much better represented than small in the formulation of codes and in their administration by industry-designated code authorities.

Business, an Almost Unwilling Groom. But you see he met her only a few days ago. (By Darling in the *New York Herald Tribune*.)

Because of this widespread criticism, Roosevelt appointed in the spring of 1934 a National Review Board under the chairmanship of Clarence Darrow, famous criminal lawyer. Greatly to the disappointment of NRA officials, the Darrow Board ignored the very considerable body of evidence showing that codes had protected small business and concentrated exclusively on assembling evidence that pointed to the contrary tendency. The result was not a judicious appraisal of the actual situation, but a blistering indictment of the whole experiment. Enemies of NRA gave great publicity to the adverse findings of this report, yet laid little stress on its most remarkable conclusion—that oppression of small businessmen was inevitable under capitalism and that the only answer was socialism.

Meantime, consumers had their own grievances against NRA. Just how much of the sharp price advances in many areas was fairly attributable to the codes and how much to other factors it is impossible to say; consumer resentment, however, was focused almost exclusively on NRA. The administration realized the seriousness of this resentment, but attempts to protect the consumer only had the effect of alienating the industrialists.

The decline in NRA's popularity was a serious matter. The agency's striking success in obtaining the initial cooperation of the business world resulted from its overwhelming public support during the first months. Fear of public opinion was likewise the most powerful force in gaining general compliance with code provisions. A threat to deprive a violator of his Blue Eagle usually brought him into line. As criticism of the NRA increased, however, more and more businessmen felt that they could abrogate code provisions with impunity. Since open defiance of the codes threatened the whole experiment, the agency was impelled to order "crackdowns" and to prosecute more and more offenders. But such attempts at coercion angered still further the agency's critics.

Whether to continue the experiment after the expiration of the original law in June, 1935, was one of the principal problems confronting Congress in the spring of that year. The President asked that the act be extended for an additional two years, asserting that the fundamental purposes and principles were sound and that to abandon them would "spell the return of industrial and labor chaos." He acknowledged, however, the need for amendments that would include a more definite statement by Congress "in order to clarify the legislative purpose and to guide the execution of the law."

Even to this reformed NRA there was strong opposition in Congress. Some kind of extension, however, would probably have been provided had not a decision of the Supreme Court on May 27, 1935, applied the *coup de grace* to the whole undertaking. In the case of A. L. A. Schechter Poultry Corporation v. United States, the Court unanimously reversed the decision of the lower courts under which the defendants had been convicted of violating the provisions of the live-poultry code. The Court declared that the National Industrial Recovery Act was unconstitutional insofar as it delegated legislative power to the President without adequate standards to guide him and insofar as it provided for Federal regulation of hours and wages in enterprises like the Schechter concern whose business was entirely intrastate in character.

From the beginning NRA had been handicapped by the incompatibility of its two main objectives—that of stimulating recovery and that of drafting rules of permanent benefit. The first called for the utmost haste; the second for caution and deliberation. Given the conditions of 1933, it is not surprising that the demands of recovery received priority. The result was that NRA made a considerable success of its short-term objectives—speeding production, increasing purchasing power, and establishing a truce on cutthroat competition. But the atmosphere of excitement and haste that contributed to immediate success was prejudicial to the achievement of the agency's long-range objectives. The codes attempted too much and contained too many ill-advised provisions. The resulting deterioration of public support even more than the Supreme Court's decision foretold NRA's eventual collapse. Nevertheless, the agency's failure was far from complete. Public opinion and subsequent legislation consolidated many of the gains that had been made: the abolition of child labor, the recognition of labor's right to organize, the establishment of certain standards of maximum hours and minimum wages, and the restraint upon ruthless exploitation of the country's natural resources.

Labor's Right to Organize

The overthrow of NRA made it essential for the Roosevelt administration to clarify its labor policy. After a long period of retreat, the unions were now attempting a militant advance. Total union membership, which had fallen below 3 million in 1933, jumped to 4.2 million in 1935. Much of this growth could be attributed to the famous Section 7-A of the National Industrial Recovery Act, which declared "employees shall have the right to organize and bargain collectively through representatives of their own choosing," and no employee "shall be required as a condition of employment to join any company union or to refrain from joining . . . a labor organization of his own choosing."

Union organizers made skillful use of this declaration of policy. In the coal mines, for example, the news was carried from pit to pit with large banners bearing the legend: "President Roosevelt wants you to join a union." The workers' response astonished even the labor leaders themselves. Not only did total membership increase rapidly, but hundreds of local unions were organized in the mass production industries where there had been practically no earlier unionization.

But labor's rejoicing proved to some extent premature. Many employers sought to fulfill the collective-bargaining stipulation of Section 7-A by encouraging company unions. These more than doubled in number between 1933 and 1935, while their membership rose from less than 1.3 million in 1932 to about 2.5 million. Moreover, despite NRA, the most resolute of anti-union employers succeeded in preventing organization altogether.

Labor protested against many of the code provisions. They asserted that in both the drafting and administering of these management was given too much power. In the wage and hour provisions, labor usually fared poorly in the unorganized industries. Innumerable disputes arose between AFL unions, unaffiliated independent unions, and company unions over the right to bargain for employees in particular plants. This led in some cases to assigning the rival unions proportional representation in a specially created bargaining agency and in others to dealing separately with majority and minority groups.

Such grievances as these, plus wage and hour demands to be expected during a period of increasing production and rising prices, led to an epidemic of strikes in 1933 and 1934. Since these threatened to retard recovery and injure the NRA experiment, President Roosevelt appointed in August, 1933, a National Labor Board, composed of three representatives of industry and three of labor with Senator Wagner of New York as impartial chairman. This body heard complaints, settled strikes, and conducted elections to determine collective-bargaining representatives. The board was a purely executive creation under the general authority of NRA, but so long as the prestige of the latter was high, the panel had a reasonable degree of success in its activities. During 1934, however, when NRA was under severe attack, the board suffered a series of defeats due to the unwillingness of management and labor to accept its jurisdiction and to abide by its decisions.

In their disillusionment, unionists dubbed NRA the "National Run Around" and demanded additional protection for their right to organize. A bill for this purpose, introduced by Senator Wagner in 1934 without the President's support, failed of passage. Reintroduced the next year, the measure won increased support in the two Houses of Congress. Such was the situation when the Supreme Court's Schechter decision destroyed NRA. Left now without even the safeguards of Section 7-A, labor redoubled its efforts. The result was the enactment on July 5, 1935, of the Wagner-Connery or National Labor Relations Act.

The law authorized the establishment of a new National Labor Relations Board (NLRB) of three members appointed by the President with the consent of the Senate. The general guarantee of Section 7-A was re-enacted in almost identical language, but it was now implemented with a series of specific rules. Five unfair labor practices were listed; employers were forbidden: (1) to interfere with employees in the exercise of the right to bargain collectively; (2) to dominate any labor organization or give financial support to it; (3) to discriminate in dealing with employees in order to encourage or discourage membership in any labor organization; (4) to discriminate against any employees who filed charges or testified before the NLRB; and (5) to refuse to bargain collectively with the representatives of their employees. The act provided that in any bargaining unit the representatives chosen by the majority should be the exclusive representatives of all the employees. In case of dispute, the NLRB was authorized to certify the proper employee representatives. To assist in this decision, the board might take a secret ballot or utilize any other suitable method. The NLRB could issue "cease and desist" orders against employers who violated the act, but these were enforceable only through petition to the Federal courts.

The National Association of Manufacturers and other business spokesmen protested vigorously against this legislation. They contended that it was one-sided since it defined unfair conduct on the part of the employers without providing parallel rules for the unions themselves. Asserting that the act was unconstitutional, most large employers determined to ignore it pending a test of the legal issues. As a result, the law was largely inoperative during the next two years. In 1937, however, the Supreme Court upheld its validity in Associated Press v. NLRB, NLRB v. Jones and Laughlin Steel Corporation, and several other cases.

With its authority supported by the courts, the NLRB became a powerful body. By the end of 1939 it had ordered the disestablishment of 340 company unions. The formation of new organizations of this type practically ceased, while the old company unions that survived were reorganized to give them more independence. Meantime, general trade-union membership continued to grow, until in 1941 about 11 million workers were affilliated with some organization. This growth was not, of course, to be attributed solely to the Wagner-Connery Act and the NLRB, but these served at least as a strong deterrent to such methods as employers had used in the past to counteract the efforts of the organizers.

Social Security

Another foundation stone of the Second New Deal was the Social Security Act of August, 1935. Behind its passage lay a reversal in prevailing American opinion. Old-age pensions, unemployment insurance, and provisions for sickness and accident benefits under government administration had been commonplace in Europe before World War I. But most Americans persisted in the belief that saving against old age and misfortune was an individual problem. The depression provided a cruel disillusionment. Thrifty citizens saw their life savings swept away by bank failures, while the average individual's inability to guarantee his own security in a complex economic system was demonstrated in many other ways as well. By 1932 there was a widespread demand for government action. The AFL passed resolutions asking unemployment insurance with compulsory payments by employers and the state—reversing its earlier hostility to the proposal—and the Democratic National Platform included a plank advocating both unemployment and old-age insurance under state laws.

But building a social security system exclusively on state legislation offered many difficulties. Each state hesitated to burden employers with payroll taxes lest factories be moved to other states where no such levies were imposed. Some Federal program to coordinate action on a national basis seemed to be required. To study the problem, President Roosevelt appointed in June, 1934, a Committee on Economic Security with Secretary of Labor Perkins as chairman and a number of advisory groups composed of technical experts. In January, 1935, the President transmitted to Congress this committee's recommendations for joint Federal-state action.

Bringing the Prodigal Home. (By Bishop in the *St. Louis Star-Times*.)

None too early was the administration taking up the problem. Local clubs throughout the country were agitating for the Townsend Old Age Revolving Pension Plan, a scheme concocted by Dr. Francis A. Townsend, under which every individual over sixty years of age was to be paid $200 each month to be entirely spent within the next thirty days. Thus at one step, so its sponsors argued, security for the aged would be provided along with perpetual prosperity for the country. Upton Sinclair's EPIC (End Poverty in California) plan would levy special taxes to pay $50 a month to the needy of sixty years of age and older. Even more extreme programs were being advanced by Senator Huey Long of Louisiana with his Share-the-Wealth plan for guaranteeing to each citizen an income of $5,000 annually and by the radio priest, Father Charles E. Coughlin of Royal Oak, Michigan, with his demands for radical inflation. In comparison with such reckless proposals as these the recommendations of the administration seemed mild. The Social Security Act passed Congress by substantial majorities and received the President's signature on August 14, 1935.

The new law dealt with old-age pensions, unemployment insurance, public assistance to the needy aged, the needy blind, and dependent children, and additional aid for maternal and child welfare services and public health facilities. The only one of these programs exclusively administered by the Federal government was that providing for old-age insurance. All employers and employees except those in certain exempted categories were required to pay a payroll tax equivalent to 1 per cent of the salary of each employee. This tax was to be gradually increased until it reached 3 per cent in 1949. These revenues would be used to build up reserves in the Federal Treasury out of which after January 1, 1942, retired workers were to receive pensions of $10 to $85 monthly, depending upon their average wages and the length of time they had been contributing.

Provision for unemployment insurance was left to the states, but in order to encourage the establishment of such plans, a Federal unemployment tax was levied upon all employers—except those in exempted categories. The employers were to be allowed a credit up to 90 per cent for any contributions made to state unemployment funds. From the 10 per cent retained in such cases, the Federal government made grants to the states to assist them with administrative expenses. This inducement proved adequate to obtain the enactment of unemployment insurance laws in all the states by July 31, 1937.

In other sections the Social Security Act provided for Federal grants-in-aid up to $15 per month for states that would match this contribution and administer a program of public assistance to old people in need of relief who were not covered by the insurance plan. Similar Federal grants were available to states for aiding the blind and dependent children. Federal aid on a somewhat different basis was extended for certain health and welfare activities and for vocational rehabilitation.

The law was criticized in various quarters. Employers complained of their new tax burdens and bookkeeping problems. Liberals were displeased because agricultural laborers, domestics, and many others had not been included and because the benefits were small. Economists considered the payroll tax as deflationary in effect and unnecessarily heavy, since the Federal government with its power to tax was not under the same necessity as private insurance companies to accumulate huge reserves.

Whatever the misgivings about details, social security in principle soon won general acceptance. Republican efforts during the campaign of 1936 to turn the workers against the law found little response, and it became apparent that the popular demand was not for repeal but for liberalization. In 1939 Congress enlarged the benefits and provided for protecting the widow and children of the worker in case of his death.

Regulation and Reform

Some of the most important New Deal legislation dealt with the protection of depositors, investors, and consumers from abuses to which the depression had called attention.

The Glass-Steagall Banking Act of June, 1933, strengthened the banking structure with three principal provisions: the Federal reserve banks were given enlarged powers to curb speculative expansion of credit by member banks; commercial banks were prohibited from engaging in investment banking or maintaining security affiliates; and a Federal Deposit Insurance Corporation (FDIC) was established to guarantee despositors against losses to the extent of $2,500. Although somewhat skeptically regarded at first, the insurance of bank deposits proved entirely feasible. The coverage was increased to $5,000 in 1934 and to $10,000 in 1950.

No area of economic life was more in need of regulation and reform than the business of trading in securities. Elementary safeguards, which would assure the investor of adequate information, had never been set up in the United States, even though England had had such laws since 1844. Shocking abuses were revealed in the investigations of the Senate Committee on Banking and Currency for which Ferdinand Pecora of New York served as counsel. The committee's hearings, which began in 1932 and continued until 1934, prepared the ground for the banking legislation just described and also for the Securities Act of 1933 and the Securities and Exchange Act of 1934.

These new laws added another regulatory body, the Securities Exchange Commission (SEC), to the galaxy of Federal agencies. Corporations whose securities were traded on the exchanges were required to register with the SEC and provide accurate and up-to-date information. These requirements were particularly stringent in the case of new issues. Although they did not guarantee the investor against loss, they did ensure that he would have access to a certain minimum of reliable information. The SEC was also given broad powers to curb manipulations and other abuses in the stock market. The Federal Reserve Board and the SEC were both given important powers in fixing margin requirements and otherwise controlling brokers' loans.

The New York Stock Exchange, jealous of its powers of self-government, regarded the new regulatory body with great suspicion. This was somewhat dissipated through the cautious policy of SEC's first chairman, Joseph P. Kennedy, who had been himself a successful trader. Under neither Kennedy nor James M. Landis, the second SEC chairman, however, did the Exchange take effective steps to reform itself. The situation came to a showdown in 1937, when William O. Douglas took over as chairman of the commission. Douglas insisted that the Exchange be completely reorganized to take control out of the hands of men who were dealing in stocks primarily on their own account and to place it with those doing business with the general public. This proposal found a sympathetic response among an insurgent faction within the Exchange itself, but was bitterly opposed by the Old Guard. At this juncture, however, came a shocking revelation of the abuses possible under the old system. Richard

Whitney, a former president of the Exchange, was indicted for grand larceny on charges of having misappropriated his customers' securities over a period of many months. Fearing new regulatory laws in the face of these disclosures, Old Guard resistance collapsed and the New York Stock Exchange was completely reorganized, with William M. Martin, Jr., who had been a leader in the reform movement, as its new president.

Additional responsibilities were entrusted to the SEC by the Public Utility Holding Company Act of 1936, which required all public-utility holding companies to register and file specified information on their corporate organization. As soon as practicable after January 1, 1938, the SEC was to require each holding company to limit its operation to a single integrated public-utility system, although permission might be granted to control more than one system if such control was necessary to economical management, was exercised over a contiguous geographical area, and did not constitute so large a combination as to impair localized management, efficient operation, or effective regulation. Even in the case of integrated systems, however, the new legislation did not allow holding companies beyond the second degree.[8]

One of the most bitter battles of the thirties was fought over this legislation. To liberals, utility abuses had been a familiar story since 1928, when the FTC began its important investigation of the industry, and the law of 1936 contained only the minimum safeguards that the situation demanded. But the corporations under attack put up a desperate defense. They protested that the outlawing of non-integrated companies and companies pyramided beyond the second degree was a "death sentence." Congress was deluged with telegrams of protest from investors, but a Senate investigation, aggressively conducted by Senator Hugo Black of Alabama, revealed that many of the messages had originated with holding-company lobbyists rather than their supposed senders.

The corporations' resistance to the measure did not end with its passage. Most of them refused to register with the SEC until the validity of this requirement was affirmed by the Supreme Court in the Electric Bond and Share case in 1938. In actually enforcing the "death sentence," the commission proceeded cautiously and sought to promote voluntary reorganization to as large a degree as possible. Less publicized but more immediately effective provisions of the law authorized the SEC to discourage the issuance of unnecessarily risky securities and the assumption of fixed charges beyond the normal earning capacity of the companies.

The principle of government regulation already established in other areas was strengthened by the establishment of the Federal Communications Commission (FCC) in 1934 to supervise the telephone, telegraph, and radio industries,

---

[8] This meant that an operating company might be controlled by a holding company and this first holding company by a second, but further pyramiding was prohibited.

and by the much expanded powers given to the Federal Power Commission by the Federal Power Act of 1935. Consumers were given greater protection through the passage of the Food, Drug, and Cosmetic Act of 1938, a considerably stronger law than the pioneer act of 1906.

Problems of the Budget

The New Deal was expensive. Between March, 1933, and December, 1936, $13.2 billion was added to the national debt, whose total rose to $33.9 billion. This sum was by no means unmanageable. As a matter of fact, through lower interest rates, the Treasury was able to reduce the annual carrying charges so that it cost the Federal government less for interest payments in 1936 than it had in 1934. The continuing deficit was, nevertheless, embarrassing to an administration that had come to power on a platform pledging economy. To emphasize the emergency character of the excess spending, Treasury reports differentiated between ordinary expenditures and such recovery and relief items as agricultural aid, relief, public works, homeowners aid, and the RFC. The point was stressed that the ordinary budget was in balance and that borrowing was necessitated entirely by the relief items. The administration argued that as national income increased, emergency expenditures could be tapered off while revenue would automatically increase until the budget was balanced again.

In his effort to keep the ordinary budget in balance, Roosevelt obtained the enactment of new tax levies and resisted pressure to restore the cuts that had been made in 1933 in the salaries of Federal employees and in benefit payments to the veterans. But on the economy issue Congress rebelled. On March 28, 1934, the Independent Offices Appropriations Act—passed over the President's veto—reduced the maximum pay cut for government employees from 15 per cent to 10 per cent from February 1, 1934, to June 30, 1934, and to 5 per cent thereafter. This final 5 per cent cut was ended on July 1, 1935. Meantime, pressure from the veterans' lobby had resulted in restoring their benefit payments.

The most serious issue involving the veterans was the increasing demand for immediate payment of the bonus. In 1935 Congress passed a measure that would have authorized the issuance of Treasury notes or greenbacks to pay the full maturity value of the certificates. Not only did Roosevelt veto the measure, but he went before Congress in person on May 22, 1935, to state his objections. His principal argument was that the government's obligation during the depression was to all the unemployed and that able-bodied veterans ought not to be entitled to special treatment. The House voted 322 to 98 to override the veto, but in the Senate the President's action was sustained, although 54 Senators favored overriding the veto to the 40 who supported it.

Roosevelt's opposition only delayed the measure's passage. In January, 1936, a new bill, the Adjusted Payment Compensation bill, passed Congress. In its latest form the project was less objectionable than the 1932 or 1935 versions since it eliminated the inflationary provision for paying the bonus in green-backs and stipulated that the veterans should receive redeemable, nine-year, interest-bearing bonds. Although the President still refused to approve the measure, it was enacted into law over his veto by overwhelming votes. Congressional generosity had made the government liable to immediate demands of about $2.4 billion,[9] and of this total the veterans collected about $1.7 billion during the course of the next few months.

The 1936 Boom

Whether as a result of the New Deal, as the administration supporters insisted, or in spite of the New Deal, as Republican critics charged, the fact was undeniable that by Election Day, 1936, the country was enjoying a substantial degree of prosperity. National income had been $41 billion in 1932; it was $64 billion in 1936. Industrial production by December, 1936, was not only double the 1932 level, but somewhat higher than it had been in the fabulous year of 1929. In October, 1936, Roosevelt was able to announce that for the first time in fifty-five years an entire twelve months had passed without a single national bank failure.

Conditions were sufficiently good to assure the triumphant re-election of the President. But New Deal policies had, nevertheless, aroused opposition in many influential quarters and bitter battles lay ahead.

[9] This was a larger sum than provided for in the 1935 bill because Congress was forgiving the interest on sums the veterans had borrowed against their certificates since 1931.

20

New Deal on the Defensive

The years 1936 to 1939 witnessed a bitter struggle between the Roosevelt liberals and their conservative critics. It was a fight that crossed party lines, with many one-time Republicans supporting the President while right-wing Democrats rebelled against his leadership. The first round of the battle, the election of 1936, was won by Roosevelt in decisive fashion, but succeeding rounds were less astutely fought. In the struggle for judicial reform, in the attempted purge of the right-wing Democrats, and in the Congressional election of 1938 the President suffered setbacks. Despite minor victories, however, the conservatives were not able to regain control of the government nor to force the reversal of any basic New Deal policy. On the contrary, new legislation during the second Roosevelt administration extended government regulation still further in several directions.

The Election of 1936

The first determined effort to unseat the Roosevelt faction was through the organization of the Liberty League in August, 1934. The Du Ponts and other wealthy industrial and financial leaders provided the movement with ample funds, while conservative Democrats like Alfred E. Smith, ex-Governor Joseph B. Ely of Massachusetts, and Jouett Shouse, former chairman of the Democratic Executive Committee, cooperated in trying to break the President's hold over his own party. Although the League's activities were unsuccessful in the Congressional election of 1934, it redoubled its efforts the next year. The climax of the campaign occurred in January, 1936, when Al Smith belabored the administration for an hour to the delight of a banquet hall full of rich Liberty Leaguers in Washington. Nevertheless, the affair had unexpected repercussions. No less than twelve members of the Du Pont family had been counted among Smith's audience, and the spectacle of the rich and privileged now making a hero of the Happy Warrior whom most of them had opposed in 1928 appeared to the rest of the country as ridiculous.

As the Liberty League lost ground, wealthy anti-New Dealers turned to other expedients. Thousands of dollars were advanced to Governor Eugene Talmadge of Georgia, spokesman for the most narrow and demagogic Southern conservatives, to organize a revolt against Roosevelt in his section. It was hoped that by feeding this and other local quarrels within the Democratic party a substantial anti-Roosevelt bloc could be sent to the national convention. But Postmaster General Farley directed an astute preconvention campaign. In all the presidential preference primaries Roosevelt's undiminished popularity with the Democratic rank and file was demonstrated.

The leading contenders for the Republican nomination were former President Hoover, Senator Borah, Senator Vandenberg of Michigan, Colonel Frank Knox, formerly a Bull Mooser and now a wealthy Chicago newspaper publisher, and Governor Alfred M. Landon of Kansas. Despite the greater prominence of the other candidates, Governor Landon won the nomination on the first ballot at the Cleveland Convention. He seemed to have many assets for leading the anti-New Deal fight in 1936. Conservatives were impressed by his success in keeping the Kansas state budget in balance, while liberals accepted him because he came from the farm belt and had been a Theodore Roosevelt supporter in 1912. His background was that of a small Midwestern businessman, and the Republican leaders believed this would dramatize their contention that the New Deal was the enemy of small business. The lack of color in the candidate's personality was obvious, but it was hoped that this might be an asset if the voters were tired of Roosevelt exuberance. Besides, the ticket was balanced by nominating the aggressive Colonel Knox for the vice-presidency.

Although hopefully undertaken, the Republican campaign was ill-starred from the beginning. The party platform and the speeches of the candidates illustrated the party dilemma. The New Deal had to be denounced as a whole while it was being accepted in most of its significant parts. Democratic violation of the Constitution, extravagance, bureaucracy, and appeal to class prejudice were cited as evidence that America was "in peril." Nevertheless, the Republicans pledged themselves to the effective regulation of business, to emergency benefit payments for farmers, to guaranteeing labor's right to organize, and to relief for the unemployed. Clear-cut issues were largely confined to pledges to balance the budget immediately, to repeal the Reciprocal Trade Agreements Act, and to seek with government assistance to sell the agricultural surplus abroad.

The Democratic convention at Philadelphia was a triumph for Roosevelt. Not only were he and Garner renominated without opposition, but the platform was a thoroughly New Deal document. "We hold this truth to be self-evident," it proclaimed, "that government in a modern civilization has certain inescapable obligations to its citizens, among which are: (1) protection of the family and the home; (2) establishment of a democracy of opportunity for all the people; (3) aid to those overtaken by disaster." And the platform pointed with pride to the administration's achievements under each of these headings, while promising more progress in the future. As another New Deal triumph, selection of party nominees by a simple majority vote was substituted for the two-thirds rule.

Once again Roosevelt appeared before the convention in person to accept the nomination. The delegates were roused to great enthusiasm by the President's condemnation of "economic royalists" and by the stirring conclusion in which he declared:

> There is a mysterious cycle in human events. To some generations much is given. Of other generations much is expected. This generation of Americans has a rendezvous with destiny.

For a time, great importance was laid on the emergence of a new third party. Old-line politicians had long feared that the admirers of Huey Long, Dr. Townsend, and Father Coughlin might join forces in a single mass movement, and the formation of the Union party in June, 1936, was intended to bring about exactly this result. But several factors contributed to making the new party much less formidable than expected. In the first place, Huey Long was dead. His had been one of the most curious careers in American politics. An enormously clever and effective demagogue, he had secured election as governor of Louisiana in 1928. His political machine was corrupt and dictatorial, but he gave better roads and schools to his poor constituents. Elected United States Senator in 1930, he gained wide publicity from the start. His speeches, both in the Senate and over the radio, were rambling and violent, yet they were highly entertaining and never lacked for auditors. His "Share the Wealth" movement with its slogan "Every Man a King" won thousands of adherents in 1935, and his ambition to gain the White House had Farley and the Democratic high command seriously worried. They did not believe that Huey could achieve his goal, but they did fear that he might win enough votes to throw the election to the Republicans. In September, 1935, however, the Louisiana politician was assassinated in his home state. The Union party chose as its standard-bearer a rather drab North Dakota legislator, Representative William Lemke, hitherto little known except as an advocate of farm relief and inflation. Father Coughlin was so confident of his own influence that he promised to retire from broadcasting if Lemke did not poll at least 12 million votes, but the priest's attempts to create enthusiasm for

"Liberty Bill" were unavailing. In the end the Union party received only 900,000 votes. Small though this was when compared with Coughlin's prediction, it was larger than the 190,000 that went to Norman Thomas, the Socialist candidate, and the 80,000 to Browder, the Communist.

The only real contest was between Roosevelt and Landon, and even that proved to be a very unequal one. Despite the fact that a number of prominent Democrats followed Al Smith in "taking a walk"—deserting their party nominee and supporting Landon—the mass of the voters moved in the opposite direction. Landon's campaigning proved ineffective, while Roosevelt's was adroit and bold. When the votes were counted, Landon found himself defeated more decisively than any previous Republican candidate for the presidency. He had carried only two states and won only eight electoral votes as against Roosevelt's 523. The popular vote was: Roosevelt, 27,476,673, Landon, 16,679,583.

The Second Inaugural

Roosevelt took the presidential oath for the second time on January 20, 1937 —the first inauguration on the new date provided by the Lame Duck Amendment. The ceremony took place in a heavy rainstorm—an appropriate setting for the first act of a tempestuous period in national politics. There was little of complacency in the inaugural address. In response to his own question—have we reached "the goal of our vision"?—the President stated:

> I see a great nation, upon a great continent, blessed with a great wealth of natural resources. . . .
> But here is the challenge to our democracy: In this nation I see tens of millions of its citizens—a substantial part of its whole population—who at this very moment are denied the greater part of what the very lowest standards of today call the necessities of life. . . .
> I see one-third of a nation ill-housed, ill-clad, ill-nourished.

Obviously the second Roosevelt administration was being dedicated to new offensives under the standard of social justice. The President's conservative opponents, speculating uneasily on where the first blow would be struck, did not have long to wait. On February 5 the Chief Executive dispatched a message to Congress calling for reorganization of the entire Federal judiciary. Even a country conditioned always to expect the unexpected was stunned by the audacity of this maneuver.

The Supreme Court and the Progressive Movement

No discussion of the President's proposals and the great debate thereby precipitated would be meaningful unless the issue were placed in its historical perspective.

The power exercised by the Supreme Court in declaring Federal and state laws unconstitutional was not explicitly granted in the Constitution, and it is debatable whether the framers of that document intended the Court to perform such a function. When under the strong leadership of John Marshall the Supreme Court actually began to invalidate Federal and state laws, there were protests but the precedents for its doing so were successfully established. Nevertheless, during the first seventy years of national history the Supreme Court declared acts of Congress unconstitutional on only two occasions.

Following the Civil War, the Court became much bolder in invalidating Federal laws, taking such action in twenty-three cases between 1860 and 1900 and in thirty-five from 1900 to 1930. One of the disallowed laws, the income-tax provision of 1894, was the embodiment of a great popular demand, and the Court's decision shocked millions of citizens. The Court was accused of using its great power to shield the wealthy against paying their proper share of Federal taxes. Such censure was all the more bitter because of the increasing frequency with which the Federal judiciary was setting aside state legislation that attempted to regulate business. Between 1890 and 1937, 228 state laws were invalidated on the ground that they deprived "persons"—frequently corporations—of property "without due process of law."

By 1900 it was already apparent that the Supreme Court provided a conservative stronghold for property interests threatened through either Federal or state legislation. The progressives became increasingly dismayed over the obstacles placed in their path by the judiciary, and the recall of judges and of judicial decisions became, as we have seen, progressive demands before World War I.

Theodore Roosevelt sought to liberalize the judiciary by new appointments. In 1902 he named Oliver Wendell Holmes, Jr., of Massachusetts to the Supreme Court largely because of Holmes's prolabor decisions as a judge in his home state. Although the Rough Rider was much disappointed when the new judge dissented from the majority decision in the Northern Securities case, Holmes soon proved a liberal influence of the greatest importance. Again and again during his thirty years as a Supreme Court justice he thrilled progressives with his bold and brilliantly phrased opinions, the most memorable of them being dissents from the decisions of his more conservative colleagues. Roosevelt's other two appointments were much less effective for his purpose.

That Roosevelt named only three men to the Supreme Court in almost eight years in the White House illustrates the good fortune of the conservatives in maintaining their dominance. The conservative Taft had six opportunities to name justices during his four-year term, while the liberal Wilson had only three during the next eight years. On the other hand, the Old Guard Harding made four appointments and his successors, Coolidge and Hoover, made one and three appointments respectively. The assumption that progressive Presidents always named progressive judges and conservative Presidents conservative judges is not always valid—as the choice of the reactionary McReynolds by Wilson and the appointments of the liberals, Stone and Cardozo, by Coolidge and Hoover illustrate. Yet in general it has proved true that the chief executives have selected judges who incline toward their own philosophy of government. The jealousy with which the conservatives regarded their control of the Court was best shown by the extreme bitterness of the fight against the confirmation of Louis D. Brandeis when Wilson named this progressive lawyer from Massachusetts to the bench in 1916.

Conservative success in keeping control of the Court showed its results in that body's decisions. In an earlier section (see Chapter 2) the judicial obstacles placed in the way of state regulation of hours of labor have been discussed. Eventually the Court gave way on this issue, but it still remained hostile to minimum-wage laws, even those intended to protect women. In the case of Adkins v. Children's Hospital (1923), the Supreme Court by a vote of five to three declared unconstitutional an act of Congress establishing minimum wages for women and children in the District of Columbia. Since the line of reasoning employed by the majority made it certain that similar state laws would be invalidated, the decision stood as an effective barrier in the way of protecting workers from sweatshop conditions.

State laws regulating child labor were not interfered with, but two attempts of Congress during the Wilson administration to pass a Federal law on the subject were invalidated by the Court.[1]

Organized labor's grievances against the judiciary have been frequently alluded to, but it should be added that the Supreme Court went to the extent of invalidating Federal and state laws that had been specifically enacted to protect the right of collective bargaining. In 1908 a Federal provision prohibiting "yellow-dog" contracts between the railroads and their employees was declared unconstitutional (Adair v. United States), while in 1915 a similar state law was invalidated (Coppage v. Kansas). The Court even denied the right of a state legislature to limit the power of its own state judges to issue injunctions in labor disputes. This latter decision, handed down in 1921 in the case of Truax v. Corrigan, provoked Justice Holmes to say in his dissenting opinion:

> There is nothing that I more deprecate than the use of the Fourteenth Amendment beyond the absolute compulsion of its words to prevent the making of social experiments that an important part of the community desires, in the insulated chambers afforded by the several States, even though the experiments may seem futile or even noxious to me and to those whose judgment I most respect.

[1] Hammer v. Dagenhart (1918) and Bailey v. Drexel Furniture Company (1922).

Even during the twenties, when the progressive movement was in eclipse, the Federal judiciary was under chronic attack because of its conservatism. The platform on which LaFollette and Wheeler ran during the third-party venture of 1924 urged a constitutional amendment under which a law declared unconstitutional by the Supreme Court might be re-enacted by Congress. Senator Borah was the author of a bill that would have required the concurrence of seven members of the Court to declare an act of Congress unconstitutional. Such proposals were doomed to failure, but in 1930 the progressive bloc was able to prevent the confirmation of the supposedly antilabor John J. Parker as a Supreme Court justice and to put up a strong, though unsuccessful, fight against the confirmation of Chief Justice Hughes.

The Supreme Court and the New Deal

Not until 1934 did cases involving the New Deal begin to reach the Supreme Court. Both friends and foes of the Roosevelt measures watched eagerly for an indication of the attitude that the justices would take. Nervous New Dealers found some reassurance in the Court's decisions upholding a Minnesota mortgage-moratorium act and a New York milk-control law (Home Building and Loan Association v. Blaisdell, Nebbia v. New York). Neither case involved a Federal measure, but both involved the powers of government to deal with an economic emergency. Realistic observers noted, however, that these were both five-to-four decisions. It was obvious that four of the justices—McReynolds, Sutherland, Van Devanter, and Butler—would view any new intervention of government into the economic sphere with extreme suspicion. Those familiar with the record of the judges were not surprised at this; the Court was readily analyzed as containing four ultraconservatives (the justices just named), three liberals—Brandeis, Cardozo, and Stone—and two middle-of-the-roaders—Chief Justice Hughes and Justice Roberts. The fate of the New Deal depended largely on how the last two exercised their balance of power.

The administration received its first serious setback on January 7, 1935, in the "Hot Oil" case (Panama Refining Company v. Ryan), in which all of the Supreme Court judges except Cardozo concurred in holding section 9-A of the National Industrial Recovery Act invalid. The grounds of the decision were important since they hinged largely on the opinion that the section violated the Constitution by delegating legislative power to the Executive—the first instance of an act of Congress being set aside for this reason. Because the delegation of emergency powers to the President had been a prominent feature of the legislation of the Hundred Days, the decision had implications of the most serious kind.

The next important New Deal measure to pass under review was the Congressional resolution of June 5, 1933, under which any clause in a public or private contract specifying payment in gold was voided and the obligation was made payable dollar for dollar in any legal tender currency. The windfall to creditors and the utter financial confusion that would have followed the invalidation of this law were obvious, yet such a disaster was only narrowly averted. By five-to-four decisions on February 18, 1935, the Court upheld the resolution as regards private contracts, but denied the power of Congress to modify the obligations of United States bonds. The plantiff was not, however, allowed to recover against the government since he had not proved any actual damage.[2]

The New Deal's "Black Monday" in court came on May 27, 1935. By three unanimous decisions the Frazier-Lemke Farm Mortgage Act of 1934 was found invalid, the President's removal of William E. Humphrey from the Federal Trade Commission was declared illegal, and the general code-making procedure under NRA was ruled unconstitutional.[3] It was the last of these decisions that the President found most upsetting. Not only did it destroy an agency from which he had hoped much good could still eventuate, but, what was more serious, the Court's opinion seemed to construe the commerce clause more narrowly than any decision for decades. "We have been relegated," Roosevelt told his press conference, "to the horse-and-buggy definition of interstate commerce."

The year 1936 was equally difficult for those who had to argue New Deal cases before the courts. On January 6, the first Agricultural Adjustment Act was declared unconstitutional, with the judges dividing six to three (United States v. Butler)—perhaps the most criticized of all the anti-Roosevelt decisions. On February 17 the government won one of its few victories when the power of the TVA to sell surplus electricity generated at Wilson Dam was recognized by all the justices except McReynolds (Ashwander v. TVA). But in June the power of the SEC was narrowly circumscribed (Jones v. SEC), while a month later the New Deal suffered another major defeat in the invalidation of the first Bituminous Coal Conservation Act (Carter v. Carter Coal Company). Hughes joined the liberal minority in dissenting from this and a subsequent decision in which the New York Minimum Wage Act (Morehead v. Tipaldo) was declared unconstitutional. The latter case emphasized the predicament in which liberals now found themselves. While on the one hand the Court was setting aside Federal laws that established minimum labor standards on the ground that they invaded the powers of the states, on the other hand it was denying the power of the state legislatures to pass similar laws on the ground that these violated the Fourteenth Amendment. A legal "no man's land" had been created where neither Federal nor state governments could act.

[2] The so-called Gold Clauses Cases—Norman v. Ohio Railroad Company, Perry v. United States, etc.

[3] Louisville Bank v. Radford, Humphrey's Executor v. United States, A.L.A. Schechter Corporation v. United States.

The extent of the administration's difficulties is not adequately indicated by this account of Supreme Court cases. The lower ranks of the Federal judiciary were also largely staffed with conservatives, and these District and Circuit Court judges were no less eager to hamstring the Roosevelt reforms. Sixteen-hundred injunctions restraining officers of the Federal government from carrying out acts of Congress were granted. A variety of legal devices were resorted to by anti-New Deal lawyers to invite judicial intervention. Such agencies as the TVA, SEC, and NLRB found themselves almost powerless to carry out the functions for which they had been created.

Fall In! (By Seibel in *The Richmond Times-Dispatch.*)

The Judicial Reorganization Bill

Behind the scenes the administration was considering ways and means of removing these judicial obstacles. This study was in progress throughout the year 1936, but it was carried on very quietly because the President wanted the campaign issue of that year to be the New Deal as a whole rather than any highly controversial new proposal. The judicial issue was avoided during the campaign not only for the sake of political expediency, but because of the difficulty of framing a concrete plan. The most logical remedy appeared to be a constitutional amendment whereby the power of Congress and the state legislatures to deal effectively with twentieth-century economic problems would be affirmed in unequivocal language, but this did not seem to be practical. The drafting of an amendment acceptable to two thirds of Congress would have been difficult in the first place; its acceptance by the three quarters of the states would have been next to impossible. Another popular proposal was that of requiring seven, eight, or all of the judges to concur in a decision before the Supreme Court could invalidate a law. Roosevelt and his advisers decided, however, that any such measure would probably itself be declared unconstitutional by the justices. To other suggestions, equally serious objections were raised and, by a process of elimination, the President and Attorney General Homer Cummings hit at length on the proposal transmitted to Congress in the presidential message of February 5, 1937.

This message on "judicial reorganization" took as its thesis the necessity for legislative action to quiet complaints over "the complexities, the delays, and the expense of litigation in United States courts." The overcrowded dockets proved "the need for additional judges" in all the ranks of the Federal judiciary. "A part of the problem of obtaining a sufficient number of judges to dispose of cases," the President asserted, "is the capacity of the judges themselves. This brings forward the question of aged or infirm judges—a subject of delicacy and yet one which requires frank discussion." He then alluded to the voluntary retirement act of 1869, which permitted judges to retire on a full pension at the age of seventy. Despite this provision, many continued on the bench long past this age. In exceptional cases they retained their full mental and physical vigor, but the less fortunate ones were "often unable to perceive their own infirmities." The President's answer to the problem was embodied in the draft bill accompanying the message. It provided that, when any Federal judge attained the age of seventy and had served as judge for at least ten years and within six months thereafter had not resigned or retired, the President should appoint with the consent of the Senate one additional judge. Not more than fifty judges might be appointed under the act, and no judge might be named to the Supreme Court if the appointment would result in more than fifteen members of that body. The rest of the bill dealt with procedural reforms, most of them not very controversial in character. From the start, debate focused on the proposal to enlarge the Supreme Court.

The message of February 5 was less ably composed than most Roosevelt documents. Its best sentence asserted: "A constant and systematic addition of younger blood will vitalize the courts and better equip them to recognize and apply the essential concepts of justice in the light of the needs and the facts of an ever-changing world." But evidence of the existing Court's failure to adapt itself to new problems was not presented. Instead, the principal stress was laid upon the alleged inability of the elderly judges to keep up with their work. In later years Roosevelt himself commented: "I made one major mistake when I first presented the plan. I did not place enough emphasis upon the real mischief —the kind of decisions which, as a studied and continued policy, had been coming down from the Supreme Court."

The blunder was a serious one. Six of the nine justices of the Court were over seventy; the effect of the bill, therefore, would be to give the President six new appointments regardless of whether the elderly incumbents chose to continue to serve or to retire. The proposal was to pack the Court,[4] and the indirection of the presidential message only made the maneuver seem more Machiavellian than it actually was.

A month later in a radio address, Roosevelt argued for his plan more effectively. He charged the Court itself with violating the spirit of the Constitution by "assuming the power to pass on the wisdom of these Acts of Congress—and to approve or disapprove the public policy written into these laws." To support the accusation he quoted the dissenting opinions of the liberal justices. Facing squarely the criticism that he would be "packing the Court," he denied that he wanted to appoint justices whom he could control on specific cases and continued:

> But if by that phrase the charge is made that I would appoint and the Senate would confirm Justices worthy to sit beside present members of the Court who understand those modern conditions; that I will appoint Justices who will not undertake to override the judgment of the Congress on legislative policy; that I will appoint Justices who will act as Justices and not as legislators—if the appointment of such Justices can be called "packing the Courts," then I say that I, and with me the vast majority of the American people, favor doing just that thing—now.

This radio address came too late to overcome the bad impression caused by the deviousness of the first move. Conservatives denounced the measure in ringing terms both in and out of Congress. They warned the country that Roosevelt was attempting to dominate the judiciary and overthrow the Constitution. It was an issue tailor-made for anti-New Dealers who had long hoped to alarm the nation and precipitate a popular rebellion against the President. In newspaper editorials, over the radio, and even from the pulpit came fierce denunciations.

Insofar as these cries of alarm originated in Republican or Liberty League circles, the President could shrug them off. Again and again he had seen similar opposition develop, only to be easily overridden when the votes were counted.

---

[4] Court-packing proposals were not entirely a New Deal innovation. The Federalists were accused of altering the number of Federal judges for party advantage in 1801; the Republicans of doing so after the Civil War.

Even the revolt of conservative Democrats like Senators Carter Glass and Harry F. Byrd of Virginia was not alarming since they had opposed New Deal measures before. What the President had not anticipated was that his proposal would antagonize a dangerously large number of legislators hitherto loyal to his program. Many of these were at heart conservative and, now that the election was past, they were anxious to assert their independence of the White House. They were shocked by the President's proposal and embittered by the fact that he had presented it to Congress without previous consultation. The most unexpected blow of all came when the leadership in the antireorganization-bill fight was assumed by Senator Wheeler of Montana, who had always been regarded as a spokesman for the extreme liberals. Wheeler's position was curious. He was bitterly opposed to the Roosevelt plan as a dangerous expansion of the powers of the Executive, but he himself was the sponsor of a more radical measure—a proposed constitutional amendment that would have permitted a two-thirds Congressional vote to overrule any decision of the Court in which an act of Congress was held unconstitutional. Conservative Republicans, having learned the bitter lesson that their prominent participation in a fight against a New Deal proposal was likely to increase rather than decrease its popularity, kept in the background while the Democrats quarreled among themselves.

Public opinion, it soon developed, was sharply divided on the issue. Even the heads of the nation's law schools were of two minds. At the hearings before the Senate Judiciary Committee, the deans of Columbia, Michigan, Fordham, and New York University law schools opposed the reorganization bill; those of Yale, Northwestern, and Notre Dame supported it; so did former deans of Pennsylvania and Duke. Six New England college presidents condemned the measure, but Professors Edward S. Corwin of Princeton and Charles Grove Haines of the University of California (Los Angeles), two of the country's leading authorities on the Constitution, defended it.

Had the issue come to a vote within the first few weeks after the presidential proposal was presented, it would probably have passed by a narrow margin. Between March and June, however, developments occurring within the Supreme Court itself profoundly affected the issue.

The New Deal Becomes Constitutional

The President's reorganization proposal gave a new solidarity to the institution under attack. Brandeis, both the oldest and the most liberal justice, resented the imputation that the age of the judges prevented them from keeping up with their business, while liberal and conservative justices alike opposed the creation of new places on the bench. In answer to an inquiry from Senator Wheeler, Chief Justice Hughes composed a letter, in which Justices Van

Devanter and Brandeis concurred, defending the Court against the charge that it was slow and inefficient.

Hughes's letter gave a mighty lift to the Wheeler faction, but an even greater one followed when Justice Roberts deserted the conservative side of the bench and voted with Hughes, Stone, Cardozo, and Brandeis to uphold the constitutionality of a Washington minimum-wage law. This important decision (West Coast Hotel Co. v. Parrish) delivered on March 29 overruled the Adkins decision of 1923 and the New York Minimum Wage case of 1936.

Additional evidence that the Court could reform itself without outside assistance was offered on April 12 when a series of five-to-four decisions upheld the National Labor Relations Act.[5] Justice McReynolds in his dissenting opinions argued that principles laid down in the Schechter and Carter cases should have been followed, but Hughes and Roberts once again sided with the liberals in asserting that the labor practices involved in these cases threatened to obstruct interstate commerce and that the Federal government therefore had the power to act. A third major New Deal victory was embodied in a series of decisions upholding the Social Security Act.[6]

The President and his advisers felt their attack upon the judiciary had already brought results. They attributed the new liberalism of Chief Justice Hughes and Justice Roberts largely to the desire of these two astute men to save the Court from unwelcome change. Most commentators have agreed that such a motive was either consciously or unconsciously guiding the judges during the 1937 session. It should be pointed out, however, that Justice Roberts' shift on the issue of minimum-wage legislation occurred before the presidential message on judicial reorganization was sent to Congress. Other factors influencing the Court may have been the conclusive results of the 1936 election and a wave of strikes, which gave impressive evidence of the need for labor legislation. Moreover, the laws of the Second New Deal were drafted in less haste than those of the First and thus provided fewer grounds for their invalidation.

As a final demonstration that the Roosevelt proposal was unnecessary, Justice Van Devanter retired in June, thus opening the way for the first new appointment in five years. The justice's action was facilitated by the knowledge that under the Supreme Court Retirement Act recently passed by Congress he could leave the bench without resigning, thereby enjoying immunity from certain taxes and being assured that his compensation could never be reduced.

Death of the Court Bill

Legislators who had been supporting the reorganization bill out of a sense of loyalty rather than conviction now advised Roosevelt to abandon his project,

[5] NLRB v. Jones and Laughlin Steel Corporation, Associated Press v. NLRB, etc.
[6] Helvering v. Davis, Carmichael v. Southern Coal Company, etc.

since it had already served the purpose of inducing the Court to take a more charitable view of New Deal legislation. The President refused, however, on the grounds that the liberal margin in the Court was too narrow and uncertain. If a Constitutional "no man's land" had been eliminated, it was only to create a "Roberts' land." Even the retirement of Van Devanter did not reassure the President, because he was committed to appointing Senator Joseph Robinson of Arkansas, Democratic leader of the Upper House, to fill the vacancy. Robinson had been a thoroughly loyal New Deal legislator, but it was feared that as a judge he was likely to revert to a more conservative philosophy.

On June 14 the reorganization bill suffered a blow of staggering proportions. Seven Democrats on the Senate Judiciary Committee joined with three Republicans in a majority report against the bill (a minority of eight committee members recommended passage) and appended their names to a scathing condemnation of the project:

> We recommend the rejection of this bill as a needless, futile, and utterly dangerous abandonment of constitutional principle. . . .
> It is a measure which should be so emphatically rejected that its parallel will never again be presented to the free representatives of the free people of America.

Convinced at last that the original bill could not pass, the President assented to a modified plan under which he would make two new appointments instead of six. But the opposition was equally determined to defeat this proposal. The Senate became involved in a heated debate, and tempers on all sides were worn thin. When Senator Robinson, his strength overtaxed by the legislative battle, fell dead in his apartment, the compromise bill received its final blow.

The last chapter was written on July 22 when the Senate, by a vote of 70 to 20, recommitted the measure to the Judiciary Committee. Eventually a law providing for procedural reforms in the lower courts, but leaving the Supreme Court strictly alone, was quietly enacted into law.

The New Deal Court

The defeat of Roosevelt's reorganization plan was a great moral victory for the opponents of the New Deal. Equally important were its implications as a revolt against the President's leadership of the Democratic party. Yet it did not prevent his securing his ultimate end—the liberalization of the Supreme Court. Within the next four years Roosevelt had the opportunity to appoint not six, but seven, justices. Justice Sutherland followed Van Devanter into retirement within seven months; Cardozo died in 1938; Butler and Brandeis both retired in 1939, to be followed by McReynolds and Hughes in 1941. By the end of the latter year, Roberts and Stone were the only pre-Roosevelt appointees still on the bench.

Roosevelt's first appointment was made in August, 1937, before the excitement of the reorganization-bill controversy had died down. The naming of Senator Hugo L. Black of Alabama, one of the most ardent New Dealers, was a bitter dose for conservatives to swallow. But the tradition of senatorial courtesy led to Black's confirmation by a vote of 63 to 16. The new justice quietly took the oath and left for a European vacation before taking up his new duties. At long last the country seemed in a position to forget the court issue, when suddenly the whole controversy was reopened by newspaper articles charging Black with membership in the Ku Klux Klan and demanding his resignation. So great was the outcry that the new justice felt compelled to cut short his vacation and return home. In a radio talk he admitted that he had once accepted membership in the Klan, but asserted that this membership had terminated long ago and that he did not hold any of the racial or religious prejudices which characterized that organization.

Black's difficulties did not end with his radio statement. An attempt was made to prevent his assuming his duties through petition to the Supreme Court itself. After this motion was rejected, the new justice became the victim of a campaign charging him with incompetence. Despite all attacks, Black stuck to his post and gradually won a large measure of respect. The irrelevance of the Klan charge was demonstrated by his strongly worded decisions upholding minority rights.

No subsequent Roosevelt appointment aroused a comparable outcry. There was some opposition to Felix Frankfurter in 1941 because of the reputation for radicalism that he had gained during the Sacco and Vanzetti case, as well as during his behind-the-scenes activities as New Deal adviser. On the bench, however, Justice Frankfurter proved to be more conservative than most of the other New Deal appointees.[7] Much of the criticism of the President's policy toward the judiciary was quieted when he elevated the widely respected Harlan F. Stone of New York to the Chief Justiceship upon the retirement of Hughes in 1941.

As might be expected, the liberal trend in Supreme Court decisions begun in 1937 continued. Such important New Deal laws as the Agricultural Adjustment Act of 1938 and the Fair Labor Standards Act were upheld.[8] The unanimous approval given to the latter in the so-called Darby case of 1941 was one of the administration's greatest judicial victories because it overruled Hammer v. Dagenhart, a barrier to Federal regulation of child labor since 1918.

[7] The other new judges were Stanley Reed of Kentucky, who was elevated from the post of Solicitor General; William O. Douglas of Connecticut from the SEC; Frank Murphy of Michigan and Robert H. Jackson of New York, both former Attorneys General; and Senator James F. Byrnes of South Carolina. When in 1942 Roosevelt decided to avail himself of Byrnes's executive abilities in the war administration, he appointed Wiley B. Rutledge of Iowa, a circuit court judge, to fill the vacant place.
[8] Mulford v. Smith, United States v. **Darby.**

Executive Reorganization

Ever since Theodore Roosevelt's day the need for reorganization of the executive branch of the Federal government had been recognized. Every President thereafter had urged that something be done. Limited steps had in fact been taken, but the task was too complex for detailed Congressional legislation. Presidents Taft, Wilson, and Hoover had been in agreement on the principle that effective reform could only be secured through a grant of authority to the President. The little that they had been able to accomplish, however, was no real answer to the problem. The rapid multiplication of government activities, indeed, made the situation increasingly worse.

Consequently, on January 12, 1937, President Roosevelt sent to Congress a special message requesting legislation for the reorganization of the executive branch of the government. The charge made against his Supreme Court plan —that it represented a hastily contrived scheme upon which no sufficient advice had been sought—could not be made against this proposal. On the contrary, the President was transmitting a plan carefully formulated by a Committee on Administrative Management consisting of three of the country's leading authorities on public administration: Louis Brownlow and Charles F. Merriam of Chicago and Luther Gulick of New York. There were five major recommendations: (1) expansion of the White House staff so that the President might have a group of able assistants to keep him in touch with administrative affairs; (2) strengthening the managerial agencies of the government, particularly those dealing with the budget, with efficiency research, with personnel, and with planning; (3) extension of the merit system "upward, outward, and downward to cover practically all non-policy-determining posts," and reorganization of the civil service system under a single responsible administration; (4) overhauling the hundred independent agencies and commissions and placing them by executive order under one or another of twelve executive departments (the ten existing departments plus two new ones—Social Welfare and Public Works); and (5) reform of the auditing procedures of the government.

Because of preoccupation with the Supreme Court fight, Congress made little progress in dealing with this proposal during the 1937 session. In 1938, however, a reorganization bill passed the Senate. There were included several safeguards and certain departures from the presidential plan: no provision was made for a Department of Public Works; the regulatory commissions like the Interstate Commerce Commission were to be left alone; all executive orders issued under the act were subject to disapproval by Congress within sixty days by joint resolution. It was difficult to see how such a grant of power to the President could undermine republican government, yet such was the accusation hurled at the bill by the anti-New Dealers. The measure was labeled "a dictator bill" and all the propaganda techniques that had been so effective in the Supreme Court fight were once again employed. The House was sufficiently impressed by this clamor to kill the measure. Once again a presidential project had been defeated through defections in the Democratic ranks.

In 1939 a modified bill was passed without serious trouble. It provided for six administrative assistants to the President and directed him to formulate plans for abolishing unnecessary government agencies or for grouping and consolidating them to promote economy and efficiency. He was to transmit these reorganization plans to Congress, after which they would become effective unless the legislature within sixty days passed concurrent resolutions disapproving them. The powers granted to the President, however, fell short of what he had originally asked by failing to provide for any new executive departments, by exempting from reorganization a number of the independent boards and commissions, by not revamping the auditing system, and by not bringing the civil service system under a single administrator.

The Recession

Meantime, new economic problems had arisen to plague the administration. For a few months in late 1936 and early 1937 the administration was actually concerned about an excess of prosperity. Industrial production was high, the stock market was buoyant, and commodity prices were rising rapidly. It was feared indeed that the country might be entering upon a period of wild speculation like that of the late twenties. The administration shifted rather abruptly to deflationary policies. The WPA rolls were greatly reduced, economy was enjoined upon the government departments, and the balancing of the budget within a year was contemplated.

After August, 1937, however, the situation radically altered. Industrial production declined and prices fell. Unemployment once again became a serious problem. This new depression—or recession as the administration preferred to call it—was short-lived. Recovery began in June, 1938, and by December much of the lost ground had been regained. While it lasted, however, the setback was serious and discouraging. Inevitably it struck a damaging blow at the prestige of the Roosevelt administration.

Many economists attributed the recession to natural factors operating quite independently of government policy. Nevertheless, in the supercharged political atmosphere of 1937 the country's new economic troubles became the subject of bitter accusations. New Dealers asserted that there was a deliberate "strike of capital," that businessmen were recklessly contributing to economic distress in order to force a change of government policy. Anti-New Dealers with similar intemperance blamed the whole situation on the administration's hostility to business.

Disagreements as to the causes of the recession led to different proposals for its cure. The conservative prescription called for a halt to government spending, tax relief to the corporations, and a recess on social legislation. Without subscribing to this whole program, right-wing New Dealers like Secretary of the Treasury Morgenthau sympathized to the extent of advising economy and budget-balancing. On the other hand, more radical advisers urged completely different measures. Attributing the recession to premature reductions in relief expenditures, they argued for an enlarged spending program. Marriner S. Eccles of the Federal Reserve Board and Harry Hopkins, the WPA administrator, were spokesmen for this philosophy. Evidently reluctant to commit himself, the President allowed the recession to continue for over eight months before he appealed to Congress for funds to expand WPA and PWA activities again. But in a message of April 12, 1938, he finally indicated his acceptance of the tenets of the spending school. The country's economic troubles he attributed to the fact that "production in many important lines of goods outran the ability of the public to purchase them." This led him to assert:

> Today's purchasing power—the citizen's income of today—is not sufficient to drive the economic system at higher speed. Responsibility of government requires us at this time to supplement the normal processes and in so supplementing to make sure that the addition is adequate. We must start again on a long steady upward incline in national income. . . .
>
> Let us unanimously recognize that the Federal debt, whether it be twenty-five billions or forty billions, can only be paid if the nation obtains a vastly increased citizen income. I repeat that if this citizen income can be raised to $80 billion a year the national government and the overwhelming majority of state and local governments will be "out of the red."

Congress responded to the presidential plea by authorizing more than $5 billion in emergency expenditures. Hopkins again showed himself a master of the art of putting such a program quickly into operation. Monthly WPA expenditures during the final months of 1938 were double what they had been a year before. The PWA, administered by Secretary Ickes, also greatly increased its activities, although this was necessarily a somewhat slower process.

Increased government expenditures were paralleled by business recovery, but whether this was cause and effect depended on the point of view. The advocates of compensatory spending said it was and added that, if the government would double or triple expenditures for public projects, the unemployment problem would be completely solved. This reasoning was anathema to conservatives who insisted that, if the government would put its financial house in order, the resulting wave of confidence would ensure a really sound business recovery. They regarded the advocacy of a policy of deficit spending as evidence that the New Deal was incapable of solving the country's problems. The acrimonious debate between these two points of view was still raging when World War II completely changed the whole economic picture.

Attempted Purge

Events since the 1936 election had given additional proof of what had long been evident—the complete lack of agreement among Democrats upon basic principles. Some Democrats were advocates of increased Federal power, others clung to traditional states-rights doctrines; some championed the right of labor to organize, others desired to curb labor unions; some sought through government intervention to broaden the opportunities of the underprivileged, others wished to fortify the position of the dominant economic and social groups.

The New Deal as Don Quixote. (By Berryman
in *The Evening Star*, Washington, D.C.)

In 1938 Roosevelt attempted the herculean task of rectifying this situation. He appealed to the Democratic voters to repudiate the party conservatives and nominate only liberals. In a radio address on June 24 he asserted: "An election cannot give a country a firm sense of direction if it has two or more national parties which merely have different names but are as alike in their principles and aims as peas in the same pod."

The boldness of the President's effort was best exemplified by his address at Barnesville, Georgia, on August 11, 1938, when he appealed to the Georgia Democrats to repudiate their Senator, Walter F. George, while the latter was sitting on the platform only a few feet away. George, Roosevelt said, was his personal friend; he was a gentleman and a scholar, but on most public questions, he and the President did "not speak the same language." With equal directness Roosevelt subsequently asked for the defeat of Senator Millard Tydings of Maryland and Representative John O'Connor of New York, while requesting the approval of Senator Alben Barkley of Kentucky. These were the only contests in which Roosevelt intervened directly, but lesser administration figures became involved in a number of other primaries.

This effort to drive the conservative Democrats out of Congress was promptly labeled "a purge" by the opposition press. Had the term been intended simply in its dictionary meaning of "a cleansing," the President would presumably have been glad to accept it as descriptive of what he was attempting. But in 1938 the connotations of the word were far more extensive and unfavorable. Hitler had consolidated his position in Germany by a so-called purge; Stalin had done the same thing in the Soviet Union. Hence the use of the term in connection with Roosevelt obviously implied that he too was involved in an undemocratic attempt to crush all who opposed him. Although the President insisted that his objection to certain legislators was on the ground of their general political philosophy, his critics charged that he was taking a mean revenge against Democrats who had opposed the Supreme Court bill. Nor did the President's opponents base their condemnation merely on the motivation of his conduct; they insisted that whatever the grounds, it was wrong for a Chief Executive to interfere in such local primary contests.

Only in New York and Kentucky was Roosevelt's intervention effective. Representative O'Connor was defeated in the Democratic primary and then defeated again in the November election when he ran as a Republican, while Senator Barkley won his primary contest. But in Georgia and Maryland the proscribed candidates won decisive victories, as did practically all the other conservative Democrats marked for retirement. The primaries had as their general result the strengthening of the anti-New Deal faction.

Roosevelt's attempt to liberalize his party was badly timed. The political tide had turned in the opposite direction. This had been demonstrated in the Supreme Court and reorganization fights, and it was given further proof by the November elections of 1938. In the Senate the Democratic majority dropped from 75 seats to 69, while the Republicans were climbing from 17 to 23. In the House the Democrats dropped from 333 to 262 seats and the Republicans rose from 89 to 169. Even more impressive were Republican gubernatorial victories in a number of key states.

The Hatch Acts

The revival of the WPA plus the unusual bitterness of the political campaign of 1938 focused attention on the potentialities of the relief administration for bribing or coercing the voters. The Senate appointed the Sheppard Committee on Campaign Practices to examine the situation; this Democrat-dominated committee reported in January, 1939, that the local WPA agents in Pennsylvania, Kentucky, and Tennessee were using the relief organization to promote the

New Deal vote. While it is difficult to say how much actual political manipulation of relief there had been, there was enough evidence of irregularities to induce Congress to pass and the President to sign the Hatch Act of August 2, 1939.

Entitled "an act to prevent pernicious political activities," this measure made it unlawful for any person to coerce any other person for the purpose of influencing his vote in any Federal election. Specifically, it was to be unlawful to deprive any person of relief on account of race, creed, color, political activity, support of or opposition to any candidate or any political party in any election. The solicitation of campaign contributions from relief workers was also forbidden. But the act went beyond prohibiting abuses in relief administration to interdict all officers or employees in the executive branch of the Federal government, except policy-making officials, from taking an active part in politics.

A second Hatch Act was passed in July, 1940, to apply to state officials who received any part of their compensation from Federal funds. It also restricted the amount any political committee might spend in a single year to $3 million, and limited the amount any single individual or corporation might contribute to $5,000.

New Programs for Agriculture

Even though public attention during the second Roosevelt administration was largely concentrated on such controversial issues as the Judicial Reorganization Bill and the attempted purge of the conservative Democrats, the New Deal was still moving ahead toward some of its objectives.

In the Hoosac Mills case (United States v. Butler, 1936), the Supreme Court had dealt a crippling blow to the first Agricultural Adjustment Administration. The issue was the constitutionality of the processing tax; a majority of the Court held that this was invalid since it had been levied, not for the general welfare, but for the purpose of regulating agricultural production. Although many AAA activities were not affected by this decision, the system of contracts under which the government promised benefit payments in return for the farmer's reduction of acreage was ruled out. AAA officials and farm leaders, convinced that the results might be disastrous, quickly brought forward an alternative policy.

On February 29, 1936, the President gave his approval to the Soil Conservation and Domestic Allotment Act, an amendment and extension of the less ambitious Soil Erosion Act of 1935. The Secretary of Agriculture was authorized to make payments to farmers who employed methods that maintained and restored the fertility of the soil and prevented erosion. Producers could qualify for these payments by decreasing the acreage planted to soil-depleting crops—cotton, tobacco, corn, wheat, and other grains—and increasing the acreage planted to soil-conserving crops—legumes and perennial grasses, or crops like soybeans and cow peas that were valuable as fertilizer when plowed under. Other conservation practices entitling the user to benefits were the application of fertilizer, the planting of trees, and the terracing and furrowing of pastures on the contour. The AAA was continued under the same name to carry out the provisions of the new law, but some of the procedures rebuked by the Hoosac Mills decision were abandoned.

Agricultural conservation had much to commend it. The folly of many of the agricultural practices of World War I and the postwar period had been dramatically illustrated during the early thirties. Parched by hot sun and scanty rainfall, millions of acres of Western land were ruined. Great dust storms blew away the thin topsoil, thousands of farms were abandoned, and hundreds of thousands of farmers were reduced to the status of migratory agricultural laborers. Consequently, the conservation program won the cooperation of two thirds of the 16.8 million farmers of the country.

But the new law did not prevent agricultural surpluses. The aggregate production of the fifty-three leading crops was larger in 1937 than in any previous year in American history. Huge surpluses of cotton, wheat, and other crops began to accumulate, and the situation threatened to develop another tragedy like that of 1932.

To meet this situation, a new Agricultural Adjustment Act of February 16, 1938, provided for a variety of procedures. Underlying the whole was the philosophy that Secretary Wallace had been urging upon the nation. Farm policy, the Secretary argued, should try not only to secure for agriculture its fair proportion of the national income, but also to guarantee to consumers an adequate food supply through years of plenty and scarcity alike. By enabling the farmer to store non-perishable staples, an "ever-normal granary" would be provided.

The act of 1938 stressed again the importance of conservation. It required that the farmer should plant no more acreage in a particular commodity than his allotment under a national quota large enough to meet normal domestic consumption and export requirements, and also to provide a reserve or carry-over supply of the commodity. If a farmer kept within his acreage allotment and otherwise followed soil-conserving policies, he qualified for benefit payments. Producers of cotton, wheat, corn, tobacco, and rice were granted certain additional protection. Growers of these staples who cooperated with the AAA program were eligible for price-adjustment or parity payments whenever Congress made appropriations available for this purpose. These payments were intended to provide the growers with a return as nearly equal to parity price as the funds so appropriated would permit.[9]

[9] Parity was defined as "that price for the commodity which will give to the commodity a purchasing power with respect to articles that farmers buy equivalent to the purchasing power of such commodity in the base period. The base period is August, 1909, to July, 1914, except for tobacco where the base period is August, 1919, to July, 1929."

Another type of assistance was available through the Commodity Credit Corporation, which was empowered to make loans on the security of certain agricultural products. Farmers cooperating in the AAA program might obtain loans ranging from 52 per cent to 75 per cent of parity. These commodity loans not only permitted the storage of grain, but had the effect of putting a floor under agricultural prices. Producers of wheat were also given an opportunity to secure crop insurance against losses due to unavoidable causes, such as drought, flood, and disease.[10]

In the case of cotton, wheat, corn, tobacco, and rice, marketing quotas might under certain conditions be imposed. All sales in excess of individual quotas were subjected to heavy penalty. Another method of dealing with the surplus problem was provided by continuing and expanding the operations already initiated by the Federal Surplus Commodities Corporation, which bought up and distributed agricultural surpluses through relief channels or through subsidized exports.

Although the Agricultural Adjustment Act of 1938 returned to a system of paying benefits to farmers who restricted their acreage, the processing tax was avoided. The program was financed by annual Congressional appropriations of $500 million for benefit payments and about $212 million for parity payments.

Agriculture had obviously joined the ranks of the subsidized industries. Many observers regretted the development, but no feasible alternative was suggested and Republican counterproposals were notoriously vague. At least it could be said that, in return for their annual contribution, the taxpayers were now being assured an ample food supply and certain minimum safeguards for the nation's soil resources.

Farm Security Administration

In 1937 the President's Special Committee on Farm Tenancy issued a disquieting report:

> For the past 55 years, the entire period for which we have statistics on land tenure, there has been a continuous and marked decrease in the proportion of operating owners and an accompanying increase in the proportion of tenants. Tenancy has increased from 25 per cent of all farmers in 1880 to 42 per cent in 1935.

Yet this growth of tenancy was only part of the problem. Agricultural insecurity was the lot not only of tenants and sharecroppers, but of farm laborers, families on submarginal land, families on holdings of inadequate size, owner-families hopelessly in debt, and young people unable to obtain farms. According to an-

10 The crop insurance plan was extended to cotton in 1942.

other study based upon the agricultural census of 1935, 1.7 million families, representing nearly 8 million men, women, and children, received net income of less than $500 per year.

To this vast company of the agricultural underprivileged, AAA had little to offer. In 1934 a rural rehabilitation division was set up as a branch of the Federal Emergency Relief Administration. The next year the Resettlement Administration was established as an independent agency to carry out a more ambitious program under Federal direction. In 1937 the Resettlement Administration was replaced by the Farm Security Administration (FSA) in the Department of Agriculture.

The FSA fell heir to numerous experimental projects dating back to the early days of the New Deal. About 160 resettlement communities and subsistence homesteads had been laid out in various parts of the country. They followed no uniform pattern. In some the colonists did full-time farming; in others they did part-time farming and worked the rest of the time either in specially established local industries or in some nearby town. In some, operations were carried on cooperatively, in others individually. Activities of this kind were fascinating social experiments, but they were extremely vulnerable to criticism. They furnished altogether too much ammunition for those who wanted to depict the New Dealers as impractical utopians or as Communists bent on destroying the American economic system. At the insistence of Congress, the FSA gradually liquidated the homestead projects, giving the settlers the first opportunity to buy.

Other FSA activities aroused less opposition. In case of flood, drought, or complete impoverishment due to erosion the agency made outright grants of money, but this was exceptional. The usual procedure was to loan money to the distressed farmer, contingent upon his accepting guidance in farm and home management intended to make him self-supporting. Under the Bankhead-Jones Act of 1937 selected tenants and laborers might be advanced sufficient funds to purchase their farms. Most of the FSA loans were more modest in size and purpose; they were short-term advances for seed, fertilizer, livestock, farming equipment, clothing, necessary medical care, repairs, and similar purposes. In the case of farmers hopelessly in debt, voluntary adjustments with the creditors were sought whereby the debt might be scaled down to manageable terms.

Considering the desperate circumstances of its clientele and the fact that its loans were made only to persons who could not obtain credit through other channels, FSA was remarkably successful in its financial operation. Up to June 30, 1945, almost 90 per cent of its loans were repaid when they fell due. This was evidence that a considerable amount of agricultural rehabilitation had actually been accomplished. Vastly more needed to be done, however, and FSA appropriations were always low as compared with those for other purposes, partly because of the suspicion with which the larger farmers viewed these efforts to improve the status of tenants and laborers.

Wage and Hour Legislation

For a while after the overthrow of NRA, the minimum-wage and maximum-hour provisions of the codes were maintained in many fields by voluntary agreement. As old abuses reappeared, however, labor began to insist on Federal legislation defining fair labor standards. A beginning toward this goal was taken in the Walsh-Healy Government Contracts Act of 1936, which required that all producers who made contracts with the Federal government involving amounts of $10,000 or more must pay not less than the prevailing rate of wages in the locality, must maintain an eight-hour day and a forty-hour week, and must not employ boys under sixteen nor girls under eighteen. Similar requirements were laid down for airlines carrying mail or passengers by the Air Transport Act of 1936.

The proposal for a general wage-hour law met with strong opposition. Southern legislators were afraid that one of the principal attractions drawing industry to their section would be lost. Northern businessmen felt that their costs might be raised, and farmers feared that higher industrial wages would increase their problems with agricultural labor. A wage-hour bill recommended by the President passed the Senate in 1937, but failed in the House. On June 25, 1938, however, the Fair Labor Standards Act was finally passed. The law applied to employees engaged in interstate commerce or in producing goods for interstate commerce, but a number of sizable groups were specifically excluded—agricultural laborers, domestic servants, and seamen, for example. The wages of all employees covered by the act were to be not less than 25 cents an hour; this minimum was to be gradually raised until it reached 40 cents an hour in 1945. Similarly, maximum hours under the law were fixed at forty-four and were to be reduced by stages until a forty-hour week was established in 1940. When the employee worked more than the maximum, he was entitled to time-and-a-half pay for the overtime. The act forbade the employment of children under sixteen years of age in most occupations and of those under eighteen in occupations found by the Children's Bureau to be specially hazardous.

The immediate result of the act was to raise the wages of about 300,000 persons who were receiving less than the 25-cent minimum and to shorten the working hours of some 1.3 million workers. As the standards were gradually raised, more and more members of the labor force benefited. Since these standards were in themselves very modest, the operation of the law reveals much about the sweating of labor that preceded its enactment.

The New Deal and Business

Toward agriculture and labor the Roosevelt administration followed policies that were, whether wise or ill-advised, reasonably consistent. The New Deal's program for dealing with business lacked the same clarity of purpose. Mr. Dooley's famous summary of the trust policy of the first Roosevelt—"On wan hand I wud stamp thim undher fut; on th' other hand not so fast"—might almost as aptly have been applied to the second.

The NRA, as has been seen, represented a departure from the philosophy of the antitrust laws toward a policy of permitting industries to protect themselves against the hazards of excessive competition. After the death of NRA, Congress enabled a number of businesses to achieve the same goal through special legislation. The Guffey-Snyder Bituminous Coal Stabilization Act of 1935 provided for the appointment of a National Bituminous Coal Commission, representative of industry, labor, and the public, with power to promulgate a code for the industry and establish minimum prices. Labor was guaranteed the right of collective bargaining, and maximum-hours and minimum-wage agreements by producers of two thirds of the tonnage and representatives of over one half of the mine workers bound the entire industry. This little NRA suffered the same fate as its parent, however, when the Supreme Court, in Carter v. Carter Coal Company, invalidated it in 1936 on the grounds that its labor provisions unconstitutionally delegated legislative powers. The following year a new measure, the Guffey-Vinson Act, by omitting the mandatory labor provisions of the original law, succeeded in putting the stabilization of the bituminous coal industry on a basis that the Supreme Court sustained in Sunshine Anthracite Coal Company v. Adkins (1940).

Although petroleum refining was concentrated in some twenty corporations, about one half of the crude oil of the nation came from the wells of small independent producers. During the depression, serious overproduction had ruinous effects on prices. The public interest was involved since chaotic conditions in the industry were resulting in serious waste of an essential natural resource. The situation led the legislatures of the oil-producing states to establish maximum quotas for the individual producers. Two problems subsequently developed: correlating the policies of the various states so that one did not profit unduly through the conservation measures undertaken by another, and the curbing of trade in so-called "hot oil," which was produced in violation of the state quotas. Since Federal assistance seemed to be required, Section 9 of NIRA had made special provision for the petroleum industry. But in the Hot Oil case (Panama Refining Company v. Ryan, 1935), that section had been declared unconstitutional even before the rest of NIRA. A substitute was provided in the Connelly Act of 1935, forbidding interstate commerce in contraband oil produced in excess of state-fixed quotas. Meantime, a mechanism for agreement upon state quotas had been worked out through interstate compacts of the oil-producing commonwealths.

Independent wholesalers and retailers, worried over the increasingly serious competition of the chain stores, also demanded protective legislation after NRA's demise. Independent druggists and other interested groups secured from the legislatures of most of the states fair-trade acts, which legalized contracts under which manufacturers bound retailers not to sell their products at less than a prescribed minimum retail price. Despite President Roosevelt's opposition, Congress cooperated in 1937 by passing the Miller-Tydings Act, which exempted such price maintenance agreements from the Sherman Antitrust Act.

But New Dealers were sharply divided among themselves on the issue of legalizing restraints on trade. Many continued to have faith in the old progressive policy of enforced competition. In this they had the support of a large section of public opinion. One of the unexpected results of the NRA experiment was to restore to the antitrust laws a portion of their old-time popularity. Throughout the twenties the laws had been under attack as based upon an outmoded and indefensible philosophy. The eagerness with which many businessmen resorted to price fixing and limiting of production under the protection of NRA codes, however, served to educate the consuming public in the merits of the Sherman Act.

Early in his administration, Roosevelt attempted to restore the Federal Trade Commission to its original functions by removing Chairman Humphrey, the Coolidge appointee whose conservative policies had been so welcome to big business,[11] and by appointing strong men to this and other posts in the agency. Still more significant efforts to revive the antitrust laws originated in the Department of Justice. In 1938 the President appointed Thurman Arnold of the Yale Law School as Assistant Attorney General in charge of the Antitrust Division. Arnold was the country's leading critic of business practices restraining competition—"bottlenecks of business" as he described them. The division now began a series of carefully prepared cases. Despite the fact that the litigation received much less publicity than the famous antitrust suits of earlier days, considerable success was achieved. Instead of a dissolution order difficult of enforcement, the outcome of Arnold's cases was frequently a "consent decree"— an agreed settlement between the government and the defendants in which the latter undertook to abstain from certain practices in restraint of competition. Reform was thus forced upon certain automobile finance corporations in 1939

[11] In Humphrey's Executor v. U. S. (1935), the Supreme Court ruled that Humphrey's removal was illegal, since Congress had specified that commissioners might not be removed except for cause. Since Humphrey had meantime died, however, the decision had no effect on Roosevelt's revitalizing of the agency.

and upon the "block-booking" practices of the motion-picture industry in 1940. Arnold was sufficiently consistent in his philosophy to attack restrictive policies of the building-trade unions as well as those of the contractors.

Meantime, one of the most significant investigations ever made of the workings of American capitalism was undertaken by the Temporary National Economic Committee (TNEC), established by Congress in 1938 upon the President's recommendation. Through public hearings and extensive research, a wealth of material was assembled relating to the degree of concentration of control in the American economic system, as well as the methods and effects of that concentration. The TNEC's reports appeared to prepare the ground for new legislation dealing with abuse of the patent laws and other matters, but the onset of war had the inevitable effect of postponing such measures.

The administration's ambition to retard the growth of big business and the accumulation of excessive private fortunes was reflected in its recommendations for tax revision. The estate-tax and gift-tax rates were increased in 1934 and 1935, making them for the first time a major source of Federal revenue. Also raised were individual surtaxes and corporation income rates, while an excess-profits levy reminiscent of World War I days was restored to the tax structure.

These changes, mostly incorporated in the Revenue Act of 1935, were much resented by businessmen. Even more disliked was the tax on undistributed corporation profits, introduced in the Revenue Act of 1936. This step was taken to discourage the accumulation of unnecessarily large corporate surpluses, a form of oversaving that, by reducing dividend payments to stockholders, destroyed purchasing power and reduced government revenues from personal income taxes. Spokesmen for business, however, defended these surpluses as a necessary insurance against hard times and as providing the funds for plant expansion.

Conservative Democrats and Republicans mustered enough strength in 1938 to modify the New Deal tax structure. In the Revenue Act of that year Congress radically reduced the tax on undistributed profits and otherwise lightened the tax burden of the corporations. The conservatives won another victory the next year when the undistributed profits tax was entirely repealed.

Transportation Policy

In dealing with the air-transport industry and the merchant marine the New Deal sought certain reforms, yet in the end fell back upon a policy of generous subsidy similar to that of preceding Republican administrations.

In 1933 the government's air-mail contracts fell under vigorous criticism. It was alleged that the Hoover administration had permitted collusive bidding, had favored the big companies, and had made excessive expenditures. Despite the depression, Federal payments to the airlines had mounted from $9.4 million in 1929 to $19.5 million in 1933. Early in 1934 Postmaster General Farley canceled the contracts and for some weeks the army flew the mail. The results were unfortunate. A series of severe February storms swept the country and the army pilots and equipment were found inadequate for these abnormal conditions. Ten flyers lost their lives within a month, causing a public outcry that largely diverted attention from the abuses of the old system. The Air Mail Act of 1934 restored contract operations, but under safeguards to assure genuinely competitive bidding. The government made a substantial saving and in 1937 Farley was able to boast that although two and a half times as much air mail was being transported as in 1932, the cost to the government was $7 million less.

But the airlines claimed that the new contracts were not adequate to maintain the industry on a profitable basis, and in 1938 Congress established the Civil Aeronautical Authority (CAA) with extensive powers not only to regulate aviation but to adjust air-mail payments to the needs of the different classes of carriers. By 1939 total payments had risen to about $18 million, but this figure was hardly comparable to that of 1933 since the volume of mail had increased very greatly.

The merchant marine subsidy program was even more vulnerable to criticism than that in the field of aviation. Despite annual payments amounting to about $29 million, the American merchant marine fleet was rapidly reaching the point of total obsolescence. By the Merchant Marine Act of 1936 a new United States Maritime Commission was created. This body was authorized to grant direct subsidies instead of the discredited mail contracts. Payments were to be of two kinds: one to promote construction and the other to assist the private owners in meeting their operating costs. If the subsidy program proved ineffective, the commission was empowered to build ships on its own account, sell or charter them if possible, and operate them itself if necessary.

Toward the railroads the New Deal undertook no radically new departures in policy. The Emergency Transportation Act of 1933 authorized the appointment of a Federal Coordinator of Transportation, a temporary post to which Roosevelt named Joseph B. Eastman of the ICC. The coordinator's recommendations for economies in operation met with resistance from both management and labor, but his advice to the government on future transportation policy had greater influence. "Theoretically and logically," Eastman pointed out, "public ownership and operation meet the known ills of the present situation better than any other remedy." In view of the practical difficulties of such a course of action, however, he recommended an extension and improvement of the existing system of Federal regulation of privately owned and operated carriers. Congress responded by extending the jurisdiction of the ICC to include motor and water carriers, the first by the Motor Carrier Act of 1935, the second by the Transportation Act of 1940.

Government-operated Business

Government competition with private enterprise, the ultimate sin in conservative eyes, advanced somewhat under Roosevelt, but not without encountering strong and bitter opposition.

One of the hardest-hit industries of the depression was that of house-building. For the New Deal to attempt to stimulate construction was an obvious step in its recovery program. To a large extent, this was done through the encouragement of private business. In 1934 Congress authorized the establishment of a Federal Housing Administration (FHA). This agency was empowered to insure loans made by private lending institutions for both the repair of old dwellings and the construction of new ones. In the former case only 20 per cent of the loan was insured, but for new construction fully insured mortgages might be written for as much as 90 per cent of the value and carrying a maturity of twenty-five years.

Although FHA stimulated the building of homes for middle-income families, it was no answer to the more desperate needs of the low-income group composing from one third to one half of the entire population. To build decent homes cheaply enough to be sold or rented to such people was apparently beyond the abilities of private enterprise. There was, moreover, a powerful landlord interest in perpetuating a situation where the poor had to live in dilapidated old properties. As early as 1933 low-cost housing and slum-clearance programs had been designated as a desirable area for expenditure under the PWA. But results were inadequate until legislation was passed in 1937 establishing the United States Housing Administration (USHA). This body was empowered to make long-term low-interest loans to state or local public-housing agencies for slum clearance and low-rent housing construction. As a Federal subsidy for these projects, the USHA was authorized to remit the interest and advance an annual sum equivalent to ½ per cent of the construction loan, provided that this grant was necessary to the maintenance of low rents and provided that the local agency was also making a contribution. By November, 1939, 296 public-housing projects were in progress under this program. These promised better homes for 650,000 persons, but this was only a fraction of the number needed. The administration appealed to Congress for authorization to expand the project, but the bill was defeated in the House.

Business feared New Deal intervention in the power industry even more than it did the public-housing policy. So enthusiastic was the President over the success of TVA that in 1937 he advocated the establishment of similar regional-planning agencies in six other areas of the country: the Atlantic Seaboard, the Great Lakes-Ohio Valley, the Missouri Valley, the Southwest, the Colorado Valley, and the Columbia Valley. Although Congress was not prepared to entertain so bold a proposal, it did provide generous appropriations for the building of large dams in various parts of the nation. Such projects as Bonneville and Grand Coulee on the Columbia, Fort Peck on the Missouri, Big Thompson on the Colorado, and the Central Valley in California, built for various purposes such as navigation, flood control, and irrigation, all contemplated the generation of public power. Another favorite Roosevelt project, the St. Lawrence Seaway, failed of realization, however, because of the opposition of private power interests and the railroads.

Farmers, to whom electricity was a servant even more useful than to city dwellers, had been largely excluded from its benefits under rugged individualism. Private companies had found it profitable to extend service to less than 8 per cent of the nation's farms. In 1936 Roosevelt sought to remedy the situation by setting up the Rural Electrification Administration (REA) and allotting to it $100 million of Emergency Relief Administration funds. The experiment was given a more secure basis the next year when Congress passed the Rural Electrification Act. Farmers were encouraged to form cooperatives that would erect transmission lines and furnish electricity to persons in rural areas not receiving central-station service. Such associations were to be assisted through low-interest loans from the REA. The administration endeavored to avoid controversy by not promoting cooperatives in areas already served by private industry and by encouraging farmers' associations to purchase electricity wholesale from the corporations rather than build their own generating plants. Even so, the utility companies did not relish distribution through cooperatives and undertook a rural electrification program of their own. The result of this wholesale competition in good works was gratifying. By 1943 more than eight hundred cooperatives were providing farmers with electricity, and their activities combined with those of purely private industry were serving the needs of 2.5 million farms, some 26 per cent of the nation's total.

A favorite conservative accusation was that the New Deal was socialistic. A review of the record reveals that this was mostly name-calling. There was a measure of socialism in the Roosevelt policies relating to electrical power and public housing, but even in these fields the application of the philosophy was strictly limited. An administration really committed to advancing socialism would certainly have proceeded very differently, particularly in dealing with the banks, the railroads, the coal mines, and the merchant marine—strategic areas of the national economy that were prostrate and dependent on government assistance in 1933. The most characteristic New Deal policies were those designed to pull private enterprise out of the ditch, refuel it with loans, and set it back on the road again with some attempt to add governors to the machinery to prevent it from again smashing up. Roosevelt conceived his mission to be to save capitalism rather than to destroy it. Whether that was a virtue or a defect depended on the point of view. And whether the steps actually taken did in the aggregate strengthen private enterprise or weaken it was a question over which men might honestly differ.

Recess on Reform

Roosevelt had crowded proposal upon proposal during his first five years in office because he was convinced that the progressive movement runs in cycles. Unless the reforms on which he had set his heart could be speedily achieved, they might be long delayed by the changing mood of the public. The soundness of this analysis was proved by the anti-New Deal reaction that set in during his second term. The results of the 1938 elections convinced the President that the time had come to go on the defensive so far as his domestic program was concerned, and during the next years no really new campaigns were begun. Some of the earlier laws, like the Social Security Act, were improved. A few untenable positions like the tax on undistributed corporation profits were surrendered. On the whole, however, the Roosevelt strategy consisted in holding the ground already won and resisting such conservative counterattacks as that directed against the National Labor Relations Act.

The President's more conservative mood was intensified by his growing preoccupation with the world situation. Developments in Europe and Asia soon overshadowed every issue of domestic politics.

21
Depression America

From 1929 to 1939 the Great Depression continued to be the most important factor in American social and cultural life. The complacency of the prosperous twenties was rudely shattered. In 1928 it had been easy to believe that poverty would soon be abolished through the beneficent workings of rugged individualism; two years later poverty's threatening shadow was looming over millions of industrious citizens who had prided themselves on their ability to provide for their own security.

As faith in the old gods of laissez faire, individual thrift, and welfare capitalism declined, Americans began increasingly to look for salvation to collective action and government intervention. The impact of these changing ideas on the political scene has already been described; no less important were the consequences in labor relations, in intellectual trends, and in the conditions under which authors and artists produced their work.

Collapse of Welfare Capitalism

On the eve of the depression, employers had reason to congratulate themselves on the unusual docility of their workers. Not only had labor union membership failed to expand during the prosperous mid-twenties, but many unions actually lost ground. William Green, who had succeeded Gompers as AFL president after the latter's death in 1924, was a mild and friendly man, dedicated to the ideal of a respectable unionism that would not frighten the business community by unseemly tactics. In contrast with the unions' apologetic and defensive behavior, management was assuming the leadership in labor relations.

Although many employers did not hesitate to show the iron hand by using labor spies, black lists, and yellow-dog contracts to combat the unions, their most effective strategy was to convince their employees that the strike and the boycott were old-fashioned weapons and that the utopia of high wages, reasonable hours, wholesome recreational programs, retirement pensions, and other benefits would be speedily achieved through cooperation with enlightened management.

But welfare capitalism, so glittering in appeal during days of prosperity, became an early victim of the depression. After an initial effort to maintain wages in response to President Hoover's appeal, employers found it necessary to cut their labor costs by every possible means. Statisticians might argue that hourly wage rates fell more slowly than the cost of living, but this afforded little consolation to the average worker. At best, he found employment uncertain and layoffs frequent; at worst, he might spend many months without any job at all. In their desperation many workers took employment in small depression-born factories that operated under sweatshop conditions.

The other pillars on which welfare capitalism had rested proved as shaky as that of high wages. Health benefits and recreational programs were often regarded as non-essentials that had to be abandoned as one of the early steps of retrenchment. Particularly unhappy were the situations in which employees had been encouraged to make regular purchases of company stock and now found the value of their holdings shrunk to a fraction of what they had paid.

The company unions, financed and dominated by management, were helpless to protect the workers against these developments. Nor could the independent unions do much more. Weak and defeatist in temperament, the union leaders were not in a position to fight against the black forces that the depression had unleashed.

In the imaginations of a few panicky businessmen and a handful of hopeful intellectuals, the situation seemed ripe for revolution. But realistic observers noted that really radical discontent was surprisingly small. Here and there demonstrations occurred among unemployed workers or veterans seeking payment of the bonus. On the whole, however, the mood was one of stunned disbelief that the depression was real and that the platitudes of prosperity had lost their meaning. As late as 1932 the AFL leadership was persisting in its opposition to unemployment insurance and pinning its hopes of recovery on a shorter work week.

But if the reaction from the cult of rugged individualism was slow in coming, it was nevertheless irresistible once it started. In politics, Roosevelt's great electoral victories and the whole New Deal program were its manifestations. On the social front, the most dramatic change was the rise of a militant labor movement.

The great expansion of unionism during the 1930's resulted only in part from the new government policy represented by the Norris-LaGuardia Act, the NRA, and the National Labor Relations Act. Important though it was to the unions to have this legal protection, the change in the laws would not in itself have swelled the union membership rolls had not the workers been eager to join.

This belated conversion of millions of Americans to a belief in unionism resulted in substantial measure from disillusionment with welfare capitalism. No longer were the workers willing to trust their destinies to the personnel policies of their employers. They now wanted the terms of their employment spelled out in union contracts. The grim experience of the depression had also taught the workers to demand more protection from government in the form of old age pensions, unemployment insurance, minimum wages, and limitation of the hours of labor.

A factor of importance in the growing labor movement was the almost complete cessation of immigration. The legislation of the twenties, strict administration of the laws, and discouraging job prospects had reduced the influx of foreigners to a mere trickle. Indeed, in some years during the thirties more people left the country than came in. This meant that after 1930 the working force contained an ever increasing proportion of second- and third-generation Americans, no longer willing to accept the conditions that had satisfied their immigrant forebears. Thoroughly Americanized, these workers demanded what they considered to be their birthright—not just life and liberty, but security in their jobs and high wages.

Rise of the CIO

For years there had been dissension within AFL ranks over the issue of industrial unionism. An aggressive faction had insisted that the mass-production industries like autos, rubber, steel, and electrical equipment would never be adequately organized except by new unions founded along industrial lines. But the established craft unions regarded with great suspicion the creation of any more industrial unions than strictly necessary. When the NRA experiment suddenly opened up an opportunity for invading the unorganized industries, the problem was postponed for the time being by chartering federal locals directly responsible to the AFL officers. This soon proved unsatisfactory. The craft unions were anxious to use such locals as recruiting agencies for their organizations and insisted upon a broad construction of their jurisdictional rights. Yet such groups as the auto workers and the rubber workers were just as insistent that they be brought together in single unions for each industry. Many of the old-line leaders, their critics charged, were not only too much concerned with protecting vested interests, but too cautious and conservative to take full advantage of new conditions.

Dissension within the AFL reached a crisis at the 1935 convention at Atlantic City. Strongly worded majority and minority reports came from the resolutions committee. Eight committee members emphasized the duty of protecting the jurisdictional rights of all trade unions organized along craft lines; six opposed this, contending that "in those industries where the work performed by a majority of the workers is of such a nature that it might fall within the jurisdictional claim of more than one craft union, . . . industrial organization is the only form that will be acceptable to the workers or adequately meet their needs." The AFL, the minority report continued, "must recognize the right of these workers to organize into industrial unions and be granted unrestricted charters which guarantee the right to accept into membership all workers employed in the industry." Sharp debate followed, climaxed by a fist fight in which John L. Lewis of the United Mine Workers knocked down William L. Hutcheson of the Carpenters' Union. But although triumphant in single combat, the burly champion of industrial unionism was short on votes. When the convention was polled, the majority report safeguarding craft unionism was adopted.

Picketing. (By Kirby. Reproduced by permission of the *New York World-Telegram*. Copyright, 1937.)

On November 9, 1935, just a few weeks after the tumultuous Atlantic City convention, eight heads of AFL international unions met at Washington and formed the Committee for Industrial Organization (CIO) of which Lewis was named chairman. The new group announced that its functions would be "educational and advisory" and professed loyalty to the AFL. But President Green and the AFL executive committee regarded the CIO's activities as rebellion against the majority decisions at Atlantic City and ordered the group to dissolve. When the group failed to do this, the AFL heads took drastic disciplinary action. In August, 1936, the executive council declared ten unions associated with the CIO guilty of dualism, insurrection, and rebellion, and ordered their suspension. With the insurgent groups unrepresented, the Tampa convention of the AFL voted to uphold the action of their executive council.

Yet the rebels remained unrepentant. All peace efforts failed and in 1938 the CIO, keeping its initials but changing its name to the Congress of Industrial Organizations, adopted a constitution and accepted its status as a separate federation of American labor unions. This was in many ways an unfortunate development because the AFL and the CIO devoted energies to fighting each other that they might better have reserved for promoting the primary interests of labor. Particularly exasperating to employers and the public were the jurisdictional disputes between the two, which frequently led to work stoppages having nothing to do with basic labor-management relations. Despite the split, however, labor was usually able to present a united front during political campaigns or when antiunion legislation was threatened. The very fact of their rivalry, moreover, led to energetic organizing efforts that greatly increased the membership of both federations. John L. Lewis provided the CIO with pugnacious leadership until 1940, when he resigned after a failure to carry the movement with him in support of Willkie in the presidential campaign. He was succeeded by Philip Murray, originally a Mine Workers' official but more recently head of the very successful Steel Workers Organizing Committee (SWOC).

Fighting for Recognition

Throughout the years 1936 and 1937 the country was plagued by strikes. This development was almost inevitable since the workers were now resolved to join trade unions and obtain contracts, while many employers were determined not to put their labor relations on this basis. Despite the prohibitions of the National Labor Relations Act, employers sought to combat unionism by using labor spies, discriminating against trade-union members, and promoting rival company unions. Angered by management's defiance of law, the workers resorted more and more to a technique which, as the courts eventually decided, was itself illegal. This was the sit-down strike in which employees, without quitting the plant, simply refused to work. Used successfully in 1933 against the Hormel Packing Company in Austin, Minnesota, the weapon was frequently resorted to during the next few years, particularly in the Detroit area. The philosophy behind this development was well expressed in the auto workers' song:

> When they tie the can to a union man,
>   Sit down! Sit down!
> When they give him the sack they'll take him back,
>   Sit down! Sit down!
> When the speed-up comes, just twiddle your thumbs,
>   Sit down! Sit down!
> When the boss won't talk don't take a walk,
>   Sit down! Sit down!

Another center where sit-down strikes were numerous was Akron, Ohio, the home of the rubber industry. Serious trouble developed at the Goodyear plants when the management attempted to lower costs by increasing hours, reducing wages, and laying off workers. A five-week strike began February 17, 1936. One of the longest picket lines in labor history was employed and there was some disorder. The strike ended without recognition of the United Rubber Workers or dissolution of the company union, yet with substantial concessions to the strikers on other issues.

The prestige of the newly organized CIO had been at stake. The Goodyear workers had been largely unorganized when the strike began, but the CIO intervened and rendered valuable help. The strike was sufficiently successful to bring the United Rubber Workers thousands of members during the next few months. In 1935 there had been only 3,000 union members in the rubber industry; the number jumped to 33,000 in 1936 and to 70,000 in 1937.

During 1936 the United Automobile Workers, CIO, also made progress despite the opposition of the large companies—an opposition that led the General Motors Corporation to spend $994,855 on private detective services between January 1, 1934, and July 31, 1936. A variety of grievances brought increasingly frequent work stoppages until finally, in January and February, 1937, one of the greatest struggles in American industrial history was fought out. Two weeks after the strike began 112,800 of the corporation's 150,000 production workers were idle.

The focal point of the conflict was Flint, Michigan, where the sit-down strategy was employed in its boldest form. For six weeks the strikers held key General Motors plants. An attempt by the Flint police to prevent food from being carried to the sit-down strikers precipitated a three-hour battle in which the police used tear gas and buckshot, while the strikers fought back with sticks, metal pipes, nuts and bolts, soda-pop bottles, coffee mugs, automobile door hinges, and cold water from the plants' hoses. After this episode Governor Frank Murphy ordered 1,500 Michigan national guardsmen into the city, but

Sit-Down Strike at the National Container Company in Philadelphia, March, 1937. (World Wide Photos.)

he refused to command them to expel the strikers from the plants and he directed that there should be no further attempt to halt the entry of food. The corporation was successful in obtaining an order from a Federal circuit court judge directing the strikers to evacuate the plants under penalty of imprisonment for contempt of court and of having a fine of $15 million—the estimated value of the plants—assessed against them. But the workers defied the order and the authorities decided against any attempt to carry it out by force.

Governor Murphy was determined to avoid bloodshed and, ignoring the legal issues involved in the strike, he bent all his efforts toward obtaining a peaceful settlement. The management at first refused to negotiate until their property was evacuated, but at length after a direct appeal from President Roosevelt it accepted Governor Murphy's mediation. On February 11, 1937, a settlement was announced. The United Automobile Workers was to be recognized for at least six months as the exclusive bargaining agent for the workers in the seventeen strike-bound plants. In all other General Motors plants the union would be recognized as the agent of its members. All strikers were to be rehired and there was to be no future discrimination against union members. The company and the union agreed to settle other outstanding grievances through negotiations leading to a signed contract. It was a CIO triumph, and after brief trials of strength the other auto plants soon fell in line. Ford attempted to hold out longer than the others, but after a ten-day strike in 1941 it too surrendered and signed a contract granting the UAW for the first time the closed shop, the check-off, and the union label.

The legality of the sit-down strike became a matter of heated controversy. The Roosevelt administration avoided any clear-cut pronouncement on the issue and Congress was divided; conservatives like Senators Vandenberg of Michigan and Tydings of Maryland condemned labor's aggressive tactics in strong terms, while liberals like Senators Wagner and Norris contended that management's sit-down against the National Labor Relations Act had given the workers ample justification. They called attention also to the hearings before the LaFollette Committee on Civil Liberties in which many unsavory details relating to the antiunion tactics of the employers were being revealed. When in 1939 the issue reached the Supreme Court in the case of NLRB v. Fansteel Metallurgical Corporation, the sit-down strike was finally pronounced illegal.

Meantime, the issue of union recognition was being fought out in the steel industry. The Steel Workers Organizing Committee, with Philip Murray as its head and a substantial portion of its expenses advanced by Lewis' United Mine Workers, waged an aggressive campaign. One of its most successful stratagems was that of winning over the leaders and rank-and-file of the company unions themselves. So strong was the movement that in March, 1937, the United States Steel Corporation, without risking a strike, recognized the SWOC and permitted the negotiation of contracts with all its subsidiaries.

Several other steel companies followed the lead of the industry's largest unit, but a group of independents elected to resist. The SWOC's struggle with Little Steel, as this group was called, precipitated the bloodiest labor battle of the thirties. At the Republic Steel Company's plants at Chicago ten strikers were killed in a fracas with the police on Memorial Day, 1937; similar incidents led to loss of life in the three Ohio cities of Youngstown, Massillon, and Cleveland. In the end the strikes against Little Steel failed, and the defeat was a serious one to CIO. Labor's aggressive tactics had brought it into disfavor with most of the American white-collar class. Tom Girdler, president of Republic Steel, received considerable acclaim for his defiance of the CIO, and John L. Lewis was widely denounced. The unpopularity of the CIO was so great in the summer of 1937 that even the President himself seemed to feel its influence. Referring to the bitter struggle between the CIO and Girdler's Republic Steel, he exclaimed: "A plague on both your houses."

A favorite allegation against the CIO was that it was a Communist outfit. This was certainly untrue so far as its high command was concerned. Neither Lewis, nor Murray, nor Sidney Hillman of the Amalgamated Clothing Workers, nor any other CIO leader of comparable prominence had any connection or sympathy with the Communist party. Among local leaders and local unions there was, to be sure, Communist infiltration, but this arose mostly out of the determination of the movement to use any organizing talent that was offered without scrutinizing its political coloring too critically. The bitterness of the great strikes of 1936 and 1937 did not result from their Communist character, but rather from the nature of the issue involved. In almost every case this was not primarily wages and hours but the life or death of the union itself.

In the long run the CIO withstood all attacks and established itself permanently not only in the rubber, auto, and steel industries, but in the electrical, textile, and canning fields as well. Even white-collar workers like newspaper reporters and store clerks organized. As remarkable as the penetration of unionism into new fields was the growth of the older unions, both AFL and CIO. Between 1933 and 1941 the United Mine Workers (CIO) and the Amalgamated Clothing Workers (CIO) both doubled in membership, while the Teamsters Brotherhood (AFL) had a sixfold increase and the Hotel and Restaurant Employees jumped over ninefold. Even Little Steel abandoned its antiunion policy and signed contracts in 1941, after the NLRB ordered the reinstatement of the workers it had discharged in breaking the union in 1937. By 1941 total union membership had risen to 10.5 million—three and a half times that of 1933.

Marx and Other Prophets

The wide prevalence of unemployment and poverty, declining faith in capitalism, and the rise of a militant labor movement appeared to give a golden opportunity to the American Communists. In a score of ways the disciples of Lenin and Marx were able to extend their influence during the thirties. Nevertheless, their efforts to create a formidable mass movement largely failed.

From 1930 until he was dumped in 1946, the leader of the American Communist party was Earl Browder, a colorless Kansan, whose principal asset in Stalin's eyes was probably his unquestioning faithfulness in expounding the current Moscow line. During the worst days of the depression the Communists played a lone hand, in the futile illusion that an American revolution was just around the corner and that they must monopolize its leadership against all possible rivals. During these years Roosevelt was denounced as a tool of Wall Street, no better than Hoover; Norman Thomas and other Socialists were condemned as "social fascists"; John L. Lewis and William Green were both damned as "labor fakers."

The intransigence of the Communists had curious consequences. Among American workers the party continued to have very little support; in 1934—despite unemployment and discontent—the official membership was only about

24,000. But Communist contempt for democratic futility did bring a response among many American intellectuals. Serious-minded people, distressed by the sufferings of the depression, exhibited increasing interest in Soviet Russia. They were impressed by news of the Five-Year Plans, by means of which the Russians seemed to be moving with giant strides toward a more rational economic system. There was, of course, another side to the picture, but reports of Russian famines, forced labor, and ruthless purges were discounted as reactionary propaganda. Thus was created a growing company of fellow travelers, individuals not willing to go all the way by accepting Communist party membership, but nevertheless disposed to wish for the success of the Soviet experiment.

In August, 1935, international Communism changed its tactics in a manner that made the path of the fellow traveler much more attractive. At the Seventh Congress of the Comintern the party officially approved the strategy of the Popular Front. Belatedly recognizing the menace of Nazism and Fascism—a menace that might never have become so great had not the Communists so persistently undermined the democracies—Moscow now ordered the party faithful to cooperate with non-Communists in combatting Fascism on both the domestic and foreign fronts.

Browder and the American Communists shifted gears with obedient promptness. Abruptly halting their attacks on New Dealers, Socialists, labor leaders, and other "social fascists," they began to present themselves as zealots for democracy. "Communism is Twentieth Century Americanism," declared a new party slogan. Browder's midwestern origin from an old-line American family was capitalized as a party asset; Communist literature glorified George Washington and Thomas Jefferson and depicted Marxists as the legitimate heirs to the Spirit of 1776. Communist orators solemnly renounced any intention of gaining power except through democratic processes.

Although these new tactics did not remove the anti-Communist prejudices of most Americans, they did make the party more nearly respectable than it had ever been before. By 1938 it had grown to a total of perhaps 100,000 members. By comparison with the less than 10,000 of predepression days this was an impressive gain; set against a total American population of 130 million it was still very small.

The Communist situation was confused, however, by its many ramifications, as represented by fellow travelers and other conscious and unconscious allies of the party. The fellow travelers were of every hue. Some followed the Moscow line so faithfully that they might as well have been party members, as indeed some of them secretly became. Others prided themselves on their independence, but willingly cooperated with the Communists on issues where they thought the latter were right. Thousands of citizens were innocent of any wish to help the Communists but joined associations devoted to worthy causes, only to discover—sometimes years later—that these associations had been under secret party control.

The success of the Communist front organizations was a reflection of the growing social consciousness of the day. Many college students, eager to demonstrate their hatred of militarism and social injustice, joined the American Student Union. Christian pacifists and other liberals found an outlet for their idealism in the League for Peace and Democracy. A score of fund-gathering committees capitalized on widespread sympathy for the Spanish Loyalists, refugees from Nazi terrorism, Negro victims of injustice, and mistreated strikers. The degree of actual Communist control over these organizations varied greatly. Non-Communists usually outnumbered Communists in their membership, but the Communist minority was highly successful in worming its way into key positions. One conspicuous result within such outfits was that the evils of Nazi totalitarianism were vigorously condemned, while those of Soviet Russia were largely overlooked.

Communist infiltration extended in many directions. Some of the party faithful occupied government positions, and a few of these were later convicted of having acted as spies for the Soviet government. Other Communists bored into the labor movement, gaining particular influence in such CIO unions as the Electrical Workers, the Maritime Union, and the Fur Workers. Individual lawyers, writers, artists, actors, and college professors occasionally fell into the Communist orbit—either as party members, conscious fellow travelers, or innocent members of front organizations.

All in all, the American Communists had pieced together a rather formidable-looking Trojan Horse. But the wooden creature was a jerry-built structure, destined to fall apart at the slightest push. Among the party membership itself there was a constant turnover. Some members had been attracted to the conspiratorial atmosphere of the party because of frustrations in their own personalities; these often renounced membership and sought to expiate their guilt by becoming rabid anti-Communists. Other Communist converts were idealists, honestly distressed by the world's ills and hopeful that Marxism would solve all problems. Such people were particularly likely to become disillusioned and leave the party when confronted by unpleasant truths like the Moscow purges or the Soviet-Nazi pact of 1939. Members of the front organizations were even less to be depended upon; so long as the Soviet Union appeared to be moving toward a more democratic system and to be sincere in its opposition to Fascism, these organizations maintained considerable popularity. Once Stalin's duplicity in secretly negotiating with Hitler was revealed, most of the organizations that had been slavishly following the Moscow line collapsed.

The Communists had in truth failed. In America they never gained the mass following that they did in most European countries. One powerful obstacle was the New Deal. Roosevelt, not Browder, was the savior upon whom most of those who had lost faith in Hoover's brand of rugged individualism now pinned their hopes. Even among the minority for whom the New Deal's program was too moderate, the Communists had too much competition for real success. The armies of discontent were moving under a confusion of separate generals and many different-colored banners. To most of the volunteers, Marx, Lenin, and Stalin were shadowy figures, less glamorous than the domestic captains who sprang up during the depression years—men like Dr. Townshend, Father Coughlin, and Huey Long.

America Discovers Keynes

Marx's appeal to the intellectuals was further blunted by rising interest in a new body of thought that seemed to give the New Deal what it very much needed—a plausible justification in economic theory.

From the viewpoint of classical economics, the New Deal had been all wrong. The older theory had been that the economic system always tended toward healthy equilibrium. Periods of falling demand and apparent overproduction would, therefore, be self-correcting. Nature's cure for depressions was ruthless but sure: liquidation of debts and wage cuts would lead to lower prices; lower prices would increase demand and restore economic activity to a normal level. For the government to intervene by creating more money, spending to help the unemployed, or protecting debtors against their creditors was, from the classical viewpoint, both mischievous and futile.

Whatever the validity of this body of doctrine, modern democratic governments simply could not steel themselves to follow it to the letter. Even under Hoover the government was committed to helping debtors hold on to their property, trying to prevent the collapse of farm prices, and making funds available for relief of the unemployed. Under Roosevelt the theory that depressions must be left to run their course was completely abandoned. To the horror of orthodox economists the New Deal seemed willing to embrace every imaginable heresy: abandonment of the gold standard, curbs on agricultural production, subsidies to farmers, government expenditures to provide work for the unemployed, an unbalanced budget, and the imposition of lower interest rates.

As the actual practice of the day departed farther and farther from classical precepts, two viewpoints were possible. Conservatives naturally argued that the whole tendency of the New Deal must be wrong, since it ran counter to the economic wisdom accumulated over many years. Liberals, on the other hand, were quick to apply the standards of pragmatism. When the government did nothing, the depression seemed to go from bad to worse; when the government took action, conditions seemed to improve. Since the theory and the facts had lost contact with each other, might not the theory be wrong?

The need for a new hypothesis gave American economists a lively interest in the writings of John Maynard Keynes, the most brilliant English student of these problems. As a young economist. Keynes had created a great impression by his book *The Economic Consequences of the Peace* (1919), in which he had accurately predicted the financial chaos that would follow from the attempt to collect reparations from Germany after World War I. Later in the twenties Keynes directed his attention to the problems created by England's prolonged postwar depression with its loss of export markets and large-scale unemployment. Keynes's studies led him to repudiate many assumptions of classical economics. Tentatively in the *Treatise on Money* (1930) and much more confidently in *The General Theory of Employment, Interest and Money* (1936), Keynes laid the basis for what came to be known as the New Economics.

Although Keynes's work was too difficult for any but well-trained economists to understand in detail, something of his viewpoint eventually worked its way into the comprehension of most well-read Americans. "Say's Law," with its assumption that the demand for goods would always automatically equate itself to the production of goods, was the first of the older axioms to fall under Keynes's assault. Demand kept pace with supply, Keynes believed, only so long as all income was spent either in consumption or investment. When either consumption or investment declined and money passed into idle savings, depressions and unemployment were inevitable. Since consumption was largely based upon personal habits, it tended to be rather stable. The critical factor in causing depressions and booms was, therefore, investment.

All of this might have seemed to be of merely academic concern had not Keynes drawn from his analysis startling conclusions as to the proper function of government. He argued that the state could no longer be regarded as merely the neutral umpire in the economic game. Whether one liked it or not, government was involved as a player. Through taxing and spending it influenced the whole economy. If it drew in more of the national income than it spent, it tended to retard economic activity. If it spent more than it took in, its influence was to accelerate the economy. Keynes argued that a nation should frame its fiscal policies to compensate for the fluctuations in private capitalism. The annually balanced budget was folly. During periods of depression the government should deliberately incur a deficit, borrowing money from idle private savings to spend in ways that would compensate for the decline of private investment. During periods of inflation, the opposite policy should prevail.

Keynes also departed from orthodoxy in advocating government policies that would tend to redistribute income. Since the wealthy tended to oversave, their income should be reduced by progressive taxes and lower interest rates. The low-income groups, on the other hand, should be benefited through government expenditures for social security and public services. Greater income at the bottom of the economic pyramid would increase the demand for goods and encourage investment.

The relation of the New Economics to the New Deal was largely indirect. When Keynes visited Roosevelt in 1934, the latter found the Englishman's mathematical analysis difficult to understand, while Keynes was disappointed to find how little the President had read in the field of economics. During the early days of the New Deal there had been, in truth, very little consistent theory, Keynesian or otherwise, in the administration's feverish attempts to deal simultaneously with a score of practical problems.

But if the New Dealers discovered Keynes after rather than before they had formulated their program, they were none the less eager to embrace a body of thought that seemed to justify so much of what they had already done. During the second Roosevelt administration, the framing of policy along consciously Keynesian lines became more common.

Meanwhile, at the academic level the Keynesian yeast was leavening the whole field of economics. Some American scholars like Seymour E. Harris and Alvin Hansen of Harvard accepted the new theories with enthusiasm; others were critical. In either case, Keynes was far too challenging to be ignored.

Heretical though the New Economics seemed from the conservative point of view, there was little in it to give aid and comfort to the Marxists. A man of great versatility, Keynes was both scholar and practical man of affairs. As adviser to the British Treasury, insurance company executive, and investment counselor, he was deeply committed to the preservation of private capitalism. To American intellectuals, therefore, Keynes served a wholesome function. No longer did the only three rational alternatives seem to be laissez faire, democratic socialism, or communism; impressive academic backing had now been given to a fourth possibility—that of a private-enterprise system whose malfunctioning could be corrected by intelligent government policy.

Literature Looks at Society

Many of the literary trends of the twenties became outmoded during the depression. Before 1930 sensitive authors had been repelled by the smugness and brashness of their prosperous fellow-Americans. Many artistic people demonstrated their disapproval by living abroad; others worked off their resentment by savage satire. During the thirties this alienation largely disappeared. The mood of cynical individualism gave way to a growing concern for the problems of contemporary society. The literature of the thirties reflected no consistent philosophy; some of it was unblushingly Marxist; some of it reflected the broadly humanitarian viewpoint of the New Deal; much of it was merely troubled or angry in tone without political implications.

One of the major literary landmarks of the decade was John Dos Passos' trilogy *U.S.A.*, composed of *The 42nd Parallel* (1930), *1919* (1932), and *The Big Money* (1936). Combining such ingenious devices as "The Newsreel" and "The Camera Eye" with sketches of figures like Carnegie, Edison, Debs, Bryan, Theodore Roosevelt, and Wilson, and case histories of a dozen fictional characters, Dos Passos surveyed American life from 1900 to 1930 in its many and varied aspects. What he portrayed was not pleasant; his more unscrupulous characters gained material success, while the few who aspired to improve the world were frustrated. Trade unionists, IWW agitators, and Communists were more sympathetically portrayed than were the figures of the bourgeois world. The novel showed a strong leaning toward Marxism, but one from which the author was in the process of disillusionment even before a first-hand view of the Spanish Civil War completed his disenchantment. Like many others who had put their hands too close to the Marxist stove, Dos Passos in his later writing became not only fervently anti-Communist, but anti-New Deal as well.

Ernest Hemingway also displayed an ambition to outgrow the narrow individualism of the twenties and to deal with some of the basic problems of his generation. In portraying the Spanish Civil War in *For Whom the Bell Tolls* (1940), Hemingway combined his old-time facility in describing scenes of bloodshed and violent action with a newly displayed talent for telling a love story of unusual tenderness and a new respect for loyalty, idealism, and human decency. Much of the book's success came, no doubt, from its timeliness, since the year of its appearance was one of catastrophic democratic defeats.

Particularly responsive to the new social climate was John Steinbeck, whose novel *The Grapes of Wrath* (1939) vividly depicted the consequences of the dust storms of the thirties, together with a revelation of the exploitation of itinerant agricultural workers. Despite the grimness of his theme, Steinbeck conveyed a belief in basic human goodness and confidence that in the long run this good would prevail.

The death of Thomas Wolfe in 1938 cut short a career of rich promise. Largely autobiographical, Wolfe's novels, *Look Homeward, Angel* (1929), *Of Time and the River* (1935), *The Web and the Rock* (1939), and *You Can't Go Home Again* (1940), portrayed his Carolina boyhood, his life at Harvard and Oxford, his teaching at New York University, and his residence in France and Germany. They combined graphic realism with passages so lyrical and rhythmic that they have been taken from their context and published as poetry.

American society in its local or regional aspects was dissected by uncompromising realists. In *Young Lonigan: A Boyhood in Chicago Streets* (1932) and its sequels, James T. Farrell drew a savage portrait of the city environment in which he himself was brought up. In *Native Son* (1940), Richard Wright showed how relentless were the forces driving a Negro boy into crime in the slums of a Northern city. In a more restrained, ironic, and satirical mood, the sterility of the so-called cultured circles in New England was laid bare by John Marquand in *The Late George Apley* (1937) and *H. M. Pulham, Esquire* (1941).

Although the traditionalism of Southern society was still viewed with nostalgic affection by conservative Southern authors, the region was very differently treated in the work of others. Erskine Caldwell depicted the degeneracy of the poor white stock in stories all the more shocking because of the broad humor of their treatment. The dramatization of Caldwell's *Tobacco Road* (first published as a novel in 1932) enjoyed a fabulously long run both on Broadway and on tour. The Mississippian, William Faulkner, was a writer of extraordinary power who intrigued students of style with boldly constructed novels like *The Sound and the Fury* (1929), a morbid story of decadent aristocracy.

These were the authors most discussed by the serious-minded. But larger royalty checks were enjoyed by writers who ignored these aspects of life and helped their readers forget contemporary problems. Detective and mystery stories continued to be the popular form of escape literature, but readers with more time derived pleasure from lengthy historical novels, which appeared in large numbers. The most sensationally successful novel of the decade was Margaret Mitchell's *Gone with the Wind* (1936). This set the style for many less able efforts, which appealed to the reader less as vehicles for learning history than for following the escapades of lovely heroines. Of more solid merit were the carefully prepared historical novels of Kenneth Roberts and Walter Edmonds.

Americans Learn About Art

During the thirties there was evidence that more Americans than ever before took a serious interest in the fine arts. Training in painting and music gained a more secure place in education. Native talent was no longer ignored, while the public lionized foreign visitors. Probably little of the artistic production of the period had any claim to greatness, but there was interest and activity, and these offered much promise for the future.

To a much greater extent than ever before the Federal government became a patron of the arts. The Great Depression bore down with particular severity upon painters, and by 1935 some four thousand were in serious straits. To relieve this group the WPA Art Project, under the direction of Holger Cahill, was organized. During the next five years about 52,000 easel paintings were created by government-paid artists and placed on permanent loan in schools, libraries, and hospitals. Even more remarkable was the stimulus given to mural painting. The WPA program resulted in the installation of over 1,500 murals in tax-supported public institutions located in every section of the country. The PWA administration also gave extensive employment to mural painters. Artists as firmly established as George Biddle, Reginald Marsh, and Boardman Robinson contributed to the decoration of the new buildings erected in Washington to house the Justice, Post Office, and Interior Departments. Government-sponsored art ranged all the way from the very fine to the worthless. Competent critics found encouragement, however, in the freshness and enthusiasm of much that was produced. Moreover, from the educational point of view, works of art placed in post offices, hospitals, and schools were much more likely to arouse the interest of the general public than pictures purchased by wealthy patrons to be hung in their own homes.

The period was characterized by great variety in style. Some artists were working with a precision of detail that was almost photographic; others painted in a mood so abstract as to bewilder those who inspected their work. Some were traditionalists following the canons of taste well formulated in the past; others were audacious innovators. Combining the thorough technical mastery of the academicians with the force and honesty characteristic of the best of the modernists was Eugene Speicher, acclaimed by many as the country's leading portrait painter. John Marin painted a variety of American scenes ranging from rocky Maine and crowded New York to the barren Southwest in a sensitive style bordering upon the abstract. A stimulating influence on American art was the infinite variety provided by the country's regional differences. Life in the midwestern prairie country found reflection in the paintings of Thomas Hart Benton, Grant Wood, and John Steuart Curry; New York City's perennial fascination for the artist was captured by Reginald Marsh and Edward Hopper; even Alaska was not beyond the scope of the restless artist, as some of the best of Rockwell Kent's work emphasized.

Radio broadcasts taught many Americans that opera and symphony concerts were less formidable than they had imagined. The moving-picture industry was somewhat more timid in promoting serious music, but it did offer employment to some of the more shapely prima donnas. The most effective medium for broadening the popular interest in music, however, was the phonograph. With better methods of recording and reproduction, recorded music achieved a degree of excellence that provoked genuine enthusiasm. Of course, neither radio nor phonograph offered compensations as rich as personal attendance in the music hall. Opportunities to enjoy this latter experience widened during the thirties and were seized by an increasing number of people. Once again government sponsorship through WPA orchestras and free concerts not only kept musicians alive during the depression, but served an educational function as well.

The American-born artist became much less of a novelty on the opera and concert stage. Grace Moore, Gladys Swarthout, Lawrence Tibbett, John Charles Thomas, and many others held their own against foreign talent in the operatic field, while Marian Anderson and Albert Spaulding proved prime drawing cards on the concert stage. Top-ranking native conductors were not so common, but Werner Janssen enjoyed a considerable success in this field during the thirties. Nor was the country so entirely dependent on European composers as formerly. Deems Taylor repeated his earlier success with the opera *Peter Ibbetson,* produced by the Metropolitan in 1931. Other notable American operas were *The Emperor Jones* by Louis Gruenberg and *Merry Mount* by Howard Hanson, staged by the Metropolitan in 1933 and 1934 respectively. Another interesting work was the folk-opera *The Devil and Daniel Webster* (1939), with music by Douglas Moore and libretto by the distinguished poet, Stephen Vincent Benét. In the field of symphonic works, John Alden Carpenter's *Sea Drift* (1934) and Daniel Gregory Mason's *A Lincoln Symphony* (1937) combined thoroughly American themes with an orthodox technique. On the other hand, modernistic efforts like the *Third Symphony* by Roy Harris and *Music for the Theatre* by Aaron Copland represented bold pioneering into new idioms.

It was perhaps this new enthusiasm for art and music that provided the most hopeful symptom for the American future. Such tastes could never, it is true, be the prime driving forces for any large percentage of the population, but they pointed to a broadening of interest. The Great Depression had dramatized the flimsiness of a civilization based excessively on material prosperity. There were hopeful signs that more Americans were perceiving the truth that making a living was not an end in itself but a means, and that really rich living depended upon a breadth of culture.

22

Gathering Clouds

President Franklin D. Roosevelt took office during troublesome times in the diplomatic world. Japan had just successfully defied the League of Nations and the Stimson Doctrine. Benito Mussolini was formulating plans for an African empire to renew the power that once was Rome's. Adolf Hitler had recently emerged as the most powerful figure in Germany and was bent on wiping out the stain of the Versailles Treaty. International trade was rapidly declining in the face of growing nationalism, and with that decline the war debts and reparations problems were becoming more difficult to solve. Moreover, international economy was disrupted by the currency situation. The seeds of chaos then being sown threatened a harvest of world-wide strife and discord.

The Attitude of the New Deal

The campaign of 1932 indicated that the Democrats were largely concerned with clearing up troubles at home. Little was said in their platform about international affairs, and then only in general terms. The platform favored reciprocal trade agreements, an international conference to consider the rehabilitation of silver and promotion of international trade, and peaceful settlement of disputes. Nothing was said about the League of Nations. Even the candidate, who had been a strong Wilsonian in 1920, refused to endanger the party's election chances by reviving the issue of American entry into the League. With the exception of the advocacy of reciprocal trade agreements, the Democratic position on international affairs was strikingly similar to the Hoover theses. As the campaign progressed, however, it became apparent that the New Deal was rejecting an international economic outlook, under which American farmers and manufacturers would have to fix their prices to compete in a world market, in favor of a planned national economy based primarily upon the readjustment of domestic costs and domestic prices.

The Decline of World Trade

Following the enactment of the Hawley-Smoot Tariff, other countries had raised their own economic barriers on the assumption that high import duties would provide a safeguard for their domestic products against the sharp fall of world prices, for their gold reserves, and for their labor situation. Even Britain, long a champion of free trade, succumbed to this trend in November, 1931.

The result was that international trade fell off sharply in the years immediately preceding Roosevelt's first inauguration. In 1929, the total value of the exports and imports of 110 countries was slightly more than $68 billion; by 1932 it had gradually dropped to $26 billion. A decline of approximately 62 per cent in three years was a cause for worry, if for no other reason than that the payment of war debts was affected; if the debtor nations did not build up their trade, they would never accrue the wherewithal to send their semiannual installments to the United States.

The London Economic Conference

Perhaps the way to solve the numerous interrelated problems was through an international conference, such as originally proposed by the European nations at the time of the Lausanne meeting. The invitation reached the United States just about the time of the Democratic convention and gave the party an opportunity to include a plank advocating American participation. President Hoover was also in agreement, and in August, 1932, the United States was represented on the Organizing Committee and the Preparatory Committee of Experts at Geneva to discuss what would be taken up at the international conference. On the proposed agenda were such problems as world unemployment, the decline of commodity prices, international trade, monetary chaos, and debts and reparations.

During April and May, 1933, Ramsay MacDonald of Britain, Edouard Herriot of France, and representatives of other countries visited President Roosevelt to discuss the impending meeting. In a "fireside chat" of May 7, the President said: "The international conference that lies before us must succeed. The future of the world demands it and we have each of us pledged ourselves to the best joint efforts to this end." Nine days later he sent an appeal to the heads of the fifty-four other nations invited in which he asserted:

The Conference must establish order in place of the present chaos by a stabilization of currencies, by freeing the flow of world trade, and by international action to raise price levels. It must, in short, supplement individual domestic programs for economic recovery, by wise and considered international action.

Despite these glowing statements, the United States had taken steps, even during the Hoover administration, that made the success of the meeting unlikely. The questions of tariffs, war debts, and reparations were ruled off the agenda of the conference. It is difficult to see how international economics could have been improved and stabilized without a discussion of these matters.

The Economic Conference opened in London on June 12, 1933. The American delegation, headed by Secretary of State Cordell Hull,[1] was anxious to achieve accord, but it was handicapped both by the prohibitions placed upon it and by the changing policy back home. The various delegation leaders started the discussion with hopeful generalities, an indication that not much had been accomplished in the preliminary meetings. Prime Minister MacDonald announced that the question of war debts, although barred from consideration at the meeting, would have to be discussed eventually. While his statement was undoubtedly true, it antagonized the American Congress, which had been largely responsible for the prohibition.

The issue of currency stabilization was the first concrete matter taken up. France, Belgium, Italy, Holland, and Switzerland wanted gold to be the medium for such stabilization. The American delegation refused to agree because the dollar was declining in international exchange; in turn, American prosperity apparently was beginning to return. Were stabilization on a gold standard adopted internationally, that hoped-for prosperity might prove only an illusion. When the conference threatened to break up, however, the American delegation accepted a compromise: the gold countries should continue the gold standard at existing parities; those that had gone off gold were to return as soon as possible and in the meantime would try to prevent speculation in currency exchange.

As soon as President Roosevelt learned of this compromise, he wired the American delegation on July 3, 1933, that he "would regard it as a catastrophe amounting to a world tragedy if the great Conference of Nations . . . should . . . allow itself to be diverted by the proposal of a purely artificial and temporary experiment affecting the monetary exchange of a few Nations only." Although this repudiation of the compromise was approved in the United States, where prices had already started to fall as a result of fears over currency stabilization, it was vigorously denounced at the London Conference. The American government was charged with bad faith, for it had shown its will-

[1] The other members were: Senators Key Pittman of Nevada and James Couzens of Michigan, Representative S. D. McReynolds of Tennessee, James Cox of Ohio, and Ralph Morrison of Texas.

ingness to agree to stabilization during earlier conferences. President Roosevelt defended his action by placing the blame on the few gold countries which, he asserted, were seeking only temporary expedients; but considering that he himself had said that international development should come before domestic economic policies and then had opposed stabilization, his step was not entirely consistent.

With the July 3 statement the London Conference really came to an end. While it is true that Secretary Hull did try to salvage something from the wreckage, his efforts were useless. The British delegation also attempted to effect some stabilization between the pound sterling and the dollar, but the Americans' hands were tied by the domestic policy of their country. Regardless of who was to blame, the failure of the London Economic Conference was a bitter blow to the betterment of international economic accord. Efforts at cooperation dwindled thereafter and economic nationalism, which had been growing for some time, was given additional impetus. Nor did recriminations help the situation to any degree. From the European point of view, however, the New Deal had started off poorly in international affairs.

The European Nations Default

Closely associated in the European mind with improvement of the international economic situation was the matter of war debts. As has been mentioned, the Lausanne Conference provided for practically canceling German reparations if the European debtors of the United States could make a satisfactory arrangement for decreasing their own obligations. The United States was not willing to cancel the war debts, but both President Hoover and President-elect Roosevelt were ready to conduct separate discussions with each debtor nation, even though they disagreed as to the medium for such discussions. By December 15, 1932, the moratorium was over and the semiannual installments were due again. Five nations defaulted, the remainder made their full payments. Britain, in an accompanying note, urged the reopening of the whole debt question as a "contribution . . . to world revival."

The Roosevelt administration consistently refused to support cancellation or a general conference to consider lowering the European obligations. The latter position was indicated clearly when the United States banned the problem from the London Economic Conference agenda.

Three days after that conference opened the next debt payments became due. The European nations were faced with three choices: paying the installment in full; deferring—or from the American point of view defaulting—in hope of reaching a new agreement; or making partial or token payment that would recognize the debt responsibility, but at the same time indicate the need for reduction. The nations that had defaulted the previous December once again failed to make any payment. Finland paid her full obligation. The remaining countries followed the lead of Great Britain in making token payments "as an acknowledgment of the debt pending a final settlement." The British argument was that full payment might interfere with the success of the London Conference, for in the past when such payments were made world prices inevitably went down; the object of the conference was to stabilize them. Thus of the nearly $144 million due the United States, less than $12 million was received.

President Roosevelt announced that "inasmuch as the payment made is accompanied by a clear acknowledgment of the debt itself . . . I have no personal hesitation in saying that I do not characterize the resultant situation as a default." He accepted the token amounts and the Treasury Department credited them to the countries concerned. As to the requests for reconsideration, the President said that they were up to Congress and he urged the token payers to send their representations to that body as soon as possible.

Congress, representing the current American opinion, was in no mood to review the war-debt issue. The emphasis placed upon domestic recovery, the "poor-sportsmanship"—as Senator Johnson called it—of the London Conference in alluding to war debts, and the fact that European nations could find money to spend on armaments, all combined to develop opposition to lowering the obligations to the United States. Consequently, the State Department did not even bother to present the requests of the token payers to the legislature. Thus the European debtors continued either to default entirely or to make partial payments—with the exception of Finland.

The Johnson Debt Default Act

It was in such a mood that Congress overwhelmingly passed the Johnson Debt Default Act in April, 1934. The original bill, sponsored by arch-isolationist Senator Hiram Johnson of California, had been introduced in 1933 to prohibit any citizen of the United States from buying or selling any securities of a country in arrears or in default of its war debt under penalty of fine or imprisonment. The State Department objected strenuously to the proposal because it would apply to bonds that had already been sold; consequently, many American investors would suffer. Therefore the bill was laid on the table until January, 1934, when it was amended to read that no loans could be made to any nations in default or in arrears, nor could such countries sell any of their securities in the United States. Although there was debate for nearly three months, the passage of the Johnson Bill was never in doubt and it was signed by President Roosevelt on April 13, 1934.

The Johnson Act did not achieve its objective of compelling the debtor nations to resume their payments. On the contrary, on the next installment date, June 15, 1934, the token payers stopped making even partial payments. Moreover, the Johnson Act checkmated any possible conferences for reducing the obligations. Its passage may have thwarted international economic recovery by preventing the possibility of American loans to foreign nations. Nor did it help the role of the United States in international affairs because Europe regarded it as vindictive. Finally, it was in line with the asserted Roosevelt policy of trying to promote better relations; the President's signature on the measure was probably motivated by his desire for Congressional support of his domestic recovery program.

The Hull Reciprocal Trade Program

While it appeared that the United States thus far had not helped the international economic situation, actually Secretary of State Hull was hard at work on a reciprocal trade program idea advocated in the Democratic platform and by Roosevelt during his campaign. The general thesis was that the existing Hawley-Smoot Tariff was in large part responsible for existing world ills because it tended to suppress international trade. Reciprocal agreements, on the other hand, would not only revive such trade but would build up international prosperity, help to stabilize currencies, and enable the European debtors to pay their obligations. Moreover, they might help to promote American economic recovery by assisting industry and agriculture in finding broader markets.

On March 2, 1934, the President asked Congress for permission "to enter into executive commercial agreements with foreign Nations" and "within carefully guarded limits, to modify existing duties and import restrictions in such a way as will benefit American agriculture and industry." He pointed out that world trade had declined 70 per cent since 1929 and that American exports had fallen off 52 per cent during the same period. "This has meant," he continued, "idle hands, still machines, ships tied to their docks, despairing farm households, and hungry industrial families." The proposal had the unqualified support of Secretary Hull, who indeed may have been the original sponsor of it, having introduced a somewhat similar plan when he was a member of Congress in 1916.

Almost immediately a bill was introduced embodying the President's plan. Attacks from numerous quarters were made. Some who opposed it were fearful lest their own special business interests would suffer; others were against it because they believed that tariff protection was necessary for national prosperity; still another faction considered it unconstitutional because it delegated both taxing and treaty-making power to the executive branch. Despite the fact that the bill encountered more opposition than any other measure thus far in the New Deal program, it was passed by substantial majorities—mainly Democratic—in both Houses and signed by the President on June 12, 1934.

Called "an Act to amend the Tariff Act of 1930," the measure was popularly known as the "Hull Trade Agreement Act." First of all, it authorized the President to negotiate trade agreements with other nations to obtain new markets for American products. To do this, he could raise or lower the Hawley-Smoot rates up to 50 per cent. A special Executive Committee on Commercial Policy was to assist the President, and all interested parties could give their criticisms and suggestions before an agreement became effective. Once arrangements between the United States and another country were completed, the President was to put the agreement into effect by executive proclamation, no action of Congress being necessary. The act was to remain in effect for three years.

Secretary Hull, who was in charge of negotiating these reciprocal agreements, strove for certain things. In the first place, he tried to speed up the exchange of commodities produced by one of the parties and needed by the other. Next, he attempted to gain special concessions for American surplus goods. Finally, he granted similar concessions in American markets for staples of the other signatory, although he seldom allowed reductions on imports that competed strongly with domestic products.

The first reciprocal agreement was signed with Cuba in August, 1934. By the time the three years were up, fifteen other nations had completed arrangements with the United States and three agreements were pending.[2] Immediately trade with these nations grew rapidly. For example, during the first year of the treaty with Belgium, American exports jumped $11 million—an increase of 24 per cent; for the first year of the Canadian agreement, the export increase was more than $60 million. And whereas American trade with non-signatories increased 25 per cent, that with signatories grew by 40 per cent. The administration consistently supported the most-favored-nation principle, and tariff reductions granted under the special agreements with individual nations were automatically extended to all other countries with which the United States had commercial treaties. Thus the effect of the Hull program was to modify greatly the whole tariff structure.

In 1937 the Trade Agreements Act was extended for another three years, during which period additional reciprocal arrangements were effected, principally with Great Britain and most of the remaining nations of Latin America. Besides helping American business, these treaties influenced other countries to conclude similar agreements with their neighbors. Thus the flow of inter-

---

[2] The other fifteen were: Belgium, Brazil, Canada, Colombia, Costa Rica, El Salvador, Finland, France, Guatemala, Haiti, Honduras, Netherlands, Nicaragua, Sweden, and Switzerland.

national trade began again, and better feeling developed among the numerous signatories. Since 1940 Congress has continued to extend the measure.

The United States likewise helped American exporters early in 1934 by establishing the Export-Import Bank, authorized under a provision of the National Industrial Recovery Act. This bank loaned money to other countries to stabilize their currencies and their exchange, which in turn would make possible more American sales. In addition, many countries received American credit so that they could buy equipment, such as rolling stock, building supplies, and machinery, in the United States.

Recognition of the Soviet Union

The Soviet government was still unrecognized when President Roosevelt took office, but American liberals were eager for a change of policy and American exporters were pressing for restoration of diplomatic relations so that their trade would be safeguarded. The initiative that led to recognition was taken by Maxim Litvinov, head of the Russian delegation to the London Economic Conference, when he proposed to Secretary Hull that differences between the two nations might be patched up.

Secretary Hull informed President Roosevelt of the olive-branch suggestion with the result that Litvinov was invited to Washington in November, 1933. Meantime, the way was being paved for restoration of friendship when the Reconstruction Finance Corporation made a loan to American exporters to facilitate the Russian purchase of American cotton.

After a series of conversations, notes were exchanged between Roosevelt and Litvinov on November 16, 1933. In these notes the Soviet emissary promised that his government would not promote propaganda in any manner in the United States nor allow any organization to develop within Soviet territory that sought the overthrow of the American government. Moreover, Americans in Russia were to be granted freedom of conscience and worship, as well as fair trials if accused of crimes. After diplomatic relations were restored, the Soviet government promised to negotiate on the issue of the debts contracted under preceding Russian regimes. As these statements of Soviet policy were satisfactory to President Roosevelt, he announced American recognition of the Soviet Union the same day.

In general, this recognition was well received by the American people, despite the fact that there were some who felt that the Red menace of post-World War I days was still great. There were high hopes of an immediate increase of American exports to Russia. Indeed, one of the reasons for establishing the Export-Import Bank was to speed up commercial relations between the two countries. The failure of the debt negotiations, however, made operative the Johnson

Debt Default Act, and no loans could be extended to the Soviet. Without loans, the expected trade boom did not materialize. As time passed, there was also the feeling in America that Russia was not living up to her no-propaganda pledge. Yet diplomatic recognition of Russia was in line with the Roosevelt inaugural promise to be a good neighbor. And perhaps behind that recognition was the administration desire to secure additional support against Japanese aggression.

The Way toward Philippine Independence

President Roosevelt took up the Philippine issue where Hoover left off. Filipino objections to the Hawes-Cutting Act were remedied in the McDuffie-Tydings Act of March, 1934. During the ten-year probationary period the provision for American control of foreign affairs was retained, all military forces in the islands might be called into American service if danger threatened, immigration differences were worked out to mutual satisfaction, and a special commission would consider the tariff situation. The Philippine Congress approved this act on May 1, 1934.

A special constituent assembly of Filipinos then drew up a constitution, which was approved both by President Roosevelt and the Filipino people by the middle of 1935. Victorious in the first election under this document, Manuel Quezon became President of the Commonwealth of the Philippines on November 15, 1935. Before the probationary period was up, however, the safety of the Philippines was dangerously challenged. The occupation of the archipelago by the Japanese from 1942 to 1945 drove Quezon into exile in the United States, where he died. But in the months after V-J Day the United States fulfilled its pledge. On July 4, 1946, the Philippines became an independent republic, with Manuel Roxas serving as president.

The Good Neighbor

The "Good Neighbor" policy of the New Deal, however, is primarily associated with American relations with Latin America. This policy was foreshadowed by an address that President Roosevelt made before the governing board of the Pan-American Union on April 12, 1933. In it he said:

> The essential qualities of a true Pan Americanism must be the same as those which constitute a good neighbor. . . . Friendship among Nations . . . calls for constructive efforts to muster the forces of humanity in order that an atmosphere of close understanding and cooperation may be cultivated. It involves mutual obligations and responsibilities. . . . In this spirit the people of every Republic on our continent are coming to a deep understanding of the fact that the Monroe Doctrine . . . was and is directed at the maintenance of independence

by the peoples of the continent. . . . It is of vital importance to every Nation of this continent that the American Governments, individually, take, without further delay, such action as may be possible to abolish all unnecessary and artificial barriers and restrictions which now hamper the healthy flow of trade between the peoples of the American Republics.

While the emphasis in this speech was placed upon increased trade and commerce, the Roosevelt administration quickly showed an interest in maintaining a policy of non-intervention and in concluding dollar diplomacy. Fulfillment of these aims was aided immeasurably by Secretary Hull, whose informal dealings with Latin-American leaders accomplished more good than strait-laced diplomacy, and by his assistant, Sumner Welles, whose knowledge of Latin-American problems furnished the basis for many moves in support of the Good Neighbor policy.

One of the first opportunities to act the part of the Good Neighbor was offered during the seventh regular Pan-American Conference held at Montevideo, Uruguay, in December, 1933. Secretary Hull, head of the American delegation, did not try to assume a commanding position in open discussions, but used behind-the-scenes diplomacy to achieve his ends. He gained tacit support for reciprocity and he prevailed upon the other republics to endorse several commitments to outlaw war. The most important action of the meeting was to approve Article VIII: "No State has a right to intervene in the internal or external affairs of another." The American backing of this article showed a definite change of heart since the Havana Conference of 1928. Another step toward peaceful relations provided for permanent bilateral commissions of inquiry and consultation. Moreover, the meeting brought a temporary truce between Bolivia and Paraguay, who had been fighting over the Gran Chaco. A number of cultural and economic questions were also amicably discussed. All in all, the Montevideo Conference ended on a note of great accord; most of the fears and suspicions that Latin Americans had of the United States were erased for the time being.

Completing the Withdrawal from Haiti

Putting the Good Neighbor policy into more practical effect in regard to Haiti, President Roosevelt found the solution which had evaded his predecessor by concluding an executive agreement with Haitian President Vincent. This "Agreement of August 7, 1933," provided for complete Haitian control of the national guard by October 1, 1934, at which time the last of the American marines would be withdrawn. In collaboration with President Roosevelt, a fiscal representative would be named by Vincent to supervise collection of customs after January 1, 1934.

Since this financial arrangement was not wholly satisfactory to the Haitians, Vincent went to Washington where, in April, he obtained a promise that a new solution would be worked out. Three months later, Roosevelt visited Haiti and, after looking over the situation, he ordered the last of the marines to be withdrawn by August 15. At the same time, provision was made for sale by the National City Bank of New York of a controlling interest in the National Bank of Haiti to the Haitian government and for the conclusion of American fiscal control. By the summer of 1935 these financial arrangements were completed and Haiti was once more in full control of all her affairs. American dollar diplomacy in the West Indies was thereby at an end.

Meantime, the United States had helped to ensure Haitian financial competence by signing a reciprocal trade agreement with her in March, 1935. Haiti could now send cocoa, rum, and fruit to the United States at considerably less than the Hawley-Smoot rates, while the insular authorities granted similar reductions on American machinery and automotive equipment.

Abrogation of the Platt Amendment

As has been stated, a tense situation had developed in Cuba during the closing days of the Hoover administration. The depression there led to political discontent directed against Dictator Machado. In an effort to end the troubles, President Roosevelt named Sumner Welles as ambassador in the early summer of 1933. Welles tried to solve the difficulties by suggesting that Machado take a leave of absence, but the Cuban executive refused to do so. Thereupon the Cubans took matters into their own hands, staged a general strike on August 4, and forced Machado to flee the country. Then followed months of tumult, with no president or *junta* able to remain long in office. Cries were also raised for the abrogation of the Platt Amendment. Although Roosevelt sent a number of warships to Cuban ports to protect American interests, he called upon the ABC powers and Mexico to assist the United States in prevailing upon the Cubans to re-establish orderly government. There was no thought of unilateral action or intervention.

Not until January, 1934, was a semblance of peace restored to the island with the coming into power of Carlos Mendieta, who was recognized promptly by the United States. Additional help was given in the form of financial credit through Export-Import Bank loans and a reciprocal trade treaty. That treaty granted Cuba concessions on sugar, rum, fruits, tobacco, and numerous other items, while she in turn allowed reductions on more than four hundred imports from the United States.

The most important token of the Good Neighbor policy, however, was the abrogation of the Platt Amendment. As early as November, 1933, President

Roosevelt had urged this step to show "by deed our intention of playing the part of a good neighbor to the Cuban people." It was not until June, 1934, however, that a treaty was ratified to provide for removal of the Platt Amendment from the Cuban constitution and the voiding of the 1903 treaty that incorporated the amendment. For defensive purposes, however, Cuba allowed the United States to continue the lease of Guantanamo Bay.

Placating Panama

In somewhat similar fashion the United States ended its protectorate over Panama. For many years Panamanians had disliked that provision of the Hay-Bunau-Varilla Treaty of 1903 which gave the United States the right to intervene to preserve order and to ensure independence. They asserted that those rights actually deprived Panama of sovereignty. The situation was complicated still more when the United States went off the gold standard and tried to pay the annual rental for canal rights in 59-cent dollars instead of the promised gold. Moreover, growing unrest in other parts of the world made the Roosevelt administration realize the need of close accord with Panama for protection of the canal.

Consequently, under a treaty of March, 1936, the United States gave up its right to intervene in Panama for the protection of the waterway, along with its right under eminent domain to obtain additional territories near the terminals. On its part, Panama agreed to cooperate with the United States in defending the canal and the adjacent territory. The United States promised to pay its annual rental in Panama money at the old gold exchange rate.

The decision of Japan to withdraw from the naval limitations agreements caused considerable worry in the United States Senate. Could the United States defend the canal adequately under the new arrangements? Many thought not. Therefore it was not until July, 1939, that this treaty, in somewhat amended form, was ratified by the American Upper House.

The Gathering Storm

Thus far the New Deal in its diplomacy had been motivated by the desire to promote world economic recovery, which in turn would help the United States fulfill its domestic program. If the rest of the world did not cooperate, then the United States could always rely upon the support of the other republics of the hemisphere that had been wooed with the Good Neighbor policy.

As the early years of the New Deal passed, however, it became increasingly evident that there was more to world unrest than simply monetary and commercial dislocation. A growing spirit of aggression—which may have had behind it economic factors, to be sure—threatened the peace of the world. Despite the fact that Roosevelt's wish to complete the domestic program of recovery took his primary attention, the increasing world tension could not be disregarded.

The Geneva Conference

Approximately a month before Roosevelt was inaugurated, the Geneva Disarmament Conference reopened its meetings. Germany, which had been seeking equality of treatment, had been placated and had returned to the meetings. Once again, however, there was failure to reach an agreement during the early weeks. Then in March, 1933, Prime Minister MacDonald offered a new proposition: the armies of the European nations should be raised through conscription, the size of each determined according to population; no army should be large; heavy guns and military planes should be kept at a minimum; Germany was to be granted proportional equality with her neighbors; and France, worried over growing German strength, was to be reassured through a meeting of signers of the Paris Pact to determine how it could be enforced. Germany did not like this British plan and sought fuller rights. When the conference refused, she threatened to build up her armaments anyway.

President Roosevelt then tried his hand at suggesting a settlement. At the same time that he urged the countries represented at the London Economic Conference to compromise on financial problems (May 16, 1933), he asked the Geneva delegation to "enter into a solemn and definite pact of non-aggression." Six days later, the new chairman of the American delegation, Norman H. Davis, told the Geneva gathering:

> We are ready not only to do our part toward the substantial reduction of armaments, but if this is effected by general international agreement we are also prepared to contribute in other ways to the organization of peace. In particular we are willing to consult the other states in case of a threat to peace with a view to avoiding conflict.

This meant that the United States would cooperate with the League of Nations in any action it took to avert war. There was an additional promise that the United States would not attempt to restrain collective efforts to bring an aggressor to terms.

While this American position heartened France, it did not bring approval of the British proposal. Germany still refused to agree that she was being fairly treated. Although Hitler professed a desire for accord, the actions of the German delegation indicated the opposite. With the meeting still deadlocked in June, an adjournment was called. Just before the conference was to reconvene in October, 1933, Germany stated that she would not attend, and, furthermore,

The Pyromaniac. (By Kirby. Reproduced by permission
of the *New York World-Telegram.* Copyright, 1933.)

announced her decision to withdraw from the League of Nations. She knew
that her plans were opposed by the United States because Hull had already
informed her ambassador that Americans would "wage a steady contest for the
disarmament of the heavily armed nations, rather than become parties to a
plan for others to proceed to rearm." While the Geneva Conference held some
abortive sessions in the spring of 1934, to all intents and purposes its efforts
were fruitless after Germany's departure. The failure of this conference increased Roosevelt's apprehensions about the possibility of new wars.

The Buenos Aires Conference

In line with this apprehension, Roosevelt announced in March, 1936, that
all the hemisphere republics had agreed to discuss at Buenos Aires the problem
of how to meet the threat of world chaos. The meeting opened on December
1, 1936, and the importance attached to it may be gleaned from the fact that
President Roosevelt went to Argentina to deliver the opening address. He said
in part:

This is no conference to form alliances, to divide the spoils of war, to partition countries, to deal with human beings as though they were pawns in the game of chance. Our purpose, under happy auspices, is to assure the continuance of the blessings of peace.

After this stirring opening speech, the conference began its search for greater accord. Secretary Hull, again heading the American delegation, gained unanimous approval for his suggestion that all the previous treaties for peace and arbitration be ratified once again. It was also agreed that when the peace and safety of the Americas were threatened externally or internally, the several republics would meet to find a cooperative solution. Moreover, approval was given to the proposal for a common policy of neutrality in the event of war outside of the hemisphere or between two or more nations within. Likewise all differences among the republics—territorial and financial—must be submitted to arbitration. The accord reached at Buenos Aires indicated that the Monroe Doctrine had in effect become multilateral.

It was partly as a result of this accord that the United States and five Latin-American republics finally found the solution to the Gran Chaco War during the summer of 1938 after the League of Nations failed. Yet the policy of nonintervention and of the Good Neighbor was sorely tried when Mexico expropriated American, British, and Dutch oil properties valued at nearly $500 million. The American companies concerned appealed to their government for redress and Secretary Hull sent vigorous notes to Mexico about seizures without adequate compensation. There was no thought of employing force against Mexico, however, and after several years of jockeying, a joint commission was set up that reached a satisfactory settlement in 1943.

The Growth of Isolation

American public opinion, primarily concerned with domestic recovery, had been apathetic toward the entire Geneva proceedings. That apathy was clearly demonstrated in connection with Secretary Hull's request of April 5, 1933, that Congress provide for the President to forbid the exportation of arms and munitions of war when such shipments "might promote or encourage the employment of force in a dispute or conflict between nations." The general purpose would be to cooperate with other peace-loving nations in preventing aggressors from obtaining additional military supplies. Hull qualified his request with the assertion that the embargo would be used "to the sole end of maintaining the peace of the world and with a due and prudent regard for our national policies and national interests."

Although the House of Representatives approved a bill incorporating the Secretary's suggestions, the Senate amended it so that the embargo would have to be applied against all belligerents, aggressor or otherwise. When the House refused to agree the measure lapsed—for the time being.

The Senate version reflected a growing spirit of isolation. The feeling was increasing that the country must not be drawn into another conflict like World War I. Norman Davis expressed the views of most Americans when he said, in May, 1934, that while the United States would cooperate in an international disarmament program, it would not "participate in European political negotiations and settlements and will not make any commitment whatever to use its armed forces for the settlement of any dispute anywhere."

But why had this spirit developed? It is impossible to place one's finger on any single factor, for there were a number of contributing elements. To many Americans, World War I had been fought in vain; the world had not been made safe for democracy. There was a growing feeling that wars were engineered by munitions makers so that they might make money. This view was so powerful that *Fortune* magazine made an investigation, which it published in its March, 1934, issue. This report appeared to be so damning that President Roosevelt asked Hugh Johnson and Bernard Baruch to try to find a formula for ending wartime profits. The Senate also set up its own investigating committee headed by Gerald P. Nye of North Dakota, an extreme isolationist. Making its report in 1937 after three years of much publicized hearings, the Nye Committee charged that American business leaders had not only profited greatly during World War I, but had evaded the payment of taxes on their ill-gotten gains. Moreover, the Army and Navy Departments had been lax to the point of corruption, political connections were important in obtaining contracts, and American bankers were instrumental in bringing the country into war to save their loans to the Allies. Although the report did not prove its points and its conclusions were not warranted by the evidence obtained, many Americans were shocked by the findings and completely converted to isolationism.

Another factor in the isolationist trend was the failure of the debtors to repay what they had borrowed during World War I. And what made it worse, Americans felt that this money was being used to build up national armaments, which would lead to future wars. The League of Nations was looked upon simply as an organization to further the interests of its members. The World Court was only a tool of the League. If the United States joined the Court, the nation might become involved in European entanglements and war. In January, 1935, President Roosevelt, following the precedent of Harding, Coolidge, and Hoover, appealed to the Senate to approve the World Court protocol, but the Upper House did not provide the necessary two-thirds vote because of isolationist opposition.[3]

Among the so-called intelligentsia the isolationist trend was also strong. The

[3] The vote was 52 in favor of adherence, 36 against.

nation was flooded with literature stressing the futility of war and playing up the need to avoid entanglements with the rest of the world. Charles and Mary Beard developed this thesis in their writings, as did Harry Elmer Barnes, himself a propagandist against the German menace prior to the entrance of the United States into World War I. It became the vogue in college classrooms to teach that the Treaty of Versailles was a harsh peace, responsible for many of the world's troubles during the twenties, and that the Allies were equally guilty with the Germans of starting the conflict. Consequently, the younger generation was imbued with the psychology of isolation; many seemed to act upon the slogan, "Peace at any price."

The Failure of Naval Limitation

This isolationist trend was given added impetus by the results of the London Naval Conference of 1935, provision for which had been made at the 1930 meeting. Preliminary to this conference, delegations from the United States, Great Britain, and Japan had gathered at London in June, 1934. The Britons urged continuation of the existing ratios, reduction in size of battleships, either abolition of the submarine or reduction in size and number, and an increase in the number of cruisers. The Americans sought a 20 per cent reduction of existing naval armaments and maintenance of existing ratios. On the other hand, the Japanese delegates wanted equality with the other two; they would agree to reduction, but only on their own terms. All efforts at compromise failed, although the British were more ready to yield to Japanese wishes than were the Americans, who were opposed to any change in the relative strength of the navies. On December 29, 1934, therefore, the Japanese government informed the other signatories of the Washington and London Naval Treaties that it would withdraw from the agreements two years later.

Thus the London Naval Conference of 1935, opening in December, began inauspiciously. Japan still insisted on equality and the United States continued to support the existing ratios. The American delegates took the position that granting of equality would be an admission that Japanese actions in the Far East were approved. Thereupon the Japanese envoys left the conference. The remaining delegations, representing France, Italy, Britain, and the United States, then tried to salvage something from the wreckage. In March, 1936, they agreed to a new London Naval Treaty, under which Britain and the United States were to continue their tonnage parity and not engage in any competitive building. The restrictions on the number of ships in each category were removed, but there were so many escalator and escape clauses that the treaty actually had little significance. Nevertheless, the United States Senate ratified the treaty without a dissenting vote. To many Americans the withdrawal of Japan from the naval limitations agreements and the fact that Britain and France were embarking on new naval construction programs meant a greater possibility of war. Country after country, large and small, was developing its land armaments. The wise thing to do, therefore, was to try to insulate the nation from these troubles.

Neutrality Legislation

Meantime, growing tension in two instances had led to actual war. Bolivia and Paraguay had resumed fighting over the Gran Chaco, and Italy, flaunting the League, had attacked Ethiopia in the fall of 1935. Because these wars, especially the Italo-Ethiopian, might broaden to embroil the United States, popular demand for American neutrality grew. Congress answered with the Joint Resolution of August 31, 1935, better known as the "Neutrality Act." This measure, the most sweeping neutrality legislation passed thus far in American history, stipulated that when war broke out between two or more foreign nations, or during the progress of such conflict, the President was directed to proclaim "such fact." Immediately thereafter, an embargo on arms, munitions, and implements of war to any of the belligerents was to become effective, the designation of such commodities to be made by the President. Control and supervision of the manufacture and sale of munitions was placed in the hands of a permanent National Munitions Control Board made up of the Secretaries of State, War, Navy, and Commerce. Also on presidential proc-

Sand. Uncle Sam, ostrichlike, tries not to see the troubles overseas.
(By Carlisle in the *New York Herald Tribune*.)

lamation, American citizens would travel at their own risk on ships owned by belligerents.

President Roosevelt approved this resolution "because it was intended as an expression of the fixed desire of the Government and the people of the United States to avoid any action which might involve us in war." He believed that "the purpose is wholly excellent," but cautioned that there were some weaknesses in the resolution that should be remedied in future legislation.

The resolution expressed the current opinion that the United States had been drawn into World War I because of American traffic in arms. Were that traffic prohibited, there would be less chance of American embroilment in future struggles. Yet to cut off arms to both the aggressor state and the victim of aggression would obviously aid the stronger party.

On October 5, 1935, President Roosevelt proclaimed "that a state of war unhappily exists between Ethiopia and the Kingdom of Italy" and declared the Neutrality Act provisions in effect. Implements of war were defined and Americans were warned against traveling on ships of the belligerents.

The new neutrality policy ended America's position as the champion of neutral rights on the high seas. Americans who dealt with either belligerent did so at their own risk; they could not count upon government assistance if, for example, their cargoes were seized. Nor did the act work out as expected. American exporters could and did send to Italy many commodities not on the prohibited list, but which could easily be converted into implements of war. This was not in line with Roosevelt's desire to weaken the aggressor nation—and Italy certainly was that.

That the President recognized the weaknesses in the measure was shown in his annual message to Congress on January 3, 1936, in which he said:

> Nations seeking expansion, seeking the rectification of injustices springing from former wars, or seeking outlets for trade . . . fail to demonstrate that patience necessary to attain reasonable and legitimate objectives by peaceful negotiation or by an appeal to the finer instincts of world justice. They have therefore impatiently reverted to the old belief in the law of the sword. . . .

Consequently, he urged greater cooperation between the legislature and Executive in promoting more effective neutrality as a means of avoiding war.

Speedy Congressional action was required because parts of the Neutrality Act of 1935 would terminate at the end of February, 1936. Moreover, the Italo-Ethiopian strife might spread to entangle more countries. Administration leaders in Congress realized that the well-rounded measure the President desired might lead to protracted debate between the isolationists and their opponents. Therefore the Neutrality Act of February, 1936, was but a stopgap to keep the original legislation alive until a more inclusive measure could be worked out. The original resolution was extended to May 1, 1937, and several amendments were added to it. No credits or loans could be extended to any belligerent nation; the measure was not to apply to other American republics involved in war with a nation outside the hemisphere; and the discretionary right of the President to extend the embargo to other countries that might become belligerents now became a mandatory order to do so.

The Spanish Civil War

This measure of 1936 also had its weaknesses—notably, it did not cover civil wars. The issue arose in July, 1936, when an internecine struggle broke out in Spain between those who wished to maintain the existing republic—the so-called Loyalists—and the factions supporting General Francisco Franco and a totalitarian regime. Unfortunately for the cause of peace, Germany and Italy backed the Franco rebels, while Russia gave aid to the Loyalists despite the fact that twenty-seven nations had established a committee to localize the hostilities and maintain the principle of non-intervention.

The Spanish Civil War aroused widespread feeling in the United States. Advocates of democracy sympathized with the Loyalists to the extent of establishing innumerable committees to provide funds, clothing, and medical supplies for them. Hundreds if not thousands of adventurous Americans joined the Loyalist armed forces. Many doctors and nurses left for Spain to help the cause. On the other hand, there were those who preferred totalitarianism to the dread Communism associated with Loyalism and countered with similar efforts to assist Franco. Many prominent prelates of the Catholic Church swung their influence to his cause. Despite the fact that the civil war quickly became a struggle between two rival ideologies that threatened to break through local barriers, the American State Department, voicing the President's wishes, announced in August, 1936:

> In conformity with its well-established policy of non-interference with internal affairs in another country either in time of peace or in the event of civil strife, this Government will, of course, scrupulously refrain from any interference whatsoever in the unfortunate Spanish situation.

At the same time, the Department tried to dissuade American exporters from sending arms to either side on the ground that the spirit of American neutrality would be violated even though there was no specific law to the contrary. In general, the shippers of arms and munitions followed administration wishes, but in December, 1936, a license was requested to export planes and war material to the Loyalist government. This request brought the issue to the fore, and early in January, 1937, Congress almost unanimously approved another Joint Resolution, which prohibited the exportation of arms and implements of war to either side in Spain. Thus the civil war was specifically brought under the 1936 neutrality legislation despite loud protests from many Americans, particularly those with Loyalist sympathies. These protests were perhaps justified, because whatever action the United States took would be beneficial to one belligerent or the other. Since Germany and Italy were already helping Franco, the extension of the neutrality legislation definitely hurt the Loyalists; in fact, it might even be called actual intervention against the Loyalists because it denied them rights customarily enjoyed by *de jure* governments.

When the temporary features of the 1936 acts were about to lapse on May 1, 1937, the troubled international picture had scarcely changed. True, the Italo-Ethiopian War was ended, but only because Italy had overrun all of the enemy territory. The contest in Spain was still being strongly waged, Hitler had defied the Locarno Pact by invading the Rhineland, and the situation between Japan and China was such that hostilities might break out at any moment. Consequently, Congress decided to place on the statute books a permanent neutrality measure.

The debate on the new neutrality bill was long and bitter, showing that while the legislators were in agreement on the principle, they were at odds over the means of achieving it. On May 1, 1937, the measure was finally passed and signed by the President. It represented a compromise between those who believed that an embargo must be proclaimed as soon as a war broke out and those who felt that the President should have a certain amount of discretion in invoking such an embargo. Much of the previous legislation was kept. The President still had the duty to proclaim when a state of war existed; and it would then become unlawful to export arms, munitions, and implements of war to any of the belligerents or to "purchase, sell, or exchange" the securities of such contestants. Nor could any American ships carry arms or implements of war to belligerents, or be armed. American citizens were forbidden to travel on ships of a country at war. Finally, under the mandatory provisions, belligerency applied as well to civil wars.

The discretionary powers of the President included the right to prohibit the use of American ports to armed merchant ships and submarines of belligerents or as bases of supply. The chief innovation was the "cash-and-carry" clause: the President could enumerate certain commodities that might not be exported to a warring country "until all right, title, and interest therein shall be transferred to some foreign government"; such goods must not be transported in American ships; in other words, the belligerent must pay for such goods and see that they were then shipped in its own vessels. The National Munitions Control Board was continued, and American republics were exempted from the workings of the measure unless they were "cooperating with a non-American State or States in such a war."

Although the Neutrality Act of 1937 contained many more mandatory and discretionary prohibitions than its predecessors, it actually could provide for what might be called unneutral actions. Undoubtedly the "cash-and-carry" feature would benefit the belligerent with money and shipping. It was supposed to be a warning to Germany and Italy that neither would have the advantage of American supplies because they lacked the wherewithal to pay for them. Actually, however, it was not much of a warning. Were either country to go to war, it would certainly be facing a stronger naval power which would prevent it from obtaining any American supplies. Therefore, were the act to be invoked under such circumstances, either Germany or Italy would be guaranteed that its enemy would be seriously handicapped in procuring American commodities. The measure also ran contrary to commitments the United States had with Latin-American countries; there were promises not to sell war material to rebels in those republics, yet the measure stipulated that in case of civil war it must be applied to the recognized administration and the challengers alike. In similar fashion, there could be no move made to distinguish between the aggressor nation and the one attacked. While international bankers were restricted in their operations, American exporters of goods not on the embargo list were not—provided the belligerent buyer had the cash. As Senator Borah said in criticism: "We seek to avoid all risks, all dangers, but we make certain to get all the profits."

The Neutrality Act was immediately proclaimed in effect for the Spanish Civil War by President Roosevelt on May 1, 1937. On the other hand, he did not invoke it after the reopening of hostilities between Japan and China on July 7, 1937, an event which has sometimes been called the beginning of World War II in the Far East. The excuse was that there had been no formal declaration of war and the institution of the Neutrality Act would make more difficult a peaceful and speedy settlement of the strife. The real reason why the measure was not put into practice, however, was because its application would have helped Japan. The administration desired to assist China and could not do so were the Neutrality Act applied to the conflict. Therefore the policy of helping a victim of aggression was placed before the law.

Nevertheless, the publicity attendant upon the contemplated shipment of nineteen planes to China aboard the government-owned Wichita in August, 1937, caused President Roosevelt to make the following proclamation on September 14, 1937:

> Merchant vessels owned by the Government of the United States will not hereafter, until further notice, be permitted to transport to China or Japan any of the arms, ammunition, or implements of war which were listed in the President's Proclamation of May 1, 1937.
>
> Any other merchant vessels flying the American flag, which attempt to transport

any of the listed articles to China or Japan will, until further notice, do so at their own risk.

The question of applying the Neutrality Act remains in *statu quo,* the government policy remaining on a 24-hour basis.

As it became increasingly apparent that the Sino-Japanese struggle was more than an incident, President Roosevelt still refused to put the Neutrality Act into effect. He left little doubt about which nation he considered to be the aggressor—even though he did not mention Japan by name—when he addressed a gathering in Chicago on October 5, 1937. After reviewing "the political situation in the world, which of late has been growing progressively worse," he pointed out that peace-loving nations would suffer unless something were done to prevent "innocent peoples, innocent nations" from "being cruelly sacrificed to a greed for power and supremacy which is devoid of all sense of justice and humane considerations." Then he continued:

> If we are to have a world in which we can breathe freely and live in amity without fear—the peace-loving nations must make a concerted effort to uphold laws and principles on which alone peace can rest secure. . . .
>
> When an epidemic of physical disease starts to spread, the community approves and joins in a quarantine of the patients in order to protect the health of the community against the spread of the disease. . . .
>
> America hates war. America hopes for peace. Therefore, America engages in the search for peace.

This so-called quarantine speech indicated that President Roosevelt was throwing off the cloak of isolation forced upon him by the Neutrality Acts. In so doing he was not seeking war, but joint action of peace-loving nations to maintain peace. The speech was probably a trial balloon sent up to test American opinion. If so, the generally hostile response warned the President that he would have to move cautiously in the face of a public opinion still overwhelmingly isolationist.

The "Panay" Incident

Meantime, American neutrality was given a severe test when Japanese planes bombed and strafed the American gunboat *Panay* and three American merchant craft on the Yangtze River near Nanking on December 12, 1937. No warning was given by the attackers, three Americans were killed, seventy-four were wounded, and the *Panay* and two of the other ships were sunk. Possibly in an effort to prevent witnesses from describing this unprovoked attack, the planes machine-gunned the boats taking the survivors to shore.

Since the *Panay* was plainly marked with two large American flags and was in the Yangtze on the legitimate business of transferring American refugees and supplies from war-torn areas, the Roosevelt administration was naturally distressed. The following day Secretary Hull informed the Japanese ambassador "that the President is deeply shocked and concerned" by the news of this indiscriminate bombing. He further sought full Japanese expressions of regret, compensation for the losses, and promises that there would be no recurrence of such attacks.

The Japanese government evidently realized that its forces had gone too far because its Foreign Minister sent prompt apology, assured the United States that indemnity would be paid, and that it would "deal appropriately with those responsible for the incident." As evidence ot good faith, the Japanese government announced ten days later that the chief of the air force had been removed and that orders had been transmitted to all Japanese forces to use the utmost caution against similar incidents "even at the sacrifice of a strategic advantage in attacking the Chinese troops." Toward the end of April, 1938, Japan made payment of more than $2 million for the deaths, injuries, and property losses sustained in the *Panay* incident.

Although there was a flurry of apprehension in the United States over this affair, there was no widespread demand for war after the prompt Japanese apology was given. Indeed, the average American did not really care what was happening in the Far East; he was primarily concerned with the financial problems at home. If too much were made of the incident, war might result—and he did not want war.

This isolationist, antiwar attitude was further shown in December, 1937, when Representative Ludlow of Indiana proposed an amendment to the Constitution that would make mandatory a national referendum before war could be declared, except in case of actual invasion. Early in January, 1938, President Roosevelt used all of the pressure at his command to defeat this Ludlow Amendment. In a letter to Speaker Bankhead he said:

> I must frankly state that I consider the proposed amendment would be impracticable in its application and incompatible with our representative form of government. . . . Such an amendment . . . would cripple any President in his conduct of our foreign relations, and it would encourage other nations to believe that they could violate American rights with impunity. I fully realize that the sponsors of this proposal sincerely believe that it would be helpful in keeping the United States out of war. I am convinced that it would have the opposite effect.

Largely as a result of this administration pressure the amendment was defeated, but only by the close vote of 209 to 188. And the American opposition to becoming involved in a Far Eastern war was indicated in a popular poll in which 54 per cent desired to have the United States withdraw entirely from China, and only 30 per cent wanted the government to compel respect for American rights there.

Thus, as World War II approached, it became increasingly evident that the American people wanted to avoid any entanglements that might embroil them in conflict. In the early years of the Roosevelt regime the President sought to improve world accord through international conferences. Both the failure of European nations to agree and the preponderant American interest in domestic recovery prevented the success of these ventures. Roosevelt, in furtherance of the Good Neighbor program, scored greater accomplishments in the Western Hemisphere, as evidenced by the Montevideo and Buenos Aires Conferences. The abrogation of the Platt Amendment and the passage of the McDuffie-Tydings Act were other actions of the Good Neighbor. But because attempts at international cooperation failed, the American people were developing an isolationist—almost peace-at-any-price—attitude as shown by the enactment of the Johnson and Neutrality Acts.

Those Neutrality Acts were based upon a misinterpretation of the reasons for American entrance into World War I and consequently upon a belief that no external danger could possibly touch the United States. Moreover, by trying to maintain a policy of extreme isolation, Congress and the people were indirectly admitting that the nation had no outside interests worth defending. Therefore the neutrality legislation amounted to a form of appeasement on the part of the United States. To President Roosevelt, however, the growing use of force by aggressor states so threatened both American and world security that by the end of 1937 he was fully convinced that a more active policy was needed. With the New Deal at home largely complete, he turned his attention more and more to the international scene.

Troublesome Times

The menace to the world's democracies was clear to the more discerning by the spring of 1938. By that time Adolph Hitler had shown his contempt for treaties by denouncing the Treaty of Versailles and by scrapping the Locarno Pact. In an effort to promote the German master race and fulfill the theories expressed in *Mein Kampf*, he had marched his troops into the Rhineland in early 1936, and during the Spanish Civil War he had tested the strength of his army, which had grown in defiance of the Versailles Treaty. Moreover, he had persecuted the Jews and other minority groups in Germany. He had arranged an agreement with Italy, known as the Rome-Berlin Axis, which gave him a freer hand in his eventual domination of Austria and in his challenging of France and Britain. He was already casting greedy glances toward neighboring Czechoslovakia. Along with Japan, Germany had resigned from the League.

The new British Prime Minister, Neville Chamberlain, believed in a policy of appeasement toward this German threat to the peace of Europe. He argued that German aggressiveness arose out of dissatisfaction with the Treaty of Versailles and the inability to obtain sufficient resources to meet the demands of a growing population. Therefore peace could be preserved by adjusting these complaints. Chamberlain's position had much support in England, where many conservatives felt that the real menace to European safety came not from German Nazis, but from Russian Communists. The so-called Cliveden set, in their conservative complacency, did not appear to realize that there was much more to the Hitlerian menace than complaints resulting from World War I.

France, convulsed by hard times and political strife, was deteriorating internally and thus was in no position to challenge Germany. The League having failed her, she was compelled to follow Britain's lead in appeasing her natural enemy. Russia was more concerned with the progress of her economic experiments than she was with what was happening in the rest of Europe. Furthermore, she realized that she herself was the object of distrust.

In the Far East Japan had once more defied the other powers by attacks on China. Evidently she was attempting to promote the "New Order" there—or the Greater East Asia Co-Prosperity Sphere—under which she would dominate that part of the world, regardless of prior commitments.

In the United States, President Roosevelt realized the gravity of the situation and, continuing the stand he had taken in his "quarantine" speech of the previous October, he took the lead in formulating American foreign policy instead of acquiescing in the prevalent isolationist point of view. In a special message to Congress in January, 1938, he said:

> We, as a peaceful Nation, cannot and will not abandon active search for an agreement among the nations to limit armaments and end aggression. But it is clear that until such an agreement is reached—and I have not given up hope of it —we are compelled to think of our own national safety.

To make that safety possible, he asked appropriations for both 1938 and 1939 to build up army antiaircraft defenses, modernize field equipment, and increase the enlisted reserve, as well as to construct naval ships of all sizes.

When isolationists in Congress balked at the proposal because it might lead the country into war and result in an entangling agreement for naval cooperation with some other nation, Secretary Hull defended the plan on February 10. He wrote that the rearmament program was vital for national defense, but was not large enough to enable the United States to enter an aggressive war. Moreover, said the Secretary, it might help the cause of peace by adding greater weight to American influence in world councils. Certainly the United States had no thought of a secret commitment with any other power. The Secretary's appeal, together with the increasing German menace, finally persuaded Congress to pass the presidential rearmament proposals in practically their original form.

Appeasement at Munich

While laying the groundwork for American defense, however, the administration did not relax its efforts to prevent a war in Europe. Convinced that Hitler's next move would be to absorb Austria, Secretary Hull told German Ambassador Dieckhoff in January, 1938, that the paramount question facing the world in general and the United States in particular was whether the principles of international law and order should be replaced by the rule of force and aggression. All countries should consistently cooperate to support the principle of law and order. This statement could be considered a mild warning to Germany against further aggression.

The gesture was fruitless, for on March 11, 1938, the legions of Hitler moved into Austria in defiance of a three-year-old pledge that the Reich would not acquire its neighbor's territory, and two days later the Fuehrer announced the union of the two countries under his control. The American attitude was quickly shown on March 17 when Hull said that the United States must not become "a self-constituted hermit state." Isolation would do no good in the present world. For the sake of its interests and security, the United States must maintain its influence in world affairs and work constantly for peace.

Germany paid little attention to the American pronouncements. Instead, during the summer of 1938, increasingly serious Nazi demands were made for the Sudetenland of Czechoslovakia. A so-called war of nerves—incessant propaganda and sword-rattling—initiated the move against this territory, which Hitler indicated he must have even though he had to go to war for it. The personal trips which Prime Minister Chamberlain made to Germany to seek a negotiated peace proved abortive.

Believing that the struggle over the Sudetenland might involve Europe in a general war, President Roosevelt sent personal messages to the leaders of Czechoslovakia, Germany, Britain, and France on September 26, 1938, in which he said:

> The fabric of peace on the continent of Europe, if not throughout the rest of the world, is in immediate danger. . . . Should hostilities break out the lives of millions of men, women, and children . . . will most certainly be lost under circumstances of unspeakable horror. The economic system of every country involved is certain to be shattered. The social structure of every country involved may well be completely wrecked.

After pointing out that the United States had no political entanglements, he asserted that his main interest was in settling disputes by peaceful means. "I am persuaded that there is no problem so difficult or so pressing that it cannot be justly solved by the resort to reason rather than by resort to force." Therefore, on behalf of the American people "and for the sake of humanity everywhere," he asked the disputants not to break off their negotiations, but to seek a pacific settlement.

The replies from three of the countries indicated their desire for peace, but Hitler's answer placed the whole burden of responsibility for the crisis upon Czechoslovakia. In brief, if she wanted peace, she could have it by turning the Sudetenland over to Germany without further ado. If she did not, then Germany would seize it.

Still the Roosevelt administration did not give up hope. American envoys everywhere were instructed to use their good offices in having the countries to which they were assigned send messages to the potential belligerents stressing the need to preserve peace. The President also sought the cooperation of Mussolini in settling the problem and sent another appeal to Hitler.

American opinion was overwhelmingly for any solution that would avoid war. Great was the relief, therefore, at the news that a last-minute conference had been arranged by Hitler at Munich. There, on September 30, Hitler, Mussolini, Chamberlain, and Daladier of France signed a Four-Power Accord whereby war was averted at the price of giving the Nazis practically a free hand in taking over the Sudetenland. Chamberlain returned to England declaring: "I believe it is peace for our time," and millions of Englishmen, Frenchmen, and Americans hoped that he was right. But this supreme effort to appease Germany soon proved a great mistake. The betrayal of Czechoslovakia destroyed the moral prestige of England and France in the eyes of smaller states. The snubbing of Russia aroused her suspicion and resentment, while Germany and Italy had only contempt for the weakness of the Western democracies. American opinion soon reversed itself and condemned the European appeasers. Illogically, however, few Americans saw that the United States shared in the responsibility. Roosevelt no less than Chamberlain had been desperately anxious to preserve peace. Much more important in the underlying situation, moreover, Congress and the country insisted on the futile policy represented by the Neutrality Acts; Hitler could therefore continue his course of aggression in the conviction that the United States would do nothing to help those who resisted him.

The Munich breathing spell was brief. France and England displayed their growing concern with the situation by a great rearmament effort, while as early as October 28, 1938, President Roosevelt declared:

> It is become increasingly clear that peace by fear has no higher or more enduring quality than peace by the sword.
> There can be no peace if the reign of law is to be replaced by a recurrent sanctification of sheer force.

There can be no peace if national policy adopts as a deliberate instrument the threat of war.

And the President was deeply shocked shortly afterward by news of even more violent persecution of the Jews; he said: "I myself could scarcely believe that such things could occur in a twentieth-century civilization." Consequently, on November 15 he ordered Ambassador Hugh Wilson to return home—an obvious rebuke to the Nazis.

The Lima Conference

It was while Europe and Asia were faced with the possibility of open war at any moment that the republics of the Western Hemisphere gathered at Lima, Peru, for their regular Pan-American Conference. Naturally, they were chiefly concerned with the means by which international law and order could be restored and, if this proved impossible, with how the republics could prevent external dangers from affecting them.

Secretary Hull, once again the chairman of the American delegation, was the most energetic worker at this December meeting and did much to promote the thesis "that national defense has now become a problem of continental defense . . . in cooperation with the other twenty republics and Canada." The result was unanimous approval of the so-called Declaration of American Principles, which reaffirmed the doctrine of non-intervention, proscribed the use of force as an instrument of national or international policy, upheld peaceful settlement of disputes, and avowed that "international cooperation is a necessary condition to the maintenance of the aforementioned principles." Perhaps the foremost action was the approval of the Declaration of Lima, which affirmed "their continental solidarity and their purpose to collaborate in the maintenance of the principles upon which the said solidarity is based." The republics also agreed "to defend them against all foreign intervention or activity that may threaten them"—an answer to the fifth-column menace.[4] Also under that Declaration, "in case the peace, security or territorial integrity of any American Republic is thus threatened by acts of any nature that may impair them, they proclaim their common concern and their determination to make effective their solidarity, coordinating their respective sovereign wills by means of the procedure of consultation. . . ." Such consultation was to take the form of meetings of the several foreign ministers when any republic believed that hemisphere safety was endangered. By this means it was hoped that totalitarian threats in both Europe and Asia would be kept from American shores and that the pressure of a solid hemisphere bloc might avert another world struggle.

[4] The "fifth column" was an expression first used during the Spanish Civil War. It refers to subversive agents who go to another country to pave the way, through undermining the confidence of the people and the like, for eventual military invasion.

The Outbreak of War

It was well that there was solidarity in the hemisphere, because war broke out in Europe before the end of 1939. That President Roosevelt anticipated this was evident from his annual message to Congress on January 4, 1939, when he said:

> All about us rage undeclared wars—military and economic. All about us grow more deadly armaments—military and economic. All about us are threats of new aggression—military and economic.

Then, asserting that the use of force by enemies of democracy made necessary the employment by peace-loving nations of weapons of defense, he called for increased appropriations for the army and navy. Moreover, he criticized the existing neutrality legislation because it might conceivably result in the United States helping an aggressor nation at the expense of the one attacked. Shortly after this message, the President sought to build up stockpiles of materials that might be important for American defense.

Such plans and suggestions were obviously the need of the hour. On March 14, 1939, Hitler invaded the remainder of Czechoslovakia, despite his pre-Munich pledge. The immediate State Department condemnation of this action as "wanton lawlessness'" did no good. On April 7 Mussolini, desirous of sharing in the spoils, attacked Albania and soon had the country under his control. Once again the State Department's verbal opposition to this threat to world peace did no good.

The democratic powers in Europe realized at last the futility of appeasement. Britain and France announced that they would go to the aid of Poland, Rumania, and Greece were they attacked. At the same time they sought agreement with Russia for a bloc to thwart the Rome-Berlin Axis.

To the United States the division of Europe into two camps boded ill for world peace. Consequently President Roosevelt sought specific assurance from Hitler and Mussolini that neither would attack or invade the remaining independent countries of Europe and the Middle East, not only for the present, "but also to a future sufficiently long to give every opportunity to work by peaceful means for a more permanent peace." Neither Hitler nor Mussolini saw fit to send a reply to Roosevelt's plea, although the Fuehrer did tell the German people that he had no thought of attacking any more of the Reich's neighbors. Had he not given them definite pledges to that effect?

How much Hitler's promise meant was indicated before the month of April was over. He demanded of Poland the return of Danzig, as well as numerous concessions along the Polish Corridor. To make his demands more effective he mobilized a large army along the Polish border. The worried British and French governments took this occasion to announce that an attack upon Poland would mean war.

Remonstrating with the German dictator was obviously futile. He understood only the language of force and this language Roosevelt was powerless to use. As a minimum contribution to strengthening the anti-Nazi front, the United States needed to repeal the arms embargo, so that in case of hostilities England and France could supplement their inadequate war-production facilities with those of America. But the President's earnest efforts to amend the Neutrality Act before Congress adjourned for the summer were unavailing. Not even a White House conference convinced Senator Borah and his fellow isolationists that war was actually imminent or that the United States had any responsibility in the situation.

Confidence that America would stand aside, therefore, was one factor encouraging Hitler to persist in his reckless course. The war of nerves against Poland continued, while mutual suspicion frustrated efforts to draw the Soviet Union into an anti-Nazi alliance with Britain and France. Instead, the democratic world was stunned when it learned on August 21 that Russia and Germany had concluded a non-aggression pact. Far from being an act of peace, this treaty released Germany from the possibility of a two-front war and revealed that it would probably be but a matter of days before the march into Poland began.

President Roosevelt once again tried to effect a peaceful settlement by appealing to King Victor Emmanuel of Italy on August 23 to cooperate with the United States to "advance those ideals of Christianity which of late seem so often to have been obscured." The next day he also sent earnest pleas to both Hitler and President Moszicki of Poland to forego the use of force and to settle their dispute through diplomacy.

The attempts were fruitless, however, because Hitler wanted no peaceful respite. The blame was placed upon Poland because of her unwillingness to accede to all the German demands. On the morning of September 1, 1939, the invasion of Poland started, and two days later France and Britain, living up to their promises, went to her assistance. World War II had begun.

23

The Prelude to Pearl Harbor

In many respects American involvement in World War II followed the pattern of World War I days. In both cases there was an attempt to remain neutral; in both cases neutrality became increasingly difficult; in both cases the United States went in on the side of England, France, and Russia against Germany and her allies. Yet there were also great differences. During World War II a complete German victory seemed much more likely to occur than it had during World War I, and the American people felt a much more serious threat to their own security. Long before hostilities began at Pearl Harbor, the United States had abandoned the pretense of neutrality and committed itself to helping the democracies with shipments of arms and naval patrols. War, when it finally came, was simply the last step plunging the nation into a conflict in which it had become more and more involved.

The Impact of War on the United States

The outbreak of World War II did not come unexpectedly to the people of the United States as had World War I. While it is true that many Americans hoped until the actual invasion of Poland that efforts to maintain peace would be successful, they had been following events in Europe closely in their newspapers and over their radios for several years. Therefore there was not the distinct shock that accompanied the war of 1914.

President Roosevelt was quick to act. After appealing to the participants on September 1, 1939, to refrain from bombing civilians, he delivered a radio talk two evenings later in which he pointed out that European events of the previous four years had "been based on the use of force and the threat of force." The primary duty of the United States should be to seek "for humanity a final peace" that would end "the continued use of force between nations." The President did not ask the people to remain neutral in thought, because "even a neutral has a right to take account of the facts." He believed the United States would be able to stay out of the conflict, but he admitted that the war would certainly affect the country in many ways. Yet "as long as it remains within my power to prevent, there will be no blackout of peace in the United States."

On September 5 the President proclaimed the neutrality laws in effect and prohibited the exportation of arms and munitions to the belligerent nations. The following day the Federal Bureau of Investigation was placed in charge of "matters relating to espionage, sabotage, and violations of the neutrality regulations." Next, Roosevelt declared a limited national emergency to safeguard American neutrality and strengthen national defense.

The Neutrality Act of 1939

Although the President's official position was one of neutrality, it was clear that he favored the democracies. His numerous utterances indicated that he desired Britain and France to win, and his efforts during the spring and summer of 1939 to obtain amendments to the existing neutrality legislation were made so that he could distinguish between the aggressor and the attacked. Moreover, he tried to effect a closer commercial relationship with Britain and France and sought to conclude arrangements for the sale of arms, munitions, and planes to them.

American public opinion (84 per cent according to one poll) undoubtedly desired an Allied victory, but also strongly believed that the United States must stay out of the war. These practically contradictory views made it difficult for the President to put into effect his program for aiding the democracies because Americans of the isolationist school, led by Senators Borah and Wheeler, held that anything but strictest neutrality would involve the nation in hostilities.

Nevertheless, on September 21, 1939, Roosevelt called Congress into special session for the specific purpose of amending the Neutrality Act, because it "so alters the historic foreign policy of the United States that it impairs the peaceful relations of the United States with foreign nations." He continued with the assertion, "I regret that Congress passed the Act. I regret equally that I signed that Act." Specifically he wanted to change the embargo provisions that prevented the sale of completed implements of war, but that allowed the selling of uncompleted ones which could be shipped on American vessels. "There in itself . . . lies definite danger to our neutrality and our peace."

Congress could no longer pigeonhole the presidential request, but the debates were heated in the extreme. Congressmen of the Nye school of thought asserted that the repeal of the arms embargo would mean a repetition of World War I days; American munitions makers would sell to the Allies, make a huge profit, and help involve the nation in war. Still another group in the opposition declared that repeal would be an unneutral step for the United States to take; the war had already begun, and a change in American policy would aid one side to the detriment of the other. And there were those who still believed that the Neutrality Act of 1937 was the best means of maintaining American isolation. Supporting the administration were those Congressmen who argued that the President was right. The existing legislation was in effect unneutral since it helped the aggressors, who knew that the countries they invaded would not be able to obtain assistance from the United States. Moreover, traditional American rights on the high seas had been given up, and the smaller and weaker countries of the world, which had previously looked to the United States for protection, could no longer do so. Some legislators advocated repeal frankly because they believed it was in the best interests of the country for the Allies to win.

Not until November 4, after about six weeks of interventionist-isolationist debate, was the Neutrality Act of 1939 finally approved.[1] The measure kept many of the supposed safeguards of earlier legislation and extended the cash-and-carry principle to all commodities. The chief changes were: now Congress, as well as the President, could proclaim that a state of war existed; the much discussed embargo on implements of war was dropped; and the President could define danger or combat zones wherein American citizens, ships, and planes could not go.

The President immediately put this new measure into effect, accompanying it with the definition of combat areas where American ships could not go. They included all the ports of the belligerents, most of the Bay of Biscay, the English Channel and the waters around the British Isles and the adjacent islands, and the Baltic and North Seas. The closing of the last two seas meant that American vessels could not reach such neutral countries as Belgium, the Netherlands, and Sweden. It was hoped, as a result of these proclamations, that there would be no incidents to involve the United States in war.

The Panama Conference

While the Neutrality Bill of 1939 was being debated, steps were taken to safeguard the hemisphere. In line with the decision made at Lima, the several

---

[1] The House vote stood 243 to 172, the Senate 55 to 24. A public-opinion poll taken at about the time of passage showed a 56 per cent approval of the measure.

foreign ministers met at Panama in late September to discuss how the war could be kept from the Americas. Unanimous approval was given on October 2 to the Declaration of Panama:

> The American republics, as long as they maintain their neutrality, have the undisputed right to conserve free from all hostile acts by any belligerent non-American nation those waters adjacent to the American continents which they consider of primordial interest and direct utility of their relations, whether such hostile act is attempted or carried out by land, sea, or air.

The declaration then provided for a safety or neutrality zone roughly 300 miles wide around the Americas, wherein no belligerent action should take place. Maritime and air patrols would see to it that the zone was maintained as a neutral area.

The foreign ministers also initiated an Inter-American Financial and Economic Advisory Committee to provide the several republics with advice and information in the fields of commerce and finance, thereby preventing a serious dislocation that might normally follow the outbreak of the European war. A General Declaration of Neutrality of the American Republics forbade the use of any American territory as bases for belligerent operations or belligerent planes to fly over hemisphere territory, established rules for internment of ships, and set up rules of search.

The United States provided most of the vessels for the patrol of the safety zone, and her representatives played prominent roles in the several committees the Panama Conference established. The warring countries, however, refused to admit the legality of the safety zone and asserted that they would pay no attention to it because their enemies would not. The most notable example of infringement of the zone concerned the German pocket battleship *Graf von Spee*, which had been attacking British and French merchantmen in the Atlantic since the opening of the war. Finally in early December, 1939, she was tracked down by three British cruisers and badly damaged in a running fight off the coast of South America. She was forced to take refuge in Montevideo. The Uruguayan government insisted that she leave after 72 hours, but rather than face the awaiting British cruisers, she was scuttled by her crew who were subsequently interned. The American republics protested vigorously against the defiance of hemisphere neutrality provisions, and the following April the Neutrality Committee announced that ports of the Americas would be closed to ships of those belligerent nations that refused to recognize the safety zone. Because of the British blockade, few German ships other than submarines reached American waters after the opening of 1940, so that there were only isolated instances thereafter.

The Fall of France

After the initial attacks of World War II and the fall of Poland, both sides settled down during the winter of 1939–40[2] along their respective western front lines—the Allies behind the Maginot Line, the Germans protected by their ever stronger Siegfried Line. To some this so-called "phony war" revived hopes of a peaceful settlement of differences. On April 9, 1940, however, Hitler suddenly struck at Denmark, despite a year-old non-aggression pact that he himself had initiated. At the same time and in similar fashion, German troops invaded Norway. Although the Norse, unlike the Danes, attempted to repel the aggressor and obtained some help from the British, the fifth-column that the Germans had organized through the efforts of the traitor, Vidkun Quisling, helped to bring defeat in a few short weeks.

May witnessed even more disastrous blows to the Allied cause as the *blitzkrieg* swept over Holland, Belgium, Luxembourg, and France. With the Maginot Line outflanked, the British forces were soon separated from their Allies and pinned against the English Channel. Only the extreme heroism of those forces and the skill and bravery of the British reserve fleet enabled their evacuation from Dunkirk. The French were subjected to an overwhelming attack, culminating in their surrender on June 22, 1940. Hitler sought to wipe out the stain of November 11, 1918, by staging the armistice conference in the same railroad car which had been used on that occasion in the same forest of Compiègne. Taking advantage of this French disaster, Mussolini had entered the war on June 10 by attacking from the east.

To Americans the power of the German *blitzkrieg* was astounding. It appeared as though the democracies, now represented solely by the British Empire, could no longer withstand the Axis poundings. Nevertheless, the administration did not give up hope and continued to extend moral support. Even more was promised. On the day that Mussolini attacked the French rear, President Roosevelt, after extending the provisions of the Neutrality Act to cover the new belligerent, made a speech in which he traced his efforts to dissuade Italy from entering the war and her refusal to consider his proposals. Instead, "the hand that held the dagger has struck it into the back of its neighbor." Because the extension of the war would threaten American rights and institutions, the President announced that the United States "must pursue two obvious and simultaneous courses": the extension of all the material resources of the country to the opponents of force and the promotion of American defense.

More and more Americans supported aid to the democracies and increased preparedness. To them the fall of France meant that the American defense

[2] The chief fighting of that winter was between Russia and Finland. American sympathies were definitely with Finland, as indicated by the loans made to her in mid-December, 1939.

frontier was no longer the Maginot Line as President Roosevelt had once intimated. It was now the English Channel and might soon be the Atlantic because the safety of the British Isles was in question after the German air *blitz* of England began in the summer of 1940. None knew whether Britain could hold out against the mounting air attacks and the invasion that was expected at any moment. Were Britain to fall, the United States might be the next object of German attack. But the United States was not prepared; the Atlantic, without the British navy, would no longer be the safeguard that had protected the country for generations. Thus, for the sake of American defense, the United States must go all out in providing aid to Britain so that she might withstand the totalitarian blows.

The first step in giving full aid to Britain had already been taken when the President made his "stab-in-the-back" speech. Using a little-known law of World War I days as authority, the administration resorted to the "trade-in" method. On June 6 the Navy Department started delivery of one-hundred "overage" scout bombers to the Curtiss-Wright factory at Buffalo, New York, for eventual trade-in for newer models. The turned-in planes were then sent at once to Britain and France. Subsequently the government by the same means sent indirectly to the democracies 100 armed attack planes, 600,000 British Enfield rifles, and 800 French 75-millimeter guns of World War I vintage, as well as other stockpiles of ammunition, machine guns, and mortars. Although the Federal government did not do the actual selling of these war implements under the trade-in arrangement, its neutral position might be open to question inasmuch as no effort was made to dispose of similar commodities to the Axis. In similar fashion, the United States helped Britain by permitting Canadian fliers to receive training at Florida fields and by allowing her warships to be repaired and refitted in American yards. Moreover, American planes were flown directly across the Canadian border for military use by the neighbor.

The Destroyer-Base Deal

These supplies were of inestimable assistance to Britain in her lone defense against the Axis, but more was deemed necessary to save her from defeat. One way of directly aiding Britain would be to strengthen her navy, and this in turn would diminish the danger of attack upon America.

Another menace developing from the fall of France and other countries was that Germany might try to take over their holdings in the New World. The United States had already taken steps at the Havana Conference (see below) to prevent that from happening, but it was essential, so President Roosevelt believed, to develop additional safeguards. Would it not be possible, therefore, to accomplish both objectives at the same time? The President thought so. Consequently, during the summer of 1940, he opened secret negotiations with British Ambassador Lord Lothian for the American lease of British bases in the Western Hemisphere, the "rental" to take the form of fifty overage destroyers, which could be recommissioned to help strengthen the British navy. The negotiations were secret because of the expected isolationist opposition in Congress, which might hold up completion of the arrangements until too late.

Before Roosevelt made the final commitment, Attorney General Jackson reported that there was no doubt of the right of the President to arrange the deal by executive agreement rather than by treaty. Moreover, he found two old laws and a decision of the Supreme Court to uphold the presidential right "to dispose of vessels of the Navy and unneeded naval material." Finally, the Attorney General concluded that the transference of the overage destroyers would not run contrary to neutrality laws because they had not been built specifically to be turned over to a belligerent nation.

On September 2, 1940, the negotiations were completed. In exchange for the fifty destroyers,[3] the United States received ninety-nine-year leases for bases in the Bahamas, Jamaica, St. Lucia, Trinidad, Antigua, and British Guiana. In addition, Britain granted the United States similar leases for Newfoundland and Bermuda as "gifts—generously given and gladly received."

The following day the President informed Congress of this deal. He justified his action by saying:

> The value to the Western Hemisphere of these outposts of security is beyond calculation. Their need has long been recognized by our country, and especially by those primarily charged with the duty of charting and organizing our own naval and military defense. They are essential to the protection of the Panama Canal. . . . For these reasons I have taken advantage of the present opportunity to acquire them.

The isolationists in Congress and throughout the country denounced the action as dictatorial, as a violation of American neutrality, as a step in defiance of traditional American policy, and as contrary to international law. But the majority of the American people, after the initial surprise had worn off, praised the action— although perhaps not the method. They showed by this approval that they were ready at last to commit the nation to all-out aid to Britain and to stronger hemisphere defense.

The Havana Conference

Meantime, an actual move to safeguard the hemisphere was taken at the second meeting of foreign ministers, held at Havana, Cuba, in July, 1940. The immediate reason for this session was fear lest Germany attempt to take over the

---

[3] The original cost of these destroyers was $75,477,348; the cost of recommissioning them was $20,478,445.

New World colonies of countries she had occupied. Moreover, in the independent South American countries, particularly in Chile, Uruguay, and Bolivia, German fifth-column activities appeared to be increasing in a way that would suggest these areas were included in Nazi plans for world domination. Latin American trade was badly disorganized by the war and the situation was particularly serious in Brazil and Chile—a situation that made German promises of vast barter deals of raw materials for postwar use particularly seductive.

The most important measure that resulted was the Act of Havana, which stated that the American republics, jointly or singly, might take over the administration of the threatened territory of non-American nations. A special Inter-American Commission for Territorial Administration was established to supervise the trusteeships.[4] Further agreements were approved for better financial cooperation among the republics, with the United States helping the cause by announcing, while the conference was in session, a $500 million increase in the lending power of the Export-Import Bank. Finally, the completion of the Pan-American Highway was to be speeded to improve the commercial interchange and defense of the hemisphere. At the conclusion of the meeting Secretary Hull said: "The agreements have cleared the decks for effective action whenever such action may become necessary."

The Campaign of 1940

Soon after the fall of France, the American people turned their attention temporarily toward the election of 1940. As in 1916, the world situation played a prominent role in the campaign. For the first time in many years, diplomatic issues took their place beside matters of domestic concern. Despite the continued efforts of the Democratic administration to keep the country at peace, many Americans believed that it was only a matter of time before the United States again would be at war with Germany. In the domestic picture, the great problem was whether the New Deal had accomplished its objectives; a growing conservative element believed that it had not and that a change to Republicanism would benefit the nation and speed the return of prosperity. Moreover, the conservatives were worried because the third-term precedent was seriously challenged for the first time.

The Republicans met in Philadelphia on June 24. The outstanding candidate for the nomination at the outset was Thomas E. Dewey, the young district attorney of New York City who had gained national fame as a racket buster. His

---

[4] Eventually the United States, Venezuela, and Brazil assumed the trusteeship of Surinam —the former Dutch Guiana—and the United States alone took over Denmark's Greenland. Guadeloupe and Martinique, both French colonies, were not placed under this plan, but the American republics kept a watchful eye on the latter because of the presence of part of the French fleet, which they did not want to fall into German hands, and because the governor, Admiral Robert, was suspected of being pro-Nazi.

major opponent in the early stages of preconvention jockeying was Senator Robert A. Taft of Ohio, isolationist son of the former President. Another Senator, Arthur H. Vandenberg of Michigan, a semi-isolationist, was a potential dark horse. As the convention approached, however, the tide of popular—rather than political—opinion swung in favor of Wendell L. Willkie, a former Democrat. Hoosier-born and bred, trained as a lawyer, but experienced as well as a teacher and farmer, Willkie had gained fame as president of Commonwealth and Southern when he obtained for his company the demanded price from the government for subsidiaries taken over by TVA. He was regarded as a liberal conservative who would offer the best opposition to the New Deal. Although the old-line politicians were cool to Willkie, he received enthusiastic support from a younger and more internationally minded group—some of them amateurs. By clever management the convention galleries were packed with noisy partisans primed to shout, "We Want Willkie!" On the first ballot Dewey had a commanding lead, but was far short of a majority, with Taft second and Willkie a poor third. From then on, however, Dewey's strength faded, while Taft and Willkie increased their totals. On the sixth ballot the Willkie band wagon was successful. For the vice-presidency, the Republicans selected Charles L. McNary of Oregon, the Senate minority leader and active spokesman for the farmers.

The Republican platform denounced the New Deal for its "shifting, contradictory, and overlapping administrations and policies," which had failed "to solve the problem of unemployment and revive opportunity for our youth." The Republicans promised "to re-create opportunity for the youth of America and put our idle millions back to work." Social security and similar New Deal reforms would be kept and extended, but in amended form and with abler administration. Waste, discrimination, and politics would be removed from the relief problem by giving most of the task back to the states. A Constitutional amendment to limit Presidents to a maximum of two terms was demanded. In foreign affairs, the Republicans were "firmly opposed to involving this nation in foreign war," but favored "the extension to all peoples fighting for liberty, or whose liberty is threatened, of such aid as shall not be in violation of international law or inconsistent with the requirements of our national defense."

During the spring of 1940 President Roosevelt remained silent about a third term, despite the fact that the party leaders had been trying to get him to commit himself during the preceding two years. Nevertheless, his name was entered in numerous state primaries, and in each of them he gained overwhelming victories. Moreover, his political managers saw to it that no other candidates grew strong enough to challenge his leadership. There were a few, however, whose presidential aspirations were obvious: Postmaster General Farley, who was vigorously against the third term and subsequently broke with the President over it, Security Administrator Paul V. McNutt, and Vice-President Garner.

Pinning a Tail on the Donkey. (By Seibel
in *The Richmond Times-Dispatch*.)

When the Democratic convention opened in Chicago in the middle of July, the President still had not broken his silence. Nevertheless, his New Deal backers, under the leadership of Harry Hopkins, had a smooth organization working in a nearby hotel, which was in constant communication with the President. Not until Permanent Chairman Alben Barkley concluded his keynote speech did he issue a special message, in which the President stated that he did not seek the nomination and was therefore releasing his delegates to vote for any candidate they might choose. Since Roosevelt did not specifically say that he would not run if drafted and since the convention was "rigged" in his favor, the delegates enthusiastically renominated him on the first ballot. Most political observers were skeptical of the President's professed reluctance to run again. They observed that, if he had wanted to, he could have eliminated himself by a firm statement at an early date. Moreover, he quickly accepted the nomination through a radio message to the assembled delegates in which he said: "My conscience will not let me turn my back upon a call to service."

Garner was not named again for the vice-presidency. He was now considered too conservative for the New Dealers. Earlier in the year the President had said that in order to win and carry on the New Deal program, two liberals would have to be on the Democratic ticket. Consequently, Secretary of Agriculture Wallace was substituted at Roosevelt's insistence, but without much enthusiasm on the part of the rank-and-file politicians.

The platform stated that "we will not participate in foreign wars, and we will not send our army, naval or air forces to fight in foreign lands outside of the Americas, except in case of attack." Aid to those fighting aggression was promised, along with preparedness. Promotion of water-power development for the use of all, the enforcement of fair labor standards, defense of "all legitimate business," and the continuance and expansion of the New Deal were likewise promised.

Willkie made an extended speaking tour in which he attacked not the basic principles of the New Deal, but the Democratic administration of it. He also found fault with the failure of the New Deal to provide adequate preparedness and urged even more aid to the democracies. Many Republican orators went beyond Willkie in denouncing the President. They accused him of trying to be a dictator—and they used the destroyer-base deal in an effort to prove that he had made secret commitments with Great Britain that would lead the country into war, that he had agreed to send American troops to foreign lands without Congressional approval, and that he had done little to promote preparedness.

As he had promised in his acceptance speech, President Roosevelt did not campaign at first in the usual sense, but devoted his time to domestic and foreign problems. Yet he did tour the country visiting navy yards, factories, and arsenals, thereby making contact with many voters. When it appeared that Willkie was gaining ground, moreover, Roosevelt made an active and direct appeal for votes. The reason he gave was that it was necessary for him "to call the attention of the nation to deliberate or unwitting falsifications of fact." In five major speeches Roosevelt stressed the reforms of the New Deal and the need of experience in office. On the war issue both Willkie and Roosevelt became irresponsible. The Republican candidate warned that the nation would be involved in hostilities within five months if Roosevelt won, while the President rashly assured father and mothers: "I have said this before, but I shall say it again and again and again. Your boys are not going to be sent into any foreign war."

On election day it was the seriousness of the world situation that swung the decision to Roosevelt. The electorate decided it would be unwise to swap horses. Nevertheless, the results were closer than in previous campaigns in which Roosevelt had run. In the popular field he received 27.2 million votes to Willkie's 22.3 million, while the electoral college gave 449 votes to Roosevelt and 82 to Willkie, who carried ten states. The general interest in the election was indicated by the nearly 50 million votes cast; a feature was the number of split ballots. The victorious President maintained his majority in Congress as the Democrats increased their House seats by 6 (for a total of 268 to the Republicans' 162), although in the Senate the Democrats dropped 3 seats (for a total of 66 to the Republicans' 28).

The Burke-Wadsworth Act

Roosevelt regarded the election of 1940 as a popular mandate to continue his policies of preparedness, hemisphere defense, and all-out aid to the democracies. Even while the campaign was under way he took steps to further his objectives. On August 18, following a meeting with Prime Minister Mackenzie King of Canada, Roosevelt announced the establishment of a Permanent Joint Board on Defense to consider "sea, land and air problems" relating to the "defense of the north half of the Western Hemisphere."

In his acceptance speech of July 19, 1940, the President said: "Because of the millions of citizens involved in the conduct of defense, most right-thinking persons are agreed that some form of selection by draft is as necessary and fair today as it was in 1917 and 1918." And while waiting for Congress to enact such a conscription act, he obtained authority on August 27 to call out the National Guard because of "the increasing seriousness of the international situation."

A bill providing for the first peacetime draft in American history had been introduced into Congress in June, 1940, by Senator Edward Burke, a Nebraska Democrat, and Representative James Wadsworth, a New York Republican. Extensive committee discussion and earnest debates in both Houses delayed its enactment; the non-interventionists asserted that its passage would surely lead the nation into war; the supporters declared that the army could not wait for voluntary enlistments to build itself up to needed strength. There were also disagreements between the two Houses over the age limits before a compromise was reached on September 14.[5] Two days later the President signed this so-called Burke-Wadsworth Act. Its passage was helped by the support that both Presidential candidates gave it.

The measure provided that all men between the ages of twenty-one and thirty-six must register for an eventual year's military service within the limits of the United States. The maximum number to receive such training in a given year was fixed at 900,000. Presidential proclamation fixed October 16 as registration day and President Clarence Dykstra of the University of Wisconsin was named as Selective Service Administrator. The first men so drafted were called for their military training in November.

---

[5] The House vote was 232 to 134; in the Senate it was 47 to 25.

Meantime, President Roosevelt had made preparedness a bipartisan matter by appointing to his cabinet two Republicans. Henry L. Stimson became the new Secretary of War, while Frank Knox took over the administration of the Department of the Navy. Both men filled their posts with marked ability and efficiency.

Lend-Lease

The President still was not satisfied with what had been done to strengthen the defense of the Americas. He knew that on September 27, 1940, Germany, Italy, and Japan had concluded the Tripartite Pact under which they agreed to assist one another in case any power then neutral—meaning the United States —entered the war against one of them. Consequently, in a radio talk to the nation on December 29, 1940, President Roosevelt described the increasing Axis menace and told of how Hitler had said: "I can beat any other power in the world." Then he reviewed the assistance the United States had given Great Britain and the need to continue and extend that aid because:

> If Great Britain goes down, the Axis powers will control the continents of Europe, Asia, Africa, Australasia, and the high seas—and they will be in a position to bring enormous military and naval resources against this hemisphere. It is no exaggeration to say that all of us, in all the Americas, would be living at the point of a gun—a gun loaded with explosive bullets, economic as well as military.

The President continued with the assertion that the policy of the nation was "to keep war away from our country and our people." To do this, the country must speed up its production along all lines so that the nations fighting aggression might obtain whatever supplies they needed. "We must become the arsenal of democracy."

This speech set the stage for further proposals in the President's annual message to Congress of January 6, 1941. After pointing out that the democracies did not need manpower, he asserted that they would soon "need billions of dollars' worth of the weapons of defense." However, they would soon be unable to pay for those weapons "in ready cash." Despite the "cash-and-carry" provision, it would not be right for the United States to say that they should therefore surrender. Instead, the President asked that the democracies be loaned war materials, for which "we shall be repaid within a reasonable time following the close of hostilities, in similar materials, or, at our option, in other goods of many kinds, which they can produce and which we need."

Were the United States to extend these material loans, the democracies would win. That victory would make possible a "world founded upon four essential human freedoms"—freedom of speech and expression, freedom of worship, freedom from want, and freedom from fear. This was Roosevelt's first expression of what might be called the victory aims of World War II.

Where the War May Be Decided. (By Herblock
in the NEA Services, Inc.)

Congress speedily took up the President's request. On January 10, 1941, H.R.
1776 was introduced, a bill "further to promote the defense of the United
States." It first of all defined "defense articles," which included weapons, munitions, ships, aircraft, and agricultural and industrial commodities. Then, "notwithstanding the provisions of any other law," the President might authorize
the head of any governmental department or agency "to manufacture in arsenals, factories, and shipyards . . . any defense article for the government of
any country whose defense the President deems vital to the defense of the
United States." The department or agency might then sell or lease such articles
to that government. These loaned defense commodities must not be convoyed
by American naval vessels, and the President must make a report to Congress
at least once every ninety days about lend-lease activities.

This lend-lease bill has been called the broadest grant of power ever given to
a President, but administration supporters asserted it was necessary in order to
assure speed and efficiency in American aid to the democracies. The non-interventionists immediately condemned the measure. Democratic Senator Clark of
Missouri declared it was a method of authorizing the President to declare war;
Republican Senator Johnson of California thought it "monstrous"; Wheeler
of Montana said that he would filibuster against it because it was a "New Deal
triple-A foreign policy; it will plow under every fourth American boy"; LaFol-

lette looked on it as "a bold attempt to create a dictatorship to govern our future foreign policy." In special committee hearings they called in "experts" like Charles Lindbergh to testify against the need of such an extreme proposal. A middle group in Congress approved the aid to Britain, but believed it could be accomplished without giving the President so much power. Secretaries Hull, Stimson, and Morgenthau, together with other prominent government officials, gave their unlimited support to the plan, while the President used his influence upon key Congressmen. The Lend-Lease Act eventually became law on March 11.[6] Congress then quickly appropriated $7 billion to put lend-lease in operation and the President ordered shipments of vital materials to the democracies at once.

The passage of the Lend-Lease Act definitely marked the end of the isolationist policy that the United States had pursued since the close of World War I. It was the logical step to take in view of the fact that the nation had committed itself to the policy of aiding opponents of aggression. Britain was naturally thankful, and Prime Minister Winston Churchill referred to the act as a "monument of generous, far-seeing statesmanship." Germany tried to play down the effects by saying that American aid would arrive too late to save Britain, but at the same time she called the measure "the most flagrant North American meddling."

The new policy greatly strengthened the antifascist cause. British dollar credits in the United States were practically exhausted, and American neutrality legislation stood as a bar to private loans. Already British purchases in the United States were being reduced—a most undesirable situation. Lend-lease was based upon the sound premise that the continuance of British and Chinese resistance to aggression would give America time to strengthen its defenses, and the further premise that the most sensible thing to do with the major portion of war implements produced in American factories was to place them as expeditiously as possible in the hands of those who would use them against America's potential enemies. Lend-lease had the additional great merit of making the United States government the sole important customer for the arms industry. Instead of a situation wherein representatives of the American armed forces were competing with the purchasing agents of the other democratic powers, the new policy gave the United States government complete power over the allocation of weapons. It could decide which should be kept in the United States and which should be sent abroad.

To be sure, lend-lease marked the end of real neutrality. The nation was

---

[6] The House approved of the bill on February 8 by a vote of 260 to 165 (135 Republicans were on the losing side), the Senate amended and passed it on March 8 by a vote of 60 to 31 (with 17 Republicans and LaFollette in the minority), and the House accepted the Senate amendments on March 11 by a vote of 317 to 71. The chief amendment terminated the President's power on June 30, 1943.

openly trying to help one side to the detriment of the other. But the question had become clearly one of American security. To be neutral in a struggle of this character was to acquiesce in the victory of nations whose hostile designs upon the Western Hemisphere were obvious—at least to most observers.

The Error Must Not Be Repeated

As has been shown, many Americans believed that the wisest policy for their country was to avoid at all costs any act which might lead it into war. These so-called isolationists had been largely responsible for the Johnson Debt Default Act of 1934 and the subsequent neutrality legislation. They hailed the findings of the Nye Committee as proof that World War I had benefited only a few selfish international bankers and munitions makers. They opposed all efforts to increase the army and navy, to enact the Selective Service Law, and to pass lend-lease because they believed such steps would develop a belligerent spirit in the United States and thereby increase the possibility of war. As in the period from 1914 to 1917, many isolationists, especially young and devout Christians, honestly believed that hostilities would be disastrous for the country.

There were other groups within the isolationist camp, however, who were not so idealistic, but who supported the movement for other, more selfish reasons. Some anti-New Dealers saw in the administration's request for pre-paredness a Roosevelt effort to turn the country's attention from the short-comings of his domestic policies. Many social reformers regarded the movement as the beginning of the end for the program of social justice. Up to the time of the German attack on the Soviet Union, American Communists proclaimed that war would benefit only the capitalists. American fascists desired neither preparedness nor war because they wanted an Axis victory, with the resulting spread of totalitarianism to the United States. Many German-Americans and Italo-Americans opposed American entrance into the war because it would spell defeat for their native lands. A few businessmen thought that appeasement of the dictators would bring profitable trade to the country, while Axis agents tried to build up a feeling of security in the United States so that lend-lease would not be granted to the enemies of Germany. Normally these diverse elements would have had little or nothing in common, but now they rallied in mutual support of their goal—to keep the country out of war.

These strange bedfellows used every means to advance their cause. In Congress there were Senators Johnson, Wheeler, Nye, and LaFollette, together with Representatives Hamilton Fish of New York and Clare Hoffman of Michigan—to mention the most prominent—who constantly spoke and voted against preparedness bills. From public platforms Charles Lindbergh and others severely condemned the Roosevelt foreign policies. Over the radio Father Charles

Coughlin preached in a fascist vein. Books, periodicals, and pamphlets such as Elizabeth Dilling's *Red Network*, Father Coughlin's *Social Justice*, and Gerald Winrod's *The Defender* promoted the isolationist viewpoint.

It was through the agency of special commitees, however, that most of the isolationist propaganda was disseminated. Some of these organizations made their appeal chiefly to those of German blood. Under the leadership of Fritz Kuhn, the members of the German-American Bund wore uniforms at their meetings, practiced military drill, and greeted one another with the Nazi salute. Financed in part by the Reich through the German diplomatic corps in the United States, these pro-German committees[7] tried to dissuade Americans from supporting preparedness measures. They also sang hymns of hate against the British and the Jews.

Many Americans, refusing to join the definitely Nazi organizations, nevertheless did become members of committees that placed their appeal on some different basis. There were more than seven hundred of these isolationist agencies in the United States at the opening of World War II; while most of them were ephemeral, some were strong and vociferous. One of the most publicized was the American Fellowship Forum to promote Nazi ideological warfare, the need for appeasement, and opposition to preparedness. Through *Today's Challenge*, the Forum made its appeal; contributors were Lawrence Dennis, a frank proponent of American fascism, Representative Fish, Senator Lundeen, and George Sylvester Viereck of World War I notoriety. Another group was William Dudley Pelley's Silver Shirts, which used *The Galilean* to urge a purge of Jews and others who Pelley asserted were un-American. The Christian Front, professed admirers of Father Coughlin, consisted of a number of platoons with a claimed membership of at least 200,000, dedicated to dominating the country by force. More than twenty isolationist Congressmen, wittingly or not, allowed their franking privileges to be used to send out literature detrimental to preparedness and to the Allied cause.

The America First Committee attempted to consolidate the membership of these numerous groups. Organized in the fall of 1940 by R. Douglas Stuart, Jr., a wealthy student at Yale, it had as its general purpose the avoidance of war at any price. The first national chairman was General Robert E. Wood, a well-known Chicago businessman. Prominent among the members or those who cooperated were Charles Lindbergh, Kathleen Norris, Henry Ford, General Hugh Johnson, and isolationist Senators like Wheeler and Nye. This committee sent out thousands of pamphlets, letters, buttons, and stickers. Hundreds of speeches were delivered, but they showed little contact with reality. For example, on April 7, 1941, Lindbergh asserted that Great Britain was a beaten nation; he con-

[7] Lesser known agencies in America were the League of Friends of New Germany, the German Legion, the German Edda Kultur League, the Homeland Regional Group, the League of German-American Writers, and the Hindenburg Youth Association.

cluded, therefore, "that we cannot win this war for England, regardless of how much assistance we extend." Six weeks later, he and Wheeler asked for a negotiated peace because, were the United States to enter the war, it would mean the end of democracy on this side of the Atlantic. In September, 1941, the eminent flier declared: "The three most important groups which have been pressing this country toward war are the British, the Jewish, and the Roosevelt Administration."

While it is impossible to say how much influence these isolationist organizations had upon the American mind, or to determine accurately their membership, their efforts were not without effect. The debates in Congress showed that opposition to war was strong, and delaying tactics did hold up preparedness measures. The antiwar spirit was also active in the colleges; thousands of students signed the Oxford Pledge not to fight under any circumstances and flooded Washington with petitions urging the administration not to repeat the mistake of 1917.

Developing a Punch. (By Hungerford in the *Pittsburgh Post-Gazette.*)

The administration did not conceal its bitterness toward these organizations. For example, President Roosevelt asserted that the isolationists were demanding that he "become a modern Benedict Arnold and betray all that I hold dear—my devotion to our freedom—to our churches—to our country." He referred to Lindbergh as an "appeaser and defeatist" in such denunciatory terms that the colonel resigned his commission in the Army Air Force. The President also implied that there was a strong similarity between the writings and speeches of the non-interventionists and the articles coming from the Reich.

Nor was the opposition to the isolationists limited to the administration. To counteract the efforts of the America First Committee and other such groups, many Americans aligned themselves with the Committee to Defend America by Aiding the Allies and the Fight for Freedom Committee. Pamphlets, speeches, radio talks, and advertisements were used by the internationalists in their fight.

Improving Hemisphere Defense

Despite the attacks of the isolationists, the United States continued to build up American defenses during the spring and summer of 1941, by giving more assistance to Britain and other countries fighting the Axis and by cutting down potential Axis influence in the Western Hemisphere. For example, just as lend-lease material began to flow from American ports in April, 1941, the United States turned over ten coast-guard cutters to Great Britain for antisubmarine warfare. This action was deemed necessary because of the staggering merchant losses the British were suffering on the seas and because the Neutrality Act prohibited the United States from convoying American supplies to belligerents.

In the same month Roosevelt and Prime Minister Mackenzie King of Canada agreed that "in mobilizing the resources of this continent each country should provide the other with the defense articles which it is best able to produce quickly, and that production should be coordinated to this end." Consequently, the United States bought strategic materials—such as aluminum—from Canada to speed up American defensive preparations, while Canada obtained essential dollar exchange to balance her unfavorable trade and enable her to buy more American goods.

Likewise in April, the United States signed a pact with the Danish Minister in Washington under which it gained the right to establish military and naval installations on Greenland. Not only was this a move to prevent the island from falling into German hands as the mother country had and to protect the hemisphere, but it meant as well that the United States might guard British merchantmen as far east as Greenland.

German protests at these steps were as nothing compared with the cries raised against the seizure of her merchant ships in American ports. On March 30, 1941, the United States Coast Guard, under orders of the Treasury Department, took over twenty-eight Italian and two German ships lying in American harbors because their crews, on instructions from their respective governments, had wrecked the machinery and engaged in other acts of sabotage. Asserting that the sabotage of ships was a menace to navigation, the United States took action under the Espionage Act of 1917. At the same time thirty-five undamaged Danish ships were brought under American control.[8]

Then arose the question of what to do with the seized ships. The President found the solution by asking Congress on April 10 to extend his authority to requisition or purchase American vessels to include the recently seized ones. On June 6 Congress gave the President the desired authority, and on the same day Roosevelt ordered the United States Maritime Commission to take over "any foreign merchant vessel which is lying idle in waters within the jurisdiction of the United States . . . and which is necessary to the national defense. . . ." Thus the German, Italian, and Danish ships, together with subsequently seized French ones—including the *Normandie*—were acquired by the United States. Later a number of these were used to carry cargoes to Britain.

Still another blow at the Axis was delivered on June 14 when the President, under the Trading-with-the-Enemy Act of 1917, froze all Axis assets in the United States. By so doing Roosevelt hoped to diminish totalitarian propaganda and sabotage in the country. To serve the same end, the State Department closed, as of July 10, twenty-four German consulates in the United States, together with the German Library of Information and other propaganda agencies because they were engaging "in activities wholly outside the scope of their legitimate activities." Subsequently, all Italian consulates were also closed.[9]

Nor was the United States finished. Acting under authority obtained through the declaration of the unlimited national emergency of May 27, 1941, the President issued a "Proclaimed List of Certain Blocked Nationals." This consisted of some 1,800 persons and firms in the Western Hemisphere who were "deemed to be acting for the benefit of Germany and Italy"—in other words, they were undermining American official policy. No American firms were to do business with the black-listed concerns, whose assets held in the United States were to be frozen. This was an unusual action for the United States to take while still a neutral, but it was further proof of the administration's insistence upon keeping Axis influence at a minimum in the hemisphere.

Meantime, the President pushed the defensive zone closer to Europe by ordering the American occupation of Iceland on July 7, because "the United States cannot permit the occupation by Germany of strategic outposts in the Atlantic to be used as air or naval bases for eventual attack against the Western Hemisphere." This pronouncement increased the ire of the isolationists, who asserted that it would be only a matter of time before the nation was involved in war. Senator Wheeler declared that American naval ships had already attacked

---

[8] Following the lead of the United States, nine Latin-American countries also seized the Axis ships within their ports.

[9] Germany reciprocated by closing American consulates and American Express offices in the Reich and occupied countries on July 15 because of "grave acts" against Germany. Shortly after, Italy followed suit and in addition froze American investments within her territory.

German submarines, a statement that brought quick denial from Secretary Knox.

But if that were not the case, German submarines at any rate were attacking American shipping. On May 21, 1941, the *Robin Moor*, clearly marked as an American merchantman, was sunk 700 miles off the coast of Brazil while on her way to Cape Town. The submarine commander made no effort to help the passengers and crew, who drifted in lifeboats for nearly three weeks before they were rescued. When the news reached the United States on June 9, an immediate protest was sent to the Reich; but the answer was not considered satisfactory: "Germany will continue to sink every ship with contraband for Britain whatever its name."

Consequently the President sent a special message to Congress on June 20 in which he said:

> We must take the sinking of the *Robin Moor* as a warning to the United States not to resist the Nazi movement of world conquest. It is a warning that the United States may use the high seas of the world only with Nazi consent. Were we to yield on this we would inevitably submit to world domination at the hands of the present leaders of the German Reich. We are not yielding and we do not propose to yield.

As definite proof that the United States was not going to yield, the administration condemned the unprovoked German attack upon Russia in June and at the same time announced that lend-lease help would be extended to the Soviet.[10] Moreover, at the request of Chief of Staff George Marshall, the President asked Congress in early July to lengthen military service for the draftees because their discharge after a year's training would disrupt plans for enlarging the army. The isolationists charged the administration with trying to break a contract made in the Burke-Wadsworth Act and declared that the nation was not in such grave peril as Roosevelt inferred. By August 12, however, Congress had complied with the President's request by adding six months to the military service of conscripted men;[11] the extra service was made more palatable through a $10-a-month pay raise after one year.

The Atlantic Charter

Despite these preparations, the Axis victories in Europe and Asia, together with continued Allied losses on the high seas, made essential more definite planning by the democracies. Therefore President Roosevelt and Prime Minister Churchill met at sea off the coast of Newfoundland August 9–12, 1941. They

[10] This decision also brought vociferous protests from the isolationists. Lindbergh said: "I would a hundred times rather see my country ally herself with England, or even Germany with all her faults, than with the cruelty, the godlessness and the barbarism that exist in Soviet Russia. The only sensible thing for us to do is to build an impregnable defense for America and keep this hemisphere at peace."

[11] The House vote was 203 to 202; the Senate approved by 45 to 30.

discussed what aid should be sent the Soviet, what policy should be followed in respect to Japan, and numerous other problems concerning lend-lease and preparedness. The most important and publicized action, however, was the agreement on broad aims and principles for the post war world. This agreement, known as the "Atlantic Charter," was made public on August 14 and contained the following provisions:

First, their countries seek no aggrandizement, territorial or other;

Second, they desire to see no territorial changes that do not accord with the freely expressed wishes of all the people concerned;

Third, they respect the right of all peoples to choose the form of government under which they will live; and they wish to see sovereign rights and self-government restored to those who have been forcibly deprived of them;

Fourth, they will endeavor, with due respect for their existing obligations, to further the enjoyment by all States, great and small, victor or vanquished, of access, on equal terms, to the trade and to the raw materials of the world which are needed for their economic prosperity;

Fifth, they desire to bring about the fullest collaboration between all nations in the economic field with the object of securing, for all, improved labor standards, economic advancement, and social security;

Sixth, after the final destruction of the Nazi tyranny, they hope to see established a peace which will afford to all nations the means of dwelling within their own boundaries, and which will afford assurance that all men in all the lands may live out their lives in freedom from fear and want;

Seventh, such a peace should enable all men to traverse the high seas and oceans without hindrance;

Eighth, they believe that all of the nations of the world, for realistic as well as spiritual reasons, must come to the abandonment of the use of force. Since no future peace can be maintained if land, sea, or air armaments continue to be employed by nations which threaten, or may threaten, aggression outside of their frontiers, they believe, pending the establishment of a wider and permanent system of general security, that the disarmament of such nations is essential. They will likewise aid and encourage all other practicable measures which will lighten for peace-loving peoples the crushing burden of armaments.

This Atlantic Charter might be called the Fourteen Points of World War II; while the Charter was less detailed than Wilson's statement, it served much the same purpose—that of establishing a postwar goal for peace and collective security. Moreover, the Charter had greater weight in that it was sponsored by the heads of two of the strongest nations in the world. It gave oppressed peoples a hope for the future and was the beginning of the United Nations. The very indefiniteness of the Charter provided a latitude lacking in the Fourteen Points.

The Shooting War

American help for Britain was, in truth, coming closer and closer to actual war. During the summer of 1941 American naval vessels were escorting British and American merchant ships as far as Iceland. Although they were forbidden to shoot unless attacked, they helped to protect the sea lanes by reporting to British destroyers and planes the positions of German submarines. In accordance with this policy, the United States destroyer *Greer* had been tracking an underseas raider for several hours on September 4 when the submarine retaliated by firing two torpedoes at its American follower. Uninjured, the *Greer* counterattacked by dropping several depth charges and pursuing the German craft until the latter finally escaped. In a radio talk to the nation President Roosevelt condemned the attack upon the *Greer* and made known his policy for the future:

> No act of violence will keep us from maintaining intact two bulwarks of defense: First, our line of supply to the enemies of Hitler, and, second, the freedom of our shipping on the high seas. From now on, if German or Italian vessels of war enter the waters the protection of which is necessary for American defense, they do so at their own peril.

Roosevelt denied it was an act of war to maintain the American patrol to protect shipping. Moreover, he warned that "American naval vessels and American planes will no longer wait until Axis submarines . . . or raiders . . . strike their deadly blow—first." This amounted to a virtual order to American ships and planes to shoot first.

The isolationists denounced this order as the beginning of a "shooting war." The Reich characterized the President as a dictatorial aggressor who was ready to involve an unwilling nation in war to satisfy his lust for power.

Amending the Neutrality Act

Within three weeks after the *Greer* incident, the President intimated that he would soon ask Congress for permission to arm American merchantmen; this would mean, of course, a partial repeal of the Neutrality Act of 1939. It is impossible to say what chance of success the repeal movement would have had under ordinary circumstances. The isolationists were still very strong in Congress, as indicated by the close House vote on extension of military training. Nor was the nation as a whole in favor of the step, even though public-opinion polls showed support for American convoying of lend-lease material if that were the only means of preventing a British defeat. However, the cause of repeal was greatly assisted by the actions of Germany herself.

On September 27 the *L. C. White*, an American-owned tanker now under Panama registry,[12] was sunk off the Brazilian bulge well within the limits of the neutrality zone. Secretary Hull characterized the incident as "another act of lawlessness, piracy and attempted frightfulness in connection with the general

[12] Many American ships changed registry to some other neutral hemisphere country in order to avoid the prohibitions of United States neutrality laws.

movement to drive people off the Atlantic Ocean, which is part of the world movement of conquest."

In a special message to Congress on October 9, the President said: "Our merchant vessels are sailing the seas on missions connected with the defense of the United States. It is not just that the crews of these vessels should be denied the means of defending their lives and their ships." Consequently, he asked for the repeal of the clause prohibiting the arming of American ships, and at the same time intimated that he wished Congress would also remove the "crippling provisions" banning American vessels from combat zones and belligerent ports.

Score Board. (By Seibel in *The Richmond Times-Dispatch*.)

Debate on amending the Neutrality Act was cut short by the news that on October 17 the destroyer *Kearney* had been hit off Iceland with resulting casualties of ten injured and eleven missing. The incident brought House passage of the bill by an overwhelming vote—259 to 138. In the Senate, three Republicans—Austin of Vermont, Bridges of New Hampshire, and Gurney of South Dakota—substituted a measure calling for total repeal of the Neutrality Act because it was "detrimental to the best interests of the United States," which could not exist in a "nazified world." This proposal had the unqualified support of Wendell Willkie, who considered the act in question an "ugly smudge of isolationism." But the Democratic majority preferred to follow the President's wishes by repealing only three sections of the act: the bans on arming of merchantmen, on entrance into combat zones, and on entering belligerent ports. Rallying their forces, the isolationist Senators, led by Wheeler and Nye, warned that repeal would be "the last step before we enter war." A filibuster—like that waged by the willful men of 1917—was threatened.

The isolationist resistance was overcome after the destroyer *Reuben James*, convoying supplies to Iceland, was sunk by the Germans with a loss of 100 lives. On November 7, the Senate approved repeal of the three clauses by a vote of 50 to 37, and six days later the House accepted the Senate version by 212 to 194.

The order for arming merchantmen was speedily given, and they were thereafter allowed to go to Allied ports with military supplies. Both these merchantmen and American naval vessels could shoot on sight in order to keep the supply lines open, to maintain freedom of the seas, and to strengthen the defense of the hemisphere. The United States was still theoretically neutral, but it was a neutrality in name only. While the isolationists continued to assert that the United States should avoid war, war had already come. By November 1 German submarines had taken a toll of eleven American merchant vessels and one destroyer. Two other destroyers and innumerable merchantment had been attacked but escaped sinking. To prevent further losses, American ships were ready to fight. Under the circumstances it could be but a matter of time before all-out hostilities developed. Strangely enough, however, the final steps were taken on the other side of the world.

Mounting Japanese Aggression

Following the *Panay* incident, most Americans turned their backs upon the Far East, while they viewed with increasing apprehension the storm clouds developing over Europe. Nevertheless, in the period from early 1938 until the Pearl Harbor attack, the Roosevelt administration realized that the Japanese menace was growing rather than diminishing. Because of isolationist sentiment, however, that menace was dealt with in words rather than deeds during most of these months.

During 1938 the State Department protested against Japanese encroachments on American rights in China and against the Japanese bombings of Chinese civilians. Moreover, the Western powers showed apprehension over reports that Japan was building a larger navy. In February, 1938, Britain, France, and the United States demanded that Japan reveal whether she was constructing any capital ships exceeding the 35,000-ton limit placed in the Washington Treaty, but Japan refused to divulge her plans. There was nothing the other nations could do about this rebuff; France and Britain were much too concerned with

Hitler's moves, while the United States did not wish to push Japan too strongly because this might mean war.

Nevertheless, the Roosevelt administration tried to restrain Japan by other means. On July 1, 1938, Secretary Hull informed the manufacturers and exporters of airplanes and aircraft parts that the government strongly opposed the sale of such equipment to any nation which used planes to attack and bomb civilian populations. Although no penalties were threatened, there was general compliance with what might be called a moral embargo. In 1939 the State Department similarly frowned upon the exportation of high-octane gasoline or of any information disclosing how to manufacture this aviation fuel. Even before this "moral" embargo was placed, the administration persuaded bankers not to extend any financial credit to Japan.

Since President Roosevelt had never proclaimed that a state of war existed in the Far East, neither the Neutrality Act of 1937 nor that of 1939 was put into effect. At first he withheld the proclamation because he hoped that the troubles between Japan and China could be settled quickly; later he realized that if the neutrality legislation became effective, China, a victim of aggression, with few ships and little money, would be unable to obtain American assistance.

These actions had little effect upon Japan, except perhaps to offer convincing proof that the United States was unfriendly toward her. Appeasement at Munich encouraged aggression in Asia as well as in Europe, and on November 3, 1938, Premier Fumimara Konoye for the first time publicly stated Japan's ambition:

> What Japan seeks is the establishment of a new order that will ensure the permanent stability of East Asia. In this lies the ultimate purpose of our present military campaign. This new order has for its foundation a tripartite relationship of mutual aid and co-ordination between Japan, Manchukuo, and China in political, economic, cultural, and other fields.

Konoye's pronouncement neglected to mention that Japan was forcing the "New Order" upon an unwilling China or to define what East Asia would include. The American State Department called attention to these omissions and protested that Japanese actions were harming American "rights and interests" in China. Since these interferences were "counter to the provisions of several binding international agreements" to which Japan and the United States were voluntary parties, the United States considered them "unjust and unwarranted." Nor did the United States consider it just for one party to draw up terms for the New Order for regions not under its jurisdiction. Hull then concluded with the assertion that his country would not countenance the abrogation of any of its rights through arbitrary methods. The United States, however, was agreeable to discussing any new and mutually satisfactory proposals.

By no means impressed by American protests, the Japanese extended their control over Hainan in February, 1939, followed two months later by the seizure of several islands only 700 miles from Singapore. Then in June she began to blockade the British and French concessions in Tientsin. As the war spread there were more American lives threatened, American property destroyed, and American rights in the Japanese-occupied sections of China interfered with. Since mere protests were ineffective, the Roosevelt administration decided to resort to more drastic steps.

On July 26, 1939, the United States gave Japan the necessary six months' notice for the termination of the 1911 commercial treaty. The cancellation of that treaty, with its most-favored-nation clauses, would remove all obstacles to an actual embargo against Japan. When the six-month period ended in January, 1940, Japanese-American trade relations were maintained on a day-by-day basis, subject to interruption at any time. But even this threat did not cause Japan to change her policies. The military forces of Japan continued to press their advantage, moving into Hunan Province in September, 1939, and capturing Nanning two months later. In this progress Japan was aided by the outbreak of the European war, which prevented Britain and France from assisting their nationals in the Far East or from supporting in wholehearted fashion the American protests.

In early June, 1940, Japan took advantage of the collapse of France to move into French Indo-China. Simultaneously she demanded that Britain close the Burma Road to all military supplies to China. Japan backed up this demand with the implied threat that if Britain did not comply, an attack would be made upon Hongkong. Britain, now facing the Reich alone and fearing an invasion, could do nothing except agree to close the road for three months starting July 18. The effect was to cut China almost completely off from the rest of the world.

On September 27, 1940, Japan openly asserted its solidarity with the European Axis. The Tripartite Pact, concluded on that date, stated in part:

> The Governments of Germany, Italy and Japan consider it the prerequisite of a lasting peace that every nation in the world shall receive the space to which it is entitled. They have, therefore, decided to stand by and cooperate with one another in their efforts in Greater East Asia and the regions of Europe respectively. In so doing it is their prime purpose to establish and maintain a new order of things, calculated to promote the mutual prosperity and welfare of the peoples concerned. . . .
>
> Accordingly, the Governments of Germany, Italy and Japan have agreed as follows:
>
> Article 1. Japan recognizes and respects the leadership of Germany and Italy in the establishment of a new order in Europe.
>
> Article 2. Germany and Italy recognize and respect the leadership of Japan in the establishment of a new order in Greater East Asia.

Article 3. . . . They further undertake to assist one another with all political, economic and military means if one of the three . . . is attacked by a Power at present not involved in the European War or in the Chinese-Japanese conflict.

Although Article 3 was certainly intended as a warning to the United States, President Roosevelt was not swerved from his position. In a radio address of October 12, 1940, he proclaimed the need for maintaining democracy in the Western Hemisphere. Then he asserted:

The core of our defense is the faith we have in the institutions we defend. The Americas will not be scared or threatened into the ways the dictators want us to follow.

No combination of dictator countries of Europe and Asia will halt us in the path we see ahead for ourselves and for democracy.

No combination of dictator countries of Europe and Asia will stop the help we are giving to almost the last free people fighting to hold them at bay. . . .

We know now that if we seek to appease them by withholding aid from those who stand in their way, we only hasten the day of their attack on us. . . .

Based on these premises, the President's policy included several main points. First of all, the United States should not seek war with Japan. Second, it must not back down on its insistence that American rights in the Far East be respected. Third, it must not withhold aid from the defenders of democracy. Fourth, all kinds of pressure, diplomatic and economic, should be used to try to force Japan to cease her aggression. And, finally, the United States was willing to confer with Japan and other nations interested in the Far East for a possible settlement of regional problems.

Additional economic and commercial pressure was already being exerted. On December 15, 1938, the first of a series of loans was made to China. On July 2, 1940, the President signed the Export Control Act, which empowered him to curtail or stop completely the export of materials considered vital to the American defense program. Almost immediately Roosevelt announced that, beginning in August, no more export licenses would be granted for shipping aviation gasoline and machine tools to Japan. This was followed in September by a similar ban on scrap iron and steel. These actions were denounced by Ambassador Horinouchi as "unfriendly acts" and "discriminatory" measures that might cause "unpredictable results." Hull's answer was sharp and critical. He could not see, he said, how Japan, which had broken so many commitments and had violated so many American rights in China, could object to the validity of the embargoes: ". . . of all the countries with which I have had to deal during the past eight years the Government of Japan has the least occasion or excuse to accuse this Government of an unfriendly act." Despite Japanese threats, the United States went on to extend the embargo before the spring of 1941 to include arms, ammunition, other implements of war, and many strategic materials.

Tension Mounts

The opening of 1941 found relations between the United States and Japan increasingly strained. The Japanese military clique was growing in strength and taking a more active part in the political affairs of the country. Members of jingoistic and terrorist societies were assassinating those who advocated peace. The chauvinistic press was attempting to sway the minds of the people in favor of the New Order. If some Japanese appeared desirous of maintaining American friendship, others were openly hostile.[13]

Japan was angered by the American refusal to recognize the New Order and by the increasing number of commodities placed on the American embargo list. Yet there was the feeling held by some that the United States would never risk war with Japan. To this feeling the isolationists in the American Congress contributed when they voted down the presidential request for appropriations to deepen the harbors at Guam and other Pacific islands.

It cannot be said that the United States was not warned of the danger that Japan might attack American soil. In testimony before the House Foreign Relations Committee on January 15, 1941, Secretary Hull pointed out that an increasing number of statements had recently been made by Japanese leaders about their plans for the domination of the Far East. The Secretary considered these "a program for the subjugation and ruthless exploitation by one country of nearly half the population of the world." This program should therefore be a "matter of immense significance, importance and concern" to America. Nine days later, Secretary of the Navy Knox became anxious about the situation as shown by his note to War Secretary Stimson:

> If war eventuates with Japan, it is believed easily possible that hostilities would be initiated by a surprise attack upon the Fleet or Naval base at Pearl Harbor. ... The dangers envisaged in their order of importance and probability are considered to be: (1) air bombing attack; (2) air torpedo plane attack; (3) sabotage; (4) submarine attack; (5) mining; (6) bombardment by gunfire.

This remarkable prediction was followed on January 27 with a report from Ambassador Grew that he had it on reliable authority "that a surprise mass attack on Pearl Harbor was planned by the Japanese military forces, in case of trouble between Japan and the United States; that the attack would involve the use of all Japanese military facilities."

Despite these warnings, American popular attention was concerned chiefly with events in Europe and the debates then going on in Congress over lend-lease. Trouble in the Far East seemed too remote to affect the United States, and the belief persisted that America would not be drawn into the imbroglio un-

---

[13] For example, on October 4, 1940, Foreign Minister Matsuoka is reported to have said: "I fling this challenge to America. If she in her contentment is going to stick blindly and stubbornly to *status quo* in the Pacific, then we will fight America."

less she herself sought war. Indeed, the opinion polls indicated that the primary potential enemy was thought to be Germany, not Japan. It was also felt that, if war were to come with Japan, the enemy could be quickly and easily defeated.

Both the United States and Japan wanted to avert an early showdown. The Roosevelt administration did not desire war, if war could be avoided. If it must come, it would be better late than soon, because the nation was not ready for hostilities either in terms of military preparation or of national unity. On their side, the Japanese were playing for time in the hope that their Axis partners would be victorious in Europe and that Japanese domination over East Asia could thereafter be achieved at a minimum price.

In January, 1941, Bishop James Walsh and Father James Drought, members of a Catholic missionary order, acted as intermediaries in bringing to Washington confidential messages from Premier Konoye. The informal talks thus initiated took on an official character with the arrival in February of a new Japanese ambassador, Admiral Kichisaburo Nomura, who had attended the Naval Academy at Annapolis in his youth.

On March 8 Nomura and Hull began a series of conferences on all outstanding difficulties. The early talks soon indicated Japan had gone so far in her military conquests that she would not consent to stop or to relinquish her gains. To both Hull and President Roosevelt Japan's course seemed likely to lead to war with the United States, but they hoped to avert hostilities as long as possible. Moreover, the other countries with a stake in the Far East were either too busy with the European struggle or were already occupied by Germany. Although an ABCD (America, Britain, China, and the Dutch) agreement for preserving the *status quo* in the Pacific was being developed during the spring, that arrangement actually did not mean much. Under the circumstances it seemed best to continue the peace talks with Nomura as long as possible.

But, even while these peace talks were going on, the United States was continuing its policy of trying to stem the Japanese advance by economic pressure. With the passage of lend-lease, further credit as well as strategic supplies were extended to China—making a total of more than $100 million since the beginning of 1940. Moreover, lend-lease aid was granted to the Dutch East Indies and Malaya.

Freezing Japanese Assets

The diplomacy of 1941 cannot be understood without a realization of the extraordinary importance of Malaya and the Dutch East Indies. Most of the world's rubber, tin, and quinine came from this area, and it also had rich supplies of petroleum. Next to the protection of its own territories, the United States held no objective of foreign policy more important than that of keeping this vital area of Southeastern Asia out of hostile hands. Fear that Japan would attack this region had compelled the Roosevelt administration to refrain from a complete embargo—one that would have deprived the Japanese war machine of American gasoline. Japanese occupation of French Indo-China in 1940 increased the threat to Malaya and the East Indies and caused Washington to apply more diplomatic pressure against the Asiatic aggressor. A crisis over the issue did not arise so long as Japanese forces in French Indo-China were small in numbers and concentrated in the northern part of the country. But in July, 1941, the situation was radically altered. The Vichy government was forced to give its assent to full Japanese control over the country, and the Japanese began to strengthen their forces and move them into the south. Such steps could hardly be called defensive; Japan was obviously building up French Indo-China as an offensive base for an attack upon Malaya and the East Indies.

Since appeasement had failed, the United States resorted to drastic action. On July 25, 1941, the President announced the freezing of all Japanese assets in the United States. The effect of this was to stop all commercial intercourse between the two countries, thus imposing at last a complete embargo. To get gasoline and other vital supplies, Japan now either had to attempt to conquer Southeastern Asia, involving herself in war with Britain, the Netherlands East Indies, Australia, and probably the United States, or else she had to induce America to resume trade relations. But the United States, now determined to stop supplying the Japanese war machine, refused to reopen trade unless Japan would abandon its policy of conquest. In such a diplomatic impasse the only outcome could be war—unless either Japan or the United States were to abandon its position.

Sumner Welles of the State Department clearly stated the American case. He asserted that the occupation of Indo-China was a definite threat to American security because it menaced procurement of raw materials vital to its defense. Moreover, the Japanese advance into Southeastern Asia was in direct defiance of the Tokyo promise to respect the Far Eastern *status quo*. Welles concluded: "The Japanese Government is giving clear indication that it is determined to pursue an objective of expansion by force or threat of force." At the same time the United States Navy heads announced that the fleet was virtually ready to back up the national policy in the Pacific.

Japan was not prepared for the showdown, however. She had partially safeguarded her position, it is true, by signing a non-aggression pact with the Soviet on April 13, thereby ensuring that there would be no attack upon her from the north. But she continued her diplomatic fencing with the United States. American firms in China were merely taken into "protective custody," with the intimation that this policy would be relaxed if the United States would reciprocate. Another example of Japanese appeasement resulted from the so-called Chungking incident. Japanese planes dropped bombs near the American gunboat *Tutuila*, anchored in the Yangtze River, causing slight damage. Without waiting for a protest to come from the State Department, Tokyo sent an apology to Washington and said full reparation would be made.

President Roosevelt refused to be swerved from his embargo policy by the Japanese actions, largely because Japan had not as yet made satisfactory pledges regarding the future of the Far East. At the meeting with Churchill that resulted in the Atlantic Charter, the dangerous Pacific situation was discussed. The Prime Minister favored a stern ultimatum to Tokyo, but Roosevelt felt that it would only serve to force war at once. Instead, he believed he could "baby them along" for some time to come.

The Failure of Peace Talks

Within the Japanese government there was a significant division of opinion. Premier Konoye and Emperor Hirohito were moderates, hoping that some peaceful settlement with the United States would prove possible. In this policy they had the support of the navy heads, who foresaw that in a long war Japan would probably be defeated. But they were strongly opposed by the more fanatical nationalists—a group that included Foreign Minister Matsuoka, War Minister Tojo, and the army leaders. For a time during the summer of 1941 the moderates appeared to have the upper hand when Matsuoka was replaced in the Foreign Ministry by Admiral Teijuro Toyada. On August 7 Premier Konoye renewed an earlier proposal that he and Roosevelt meet somewhere in the Pacific to seek a way out of the impasse.

The President was at first inclined to accept this invitation, but Secretary Hull advised against such a meeting unless the two governments came to an agreement on basic issues. On September 4 Roosevelt personally repeated to Nomura four essential principles which Hull had developed during earlier negotiations: (1) both parties should respect the political independence and territorial integrity of all nations; (2) neither should interfere in the other's affairs; (3) the equality of all countries should be upheld; and (4) there should be no change in the *status quo* in the Pacific except by peaceful means. The Japanese did not reject the Hull principles, but hedged on how they should be applied in China and other areas.

For several weeks the diplomatic exchange continued. Ambassador Grew, convinced of Konoye's sincerity, urged that Roosevelt consent to an early meeting. The President's chief advisers, Hull and Stimson, opposed this as likely to lead to a Far Eastern Munich at the expense of the hard-pressed British and Chinese.

Diplomatic historians have divided sharply over the President's failure to meet directly with the Japanese Premier. Critics argue that the door was thus slammed shut on America's best opportunity to settle Far Eastern problems through diplomacy and thus avoid a costly war. Roosevelt's defenders doubt that Konoye was in a position to withdraw Japanese forces from China and Indo-China and break with the Axis—the only honorable conditions that the United States could have accepted in return for aiding Japan in its economic difficulties.

The situation grew worse rather than better. On October 16 Konoye had to resign, and the more aggressive General Tojo became Premier. Although less ready than Konoye to make substantial concessions to the United States, the Tojo government still delayed a final decision on peace or war. On November 5 the Japanese Privy Council decided to make a final offer to the United States and then to attack if these terms were rejected. A special envoy, Saburo Kurusu, was sent to Washington to join with Nomura is the final negotiations.

On November 20 Kurusu and Nomura proposed a *modus vivendi*, or temporary agreement, covering the following points: (1) Japan and the United States would not move their armed forces into any region in Southeastern Asia or the Southern Pacific except the parts of Indo-China already occupied by the Japanese; (2) Japan would evacuate Indo-China either upon the restoration of peace between Japan and China or upon a general Pacific area settlement; (3) Japan and the United States would cooperate in obtaining needed commodities from the Netherlands East Indies; (4) Japan and the United States would restore their commercial relations and the United States would supply Japan with oil; and (5) the United States would refrain from measures prejudicial to the establishment of peace between Japan and China.

The last two points were quite unacceptable to Roosevelt and Hull because they would have required the United States to reverse its support of China and become a partner of Japan. Nevertheless, Roosevelt at first hoped that a *modus vivendi* on fairer terms might be arranged. In the end, however, he decided against this procedure, being influenced, on the one hand, by British and Chinese warnings against appeasement, and, on the other, by intercepted code messages from Japan indicating that some warlike move was imminent. On November 26 Hull handed the Japanese envoys a document stating in stronger terms than ever the fundamental American position. Among other things, the United States asked Japan to evacuate China and Indo-China, to support no other Chinese government than Chiang Kai-shek's, and to join in a multilateral nonaggression pact to insure peace in the Pacific area.

Hull's action of November 26 reflected his conviction that further negotiation was probably hopeless and that all the United States could do was deal with Japanese aggression in whatever new form it took. For eleven days more the diplomatic stage play continued, but the Japanese war machine was already in action. On November 25 the Japanese fleet had begun to move in utmost secrecy toward Hawaii, and on December 1 the Japanese Privy Council made the final decision for war.

Although the Roosevelt administration was certain that Japan was up to something, the general conviction was that she would not want to consolidate American public opinion by a direct attack upon American territory. Warnings to be on the alert were sent to American commanders throughout the Pacific area, but they were lacking in urgency. The real expectation was that Japan would invade either Siam or Malaya as the first step toward grabbing the oil and rubber she desperately needed. What the United States should do to oppose this was a matter of earnest discussion behind the scenes. To allow the Japanese to overrun Southeastern Asia was dangerous to American economic interests and would expose the Philippines to attack; yet to go to war because Japan had invaded some distant territory like Siam or Malaya would bring the full weight of isolationist wrath down on the administration's head. Unable to answer the basic question, Roosevelt decided upon three immediate steps: (1) to address a general appeal for peace to Emperor Hirohito; (2) to explain the situation in a speech to Congress; and (3) to warn the Japanese government against further aggression.

Only the first of these steps was taken before the Pearl Harbor attack. On December 6 President Roosevelt cabled a personal appeal to Emperor Hirohito, reviewing the historic friendship between Japan and the United States and appealing to the Emperor to join with him in preventing "further death and destruction in the world." No reply to this appeal was forthcoming; instead the Japanese said their last word when Nomura and Kurusu called on Secretary Hull on December 7 at 2:20 P.M. and handed him their government's arrogant rejection of his note of November 26. Angered both by the contents of the note and by the news from Pearl Harbor, which had begun to come into Washington just before this interview, Hull denounced Japanese conduct in sharp terms. "In all my fifty years of public service," the Secretary declared, "I have never seen a document that was more crowded with infamous falsehoods and distortions on a scale so huge that I never imagined until today that any government on this planet was capable of uttering them." The two Japanese left in silence.

Pearl Harbor

War had already begun when the envoys presented the Tokyo rejection. At 7:50 A.M., Hawaiian time (1:20 P.M., E.S.T.), on that fateful December 7, 1941, planes from Japanese carriers began dropping bombs on Pearl Harbor. The American military forces commanded by General Walter C. Short and the fleet under Admiral Husband E. Kimmel were caught napping, despite the warnings given of the possibility of a surprise attack. The resulting casualties were great: 2,117 navy and marine personnel were killed, 960 were missing and 860 wounded; the army had 226 officers and men killed or mortally wounded and 396 less seriously wounded; there were 80 naval planes destroyed and 70 disabled out of 202; the army lost 97 of its 273 planes; either sunk or severely damaged were five battleships—the *Arizona, Oklahoma, California, Nevada,* and *West Virginia,* along with three destroyers, a mine layer, and a target ship; damaged were three battleships, three cruisers, a seaplane tender, and a repair ship.

Several investigations have failed to lay the blame conclusively at anyone's door. The first investigation committee, headed by Justice Roberts, which met early in 1942, blamed General Short and Admiral Kimmel for not taking necessary precautions in the face of numerous warnings from Washington. In the summer of 1945 the Army and the Navy made public their special findings. Blame was divided between the two Pacific commanders and the authorities in Washington. The longest investigation, that made by the joint Congressional Investigating Committee and lasting for ten weeks beginning November 15, 1945, resulted in the following majority report: (1) the responsibility for the well-planned and executed attack rested upon Japan; (2) the President and other high government officials in Washington tried their best to avert war with Japan; (3) despite the warning from Washington, the Pacific commanders failed to have their forces sufficiently alerted; and (4) the War Department erred in not making certain that the Hawaiian Department was ready. A minority report of this committee found: (1) that the Washington messages to Hawaii were so indefinite and conflicting that they failed to give the impression of need for wartime alert; (2) President Roosevelt did not effect sufficient cooperation among the several branches in evaluating the information gained through cracking the Japanese code.

War Is Declared

That Sunday evening—it was Monday, December 8, in Tokyo—Ambassador Grew was notified by the Japanese government "that there has arisen a state of war between Your Excellency's country and Japan beginning today." This was the formal announcement of what had begun twelve hours earlier, and the note went on to assert that the United States was responsible for what had happened.

President Roosevelt was quick to reply. Shortly after midday on December 8, he appeared before the whole Congress, specially convened for the purpose, to deliver his war message. The President began with the solemn words:

> Yesterday, December 7, 1941—a date which will live in infamy—the United States of America was suddenly and deliberately attacked by naval and air forces of the Empire of Japan.

Then he went on to show that peace negotiations were still going on when the Pearl Harbor attack occurred and that the attack must have been planned "many days or even weeks ago." The President also announced that the Japanese had attacked Malaya, Hongkong, Guam, the Philippines, and Wake and Midway Islands.

> No matter how long it may take us to overcome this premeditated invasion, the American people in their righteous might will win through to absolute victory.
>
> I ask the Congress to declare that since the unprovoked and dastardly attack by Japan on Sunday, December seventh, a state of war has existed between the United States and the Japanese Empire.

Congress acted just as speedily. Within four hours the war declaration was approved, first by the Senate 82 to 0, then by the House 388 to 1.[14] This declaration authorized the President to use all the forces and resources of the United States to "bring the conflict to a successful conclusion." And before the day was over, Britain, true to an earlier promise, also declared war against Japan.

Three days later—December 11—Germany and Italy, in conformance with the Tripartite Agreement and because of numerous American "provocative" acts, declared war against the United States. On the same day, President Roosevelt sent another war message to Congress, and both Houses then passed war declarations against Germany and Italy without a dissenting vote.[15]

Meantime, on the evening of December 9, the President, in a radio talk to the nation, gave the general purposes of American participation in the war:

> The true goal we seek is far above and beyond the ugly field of battle. When we resort to force, as now we must, we are determined that the force shall be directed toward ultimate good as well as against immediate evil. We Americans are not destroyers—we are builders.
>
> We are now in the midst of a war, not for conquest, not for vengeance, but for a world in which this Nation, and all that this Nation represents, will be safe for our children. . . .
>
> And in the dark of this day—and through dark days that may be yet to come— we will know that the vast majority of the members of the human race are on our side. Many of them are fighting with us. All of them are praying for us. For, in representing our cause, we represent theirs as well—our hope and their hope for liberty under God.

[14] Jeanette Rankin of Montana, who also voted against American entrance into World War I, was the sole dissenter.

[15] Bulgaria, Hungary, and Rumania declared war on the United States on December 12. The United States did not retaliate until June 5, 1942. Previously, a declaration against Thailand was passed on January 25, 1942.

24

The Global War

World War II was a global war in the truest sense of the word. Rival military forces faced each other in battle on the continents of Europe, Asia, and Africa, as well as upon hundreds of islands in the Pacific. Naval encounters were fought literally on the seven seas. The number of men involved in actual combat, as well as the number of civilians affected, reached the highest total in world history. The amount of property destroyed reached astronomical figures. Considering the scope of this global contest, the following account of World War II will be primarily concerned with the major exploits of the American armed forces.

The Rival Forces

The major countries involved in this epic struggle were: on the Allied side, the United States, Great Britain, Russia, and China, with considerable help from the Netherlands East Indies; on the Axis side, Germany, Italy, and Japan, with assistance from Hungary, Finland, Bulgaria, and Rumania. The combined Allied military strength in December, 1941, has been estimated at from 9.7 million men to 15.7 million; that of the Axis, at from 10.6 million to 13.6 million. The Allied air power is estimated to have been between 12,100 and 15,-300 planes to the Axis's 13,200 to 18,400. As for the naval ships in operation or under construction on each side, the estimate for the Allies was 1,394, and for the Axis, 790.

In the beginning, the Axis had numerous advantages. Both in Europe and in Asia it was fighting along interior lines and nearer the home front; thus the supply lanes were shorter and the deficit in sea transportation facilities was not too severe a handicap. Moreover, both Germany and Japan opened their attacks unexpectedly and, while they had been preparing for many years, their foes were largely unready. They were both able thereby to overrun large areas from which they obtained supplies needed to continue their war efforts. Their ruthless destruction of people and property tended to cow large sections, and the very speed and daring of their original onslaughts swept aside all resistance.

The Allies, with their long lines of communication, were at a disadvantage. For example, the United States was approximately 3,000 miles away from the European arena and more than twice as far from the Far Eastern front. The problem of logistics had to be solved before the full American weight could be used. Moreover, the speedy Japanese attacks early in the war deprived the Allies of numerous essential materials, such as rubber and tin, while the German advance conquered important agricultural, mineral, and oil areas.

What the Axis did not count upon, however, was the Allied will to win. The sneak attack upon Pearl Harbor, which almost destroyed the American Pacific fleet, did not break American morale. Instead, the United States immediately began to mobilize its fighting and industrial strength to wipe out the stain. And England was able to withstand the terrible air *blitz* following the fall of France and show the stamina of a bulldog, while Russia survived the initial German attack and was starting to show its immense recuperative power. Through excellent cooperation, the Allies gradually formulated plans for attack and, aided by the increasing supplies of men, money, and equipment that the United States threw into the struggle, the Axis advantages were slowly but surely wiped away. Indeed, fighting along the interior line in the long run proved a disadvantage because the Allies directed their full power against the concentrated areas held by the enemy and because Axis supplies ran short in the long and furious contest.

A Black Beginning

In the Pacific theater the six months following Pearl Harbor were indeed dark days for the Allies. Before the end of 1941 the Japanese had taken Thailand, moved into Malaya and seized Hongkong on the Asiatic mainland, captured Guam, Wake, and the northern Gilbert Islands, and made several landings in the Philippines. Moreover, during the Malayan campaign, they dealt another disastrous blow at Allied seapower by sinking two powerful British warships, the *Prince of Wales and the Repulse*.

January, 1942, witnessed additional Japanese victories. They moved closer to Burma on the west, pushed deeper into the Philippines where they seized Manila and the important naval base of Cavite, and invaded the rich and strategic Netherlands East Indies. The Allies were beginning to strike back, however, as American troops arrived in Australia and occupied the Fiji Islands to form a ring through which the Japanese could not penetrate. A sharp blow was struck at a Japanese transport fleet in the Strait of Macassar, but without permanently stopping the enemy advance into Borneo.

The following month brought more bad news to the Allies. On February 15 the great British naval base at Singapore fell. Furthermore, the Allied hope of holding the remainder of the Dutch East Indies faded when their fleet lost the battle of the Java Sea (February 27—March 1). Batavia and Java fell before the middle of March and Japanese landings were made in the Solomons. On the continent of Asia the enemy seized Rangoon, thus threatening the vital supply route to China.

By this time, however, American defense was improving and counterattacks took more definite form. The navy, under Admiral Chester W. Nimitz and Vice Admiral William F. Halsey, Jr., was striking back. Task forces with carrier planes had already raided the Marshalls, Gilberts, and Wake as well as numerous Japanese-occupied bases in New Guinea. The army, led by General Douglas MacArthur, was establishing a base in Australia.

Yet the worst news of all was soon to come. Americans had been watching the desperate battles in the Philippines put up by outnumbered American and Filipino troops.[1] The multipronged Japanese invasion could not be stemmed, and their control of the seas prevented reinforcements and supplies from reaching the hard-pressed defenders. On Christmas Day MacArthur declared Manila an open city to save the more than 600,000 civilians from attack, but two days later the Japanese disregarded the proclamation by staging a disastrous bombing. On January 2, 1942, the city fell, as well as the nearby naval base of Cavite. The Americans retreated to the Bataan Peninsula, where they put up an historic defense. Although constantly pounded from land and air they held out day after day. Help could not reach the beleaguered men. President Roosevelt, believing defeat inevitable, ordered MacArthur to go to Australia, leaving General Jonathan Wainwright in command. On April 9 Bataan finally fell, but those who could escaped to the island of Corregidor. Then there started another round-the-clock bombing until the occupants of the Rock, as the Corregidor fortress was called, worn out by sleeplessness, suffering from malaria for which no quinine was available, and weakened by scarcity of food, had to give up on May 6, thereby bringing organized resistance in the Philippines to an end. Many of the more than 30,000 troops and a similar number of civilians who were captured perished during the infamous "death march" of Bataan. The heroic defense of both Bataan and Corregidor was not in vain, however, because it up-

[1] MacArthur had been in the Philippines since the middle 1930's building up the Filipino armed forces. When the war clouds began to gather, President Roosevelt placed him in command of a joint American-Filipino army. Although MacArthur did an excellent job, the troops were not sufficiently numerous nor well enough equipped to cope for long with the larger Japanese forces.

set the Japanese timetable and gave the Allies a valuable breathing spell in which to organize the outer defense ring to check the Japanese advance.

There were a few bright spots in the Allied picture. On April 15, 1942, General James Doolittle and his band of daring aviators took off from the deck of the *Hornet*—referred to by Roosevelt as Shangri-La—and bombed the city of Tokyo.[2] Three weeks later an American squadron prevented Japan from breaking the line of communication to Australia by winning the battle of the Coral Sea.[3] On May 5 British troops landed on Madagascar, which they eventually subdued, to end Japanese expansion in that direction.

On the whole, however, the period up to the beginning of June, 1942, was one of important Japanese victories. The enemy had gained control of Thailand, Malaya, Burma, the Dutch East Indies, and the islands of the western Pacific, and was threatening Australia. And in so doing the Japanese had gained not only important strategic advantages, but immensely valuable economic resources—petroleum, rubber, and tin. Despite the darkness of the picture, the Allies were confident that they could prevent further Japanese advances and, with growing military, naval, and air strength, could start hitting back. Consequently, the attention of the Allies shifted to the European and African theaters and the effort to crush Hitler and Mussolini.

The Invasion and Conquest of Africa

At a White House conference between President Roosevelt and Prime Minister Churchill toward the close of December, 1941, it was agreed that the major Anglo-American objective should be the defeat of the European members of the Axis. The first important assignment for American troops would be in North Africa, where British and Italo-German forces had been struggling for supremacy since the summer of 1940.

This African arena was of vast importance to the Allies. Control of it meant the maintenance of British domination of the Mediterranean and of the lifeline to India and the Far East. To the United States victory was important because German occupation of the west coast of Africa, and of Dakar in particular, would bring the Axis within 1,600 miles of Brazil and threaten the Western Hemisphere. Moreover, an Allied victory would pave the way for an invasion of the European fortress from the south.

Plans for an Allied invasion were only in the formative stage when alarming news arrived in June, 1942, that General Erwin Rommel's Afrika Korps had captured Tobruk and had swept on to a position approximately 50 miles from

---

[2] This raid was more of a morale booster than anything else. Actually, it was a bad maneuver from the tactical point of view because it served only to make the Japanese strengthen their air defenses.

[3] In this battle, lasting from May 4 to May 8, the United States lost the carrier *Lexington* and the *Yorktown* was badly hit, but several large Japanese ships were sunk.

Alexandria. It seemed that nothing could prevent Egypt and the Suez Canal from falling into Axis hands. But the victory-shouting Germans did not count upon the cooperation that followed. General Bernard Montgomery and his British Eighth Army dug in at El Alamein to hold the line until Australian troops, American planes and heavier tanks, and other additional equipment poured in.

In October, 1942, Montgomery's men opened the counterattack that was to drive the enemy back and virtually destroy the Italian army in Africa. Yet the Montgomery offensive was but one arm of the pincer movement in this final campaign. Roosevelt and Churchill had been conferring in Washington when the gloomy news of the fall of Tobruk reached them. Then and there they laid plans for an Anglo-American invasion of Africa from the northwest calculated to hem in the Axis troops and force their surrender.

The first step in the invasion plans followed shortly after that conference was over. American agents in Africa negotiated with several French officers to loosen their Vichy ties, and efforts were also made to deal with the anti-Vichy leaders. In mid-October, 1942, General Mark Clark and a group of Commandos landed secretly on the North African coast to complete arrangements for the actual invasion without French interference.

Finally, on November 8, a large armada of British and American ships landed some 400,000 men at Casablanca, Oran, and Algiers. Under the command of General Dwight D. Eisenhower, the invaders faced some opposition from both Germans and French, but the three towns quickly fell. The surrender of most of the French forces followed speedily, helped by the fact that Admiral Jean Darlan, hitherto of the Vichy regime, fell into American hands early in the invasion and agreed to give the "cease fire" order. Despite much criticism, Eisenhower appointed Darlan as political head of the occupied territories. Dakar gave up before the end of the month, thereby ending the potential menace against the Western Hemisphere.

The primary objective of the invasion, however, was to pinch off the Rommel forces in North Africa. Therefore the Allied troops that had landed at Algiers immediately opened their eastward drive into Tunisia with the hope of seizing naval and air installations at Bizerte and Tunis. They were beaten to these goals by the Germans, however, who sent troops by air from Europe to meet the situation. The German opposition, plus the deep mud, held up the Allied advance for several months. Meantime, Montgomery rolled forward swiftly from the east and finally, in January, 1943, forced the Afrika Korps into Tunisia, which was protected by the Mareth Line. General Henri Giraud, who had succeeded Darlan after the latter's assassination, gave additional help to the Allied cause when an army of Fighting French pushed northward to join the British and Americans.

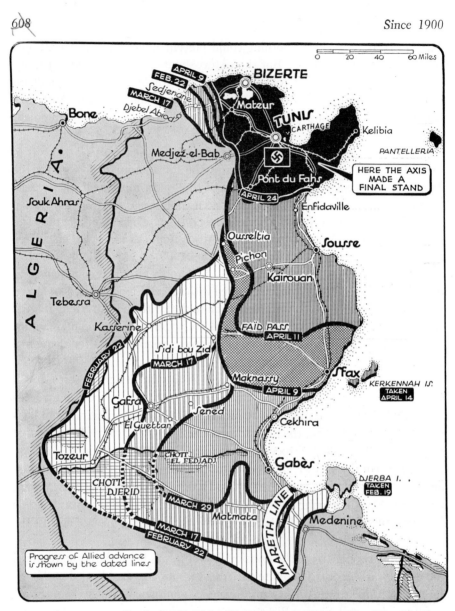

Battle for Tunisia. (From Francis Brown, *The War in Maps*. By permission of Oxford University Press, New York.)

Yet victory was not easy. In February the Germans forced the Americans back through Faid Pass, and then won the bloody battle of Kasserine Pass. This counterattack regained nearly 4,000 square miles of territory and drove the Americans back into Algeria. Despite these victories, Rommel was unable to cut off Americans from the British forces in the north.

The American defeat was partially offset by the fact that the troops had received their first real baptism of fire and, although compelled to retreat, had not broken. Moreover, the leaders realized that a mistake had been made in training too many men for mechanical warfare and not enough for the infantry. Throughout February, 1943, the American army was regrouped and reinforcements and additional equipment arrived. Then toward the close of the month, Kasserine Pass was regained after another bitter struggle. The Mareth Line crumbled to enable the British to seize Sfax and Sousse, and the Afrika Korps was forced into the Tunis-Bizerte pocket where it united with the German troops under General Jurgen von Arnim.

Once in this pocket it was but a question of time before the Germans had to surrender. American bombers pounded the steadily contracting trap and at the same time prevented German transports from carrying away many of the beleaguered men. Allied artillery smashed the defenses, while the infantry infiltrated the enemy lines. Yet not until the end of April were there signs of a break as the combined Allied divisions redoubled their efforts. Finally, on May 7, the British First Army stormed into Tunis and the American Second Corps under General Omar Bradley compelled the surrender of Bizerte. Those victories, gained through full cooperation among the Allied armies and their respective ground, sea, and air arms, brought German resistance in Africa to an end, and on May 9 what remained of the Axis troops on that continent surrendered unconditionally.

The fall of Africa was the first great Allied victory in which Americans participated. Although the cost in men had been high—there were 70,000 casualties—the results justified it. Not only were nearly 350,000 Italians and Germans killed or captured and 200,000 tons of enemy material seized or destroyed, but the successful campaign rescued the Mediterranean lifeline from Axis control. Moreover, since from anywhere along the thousands of miles of North Africa coast the Allies might open an assault against southern Europe, German attention was diverted from Russia and the English channel.

The Invasion of Sicily and Italy

In anticipation of the North African victory, Roosevelt and Churchill mapped out the next move while they were conferring at Casablanca in January, 1943. A message was forwarded to General Eisenhower "that an attack against Sicily will be launched in 1943 with the target date as the period of the favorable July moon." There was a dual reason for this project: to open the Mediterranean to Allied commerce of all descriptions, thereby saving a 12,000 mile trip around the Cape of Good Hope; and to regain a foothold on the European continent preparatory to the eventual assault upon the Reich itself.

Completion of the plan required time, but Eisenhower showed marked administrative ability in supervising the mobilization of men and supplies for the undertaking. The prelude to actual invasion was the bombing of both Sicily and Italy to soften up the enemy possessions. This move began in mid-May while the cleaning up of North Africa was still going on. Toward the end of the month Allied aviators concentrated their attention upon the island of Pantelleria and, after twenty days of almost continuous bombing, ten-thousand troops there were compelled to surrender—the first time such a victory was achieved through air power alone. Shortly after, the islands of Lampedusa, Linosa, and Lampione were also conquered to end a menace to Allied shipping in the Mediterranean and to provide steppingstones to Sicily.

It was on July 9, 1943, that the invasion of Sicily began with the landing of American airborne troops, followed quickly by the debarkation of more than 150,000 Allied infantry, artillery, and tank groups. The two main forces were the British Eighth Army under Montgomery and the American Seventh under General George S. Patton, Jr., which had gained fame in the African campaign. Patton was a fearless and rough-tongued leader who was referred to as "Old Blood and Guts"; he was, moreover, an expert in tank warfare. In thirty-eight days of vicious fighting, during which Allied cooperation in all branches was again shown, the island was overrun and the enemy forced to surrender. A feature of the victory was the strategy of General Patton in using his tanks to divide the opposition. Total Allied losses were approximately 25,000, those of the Germans and Italians, more than 150,000—or nearly half the number in Sicily at the time of the original attack.

While the Sicilian campaign was being fought, the Allies were pounding the Italian peninsula from sea and air, directing their bombs and shells toward ports and military installations. Even Rome itself did not escape, for on July 19 more than 500 American bombers dropped 1,000 tons of missiles on railroad yards and airfields within the city.[4] An Italian appeal to Hitler for more support was turned down. Indeed, the Fuehrer insisted that the Italian boot as far north as the Po River must be evacuated by the Axis. When Mussolini gave in to Hitler's wish, he was replaced as prime minister by Marshal Pietro Badoglio in July 1943. Although Badoglio proclaimed that Italy would continue fighting, the populace was now demanding peace.

The continued pounding of Italy by Allied airmen brought increased grumbling from the inhabitants. Consequently, Badoglio made secret arrangements with General Eisenhower for an Italian surrender, which he hoped could be consummated without Hitler's knowledge. Eisenhower had instructions to accept only unconditional surrender, thereby making terms of the greatest

---

[4] Up to this time every effort had been made to spare attacks on Rome because of its religious importance. Now, however, the Allies realized it had become vital as a military and communications center. When the pleas to have it declared an open city were turned down by the Italians and Germans, the fliers were rigidly briefed so that when they did attack they avoided Vatican City and destroyed practically no religious shrines. The Germans raised the cry of vandalism, ignoring what they themselves had done to churches in Allied countries.

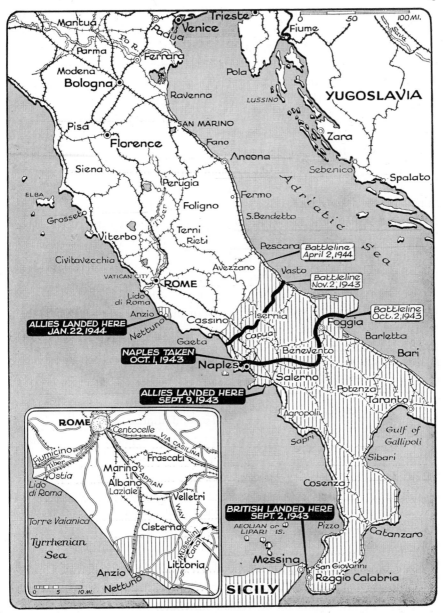

Invasion of Italy. (From Francis Brown, *The War in Maps*.
By permission of Oxford University Press, New York.)

advantage to the Allies. While the negotiations were being conducted, General
Montgomery and his Eighth Army on September 3 gained a comparatively
easy beachhead at Reggio Calabria on the toe of the Italian boot, and started
northward.

This maneuver speeded the Italian decision to withdraw from the war, and on the same day an armistice was signed, with Eisenhower announcing the unconditional surrender on September 8.[5] Although Allied morale was considerably raised by this act that eliminated one member of the Axis, the material advantage was not great because German forces occupied most of Italy and continued to dispute the Allied invasion. On September 9, a second beachhead was established by General Mark Clark, at Salerno, near Naples. The specific purpose was to seize the important base and port of Naples and subsequently to form a junction with Montgomery's men pushing through Calabria, thereby cutting off the Germans in southern Italy. It was easier said than done, however, because the enemy took full advantage of the natural fortifications and heavily mined roads to slow the Allied advance. Not until September 16 did the American Fifth and the British Eighth link up, and then most of the Germans had succeeded in escaping the trap. The following day a third invasion unit landed at Taranto on the Italian heel. Still the Germans refused to turn and run, so that it was October 1 before Naples fell.

The surrender of that base, plus the Allied seizure of Sardinia and Corsica, were bitter blows to the enemy, but the Germans continued to maintain a stiff resistance. They were aided by the very severe winter of 1943–1944 and by the short battle line across the Italian peninsula, which enabled them to concentrate their forces. The Reich armies retreated slowly until they reached the Gustav Line, whose main stronghold was Cassino, where they held out for many weeks. During the stalemate General Eisenhower was called back to Britain to organize the strategy for the real second front.

An effort was made to break the Gustav Line in January, 1944, when a combined force under General Clark landed to the north at Anzio, only twenty miles below Rome. The Germans apparently expected such a maneuver, however, and the invaders were unable to break the ring around the beachhead. For several months it was a question whether the Anzio spearhead could be maintained, as Clark met with difficulty in landing reinforcements and the small foothold was the target of constant bombing. Not until early May was the German encirclement broken through, aided by a coordinated attack on the Gustav Line from the south; that line crumbled when Cassino fell on May 18. The Allied forces then moved swiftly on Rome, which was taken without serious opposition on June 4.

[5] Although the document was secret, subsequent events proved that the following must have been among its provisions: that Italy cease hostilities immediately and try to prevent Germany from using Italian equipment, etc., against the Allies; that all Allied prisoners in Italian hands be released at once; that the Italian fleet, merchant marine, and airfields be turned over to the Allies as quickly as possible; and that Corsica and other islands be made available for Allied operations. When Germany refused to evacuate Italy, the latter declared war on the Reich, October 13, 1943, and was recognized as a cobelligerent by the Allies, but was not granted Allied status.

Starting on the Long Road Back

While these successes in Africa and Italy were being achieved, the tide of battle was turning in the Pacific. Although the Japanese did attack the Aleutians from the air in June, 1942, and subsequently made landings on the islands of Kiska, Attu, and Agattu, they were never able to penetrate deeper into the North American continent because of the activity of the American naval and air forces.[6]

The temporary loss of part of the Aleutians was more than offset, however, by the American victory in the Battle of Midway, June 3–6, 1942, helped in no small part by the vital fact that Naval Intelligence had cracked the Japanese code even before Pearl Harbor. Over a hundred Japanese ships, prepared to assault and occupy strategic Midway Island, were intercepted and forced to flee after a three-day encounter fought over hundreds of miles of ocean. American land and carrier-based bombers destroyed four Japanese carriers, one cruiser, and 258 planes. The American losses were the carrier *Yorktown*, the destroyer *Hammann*, and 150 planes. This battle was the most crippling defeat inflicted on the Japanese navy up to that time. Combined with previous losses, Midway left the enemy too weak to match the ever growing American armada in the Pacific. Consequently, plans to start toward Tokyo could be put into operation and, with the Japanese naval threat ended, more American strength could be released to the European theater.

The first great blow at Japanese conquests was delivered when the marines, under General Alexander A. Vandegrift, opened their assaults upon the islands of Tulagi, Gavutu, and Guadalcanal of the Solomon group. The first two objectives were attained fairly quickly, but on Guadalcanal there was fierce resistance, which was not wiped out until February, 1943. The struggle almost ended in disaster for the Americans at the very outset as the Japanese fleet made a surprise attack on the night of August 9 to sink four Allied heavy cruisers in the Battle of Savo Island, an encounter that temporarily prevented the landing of needed Allied supplies. The marines were not to be denied, however, and they soon gained control of the island's main airstrip. This was of untold advantage because it enabled the Americans to put their airpower to good use in later phases of the struggle. In addition to the severe land and air fighting, in which casualties on both sides were high, there were fought four sea battles, culminating in the so-called Battle of Guadalcanal. In these several encounters the enemy lost at least 47 important ships, while they in turn sank the carriers *Wasp* and *Hornet*, together with numerous destroyers and cruisers. By eventu-

---

[6] In May, 1943, the Americans began their real counterattack by seizing Attu and Agattu after a heavy bombardment. Thus Kiska was bypassed and the Japanese withdrew secretly in August just before the Americans were ready to stage their all-out move to drive the enemy out.

ally winning Guadalcanal, the Americans gained more than simply a small island in the Pacific. They learned valuable lessons in jungle fighting that served in good stead later on; they learned as well the value of naval and air cooperation with invasion forces; they had a steppingstone for future conquests; and they had dealt grievous losses to the Japanese navy.

During this long struggle over Guadalcanal, General MacArthur was striking at the enemy from another direction. The Japanese had gained control of the larger part of New Guinea and were moving uncomfortably close to Port Moresby, a potential jumping-off spot for the invasion of Australia. The Australians checked the advance in September and opened a counterattack with the help of the Amercan air forces, which brought in supplies and prevented the enemy from landing reinforcements. American troops then added their strength and by the end of the year Gona and Buna had been recaptured. It required another year of desperate fighting before New Guinea was effectively dominated.

Throughout that year of 1943 American marines, fliers, and fleet put into practice the lessons learned at Guadalcanal. The most important encounters were the mopping up of the rest of the Solomons, the conquest of the Gilberts in November after the bloody battles of Makin and Tarawa (November 21–23), and the invasion of New Britain in December. Several naval battles were fought as well—Bismarck Sea (March 2–6), Kula Gulf (July 5–6, 12–13), and Vella Gulf (August 6–7)—in all of which the Japanese losses far exceeded the American.

By the end of 1943 the Americans had their invasion pattern well worked out. The first move was usually a series of reconnaissance flights to obtain pictures of the objectives. This was followed by a heavy air bombardment aimed at wrecking airfields and destroying military supplies and installations. Then a task force[7] would arrive on the scene and set the stage for the actual invasion by attacking the objective from sea and air to prevent the enemy from either escaping or sending in reinforcements and to wreck coastal defenses and sear the beaches. With preparations complete, the invasion forces, usually headed by marines, would be landed from new types of naval craft—such as landing-craft infantry and amphibious tractors, to be joined quickly by tanks. The navy stood off shore and planes flew overhead to shell and bomb ahead of the advancing troops.

It was this attack pattern that won for the Americans in 1944 the Marshalls, where the initial campaign was directed against Kwajalein on January 31, the Admiralty Islands (February), the Mariannas (the struggle for Saipan lasted from June 15 to July 9), Guam (August-September), and Palau and Halmahera (September), the last Japanese bases in the open Pacific. Moreover, these

---

[7] The most famous was Task Force 58 under Admiral Marc Mitscher.

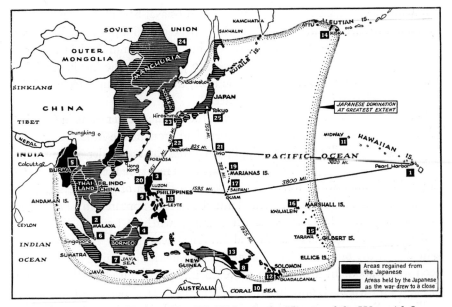

Twenty-Five Highlights in the History of the War with Japan.
(Courtesy of the *New York Times*.)

1941   1 Dec. 7—Japanese planes attack Pearl Harbor
        2 Dec. 8—Malay campaign launched by Japanese
        3 Dec. 10—Landings made on Luzon
        4 Dec. 22—Borneo invasion begun

1942   5 Jan. 19—Conquest of Burma begun
        6 Feb. 15—Singapore falls to Japanese
        7 Feb. 27—Allies routed in Battle of Java Sea
        8 Mar. 8—First Japanese landings in New Guinea
        9 May 6—Surrender of Corregidor
       10 May 4–8—Japanese defeated in Battle of Coral Sea
       11 June 3–6—Japanese turned back in Battle of Midway
       12 Aug. 7—American forces land on Guadalcanal   *SOLOMANS*

1943   13 Mar. 5—Japanese routed in Battle of Bismarck Sea
       14 Aug. 15—Allied forces retake Kiska
       15 Nov. 20–24—Tarawa and Makin Islands recaptured   *GILBERTS*

1944   16 Feb. 1—First Japanese territory invaded at Kwajalein
       17 June 14—Invasion of Marianas begun
       18 Oct. 20–26—Landings on Leyte, Battle of Leyte Gulf
       19 Nov. 24—First B–29 raids from Marianas bases

1945   20 Jan. 9—American forces land on Luzon   *PHILIPPINES*
       21 Feb. 17—Landing on Iwo Jima   *BONINS*
       22 April 1—Invasion of Okinawa begun   *Ryukyus*
       23 Aug. 6—First atomic bomb dropped on Hiroshima
       24 Aug. 9—Russia invades Manchuria following war declaration
       25 Aug. 11—Tokyo learns Allied answer to surrender offer

conquests practically neutralized the prominent naval base at Truk, which was no longer able to obtain supplies as the Japanese communication lines were cut. The Japanese navy was being slowly but surely diminished in size, and what remained of it retired to home bases to prepare for the inevitable Allied attack upon Japan proper.[8] At the same time, the Japanese air force was being whittled down despite its strong resistance.

One of the most heartening incidents in the Pacific theater came in October, 1944. The attacks on Palau and Halmahera had brought the Americans within several hundred miles of the Philippines. During the remainder of September and in the first weeks of October American fliers regularly bombed and strafed the archipelago, and the navy helped to sweep the sea of Japanese naval and merchant craft. Although the natural initial objective appeared to be the island of Mindoro, on October 19 MacArthur struck swiftly at Leyte in the central part of the Philippine chain. Several landings were quickly made, footholds gained, and the principal airstrip seized. The American promise to return had been made good. In a desperate move to isolate the invaders, the Japanese brought up their fleet, only to suffer their greatest naval defeat. In the second Philippine Sea engagement, Admiral Thomas Kinkaid, with his Seventh Fleet, and Admiral William Halsey, with his Third, destroyed or badly damaged some thirty ships during a running two-day battle (October 23–24). The announced American losses totaled only a fraction of that number.

Mopping up on Leyte proved slow work because typhoons, heavy rains, and deep mud slowed up the American advance. Moreover, 10,000 Japanese reinforcements were brought to the island by the "Tokyo Express"—a large, speedy transport system. Consequently, it was not until Christmas time that the numerous prongs of the American invaders closed in on the enemy and ended its opposition. Meantime, additional landings were made on Samar and Mindoro, while planes from Saipan and from carriers blasted at Tokyo, Formosa, Okinawa, and Iwo Jima, and the American navy cut deeper into the communications lines between Japan and her outlying conquests.

With the opening of 1945 the combined American land, sea, and air arms were poised to complete the destruction of the enemy. On January 5 MacArthur's men landed at Lingayen Gulf on Luzon and immediately started their push toward Manila, only 100 miles away. Aided by the navy, which thwarted the Tokyo Express, and by fliers who destroyed Japanese installations, the land forces captured the Philippine capital on February 5, followed within two weeks by the seizure of Bataan and Corregidor—with the help of paratroops. Gradually the other islands of the archipelago were brought under American

---

[8] The later conquests were aided by the first Philippine Sea victory (June 19–20) in which four Japanese carriers, three cruisers, three destroyers, one battleship, four tankers and more than four hundred planes were destroyed. In comparison, American losses under Admiral Spruance were negligible.

control, and on July 5, 1945, MacArthur proclaimed that the Philippines were liberated and his campaign there was "virtually closed."

Other Allied maneuvers, however, endangered the Japanese homeland more directly than did the fall of the Philippines. For example, in the middle of February the invasion of the Bonins opened. Iwo Jima was needed as an airfield for emergency landings of planes bombing Japan from the Mariannas and for the planned invasion of Japan itself. The marines gradually overcame the stubborn opposition, captured Mount Suribachi on February 23, and three weeks later (March 17) the complete conquest of the island was announced. The American casualties were high—approximately 20,000—grim evidence of the fury of the opposition. Furthermore, suicidal attacks by kamikaze[9] fliers damaged or sank many American naval craft.

Still more furious was the struggle for Okinawa in the Ryukyus, about half-way between Iwo and Japan. After a ten-day bombardment, General Simon Buckner's Tenth Army and some marine divisions made simultaneous beachheads to open a contest that was to last for ten weeks. The Japanese troops were ordered not to surrender because the home government realized that its hope of escaping defeat was "anchored solely on Okinawa." In the face of this resistance, the Americans had to cut the enemy lines into several segments and defeat each before final victory was achieved on June 21. The losses on both sides were stupendous: for example, the Japanese dead alone numbered more than 100,000, while the American casualties neared 80,000. Moreover, kamikaze attacks sank 33 American ships and damaged 45 more; aircraft destruction reached the astounding figure of at least 3,000 Japanese planes and 1,000 American. In the face of these losses there was a promising note: in spite of indoctrination and orders, nearly 8,000 Japanese surrendered. This was a definite sign that the enemy was starting to crack as the homeland was endangered.

On another Far Eastern front—the China-Burma-India theater—the tide was also turning. After the Americans under General Joseph Stilwell, along with British, Indian, and Chinese troops, had been driven out of Burma and into India in 1942, conditions looked very black. Not only was the loss of territory and prestige great, but the Allies found it much more difficult to send aid to the Chinese forces under Chiang. Throughout 1943 there were no conclusive battles and neither side gained material advantage. In 1944, however, the Allies moved slowly back into Burma in the face of strong Japanese resistance and a very difficult terrain. A three-month siege was required before Myitkina fell in August, and Akyab, Rangoon, and Lashio did not come into Allied hands until the early months of 1945. The capture of Lashio reopened the Burma Road and

[9] Kamikaze fliers were fanatical Japanese who flew their planes at terrifying speed directly at an objective, such as a ship, with the hope that in the resulting crash the objective would be destroyed, even though they themselves were killed. The losses from these attacks were great for American airmen, and gunners found it difficult to cope with such tactics.

permitted more supplies to be sent to the Chinese, who were going through periodic reverses and victories.[10]

The turn in the tide also enabled the superfortresses—the B-29's—to open their attacks on Japan proper from CBI bases. The first raid (June 15, 1944) was largely a test of the giant bombers, and the test was satisfactory. Despite the difficulty in obtaining the necessary gas, oil, and other supplies, in the following autumn the B-29 raids became quite regular, and the damage to Japanese home bases and factories increased when the conquest of the Mariannas gave the Americans bases from which to launch attacks on Japan from the east as well. The ruin of Japanese industrial cities mounted with each passing month of 1945.[11] With her air force largely depleted, her navy forced under cover, her conquests—with the exception of those in China and Manchuria—almost entirely lost, with her homeland subjected to almost constant bombing, and with morale beginning to crack, Japan faced a dismal future, a future made darker by the fact that on April 5 Russia gave the necessary one-year notice for the cancellation of her neutrality pact with Japan—a prelude to war. Slighty more than a month later the news of the unconditional surrender of Germany reached Tokyo.

Preparation for D Day

Events leading to that German disaster began with the opening of the long-awaited second front in Europe. Since the entrance of the United States into the war, Russia had insisted that such an operation be conducted. A second front, she asserted, was the only way to defeat Germany, and the sooner it was opened the better. Churchill urged delay, however, and it was not until Stalin, Roosevelt, and Churchill met at Teheran in December, 1943, that agreement was reached. Then Eisenhower received the following message:

> You will enter the continent of Europe and, in conjunction with the other Allied Nations, undertake operations aimed at the heart of Germany and the destruction of her armed forces.

The task of getting men, supplies, and transportation facilities ready for this gigantic operation was tremendous. Although the first American troops had arrived in North Ireland in January, 1942, most of them, together with those who landed in the ensuing months, had been used in the African and Italian

---

[10] Until the reopening of the Burma Road, supplies had to be sent by way of the Ledo Road, largely constructed by American engineers, or by plane over the dangerous "hump" as the Himalayas were called by the fliers.

[11] Between November 24, 1944, and August 1, 1945, 311 bombing missions were conducted by the B-29's. Eighty-two industrial targets were hit in 62 cities, 158 square miles of urban industrial regions were burned, and more than 8 million persons were rendered homeless. The major targets were Tokyo, Osaka, Nagoya, and Kobe. In addition, the fliers laid mines in 44 sea areas.

campaigns. Thus, in the midsummer of 1943 there was only one American division (about 15,000 men) in the British Isles. From that time on, however, the influx was rapid, helped by the fact that the Mediterranean needs were not so great and the Japanese menace was dwindling. Consequently, transportation facilities were concentrated on building up the necessary stockpiles for the continental invasion. By the first of June, 1944, the American army personnel in Britain numbered 1,533,000, and supplies were so abundant that within a month after landing each man was fully equipped.

The softening up of Germany through air bombardment had begun in 1942, but not until July, 1943, when Marshal Harris' Royal Air Force swept over Germany at night while General Eaker's American Eighth Air Force took over during the day, did round-the-clock attacks begin. With the passing months the number of raids, planes included in those raids, and tonnage of missiles dropped increased greatly. For example, on June 6, 1944, the American strength stood at 3,000 heavy bombers, and 6,500 planes of other types; and in the 33 months after August, 1942, the Eighth Air Force rained 1.5 million tons of bombs on the continent.

The main objectives were communications centers, munition plants, synthetic-oil factories, submarine pens, dams, and rocket-bomb stations. German industry withstood this rain of destruction remarkably well. Until 1944, indeed, the enemy war production continued to rise. In the end, however, the Allied attack took a terrible toll.

Up until February, 1944, the German *Luftwaffe* put up a desperate resistance. Then, however, the German fliers were ordered to make an all-out attack against the invaders. During a week of raging battle over the industrial centers of Germany, a large portion of the German air fleet was destroyed. This setback, added to the dwindling German gasoline and oil reserves, made subsequent Allied air attacks less dangerous, although the flak sent up from German ground guns still took its toll. Also contributing to the softening-up process was the inauguration of shuttle bombing, in which planes from England continued on to occupied sections of Italy after bombing their objectives, thus avoiding a trip back over the target. A second shuttle run was instituted just before D Day between Italy and Russia, and shortly thereafter a third was begun between England and Russia.

D Day

In addition to getting men, ships, and supplies ready and softening up the enemy, General Eisenhower and his staff had to consider where and when the beachhead should be established. After considerable study, Normandy was selected as the site and June 5, 1944, as the most favorable time in terms of tide, wind, and moonlight—an essential for the airborne troops. An unexpected

United States Troops Storming Normandy Beaches,
D Day, 1944. (Brown Bros.)

storm, however, caused a sudden change in plans and the second front actually opened a day late—on June 6. At 2 A.M. American and British airborne troops were landed to gain control of strategic areas inland from the invasion beaches. An aerial attack started about an hour later, followed at six o'clock by a naval bombardment. Then at six-thirty assault troops, carried in a variety of crafts, went ashore in the face of enemy fire, mines, barbed wire, and underwater entanglements. The American First Army, commanded by General Bradley, eventually gained beachheads in the Carentan-Bayeau area, while the British and Canadians under General Miles Dempsey found their footholds in the Bayeau-Caen region. Despite determined enemy resistance, reinforcements and supplies piled ashore all day. Within twenty-four hours the beachheads were secure, and the greatest amphibious operation in history was a success.

Again only cooperation could have achieved the result. The credit belongs equally to the staff of experts who planned the maneuver, the weather experts, those who found the proper place to attack, the navies that carried the men to the Normandy beaches and then stood by to protect them, the air forces that had been steadily pounding the interior and that helped to prevent the Germans from bringing up supplies, the airborne infantry that led the actual invasion, the divers who removed the undersea obstacles, the sappers who destroyed many of the mines, the supply and ordnance branches that helped to make everything ready, and the ordinary soldiers who resolutely carried out their assignments.

The movement into the interior might have been speedy had the invaders been able to gain a large port where additional reinforcements of all types could be landed quickly and easily. But due to stubborn enemy defense of Cherbourg, special docks or breakwaters had to be floated across the Channel, as substitutes. Even though Cherbourg finally fell on June 27, it was so badly damaged by air attack and enemy explosives that it was of little use as a port of debarkation.

On July 5 Eisenhower attributed the slowness of the advance to three factors: the stubborn fighting of German infantrymen, the nature of the countryside, and the bad weather that prevented the Allied air arm from attacking and engaging in reconnaissance work. By the end of July, however, conditions were brighter. An average of 30,000 troops were being landed daily, along with 30,000 tons of supplies. General Bradley was completing the organization of the armies under his command: the American First, headed by General Courtney Hodges, and the Third under General Patton. At the same time General Montgomery was consolidating the Canadian First under General Crerar and the British Second commanded by General Dempsey.

After a heavy bombardment, Bradley finally broke out of the beachhead before the end of the month by seizing St. Lo, while the Montgomery forces took the strongly held Caen. Then General Patton showed the initiative and daring for which he was famous. In August his tank corps stormed through a breach at Avranches into Brittany, and from there he continued on his way toward Paris. Meantime, the Allies protected his flank by moving deeper inland; a pincers developed to form the Falaise pocket, in which approximately 100,000 of the enemy were captured. The stubborn defense of Panzer units prevented the pocket from closing completely, but the Germans who escaped through the narrow corridor fled from Normandy in confusion.

The Overrunning of France

The harassed Germans soon faced another front in France, General Alexander Patch's American Seventh Army having landed in the south on August 15 against unexpectedly weak resistance. Marseilles, Cannes, and Toulon were occupied within two weeks and then Patch moved northward to join up eventually with Patton, who had run roughshod through Chartres, Tours, Troyes, and numerous other cities to flank Paris.

While this junction was being effected, Bradley and Montgomery rushed

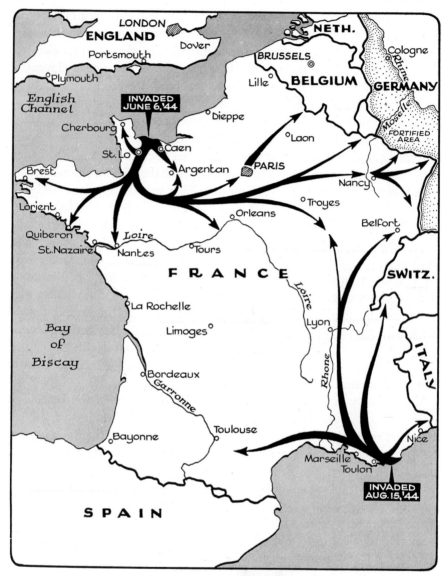

Battle of France. (From Francis Brown, *The War in Maps*.
By permission of Oxford University Press, New York.)

along the Seine to force the surrender of Paris on August 25, aided by the
activities of two underground factions, the French Forces of the Interior (FFI)
and the Maquis. Actually the fall of Paris in itself was not important, except to
morale, because the Germans were retreating at such a fast pace that the city
was soon far behind the lines. Not only were the Germans losing territory,
but men and equipment as well. By the end of August, at least 400,000 men had

been killed or captured, while 1,500 pieces of artillery, more than 1,000 tanks, and approximately 20,000 motor transports and other mobile equipment either had fallen into Allied hands or had been destroyed.

As September progressed, practically all of France, with the exception of some of the coastal towns, was freed from German control, and Allied armies were moving rapidly through Luxembourg and Belgium. On the eastern flank Patton's Third Army was laying siege to Metz, while Patch's Seventh Army, after its successful march from the Mediterranean, was probing at the Belfort Gap. These rapid maneuvers toward the Reich threatened to isolate the German forces in Italy, thereby aiding the Allied movements north of Rome.

Piercing the Siegfried Line

The first major attack on the Siegfried Line was a flanking movement. In the third week of September, British and American airborne troops attempted to bridge several rivers that made up the Rhine delta in Holland. Despite the fact that this maneuver was the largest airborne effort of the war—2,800 planes and 1,600 gliders were used—the British failed, although the Americans did manage to retain control over several crossings of the Waal and the Meuse. Two weeks later came an attack by Hodges on well-defended Aachen. When the request for surrender was rejected, the Allies subjected the town to two days of the most methodical and destructive bombing of the war, followed by a storming which brought capitulation on October 21.

The winter offensive opened in early November, with seven Allied armies moving forward. It might have been more successful had the weather been better and if the supply lines had been able to keep up with the advancing troops. Moreover, Eisenhower had to weaken part of the front line by putting in "green" divisions, so that the hammer blows might be continued against the main points of attack.

The Battle of the Bulge

The Germans under General von Runstedt discovered one of these weak links and, aided by a heavy fog, massed 24 divisions along a 75-mile front between Trier and Monschau. On December 16 his sudden counterattack broke through in an effort to reach the coast. For a time it appeared that this move would be successful. The enemy overan 700 square miles of Belgium and Luxembourg territory and came within 4 miles of the Meuse before the Allies rallied. General Montgomery on the north prevented the bulge from widening in that direction, while Patton used his Third Army to hold the southern flank. Providentially, the 82nd and 101st airborne divisions were speeded from Reims to

"Just as We Were about to Take a Snooze." (By Carlisle
in the New York Herald Tribune.)

pinch the bulge.[12] By Christmas the worst danger was over as a change in the weather enabled Allied airmen to cooperate with ground troops in turning the tide. This Battle of Ardennes, better known as the Battle of the Bulge, was the last important German offensive of the war. The German reserve strength was ebbing rapidly, the oil supply was dwindling, communications were more and more disrupted by Allied bombing, and the Russians were staging a great drive on their front.

The Surrender of Germany

As 1945 opened, it became apparent that Germany could not hold out much longer. By the middle of January most of the Ardennes Bulge had been wiped out, and by the end of the month the Westwall was thoroughly pierced. In February, Holland was largely in Allied hands and the attack on the Saar Basin opened. By early March four Allied armies were on the bank of the Rhine. Germany was losing her industrial regions—a blow just as telling as the military defeats. Cologne fell to the First Army on March 6, and the following day the Allies enjoyed a bit of unexpected good luck when the undamaged Ludendorff Bridge across the Rhine at Remagen was captured to allow an easy Allied crossing. When the Germans rushed reinforcements to minimize this bridgehead, the Allies spanned the river at other points.

As March progressed, city after city in the Ruhr capitulated; the Allied armies linked up for the final drive, and sent out spearheads that made the German confusion greater. Many of the enemy, especially the old men and boys who had been hastily recruited to defend the Fatherland, surrendered—at the rate

[12] The 101st gained fame by holding Bastogne against overwhelming odds. General McAuliffe refused to surrender the town, replying to the German request with the answer: "Nuts!" Eventually he was relieved by Patton's great dash. The 82nd, less publicized, held open the gap on the west to allow the entrapped divisions of the First Army to escape.

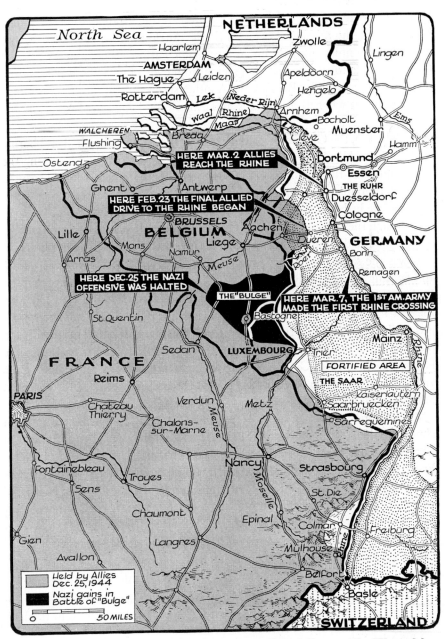

Battle of the Rhine. (From Francis Brown, *The War in Maps*.
By permission of Oxford University Press, New York.)

of more than 25,000 a day. The Western front moved ahead as rapidly as did the Russians from the east. The German pocket grew smaller and smaller as Hanover, Stuttgart, and other key cities fell during April before the Allied *blitzkrieg*. By the middle of the month the Anglo-American forces were not more than 50 miles from Berlin. A week later Patton's speedy tanks reached Czechoslavakia to cut the Austrian region from contact with the Reich capital, which was already under Russian fire. Another successful cut through the Reich was completed when the Russians and Americans joined at Torgau on the Elbe on April 27.

In Italy, too, the Germans were facing defeat. Although they had stubbornly contested the Allied drive northward and had held the Gothic Line along the Po for months, they could not stem the coordinated attack which began in April, 1945. Italian partisans, sensing Allied victory, seized and executed Mussolini before he could escape to Switzerland. The German troops could not get out through the Brenner Pass, and on May 2 they surrendered unconditionally, along with the divisions in Austria that had been trapped by Patton's lunge.

It was the same day, May 2, that Berlin, largely gutted by air attack, fires, and fighting, came into Russian hands. The day before, the suicide of Adolph Hitler, who had refused to face defeat, was announced. Admiral Karl Doenitz, the new Fuehrer, declared that he would continue the war, but such a promise was futile. On May 4 German forces in Denmark capitulated, northern Germany gave in, and Norway, a potential German refuge, was isolated from the Reich. Moreover, the German forces were cut into smaller segments by the victorious Allies, while the German people showed increasing signs of unrest. Surrender was the only surcease.

As the various German army groups continued to lay down their arms in almost wholesale fashion, Admiral Doentiz realized the folly of continuing. On May 6 he sent a secret delegation to confer with General Walter Bedell Smith, Eisenhower's Chief of Staff, at a little red schoolhouse in Reims. The Germans at first refused the unconditional surrender terms of the Allies, but with the arrival of German Chief of Staff General Gustav Jodl early on the morning of May 7, they gave in and signed the Act of Military Surrender.[13] The following day formal surrender terms were concluded at Berlin with representatives of the Allied powers, the terms becoming effective at 12:01 A.M. (European time) on May 9. The most important clause in the surrender document was:

> We . . . agree to unconditional capitulation of all our armed forces on land, sea and air, and also all forces at present under German command, to the high command of the Red Army and at the same time to the Allied Expeditionary Forces.

[13] After signing the unconditional surrender document, Jodl is reported to have said: "With this signature the German people and armed forces are for better or worse delivered into the victors' hands. In this war, which has lasted more than five years, both have achieved and suffered more than perhaps any other people in the world."

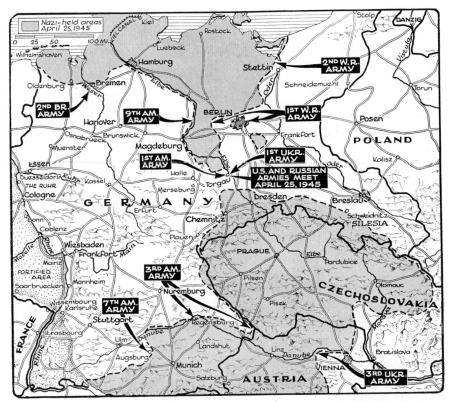

Germany's Collapse. (From Francis Brown, *The War in Maps.* By permission of Oxford University Press, New York.)

Although some fighting still continued, World War II was at an end as far as Germany was concerned. News of the surrender was followed by celebrations in all parts of the Allied world. Yet there was an undercurrent of sadness because President Roosevelt, who had died on April 12, could not witness the triumph for which he had worked so long and hard.

The End of the Axis: Victory over Japan

By the Potsdam Proclamation of July 26, 1945, the United States, Britain, and China threatened Japan with utter destruction unless she surrendered unconditionally. Although the Japanese cabinet, confronted by increasingly disastrous air attacks and encirclement by Allied naval forces, wanted to bow to this ultimatum, the die-hard army leaders insisted on fighting on.

Redoubled Allied attacks by land, sea, and air showed that the warning of destruction was no empty threat. When Japanese resistance continued, the Allies decided to play their ace—a new weapon of revolutionary significance. On

August 6 a superfortress dropped an atomic bomb on Hiroshima, virtually destroying the entire city at a single blow. Scarcely had Japan recovered suffi- ciently to realize the implications of this event when she faced another sharp blow; on August 8 Russia, in conformity with the Yalta Agreement, informed Japan that the next day war would begin between the two countries. Soviet troops swiftly invaded Manchuria and Korea to remove all possibility that Japanese troops on the Asiatic mainland could hold out. On that same fateful day (August 9) Nagasaki was destroyed by a second and deadlier atomic bomb, while B-29's ravaged the home islands from tip to tip.

Finally comprehending that further resistance would be futile, the Japanese government announced on August 10 its willingness to start surrender negotia- tions, provided Emperor Hirohito were allowed to keep his throne. In answer the Allies asserted that the emperor's position could not be guaranteed. He could continue on the throne only until the Allies fully occupied Japan and the unconditional surrender terms were fulfilled. Then there must be a free election under Allied supervision to determine the future leader and type of government. A three-day delay followed, but finally, at 7 P.M. on August 14, President Truman announced that Japan had accepted the Allied terms. The wild celebra- tion which followed surpassed those of VE Day and Armistice Day, 1918. Five days later a Japanese delegation signed the preliminary surrender document at Manila, with General MacArthur acting for the victors. Then on September 2, aboard the American battleship *Missouri* anchored in Tokyo Bay, the formal surrender occurred.

These terms provided for the surrender of Japanese forces everywhere, with prompt demobilization and the turning over to the Allies—or the destruction— of all military supplies and equipment. Moreover, the emperor and the govern- ment agreed to obey all orders of the Allied Supreme Command, which, under General MacArthur, would supervise the occupation of Japan. Provision was also made for the trial of war criminals, for the establishment of democratic institutions, and for the regulation of the Japanese economy.

Although many Japanese divisions in outlying regions continued fighting for some time, to all intents and purposes World War II had ended. Lasting nearly six years, with the United States participating for three years and nine months, it was the greatest, the most widespread, the most destructive, and the most costly war in history. Victory was gained by the Allies in large part through co- operation, not only among themselves, but among the various branches of their respective services. Naval power played no small part in the Allied triumph, for World War II was the greatest naval war in history; in the struggle for control of the Pacific the American navy was of paramount importance. Logistics also played a prominent role; the Allied ability to transport supplies many thou- sands of miles gradually offset the shorter lines of the Axis, and the members of the respective merchant marines deserved no less credit for ultimate victory than those in the fighting forces.

It has been estimated that more than 80 million men were under arms at one time or another during the course of the war. Of these, 14 million were killed and millions more wounded. Civilian populations also suffered greatly from the direct and indirect effects of the struggle. Many communities were wiped out or badly damaged by air assault, V-bombs,[14] shellfire, fires, and infantry attack. Large industrial and agricultural areas were destroyed in both Europe and Asia. The estimated cost of the war reached nearly the trillion dollar mark.

As for the United States, the casualties were much greater than in World War I. The Army figures revealed that 318,274 were killed and 565,861 wounded. The Navy report, including the marines and coast guard, listed 89,345 killed and 105,953 wounded. The total casualty list was around the 1.1 million mark. The naval ship losses totaled 696 craft in all categories, and merchant ships sunk numbered 538. The monetary cost was around $330 billion. Moreover, the United States was compelled to draw on future reserves of iron, tin, rubber, oil, wood, and numerous other commodities that could have been better used for the peacetime needs of present and future generations. Millions of Americans pondered whether victory was worth the cost. Defeat, they realized, would have cost eternally more; but merely to have escaped defeat was not enough. A just and lasting peace would be the only gain sufficiently precious to balance the great sacrifice.

[14] In 1944 and 1945 Germany launched the V-1 and the more destructive and powerful V-2 rocket-robot bombs against England. Thousands of lives were lost and many homes destroyed by these missiles.

25

The Home Front

The Pearl Harbor blow came as a stunning shock to the American people. Nevertheless, that shock was of immediate value in one respect; it effected a unity that had been lacking for years. The attack upon American soil and the danger of invasion of the United States itself ended the bitter debate that had been raging between the internationalists and the isolationists. Both groups now established common cause, as did Democrats and Republicans, industrialists and labor. Overnight the American people became united in the conviction that they must help to wipe out the totalitarian threat. This, they now realized, could be done only by girding the United States with full military regalia and making a supreme effort to ensure national survival.

Rallying Round the Flag

As concrete proof that partisanship was put aside, outstanding Republicans like Hoover and Landon, together with the minority leaders in Congress, pledged their support to the all-out war effort. Through William Green and Philip Murray, labor quickly promised full cooperation and, with capital, agreed that industrial disputes, especially in essential fields, must be kept at a minimum. John L. Lewis declared: "When the nation is attacked every American must rally to its support. . . . All other considerations become insignificant."

Isolationists either abruptly changed their position or became silent. The carping *Chicago Tribune* suddenly ended its criticism of the administration's foreign policy in favor of "our country, right or wrong." The America First

Committee likewise ceased its efforts to obstruct the preparedness movement and most of its leaders resigned.

This unity made possible a mobilization program unparalleled in the history of the world. The army, navy, and air forces were quickly expanded; industry, on a round-the-clock schedule, turned out equipment—planes, guns, tanks, ammunition, uniforms—in numbers and amounts hitherto undreamed of. The government quickly went on a wartime footing and established agencies to deal with every phase of the emergency. Civilians, both men and women, cheerfully did without many commodities needed primarily for the military.

Raising an Army

Pearl Harbor found the United States still in the preparatory stages as far as the army was concerned. Army personnel numbered nearly 1.6 million on December 7, 1941, and by far the largest percentage of this total consisted of men serving under the Burke-Wadsworth Act and therefore not eligible for overseas service. Many were unacquainted with either the implements or the strategy of modern warfare. Yet less than four years later, on August 15, 1945, the army had an efficient fighting force of 8.3 million, equipped with the finest implements in the world. How this was done is a story in itself and only the highlights can be dealt with here.

On the day after Pearl Harbor, recruiting offices throughout the country were literally flooded with men and youths seeking to enlist voluntarily. Although volunteers were accepted for some services throughout the war, army officials could not rely upon this unpredictable source. Consequently, the primary dependence for enlarging the army was placed upon conscription. On December 13, 1941, Congress removed the ban on using drafted men for overseas service, and a week later the time of such service was extended to the duration and six months. Then in February, 1942, all previously unregistered males within the twenty to forty-four age group were placed within the draft category, and two months later those between the ages of forty-five and sixty-five were ordered to register, not for military service, but as potential draftees for work in essential industries. The final amendment of the Burke-Wadsworth Act in June, 1942, lowered the conscription age for military service to eighteen.

The task of calling up those who had registered was a mighty one. Now under the supervision of General Lewis B. Hershey, the draft was taken care of by 54 state agencies, 515 boards of appeal, and 6,443 local boards, manned by more than 200,000 workers, mostly volunteer. In general, the local draft agencies tried to prevent undue hardship. The call of married men with children or other dependents was delayed as long as possible. Naturally, however, the system was not uniform because conditions in each draft area varied. Some had a large pool of young, unmarried men with no dependents; in others that pool was small. In the latter case, married men were called more quickly. Although there were some complaints over interpretation of orders from Hershey head-quarters, the draft on the whole worked well.

In similar fashion the navy complement grew. The number of men in the navy at the time of the first Japanese attack was 325,000; at the conclusion of hostilities there were nearly 3.4 million. The marine forces grew from 28,300 to 477,000 during the same period, while the coast guard expanded from 14,000 to 171,000. The total of naval combat ships showed the same remarkable in-crease.[1] For ships of all types under the control of the Navy Department, the number multiplied from 4,500 in 1941 to 91,209 at the end of the war. Of the newer types added, perhaps the most unusual were those for landing infantry (LCI) and tanks (LCT). The time needed to construct combat craft was materially reduced as the war progressed: battleships could be built in 32 months as compared with the 39 months of pre-Pearl Harbor days; aircraft carriers in 16 months instead of 32; submarines in 7½ months rather than in 14; and destroyers in 5½ months instead of 13.

Of the specialized branches, the air arms of both army and navy showed the most spectacular improvement. In December, 1941, the number of pilots was pitifully small; by the end of the war the naval branch, including marines, had nearly 50,000 pilots, together with ground crews and other personnel to the number of more than 500,000; for the army, in 1943 alone 65,000 pilots were graduated by the training command, along with nearly 14,000 navigators, 14,000 bombardiers, 82,000 aerial gunners, and approximately 530,000 tech-nicians of various types—indeed, the army air forces ultimately totaled about 3 million. Closely associated with the army air arm were the airborne troops, both parachute and glider battalions, which did such excellent work during the invasions, in the Battle of the Bulge, and in the all-out drive to final victory in Europe. As for planes, in 1941 the combined army and navy air arms included about 8,000, of which a goodly percentage were obsolete. By VJ Day, the navy had close to 40,000 and the army had approximately twice that number. The planes were constantly being improved in range, fire power, bomb loads, speed, and fighting ability. Perhaps the most notable advances were made in jet propulsion and in size. Radar and the bomb sight were of inestimable value, too, in American air and bombing progress.

To train this vastly increased armed personnel, 1,200 camps, cantonments,

---

[1] The chief advocates of a bigger and better navy during the thirties were President Roose-velt and Representative Carl Vinson of Georgia. The first move to build up the navy to Wash-ington Treaty strength came when the President used funds appropriated under the National Industrial Recovery Act for that purpose. Virtually each year from 1934 on Vinson intro-duced naval construction bills. The most successful was the one of 1938, passed only after long opposition from the isolationists, which provided for the largest building program since World War I. With the outbreak of hostilities in Europe, President Roosevelt obtained Congres-sional approval for a two-ocean navy. This construction was just getting under way at the time of Pearl Harbor.

and stations were established throughout the country. An intensive basic training course lasting from 12 to 17 weeks was given the new men, after which there was a possibility of attending specialized schools in such fields as gunnery, mechanized warfare, amphibious operations, radar, communications, and officer training. The various branches of the armed services also used many colleges and universities to train their men in such specialties as air-force training, engineering, radio and radar, meteorology, and language-and-area studies. Moreover, many college graduates were schooled for positions in various phases of military and civilian government in anticipation of the occupation of enemy countries during and after the war.

Beginning June 1, 1942, the pay of the various branches was increased. That of the private and the ordinary seaman was raised from $21 a month to $50, with higher ranks increased in proportion. In the same year the Service Men's Allotment Act was passed to provide dependency payments for the servicemen's wives and children. In anticipation of the discharge of military men, the President signed on June 22, 1944, the measure popularly called the G. I. Bill.[2] First of all, this act provided for 52 weeks of unemployment compensation at $20 a week, together with adjusted compensation for self-employed veterans returning to their old business. Next, the government guaranteed 50 per cent of loans up to $2,000 to veterans who were buying homes or setting themselves up in business. Half a billion dollars was appropriated for the construction of hospitals for veterans and for expansion of the United States Employment Service to help get them jobs. Finally, veterans going to college might obtain $500 a year for four years to be used for tuition and books, plus $50 a month ($75 if married) for subsistence.[3]

An unusual feature of the mobilization for World War II was the enlistment of women. In May, 1942, Congress established the Women's Auxiliary Army Corps (WAAC) under the command of Major—later Colonel—Oveta Hobby; on July 1, 1943, the members of the WAAC were incorporated into the regular army as the Women's Army Corps (WAC). More than 100,000 Wacs served as clerks, stenographers, cryptographers, weather observers, link training instructors, laboratory technicians, truck drivers, and small-arms repairers. Although most of the Wacs were stationed in the United States, some 15,000 saw service in the various overseas fields of operations. The navy also had its women's branch, the WAVES (Women Accepted for Volunteer Emergency Service), organized in July, 1942, under Lieutenant Commander Mildred McAfee. A total of 86,000 women joined up. Until the fall of 1944 they did not

---

[2] The term "G.I." first referred to anything issued by the government (Government Issue). Gradually it was applied to the enlisted men themselves and is comparable to the doughboy of World War I. Toward the close of World War II the expression became "G.I. Joe."

[3] In December, 1945, the subsistence rates were increased to $65 and $90 respectively.

serve outside of the United States. Thereafter, some 4,000 were on duty in Hawaii, with lesser numbers in Alaska, Puerto Rico, and Bermuda.[4]

Not to be forgotten in the mobilization story were the thousands of doctors, dentists, nurses, medical corpsmen, and pharmacists' mates who performed invaluable service in taking care of the wounded men.

Civilians and the War

Despite the long hours of regular work which the war entailed, millions of Americans found time to contribute volunteer services. After the attack on Pearl Harbor, the possibility that mainland cities of the United States might be subjected to air raids no longer seemed fantastic. The Office of Civilian Defense (OCD), established several months earlier, suddenly took on vital significance. Five and a half million persons were trained for special duties as neighborhood air-raid wardens, auxiliary firemen, emergency first aid workers, and aircraft warning personnel. Cities established their own air-raid signals, and practice blackouts educated not only the OCD force but the general public in the grim possibilities of modern warfare. Most OCD activities came to seem unrealistic after the Axis powers were thrown on the defensive, but the services performed by 77,000 nurses' aides in the dangerously understaffed hospitals were of vital importance.

Other essential work was carried out under the auspices of the Red Cross. Women sewed or knitted as they had during World War I. Much more significant, however, was the blood-donation service. Techniques had been discovered for extracting the plasma from blood and processing it in such a form that it could be sent to battlefields throughout the world. There, mixed with sterile water, the plasma was available to give lifesaving transfusions to wounded servicemen. This procedure more than any other single factor accounted for the remarkable achievement of World War II in cutting down mortality from wounds.[5]

Local draft and rationing boards required long hours of volunteer work, while the efforts of thousands of unpaid workers in the USO (United Service Organization) centers brightened the off-duty hours of millions of lonely servicemen. Even the housewife in her kitchen helped the war effort as she

[4] There was also the United States Marine Corps Women's Reserve under Colonel Ruth Streeter. Organized in February, 1942, about 19,000 enlisted in this branch. After January, 1945, some 5,000 were sent to Hawaii. The SPARS, the women's branch of the Coast Guard, started in November, 1942, and numbered 10,000 under command of Captain Dorothy Stratton. The WAFS (Women's Auxiliary Ferrying Service) did not continue throughout the war.

[5] General Paul Hawley, chief surgeon of the American forces in the European theater, announced that 96.1 per cent of the 1,375,000 Americans wounded had been saved. He attributed this achievement to the use of plasma, sulfa, penicillin, and to the fact that the men were bigger and stronger than the soldiers of World War I.

carefully saved waste fats, tin cans, and waste paper for the salvage drives, while the entire family hoed the victory gardens—numbering some twenty million—which were to be found on virtually every vacant lot.

Signs of the Times. (By Summers in the *Buffalo Evening News*.)

It proved easier to contribute war work of a positive nature than to accept cheerfully the numerous disruptions in normal living that the war made necessary. Rationing was a nuisance to all concerned, not only because of the need to stand in line to obtain ration books, but because of the added time spent in marketing. Even more annoying was the difficulty in locating such periodically scarce items as butter, coffee, sugar, meat, cigarettes, women's stockings, and men's underwear. These scarcities led to the establishment of black markets where unpatriotic—although they would be the last to admit it—citizens could buy such commodities without coupons at more than ceiling prices. Such shortages, together with overcrowded transit facilities and crowded housing conditions, were the hardships of the home front over which civilians delighted to grumble, but which did not greatly impress the men in the armed services familiar with conditions in other countries.

Mobilization of Industry

It was obvious that the country's greatest advantage over the enemy lay in its gigantic industrial potential. Yet the problem of converting factories from peace to war manufacture, of building new plants, and of establishing priorities for the use of raw material and manpower, required central planning and direction to a degree unprecedented in democratic America.

The government profited by the experience of World War I and also by several later studies of the war mobilization problem. Despite this, however, many World War I mistakes were repeated, many new ones made, and it required a long period of trial and error before the final organization was evolved and a competent personnel recruited. Impatient critics emphasized the President's deficiencies as an administrator; they pointed out that the jurisdictions of the various defense agencies overlapped, that jurisdictional and intra-agency feuds were frequent, and that the Chief Executive was altogether too prone to resolve such difficulties by creating still another coordinating board instead of simplifying and clarifying the lines of authority. All this was true. Yet in a more important sense Roosevelt did a remarkable job. He challenged the nation with seemingly impossible production goals, he assembled a hard-working team, and despite the appearance of muddle the most remarkable record of industrial production in the world's history was achieved.

One reason for the unsatisfactory results obtained by the earlier defense agencies was that they were established before Pearl Harbor while the nation was not ready to accept the drastic steps that a war economy would have required.[6] Not until President, Congress, and nation were shocked into drastic action by Pearl Harbor did really effective administrative organization evolve. The First War Powers Act of December, 1941, authorized the President to redistribute the tasks of the several boards and agencies in the interests of the most efficient prosecution of the war—a counterpart of the Overman Act of World War I. Existing laws were liberalized to facilitate government procurement of essential supplies, while the Trading-with-the-Enemy Act of 1917 was brought up to date to give the President control over all communications and the right to use property confiscated from the enemy.

Under his new authority Roosevelt in January, 1942, placed Donald Nelson, a Sears Roebuck executive, in charge of the War Production Board (WPB). Occupying a post similar to that of Bernard Baruch in 1918, Nelson was answer-

---

[6] Insufficient authority handicapped the activities of the Council of National Defense, established in May, 1940, and the Office of Production Management (OPM) and the Office of Emergency Management (OEM), set up early in 1941. Nor did the first attempts to control prices or to settle labor disputes through such overlapping agencies as the Office of Price Administration and Civilian Supply (OPACS), the National Defense Mediation Board (NDMB), the Economic Defense Board (EDB), and the Supply Priorities and Allocations Board (SPAB), prove effective.

able only to the President in his efforts to procure adequate supplies and to increase output. The agency was organized into six major divisions: purchases,
production, materials, industry operations, labor, and civilian supply, each
under a competent director. Following the Baruch precedent, more than 200
Industry Advisory Committees were established. The antitrust laws were
tacitly suspended while the concerns in each industry pooled their patents and
divided available government contracts. Also sponsored by the WPB were
over 5,000 labor-management committees formed in individual war plants.
Through these channels thousands of practical suggestions for improving techniques and for saving time were received from the workers.

Both to utilize plant equipment and to conserve vital material, all production
for civilian use of automobiles, radios, mechanical refrigerators, vacuum cleaners,
washing machines, and most electrical appliances was halted during the early
months of 1942. Manufacture of hundreds of other metal goods was either
stopped entirely or drastically curtailed, while practically all home construction
except that approved for defense workers by the National Housing Agency
ceased. Many small industries were hard hit by this transition, but an effort
was made to protect their interests through the Smaller War Plants Corporation (SWPC), which gave out and financed war contracts to small business
and assisted them with their engineering problems.

Japanese conquest of 90 per cent of the world's rubber supply during the
three months following Pearl Harbor created a most serious crisis. A belated
effort at laying in a stockpile of rubber had begun in 1941, but less than a year's
supply was accumulated before Malaya and the Netherlands East Indies fell
into enemy hands. The sale of new tires except on a strict rationing basis was
prohibited on January 5, 1942, and a program was adopted for conserving
rubber which involved gasoline rationing, a 35-mile-an-hour speed limit on the
highways, and periodic tire examination. A vast expansion of synthetic rubber
production was called for, to be organized under the WPB. In harmony with
this suggestion, Roosevelt appointed William M. Jeffers, an executive of the
Union Pacific Railroad, as Rubber Administrator.

Modern war demands global strategy in economic planning as well as in
military operations. To pre-empt vital supplies, to keep them out of enemy
hands, to implement foreign policy with rewards and penalties in the form of
purchases and sales to particular countries, were all important American activities. During the earlier years of the conflict numerous agencies were dealing
with such problems, and inevitable clashes of policy resulted. The most
publicized of these was the feud between Vice-President Wallace, the head of
the Board of Economic Warfare (BEW), and Secretary of Commerce Jesse
Jones, whose RFC advanced the funds for many of the country's strategic
imports. In July, 1943, the President was compelled to intervene by abolishing

the BEW and transferring its functions, together with many of those of the RFC subsidiaries, to a new Office of Economic Warfare (OEW) headed by Leo Crowley. This agency in turn was later consolidated with others, including the Office of Lend-Lease Administration, into the Foreign Economic Administration (FEA), which became one of the key agencies for the waging of total war.

Later sections of this chapter will describe how the Office of Price Administration (OPA) struggled to ration scarce items and keep a ceiling on prices and rents, how the National War Labor Board (NWLB) handled disputes over wages, and how the War Food Administration (WFA) worked to increase agricultural production. One of the great needs was for the effective coordination of these activities. Obviously, what was done by OPA affected both industrial production and farm production, while the problems of wage rates and prices were interrelated at every point.

Acting under the Anti-Inflation Act of October, 1942, the President established the Office of Economic Stabilization (OES), under the chairmanship of James F. Byrnes of South Carolina, who resigned from the Supreme Court to take over this important post. He was given control over "civilian purchasing power, prices, rents, wages, salaries, profits, rationing, subsidies, and all related matters."

Although the OES did some excellent work in supervising the improvement of production and in holding the line against inflation, there were an increasing number of critics who asserted that Stabilizer Byrnes was loaded down with too much detail, thus impairing the efficiency of OES. These critics demanded the establishment of an agency comparable to Wilson's War Cabinet, which had dealt so effectively with problems of coordination and jurisdictional disputes during World War I. The presidential answer was the organization of the Office of War Mobilization (OWM) on May 28, 1943, which was referred to as "the nearest thing to an orderly planning committee for the home front that has yet been devised." Roosevelt placed the new agency under the direction of Byrnes, whose powers now became so great that he was popularly referred to as the "Assistant President." Associated with him were Secretary of War Stimson, Secretary of the Navy Knox, Chairman of the Munitions Assignment Board Harry Hopkins, Chairman of the War Production Board Donald Nelson, and Byrnes's successor as Economic Stabilizer, Judge Fred M. Vinson of Kentucky.

The machinery of economic mobilization often seemed cumbersome. There were terrifying noises emanating from Washington when the gears appeared to clash and angry recriminations were exchanged.[7] As always in wartime, there was much Congressional denunciation of the incompetence of the executive

---

[7] Such friction, for example, brought about the resignation of Donald Nelson as WPB head and the appointment of Julius Krug to succeed him.

departments. But much more judicious than the work of most such bodies was that performed by the special Senate committee to investigate the national defense program. Ably led by Senator Harry S. Truman of Missouri, hitherto inconspicuous as a legislator, the committee uncovered cases where excess profits had been allowed to contractors and where production schedules had not been met.

Despite occasional evidences of administrative confusion and profiteering, the task of economic mobilization was magnificently carried through. In 1940 American war production was insignificant; in 1942 it had jumped to a volume equaling that of Germany, Italy, and Japan combined. But this was only the beginning. In 1943 it was one and a half times as great as total Axis war production, and in 1944 twice as great. Stalin himself paid tribute to this record at the meeting of the Big Three at Teheran when he proposed a toast to American war production, without which the enemy could not have been defeated.

The Problem of Price Control

Gigantic government expenditures and full employment, during a time when civilian goods were becoming increasingly scarce, threatened to bring about America's greatest inflation since the War for Independence. Yet, although the danger was recognized on all sides, government price fixing was against American tradition and its imposition was long delayed. The impact of war in Europe had already resulted in a sharp rise in the cost of living before the United States became directly involved. Only after six months of discussion did Congress finally approve the Price Control Act on January 30, 1942. This law established an Office of Price Administration (OPA) and empowered its administrator to fix fair maximum prices on commodities whenever they rose or threatened to rise unduly. Ceiling prices of farm produce, however, could not be set below 110 per cent of parity and any action had to have the approval of the Secretary of Agriculture. The administrator was also authorized to recommend the stabilization or reduction of rents in defense areas, while his rationing power covered all commodities sold for personal needs.

The scope of rationing was gradually expanded over the next several months to include sugar, meat, butter and other fats, canned goods, coffee, shoes, gasoline, and fuel oil. The most ambitious step in the price-control program was the issuance on April 28, 1942, of the General Maximum Price Regulation, which imposed wholesale and retail ceiling prices on almost all commodities. The general principle was that prices were not to exceed their highest level during March, 1942. An important omission made necessary by Congress was in the control of most food prices. Not until the original law was amended in October did OPA establish ceilings in this area.

The price control agency became a favorite whipping boy for harassed civilians, both those with things to sell and things to buy. Its first administrator, Leon Henderson, was a vigorous executive and a forceful personality. But his very energy aroused the hostility of Congress and, to save the agency, the President allowed him to resign in December, 1942, and appointed in his place the more diplomatic Prentiss Brown, formerly Senator from Michigan. Although Brown restored peace between OPA and Congress, the agency's less rigorous enforcement policies threatened to defeat its purpose. Congress, moreover, insistently demanded personnel with greater business experience. In October, 1943, therefore, Chester Bowles, a prominent New York advertising executive who had proved a successful OPA official at the state level, succeeded Brown. The new head proved a good choice. In one of the war administration's most difficult and unpopular posts Bowles achieved a very creditable record.

Advice from the Corner. (By Summers in the *Buffalo Evening News*.)

In May, 1943, the need for more drastic price-control policies became evident because the cost of living had advanced almost 8 per cent since May, 1942. This, combined with earlier increases, meant a 27 per cent rise since the outbreak of war in 1939. One step to combat the situation was the extension of rent control over the whole nation in October, 1942. Another was the so-called Hold-the-Line order issued by the President on April 8, 1943. An effort was made to freeze all items affecting the cost of living. Except in exceptional circumstances, wage and salary increases were to be prohibited, workers were not to be permitted to change jobs for higher pay, and government agencies regulating common carriers and public utilities were to prevent rate increases. Its hand thus strengthened, OPA was successful in restricting the rise of living costs during the next two years to 1.4 per cent. The total increase in the cost of living of less than 29 per cent up to VE Day may be compared with the 63 per cent rise that took place between the outbreak of World War I and the armistice, or the more than 100 per cent increase represented by the prices of 1920.

The validity of the cost-of-living indexes was often challenged, particularly by labor spokesmen seeking wage boosts. This was natural because to the average citizen the increase in living costs seemed much greater. In the first place, high wartime withholding taxes took a very sizeable sum. To this should be added the substantial deduction which many workers had authorized for war bonds. There was thus a wide gap between what was earned and what was actually received. Moreover, prices had risen in unequal degree and the consumer was most conscious of those that had gone up sharply. He thought very little, for example, about the fact that rents had risen less than 4 per cent since 1939, but he never forgot that food prices had advanced by 50 per cent. Even more distressing to the consumer was the 40 per cent rise in clothing prices.

Statistics were also deceiving because they failed to take into account the very considerable volume of above-ceiling price transactions; the OPA itself admitted that some 12 per cent of the items in food stores were sold at higher than ceiling prices. Yet even though the degree of inflation occurring between 1939 and 1945 was larger than government figures indicated, economic controls had saved billions of dollars for both the government and the consuming public. The OPA served as a brake. It did not entirely stop inflation, but slowed it down until it was no longer dangerous to the war effort.

The Problem of Transportation

Total mobilization and global war involved enormous strain on railroad and shipping facilities. Instead of bringing the railroads under government operation as in World War I, the lines, left under private management, were closely supervised by the Office of Defense Transporation (ODT) directed by the experienced Joseph B. Eastman. Men, material, and supplies were moved about the country in much greater volume and with less confusion than during World War I—a remarkable achievement since the railroads had less equipment and fewer employees. This was not accomplished without paying a price, however. A number of tragic accidents testified to the strains the war was placing upon both equipment and personnel.

More vital than the coordination of the railroads was the efficient use of every precious unit of shipping. In February, 1942, the War Shipping Administration (WSA), headed by Vice Admiral Emory S. Land, assumed all the property and powers of the United States Maritime Commission. In addition to the ships thus obtained, the WSA acquired title to or the use of practically all the nation's privately owned seagoing vessels as well as a large proportion of the smaller craft. To this great fleet were added more than four thousand newly constructed ships. Many World War I building records were beaten. The most remarkable exploit perhaps was the construction of a 10,000-ton ship in 78 days, one third of the time required for a similar project during the earlier conflict. This was made possible by radically new techniques, developed particularly in the shipyards of Henry J. Kaiser.

Although shipping was necessarily more highly regimented than railroad transportation, the actual operation of the merchant marine was through some 130 privately owned companies. An extensive training program provided additional officers and men for the crews. The latter composed some of the war's unsung heroes. Enemy attacks by submarine and plane resulted in approximately 6,000 casualties. Several routes like those to ports of Northern Russia were particularly arduous and dangerous. Despite many difficulties, however, the merchant marine accomplished its mission of delivering the weapons of war to every theater.

Transocean air travel and transport, still in their infancy when the war began, were enormously expanded. Presidents, prime ministers, and key personnel hopped from continent to continent with surprisingly few mishaps, while air transport for less dramatic missions became routine.

The Farmers and the War

No individual in World War II played as powerful a role as had Herbert Hoover in World War I. The War Food Administration (WFA), headed by Judge Marvin Jones, was only a pale copy of its famous predecessor. Whereas Hoover had reduced civilian food consumption through a great propaganda campaign, this end was now achieved by an extensive system of OPA-administered rationing. The increased production that Hoover had gained through the incentive of guaranteed high prices was this time achieved through a system of subsidies designed in combination with ceiling prices to protect consumers.

Heated debate raged over the merits of the ceiling price-subsidy system. The farmers argued that subsidies placed a burden upon the taxpayer which rightly belonged on the consumer; they demanded that ceilings and subsidies be abandoned and prices allowed to seek their natural levels. But the administration firmly opposed this policy. Food prices had already risen sufficiently to make the workers restless; a further jump would precipitate a wholesale outbreak of strikes, a series of pay raises, and an upward spiral of inflation. Subsidies admittedly added to the national debt, but they did not increase it nearly so rapidly as would runaway prices during a period when the government was making tremendous purchases. Although Congress twice passed bills that would have killed the subsidy program, they were vetoed by the President.

Farmers had other grievances than price controls. Livestock raisers and dairy farmers found feed scarce and expensive. Agricultural machinery was difficult to obtain. The armed services and the war industries drew away agricultural manpower and labor costs shot up.

Despite all these handicaps, the farmers achieved a remarkable production record. Favored during most of the war years with good weather, they harvested the largest crops in American agricultural history. More than a billion bushels of wheat were produced in 1944, while the corn crop exceeded 3 billion bushels for three years in a row (1942–1944). Meat production kept pace, going over the 20 billion-pound mark annually for the three years of 1942–1944, and reaching 25 billion pounds in the latter year.

Farm income, including government payments, doubled between 1940 and 1943, exceeding $20 billion in the latter year—a far cry from the 1932 situation when total farm income was less than $5 billion. Income continued to exceed $20 billion annually in 1944 and 1945. To be sure, the increasing cost of things that the farmers had to buy absorbed much of this rise, yet there was a large net gain and there could be little doubt that agriculture was more prosperous than it had been for a generation. One of the healthiest signs was the shrinking agricultural debt. Total farm-mortgage debt which had risen to almost $8.5 billion in 1920 and to $9.6 billion in 1930, had fallen to less than $5.3 billion by 1945. Farmers were obviously facing the new postwar era in much sounder financial condition than they had the decade of the twenties.

Labor and the War

Throughout the thirties the nation had struggled with the problem of unemployment. After Pearl Harbor the situation was transformed. With 12 million men eventually taken into the armed services, where was the labor to be obtained to man the nation's industries? The answer was found in the entry into the factories of millions who had never been wage workers—many of them women. The number of persons gainfully employed rose from 45 million in 1940 to more than 60 million in 1944. A further contribution was provided by millions of hours of overtime work performed in every community.

Less than a week after the United States entered the war a labor-management conference, meeting at the President's call, agreed to refrain from strikes and lockouts affecting essential industry during the war, to settle all labor differences by peaceful means, and to accept the jurisdiction of a war labor board.

Accordingly, in January, 1942, Roosevelt established the National War Labor Board (NWLB) composed of twelve members giving equal representation to the public, the workers, and the employers. William H. Davis of New York was designated as chairman. The board acted only on cases where a dispute had failed of settlement through ordinary channels of collective bargaining and the conciliation services of the Department of Labor.

During the first year the new system worked quite effectively. Although almost 3,000 strikes occurred, they were quickly settled and the number of man-days of labor lost was the smallest since 1930. About 400 of these disputes went to the NWLB; in all but four of these the parties complied with the findings of the board; the cases of non-compliance in essential plants were handled by government seizure and operation. In July, 1942, the board settled a strike in the lesser steel companies' plants by allowing a 15 per cent pay increase to compensate for the rise in the cost of living since January, 1941. This became known as the Little Steel formula and served as a yardstick for wage scales during the balance of the war.

The strike record was not as good in 1943. Workers were distressed by the increased cost of living, which, despite OPA, continued until the Hold-the-Line order of May, 1943. Jurisdictional disputes increased, as did work stoppages over questions of factory discipline. Many strikes were "wildcatters"—unauthorized by the unions. Employers and employees blamed each other for the situation. The former accused the workers of infringing upon the prerogatives of management; the latter asserted that the employers were trying to discredit unionism with the public by provoking work stoppages through petty acts of tyranny. In all there were 3,752 strikes in 1943 involving the loss of 13.5 million man-days of labor—three times the amount of time lost the previous year.

The most serious trouble came in work stoppages by John L. Lewis' coal miners. The struggle lasted throughout the greater part of the year, during which Lewis defied the NWLB, Fuel Administrator Ickes, and the government generally. Although the administration refused to admit it, Lewis in effect broke the Little Steel formula by obtaining premium pay and additional overtime work.

Congressional concern over the situation led in June, 1943, to the passage of the Smith-Connally War Labor Disputes Act against the opposition of the unions and over the President's veto. Increased powers were granted to the NWLB; thirty days' notice had to be given before a union could take a strike vote; explicit sanction was given to presidential seizure of war industries where production was interrupted by labor disputes; and it was made a criminal offense to instigate, direct, or aid strikes in government-operated plants or mines. A final provision, particularly resented by labor, prohibited union contributions to political campaign funds. Several states in the South and West passed laws restricting union activities still more stringently.

The strike record of 1944 was somewhat better. While there were more work stoppages—4,956—they were for the most part quickly settled and the number of man-days lost fell to 8.7 million.

The most serious strikes inevitably made the newspaper headlines[8] and provoked condemnation of the groups involved. The situation, however, was never actually dangerous, except possibly in connection with the coal strikes. The number of man-days lost was less than 1 per cent of the amount worked. Every time the laborers worked on a legal holiday, as they usually did, the contribution to the war effort was greater than the labor lost through work stoppages for many months. Yet at the same time, the percentage of time lost was not always a true yardstick because the stoppages frequently caused tie-ups in other fields that were not indicated in the Department of Labor statistics.

War Finance

The cost of waging modern warfare has reached figures formerly considered astronomical. By VJ Day, World War II had made necessary United States government expenditures of more than $300 billion—a staggering sum when contrasted with the total American World War I expenditures of some $32 billion.

Despite this huge outlay, the American public raised a larger proportion of war costs out of taxation than ever before. Between Pearl Harbor and VJ Day the United States collected about $123 billion in revenues, or approximately 40 per cent of its expenditures. This contrasted with 33 per cent during World War I. The record for the fiscal year ending June 30, 1945, was particularly good. Expenditures for that period reached $100 billion, but net receipts were $46.5 billion or 46 per cent of the outlay.

There was general agreement on the necessity of high wartime taxes. They were essential to preserve government solvency, to prevent unjustifiable enrichment of those profiting from the booming wartime economy, and perhaps most of all to reduce the threat of inflation. The actual rates to be fixed for the various income brackets, however, were matters for heated debate. Months of such controversy were the prelude to the enactment in October, 1942, of "the greatest tax bill in history." The tax base was broadened to require payment of income taxes by all persons receiving more than $1,200 if married and

---

[8] One of the most publicized, although not particularly serious, disputes involved the government seizure of Montgomery Ward and Company, whose head, Sewall Avery, refused to follow the orders of the NWLB. Avery denied that his concern was engaged in war work, but President Roosevelt insisted that the strike affected the morale of the nation. In another case James Petrillo, head of the musicians' union, also defied the government, but was not punished. This resulted in much criticism of the administration's position.

$500 if single. The normal tax rate was increased from 4 to 6 per cent, but this sum was an insignificant burden compared with the imposition of surtaxes ranging from 13 per cent on the first $2,000 of taxable income to 82 per cent on incomes exceeding $200,000. Nor was this all; income exceeding $624 in the case of a single person and a somewhat larger figure for a married individual was subjected to a 5 per cent "Victory tax" withheld by the employer.

These new rates represented a revolution in taxation. The number of people paying income taxes to the Federal government had been only 4 million in 1939 and 17 million in 1941, but the direct taxes levied under the 1942 legislation reached 50 million persons. Under the 1939 rates a childless couple having $3,000 gross income had paid little if any income tax; under the 1941 rates such a couple paid about $109; under the 1942 rates the tax was $340. Corporation taxes were also raised so that the maximum normal and surtax rates on the largest incomes totaled 40 per cent. In addition to this, excess profits were taxed at the rate of 90 per cent—subject, however, to certain postwar rebates to aid reconversion.

These taxes, plus either new or increased excise levies on liquor, beer, telephone service, travel tickets, amusements, and telegraph messages, greatly increased the revenues of the government, but they involved many annoyances and inconveniences. The income-tax forms had become almost impossibly complicated to fill out, the Treasury Department's problem of enforcement had become unmanageable, and the system of collecting these huge sums after the completion of the year on which the tax was levied threatened to result in wholesale defaults. In support of a much-needed reform, Beardsley H. Ruml, a New York financial expert, became the leading proponent of a "pay-as-you-go" plan, under which employers would withold the Federal income tax from wages and salaries as they were paid. In order to put all taxpayers on a current basis, Ruml insisted that the government forgive the 1942 tax. The latter proposal was unsatisfactory to the Roosevelt administration, but public demand led in June, 1943, to the passage of a Revenue Act that represented a modified version of the Ruml plan. Taxpayers had to file returns for both 1942 and 1943 income, but 75 per cent of their tax for whichever year was smaller was forgiven. Beginning July 1, 1943, income-tax payments were put on a current basis; wage and salary earners had their taxes deducted at the source; those with incomes from other sources had to estimate their income and make quarterly payments to the Treasury.

Despite these large taxes, net corporate income was at record heights, as were many individual incomes. In view of this wartime prosperity, President Roosevelt asked early in 1944 for additional taxes to the amount of $10.5 billion. Wendell Willkie also urged higher taxes to curb inflation and lessen the burden of debt to be left for the postwar generation. The majority of Congressmen believed, however, that the existing burdens were as heavy as the country could bear. Although they consented to increase the excise levies and raise the excess profits tax to approximately 95 per cent, the new bill provided only about $2.2 billion in additional revenue, and the net result was considerably less because Congress had frozen the Social Security levy at 1 per cent instead of permitting it to jump to 2 per cent as provided by earlier law. To show his strong disapproval of the Congressional action, the President took the unusual step of vetoing a revenue measure with a message so strongly worded that the Democratic leader in the Senate, Alben Barkley of Kentucky, angrily demanded that the veto be overridden. Barkley's advice was followed in a vote of 299 to 95 in the House and 72 to 14 in the Senate, while the rebellious leader was unanimously re-elected to the post from which he had resigned in protest over the President's message. Roosevelt attempted to smooth the ruffled feathers of the legislators by a telegram to Barkley denying his intention of attacking the integrity of Congress.

Even after the pay-as-you-go innovation, the income-tax structure was still so complicated that popular protest led to the passage in May, 1944, of the Individual Income Tax Act, sometimes called the Tax Simplification Act. The new law relieved millions of taxpayers receiving income exclusively from wages or salaries of the necessity of filing returns, it simplified the forms for other taxpayers, and it merged the troublesome Victory tax with the regular levies.

Though the tax burdens laid on the country were as great as Congress believed could be borne, there still remained a huge deficit. The public debt, which stood at $49 billion on June 30, 1941, climbed to nearly $259 billion by June 30, 1945. Every effort was made to borrow as much as possible from individual citizens. This was not essential to raise the money, since the banks readily subscribed whatever sums were asked of them. But government borrowing from banks, as it increased the amount of money in circulation, was highly inflationary. Bond purchases by individuals, on the other hand, decreased the volume of money and was one of the best safeguards against inflation.

During the great war-bond drives, thousands of volunteer solicitors conducted house-to-house canvasses: banks, theaters, and department stores set up booths where bonds could be purchased; and newspapers, magazines, radio stations, and movie houses appealed to the public to buy. A particularly effective technique was to induce wage earners and salaried workers to authorize regular deductions from their pay checks for bond purchases—a method that had the special advantage of selling bonds even when the special drives were not being conducted. In the single month of April, 1945, 25 million persons bought $485 million worth of bonds in this way. The sale of "E" Bonds, the type particularly designed for the small investor, totaled about $40 billion between May 1, 1941, and December 31, 1945.

One of the most interesting developments of the war years was the vast accumulation of savings of all types. Despite much easy spending of war earnings, the liquid savings of the American public were estimated at $129 billion by the spring of 1945. This helped to keep down prices during the war and created a backlog of purchasing power for the postwar years, but its unusual volume held at the same time future inflationary dangers.

Censorship and Information

By executive order of December 29, 1941, President Roosevelt established the Office of Censorship to censor all communications between the United States and foreign countries. The task of censoring mail was a huge one, requiring the services of 10,000 employees who deleted all mention of troop and ship movements, details of war production, descriptions of fortifications, air-raid preparations, and weather reports.

The newspapers and radio also agreed to a system of voluntary censorship. Codes of wartime practices were prepared after consultation between government officials and broadcasting industries. Unless it was given out by the appropriate government authorities, the newspapers and radio stations were asked not to reveal information regarding troop and ship movements, attacks by air upon the United States, airplanes' characteristics and activities, fortifications, production, weather, maps and photographs of the foregoing, and movements of the President or other high military and diplomatic officials. The Director of Censorship was Byron Price, a veteran journalist and Associated Press executive, who handled his delicate task in competent fashion, and violations of the letter or spirit of the code were few.

It will be noted that the newspapers had been asked not to publish information involving military security unless cleared with the proper authorities. This made the War and Navy Departments the real arbiters in most cases of what might or might not be released. Their tendency, particularly during the earlier months of the war, was to err on the side of overcaution. Consequently, censorship appeared to be sometimes used to shield the reading public from bad news, like the full truth about Pearl Harbor, or from any mention of military blunders—such as the incident in which American gunfire shot down American paratroopers in the attack on Sicily.

On June 13, 1942, partly as the result of pressure from writers and publishers, the Office of War Information (OWI) was established with Elmer Davis, a widely respected essayist and radio commentator, the director.[9] The OWI was authorized to utilize the press, radio, motion pictures, and other facilities to

---

[9] An earlier agency, the Office of Facts and Figures (OFF), under the direction of Archibald MacLeish, had not had sufficient power to coordinate the informational material emanating from the various government bureaus.

develop an informed and intelligent understanding, both at home and abroad, of the status and progress of the war, and of the war policies and aims of the government. It was hoped that the Davis agency would make accessible larger rations of war news. Strict censorship policies by the War and Navy Departments, however, continued to defeat this end. OWI's domestic branch was largely liquidated in 1943 when Congress, suspicious that the agency would serve a political purpose during the presidential campaign the next year, cut its appropriations. But the foreign branch, engaged in propaganda in enemy and neutral countries, survived Congressional attacks and conducted an intensive program through all available media. Particularly notable were its short-wave radio activities. It operated 16 transmitters and sent out 2,700 programs weekly in 24 different languages. It discovered that the most effective propaganda in a news-starved world was straight factual material about war developments, American war production, and plans for postwar reconstruction. Unquestionably the weapon of psychological warfare undermined the enemy's will to resist and was especially effective in hastening the surrender of Italy.

Dealing with Disloyalty

On the whole, the war period resulted in little interference with freedom of opinion in the United States. The President and the various war administrations were subjected to frequent and at times violent criticism. Some of the attacks represented mere partisanship, but on other occasions they revealed honest points of difference. Often freedom of speech proved a source of positive democratic strength since it led to the improvement of weak points in the defense organization and the rectification of mistakes.

There was much less of the witch-hunting atmosphere than during World War I. This reflected, in part, the moderation and good judgment of Attorney General Biddle. It resulted, too, from the circumstance that Communists and Socialists did not follow the extreme antiwar line that they had in 1917. The former, because of the German attack upon Russia, urged the subordination of every other end to the winning of the war. The Socialists were not so strongly prowar, but after Pearl Harbor they could hardly condemn the struggle as merely another instance of capitalist imperialism.

The administration did not jail radicals simply because they had unpopular economic or social philosophies; but it did proceed against certain individuals and groups whose activities threatened the war effort by promoting racial hatred, encouraging evasion of military service, or disseminating enemy propaganda. Newspapers like Father Coughlin's *Social Justice* were barred from the mails, while George Sylvester Viereck, a paid Nazi agent, and various domestic fascists like William Dudley Pelley, George Christians, and Ralph Townsend were arrested, some of them receiving prison sentences under the espionage laws. But the government's most ambitious project—a mass sedition trial of 28 pro-Nazis—miscarried. The death of the presiding judge after many weary weeks of court proceedings, enlivened principally by the antics of the defendants and their lawyers, resulted in a mistrial. Although the whole group never again came to trial on the conspiracy charge, several members were tried and punished on other grounds. Such individuals, however, were few in number and the country supported the war with greater unanimity than in any previous conflict. The enemy made occasional efforts to land agents and saboteurs by submarine, but these were frustrated through the vigilance of the FBI.

The Special Committee to Investigate Un-American Activities, the so-called Dies Committee, first authorized by the House of Representatives in 1938, was active throughout the war. Its efforts were approved by a majority of Congressmen and it received generous appropriations. Its supporters claimed for it important achievements in exposing subversive movements, but the committee was under continual fire from liberals. Its chairman, Martin Dies of Texas, was accused of being much more alive to the dangers of communism than of fascism, and of applying the brand of Communist recklessly to every liberal or labor leader whom he disliked.

The most shameful violation of civil liberties was the treatment of Japanese-Americans. Early in 1942 the army removed all persons of Japanese descent from three West Coast states and lodged them in relocation centers farther inland. This drastic step was taken on the contention that it was necessary to prevent spy activities and sabotage in an essential military zone, even though two thirds of the 110,000 evacuees were American citizens. The Supreme Court finally held in December, 1944, that the mass evacuation had been legal under the war powers of the President, but that American citizens against whom no charge had been filed and whose loyalty was not questioned could not be detained after removal from the military zone. Meantime, the War Department repealed its ban against the return of loyal evacuees to the coast, but certain elements of the Western public bitterly opposed the return of the Japanese-Americans. Over the course of the next eighteen months, no less than 59 acts of violence were committed to terrorize the returning evacuees. Although West Coast opinion in the main condemned such tactics, many Japanese-Americans decided to find new homes elsewhere. The harsh treatment of this group was perhaps inevitable, considering the shock of the Pearl Harbor attack and the revulsion against all things Japanese. But it is only just to the Japanese-Americans to stress that 17,600 of them served with the United States armed forces, that Japanese-American battle units had outstanding records in action, and that no Japanese-American was convicted of either sabotage or espionage during the war.

German and Italian groups were dealt with less rigorously. Citizens were not molested unless accused of specific acts of disloyalty. All enemy aliens over fourteen years of age, however, were required to register and to obtain "certificates of identification." They were barred from all vital defense areas and ordered to surrender their firearms, ammunition, cameras, and short-wave radios. Alien enemies considered dangerous were interned; but only 1,228 Germans and 232 Italians were so treated as compared with 2,151 Japanese. By early 1944, most Italians had been released, but German internees were kept under guard until the end of the war.

Politics as Usual

Unlike the unwritten British Constitution, the Constitution of the United States did not permit postponement of elections during wartime. To many observers this seemed unfortunate; political campaigns were regarded as a dangerous democratic luxury during a compelling national emergency. On the other hand, elections in wartime had much to be said for them. They provided an important popular referendum on the civilian direction of the war. More important, freedom of political debate and honest elections gave impressive evidence of the democratic values that America was fighting to preserve.

The Congressional election of 1942 came at a dark moment of the war. For eleven months after Pearl Harbor, the United States had been on the defensive and had suffered the humiliation of losing all her possessions in the western Pacific. On the home front civilians were undergoing the inconveniences of shortages and rationing, of rising prices and increased taxes, and of numerous bottlenecks in industry and transportation. Under the circumstances it was not surprising that the mid-term elections showed a strong anti-administration trend. Democratic strength in the House declined from 267 to 222, while the Republicans were rising from 162 to 209. In the Senate the Democrats fell from 66 seats to 57, while the Republicans rose from 28 to 38. One of the 1942 casualties was the famous independent, Senator George Norris of Nebraska, whose seat was captured by the conservative Republican, Kenneth S. Wherry.

The results of the election were actually more serious for the President than the statistics indicated. The dwindling Democratic majorities in both Houses gave the balance of power to conservative Southern Democrats, who often allied themselves with the Republicans. This coalition was no less determined than the New Deal Democrats to gain complete victory over the Axis. It accepted also the principle that the United States must support international machinery to maintain peace in the future. But on domestic issues the coalition was rebellious. The attacks upon the OPA and OWI have already been noted, as well as passage of the Smith-Connally Act and rejection of the administration's tax recommendations in 1944. Contending that they were no longer needed, the conservative coalition liquidated such relief agencies as the CCC, the WPA, and the NYA. Only for the last of these agencies did the New Dealers put up a fight, asserting that it should be continued as a training program for the war industries. One of the most disturbing victories of the anti-New Deal coalition was the killing of the National Resources Planning Board, an agency attempting to formulate a well-coordinated program for the postwar period. In the interests of national unity, President Roosevelt announced that "Dr. New Deal" had been dismissed and that "Dr. Win-the-War" was now in charge, but this gesture of appeasement resulted principally in distressing the President's liberal supporters without reconciling the conservatives.

The Election of 1944

In November, 1944, the first wartime presidential election in the United States since 1864 was held. Wendell Willkie made a spirited fight to win a second Republican nomination. He had become one of the country's most evangelical advocates of internationalism following a trip around the world by air in 1942. He poured out his convictions in the short but persuasive book, *One World*, which sold two millon copies during the next two years and headed the best-seller list for sixteen consecutive weeks. On domestic issues he also did some effective writing, impressing many who had not voted for him in 1940 with the genuineness of his liberalism. But Willkie's frankness and courage were in the end his undoing. He staked everything on capturing the Wisconsin primary in April, 1944, hoping to defeat isolationism in a traditional stronghold. He was badly beaten, however, and retired from the race despite his strong position in public-opinion polls.

Meantime, Dewey's star rose steadily. His greatest asset was his record as a vote getter in the pivotal state of New York. His election as governor in 1942 was the first such Republican victory since 1920 and offered hope that he might defeat Roosevelt in the latter's home state. The governor's other advantages were his youth, his reputation for efficiency, and his wide fame as a prosecutor of racketeers and corrupt politicians. Two other Republican governors, John Bricker of Ohio and Harold Stassen of Minnesota, were prominently mentioned for the nomination, but they could not overtake their New York rival.

In June, the National Convention, meeting in Chicago, nominated Dewey on the first ballot and selected Bricker as his running mate. The platform incorporated the so-called Mackinac Declaration, agreed to by the party leaders the previous year, which called for "responsible participation by the United States in a postwar organization among sovereign nations to prevent military aggression and to obtain permanent peace with organized justice in the world." The platform pledged the party not only to prosecute the war to total victory, but to bring home at the earliest possible time after cessation of hosilities all members of the armed forces who did not have unexpired enlistments and who did not volunteer for further overseas duty. The party devoted itself "to re-establishing liberty at home," to taking the government out of competition with private industry, and to terminating rationing, price fixing, and all other emergency powers after the close of the war.

Roosevelt's renomination by the Democrats was inevitable. Millions of citizens regarded the President's continuance in office as essential to prevent interruption of the war effort and to provide experienced leadership for the postwar period. From the standpoint of party expediency, moreover, it was unlikely that any other Democrat could win the November election. Serious anti-Roosevelt sentiment in the party was confined to Texas and other areas of the South, where New Deal policies benefiting organized labor, tenant farmers, and Negroes were bitterly resented. Only one man, however, could have prevented the renomination of Roosevelt and that was Roosevelt himself. After he announced his willingness to run again on the eve of the Chicago Convention, the only question was how large the anti-Roosevelt vote would be. The answer was provided on the first ballot, when Senator Harry Byrd of Virginia received 89 votes and James Farley 1 vote, while the President was rolling up a total of 1,066.

The real fight was waged over the second place on the ticket. Vice-President Wallace had not been the inconspicuous figure that tradition associated with that office. Instead, he had become a prominent public character through his vigorous championship of the rights of the underprivileged. In the columns of the opposition press, Wallace was portrayed as the embodiment of all that was most impractical and visionary in the New Deal. Yet the idealism that had aroused the hostility of conservatives won the enthusiastic support of many liberals.

Such was the opposition to Wallace among the Southern Democrats and the machine politicians of the North that his renomination could have been won only if Roosevelt had vigorously insisted upon it. This the President, striving for party harmony, refrained from doing. In a letter made public shortly before the convention, he testified to his admiration for Wallace and stated that, if he were a delegate, he would vote for Wallace; but he disclaimed any intention of dictating to the convention. The first choice of the party conservatives would have been War Mobilizer Byrnes, but the CIO's hostility to this suggestion made the choice of some compromise candidate essential. The President suggested either Supreme Court Justice William O. Douglas or

Senator Harry S. Truman of Missouri. With this help Senator Truman was nominated on the second ballot.

The preamble of the platform read: "The Democratic party stands on its record in peace and in war. To speed victory, establish and maintain peace, and guarantee full employment and provide prosperity—this is its platform. We do not detail scores of planks. We cite action." This was the keynote of the Democratic campaign. The country was asked to give the President a vote of confidence to continue the international and domestic policies with which he had become identified.

The contest was not lacking in bitterness. The most active workers in the Roosevelt cause were to be found in the Political Action Committee, organized by the CIO and supported by special contributions from union members, since the direct use of union funds was forbidden by the Smith-Connally Act. Astutely led by the veteran unionist, Sidney Hillman, the PAC waged an energetic campaign, based on effective publicity and house-to-house activity by thousands of enthusiastic amateurs to get out the vote. But these aggressive tactics—so sharply different from the traditional ones of the AFL—were bitterly denounced by the Republicans. The fact that Roosevelt had ascertained the attitude of the PAC on Truman before giving the latter his endorsement was twisted to mean that the unionists had captured the Democratic party. "Clear it with Sidney" was the taunt repeatedly thrown against the administration, but the attack upon Hillman boomeranged to a certain extent since many foreign-born and Jewish voters felt the Republicans were playing upon racial prejudice. Governor Dewey toured the country and attacked the administration in a series of vigorous speeches. He asserted that the government was in the hands of "tired old men" and called for a thorough "housecleaning." The President responded with much of his old-time fire, lashing out at his critics in one particularly aggressive speech before the Teamsters' Union in Washington.

The election provided another Democratic triumph. Roosevelt carried 36 states and gained 432 electoral votes as against Dewey's 12 states and 99 electoral votes. The popular vote was much closer, with Roosevelt receiving 25.6 million, Dewey, 22 million[10]—the closest margin of victory since 1916. The new Senate contained 57 Democrats, 38 Republicans, and 1 independent—the same division of strength as in the old—but the House received a reinforcement in the Democratic ranks, 242 of the administration party being elected to 190 Republicans and 2 independents. Isolationism was strongly rebuked by the voters; Senator Gerald Nye of North Dakota, Senator Bennett Clark of Missouri, Representative Hamilton Fish of New York, and Representative Stephen Day of Illinois all failed of reelection.

[10] The minor party vote was insignificant. Thomas, Socialist, received 80,419; Watson, Prohibition, 74,758; and Teichert, Socialist-Labor, 45,335.

Death of a Warrior

The fourth term was brief. On January 20, 1945, simple inauguration cere-
monies appropriate to wartime were conducted on the White House grounds.
"We have learned that we cannot live alone . . ." Roosevelt asserted in his
inaugural address. "We have learned to be citizens of the world, members of
the human community." Within a few days he embarked for the Crimea,
where he participated in the important Yalta Conference with Churchill and
Stalin. Upon his return he appeared before Congress to explain some of the
decisions taken there and to appeal for strong support for the forthcoming
San Francisco Conference at which the Charter of the United Nations Organization would be drafted.

Meantime, a sharp controversy over domestic issues had been precipitated
when the President dismissed the conservative Secretary of Commerce Jones
and nominated Henry Wallace to replace him. The whole conservative-liberal
battle was reopened in aggravated form, because the post now had connected
with it vast powers over the RFC and other Federal lending agencies. Inheritance of the whole kingdom over which Jesse Jones had reigned would give
the ex-Vice-President a magnificent opportunity to push his own program for
the achievement of full employment in the postwar economy. A bitter struggle
in Congress[11] resulted in neither side winning a clear decision. Wallace
achieved confirmation as Secretary, but the post was divested of all power over
the Federal lending agencies.

This, however, was the last important battle of the Rooseveltian period.
The strain of war had levied a heavy toll on the President's health. He had
spent his energies with characteristic prodigality during the presidential campaign, even driving in an open car through the rain in New York City as if to
answer the charge that he was a tired old man. But these exertions, followed
by the hard trip to Yalta, exhausted him. Seeking to renew his strength, Roosevelt went to Warm Springs, Georgia, for a spring vacation. There, resting and
working in an environment that he loved, he was unexpectedly stricken with a
cerebral hemorrhage on April 12, 1945, and died within a few hours. Released
after his death was a speech he had been working upon during these last days;
its closing words afforded an appropriate valedictory from the fallen war leader
to the nation:

> The only limit to our realization of tomorrow will be our doubts of today. Let
> us move forward with strong and active faith.

[11] The bitterness was accentuated by the belief in certain quarters that Jones was being
punished for his supposed part in the Texas revolt and because Roosevelt admitted that Wallace was being rewarded for his loyalty in the 1944 campaign.

26

The Mirage of Peace

During World War II the nation found strength in the hope that this time a better world would really emerge from the battlefield. The rejection of isolationism after the shock of Pearl Harbor seemed complete. The United States and its allies buried their ideological differences to concentrate on defeating the enemy. Out of this new climate of opinion there evolved the idea of the United Nations—a new international association to take the place of the more or less discredited League of Nations.

But cooperation in wartime proved much easier to maintain than postwar harmony. Between the Communist and the non-Communist nations a hostility developed that increased in bitterness as time went on. Discouraged Americans had reason to wonder whether the stable world society of which they had dreamed would ever be established.

Comrades in Arms

Under the lash of Axis aggression, the United States, Great Britain, and Russia achieved sufficient cooperation to win the war. Between the United States and Great Britain the relation was particularly close. Soon after Pearl Harbor Prime Minister Churchill flew to Washington to confer with President Roosevelt upon a plan of action. This direct approach was so successful that the two chiefs of state conferred on several other occasions—at Washington, at Casablanca, and at Quebec. At these meetings the great strategic decisions were made that led to the invasions of North Africa, Sicily, Italy, and France.

Day-to-day planning was conducted in Washington by the Anglo-American
Joint Chiefs of Staff, while on the European front English and American officers cooperated under the command of General Eisenhower.

Churchill, Roosevelt, and Stalin at Yalta, 1945. (Acme.)

With the Soviet Union, relations were less cordial. Bearing the brunt of
German attacks for many months, the Russians complained at the Anglo-
American delay in establishing a second front. Despite such recriminations, a
better understanding took shape during the latter months of the war. In Octo-
ber, 1943, Secretary of State Hull journeyed to Moscow to confer with Russian
Foreign Minister Vyacheslav Molotov and British Foreign Secretary Anthony
Eden. A month later the Big Three—Roosevelt, Stalin, and Churchill—met
at Teheran, Persia, to work out plans for a second front.[1]

The second conference of the Big Three was held at Yalta in the Crimea
during February, 1945. In the communiqué made public at the time, the
leaders announced their agreement on such important issues as the postwar

[1] Churchill and Roosevelt conferred with Chiang Kai-shek at Cairo, Egypt, just prior to the
Teheran Conference to coordinate action against Japan.

occupation of Germany, the fixing of reparations, the right of liberated peoples to establish governments of their own choice, and the reorganization of the provisional governments of Poland and Yugoslavia. These provisions were warmly applauded in America as evidence that Russia and the West had achieved a good understanding. But the Yalta Conference resulted in certain other decisions, kept temporarily secret for military reasons, which provoked sharp controversy when they were eventually revealed. The most important of these concerned the Far East. The Soviet Union pledged itself to enter the war against Japan after the surrender of Germany. As a reward, Russia was to receive the Kurile Islands, the southern half of Sakhalin, and the lease of Port Arthur as a naval base; the port of Dairen was to be internationalized and there was to be joint Russo-Chinese operation of the Chinese Eastern and Southern Manchurian railroads. Most of these privileges had been held earlier by Russia and lost as a result of the Russo-Japanese War.

After the full record of the Yalta Conference became known—months after Roosevelt's death—the wartime President was severely criticized for his "surrender" to Soviet demands. These fatal concessions, so the argument ran, gave Russia control of Manchuria, made the Chinese Reds' victory over Chiang Kai-shek inevitable, and led to Communist aggression in Korea. Roosevelt was also condemned for consenting to Russian occupation of Berlin and Eastern Germany and for acquiescing in Communist-controlled governments in the liberated countries of Eastern Europe. Most of these criticisms appear to be based more upon a desire to find a scapegoat for the nation's postwar troubles than upon an accurate understanding of the military situation in February, 1945. When the Big Three met at Yalta, American troops had not yet crossed the Rhine nor completed the conquest of the Philippines. The feasibility of the atom bomb was still to be proved. Decisions at the conference were made upon military estimates that assumed many months of hard fighting still lay ahead. The Chiefs of Staff were particularly eager to bring Russia into the war against Japan, thereby tying up Japanese troops on the continent of Asia and saving the lives of American soldiers when the invasion of the Japanese home islands began. Whether or not Roosevelt's diplomacy at Yalta was wise, the record seems clear that it was based on what he believed to be a realistic view of the military situation. The idea that the President was senile or pro-Communist when he entered upon these arrangements has little to support it.

The United Nations

At the Yalta Conference the Big Three agreed upon "the earliest possible establishment . . . of a general international organization to maintain peace and security." A meeting for this purpose was to be convened at San Francisco on April 25, 1945. Behind these decisions lay many months of discussion.

In a sense the seed had been planted in August, 1941, when Roosevelt and Churchill expressed in the Atlantic Charter their aspiration for a postwar "system of general security." The plant began to grow in the United Nations Declaration of January 1, 1942, in which the United States, Great Britain, China, and Russia pledged themselves to employ their full resources against the Axis, to cooperate with each other, and make no separate peace with the enemy. The declaration provided that other nations that rendered material assistance in the war against Hitlerism might adhere to this agreement. The following day, twenty-two other countries ratified the pact, and by January 1, 1945, nine more countries had done so. At the Yalta Conference the Big Three decided that only signatories of this document could be represented at San Francisco, a decision that resulted in eleven more states declaring war against the Axis and signing the declaration.[2]

Most striking was the change in American opinion. Instead of regarding the idea of a new world organization with suspicion, Congress appeared to be rushing ahead of the Roosevelt administration. In March, 1943, Republican Senators Joseph Ball of Minnesota and Harold Burton of Ohio joined Democratic Senators Carl Hatch of New Mexico and Lister Hill of Alabama in sponsoring the so-called B_2H_2 resolution, which urged the broadening of the United Nations into a postwar agency for the maintenance of peace. Regarded as premature by President Roosevelt, this proposal was not acted upon, but in September, 1943, the House of Representatives adopted by a vote of 360 to 29 a resolution introduced by James Fulbright of Arkansas, favoring the creation of "appropriate machinery with power adequate to establish and maintain a just and lasting peace among the nations of the world."

The Senate, apparently jealous of its prerogatives in foreign affairs, declined to concur in the Fulbright Resoluton, but in November, 1943, it voted 85 to 5 to approve the formula agreed upon in the recent Moscow Conference of Foreign Ministers:

> That they recognize the necessity of establishing at the earliest practicable date a general international organization, based on the principle of the sovereign equality of all peace-loving states, and open to membership by all such states, large and small, for the maintenance of international peace and security.

Although the Senate added the proviso that a two-thirds vote of that body would be required before the United States could enter such an organization, it was evident that the emerging United Nations was being greeted in a very different spirit than Wilson's League of Nations had been.

---

[2] Argentina signed after the Yalta deadline, but an American plea brought her an invitation to San Francisco.

New Areas of International Cooperation

The advocates of postwar cooperation realized that more was needed than simply an organization to prevent aggression; there must be cooperation as well to promote the Four Freedoms and to help the millions of civilians whose property had been ravaged by war. Consequently, forty-four nations met at Hot Springs, Virginia, in May, 1943, where they established the Food and Agricultural Organization (FAO) to determine what foods were needed for a good diet in various parts of the world.

Much more significant were the various problems of relief and rehabilitation, which involved not only the humanitarian issue but the military and economic as well. To meet these needs, the United Nations Relief and Rehabilitation Administration (UNRRA) was organized late in 1943 with funds contributed by the member nations on the basis of their relative national incomes—the quota of the United States was nearly 75 per cent. First under the leadership of former Governor Herbert Lehman of New York and then under Fiorello La Guardia, former mayor of New York City, UNRRA expended more than $4 billion to send food to destitute countries of Europe and Asia to prevent millions of unfortunates from dying of starvation.[3]

It was also realized that war-torn countries would face economic problems after the war; their industries must be rebuilt and their currencies stabilized to prevent a recurrence of the troublesome days of the 1930's. Therefore at the Bretton Woods (New Hampshire) Conference in the summer of 1944 provision was made for an International Monetary Fund of $8.8 billion (the American quota being $2.75 billion) to stabilize the currencies of the world, and for an International Bank of Reconstruction, with capitalization of $9 billion (the quota of the United States was slightly more than $3 billion), which would make direct loans to member nations for reconstruction of their industry and agriculture.

The San Francisco Conference

Even while these plans for humanitarian and economic rehabilitation were being formulated, the great powers were moving toward a general United Nations organization. The idea had been accepted in principle at the Moscow Conference of Foreign Ministers in October, 1943. The following August United States Undersecretary of State Edward B. Stettinius met with Sir Alexander Cadogan and Andrei Gromyko, representing Britain and the Soviet, at Dumbarton Oaks (outside of Washington, D.C.) where they drafted prelimi-

[3] Unfortunately, there were charges that some of this relief was used for political purposes in several countries. Consequently, the United States refused to support UNRRA after 1946.

nary plans for an association of nations. Final arrangements for a full United Nations Conference were made, as has been said, at Yalta in February, 1945.

Although President Roosevelt died before the San Francisco Conference opened, he contributed substantially to its success. Profiting from Wilson's mistakes, Roosevelt appointed an American delegation in which Republicans had equal recognition with Democrats and in which senators and representatives had important posts.[4] During the last months of his life Roosevelt laid the foundations for the bipartisan foreign policy that Truman continued successfully for several years. On the Republican side, the greatest contribution was made by Senator Arthur Vandenberg of Michigan, once an isolationist but now a strong champion of international cooperation.

When the conference opened on April 25, 1945, forty-eight nations were represented. Since the Dumbarton Oaks plan provided only a rough outline, there was ample opportunity for disagreement over details. On several issues the Russians took stubborn positions from which they were moved with difficulty —if at all. Indeed, at one point in the proceedings Soviet intransigence threatened to break up the meeting. To deal with this crisis, President Truman sent Harry Hopkins to Moscow for direct conversations with Stalin. In the end the great powers found acceptable compromises on such troublesome issues as the admission of White Russia and the Ukraine as independent members,[5] the admission of Argentina, the exclusion of Spain, trusteeships, and the voting and veto rights of the great powers.

The United Nations Charter

According to the preamble of the completed Charter, the peoples of the United Nations, in order "to save succeeding generations from the scourge of war," "to establish conditions under which justice and respect for the obligations arising from treaties and other sources of international law can be maintained," and to ensure "that armed force shall not be used, save in the common interest," had combined their efforts to accomplish these aims. The charter members were the forty-eight nations represented at San Franciso, plus White Russia and the Ukraine, which were admitted during the session. Provision was also made for including Poland after a reorganization of its government. Other

---

[4] The American delegation included: Secretary of State Stettinius, who had succeeded Cordell Hull in November, 1944, Senators Connally and Vandenberg, Representatives Bloom and Eaton, Commander Harold Stassen, former governor of Minnesota, and Dean Virginia Gildersleeve of Barnard College.

[5] At the Yalta Conference, Roosevelt had agreed to support Russia's demand for three votes in the Assembly, with the understanding that the United States might request a similar number. When this agreement became public, the idea of demanding three seats for the United States aroused so much opposition in American public opinion that it was dropped. The Soviet Union, however, demanded and received separate seats for two of her subordinate republics.

"peace-loving" states might be admitted by vote of the General Assembly on recommendation of the Security Council. Members violating the provisions of the Charter might be suspended or expelled by a similar procedure.

The General Assembly, made up of delegates from each member state, might discuss "any questions or any matters within the scope of the present Charter or relating to the powers and functions of any organs provided for in the present Charter, and . . . make recommendations to the Members of the United Nations or to the Security Council or to both on any such questions or matters." The only restriction concerned disputes already being considered by the Security Council. The Assembly had the right to initiate studies concerning the strengthening and codification of international law, the solution of social, cultural, educational, health, and economic problems, and to recommend measures for the peaceful adjustment of any situation likely to cause trouble. On important matters, a two-thirds vote was required.

Much more powerful was the Security Council of eleven members. Five of these—the United States, Britain, China, France, and Russia—held permanent seats. The other positions were filled by vote of the General Assembly for two-year terms. For approval of any action the vote of seven members was needed and, on important issues such as the use of military power, the Big Five must be unanimous. It was here that the disputed veto power came in; although a permanent member could not prevent consideration of a dispute in which it was involved, it could use its veto to prevent the imposition of economic or military sanctions.

Directly under the jurisdiction of the Security Council was the Military Staff Committee, consisting of the chiefs of staff of the Big Five. This committee could call out whatever armed forces the United Nations agreed to place at the organization's disposal when the Security Council deemed it necessary.

Another agency of the UN was an Economic and Social Council elected by the General Assembly to report on "international economic, social, cultural, educational, health, and related matters." Among the specialized agencies under its supervision were the International Bank, the International Stabilization Fund, the International Labor Organization (ILO), the United Nations Educational, Scientific, and Cultural Organization (UNESCO), and the Food and Agricultural Organization.

The Charter likewise provided for a Trusteeship Council to supervise territories already held under mandate, those lands gained from the Axis in World War II, and the regions voluntarily placed in trusteeship by the nations administering them. The International Court of Justice, to meet at the Hague, was made up of fifteen judges elected by the Assembly. Finally, there was a permanent Secretariat to keep the records and assemble the data needed by the UN.

In the effort to maintain peace, the UN was to function in a more or less prescribed manner. When a dispute arose that might endanger international peace, the parties to it were expected to seek a solution by peaceful means. If such negotiations appeared to be failing, the issue could be presented to either the General Assembly or the Security Council for investigation and recommendations for settlement. In the event of a breach of the peace, the Security Council was empowered to order economic sanctions against the offenders; if these were insufficient, the Military Staff Committee could be called upon to end the disturbance through armed force.

The Charter was criticized on various grounds. The small states deplored the dominating position given to the major powers, but the Big Five answered that they would have heavier responsibilities for maintaining peace than their smaller neighbors and must therefore have greater weight in UN councils. For the veto power exercised by the Big Five in the Security Council there was less defense; yet the United States and Britain were no less insistent than Russia upon this safeguard to their interests. From the beginning it was obvious that if the wartime allies could maintain a general unity of purpose, the UN would succeed. If these great powers quarreled among themselves, the new organization would find itself in serious difficulties.

Provision was made that the Charter would become effective when the Big Five and a majority of the remaining members ratified the document. Nicaragua was the first to act favorably, but the United States was the initial Big Five member to give approval. The Senate, after remarkably little debate, approved of American membership before the end of July, 1945, by the decisive vote of 89 to 2.[6]

The Potsdam Conference

The establishment of the UN was but one phase of the effort to prevent future conflicts. In 1945 the principal danger appeared to lie in the revival of a strong and revengeful Germany. During the war, decisions had already been made for the subjugation of the Reich, and the implementation of these policies was arranged at a Big Three conference, convened at Potsdam outside of Berlin, two months after the German surrender. Representing the victorious powers were President Truman, Prime Minister Churchill (who was replaced during the meeting by Clement Atlee, his successor as a result of a British election), and Marshal Stalin. The Potsdam Declaration of July 25, 1945, provided for the complete disarming of Germany. This action was to be strengthened by wiping out the Nazi organization from top to bottom, by the trial of war criminals, by breaking up cartels and supervising German industry, and by the establishment

---

[6] Senators William Langer of North Dakota and Henrik Shipstead of Minnesota, both Republicans, were the only dissenters.

of democratic institutions. Germany was divided into four occupation zones, respectively allocated to the Russians, British, French, and Americans. The American zone was located in the southern area, bordering on Austria and Czechoslovakia.

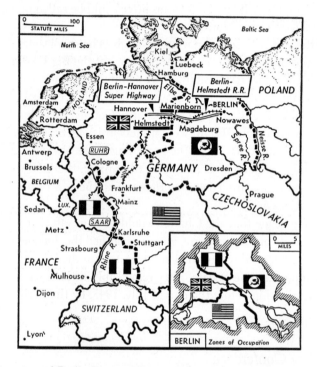

German and Berlin Zones of Occupation. (Press Association, Inc.)

The Potsdam meeting was not a peace conference, nor was a formal congress to deal with all the manifold problems of world settlement after the fashion of the Paris Conference of 1919 in immediate prospect. Indeed, the procedure laid down was to postpone a general settlement, while clearing the ground through special agreement on specific issues. Treaties for Germany and Austria were not to be considered until those with Italy, Finland, Hungary, Bulgaria, and Rumania had been signed.

Pending final decisions regarding Germany, the Potsdam Declaration laid down a provisional boundary. East Prussia was divided between Russia and Poland, while large additional territories in eastern Germany were allotted to Poland to compensate for her land given up to the Soviet Union.

Occupation Problems: Germany

The governing of vanquished Germany was no easy task. Nazi recruitment of slave labor and imprisonment of potential resistance leaders had torn millions of Europeans from their homes and left them at the war's end stranded and destitute hundreds of miles from home—if any home still survived. The rehabilitation of these displaced persons was a gigantic task and one that was enormously complicated by the migration of millions of Germans rendered homeless by Allied bombing or expelled from territories allotted to Poland, Czechoslovakia, or Russia. All European economic life was disorganized, and the mobilization of sufficient food to prevent starvation was difficult.

Specially trained military government teams wrestled with these and a thousand other problems. Administration at the local and provincial level had to be entrusted to German personnel, and the selection of individuals who were both competent and politically reliable was far from easy. The general principle laid down was that no Nazi sympathizer should be employed in any administrative capacity either in government or industry. For some time, however, this rule was subject to wholesale violation. Military government officers often allowed former Nazis to hold important posts on the ground that they were the only persons available with the requisite experience. Or reactionaries close to the old regime were utilized because some American officers were reluctant to employ trade unionists or Socialists. This situation led to a showdown in October, 1945, when strict orders were issued for a thoroughgoing purge of Nazi sympathizers.

The occupying powers sought to inculcate democracy by extending freedom of the press, of speech, and of religion. Schools were reopened with denazified teaching staffs and books. Once again German political parties of various shades of opinion found themselves free to operate. Elections to local councils took place in the American zone in January, 1946, while elections to higher representative bodies were conducted later in the year. But Soviet and French opposition led to delay in setting up any German-staffed administration for the whole country. The practical effect of the occupation policies was to divide the Reich into four almost completely separate countries, thus adding greatly to the problem of economic reconstruction.

The Potsdam Declaration had called not only for the complete dismantling of the German armament, aircraft, and shipbuilding industries, but for drastic reductions in such potentially dangerous fields as steel and chemicals. It had also been agreed that the Reich's factories and machinery should be available for removal as reparations. Serious controversy arose as to how this should be done. Since Germany with its new boundaries would be unable to feed itself, a minimum of industrial production for export would have to be permitted in order to pay for essential imports. Russia argued for reducing German potential to the lowest possible level, regardless of the effect; the British, desperately needing a market in Germany, urged a measure of leniency. American experts differed on the problem, but the tendency was for the American government to take a middle position.

On one proposition there was substantial agreement: the punishment of German war criminals. Such Nazi ringleaders as Hitler, Himmler, and Goebbels cheated the gallows by commiting suicide, but Goering and some twenty other German leaders were the defendants in a unique trial opening at Nuremberg in November, 1945. On the bench sat an international military tribunal of distinguished jurists from the Big-Four powers; the same nations were represented in the corps of prosecutors. The Americans most prominent in the proceedings were former Attorney General Francis Biddle, who served as one of the judges, and Supreme Court Justice Robert H. Jackson, chief United States prosecutor. The trial established important precedents, both because of its international character and because of the charges included in the indictment. The German leaders were accused not only of violating the laws of war and humanity, but of plotting and waging aggressive war. Critics of the trial contended that this was *ex post facto* procedure—that plotting aggression had been defined as a crime after the deed was done. Justice Jackson argued, however, that since the Kellogg-Briand Pact of 1928 and other treaties had condemned recourse to war, the activities carried on by German political and military leaders had been clearly illegal. The trial lasted more than ten months and resulted in the conviction of all but three of the defendants. Eleven were sentenced to death by hanging; eight were given prison terms. Although Goering escaped execution by a last-minute suicide, the other death sentences were carried out on October 16, 1946.

Lesser criminals were also tried and punished. Thirty-six officials and guards from the infamous Dachau concentration camp were brought before an American military tribunal and condemned to death, while several German civilians who had participated in the murder of American aviators met a similar fate. In the end, nearly three hundred Germans were executed for war cimes by United States authorities.

Occupation Problems: Japan

The postwar situation in Japan differed from that in Germany in certain important particulars. In the first place, the surrender negotiations had resulted in an Allied agreement to retain the emperor and govern through him, with the eventual decision regarding his status being left to the Japanese people. Secondly, Japan was occupied for the most part by American forces, and American officials had the principal authority in formulating occupation policy.

As Supreme Allied Commander, General Douglas MacArthur exercised enormous powers over the defeated enemy. During the crucial first weeks of the occupation, this authority was controlled only by MacArthur's superiors in Washington. The protests of Russia and other Allies resulted in some modification of the situation by the end of 1945. The foreign ministers of the Big-Three powers, meeting in Moscow in December, agreed to the establishment of a Far Eastern Commission composed of representatives of eleven nations. This body with its headquarters in Washington could formulate principles to govern the control of Japan. Another group, the Allied Council, with representatives of the United States, the Soviet Union, China, and the British Commonwealth, was to sit in Tokyo to advise the Supreme Commander on the spot. But the terms of the Moscow agreement were so drawn as to leave the substance of power still very largely in American hands.

MacArthur acted speedily to dissolve the Imperial General Staff and to demobilize the army. The jingoistic Black Dragon society was liquidated, and the Japanese press was freed from Japanese censorship, although subjected to American controls. Political prisoners were released and civil liberties proclaimed. The secret police was abolished. No elaborate system of military government comparable to that in Germany was set up. MacArthur with a relatively small corps of advisers operated through directives to the emperor and the Japanese cabinet.

Japanese political institutions were substantially altered by a new constitution, drafted with MacArthur's approval in March, 1946. This defined the emperor's power as derived from "the sovereign will of the people," and required the advice and approval of the cabinet for all acts of the emperor in matters of state. The Diet, elected by universal suffrage, was to appoint the premier and the Supreme Court, as well as to exercise supreme legislative power. The new document renounced war and the use of force and forbade the maintenance of an army, navy, or air force.

In other particulars the treatment of Japan followed the German precedent more closely. Similar provision was made for collecting reparations by confiscating external assets and removing factories and machinery. The arrest and trial of war criminals were likewise stipulated. American military tribunals tried Generals Yamashita and Homa and ordered their execution after hearing testimony of Japanese atrocities in the Philippines under the defendants' commands. Numerous lesser criminals were punished, while former Premier Tojo and other major leaders were brought before a special international tribunal like that at Nuremberg, which imposed the death penalty.

The Iron Curtain

The defeat of the Axis had for the time being ended all threat of aggression from Germany and Japan, but grave new problems arose out of the power vacuum left by these two great nations. With France and Britain too much weakened by the war to play the important part in world politics that they had in earlier generations, only two major powers remained: Soviet Russia and the United States.

Neither the American people nor their government at first realized the full implications of the new situation. They had renounced isolation to be sure, but they were thinking of American participation in world affairs as confined largely to temporary occupation duties in the defeated countries and long-range co-operation with the UN. Under clamorous pressure to "Bring Daddy Home," American forces were withdrawn from distant bases and demobilized at a rapid rate. The army and navy that totaled over 12 million men in June, 1945, had shrunk to about 2 million men a year later.

As the American turtle withdrew into its shell, its Russian counterpart stretched out its neck more and more boldly. Even before Roosevelt died, he and Churchill protested to Stalin against imposing a Communist government in Poland in violation of the Yalta pledge that there would be "free and un-fettered elections." What happened in Poland was only one in a chain of simi-lar episodes. Taking full advantage of European chaos, the Soviet Union moved steadily to expand its influence by incorporating the prewar Baltic states and part of Poland within its own boundaries, and by supporting Communist or pro-Russian regimes in the neighboring states of eastern Europe and the Bal-kans. The United States protested repeatedly against the undemocratic charac-ter of these governments and their violation of American property rights.

Similar concern was aroused over Soviet policy in other parts of the world. The Russians were accused of using their occupation of Germany and Austria to promote the interests of local Communist parties, of seeking to coerce Tur-key into surrendering control of the Dardanelles, and of intriguing in the poli-tics of Iran and other Middle Eastern countries. Suspicion extended to the Far East, where the Soviet shadow fell menacingly over China, Manchuria, and Korea.

Even the rapidly accumulating evidence of Russian imperialism failed to im-press many Americans, who were reluctant to believe that their recent ally was engaged in anything more sinister than defensive steps based upon an exag-gerated estimate of her security needs. American public opinion at first gave a rather tepid response to Winston Churchill's grim warning during a speech at Fulton, Missouri, in March, 1946. "From Stettin in the Baltic to Trieste in the Adriatic," Churchill declared, "an iron curtain has descended across the conti-nent." Condemning the "police governments" of the Russian sphere, he called for Anglo-American cooperation against the growing menace.

President Truman, who had been present when Churchill made his Iron Curtain speech, needed little convincing of the need for stronger resistance to Communist expansion. The experience of the American government in attempting to negotiate with the Soviet Union on a variety of issues had been a continuing disillusionment. Throughout 1946 and early 1947 events moved relentlessly toward the formation of two hostile camps in world politics: one centered around the Soviet Union, the other around the United States.

Diplomatic Bickering

Drafting peace treaties in this atmosphere was a long and arduous task. Throughout 1946 the foreign ministers of the victorious powers struggled with the drafting of treaties for Italy, Bulgaria, Rumania, Hungary, and Finland. Three questions aroused particular controversy: the disposition of the Italian colonial empire; the rival claims of Italy and Yugoslavia to Trieste and Venezia Giulia; and the control of navigation on the Danube. Each issue involved the relations of the Soviet Union and the Western powers. The colonial problem was compromised fairly early by agreement that the colonies should continue under British administration for one year and that their final status should be determined by the Big Four or by the UN Assembly if the Big Four were unable to agree. The debate over Trieste provoked the greatest bitterness. Control over this strategic port was regarded as vital by both the Russian and the anti-Russian blocs. Final agreement provided for the establishment of a Free Territory of Trieste and its immediate environs under a governor responsible to the UN Security Council, while most of Venezia Giulia was to be ceded by Italy to Yugoslavia.[7] The United States put up a strong fight for the principle of free navigation of the Danube; the Russians opposed this as a covert form of economic imperialism. In the end the United States succeeded in having the free navigation principle written into the treaties.

In his long struggle with the Russian diplomats, Secretary of State Byrnes counted heavily on the support of Senators Connally and Vandenberg, who accompanied him to all the important conferences. Thus did the Truman administration seek to ensure itself against any repetition of Wilson's unhappy experiences with the Senate.

Bipartisan support for Byrnes did not mean that his activities escaped criticism. In a speech at New York in September, 1946, Secretary of Commerce Wallace condemned those who would base American policy on "getting tough" with Russia and expressed his conviction that the United States had no more business in the political affairs of Eastern Europe than Russia had in the West or in the Americas. Wallace's words were resented by Byrnes, Connally, and Vandenberg as an intolerable criticism of their efforts at a time when critical negotiations were in progress. Faced with the unhappy alternative of choosing between his Secretary of State and his Secretary of Commerce, President Tru-

---

[7] By direct negotiations between Yugoslavia and Italy, the Free Territory of Trieste was partitioned between the two in 1954.

man asked for Wallace's resignation—despite the embarrassing fact that the President had previously given the Wallace speech his public approval.

The completion of the satellite treaties cleared the way for consideration of the future of Germany and Austria. The Big Four foreign ministers met for this purpose at Moscow in March, 1947. By this time poor health had caused Byrnes to resign as Secretary of State and the burden of speaking for the United States fell upon his successor, General George C. Marshall. After forty-six days the conference broke up without agreeing on either a German or an Austrian treaty. Among the controversies that led to this deadlock, the reparations issue was the most important. As compensation for the unparalleled damage wrought by the Nazis on Russian soil, the Soviets demanded $10 billion. Since the Potsdam formula for payment through the seizure of external assets and industrial equipment would not cover so large a bill, the Russians asked for payment in goods produced by German industry. The American and British delegations opposed this because it would so burden German economy that the population would be unable to pay for essential food imports. Another source of controversy was the form of government to be permitted in Germany. Marshall advocated a federal republic with a very weak central government, while the Russians, fearing that this would open the way for attaching the industrially rich western parts of Germany to an anti-Russian bloc in western Europe, insisted upon a centralized government. The Secretary of State bluntly stated his suspicion of this proposal in a subsequent radio address to the American people:

> Agreement was made impossible because the Soviet Union insisted upon proposals which would have established in Germany a centralized government, adapted to the seizure of absolute control of a country which would be doomed economically through inadequate area and excessive population and would be mortgaged to turn over a large part of its production as reparations.

Thus mutual suspicion had made it impossible to map out the future of Germany. Yet until a German treaty was completed, order and security could hardly be restored in Europe.

Frustrations in the United Nations

When the UN began operations, most Americans still hoped that the One World ideal of World War II days could be achieved. To the organization meeting at London in January, 1946, the United States sent a distinguished delegation composed of Secretary of State Byrnes, former Secretary Stettinius, Senators Connally and Vandenberg, and Mrs. Eleanor Roosevelt. American interest in the new experiment was intensified when the Security Council began the continuous functioning for which the Charter provided. First in temporary

New York quarters, and later in the beautiful buildings constructed in New York City on an East River site contributed by John D. Rockefeller, Jr., the UN sessions became a favorite spectacle for sightseers.

The Headquarters of the United Nations
in New York City. (United Nations.)

Despite this hopeful beginning, the UN was at once dangerously involved in the great contest for power between the Soviet Union on one side and the United States on the other. Russian diplomats condemned the evidences of British imperialism that they professed to see in Syria, Indonesia, and Greece, while Britain and the United States denounced Soviet conduct in Iran. This last problem assumed explosive proportions when the Iranian government protested to the Council over continued occupation of northern Iran by Russian troops, in violation of a treaty under which British, American, and Soviet forces were all to be withdrawn by March, 1946. Russia objected to consideration of the dispute on the ground that it was a matter for direct settlement between the two parties. When her request for posponement was voted down, Soviet Representative Gromyko walked out of the Security Council and refused to attend subsequent sessions in which the issue was discussed. Undeterred by this gesture of Russian displeasure, Secretary Byrnes strongly upheld the right of Iran and other small nations to be heard before the Council. Tension subsided when Soviet troops were at length withdrawn and outstanding controversies between Russia and Iran were compromised in an agreement negotiated directly by the two countries.

Those interested in the success of the UN felt encouraged by the outcome of the Iranian episode, which seemed to suggest that the mobilization of world opinion through the new organization might serve to protect small nations against the aggressive designs of powerful neighbors. The UN also helped in settling other troublesome issues. When the newly founded state of Israel became involved in war with her Arab neighbors in 1948, hostilities were finally terminated through the skillful efforts of the UN mediator, Ralph Bunche, an American Negro. The world organization similarly employed its good offices in mediating between the Netherlands government and its recently emancipated colony, the Republic of Indonesia. Optimists could also obtain comfort from the progress made in many non-political UN activities: the negotiation of international agreements outlawing genocide (race-murder) and defining basic human rights, the study of international economic problems, the promotion of cultural exchange, the control of trade in narcotics, and the provision of emergency aid for afflicted children in backward countries.

All such UN success was overshadowed, however, by increasing evidence of conflict between the Communist bloc and the Western powers. By the end of 1950 the Soviet Union had employed its Security Council veto fifty times; when the Council instituted discussions that could not be vetoed, Russian delegates resorted to boycotts, sometimes absenting themselves from deliberations for many weeks. The Soviet Union refused to participate in the Food and Agriculture Organization, the International Bank, and several other UN agencies. Russian obstructionism prevented the organization of the UN military force provided for in the Charter.

The Problem of Disarmament

Among the problems with which the UN struggled, none was more significant than that of mounting armaments. Heavy military expenditures were a burden upon the world economy, and the development of new weapons monopolized the efforts of scientists and engineers to the exclusion of more constructive tasks. Most serious of all, the development of the atomic bomb was a warning that, unless controlled, the new means of destruction might wipe out the human race.

The United States made an earnest effort to safeguard the world from the horrors of nuclear warfare. At the opening session of the UN Atomic Energy Commission in June, 1946, Bernard Baruch presented the American proposal for the establishment of an international authority to control all atomic-energy activities potentially dangerous to world security. The atomic bomb itself should be outlawed, and the international authority should have power to punish violations of the agreement. The United States promised to stop manufacturing bombs, dispose of its stock of bombs, and make available its scientific information, but only after the international authority was in effective operation. The choice, as Baruch grimly presented it, was between "World Peace or World Destruction."

To most nations, the American offer to lay aside the terrible new weapon seemed generous indeed, but the Soviet Union viewed it with great suspicion. She opposed the broad international control advocated by the Baruch Plan and particularly the stipulation that no veto of the acts of the new atomic authority should be permitted. The first Russian counterproposal was for a simple renunciation of atomic weapons by all the powers without provision for international controls or inspection. In subsequent UN debates the Russian position changed somewhat: the need of an international authority and some form of international inspection was conceded. But fundamental differences remained. The Soviet government insisted that, as a prerequisite to international control, atomic bombs should be prohibited by international treaty and all atomic energy plants turned over to international management. The United States refused to take such steps until the system of international control had actually been made effective. The United States wanted the international authority's power of inspection to be broad and exempt from veto; the Russians wanted to define it more narrowly. Finally and most important, the United States asserted that once a treaty had been approved, there should be no legal right, by veto or otherwise, whereby a willful violater could escape punishment. The Russians wanted to retain enforcement within the framework of the Security Council where each of the Big Five representatives had a veto.

Meanwhile, negotiations for a general disarmament marked time. By unanimous agreement in December, 1946, the UN Assembly accepted a sweeping resolution calling for the formulation of practical measures for disarmament to be submitted to a special Assembly session, for the elimination of atomic and other weapons of mass destruction, for international inspection and safeguards against violations of disarmament agreements, for the speedy establishment of an international police force, for balanced withdrawal of troops stationed in ex-enemy countries, and for the progressive reduction of national armed forces. But disagreement developed over the steps to implement these pledges. The Soviet government wanted to consider the atomic energy problem as simply one phase of the whole problem of disarmament; the United States insisted that the atomic energy issue must have priority. Whatever the relative merits of these two lines of procedure, it was obvious that no realistic disarmament could be achieved until Russia and America worked out their differences, not only on the problem of the bomb but on other issues as well.

The Truman Doctrine

Growing concern was felt in Britain and the United States as more and more of Europe fell under control of pro-Russian governments. By the spring of 1947 these included Finland, Poland, Hungary, Czechoslovakia, Yugoslavia, Rumania, and Bulgaria, as well as Russian occupation zones in Germany and Austria. In Italy and France, moreover, there were large and powerful Communist parties.

Greece had an anti-Communist government, but its hold upon the country was insecure. Economic conditions were desperately bad, and numerous guerrillas, particularly in northern Greece, were attempting to overthrow the royalist regime. It was feared that a rebel victory would extend Russian influence over yet another country and one of critical importance because of its position near the strategic Dardanelles and the oil-rich Middle East. Britain under Churchill had undertaken a policy of providing military and economic support to the threatened regime, and the succeeding Labor government continued this policy.

But in March, 1947, a crisis developed. England's own economic position was so precarious that her statesmen decided she must withdraw her help from Greece at the end of the month. The Truman administration decided to take over the responsibility. On March 12 the President asked Congress to approve a $400 million program of economic and military aid not only for Greece, but for Turkey as well. The request had broad implications as the President gravely acknowledged. In what was promptly dubbed the "Truman Doctrine," he said:

> I believe that it must be the policy of the United States to support free peoples who are resisting attempted subjugation by armed minorities or by outside pressures.
> I believe that we must assist free peoples to work out their own destinies in their own way.
> I believe that our help should be primarily through economic and financial aid which is essential to economic stability and orderly political processes.

Not since Pearl Harbor had there been such widespread controversy over American policy as the Truman Doctrine provoked. Many Americans supported it strongly as a much needed step toward checking the expansion of Soviet influence. Others criticized it as a form of economic imperialism, an interference with the domestic affairs of other nations, and the beginning of a dangerous adventure in power politics that might end in war. It was asserted that this attempt to safeguard democracy was being made by governments that were themselves antidemocratic. Henry Wallace, no longer in public office, was the sharpest critic of the new policy.

Many who did not go as far as Wallace did regretted that the United States had taken unilateral action without at least attempting to utilize the machinery of the UN. Truman defended himself on the ground that the UN was not yet equipped to deal with such problems, and Warren Austin, the United States representative on the Security Council, argued that the American action was intended to strengthen, not weaken, the principle of collective security. Nevertheless, the supporters of the program thought it best to accept the so-called Vandenberg amendment, under which Congress directed the President to withdraw any or all of the aid if the Security Council found that action by the UN made its continuance unnecessary or undesirable. The United States waived its right of veto on the issue.

After hot debate, the proposal to expend $400 million on Greek and Turkish aid was approved by Congress in May, 1947, and later appropriations made it possible to continue the policy. In many ways the Truman program achieved striking success. The Greek government was sufficiently strengthened to defeat its enemies. In October, 1949, the long civil war was finally brought to an end as a result not only of American aid, but of the action of Marshal Tito, who closed the frontier of Yugoslavia to Communist guerrillas after his break with Stalin. Furthermore, the economic rehabilitation of the ravaged country had made good progress with the repair of highways, bridges, and railroads, the resettlement of refugees, the expansion of agriculture, and a health program that reduced malaria from more than one million to less than 50,000 cases a year.

European Recovery Program

Needless to say, Greece and Turkey were not the only areas urgently needing economic assistance. At the same time that the aid plan for those two countries was adopted, Congress appropriated $350 million for relief supplies for Italy, Austria, Poland, China, Trieste, and Greece. Earlier than this, Great Britain, France, and Italy had successfully applied to American sources for postwar loans. The Soviet Union had also sought a large American credit to finance imports, but negotiations for this made no progress because of the strained relations between the two countries.

By June, 1947, it was clear that the whole question of American financial assistance to Europe and the rest of the world required review and clarification. How much would the United States need to spend for such purposes? Should its assistance be available to all European countries or only to those shunning Communism? On June 5, in an address at Harvard University, Secretary of State Marshall announced a healthy new approach to the problem:

Our policy is not directed against any country or doctrine, but against hunger, poverty, desperation and chaos. Its purpose should be the revival of a working economy in the world so as to permit the emergence of political and social conditions in which free institutions can exist. Such assistance I am convinced must not be on a piecemeal basis as various crises develop. . . . The initiative I think must come from Europe. . . . The program should be a joint one, agreed to by a number of, if not all, the European nations.

Great Britain and France accepted this suggestion with alacrity. They promptly initiated steps to formulate a broad program for European rehabilitation and urged the Soviet Union to join them in the enterprise. But Russia, feeling unable to cooperate in a project that would require the exchange of statistical information and give American capitalism a dominant position in the European economy, took a hostile stand. An invitation to a general conference of all European nations was rejected by the Soviet Union and eight of its satellites. Representatives of sixteen other countries met at Paris from July to September, 1947. Promising to help themselves as much as possible, they formulated a four-year program for European recovery that would require some $15 billion in American aid.

On the American side, the Marshall Plan was subjected to careful scrutiny. Senator Taft and certain other leaders questioned whether the United States could do what was asked without regimenting and weakening its own economy. But Congressional misgivings were largely forgotten after the Communists seized control of Czechoslovakia in February, 1948, in a coup that particularly shocked American opinion. On April 3, President Truman signed the Foreign Assistance Act of 1948, which appropriated $5.3 billion for the first year of Marshall Plan aid to sixteen European countries[8] and Western Germany, and also included additional military aid to Greece and Turkey and assistance to Nationalist China.

To head the Economic Cooperation Administration (ECA) charged by Congress with responsibility for making grants and loans under the European Recovery Program (ERP), President Truman appointed Paul G. Hoffman, the progressive president of the Studebaker Corporation. Into Europe now flowed goods vitally needed to restore the economies of the cooperating countries— grain to alleviate hunger, coal, petroleum products, cotton, and other raw materials to feed lagging industries, and machinery to increase future production. This flood of exports had, of course, a highly stimulating influence on the American economy as well.

The economic problems of Europe were serious. To the devastations of war were added exasperating difficulties growing out of the postwar situation. The

[8] They were Great Britain, France, Italy, Belgium, the Netherlands, Luxembourg, Norway, Sweden, Denmark, Austria, Greece, Portugal, Switzerland, Turkey, Ireland, and Iceland.

continuing hostility between Western Europe and Soviet-dominated Eastern Europe disrupted normal trade relations between the industrialized and the agricultural regions of the Continent. The continued partition of Germany was a disrupting factor of especial importance. To add to the trouble, independence movements in the colonial empires of Western European states reduced the flow of badly needed raw materials and revenues. All of these conditions contributed to Europe's extraordinary dependence on imports from the Western Hemisphere. Since the war-ravaged continent could produce little for export and since American tariff policy still restricted the sale of foreign goods in the United States, the problem of finding dollars to pay for imports was a most perplexing one. American aid under ERP permitted the temporary bridging of this "dollar gap," but the permanent solution of the problem depended on increasing European exports and decreasing imports until trade was in reasonable balance. This was the long-range objective of the European Recovery Program.

Optimistic Americans hoped that under the spur of necessity the nations of Western Europe might merge their economies by eliminating tariff barriers and trade quotas and adopting a uniform currency. Economic nationalism proved, however, to be too deeply rooted to permit any such immediate reforms. The various countries continued to follow policies that sometimes conflicted with the interests of their neighbors and those of Western Europe as a whole.

Despite such disappointments, ERP was on the whole a distinct success. Congress continued to support the plan, appropriating some $11 billion during the first three years of the program. A report of ECA in 1951 stressed such impressive gains as the following: over-all industrial production in Western Europe was running 40 per cent higher than in 1938; harvests were about 10 per cent above their prewar levels; economic recovery in Britain and Ireland had advanced to the point where those two nations felt able to get along without further aid.

A principal objective of American economic aid was to strengthen democratic regimes and to halt the spread of Communism. This aspect of ERP also appeared to succeed. The turning point was the Italian election of April, 1948. Backed by a militant party membership of 2.3 million—probably the largest European Communist group outside of Russia—the Italian Reds threatened to gain control of the Chamber of Deputies, or at least to make such a show of strength that they could seize power as they had only a few weeks before in Czechoslovakia. To prevent this development, American weight was thrown unhesitatingly into the balance. Secretary Marshall warned that a Communist Italy would receive no help from the ERP; Italo-Americans wrote thousands of letters to relatives and friends in the old country seeking to influence their votes. This pressure, together with the active intervention of Roman Catholic bishops and priests, resulted in a victory for the conservative de Gasperi government and a setback for the Communists. Subsequent elections in France and Western Germany marked similar checks to Communist voting strength.

Struggle for Germany

As the cold war between the Communist and anti-Communist blocs became increasingly bitter, the importance of Germany became obvious. With its large population, heavy industry, and scientific knowledge, a reunited Germany would give an overwhelming preponderance to whichever side gained its support. Throughout 1948 and early 1949 a dangerous contest to win the upper hand in Germany was in progress.

Unable to reach agreement with the Soviet Union, statesmen from Britain, France, and the United States, together with those from the Benelux countries (Belgium, the Netherlands, and Luxembourg), met in London from February to June, 1948, to break the stalemate on German policy. They decided to merge the French, British, and American occupation zones in a new West German State. To minimize the danger of future German aggression, they planned the establishment of a federal rather than a centralized government and stipulated that the strategic Ruhr industries be controlled by an International Authority. With these safeguards, the economic revival of Western Germany was to be encouraged as a necessary condition to Marshall Plan success. As a first step, the Western powers instituted currency reform by substituting new "West marks" for the almost worthless reichsmarks then flooding the country.

The Soviet government denounced these measures as contrary to the Potsdam Agreement. To counter the new currency, the Russians issued their own East marks, through whose manipulation they sought to dominate the economic life of Berlin. Then, under the pretext that the introduction of the West marks into the city made drastic control measures necessary, the Soviet authorities in April, 1948, began interfering with railroad, highway, and canal traffic from the Western occupation zones across the hundred-mile Soviet-controlled corridor to Berlin. Finally, on June 24, all traffic over that route was stopped. The probable purpose of this Berlin blockade was to exert such pressure that the Western powers would abandon their plans for a West German State and agree to unify the country on Russian terms. Failing this, the Soviet leaders hoped at least to force their rivals out of Berlin. If the Russians could win undisputed control of the historic capital, it would give them a great psychological advantage in the struggle for all Germany.

Within the three Western sectors of Berlin, more than two million persons, now deprived of essential food and fuel, looked to the Western powers for help. A counterblockade of the Soviet zone was promptly imposed. Much more spectacular, however, was the organization of a gigantic effort to supply Berlin by air. Pressing into use every available cargo plane, courageous pilots carried into the city some 4,000 tons of food and other necessities each day.

At first few observers believed that the airlift could long succeed. It was regarded as a makeshift, pending some diplomatic solution of the controversy. A few impatient Americans called for military action to convoy trains and highway caravans into the city, but responsible statesmen ruled out any step that might plunge the world into war. Instead, the airlift was continued week after week with increasing effectiveness. Despite predictions that bad flying weather and heavy coal loads would defeat the operation during the winter, the flights continued successfully.

The arduous service of the airlift pilots won an important victory for the Western powers. Instead of demonstrating to the hapless Berliners their dependence on Russia, the blockade intensified the anti-Communist feeling of all Germans not under Soviet control and impressed them with the determination of the Western powers to resist coercion. Recognizing the failure of its policy, the Soviet government finally lifted the blockade on May 12, 1949, after secret discussions with American officials.[9] The Western powers thereupon agreed to a new conference of the Big Four foreign ministers on the whole German problem. But this meeting was no more successful than earlier ones in solving the problem.

Plans for the West German State continued to go forward. From September, 1948, to May, 1949, delegates from the three Western zones met at Bonn to frame a constitution. The original members of the federal republic were to be the eleven states included within the British, French, and American zones, but provision was made for the admission of others in the hope that the five states of the Soviet zone would eventually join. The relations of the new West German State with Britain, France, and the United States were defined in an Occupation Statute. Occupation troops were to remain in their three respective zones, but Allied military government was to be replaced by an Allied High Commission, composed of civilians.

To counter the establishment of this West German State—officially known as the Federal Republic of Germany—the Communists of the Soviet occupation zone proclaimed a German Democratic Republic, with its capital at Berlin. The effect of four years of military occupation was thus to divide Germany into two nations, each desirous of absorbing the other on its own terms. Although the West German State had more than twice the population of its rival, as well as much greater resources in coal, steel plants, and other industries, the East German State was not without advantages of its own. More than half of

---

[9] During the course of the airlift, Western pilots made 277,264 flights to Berlin and carried 2,343,315 tons of necessities to the inhabitants.

the prewar German food production came from this area. Moreover, a government with its capital at Berlin had important advantages in appealing to German nationalism.

The longer tension persisted between the Soviet Union and the Western democracies, the more each side modified its German policy. No longer was the principal objective that of keeping the former enemy weak and incapable of military action. Instead, the major consideration was how German resources and manpower might be brought to bear in a future conflict between the East and the West. In this dangerous game of wooing the Germans, the Soviet occupation authorities played one card by granting a general amnesty to former Nazis and officers of Hitler's army, while the Western policymakers played another by curtailing their program for dismantling German war industries. In the Soviet zone the core of a future East German army was created through the organization of an efficient, well-armed, and thoroughly loyal Communist police force of some 50,000 men. This development stimulated American officials to discuss openly the advisability of permitting the rearmament of the West German State.

Senators Arthur Vandenberg and Tom Connally Conferring with
Secretary of State Dean Acheson. (World Wide Photos.)

Defense in the West

Believing that democratic failure to make a united stand had been an important cause of World War II, Western statesmen attempted to avoid the same error in dealing with the new Communist imperialism. In January, 1948, Great Britain gave up its traditional effort to maintain a free hand in dealing with continental European affairs and offered to enter a defensive union with its neighbors across the Channel. The February coup of the Communists in Czechoslovakia added urgency to the British overture, and in March, 1948, the foreign ministers of Britain, France, and the Benelux countries signed a fifty year military and economic assistance treaty at Brussels.

Realists both in Europe and America realized that the Brussels Pact was only a first step toward adequate security. Whether united or divided, Western Europe was indefensible against Soviet armed attack without strong help from America. Would the United States complete its renunciation of isolationism by promising to aid foreign nations resisting aggression? To be sure, a general obligation of this character had been undertaken in the United Nations Charter, but Soviet obstructionism had made the UN an uncertain factor in international affairs. The Senate acknowledged that something more was needed when, on June 11, 1948, it adopted by a 64 to 4 vote a resolution offered by Senator Vandenberg, authorizing the government to develop collective defense arrangements within the UN Charter and to associate the United States with them. Although the issue was somewhat overshadowed by the presidential campaign during the latter half of 1948, the blockade of Berlin and other Communist activities made the need for a Western defense system more and more obvious. President Truman, in his inaugural address, pledged his second administration to this objective.

Such were the circumstances behind the negotiation of the North Atlantic Treaty, signed at Washington on April 4, 1949. The twelve signatory nations[10] agreed

> that an armed attack against one or more of them in Europe or North America shall be considered an attack against all of them and that in the exercise of the right of individual or collective self-defense, recognized by Article 51 of the United Nations Charter, they will take such action as deemed necessary, including the use of armed force, to restore and maintain the security of the North Atlantic area. The attack and counter-measures shall immediately be reported to the United Nations Security Council, and action shall be terminated when the Council has taken measures to restore international peace.

Although care had been taken to reconcile the new pact with the UN Charter, many Americans regretted the treaty as a step toward substituting regional de-

[10] United States, Canada, Great Britain, France, Belgium, the Netherlands, Luxembourg, Norway, Denmark, Iceland, Italy, and Portugal.

fense arrangements for the general security of a world organization. From another point of view, the treaty was criticized by Senator Taft and other Republicans who disapproved the implied obligation to supply arms to the new allies. But ratification was strongly urged by such Republican Senators as Vandenberg and Dulles. On July 21, 1949, the Senate finally approved the North Atlantic Treaty by a vote of 82 to 13.

As predicted, the next urgent question was that of supplying American arms to the other members of the North Atlantic Treaty Organization (NATO). Although many legislators were dismayed by the prospect of new expenditures and enlarged power for the President, the pressure of world events crumpled all opposition. President Truman's announcement on September 23, 1949, that Russia also possessed the secret of the atomic bomb shattered any illusion that American monopoly of this weapon was a sufficient guarantee against Soviet attack. On September 27 both Houses of Congress passed by heavy majorities the Mutual Defense Assistance Act, authorizing expenditures of $1 billion for arming Western Europe and $314 million for threatened areas elsewhere.

The first shipments of American arms reached France and Italy in April, 1950, without serious incident, despite Communist threats to halt their movement through strikes and sabotage. Throughout 1950 Communist tactics featured "peace congresses" and "peace petitions" to convince the peoples of Western Europe that the Soviet Union had no aggressive designs and that "capitalist warmongers" in the United States were the real threat to world peace. Such propaganda was not without its appeal to war-weary peoples fearful lest their countries once again become the battleground of the nations.

Despite these obstacles, plans for the defense of Western Europe became more definite during 1950 and 1951. In September, 1950, the North Atlantic Council announced its decision to create "in the shortest possible time, an integrated military force adequate for the defense of the freedom of Europe." Two months later General Eisenhower was appointed NATO Supreme Commander.

Plans for the defense of the North Atlantic area largely hinged on the extent to which the allies could count upon the resources and manpower of West Germany. Secretary Acheson urged the recruitment of ten German divisions for the Atlantic Pact army, but this proposal was strongly opposed in France, where memories of three German invasions within a period of seventy years were still vivid. Alternative plans that would have dispersed German combat units through the NATO army were rejected by the Adenauer government, which was reluctant to rearm unless German nationalism was satisfied through the creation of German divisions. The West German government was in the advantageous position of being asked to rearm and being able to exact concessions from the victorious powers. This problem was still unresolved when the Truman administration ended, but certain intermediate steps had been taken. In October, 1951, Congress passed a resolution declaring an end to the state of war between the United States and Germany. In 1952 the Bonn government was granted almost complete sovereignty. Formal military occupation by American, British, and French troops was ended, although the Western powers continued, with Bonn's consent, to keep troops at German bases as a deterrent to Russian aggression.

Strange Bedfellows

The efforts of the United States to check Soviet imperialism brought a change of policy toward two other European countries. Although Yugoslavia was one of the nations where the Communists seized power after World War II, Marshal Tito, the local Communist leader, proved much less manageable than puppet heads in other Soviet-dominated countries. The Cominform—the Communist International in its postwar reincarnation—denounced Tito in an obvious attempt to overthrow his leadership. Despite hostile propaganda, trade boycotts, and threats of war, Tito clung to power and maintained the independence of his country. The American government encouraged Tito's defiance through trade deals and relief to prevent famine. Although aid to Yugoslavia had obvious advantages in preventing complete Russian domination of the Balkans and in encouraging defiance of Moscow by other Communist regimes, the policy did not escape criticism by Americans who condemned the Tito government as both totalitarian and antireligious. Even more sharply criticized was the trend toward closer American relations with Spain, where the notorious General Franco, once the protégé of Mussolini and Hitler, still maintained a dictatorial regime. Once again the desire of the United States to strengthen the defense of Europe against Soviet aggression overrode objections to helping an antidemocratic government to survive.

In Latin America, too, the United States had to choose between greater and lesser evils. During World War II Argentina, from the point of view of the United States, behaved very badly. While the other Latin-American states gave moral and material support to the UN cause by declaring war, curbing Axis activities, and supplying strategic materials, Argentina refused to cooperate. A fierce competitor with the United States in agricultural exports and jealous of the North American nation's leading role in hemisphere affairs, she had become strongly nationalistic. Many of her wealthy leaders believed in totalitarian government and sympathized with the Axis.

Fear of economic sanctions by the United States and Great Britain did induce President Pedro Ramirez to sever relations with Germany in January,

1944, but this step proved unpopular with the Argentine military. Toward the end of February, the so-called Colonels' Clique overthrew Ramirez and placed Edelmiro Farrell in the presidency, with the real power in the hands of Colonel Juan Perón. The United States refused to recognize this new regime and later withdrew its ambassador, froze Argentine credits, and barred American ships from Argentine ports.

All the republics except Argentina were represented at a conference held in anticipation of the approaching end of the war at Mexico City in February and March, 1945. Here was framed the Act of Chapultepec, which read in part:

> That every attack of a State against the integrity or the inviolability of the territory or against the sovereignty or political independence of an American State, shall . . . be considered as an act of aggression against the other States which sign this act. . . .
> That in case acts of aggression occur, or there may be reasons to believe that an aggression is being prepared by any other State against . . . an American State, the States signatory to this act will consult amongst themselves in order to agree upon the measures it may be advisable to take.

Since the act covered aggression both from without and within the hemisphere, it was interpreted as being largely directed against Argentina. Moreover, the willingness of other American states to rely upon the army and navy of the United States indicated that the old fear of *Yanqui* imperialism was largely gone.

The Mexico City conference also provided for cooperation in the postwar period and support of the proposed United Nations. Although Argentina's recent pro-Axis policies were deplored, the door was left open for her to resume her place in the hemisphere family by declaring war against the Axis and approving the conference resolutions. These steps the Farrell-Perón government took in a last-minute effort to escape from its isolated position. Despite Soviet objections, the United States thereupon obtained a place for Argentina among the charter members of the UN.

Events during the succeeding months gave the United States reason to doubt the sincerity of Argentina's conversion. The Perón regime continued its undemocratic policies and took no effective steps to prevent Axis exiles from finding a haven on Argentine soil. The United States consequently reverted to a policy of throwing its weight against the dominant faction. The high point of this campaign was reached in February, 1946, when the American government made clear its hope that Perón would be defeated in his attempt to win the Argentine presidency. A "Blue Book" released by the State Department provided damning evidence of the pro-Axis course that Perón and his associates had followed so long as it seemed safe to do so. Despite this record, however, the South American strong man obtained a decisive victory at the polls.

There followed a long debate as to the future course that the United States should take. One State Department faction advocated continuing the anti-Perón policy; another favored acceptance of Perón in order to bring Argentina once again into full participation in inter-American affairs. The latter point of view eventually prevailed: in June, 1947, President Truman announced that the United States was now satisfied with Argentina's compliance with the anti-Nazi provisions of the Act of Chapultepec and was ready to include her in discussions for a Western Hemisphere defense pact.

On September 2, 1947, Argentina and eighteen other American states, including the United States, signed the Treaty of Rio de Janeiro. Implementing the Act of Chapuletpec, this Rio Pact stated that an armed attack on any American nation would be considered an attack on all American states. The signatories undertook to go to the assistance of the victim of aggression in conformity with Article 51 of the UN Charter, which recognized the right of individual or collective self-defense.

A further step of integration was taken at the Inter-American Conference held at Bogotá, Colombia, during the spring of 1948. Here was drafted the Bogotá Charter, establishing the Organization of American States (OAS). Provision was also made for regular Inter-American conferences and consultations of foreign ministers, for an Advisory Committee, and for a Council of the Organization, consisting of one representative from each of the twenty-one member states, with headquarters at Washington. The OAS as a whole was integrated with the UN as one of the regional associations provided for in the UN Charter.

As the United States government swallowed its distaste for Perón and sought to integrate Argentina into its Western Hemisphere defense plans, it was more obvious than ever that American foreign policy had undergone a significant reorientation, being primarily shaped now by fear of Communism rather than of Fascism.

Troubles in Asia

The principle of "containment," upon which the Truman administration had based its policy toward the Soviet Union,[11] was much more difficult to apply in Asia than in Europe. In the West there were old, established democratic states, which, even though weakened by war, could be used as bastions of a defense system. In the East, all was in flux. The old militaristic Japan had been destroyed, and no one yet knew just what the new Japan would be like. China, freed from the grip of Japanese invaders, was now tragically involved in

---

11 The word first came to public attention in an article attributed to "X," in *Foreign affairs* in July, 1947. The anonymous author was well known to be George F. Kennan, a member of the State Department. He wrote that "the main element of any United States policy toward the Soviet Union must be that of a long-term, patient but firm and vigilant containment of Russian expansive tendencies."

a renewal of the civil war between the Nationalists and the Communists. Elsewhere the vast populations that had been under colonial rule were demanding and achieving independence.

Fortunately for the United States, the decision to grant independence to the Philippines had already been made before World War II, and it was possible to carry the policy through with a minium of the bad feeling that accompanied the separation of the European nations from their Asiatic colonies. On July 4, 1946, President Truman formally recognized the independence of the Philippines as a separate and self-governing nation. The new republic readily agreed to maintain close relations with the United States. Under a 99-year agreement made in 1947, the Filipinos consented to the continuance of American military and naval bases in the islands.

Most of the other Asiatic nations, however, followed the example of India in resisting close ties with either the Communist or anti-Communist blocs. Jealous of their recently achieved independence and fearing a revival of Western imperialism as much as they did Soviet aggression, they clung to a policy of neutrality.

What happened in China was particularly unwelcome to American opinion. Under the Yalta agreement, the Soviet Union was to enter the war against Japan and take over certain Japanese privileges in Manchuria as compensation. As a result of this arrangement, the Russians were able to arrange matters so that most of the captured Japanese war material fell into the hands of Chinese Communists rather than their Nationalist rivals. This was only one of many factors in the situation tending to strengthen the Reds and weaken Chiang Kai-shek in the months immediately following World War II.

The Truman administration believed that continued civil war not only would be a tragedy for the Chinese, but would threaten the peace of the world if the United States and the Soviet Union became involved in aiding the two factions. In December, 1945, Truman sent General Marshall as a special envoy to China to attempt to mediate between the warring factions. For a time it seemed that he would be able to persuade them to stop fighting and form an all-party government, but in the end any such compromise proved unacceptable to the extremists in both camps.

In January, 1947, the United States terminated its mediation efforts and withdrew virtually all of the 12,000 American military personnel that had been kept in China since VJ day. Although determined not to risk American troops in the Chinese caldron, the Truman administration still helped the battered Nationalist forces with arms and supplies.

The war continued to go badly for the Nationalists, and in 1949 their whole front collapsed. Driven from one temporary capital after another, the Chiang regime finally abandoned the mainland in December, 1949, and established itself on the island of Formosa. Virtually all of China thus fell under the rule of Mao Tze-tung.

The collapse of Nationalist China posed problems of fundamental importance to the Truman administration. Should the United States increase its assistance to Chiang, supply more arms and technical aid, and even send American troops to defend Formosa and help reconquer the mainland? Such was the policy advocated by certain influential Congressmen and publishers, together with the so-called China lobby—a somewhat mysterious, but apparently well-financed pressure group. Or would the United States accept the finality of the Communist victory, recognize Mao's government, let it represent China in the UN, and hope that Chinese nationalism would prevent Red China from becoming completely subservient to Moscow? This was the policy favored by the British government, which recognized the Communists soon after Mao completed his conquest of the mainland.

Reassessing its China policy during the Nationalist debacle, the Truman administration decided against both alternatives. A voluminous White Paper, issued by the State Department in August, 1949, revealed the discouraging record of American efforts to aid Chiang Kai-shek and bring an end to the civil war. Between 1945 and 1949 the United States had given $3 billion worth of assistance to the Chinese Nationalists, but this had been largely wasted through the inefficiency and corruption of the Chiang government. A major share of the American arms was easily captured by the Communists. The Chiang regime, moreover, stubbornly resisted American political and military advice and suggestions for reform. On the basis of this experience, Truman decided against further aid to the Nationalists and rejected Republican suggestions that American troops be sent to help defend Formosa. On the other hand, the administration refused to recognize the Chinese Communist government. Any inclination that might have been felt to follow the British example was killed by the unfriendliness of the Chinese Reds, who declined to exchange ambassadors with Britain, seized American consular property, and signed a treaty of alliance with the Soviet Union. Persisting in a policy of non-recognition, the United States took the lead in opposing all suggestions that China's seat in the UN be transferred to the Communist government.

The Communist victory in China was a staggering setback for the anti-Communist cause. Was the disaster inevitable, or could it have been prevented by greater foresight and wisdom? The Republicans blamed the Democrats for what had happened. The mischief, they alleged, had begun with Roosevelt's folly at Yalta; it had been continued by the blindness of Truman, Marshall, and Acheson in failing to recognize the seriousness of the Communist threat in China and withholding from Chiang full American support. The Democrats deplored what had happened, but argued that the United States had given

Chiang as much aid as it could, short of an all-out military effort that the American people would not have supported. They insisted that the Nationalists had been largely responsible for their own defeat.

War in Korea

On June 25, 1950, the most serious international crisis since the end of World War II suddenly developed with the invasion of South Korea by the Communist armies of North Korea. The existence of these two Korean states was another unfortunate result of Soviet-American hostility. Korea, liberated in 1945 after thirty-five years of Japanese rule, had been divided into two occupation zones. Soviet troops occupied the country north of the thirty-eighth parallel; United States troops occupied the area to the south. As in Germany, mutual suspicion of the occupying powers led to the establishment of two governments, each claiming to be the legal authority for the whole nation. The South Korean government, headed by Syngman Rhee, was established under the observation of a UN committee and therefore possessed superior credentials in all but Communist eyes. By July, 1949, the Soviet Union and the United States had both withdrawn their occupation troops, but they continued to give aid and advice to the two Korean governments.

Under these circumstances, the North Korean invasion across the thirty-eighth parallel was a particularly flagrant defiance of the United Nations. The Truman administration had to decide quickly whether the United States should stand aside and allow South Korea to defend itself as best it could, or take the lead in proposing strong UN countermeasures. On the very day of the North Korean invasion, the Security Council by a vote of 9 to 0, with Yugoslavia abstaining, adopted a resolution proposed by the United States, condemning the North Korean action and calling for withdrawal of North Korean forces. Ironically, a Soviet boycott of the Council on the China issue made it possible for this important action to be taken without a Russian veto.

But news from the Korean battlefields soon demonstrated that no paper declaration could save the South Korean Republic. Well disciplined and well equipped with Russian guns and tanks, the Communist armies rapidly overran the South Korean defenses. If aggression were to be repelled, it would require the use of American arms. On June 27, 1950, President Truman announced that he had ordered the United States air and sea forces to support the hard-pressed armies of the invaded country. He also announced a significant change in American policy toward Formosa. Since Communist seizure of that island would threaten United States forces in Korea, he ordered the Seventh Fleet to neutralize the area by preventing both Communist attacks on the island and Nationalist forays against the mainland. Once again the United States was firmly supported by the UN Security Council. By a vote of 7 to 1, the Council adopted a resolution calling upon UN members to give military assistance in repelling the North Korean invasion. Hope that military aid could be restricted to air and naval support soon ended with the news of further South Korean defeats. On June 30 the President authorized the dispatch of American ground troops, and the first small units were flown into Korea from Japan.

Truman's prompt measures seemed to have the support of almost all Americans except the Communists and their fellow travelers. Republicans who had been sharply critical of the Truman-Acheson China policy applauded this stiffer attitude toward Communist expansion in Asia. Henry Wallace, long a critic of the administration, announced his support of the UN action.

Within the UN itself the situation became more difficult in August, 1950, when the Soviet Union ended its boycott and returned to a policy of obstructionism in the Security Council. During the fall session of the Assembly, however, Secretary Acheson obtained an enlargement of the powers of the Assembly that largely circumvented the ability of the Soviet Union to prevent UN action through its veto.

Although this decision to combat aggression in Korea had strong national and international support, the military problems involved were serious. The UN army, under the command of General Douglas MacArthur, eventually included units from a dozen or more countries, but the major burden had to be borne by the United States. American occupation troops from Japan were poorly equipped for savage fighting in the mountainous Korean terrain. Reinforcements had to be drawn from an American homeland ill prepared for war. Under these conditions, South Korean and American forces suffered a series of defeats that threatened disaster. In August, 1950, the UN army held only a small stubbornly defended bridgehead, about the size of Connecticut, around the South Korean port of Pusan.

On September 15 MacArthur suddenly seized the offensive with an amphibious landing at Inchon on the west coast, near the former South Korean capital of Seoul. This bold maneuver surprised and disorganized the enemy and was followed by rapid UN Advances. Within two weeks MacArthur's forces had cleared South Korea up to the thirty-eighth parallel. Although South Korean troops pushed across into North Korean territory as early as October 1, the main UN forces halted temporarily to reorganize and await a clear mandate from the UN. There was some opposition to authorizing MacArthur to cross the parallel. The government of India, which maintained diplomatic relations with Peiping, warned that an invasion of North Korea might bring Communist China into the war; but spokesmen for the United States and other Western nations minimized this possibility. They advocated a complete conquest of North Korea in order to unify the country and prevent a renewal of aggression. On October 7 the UN Assembly overwhelmingly recommended that "all appropriate steps be taken to ensure conditions of stability throughout Korea," and provided for future elections and economic rehabilitation under UN supervision.

MacArthur made the most of his new authority. North Korean resistance largely collapsed and UN forces swept northward, capturing the Communist capital, Pyongyang, on October 20, 1950. This period of easy victories ended six days later when, for the first time, the UN army found itself opposed by Chinese Communist "volunteer" units. After sharp fighting with this new enemy, the UN forces fell back from 50 to 100 miles. The China Communists did not press their offensive on this occasion, but withdrew to the north, arousing hope that their intervention was of a limited character.

Rigors of the Korean War. (World Wide Photos.)

The question of what to do next in Korea aroused serious disagreement among British, French, and American policymakers. The Europeans, alarmed by the Chinese Communist intervention and fearing that the Korean war might broaden into general hostilities, wanted no further UN advance until a serious effort could be made to settle the issue by diplomacy. Although Communist China rejected an invitation to explain its action in Korea, it did send a delegation to the UN to present charges that the United States had been guilty of aggression against Formosa. Despite the limited powers of this group, it was hoped that the establishment of contact with the Mao regime might open the way for a Korean settlement.

But events took a turn that ended all hopes for a quick peace. On November 24, 1950—the very day that the Chinese Communist delegation arrived at New York—General MacArthur ordered a full-scale offensive north to the Yalu River, the boundary between Korea and Manchuria. This, the general announced, was an action to end the war and permit the prompt withdrawal of UN forces. Hostilities, it was intimated, might be over before Christmas.

MacArthur's "end-the-war" offensive resulted in near-disaster to his army. Instead of the less than 100,000 men estimated in UN intelligence reports, two or three hundred thousand Chinese troops had moved secretly across the border and were massed in the mountains of North Korea. For two days the Communists allowed the UN forces to press forward until they were within fifty miles of the frontier. Then the trap was sprung in a huge counteroffensive. The Communists broke through the center of the UN line, splitting the Tenth Corps in the northeast from the Eighth Army in the west. The Eighth Army began a long retreat back to the thirty-eighth parallel. The Tenth Corps, fighting desperately to avoid encirclement, was finally evacuated from the North Korean port of Hungnam and taken by sea back to South Korean territory, where it was eventually incorporated with the Eighth Army in a new defensive line.

China's full-scale intervention and the great UN defeat plunged public opinion in the United States and Europe from rosy optimism to bleakest pessimism. MacArthur was bitterly criticized for carrying the war provocatively near the Chinese frontier, for proceeding on faulty intelligence reports, and for deploying his forces in such a way that they were easily split by the enemy. But recriminations about the past were outweighed by anxieties for the future. The Peiping radio boasted of the Chinese intention to drive the UN forces into the sea, and such a disastrous outcome to the Korean war indeed seemed a possibility when 1951 opened. Plans were openly discussed for an evacuation to Japan if worst came to worst.

On the diplomatic front things were just as bad. The Chinese Communist delegation to the UN went home after elaborating on the wickedness of American imperialism and demanding UN evacuation of Korea, Communist control of Formosa, and representation for Communist China in the UN. Still hoping for peace, the UN Assembly appointed a three-man truce committee, but all overtures were defeated. American representatives at the UN pressed for a resolution branding Communist China an aggressor. Fear lest this condemnation should close the door to peace delayed UN action, but finally on

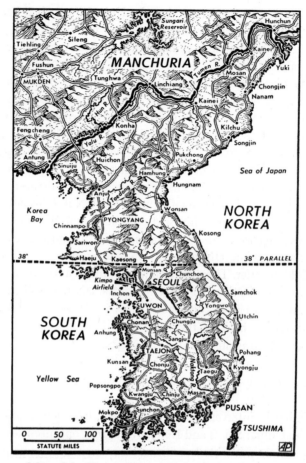

Map of the Korean War. (Wide World Photos.)

February 2, 1951, the Assembly found Communist China guilty of aggression in Korea.

By the end of January fear that the Communist armies could push the UN forces into the sea largely disappeared. Passing again to the offensive, the UN army had recaptured Inchon and Seoul in a campaign whose announced objective was not so much to capture territory as to wear down the enemy. But if the fear of disastrous UN defeat lessened, belief in the possibility of decisive victory did not revive.

Truman versus MacArthur

The recess on domestic politics that had followed the outbreak of the Korean War did not last long. As the conflict dragged on month after month with lengthening casualty lists, the public found an outlet for its frustrations in blaming the Truman administration for the situation. The Republicans pointed the way by charging that the Communist attack had been invited by the weakness of American foreign policy toward Asia. Truman and Acheson were further blamed for fighting a limited "police action," instead of the full-scale war that might bring decisive victory.

The controversy over strategy became dramatized as a personal struggle between President Truman and Douglas MacArthur. Evidence of friction between the commanding general and his superiors in Washington had been accumulating since the start of the Korean War. Truman had emphasized that the neutralization of Formosa by United States forces was intended as a temporary policy and that the final disposition of the island would be left to the UN. The general's disapproval of this was expressed in a message that he prepared in August, 1950, for a meeting of the Veterans of Foreign Wars. Learning of the message shortly before it was to be delivered, the President ordered its withdrawal, but it was too late to prevent wide publication of MacArthur's views. Describing the Truman position as "the threadbare argument by those who advocate appeasement and defeatism in the Pacific," MacArthur implied that Formosa should be permanently held by the United States or some friendly ally as an essential link in the nation's Pacific defenses. In an effort to improve relations between himself and the strong-willed commander, Truman flew to Wake Island for a personal conference in October.

The reconciliation was short-lived. MacArthur's refusal to confine himself to military matters was a chronic embarrassment to the administration. Many Asiatics regarded the general as a symbol of American imperialism and were particularly displeased by his close relations with the discredited Chiang regime. Europeans feared that MacArthur's impetuous statements and actions would involve the United States in a full-scale war against Communist China and the Soviet Union, committing American forces to Asia while Europe was left defenseless. On December 6, 1950, the general was sternly ordered to clear all foreign or military policy statements with Washington before issuing them to the public.

The final break came in the spring of 1951. On March 20 the Joint Chiefs of Staff informed MacArthur that a new Korean policy statement was being prepared. Instead of waiting for this, MacArthur issued another of his unauthorized statements, in which he combined an announcement that he was ready to meet the Chinese military commander on the field of battle and arrange a truce, with a warning that an expansion of military operations against Chinese coastal areas and interior bases would doom the Communist government. Angered by MacArthur's act in transforming a proposed peace gesture into a kind of ultimatum, the President again warned the general against making policy statements without clearing them. MacArthur defied the new order with audacious promptness. On April 5, Representative Joseph W. Martin, Republican leader in the House, read a message from the general, calling, in effect, for a completely new foreign policy: landing of Chiang's Formosa-based troops on the mainland to open up a second front against the Chinese Communists and the concentration of American power in Asia rather than in Europe.

On April 11, 1951, the nation was stunned by the news that the President had relieved General MacArthur of his command and designated General Matthew B. Ridgway to succeed him. At UN headquarters and in European capitals Truman's decision was received with elation. The American reaction was very different. For millions MacArthur was the greatest of World War II heroes, who had added to his laurels by brilliant feats during the occupation of Japan and the Korean War. City after city arranged triumphal welcomes for the homecoming commander, while a few of the more irresponsible Republicans talked of impeaching the President. Excitement reached its peak on April 19, when MacArthur addressed a joint session of Congress. The speech was a remarkably effective one. Asserting that "in war there is no substitute for victory," MacArthur presented his formula for bringing the conflict to a victorious conclusion: intensification of the American economic blockade against Communist China; imposition of a naval blockade against the China coast; removal of restrictions on air reconnaisance over China's coastal area and Manchuria; removal of restrictions on Chinese Nationalist forces on Formosa, "with logistical support to contribute to their effective operations." Recalling the line from the old West Point ballad that "old soldiers never die, they just fade away," the general ended on a strongly emotional note.

The old soldier faded rather slowly, however. Three months after his dismissal, MacArthur was still making triumphal visits to American cities and delivering impassioned attacks on the Truman foreign policy. Meantime, the general's dismissal became a matter of investigation by a Senate committee. MacArthur developed his views with his usual vigor, while the case against the general was clarified by Secretary of Defense Marshall, Secretary Acheson, and other witnesses. Although the dismissed general continued to have strong emotional support, not many politicians were ready to commit themselves wholly to his policy. The real issue seemed to be whether the United States should bomb Chinese territory and support Chinese Nationalist attacks upon the mainland despite the risk that this might precipitate World War III by involving the Soviet Union, or whether the United States should strive to limit the war in Korea while it built up its own armed strength and that of its allies to the point where Communist aggression need no longer be feared. In the heated political atmosphere, it was not to be expected that Democrats and Republicans would agree on whether or not MacArthur's dismissal had been justified, but the hearings did serve some purpose in clarifying American policy. Secretary

Marshall and other administration spokesmen expressed determination to keep Formosa out of Communist control and to oppose Red China's "shooting her way" into membership in the UN. In addition, the United States began to increase its aid to the Nationalist government on Formosa, thus moving somewhat closer to the China policy advocated by the Republicans, although avoiding the bombing of Chinese territory and other extreme measures advocated by the MacArthur faction.

Diplomatic Tug of War

On June 23, 1951, Jacob A. Malik, Soviet delegate to the UN, suggested in a radio speech that it might be possible to end the Korean War by an armistice providing for the mutual withdrawal of forces from the thirty-eighth parallel. This unexpected overture was followed by an exchange of cease-fire suggestions between General Ridgway and Communist headquarters in North Korea. On July 10 truce negotiations began at Kaesong, a city lying near the battle front in western Korea.

Hope that these talks would bring a speedy end to hostilities was soon dashed, as the negotiators became involved in a succession of tedious wrangles. Sometimes the issues between the two parties seemed to be genuine; sometimes the debates appeared to be mere struggles for propaganda advantage. The first controversies involved the neutralization of the meeting place. Charges and countercharges of violations of the neutral zone resulted in a total suspension of negotiations from August 23 to October 25, 1951, when they were finally resumed at Panmunjom, six miles to the southeast of Kaesong.

The Communists at first demanded that a buffer zone between the opposing forces be established at the thirty-eighth parallel, but the UN delegation opposed this because the earlier invasion had proved this line to be indefensible. Instead, they demanded that the armistice line follow the actual battle front, which for the most part lay some distance to the north of that parallel. Eventually the Communists conceded this point, but they were more persistent in their stand on the exchange of prisoners and policing of the armistice. The prisoner question involved an issue of grave moral significance. The Communists demanded the repatriation of all prisoners of war held by either side; the UN negotiators insisted that repatriation be voluntary, since they knew that many Chinese and North Korean prisoners were non-Communists who feared death or torture if they went home. After months of futile debate on this point, the truce negotiations again broke down completely in October, 1952.

The Truman administration's inability to bring these negotiations to a satisfactory conclusion was a heavy burden to the Democrats in the presidential election of 1952. Republican denunciations of President Truman and his harassed Secretary of State, Dean Acheson, naturally reached a crescendo during the political campaign.

Yet the Truman-Acheson record in foreign affairs was much better than these partisan criticisms made it appear. In Europe a series of bold and imaginative steps that included the Truman Doctrine, the Marshall Plan, the Berlin airlift, and NATO had saved western Europe from the threatened Communist seizure of power. In Asia, to be sure, the score for the West was not so favorable: China and North Korea had been lost to the Communists; and South Korea's rescue had been effected at a sickening cost. Yet in Asia, too, the Truman administration had served the historic function of reorienting American foreign policy to meet radically new conditions.

Just as the change of policy toward Germany had been forced by the Soviet threat in the West, so an altered policy toward Japan was hastened by Communist aggression in the East. On September 8, 1951, the United States and forty-seven other nations signed a treaty of peace with Japan. During the year of delicate negotiations that preceded this event, John Foster Dulles, a Republican foreign affairs expert, acted as special representative of President Truman. Warned by the difficulties that had embarrassed conferences on European problems, the State Department ignored Russian demands that the Japanese treaty be prepared by the four principal Far Eastern powers—Great Britain, the United States, China, and the Soviet Union. Instead, Dulles conferred separately with the various governments concerned. Since neither the Communist nor the Nationalist regime had an undisputed right to speak for China, that country was left out of the negotiations with the undersanding that Japan would eventually make a separate treaty with its neighbor. Although consulted in the preliminary discussions, the Soviet Union would have nothing to do with the negotiations.

Having won the support of forty-nine nations for its program of action, the United States served as host at the formal peace conference which opened at San Francisco in September, 1951. Andrei Gromyko, representing the Soviet Union, tried to disrupt proceedings by insisting that Red China be invited to participate and by denouncing the draft treaty as an instrument of American imperialism, whereby Japan would be remilitarized for aggression against the Communist nations. Under the skillful presidency of Secretary Acheson, however, Russian obstructionism was squelched, and the conference moved smoothly to its culmination in the approval and signing of the treaty.

Under the peace treaty Japan was compelled to recognize the independence of Korea, to renounce all claim to Formosa, the Kurile Islands, and South Sakhalin, and to concur in an American-administered UN trusteeship over the Ryukus, the Bonins, and other Pacific islands. Japan agreed to abide by the UN provisions for the peaceful solution of international disputes and to assist the

UN in any action it might undertake; in return, Japan was to possess the right of a sovereign power to "individual or collective self-defense," a stipulation that would permit her to rearm and to seek allies. Occupation troops were to be withdrawn, but foreign armed forces might be stationed on Japanese territory under special agreement with the Japanese government. Although it was recognized that Japan ought to pay for the extensive damage her aggressions had caused, it was also realized that Japanese resources were insufficient to make complete reparation. Some provision was made for confiscation of Japanese assets in foreign countries, and a plan was outlined for the payment of partial reparations through Japanese manufacture of consumer goods and industrial equipment out of raw material supplied by claimant states. On the whole, the treaty was a generous one—at least in comparison with the harsh terms that had become traditional in dealing with vanquished countries during the twentieth century.

Although the United States had achievd a major diplomatic victory in gaining the support of so many nations for the Japanese peace settlement, its policy did not escape sharp criticism. In refusing to sign the treaty, the Soviet Union had the support of its satellites, Poland and Czecoslovakia. India and Burma, professing fear that American bases in Japan and in the trusteeships would cause future trouble, refused to participate in the San Francisco Conference. The rival governments of China both protested against their exclusion from the negotiations. Even among the signatories there were misgivings. The Philippine government criticized the inadequacy of the reparations clauses and feared a revival of Japanese imperialism. To quiet these apprehensions and also to strengthen the defenses against international Communism, the United States signed mutual defense pacts with the Philippines, Australia, and New Zealand. To complete this security system, the United States concluded a security treaty with Japan immediately after the signing of the peace treaty. This authorized the maintenance of American land, air, and sea forces in and around Japan "so as to deter armed attack upon Japan."

Thus to the sea walls the United States had helped to erect against the Communist tide in Europe were now added such feeble dikes as could be improvised in Asia out of the materials at hand.

27

Tribulations of Truman

Not only in foreign relations but in domestic affairs as well, troubled seas prevailed during the almost eight years of the Truman Presidency. To reconvert the national economy from a wartime to a peacetime basis involved vexing problems, for whose solution advocates of national planning counseled one course of action and champions of rugged individualism another. Labor-management relations went through a succession of crises, in which the unionists' aggressive tactics played into the hands of those who wished to place legal curbs on union activities. Even more persistent was the loyalty issue. The Soviet threat abroad aroused fear of subversion at home, and the Truman administration found itself under attack both from those who charged that it was coddling Communists and from those who complained that it was persecuting them. In 1948 Truman rode out the storm to win unexpected re-election, but he found no calm waters ahead. On the contrary, the frustrations of the Korean War and revelations of wrongdoing among the lesser officeholders intensified the lightning flashing around the presidential shoulders.

The New Team

Roosevelt's death had brought to the White House a man of very different background. Born on a Missouri farm in 1884, Harry S. Truman received no more than a high-school education. After holding minor clerical jobs in Kansas City, he returned to the farm until the United States entered World War I. Here he achieved his first minor distinction. His long service with the Missouri National Guard enabled him to gain a captaincy in the field artillery.

Truman at the Helm. (By Berryman in *The Evening Star,*
Washington, D.C.)

He won commendation for his coolness under fire and returned from France a major. A postwar venture in the haberdashery business failed, but a modest start in politics was achieved in 1922 when he was elected judge of the Jackson County Court, an administrative board. He was defeated for re-election, but in 1926 returned to the court as presiding judge. In 1934 the notorious Kansas City boss, Tom Pendergast, engineered Truman's election as United States Senator. Despite an undistinguished beginning, Truman emerged as one of the most respected members of Congress—in large part because of the energy he displayed as chairman of the special committee to investigate the national defense program.

Like most vice-presidential candidates, Truman had been selected more for the political strength he would give the ticket than on the basis of his qualifications for chief executive. When he suddenly assumed the highest position in the government, the country had to appraise his qualities in a new perspective. There were some misgivings. Truman's early connection with Pendergast was disturbing, as were his provincial background and limited acquaintance with broad issues. Yet friends pointed out that Truman's integrity had never been challenged, that he was a hard and earnest worker, and that he had a sincere desire to do the right thing. Perhaps his most impressive asset seemed to be his friendships in Congress, which it was hoped would lead to closer cooperation between the executive and legislative branches than had obtained during Roosevelt's later years.

As was customary, the new President promised to carry out the policies of his predecessor and requested the cabinet members to remain at their posts.

Anti-New Dealers hoped that Truman would hold to this line of conduct only briefly and that he would soon move sharply to the right. In this they were doomed to disappointment. No abrupt repudiation of the New Deal ensued; indeed, Truman's recommendations for legislation followed closely his predecessor's program. In the personnel of government, however, important shifts were made. One cabinet change followed another until by the end of 1945 Secretary of the Navy Forrestal, Secretary of the Interior Ickes, and Secretary of Commerce Wallace were the only holdovers.[1] The most trusted advisers of the new President were Secretary of State Byrnes, Secretary of the Treasury Vinson, and John F. Synder, a St. Louis banker who was chosen to head the important Office of War Mobilization and Reconversion (OWMR), the successor to OWM. Vinson and Snyder achieved additional prestige in June, 1946, when the former became Chief Justice of the United States after the death of Harlan Stone and the latter succeeded to the post of Secretary of the Treasury.

Although the initial shake-up was well received, some of Truman's later appointments encountered sharp criticism. This came to a head early in 1946, when President Truman asked the Senate to confirm the appointment of Edwin M. Pauley, a wealthy California oil operator, as Under Secretary of the Navy. Pauley had been treasurer of the Democratic National Committee during the 1944 campaign, and opponents of his nomination accused him of attempting to use his influence to stop Federal litigation opposed to the interests of the California oil magnates. The star witness for the opposition was Secretary of the Interior Ickes. When the President supported Pauley and suggested that Ickes had been mistaken in his allegations, the veteran Secretary resigned. Convinced at last that Pauley could not be confirmed, Truman withdrew the nomination. The retirement of Ickes under these circumstances was a damaging blow to the administration, but the President retrieved some of his lost ground by appointing to the Interior post Julius A. Krug of Wisconsin, who had won respect for his effective work on the War Production Board.

[1] The various cabinet changes under Truman were: Secretary of State, James F. Byrnes of South Carolina, followed by George Marshall of Virginia in 1947, and by Dean Acheson of the District of Columbia in 1949; Secretary of the Treasury, Fred M. Vinson of Kentucky, followed by John W. Snyder in 1946; Secretary of War, Robert Patterson of New York, followed by Kenneth Royall of North Carolina in 1947; Secretary of the Navy, James Forrestal of New York, who became the first Secretary of Defense when that department was established in 1947, to be followed by Louis Johnson of West Virginia in 1949, and by George Marshall in 1950; Attorney General, Tom Clark of Texas, followed by J. Howard McGrath of Rhode Island in 1949 and by J. P. McGranery of Pennsylvania in 1952; Postmaster General, Robert Hannegan of Missouri, followed by Jesse Donaldson of Illinois in 1947; Secretary of the Interior, Harold Ickes of Illinois, followed by Julius Krug of Wisconsin in 1946, and by Oscar Chapman of Colorado in 1949; Secretary of Agriculture, Clinton Anderson of New Mexico, followed by Charles Brannan of Colorado in 1948; Secretary of Commerce, Henry Wallace, followed by W. Averell Harriman of New York in 1946, and by Charles Sawyer of Ohio in 1948; and Secretary of Labor, Lewis Schwellenbach of Washington, followed by Maurice Tobin of Massachusetts in 1948.

Demobilization

The American soldier had fought with determination and courage not because he loved war, but because he hated it. No desire was stronger than to do the disagreeable job as quickly and efficiently as possible so that he might go back home. Inevitably the defeat of the enemy first in Europe and then in the Pacific brought an overwhelming demand for as rapid and complete a demobilization as possible.

The first step in this direction was taken in May, 1945, just after VE Day. A point system for the discharge of enlisted men was announced, under which such factors as length of service, time overseas, decorations and battle stars, and number of children were counted. The unexpectedly rapid collapse of Japan made it possible to liberalize the system in September. Under pressure from Congress and the public, the services speeded up demobilization; by the end of the year there had been 5 million discharges from the army and 1.5 million from the navy.

In January, 1946, however, a change of policy became necessary. The occupation of conquered countries, as well as the garrisoning of bases throughout the world, required large forces. With new enlistments lagging and draft boards following more lenient policies, the nation was threatened with a shortage of manpower. The army therefore announced that the number of monthly discharges would be sharply curtailed. The order resulted in serious demonstrations by bored and homesick soldiers in places as far removed as Manila, Yokohama, Vienna, and Frankfort. Congress was beset with letters and deputations from "Bring Daddy Back Home" clubs. The uproar quieted down after General Eisenhower, now Chief of Staff, clarified army policy. After this flare-up, demobilization proceeded with reasonable smoothness. Plans called for an army of 1.5 million men and a navy of 700,000 by July 1, 1946, as compared with 8.3 million and 4 million in the two services on VE Day.

A continuance of the policy of discharging soldiers after 24 months of service would reduce the army by December, 1946, to half a million less than the 1.5 million considered necessary for America's immediate postwar commitments. To meet this situation, President Truman asked that the draft be continued beyond May 15, 1946, when it was scheduled to expire. On this issue, as in its discharge policy, Congress was sensitive to the outspoken hostility of millions of voters to conscription in peacetime. Extensions to the draft were provided grudgingly until March 31, 1947, when selective service was for the time being terminated.

Growing tension between the United States and Russia soon compelled the Truman administration to appeal to Congress for a new conscription law. The resulting Selective Service Act of June, 1948, made men from 19 through 25

Secretary of State Byrnes, President Truman, and
Secretary of Commerce Wallace. (Acme.)

eligible for induction, but most veterans of World War II were exempted,
while 21 months became the limit of service for draftees.

Reconversion

The soaring national debt, as well as the pressing need for civilian goods,
dictated a rapid reconversion of American industry from war to peace production. Victory in Europe permitted the first cutbacks, but wholesale reconver-

sion did not commence until shortly after the surrender of Japan. Then the Army and the Navy promptly canceled $35 billion worth of war contracts, while 229 WPB controls were removed. The 150 that were retained dealt with commodities still critically scarce, like tin, rubber, lumber, paper pulp, and textiles. Sale of surplus government property was speedily organized. The extent of this operation is suggested by the fact that 252 factories and plants built by the government at a cost of nearly $1.5 billion were placed on sale, to say nothing of a tremendous quantity of machine tools, trucks, jeeps, and miscellaneous equipment of all types.

Both harassed businessmen and individual wage earners were eager for relief from wartime tax burdens. In November, 1945, Congress passed a new revenue act estimated to reduce taxes by almost $6 billion. All excess-profit levies were eliminated, while corporation income-tax rates were reduced from 6 to 4 per cent. Extending the $500 exemption for taxpayers and dependents to normal as well as surtaxes released about 12 million individuals from the necessity of paying any income tax whatsoever. For 36 million other individuals the tax burden, though still heavy, was reduced through the scaling down of surtax rates and a 5 per cent over-all reduction.

In October, 1945, Director Snyder had predicted many serious reconversion problems. Unemployment would rise, he feared, until there might be as many as 8 million out of work by the next spring. This picture proved unnecessarily gloomy. In April, 1946, Snyder was able to report that unemployment had apparently passed its peak and was down to about 3 million. Production of civilian goods had reached the rate of $150 billion a year—18 per cent more than on VJ Day and 26 per cent more than in 1939.

For the time being there was an almost insatiable market. Savings of more than $140 billion were available for the purchase of new homes, new cars, new radios, more clothing, and more food. The principal postwar grievance was that production, though statistically impressive, still fell far short of demand. Black markets continued to flourish in the scarce fields.

Particularly acute was the housing shortage. Millions found it necessary to purchase real estate at sharply inflated prices in order to obtain shelter. New construction languished for many reasons, but particularly because of an acute lumber shortage. To the difficult post of Housing Expediter the President appointed Wilson Wyatt, former mayor of Louisville, Kentucky. Wyatt called for the building of 1.2 million homes in 1946 and 1.5 million in 1947. The Patman Bill embodying his recommendations became law in April, 1946. Congress also passed an emergency measure appropriating $254 million for temporary homes—trailers and converted military barracks and war housing— to meet the desperate immediate needs of veterans and the families of men still in the services. Many of these were located near colleges and universities to house the veterans who had resumed their education under the GI Bill of Rights.

Strikes

The greatest reconversion problem proved to be labor unrest—as might have been predicted either from the experience of 1919 and 1920 or by an analysis of the powerful forces being built up during the war years. Labor unions were stronger than ever before. In 1935 there had been less than 4 million union members; that number had risen to 11 million by 1941 and to 14.5 million by 1945. The workers had enjoyed heavy earnings during the war, largely through overtime pay and bonuses. The national average for factory workers increased from $23.19 weekly in 1939 to $47.16 in 1945. With the coming of peace, labor feared that its income would be sharply reduced unless it could force raises to compensate for the loss of overtime. Such a reduction in take-home pay would be a serious blow at a time when prices were 33 per cent higher than in 1941. All over the country workers began to demand a raise of 30 per cent—which would give as much pay for 40 hours of work as had been received for 48 hours during the war. Management pronounced this unreasonable and inflationary. Any such pay raise would throw business into the red unless price increases were made—and these were forbidden by OPA.

On November 21, 1945, some 180,000 workers walked out of General Motors plants in twenty different states. The strike was fought out along far different lines than the conflict of 1937. On labor's side there was no attempt to take possession of corporate property; on management's side there was no aggressive strikebreaking. Spokesman for the workers was Walter Reuther, UAW vice-president, who employed ingenious tactics. The workers' demand for a 30 per cent raise was accompanied by an elaborate brief, which argued that the corporation could make this concession without increasing prices on its products and still earn almost double the annual profit it had made during the 1935–1939 period. The company refused to permit investigation of its accounts and countered with an offer of a 10 per cent raise with a 45-hour week—to increase the employees' take-home pay to 6 per cent above wartime levels. This exchange provided ammunition for a campaign on both sides to enlist the support of public opinion. Pickets of the UAW stressed the failure of General Motors to open its books, while the company purchased advertising space to denounce Reuther's challenge to private enterprise.

The President appointed a fact-finding commission, but this body's recommendation of a wage increase of 19.5 cents an hour (a little over 17 per cent) was refused by the company. Not until March, 1946, was a settlement finally reached on the basis of an 18.5-cent pay raise and liberal vacation allowances.

Comparable concessions had already been granted by Ford and Chrysler without strikes.

The Bulge in the Line

The General Motors strike was only one of the major struggles fought out early in 1946. By the last week in January approximately 1.6 million men were on strike and the whole reconversion effort was threatened with paralysis. Congress began to talk in terms of drastic legislative remedies, while the Truman administration hunted feverishly for some magic formula that would dispel the conflict.

Greatest in size and seriousness was the tie-up in steel, which reduced output to 89,000 tons a week as compared with the 88 million-ton rate achieved during the war. The issue had been defined early the preceding fall when Philip Murray, the union leader, demanded a 25-cent-an-hour wage increase to hold pay at its wartime level. Benjamin F. Fairless, president of the United States Steel Corporation and spokesman for the entire industry, would not discuss wage adjustments unless the government consented to a $7.00 per ton rise in the price of steel. President Truman sought to avert the strike by announcing that the government would permit a price increase of about $4.00 a ton if the industry would settle its labor controversy. When Murray and Fairless were unable to come to terms, the President then suggested an 18.5-cent-an-hour raise as a reasonable compromise. Murray accepted this recommendation, but Fairless rejected it and the strike became inevitable. Although some 800 plants in 250 cities and 25 states were involved, there was comparatively little violence; just as in the General Motors strike, both sides appealed for the support of public opinion.

Government price policy was the major factor involved. To what extent should prices be allowed to rise to enable management to pay higher wages and still make a fair profit? Chester Bowles, head of OPA, opposed any major price change. He contended that wages could be raised and industry still could make a profit because of the repeal of the excess-profits tax and the assured market for a large volume of goods. Price raises, on the other hand, would lead the country into a disastrous spiral of inflation. But another group of administration advisers, headed by Reconversion Director Synder, advocated relaxation on the price line in order to stimulate a large volume of production as the best weapon against inflation. A compromise between these two points of view was embodied in the policy announced by President Truman on February 14, 1946. He decided that labor was entitled to wage increases to match the 33 per cent rise in the cost of living since January, 1941. If such raises would bring company earnings below their prewar averages, price increases would be permitted, but the wage raises would require approval of the Wage Stabilization Board. Truman described his new policy as "a bulge in the line."

The new formula was first employed to settle the steel strike. The government permitted a $5 per ton price raise, whereupon the industry conceded the 18.5-cent pay increase that the President had recommended. The new wage pattern was widely copied. Strikes in the electrical industry and elsewhere were settled, and wage increases were made by many other companies after peaceful negotiation. The amount granted was usually from 18 to 20 cents an hour. Combined with the 15 per cent that most workers had received during the war under the Little Steel formula, the total raise since 1941 approximated the 33 per cent increase in living costs during this period.

The May Crisis

The improved situation of March, 1946, was a false dawn. The most difficult labor problems still lay ahead. The first of the new challenges came from that militant veteran, John L. Lewis. Enemies—of whom Lewis had a legion, within the labor movement as well as outside of it—asserted that the miners' chieftain was piqued by the gains Philip Murray had won for the steelworkers and was eager to capture the center of the stage once again for himself. But whatever part personal ambition may have played in motivating his conduct, Lewis was without doubt sincere in his desire to seize a supreme opportunity to win better working conditions for one of the nation's most hazardous occupations.

Negotiations for a new bituminous contract to replace the one that would expire on March 31, 1946, broke down completely. Lewis postponed any discussion of wage rates while he fought to win from the operators stricter safety rules and contributions to a huge health and welfare fund to be administered by the union. He quoted impressive statistics to support his demands: according to the United States Bureau of Mines, 17,626 persons had been killed and 855,056 injured in mine accidents in 14 years, while insurances rates for miners were 277 per cent above standard. The fund, according to Lewis, would permit modern medical service, standardized hospitalization, and insurance at reasonable premiums. The operators objected, however, to turning over money that might run as high as $70 million annually to Lewis' exclusive control.

The deadlock had its inevitable result when 400,000 bituminous miners went out on strike on April 1. During the next six weeks the situation became steadily more serious. By early May steel output dropped to 57 per cent of capacity; Detroit's auto factories closed down, throwing 350,000 out of work; Chicago and other cities adopted "brown-out" restrictions to conserve electricity; the railroads curtailed their passenger service by 25 per cent; and the Office of Defense Transportation imposed a drastic freight embargo allowing only the most vital commodities to move. At last when a complete industrial shut-down threatened, Lewis relaxed his pressure and sent the miners back to work on May 13 for a twelve-day truce.

By this adroit move Lewis sidestepped an avalanche of public resentment and allowed its impact to be taken by another branch of the labor movement—the Brotherhoods of Locomotive Engineers and Railroad Trainmen, who took the unprecedented step of tying up the nation's railroads on May 23. The dispute leading to this crisis began in July, 1945, when all twenty of the railroad brotherhoods served demands upon the carriers for wage increases averaging $2.50 a day and for changes in the working rules. When no settlement was reached, eighteen of the brotherhoods agreed to an arbitration of the dispute. The trainmen and engineers, however, refused this solution. President Truman averted an immediate showdown by appointing a fact-finding board as provided in the Railroad Labor Act of 1926. On April 18, 1946, the board recommended a wage increase of $1.28 a day (16 cents an hour) and seven changes in working rules. The two brotherhoods rejected these proposals as unsatisfactory and issued a strike call.

On May 17 President Truman ordered government seizure of the lines. Five days later he suggested a wage increase of 18.5 cents an hour with no

Are You Sure You Didn't Miss Anything?
(By Herblock in *The Washington Post*.)

change in the working rules for a year. The compromise was accepted and incorporated in a contract between the carriers and all the other brotherhoods, but the trainmen and the engineers continued to demand rule changes.

On May 23 these two dissident brotherhoods went out on strike. They would handle only milk, army hospital, and troop trains. Supervisory personnel ran a few other special trains, but otherwise the tie-up was complete, with neither passengers nor freight able to move except through the overstrained facilities of buses, taxis, trucks, and planes. Improvised relays of mail trucks kept first-class mail moving, but an embargo on all other mail became necessary.

Such a complete paralysis of the nation's economic life was intolerable, and the President resorted to vigorous action. On the evening of May 24 he made a radio address, asserting his determination to use every power at his disposal to get the trains moving unless the strike were ended by the next afternoon. To back up this threat he called upon the army and obtained a promise of cooperation from the eighteen non-striking brotherhoods. But his greatest weapon was public opinion, now thoroughly aroused. A few minutes before the deadline on the twenty-fifth, A. F. Whitney and Alvaney Johnson, the heads of the striking brotherhoods, surrendered. They accepted the presidential recommendations, and the strike was over.

John L. Lewis, a better strategist than the inept Whitney and Johnson, managed to win a substantial victory. On May 22, near the end of the twelve-day truce, the government took over the mines; a week later Secretary of the Interior Krug and Lewis signed a contract providing for a wage increase of 18.5 cents an hour, increased vacation pay, and much stricter safety rules. The controversial welfare-fund issue was compromised by an agreement that 5 cents on each ton of bituminous coal mined should be assigned to a "welfare and retirement" fund to be administered by a board representing both the operators and the unions, but that a separate medical fund should be managed by the union alone.

Congress and the Labor Issue

Inevitably the great strikes strengthened the hand of those who wanted to regulate the unions. The President himself was sufficiently disturbed to suggest new legislation. In December, 1945, he proposed that the principle of the Railroad Act of 1926 be extended to other important industries: there should be a cooling-off period of thirty days between a breakdown in collective bargaining and the commencement of a strike or lockout; during this period the issues should be presented to a fact-finding commission appointed by the President. On May 25, 1946—the day on which the railroad strike reached its climax—Truman appeared before Congress to ask for drastic legislation: if the workers in any essential industry taken over by the government under its wartime powers ignored the President's appeal to return to work, their union leaders might be subjected to injunction proceedings, recalcitrant union leaders and employers might be subjected to criminal penalties, strikers might be deprived of their seniority rights and drafted into the armed forces; and when an industry was being operated by the government during such an emergency, its net profits would go to the United States Treasury. So great was the excitement over the railroad tie-up that the House passed a bill embodying these emergency powers by a vote of 306 to 13 within an hour after the presidential message. But the Senate, disliking both the drafting of workers and the confiscation of profits, was more cautious. The administration bill was radically amended and sent back to the House, where it was allowed to languish along with the President's earlier request for fact-finding machinery.

Congress finally determined on an independent course of action. Despite loud protests by all branches of organized labor, the legislators passed in May, 1946, the so-called Case Federal Mediation Bill. In a long veto message, President Truman stated the reasons for his disapproval: the measure, he said, struck at symptoms rather than causes and would have prevented none of the big strikes of 1946. An attempt to override the veto failed in the House by 5 votes and, with this impasse, the effort to write major labor legislation was over for the moment, although Congress and the President did agree in July upon the so-called Hobbs Act, providing penalties up to a $10,000 fine and 20 years' imprisonment for interference by threats of violence or by robbery or extortion with the movement of goods in interstate commerce.

Truman and Congress

The deadlock between Congress and the President on strike legislation was paralleled by disagreements on many other issues. Truman's honeymoon was of short duration, and before many months he found himself involved in the conflicts with the legislative branch so characteristic of the American system of government. His recent graduation from the Senate seemed only to encourage his former colleagues to match their judgments against his without any inhibitions.

The President's difficulties with Congress at first concerned domestic issues. In the field of international affairs he had for the time being remarkable backing. The legislators ratified the United Nations Charter, as well as the Bretton Woods agreement, and renewed the Reciprocal Trade Agreements in a form that permitted the President to make concessions as great as 50 per cent on the rates embodied in earlier agreements. Congress postponed action, however, on domestic measures urged by the President soon after taking office—measures

I Do My Best to Save Them. (By Herblock in *The Washington Post*.)

authorizing governmental planning to ensure full employment, increased unemployment benefits, and the extension of the Selective Service Act.

On September 6, 1945, Truman sent his first fully articulated program to the Capitol. It was a distinctly New Deal document reiterating the earlier requests which Congress had failed to act upon and calling for an increase in the legal minimum wage from 40 to 65 cents an hour, an expanded and liberalized social security plan to include health insurance, a national housing and slum clearance program, long-range planning to develop natural resources and to carry on essential public works, assistance for the farmer and the small businessman, a permanent Fair Employment Practices Act, and government assistance and direction for scientific research. For the transitional period he requested a continuance of his war powers, of price and wage control, and also of selective service.

In seeking to achieve his so-called Fair Deal, Truman soon discovered what Roosevelt had had to contend with during his later years. The Democratic majority in the two Houses was deceptive. Conservative Southern Democrats—many of them holding strategic committee posts—were ready to cooperate with Republicans in blocking the presidential program. Where they lacked votes for a frontal attack, they were successful in amending bills until they bore little resemblance to the administration proposals. The President found it hard to overcome the coalition, even though on some issues he had the support of liberal Republicans.

Full Employment Bill

America's wartime economy fascinated imaginative citizens. The achievement of huge production goals, the expansion of plants, and the disappearance of unemployment were immensely impressive. Why could not the peacetime economy make full use of the nation's enormous productive capacity and afford employment to all who were able and willing to work? Practical men as well as idealists were forced to think along these lines. As a matter of realistic finances, how could a national debt of $270 billion be carried unless the national income were raised to a figure that would have been considered fantastic in 1939?

Before the war was over, such economists as Alvin Hansen, Seymour Harris, and Stuart Chase had written extensively on the theme of full employment. Although private enterprise must bear the major responsibility for postwar prosperity, these economists emphasized the need to maintain government controls until the danger of inflation was past, and urged government spending to take up the slack in case private investment declined and unemployment threatened. These Keynesian ideas influenced the politicians. During the election of 1944, the Democratic platform, the speeches of President Roosevelt, and the literature of the CIO Political Action Committee all stressed the full-employment theme. The Truman administration accepted this legacy gladly.

Many Americans accepted the aspiration of full employment without subscribing to the idea that government planning was necessary to achieve it. Governor Dewey and the Republicans fought their 1944 campaign on the contention that the principal danger to peacetime prosperity was excessive government interference. The Bible of the anti-New Dealers became Friedrich Hayek's *The Road to Serfdom*, in which a distinguished Austrian emigré economist warned that governmental planning and intervention in the economic sphere led inevitably to totalitarianism. The National Association of Manufacturers proclaimed the necessity of removing wartime controls as speedily as possible in order to achieve full production and maximum employment.

The Fair Deal formula for postwar planning was incorporated in the Murray-Wagner Full Employment Bill. As originally drafted this was a far-reaching proposal. The obligation of the Federal govenment to maintain full employment was recognized, provision was made for the appointment of a board of economists who would draw up a national production and employment budget showing how much of a contribution would be required from governmental spending, and Congess was assigned to provide adequate Federal funds to meet these needs.

In this form the bill was highly unpalatable to conservatives of both parties.

The implication that Federal spending to prevent unemployment should be accepted as a fixed policy raised specters of continued deficit spending, while the production budget spoke in the hateful language of economic planning. On the other hand, conservatives could not afford to put themselves on record as opposed to the measure's basic purpose. Attack therefore took the form of weakening amendments.

As finally passed and signed by the President on February 20, 1946, the Maximum Employment Act was a compromise. It set a goal of "maximum" rather than "full" employment; it eliminated the national production budget and substituted an "economic report" to be prepared annually by a board of three economists; instead of committing Congress "to provide Federal expenditure" to maintain full employment, it called upon the Federal government to "coordinate and utilize all its plans, functions, and resources" to this end. Approved by overwhelming majorities, the measure was recognized to mean much or little according to the interpretation placed upon it. Conservatives accepted it as a harmless "New Year's resolution" that left Congress entirely free to do what it pleased; liberals hailed it as a landmark, a recognition of a basic new responsibility of government.

Price Control

The debate over economic policy assumed a more acute form in the controversy over the continuance of price control. In magazine articles, in radio talks, and in statements before Congressional committees, Chester Bowles, first as head of OPA and then as Economic Stabilizer, argued that only price control stood between the country and a repetition of the economic pattern of 1919 and 1920—runaway inflation followed by depression. So long as the demand for goods ran far in advance of supply, OPA was necessary. When full production was achieved, controls could be gradually relaxed. As always, however, consumers' interests were pressed upon the government with less effectiveness than were the interests of special pressure groups. The National Association of Manufacturers engaged in a huge advertising campaign to convince the public that the best way to combat inflation was to remove price controls. Higher prices, so the argument ran, would stimulate higher production; the law of supply and demand, if allowed to operate, would soon correct unreasonably high prices. Price ceilings, on the contrary, denied to the manufacturer a reasonable profit and deterred production or diverted it to the black market, thereby contributing to inflation. The argument was persuasive, but OPA defenders rejected some of its premises; they denied that businessmen were being required to operate at a loss or that price control did in fact deter production.

Other groups also attacked OPA. Spokesmen for agriculture contended that the high cost of farm labor, of feed, and of other necessities made price increases imperative. They wanted an end to the subsidy system and a removal of price controls on agricultural commodities. If that could not be achieved, they wanted new legal definitions of parity that would compel a substantial increase in price ceilings. Congressmen were particularly impressed by the farm demands because of the shortage of meat, butter, and cooking fats, and the growing black market in these items.

The OPA would expire on June 30, 1946, unless Congress gave it a new lease on life. For six months before this date President Truman urged prompt action in order to end uncertainty and the withholding of goods in hope of higher prices. But the debate in Congress was long and bitter. Legislators willing to continue the agency with all its wartime powers and legislators wanting to kill it completely were both in a minority; the majority favored extension—but with provisions limiting the agency's authority. No until three days before the June 30 deadline did Congress finally extend the Price Control Act for another year, but with a number of what Bowles called booby-trap amendments.

The President was under great pressure from his Congressional leaders to sign this measure, but the government officials most concerned with the battle against inflation urged a veto. In order to emphasize his disapproval of the measure as well as to answer critics who asserted that he was trying to perpetuate himself in power, Chester Bowles resigned. The President's final decision caught the country by surprise. On June 29 he vetoed the OPA bill because it was an "impossible" measure that provided "a sure formula for inflation."

The result of the Congressional delay and the presidential veto was a three weeks' period during which OPA was without legal powers while the legislators debated their next step. Despite appeals to hold the line on a voluntary basis, sharp price increases occurred all over the country. Some of these were inevitable since Federal subsidies had been terminated along with price control on June 30. But steak and butter at from $0.80 to $1.00 a pound reflected a shrewd estimate of what the market would bear rather than a minimum raise to cover increased cost of production. Consumer resistance brought down some of the unreasonable prices, and the restraint of manufacturers who did not want to strengthen the arguments of the price-control advocates held down others. Yet the danger of runaway inflation was enough to induce Congress to pass a compromise measure extending the life of OPA until June 30, 1947, and restoring controls over rents and most commodities. The new law required an adjustment of price ceilings to permit the same margin of profits enjoyed by manufacturers in 1940; meat, poultry, grains, dairy products, and a number of other key commodities were to be exempted from control until August 20; and a three-man "decontrol" board was created with power to lift ceilings and to recontrol commodities when necessary. On July 25 the President signed the new bill despite

Political Dilemma. (By Berryman in *The Evening Star,*
Washington, D.C.)

the fact that it was scarcely more workable than the measure he had vetoed
earlier.

A worse formula for dealing with the meat situation could scarcely have been
devised. For almost two months livestock raisers hurried their product to
market, impelled by high prices and uncertainty as to what the decontrol board
would do on August 20. Following the mandate of Congress, the new board
studied the problem and decided that since prices had risen unreasonably and
meat was in short supply, controls should be restored. With the reimposition
of price control, meat practically disappeared from the market to the vast discontent of consumers. Producers simply held their stock, fattening them up
against the day when they might force a relaxation of government policy.

The President's first inclination was to stand firm, but Democratic politicians, nervous at the impending Congressional elections, implored the administration to give the voters meat. On October 14, Truman gave up. In a radio
address to the nation he announced not only the immediate termination of meat
controls, but abandonment of all price ceilings except on rents as rapidly as
was "compatible with economic security." The step was inevitable. Events had
proved the near impossibility of holding some prices down and not others.
Premature relaxation of rationing after VJ Day, the "bulge-in-the-line" policy,
Congressional failure to pass adequate legislation, and contradictions in execu-

tive policy had all contributed to the situation that confronted the nation in October, 1946.

Republican Landslide

Truman's retreat on the price control issue did not save his party from a bad mauling in the elections of November, 1946. Ever since 1938 the Republicans had been demonstrating increased strength; only the war emergency and Roosevelt's great personal hold on the voters had prevented more decisive opposition gains. With the termination of both these influences, a strong swing to the Republicans was to be expected. The Democrats were blamed—sometimes with reason, sometimes without—for every postwar annoyance—for shortages of housing and civilian goods, for the unbalanced Federal budget and heavy taxes, for the activities for the Communists, and, above all, for the nation's labor troubles. To sum up the whole opposition case, some inspired partisan coined the slogan: "Had enough? Vote Republican."

When the November votes were counted, the full extent of the Republican swing was revealed. Democratic strength in the House was cut from 241 to 188, while the Republicans increased their representation from 192 to 246. The new Senate contained 51 Republicans and 45 Democrats as compared with 39 Republicans and 56 Democrats in the old. The Republicans now had control of both branches of the legislature for the first time since 1930. Governor Dewey, the Republican standard-bearer in 1944, gained new prestige by rolling up an extraordinary 680,000 vote majority in the New York gubernatorial contest, while Senator Arthur Vandenberg of Michigan and Senator-elect John Bricker of Ohio, two other possibilities for the 1948 Republican nomination, enjoyed decisive electoral victories.

Revival of Laissez Faire

President Truman obviously accepted the election returns as evidence that the country had "had enough" of wartime regulation. Four days after the election he issued an executive order dropping all controls on prices and wages, but continuing rent control and the rationing of sugar and rice. The OPA began a process of gradual liquidation. Meantime, because the President was unwilling to give him adequate support, Wilson Wyatt resigned as National Housing Expediter. On December 14 Truman swept away the priorities system and removed the $10,000 sales ceiling for new homes, as well as the $80 maximum rental. This represented a virtual abandonment of the administration's effort to compel the construction industry to concentrate on the building of modest homes at prices the veterans could afford to pay. Additional steps in the lifting of controls were the presidential proclamation of December 31, 1946, announcing the end of hostilities, and the executive order of June 11, 1947, terminating sugar rationing. Congress provided for a continuance of rent control, but landlords and tenants were permitted to agree upon leases for as much as 15 per cent higher rent than the previous ceiling.

The country paid heavily for its eagerness to return to laissez faire. Effective price control had broken down on June 30, 1946, and in the next ten months wholesale prices rose 31 per cent—nearly four times the rise of the preceding 37 months of stringent control. Finding its 18.5-cent wage increase of 1946 canceled by the soaring cost of living, labor pressed new wage demands. A "second round" of raises became necessary in 1947 and a third in 1948 as prices continued to rise. The spiral of inflation seemed inexorable. The rising cost of living led to new wage demands, while wage raises led in their turn to higher prices. Managers, workers, and farmers each laid the blame on the shoulders of the other groups. As in all periods of inflation, those able to speculate often reaped fortunes, while recipients of pensions or fixed incomes suffered seriously.

Curbs on Labor

The Republican victory of November, 1946, was generally interpreted as a rebuke to the labor unions, whose aggressiveness had alarmed many sections of the public. That the Truman administration shared this impatience was evident from its handling of the coal crisis soon after the election. Nominal government control of the bituminous mines had been retained since May, 1946, because of the unwillingness of some of the operators to accept the terms of settlement negotiated by Secretary of the Interior Krug with the UMW. In November Lewis attempted to reopen the contract and, when the government refused, the Mine Workers declared the contract terminated, thus giving the signal for a new walkout of the miners. Lewis' action was in defiance of a temporary injunction that the government had obtained from Federal District Court Justice T. Alan Goldsborough. After a stormy trial, Lewis and the UMW were found guilty of contempt of court; on December 4 Goldsborough fined the former $10,000 and the latter $3.5 million.

While the government wrestled with the union, economic activity throughout the country slowed down alarmingly. Factories closed for lack of coal, blast furnaces were shut down, railroad passenger service was sharply curtailed, a rigid freight embargo was ordered, and communities reverted to the "brown-outs" of wartime. Great was the nation's relief, therefore, when on December 7 Lewis suddenly changed his tactics and ordered the miners to resume work, while the legal issues were considered by the Supreme Court.

On March 6, 1947, the Supreme Court finally announced its decision. By a 7-to-2 vote Judge Goldsborough's verdict that Lewis and the union were guilty of contempt of court was upheld. By a narrower margin, 5-to-4, the Court ruled that the Norris-LaGuardia Act did not apply to labor disputes between the government and its employees. The gargantuan fine against the union, however, was reduced to $700,000, with the proviso that the full $3.5 million would have to be paid if the union failed to comply with the lower court's restraining order.

The Taft-Hartley Act

The protracted struggle between the miners' chieftain and the Truman administration strengthened the case of those demanding drastic legislation regulating the labor unions. The Republicans were in control of Congress, and the unions had lost favor with the public through the postwar strikes. A bill passed in the House under the leadership of Fred A. Hartley, Jr., of New Jersey went too far to win the support of the Senate, which drafted a somewhat more moderate plan. Senator Taft took the most prominent role in the deliberations of the Upper House and also in the conferences where the two branches of the legislature reached a compromise.

As finally sent by Congress to the President on June 9, 1947, the Taft-Hartley Labor-Management Relations Bill amended the Wagner Act in many particulars. To the prohibited labor practices of employers were now added such unfair union practices as coercing non-members, refusing to bargain collectively, and engaging in secondary boycotts or jurisdictional strikes. The closed shop in which employers agreed to hire only union members was prohibited; the union shop, wherein employees might be compelled to join a union after they were hired, was permitted—but only under rigid safeguards. Unions might be sued by employers for breach of contract, or by third parties for injuries suffered through secondary boycotts or jurisdictional strikes. Unions were required to publish financial statements and were debarred from making contributions for political purposes. Officers of unions were required to sign affidavits that they were not members of the Communist party and did not support any organization advocating overthrow of the United States government. Employers or unions wishing to terminate or modify a contract were required to give 60 days' notice; employees striking during this "cooling-off" period lost their rights under the act. The government was empowered to obtain injunctions prohibiting for 80 days strikes or lockouts that threatened national health or safety.

President Truman vetoed the bill in a long and caustic message, which left no doubt of his emphatic disapproval:

> The bill taken as a whole would reverse the basic direction of our national labor policy, inject the Government into private economic affairs on an unprecedented scale, and conflict with important principles of our democratic society. Its pro-

visions would cause more strikes, not fewer. It would contribute neither to industrial peace nor to economic stability and progress. It would be a dangerous stride in the direction of a totally managed economy. It contains seeds of discord which would plague this nation for years to come.

But Congress was unimpressed. On the very day of the veto, June 20, the House voted to override by 331 to 83, and three days later the Senate repassed the measure by a vote of 68 to 25. The Democrats split, with only 22 Senators supporting the President and 20 opposing him. On this issue the Southern conservatives had much more in common with the Republicans than with the Northern Democrats.

Labor leaders refused to concede that the battle was lost. Although divided in other matters, the AFL, the CIO, the Railroad Brotherhoods, and various unaffiliated unions combined in condemning the new law and calling for its repeal. The non-Communist affidavit, regarded as an insult to labor since no comparable pledge was exacted from employers, provided an issue on which some leaders thought it advisable to make the first stand. John L. Lewis, who had led the UMW out of the CIO after his unsuccessful support of Willkie and back into the AFL in 1946, now tried to get other Federation officials to join him in a policy of refusing to file the non-Communist statements. Outvoted on the issue, Lewis with characteristic stubbornness again led his union out of the Federation to resume independent status. Within the CIO there was a similar division of opinion over signing this affidavit. In the end, however, most union officials complied because the penalty for refusal was forfeiture of rights before the NLRB—a very serious matter now that government played so important a role in labor-management relations.

Eventually labor leaders settled on a policy of obeying the new law, while attempting to obtain its repeal through defeating those Congressmen who had voted for it. In practice the measure proved somewhat less damaging to the unions than they had feared. Most employers were reluctant to provoke serious strife by using the law to harass the unions during a period of prosperity. Some labor leaders like Lewis were adept at obtaining contracts that afforded immunity from certain Taft-Hartley provisions. But the unions were fearful that the new act might weaken their bargaining power in a future depression and handicap their organizing campaigns in the South.

The Eightieth Congress

The Taft-Hartley Act was the major legislative achievement of the Republican Congress elected in 1946. Even less than its predecessor was this Congress disposed to enact into law any substantial portion of President Truman's proposed Fair Deal. Instead of broadening the coverage and increasing the benefits of the social security laws, Congress excluded certain groups hitherto covered. Proposals for national health insurance and Federal aid to education were rejected, together with presidential recommendations for raising the minimum hourly wage from 40 to 75 cents. Truman's request for a long-range housing program was answered by legislation providing limited government aid to private construction, but no funds for public housing and slum clearance.

Republican leaders in Congress devoted major attention to an attempt to cut government expenditures and reduce taxes. President Truman's budget for the year ending June 30, 1948, fell under speedy attack. Although it contemplated lower expenditures than had been possible for the six previous years, the total of $37.5 billion was still huge by prewar standards. Even the largest pre-World War II budgets had not exceeded $9 billion. The House of Representatives resolved to cut the President's recommendations by $6 billion; the Senate more realistically set a goal of a $4.5 billion reduction. Even this latter cut was difficult to achieve when Congress began consideration of specific items. The largest categories of expenditure were for national defense, veterans' services, and interest on the public debt—items that even the thriftiest legislators were reluctant to attack. In the end, Congress was able to slash less than $3 billion from the Truman budget.

Despite the fact that budget cuts were less extensive than first promised, the Republicans believed that it was feasible to reduce taxes. Postwar prosperity brought into the Treasury such a volume of revenues[2] that it seemed possible to repeat the Republican financial formula of the twenties—balance the budget, reduce the public debt, and still cut taxes. Congress and the President could not agree, however, on a tax reduction measure. In June, 1947, the legislators passed a bill to cut income tax rates in all brackets, but Truman vetoed the measure, saying: "The right kind of tax reduction, at the right time, is an objective to which I am deeply committed. But I have reached the conclusion that this bill represents the wrong kind of tax reduction, at the wrong time." It was the wrong time, he believed, because of inflation; it was the wrong kind because it failed to give major relief to the small taxpayers who needed it most. A Republican attempt to override the veto failed in the House by two votes. In July Congress passed another tax reduction bill, only to have Truman kill it in similar fashion.

The Republican majority finally had its way in April, 1948. For the third time Congress presented the President with a bill to reduce personal income taxes; for the third time he vetoed the measure on the grounds that tax reduction would contribute to inflation, undermine the soundness of government finances, and benefit the rich more than the poor. This time, however, 84 Democrats in the House and 27 in the Senate joined the Republicans to

[2] During the fiscal years ending June 30, 1947, and June 30, 1948, the Federal government enjoyed its first surpluses in 17 years.

provide the two-thirds majorities necessary to override the veto. By the new law personal exemptions were increased from $500 to $600, married couples were permitted to split their incomes for tax-filing purposes, and levies were reduced on a sliding scale from 12.6 per cent in the low brackets to 5 per cent in the high.

On issues of foreign policy there was less evidence of partisanship than on domestic issues. Through the assistance of Senator Vandenberg, the Truman administration was able to count upon enough Republican votes to carry through the policies of aid to Greece and Turkey and the European Recovery Program. The Eightieth Congress also assented to an extension of the Reciprocal Trade Agreements Act, revived the draft, and passed necessary appropriations for national defense.

Election of 1948

Rarely in their history had the Republicans prepared for a presidential election with more confidence than they did for that of 1948. The election of 1946 indicated an apparent Republican trend, while events during the following two years seemed to increase the likelihood of Democratic defeat. Growing fear of Communism favored the Republicans, who had long charged their political opponents with radicalism. The Democrats, moreover, appeared to be badly divided. Henry Wallace's quarrel with the Truman administration became increasingly bitter. The former Vice-President condemned the Truman Doctrine and the European Recovery Program as forms of American imperialism, advocated better relations with Russia, and urged bolder domestic reforms. Thousands of Americans with similar views joined in organizing the Progessive Citizens of America. No secret was made of their intention to launch a third-party movement in 1948 with Wallace as the candidate for President. While the Wallace movement threatened to attract a wide following from the Democratic left wing, conservative Democrats in the South were preparing a rebellion of their own. Angered by the President's advocacy of a civil rights program to promote Negro equality in employment, education, and voting, Southern Democratic leaders threatened to desert the party if Truman were renominated.

Cheered by all these favorable omens, several Republican hopefuls sought the party nomination. Senator Taft of Ohio, the most conspicuous legislator in the Eightieth Congress, was an obvious possibility, as was Governor Dewey. A third vigorous contender was Harold E. Stassen, former governor of Minnesota and an advanced internationalist. A grass roots movement to draft General Eisenhower gained ground until the hero of the North African and European campaigns firmly eliminated himself.

When the Republican National Convention convened in Philadelphia in

June, it was obvious that more delegates were committed to Governor Dewey than to any other candidate. Taft and Stassen made a belated attempt to combine forces in a stop-Dewey movement, but this was futile since neither wished to step aside in favor of the other. On the first ballot, Dewey received 434 votes to Taft's 224 and Stassen's 157, with smaller votes going to Senator Vandenberg, Governor Earl Warren of California, and other favorite sons. On the second ballot, Dewey's vote increased to 515—only slightly less than the necessary majority. Dewey's nomination was made unanimous on the third ballot, and the ticket was completed by the nomination of Governor Warren for Vice-President. In its platform the party pledged itself to continued support of the United Nations and the European Recovery Program, but urged reduction of government expenses and taxes, as well as new legislation to root out domestic Communism.

Within the Democratic party there was some talk of shelving Truman in favor of a less controversial figure. Despite Eisenhower's disavowal of presidential aspirations, a number of Democratic leaders, both liberals and conservatives, urged the general's nomination on the Democratic ticket. This strange balloon was punctured by the general's unequivocal refusal to allow his name to be considered. Some of the party progressives tried then to shift support to Supreme Court Justice William O. Douglas, but he too announced that he would refuse the nomination. Without any outstanding rival, Truman was nominated on the first ballot. The vice-presidential nomination went to Alben W. Barkley, veteran Senator from Kentucky.

Much of the excitement of the Philadelphia convention centered on the framing of the platform. To appease the Southern wing, the platform committee had drafted a weak civil rights plank, but this was rejected in favor of a strong resolution, championed by Mayor Hubert H. Humphrey of Minneapolis and other liberals, many of them associated with Americans for Democratic Action (ADA), a progressive pressure group uniting a number of former New Dealers. In its fight for a strong civil rights plank the ADA had the support of several city bosses anxious to win the Negro vote. The liberal victory—won by the close vote of 651½ to 582½—was followed by an ominous withdrawal of 35 delegates from Mississippi and Alabama. In its other planks, the Democratic platform called for support of the Truman foreign policy and a consummation of his Fair Deal program.

The new protest parties speedily took the field. On July 17, just two days after the end of the Democratic Convention, the Southern rebels, popularly dubbed the "Dixiecrats," held a States Rights Convention at Birmingham, Alabama, where they condemned the civil rights program and called for continued segregation of Negroes. They nominated Governor J. Strom Thurmond of South Carolina for President and Governor Fielding Wright of Mississippi for Vice-President. Later in the month the new Progessive party[3] named Henry Wallace as its candidate for President and Senator Glenn H. Taylor, radical Democrat from Idaho, for Vice-President. The platform called for peace with Russia, destruction of all atom bombs, repeal of conscription, and far-reaching domestic reforms.[4]

All these events confirmed the Republican leadership in its conviction that victory was certain. Much of the Southern electoral vote was expected to go to Thurmond. The anticipated Wallace vote of five or six million would so diminish the Truman vote in the large cities that the pivotal states would go to Dewey. Confident in this analysis and relying upon the predictions of public opinion experts and poll-takers, Governor Dewey conducted a quiet campaign. He avoided controversial issues and stressed such safe principles as the need for national unity.

President Truman refused to concede that his cause was hopeless. In an attempt to demonstrate that Republican pledges were hollow, he called the Eightieth Congress back into special session on July 26 to deal with inflation, housing, and civil rights. The Republican majority denounced this maneuver as a political trick and passed only a few measures before adjourning on August 7. This provided ammunition for Truman's most effective argument—that the Eightieth Congress had been a "do-nothing" body that had refused to enact the measures needed to curb inflation and advance the welfare of the people. The President proved an indefatigable campaigner, visiting every section of the country and arguing his case in informal speeches from station platforms.

Following many hours of uncertainty after the polls closed, the election results finally became clear. Truman obtained 304 electoral votes; Dewey, 115; Thurmond, 38. In the popular vote, Truman had over 24,000,000; Dewey, not quite 22,000,000; Thurmond, 1,168,000; and Wallace, 1,138,000. In the new Congress, the Democrats won 262 House seats to the Republicans' 171 and the American Labor party's 1; in the Senate there were 53 Democrats and 43 Republicans.

A number of factors contributed to Truman's unexpected victory. Republican overconfidence played a major part; since Dewey's total vote in 1948 was less than in 1944, it was obvious that many Republicans had neglected to vote. A decline in farm prices and fear that the Republicans would not give adequate aid cost Dewey the electoral votes of such farm states as Iowa, Wisconsin, and Minnesota. In several states the Truman candidacy was strengthened by excel-

[3] This is not to be confused with earlier parties bearing the same name. The first Progressive party lasted from 1912 to 1916; the second existed as a national party for only the 1924 campaign, although the LaFollette family led a local Progressive party for many years in Wisconsin state politics.

[4] Other nominations for the 1948 election were: Norman Thomas, Socialist; Edward A. Teichert, Socialist Labor; Claude A. Watson, Prohibition. The Communist party nominated no candidate of its own, but endorsed the Progressive ticket.

lent Democratic nominations for Congressional and state offices—like that of Professor Paul Douglas of the University of Chicago for Senator from Illinois and of Mayor Humphrey for Senator from Minnesota. Of crucial importance was the relative failure of the Wallace candidacy. Although not many voters doubted the loyalty and idealism of the former Vice-President, they were disgusted by the noisy Communist activity in his behalf. Most of the key labor union leaders were particularly careful to avoid commitment to the new party. After all other factors have been recognized, however, it remains true that Truman made a major contribution to his own victory: thousands of doubtful voters were won over by the President's courageous campaign and willingness to debate issues that Dewey appeared to be avoiding.

The Second Administration

On January 20, 1949, President Truman was inaugurated for his second term. Prophetically he declared: "Today marks the beginning of a period that will be eventful, perhaps decisive, for us and the world." He condemned Communism in strong terms and outlined a four-point program for combatting this "false philosophy" on a world-wide scale. The first three of the proposed points were support of the United Nations, new appropriations for the European Recovery Program, and negotiation of a North Atlantic Security Pact—all ideas familiar to the nation. Point Four, however, incorporated an important new proposal. "We must," the President asserted, "embark on a bold new program for making the benefits of our scientific advances and industrial progress available for the improvement and growth of undeveloped areas." Despite wide agreement that Truman had pointed out one of the major world needs—that of extending American technical and financial assistance to underdeveloped areas in Asia, Africa, and Latin America—the actual implementation of the idea progressed slowly.

To direct American foreign policy through this troublesome period, President Truman had to choose a new Secretary of State. General Marshall, whose great prestige had strengthened the administration during two critical years, was compelled to resign because of ill health. In his place the President appointed Dean Acheson, who had served earlier as Under Secretary of State. With an intimate knowledge of foreign affairs and wide experience in government, Acheson appeared to be an excellent choice. But the new Secretary of State had from the beginning many critics, who accused him of tolerating Communists in the State Department and favoring appeasement with Russia.

Government Reorganization

To deal with increasingly complex problems both in the foreign and the domestic fields, Democrats and Republicans agreed on the necessity for achieving greater government efficiency. Efforts to accomplish this goal, which had begun with the Roosevelt administration, continued under Truman. In December, 1945, Congress granted him more extensive powers than had been given to Roosevelt or any other predecessor to reorganize the executive departments. Only the Interstate Commerce Commission, the Federal Trade Commission, the Securities Exchange Commission, and a few other independent boards were exempted. The need for improving the machinery of government was recognized in another form when, in August, 1946, the Legislative Reorganization Act raised the salaries of Congressmen to $12,500 and allowed them $2,500 for expenses, provided for more regular consultation between the executive and legislative branches, and—most important—for simplifying the complex and overlapping Congressional committee system.

After the experiences of World War II, there was wide recognition of the necessity of unifying the armed services. In July, 1947, the President placed his signature on a law purporting to attain this objective. To head the new National Military Establishment there was to be a Secretary of Defense with cabinet rank, supported by three subsidiary Secretaries of the Army, Navy, and Air Force. Integrated defense plans were to be prepared by the Joint Chiefs of Staff composed of the Army Chief of Staff, the Chief of Naval Operations, the Chief of Staff of the Air Force, and the Chief of Staff assigned to the President. The new law also provided for such important coordinating agencies as the National Security Council, the National Security Resources Board, and the Central Intelligence Agency.

The first Secretary of Defense was James V. Forrestal, who had served efficiently as Secretary of the Navy under the old organization. He found his new position a difficult one. The various services could not forget their traditional jealousies of one another. Genuine unification was hampered by constant bickering between officials trying to obtain maximum appropriations for their particular branches. Forrestal's difficulties were increased by deficiencies in the new law, which granted too much autonomy to the subsidiary secretaries and provided no single Chief of Staff. His health broken by nerve-racking overwork, the first Secretary of Defense resigned his post in March, 1949. Forrestal's suicide two months later shocked the nation and underlined the need for legislation to enlarge the powers of the new Defense Secretary, Louis A. Johnson. In August, 1949, Congress increased the authority of the Secretary of Defense over the three armed services and provided for a non-voting chairman for the Joint Chiefs of Staff to help break stalemates in their discussions—a post given to the widely respected General Omar Bradley. Johnson's vigorous personality soon made enemies. Spokesmen for the navy bitterly complained that their plans for an expansion of the naval air force had been overridden, while all the services objected to attempts to impose economy upon them.

Under attack from many quarters, Johnson resigned in September, 1950. To succeed him in this critically important post President Truman called General Marshall out of retirement.[5]

Meantime, government reorganization was proceeding with less excitement in other departments. In 1947 Congress had unanimously authorized the appointment of a Commission on Organization of the Executive Branch of the Government. The non-partisan character of the project was emphasized by the fact that the commission was composed of six Democrats and six Republicans, with former President Herbert Hoover as chairman and future Secretary of State Acheson as vice chairman. Most of the detailed work was done by 300 experts employed to make exhaustive studies of the actual functioning of the government. The Hoover Commission issued 18 reports between February 7 and April 1, 1949. Among its recommendations were that the number of government departments and agencies be reduced from the existing 65 to 22 or 23, that uniform budgeting and accounting systems be introduced, that the State Department be given authority over other government units engaged in foreign affairs, that the Post Office be taken out of politics and operated on a business basis to eliminate its chronic deficit, and that a cabinet rank department be established to deal with problems of social security and education. It was estimated that annual savings of some $3 billion could be achieved through adoption of these reforms.

In June, 1949, Congress passed a Reorganization Act giving general approval to the Hoover Commission reports and authorizing the President to prepare specific proposals for carrying out the recommendations. These plans would go into effect unless disapproved by either House within 60 days after they were submitted by the President. Of the first seven plans submitted under this procedure, all were allowed to stand except one. Fearing that the establishment of a Department of Welfare with a Secretary of cabinet rank would strengthen the demand for national health insurance, this proposal was killed in the Senate by a coalition of Republicans and Southern Democrats. Several other Truman proposals were disapproved the next year. Despite these setbacks, the President was able to make many salutary changes, clarifying lines of authority and improving accounting practices.

Truman also obtained from Congress requested legislation dealing with the important matter of presidential succession. An act of July 18, 1947, provided that if, by reason of death or other cause, there was neither a President nor Vice-President to discharge the duties of the Chief Executive, the Speaker of the House of Representatives should act as President. Thereafter the succession passed through the President pro tempore of the Senate and the cabinet officers in order of rank. Truman advocated this plan of succession in place of

[5] Upon Marshall's resignation in September, 1951, he was succeeded by Robert A. Lovett of New York.

the older provision under which the Vice-President was followed by the Secretary of State, because he believed that the Presidency should pass to elective officers like the Speaker of the House before it passed to the purely appointive officers of the cabinet.

Another major step pleased the President much less. In 1947 the Republican-controlled Eightieth Congress mustered the two-thirds majorities necessary to approve the following amendment to the Federal Constitution:

> No person shall be elected to the office of the President more than twice, and no person who has held the office of President, or acted as President for more than two years of a term to which some other person was elected President shall be elected to the office of the President more than once . . .

Widely regarded as little more than a futile rebuke to the late Franklin Roosevelt, the proposed amendment received much less attention than it deserved in view of the fact that its passage might tie the hands of the electorate in some grave future emergency. With little debate or public discussion, the Twenty-second Amendment was approved by one state legislature after another. At first its support was primarily Republican, but the final push came largely from Southern Democrats as a gesture of defiance to Truman. The new amendment went into force in February, 1951. Although President Truman was specifically exempted, it was believed the amendment would greatly diminish his chances of election to a third term.

Progress of the Fair Deal

Many Truman supporters believed that the Democratic triumph in the 1948 campaign would result in speedy enactment of the Fair Deal program. Yet events soon proved that the situation of earlier years had not materially changed. Much of the Truman domestic program was unacceptable to the Dixiecrat faction of his own party. By loose alliance with the Republicans, the Southern Democrats were able to obstruct many proposals. Their position was particularly strong because they headed key committees through seniority.

Illustrative of the situation was the fate of the civil rights program. This issue had become increasingly important during the first Truman administration. In 1947 a distinguished Committee on Civil Rights, appointed by the President, had recommended a number of measures to protect the rights of Negroes and other minorities. These included the enactment of laws to make lynching a Federal crime, to end poll tax requirements for voting, to enforce fair employment practices, to prohibit discrimination or segregation on interstate trains, buses, and other means of transportation, and to make non-discrimination a condition for all Federal grants-in-aid for housing, education, and the like. President Truman had accepted the major recommendations of this committee and urged Congress to pass the necessary legislation—thereby precipitating the Dixiecrat revolt of 1948.

Since the Republican national platform had also advocated civil rights legislation, the outlook for enactment of such measures seemed bright. But Southern legislators still had a potent weapon of opposition. Senate rules permitted unlimited debate except when closure was imposed by a two-thirds vote. Through filibusters, therefore, Southern Senators could not only block all civil rights bills, but could hold up all other Senate business as long as such proposals were under consideration. In March, 1949, the Truman administration tried to obtain a reform in the closure rules to make it easier to limit debate. This move, however, was opposed by an alliance of Republicans and Southern Democrats. A new rule was adopted, but its effect was merely to clear up certain ambiguities in the old. Defeat on this issue placed an almost insuperable obstacle in the path of the Truman civil rights proposals. On a test vote in May, 1950, supporters of the Fair Employment Practices Bill were twelve votes short of the two-thirds necessary to impose closure.

Attempts to carry out the Democratic pledge to repeal the Taft-Hartley Labor Relations Act were similarly unsuccessful. An administration bill failed by close votes in both Houses during the spring of 1949. Senator Taft proposed to amend the law by modifying the injunction provisions and making a few other concessions, but his bill died in the House after passing the Senate. In 1951, however, the controversial labor relations act was amended to permit the negotiation of union-shop agreements without special vote of the workers.

Other Fair Deal failures followed. Plans to set up a national health insurance system, under which citizens would receive prepaid medical, dental, and hospital services to be financed by payroll taxes and government subsidies, were vigorously opposed by most doctors. Condemning the proposal as "socialized medicine," the American Medical Association raised a $3 million fund to oppose it. Congress took no action on this or various proposed substitutes, but did vote enlarged appropriations for construction of hospitals, medical research, and medical education. Despite wide demand for Federal aid to the states to equalize educational opportunities, all measures for this purpose failed, largely because of disagreement on whether such aid should be restricted to public schools or should include funds for bus transportation and other services for parochial school children.

The problem of devising a postwar agricultural program was not easily solved. The administration felt two conflicting obligations: one to the farmers to prevent any such drop in farm income as had followed World War I, and a second to the workers and other consumers who resented soaring food prices. Secretary of Agriculture Charles F. Brannan attempted to reconcile this conflict of interests by a plan that would have changed the parity formula for stor-

able staples and allowed the prices of perishable commodities to be determined by supply and demand, with government subsidies to guarantee minimum returns to producers. The Brannan Plan was viewed with suspicion by
the American Farm Bureau and other major farm organizations, which considered it more favorable to the small farmers than to the large. Consequently,
Congress rejected the Brannan program in favor of a continuance of the
existing price support system. The Commodity Credit Corporation continued
to make extensive crop loans to protect producers against falling prices. By the
Agricultural Act of 1949 prices on such basic commodities as corn, wheat,
cotton, tobacco, rice, and peanuts were to be supported on a sliding scale: 90
per cent of parity through 1950, not less than 80 per cent in 1951, and thereafter between 75 and 90 per cent as needed. Flexible price supports were
provided for butter, milk, and other perishable items. Since industrial prices
continued to go up, the prices guaranteed to the farmers went up with them.

Despite these setbacks, the Truman Fair Deal achieved some of its legislative
goals. In 1949 over a million workers benefited by an amendment to the Fair
Labor Standards Act raising the minimum wage from 40 to 75 cents an hour.
The Reciprocal Trade Agreements Act was extended for another three years
without the restricting amendments that had been voted by the Republican
Congress in 1948. In July, 1949, Congress passed a National Housing Act,
authorizing the construction of 810,000 units of public housing over the next
six years.

In August, 1950, President Truman signed a new Social Security Act that
increased the number of persons eligible for benefits from 35 million to about
45 million. Among those newly covered were self-employed workers, farm
workers, domestic servants, and college professors. Pensions and other benefits
were substantially increased at the same time.

Truman also achieved a liberalization of the Displaced Persons legislation
passed by the Eightieth Congress. Since World War II, much sympathy had
been aroused by the plight of some 850,000 Europeans who had lost their
homes through the international upheaval. Many were Jews who had lost
everything through Nazi and Polish persecution; other were Germans expelled
from Czechoslovakia and Poland in reprisal for indignities earlier suffered by
the nationals of those countries; still a third group consisted of Poles, Lithua-
nians, and other Baltic peoples unwilling to return to homelands now annexed
by the Soviet Union. Since immigration quotas assigned to these European
countries had not been filled during the war years, there was wide support for
temporarily relaxing the annual quotas to permit a portion of these displaced
persons to find American homes. In June, 1948, Congress enacted a measure
that would admit some 205,000 of them. Although the President signed the
bill, he vigorously condemned certain provisions as discriminatory against Jews

and Catholics. The deficiencies of the law became more apparent as time went on. Because of its restrictive provisions, only 140,000 displaced persons were actually admitted over the course of the next two years. In June, 1950, Congress finally liberalized its policy to admit a total of 415,000 without discrimination.

Impact of the Korean War

The outbreak of the Korean War multiplied the problems of the administration. The new situation demanded a return to the policies of World War II days, yet the nation was reluctant to suffer again the inconveniences of large-scale conscription, economic mobilization, price controls, and the like. The growing unpopularity of the conflict was reflected in an unwillingness to give full cooperation to national policy.

Even before North Korea began its invasion, Truman's budget requests had reflected the worsening world situation. In January, 1950, he asked Congress for $40.4 billion, of which $12.8 billion would be for defense and $5 billion for foreign aid. But even these large figures appeared inadequate after the outbreak of the Far Eastern war. By the time Congress adjourned in September, 1950, it had appropriated over $53.2 billion—almost $25 billion for defense and over $10 billion for foreign aid. Still larger budgets followed in 1951 and 1952, as defense production shifted into high gear.

Chinese intervention in Korea and subsequent UN defeats created an atmosphere of crisis. On December 16, 1950, President Truman declared a state of national emergency and announced that the nation's armed forces would be increased to 3.5 million men, with a rapid speed-up in the production of military equipment. To direct the new Office of Defense Mobilization, the President appointed Charles E. Wilson, a former president of the General Electric Company and vice-chairman of the War Production Board during World War II. To supply the manpower needs of the armed services, Congress extended and revised the Selective Service Act in June, 1951.

Large new orders for war equipment greatly increased the inflationary pressures that had been forcing prices up with only brief leveling-off periods since the end of World War II. The need for economic controls had been recognized in the passage of the Defense Production Act in September, 1950, which authorized the President to encourage voluntary action to prevent inflation and to issue ceilings on prices and wages where necessary. Reluctant to involve the nation once again in full price control, the administration attempted to rely upon voluntary cooperation. By December, 1950, the need for stronger measures seemed obvious, but the imposition of controls proved very difficult. Manufacturers strenuously objected to ceilings on their prices unless wages were controlled. Union leaders insisted that it was unjust to the workers to freeze their wages unless the cost of living were stabilized through general price control. In January, 1951, the difficulties of the situation led to the resignation of Alan Valentine as Economic Stabilization Director and his replacement by Eric Johnston, a well-known industrialist. The two principal officers serving under Johnston were Michael DiSalle, Director of Price Stabilization, and Cyrus Ching, chairman of the Wage Stabilization Board.[6] On January 26, 1951, the new team announced the imposition of a general price ceiling at the highest level charged between December 19, 1950, and January 25, 1951. Wages were not to be raised beyond their January 25 level without prior authorization of the Wage Stabilization Board.

In the spring of 1951, President Truman requested a strengthening of the Defense Production Act to permit greater control over food prices, installment credit, and rents. But these requests met much opposition. There was strong pressure upon Congress not only to refuse to grant additional powers, but to modify some of the policies already initiated. Particularly controversial was Price Stabilizer DiSalle's order requiring a series of rollbacks in beef prices.

On July 31, 1951, Congress finally passed a measure amending and extending the Defense Production Act for eleven months. Price control was weakened by provisions prohibiting the establishment of slaughtering quotas for livestock and limiting the imposition of rollbacks. By the controversial Capehart amendment, manufacturers were entitled to apply for price increases to cover increased expenses that might have arisen in their business since the outbreak of the Korean War. The bulwarks against inflation were further weakened by a relaxation of the strict terms that had been required for installment purchases. President Truman described the bill as the "worst I ever had to sign." It would, he was convinced, push prices up and lead to new wage demands.

The resistance to strict economic controls and higher taxes arose in large part from the fact that, despite all warnings, the nation did not feel the same urgency to close ranks and to accept sacrifice that a full state of war would have brought forth. Perhaps by design, Communist leaders alternated menacing actions with gestures toward conciliation. Although Soviet peace moves did not divert the nation from rearmament, they did perceptibly ease tension and stiffen opposition to full mobilization.

The Question of Loyalty

War in Korea and the threat of possible conflict with the Soviet Union heightened concern over the problem of internal security. Under existing conditions American Communists could hardly be regarded merely as members of a political faction. Evidence was all too clear that most Communists placed

---

[6] Upon Johnston's resignation in November, 1951, he was succeeded by Roger Putnam of Massachusetts. DiSalle was succeeded by former Governor Ellis Arnall of Georgia in February, 1952.

loyalty to party above all other loyalties and that they were closely controlled from Moscow. The danger that they might infiltrate government bureaus and pass on secret information to Russian agents, or that they might cause trouble in defense industries through control of key labor unions was a real one. In 1947 President Truman had initiated steps to deal with the situation by ordering a loyalty check of all government employees and dismissal of any found to have subversive affiliations. Labor union leaders took measures of their own to purge Communists from positions where they might control union policy. Under the leadership of right-wing heads like Philip Murray and Walter Reuther, the CIO expelled Communist-dominated unions and organized new ones.

A powerful faction in Congress believed that such measures as these did not go far enough. Through sensational investigations they sought to convince the country that the executive branch of the government was honeycombed with Reds and that subversive influences were dangerously at work, not only in the labor unions but in the entertainment world and in schools and colleges. The leading Red-hunter in the Republican-controlled Eightieth Congress was Representative J. Parnell Thomas of New Jersey, chairman of the House Committee to Investigate Un-American Activities. Like Martin Dies, who had won earlier notoriety in this post, Thomas attempted to keep his name in the headlines through reckless charges. Many citizens regarded the dictatorial methods of the Committee as themselves un-American.

When Representative Thomas was tried and sentenced to prison for graft, there was some hope that the loyalty issue would be handled more judiciously in the future. But a number of episodes soon combined to alarm the public and lend color to the wildest charges of Communist infiltration. In June, 1949, Judith Coplon, an employee of the Justice Department, was convicted of taking secret government documents with the intention of passing them on to a Russian agent.[7]

This was a minor sensation, however, compared with the case of Alger Hiss. Slender and handsome, Hiss seemed to represent the finest type of young intellectual drawn into government service during the New Deal era. A graduate of Johns Hopkins and Harvard Law School, he had once served as secretary to the famous Justice Oliver Wendell Holmes. He was given a position in the State Department in 1936. Subsequently he held a minor post in the delegation sent to the Yalta Conference and served as secretary general of the United Nations Charter Conference in San Francisco. After leaving government service in 1946, he became president of the Carnegie Endowment for International Peace.

The first public charges that Hiss was a Communist were made in testimony

[7] Miss Coplon's conviction was eventually reversed on technical grounds.

before the Un-American Affairs Committee by Whittaker Chambers, a confessed former Communist who had left the party in 1938. To prove his contentions, Chambers produced copies of secret State Department documents
that, he alleged, had been given to him by Hiss in 1937 and 1938. When the
former State Department official denied before a Federal Grand Jury that he
had given any documents to Chambers or that he had even met him after
January 1, 1937, he was indicted for perjury.[8]

The first Hiss trial ended in July, 1949, with the jury unable to agree on a
verdict. The defendant had impressive character witnesses, including Supreme
Court Justices Frankfurter and Reed, but evidence that some key documents
were in his handwriting and others were written on the same kind of typewriter
as his counted heavily against him. Brought to trial a second time, Hiss was
found guilty in January, 1950, and sentenced to five years' imprisonment.[9]

As fear of Communists increased, there was a sharp division of opinion on
the question of whether the party itself should be outlawed. Proponents of such
legislation argued that the Communist party was not a party in the American
sense of the term, but a conspiracy controlled by a foreign power and committed
to the overthrow of the government. Opponents contended that to outlaw a
political party was a gross violation of American civil liberties and that such a
measure would be ineffective in any case, since it would simply halt open Communist activity while undercover intrigues would be harder than ever to control.

The outbreak of the war in Korea intensified the demand for anti-Communist
legislation. In September, 1950, Congress passed the McCarran Internal Security Bill, which required registration with the Attorney-General of all Communist
and Communist-front organizations and all individual members of such groups.
Such members were prohibited from receiving passports or from working for the
government or any defense industry. Aliens who had ever belonged to Communist or other totalitarian parties were forbidden to enter the country as
immigrants, while similar safeguards were established for naturalization. Finally,
the bill empowered the government in case of war to hold Communists and
other potential saboteurs in detention camps. President Truman vetoed the
bill with a strong message pointing out the dangerous looseness of its definition
of Communist-front activities. "In a free country," the President declared, "we
punish men for the crimes they commit, but never for the opinions they have."
Congress was not deterred, however, by such admonitions. Before the month
was over the veto was overridden by large majorities in both Houses, and the
Internal Security Bill became law.

Meantime, the Communist party had been strongly attacked from a different
quarter. In July, 1948, a Federal Grand Jury indicted William Z. Foster, Eugene

---

[8] Statutory limitations prevented Hiss's indictment on a direct charge of espionage.

[9] A somewhat similar case in 1953 resulted in the conviction of William W. Remington, a
former Commerce Department employee, for perjury in denying Communist activities.

Dennis, and ten other leading American Communists for violating the Smith Alien Registration Act of 1940, a little-known statute that had among other things made it unlawful for any person to teach the desirability of overthrowing any government in the United States by force or violence, to print or circulate written matter aimed at causing such an overthrow, or to help organize or have membership in any group that advocated the doctrine of violent overthrow. The precarious condition of Foster's health made it necessary to defer his trial, but the other eleven Communists were the principals in a long court battle lasting from January to October, 1949. In the end the jury found the eleven guilty and Judge Harold Medina imposed prison terms ranging from three to five years.

Not until June 4, 1951, did the Supreme Court rule upon the constitutionality of the Smith Act as applied in the case of the eleven Communists. A majority, composed of six justices, upheld the conviction. The Smith Act, according to Chief Justice Vinson, did not violate the guarantee of free speech in the First Amendment because of the clear and present danger involved in Communist activities. "Overthrow of the Government by force and violence is certainly a substantial enough interest for the Government to limit speech." Strong dissents were written by Justices Black and Douglas, who saw no clear and present danger that Communist advocacy might succeed. "There is hope," said Black, "that in calmer times, when the present pressures, passions, and fears subside, this or some later court will restore the First Amendment liberties to the high preferred place where they belong in a free society."

The effect of the Smith Act, as interpreted by the Supreme Court majority, was to outlaw practically all Communist activity. The decision was followed by arrests of many other party leaders on charges of conspiring to advocate the overthrow of the government.

The most serious case of actual espionage was one involving the development of the atomic bomb. In February, 1950, Dr. Klaus Fuchs, one of the key scientists employed on atomic research by the British during World War II, was arrested in England and confessed to supplying Soviet agents with vital data. Interrogation of Fuchs led to the arrest of a group of Americans who had also spied for the Russians, providing the information the Communist government needed to produce its own atomic bomb so promptly. Convicted of espionage in April, 1951, Julius and Ethel Rosenberg were sentenced to death, while Morton Sobell and David Greenglass were given long prison sentences.

Not to be outdone by Federal Congressmen, many state legislators worked the loyalty issue for all it was worth. Committees were established to investigate alleged subversive activities, and laws were passed forbidding state employment of Communists. A number of states required special loyalty oaths from state employees.

Among the politicians who sought to ride the anti-Communist wave, none was more extravagant in his accusations than Republican Senator Joseph R. McCarthy of Wisconsin. In a political speech in February, 1950, he charged that there were "at least fifty-seven" Communists in the State Department. In a subsequent Senate speech, McCarthy described eighty-one State Department officials, past or present, as bad security risks. In March, a subcommittee of the Senate Foreign Relations Committee, under the chairmanship of Democratic Senator Millard Tydings of Maryland, began hearings on these charges. It soon became apparent that the Wisconsin Senator was unable to name a single Communist party member in the Department. He did, however, make vague accusations of left-wing tendencies against various officials. His most vigorous attack was upon Professor Owen Lattimore of Johns Hopkins University, whom he described as Russia's "top espionage agent in America" and the "architect" of the American Far Eastern policy, which had resulted in the "betrayal" of Nationalist China. The Tydings Committee gave McCarthy full opportunity to support his charges and Lattimore an equal chance to refute them. The professor denied that he was ever a Communist or Communist sympathizer, or that he had had more than an occasional consultative connection with the State Department. After four months of hearings, the Democratic majority on the investigating committee reported that McCarthy had failed to prove a case against a single individual in the State Department and that his charges constituted "the most nefarious campaign of half-truths and untruth in the history of the Republic." In a minority report, Senator Henry Cabot Lodge, Republican from Massachusetts, conceded that McCarthy had not proved his charges, but criticized the investigation as superficial and inconclusive. Senator Bourke Hickenlooper of Iowa, the other Republican on the committee, refused to sign either report, but left little doubt that his sympathies were with McCarthy.

Fear of subversion was readily translated into a fear of aliens. In June, 1952, Congress passed over President Truman's veto the McCarran-Walter Act, a codification and revision of Federal immigration laws. Although the new measure did repeal the unfortunate Asiatic exclusion clause that had damaged American prestige in the Far East since 1924, it was the reverse of liberal in most of its other provisions. The discriminatory national origins quotas were retained, and strict new barriers were added to exclude aliens who might at any time have been affiliated either with Communist or Communist-front groups or with any other totalitarian party.

Republican Upsurge

The heavy atmosphere of party politics that hung over the loyalty issue pervaded an ever larger area of public discussion. The Congressional election of 1950 was bitterly contested, with the Democrats claiming exclusive credit for saving the world from Communist domination and the Republicans charging that their opponents were leading the nation into disaster by domestic "socialism" and foreign appeasement. "Acheson Must Go" was a favorite Republican slogan. The attack upon the Secretary of State probably derived in part from his reputation for aloofness and unpopularity with the politicians, but the professed reasons largely concerned his Far Eastern policy, which was blamed for the Communist victory in China and American involvement in Korea.

The election resulted in heavy Republican gains. Although the opposition party failed to win control of Congress, its representation in the Senate rose from 42 to 47 seats and in the House from 171 to 199. Two contests had particularly significant results. Senator Taft's prestige was much increased by his great majority in the Ohio senatorial election. Organized labor had announced its intention of punishing the sponsor of the controversial Taft-Hartley Act, but the attempt failed—in part because of the weak candidacy of Taft's Democratic opponent, and in part because of an apparent determination of many voters to resist labor union dictation. In a bitter contest in Maryland, the veteran Senator Tydings was defeated by Republican John M. Butler. This upset was generally attributed to the Republican charge that Tydings, as chairman of the special committee investigating Senator McCarthy's accusations, had "whitewashed" the Truman administration and had protected the "Reds." A faked photograph showing Tydings in earnest conversation with the Communist leader, Earl Browder, was widely circulated. In view of the fact that Tydings was a well-known conservative whom President Roosevelt had tried to "purge" as an anti-New Dealer in 1938, these charges appeared absurd, but they apparently counted with many Maryland voters. The result of this selection was to increase the influence of Senator McCarthy in Republican party circles, despite the fact that several fair-minded Republicans like Senator Margaret Chase Smith of Maine publicly condemned his tactics.

These and other striking Republican victories in 1950 aroused party hopes for the presidential election of 1952. Although determined never again to underestimate Truman as they had so disastrously in 1948, the Republicans gained confidence through numerous episodes that appeared to diminish the prestige of the administration. Although the President's personal honesty was seldom questioned, his tact definitely was. Much more damaging to the administration was the fact that men close to the White House were accused of accepting gifts and favors in return for influencing the decisions of government agencies on contracts and loans. In 1949 an investigation of the so-called 5 percenters—political fixers who undertook to obtain government contracts for small businessmen for a fee—resulted in a jail sentence for John Maragon, a crony of Major General Harry Vaughan, the President's military aide. In 1951, Senator Fulbright of Arkansas, himself a Democrat, charged that the Reconstruction Finance Corporation had been influenced in the making of loans by a ring of fixers with connections in the White House and in the RFC itself. A key figure was alleged to be E. Merl Young, husband of a White House stenographer. Some of the testimony heard by the Senate Banking Subcommittee, of which Fulbright was chairman, involved the mysterious gift of a $9,540 mink coat to Mrs. Young. Seeking to restore public confidence in the integrity of the RFC, President Truman adopted a plan recommended by the Fulbright Committee for reorganizing the agency under a single administrator instead of a board of five directors. Despite strong opposition by Republicans, who believed the RFC should be entirely liquidated because its original objective had been fulfilled, the President's reorganization plan was allowed to stand by a narrow vote in Congress.

The Truman administration was further weakened by the end of 1951 by revelations of widespread irregularities in the Internal Revenue Bureau. Prosecutions for income tax frauds had been squelched through bribes and "gifts" to the officials of the bureau, while the latter had sometimes used their positions to extort money from taxpayers who had reason to fear investigation. As the President ordered a belated housecleaning, dismissals and sudden resignations swept the country. Seven out of 64 collectors gave up their posts, and almost 200 other subordinates in the Bureau resigned or were dismissed. The scandal even touched the Justice Department when Assistant Attorney General T. Lamar Caudle was ousted for accepting favors from tax delinquents.[10] Seeking to restore public confidence in a branch of government that touched every taxpayer, Truman submitted to Congress a plan for a completely different organization of the Bureau under the Reorganization Act. But the President's reform steps were taken too falteringly to save his prestige.

The Republicans also found campaign ammunition in the widely publicized hearings of the Senate Special Crime Investigation Committee, under the chairmanship of Estes Kefauver of Tennessee. These revealed a close tie between underworld elements and local politicians in many Democratic-controlled cities.

Republican administrations like those of Grant and Harding, when besmirched by scandal, had been able to brazen out the situation and hold on to power. That the voters punished the Democrats more sternly did not mean that the Democratic misdeeds were more heinous than the Republican had been, or that the country was more virtuous. The revelations of wrongdoing under Truman came at just the opportune moment to accentuate the swing to the Republicans, a swing already strongly apparent because of popular resent-

---

[10] In 1956 Caudle and Matthew J. Connelly, who had been Truman's appointments secretary, were convicted in Federal court of having conspired to help a defendant accused of tax evasion.

ment over the Korean War, over the bad relations with Russia, and over Communist infiltration of government—both imaginary and real. Under the circumstances, any Republican candidate for President would have been a strong contender in 1952, and the popular hero, Dwight D. Eisenhower, was a sure winner.

28

Changing America

During the 1940's and 1950's the conditions of American life were strikingly different from those that had prevailed during the '30's. To a new generation, stories of collapsing prices, wholesale foreclosures, and mass unemployment seemed as remote and unreal as though these recent misfortunes had been suffered on another planet. War and the threat of war kept industrial activity at a high peak; full employment and good wages laid the basis for a high standard of living despite high prices. And yet, although it was an age of prosperity, it was not a complacent age like the twenties. The possibility of nuclear war hung over life like a threatening shadow, interdicting the kind of irresponsible individualism that had prevailed in the post-World War I decade. Because it was an age of anxiety, it was an age that feared the unfamiliar. The man who got ahead was the man who avoided eccentricities of opinion and behavior and conformed to established patterns.

The New American Capitalism

The American economic system was still in process of evolution. The form it was taking was not easy to describe. Certainly it bore little resemblance to the stereotype of capitalism denounced in Marxist propaganda. On the other hand, it was not much like the free competitive system described in the older American textbooks either.

The tendency toward what the economists called oligopoly, already evident during the twenties, continued. In most leading industries a few major corporations dominated the field. The general situation was neatly illustrated in the automobile industry. During World War II, when war production forced the cessation of all pleasure vehicle manufacturing, the magazines and newspapers contained frequent stories about the new automobile companies and bold new car designs to be expected after the war. In the cold postwar dawn, however, all these dreams evaporated. Despite the sale of millions of dollars of stock to hopeful investors, the Tucker—heralded as a marvel of advanced design—never went into production at all. The Kaiser and the Henry J survived the perils of birth, but succumbed during infancy despite the fact that they were promoted by Henry J. Kaiser, who had made an outstanding wartime success in shipbuilding.

Even the older independents held on with difficulty. In 1954 the American Motors Corporation was organized to merge the Hudson and Nash companies. Later in the same year the remaining two independent companies united forces in the Studebaker-Packard Corporation. But these reorganizations could not greatly alter the basic elements in the situation. The big three—General Motors, Ford, and Chrysler—continued to enjoy overwhelming advantages in acquiring the best plants and machinery, the ablest personnel, the best contracts with suppliers, and ample working capital. Particularly in the field of distribution, the older independents competed only with difficulty and the newer ones found the situation impossible. The mass sale of cars depended upon a nation-wide network of enterprising dealers and a loyal following among the buying public.

In 1955, when total production of passenger cars reached an unprecedented 7.9 million, more than half this business went to General Motors; Ford's and Chrysler's shares were respectively 28 and 17 per cent. This left for the struggling independents only a little more than 4 per cent of the market.

The automobile situation was by no means unique. In the manufacture of steel, chemicals, gasoline, cigarettes, and a score of other products, a few firms were the leaders, and the smaller companies survived as best they could. According to one authority, 135 corporations owned 45 per cent of the industrial assets of the United States; this was almost one quarter of those of the entire world. Some experts believed that the situation had now stabilized itself and that big and small business would henceforth continue to exist in roughly the same ratio, although the aggregate of production, of course, would continue to grow.

Aggressive price competition was not a characteristic of the new capitalism. The standard brands of cigarettes always sold for the same price; the price per ton of steel was customarily the same, from whatever company it was purchased; the price differential among Chevrolets, Fords, and Plymouths was never large. Obviously, some force other than conventional supply and demand was at work. The large corporations administered their prices on the basis of careful calculations of costs at given levels of production, desired margins of profit, potential markets, public relations, and other highly sophisticated considerations.

This did not mean that competition had disappeared. The rivalry between Chevrolet and Ford, or between Camels and Luckies, was obviously acute, but it took the form of appeals to the consuming public based upon supposed differences in quality rather than price. In the automobile market the struggle was to a large extent fought out on the drafting board, where the annual models were designed. To anticipate the trends in popular tests, to gain an advantage in placement of headlights, curvature of windshield, or shape of fenders, was worth millions of dollars. Out of this competition the postwar car evolved as a longer, wider, shinier, and faster model than its prewar predecessors. Most of the public apparently loved the illusion of luxury provided by 120-inch wheelbases and 200-horsepower engines, but a rebellious minority expressed disapproval by buying smaller and more economical cars imported from Europe.

If feminine purchasers in particular often seemed more interested in car bodies than in engines, the same tendency could be seen throughout the merchandising world. As self-service drug stores, hardware emporiums, and other wait-on-yourself establishments followed in the path of the already triumphant supermarkets, attractive packaging often seemed the most important competitive advantage that a product could have.

An even greater asset, however, was a familiar brand name that customers would ask for instinctively. To implant these desired responses, industry spent increasing sums that reached a total of some $10 billion in 1956. The writing and placing of the advertising became a highly specialized business, centering on Madison Avenue, New York. In planning their sales strategies, the experts conducted ambitious market surveys and even experimented with appeals suggested by Freudian psychology.

The Managers

The death of Henry Ford in 1947 was a symbolic event. Even during his lifetime Ford had become an anachronism, and after his passing this species of industrial tycoon became almost extinct. The poorly educated, erratic genius, who made millions through native shrewdness and flashes of intuition, was well equipped to build an economic empire, but not to administer it. Business leaders were now usually college-educated men who had spent many years with their particular companies, where they had gradually made their way up the managerial ladder until they reached the top. The new managerial class looked for its financial rewards, not through appropriating a lion's share of the profits, but through substantial salaries and retirement benefits. Its most important incentive was perhaps not financial at all, but professional pride in the progress of the corporation.

The successful business executive was no longer a man of dictatorial temperament who handed down commands to subservient lieutenants. He was more
likely to have the qualities of a good team captain, able to inspire the loyalty of
his fellow executives and to keep the multiple wheels of a complex organization
running smoothly. Not one man, but groups of men, generally worked out the
key company policies. To supply the data for these decisions, large research departments were employed, as well as efficient squads of accountants, lawyers,
and engineers.

The result of these changes was paradoxical. In the old days everyone had
known about John D. Rockefeller, or Andrew Carnegie, or George Westinghouse; now relatively few people could have identified the men who were
managing General Motors, Standard Oil of New Jersey, or U. S. Steel. Yet the
new corporations were much more powerful than the old ones had been. Management decisions might affect the welfare of whole communities; they might
contribute to or combat the inflation of the national economy; they might
involve American foreign relations in remote sections of the globe. Almost any
management policy of a billion-dollar corporation had limitless ramifications.

Who chose these men of power? In theory, the corporation stockholders
elected the board of directors; and the board in turn fixed the major policies and
hired the managers to run the company in its day-to-day operations. In practice,
however, the stockholders had little influence. The large corporation had so
many stockholders, and even large stockholders held so small a proportion of
the entire stock, that ownership meant little except a right to receive whatever
share in the profits the directors voted to distribute. In the election of directors
and other matters that the stockholders were entitled to decide, the vote was by
proxy, and under normal circumstances only the existing management had the
necessary facilities for soliciting and collecting these proxies. This meant that,
except in the case of a major revolt, the management was self-perpetuating.

At least in the case of the largest corporations, finance capitalism which had
seemed so powerful in 1900 exerted much less influence a half century later. The
vast sums needed for business expansion were largely raised through channels
independent of the investment banker. According to one study, 64 per cent of
the $150 billion spent in capital expenditure in the United States between
1946 and 1953 came from "internal sources"—that is, by plowing back a share
of the profits of the corporations themselves. Of the remainder, 36 per cent was
raised by current borrowing, 12 per cent by the issue of bonds, and 6 per cent by
the issue of stock. Even in the cases where bonds and stock were issued to
raise capital, the corporations were sometimes strong enough to sell the new
securities directly to their own stockholders without depending upon Wall
Street syndicates. This ability to find their own money was another bulwark of
strength to management.

Management control encountered some criticism from stockholders who grumbled because more of the corporate profits were not distributed as dividends, or accused the company executives of rewarding themselves too generously with high salaries, retirement benefits, and stock option plans. The shrewder managements were able to keep such discontent at a minimum and to instill in their stockholders a sense of pride in the accomplishments of the company. The annual report, once a dreary compilation of unexplained statistics and dull prose, now blossomed forth as an attractively printed brochure with glossy covers, pictures, and down-to-earth explanations of company policies. The Standard Oil Company of New Jersey encouraged a large attendance at its annual meetings, where stockholders happily munched sandwiches and addressed questions to company executives. Other large corporations copied Standard Oil in erasing the popular image of the annual meeting as an anachronistic formality and substituting that of a happy gathering combining the spirit of the family reunion and the college pep fest.

This urgent need to humanize the corporations extended far beyond the relationship of the managers with their own stockholders. Each company had its public relations officers alert to obtain favorable publicity. Schoolteachers were provided with educational movies and other free teaching material. Rotary clubs and other luncheon groups found a convenient source of free speakers. Enthusiastic support was given to community chest drives and other local charities. Just how far corporate responsibility extended in the direction of philanthropy was a serious question. Many progressive industrialists believed that the corporations should make generous annual gifts to colleges, hospitals, and research organizations; conservative businessmen feared that such a policy would subject them to stockholder criticism and involve them in controversial issues.

Whether or not the corporations had a direct obligation to practice philanthropy, wealthy men did feel increasing responsibility to make personal gifts. The earlier examples of Carnegie and Rockefeller were followed by the establishment of a long list of charitable foundations. Greatest of all these public trusts was the Ford Foundation, established in 1936 but receiving most of its assets after the death of Henry Ford in 1947. Endowed with over 3 million shares of stock in the Ford Motor Company, the new foundation was in a position to distribute princely sums, particularly in the field of education. In part, the rise of the great foundations was to be explained in terms of the greater responsibility toward society felt by wealthy families; in part, the gifts reflected the influence of heavy taxes on income and inheritance. The choice confronting rich men was often not between keeping or giving away their money, but between redistributing the major portion of their fortunes through the agency of government or through private trustees.

Labor Seeks Security

In one of the most penetrating analyses of the new American capitalism, Professor John K. Galbraith of Harvard put forth a theory of countervailing power. The huge economic power of the giant corporations, Galbraith observed, was held in check both by the countervailing power of other corporations that purchased their products (as, for example, the automobile companies bought steel) and by the growing power of government and labor unions.

Despite labor's dislike for the Taft-Hartley Act and state right-to-work laws, the unions suffered no real diminution of power, at least in the economic sphere. The American public now accepted it as part of the normal course of events that union contracts with management would periodically run out and have to be renewed. Whenever this happened, the labor leaders invariably requested not only substantial pay raises, but a growing variety of other benefits. Management always offered less than labor demanded. This set the stage for feverish bargaining sessions and sometimes for strikes—although after 1946 these were seldom as serious as the immediate postwar strikes had been. The principal reason was the prevailing prosperity, which encouraged employers to grant much of what labor demanded in order to keep production rolling. The relation of these successive wage increases to inflation was a matter of dispute. The workers claimed they were demanding no more than they needed to meet rising prices; management retorted that the increased cost of labor was one of the principal causes of these higher prices.

As much of the old-time blood and thunder passed out of labor-management relations, hopeful new formulas were evolved to make strikes less frequent. In 1948 General Motors and the United Automobile Workers (UAW) signed a contract containing a so-called "escalator clause," under which wage rates were tied to the Bureau of Labor Standards cost-of-living index. When living costs went up, automatic wage increases would go into effect; when costs went down, wages would be reduced. Many other companies accepted the escalator clause— to the general satisfaction of the workers in a period of rising prices.

An even more important precedent was provided by the contract signed by General Motors and the UAW in 1950. Instead of the usual one-year term, the new agreement was to run for five years with annual wage increases, cost-of-living adjustments, and a variety of fringe benefits. Once again the example of General Motors was followed by other companies, and the one-year contract— with its unsettling effects—became less common.

By this time the general public had become accustomed to the idea that the automobile industry was likely to be the testing ground for new strategies on the part of both management and labor. Therefore it was no surprise when Walter Reuther, the peppery head of the UAW, began in 1955 to push a demand for what was called the guaranteed annual wage. Intended as security against unemployment and seasonal layoffs, this would have obligated the automobile companies to supplement state unemployment benefits so that unemployed workers would be guaranteed 80 per cent of their pay for 52 weeks. In its original form the guaranteed annual wage was unacceptable to management, but first Ford and then the other companies granted a modified version, called Supplementary Unemployment Benefits (SUB). This provided that the companies would set up funds out of which state unemployment benefits would be supplemented, so that laid-off workers would receive 65 per cent of their take-home pay for 4 weeks and 60 per cent for 22 more weeks. As other companies conceded the SUB, labor felt encouraged to believe that the new policy would not only insure greater justice to the unemployed worker, but would spur management to plan its production schedules so that seasonal lay-offs would be reduced to a minimum.

All labor contracts showed an increasing emphasis on the so-called fringe benefits—retirement pensions, vacations and holidays with pay, group life insurance, accidental death payments, and hospitalization and medical plans. Sometimes these benefits were administered through union welfare funds, to which the employers agreed to make regular contributions. In 1946, for example, the United Workers under John L. Lewis' aggressive leadership won a royalty on each ton of bituminous coal to be paid into a welfare and retirement fund. Although there were occasional charges of mismanagement of the miners' fund, much good was done through the building of hospitals and the provision for medical care in many isolated mining communities that had never had such services before.

In 1955 the AFL and CIO buried their twenty-year quarrel and merged under the name of the American Federation of Labor and Congress of Industrial Organizations (AFL–CIO). The two main branches of the labor movement had been moving toward reunion for several years. Both had been under new leadership since November, 1952, when by strange coincidence Philip Murray of the CIO and William Green of the AFL died within two weeks of each other. Walter Reuther, the new CIO executive, and George Meany, who now headed the AFL, patiently laid the groundwork for reconciliation. In 1954 the two federations agreed to a "no-raiding" pact, and in December, 1955, the merger was finally consummated at a convention in New York City. Total membership in the new AFL–CIO was about 15 million—10 million contributed by the old AFL and 5 million by the CIO. Meany was elected president; Reuther became vice president in charge of the Industrial Department.

Many serious problems confronted Meany and Reuther. The old quarrel had left many unhealed wounds. Moreover, the labor movement was not yet completely unified. Some 2 million workers belonged to independent unions like the United Mine Workers and the Railroad Brotherhoods. Since three quarters of American labor still did not belong to any union, the new federation pledged itself to a vigorous organizing campaign, but workers in the 1950's proved much more difficult to recruit than they had during the 1930's and 1940's. Prosperity had brought so much improvement in working conditions that the gnawing discontent that made for swift unionization was no longer prevalent.

Labor's Bad Boys

Although Meany and Reuther believed in an aggressive unionism, they wanted a labor movement that was kept clean of Communist infiltration and unwholesome connections with the criminal world. The battle to throw out the Communists had been largely won before the merger, but the battle against union corruption was just beginning.

The dangers of corrupt unionism were well illustrated by the situation along the waterfronts of New York City and other Eastern ports. The rough and unruly workers upon whom the ports depended to load and unload ships belonged to the International Longshoremen's Association, AFL. In December, 1952, an investigation by a special New York Crime Commission revealed that the ILA was dominated by racketeers, many of them with criminal records. These thugs ruled the waterfront by terroristic methods. By controlling the hiring halls they arbitrarily decided which longshoremen would have jobs and thereby kept the men in subjection. By threatening strikes and slowdowns they forced shipping lines to pay tribute that went directly into their own pockets. So long as these extortions were not too outrageous, the shipping companies found it more advantageous to go along with the system than to try to buck it. The New York investigation also revealed that the waterfront rackets had gained protection by tieing in with corrupt politicians in New York City and Jersey City. The prize-winning movie "On the Waterfront" gave wide publicity to the situation.

Despite all this adverse publicity, the ILA defended itself successfully against all who tried to destroy it. The state governments of New York and New Jersey established a joint Waterfront Commission to attack the abuses, and the AFL cooperated by expelling the ILA and chartering a new union, the International Brotherhood of Longshoremen. But when NLRB elections were held in 1953, 1954, and 1955, the independent ILA defeated its AFL-chartered rival on each occasion—either because the longshoremen actually preferred the old union or because they did not dare to vote against it. During the long struggle the ILA weathered major strikes, Taft-Hartley injunctions, and convictions for contempt of court. But if this tough union refused to die, it did at least submit to face-washing. Under pressure from the Waterfront Commission the worst abuses of the hiring system were corrected, and to compete successfully with its AFL rival the ILA felt compelled to deal somewhat more fairly with its own membership.

The ILA was a relatively small union with only 60,000 members. Its great importance lay in its ability to tie up shipping in Eastern ports. To the honest labor movement a still greater challenge was posed by the International Brotherhood of Teamsters. With its 1.4 million members, this giant had displaced the United Automobile Workers for the distinction of being the largest American union. In economic power the Teamsters had no rival. Controlling practically all the truckdrivers of the nation, the union was in a position to tie up the business of almost any city or region. The success or failure of other unions' strikes often depended on whether or not the Teamsters would respect their picket lines. Yet a series of revelations in 1957 showed that the leadership of the Teamsters was shockingly corrupt.

Unsavory disclosures concerning the Teamsters resulted from the investigations of a special Senate Committee on Improper Activities in the Labor or Management Field under the chairmanship of Senator John L. McClellan, an Arkansas Democrat. The committee employed as special counsel 31-year-old Robert Kennedy, brother of Massachusetts Senator John Kennedy. Under Kennedy's probing the special committee learned many things about the Teamsters' high command despite mysterious disappearances of key witnesses, burning of records, lapses of memory, and refusals to answer questions that might tend to incriminate. Through connections with local politicians, it appeared that Teamster officials had controlled a string of taverns, gambling joints, and houses of prostitution in Portland, Oregon. Dave Beck, the portly union president, had become wealthy by exploiting his position. Not content with a princely salary and the privilege of living rent-free in a Seattle mansion purchased with union funds, Beck had made highly profitable investments, using not only his own money but money improperly "borrowed" from the union welfare fund. Particularly unethical was Beck's practice of borrowing money from companies with which the union had labor contracts, thereby playing both sides of the table.

To the AFL–CIO leadership, Dave Beck was a serious problem. Unless energetic steps were taken to clean house, the whole labor movement might be injured through public resentment and demands for anti-union legislation. Yet under the constitution of the federation, unions enjoyed almost complete autonomy. Unless the Teamsters themselves elected new leaders, Meany and his associates could only reprimand the wrongdoers and threaten the union with expulsion. What could be done was done. In February, 1957, the AFL–CIO executive council, meeting at Miami, adopted a strict code of ethics, condemning such abuses as those that had developed in the Teamsters union. In May

Beck was removed from his AFL–CIO vice-presidency after a hearing in which he was found guilty of "gross misuse of union funds."

The convergence of heat from Congressional investigation, AFL–CIO condemnation, and Federal indictment for income tax evasion was sufficient to convince Beck that he should not run for re-election to the Teamster presidency. But the heir-apparent to Beck's crown, Jimmy Hoffa, was, in the opinion of many observers, an even more sinister figure than Beck himself. A cocky and aggressive young man, Hoffa had the same reputation for using union funds for business speculations that Beck did and, in addition, was alleged to have close ties with New York's notorious Johnny Dio and the gangsters of many other cities.

In what appeared to be a coordinated drive to prevent Hoffa's election to the Teamster presidency, the McClellan Committee subpoenaed him to testify concerning his activities, the AFL–CIO executive council charged the union with being dominated by corrupt influences and gave it an ultimatum to clean up, and a rival faction within the Teamsters appealed to the Federal courts to halt the union election on the grounds that Hoffa had rigged it through the chartering of "paper" locals and other irregularities. But at their October, 1957, convention, the defiant Teamsters resisted all these pressures and gave the presidency to Hoffa by an overwhelming vote. The new head warned the AFL–CIO not to interfere, but promised that he himself would eliminate union corruption and make the Teamsters a "model of trade unionism."

In its December, 1957, convention, the AFL–CIO carried its campaign to eliminate union corruption a step farther by voting to expel the Teamsters and several smaller unions where similar conditions had been uncovered.

Rise of the Negro

In no area was the long view more required than in considering the position of the Negro in American life. Disenfranchisement, discrimination, poverty, and lack of opportunity were often the black man's lot. Yet there are degrees in misfortune and the Negro's situation had improved in many ways since 1900.

Americans have always believed in education as the most valuable key to every problem, and in this area real progress had been made. In 1910 30 per cent of the Negroes had been illiterate; only 8 per cent were thus handicapped in 1940. As late as 1915 there had been only 64 Negro high schools in the country; by 1940 the number had risen to 2,500. Almost 20,000 Negroes were graduated from colleges during the decades of the thirties—more than twice the number of the more prosperous twenties. After World War II these educational trends were accelerated.

Mob violence, so terrifying to the Negroes and so degrading to the whites, was diminishing. More than 100 Negroes had been lynched in each of the first two years of the century, and there were between 50 and 100 such incidents annually thereafter until 1917. The relatively good record of only 35 lynchings of Negroes in that year was not maintained; in 1919 there were 76—but thereafter the annual number dropped until in 1929 it fell to 7. Once again the gain was not permanent and in 1933 there were 24; but there were never more than 8 in any year after 1936. In 1952, 1953, and 1954 there were no lynchings at all.

During World War II Americans were shocked by several race riots. Detroit, whose war industries had attracted both Negroes and Southern whites, was the scene of strife in 1942 and again in 1943. Similar if less serious clashes occurred in the Harlem district of New York City and in Los Angeles. Several fatalities took place in the South when trouble arose between Negro soldiers and white police or civilians, while an ugly clash between white and Negro soldiers occurred at Fort Dix, New Jersey. Disquieting as these incidents were, there was much less violence than in the terrible year of 1919, when race riots had taken place in 26 American cities. More important than the smaller number of riots during World War II—which might be ascribed principally to good fortune—were the positive steps taken in scores of American communities to prevent race relations from deteriorating to the point where there was danger of such incidents. Such diverse institutions as churches, schools, police departments, and labor unions undertook educational projects and other programs intended to reduce misunderstanding between whites and Negroes.

As the Negro came to enjoy somewhat more security against mob violence, he became more concerned over the problem of "legal lynching"—the practice in many states of dealing more drastically with blacks accused of crime than with whites. Nation-wide publicity was attracted to the so-called Scottsboro case, in which an Alabama court sentenced to death nine Negroes charged with attacking two white women. The Federal Supreme Court overruled a first conviction in 1932 on the ground that the defendants were not permitted to have adequate counsel, and a second conviction in 1935 because the Negroes had been systematically excluded from the jury lists. Despite the rulings of the Supreme Court, however, the tacit exclusion of Negroes from jury service continued to be the practice in most rural courts of the South.

Negroes with outstanding talent received an increasing degree of recognition. Upon the death of George Washington Carver in 1943, impressive tribute was paid to his achievements as a scientist. Marian Anderson was acknowledged to belong in the company of the greatest singers of her generation, while the extraordinary musical talent of Roland Hayes and Dorothy Maynor was given due praise. An increasing number of Negroes achieved distinction in literature and the arts. Acclaimed by both white and black sports lovers were such out-

Marian Anderson. (Brown Bros.)

standing Negro athletes as heavyweight champion Joe Louis, fleet-footed Jesse Owens, the hero of the 1936 Olympic games, and Jackie Robinson, the first Negro in big-league baseball.

Not so promising, however, were the prospects for Negroes of only ordinary ability. In the vital matter of earning a living, the black man found himself seriously handicapped by racial prejudice. The lot of the sharecropper and tenant in the South tended to deteriorate. Negroes left the land and moved to the cities, particularly those of the North. Yet here they encountered the prejudice not only of the employers but of workers who frequently admitted only whites to their labor unions. The CIO sought to encourage more liberal policies, but was by no means able to break down the barriers in all local unions. Negroes usually had to accept the menial tasks that no one else wanted. They were the last to be hired in boom days and the first to be let out when business lagged. No group suffered more during the Great Depression.

Some New Deal policies hurt the Negro. This was true of the crop restriction efforts of the early AAA and of some aspects of the NRA that resulted in Negro employees being discharged rather than being given minimum-wage rates. But other policies were of great benefit. Employment under WPA and other forms of relief saved many Negro families from disaster, while PWA and USHA housing projects were of particular value to a group that had hitherto had to dwell almost exclusively in the slums. On the balance, most Negroes approved the New Deal, and thousands in the Northern cities changed their political allegiance—temporarily at least—from the party of Lincoln to that of Franklin Roosevelt.

As the Negro vote became independent, politicians became more acutely conscious of Negro demands. Although filibusters by Southern Senators prevented votes on the Federal anti-lynching bills that came before Congress in the thirties and the anti-poll-tax measures of the forties, these proposals showed impressive strength. Federal intervention undoubtedly contributed to significant changes of opinion in the South. Lynching fell under almost universal public condemnation. A few states repealed the poll-tax laws that had served to exclude the Negro from the ballot. On this issue, however, Southern opinion was still conservative, and various legal obstacles as well as extralegal forms of coercion prevented many Negroes in the South from exercising their constitutional right to vote. This continued to be so even after 1944, when the Supreme Court struck down one of the principal white bulwarks by ruling that Negroes might not be excluded from voting in primary elections.

An impressive victory for the Negro race was won when President Roosevelt on June 25, 1941, issued Executive Order 8802, which declared:

> . . . the policy of the United States [is] to encourage full participation in the national defense program by all citizens of the United States, regardless of race, creed, color, or national origin, in the firm belief that the democratic way of life within the Nation can be defended successfully only with the help and support of all groups within its borders.

Such affirmations of principle had been made before; what made this one more than mere words was the appointment of a Fair Employment Practices Committee (FEPC) to investigate complaints and to take steps to redress grievances. The FEPC conducted public hearings and focused publicity on employers and unions practicing discrimination. The effort to open up new areas of employment for the Negroes was well timed since war production provided an almost unlimited demand for labor of all kinds. Between 1940 and 1944 the number of Negroes employed in manufacturing and processing increased from 500,000 to around 1.2 million; in government service from 60,000 to 200,000. President Truman advocated the continuance of FEPC as a permanent postwar agency, but the proposal was defeated by the filibustering tactics of Senator Bilbo of Mississippi and other Southern legislators.

Despite this setback, the antidiscrimination cause made progress. The struggle, first against fascism, then against communism, quickened the conscience of many whites; the inconsistency of waging war against totalitarian government abroad while denying racial equality at home was obvious. Moreover, the injustice of demanding from Negroes the full obligation of citizenship in the way of military service while denying them many of its privileges became clear to more and more Americans. Governor Dewey of New York succeeded in obtaining an excellent antidiscrimination law from the state legislature in 1945, and similar measures were enacted in other states and municipalities.

A series of Supreme Court decisions threatened to overturn the whole system of segregation in Southern education. Earlier interpretations of the Fourteenth Amendment had permitted segregation, provided the facilities available to Negroes were "separate but equal" to those available to whites. The new decisions laid much stronger stress on equality. Negroes, it was ruled, did not enjoy equal educational facilities if their tuition was paid at out-of-state schools while white students were provided with higher education in state-supported institutions within the state. The issue was particularly acute in law, medicine, and other expensive forms of graduate instruction. The Court ruled that equal facilities were not provided when special graduate schools for Negroes were demonstrably inferior in faculty and equipment to state-supported white institutions, and when Negroes were permitted to attend classes along with whites in state schools but were required by law to sit apart in classroom and library and take their meals at a different time. Confronted by these decisions, a number of Southern state universities abandoned segregation at the graduate level. At the undergraduate level there were fewer changes in the old system; in elementary and secondary schools, none at all. But intelligent Southerners now recognized that segregation in education could be retained, if at all, only through such radical improvement in Negro schools that their "separate but equal" status would be an actuality.

The final overthrow of the "separate but equal" doctrine came in a Supreme Court decision of May 17, 1954 (Brown v. Topeka). Chief Justice Earl Warren, whom President Eisenhower had appointed in 1953 after the death of Chief Justice Vinson, spoke for a unanimous court in ruling that separate facilities were inherently unequal and that laws requiring Negroes to attend separate public schools violated the Fourteenth Amendment by denying to persons "the equal protection of the laws." Thus at one stroke the Supreme Court destroyed the whole legal structure by which segregated education was required in seventeen states and permitted in four others.

Unequivocal though the decision was, the tribunal recognized that school segregation could not be eliminated overnight. Not until a year later, in May,

1955, did the Court, after hearing arguments from all interested parties, lay down the principles that should guide compliance. Responsibility for integrating schools was placed upon the shoulders of local school authorities, but the Federal district courts were to see that the task was done. The elimination of segregation should proceed with what the Court called "deliberate speed." The district courts were to see that "a prompt and reasonable start" was made, but they might allow additional time for meeting specific local problems.

The way in which the various states responded to the Supreme Court's directive differed greatly. The District of Columbia integrated its schools promptly, and such border states as Maryland, Delaware, Kentucky, Missouri, and Oklahoma at once began the gradual process that the Court had recommended. In a second ring of states including Tennessee, Arkansas, Texas, and North Carolina, integration proceeded much more slowly, and the greater proportion of the schools were still segregated three years after the historic decision. In the remainder of the South—in Virginia, South Carolina, Florida, Alabama, Louisiana, Mississippi, and Georgia—the universal attitude was one of stubborn non-compliance. The politicians sought to prevent integration by a network of legal obstacles. Some state legislatures declared the Supreme Court's decision to be itself unconstitutional and affirmed their right to "interpose"—whatever this vague term might mean—to prevent enforcement of the ruling. Other states passed laws authorizing officials to abolish the public school system if segregation were required, to cut off state funds from any district that integrated its schools, and to use state funds for the support of private segregated schools. In several states the National Association for the Advancement of Colored People, which had taken the lead in the fight against segregation, was harassed by new laws and litigation.

Even more serious was the increasing resort to racial hatred and mob action. In some communities the Ku Klux Klan was revived; in others, so-called Citizens Councils encouraged economic reprisals and mass demonstrations against Negroes who tried to assert their rights. Not all the fomenters of trouble were Southerners; one of the most notorious rabble-rousers was John Kasper, a native of New Jersey.

With the stiffening of die-hard opposition on the segregation issue, it was obviously only a question of time before Federal and state authority would clash in a more dramatic way than they had since Reconstruction days. The next chapter will describe how this showdown came during the second Eisenhower administration.

Women and the Family

During World War II more than three million women took jobs who would not have done so otherwise. In addition, millions of farm wives did outside chores which had always been considered men's work. A quarter of a million women enlisted in the WACS, the WAVES, or some other service. It was convincing proof of women's ability to perform any task that did not involve extraordinary physical strength. The effect of the war, however, was not to institute a new trend so much as to accelerate one already strongly established. In 1880, 2.5 million women had worked; the number had increased to 5 million by 1920 and to 11 million by 1940.

After the war it became even more common for women to become wage and salary earners. By 1957 the number of females over 14 gainfully employed had risen to over 22 million—twice the number in 1940. Prosperity opened up the jobs; electric appliances lightened the housework that had bound wives to the home; and inflation provided the spur to seek extra income for the family.

Typical of the new woman was Eleanor Roosevelt. Impatient with the purely social duties traditionally imposed upon the First Lady, Mrs. Roosevelt carried on an extraordinary number of activities. At various times she accepted employment as a teacher, lecturer, radio commentator, magazine feature writer, and columnist for the daily press. Her unpaid activities were even more extensive. The First Lady's zeal made her a figure scarcely less controversial than her husband. Many Americans asserted that Mrs. Roosevelt's activities should be confined to the White House, that her restless traveling was both undignified and meddlesome. On the other hand, she had millions of admirers and defenders; to them she was a great person in her own right, giving herself without stint to causes in which she believed. After her husband's death, Mrs. Roosevelt gained new respect as a courageous advocate of human rights in the Assembly of the United Nations.

Women gained distinction in many different lines of endeavor. Within the field of government they achieved administrative posts, seats in the Senate and the House, governorships, and important diplomatic missions. In the field of literature they may be said to have gained equal recognition with men. Few journalists commanded more respect than Dorothy Thompson, Anne O'Hare McCormick, Marguerite Higgins and Freda Kirchwey.

The extent to which women's ambition for a career undermined the stability of the family was a matter of dispute. An increasing number of women, confronted with the choice of marriage or a job, elected to take both. Critics connected the practice with the rising divorce rate and increasing juvenile delinquency, but it was difficult to prove that the woman who worked was necessarily a worse wife and mother than the woman who stayed in the home.

Whatever its perils, marriage was hardly declining in popularity. In 1910, 59 per cent of all women over the age of 15 were married, while 30 per cent were single; in 1950, 66 per cent were married, while only 20 per cent were single. The war years were characterized by an unusually large number of youthful marriages. The depression of the early thirties had caused the marriage rate to drop to 7.9 per thousand population in 1932, but it climbed to 12.1 by 1940, the highest rate since 1920. The rate rose to 13.1 in 1942. For the next three years the rate was lower, but in the first postwar year, 1946, the marriage rate jumped to 16.4, the highest of the twentieth century. Many war marriages were entered upon in haste and were strained by separation and the tensions of wartime living. The divorce rate, which had climbed from 0.73 per thousand population in 1900 to 2.0 in 1940, jumped to an abnormal 4.3 in 1946 and then fell back to about 2.5 per thousand in 1950.

The decline in the birth rate, which had disturbed some observers during the twenties and early thirties, was at least temporarily arrested. In the depression year of 1933 the rate had fallen to 16.6 per thousand population; better times brought it up to 17.9 in 1940, while the war resulted in its rising to 21.5 in 1943—the highest since 1925. Youth's eagerness to marry and have children during the darkest period of the war seemed to indicate that it had little fear of the future. The new trend continued during the postwar years with a birth rate of 25.8 in 1947 and 24.6 in 1955.

Wartime conditions brought many parental problems. The juvenile-delinquency rate, which had shown a gratifying decline during the thirties, jumped up sharply. In 1944 there were 56 per cent more court cases than in 1939. The increase in the rate of delinquency was greater for girls than for boys, although the actual number of boy delinquents continued to be larger than the number of girls. During the 1950's the rate of delinquency in proportion to population declined somewhat, but evidences of serious maladjustment still continued. City schools transformed into "blackboard jungles" by vicious juveniles, youthful gang wars which resulted in killings and mutilations, and teen-age drug addiction and sex orgies provided sensational material for newspaper accounts and periodic legislative investigations. Less publicized were the earnest efforts being made in many communities to get to the root of the problem and provide facilities for extending psychiatric care to the worst adjusted youngsters, as well as wholesome activities for those whose principal trouble appeared to be a combination of high spirits and too much idle time.

Religion and Morals

The troubles of the depression, the long agony of the war, and the anxieties of the postwar period caused many Americans to return to the shelter of the church. Books from the warfronts testified to the comfort that religion had provided for men adrift in the Pacific or flying on dangerous missions. Many servicemen were impressed by the sacrificial spirit and the fine teamwork of Catholic, Protestant, and Jewish chaplains. The mythical exploits of one of these at Pearl Harbor provided the theme for one of the war's popular songs:

"Praise the Lord and Pass the Ammunition." The greater interest in religion continued into the postwar period, as evidenced by the extraordinary popularity of such inspirational books as Lloyd Douglas' *The Robe* (1943), Thomas Merton's *Seven-Storey Mountain* (1948), Joshua Liebman's *Peace of Mind* (1946), and Norman Vincent Peale's *Power of Positive Thinking* (1952).

The Roman Catholic Church appeared to be vigorously alive. The eloquent Bishop Fulton J. Sheen exerted a widening influence. Through his personal contacts a number of prominent converts, including the journalist Heywood Broun, the industrialist Henry Ford II, and the playwright-politician Claire Booth Luce were won to the Church, while his TV appearances touched the lives of millions of other Americans. The membership of the Church grew rapidly, largely through births but with a substantial flow of conversions as well. Catholic strength was manifest in the increasing enrollment in parochial schools, in the building of churches, and in the organization of new suburban parishes.

Convincing vitality also marked the Protestant churches. Some of the excessive denominationalism that had characterized the nineteenth century disappeared. The union of various Lutheran bodies resulted in the organization of the United Lutheran Church in 1918 and the American Lutheran Church in 1931. Another merger in 1934 brought the establishment of the Evangelical and Reformed Church with nearly a million members. In 1931 the historic Congregational Church joined with the Christian Church, while in 1939 the largest of all these mergers united eight million members in the Methodist Church. Churches not formally united showed an increasing degree of cooperative enterprise. Interdenominational cooperation was carried further than ever before with the organization in 1950 of the National Council of the Churches of Christ in the United States. This body, supported by 26 Protestant denominations and 4 Eastern Orthodox groups, represented nearly 32 million church members and brought within a common framework such hitherto separate agencies as the Federal Council of Churches, the Foreign Missions Conference, and the International Council of Religious Education.

Many Protestant clergymen, ashamed of the church's excessive zeal in whipping up war fever during World War I, swung over to radical pacifism. Of 19,000 ministers polled in 1931, 62 per cent expressed a conviction that the church should refuse to sanction or support any future war. Such sentiment became particularly characteristic of Christian young people and students. Indeed, the sentiment was so widespread as to contribute materially to the isolationism of the thirties. When war finally came, a sizable group stuck to these convictions and suffered internment in conscientious objectors' camps rather than submit to conscription into the armed forces. The great majority, however, considered the moral issues of the conflict important enough to override all other considerations. They pinned their hopes for the future upon victory in a just war and the promotion of good will in the postwar world.

The Billy Sunday type of evangelism was no longer in vogue among the older Protestant bodies, which preferred to expand their membership by less bombastic means. This conservatism of appeal seemed defeatist to many more emotional Christians. One of the phenomena of the war years was a series of massive Youth-for-Christ rallies conducted in various parts of the country. During the postwar years revivalism had a strong resurgence, particularly in the person of Billy Graham, a handsome young Southerner, whose sincerity and earnestness drew huge crowds to his services, whether they were held in Scotland, in India, or in supposedly blasé New York City. Another evidence of revolt against religious intellectualism was the remarkable growth of such groups as the Pentecostal and Holiness sects, the Assemblies of God, the Church of the Nazarene, and Jehovah's Witnesses. Entirely different in its appeal was the Oxford Group or Moral Re-Armament movement, which stimulated many rich and well-educated people to a new interest in religion.

Religious statistics for 1956 recorded church membership at over 100 million. This included 58.5 million Protestants, 33.5 million Catholics, and 5.5 million Jews. Only 39 per cent of the population were non-members, as compared with 65 per cent in this category in 1900.

Despite this impressive evidence of church growth, many observers believed that church membership was more often merely nominal than in earlier days and that the proportion of the population deeply motivated by religion was declining. At all events, evidence in dismaying abundance was at hand to prove that many Americans had foggy notions of right and wrong. Early in 1951 millions of Americans watched by television the hearings of a special Senate crime investigating committee under the chairmanship of Estes Kefauver of Tennessee. The testimony clearly revealed the existence of great crime syndicates controlling gambling resorts, houses of prostitution, and other illegal establishments in cities across the country. Even more shocking than this demonstration that American crime was still big business was the realization that these conditions could not exist without the protection of complaisant politicians. Much of the ultimate responsibility rested upon ordinary citizens who gave their patronage to gambling agencies and voted for corrupt political machines. The Kefauver investigation inspired many similar inquiries at the state level. One of the most disturbing of these revealed the extent to which New York City youngsters of high-school age had been debauched by dope peddlers.

The Challenge of Science

The atomic bomb dropped on Hiroshima on August 6, 1945, had intellectual repercussions not less impressive than its material results. Intelligent Americans suddenly realized that the advance of science had been so rapid and revolutionary as to require fundamental readjustments in all political and social relationships. Yet the bomb represented the culmination of merely one line of recent research. Science had made less dramatic but scarcely less significant progress in the fields of aviation, electronics, chemicals, and medicine.

Even before the war it was obvious that America was becoming increasingly science-minded. The number of industrial research laboratories in the country increased from around 400 in the early twenties to approximately 2,400 in the late thirties. During the latter decade, $300 million was being expended for such industrial research each year. One center alone, the Mellon Institute for Industrial Research at Pittsburgh, employed 142 investigators and 76 assistants. Giving valuable support and direction to scientific work throughout the country was the National Research Council, organized in 1916.

The general public accepted as a matter of course the assumption that daily life would be more and more transformed by science. Women wore clothing made of synthetic fabrics and used innumerable gadgets made of plastic in the home. Newspapers printed photographs flashed through space, and householders eagerly purchased television sets. Each year saw new knowledge in the field of nutrition, and the manufacture and sale of vitamins became big business. Many serious diseases lost much of their terror when treated with sulfa drugs or other new miracle workers like penicillin, aureomycin, and cortisone. Meanwhile, preventive medicine continued to advance—quietly as a rule, but sometimes with extraordinary fanfare as in the 1955 announcement of the successful testing of the Salk polio vaccine.

The necessities of war telescoped into a few years developments that might have been expected over a generation. Not only did the use of blood plasma transform the treatment of the wounded, but it led to an intensified study of the proteins contained in the plasma. From these investigations came the discovery of serum albumin for the treatment of shock, fibrinogen to combat excessive bleeding, and globulins for the treatment of measles and jaudice. Another line of research led to the production of DDT, an insecticide whose use during the war cut down malaria during the Pacific island campaigns and checked the spread of typhus in Italy.

No less impressive was progress in electronics and aviation. Radar permitted antiaircraft gun crews to detect the approach of planes in the darkest night 100 miles away, it enabled plane crews to observe the nature of the terrain beneath them through darkness or cloud or fog, and it made marine navigation safer. Aeronautical engineering more than doubled the speed of aircraft and made it possible for them to fly at much higher ceilings. Turbine and jet engines destined to revolutionize transportation were developed.

The great importance placed by the government on wartime science was evidenced by the establishment of the Office of Scientific Research and Development (OSRD) under the direction of Dr. Vannevar Bush of the Carnegie Institution. The war was unquestionably shortened by many months through the activities of this agency; indeed, had the enemy been allowed to pre-empt the field of scientific research, United Nations victory might not have been achieved.

The internationalism of science under normal conditions is evidenced by a listing of the key discoveries that laid the theoretical groundwork for the development of the atomic bomb. In 1905, Albert Einstein, a German by birth but residing in Switzerland, opened up a new line of scientific thought with his hypothesis that matter might be converted into energy. Some five years later, Lord Rutherford in England and Professor Nagaoka in Japan theorized that the chemical atom was not a hard massy particle, ultimate and indivisible, but had a nucleus at the center containing concentrated matter and energy. Rutherford later demonstrated that bombardment with rays of radium could convert atoms of one element into atoms of other elements. Dr. Enrico Fermi in Rome showed that such conversion could be effectively obtained by using small atomic fragments called neutrons. This line of research culminated in an epochal experiment in 1939 when Dr. Otto Hahn and Miss Lise Meitner of Berlin, working at the Kaiser Wilhelm Institute, bombarded uranium atoms with neutrons and caused them to divide and fly apart with a velocity of 200 million electron-volts. However little this news might mean to the man in the street, it was of world-shaking significance to the world's physicists. Nuclear matter had been transformed into nuclear energy, energy higher than had ever been attained by man before.

The absence of American names in the foregoing list does not mean that the United States was behind the rest of the world in the study of nuclear physics. On the contrary, the invention of the cyclotron or atom-smasher by Dr. Ernest O. Lawrence of the University of California won him the Nobel Prize in Physics in 1939, while equally important landmarks were the discovery of deuterium or heavy hydrogen by Dr. Harold C. Urey of Columbia and that of U-235, a rare form of uranium, by Professor Arthur J. Dempster of the University of Chicago. The onset of war found the country with a company of brilliant scientists already well grounded in the fundamentals of nuclear physics. American science was immeasurably strengthened when three of the world's greatest physicists—Lise Meitner, Niels Bohr, and Enrico Fermi—found refuge in the United States after being forced out of Germany and Italy.

The possibility of using atomic power for military purposes was brought to President Roosevelt's attention late in 1939 and resulted in the appointment of a committee to survey the problem. Two years later it was decided to expand

Cloud Produced by Explosion of Atomic Bomb
at Nagasaki, August 9, 1945. (Brown Bros.)

the research program. At Roosevelt's suggestion British and Canadian scientists working on the problem came to the United States and joined forces with the Americans directed by Dr. Bush in the OSRD. Needs of military security led to the transfer of a major part of the program to the War Department in June, 1942, and Major General Leslie R. Groves was placed in charge.

Extraordinary secrecy shrouded the so-called Manhattan Project. Thousands of persons were employed, but the work was so compartmentalized that only a few highly placed men in government and science knew the whole story.[1] Congress cooperated by making almost $2 billion available without asking embarrassing questions. Key plants were erected in areas as remote from each other as Tennessee and Washington, while the country's newest and best-equipped physics laboratory was built at Los Alamos, New Mexico. Dr. J. Robert Oppenheimer of the University of California was in charge of the Los Alamos project, and the *émigrés* Bohr and Fermi gave valuable technical assistance. Near there, on June 16, 1945, the first atomic bomb was dropped, causing an explosion felt 200 miles away and seen for over 100 miles. Two months later, atomic-bomb destruction in Hiroshima and Nagasaki hastened Japanese surrender.

This highly publicized event brought problems of the utmost gravity to American statesmen. Should the secret of the bomb be kept or shared with the Soviet Union and other partners at arms? Should the bomb's use be outlawed or should it be entrusted to the UN for use in preserving peace? Should the control of atomic power within the country remain in military hands or should it be transferred to civilians? What peacetime uses had this new source of energy? Should this energy be exploited under private ownership or should it be socialized? Despite the large amount of discussion, it was doubtful whether Americans generally realized the urgency of the new problems posed by scientific progress.

Failure to achieve effective international control of atomic power resulted in an expensive and dangerous race in developing new weapons. Early in 1950 President Truman ordered American scientists to try to develop a hydrogen bomb. Thereafter, the United States and Russia matched strides. In November, 1952, the United States exploded what was described as an H-bomb prototype; in August, 1953, Russia countered with the testing of what may have been the first true H-bomb. Subsequently both powers undertook periodic trials of their newest nuclear weapons, and in 1957 Britain joined the race by testing its first H-bomb. Some scientists warned that nuclear tests were likely to prove injurious to the human race, while others minimized the danger. The issue became serious enough to play a part in the presidential campaign of 1956.

The rival powers also enlisted their scientists in an effort to develop long-range missiles. In October, 1957, the American public was shocked to learn that Russian scientists had gained a jump on their American counterparts by being the first to launch an earth satellite. This so-called *Sputnik* was without military significance in itself, but it warned of Russian progress in the rocket field, upon which not only artificial satellites but intercontinental ballistic missiles were dependent.

[1]Despite these elaborate precautions, Soviet secret agents were able to obtain vital data on the atomic bomb. See Chapter 27.

Boom in Education

Mathematics, chemistry, physics, and foreign languages had other uses than to train nuclear physicists and ballistics experts. During the war years thousands of young Americans came to a new realization of the utility of higher learning. Many of the most desirable branches of the services were reserved to those who had been to high school or college. Many promising soldiers and sailors were sent to college for short terms; some of the most able received a complete training in medicine or engineering. This taste of college life, together with the provisions of the G.I. Bill, contributed to the extraordinary situation that prevailed six months after VJ Day when almost every college in the country was filled to overflowing with returned veterans. In the fall of 1949 college enrollments exceeded 2.4 million as compared with 1.4 million in 1939.[2]

Number subsidized for college	2,200,000
Number subsidized below college	3,500,000
On-the-job training	1,400,000
On-the farm training	700,000
	7,800,000

Educational benefits extended to veterans of the Korean War resulted in further training for about 1.5 million men—about half of whom went to college.

Once again the result of war was to accentuate a trend already well established. In 1900 only 11 per cent of American young people between the ages of 14 and 17 were to be found enrolled in full-time high schools. The percentage had risen to 73 by 1940. During the same period the number of American colleges had risen from around 500 to three times that number, while college enrollment had increased eightfold.

During the 1950's these educational trends continued. The Korean War reduced college attendance for a year or two, but the campus flood soon began again. In the fall of 1955 enrollment at colleges and universities reached 2.7 million. The prospect for the future was a still more rapid expansion. With the higher birthrate and the larger proportion of young people seeking higher education, the colleges were confronted with challenging questions. Should standards for admission remain constant; or should they be raised to screen out those least qualified for further study? How were the new classroom buildings, laboratories, and libraries needed for swollen enrollments to be provided? Would alumni and other individuals provide the funds for this capital expansion? Would business corporations accept this as one of their new responsibilities? Or must the necessary funds come from the state and Federal governments?

A particularly critical problem arose out of the faculty salary situation. Postwar inflation tended to increase the cost of living faster than the colleges could adjust professors' salaries, even with frequent tuition raises. In some fields a

[2] Up to July, 1951, the G.I. education program had involved expenditures of $14.5 billion and had benefited almost 8 million veterans, as follows:

UNPRECEDENTED
DEMAND FOR COLLEGE
EDUCATION —

AMERICAN
COLLEGES

AVAILABLE
FACILITIES

The Camel and the Needle's Eye. (By Messner
in the *Rochester Times-Union.*)

drift away from teaching into better-paid professions was already taking place.
How then could the additional teachers needed for anticipated enrollments be
found? In December, 1955, the Ford Foundation showed its concern both with
this problem and with the nation's growing shortage of medical facilities by
granting $500 million, the largest gift in the history of philanthropy, to colleges
and hospitals. The grant to the colleges was specially earmarked for the improvement of salaries. Even with this help, however, the faculty salary problem was
far from solved.

Along with the rapidly expanding university enrollment went a bewildering
growth in course offerings. An attempt was made to prepare students for more
and more special vocations, while the elective system made it possible to obtain
an A.B. degree for almost any combination of courses that appealed to the
fancy of the student. Many authorities became alarmed. As early as 1930,
Abraham Flexner had asserted that there was in the United States no university
in the real sense of the term—"no institution, no seat of learning devoted to
higher teaching and research. Everywhere the pressure of undergraduates and
vocational activities hampers the serious objects for which universities exist."

More emphatic still were the judgments passed on the colleges and universities by President Robert Maynard Hutchins of the University of Chicago. The great criminal in the educational field, according to Hutchins, had been President Eliot of Harvard who "applied his genius, skill, and longevity to the task of robbing American youth of their cultural heritage." President Hutchins urged that the liberal arts college be restricted to general education based upon the study of the greatest books of the Western world and the arts of reading, writing, thinking, and speaking, together with mathematics. He called for a reorganization of American education so that the last two years of high school and the first two years of college might be combined in a well-integrated course of studies leading to the A.B. degree at about the age of 20. Thereafter, the more competent students would be accepted in the university proper, where they would study metaphysics, social science, and natural science.

Hutchins' ideas were hotly debated both at the University of Chicago and in the educational world generally. At his own institution he succeeded in having some, although by no means all, of his principles carried out. A more radical experiment based upon his philosophy was undertaken at St. John's College at Annapolis, Maryland, in which all the students were required to read in their entirety a long list of important books ranging from Homer's *Iliad* to Veblen and Young's *Projective Geometry*.

The idea of directing education back to the so-called Great Tradition was rejected in most quarters. In fact, such new colleges as Bennington and Sarah Lawrence, with their emphasis on the cultivation of the fine arts and their highly individualized programs, were experiments in the opposite direction. Most institutions avoided the two extremes. There was much modification of the curriculum, with an increasing emphasis on broad survey or general-education courses during the freshman and sophomore years and some departure from narrow departmental majors. In general, it appeared that the complexity of contemporary political and social problems had compelled much hard thinking about the objectives of education, and that most institutions were striving to reorganize their programs of study in the light of these studies. The Russian launching of its *Sputniks* in 1957 focused attention on the need for greater emphasis on science at all levels of American education.

Newspapers, Magazines, Radio, and Television

In the financial organization of the newspaper field, trends already noted continued. No new national chains as extensive as the Hearst or Scripps-Howard developed (and the Hearst empire had begun to break up) but the smaller chains flourished, while consolidation reduced the number of papers published in most cities. Newspapers became increasingly dependent on the Associated Press and the United Press for their news; as a result, the Supreme Court ruled in 1945 that it was a violation of the antitrust laws for the Associated Press to reject arbitrarily an application for membership because of the veto of a rival journal.

The amount of space devoted to syndicated features also continued to increase. The thirties and forties witnessed a great rise in the popularity of the columnists. The widely printed opinions of Walter Lippmann, David Lawrence, Westbrook Pegler, Drew Pearson, and Walter Winchell had an influence far greater than the ideas expressed in the editorials of the individual newspapers. Indeed, the dwindling prestige of the editorial page was frequently commented upon.

American newspapers of the forties and fifties differed from those of the early years of the century in the much larger coverage given to foreign affairs. From being poorly informed on such matters the American public had become perhaps the best informed of all peoples. A generation of intelligent reporting of world affairs did much to educate Americans for new responsibilities in the postwar world.

The intense interest of many Americans in the news led to the establishment in 1923 of the magazine *Time*. The enormous success of this weekly venture encouraged the founding of *Newsweek* and other periodicals devoted to briskly written presentation of current events. The same Henry Luce who made a fortune out of *Time* hit upon another winning formula in 1936 when he purchased *Life* and transformed it from a humorous magazine to one featuring interesting pictures so arranged as to tell a story. This also brought a large number of imitators and competitors into the field, the most successful of which was *Look*. The greatest money-maker of all was the *Reader's Digest*; guided by the intuition of Dewitt Wallace, this pocket-sized magazine was so perfectly tailored to suit the taste of the average middle-class American that it achieved a monthly circulation of around eight million by the end of World War II. Once again many imitators entered the field, but none gained anything like the popularity of the prototype.

Meantime, the radio became increasingly important as a medium through which history was both made and reflected. Roosevelt's success in winning four elections and achieving many of his goals was to be credited in considerable degree to the influence he gained by speaking directly to the people over the radio. Moreover, the American people had a sense of direct participation in great events when they listened to the ranting speeches of Hitler, the magnificent oratory of Churchill, or the solemn voice of MacArthur presiding over the Japanese surrender ceremony. During the most critical periods of the war, listeners turned to their radios almost hourly for the latest reports from the fronts. Of the total broadcasting time on the NBC Network, only 3.6 per cent was devoted to news in 1939, but by 1944 it was 20.4 per cent.

Radio provided a varied fare. In addition to news, there were opera and symphony broadcasts for music lovers, a galaxy of high-priced comedians and quiz programs for family entertainment, exciting adventure stories for young-sters, and sentimental serials known as "soap operas" for bored housewives. In many quarters it was asserted that broadcasting was excessively commercialized and that the system of chain broadcasting provided too few programs of an educational or informational character, as well as too little material reflecting the needs and interests of the local community.

Television was developed as a medium for mass communication much more rapidly than had been anticipated. Although receiving equipment was expen-sive, high postwar earnings enabled large numbers of people to buy sets as soon as broadcasting began in any section of the country. Rather than being a luxury monopolized by the rich, television became the proud possession of thousands of families that would have been considered underprivileged during the 1930's. Some 9.8 million American homes had television sets in use at the close of 1950. Even more than radio, television became a matter of sharp con-troversy. Critics lamented the large number of programs devoted to Western melodrama, pseudoscientific adventure serials, and horror stories—all of which they regarded as a bad influence on children, for whom television had a par-ticular fascination. Book publishers complained that TV addicts were in danger of forgetting how to read; film producers and exhibitors were hard hit by reduced attendance at movies. Since the medium was an expensive one, the time devoted to advertising was even greater than on radio, while the propor-tion of programs devoted to good music or education was smaller. But the cultural results were by no means all bad. The eagerness with which television audiences followed the deliberations of the United Nations on the Korean issue or the Kefauver crime hearings demonstrated that the new invention might give Americans a new sense of direct participation in world and domestic politics.

Books

From the standpoint of the serious reader the literary production of the 1940's and 1950's was disappointing. Most of the bright young authors of the 1920's and 1930's failed in middle age to sustain their earlier reputation for originality and power. Of Ernest Hemingway's later books, only *The Old Man and the Sea* (1952), a short novel glorifying man's heroism in fighting against impossible odds, found general favor. William Faulkner's *A Fable* (1954) was an ambitious protest against the futility of war, but its intricacy of style and symbolism defeated many hopeful readers. Similarly, John Steinbeck's *East of Eden* (1952) seemed unsatisfactory to most critics, despite its high intentions. Others of the earlier generation showed an even greater falling off of powers.

Sinclair Lewis died in 1951 with reputation sadly damaged by the mediocrity of his later books, while John Dos Passos seemed to be doing some kind of painful penance for his earlier flirtation with radicalism.

The younger generation of writers included many men of talent but few, if any, who seemed to be destined for permanent fame. In such novels as *A Rage to Live* (1949) and *Ten North Frederick* (1955), John O'Hara described with sharp penetration the political and social activities of the well-to-do set in small-city Pennsylvania. In dealing with sex, O'Hara wrote with an explicitness that demonstrated the extent to which the standards of literary propriety had changed since the furor aroused by the early novels of Theodore Dreiser. This same unvarnished realism characterized two of the most widely read novels dealing with World War II: Norman Mailer's *The Naked and the Dead* (1948) and James Jones's *From Here to Eternity* (1951).

Yet there were opposing literary tendencies with signs of a reaction toward idealism and the re-emphasis of traditional values. Herman Wouk's *The Caine Mutiny* (1951) dealt with the Navy during World War II with a respect for authority that contrasted sharply with the cynicism of Mailer and Jones. Wouk made an even more explicit defense of traditionalism in *Marjorie Morningstar* (1955). An impressive vein of realism also ran through the works of John Hersey, particularly in *The Wall* (1950), a novel depicting the stubborn heroism of the Jewish community in Warsaw during World War II. This increased respect for man's basic decency was reflected in Robert Penn Warren's *Band of Angels* (1955), Mackinley Kantor's *Andersonville* (1955), and James Gould Cozzens' *By Love Possessed* (1957).

The most exciting trend in the world of books was the rise of the paper backs. Enterprising promoters discovered that by publishing books in cheap editions and selling them through unconventional channels like drugstores and newsstands a vast new market could be reached. At first the paper backs were mostly mystery stories or sensational novels whose sales appeal arose from provocative titles and pictures of scantily clad damsels. Further experimentation demonstrated that, while good books might not sell as well as bad, they nevertheless would sell well enough to justify republication. The thrifty reader with serious tastes could now afford to own not only the writings of modern authors like Hemingway and Fitzgerald, but older classics by Emerson, Whitman, Melville, Thoreau, and many others.

If the popularity of the high-class paper backs seemed inconsistent with the low level of popular taste reflected in other newsstand literature, it simply provided one more proof of the variety of American society. Despite the tendency toward conformity, a nation of 175 million people and continental size could provide a market for many different levels of taste. The phonograph industry that could furnish a princely income to the swivel-hipped Elvis

Presley could also give to thousands of music lovers the symphonic interpretations of Arturo Toscanini.

America was changing—but it was changing in more than one direction. Pessimists, convinced that things were getting worse and worse, could wring their hands over the decline of economic individualism, the blatancy of advertising, the racketeering labor unions, race prejudice, and schools where no one learned to spell. But optimists could nourish their faith by noting the rising standard of living, the greater security of the workingman, the improved status of minority groups, the progress of medicine and science, and an abundance of other hopeful signs. To men of faith, the American dream shone as brightly as ever.

29

Eisenhower Republicanism

On one occasion Dwight D. Eisenhower asserted that Republicans should be "progressive moderates"; another time he defined the party goal as "dynamic conservatism." By such verbal combinations the man who entered the White House in January, 1953, tried to stake out a political position that would borrow from the New and Fair Deals a concern for human welfare, but would temper this with deference to states' rights and economic individualism. In avoiding the extremes of either left or right, Eisenhower had the support of a majority of Americans. Although not exciting, the middle of the road appeared to be quiet and safe.

Eisenhower versus Taft

Although Truman's surprise victory of 1948 warned the Republicans against overconfidence, the party's prospects for 1952 looked sufficiently bright to inspire a vigorous struggle for the presidential nomination. Long before the convention it was obvious that Taft and Eisenhower were far in the lead and that such other Republican hopefuls as Warren, Stassen, and MacArthur would have a chance only if the front-running two ended in a dead heat.

With customary candor Taft made no mystery of the fact that he wanted the nomination. Supporting his candidacy were thousands of conservative Republicans who admired the Ohio Senator for his stubborn opposition to the New and Fair Deals. The Taftites remembered with bitterness how their hero had been passed over for Willkie in 1940 and for Dewey in 1944 and 1948. They blamed "me-tooism"—that is, Republican acceptance of many of the

New Deal social welfare goals—for the recent party defeats and demanded a return to old-fashioned Republicanism. On foreign policy the Taft admirers tended toward isolationism. They regarded the UN and NATO with suspicion; they distrusted England and France and wanted to give priority to Asia in the struggle against Communism. Already strong in the Midwest, the conservatives hoped to pick up many delegates from the South, where the Republican rank-and-file was negligible and party hacks normally controlled the state organizations.

Although Taft had many admirers in the East, Governor Dewey of New York, Senator Henry Cabot Lodge, Jr., of Massachusetts, and Senator James H. Duff of Pennsylvania were not among them. They and other Eastern leaders believed that the nomination of the Ohio Senator would be a fatal mistake, dooming the party to defeat. They wanted to retain the social gains of the New Deal but with greater economy and efficiency of administration; even more did they want to preserve continuity of foreign policy by renouncing isolationism and giving strong support to the UN and NATO. Here again their complaint was not so much that the Democrats were doing the wrong thing, as that they were doing the right thing badly. This moderate Republicanism had wide support among party amateurs, especially among business executives.

The anti-Taft Republicans found an ideal candidate in General Eisenhower. As commander of the NATO army, he knew the realities of the world situation. On domestic issues he was for the most part uncommitted and open-minded. Most important of all, Eisenhower's military fame and affable personality had given him enormous popularity among all sectors of the American public.

Despite its potential strength, the Eisenhower candidacy got off to a faltering start. Since the general had firmly rejected overtures from both Republicans and Democrats in 1948, no one knew whether he was now available. Finally, in January, 1952, he announced that he would accept the Republican nomination if proffered, but that he would remain at his NATO post and not actively participate in the scramble for delegates.

The Eisenhower announcement served to stir the Taft faction to new activity. It became obvious that Taft could be beaten only if Eisenhower abandoned his aloofness and fought for the nomination. In June, therefore, the general returned from Europe, took off his uniform, and plunged into politics.

The Taft-Eisenhower fight was strongly reminiscent of the 1912 struggle between William Howard Taft, the Senator's father, and Theodore Roosevelt. In both cases the Taft conservatives were accused of trying to steal the nomination by manipulating the Southern delegations. Yet there was a significant difference: in 1912 the Taft faction was able to control the convention machinery and seat its challenged delegates; in 1952 the conservatives tried similar tactics but were defeated. When the Republican National Committee awarded temporary seats to the challenged Taft delegates, the Eisenhower forces retaliated immediately. Twenty-three out of twenty-five Republican governors attending a governors' conference at Houston, Texas, protested against the National Committee action.

Charges and countercharges were intensified when the National Convention convened at Chicago in July. The Eisenhower faction demanded that the contested delegates be excluded from voting not only on their own cases but on all others as well. The Taftites countered with a compromise proposal, but were voted down. This fight was only a warm-up for the decisive struggle over seating the Georgia and Texas delegations. Reluctant to attack the popular Eisenhower, the Taft faction centered its fire on Governor Dewey, whom it accused of master-minding the anti-Taft movement. The bitterness of the conservatives resulted from the knowledge that they were losing; in the crucial case, Eisenhower delegates from Georgia were seated in place of the Taft delegates by a vote of 607 to 531.

The rest of the convention was anticlimactic. On the first ballot the initial standing was Eisenhower 595 and Taft 500, but subsequent switches gave Eisenhower 845 votes and the nomination without the need of a second ballot. The general chose as his running mate Senator Richard Nixon of California, whose prominence in the Alger Hiss investigation had made him popular with the more nationalistic elements in the party. The Republican platform attempted to take a middle ground between the Europe-first and Asia-first partisans by pledging vigilance in both areas and condemning Democratic failures. Reciprocal trade agreements were favored, but with the proviso that they must "safeguard our domestic enterprises." The Taft-Hartley Act was supported, but amendments to meet labor criticism were promised. On civil rights the party took a weaker position than in 1948; on farm policy the pledges were more specific: "full parity prices for all farm products," adequate storage and credit facilities, and farm loans.

Although the Taft-Eisenhower feud left deep wounds within the party ranks, it by no means injured Republican prospects in the ensuing campaign. For most of the vast TV audience watching the convention Eisenhower had been cast in the role of hero and Taft as villain. When virtue proved triumphant, the viewers were delighted, and the Republicans were off to a magnificent start before the Democrats had even chosen their candidate.

Eisenhower versus Stevenson

When the Democratic Convention met at Chicago there was still great confusion as to who would be the candidate. All talk of a third term for Truman had been ended in March when the President removed himself from the running.

Truman's first choice for the succession was reported to be Governor Adlai Stevenson of Illinois, but Stevenson, insisting that he still had important work to do in his state administration, declined to cooperate. Truman then transferred his backing to Vice President Barkley, but some of the CIO allies of the party vetoed this suggestion because they thought Barkley at 74 was too old for the position. In the preconvention primaries Senator Kefauver had been more successful than any of his rivals, but he was disliked by Truman and most of the party leaders because of the embarrassing disclosures that had come out of his highly publicized crime investigation. Each of the other potential candidates had some fatal weakness: Senator Russell of Georgia would alienate the Negro vote; Averell Harriman was too wealthy and too closely identified with the New Deal; and Senator Robert Kerr of Oklahoma aroused little enthusiasm except in his own section.

On the first two convention ballots Kefauver led, but his totals fell short of the number needed for the nomination. On the third ballot, the delegates turned to Governor Stevenson, who had indicated that he would not resist a genuine draft. To balance the ticket, Senator John Sparkman of Alabama was nominated for Vice President. The platform pledged the party to the ideals of the Fair Deal: high price supports for agriculture, strong civil rights legislation, repeal of the Taft-Hartley Act, and international cooperation to resist Communism and to preserve peace.

Once nominated, Stevenson cast off his cloak of reluctance and conducted an aggressive campaign. His speeches were eloquent and witty, but they did not win the enthusiastic following that a relatively little known man needed to deflect the spotlight from a great national hero. Meanwhile, Eisenhower was proving a better campaigner than might have been expected. Wherever he went, huge crowds turned out to greet him. His speeches impressed thousands by their vigor and sincerity.

Except for President Truman, who criticized Eisenhower with charateristic sharpness, the Democrats avoided the risks of attacking the popular general directly. They hoped to find a more vulnerable target in Nixon, whom they disliked for the allegedly unfair tactics he had used in defeating his New Deal rivals in earlier California elections. Great was the Democratic jubilation, therefore, when the New York *Post* uncovered the fact that over the course of two years California businessmen had contributed over $18,000 to help Nixon with his travel and hotel bills and other expenses incident to a political career. These revelations threatened to be so damaging that a few timid leaders urged Nixon to yield his place on the party ticket to someone else. But the party high command turned back the Democratic attack with an adroit counteroffensive. They charged that Stevenson's subordinates in the Illinois state government had been aided by similar funds. Even more effective was a nationwide television broadcast in which Nixon defended the purity of his conduct in highly emotional terms.

Democratic efforts to stem the Republican tide were futile. The returns gave Eisenhower 442 electoral votes to Stevenson's 89; the popular vote was 34 million to 27 million. Stevenson carried no state outside the South, and even in that traditionally Democratic region he lost Tennessee, Texas, Florida, Oklahoma, and Virginia. The election seemed to be more of a personal triumph for Eisenhower, however, than a vote of confidence for his party. Indeed, the Republicans won control of Congress only by the slimmest of margins. In the new House there were 221 Republicans, 213 Democrats, and 1 independent. In the Senate the balance was razor-thin; there were now 48 Republicans, 47 Democrats, and 1 independent.

While Eisenhower's victory resulted in major part from the overwhelming sentiment summed up in the slogan "I Like Ike," he also benefited from other factors. There was widespread belief that the Democrats had been too long in power and that the country would benefit by a change. This was closely related to popular resentment over recently revealed scandals in the Truman administration. Particularly damaging to the Democrats were the Korean War and the stalemated peace talks. One of Eisenhower's most effective promises was that he would make a trip to the Far East to investigate the situation.

New Faces in Washington

On January 20, 1953, the capital city was jammed with joyful Republicans eager to celebrate the termination of twenty black years of Democratic rule. Eisenhower's inaugural address, dealing largely with foreign affairs, was solemn in spirit and moderate in tone. The Democrats found little in it to criticize, and the only words of disapproval came from the extreme nationalist wing of the Republicans.

The inaugural promised no abrupt changes of policy, and, for the most part, there were none. The new administration differed from the old most strikingly in personnel. Under Truman the key offices were usually held by men who had gained their experience in politics and government; under Eisenhower the posts were more likely to go to businessmen.

The new President came from a background far different from that of any of his twentieth century predecessors. Born in Denison, Texas, in 1890, Eisenhower had spent his formative years in Abilene, Kansas, where his family moved when he was one year old. After graduating from the Abilene High School, Dwight received an appointment to the United States Military Academy at West Point. In 1915 Eisenhower began his military career with the usual second lieutenant's commission and made his way up the hierarchy of rank until the eve of American participation in World War II, when he was a major general and Chief of Staff of the Third Army. Up to this time his military record had been good but not extraordinary. Eisenhower's more rapid push to the top followed the Louisiana maneuvers of 1941, in which his capacity for leadership made a deep impression on his superiors. He was brought to Washington, where he became a trusted subordinate of General Marshall, the Chief of Staff. Eisenhower's first major opportunity came when he was given command of the American forces that invaded North Africa in 1942; success in this campaign and in the conquest of Sicily and southern Italy led to the most important assignment of all. In January, 1944, he was transferred to England to direct the triumphant second front invasion. After the war he served for three years as Army Chief of Staff, for two more as president of Columbia University—a strange and not altogether happy interlude—and finally from December, 1950, to June, 1952, he was supreme commander of the new NATO army.

Eisenhower's great military success was based upon certain traits of personality. He was not a brilliant general after the fashion of Napoleon or Douglas MacArthur. The grand strategy of the Allied campaigns was devised far from the battle fronts, and Eisenhower merely carried it out. Nor was he a hard-driving field commander like General Patton. Eisenhower's talents were those of a team captain. In coalition warfare it was a difficult task to reconcile the conflicting ideas and clashing temperaments of high-ranking officers from different services and different countries. Simple and direct in manner with an unusual ability to listen patiently to every shade of opinion, Eisenhower inspired trust and affection and was therefore able to coordinate the vast war effort.

As President, Eisenhower directed the government in similar fashion. He sought to recruit a competent team of administrators and trust them with the task of formulating policy and carrying it out. He kept himself as free as possible from the day-to-day routine of government so that he could concentrate his attention on major issues. He conducted his relations with Congress on the same basis, making recommendations and signing or disapproving bills that came to his desk, but leaving the legislators free to act without constant pressure from the White House.

Eisenhower's reluctance to play the role of strong executive made his cabinet appointments highly important. John Foster Dulles, the new Secretary of State, was a New York corporation lawyer and specialist in international affairs, who had been a State Department consultant during the Truman administration. George Humphrey, the Secretary of the Treasury, was a highly successful Ohio industrialist with extensive interests in coal and steel. Charles E. Wilson, the Secretary of Defense, had been president of the General Motors Corporation. These three men became the most influential figures in the new administra-

Secretary of State John Foster Dulles Conferring with
President Eisenhower. (World Wide Photos.)

tion; their cabinet colleagues came mostly from the same kind of business or legal background.[1]

Even Senator Taft was troubled by the economic complexion of the administration. "I'm not at all sure," he said, "that all these businessmen are going to work out. I don't know of any reason why success in business should mean success in public service." Reluctant to sell his General Motors stock in conformity with the conflict-of-interest laws, Wilson assured a Congressional committee that "what was good for the country was good for General Motors and vice versa." For this and subsequent blunt statements, Wilson became a frequent center of controversy. Other businessmen-in-government behaved more discreetly, but a succession of minor incidents illustrated the pitfalls inherent in

[1] Other Eisenhower cabinet officers were: Attorney General, Herbert Brownell, Jr., of New York, succeeded in 1957 by William Rogers of New York; Postmaster General, Arthur Summerfield of Michigan; Secretary of the Interior, Douglas McKay of Oregon, succeeded in 1956 by Fred A. Seaton of Nebraska; Secretary of Agriculture, Ezra Taft Benson of Utah; Secretary of Commerce, Sinclair Weeks of Massachusetts; Secretary of Labor, Martin Durkin of New York, succeeded by James P. Mitchell of New York in 1953; Secretary of Health, Education and Welfare, Oveta Culp Hobby of Texas, succeeded by Marion B. Folsom of New York in 1955. Humphrey left the cabinet in 1957 and was succeeded as Secretary of the Treasury by Robert B. Anderson of Texas; Wilson also resigned in 1957 and was followed by Neil H. McElroy of Ohio.

the situation. In 1955, Harold E. Talbott, Secretary of the Air Force, resigned under fire after disclosures that he had used his position to promote personal business interests. Two or three less prominent officials encountered the same kind of trouble.

Eisenhower's policy of saving his energies for major concerns required heavy reliance on his assistants in the White House. The post of Assistant to the President was entrusted to Sherman Adams, a taciturn, hard-working former governor of New Hampshire. Adams acted as a chief of staff, mediating between feuding administrators, assuming personal responsibility for many matters, and carefully organizing the data that the President needed for final decision. Not the least of Adams' functions was to divert criticism from Eisenhower; when conservative Republicans disliked the presidential policies, they usually found it more discreet to attack the king's minister rather than the king himself.

One of Eisenhower's greatest needs was Congressional leadership thoroughly committed to his brand of Republicanism. Instead, he found himself compelled to work with right-wing leaders who were unsympathetic to many aspects of the administration program. Despite disappointment over failure to get the nomination and a feeling that the President had not consulted him adequately on appointments, Senator Taft demonstrated magnimity and a desire to cooperate in achieving a good record for the administration. Consequently, Eisenhower suffered a serious loss when Taft died after a short illness in July, 1953. Taft's successor as Republican Senate leader, William Knowland of California, was an honest but stubborn man, who did not hesitate to oppose the President when he thought him wrong. Knowland was particularly opinionated in the field of foreign policy. Eisenhower found much more consistent support from Eastern legislators like Senators Clifford Case of New Jersey and Irving Ives of New York, but these liberals had less influence in Republican circles than the conservatives. Consequently, the administration's success in achieving its objectives often hinged on its ability to gain Democratic votes.

Balancing the Budget

A businessman's administration naturally felt that its first responsibilities were to balance the budget and halt inflation. Eager to impose efficiency on official Washington, new departments heads warned their subordinates against tardiness, coffee breaks, and all the other time-wasting artifices familiar to office workers. Meanwhile, the administration leaders addressed themselves to the more serious business of cutting the budget that Truman had submitted just before leaving office. With proposed expenditures of $78.6 billion—about $10 billion more than anticipated revenues—the Truman estimates seemed final proof to the Republicans of Democratic recklessness.

The Republicans soon discovered, however, that their ideal of a balanced budget could not be achieved overnight. Many items of expenditure like interest on the public debt and veterans' benefits were required under earlier laws. Of the other items, the amounts to be saved through greater efficiency never proved to be as large as they had seemed to enthusiastic campaigners. Between 1952 and 1956 the Republicans were able to reduce the number of Federal employees from over 2.4 million to less than 2.2 million, but the limit of such economies was soon reached.

The hard truth was that two thirds of the budget was for security items—defense and foreign aid—and it was here that cuts must be made if major savings were to result. Secretary of Defense Wilson made a significant overhaul of defense policy. Instead of continuing a herculean effort to bring the nation to a high state of readiness by 1954—likely to be a crucial year according to Truman's advisers—Wilson advocated a stretch-out of preparation over a longer period. He also believed it possible to get "a bigger bang for a buck"—that is, to save money by concentrating on nuclear weapons at the expense of conventional armaments. Despite Democratic charges that this involved a gamble with national security, the Republicans were able to reduce defense appropriations considerably. Total expenditures for the fiscal year 1954 were $67.8 billion—almost $11 billion less than Truman had recommended—and the deficit was only $3 billion instead of the almost $10 billion that had been estimated. The final achievement of a Korean armistice in July, 1953, helped Republican finances substantially.

Eisenhower hoped to balance the budget before redeeming the Republican campaign pledge to cut taxes. During his first year in office he even induced a reluctant Congress to continue for six months the excess profits tax due to expire on June 30, 1953. In 1954 with Congressional elections approaching, however, the demand for tax reduction was too strong to be resisted. Moreover, it was hoped that a cut might help to halt a threatened depression. Therefore Congress gladly allowed the excess profits tax to die and a previously authorized income tax cut to go into effect. More important, the legislators thoroughly revised the income tax laws, allowing large deductions to heads of households, widows and retired persons, farmers, and businessmen. The Democrats charged that the measure unduly favored the higher income groups, particularly stockholders, because it exempted the first $50 in dividends from taxation and reduced the rate on dividends above that figure. The Republicans retorted that the exemption would benefit small stockholders more than large and was an act of justice to relieve investors from a form of double taxation.

By lowering rates and otherwise amending the revenue laws, Congress reduced taxes by $7.4 billion—the largest cut ever provided in a single year. Welcome though this was, it delayed the achievement of a balanced budget. For fiscal year 1955 there was a deficit of over $4 billion despite further reduction in expenditure. A year later the picture was quite different. For the twelve months ending June 30, 1956, the government took in $1.75 billion more than it paid out—the first surplus since 1948. The balancing of the budget was achieved not by new economies, but by larger revenues—the by-product of a new wave of prosperity. Indeed, after 1955 the Eisenhower administration spent more freely, both for defense and for social welfare.

During the second Eisenhower administration the budget problem provoked serious controversy. On one side were the conservatives, insistent on holding down expenditures and providing further tax cuts; on the other were the liberals, acutely conscious of the need for continued foreign aid, rapid development of new weapons, and increasing Federal activity in such fields as health and education.

For the first eight months of 1957 the budget problem was hotly debated. When Eisenhower sent his recommendations to Congress in January, the proposed expenditures for fiscal 1958 were $71.8 billion, larger than any previous peacetime budget. Secretary of the Treasury Humphrey took the unusual step of criticizing the budget in a press conference. Unless government expenditures were curtailed and taxes cut, he predicted a depression "that will curl your hair." Humphrey's statement and subsequent comments by the President appeared to put the responsibility for cutting the budget upon Congress, but the legislature, where the Democrats now had a majority in both Houses, tried to throw the burden back upon the administration. Eventually Eisenhower did suggest ways in which $1.8 billion could be saved, but most of this was criticized as mere juggling of the books. A bipartisan economy bloc began cutting away at the Eisenhower budget so ferociously that the President had to put up a vigorous fight to save his program. Even so, Congress appropriated some $5 billion less than Eisenhower had originally asked. The whole episode seemed to prove that the days of Calvin Coolidge and Andrew Mellon were past; the conservative goals of drastic economy, reduction of the national debt, and tax cuts were almost impossible to achieve so long as the nation felt seriously menaced by Communist imperialism.

The Fight against Inflation

Secretary Humphrey, it may safely be assumed, did not consider John Maynard Keynes his patron saint. Humphrey would not have conceded that the government should adjust its spending and taxing policies to the ups and downs of the economic cycle, or that it had an obligation to provide massive public investment when private investment failed. Yet Humphrey was not afraid to use government weapons of a more conservative type.

When the administration took office, inflation, fed by the Korean War and rearmament, was a serious problem. Eisenhower and his advisers fought the fire, not with more regulation, but with less. Price and wage controls were terminated, and the economy was left largely free in accordance with conservative doctrine. On the other hand, Secretary Humphrey believed that to tighten credit was a legitimate anti-inflation policy. By raising the interest rate on new issues of government bonds, the Treasury deliberately undertook to attract investment funds and make it harder for private borrowers to obtain loans. Thus was initiated the administration's controversial "tight money" policy, in which the Treasury and the Federal Reserve Board were close allies.

During the fall of 1953 and the spring of 1954 concern over inflation gave way to fear of another depression. Between July, 1953, and March, 1954, industrial production declined 10 per cent and the number of unemployed grew to a disturbing 3.75 million. The Republicans had cause for alarm because memories of 1929 had been one of the party's major handicaps for twenty years. The Eisenhower administration met the situation by relaxing its tight-money policy, allowing tax cuts to go into effect, and postponing its attempts to balance the budget.

Whether these moderate steps would be enough to stem the depression was by no means certain. Both the CIO and the AFL criticized Eisenhower for inaction, and former President Truman urged the expenditure of $3 billion for emergency public works and welfare. Within the Eisenhower cabinet, counsels were divided: the more politically minded advisers wanted to expand government spending, but Secretary Humphrey and the conservatives opposed hasty action. Taking his characteristic middle position, the President moved slowly, but ordered that plans for highway construction and other public works should be ready in case the situation became worse.

To the Republicans' great relief, the economic picture brightened during April and May, 1954. By mid-year the recovery was almost complete. Conservatives and liberals drew conflicting lessons from what had happened. The former emphasized the fact that the Eisenhower administration had kept its head, avoided rash action, and thus contributed to a restoration of business confidence. Liberals, on the other hand, believed that serious depression had been avoided by Eisenhower's prompt resort to certain government remedies and his apparent determination to take whatever additional action might be necessary. Whichever was the better explanation, it seemed obvious that no future administration, either liberal or conservative, would allow a depression to develop very far without attempting to halt it by government action.

With the passing of these economic clouds the country entered a period of impressive prosperity. Between 1953 and 1956 gross national product increased from $363.2 billion to $412.4 billion. Employment in 1956 reached a new high of 65 million—a rise of 3.7 million over 1953. The farmers failed to share in this prosperity, but most other groups enjoyed a substantial increase in income.

Despite this boom, the Eisenhower administration was able to boast during its first three years in office that inflation had been halted. From 1953 until early 1956 the consumers' price index remained relatively stable. Thereafter, however, prices started to push up again. During 1956 the cost of living rose 3 per cent, and this upward trend continued through most of 1957. Management blamed labor for the new inflation; union pressure, so the argument ran, had pushed wages up faster than productivity, thus increasing industrial costs and making higher prices necessary. Labor denied this and attributed the rising cost of living to excessive corporate prices.

Undoubtedly Secretary Humphrey believed that heavy government spending and high taxes were major factors in this inflation, but he could do little about these things so long as the world situation remained critical. The administration's principal anti-inflation weapon had to be its tight money policy. The Federal Reserve Board, with Treasury blessing, applied the brakes with increasing pressure. The effect was felt throughout the country as borrowers, both large and small, found it harder to obtain money and were charged higher interest rates. The wisdom of the tight money policy was a matter of controversy. Hostile critics blamed it for hampering small business and home construction and for adding to the difficulties of states and municipalities in building new schools. Despite criticism the administration stuck to the tight money policy until November, 1957, when declining business activity and falling stock prices resulted in a relaxation.

The Changing Farm Problem

To head the Department of Agriculture, President Eisenhower named Ezra Taft Benson of Utah, a high dignitary in the Mormon Church and a leader in the farmers' cooperative movement. The President also gave great weight to the advice of his own brother, President Milton Eisenhower of Pennsylvania State University.

The new regime inherited from the Truman administration a disturbing farm situation. During the year before Eisenhower took office, both agricultural prices and total farm income had been falling. Benson blamed the trouble on bad government policy. Although the Agricultural Act of 1949 had provided for a transition from rigid price supports to flexible ones, farm belt pressure resulted in an extension of the supports at 90 per cent of parity through 1954. This government guarantee, Benson believed, encouraged the farmers to overproduce, necessitated large government expenditures, and piled up unsalable surpluses in government warehouses. The Secretary urged that rigid price supports be abandoned in favor of flexible supports; in this way the law of supply and demand would have a chance to operate, and farmers would divert acreage from unprofitable staples to other crops.

The Benson program involved some change of position for Eisenhower, who had spoken in favor of full parity during the 1952 campaign, but the general idea of lessening government regulation appealed to him and he gave his Secretary full support. As a result, the Agricultural Act of 1954 was forced through Congress after a sharp fight. The new law provided flexible supports —from 82½ per cent to 90 per cent in 1955, and from 75 to 90 per cent thereafter—on five basic crops: wheat, corn, cotton, rice, and peanuts. Other parts of the act revised the parity formula, offered incentives for the expansion of wool production, and provided modified price supports for tobacco, milk, and certain other commodities.

Benson's victory was impressive, but it involved political risks for the Republicans if the farm situation continued to deteriorate. After their victory in the 1954 Congressional elections, the Democrats tried to win favor with the farmers by restoring rigid 90 per cent supports. Congress passed such a bill in the spring of 1956, but Eisenhower vetoed it. To soften the blow, the administration fixed supports for wheat, cotton, and corn at 82½ per cent for another year, instead of cutting them to 75 per cent as the law permitted. The President also found bipartisan backing for the so-called soil-bank plan, a scheme for reducing the surplus by paying the farmers to take acreage out of production and convert it into pasturage or forest. In May, 1956, Congress appropriated $1.2 billion for the soil-bank program.

As the second Eisenhower administration began, the farm situation continued to be unsatisfactory. Farm prices stopped their decline and pushed upward a little—although not as much as other prices, so that the parity index continued to fall. Despite his distaste for regimentation, Secretary Benson had to insist that the farmers accept acreage allotments on staple crops in order to qualify for price supports. Everyone was unhappy: the Republican administration because it found itself involved in continuing policies for which it had criticized the Democrats; the Midwestern farmers because they resented Benson's lower support prices and production restrictions; and consumers because they paid for the government program both in higher food prices and in higher taxes.

Ironically, neither the shift to flexible supports nor acreage restrictions sufficed to eliminate the agricultural surplus. Better methods had so increased the farmer's efficiency that government efforts to reduce production were largely nullified. Indeed, the harried Commodity Credit Corporation found itself loaded with greater surpluses than ever.

Straws in the political wind indicated that Benson's farm policies were a serious liability to the party in the Midwest. When traditionally Republican Wisconsin elected a Democrat, William E. Proxmire, to fill the vacancy left by the death of Senator McCarthy in 1957, the upset was generally attributed to the discontent of the state's dairy farmers. Despite such incidents, however, there was evidence that the farm bloc was no longer the force in politics that it had been during the twenties and thirties. The number of farmers in proportion to total population was going down; even in the South only 22.2 per cent of the population was living on farms in 1954, as compared with 51.3 per cent in 1930. The big competition for votes was now in the fast-growing urban suburbs, where high price supports for agriculture were unpopular. Farmers themselves were divided; Eastern farmers who had to buy feed for chickens and livestock had obviously different interests than the Western wheat and corn growers. And even among the latter there was more grumbling than open revolt over the Benson program. Even though farm profits were not what they had been during World War II days, the more efficient producers were able to make a respectable living. Some authorities believed that the most helpful policy for the future would be to cut marketing costs in the interests of both farmers and consumers and to induce marginal producers to move off the land.

Power and Natural Resources

One of the few issues on which there was a clear-cut conflict of philosophy between Eisenhower Republicanism and New Deal Democracy was that of public versus private power. Under Roosevelt and Truman vast Federal power projects had been built in the Tennessee Valley and in the Pacific Northwest, and plans had been pushed for similar developments elsewhere. Eisenhower and his Secretary of the Interior, Douglas McKay, advocated the so-called "partnership" principle, under which the primary responsibility for power would rest upon "the people locally"—that is, upon the states, municipalities, and private companies. The Federal government would act only in exceptional cases where the necessary projects were too large for local action.

The new approach to the power issue was illustrated by Eisenhower's policy toward the Hell's Canyon question. This deep gorge on the Snake River at the Idaho-Oregon boundary was one of the best remaining power sites in the country. The Truman administration had developed a plan for building a high multipurpose dam there as a Federal project; the Idaho Power Company had offered an alternative plan for constructing three small dams with private capital. The Eisenhower administration rejected the high-dam plan, and the Federal Power Commission granted the requested license to the private utilities company. The public-power advocates made a determined fight to upset this decision. In 1956 most of the Congressional Democrats supported a bill to substitute the Federal project, but Eisenhower marshalled enough support to defeat the measure. Still unwilling to give up the fight, the public-power faction attempted to persuade the Supreme Court to annul the FPC license for the private development, but this maneuver also failed.

The Dixon-Yates Controversy

A major struggle developed over TVA—an enterprise which Eisenhower in an unguarded moment had once characterized as "creeping socialism." This great public agency had attracted so much industry to the region that it had to supplement its hydroelectric generating facilities with steam plants. To further expansion of this kind the private power advocates were opposed. They claimed that the growing proportion of steam-generated power showed how far TVA had moved from its original purposes. They argued that TVA competition was unfair because the public agency's payments in lieu of taxes fell far short of the taxes being imposed upon the private utilities. The Republican Eighty-third Congress refused to appropriate funds for TVA expansion.

This unwillingness to build new TVA steam-generating plants involved the Eisenhower administration in a hornet's nest. By a complicated arrangement the Atomic Energy Commission contracted with Edgar H. Dixon and Eugene A. Yates, the executives of two private utility companies, to have a new private generating plant built in Arkansas, across the Mississippi River from Memphis, Tennessee. The AEC would then supply the city of Memphis with power from the Dixon-Yates plant, and the TVA, relieved of responsibilities at Memphis, would continue to deliver power to various atomic energy plants.

Public power advocates denounced the Dixon-Yates contract as a conspiracy to weaken the TVA. They charged that the deal had been made by the AEC through secret negotiations on terms unfavorable to the government. Disliking an arrangement that might result in higher electric rates, the city of Memphis decided to build its own municipal generating plant. The Eisenhower administration accepted this solution as being consistent with its partnership policy and canceled the Dixon-Yates contract.

But the last had not been heard of the Dixon-Yates affair. The Democrats, scenting campaign material, demanded a Congressional investigation. The resulting hearings were full of embarrassment for the administration. It was revealed that Adolphe Wenzell, a vice president of the First Boston Corporation, had been employed by the government as a consultant in negotiating the Dixon-Yates contract, and that the First Boston Corporation had subsequently acted as financial agent for the Dixon-Yates group. The AEC declared that this conflict of interest voided the contract and refused to compensate Dixon-Yates for expenditures already made when the project was canceled. The utilities group retaliated by suing the government.

Although the administration continued to oppose TVA expansion, it did demonstrate the other side of its partnership policy. On the grounds that the projects were too costly and complex for local enterprise, the Republicans supported plans to produce public power by a dam on the Upper Colorado River and by a tunnel between the Fryingpan and Arkansas Rivers.

While the nation's resources in water power, coal, and oil made it unlikely that atomic power would really be needed for generating electricity in the near future, a jockeying for advantage between the public and private power factions developed in this field as well. The Atomic Energy Act of 1946 had vested full control over both the military and civilian development of atomic power in the AEC. Eisenhower asked Congress to amend this provision, so that the AEC might license private agencies to develop nuclear energy for peaceful uses. Most of the President's recommendations were incorporated in the Atomic Energy Act of 1954, but the public power advocates were able to add safeguards to prevent private monopoly of atomic patents and nuclear-generated electricity.

Offshore Oil

Paralleling the controversies between the public and private power factions was a series of disputes involving conservation policy. Roosevelt and Truman had been jealous guardians of the national domain; Eisenhower favored turning over much of the responsibility to the states.

This issue came to focus early in the administration over the question of the offshore oil resources. In 1946 Congress had attempted to vest in the states full control over the underseas resources lying off their coasts, but President Truman, believing in Federal control, vetoed the bill. In 1947 and 1950 the Supreme Court upheld the paramount rights of the Federal government over the submerged lands. Congress countered with a bill to transfer title to the states, but Truman once again interposed with a veto.

During the 1952 campaign Eisenhower came out in favor of state control of the offshore resources, and early in his administration this pledge was fulfilled. On May 22, 1953, the President signed an act transferring to the coastal states all rights to the oil, natural gas, and other resources lying within their historic limits—3 miles, in most instances, and 10½ miles in the cases of Texas and Florida. Upon the President's recommendation a second law was passed retaining for the Federal government all control over the continental shelf beyond those limits. Particularly in the Gulf of Mexico the potential wealth to be drawn from this outer rim was enormous.

The transfer of offshore rights to the states was supported by a coalition of Democrats and Republicans—some because their states had an immediate interest, others because of a general desire to defend states' rights; the opposition came from Northern Democrats eager to extend the Federal conservation policy. Something of the same division of forces occurred in 1956 over the question of exempting natural gas going into interstate pipelines from price regulation by the Federal Power Commission. In fighting to curb Federal control, Democratic legislators from Arkansas, Texas, and other natural-gas producing states had the support of many conservative Republicans, but they were opposed by Northern Democrats and Republicans from heavily urbanized states where consumers might be hurt by higher gas rates. The states-righters would probably have been victorious had not the lobbyists overplayed their hand. Senator Francis P. Case, a Republican from South Dakota, disclosed that an oil-company lawyer had given an unsolicited $2,500 to Case's campaign fund in the expectation that the Senator would vote for the natural-gas bill. Case returned the money, and voted against the measure. Following the sensation caused by Case's revelation, the measure passed Congress but was vetoed by Eisenhower, who announced that he favored its purpose but was shocked by the "arrogant" manner in which private persons had been seeking "to further their own interests."

Senator Wayne Morse of Oregon, a former Republican who had now changed his affiliation to the Democratic party, was a leader of the conservation faction. He and other Democrats opposed the administration not only on the public power issue but upon a variety of other matters. They charged that unfriendly subordinate officials in the Interior Department had sacrificed the national domain by awarding timber contracts to privileged operators, allowing the exploitation of oil deposits within national wild life preserves, and similar devices.

The St. Lawrence Seaway

Democratic attacks on the Republican "giveaways" tended to be ineffective because, for one thing, Southern Democrats had been so prominent in the off-shore oil and natural gas bill fights. Moreover, the Republicans' record on development of national resources had its bright, as well as dark, spots. Particularly impressive was Eisenhower's victory in obtaining Congressional approval for the St. Lawrence Seaway—a proposal that five previous Presidents had advocated without success. Earlier attempts to link the Great Lakes to the Atlantic Ocean had been blocked through the opposition of the railroads, the Eastern seaports, and the coal miners, but compelling new reasons for the waterway had arisen. Rapidly depleting ore deposits within the United States made it imperative that the Midwestern steel mills gain access to new sources of supply in Laborador and elsewhere. For this and other reasons connected with national defense, the Eisenhower administration gave the Seaway strong backing. Moreover, Canada, weary of the long delay, indicated that it would build the project alone if the United States did not act promptly. On May 13, 1954, the President signed a bill authorizing joint construction by Canada and the United States. The American share was to be built by a government corporation, which would raise $105 million by selling its bonds to the United States Treasury. Construction and control of hydroelectric installations were entrusted to the New York State Power Authority and the Ontario Hydro-Electric Commission—in conformity with Eisenhower's "partnership policy."

Labor and Welfare

When Eisenhower chose as his Secretary of Labor Martin P. Durkin, president of the Plumbers' Union and a Stevenson supporter, most Republicans disapproved. With characteristic bluntness, Senator Taft called the appointment "incredible." Yet Eisenhower's good intentions were obvious. By appointing a prominent union leader, he wanted to assure organized labor that he was no enemy to its legitimate rights. Durkin, with equal good faith, accepted the post in the hope that he could achieve one of labor's principal goals—a revision of the Taft-Hartley Act.

Durkin lasted only nine months. He had worked out nineteen Taft-Hartley amendments that he hoped the President would recommend to Congress. Republican conservatives opposed his program, however, and Eisenhower withheld his approval. In September, 1953, Durkin resigned, charging that the President had broken his word—a contention that the White House emphatically denied.

To succeed Durkin, Eisenhower appointed James P. Mitchell, a man of very different background, whose knowledge of the labor problem came from management rather than union experience. Respected by labor as honest and fair, Mitchell was able to salve the wounds left by the Durkin resignation. The new Secretary enforced the Federal minimum wage vigorously and called for higher standards. In 1956 Eisenhower recommended raising the minimum from 75 cents to 90 cents an hour. The Democratic Congress went the administration one better by fixing the standard at $1.00 an hour.

On the whole, the Eisenhower administration and organized labor got along better than had been expected. Despite union complaints that the National Labor Relations Board had been packed in the interests of management, labor resentment remained moderate. General prosperity, rising wages, and the extension of fringe benefits were adequate to keep the workers reasonably contented.

In April, 1953, Congress created a Department of Health, Education, and Welfare. Mrs. Oveta Culp Hobby, whom Eisenhower appointed to the new cabinet post, was a Texas Democrat, well-known both through her command of the Women's Army Corps during World War II and her career as publisher of the *Houston Post*. Mrs. Hobby followed a cautious course, partly because of personal conservatism, partly as a matter of policy to allay the suspicion that the new department meant Federal encroachment in the field of medicine and education. In the spring of 1955, Mrs. Hobby was sharply criticized for not having made adequate plans for the distribution of the new Salk polio vaccine. When some 56 cases of polio were traced to the faulty vaccine produced by a particular manufacturer, the department was further condemned for having set up an unsatisfactory testing program. In July, 1955, Mrs. Hobby resigned, giving her husband's illness as her reason.

To fill the vacant post, the President appointed Marion B. Folsom, an Eastman Kodak Company executive who had had extensive business and government experience in the welfare field. Folsom plunged ahead along paths where Mrs. Hobby had feared to tread, developing a positive program for extending social security, facilitating medical care, and extending the nation's educational plant.

Without going as far as Truman had in his Fair Deal program, Eisenhower sponsored a variety of welfare proposals. In August, 1954, the Republican Congress extended the Social Security Act to cover about one million more persons, including farmers, state and local government workers, and clergymen. Old age pensions were raised and more liberal rules for pensioners were adopted. In 1956 a Democratic Congress made the system still more generous by lowering the eligibility age for women to 62 and that for disabled workers to 50.

The Housing Act of 1954 was intended to promote homebuilding, not only as a desirable goal in itself but as a stimulus to drooping business activity. Private construction was encouraged by reducing down payments and extending the amortization period of FHA-insured loans. In support of the "urban renewal" movement, the FHA was empowered to insure loans for the renovation of older dwellings. Eisenhower had recommended that the government be granted authority to build 140,000 public housing units over a period of four years, but on this the Republican Eighty-third Congress balked, limiting its authorization to 35,000 units for one year. The Democratic Eighty-fourth Congress was more favorable to public housing, but was unable to do much more than to keep the program alive. By steering between those who demanded a bold public housing policy and those who wanted no public housing at all, Eisenhower once more demonstrated his preference for the middle course.

The Republicans displayed much more enthusiasm for road building. Here the need for action was obvious. Because of depression and war, highway construction had fallen far behind the multiplying motor traffic of the nation. In 1956 Congress, acting upon a presidential recommendation, authorized the expenditure of $33.5 billion to construct 41,000 miles of modern superhighways over a period of 16 years. The states were to do the building, but the Federal government would bear 90 per cent of the costs. Federal excise taxes on gasoline and tires were raised to provide the necessary funds.

Eisenhower recommended additional Federal expenditure for the building of hospitals and public health research. More controversial was his proposal for a $25 million reinsurance fund to encourage private and non-profit health insurance organizations to offer broader protection. This recommendation fell under attack from both the left and the right. Those who believed in national health insurance condemned the Eisenhower program as hopelessly inadequate; on the other hand, the American Medical Association opposed it as a dangerous step toward "socialized medicine." As a result, Congress enacted only the non-controversial recommendations and left the reinsurance proposal strictly alone.

Aid for Education

Similar frustrations resulted from the President's attempts to aid education. The higher birth rate had increased the school-age population much more rapidly than expected, and state and local governments were therefore confronted with a serious shortage of both classrooms and teachers. Eisenhower was torn between a desire to act and a fear of Federal interference with local affairs. A first step was taken in 1953 when Congress authorized Federal grants to help build schools in districts where defense industry had resulted in an abnormal growth of population. In 1955 the President proposed outright grants of $200 million to construct schools in hardship areas, and authority for the Federal government to purchase local school district bonds up to $750 million more. Northern Democrats criticized the measure as a "do-it-yourself" program; Southern Democrats feared any action that might undermine racial segregation in the schools. Hence Congress did nothing.

In November, 1955, a White House Conference on Education, attended by 2,000 educational and community leaders, concluded that national expenditures for education would have to be doubled within ten years and that Federal aid for school construction was necessary. Using these findings, the President recommended to Congress in 1956 a program under which the Federal government would make outright grants of $1.25 billion over a five-year period and would provide $750 million more through the purchase of local school construction bonds. The President's proposal was killed in the House by a complicated series of maneuvers involving both Republicans and Democrats. First, a coalition of Republicans and Northern Democrats passed an amendment proposed by Representative Adam Clayton Powell, a Negro Democrat from New York City, which would have denied Federal aid to school districts not complying with the Supreme Court antisegregation ruling. Then conservative Republicans joined with Southern Democrats to kill the bill itself. The President's failure to hold the support of his own party was again illustrated in 1957, when the House once more voted down the school construction program with most of the Republicans and Southern Democrats in opposition.

Challenge from McCarthy

Although the Truman administration had undertaken a security program to purge disloyal persons from sensitive government posts, the Republicans were convinced that not enough had been done. In April, 1953, President Eisenhower ordered a far-reaching revision of the system. Government employees were now to be dismissed not merely for disloyalty, but for any other cause, such as alcoholism, drug addiction, or immoral conduct, that might make them security risks. The old Loyalty Review Board was abolished, each agency head was made responsible for his own personnel, and the right of arbitrary dismissal was extended from sensitive to non-sensitive posts.

The administration took vigorous action under the new directive. Between May, 1953, and October, 1954, there was a total of 6,926 "security separations," a fact on which Vice President Nixon and other Republican orators harped during the Congressional election of 1954. The Democrats indignantly charged their opponents with playing a "numbers game," in which dismissals and voluntary resignations were lumped together and no indication was given of how many employees had been found guilty of disloyalty and how many were fired merely for drinking or talking too much, or even of how many were Truman holdovers and how many were Eisenhower appointees.

The difficulties inherent in the security problem were dramatized by the case of Dr. J. Robert Oppenheimer, who had directed the manufacture of the first atomic bombs at Los Alamos and was now employed as an adviser to the Atomic Energy Commission. After considering charges that Oppenheimer had associated with Communists and had obstructed the development of the hydrogen bomb, a special investigating board recommended by a 3 to 2 vote that his security clearance be withdrawn. Upholding this decision by a vote of 4 to 1, the AEC ruled that although the famous scientist was not disloyal, he had "fundamental defects" of character and had associated with Communists "far beyond the tolerable limits of prudence and restraint." Many Americans were distressed that in an age when scientific knowledge was at a premium, the government had deprived itself of the services of one of its most brilliant minds.

By vigorous action on government security risks and by further prosecutions of Communist leaders under the Smith Act, Eisenhower hoped to make unnecessary the blunderbuss tactics by which Congressional committees had been carrying on their investigations. But Senator McCarthy showed no disposition to turn over his Red-hunting mission to the President. With the Republicans in control of the Eighty-third Congress, McCarthy assumed the chairmanship of the Government Operations Committee and its strategic Permanent Sub-committee on Investigations. Determined to keep his name in the headlines, McCarthy brushed aside the housecleaning efforts of the executive branch and directed sensational assaults upon the Voice of America overseas radio pro-gram, American libraries in foreign countries, and the Central Intelligence Agency—in all of which he professed to see evidence of Communist infiltration.

McCarthy's ruthless tactics were condemned not only by the Democrats, but by many Republicans who feared that the Wisconsin Senator was attempt-ing to seize the party leadership. Despite these warnings, Eisenhower followed a cautious policy. Occasionally he seemed to criticize McCarthy, as at Dart-mouth College in 1953 when he admonished the graduating class not to join the "book-burners." Yet he shrank from an open fight with the powerful poli-tician and directed his subordinates to cooperate in the McCarthy investi-gations.

Cooperation had its own risks, however, as Secretary of the Army Robert E. Stevens discovered. When the McCarthy subcommittee began an investiga-tion of alleged Communist infiltration into the Army, Stevens volunteered to help. Rather naively, the Secretary hoped that McCarthy would point out the areas of suspected infection and then allow him to clean them out. But any such sensible division of labor proved impossible. The break between Stevens and McCarthy came over the case of Dr. Irving Peress, a New York dentist who had been drafted into the army in 1952. Peress was granted a commission and promoted according to normal army procedures until he became a major. In December, 1953, army officials decided that Major Peress had Communist sympathies and that the simplest way of getting rid of him was to give him an honorable discharge. Secretary Stevens acknowledged that the Peress case had been badly handled and promised McCarthy that better procedures would be followed in the future. But McCarthy was determined to exploit the affair for all it was worth. When General Ralph Zwicker refused, on orders from above, to reveal the names of those who had handled the Peress case, McCarthy denounced the officer as not having the brains of a five-year-old child and being unfit to wear his uniform. This abuse of a many-times decorated World War II hero provoked a storm of resentment in the Army. Secretary Stevens first announced that he had directed General Zwicker not to reappear before the committee that had mistreated him, but later retreated ignominiously from this stand.

Stevens' apparent surrender was so disastrous to morale that the Army felt compelled to fight back by publishing sensational charges against McCarthy and his two chief associates, Roy Cohn, the committee counsel, and Francis P. Carr, the executive director. It was alleged that this trio had used the threat of hostile investigation as a weapon to get special privileges for Cohn's close friend, David Schine, a former committee consultant who had been drafted as a humble private, much to his own and Cohn's distress. McCarthy and his assistants retaliated by charging that the Army was using the unhappy Schine as "a hostage" to try to force the subcommittee to halt its probe.

Some neutral group should have been given the task of determining the truth or falsity of these conflicting charges, but the Permanent Subcommittee insisted on doing the job itself. McCarthy temporarily surrendered the chairmanship to Senator Karl Mundt, a South Dakota Republican, and for thirty-six days in the spring of 1954 hearings were held under the curious stares of television cameras. The millions of Americans in the unseen audience were never forgotten as Republican and Democratic subcommittee members wrangled over points of procedure and scrambled for party advantage. The hearings were almost equally damaging to both sides in the controversy. The Republican members of the subcommittee made no effort to defend the Army; the Democrats were much more sympathetic, but even they found it difficult to approve Secretary Stevens' vacillating conduct. On the other hand, the Democrats tended to be hostile to McCarthy, while the Republicans stood by him. But the Wisconsin Senator injured himself by asserting a right to extract material from FBI files and other confidential sources and to receive secret information from military personnel and government employees in defiance of presidential orders. Television viewers could see for themselves the arrogance and self-righteousness that McCarthy displayed even toward Eisenhower himself.

The subcommittee's findings reflected its initial prejudices: the Republican majority exonerated McCarthy of serious misconduct; the Democrats condemned him for condoning Cohn's improper activities in behalf of Schine. Both sides were severely critical of Secretary Stevens and his Army associates. Cohn resigned immediately after the hearings; Stevens held on for a decent interval but retired to private life a year later.

If the Army-McCarthy hearings appeared to have ended in a draw, the outcome was deceptive. McCarthy had gone too far, and many legislators, both Democratic and Republican, were now ready to take disciplinary action. Senator Ralph E. Flanders, Vermont Republican, Senator William Fulbright, Arkansas Democrat, and Senator Wayne Morse, Oregon independent, preferred formal charges of misconduct, and a special committee of three Republicans and three Democrats conducted hearings. In sharp contrast to the Army-McCarthy soap opera, Chairman Arthur Watkins, a conservative Utah Republican and former Federal judge, insisted upon orderly proceedings without irrelevant appeals to the galleries. The Watkins Committee recommended formal Senate censure of McCarthy, partly on the basis of his abusive treatment of General Zwicker and partly because of the Senator's contempt toward an earlier Senate committee that had attempted to investigate his finances and campaign tactics.

McCarthy characteristically fought back by calling Watkins cowardly and stupid and denouncing the hearings as a "lynch-party." But the tide was now running strongly against the Senator. By a vote of 67 to 22 the Senate voted to "condemn" McCarthy both for his earlier conduct and his more recent slurs upon the Watkins Committee. The Democrats voted unanimously for the condemnation; the Republicans were evenly split—22 for condemnation, 22 opposed. The President added his vote against McCarthy by publicly complimenting Watkins for a "splendid job." McCarthy retaliated by apologizing to the American people for having urged Eisenhower's election.

After this defeat McCarthy's star sank fast. When the Democrats gained control of the Eighty-fourth and Eighty-fifth Congresses, the Wisconsin Senator lost his committee chairmanships. In 1957 he died, a bitter and frustrated man of 48.

The repudiation of McCarthyism did not mean that Congress was relaxing its hostility to the Communists. On the contrary, antisubversion laws continued to be added to the statute books. Persons convicted of conspiring to overthrow the government by force now lost their citizenship, and the crime of peacetime espionage was made punishable by death. In 1954 the Democrats— obviously eager to prove that they were just as patriotic as the Republicans— took the initiative in pushing through a measure formally outlawing the Communist party.

All this zeal to annihilate the Communist conspiracy involved a danger that the government would jeopardize constitutional guarantees of fair trial and orderly procedure. In a number of significant cases during 1956 and 1957 the Supreme Court attempted to prevent this. In the Jencks case, the Court ruled that when the government used the testimony of witnesses interrogated by the FBI, the defense was entitled to examine the FBI files to see whether what the witness had said on earlier occasions was consistent with his testimony in open court. In the Watkins case, the Court overruled the conviction of a witness who had refused to answer certain questions put to him by the House Committee on Un-American Activities. The Court asserted that Congress must delineate the area a committee was authorized to investigate and that the questions must be pertinent to this area of inquiry. By other decisions the Court restricted the government's security-risk program to sensitive posts and placed a strict interpretation upon that clause in the Smith Act making it a crime to "organize" any group that advocated the violent overthrow of the government.

The Court, already under attack in the South for its antisegregation decisions, was bitterly denounced in many conservative quarters for seeming to hamper the anti-Communist program. Several bills, which would have served to nullify the decisions, were introduced into Congress in 1957, but only one— a measure requested by the Justice Department—to limit the application of the Jencks decision and to safeguard, as much as possible, the confidential character of the FBI files was passed. Congressional acquiescence in the other rulings gave further evidence that McCarthyism was on the wane.

Middle-of-the-Road Politics

Two facts dominated the politics of the Eisenhower age. One was the extraordinary popularity of the President himself; the other was the strange inability of the Republicans to derive the full political advantage from this popularity. The Eighty-third Congress was only narrowly Republican; the Eighty-fourth and Eighty-fifth were Democratic.

The Republicans suffered their first disappointment in the Congressional election of 1954. Throughout the campaign Vice President Nixon was an active participant, warning the country that a Democratic victory might restore "Trumanism," which he identified with "Korea, Communism, corruption, and controls"—language which the opposition party deeply resented. Eisenhower himself took to the road, campaigning more actively than any previous President had done in midterm elections. The Democrats retaliated with charges that the Eisenhower administration favored big business, was unsympathetic to the plight of farmers and unemployed workers, and was giving away the national resources. The election resulted in no strong trend for either party. The new Senate lineup was: Democrats 49, Republicans 47; the House division was: Democrats 232, Republicans 203. The Republicans could console themselves with the thought that their loss of 2 Senate and 16 House seats was smaller than that commonly suffered in midterm elections by the party in power.

Despite predictions that the election of a Democratic Congress would result in deadlock, the executive and legislative branches did not indulge in much open feuding. The Senate majority leader, Lyndon Johnson, advocated a policy of moderation, and his fellow-Texan, Speaker Sam Rayburn, exercised a similar restraint upon the House. On issues involving international cooperation Eisenhower often gained stronger support from the Democrats than from the Republicans; on domestic issues he was less fortunate, but here party lines were frequently crossed and the President achieved at least some of his goals.

With the death of Taft and the eclipse of McCarthy, Eisenhower's leadership of the Republican party was now unchallenged. The lesson of the 1954 election was clear even to right-wing Republicans: the renomination of Eisenhower was absolutely vital to party success in the 1956 campaign. Great was the consternation, therefore, when the President suffered a "moderate" heart attack on September 24, 1955, while on vacation at Denver, Colorado. Most Americans assumed that even if Eisenhower recovered, this serious illness would put an end to his political career. Reflecting the alarm of the business community, the stock market suffered its sharpest decline since 1929.

Fortunately, the crisis came at a quiet moment in national affairs, and routine business continued under the informal direction of the Eisenhower team of Nixon and Adams. For seven weeks the President remained in a Denver hospital, then he spent five weeks of further convalescence at his farm in Gettysburg, Pennsylvania. In February, 1956, the President's doctors delighted the Republican leaders with the verdict that he was probably good for "five to ten years" more of active service. On February 29 he announced his willingness to run for re-election.

The possibility that Eisenhower might have to reverse this decision was raised when he once again became a hospital patient in June—this time because of an intestinal obstruction caused by ileitis. An emergency operation was successful, however, and on July 10 he reaffirmed his intention to run again.[2]

The Election of 1956

Contrary to custom, the Democratic National Convention of 1956 was held earlier than the Republican. When the convention opened at Chicago, the renomination of Adlai Stevenson appeared almost certain. Showing none of his 1952 reluctance, Stevenson had entered actively into the preconvention campaign and had gained the pledges of more delegates than any of his rivals. The Illinois man's reputation for moderation was particularly valuable because the party leaders were looking for a standard bearer who could hold the party together despite serious North-South frictions. Neither of the other leading possibilities was acceptable to the South: Governor Averell Harriman of New York was strongly New Deal in background; Senator Estes Kefauver of Tennessee was distrusted for his liberalism on the civil rights issue and other matters. Stevenson's chances were further improved just before the convention when Kefauver withdrew from the race. Harriman remained in the contest with strong support from former President Truman, but the outcome was never seriously in doubt. Stevenson was nominated on the first ballot, receiving 905½ votes to Harriman's 210.

A much more exciting contest developed for second place on the ticket.

[2] These two illnesses, plus a mild stroke in November, 1957, again raised the question of when a President's disability warranted the succession of the Vice President. The related question was who should determine this problem. While there was much discussion of this important issue, nothing was done to solve it.

Stevenson broke with precedent by expressing no preference and allowing the delegates a free hand. The leading candidates on the first ballot were Senator Kefauver and Senator John Kennedy of Massachusetts. Although a Catholic, Kennedy won an extraordinary degree of support from the Southern delegations. For most of the second roll call he seemed to be ahead, but a few strategic shifts from favorite sons to Kefauver gave the nomination to the Tennessee Senator.

The party platform condemned Republican farm policy and advocated a return to 90 per cent of parity supports, accused the Eisenhower administration of allowing private interests to pillage national resources, and criticized the State Department's conduct of foreign affairs as "inept and vacillating." On civil rights the Democrats took a cautious position in an effort to avoid a party split.

When the Republicans met at San Francisco, all the important decisions had already been made. Eisenhower had no opposition for the first place on the ticket. Sentiment for Nixon was not equally unanimous. Some Republicans, knowing that the Vice President was disliked by many independents, hoped that the nomination would go to someone else. A month before the convention, Harold Stassen, the President's Adviser on Disarmament, announced that private polls had shown that a ticket headed by Eisenhower and Governor Christian Herter of Massachusetts would run substantially better than an Eisenhower-Nixon one. Conservative Republicans denounced this Stassen maneuver, and Eisenhower, who had already said that he would be "delighted" to have Nixon again, gave it no encouragement. Governor Herter disavowed the movement in his behalf by accepting an invitation to put Nixon's name in nomination at the convention. Even after this blow, Stassen continued to boost Herter until just before the convention opened, when he finally gave up and promised to make a seconding speech for Nixon.

With this issue settled, the convention took on the aspect of a monster Eisenhower rally. The drama reached its high point when the President appeared in person to acknowledge the cheers of the delegates and accept the nomination in a speech that avoided bitter partisanship. "Let us quit fighting the battles of the past," Eisenhower urged, "and let us turn our attention to these problems of the present and the future, on which long-term well-being of our people so urgently depends." The Republican platform was thoroughly an Eisenhower document, praising the administration for having achieved prosperity and peace and commending the "partnership" policy on natural resources. On civil rights the Republicans explicitly accepted the Supreme Court's decision that segregation must be "progressively eliminated."

Stevenson and Kefauver campaigned vigorously, criticizing the Eisenhower record both in domestic and foreign affairs. Stevenson's boldest move was to advocate that further testing of hydrogen bombs be banned by international agreement. This step was needed, he declared, to save mankind from the injurious effects of radioactive fallout. It would ease dangerous tensions in the world and would involve no risk to the United States because any violation of such an agreement could be easily detected. Eisenhower condemned the proposal as dangerous to national security in the absence of an adequate inspection system. Since the scientists themselves were divided on the question of whether the tests involved a threat to health, most voters found the issue completely confusing.

Actually, there was little that the Democrats could do to halt the Eisenhower sweep. The President's health was one of the most important issues, but Stevenson's few attempts to discuss the matter were condemned as unsportsmanlike. For most voters the President's vigorous participation in the campaign was the best answer to suggestions that he might not survive four more years in the White House.

A week before the election a sudden threat to world peace developed when first Israel and then England and France invaded Egyptian territory. Stevenson charged that the Middle East crisis demonstrated the bankruptcy of Republican foreign policy, but this last attempt to win votes failed. The gathering war clouds only increased the determination of the majority to entrust the nation's safety to Eisenhower for another term.

Eisenhower's victory was more sweeping than in 1952. His popular vote was 35.3 million to Stevenson's 25.8 million. By carrying 41 states Eisenhower won 457 electoral votes to Stevenson's 73.[3] Florida, Virginia, Texas, Tennessee, Oklahoma, and Louisiana were all in the Republican column. Not since Franklin Roosevelt defeated Landon in 1936 had a presidential candidate won so decisively.

But even the President's coattails could not carry the Republicans back into control of Congress. In the Senate the Democrats exactly held their own with 49 seats to the Republican 47; in the House they increased their margin by winning 235 seats to the Republican 200. The Republican defeat that rankled most occurred in Oregon, where former Secretary of the Interior McKay was beaten by Senator Wayne Morse, the former Republican who had shifted to the Democratic party because of disillusionment with Eisenhower.

Focus on Civil Rights

With the parties so nearly equal in strength the Negro vote had become increasingly important. Historically Republican, this vote had become overwhelmingly Democratic during the Roosevelt and Truman years in response

[3] Under normal circumstances Stevenson's electoral vote would have been 74, but one Democratic elector from Alabama exercised his constitutional right of voting for someone other than the party nominee—in this case, for Judge Walter B. Jones, also of Alabama.

to relief agencies and other reforms that helped the lower income groups. By 1952, however, many Negroes had become somewhat disillusioned with the Democrats. Of what use, they were beginning to ask, were strong presidential recommendations for civil rights legislation and Northern Democratic support for such measures if the bills were invariably filibustered to death by Southern Democratic Senators or pigeon-holed in committees headed by Southern Democratic chairmen under the seniority system? In the 1952 election there were signs that the Negro vote was beginning to trickle back to the Republicans.

Without fanfare President Eisenhower did much to promote the ideal of equality. During his first year and a half in office he appointed Negroes to 47 important positions—27 of them posts that had never before been held by Negroes. Through administration action the color line was abolished in schools serving military bases, in veterans' hospitals, and in naval installations. The policy of integrating the armed services, begun under Roosevelt and Truman, was completed. The President's Committee on Government Contracts succeeded through methods of persuasion in largely eliminating job discrimination in firms working on government orders. In the city of Washington itself Eisenhower's influence was extended toward ending discrimination in restaurants and places of amusement.

Although Northern Democrats criticized the President for not doing enough for civil rights, many Negro leaders credited him with having made an excellent record. In the 1956 election Representative Adam Clayton Powell of New York, one of the most prominent Negro Democrats, announced his support of Eisenhower, and there were other signs that the Republicans were gaining strength in Negro quarters.

Although Eisenhower had shown no enthusiasm for the kind of sweeping civil rights legislation that Truman had recommended, he did send to Congress in 1956 a moderate program formulated by Attorney General Brownell. This would create a special commission to study the civil rights situation and make recommendations, provide an additional Assistant Attorney General to supervise Justice Department activities in the civil rights field, reinforce an old Reconstruction era statute by permitting the Attorney General to apply for a Federal court injunction against anyone violating another person's rights, and also authorize the Attorney General to go to the courts for help in protecting citizens in their right to vote.

In its first encounter with Congress the Eisenhower civil rights program met the fate of so many of its predecessors: it was passed by the House but never came to a vote in the Senate. A year later, however, events developed quite differently. For one thing, many more Americans were coming to the belief that the cold war with Communism made it imperative for the nation to move more strongly against racial discrimination. For another, the 1956 election results had quickened Republican interest in the Negro vote and had warned the Northern Democrats that they could not rest their case upon past achievements.

When the House once more passed the Eisenhower civil rights bill in 1957, Senator Knowland, the minority leader, used an unusual parliamentary maneuver to bypass the hostile Judiciary Committee headed by Mississippi Senator Eastland and place the bill upon the Senate calendar. The move was aided by a favorable ruling from Vice President Nixon and the votes of 34 Republicans and 11 Democrats. Thus outflanked, the Southern Senators would usually have resorted to filibustering, but they were persuaded by Senator Lyndon Johnson, the majority leader, that this would be a mistake. Instead, they reconciled themselves to allowing the bill to come to a vote, but only after weakening it by amendments. The Northern Democrats were placed in a cruel dilemma. Some of them favored compromise with the Southern Democrats, both in the interests of party harmony and because they believed that only in this way could the bill be passed; others voted against compromise to demonstrate that they wanted a strong civil rights measure or none at all. On the crucial issue of whether to provide jury trial for persons accused of defying court injunctions, the weakening amendment passed the Senate by a vote of 51 to 42, with 12 Republicans and 39 Democrats favoring it and 33 Republicans and 9 Democrats opposed.

After the Senate passed a decidedly weak version of the bill, a House-Senate conference worked out the compromise under which the Civil Rights Act of 1957 finally became law. In its ultimate form the new statute followed the Eisenhower recommendations in providing for a Civil Rights Commission and the appointment of a new Assistant Attorney General. The government did not receive the right to apply for Federal court injunctions on all civil rights issues, but only in instances where there had been a denial of the right to vote. In most such cases the judge retained his usual power to enforce such orders without a jury trial; only in cases of criminal contempt, where the penalty imposed was more than 45 days in jail or a $300 fine, could the defendant demand a new trial with jury.

Although the measure represented only a modest victory for civil rights, most observers believed that the Republicans had profited and the Democrats lost in the complicated battle. Just how much effect the law would have in increasing the Negro vote in the South remained to be seen.

Clash at Little Rock

Any hope that Eisenhower's great prestige and instinct for conciliation might effect a peaceful solution of racial problems was shattered during the fall of

1957. Although school districts in northern Arkansas had been integrated without incident, the prosegregationists stirred up serious trouble when the same thing was attempted at Little Rock, the state capital. At first all seemed to be moving in accordance with the Supreme Court directive of 1955: the Little Rock Board of Education had set up a timetable to end segregation at the senior high school level in 1957, in junior high schools in 1960, and in elementary schools in 1963. This plan was approved by the Federal District Court, and all was in readiness for admitting carefully selected Negro students to Central High School in September, 1957.

At this point Arkansas Governor Orval Faubus, hitherto considered a moderate on the racial issue, began to make trouble. His first hostile move was to appear as a witness before the State Chancery Court, where a white mothers' organization was trying to block integration. Faubus testified that the great majority of Little Rock inhabitants were opposed to the policy and that bloodshed and mob violence were certain to follow any attempt to open white classes to Negroes. The state court thereupon issued the requested injunction, but was immediately overruled by Federal District Judge Ronald N. Davies, who enjoined all persons from hindering the integration program.

The governor's next move was to order the National Guard to surround Central High School "to maintain order." When Negro children tried to enter the school, they were turned back by the soldiers. The Board of Education now asked Judge Davies for a delay in the integration program, but the jurist refused to back down. He said that no proof had been offered that the governor's action had been necessary and ruled that his earlier decrees must be carried out. When the National Guard, on Faubus' orders, continued to bar the Negro students, Judge Davies summoned the governor to appear before him on September 20.

During the ten days between this summons and the hearing, an attempt was made to avert the growing clash of authority. Faubus discussed the situation with Eisenhower at Newport, Rhode Island, where the President was on vacation. Although the conference was apparently inconclusive, Faubus avoided a final showdown. He did not personally appear at the September 20 hearing, but he complied with a new injunction ordering him to remove the state troops. The governor then announced that he would confine his further opposition to litigation in the courts.

On Monday, September 23, with the National Guard gone, the approaches to Central High School were manned by Little Rock city police. By a ruse nine Negro children were smuggled into the building without incident, but news of what had happened infuriated the prosegregation mob that had gathered in the vicinity. Negro newspapermen were beaten, and the police had difficulty in turning back an effort to invade the building. Within the school

The Present Impasse: "Where Do We Go From Here?"
(By Pletcher in *The Sioux City Journal*.)

some of the Negro children were roughly handled by white students. After three hours of disorder the local authorities removed the Negro children to save them from harm. Friends of Governor Faubus naturally cited the day's happenings as proof that he had been right in his contention that integration would bring inevitable violence; Faubus' critics retorted that the disorder would not have occurred if the governor had not excited racial prejudices.

The next move was up to President Eisenhower. Hitherto he had shown great reluctance to use strong measures in the civil rights struggle. Indeed he had been sharply criticized for allowing the Little Rock situation to develop for three weeks without taking a decisive stand; Louis Armstrong, the famous Negro jazz musician, had publicly expressed his disgust at the President's lack of "guts." But the challenge to Federal law had now become flagrant, and Eisenhower took decisive action. Denouncing "the disgraceful occurrence" at Little Rock, he issued a proclamation commanding all persons engaged in obstruction to Federal law and Federal court orders "to cease and desist therefrom and to disperse forthwith."

When a prosegregation mob reappeared at Central High School in defiance of his proclamation, the President ordered a thousand United States Army paratroopers into Little Rock and federalized the National Guard of the state, thereby removing it from the governor's control. On September 25, the nine Negro students returned to school, this time arriving in an army station wagon convoyed by troop-laden jeeps. Outside the school a cordon of troops armed with rifles and bayonets cowed the crowd. One segregationist who allegedly grabbed at a soldier's rifle was clubbed with the gun butt; another who refused to move was pricked with a bayonet. More soldiers stood on guard within the classrooms and corridors of the school. The full authority of the Federal government was finally being exercised to protect Negro children in their constitutional right to attend non-segregated schools.

Governor Faubus protested at what he called the "military occupation" of Arkansas and the "warm red blood of patriotic American citizens" being shed by "cold, naked, unsheathed knives." On October 1 the governors of North Carolina, Tennessee, Florida, and Maryland—all moderates on the racial issue —conferred with the President in an effort to devise a formula, under which Eisenhower would agree to withdraw the troops and Faubus would promise to prevent obstruction of the Federal court orders. An agreement appeared to have been reached, but Faubus rewrote the proposed statement in a way that the White House would not accept and the negotiations collapsed. Although the governor promised not to interfere with integration personally, he would not agree to protect the Negro children against others. Instead, he continued to insist that the only solution would be for the Negro students to withdraw from the school.

The excitement at Little Rock finally subsided. The paratroopers were gradually withdrawn until on December 2, 1957, the nine Negro students attended classes for the first time without military protection. But the episode threw into dramatic highlight the whole civil rights problem. Sober warning had been given that the era of relatively good feelings that had characterized the first Eisenhower administration might not continue through the second.

30

The United States in a Troubled World

Although the Republicans had been severely critical of Democratic handling of foreign affairs, they found no easy road of their own through the jungle of world politics. In speeches and diplomatic notes, Secretary of State Dulles tried to impress upon both the Soviet rival and the NATO allies that the American government was now in more vigorous hands. Yet the difference between Acheson and Dulles was largely in the area of words. As a matter of practical necessity, the Eisenhower foreign policy had to be built upon the Truman foundations. The United States continued to counter Soviet attempts at domination by granting aid to the nations that resisted Communist threats and blandishments, and by building a ring of defensive alliances and bases around the periphery of the Communist world. Although the Soviet Union and the United States both professed a desire to ease international tensions and to negotiate a disarmament treaty, they found it impossible to agree except on minor issues, and the alarming race to develop ever more destructive weapons continued.

Internationalists versus Nationalists

The struggle between the internationalist and the nationalist wings of the Republican party was sharply fought during Eisenhower's early months in office. Many Republicans were eager to bring about a dramatic reversal of the Roosevelt and Truman policies, but the President, fresh from his NATO experience, proceeded cautiously.

The Republican platform of 1952 had promised that the United States "under Republican leadership, will repudiate all commitments contained in secret understandings such as those of Yalta, which aid Communist enslavements." The President undertook to soften this by suggesting to Congress in February, 1953, a resolution that would reject "any interpretations or applications" of secret agreements "which have been perverted to bring about the subjugation of free peoples." Since this did not repudiate the Yalta agreement itself, but only its perversion by Russia, and implied no condemnation of Roosevelt, the Republican nationalists were unhappy. The Senate Foreign Relations Committee, therefore, added a clause stipulating that the resolution did not constitute "any determination by Congress as to the validity or invalidity" of the agreement. Resenting the intended slap at Roosevelt in the word "invalidity," the Democrats opposed the resolution, and the whole matter was allowed to drop—to Eisenhower's great relief.

The President had two strong reasons for refusing to go along in an outright repudiation of the Yalta agreement. By acting upon the assumption that such agreements could be repudiated at will by one of the parties, the United States would lose its right to insist that Russia do what she had promised to do, both at Yalta and elsewhere. Moreover, because of divisions within his own party, Eisenhower was from the beginning dependent upon Democratic votes to carry out many aspects of his foreign policy. He could not expect the Democrats to cooperate if he collaborated in partisan moves to impugn the patriotism of his Democratic predecessors.

The Bricker Amendment

The so-called Bricker Amendment, which was before Congress for many months in 1953 and 1954, involved more complex issues. Ostensibly it was intended to deal with two alleged dangers to the American constitutional system: first, the secret executive agreement, like Yalta, under which a President committed the nation without Congressional approval; and secondly, the kind of treaty that involved Federal regulation of matters ordinarily reserved to the states. The latter problem had been recognized as early as 1920, when the Supreme Court in Missouri v. Holland upheld the validity of a Federal migratory bird law, passed in conformity with an Anglo-American treaty, despite the fact that such legislation would under other circumstances have been invalid. To meet the first danger, the constitutional amendment proposed by Senator John W. Bricker of Ohio would give Congress power to regulate all executive agreements; to meet the second, it stipulated that a treaty should become "effective as internal law in the United States only through legislation which would be valid in the absence of a treaty."

The Bricker Amendment gained formidable support from organizations as diverse as the American Medical Association, the Daughters of the American

Revolution, and the Vigilant Women for the Bricker Amendment—a "volunteer organization of housewives and mothers of boys overseas." In a revival of isolationism, alarmists warned that the United States might sign UN-sponsored treaties which would invade national sovereignty. One group attached stickers to its mail reading: "Wake up, Americans! Get the U.S.A. out of the United Nations. Get the United Nations out of the U.S.A. Pass the Bricker Amendment." On the other hand, the League of Women Voters and many other serious-minded citizen organizations opposed the amendment.

Although President Eisenhower at first sympathized with the broad objectives of the Bricker Amendment, advice of the State Department and further study on his own part convinced him that the proposal would dangerously limit the Executive. In a letter to Senate Majority Leader Knowland in January, 1954, the President warned that the amendment would

> . . . so restrict the conduct of foreign affairs that our country could not negotiate the agreements necessary for the handling of our business with the rest of the world. . . . Adoption of the Bricker amendment in its present form . . . would be notice to our friends as well as our enemies abroad that our country intends to withdraw from its leadership in world affairs.

While the President's opposition proved decisive in killing the unadulterated Bricker Amendment, there was still a strong possibility of some less drastic action. Administration supporters introduced a wording acceptable to Eisenhower, but this did not satisfy the nationalists. The final showdown came on a version proposed by Democratic Senator Walter George of Georgia. Despite the President's opposition, this received 60 votes to 31 opposed—thus coming within one vote of the necessary two-thirds. Senator Knowland and 31 other Republicans, as well as 28 Democrats, voted for the amendment, while 14 Republicans and 17 Democrats stood with the President in opposing it.

This showdown of February, 1954, represented high tide for the nationalists; thereafter Eisenhower's leadership in foreign affairs was not seriously challenged as far as major issues were concerned. On smaller matters, however, nationalist hostility continued to be evident. Among both Republicans and Democrats there was considerable opposition to continued foreign aid, and a battle developed each year over these items in the budget. Although aid was continued, the recommended amounts were often whittled down—particularly economic aid, which was much more vulnerable than military. Another point of friction was tariff policy. The Eisenhower administration supported a continuance of the reciprocal trade agreements program, but Congress tended to load the extension bills with restrictive amendments. This was no longer strictly a party issue; within the Republican party, the traditional protectionists were now balanced by many of the large exporting corporations that favored a liberal trade policy, while within the Democratic party the older free-trade tendencies had been greatly modified by recent industrialization of the South. President Eisenhower attempted to follow his favorite middle-of-the-road tactics; in the interest of international good will and economic prosperity he maintained a generally liberal position on foreign trade, but he permitted such concessions to protectionism as increased duties on foreign watches and bicycles.

Korean Armistice

Although the Republican right wing hoped that Eisenhower would embrace the MacArthur program for winning total victory in Korea, the President soon decided against this. Such an operation would require the use of large forces, involve huge expenditures, antagonize America's European allies, and risk war with Russia. Discussing the situation with Dulles and other advisers after his post-election trip to the Far East, Eisenhower decided to continue Truman's effort to obtain an armistice.

Even though the administration wanted peace, it made a few big-stick gestures in the hope of jolting the stalled negotiations back into motion again. Such was the principal motive of the President in publicly ordering the Seventh Fleet not to continue to "shield Communist China" from attack by Nationalist Formosa. The "Asia First" faction applauded this implied rebuke to Truman, but actually it had little meaning because Chiang Kai-shek was too weak to do more than make pin-prick raids against the mainland, and these the Seventh Fleet had already been permitting for many months. It was hoped, however, that the "deneutralization" of Formosa would stir Communist fears that American troops might be sent to aid Chiang in a real offensive.

As additional measures to bring pressure upon the Communists, the United States dispatched more Sabre jet fighter planes to the Korean front and otherwise strengthened the UN forces. Atomic missiles were also sent to Okinawa. During a visit to India in May, 1953, Dulles impressed upon Premier Nehru the idea that the United States wanted an honorable Korean peace, but that if the Communists continued to stall, American planes would bomb the Chinese Manchurian bases north of the Yalu River. No doubt this warning reached Peiping—as it was intended to.

Meanwhile, the world situation had been altered by the death of Stalin on May 5, 1953. Just how this event would change Communist policy was by no means certain, but under the dictator's first successor, Georgi Malenkov, there appeared to be some softening of tactics. On March 28 the Chinese and North Korean commanders accepted an earlier American proposal for the exchange of sick and injured prisoners of war and suggested that the general armistice negotiations, suspended since the previous September, should be resumed.

The UN accepted the Communist overture, and on April 11 negotiators at Panmunjom agreed on terms for the injured prisoner exchange. It still required three months of wrangling to hammer out a general armistice. Although the Communists had abandoned their earlier insistence upon the repatriation of all prisoners, it was difficult to decide just what should be done with those who refused to go home. Early in June, the two sides agreed that this group should be turned over to a Neutral Nations Repatriation Commission with members from India, Sweden, Switzerland, Czechoslovakia, and Poland. Under the supervision of this agency, Communist and UN representatives were to have 90 days in which to "explain" to the prisoners why they should go home. If they still refused, they should be held for 30 days more while a political conference considered what should be done with them. If no decision were reached, the prisoners were to be released and helped to find sanctuary.

With agreement on this issue it was hoped that all remaining problems might soon be solved. At this point, however, South Korean President Syngman Rhee almost torpedoed the negotiations. Angry because the proposed truce would end the war without unifying his country, Rhee secretly ordered the South Korean prison guards to open the stockades, thus releasing some 27,000 North Korean prisoners of war without waiting for any of the repatriation plans to go into effect. South Korea was also threatening to reopen hostilities unless its terms were met. Walter S. Robinson, an Assistant Secretary of State, flew to Seoul, where he spent two weeks bringing Rhee into line. At last the South Korean government agreed to respect the proposed armistice in return for assurances that the United States would go to South Korea's assistance if she were again attacked by the Communists.

Although the enemy had at first demanded the recapture of all the prisoners released by Rhee, it fortunately did not insist upon this impossible condition, and on July 27, 1953, the armistice was finally signed. Besides incorporating the agreement on exchange of prisoners, the document provided for a truce line running somewhat north of the 38th parallel for most of its distance, but dropping to the south of the parallel at its western end. Along this line a demilitarized zone 2½ miles wide was established. Each side promised not to take advantage of the armistice to strengthen its armed forces within Korea. A Neutral Nations Supervisory Commission, representative of Sweden, Switzerland, Poland, Czechoslovakia, was to see that these pledges were kept.

The Korean armistice had a somewhat chilly reception in America. Despite Republican criticism of Democratic softness toward the Communists, Eisenhower had accepted less favorable terms than those Truman had been demanding. Asked if he considered this a "truce with honor," Senator Knowland replied that he did not think so. Yet if the armistice fell short of the decisive victory that American nationalists had demanded, it did put an end to the bloodshed. Although the Communist tide had not been rolled back, it had been halted at a strategic point. Most Americans were sufficiently grateful to have the guns silenced not to criticize the terms; and, in the long run, the fact that he had ended the Korean War became one of Eisenhower's greatest political assets.

"Operation Big Switch" for the voluntary repatriation of prisoners was completed early in September, 1953. Thereafter, attention was focused on those who declined to return. About 22,500, or some 23 per cent of the total, refused to go back to North Korea or Red China, as compared with only 359, or less than 3 per cent, on the UN side who did not go home. Despite feverish Communist efforts during the "explanation" period, only 333 of their nationals changed their minds, while 8 on the other side did so. Most of the 22 Americans who elected to stay behind the Iron Curtain probably feared to return because of collaboration with the enemy or other misconduct that might subject them to punishment. In time most of these became disillusioned with the Communist Utopia and returned to America, reconciled to accepting whatever penalties might await them.

The Korean armistice still left unsettled the basic divisions that had caused the war in the first place. Subsequent efforts to negotiate a real peace treaty failed, and Korea, like Germany, continued to be a divided country. The presence of Chinese Communist soldiers to the north of the truce line and UN forces to the south warned that a renewal of the war was by no means impossible. On August 8, 1953, the United States and Korea signed a mutual defense treaty.

The China Problem

What to do about Red China proved to be as difficult a problem for Eisenhower as it had been for Truman. The naive hope of earlier days that the Chinese Communists were not Communists at all but agrarian radicals was no longer tenable. Mao Tse-tung proved himself a true Communist by maintaining close ties with Moscow, ruthlessly imposing social and economic change upon China, and liquidating all opposition. The task of industrializing this vast, backward nation was of herculean proportions, but with the aid of Soviet technicians, substantial progress was made. And as China became month by month a stronger and more unified nation, it cast an increasingly ominous shadow across the Far East.

To most Europeans the path of realism suggested that the Chinese Communist regime should be recognized as the true government of China and admitted to the UN. With this question settled, it was hoped that Chinese nationalism might assert itself and Mao Tse-tung might follow the example of Yugoslavia's Tito and refuse slavishly to follow the Moscow line. But the Eisenhower administration could not have adopted such a policy even if it had so desired. The American nationalists strenuously opposed any relaxation of policy toward Red China, and in this they were supported by general

American opinion, embittered by Red China's role in the Korean War and her continued imprisonment of American airmen and other citizens. Whenever the question of Red China's admission was raised at the UN, the United States insisted that its friends vote against it. Meanwhile, it continued to give military and economic aid to the Nationalist regime on Formosa.

Although the United States had made clear its determination to resist any Communist attempt to capture Formosa, would it also help the Nationalists maintain their hold on certain other islands close to the China mainland? This issue became suddenly important in September, 1954, when the Communists began a heavy bombardment of Quemoy, only five miles off the coast. Fearing that an attempt at invasion was close at hand, Admiral Radford, Chairman of the Joint Chiefs of Staff, and certain other military leaders, proposed that American planes join with Chiang's in bombing the Communist mainland bases. This plan was opposed by General Ridgway, the Army Chief of Staff, as likely to involve the United States in a futile war. Beset by conflicting counsels, President Eisenhower sided with the moderates in opposing not only air attacks but the proposed blockade of the China mainland.

On December 1, 1954, the United States and Nationalist China clarified their relations in a mutual defense treaty, in which the former gave an explicit pledge to go to Chiang's assistance in case of a Communist attack upon Formosa and the Pescadores. No such assurance was given concerning the offshore islands, although the door was left ajar with a provision that additional territories might be brought under the treaty by mutual agreement. In an accompanying exchange of notes, the State Department extracted from Chiang a promise not to attack the mainland without prior consultation with Washington. In effect, therefore, Formosa, which had been "unleashed" with such a flourish in 1953, was now "released."

Communist China denounced the new defense pact and continued to exchange blows with the Nationalists in the Formosa Strait. In January, 1955, the Communists began to move into the Tachens, the northernmost of the Nationalist-held offshore islands. Although this was a region of little strategic value, it raised anew the problem of where the United States intended to draw the line. The British emphasized the legal distinction between Formosa and the Pescadores, which Japan had ruled from 1895 to 1945, and the offshore islands which had always been part of China. Although recognizing this difference, the American government was reluctant to concede the islands to Communist China unless the latter would promise not to use them as bases for attack against Formosa.

Once again the administration was caught in the cross fire of nationalists like Senator Knowland, who demanded strong support for Chiang Kai-shek, and moderates who wanted strictly limited American commitments in this

Far Eastern trouble spot. In the end, a middle path was chosen. Eisenhower limited immediate American aid to helping the Nationalist troops evacuate the Tachens. At the same time the Communists were solemnly warned by a Congressional resolution of January 28, 1955, authorizing the President to employ the armed forces of the United States "as he deems necessary for the specific purpose of securing and protecting Formosa and the Pescadores against armed attack, this authority to include the securing and protection of such related positions . . . as he judges to be required or appropriate in assuring the defense of Formosa and the Pescadores." Although purposely vague, the resolution seemed to leave it in the President's discretion to help the Nationalists defend the offshore islands if he thought it necessary.

The Communists spurned UN efforts to negotiate a cease-fire in the Formosa Strait, but they did not attempt further invasions of the offshore islands. Formosa, like Korea, continued to be a pivotal point in the world balance of power. For the moment it had acquired an uneasy equilibrium that might be joggled into violent action at any moment.

Achilles Heel in Southeast Asia

Since 1945 French control over Indo-China had been seriously threatened by native nationalist movements. In Vietnam, the largest of the three constituent states, the so-called Vietminh faction, led by the Communist Ho Chi Minh, was particularly formidable. The French tried to suppress the Vietminh by a combination of military and political measures. To appease nationalist sentiment, they bestowed limited powers of self-government upon a non-Communist regime, headed by Bao Dai, a former Vietnamese emperor. But Bao Dai was scorned by most Asiatics as a mere French puppet, and anticolonial sentiment rallied around Ho Chi Minh. By 1953 French prospects were becoming increasingly bleak. Communist control had been extended over much of northern Indo-China and was threatening the rest; French public opinion, moreover, was greatly upset by Indo-China's enormous drain upon the mother country's money and manpower.

Eisenhower and Dulles believed that a Communist victory in Indo-China would be a terrible disaster for the free world. With the military and psychological momentum thus gained, the Communists were likely to roll over neighboring Burma, Thailand, Malaya, and Indonesia—areas whose great significance for the world economy had been underlined during World War II. To bolster French assistance, the United States gave increasing aid. By 1954 American money was paying three fourths of the war costs. American transport planes were carrying French troops to the fighting fronts, American fighting planes were being turned over to the French, and American technicians were being sent to service the planes. On the other hand, the Vietminh were undoubtedly obtaining aid from Communist China—although how much it was difficult to determine.

In the spring of 1954 it became obvious that without stronger measures the Communists could not be turned back. The French proposed that the United States air force be used in a massive raid to paralyze the Vietminh armies converging on Dienbienphu, where the French had concentrated their defenses in northwestern Indo-China. Although Admiral Radford favored the idea, other high administration leaders opposed it as sure to provoke a storm in Congress and in American relations with other nations. Instead Secretary Dulles urged that the Communist advance in Indo-China be halted by joint military action of the United States and other nations. In view of Republican criticism of Truman's Korean War policy, this was a drastic proposal, but Dulles conditioned it upon prior authorization by Congress and a promise by other nations to share the burden.

In April, 1954, the administration undertook to sell the Dulles plan, both to Congress and to American allies abroad, but the results were discouraging. American public opinion was cool to the prospect of sending American troops into the jungles of Southeast Asia, and even more strongly opposed was the British government. Moreover, so far as Asiatic opinion was concerned, the course urged by Dulles would be bitterly condemned as an attempt to perpetuate Western colonialism. France itself opposed the American proposal, because it might protract the Indo-China war indefinitely.

France and Britain hoped that a way out of the tangle would be found at the forthcoming Geneva Conference, where by earlier agreement Communist China was to be represented and both Korea and Indo-China were to be discussed. French determination to seek settlement became overwhelming after the fall of Dienbienphu and the consequent cabinet crisis which brought Pierre Mendes-France to the Premiership. Fearing a Far Eastern Munich, the Eisenhower administration had as little as possible to do with this conference.

On July 21, 1954, the Geneva talks produced an armistice under which the Indo-Chinese states of Cambodia and Laos were recognized as independent, and the third state, Vietnam, was divided at the seventeenth parallel with the Communists in control of the north and the anti-Communists, the south. The armistice provided for elections under international supervision to determine the future of the country, but these were never held, and Vietnam, like Germany and Korea, continued to be a divided country.

Although the Eisenhower administration believed that the threat of American intervention had halted the Communists temporarily, it took a gloomy view of the future. The armistice was regarded as only a first step in the probable extension of Communist influence over more and more territory in the region.

But the sequel in Indo-China was not as disastrous as had been predicted.

With American backing the militant nationalist, Ngo Dinh Diem, overthrew the French puppet, Bao Dai, and became the president of a South Vietnam republic. The United States took over from the French the training of the Vietnamese army and extended generous financial aid not only to Diem's government but to Laos and Cambodia as well. Thus bolstered, the new nations achieved greater stability than had been expected—although by its paternal policy the United States inherited some of the anticolonial hostility earlier directed against France.

Despite the Geneva setback Secretary Dulles continued to seek a regional security pact. On September 8, 1954, the South East Asia Treaty Organization (SEATO) came into being with the United States, Britain, France, the Philippines, Australia, New Zealand, Thailand, and Pakistan as charter members. The SEATO allies bound themselves to regard any attack upon the territory of one of them as a threat to all and to "act to meet the common danger in accordance with its constitutional processes." By a separate protocol this guarantee was also extended to Laos, Cambodia, and South Vietnam.

As a Pacific counterpart to NATO, the new SEATO was anemic. Not only did it lack the military power that made the North Atlantic organization formidable, but it failed to win the support of the major independent nations of the region. A mutual security system in which India, Burma, Ceylon, and Indonesia had no place was seriously handicapped.

India, under Prime Minister Jawaharlal Nehru, followed a persistently independent policy. Deploring the division of the world into Communist and anti-Communist camps, Nehru chose the path of neutralism, attempting to maintain friendly relations with both sides. This situation placed a serious strain on Indian-American relations. American politicians, believing that Nehru was too soft in dealing with the Communists, voted much less in economic aid to India than to such "committed" regimes as Korea, South Vietnam, and Nationalist China, despite India's huge needs. On the other hand, Nehru and other Indian leaders condemned the rigidity of American policy and particularly resented the close ties the Eisenhower administration built up with Pakistan, India's chief rival.

Problems in NATO

In the West the attempt to build an anti-Communist front still hinged on Germany. If the former enemy were remilitarized and incorporated into NATO, there would be a fair chance to restrain Soviet expansion. Otherwise the NATO army would be no match for Russian power. The need was increased by the weakening of France due to colonial troubles and domestic financial problems.

Yet not only to France but to other nations that had undergone Nazi invasion, the remilitarization of Germany seemed a painful remedy for Europe's maladies. If it were to be accepted, it must be hedged with careful safeguards. Such had been the French intention in the so-called Pleven Plan, in which the European Defense Community (EDC) had been first proposed. By incorporating national combat units from West Germany, France, Italy, Belgium, Luxembourg, and the Netherlands within a multinational army, it was hoped to gain the strength of German manpower without permitting the creation of a German national force. In May, 1952, an EDC treaty had been negotiated, although on a basis that conceded much more to German nationalism than the French had wanted.

Despite its French origins, EDC was opposed by many sectors of French opinion. The plan was condemned both by the Communists who naturally disliked any strengthening of the anti-Soviet front and by the De Gaullists who regarded EDC as a sacrifice of French sovereignty. Frenchmen feared that EDC might provide Britain and the United States with an excuse for cutting their commitments to defend Western Europe.

For many months the Eisenhower administration based its European policy on the premise that EDC must be ratified. When the French government resorted to a policy of delay, Secretary Dulles demonstrated his displeasure more and more openly. In December, 1953, he asserted that rejection of EDC would compel "an agonizing reappraisal" of United States policy, but this threat to cut off military aid only antagonized the French still further. In August, 1954, Premier Mendes-France finally submitted the EDC treaty to the French Assembly, which rejected it by a 319 to 264 vote.

At first, the death of EDC seemed to imperil the whole policy of Western defense under which both Truman and Eisenhower had operated. Fortunately, a way out of the difficulty was discovered through the patient diplomacy of British Foreign Secretary Anthony Eden. French fear of Germany was reduced by a new British pledge to keep four divisions and a tactical air force in Europe as long as the allies wanted them. Britain also committed itself to defend these allies not only against Russia, but against other aggressors as well. The United States did not go as far as this, promising only to maintain troops in Europe for the time being.

With these matters clarified, the various nations agreed on October 3, 1954, to a Paris Pact with far-reaching provisions. West Germany was granted full sovereignty and was linked with France, Italy, and the Benelux countries in a Western European Union (WEU). Through this agency West Germany was to provide twelve divisions to the NATO army, but she was not to carry her remilitarization beyond this level without the consent of her WEU partners. At the same time, West Germany and France took the first steps toward an amicable settlement of the Saar Basin dispute—a hopeful augury of genuine reconciliation between the ancient enemies.

Despite the admission of Germany and the generally improved political relations of 1954, NATO's military potential grew less rapidly than its proponents had hoped. Troubles in her North African dependencies drained off so much of France's military and financial strength that she had to reduce her contributions. In West Germany, meanwhile, remilitarization was not particularly popular and proceeded slowly. Britain found her defense expenditures a serious drain upon her struggling economy, and even the United States, under the budget-conscious Republicans, was in a mood to cut back rather than to expand military programs.

The Summit Conference

Many Europeans continued to hope that the tensions of the cold war could be reduced if only the heads of state from East and West would meet each other face to face. Prime Minister Winston Churchill deeply desired to round out his historic career with such a "summit conference," but finally retired in April, 1955, without having achieved it.

For many months President Eisenhower poured cold water on such a meeting. Exaggerated charges that Roosevelt had sacrificed American interests at Yalta had conditioned the American public to distrust all such high-level diplomatic bargaining. Moreover, Eisenhower shared with Dulles a conviction that the Russians were more likely to turn a summit conference into a propaganda battle than to make an honest effort to settle outstanding issues.

Despite these misgivings, Eisenhower found himself forced by circumstances to change his position. After Stalin's death in 1953, Soviet diplomacy had become more flexible, fluctuating between a tough and a moderate line. One result was the signing of an Austrian peace treaty on May 15, 1955, under which foreign forces were evacuated and Austria was restored to her pre-1938 boundaries. To reassure both East and West, Austria promised to follow a neutral policy and not permit the establishment of foreign bases upon her soil. This settlement revived hopes that the much more complex German problem might be solved. In anticipation of the approaching British elections the Conservatives promised the voters to seek a summit meeting, and French politicians made similar pledges in obtaining the approval of the French Assembly for the pacts admitting West Germany to NATO. Even in the United States opinion shifted toward the high-level conference idea. In March, 1955, Senator Walter George, Democratic chairman of the Foreign Relations Committee, urged such a meeting.

On May 10, 1955, the British, French and American governments jointly invited the Soviet Union to a meeting of heads of state, and the Russians promptly accepted. Although Eisenhower warned the nation against pinning too much hope on the conference, he himself showed rising optimism as the event approached. An attempt by Senator McCarthy to tie the President's hands was defeated by a decisive 77 to 4 vote.

Premier Bulganin, President Eisenhower, Premier Faure, and Sir Anthony Eden at the Geneva Conference, July, 1955. (Associated Press Photo.)

The much-publicized Summit Conference, attended by President Eisenhower, British Prime Minister Anthony Eden, French Premier Edgar Faure, and Russian Premier Nikolai Bulganin, opened at Geneva, Switzerland, on July 18, 1955. In the early sessions the President's sincere pleas for peace made a deep impression. In an effort to assure Russia that NATO was purely defensive in character, Eisenhower declared: "The United States is a fairly important member of NATO, and I can assure you that under no circumstances is the United States ever going to be a party to aggressive war—against any nation." Bulganin's reply was simple and direct: "We believe you." By this and similar friendly exchanges the Geneva Conference lowered international tension.

But the Big Four were unable to translate these peaceful professions into solutions to concrete problems. Bulganin urged that the powers agree on a collective security pact, which would obviate the need for NATO and WEU on the one side, and for the Warsaw Pact between Russia and her satellites on the other. Eisenhower contended that such an agreement would be futile unless the German question were first settled by a reunification of the country and free elections.

Both sides professed to want disarmament. Bulganin revived an earlier Russian program for limiting the armed forces of all the powers and abolishing nuclear weapons. Eisenhower fell back on the familiar American objection that a foolproof system of inspection must be established before the West could afford to give up its new weapons, but he contributed the most important new suggestion of the Summit Conference in his so-called "open-skies plan." He proposed that the two sides exchange complete blueprints of all their military establishments and provide each other with ample opportunities for aerial reconaissance to assure that neither was preparing a surprise attack.

Since plans for the Summit Conference had emphasized that the Big Four would limit themselves to an exchange of views and leave final settlements to a later conference of foreign ministers, the general reaction to the Geneva meeting was enthusiastic. Particularly in impressing the world with the American desire for peace and disproving Communist charges of capitalist war-mongering, Eisenhower seemed to have achieved one of his greatest triumphs.

Unfortunately, the aftermath brought a large measure of disillusionment. When the foreign ministers met at Geneva in the fall, the Soviet Union seemed to have relapsed into its earlier mood of suspicion and obstructionism. Although the West offered a security pact that would pledge NATO to go to Russia's defense if she were attacked by a reunited Germany, even this assurance did not remove Communist objections to free elections in East Germany—probably because such a course would not only roll back the Iron Curtain in that area but might promote unrest in the other satellites. Thus the cold war continued— but with somewhat less vituperation.

Storm Clouds in the Middle East

In the post-Summit Conference period both the Communist and non-Communist blocs made stronger efforts to win over the uncommitted nations. In this category were to be found not only South Asian states like India and Burma but the Arab nations of the Middle East. This region was vital because of its strategic relation to the Suez Canal and air routes between Europe and Asia and even more because of its tremendous oil resources. Between 1938 and 1955 Middle Eastern oil production increased from 6 million to 163 million tons a year. All western Europe was dependent on this source; in the future even the United States might need it, because the Middle Eastern fields contained almost 65 per cent of the world's known reserves.

Eager to win Arab support in the power struggle with Russia, Secretary

Dulles took a benevolent attitude toward Colonel Abdul Gamel Nasser, the Egyptian strong man who master-minded the deposition of King Farouk in 1952 and became premier in 1954. The State Department encouraged the British to bid for Nasser's friendship by hastening the withdrawal of British troops from the Suez Canal Zone. As a further friendly gesture, Britain and the United States promised to contribute $70 million toward the building of a high dam and hydroelectric plant at Aswan on the Nile—a project for which the World Bank was to advance $200 million more and Egypt itself was to provide $900 million in services and materials.

But the effort to win Egyptian friendship failed. Nasser's ambition to revenge the Arab world against Israel and perhaps ultimately to be the Bismarck who would create a united Arab state impelled him to play the West against the East, getting what he could from both sides.

When Egypt and other Arab countries declined Dulles' invitation to join in a Middle Eastern Defense Organization to parallel NATO and SEATO, the American Secretary of State encouraged the formation of an alternative grouping, the so-called Baghdad Pact. This agreement, made in November, 1955, linked Iran, Iraq, Pakistan, and Turkey—the so-called northern tier states— with Britain in a defensive alliance. Nasser bitterly opposed the Baghdad Pact for a variety of reasons. For one thing, it increased the prestige of Iraq, Egypt's principal rival for Arab leadership; for another, it included Turkey and other non-Arab countries, which had little concern in the Israeli problem; for a third, by including Britain directly and the United States indirectly, the Pact appeared to be an instrument of Western imperialism. Other Arab states like Syria, Jordan, and Saudi Arabia joined Egypt in hostility to the alliance.

In addition to dividing the Arab world, the Baghdad Pact provoked Russia into a much more active Middle Eastern policy than she had been following. The Communists found their opportunity in Egypt's rising hostility to Israel, evidenced by reprisals and counterreprisals along the armistice line. Egypt was eager to purchase modern arms, but England, France, and the United States stuck to their 1950 decision not to sell offensive weapons to either Israel or her Arab neighbors. Great was Western indignation, therefore, when in September, 1955, Nasser announced an arms deal under which Egypt would get weapons from Communist Czechoslovakia in exchange for cotton. By this and other agreements with Russia herself, Egypt obtained over the next year substantial deliveries of planes and tanks. Syria also received Communist munitions. Alarmed to find its neighbors making these preparations, Israel too sought more weapons but, except for small deliveries from France, the Western powers refused to sell, believing that to do so would intensify the arms race and the threat of war.

During 1956 Nasser continued to flirt with the Communists and to make

"Say, What If She Doesn't Want Her Honor Protected?"
(By Herblock in *The Washington Post,* 1957.)

trouble for England and France. Apparently determined to discipline the
Egyptian leader, Dulles announced on July 19, 1956, that the United States
was withdrawing its offer to help finance the Aswan Dam, and Britain took
similar action the next day. Since the World Bank loan was contingent upon
American and British participation, this too was nullified.

Dulles' abrupt change of policy was intended as a lesson to Nasser in the
limitations of Soviet aid, and Russia, as was expected, made no move to take
over the financing of the dam. The American and British leaders probably also
hoped that by killing the project they could speed Nasser's overthrow. If so,
this was the most serious of the Western leaders' many miscalculations in
dealing with the Middle Eastern hornet's nest.

On July 26, Premier Nasser delivered a shattering counterblow by announcing Egyptian nationalization of the Suez Canal, whose revenues were now to be used to build the Aswan project. Nasser promised that stockholders in the old Suez Canal Company would be compensated and that a new all-Egyptian company would be organized to operate the canal in conformity with the Constantinople Convention of 1888, which stipulated that the waterway should remain open to the ships of all nations. Placing no confidence in the wily Nasser's promises and bitterly opposed to exclusive Egyptian control of an artery so vital to their economic health, Britain and France condemned the nationalization order as a breach of international law.

During the next three months a tangled web of diplomacy was spun around the canal issue. Eighteen out of the twenty-two nations that were represented at a London conference in August backed a plan proposed by Dulles for an international operating board, but Nasser rejected this. Dulles next came up with a scheme for a Suez Canal Users Association. Fifteen nations joined this project, but it was still a matter of dispute as to how the Association should function—whether it should impose its will on Egypt by force or try to induce Egyptian concessions by diverting traffic away from the canal and around the Cape of Good Hope.

Early in October the UN Security Council took up the canal question. With Egypt's approval the Council unanimously adopted a set of six principles, which included open transit of the canal, Egyptian sovereignty, fair tolls, and other safeguards. But the negative votes of Russia and Yugoslavia killed a resolution that would have added the principle of international control.

The Suez Fiasco

Meanwhile, border incidents between Israel and the Arab states had been multiplying. Much of the trouble had been on the Jordanian frontier, and an outbreak of serious trouble seemed likely at any moment. On October 29, 1956, Israel struck, not against Jordan as had been expected, but against Egypt, her most dangerous enemy. Advancing rapidly, the Israelis easily defeated the Egyptian armies in the Sinai Peninsula, taking a large bag of prisoners and equipment—much of it Russian and Czech in origin.

On October 30, Britain and France issued an ultimatum demanding that Israel and Egypt withdraw their forces from the vicinity of the Suez Canal and allow French and British troops to occupy key positions along the waterway. Nasser indignantly rejected these demands, and British and French air attacks upon Egypt began the next day.

Deeply shocked by the British and French decision, taken without any consultation with Washington, the Eisenhower administration used UN machinery to oppose the aggression. Two Security Council resolutions, one offered by the United States and one by Russia, were vetoed by France and England, but in the Assembly, where the veto did not apply, the outcome was different. On November 1, the UN members approved by a vote of 64 to 5 an American-proposed resolution calling for an immediate cease-fire and the withdrawal of Israeli and Egyptian forces behind the 1948 armistice lines. Only Australia and New Zealand lined up with Britain, France, and Israel in opposing the action.

Britain and France refused to abide by the cease-fire resolution unless the UN itself policed the canal zone. By thus defying world opinion, antagonizing their powerful American ally, and uniting the Arabs against them, the British and French were obviously choosing a perilous course. What they hoped to obtain was the overthrow of Nasser and the internationalization of the canal. They might have succeeded if their invasion and conquest could have been carried out with lightning speed. Instead, the invasion was a cumbersome operation in which the first troops did not land at Port Said until November 5. Not only did the Egyptians have ample time to block the canal by blowing up bridges and scuttling ships, but so much pressure was mobilized against Britain and France that they had to back down and agree to the cease-fire on November 6, the day after the landings. Egypt and Israel had already promised to abide by the UN order.

The humiliation of Britain and France was brought about by many forces. In the Arab world even Iraq and other anti-Nasser governments rallied to Egypt's cause, sabotaging British-owned pipelines within their borders and threatening to expel Britain from the Baghdad Pact. Except for Australia and New Zealand, British policy found no support within the British Commonwealth of Nations: India's condemnation was to be expected, but Canada's disapproval was almost as strong. In England Prime Minister Eden's position was bitterly condemned by the Laborites and even by a faction of his own Conservative party. The most decisive steps were taken, however, by the United States and Russia. American disapproval of British and French aggression was expressed not only within the UN, but behind the scenes where the recalcitrant allies were threatened with economic reprisals. For Russia, the Suez crisis provided a golden opportunity to pose before the world as the champion of peace, to win favor among the Arabs, and to counteract the very bad publicity that the Communists were then receiving because of their ruthless suppression of Hungary.

To Britain, France, and Israel, Bulganin dispatched stern warnings on November 5, and at the same time he proposed to Eisenhower that the Soviet Union and the United States take joint action to halt the invasion. The President replied immediately, calling the proposal unthinkable and warning that the United States would oppose "the introduction of new forces" into the

Middle East. He accused Bulganin of trying to divert attention from the Russian army, which was "brutally repressing the human rights of the Hungarian people." The Anglo-French decision to halt their campaign was probably more the result of American disapproval than of Russian threats, but the Communists obtained enormous propaganda advantage from the widespread Arab conviction that Russia had played the decisive part.

Although the decision of November 6 had resulted in quieting the guns along the Egyptian front, Israeli troops were still occupying the Sinai Peninsula and Anglo-French forces controlled about one quarter of the Suez Canal. The invaders were reluctant to withdraw until the questions that had brought about the crisis were settled. Israel wanted Egypt to permit Israeli ships to use the canal, to end the blockade of Israeli ports on the Gulf of Aquaba, and to make a definitive peace treaty recognizing Israel's legal existence. Britain and France still clung to the hope that Egypt would be compelled to accept international control over the canal. These demands might have been legitimate enough under other circumstances, but world opinion was opposed to allowing the aggressors to reap any dividends from their venture. Therefore the United States backed UN demands for the complete withdrawal of the invading forces without preconditions. At Canada's suggestion, the UN organized a police force composed of units from the smaller countries to patrol the Israeli-Egyptian border and prevent further clashes.

Several months were required to restore the situation to as near normal as that troubled region could be. By Christmas, 1956, the British and French forces had completely evacuated the canal zone. The Israelis retreated much more reluctantly and held on in the Gaza Strip and along the Gulf of Aquaba until March, 1957. Their final decision to withdraw was a great relief to Eisenhower because it released the administration of the painful necessity of deciding whether or not to support UN sanctions. The Israelis coupled their promise to withdraw with a threat to take action again unless UN police prevented raids against their territory from the Gaza Strip, and unless their ships were allowed to use the Gulf of Aquaba—and the United States supported Israel on these issues.

The Suez episode was a severe blow to the Western alliance. Even though the United States had stood by Britain and France to the extent of warning Russia not to intervene, the Americans bitterly condemned the aggressors. Eisenhower and Dulles were distressed because the Anglo-French resort to force made Western objections to Soviet aggression seem insincere, and because the allies had undertaken their dangerous policy without informing the American government of their intentions. Although it could not be proved, Washington suspected that the original Israeli invasion had been made with the connivance at least of France, if not of Britain as well. But if the British and French had behaved badly, they in turn felt that Dulles' diplomacy had amounted to bungling. By encouraging the Baghdad Pact and then failing to join it, by professing friendship both for Israel and Israel's enemies, by building up Nasser and then slapping him down, and by blowing hot and cold on proposals to enforce international control over the Suez Canal, the United States had followed such a vacillating course that no one knew just where it stood.

The Eisenhower Doctrine

When Anglo-French troops pulled out of Egypt in December, 1956, their withdrawal symbolized the almost complete collapse of the powerful influence which Britain and France had so long exercised in the Middle East. Unless the United States assumed far greater responsibilities, Russia might be expected to fill the vacuum of power in the region.

On January 5, 1957, President Eisenhower appeared before Congress to ask authority to extend economic and military aid to any Middle Eastern country that desired it and to employ United States armed forces "to secure and protect the territorial independence of such nations . . . against overt armed aggression from any nation controlled by international communism." The Eisenhower Doctrine, as the new policy was promptly designated, provoked a long discussion in Congress—not so much over its purpose as over its form. Believing that the President was trying to force Congress to share a responsibility that was primarily his, the Democrats insisted upon an amendment which would show general Congressional backing for the Eisenhower Doctrine but leave it to the President to decide when the use of American forces was required. In the same resolution of March 9, 1957, Congress authorized the expenditure of $200 million for economic and military aid in the Middle East.

By sending former Democratic Congressman James P. Richards on a special mission to offer American aid to the Arab nations and by entertaining King Saud of Saudi Arabia and other Arab visitors, the Eisenhower administration worked energetically at the task of combatting Russian influence. In most of the Arab countries—especially where the ruling regimes most feared the Communists—the Eisenhower Doctrine won a measure of support. In March, 1957, American influence helped pro-Western King Hussein of Jordan crush an attempted coup by admirers of Nasser.

Whatever success the Eisenhower Doctrine achieved was of modest proportions. Egypt, showing little gratitude for American policy during the Suez crisis, continued to incline toward Moscow. In Syria, too, anti-Western elements controlled the government, following policies that were militantly anti-Israeli and anti-Turkish. Elsewhere the American policy had many weaknesses. It depended too much on the support of narrow governing cliques and offered too little to the Arab masses. It was aimed at a threat of external Soviet agression, while the real problem seemed to be the internal danger of growing anti-Western sentiment. Finally, it left unhealed the major sore spot in the Middle East—the continued hostility between Israel and her Arab neighbors.

Beyond the Iron Curtain

American diplomacy would have been easier if it had been possible to make a firm estimate of the Communist world's strength and weaknesses, but all attempts to measure the opponents' muscles seemed futile. Again and again news of feuds within the Soviet ruling clique, economic failures, or uprisings in the satellite states would lead to optimistic predictions of Communist collapse; the next month the Soviet crisis would be over and the free world would enter a new period of pessimism.

After Stalin's death in March, 1953, the rotund figure of Georgi Malenkov was for a time dominant in the Kremlin hierarchy, but in February, 1955, Malenkov resigned and the goateed and dignified Nikolai Bulganin became Premier. From the first, however, it was obvious that the real strong man of the new regime was the shrewd and tough Nikita Khrushchev, the boss of the Russian Communist party. In February, 1956, Khrushchev astounded the world by a four-hour tirade to a Communist party congress in which he denounced the hitherto venerated Stalin as a vain and power-thirsty ruler who had sent to death thousands of "honest and innocent Communists."

Under the guise of "de-Stalinization," Bulganin and Khrushchev made bewildering shifts of policy both in domestic and foreign affairs. In little matters —in permitting more foreigners to enter Russia and in relaxing some of the internal regimentation—the new regime seemed less tyranical than the old; yet the iron hand still hovered over the scene ready to pounce upon any opposition. During the 1957 the veteran Foreign Minister Vyacheslav Molotov and Defense Minister Georgi Zhukov, a friend of Eisenhower from World War II days, were both demoted. In March, 1958, Bulganin himself was pushed aside, and Khrushchev assumed the premiership.

Part of the Bulganin and Khrushchev line was to allow more liberty to the satellites. Yugoslavia, where Tito had maintained an independent Communist government since he quarreled with Stalin in 1948, was welcomed back into the fold, and Poland, where Wladyslaw Gomulka had established a Tito-like regime against Moscow's wishes in 1956, was allowed to go unpunished.

In Hungary, however, events took a different and tragic course. Inspired by the examples of Yugoslvia and Poland, the Hungarians revolted against Moscow domination. Once started, however, the movement could not be kept within the limits of so-called national communism. Liberty-intoxicated crowds, including many teen-age boys and girls, roamed the streets of Budapest, burning Communist literature, destroying Red Army monuments, killing members of the hated secret police, and otherwise showing their determination to stamp out Communism, root and branch. Confronted with such a challenge, Bulganin and Khrushchev quickly tore off their smiling masks and ordered the Soviet army to put down the rebellion with ruthless thoroughness.

The suppression of the Hungarian insurrection horrified the West, but nothing could be done to help the patriots except to offer asylum to almost 200,000 refugees who fled across the border into Austria. There was little likelihood that the Western nations would have attempted to intervene under any circumstances, but the revolt broke out at the worst possible time when the Western alliance was at odds over the Suez crisis. The UN condemned Soviet action and called for the withdrawal of Russian troops from Hungarian soil, but was powerless to enforce its orders. Nevertheless, the Communists suffered seriously in world opinion. Prime Minister Nehru and other neutralist leaders eventually criticized the Soviet conduct in Hungary, although Western leaders complained that the Asiatic reaction on this issue was not as prompt and vigorous as in condemnation of the Anglo-French aggression against Egypt.

The Hungarian tragedy was a sobering lesson in the realities of world politics for the American people. During the campaign of 1952 Republican orators had denounced Truman for basing his foreign policy on "containment" of the Soviet threat; the true goal, it was intimated, should be the "liberation" of the captive peoples. While Eisenhower and Dulles had been careful not to make explicit pledges to the satellite populations, the purpose of propaganda broadcasts across the Iron Curtain nonetheless seemed to be to encourage resistance to and revolt against Communist rule. It was understandable, therefore, that the Hungarian rebels felt bitter toward the West when their frantic appeals for help were answered only with resolutions of sympathy. It was obvious that if the subject peoples made a bid for freedom, they did so at their own risk.

The Arms Race

The United States and the Soviet Union continued to deplore the development and stockpiling of ever more deadly weapons and the expenditure of vast sums for military preparations. Both claimed to desire disarmament, but repeated efforts to agree upon practical measures brought no result.

Stymied on the major problem, President Eisenhower tried to achieve more modest goals with his atoms-for-peace plan, proposed in an address before the UN Assembly on December 8, 1953. After painting a horrendous picture of the dangers of atomic warfare, Eisenhower again emphasized America's willingness to cooperate in effective international control of the new weapons. It was not enough, however, to take this source of energy out of the hands of soldiers. "It must be put into the hands of those who will know how to strip its military casing and adapt it to the arts of peace." He proposed that the various nations contribute uranium and other fissionable materials to an International Atomic Energy Agency, which would make it available for electric power, medicine, and other peaceful activities.

Although the atoms-for-peace plan was enthusiastically applauded by most of the world, it was received with the usual suspicion both by spokesmen for Russia and by the nationalist wing of the Republican party. Eventually, however, the American project won general acceptance. In April, 1956, the United States, the Soviet Union, and ten other nations drafted the charter of an International Atomic Energy Agency; this document was unanimously approved by the representatives of 82 nations the following October—to go into effect when ratified by 18 of them. By the summer of 1957, both Russia and the United States had ratified, and the latter had already made fissionable materials and technical knowledge available for power projects and other peaceful atomic energy uses by other nations.

However commendable atoms-for-peace might be, the threat of atoms-for-war increased in seriousness rather than lessened. A UN Disarmament Commission had been intermittently at work since 1951, but the Soviet Union and the United States still remained far apart on fundamental issues. President Eisenhower's "open-skies" proposal at the Summit Conference of 1955 provided a new basis for discussion, yet Russia would accept only a limited version of it. During 1956 there were suggestions from many quarters that the powers should at least agree to ban further testing of nuclear weapons; this proposal also failed because Britain and the United States were not satisfied with the limited control that the Soviet Union was willing to accept.

During the summer of 1957 Harold Stassen, the President's Disarmament Adviser, was involved in long UN negotiations at London. For a time there was hope that more flexible positions in Moscow and Washington would make it possible to achieve arms limitation by a succession of stages. By September, however, the limit of concessions had been reached on both sides and the conference broke up in failure. The Russians had proposed an immediate two-year ban on nuclear testing without conditions and an open-skies inspection plan that would apply to a limited zone on either side of the Iron Curtain, thereby excluding most of industrial Russia and the eastern United States. The United States and its allies had countered with a promise to accept the two-year ban on nuclear tests but only as part of a larger package that would include a prohibition on further manufacture of nuclear weapons, an adequate compliance organization, and a much more extensive inspection system than the Russians were willing to concede.

Although the safeguards demanded by the Western nations were vital to their security, the disarmament issue helped to serve the propaganda interests of the Communists. It was easy to court popularity in the uncommitted countries of Asia and Africa by proposing simple formulas like "Ban the Bomb" or "Stop the Tests," and then letting the Western nations be blamed for rejecting them because no means of enforcement had been provided.

The brusqueness with which the Russians rejected the West's final offer at the London Conference of 1957 probably reflected Communist confidence that they were forging ahead in the arms race and had more to lose than to gain by accepting disarmament. The speed with which Russia progressed in this field upset all the premises upon which the Eisenhower administration had been proceeding. The New Look in defense policy had been based upon the assumption that American scientific and technological superiority made it feasible to economize on ground troops and conventional armaments, while concentrating on air power and nuclear weapons.

In January, 1954, when American confidence in the superiority of its weapons was at a peak, Secretary Dulles said in a public speech:

> Local defense will always be important. But there is no local defense which alone will contain the mighty land power of the Communist world. Local defenses must be reinforced by the further deterrent of massive retaliatory power. A potential aggressor must know that he cannot always prescribe battle conditions that suit him. . . .
>
> The basic decision is to depend primarily upon a great capacity to retaliate, instantly, by means and at places of our choosing. . . .

The policy of "massive retaliation" caused great concern to America's allies, who interpreted it as meaning that the United States had decided not to fight any more limited, or "brush-fire" wars like that in Korea. Instead, a Communist attack against Formosa or some other Free World outpost might be countered by dropping hydrogen bombs on Moscow or Peiping. Since the Russians were in a position to do some retaliating of their own, the American policy seemed to threaten to turn every small conflict into a major war of terror. The allies also feared that the new emphasis on massive retaliation might mean a drastic reduction in the American contribution to NATO ground forces.

As frequently happened, Dulles's actual policies proved to be less rash than his language. He sought to reassure world opinion that the United States meant no more than that it would retaliate in kind. In dealing with the actual situations that developed in Indo-China and the Formosa Strait, moreover, the United States made no move toward putting "massive retaliation" into effect.

Actually, the rapid development of new weapons made the problem of military planning very difficult. If the wars of the future were to be fought with nuclear weapons, the maintenance of vast ground forces, armed with conventional weapons, appeared to be a waste of money. Yet there was danger in the other alternative; if ground forces were neglected and the nation prepared only for nuclear war, this might open the way for the enemy to nibble away at free territory under such circumstances that world opinion would not tolerate retaliation with total war. Many observers believed that the two sides were moving toward a balance of terror, or atomic stalemate, in which neither would dare to risk hostilities.

Even in rich America the cost of maintaining both nuclear and conventional armaments was so great that the United States was continually having to get along with less of one or the other than extreme advocates of preparedness approved. For the poorer NATO allies, the necessity of sacrificing one military arm to support the other became imperative. In April, 1957, Britain announced that she was concentrating on nuclear weapons and was cutting back the size of her air and ground forces, and even her naval strength. This decision was hastened by the Suez fiasco, which served both to illustrate the weakening of the older forms of military power and to injure the British economy to the point where strong remedies became necessary.

It was this increasing dependence of the West upon the new weapons that caused such great dismay when Russia launched two *Sputniks* or earth satellites in October and November, 1957. Although the satellites themselves posed no threat to the free world, they dramatized unpleasant facts both for the present and the future. They completely exploded the American assumption that the United States was superior to all other nations in scientific and engineering ability and that the Russians had developed atom and hydrogen bombs only by stealing American secrets. Particularly after an American attempt to launch a much smaller satellite ended in humiliating failure in December, 1957, it became clear that in the field of rocketry, at least, the Soviet Union was ahead.[1]

The *Sputnik* crisis brought about a sober reappraisal of the whole military situation. The Russians' success in launching a satellite was convincing proof that their earlier boast of possessing an intercontinental ballistic missile (ICBM) was not mere propaganda. However, since it appeared probable that the Russian ICBM was not yet sufficiently perfected to be aimed at particular American targets, there was still hope that the United States could catch up. The more immediate problem was the intermediate range ballistic missile (IRBM). Here, too, the Russians appeared to be ahead of the United States and were already probably in a position to destroy London and Paris, while the American IRBM's, although successfully tested, were not yet being produced in quantity. Because the Russians were also producing long-range bombers at a faster rate than the United States, the picture was a gloomy one.

Yet the situation was not quite as desperate as the more pessimistic commentators made it appear. The United States Strategic Air Command (SAC), with bases in England, Western Europe, and North Africa, was prepared to drop hydrogen bombs on Russian targets on a moment's notice. Despite the

[1] American success in orbiting three small satellites early in 1958 did much to salve American pride, but did not alter the basic factors in the rocketry situation.

About Time They Went Into a Huddle. (By Hungerford
in the *Pittsburgh Post-Gazette*.)

rapid progress of Communist armament, the West retained its power of massive retaliation.

Even so, however, the United States felt that it was imperative to establish missile bases in the NATO countries. The best deterrent to Soviet ICBM attacks on New York or Detroit would be an ability to retaliate with IRBM's against the industrial centers of Russia. On the diplomatic front, therefore, Eisenhower's most important move in the *Sputnik* crisis was to join with Prime Minister Macmillan of England in arranging a meeting in Paris of the NATO heads of state to discuss the new defense problem.

The mild stroke suffered by the President on November 25, 1957, made it seem for a time that Vice President Nixon would have to substitute for him at the vital NATO conference. Eisenhower made a good recovery, however, and courageously went to Paris himself for the meetings that opened on December 16.

American proposals for missile bases in the NATO countries encountered opposition. Communist warnings to countries permitting anti-Russian bases to be constructed were not to be taken lightly in view of the Soviet's apparent superiority in the newest weapons. With characteristic carrot-and-stick tactics. Bulganin and Khrushchev linked grim threats with tempting offers to negotiate. The Russians promised not to station missile and other atomic weapons in East Germany, Poland, and Czechoslovakia if the United States agreed to the same restrictions in West Germany; they suggested stabilization of the Middle East by mutual pledges of non-interference; they proposed a ban on nuclear testing and a new summit conference to discuss other issues.

Although the United States condemned the Russian overture as a propaganda attempt to divide the Western allies with a rehash of old proposals, most of the NATO countries wanted to leave the door open to negotiations. In the end, therefore, the Paris NATO meeting ended in compromise. It was agreed that the United States would give intermediate-range missiles to those NATO countries willing to accept them, but that an attempt would be made to negotiate a disarmament agreement with the Soviet Union.

On the domestic front, the Republicans and Democrats engaged in minor recriminations, each side trying to blame the other for the American delay in the missiles race. Yet the situation was too serious for a major political battle. By spending more money on missiles research and development and by long-range steps to encourage education in science and technology, the nation hoped to preserve the balance of power upon which the peace of the world depended.

Thoughtful citizens knew that military power would not be enough. The nation's problems had grown more rapidly than its resources and its knowledge. The formulation of national policies which would "form a more perfect union, establish justice, insure domestic tranquility, provide for the common defense, promote the general welfare, and secure the blessings of liberty" was now more complex and more difficult than ever before. Nor could these benefits of civil society be enjoyed by the United States in isolation. Until justice, liberty, and economic security prevailed in the world at large, their permanence in America could not be assured. This was the great lesson of recent United States history.

Suggestions for Further Reading

GENERAL. Suggestive and stimulating are the interpretations given to various aspects of recent American history in Charles A. and Mary Beard, *The Rise of American Civilization*, 4 v. (Macmillan, N.Y., 1927–1942). Mark Sullivan, *Our Times: The United States, 1900–1925*, 6 v. (Scribners, N.Y., 1926–1935), is lively reading throughout and particularly valuable for its intimate picture of politics during the Roosevelt, Taft, Wilson, and Harding administrations. Interesting popular surveys are Lloyd Morris, *Postscript to Yesterday: The Last Fifty Years* (Random House, N.Y., 1947), and Gerald Johnson, *Incredible Tale: The Odyssey of the Average American in the Last Half Century* (Harper, N.Y., 1950). Many of the chapters in Allan Nevins and Louis Hacker, eds., *The United States and Its Place in World Affairs, 1918–1943* (Heath, 1943), are excellent, particularly those dealing with economic trends. The game of politics has an interesting description in Wilfred E. Binkley, *American Political Parties: Their Natural History* (Knopf, N.Y., 1943). Richard Hofstadter, *The American Political Tradition and the Men Who Made It* (Knopf, N.Y., 1948), is a stimulating interpretation.

FOREIGN RELATIONS. Thomas A. Bailey, *A Diplomatic History of the American People* (Appleton-Century-Crofts, 1955), is successful in demonstrating the influence of public opinion on American foreign policy. Samuel F. Bemis, *A Diplomatic History of the United States* (Holt, N.Y., 1955), combines thorough scholarship with keen interpretation. Also thoroughly competent is Julius W. Pratt, *A History of United States Foreign Policy* (Prentice-Hall, N.Y., 1955). More concise in treatment are L. Ethan Ellis, *A Short History of American Diplomacy* (Harper, N.Y., 1951), and Foster Rhea Dulles, *America's Rise to World Power, 1898–1954* (Harper, N.Y., 1955). George F. Kennan, *American Diplomacy, 1900–1950* (Univ. of Chicago Press, Chicago, 1951), is a critical commentary. Robert E. Osgood, *Ideals and Self-Interest in America's Foreign Relations: The Great Transformation of the Twentieth Century* (Univ. of Chicago, Chicago, 1953), is a thoughtful analysis.

SOCIAL AND CULTURAL. The three volumes in *The History of American Life* series dealing with this period are Harold U. Faulkner, *The Quest for Social Justice, 1898–1914* (Macmillan, N.Y., 1931), Preston W. Slosson, *The Great Crusade and After, 1914–1928* (Macmillan, N.Y., 1931), and Dixon Wecter, *The Age of the Great Depression, 1929–1941* (Macmillan, N.Y., 1948). Like other books in this series, these combine sound scholarship, lively subject matter, and an easy style, and contain excellent bibliographies. Brief but stimulating are the chapters dealing with this period in Thomas Cochran and William Miller, *The Age of Enterprise: A Social History of Industrial America* (Macmillan, N.Y., 1942).

ECONOMICS. On the nation's economic development the following surveys are outstanding: Harold U. Faulkner, *American Economic History* (Harper, N.Y., 1943), Edward C. Kirkland, *A History of American Economic Life* (Appleton-Century-Crofts, N.Y., 1951), and Fred A. Shannon, *America's Economic Growth* (Macmillan, N.Y., 1951).

RELIGIOUS TRENDS. A good survey of religious trends is William W. Sweet, *The Story of Religion in America* (Harper, N.Y., 1939). Herbert W. Schneider, *Religion in 20th Century America* (Harvard Univ. Press, Cambridge, 1952) is more interpretive.

INTELLECTUAL HISTORY. On intellectual history, Merle Curti, *The Growth of American Thought* (Harper, N.Y., 1943), is indispensable. Also excellent are Oscar Cargill, *Intellectual America: Ideas on the March* (Macmillan, N.Y., 1941), Ralph H. Gabriel, *The Course of American Democratic Thought* (Ronald, N.Y., 1940), and Henry S. Commager, *The American Mind* (Yale, New Haven, 1950). Although penetrating in its comments, Vernon L. Parrington, *Main Currents in American Thought*, 3 v. (Harcourt Brace, N.Y., 1927–1930), is unfortunately incomplete for this period. It must be supplemented with Robert E. Spiller and others, eds., *Literary History of the United States*, 3 v. (Macmillan, N.Y., 1948), Alfred Kazin, *On Native Grounds: An Interpretation of Modern American Prose Literature* (Reynal and Hitchcock, N.Y., 1942), and Fred L. Pattee, *The New American Literature, 1890–1930* (Century, N.Y., 1930). On science, see Bernard Jaffe, *Men of Science in America: the Role of Science in the Growth of Our Country* (Simon and Schuster, N.Y., 1944). Useful material is in Merle Curti, ed., *American Scholarship in the Twentieth Century* (Harvard Univ. Press, Cambridge, 1953).

EDUCATION. Important in tracing educational trends are Merle Curti, *The Social Ideas of American Educators* (Scribners, N.Y., 1935), and Adolph E. Meyer, *The Development of Education in the Twentieth Century* (Prentice-Hall, N.Y., 1939). For journalism, see Frank L. Mott, *American Journalism: A History of Newspapers in the United States* (Macmillan, N.Y., 1941).

THE ARTS. Standard works on the arts are: Samuel Isham and Royal Cortissoz, *History of American Painting* (Macmillan, N.Y., 1936), Lorado Taft, *The History of American Sculpture* (Macmillan, N.Y., 1924), and Thomas Tallmadge, *The Story of Architecture in America* (Norton, N.Y., 1927). An excellent survey of all the arts is Oliver W. Larkin, *Art and Life in America* (Rinehart, N.Y., 1949).

Chapter 1. Looking Backward

In addition to the books listed above the following are recommended:

IMMIGRATION. The most scholarly general treatment of the subject is Carl Wittke, *We Who Built America: the Saga of the Immigrant* (Prentice-Hall, N.Y., 1940). Louis Adamic, *A Nation of Nations* (Harper, N.Y., 1945), contains some exaggeration, but is stimulating and well written.

BUSINESS AND INDUSTRY. Well-balanced and authoritative is A. A. Berle, Jr., and Gardiner C. Means, *The Modern Corporation and Private Property* (Commerce Clearing House, N.Y., 1932). Historically important discussions of the trust problem, reflecting the viewpoints of three different decades are: John Moody, *The Truth About Trusts, a Description and Analysis of the American Trust Movement* (Moody, N.Y., 1904), William Z. Ripley, ed., *Trusts, Pools, and Corporations* (Ginn, Boston, 1916), J. W. Jenks and W. E. Clark, *The Trust Problem* (Doubleday Doran, Garden City, 1929), and H. R. Seager and C. A. Gulick, *Trust and Corporation Problems* (Harper, N.Y., 1929). The role of the bankers is explored in George W. Edwards, *The Evolution of Finance Capitalism* (Longmans Green, N.Y., 1938), and in more popular form in Frederick L. Allen, *The Great Pierpont Morgan* (Harper, N.Y., 1949), and the same author's *The Lords of Creation* (Harper, N.Y., 1935). Allan Nevins, *Study in Power: John D. Rockefeller, Industrialist and Philanthropist*, 2 v. (Scribners, N.Y., 1953), is scholarly and well-balanced. An outstanding business history is Ralph W. and Muriel E. Hidy, *Pioneering in Big Business, 1882–1911: A History of Standard Oil Company (New Jersey)*, (Harper, N.Y., 1955).

LABOR. Excellent standard works are Selig Perlman and Philip Taft, *History of Labor in the United States, 1896–1932* (Macmillan, N.Y., 1935), and Leo Wolman, *Ebb and Flow in Trade Unionism* (Nat'l Bureau of Econ. Research, N.Y., 1936). The most readable survey is Foster R. Dulles, *Labor in America: A History* (Crowell, N.Y., 1949). Indispensable is Samuel Gompers, *Seventy Years of Life and Labor: an Autobiography*, 2 v. (Dutton, N.Y., 1925). An outstanding monograph is Paul H. Douglas, *Real Wages in the United States: 1896–1926* (Houghton Mifflin, Boston, 1930).

AGRICULTURE. Fred A. Shannon, *The Farmer's Last Frontier: Agriculture, 1860–1897* (Farrar & Rinehart, N.Y., 1945), is an outstanding study. Brief but excellent is Solon J. Buck, *The Agrarian Crusade* (Yale Univ. Press, New Haven, 1920). Solon J. Buck, *The Granger Movement* (Harvard Univ. Press, Cambridge, 1913), and John D. Hicks, *The Populist Revolt: A History of the Farmers' Alliance and the People's Party* (Univ. of Minnesota Press, Minneapolis, 1931), are much more detailed.

SOCIAL THOUGHT. For the dominant ideas, see Richard Hofstadter, *Social Darwinism in American Thought, 1860–1915* (Univ. of Pennsylvania Press, Philadelphia, 1945). On the rise of pragmatism, consult Morton G. White, *Social Thought in America; the Revolt against Formalism* (Viking, N.Y., 1952); Ralph B. Perry, *The Thought and Character of William James*, 2 v. (Little Brown, Boston, 1936); and Sidney Hook, *John Dewey, an Intellectual Portrait* (John Day, N.Y., 1939).

Chapter 2. The Passion for Reform

GENERAL.   Excellent recent studies are Eric Goldman, *Rendezvous with Destiny: A History of Modern American Reform* (Knopf, N.Y., 1952); Richard Hofstadter, *The Age of Reform: From Bryan to F.D.R.* (Knopf, N.Y., 1955); and Russell B. Nye, *Midwestern Progressive Politics: A Historical Study of Its Origins and Development, 1870–1900* (Michigan State College, Lansing, Mich., 1951). Although written in a spirit of disillusionment, John Chamberlain, *Farewell to Reform: The Rise, Life and Decay of the Progressive Mind in America* (Day, N.Y., 1933), is valuable for its emphasis on progressivism as a broad cultural movement. Matthew Josephson, *The President Makers . . . 1896–1919* (Harcourt Brace, N.Y., 1940), is provocative and well written. The best description of the muckrakers is in Louis Filler, *Crusaders for American Liberalism* (Harcourt Brace, N.Y., 1939). Also good is Cornelius C. Reiger, *The Era of the Muckrakers* (Univ. of North Carolina, Chapel Hill, 1932).

SOCIALISM.   The American movement has been extensively examined in the following: Ira Kipnis, *The American Socialist Movement, 1897–1912* (Columbia Univ., N.Y., 1952); Howard H. Quint, *The Forging of American Socialism: Origins of the Modern Movement* (Univ. of South Carolina, Columbia, S.C., 1953); David A. Shannon, *The Socialist Party of America: A History* (Macmillan, N.Y., 1955); Donald D. Egbert and Stow Persons, eds., *Socialism and American Life*, 2 v. (Princeton Univ., Princeton, 1952).

BIOGRAPHICAL MATERIAL.   The personalities of this period are unusually interesting. Several of them have left fascinating estimates of their own achievements. Robert M. LaFollette, *Autobiography* (LaFollette Co., Madison, Wis., 1913), and William Jennings Bryan, *Memoirs* (Winston, Phila., 1925), derive their importance from the prominence of their authors. Better written and more reflective are the memoirs of lesser figures like *American Chronicle, the Autobiography of Ray Stannard Baker* (Scribners, N.Y., 1945), Frederic C. Howe, *The Confessions of a Reformer* (Scribners, N.Y., 1925), Tom L. Johnson, *My Story* (Huebsch, N.Y., 1911), *The Autobiography of Lincoln Steffens* (Harcourt Brace, N.Y., 1931), Oswald Garrison Villard, *Fighting Years* (Harcourt Brace, N.Y., 1939), Brand Whitlock, *Forty Years of It* (Appleton, N.Y., 1925), Allan Nevins, ed., *Letters and Journal of Brand Whitlock*, 2 v. (Appleton-Century, N.Y., 1936), *The Autobiography of William Allen White* (Macmillan, N.Y., 1946). Among the better biographies are: Belle and Fola LaFollette, *Robert M. LaFollette, June 14, 1855–June 18, 1925*, 2 v. (Macmillan, N.Y., 1953); Claude Bowers, *Beveridge and the Progressive Era* (Houghton Mifflin, Boston, 1932); Alpheus T. Mason, *Brandeis: A Free Man's Life* (Viking, N.Y., 1946); Joseph Dorfman, *Thorstein Vablen and His America* (Viking, N.Y., 1935); Ray Ginger, *The Bending Cross: A Biography of Eugene Victor Debs* (Rutgers Univ., New Brunswick, N.J., 1949).

PROGRESSIVISM IN THE STATES.   Excellent studies are George E. Mowry, *The California Progressives* (Univ. of California, Berkeley, 1951); Ransom E. Noble, Jr., *New Jersey Progressivism Before Wilson* (Princeton Univ., Princeton, 1946); and Robert S. Maxwell, *LaFollette and the Rise of the Progressives in Wisconsin* (State Hist. Soc. of Wisc., Madison, 1956).

Chapter 3. Theodore Roosevelt in the Saddle

GENERAL.   The general works for Chapter 2 are still useful. An outstanding treatment is George E. Mowry, *The Era of Theodore Roosevelt* (Harper, N.Y., 1958).

BIOGRAPHICAL.   Theodore Roosevelt, *An Autobiography* (Scribners, N.Y., 1924), is an interesting self-appraisal, but must be used with caution. *The Letters of Theodore Roosevelt*, ed. by E. E. Morison, 8 v. (Harvard, Cambridge, 1951–1954), contain a mine of information. The best biography is Henry F. Pringle, *Theodore Roosevelt, a Biography* (Harcourt Brace, N.Y., 1931). John M. Blum, *The Republican Roosevelt* (Harvard, Cambridge, 1954), is a shrewd appraisal. Hermann Hagedorn, *The Roosevelt Family of Sagamore Hill* (Macmillan, N.Y., 1954), provides an attractive picture of Roosevelt's personal life. For other leading figures, consult Herbert Croly, *Marcus Alonzo Hanna: His Life and Work* (Macmillan, N.Y., 1912); Nathaniel W. Stephenson, *Nelson W. Aldrich, a Leader in American Politics* (Scribners, N.Y., 1930); Philip C. Jessup, *Elihu Root*, 2 v. (Dodd Mead, N.Y., 1938); Richard W. Leopold, *Elihu Root and the Conservative Tradition* (Little Brown, Boston, 1954); Blair Bolles, *Tyrant from Illinois: Uncle Joe Cannon's Experiment with Personal Power* (Norton, N.Y., 1951).

KEY ISSUES.   On trust-busting, consult Seager and Gulick, *Trust and Corporation Problems*, cited above. On the railroads, William Z. Ripley, *Railroads: Rates and Regulation* (Longmans Green, N.Y., 1913), is a standard authority. For the coal strike, see Elsie Gluck, *John Mitchell, Miner; Labor's Bargain with the Gilded Age* (Day, N.Y., 1929). On conservation, consult Gifford Pinchot, *Breaking New Ground* (Harcourt Brace, N.Y., 1947); Benjamin H. Hibbard, *A History of the Public Land Policies* (Macmillan, N.Y., 1924); and Charles R. Van Hise, *The Conservation of Natural Resources in the United States* (Macmillan, N.Y., 1926).

Chapter 4. Taft and the Battle of the Progressives

Most of the titles recommended for Chapter 3 are still useful for the Taft period. These should be supplemented with two outstanding recent studies: Kenneth W. Hechler, *Insurgency: Personalities and Policies of the Taft Era* (Columbia Univ., N.Y., 1940), and George E. Mowry, *Theodore Roosevelt and the Progressive Movement* (Univ. of Wisconsin, Madison, Wis., 1946). The best biography of Taft is Henry F. Pringle, *The Life and Times of William Howard Taft*, 2 v. (Farrar and Rinehart, N.Y., 1939).

One of the best ways of understanding the ideals of the progressives is through a reading of such contemporary documents as Louis D. Brandeis, *Other People's Money* (National Home Library, Washington, 1933), Louis D. Brandeis, *The Curse of Bigness* (Viking, N.Y., 1934), Herbert Croly, *The Promise of American Life* (Macmillan, N.Y., 1909), Walter E. Weyl, *The New Democracy* (Macmillan, N.Y., 1912), Charles McCarthy, *The Wisconsin Idea* (Macmillan, N.Y., 1912), J. W. Davidson, ed., *A Crossroads of Freedom: The 1912 Campaign Speeches of Woodrow Wilson* (Yale Univ., New Haven, 1956).

On key issues consult Alpheus T. Mason, *Bureaucracy Convicts Itself: The Ballinger-Pinchot Controversy of 1910* (Viking, N.Y., 1941), and L. Ethan Ellis, *Reciprocity, 1911: A Study in Canadian-American Relations* (Yale Univ., New Haven, 1939).

Chapter 5. The American Empire

GENERAL. The diplomatic histories by Bailey, Bemis, Pratt, and Ellis cited above should be supplemented with the more detailed treatment of Howard K. Beale, *Theodore Roosevelt and the Rise of America to World Power* (Johns Hopkins, Baltimore, 1956). A. L. P. Dennis, *Adventures in American Diplomacy, 1896–1906* (Dutton, N.Y., 1928), combines an account of some of the principal episodes of the period with a publication of the text of interesting documents. Tyler Dennett, *John Hay: From Poetry to Politics* (Dodd Mead, N.Y., 1933), is an excellent biography of a key figure. The best studies of imperialism are Julius W. Pratt, *Expansionists of 1898* (Johns Hopkins, Baltimore, 1936), and *America's Colonial Experiment* (Prentice-Hall, N.Y., 1950). An entertaining account of the role of newspapers in bringing on the Spanish-American War is Walter Millis, *The Martial Spirit* (Riverside, Cambridge, 1931). W. D. Puleston, *Mahan: The Life and Work of Captain Alfred Thayer Mahan* (Yale Univ., New Haven, 1939), traces the career of a figure having great influence, while hitherto neglected areas of history are illuminated by Harold and Margaret Sprout, *The Rise of American Naval Power, 1776–1919* (Princeton Univ., Princeton, 1939).

CUBA AND THE DEPENDENCIES. A good over-all view is contained in William H. Haas, ed., *The American Empire: a Study of the Outlying Territories of the United States* (Univ. of Chicago, Chicago, 1940). Critical discussions of relations with particular areas are Leland H. Jenks, *Our Cuban Colony, a Study in Sugar* (Vanguard, N.Y., 1928), Russell H. Fitzgibbon, *Cuba and the United States, 1900–1935* (Banta, Wis., 1940), Moorfield Story and Marcial Lichauco, *The Conquest of the Philippines by the United States, 1898–1925* (Putnam, N.Y., 1926), Joseph Hayden, *The Philippines, a Study in National Development* (Macmillan, N.Y., 1942). On one of the key figures, consult Hermann Hagedorn, *Leonard Wood, a Biography*, 2 v. (Harper, N.Y., 1931).

THE FAR EAST. The best study of the period is A. Whitney Griswold, *The Far Eastern Policy of the United States* (Harcourt Brace, N.Y., 1938). For essential background see Tyler Dennett, *Americans in Eastern Asia* (Macmillan, N.Y., 1922). For a general survey, Foster R. Dulles, *Forty Years of American-Japanese Relations* (Appleton-Century, N.Y., 1937), is valuable. Outstanding studies of special phases are Tyler Dennett, *Roosevelt and the Russo-Japanese War* (Doubleday Doran, Garden City, 1925); Thomas A. Bailey, *Theodore Roosevelt and the Japanese-American Crises* (Stanford Univ., Calif., 1934); Eleanor Tupper and George McReynolds, *Japan in American Public Opinion* (Macmillan, N.Y., 1937); Charles Vevier, *The United States and China, 1906–1913: A Study of Finance and Diplomacy* (Rutgers, New Brunswick, N.J., 1955).

Chapter 6. Search for Security and Peace

GENERAL. The general works recommended for Chapter 5 are still useful. Also two excellent biographies of leading diplomatists: Jessup, *Elihu Root*, cited above, and Allan Nevins, *Henry White: Thirty Years of American Diplomacy* (Harper, N.Y., 1930).

RELATIONS WITH LATIN AMERICA.   The best interpretive study is Samuel F. Bemis, *The Latin American Policy of the United States, an Historical Interpretation* (Harcourt Brace, N.Y., 1943). Older but still useful is William S. Robertson, *Hispanic American Relations with the United States* (Oxford, N.Y., 1923). On the fundamental policy underlying American action, the indispensable authority is Dexter Perkins, *The Monroe Doctrine, 1867–1907* (Johns Hopkins, Baltimore, 1927); more general is the same author's *Hands Off: A History of the Monroe Doctrine* (Little Brown, Boston, 1941). Howard C. Hill, *Roosevelt and the Caribbean* (Univ. of Chicago, Chicago, 1927), Wilfrid H. Calcott, *The Caribbean Policy of the United States, 1890–1920* (Johns Hopkins, Baltimore, 1942), and Chester Jones, *The Caribbean since 1900* (Prentice-Hall, N.Y., 1936), are able monographs. A more general discussion is Dexter Perkins, *The United States and the Caribbean* (Harvard Univ., Cambridge, 1947).

An outstanding study of canal diplomacy is Dwight C. Miner, *The Fight for the Panama Route* (Columbia Univ., N.Y., 1940). An historically important indictment of American policy is Sumner Welles, *Naboth's Vineyard: the Dominican Republic, 1844–1924,* 2 v. (Payson and Clark, N.Y., 1928).

ANGLO-AMERICAN RELATIONS.   Lionel M. Gelber, *The Rise of Anglo-American Friendship: a Study in World Politics, 1896–1906* (Oxford, N.Y., 1938), is scholarly but narrowly diplomatic in treatment. Of more general interest are Forrest Davis, *The Atlantic System: The Story of Anglo-American Control of the Seas* (Reynal and Hitchcock, N.Y., 1941), and Charles S. Campbell, Jr., *Anglo-American Understanding, 1898–1903* (Johns Hopkins, Baltimore, 1957).

Chapter 7. The Good Old Days

GENERAL.   The most useful survey of economic and social history for this period is Faulkner, *The Quest for Social Justice, 1898–1914,* cited above.

IMMIGRATION.   In addition to Wittke, *We Who Built America,* cited above, see George M. Stephenson, *History of American Immigration, 1820–1924* (Ginn, Boston, 1926), and Oscar Handlin, *The Uprooted; the Epic Story of the Great Migration that made the American People* (Little Brown, Boston, 1951).

THE NEGRO.   The best general accounts are John H. Franklin, *From Slavery to Freedom: A History of American Negroes* (Knopf, N.Y., 1948) and E. Franklin Frazier, *The Negro in the United States* (Macmillan, N.Y., 1949). The viewpoint of the Negro conservatives is reflected in Booker T. Washington, *Up from Slavery* (Doubleday Doran, Garden City, 1909). The more militant movement is described in Robert L. Jack, *History of the National Association for the Advancement of Colored People* (Meador Publishing Co., Boston, 1943).

ECONOMIC PROGRESS.   The best account is Harold U. Faulkner, *The Decline of Laissez Faire, 1897–1917* (Rinehart, N.Y., 1951). Two meteoric careers are covered in George Kennan, *E. H. Harriman,* 2 v. (Houghton Mifflin, Boston, 1922), and Allan Nevins, *Ford,* (Scribners, N.Y., 1954–1957).

LABOR. In addition to Perlman and Taft, *History of Labor in the United States, 1896–1932*, and Dulles, *Labor in America*, cited above, see L. I. Lorwin and J. A. Flexner, *The American Federation of Labor* (Brookings Institution, Washington, 1933), Paul F. Brissenden, *The I.W.W.: A Study of American Syndicalism* (Columbia Univ., N.Y., 1919), and Marguerite Green, *The National Civic Federation and the American Labor Movement, 1900–1925* (Catholic Univ., Washington, 1956).

RELIGION. In addition to Sweet, *The Story of Religion in America*, and Schneider, *Religion in 20th Century America*, cited above, see Gaius G. Atkins, *Religion in Our Times* (Round Table, N.Y., 1932), and Winfred E. Garrison, *The March of Faith: The Story of Religion in America Since 1865* (Harper, N.Y., 1933). The social gospel movement is discussed in Charles H. Hopkins, *The Rise of the Social Gospel in American Protestantism, 1865–1914* (Yale Univ., New Haven, 1940), and Henry F. May, *Protestant Churches and Industrial America* (Harper, N.Y., 1949). Another controversial trend is covered in Frank H. Foster, *The Modern Movement in American Theology* (Revell, N.Y., 1939). For the Catholic Church, consult Theodore Maynard, *The Story of American Catholicism* (Macmillan, N.Y., 1942), and John T. Ellis, *The Life of James Cardinal Gibbons: Archbishop of Baltimore, 1834–1921*, 2 v. (Bruce Publishing Co., N.Y., 1952). On the prohibition movement, see Peter Odegard, *Pressure Politics, the Story of the Anti-saloon League* (Columbia Univ., N.Y., 1928).

SCIENCE AND THOUGHT. In addition to Jaffe, *Men of Science in America*, cited above, Richard H. Shryock, *The Development of Modern Medicine* (Knopf, N.Y., 1947), and Simon and J. T. Flexner, *William Henry Welch and the Heroic Age of American Medicine* (Viking, N.Y., 1941). On the main intellectual trends, Curti, *Growth of American Thought*, Commager, *The American Mind*, and White, *Social Thought in America*, cited above, are all excellent. See also Max Lerner, ed., *The Mind and Faith of Justice Holmes* (Little Brown, Boston, 1943), and Felix Frankfurter, ed., *Mr. Justice Brandeis* (Yale Univ., New Haven, 1932).

EDUCATION AND THE PRESS. See Curti, *Social Ideas of American Educators*, Meyer, *The Development of Education in the Twentieth Century*, and Hott, *American Journalism*, all cited above. Also Richard Hofstadter and Walter P. Mezger, *The Development of Academic Freedom in the United States* (Columbia Univ., N.Y., 1955).

LITERATURE AND THE ARTS. The most useful works are Spiller and others, *Literary History of the United States*, Kazin, *On Native Grounds*, and Larkin, *Art and Life in America*, all cited above.

Chapter 8. The New Freedom

GENERAL. The best studies of the period are Frederic Paxson, *American Democracy and the World War*, 3 v. (Houghton Mifflin, Boston, 1936–1948), and Arthur S. Link, *Woodrow Wilson and the Progressive Era* (Harper, N.Y., 1954). Wilson's own speeches and letters are indispensable sources upon his ideals and his political methods. For these, consult Ray S. Baker and William E. Dodd, eds., *The Public Papers of Woodrow Wilson*, 6 v. (Harper, N.Y., 1925–1926), and Ray S. Baker, *Woodrow Wilson, Life and Letters*, 8 v. (Doubleday Doran, Garden City,

1927–1938). Of the numerous biographies of Wilson, the most useful are William E. Dodd, *Woodrow Wilson and His Work* (P. Smith, N.Y., 1932), Arthur S. Link, *Wilson*, 2 v. (Princeton Univ., Princeton, 1947–1956), Herbert C. F. Bell, *Woodrow Wilson and the People* (Doubleday Doran, N.Y., 1945), John A. Garraty, *Woodrow Wilson: A Great Life in Brief* (Knopf, N.Y., 1956), John M. Blum, *Woodrow Wilson and the Politics of Morality* (Little Brown, Boston, 1956). For an unusual psychological study, see Alexander L. and Juliette L. George, *Woodrow Wilson and Colonel House: A Personality Study* (John Day, N.Y., 1956).

MEMOIRS.   Wilson's secretary provides an intimate portrait in Joseph Tumulty, *Woodrow Wilson as I Knew Him* (Doubleday Page, Garden City, 1925). His son-in-law and Secretary of the Treasury deals with the period in William G. McAdoo, *Crowded Years* (Houghton Mifflin, Boston, 1931). Important memoranda on cabinet discussions are provided by the Secretary of Agriculture, David Houston, *Eight Years with Wilson's Cabinet* (Doubleday Page, Garden City, 1926). Personalities and politics are engagingly discussed in the memoirs of Wilson's Secretary of the Navy, Josephus Daniels, *The Wilson Era: Years of Peace* (Univ. of North Carolina, Chapel Hill, 1944).

REFORM LEGISLATION.   Two key figures in the creation of the Federal Reserve System discuss its origin in Carter Glass, *An Adventure in Constructive Finance* (Doubleday Doran, Garden City, 1915), and H. P. Willis, *The Federal Reserve: A Study of the Banking System of the United States* (Doubleday Page, Garden City, 1915). The functioning of the system is elucidated in Edwin W. Kemmerer, *The ABC of the Federal Reserve System* . . . (Princeton Univ., Princeton, 1938). An outstanding monograph is Thomas C. Blaisdell, Jr., *The Federal Trade Commission: an Experiment in the Control of Business* (Columbia Univ., N.Y., 1932).

FOREIGN AFFAIRS.   Wilson's basic attitudes and principles are discussed in Harley Notter, *The Origins of the Foreign Policy of Woodrow Wilson* (Johns Hopkins, Baltimore, 1937), and Edward H. Buehrig, *Woodrow Wilson and the Balance of Power* (Indiana Univ., Bloomington, Ind., 1955). Bryan's role is sympathetically related in Merle Curti, *Bryan and World Peace* (Smith College, Northampton, Mass., 1931). For American policy in key areas, see J. Fred Rippy, *the United States and Mexico* (Knopf, N.Y., 1926), Howard F. Kline, *The United States and Mexico* (Harvard Univ., Cambridge, 1953), Charles C. Tansill, *The Purchase of the Danish West Indies* (Johns Hopkins, Baltimore, 1932), and Ludwell L. Montague, *Haiti and the United States, 1900–1935* (Duke Univ., Durham, N.C., 1940).

Chapter 9. The Road to War

GENERAL.   For an understanding of how World War I issues presented themselves to the Wilson administration, the most useful works are Baker, *Wilson, Life and Letters*, cited above, Charles Seymour, *American Diplomacy During the World War* (Johns Hopkins, Baltimore, 1935), and the same author's *American Neutrality, 1914–1917* (Yale Univ., New Haven, 1935). The pioneer revisionist work on American policy is C. Hartley Grattan, *Why We Fought* (Vanguard, N.Y., 1929). A highly readable account, but with overemphasis on the role of newspapers and propaganda is Walter Millis, *Road to War: America, 1914–1917* (Houghton Mifflin, Boston, 1935). Critical of Wilson's policies is Alice M. Morrissey, *The American*

Defense of Neutral Rights, 1914–1917 (Harvard Univ., Cambridge, 1939). Most complete of all these studies is Charles C. Tansill, *America Goes to War* (Little Brown, Boston, 1938). For intelligent summaries, see Newton D. Baker, *Why We Went to War* (Harper, N.Y., 1936), and Dexter Perkins, *America and Two Wars* (Little Brown, Boston, 1944).

PROPAGANDA.   An important study is Horace C. Peterson, *Propaganda for War, the Campaign against American Neutrality, 1914–1917* (Univ. of Oklahoma, Norman, 1937). Interesting, but to be used with great caution because of its author's record as a German propagandist in two wars is George S. Viereck, *Spreading Germs of Hate* (Liveright, N.Y., 1930). See also Arthur Willert, *The Road to Safety: A Study in Anglo-American Relations* (British Book Centre, N.Y., 1953), and Armin Rappaport, *The British Press and Wilsonian Neutrality* (Stanford Univ., Palto Alto, 1950).

MEMOIRS.   The influence upon policy of key United States officials may be traced in Charles Seymour, ed., *The Intimate Papers of Colonel House*, 4 v. (Houghton Mifflin, Boston, 1926–1928), Burton J. Kendrick, ed., *The Life and Letters of Walter Hines Page*, 3 v. (Houghton Mifflin, Boston, 1924–1925), James W. Gerard, *My Four Years in Germany* (Doran, N.Y., 1920), Robert Lansing, *War Memoirs* (Bobbs Merrill, N.Y., 1935). The activities of the British Embassy may be followed in Stephen Gwynn, ed., *The Letters and Friendships of Sir Cecil Spring-Rice*, 2 v. (Little Brown, Boston, 1929), while the problems of the German ambassador are discussed in Count J. H. von Bernstorff, *My Three Years in America* (Scribners, N.Y., 1920), and in *Memoirs of Count Bernstorff* (Random House, N.Y., 1936).

Chapter 10. The War for Democracy

GENERAL.   Of works cited above, Slosson, *The Great Crusade and After*, and volume 2 of Paxson, *American Democracy and the World War*, are of particular value for this period. John S. Bassett, *Our War with Germany: A History* (Knopf, N.Y., 1919), and John B. McMaster, *The United States in the World War*, 2 v. (Appleton, N.Y., 1918–1920), are the work of well-established historians, but are too nearly contemporary with the event to be definitive. For the policies of Wilson's Secretaries of War and Navy, see Frederick Palmer, *Newton D. Baker: America at War*, 2 v. (Dodd Mead, N.Y., 1931), and Josephus Daniels, *The Wilson Era: Years of War and After, 1917–1923* (Univ. of North Carolina, Chapel Hill, 1946).

ECONOMIC MOBILIZATION.   The report of the War Industries Board is included in Bernard M. Baruch, *American Industry in the War* . . . (Prentice-Hall, N.Y., 1941). See also Baruch, *My Own Story* (Holt, N.Y., 1957), and Margaret L. Coit, *Mr. Baruch: The Man, the Myth, the Eighty Years* (Houghton Mifflin, Boston, 1957). Extensive but uncritical is Benedict Crowell and Robert F. Wilson, *How America Went to War*, 6 v. (Yale Univ., New Haven, 1921). Less detailed is Grosvenor B. Clarkson, *Industrial America in the World War* (Houghton Mifflin, Boston, 1923). Two wartime railroad administrators tell their stories in McAdoo, *Crowded Years*, and Walker D. Hines, *War History of the American Railroads* (Yale Univ., New Haven, 1928).

MOBILIZATION OF THOUGHT.   George Creel's own account is in his *How We Advertised America* (Harper, N.Y., 1920). More objective are Harold D. Lasswell, *Propaganda Technique in the World War* (Whittlesey House, N.Y., 1927), and James R. Mock and Cedric Larson, *Words That Won the War: Story of the Committee on Public Information* (Princeton Univ., Princeton, 1940). For the antiwar movement, see H. C. Peterson and G. C. Fite, *Opponents of War, 1917–1918* (Univ. of Wisconsin, Madison, 1957).

THE WAR FRONTS. Most authoritative account of the A.E.F. is John F. Pershing, *My Experiences in the World War*, 2 v. (Stokes, N.Y., 1931). Also good is James G. Harbord, *The American Army in France, 1917–1919* (Little Brown, Boston, 1936). For the war at sea, Thomas G. Frothingham, *The Naval History of the World War*, 3 v. (Harvard Univ., Cambridge, 1925–1926), is recommended. On intervention in Russia, see William S. Graves, *America's Siberian Adventure, 1918–1920* (P. Smith, N.Y., 1941), and Betty P. Unterberger, *America's Siberian Expedition, 1918–1920: A Story of National Policy* (Duke Univ., Durham, N.C., 1956).

Chapter 11. The Treaty of Versailles—Made and Rejected

GENERAL. An excellent study is Harry R. Rudin, *Armistice 1918* (Yale Univ., New Haven, 1944). Basic documents for tracing the peace negotiations are in H. W. V. Temperley, *A History of the Peace Conference of Paris*, 6 v. (Hodder and Stoughton, London, 1920–1924), and Ray S. Baker, *Woodrow Wilson and the World Settlement*, 3 v. (Doubleday Doran, Garden City, 1922). An interpretive study favorable to Wilson is Paul Birdsall, *Versailles Twenty Years After* (Reynal and Hitchcock, N.Y., 1941). Many contrary judgments are in Thomas A. Bailey, *Woodrow Wilson and the Lost Peace* (Macmillan, N.Y., 1944).

MEMOIRS AND LETTERS. Highly critical of Wilson is Robert Lansing, *The Peace Negotiations: A Personal Narrative* (Houghton Mifflin, Boston, 1921). Less controversial accounts are given by the other members of the American delegation: Seymour, *Intimate Papers of Colonel House*, Nevins, *Henry White*, Frederick Palmer, *Bliss, Peacemaker: The Life and Letters of General Tasker Howard Bliss* (Dodd Mead, N.Y., 1934). Behind-the-scenes information of some importance is to be found in Stephen Bonsal, *Unfinished Business* (Doubleday Doran, Garden City, 1944), and his *Suitors and Suppliants* (Prentice-Hall, N.Y., 1946). Other informative works by Americans attached to the peace commission are David H. Miller, *The Drafting of the Covenant*, 2 v. (Putnam, N.Y., 1938), Bernard M. Baruch, *The Making of the Reparations and Economic Sections of the Treaty* (Harper, N.Y., 1920), James T. Shotwell, *At the Paris Peace Conference* (Macmillan, N.Y., 1937). One of the liveliest portraits of the conference is the memoir of an English diplomat, Harold Nicolson, *Peacemaking, 1919* (Harcourt Brace, N.Y., 1939).

THE TREATY FIGHT. The most extensive account, highly sympathetic to Wilson, is Denna Frank Fleming, *The United States and the League of Nations, 1918–1920* (Putnam, N.Y., 1932). More critical is Thomas A. Bailey, *Woodrow Wilson and the Great Betrayal* (Macmillan, N.Y., 1945). The conduct of the Senate is analyzed in W. Stull Holt, *Treaties Defeated by the Senate: A Study of the Struggle between President and Senate over the Conduct of Foreign Relations* (Johns Hopkins, Baltimore, 1933), and Kenneth Colegrove, *The American Senate and World Peace* (Vanguard, N.Y., 1943). Wilson's most dangerous antagonist defends his course of action in Henry Cabot Lodge, *The Senate and the League of Nations* (Scribners, N.Y., 1925). John A. Garraty, *Henry Cabot Lodge: A Biography* (Knopf, N.Y., 1953), is excellent. For an unfriendly view, see Karl Schriftgiesser, *The Gentleman from Massachusetts: Henry Cabot Lodge* (Little Brown, Boston, 1944). On the tragic failure of Wilson and the pro-League Republicans to make a workable alliance, consult Ruhl J. Bartlett, *The League to Enforce Peace* (Univ. of North Carolina, Chapel Hill, 1944).

Chapter 12. Problems of the Postwar Period

The best studies of the period are Frederic Paxson, *American Democracy and the World War*, vol. 3, James R. Mock and Evangeline Thurber, *Report on Demobilization* (Univ. of Oklahoma, Norman, 1944). The excesses associated with the Red scare are discussed in Zechariah Chafee, Jr., *Free Speech in the United States* (Harvard Univ., Cambridge, 1941). For an outstanding account of the radical movement, consult Theodore Draper, *The Roots of American Communism* (Viking, N.Y., 1957). The disintegration of the radical labor movement is described in John S. Gambs, *The Decline of the I. W. W.* (Columbia Univ., N.Y., 1932). On the most critical industrial dispute of the period, see William Z. Foster, *The Great Steel Strike and Its Lessons* (Huebach, N.Y., 1920); Commission of Inquiry, The Interchurch World Movement, *Report on the Steel Strike of 1919* (Harcourt Brace, N.Y., 1920); Marshall Olds, *Analysis of the Interchurch World Movement Report on the Steel Strike* (Putnam, N.Y., 1923).

Chapter 13. The Republican Restoration

GENERAL. Very useful are James C. Malin, *The United States After the World War* (Ginn, Boston, 1930), Louis M. Hacker, *American Problems of Today: A History of the United States Since the World War* (Crofts, N.Y., 1938), and Harold U. Faulkner, *From Versailles to the New Deal* (Yale Univ., New Haven, 1950). Highly critical is Karl Schriftgiesser, *This Was Normalcy: An Account of Party Politics During Twelve Republican Years* (Little Brown, Boston, 1948). Indispensable for this period is volume 6 of Sullivan, *Our Times*. Entertaining and shrewd is Samuel Hopkins Adams, *Incredible Era: the Life and Times of Warren Gamaliel Harding* (Houghton Mifflin, Boston, 1939). Calvin Coolidge, *Autobiography* (Cosmopolitan Book Co., N.Y., 1929), is of very limited usefulness, but Claude M. Fuess, *Calvin Coolidge, the Man from Vermont* (Little Brown, Boston, 1940), and William Allen White, *A Puritan in Babylon* (Macmillan, N.Y., 1938), are excellent.

THE PROGRESSIVE OPPOSITION. On the most significant liberal of the twenties, see George W. Norris, *Fighting Liberal* (Macmillan, N.Y., 1945), Alfred Lief, *Democracy's Norris: The Biography of a Lonely Crusade* (Stackpole, N.Y., 1939), R. L. Neuberger and S. B. Kahn, *Integrity: the Life of George W. Norris* (Vanguard, N.Y., 1937). For the 1924 third party movement, see Kenneth C. MacKay, *The Progressive Movement of 1924* (Columbia Univ., N.Y., 1947).

THE FARM PROBLEM. The best introduction to the farm problem is Wilson Gee, *The Social Economics of Agriculture* (Macmillan, N.Y., 1942). See also John D. Black, *Agricultural Reform in the United States* (McGraw-Hill, N.Y., 1929),

E. Seligman, *The Economics of Farm Relief; a Survey of the Agricultural Problem* (Columbia Univ., N.Y., 1929), Murray D. Benedict, *Farm Policies of the United States, 1790–1950* (Twentieth Century Fund, N.Y., 1953), James H. Sheidler, *Farm Crisis, 1919–1923* (Univ. of Calif., Berkeley, 1957), Theodore Saloutos and John D. Hicks, *Agrarian Discontent in the Middle West, 1900–1939* (Univ. of Wisconsin, Madison, 1951), and Gilbert C. Fite, *George N. Peek and the Fight for Farm Parity* (Univ. of Oklahoma, Norman, 1954).

OTHER ISSUES. On the election of 1920, see William T. Hutchinson, *Lowden of Illinois: The Life of Frank O. Lowden*, 2 v. (Univ. of Chicago, Chicago, 1957), and James M. Cox, *Journey Through My Years* (Simon and Schuster, N.Y., 1946). Immigration legislation is discussed in Wittke, *We Who Built America*, George M. Stephenson, *A History of American Immigration, 1820–1924*, Roy L. Garis, *Immigration Restriction: A Study of the Opposition to and Regulation of Immigration into the United States* (Macmillan, N.Y., 1927). On the bonus, see Marcus Duffield, *King Legion* (Cape and Smith, N.Y., 1931). Facts revealed in the investigation of oil-reserve scandals are in M. E. Savage, *The Story of Teapot Dome* (New Republic, N.Y., 1924). For various aspects of the power controversy, Stephen Raushenbush, *The Power Fight* (New Republic, N.Y., 1932), and Ernest Gruening, *The Public Pays: a Study of Power Propaganda* (Vanguard, N.Y., 1931), are recommended. On tax policy, Sidney Ratner, *American Taxation: Its History as a Social Force in Democracy* (Norton, N.Y., 1942), is authoritative.

Chapter 14. Foreign Affairs, 1921–1929

GENERAL. The diplomatic histories by Bemis, Bailey, Ellis, and Pratt, cited in the first section of the suggested readings, are still very useful and may be supplemented with the interpretive study, Frank H. Simonds, *American Foreign Policy in the Post-War Years* (Johns Hopkins, Baltimore, 1935). A concise summary is Allan Nevins, *The United States in a Chaotic World* (Yale Univ., New Haven, 1950).

INTERNATIONAL COOPERATION. Competent discussions are Denna F. Fleming, *The United States and World Organization, 1920–1933* (Columbia Univ., N.Y., 1938), and Russell M. Cooper, *American Consultation in World Affairs* (Macmillan, N.Y., 1934). The amazing irresponsibility of the Senate is emphasized by Denna F. Fleming, *The United States and the World Court* (Doubleday Doran, Garden City, 1945). A more creditable record is that discussed in Benjamin H. Williams, *The United States and Disarmament* (McGraw-Hill, N.Y., 1931), and Merze Tate, *The United States and Armaments* (Harvard Univ., Cambridge, 1948). Also important for an understanding of the disarmament issue are Raymond L. Buell, *The Washington Conference* (Appleton, N.Y., 1922), and Harold and Margaret Sprout, *Toward a New Order of Sea Power: American Naval Policy and the World Scene, 1918–1922* (Princeton Univ., Princeton, 1940). On the Paris Pact, the most valuable authorities are James T. Shotwell, *War as an Instrument of National Policy and Its Renunciation in the Pact of Paris* (Harcourt Brace, N.Y., 1929), David Bryn-Jones, *Frank B. Kellogg, a Biography* (Putnam, N.Y., 1937), and Robert H. Ferrell, *Peace in Their Time: The Origins of the Kellogg-Briand Pact* (Yale Univ., New Haven, 1952). Two outstanding economists discuss the debts issue in Harold G. Moulton and Leo Pasvolsky, *War Debts and World Prosperity* (Century, N.Y., 1932).

SPECIAL AREAS. The background of Soviet-American relations is discussed in volume 1 of George F. Kennan, *Soviet-American Relations, 1917–1920* (Princeton Univ., Princeton, 1956). For the non-recognition policy, consult Robert P. Browder, *The Origins of Soviet-American Diplomacy* (Princeton Univ., Princeton, 1953), Frederick L. Schuman, *American Policy toward Russia since 1917* (International Publishers, N.Y., 1928), and Foster Rhea Dulles, *The Road to Teheran: The Story of Russia and America, 1781–1943* (Princeton Univ., Princeton, 1944). The leader of the Philippine independence movement tells his story in Manuel Luis Quezon, *The Good Fight* (Appleton-Century, N.Y., 1946). On relations with Latin America, Graham H. Stuart, *Latin America and the United States* (Appleton-Century, N.Y., 1938), and Herbert Feis, *The Diplomacy of the Dollar: First Era, 1919–1932* (Johns Hopkins, Baltimore, 1950), are useful. Essential to an understanding of the Nicaraguan affair are Isaac J. Cox, *Nicaragua and the United States* (World Peace Foundation, Boston, 1927), and Henry L. Stimson, *American Policy in Nicaragua* (Scribners, N.Y., 1927). On the easing of the crisis in Mexican-American relations see the excellent biography, Harold Nicolson, *Dwight Morrow* (Harcourt Brace, N.Y., 1935). For the Japanese-American crisis of 1924, see Rodman W. Paul, *The Abrogation of the Gentlemen's Agreement* (Harvard Univ., Cambridge, 1936).

Chapter 15. Reactionaries and Rebels

GENERAL. Slosson, *Great Crusade and After*, Sullivan, *Our Times*, v. 6, Beard, *Rise of American Civilization*, v. 2 and 3, are excellent on the period of the twenties. A treasury of stimulating data and comment is provided by President's Research Committee, *Recent Soviet Trends in the United States*, 2 v. (McGraw-Hill, N.Y., 1933). Highly entertaining is Frederick L. Allen, *Only Yesterday* (Harper, N.Y., 1931). A harsher judgment of the period is Henry M. Robinson, *Fantastic Interim: a Hindsight History of American Manners, Morals and Mistakes between Versailles and Pearl Harbor* (Harcourt Brace, N.Y. 1943). Robert S. and Helen M. Lynd, *Middletown: A Study in Contemporary American Culture* (Harcourt Brace, N.Y., 1929), is a well-known sociological study of Muncie, Indiana, during the twenties. An interesting comparison is with Angie Debo, *Prairie City: the Story of an American Community* (Knopf, N.Y., 1944). A good contemporary picture is André Siegfried, *America Comes of Age, a French Analysis* (Harcourt Brace, N.Y., 1927). Severely critical judgments are contained in Harold E. Stearns, ed., *Civilization in the United States: An Inquiry by Thirty Americans* (Harcourt Brace, N.Y., 1922).

SPECIAL PHASES. The problems of organized labor are discussed in Perlman and Taft, *Labor Movements*, and in L. L. Lorwin and J. A. Flexner, *The American Federation of Labor* (Brookings Institution, Washington, 1933). Important on issues involving civil liberties are Chafee, *Free Speech in the United States*, and Arthur Garfield Hayes, *Let Freedom Ring* (Boni Liveright, N.Y., 1928); see also Felix Frankfurter, *The Case of Sacco and Vanzetti* (Little Brown, Boston, 1927), and G. Louis Joughin and Edmund M. Morgan, *The Legacy of Sacco and Vanzetti* (Harcourt Brace, N.Y., 1949). An interesting popular account is Herbert Asbury, *The Great Illusion: An Informal History of Prohibition* (Doubleday, Garden City, 1950). Outstanding contemporary studies were John M. Mecklin, *The Ku Klux Klan: a Study of the American Mind* (Harcourt Brace, N.Y., 1924), Herman Feldman, *Prohibition, Its Economic and Industrial Aspects* (Appleton, N.Y., 1927),

Charles Merz, *The Dry Decade* (Doubleday Doran, Garden City, 1931). On religious issues, see Paul A. Carter, *The Decline and Revival of the Social Gospel: Social and Political Liberalism in American Protestant Churches, 1920–1940* (Cornell, Ithaca, N.Y., 1956), and Stewart G. Cole, *The History of Fundamentalism* (Richard R. Smith, N.Y., 1931). On architecture, see W. A. Starett, *Skyscrapers and the Men Who Build Them* (Scribners, N.Y., 1928), and Frank Lloyd Wright, *An Autobiography* (Longmans Green, N.Y., 1932). On literature and the arts, see titles listed in the first section of the reading suggestions; also Joseph Beach, *American Fiction, 1920–1940* (Macmillan, N.Y., 1941).

Chapter 16. Prosperity

GENERAL.   The economic histories by Shannon, Faulkner, and Kirkland, recommended above, contain good discussions of this period. For a more detailed account, see George Soule, *Prosperity Decade: From War to Depression, 1917–1929* (Rinehart, N.Y., 1947). A contemporary study of great importance is *Recent Economic Changes in the United States*, 2 v. (McGraw-Hill, N.Y., 1929). A useful summary of this is Edward E. Hunt, *An Audit of America* . . . (McGraw-Hill, N.Y., 1930). Brief but highly suggestive is Stuart Chase, *The Road We Are Traveling, 1914–1942; Guide Lines to America's Future* (Twentieth Century Fund, N.Y., 1942). A Marxian interpretation is Lewis Corey, *The Decline of American Capitalism* (Covici Friede, N.Y., 1934). Important monographs by economists are Simon Kuznets, *National Income and Capital Formation, 1919–1935: A Preliminary Report* (National Bureau of Economic Research, N.Y., 1937), and Spurgeon Bell, *Productivity, Wages and National Income* (Brookings Institution, Washington, 1940). On the intellectual climate, see James W. Prothro, *The Dollar Decade: Business Ideas in the 1920's* (Louisiana State Univ., Baton Rouge, 1954).

SPECIAL INDUSTRIES.   J. G. Glover and W. B. Cornell, eds., *The Development of American Industries: Their Economic Significance* (Prentice-Hall, N.Y., 1932), and H. T. Warshaw, ed., *Representative Industries in the United States* (Holt, N.Y., 1928), have chapters on each major industry written by spokesmen for the industry; they contain much valuable information as well as a generous measure of special pleading. An excellent popular history of the automobile, movie, and radio industries is Lloyd Morris, *Not So Long Ago* (Random House, N.Y., 1949). Ralph C. Epstein, *The Automobile Industry: Its Economic and Commercial Development* (A. W. Shaw Co., Chicago, 1928), contains valuable statistical material, while David L. Cohn, *Combustion on Wheels: An Informal History of the Automobile Age* (Houghton Mifflin, Boston, 1944), is a popular account. Nevins, *Ford*, is a major work of scholarship. Henry Ford, *My Life and Work* (Garden City Publishing Co., Garden City, 1922), reveals Ford's economic philosophy. A well-written account of the origins of aviation is in Fred C. Kelley, *The Wright Brothers* (Harcourt Brace, N.Y., 1943), while a critical and informative study of the whole industry is Elsbeth F. Freudenthal, *The Aviation Business: From Kitty Hawk to Wall Street* (Vanguard, N.Y., 1940).

The perplexities arising out of the merchant marine problem are illuminated by Paul M. Zeis, *American Shipping Policy* (Princeton Univ., Princeton, 1938). On the movies, see Margaret F. Thorp, *America at the Movies* (Yale Univ., New Haven, 1939), and Lewis Jacobs, *The Rise of the American Film; a Critical History* (Harcourt Brace, N.Y., 1939); on radio, see A. N. Goldsmith and Austin C. Lescarboura, *This Thing Called Broadcasting* (Holt, N.Y., 1930), Paul Schubert, *The Electric World: the Rise of the Radio* (Macmillan, N.Y., 1928). On the railroads, see Sidney L. Miller, *Inland Transportation: Principles and Policies* (McGraw-Hill, N.Y., 1933).

ISSUES OF PUBLIC POLICY. Thoughtful studies are William Z. Ripley, *Main Street and Wall Street* (Little Brown, Boston, 1927), W. E. Mosher and F. G. Crawford, *Public Utility Regulation* (Harper, N.Y., 1933), Twentieth Century Fund, *The Power Industry and the Public Interest* (Twentieth Century Fund, N.Y., 1944), Corporation Survey Commission, *Big Business: Its Growth and Its Place* (Twentieth Century Fund, N.Y., 1937), and Thurman W. Arnold, *The Folklore of Capitalism* (Yale Univ., New Haven, 1937).

Chapter 17. Hoover and the Depression

GENERAL. Hoover's record is sturdily defended in William S. Myers and Walter Newton, *The Hoover Administration: a Documented Narrative* (Scribners, N.Y., 1936). Hoover's own writings reveal both his assets and limitations as statesman, see Herbert C. Hoover, *Memoirs*, 3 v. (Macmillan, N.Y., 1952); William S. Myers, ed., *The State Papers and Other Public Writings of Herbert Hoover*, 2 v. (Scribners, N.Y., 1934), and Ray Lyman Wilbur and Arthur M. Hyde, eds., *The Hoover Policies* (Scribners, N.Y., 1937). Theodore Joslin, *Hoover Off the Record* (Doubleday Doran, Garden City, 1935), is a memoir by his secretary. Useful, but not definitive, biographies are provided in Eugene Lyons, *Our Unknown Ex-President, a Portrait of Herbert Hoover* (Doubleday, Garden City, N.Y., 1948), and Harold Wolfe, *Herbert Hoover, Public Servant and Leader of the Opposition* (Exposition, N.Y., 1956). For the election of 1928, see Edmund A. Moore, *A Catholic Runs for President: The Campaign of 1928* (Ronald, N.Y., 1956).

THE DEPRESSION. The best studies are Broadus Mitchell, *Depression Decade: From New Era through New Deal, 1929–1941* (Rinehart, N.Y., 1947), and John K. Galbraith, *The Great Crash, 1929* (Houghton Mifflin, Boston, 1955). Vivid descriptions are in Allen, *Only Yesterday*, and its sequel, F. L. Allen, *Since Yesterday* (Harper, N.Y., 1940), the Beards, *America in Midpassage* (vol. 3 of *The Rise of American Civilization*), and Gilbert Seldes, *The Years of the Locust* (America, 1929–1932) (Little Brown, Boston, 1933). A historically important interpretation is that of the Harvard economist, Alvin Hansen, *Fiscal Policy and Business Cycles* (Norton, N.Y., 1941). Problems of government policy are discussed in Josephine C. Brown, *Public Relief, 1929–1939* (Holt, N.Y., 1940). For a highly critical discussion of Republican policies, consult Arthur M. Schlesinger, Jr., *The Crisis of the Old Order, 1919–1933* (Houghton Mifflin, Boston, 1957). See also the economic histories by Shannon, Faulkner, and Kirkland.

Chapter 18. Hoover's Quest for World Stability

GENERAL. Laudatory of Hoover is William S. Myers, *The Foreign Policies of Herbert Hoover* (Scribners, N.Y., 1940). A more balanced account is to be found in the diplomatic histories by Bailey, Bemis, Pratt, and Ellis. Valuable contemporary interpretation together with much documentary material is in U. S. State Department, *Press Releases* (after 1939 called *The Department of State Bulletin*), Council on Foreign Relations, *Survey of American Foreign Relations, 1928–1931*, 4 v. (Yale Univ., New Haven, 1928–1931), Foreign Policy Association, *Foreign Policy Reports* (N.Y., 1925 to date).

SPECIAL PHASES. On the London Naval Conference, much valuable information is to be found in Charles G. Dawes, *Journal as Ambassador to Great Britain* (Macmillan, N.Y., 1939). The official record is to be found in State Department Conference Series No. 6, *Proceedings of the London Naval Conference and Supplementary Documents* (Govt. Printing Off., Washington, 1931). An important reorientation of American policy may be traced in Bemis, *Latin American Policy of the United States*, and Alexander De Conde, *Herbert Hoover's Latin-American Policy* (Stanford Univ., Stanford, 1951). Good discussions of the Far Eastern problem are T. A. Bisson, *American Policy in the Far East, 1931–1940* (Institute of Pacific Relations, N.Y., 1940), Griswold, *Far Eastern Policy of the United States*, Robert Langer, *Seizure of Territory: The Stimson Doctrine and Related Principles in Legal Theory and Diplomatic Practice* (Princeton Univ., Princeton, 1947), Reginald Bassett, *Democracy and Foreign Policy, the Sino-Japanese Dispute, 1931–33* (Longmans Green, N.Y., 1952), and Richard N. Current, *Secretary Stimson, a Study in Statecraft* (Rutgers, New Brunswick, N.J., 1954). Hoover's Secretary of State has provided an important memoir in Henry L. Stimson, *The Far Eastern Crisis: Recollections and Observations* (Council on Foreign Relations, N.Y., 1936).

Chapter 19. New Deal Triumphant

GENERAL. Indispensable not only for documentary material but for Roosevelt's subsequent comments on events is Samuel I. Rosenman, comp., *The Public Papers and Addresses of Franklin D. Roosevelt*, 13 v. (Random House, Macmillan, and Harper, N.Y., 1938–1950). Particularly stimulating on this period are Beard, *America in Midpassage*, and Charles A. Beard and George H. E. Smith, *The Old Deal and the New* (Macmillan, N.Y., 1940). Other leading historiance provide generally sympathetic accounts in Arthur M. Schlesinger, *The New Deal in Action, 1933–1938* (Macmillan, N.Y., 1939), and Denis W. Brogan, *The Era of Franklin D. Roosevelt* (Yale Univ., New Haven, 1950). The most detailed discussion is Basil Rauch, *The History of the New Deal* (Creative Age, N.Y., 1944). On Roosevelt, the most complete and competent work is Frank B. Freidel, *Franklin D. Roosevelt* (Little Brown, Boston, 1952–), of which three volumes have now been published. Among numerous shorter studies, the following are recommended: Alden Hatch, *Franklin D. Roosevelt, an Informal Biography* (Holt, N.Y., 1947), James M. Burns, *Roosevelt: The Lion and the Fox* (Harcourt Brace, N.Y., 1956), Noel F. Bush, *What Manner of Man* (Harper, N.Y., 1944), John Gunther, *Roosevelt in Retrospect* (Harper, N.Y., 1950). For hostile studies see John T. Flynn, *The Roosevelt Myth* (Garden City Publishing Co., Garden City, 1949), and Edgar E. Robinson, *The Roosevelt Leadership, 1933–1945* (Lippincott, Philadelphia, 1955).

MEMOIRS. Of the rapidly growing mass of this type of material, the most valuable contributions so far are Frances Perkins, *The Roosevelt I Knew* (Viking, N.Y., 1946), Robert E. Sherwood, *Roosevelt and Hopkins: An Intimate History* (Harper, N.Y., 1948), Samuel I. Rosenman, *Working with Roosevelt* (Harper, N.Y., 1952), and *The Secret Diary of Harold L. Ickes*, 3 v. (Simon & Schuster, N.Y., 1953–54). A biased but highly informative account of the early New Deal is Raymond Moley, *After Seven Years* (Harper, N.Y., 1939). *The Memoirs of Cordell Hull*, 2 v. (Macmillan, N.Y., 1948), is particularly important for foreign affairs, but contains interesting estimates of New Deal personalities. James A. Farley, *Behind the Ballots: The Personal History of a Politician* (Harcourt Brace, N.Y., 1938), is very useful for the 1932 and 1936 political campaigns. Its sequel, *Jim Farley's Story: The Roosevelt Years* (Whittlesey House, N.Y., 1948), is a record of disillusionment. Excellent on the activities of the Federal Reserve Board is Marriner S. Eccles, *Beckoning Frontiers: Public and Personal Recollections* (Knopf, N.Y., 1951).

RELIEF AND RECOVERY. The best discussion of the activities of the various New Deal agencies is Merle Fainsod and Lincoln Gordon, *Government and the American Economy* (Norton, N.Y., 1941). Valuable factual findings are in Twentieth Century Fund, *Debts and Recovery: A Study of Changes in the Internal Debt Structure from 1929 to 1937 and a Program for the Future* (Twentieth Century Fund, N.Y., 1938). On special phases, see Donald S. Howard, *The PWA and Federal Relief Policy* (Russell Sage, N.Y., 1938), and Harold L. Ickes, *Back to Work: The Story of PWA* (Macmillan, N.Y., 1935).

NRA. Indispensable for understanding the point of view of NRA's most important administrator is Hugh S. Johnson, *The Blue Eagle from Egg to Earth* (Doubleday Doran, Garden City, 1935). Johnson's successor adds his comment in Donald R. Richberg, *The Rainbow* (Doubleday Doran, Garden City, 1936). A contemporary appraisal by competent economists is Leverett S. Lyon, *et al.*, *The National Recovery Administration* (Brookings Institution, Washington, 1935). An important post-mortem is President's Committee of Industrial Analysis, *The National Recovery Administration* (Washington, 1935).

TVA AND THE UTILITIES ISSUE. The broad objectives and administrative philosophy of TVA are lucidly set forth by its principal director, David E. Lilienthal, *TVA: Democracy on the March* (Harper, N.Y., 1944). Interesting illustrative material is available in R. I. Duffus, *The Valley and Its People, a Portrait of T. V. A.* (Knopf, N.Y., 1944). An outstanding scholarly study is C. Herman Pritchett, *The Tennessee Valley Authority, a Study in Public Administration* (Univ. of North Carolina, Chapel Hill, 1943). An English estimate is Julian Huxley, *TVA, Adventure in Planning* (Architectural Press, Cheam, Surrey, 1944). On the explosive general issue of utilities' policy see Bernhard Ostrolenk, *Electricity: For Use or For Profit* (Harper, N.Y., 1936), and M. L. Ramsay, *Pyramids of Power: The Story of Roosevelt, Insull and the Utility Wars* (Bobbs-Merrill, Indianapolis, 1937).

FISCAL AND MONETARY POLICY. Important scholarly discussions are G. Griffith Johnson, *The Treasury and Monetary Policy, 1933–1938* (Harvard Univ., Cambridge, 1939), Sherwood M. Fine, *Public Spending and Postwar Economic Policy* (Columbia Univ., N.Y., 1944), Henry H. Villard, *Deficit Spending and the National Income* (Farrar and Rinehart, N.Y., 1941), Gerard Colm and Fritz Lehmann, *Economic Consequences of Recent American Tax Policy* (New School for Social Research, N.Y., 1938), Ratner, *American Taxation*, Harold M. Groves, *Production, Jobs and Taxes* . . . (McGraw-Hill, N.Y., 1944).

AGRICULTURE. A wealth of interesting material is to be found in the Yearbooks of the Department of Agriculture. The philosophy of the New Deal Secretary of Agriculture is in Henry A. Wallace, *New Frontiers* (Reynal and Hitchcock, N.Y., 1934). Severely critical on many phases are Joseph S. Davis, *On Agricultural Policy, 1926–1938* (Food Research Institute, Stanford Univ., 1939), and Edwin G. Nourse, *Government in Relation to Agriculture* (Brookings Institution, Washington, 1940). The politics underlying farm relief are discussed in Wesley McCune, *The Farm Bloc* (Doubleday Doran, Garden City, 1943). The need for conservation is emphasized in Stuart Chase, *Rich Land, Poor Land: A Study in the Natural Resources of America* (McGraw-Hill, N.Y., 1936). On the problems of the rural underprivileged, see Carey McWilliams, *Ill Fares the Land: Migrants and Migratory Labor in the United States* (Little Brown, Boston, 1942), and Department of Agriculture, *Toward Farm Security* (Govt. Printing Off., Washington, 1941). On all phases, Gee, *Social Economics of Agriculture* (Cited for Chapter 13), is excellent.

Chapter 20. New Deal on the Defensive

GENERAL.   See titles listed under Chapter 19.

SUPREME COURT CRISIS.   For essential background, Carl B. Swisher, *American Constitutional Development* (Houghton Mifflin, Boston, 1943), and Alfred H. Kelly and Winfield A. Harbison, *The American Constitution: Its Origins and Development* (Norton, N.Y., 1955), are good. An appreciative study of the most famous jurist of the modern period is Francis Biddle, *Mr. Justice Holmes* (Scribners, N.Y., 1942). A leading authority on the Supreme Court criticizes its conduct in Edward S. Corwin, *The Twilight of the Supreme Court: a History of Our Constitutional Theory* (Yale Univ., New Haven, 1934), and *Court over Constitution; a Study in Judicial Review as an Instrument of Popular Government* (Princeton Univ., Princeton, 1938). An irreverent portrait of the court is Drew Pearson and Robert Allen, *The Nine Old Men* (Doubleday Doran, Garden City, 1936). The best account of the court controversy from the New Deal point of view is Robert H. Jackson, *The Struggle for Judicial Supremacy: A Study of a Crisis in American Power Politics* (Knopf, N.Y., 1941). Detailed and well-informed, although unsympathetic to Roosevelt, is the account of the fight over the Judicial Reorganization Bill in Joseph Alsop and Turner Catledge, *The 168 Days* (Doubleday Doran, Garden City, 1938). The role of Chief Justice Hughes may be studied in Merlo J. Pusey, *Charles Evans Hughes*, 2 v. (Macmillan, N.Y., 1951), and Samuel Hendel, *Charles Evans Hughes and the Supreme Court* (King's Crown Press, N.Y., 1951). The sequel of the controversy is dealt with in Edwin S. Corwin, *Constitutional Revolution, Ltd.* (Pomona College, Claremont, Calif., 1941), C. Herman Pritchett, *The Roosevelt Court* (Macmillan, N.Y., 1948), Samuel J. Konefsky, *Chief Justice Stone and the Supreme Court* (Macmillan, N.Y., 1945), and Alpheus T. Mason, *Harlan Fiske Stone, Pillar of the Law* (Viking, N.Y., 1956).

OTHER ISSUES.   The neurotic fringe in American politics is studied in Alfred M. and Elizabeth B. Lee, eds., *The Fine Art of Propaganda: A Study of Father Coughlin's Speeches* (Harcourt Brace, N.Y., 1939), and Harnett T. Kane, *Louisiana Hayride: The American Rehearsal for Dictatorship* (Morrow, N.Y., 1941). The so-called spending theory is expounded in Alvin H. Hansen, *Full Recovery or Stagnation* (Norton, N.Y., 1938), and Stuart Chase, *Idle Men* (Harcourt Brace, N.Y., 1940). Reasons for Federal intervention in the housing field are discussed in Michael W.

Strauss and Talbot Wegg, *Housing Comes of Age* (Oxford, N.Y., 1938), and Nathan Strauss, *The Seven Myths of Housing* (Knopf, N.Y., 1944).

Chapter 21. Depression America

GENERAL. The best survey of social trends during the 1930's is Wechter, *The Age of the Great Depression, 1929–1941*. See also Mitchell, *Depression Decade*. "Recent Social Trends," *American Journal of Sociology*, XLVII (May, 1942), 803–980, does for the thirties what the more extensive work of the same name did for the twenties. A brilliantly written survey is Frederick L. Allen, *Since Yesterday* (Harper, N.Y., 1940). Harold F. Stearns, ed., *America Now: An Inquiry into Civilization in the United States By Thirty-Six Americans* (Literary Guild, N.Y., 1938), give a more optimistic picture than the similar survey under Stearns' editorship of 1922 (cited for Chapter 15). Robert and Helen Lynd, *Middletown in Transition: A Study in Cultural Conflicts* (Harcourt Brace, N.Y., 1937), provides an important sequel to the Lynds' earlier study. A thoughtful commentary is Simeon Strunsky, *The Living Tradition: Change and America* (Doubleday Doran, Garden City, 1939).

LABOR. Good general discussions are in Dulles, *Labor in America*, and Herbert Harris, *American Labor* (Yale Univ., New Haven, 1939). On legislation, see John B. Andrews, *Labor Laws in Action* (Harper, N.Y., 1938), Joseph Rosenfarb, *The National Labor Policy and How It Works* (Harper, N.Y., 1940), and Harry A. Millis and E. C. Brown, *From the Wagner Act to Taft-Hartley: A Study of National Labor Policy and Labor Relations* (Univ. of Chicago, Chicago, 1950). Important studies are the three by Robert R. R. Brooks, *When Labor Organizes* (Yale Univ., New Haven, 1938), *Unions of Their Own Choosing* (Yale Univ., New Haven, 1939), and *As Steel Goes . . .: Unionism in a Basic Industry* (Yale Univ., New Haven, 1940). Black aspects are emphasized in Harold Seidman, *Labor Czars: A History of Labor Racketeering* (Liveright, N.Y., 1938). On the rise of the CIO, see J. Raymond Walsh, *C.I.O., Industrial Unionism in America* (Norton, N.Y., 1937), Edward Levinson, *Labor on the March* (Harper, N.Y., 1938), Herbert Harris, *Labor's Civil War* (Knopf, N.Y., 1940). On the most controversial figure in the labor movement, see James A. Wechsler, *Labor Baron, a Portrait of John L. Lewis* (Morrow, N.Y., 1944), and Saul D. Alinsky, *John L. Lewis: An Unauthorized Biography* (Putnam, N.Y., 1949). Matthew Josephson, *Sidney Hillman, Statesman of American Labor* (Doubleday, Garden City, N.Y., 1952), is a friendly portrait. Nels Anderson, *Men on the Move* (Univ. of Chicago, Chicago, 1940), discusses the migrant problem.

COMMUNISM. James Oneal and G. A. Werner, *American Communism: A Critical Analysis of Its Origins, Development and Programs* (Dutton, N.Y., 1947), tells the story from the viewpoint of an anti-Stalinist radical. Eugene Lyons, *The Red Decade, the Stalinist Penetration of America* (Bobbs-Merrill, Indianapolis, 1941), is informative but somewhat overdrawn. Whittaker Chambers, *Witness* (Random, N.Y., 1952), is the confession of a remorseful ex-Communist.

SPECIAL PHASES. On the revolution in economic thought, see Seymour E. Harris, ed., *The New Economics: Keynes' Influence on Theory and Public Policy* (Knopf, N.Y., 1947). On literature, the titles listed in the first section of this bibliography may be supplemented with Henry S. Canby, *Seven Years' Harvest: Notes on Contemporary Literature* (Farrar and Rinehart, N.Y., 1936), Halford E. Luccock, *American Mirror: Social, Ethical, and Religious Aspects of American Literature, 1930–1940* (Macmillan, N.Y., 1940), David Ewen, *Music Comes to America* (Crowell, N.Y., 1942), John T. Howard, *Our Contemporary Composers: American Music in the Twentieth Century* (Crowell, N.Y., 1941), Homer Saint-Gaudens, *The American Artist and His Times* (Dodd Mead, N.Y., 1941).

Chapter 22. Gathering Clouds

GENERAL. For competent accounts, see Bailey, Bemis, Pratt, and Ellis in their diplomatic histories. An excellent account is Allan Nevins, *The New Deal and World Affairs* (Yale Univ., New Haven, 1950). The official defense of American policy is State Department, *Peace and War: United States Foreign Policy, 1931–1941* (Govt. Printing Off., Washington, 1943). For contemporary items see State Department, *Press Releases*, *Foreign Policy Association Bulletins* and *Reports*, and W. H. Shepardson, et. al., eds., *The United States in World Affairs, 1933, 1934–35, 1936, 1937, 1938, 1939* (Council on Foreign Relations, N.Y., 1934–1940). Pronouncements of presidential policy are to be found in *Public Papers and Addresses of Franklin D. Roosevelt*; also in Wilfred Funk, ed., *Roosevelt's Foreign Policy, 1933–1941* (Funk, N.Y., 1942). *The Memoirs of Cordell Hull* is indispensable. A critical review of New Deal foreign policy is Charles A. Beard, *American Foreign Policy in the Making, 1932–1940: A Study in Responsibilities* (Yale Univ., New Haven, 1946). For a more sympathetic view, consult William L. Langer and S. Everett Gleason, *The Challenge to Isolation, 1937–1940* (Harper, N.Y., 1952).

SPECIAL PHASES. Contemporary academic support for isolationism was provided by Charles A. Beard, *The Open Door at Home: a Trial Philosophy of National Interest* (Macmillan, N.Y., 1934), and Edwin Borchard and William P. Lage, *Neutrality for the United States* (Yale Univ., New Haven, 1937). On one phase of isolationism, see F. Jay Taylor, *The United States and the Spanish Civil War, 1936–1939* (Bookman Associates, N.Y., 1956).

On New Deal trade policy, see Raymond L. Buell, *The Hull Trade Program* (Foreign Policy Assn., N.Y., 1938), and Herbert Feis, *The Changing Pattern of International Economic Affairs* (Harper, N.Y., 1940). Important memoirs throwing light on the problems of American diplomacy in three critical areas are Joseph E. Davies, *Mission to Moscow* (Simon and Schuster, N.Y., 1941), William E. Dodd, Jr., and Martha Dodd, *Ambassador Dodd's Diary, 1933–1938* (Harcourt Brace, N.Y., 1941), and Joseph C. Grew, *Ten Years in Japan* (Simon and Schuster, N.Y., 1944). Further information on relations with Russia is in Meno Lovenstein, *American Opinion of Soviet Russia* (Washington, 1941).

On the Philippines, see *Joint Preparatory Committee on Philippine Affairs: Report of May 20, 1938,* 3 v. (Govt. Printing Off., Washington, 1938), and Kirk L. Grayson, *Philippine Independence: Motives, Problems and Prospects* (Farrar and Rinehart, N.Y., 1936). On Latin America, see Bemis, *Latin American Policy of the United States*, Stuart, *Latin America and the United States*, and Edward O. Guerrant, *Roosevelt's Good Neighbor Policy* (Univ. of New Mexico, Albuquerque, 1950).

Suggestions for Further Reading

Chapter 23. The Prelude to Pearl Harbor

GENERAL. The titles recommended for Chapter 23 may be supplemented with *Documents on American Foreign Relations*, v. 1. (World Peace Foundation, Boston, 1939–1942, and *The United States in World Affairs, 1939, 1940, 1941.* The most scholarly study is William L. Langer and S. Everett Gleason, *The Undeclared War, 1940–1941* (Harper, N.Y., 1953). Roosevelt's policies are defended in Basil Rauch, *Roosevelt, From Munich to Pearl Harbor* (Creative Age, N.Y., 1950), and Herbert Feis, *The Road to Pearl Harbor* (Princeton Univ., Princeton, 1950). Roosevelt's policies are severely criticized in Charles A. Beard, *President Roosevelt and the Coming of the War* (Yale, New Haven, 1948), and Charles C. Tansill *Backdoor to War, The Roosevelt Foreign Policy, 1933–1941* (Henry Regnery, Chicago, 1952). A balanced account is Donald F. Drummond, *The Passing of American Neutrality* (Univ. of Michigan, Ann Arbor, 1955). Two exceptionally well-informed journalists provide their account in Joseph Alsop and Robert Kintner, *American White Paper: the Story of American Diplomacy and the Second World War* (Simon and Schuster, N.Y., 1940). American policy during the first years of the war is ably discussed by Sumner Welles, *The Time for Decision* (Harper, N.Y., 1944).

POLICY DEBATE. Much valuable information is contained in the account of the Lend-Lease administrator, Edward R. Stettinius, Jr., *Lend Lease, Weapon for Victory* (Macmillan, N.Y., 1944). The controversy between the interventionists and the isolationists may be traced in Charles A. Beard, *A Foreign Policy for America* (Knopf, N.Y., 1940), Allen W. Dulles and H. F. Armstrong, *Can America Stay Neutral?* (Harper, N.Y., 1939), Raymond L. Buell, *Isolated America* (Knopf, N.Y., 1940), Charles G. Fenwick, *American Neutrality, Trial and Failure* (New York Univ., N.Y., 1940), Walter Johnson, *The Battle Against Isolation* (Univ. of Chicago, Chicago, 1944), Harold Lavine and James Wechsler, *War Propaganda and the United States* (Yale Univ., New Haven, 1940), and Wayne S. Cole, *America First, the Battle against Intervention, 1940–1941* (Univ. of Wisconsin, Madison, 1953).

THE FAR EAST. Essential background for understanding the issues of diplomacy between the United States and Japan is provided in C. A. Buss, *War and Diplomacy in Eastern Asia* (Macmillan, N.Y., 1941), W. C. Johnstone, *The United States and Japan's New Order* (Oxford, N.Y., 1941), Harold S. Quigley, *Far Eastern War, 1937–1941* (World Peace Foundation, Boston, 1942), and Griswold, *Far Eastern Policy of the United States.* Ambassador Grew's *Ten Years in Japan* may be supplemented with his *Turbulent Era, a Diplomatic Record of Forty Years*, 2 v. (Houghton Mifflin, 1952).

PEARL HARBOR. In addition to the discussion provided in the general works listed above, consult Walter Millis, *This is Pearl! The United States and Japan—1941* (Morrow, N.Y., 1947), and Walter Lord, *Day of Infamy* (Holt, N.Y., 1957).

Roosevelt's policy is indicted in George E. Morgenstern, *Pearl Harbor, the Story of the Secret War* (Devin-Adair, N.Y., 1947), and Robert A. Theobold, *Final Secret of Pearl Harbor: the Washington Contribution to the Japanese Attack* (Devin-Adair, N.Y., 1954).

Chapter 24. The Global War

GENERAL. Trained historians have been employed by the various services to collect materials and prepare a comprehensive account of the conflict. The Army series alone will contain about one hundred volumes. Among the volumes already available in *The United States Army in World War II*, vols. I– (Historical Division, Dept. of the Army, Washington, 1947–   ), are: *The Army Ground Forces: The Organization of Ground Combat Troops; The War in the Pacific: Guadalcanal: The First Offensive; The Army Ground Forces: The Procurement and Training of Ground Troops; The War in the Pacific: Okinawa: The Last Battle; The European Theater of Operations*. Also in progress is Wesley F. Craven and James L. Cate, eds., *The Army Air Forces in World War II*, vols. I– (Univ. of Chicago, Chicago, 1948–   ). The history of the war at sea has been rapidly carried forward by one of the nation's leading historians: see Samuel E. Morison, *History of United States Naval Operations in World War II*, vols. I–XI (Little Brown, Boston, 1947–1957). Separate from the major projects are a number of brief popular accounts published by the Army historians under the general title, *American Forces in Action*. Useful summaries based upon the early published sources are: Roger W. Shugg and H. A. DeWeerd, *World War II: A Concise History* (Infantry Journal, Washington, 1946), Walter P. Hall, *Iron Out of Calvary: An Interpretive History of the Second World War* (Appleton-Century, 1946), Francis T. Miller, *History of World War II* (Winston, Philadelphia, 1946), and Fletcher Pratt, *War for the World* (Yale Univ., New Haven, 1950). For a good pictorial record, see *Life's Picture History of World War II* (Time, Inc., N.Y., 1950). Allied strategy is criticized in Hanson W. Baldwin, *Great Mistakes of the War* (Harper, N.Y., 1950), and in Chester Wilmot, *The Struggle for Europe* (Harper, N.Y., 1952).

REPORTS AND MEMOIRS. The clearest as well as the most authoritative brief account of the climactic phase of the war is *General Marshall's Report: The Winning of the War in Europe and the Pacific . . .* (Simon and Schuster, N.Y., 1945). On the European campaign from D Day to the surrender of Germany, an essential source is Dwight D. Eisenhower, *Report by the Supreme Commander to the Combined Chiefs of Staff on the Operations in Europe of the Allied Expeditionary Force 6 June 1944 to 8 May 1945* (Govt. Printing Off., Washington, 1946). On naval operations, see Ernest J. King, *U.S. Navy at War, 1941–1945, Official Reports to the Secretary of the Navy* (U.S. Navy Dept., Washington, 1946), and Walter Karig and Welbourn Kelley, *Battle Report: Pearl Harbor to Coral Sea* (Farrar and Rinehart, N.Y., 1944). The wartime Secretary of War contributed an important memoir in Henry L. Stimson and McGeorge Bundy, *On Active Service in Peace and War* (Harper, N.Y., 1947). Several of the major commanders have written accounts of their experiences: Dwight D. Eisenhower, *Crusade in Europe* (Doubleday, Garden City, 1948); Omar N. Bradley, *A Soldier's Story* (Holt, N.Y., 1951); Henry H. Arnold, *Global Mission* (Harper, N.Y., 1949); Lewis H. Brereton, *The Brereton Diaries* (Morrow, N.Y., 1946); Theodore H. White, ed., *The Stilwell Papers* (Sloane, N.Y., 1948). A fascinating document, part memoir, part history in the grand manner is Winston Churchill, *The Second World War*, 6 v. (Houghton Mifflin, 1948–1953).

WARTIME DIPLOMACY. The *Memoirs of Cordell Hull*, and Sherwood, *Roosevelt and Hopkins*, are indispensable. See also Sumner Welles, *Seven Decisions*

That Shaped History (Harper, N.Y., 1951), William D. Leahy, *I Was There: The Personal Story of the Chief of Staff to Presidents Roosevelt and Truman* (Whittlesey House, N.Y., 1950), Carlton J. H. Hayes, *Wartime Mission in Spain, 1942–1945* (Macmillan, N.Y., 1945), William Langer, *Our Vichy Gamble* (Knopf, N.Y., 1947), and Herbert Feis, *Churchill, Roosevelt, Stalin: The War They Waged and the Peace They Sought* (Princeton Univ., Princeton, 1957).

Chapter 25. The Home Front

Nevins and Hacker, *The United States and Its Place in World Affairs*, has excellent chapters on the wartime economy. The most important authority for industrial mobilization is the memoir of WPB chief, Donald Nelson, *Arsenal of Democracy: The Story of American Production* (Harcourt Brace, N.Y., 1946). Jack Goodman, ed., *While You Were Gone: A Report on Wartime Life in the United States* (Simon and Schuster, N.Y., 1946), is uneven in quality, but has good chapters. Mercedes Rosebery, *This Day's Madness: A Story of the American People Against the Background of the War Effort* (Macmillan, N.Y., 1944), is chaotic and impressionistic in treatment, but captures something of the spirit of the times. Valuable contemporary accounts are provided in Selden Menefee, *Assignment: U.S.A.* (Reynal and Hitchcock, N.Y., 1943), and John Dos Passos, *State of the Nation* (Houghton Mifflin, Boston, 1944). On wartime economic problems, see Seymour E. Harris, *Economics of America at War* (Norton, N.Y., 1943), and the same author's *Price and Related Controls in the United States* (McGraw-Hill, N.Y., 1945). On the war's most serious infringements of civil liberties, see Carey McWilliams, *Prejudice; Japanese-Americans: Symbol of Racial Intolerance* (Little Brown, Boston, 1944).

Chapter 26. The Mirage of Peace

GENERAL. The best accounts are in the annual volumes, *The United States in World Affairs, 1945–1952*. See also *Documents on American Foreign Relations, 1945–1952*.

INTERNATIONAL ORGANIZATION. The revival of internationalism in the United States led to the publication of many books and periodical articles. See, for example, Wendell Willkie, *One World* (Simon and Schuster, N.Y., 1943), Henry A. Wallace, *The Century of the Common Man* (Reynal and Hitchcock, N.Y., 1943), Clarence K. Streit, *Union Now: The Proposal for Interdemocracy Federal Union* (Harper, N.Y., 1941), Herbert Hoover and Hugh Gibson, *The Problems of a Lasting Peace* (Doubleday Doran, Garden City, 1942), Walter Lippmann, *U.S. Foreign Policy: Shield of the Republic* (Little Brown, Boston, 1943), Emery Reeves, *The Anatomy of Peace* (Harper, N.Y., 1945). The genesis of the United Nations Organization is well traced in Vera M. Dean, *The Four Cornerstones of Peace* (Whittlesey House, N.Y., 1946).

YALTA CONFERENCE. For a criticism of Roosevelt's concessions to the Russians, see Baldwin, *Great Mistakes of the War*, and William H. Chamberlin, *America's Second Crusade* (Regnery, Chicago, 1950). Roosevelt's conduct is defended in Sherwood, *Roosevelt and Hopkins*, James F. Byrnes, *Speaking Frankly* (Harper, N.Y., 1947), Edward R. Stettinius, *Roosevelt and the Russians: The Yalta*

Conference (Doubleday, Garden City, 1949), Feis, *Churchill, Roosevelt, Stalin,* and John L. Snell, ed., *The Meaning of Yalta: Big Three Diplomacy and the New Balance of Power* (Louisiana State Univ., Baton Rouge, 1956).

OCCUPATION PROBLEMS. On the occupation of Germany, see Julian Bach, Jr., *America's Germany: An Account of the Occupation* (Random House, N.Y., 1946), Saul K. Padover, *Experiment in Germany: The Story of an American Intelligence Officer* (Duell, Sloan, and Pearce, N.Y., 1946), James P. Warburg, *Germany —Nation or No-Man's Land* (Headline Series, No. 60, Foreign Policy Assoc., N.Y., 1946). The chief American prosecutor at the Nuremberg trial makes his accusations in Robert H. Jackson, *The Nürnberg Case* (Knopf, N.Y., 1947). On Japan, see Richard Hart, *Eclipse of the Rising Sun* (Headline Series, No. 56, Foreign Policy Assoc., N.Y., 1946), Thomas A. Bisson, *Prospects for Democracy in Japan* (Macmillan, N.Y., 1949), and Edwin O. Reischauer, *The United States and Japan* (Harvard Univ., Cambridge, 1950). Recent American policy in the Philippines is criticized in Hernando Abaya, *Betrayal in the Philippines* (A. A. Wyn, N.Y., 1946). An equally serious criticism of American policy in China is in White and Jacoby, *Thunder Out of China*.

POSTWAR FRICTIONS. Relations of the United States with the other victorious powers are discussed in William T. R. Fox, *The Super-Powers, the United States, Britain, and the Soviet Union* (Harcourt Brace, N.Y., 1944), David Dallin, *The Big Three: the United States, Britain, and Russia* (Yale Univ., New Haven, 1945), Vera M. Dean, *Russia—Menace or Promise* (Headline Series, No. 58, Foreign Policy Assoc., N.Y., 1946). The difficulties involved in dealing with the Russians are related in Byrnes, *Speaking Frankly*, and W. Bedell Smith, *My Three Years in Moscow* (Lippincott, Philadelphia, 1950). Drew Middleton, *The Struggle for Germany* (Bobbs-Merrill, Indianapolis, 1949), is the work of a well-informed journalist. Joseph M. Jones, *The Fifteen Weeks, February 21—June 5, 1947* (Viking, N.Y., 1955), deals with the Truman Doctrine and the Marshall Plan. Concise and informative is Halford L. Hoskins, *The Atlantic Pact* (Public Affairs Press, Washington, 1949). Glimpses behind the scenes are provided in Walter Millis, ed., *The Forrestal Diaries* (Viking, N.Y., 1951), and *The Private Papers of Senator Vandenberg,* ed. by Arthur H. Vandenberg, Jr. (Houghton Mifflin, Boston, 1952). The objectives of the Truman foreign policy are set forth in Department of State, *Strengthening the Forces of Freedom: Selected Speeches and Statements of Secretary of State Acheson, February 1949–April 1950* (Govt. Printing Off., Washington, 1950).

CHINA AND KOREA. Essential to an understanding are Herbert Feis, *The China Tangle: The American Effort in China from Pearl Harbor to the Marshall Mission* (Princeton Univ., Princeton, 1953), and John K. Fairbank, *The United States and China* (Harvard Univ., Cambridge, 1948). On Korea, consult Leland M. Goodrich, *Korea: A Study of U.S. Policy in the United Nations* (Council on Foreign Relations, N.Y., 1956). On MacArthur's controversial role in Korea, see Richard H. Rovere and Arthur M. Schlesinger, Jr., *The General and the President, and the Future of American Foreign Policy* (Farrar, Straus, & Young, N.Y., 1951), and Courtney Whitney, *MacArthur: His Rendezvous with History* (Knopf, N.Y., 1956). The last phase of the Korean War is described in Mark W. Clark, *From the Danube to the Yalu* (Harper, N.Y., 1954).

Chapter 27. Tribulations of Truman

GENERAL. Eric F. Goldman, *The Crucial Decade: America, 1945–1955* (Knopf, N.Y., 1956), is a well-written summary. Harry S. Truman, *Memoirs*, 2 v. (Doubleday, Garden City, 1955–1956), is a forceful statement of the author's case. William Hillman, *Mr. President* (Farrar, Straus & Young, N.Y., 1952), contains interesting Truman material. Jonathan Daniels, *Man of Independence* (Lippincott, Phila., is a friendly portrait.

THE LOYALTY ISSUE. A temperate discussion is Nathaniel Weyl, *Battle against Disloyalty* (Crowell, N.Y., 1951). Popular hysteria is condemned in Carey McWilliams, *Witch Hunt: The Revival of Heresy* (Little Brown, Boston, 1950), and Alan Barth, *The Loyalty of Free Men* (Viking, N.Y., 1951). A prominent ex-Communist makes his accusations in Louis F. Budenz, *Men Without Faces: The Communist Conspiracy in the U.S.A.* (Harper, N.Y., 1950). Ralph de Toledano and Victor Lasky, *Seeds of Treason: The True Story of the Hiss-Chambers Tragedy* (Funk & Wagnalls, N.Y., 1950), is anti-Hiss; Earl Jowitt, *The Strange Case of Alger Hiss* (Doubleday, N.Y., 1953), is a defense of Hiss; more objective is Allistair Cooke, *A Generation on Trial: U.S.A. v. Alger Hiss* (Knopf, N.Y., 1950). The two protagonists tell their stories in Chambers, *Witness*, and Alger Hiss, *In the Court of Public Opinion* (Knopf, N.Y., 1957). Owen Lattimore, *Ordeal by Slander* (Little Brown, Boston, 1950), is a vigorous defense of the author and counter-offensive against Senator McCarthy.

OTHER ISSUES. To understand the issues involved in the civil rights controversy, the essential document is *To Secure These Rights: The Report of the President's Committee on Civil Rights* (Govt. Printing Off., Washington, 1947). The essence of the Hoover Report on government reorganization is in *The Hoover Commission Report on Organization of the Executive Branch of the Government* (McGraw-Hill, N.Y., 1949). On economic policy, see George A. Steiner, *Government's Role in Economic Life* (McGraw-Hill, N.Y., 1953). On labor policy, consult Millis and Brown, *From the Wagner Act to Taft-Hartley*.

Chapter 28. Changing America

RECENT ECONOMIC TRENDS. A popular explanation of the new capitalism is Frederick L. Allen, *The Big Change: America Transforms Itself, 1900–1950* (Harper, N.Y., 1952). See also David Lilienthal, *Big Business: A New Era* (Harper, N.Y., 1953), and Herrymon Maurer, *Great Enterprise: Growth and Behavior of the Big Corporation* (Macmillan, N.Y., 1955). More thoughtful interpretations are Adolph A. Berle, Jr., *The 20th Century Capitalist Revolution* (Harcourt Brace, N.Y., 1954), and John K. Galbraith, *American Capitalism* (Houghton Mifflin, Boston, 1956). Lewis H. Kimmel, *Share Ownership in the United States* (Brookings Inst., Washington, 1952), is a scholarly study. On the characteristics of the labor leaders, consult C. Wright Mills, *The New Men of Power: America's Labor Leaders* (Harcourt Brace, N.Y., 1945).

THE NEGRO. The most complete and objective study is the work of a Swedish sociologist, Gunnar Myrdal, *An American Dilemma: The Negro Problem and Modern Democracy*, 2 v. (Harper, N.Y., 1944). Outstanding discussions by American scholars are Horace R. Cayton and George S. Mitchell, *Black Workers and the New Unions* (Univ. of North Carolina, Chapel Hill, 1939), Rayford W. Logan, ed., *What the Negro Wants* (Univ. of North Carolina, Chapel Hill, 1944), Robert C. Weaver, *Negro Labor: A National Problem* (Harcourt Brace, N.Y., 1946), *Minority Peoples in a Nation at War*, vol. 223 of *Annals of American Academy of Political Science* (Sept., 1942). Dynamic forces in the present situation are explained in Edwin R. Embree, *Brown America: The Story of a New Race* (Viking, N.Y., 1931), and Roi Ottley, *'New World A-Coming'; Inside Black America* (Houghton Mifflin, Boston, 1943), Arnold M. Rose, *America Divided, Minority Group Relations in the United States* (Knopf, N.Y., 1948), Carl T. Rowan, *South of Freedom* (Knopf, N.Y., 1952). On the legal battle against segregation, see C. Herman Pritchett, *Civil Liberties and the Vinson Court* (Univ. of Chicago, Chicago, 1954), Harry S. Ashmore, *The Negro and the Schools* (Univ. of North Carolina, Chapel Hill, 1954), Albert P. Blaustein and Clarence C. Ferguson, *Desegregation and the Law* (Rutgers Univ., New Brunswick, N.J., 1957).

SCIENCE AND THOUGHT. James P. Baxter, 3d, *Scientists Against Time* (Little Brown, Boston, 1946) is a fine account of the organization of the American scientific effort in World War II. On nuclear research, see George Gamow, *Atomic Energy in Cosmic and Human Life; Fifty Years of Radioactivity* (Doubleday, N.Y., 1948), and Daniel Lang, *Early Tales of the Atomic Age* (Doubleday N.Y., 1948), and Donald J. Hughes, *On Nuclear Energy: Its Potential for Peacetime Uses* (Harvard, Cambridge, 1957). A stimulating discussion of the challenge of modern science is Vannevar Bush, *Modern Arms and Free Men* (Simon and Schuster, N.Y., 1949). For criticism of educational practices, see Arthur E. Bestor, *Educational Wastelands: The Retreat from Learning in Our Public Schools* (Univ. of Illinois, Urbana, 1953). General discussions of the problems of higher education are R. Freeman Butts, *The College Charts Its Course: Historical Conceptions and Current Proposals* (McGraw-Hill, N.Y., 1939), and Robert L. Kelly, *The American Colleges and the Social Order* (Macmillan, N.Y., 1940). For important opposing points of view, see Robert M. Hutchins, *The Higher Learning in America* (Yale Univ., New Haven, 1936), and Harry D. Gideonse, *The Higher Learning in a Democracy: A Reply to President Hutchins' Critique of the American University* (Farrar and Rinehart, N.Y., 1937). One of the best examinations of the problem is *General Education in a Free Society: Report of the Harvard Committee* (Harvard Univ., Cambridge, 1945).

Chapter 29. Eisenhower Republicanism

GENERAL. Robert J. Donovan, *Eisenhower: The Inside Story* (Harper, N.Y., 1956) is a well-written account based on cabinet records and other confidential sources. Merle J. Pusey, *Eisenhower the President* (Macmillan, N.Y., 1956), is informative, but lacking in critical balance. Richard H. Rovere, *Affairs of State: The Eisenhower Years* (Farrar, Straus and Cudahy, N.Y., 1956), consists of material originally published in *The New Yorker*—some of it of ephemeral interest but much of permanent value for its shrewd analysis and commentary. A. Merriman Smith, *Meet Mr. Eisenhower* (Harper, N.Y., 1955), is the pen portrait by a veteran White House reporter. For a persuasive statement of the New Republicanism, see Arthur Larson, *A Republican Looks at His Party* (Harper, N.Y., 1956). William S. White,

The Taft Story (Harper, N.Y., 1954), is a sympathetic study of Senator Robert A. Taft.

SPECIFIC ISSUES. For a lively account of the Army-McCarthy hearings, see Michael Straight, *Trial by Television* (Beacon, Boston, 1954). James Rorty and Moske Decter, *McCarthy and the Communists* (Beacon, Boston, 1954), attacks McCarthy; William F. Buckley and L. Bent Bozell, *McCarthy and His Enemies, the Record of Its Meaning* (Regnery, Chicago, 1954), defends him.

Chapter 30. The United States in a Troubled World

GENERAL. Indispensable for the recent period are the annual publications of the Council on Foreign Relations, *The United States in World Affairs, 1953–1956,* and *Documents on American Foreign Relations, 1953–1956.* Donovan, *Eisenhower: The Inside Story,* Pusey, *Eisenhower the President,* and Rovere, *Affairs of State,* all deal extensively with foreign policy. For a criticism, see Dean Acheson, *Power and Diplomacy* (Harvard, Cambridge, 1958). William G. Carleton, *The Revolution in American Policy,* rev. ed. (Random House, N.Y., 1957), provides intelligent analysis.

SPECIFIC AREAS AND PROBLEMS. Useful recent books are Harold M. Vinacke, *Far Eastern Politics in the Postwar Period* (Appleton-Century-Crofts, N.Y., 1956). Amry Vandenbosch and Richard A. Butwell, *Southeast Asia Among the World Powers* (Univ. of Kentucky, 1957); Guy Wint and Peter Calvocoressi, *Middle East Crisis* (Penguin Books, Harmondsworth, England, 1957); Henry A. Kissinger, *Nuclear Weapons and Foreign Policy* (Harper, N.Y., 1957). On the Korean armistice, see Charles T. Joy, *How Communists Negotiate* (Macmillan, N.Y., 1955).

Index

i

The New York Times.

"All the News That's Fit to Print."

5 A.M. EDITION
WEATHER—Rain today; tomorrow fair and colder.

VOL. LXXXII....No. 27,318.   NEW YORK, WEDNESDAY, NOVEMBER 9, 1932.   * * * * *   TWO CENTS in New York | THREE CENTS | FOUR CENTS Elsewhere

ROOSEVELT WINNER IN LANDSLIDE!
DEMOCRATS CONTROL WET CONGRESS;
LEHMAN GOVERNOR, O'BRIEN MAYOR

| BIG VOTE FOR M'KEE | THE GOVERNOR-ELECT. | STATE VICTORY SOLID | The President's Message To the President-Elect | OVERTURN IN SENATE | THE PRESIDENT-ELECT. | SWEEP IS NATIONAL |

Weather Forecast

THE   SUN

Hull's Statement On Japanese Attack ...Page 7

Vol 210—No. 19-D   317,773   Sunday 233,019   BALTIMORE, MONDAY DECEMBER 8 1941   23 Pages   3 Cents

JAPANESE BOMB PHILIPPINES;
KILL 104 IN HAWAII; RAID
MALAY; CONGRESS ACTS TODAY

SPECIAL WAR MESSAGE DRAFTED BY PRESIDENT; MAY ASK DECLARATION

Extraordinary Joint Cabinet And Congressional Conference Held At White House To Map Action By U. S. Against Japan

BULLETINS

7 KILLED, MANY INJURED BY BOMBS IN HONOLULU; FIRES SET IN CITY AREA

Japanese Planes Strafe Streets Of Wahiawa Two Shot Down—Fifty Raiders Counted—M Day Defense Measures Put Into Effect

---

THE WEATHER

NEW YORK
Herald Tribune

LATE CITY EDITION

Vo. CV No. 35,943   FRIDAY, APRIL 13, 1945

President Roosevelt Is Dead;
Truman Sworn In as Successor

ALL THE NEWS ALL THE TIME

Los Angeles Times

IN TWO PARTS

PART I — GENERAL NEWS

VOL. LXIV   CC   TUESDAY MORNING, AUGUST 7, 1945   DAILY, FIVE CENTS

ATOMIC BOMB HITS JAPAN